Encyclopedia of Alzheimer's Disease

SECOND EDITION

Encyclopedia of Alzheimer's Disease

With Directories of Research, Treatment and Care Facilities

SECOND EDITION

Elaine A. Moore

with Lisa Moore

Illustrated by MARVIN G. MILLER

Foreword by DAVID PERLMUTTER, M.D.

McFarland & Company, Inc., Publishers
Jefferson, North Carolina, and London

ALSO BY ELAINE A. MOORE AND FROM MCFARLAND

The Amphetamine Debate: The Use of Adderall, Ritalin and Related Drugs for Behavior Modification, Neuroenhancement and Anti-Aging Purposes (2011), *Hepatitis: Causes, Treatments and Resources* (2006), *Autoimmune Diseases and Their Environmental Triggers* (2002)

WITH LISA MOORE

Encyclopedia of Sexually Transmitted Diseases (2005; paperback 2009), *Graves' Disease: A Practical Guide* (2001)

WITH SAMANTHA WILKENSON

The Promise of Low Dose Naltrexone Therapy: Potential Benefits in Cancer, Autoimmune, Neurological and Infectious Disorders (2009)

This book is intended as an educational resource and not as a substitute for treatment. Before making any therapeutic changes, the procedures and therapies described in this book should be discussed with a medical professional.

LIBRARY OF CONGRESS CATALOGUING-IN-PUBLICATION DATA

Moore, Elaine A., 1948–
Encyclopedia of alzheimer's disease; with directories of research, treatment and care facilities / Elaine A. Moore with Lisa Moore ; illustrated by Marvin G. Miller ; foreword by David Perlmutter, M.D.— 2d ed.
p.   cm.
Includes bibliographical references and index.

ISBN 978-0-7864-6458-6
softcover : acid free paper ∞

1. Alzheimer's disease — Encyclopedias.
2. Alzheimer's disease — Directories.
I. Moore, Lisa, 1973–   II. Title.
RC523.M665 2012   616.8'31003 — dc23   2011046545

BRITISH LIBRARY CATALOGUING DATA ARE AVAILABLE

Manufactured in the United States of America

McFarland & Company, Inc., Publishers
Box 611, Jefferson, North Carolina 28640
www.mcfarlandpub.com

Table of Contents

Acknowledgments
viii

Foreword by David Perlmutter, M.D.
1

Preface
3

The Encyclopedia
7

Long Term and Day Care Treatment Centers, by State
183

Research Facilities
387

Resources
393

Index
413

Acknowledgments

The second edition of the *Encyclopedia of Alzheimer's Disease* would not have been possible without the help of many people. I would especially like to thank David Perlmutter, M.D., for writing the foreword and alerting me to new information in neurology. Special thanks also go to my co-author, Lisa Moore, for taking time from her busy schedule to assist me with this project and to my clinical chemist friend, Marv Miller, for his insightful illustrations. I'm also grateful to Brett Moore for his contributions in updating the resources and nursing homes and assisting me with technical issues. And thanks to Valerie Sosnow for her proofreading skills and for keeping me focused when interruptions threatened to delay the projects.

I would like to specifically thank Sandy Clarke, director of Namaste Alzheimer's Center in Colorado Springs, Colorado, for her generous sharing of information. I would also like to thank Namaste, one of the top nursing home facilities for Alzheimer's patients in the United States, for allowing me to work as a volunteer while researching gerontology in the graduate sociology program at the University of Colorado. My interactions with both the patients and staff provided me with valuable insights. Most importantly, I'd like to thank my husband Rick for his help, encouragement, and support. Having him in my life makes everything go smoother. — E.A.M.

Foreword

by David Perlmutter, M.D.

In so many unexpected ways a lot has happened in our understanding of Alzheimer's disease since the 2002 edition of the *Encyclopedia of Alzheimer's Disease* was published. Alzheimer's has become a virtual epidemic in our country. With more than 5.3 million Americans diagnosed with the disease and that number expected to double by 2030, scientists are now gaining evidence that we may very well be able to reduce our chances of this disease. And this is a disease for which despite millions of dollars in research, there is no cure, nor any meaningful pharmaceutical treatment to slow its relentless progression. According to a recent *Medscape* report, the costs associated with Alzheimer's disease globally are staggering at an estimated $604 billion, or a full one percent of the world's gross domestic product. But looking beyond the economic impact, the emotional costs borne by the families of Alzheimer's patients are incalculable.

The very good news is that many of our most well respected peer-reviewed medical journals dealing with Alzheimer's disease are now publishing reports demonstrating in great detail who is at risk for the disease. For example, at the 2006 meeting of the American Academy of Neurology, Dr. Rachel Whitmer, a research scientist at Kaiser Permanente of Northern California, showed that individuals with high amounts of body fat had a risk of Alzheimer's increased by 293 percent compared to low body fat when followed up to 27 years after their initial evaluation. Another

study following 1,200 people from 1986 until 2006 found that those who exercised regularly saw a decreased risk for developing Alzheimer's disease by about 40 percent. This study joins countless others relating exercise to reduced risk for the disease and is bolstered by a 2011 report in the *Proceedings of the National Academy of Science* showing actual increase in size of the brain's most important memory structure, the hippocampus, induced by aerobic exercise. This is critically important, as this is the area of the brain that first degenerates in Alzheimer's disease. As the authors stated, "Exercise training increased hippocampal volume by two percent, effectively reversing age-related loss in volume by one to two years."

Homocysteine is an amino acid compound that is toxic to the brain much as cholesterol damages the coronary arteries. But unlike the drugs used to lower cholesterol, homocysteine is lowered to normal levels with nonprescription B vitamins. Research has shown that even mild elevations of homocysteine have a dramatic role in increasing Alzheimer's risk. A level of just 14 was associated with doubling of the risk for the disease as described in the prestigious *New England Journal of Medicine*, and reviewed in a *National Institutes of Health* press release stating, "People with elevated levels of homocysteine in the blood had nearly double the risk of developing Alzheimer's disease, according to a new report from scientists at Boston University. The findings, in a group of people participating in the long-running

Framingham Study, are the first to tie homocysteine levels measured several years before with later diagnosis of AD and other dementias." Other studies looking back to determine risk have overwhelmingly demonstrated the protective effects of higher education, engagement in leisure activities and higher levels of the omega-3 fatty acid, DHA.

As a practicing neurologist dealing with Alzheimer's disease on a daily basis, I believe we need to expand the public awareness that modifiable lifestyle factors have a profound role to play in determining who will or won't get this disease, and it is a blessing to all that this information is contained in these pages. While some may adopt an attitude of living their lives, come what may, with hopes of a pharmaceutical miracle when an illness befalls them, this second edition of the *Encyclopedia of Alzheimer's Disease* is written for those looking to empower themselves well beyond the status quo.

David Perlmutter is a board-certified neurologist and fellow of the American College of Nutrition. A practicing neurologist in Naples, Florida, Dr. Perlmutter also serves as adjunct instructor at the Institute for Functional Medicine in Gig Harbor, Washington. He received the 2002 Linus Pauling Award for his pioneering work in innovative approaches to neurological disorders.

Preface

When I was first asked to write a second edition of this book, I balked and procrastinated for two years. What new was there to report other than the 2003 addition of memantine, a drug long used in Europe, to the U.S. pharmacopoeia? Since 1991, only five new drugs had been approved for the treatment of Alzheimer's disease. At the Clinical Trials for Alzheimer's Disease (CTAD) meeting in Toulouse, France, on November 4, 2010, clinicians and researchers expressed disappointment about the failures of several recent drug trials, but vowed to learn from these trials.

However, it didn't seem as though much had changed since my mother's diagnosis of Alzheimer's disease in 1980 with the exception of several interesting studies by researchers affiliated with the National Center for Complementary and Alternative Medicine (NCCAM) and some diagnostic testing advances. Deciding I could at least update the nursing home section of the book, I agreed to tackle the project. Shortly after I began my research, I was struck by how many studies that I described with enthusiasm a decade ago had been halted or stonewalled or were still in process.

Hundreds of studies seemed to follow a similar theme in that they either investigated intricate biochemical changes that contributed to beta amyloid deposits and plaque formation or they involved the use of synthetic chemicals that might inhibit these processes without interfering with other essential biological functions. Too often, side effects led to discontinuation of these studies. While much had been learned about brain plasticity (yes, brain cells can regenerate) and the genes involved in signaling mechanisms, not many investigational therapies appeared promising.

My impressions were validated when I read an August 28, 2010, *New York Times* article, "Years Later, No Magic Bullet Against Alzheimer's Disease," in which Gina Kolata summarized the findings of 15 scientists who concluded that while there wasn't much in the way of new therapies and that the drugs in use weren't particularly effective, they felt studies describing risk factors for Alzheimer's disease weren't up to the gold standard for scientific scrutiny. This was an "aha" moment for me as it became clear that the only promising reports I'd seen were ones that dealt with risk factors for Alzheimer's disease. I was encouraged to read that at least some of the Duke researchers on the panel saw value in the studies describing preventive measures.

Intrigued by several holistic studies making headlines, I decided to further scrutinize the preventive measures that had been discussed by the team of researchers along with alternative therapies from the NCCAM that appeared to offer promise. In the course of this research, I found that several American experts, such as neurologist David Perlmutter, had dedicated their careers to identifying risk factors for Alzheimer's disease and finding beneficial holistic therapies, which they routinely used in their practices. I was also encouraged to read about the Prevent Alzheimer's Disease by 2020 (PAD2020) initiative, an international panel of researchers collaborating to find ways to prevent Alzheimer's disease.

I also learned that despite all the research dedicated to reducing production of beta amyloid deposits and neurofibrillary tau tangles, not all researchers found beta amyloid to be the cause of Alzheimer's disease. I found that Dr. Stephanie Soscia and her team at Harvard had discovered evidence that beta amyloid production occurred in response to Herpes Simplex I viral infection and was actually the enemy of the enemy or a friend. This is a novel but perfectly plausible idea that would fit with AIDS dementia and the number of cases of Alzheimer's disease in people who survived polio.

Consequently, the second edition of the *Encyclopedia of Alzheimer's Disease* not only includes many more nursing home facilities, it includes more information regarding prevention, holistic therapies, and novel theories. For instance, the herb curcumin, which has long been known to reduce inflammation, has been found to lower the risk of developing Alzheimer's disease. The use of curcumin-rich turmeric is thought to be responsible for the lower incidence of Alzheimer's disease in India. In addition, the B vitamin niacinamide has been shown to completely reduce symptoms in mice with experimentally-induced Alzheimer's disease. These and similar findings suggest that dietary interventions might play a larger therapeutic role than previously suspected. Much has also been learned about risk factors and their role in disease development.

Thanks to tremendous advances in the field of neurology, the genetic and environmental causes of Alzheimer's disease are no longer the mystery they were for Dr. Alois Alzheimer when he first described Alzheimer's disease in 1906. Consequently, in the second edition, the reader will find more information regarding environmental triggers along with information on drugs and vaccines undergoing clinical trials; and natural therapies such as Cerebrolysin, vinpocetine and phosphatidylserine that are approved for treating Alzheimer's disease in Europe.

The *Encyclopedia* is a comprehensive reference work intended for anyone involved in the care, treatment, and day-to-day concerns of patients with Alzheimer's and related disorders. It is also intended for those interested in learning more about the genetic and environmental factors that contribute to both early and late onset Alzheimer's disease.

In the encyclopedia section of this edition, I have attempted to cover the many topics relevant to an understanding of the development, care, prevention, and treatment of Alzheimer's disease. Following the encyclopedia section is a representative list of long-term and day care treatment facilities that have specifically noted that they care for Alzheimer's disease patients. I listed these entries by state and city, although space prohibited including very small towns. Each entry includes helpful information, such as number of beds, certifying agencies and primary insurance carriers, and whether it offers provisions for day care and home health care.

Because many nursing homes care for Alzheimer's disease patients but do not specifically advertise as such, I may have failed to list some facilities that do indeed care for Alzheimer's disease patients. And because policies at nursing homes often change over time, I suggest calling prospective nursing homes and verifying information before arranging to visit specific facilities.

While there is information for evaluating nursing homes in the Resources section, I'd also like to suggest making at least two personal visits before selecting a long-term care facility. These visits provide an opportunity to observe both the staff members and the residents and how they relate to one another. When visiting nursing homes, family members should make sure that the safety and well-being of patients are top priorities and that there is sufficient staff to take care of the individual needs of all patients. The institution should also be clean, organized, secure, and cheerful.

It is also important to consider what features of a nursing home would be most appreciated by patients and what extra amenities might be most attractive. Even patients in the late stages of Alzheimer's disease have likes and dislikes and the capacity for enjoyment. As an example, some nursing homes have greenhouses and gardens and some allow visits from family pets. If these are particularly attractive features, they should be taken into consideration during the process of selecting a long-term or day care facility. It is also important to review deficiencies and violations that have been reported at prospective nursing homes using websites listed in the Resources section.

The following section on research facilities lists the many government and university affiliated research centers in the United States that specialize in Alzheimer's disease research. Most of these centers conduct clinical trials, and different centers usually focus on specific aspects of Alzheimer's disease. Because some of the newer experimental therapies are designed to prevent further deterioration as well as reduce symptoms, all Alzheimer's disease patients can benefit from participating in these programs. Most programs are geared toward outpatients but some university programs are affiliated with specific nursing homes.

The final section, Resources, lists a wide selection of available books, journals, national and local organizations, Internet sources, support groups, and government resources as well as information on legal and minority services. The State Ombudsman listing provides contact information for anyone who needs help locating a suitable nursing home. The state ombudsman programs are also instrumental in resolving problems with nursing homes should they occur.

With the many evolving changes in healthcare, knowledge, including a review of medical records (which patients and authorized family members have a right to through HIPAA), is especially empowering. It is important for Alzheimer's disease patients and their family members to know that there are many treatments today that not only ameliorate but also help prevent symptoms. While changes may not become apparent overnight, recent studies have demonstrated beneficial effects from herbs, dietary changes, hormones, stress reduction techniques such as massage, and anti-inflammatory agents. Although advances in pharmacotherapy have seemingly stalled, Alzheimer's disease is not the bleak disorder it was a decade ago. With awareness of risk factors and preventive measures, the goals of PAD 2020 can become a reality. Alzheimer's disease and related disorders are now easier to diagnose, and, with early diagnosis, easier to manage and sometimes keep from progressing. It is important for caregivers to be aware of all available and investigational treatments, both conventional and holistic, which offer hope for Alzheimer's disease. Numerous resources, including opportunities for respite care, are now available for caregivers and can be found in the resource section of this book. For instance, Medicaid waivers are available to help cover respite services for individuals eligible for nursing home coverage who opt to be cared for at home. Studies show that caregivers who are given training and support are better equipped to care for Alzheimer's disease patients, and trained caregivers are able to provide home care for longer periods of time. The goal in writing the second edition is to empower patients, their family members, and their caregivers.

The Encyclopedia

A2M. A2M is a possible susceptibility gene for Alzheimer's disease located on chromosome 12. A2M was first discovered by Rudolph Tanzi, a geneticist from Harvard University, and it was suspected of controlling the rate at which neurons produce beta amyloid protein. A number of recent studies suggest that this genetic mutation is not involved with the development of Alzheimer's disease.

Abeta (Aβ). Abeta (Aβ) is an acronym for β-amyloid protein, a characteristic feature of the senile plaque deposits seen in the brain of patients with Alzheimer's disease. *See* Amyloid beta protein.

Aβ 42. Aβ 42, a form or subtype of Aβ ending at amino acid 42, is the earliest species of Aβ deposited in the neuritic plaques riddled through the brain of Alzheimer's disease patients. These plaques are almost exclusively composed of Aβ 42. Shifts in the metabolic pathways that produce Aβ 42 are suspected of influencing Alzheimer's disease development. Laboratory tests for Aβ 42 are available, but their use as a diagnostic marker for Alzheimer's disease has not been established. Aβ 42 is decreased in the spinal fluid of patients with Alzheimer's disease, presumably because of its aggregation in brain lesions. (Check, William, Ph.D. "Puzzling out a role for Alzheimer's tests," *CAP Today, In the News*, publication of the College of American Pathologists, June 1998. Lewczuk, P. et al., "Neurochemical diagnosis of Alzheimer's dementia by CSF Abeta42, Abeta42/Abeta40 ratio and total tau," *Neurobiology of Aging*, 2004 Mar 25 (3): 273–81. Pub Med Abstract http://www.ncbi.nlm.nih.gov/pubmed/15123331, accessed Jan 1, 2011)

Abstract reasoning. Abstract reason is evaluated in diagnostic workups for Alzheimer's disease. Abstract reason is tested by asking the patient to explain a few common proverbs, such as "The early bird catches the worm." The answers are then evaluated in terms of relevance. A tendency to interpret these sayings in literal, concrete terms may indicate organic brain disease, schizophrenia, or mental retardation. However, a limited education can also cause patients to offer literal explanations.

Acetyl-L-Carnitine (ALCAR). Individuals with Alzheimer's disease have been found to have low levels of the antioxidant-rich amino acid acetyl carnitine. Levels can be increased with dietary changes and with the dietary supplement acetyl-L-carnitine (ALCAR). Although a daily dose of 500 mg to 2,000 mg is generally recommended, the amount needed for improvement in Alzheimer's disease has not yet been determined. In several studies, acetyl-L-carnitine was found to enhance cellular adenosine triphosphate (ATP) production (the body's source of energy), and to prevent pesticide-induced injury in rats.

Furthermore, ALCAR has been reported to reduce production of mitochondrial free radicals, help maintain transmembrane function, and enhance electron transfer. The National Institute of Health is currently doing clinical trials using ALCAR. Side effects of this supplement include increased appetite, body odor, and rashes. Research suggests that the progression of Alzheimer's disease can be slowed by increasing ALCAR levels. In one study of patients showing a poor response to cholinesterase inhibitors, the addition of ALCAR brought improvement. (Brooks, J. et al. "Acetyl L-carnitine slows decline in younger patients with Alzheimer's disease: A reanalysis of a double-blind placebo-controlled study using the trilinear approach" *International Journal of Psychogeriatrics*, June 1998; 10(2): 193–203. Bianchetti, A., et al. "Effects of Acetyl-L-Carnitine in Alzheimer's disease patients unresponsive to Acetylcholinesterase inhibitors," *Current Medical Research and Opinion* 2003, 19(4): 350-3. Veracity, Dani. "How Acetyl-L-Carnitine prevents Alzheimer's disease and dementia while boosting brain function." *Natural News,* Dec 7, 2005, http://www.naturalnews.com/015553.html, accessed Dec 1, 2010)

Acetylcholine. The first neurotransmitter discovered, acetylcholine is a messenger chemical produced by the nervous system. Neurotransmitters are chemicals that allow cells to communicate with one another. This communication is necessary for thought and learning processes.

Acetylcholine levels are consistently decreased in the brains of Alzheimer's disease patients, with the amount of this reduction correlating to disease severity. Rather than a primary cause, acetylcholine reduction is a secondary event, resulting from the destruction of neurons in the parts of the forebrain rich in acetylcholine. The enzyme choline acetyltransferase (CAT), which synthesizes or produces acetylcholine, is reduced by up to 90 percent in Alzheimer's disease patients.

Acetylcholine is found at the neuromuscular junction (which connects nerve cells to muscle cells) in autonomic ganglia and at parasympathetic nerve endings. In the neuromuscular junction, the endings of motor neurons release acetylcholine. Acetylcholine diffuses across the cleft between neuronal endings and muscle fibers and attaches to receptor molecules in the muscle fiber membrane, initiating permeability changes and consequent depolarization. Without acetylcholine, the nervous system cannot communicate with muscle cells.

Acetylcholine is produced by cholinergic neurons, which are concentrated in certain areas of the nervous system, particularly the basal forebrain and the striatum. The physiological action of acetylcholine is different at central and peripheral nerve endings. In the peripheral nervous system, its action is brief and spatially precise.

In the central nervous system, its actions are slower and more diffuse.

Acetylcholine also helps brain cells communicate with each other by facilitating communication from the basal forebrain to the cerebral cortex and hippocampus, aiding the learning and memory processes. In addition, acetylcholine regulates sleep and facilitates higher cognitive functions. Acetylcholine deficiency can predispose a person to a wide range of neurological diseases, including Alzheimer's disease and stroke. The effect of acetylcholine is limited by the enzyme acetylcholinesterase and by the number of protein receptors able to bind with acetylcholine. Normally, acetylcholinesterase destroys any acetylcholine remaining after it is initially used.

In the early stages of Alzheimer's disease, a select group of neurons become deficient in acetylcholine. Studies indicate that there is a dramatic loss of acetylcholine in the cortex and hippocampal formation of Alzheimer's patients. The hypothesis that memory and cognitive deficits are caused by decreased acetylcholine activity in the brain has shaped pharmacological research. Drugs that block or inhibit acetylcholinesterase increase the amount of acetylcholine available for neurotransmission. Although acetylcholine deficiency is still considered an important step in the pathogenesis of Alzheimer's disease, the fundamental basis of the neuronal degeneration is thought to be more significant.

Acetylcholine receptor, muscarinic 1-5 *see* Muscarinic acetylcholine receptor

Acetylcholine receptor, neuronal nicotinic *see* Nicotinic acetylcholine receptor

Acetylcholinesterase. Acetylcholinesterase, which is also known as cholinesterase, is an enzyme that destroys the neurotransmitter acetylcholine after it has been used in signal transmission. Normally present in the body, acetylcholinesterase limits the amount of acetylcholine present in the circulation. An increase in acetylcholinesterase causes a reduction in available stores of acetylcholine. Drugs designed to inhibit the production of acetylcholinesterase cause a rise in the body's levels of available acetylcholine.

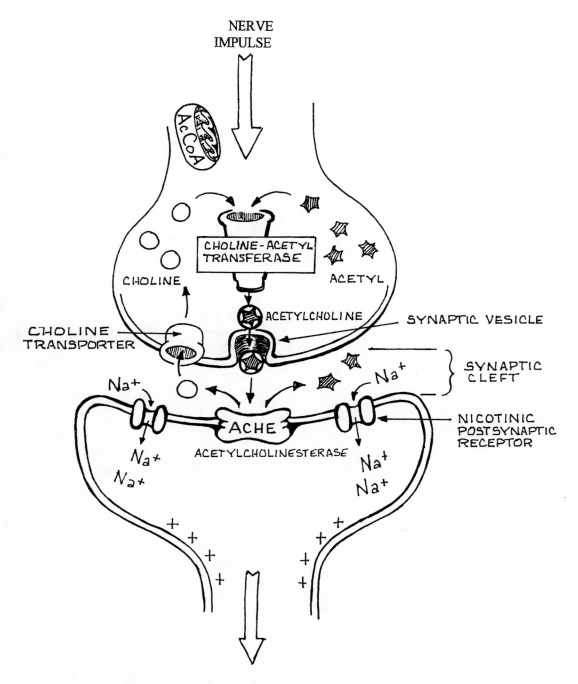

Acetylcholine (illustration by Marvin G. Miller).

Acetylcholinesterase inhibitors. Acetylcholinesterase inhibitors, which are also known as cholinesterase inhibitors, are a class of drugs widely employed in the treatment of Alzheimer's disease. Introduced in the early to mid–1990s, acetylcholinesterase inhibitors are designed to improve cognitive function. Acetylcholinesterase is an enzyme present in the brain that hydrolyzes or breaks down the neurotransmitter acetylcholine. Acetylcholinesterase also inhibits dopamine release in cells in the substantia nigra, mediates the activity of bronchioles in the lungs, and influences bladder function. There is also evidence to suggest that acetylcholinesterase inhibitors reduce the development of neuritic plaques indirectly by interfering with normal amyloid precursor processing.

Cholinesterase inhibitors are only effective in improving cognitive function if the acetylcholine receptors and postsynaptic neurons in the brain remain intact. Once the non-cholinergic neurons begin to degenerate, there is little hope of slowing disease progression. Therefore, it is important that treatment with acetylcholinesterase inhibitors be instituted as early as possible. At the XVII World Congress of Neurology in June 2001, researchers explained that there are still controversies surrounding cholinesterase inhibitors, particularly because it is difficult to predict who will improve and how significant the improvement will be in a particular person.

Cholinesterase inhibitors include tacrine, donepezil, rivastigmine, galantamine and metrifonate. Because acetylcholinesterase has other functions besides nerve transmission, drugs that inhibit it may cause unwanted side effects. Available cholinesterase inhibitors have different selected functions and different side effects so while one drug may not prove effective or have too many side effects, a different drug may prove beneficial. All of the cholinesterase inhibitors available have been shown to improve cognition by a median two points or more on the Alzheimer's Disease Assessment Scale-Cognitive Subscale. In some trials, patients showed as much as a seven-point improvement. Preliminary data on tacrine and donepezil indicate that both drugs may be useful in treating apathy, disinhibition, pacing and hallucinations in patients with Alzheimer's disease. After about six months of therapy, nearly all patients begin to regress. However, the rate of decline is slower after treatment than before treatment.

Not all Alzheimer's patients respond to cholinesterase inhibitors. It is reported that only 25–30 percent of patients show improvement. Some researchers suspect that response is dependent on which cholinergic receptor system is primarily affected. ("Alzheimer's disease management: Update on diagnosis, treatment, and outcomes, assessment," American Society of Clinical Pharmacists, Medical Association Communications, 2000)

Acquired immune deficiency syndrome (AIDS) dementia. Acquired immune deficiency syndrome (AIDS), a condition caused by the human immunodeficiency virus (HIV), is often associated with cognitive impairment. Cognitive impairment may precede the development of other signs of infection. Patients with AIDS dementia complex present with forgetfulness and poor attention, typically over several months duration. The memory impairment is typically less striking than that seen in Alzheimer's disease.

Activation imaging. Activation imaging refers to a method of functional or structural magnetic resonance imaging (MRI) in which changes in brain activation are studied. Activation imaging compares the level of brain activity while subjects perform a task to the level of brain activity in the resting state. Activation imaging may reveal subtle alterations in brain function that may appear before the emergence of mild memory impairment. In activation imaging, subjects perform a learning task involving unrelated pairs of words. This test is particularly sensitive for identifying damage to the medial temporal lobe. The learning tests are followed by periods of rest. During periods of recall, the patients are told the first word and asked to recall the associated word.

Activation imaging provides measures of signal intensity associated with relative cerebral blood flow during tasks requiring memory or other types of cognitive skills. Similar to positron emission topography (PET), activation imaging has the advantage of producing more detailed pictures in less time and does not subject the patient to radiation.

Activities of daily living (ADL). The term "activities of daily living" (ADL) refers to activities such as bathing, eating, grooming, toileting, and dressing that are part of one's personal self-care. People with dementia may not be able to perform these functions without assistance. Clinicians often measure a person's ADL to see if these functions have improved in response to different therapies. *See also* Reisberg's seven stages of Alzheimers's disease.

Activity as a form of therapy. Activities offer stimulation and provide an opportunity to learn new tasks. Activities are beneficial in that they help sustain social skills, and they encourage hand-eye coordination. Patients with Alzheimer's disease, whether cared for at home or in institutional settings, benefit from a variety of activities, including crafts, music groups, shopping trips, exercise, small discussion groups, games such as bingo, and field trips to fairs, festivals and community events. Other recommended activities include reading, puzzles and card playing. Individuals with Alzheimer's disease frequently enjoy personal hobbies such as sorting beads or rearranging their possessions. As long as these activities are not disruptive, they should be encouraged.

Acupuncture. Small studies have shown that transcutaneous electrical nerve stimulation (TENS), a form of acupuncture, may improve memory and daily living skills in patients with Alzheimer's disease. Small studies presented at the 2000 World Conference on Alzheimer's Disease, suggest that acupuncture offers complementary benefits although more studies are needed. ("Alzheimer's disease and acupuncture: Treatment appears to improve mood and cognitive functions," *Acupuncture Today*, September 2000, Vol. 01, Issue 09: http://acupuncturetoday.com/mpacms/at/article.php?id=27681)

Acute illness. Acute illnesses are illnesses that emerge suddenly and are of short duration. Unlike chronic illnesses, which persist indefinitely, acute illnesses, such as muscle sprains, are self-limiting.

Acute organic brain syndrome. Acute organic brain syndrome is a general term used to describe sudden-onset cognitive dysfunction characterized by symptoms of memory impairment and disorientation, which may progress to delirium. The prevalence of this disorder increases with age and commonly occurs in the presence of pneumonia, systemic infections, congestive heart failure, high fever, fluid and electrolyte imbalances, stroke, the postoperative state, and intoxication with drugs or alcohol. Other common clinical features include a depressed or fearful mood, apathy, irritability, impaired judgment, suspiciousness, delusions, hallucinations, and combative, uncooperative, or frightened behavior. Alzheimer's disease is the most common cause of organic brain syndrome, but in Alzheimer's disease, dementia is not acute. Rather, symptoms progress slowly over time and do not improve. In acute organic brain syndrome, symptoms subside as the underlying abnormalities are corrected. *See also* Rapidly progressive dementia

AD7c. AD7c is a protein found in neuronal threads. A laboratory test to measure levels of AD7c in spinal fluid and urine is available, and its use as a diagnostic marker for Alzheimer's disease has been established. The test is available in the United States and in Europe. (Information on the AD7c level in cerebrospinal fluid available at https://ssl.adam.com/content.aspx?productId=49&pid=49&gid=150319&site=welldynerx.adam.com&login=well1815, accessed Feb 4, 2011)

Administration on Aging (AoA). The Administration on Aging (AoA) is a branch of the National Institute of Health. The AoA supports numerous studies on Alzheimer's disease and provides educational and support resources for the elderly. The AoA works with the Health Care Financing Administration, the Health and Human Services Department of the Inspector General, the Department of Justice, Medicare contractors, health care providers and others to develop programs that train volunteer retired professionals such as doctors, nurses, accountants, attorneys and teachers to serve as resources and educators for older people in their communities.

Adult day care centers. Adult day care is a service offered through many nursing homes, senior service centers and a number of non-profit agencies. The center providing adult day care may provide transportation as an additional service. Patients at adult day care centers participate in various activities, and they receive meals as well as their medications if arranged. Adult day care provides respite for caregivers of dementia patients, and patients benefit from the stimulation and the interaction with others. Adult day care and respite care are often available through community groups, sometimes on a sliding fee schedule. Some insurance policies cover day care.

Advance directives. Advance directives (advance care planning directives) are care provisions written and signed in advance of their need that are available in the event the patient later becomes incompetent to make these decisions. Advance directives include the following points: whether and when cardiopulmonary (CPR) and do not resuscitate (DNR) orders should be withheld or put into place, the circumstances under which other-life-supporting measures, such as feeding tubes, antibiotics, hospitalization and surgical procedures, would be desired, and who should be legally designated as durable power of attorney for health care decisions and to assist the physician and family in determining what the patient's wishes would have been in case the patient becomes unable to indicate this. With good advance care planning, patients have communicated with their physician, and understand their diagnosis, prognosis and the likely outcomes of the care directives they have mandated. Advance care directives should also include appropriate contingency plans to ensure that the patient's preferences are honored.

A written legal document called an advance directive (living will or durable power of attorney) can be used to list all the provisions of one's advance care directive. Advance care directives are documented when patients are admitted to a hospital or long-term care facility. Advance care directives ensure that a patient's decisions are honored.

Adverse reaction. An adverse reaction refers to undesirable effects caused by therapeutic intervention. This term usually refers to the adverse effects of medications although adverse reactions can be related to other treatments or their improper use. In controlled trials conducted before drugs are put on the market, drugs are evaluated for a number of different adverse effects.

Advocacy. Because patients with Alzheimer's disease may eventually lose their ability to make decisions, it's important at the time of diagnosis for the patient and his or her family to arrange for an advocate who can make decisions for the patient, including those regarding living wills and trusts, power of attorney and guardianship. The determination of power of attorney or guardianship is fundamental to making eco-nomic or ethical decisions regarding patient care. Many patients with mild cognitive impairment are legally competent to execute a valid power of attorney, giving another person the power to make decisions regarding his or her health and estate. Guardianship must be imposed upon a patient who has become incompetent to render informed consent.

Affect. Affect refers to an individual's outwardly or externally expressed emotion. This may or may not be appropriate to the individual's reported mood and content of thought. For example, a patient who appears angry when relating a happy event would be described as having an inappropriate affect. Affect may be referred to as flat. This means that the patient's expression is absent or neutral. A flat affect may be caused by neuroleptic drugs, and is occasionally seen in schizophrenia. A labile affect is one characterized by rapid fluctuations between manifestations of happiness, sadness, and other emotions. Labile affect is often seen in patients with organic brain disorders.

Affective disorders. Affective disorders are defined by the American Psychiatric Association as mood disorders. Depression and euphoria are the primary symptoms of affective disorders, but not the only ones. Other symptoms include insomnia, anorexia, melancholia, suicidal thoughts, and feelings of worthlessness or being a bother to others. Euphoria is often associated with symptoms of hyperactivity and flight of ideas. Affective disorders are characterized by prolonged disturbances of mood, accompanied by a full or partial manic or depressive syndrome not due to any other physical or mental disorder.

Afferent nerve fibers. Afferent, or sensory, nerve fibers are nerve fibers originating in the posterior root of the spinal cord and are situated in a welling in the posterior root called the posterior root ganglion. Afferent fibers carry nervous impulses back to the nervous system, transmitting information about sensations of touch, pain, temperature, and vibration.

Age. Alzheimer's disease is very rarely seen in younger patients (early-onset Alzheimer's disease). Most cases are late-onset, with the incidence of developing it increasing with advancing age. Up to the age of 65, Alzheimer's disease develops in only 1 person in 1000. However, approximately 5 percent of people older than 65 are affected, and although there are reports that 25–45 percent of individuals older than 85 are affected by dementia, statistics show that 20 percent of people older than age 80 develop Alzheimer's disease and 26 percent of people older than age 85 develop Alzheimer's disease. (Munoz, David and Howard Feldman, "Causes of Alzheimer's Disease," *Canadian Medical Association Journal*, 2000 162; 65–72)

Age-associated memory impairment. While it has long been suspected that memory loss is a normal part of aging, researchers at Washington University's Alzheimer's Disease Research Center conducted studies that prove otherwise. The results of their research indicate that individuals who show signs of age-associated memory impairment eventually go on to develop dementia, suggesting that these symptoms may represent a dementia prodrome rather than a benign variant of aging. (Department of Neurology and the Alzheimer's Disease Research Center, Washington University, St. Louis Missouri, 2001)

Agency for Healthcare Research and Quality (AHRQ). The Agency for Healthcare Research and Quality works to improve the quality, appropriateness, and effectiveness of health care, and to improve access to health services. One of its chief responsibilities is the dissemination of research-based information to medical practitioners, consumers and other healthcare professionals. The agency funds a number of research projects and sponsors 12 Evidence-Based Practice Centers to aid clinicians, health plans and health insurance purchasing groups. The AHRQ website offers a large library of current articles on Alzheimer's disease and its treatment, http://www.ahrq.gov.

Aggression. Aggression refers to hostile, injurious or destructive behavior or outlook especially when caused by frustration. Aggression, agitation or psychosis occurs in the majority of people with dementia at some point in the illness. Temporary pharmacological therapies are used to reduce symptoms of aggression but because psychotropic medications can cause cardiovascular risks their use is not generally recommended as part of a therapeutic protocol. (Ballard, C., and J. Waite. "The effectiveness of atypical antipsychotics for the treatment of aggression and psychosis in Alzheimer's disease," *Cochrane Database Systematic Review*, Jan 2006 (1): CD003476)

Aging process. Aging is the major risk factor of Alzheimer's disease in the general population. The aging process also causes certain changes that contribute to the development of Alzheimer's disease in genetically susceptible individuals. Some pathogenic factors directly associated with aging include oxidative damage from free radicals and mutations in messenger RNA that impair neurotransmitters and growth factors. Some of the histological changes seen in the brains of patients with Alzheimer's disease, such as beta amyloid plaque formation, are also seen in the elderly, although to a lesser extent. *See also* Taub Institute for Research on Alzheimer's Disease and the Aging Brain

Agitation. Agitation refers to an incessant condition of being bothered, disturbed or troubled. Agitation is characterized by an inability to sit still or concentrate. In Alzheimer's disease, agitation may be triggered by fear, fatigue, a change in environment, or by an infection or another medical problem. Therefore, it is important to receive a medical evaluation to look for treatable causes of agitation. If a medical problem does not exist, then the agitation can be managed using medication and behavioral techniques to simplify the patient's routine and distract him or her from the stress that caused the problem. Drugs used to treat agitation include anti-psychotic, anti-anxiety, and antidepressants. ("Treating agitation in Alzheimer's disease patients," Web MD, 2009, http://www.webmd.com/alzheimers/guide/treating-agitation, accessed Dec 15, 2010)

Agnosia. Agnosia is a condition characterized by the inability to recognize objects when using a given sense such as sight, even when that sense is intact. Agnosia is derived from the Greek word for lack of knowledge. A person with visual agnosia would not be able to recognize objects by sight although he may be able to recognize them by hearing. In neuropsychological testing, visual, auditory, and tactile recognition abilities are measured in a test of cerebral cortex function.

Agoraphobia. Agoraphobia is a condition of anxiety about being in places or situations from which escape may be perceived to be difficult or impossible. Agoraphobia often leads to an unwillingness to leave the home setting. Agoraphobia may occur alone or in conditions of panic disorder.

Agraphia. Agraphia is a condition of expressive writing dysfunction, indicating a lesion at the posterior-frontal area of the brain. Patients with agraphia are unable to express themselves in writing.

Aisen, Paul. Paul Aisen, M.D., is the current director of the Alzheimer's Disease Cooperative Study. Since 2007 he has worked as a professor in the Department of Neurosciences, University of California, San Diego. A graduate of Harvard University and Columbia Medical School, Aisen served in 1999 as the director of the Department of Neurology, Georgetown University Medical Center in Washington, DC where he established the Memory Disorders Program. In February 2011, Dr. Aisen was appointed to the Scientific Advisory Board of Anavex Life Sciences Corporation, the developer of Anavex 2-73, which is being studied for Alzheimer's disease and is scheduled to enter Phase I clinical trials in early 2011.

Akathisia. Akathisia is a condition of restlessness in which patients cannot sit still and feel compelled to walk or pace. Akathisia is a clinical feature of Alzheimer's disease that can also occur as a side effect of neuroleptic drugs.

Alexia. Alexia is a condition of visual receptive aphasia, indicating parietal-occipital disease. Patients with alexia are unable to understand written words.

Allele. An allele is one of the possible forms of a gene. For instance, the Apolipoprotein E gene has three forms, or alleles, known as 2, 3, or 4. Individuals have 2 alleles for each gene, one from each parent. Various alleles are known to cause a greater susceptibility to or protection against various diseases.

Alpha lipoic acid. Alpha lipoic acid is a naturally occurring antioxidant that is also available as a dietary supplement. Alpha lipoic acid has been reported to offer neuro-protection in neurodegenerative diseases. It demonstrates excellent blood-brain barrier penetration and acts as a metal chelator for ferrous iron, copper and cadmium and also participates in the regeneration of endogenous antioxidants, including the body's natural stores of vitamins E and C and glutathione. *See also* Dietary supplements used for the treatment of Alzheimer's disease

Alpha secretase enzyme. Alpha secretase in an enzyme found in nerve cells that competes with beta secretase in splicing amyloid precursor protein. When alpha secretase makes the first cut in the precursor protein, another enzyme, gamma secretase, produces a second cut that results in an innocuous protein fragment known as P3. When beta secretase makes the first cut, beta amyloid protein is produced. For this reason, alpha secretase is considered protective against the development of Alzheimer's disease.

Alpha synuclein. Alpha synuclein is a protein that builds up in the brains of individuals with Parkinson's disease. In studies, mice with both beta amyloid and alpha synuclein deposits develop Lewy body dementia and movement problems sooner than mice with only alpha synuclein. (Proceedings of the National Academy of Sciences 2001, 10.1073)

Alternative medicine. Alternative medicine refers to a number of therapies such as massage, acupuncture, dietary supplements, and herbal medicine therapies that are used either alone or as complementary treatments to enhance conventional therapies. In the United States, the National Center for Complementary and Alternative Medicine (NCCAM) offers detailed information on various alternative medicine therapies that have been tested in clinical trials. Information on alternative medicine is available at http://nccam.nih.gov/health/alzheimer/, website last updated in Jan 2011 and accessed Feb 5, 2011. The Life Extension Foundation at www.lef.org also has extensive information on natural therapies, including herbal therapies that are used as prescription drugs for Alzheimer's disease in Europe and as dietary supplements in the United States such as phosphatidylserine. *See also* Acupuncture; Herbal therapy; Niacinamide

Aluminum deposits. Early research suggested a causative association between aluminum deposits and Alzheimer's disease. However, the matter is still up for debate. A number of studies have failed to establish a definitive connection. When aluminum is injected into an animal brain, it produces an acute encephalopathy accompanied by neuronal inclusions that resemble neurofibrillary tangles. These aluminum-induced tangles are now known to be of a different composition when compared to the neurofibrillary tangles characteristically seen in Alzheimer's disease. However, a number of studies have found that increased levels of aluminum in drinking water are associated with Alzheimer's disease, and aluminum plays a pivotal role in beta amyloid production.

An important reason aluminum is suspected of contributing to Alzheimer's disease is the dementia commonly seen in dialysis patients who are exposed to aluminum as part of their treatment. The acute encephalopathy of dialysis patients has indeed been traced to the aluminum in dialysis water, confirming that aluminum is neurotoxic for humans if it reaches the brain, but, neither the clinical syndrome nor the pathological changes in dialysis patients resemble those seen in Alzheimer's disease. Furthermore, a number of studies of aluminum in tap water, the ingestion of antacids containing aluminum, and workers exposed to aluminum dust and fumes show no increased risk of developing Alzheimer's disease.

Although aluminum ingestion has not been proven to contribute to Alzheimer's disease development, studies show that the concentration of aluminum in the brains of individuals with Alzheimer's disease is high and its distribution is non-uniform. Therefore, the problem is suspected by some researchers to be one of faulty metabolism, rather than increased ingestion of aluminum. Aluminum causes the development of free radicals that injure the brain and promote inflammation. Researchers at the University of Toronto found a 250 percent increased risk of aluminum exposure in individuals who had been

drinking water with high levels of aluminum for ten years. Experts emphasize the importance of reducing exposure to aluminum by avoiding deodorants that contain aluminum, especially aerosols; aluminum cookware; and antacids with aluminum hydroxide.

Researchers at the University of Tennessee in Knoxville hypothesize that a critical mass of metabolic errors co-localized in specific areas of the brain is essential to produce Alzheimer's disease. Aluminum is a known neurotoxin, which has been shown to participate in formulating this critical mass by interfering in the metabolism of glucose and iron, and by proteolytic processing of beta-amyloid precursor protein. (Joshi, Jayant et al. "Iron and Aluminum Homeostasis in Neural Disorders," *Environmental Health Perspectives* 102, Supplement 3, September 1994)

Alz-50. Alz-50 is a protein antigen seen in increased levels in the neurons of patients with Alzheimer's disease. Alz-50 is a suspected marker for neurons that will eventually exhibit tangles. Antibodies to Alz-50 react with the brain tissue of Alzheimer's disease patients. As a reagent used in laboratory studies, Alz-50 is used as a monoclonal antibody to help stain autopsy specimens in an effort to help diagnose Alzheimer's disease.

Alzheimer, Alois (*b.* Markbreit, Germany, 1864; *d.* Frankfurt am Main, Germany, 1915). The German physician Alois Alzheimer is the first physician to recognize and document the disease named after him. Excelling in science, Alois Alzheimer studied medicine in Berlin, Tubingen, and Wurzburg where he graduated in 1887. He began work in the state asylum in Frankfurt am Main primarily studying the cortex of the human brain. He eventually created a brain research laboratory at the Munich Medical School.

Alzheimer published many papers on brain disease, and in 1906 he presented a lecture that made him famous. In this lecture, Alzheimer described a woman identified as Auguste D. with an unusual disease, exhibiting symptoms of memory loss, disorientation, hallucinations, and premature death at age 55. When Alzheimer first examined Auguste in 1901, the patient, described as appearing healthy although underweight, had a history of neglecting household chores, hiding objects, becoming fearful of acquaintances, and aimlessly pacing around her apartment. Alzheimer noted that the patient, while primarily articulate, was spatially and temporally disoriented and over time her symptoms worsened. At autopsy, the woman's brain was found to have deposits of plaque and neurofibrillary tangles. Alzheimer attributed her symptoms to a disease of the cerebral cortex, and Dr. Kraepelin, a renowned neurologist, named the disease after Alzheimer. Alzheimer was appointed to chair the department of psychology at the Friedrich-Wilhelm University in 1913, and developed a severe cold complicated by endocarditis, from which he never fully recovered.

Alzheimer Research Forum. The Alzheimer Research Forum in an Internet organization devoted to advances, research publications and news about Alzheimer's disease. http://www.alzforum.org/, accessed Feb 27, 2011.

Alzheimer's Association. The Alzheimer's Association, which is also known as The Alzheimer's and Related Disorders Association, is the largest national voluntary health organization committed to finding a cure for Alzheimer's and helping those affected by the disease. The twin goals of the association are protecting individuals with dementia who participate in research and encouraging dementia research to go forward. One or more chapters of the national organization are located in almost every city in the United States. Chapters regularly sponsor educational activities that are open to the public. The Alzheimer's Association uses a two-person logo symbolizing help and hope for those impacted by the disease. The Alzheimer's Association also sponsors an annual National Alzheimer's Disease Education Conference where researchers can exchange ideas on practical yet innovative approaches to Alzheimer's care. Website offers online courses, research publications, information on housing, and caregiving. (http://www.alz.org/index.asp, accessed Jan 3, 2011)

Alzheimer's Disease Anti-inflammatory Prevential Trial (ADAPT). The Alzheimer's Disease Anti-inflammatory Prevential Trial (ADAPT) was a 2001 National Institutes of Health funded project designed to evaluate the use of the anti-inflammatory agents naproxen

and celecoxib to protect the brain and prevent the onset of Alzheimer's disease in first-degree relatives of patients with Alzheimer's disease. Enrollment began in March 2001 and ended in December 2004 when treatments were suspended because of concerns regarding cardiovascular safety of the treatments. Follow-up ranged from 1 to 46 months. The achieved enrollment was 2,528. Recruitment was achieved primarily via mailings to people aged 70+ living in the catchment areas of the six field sites. (ADAPT Research Group. "Alzheimer's disease anti-inflammatory prevention trial: Design, methods, and baseline results," *Alzheimer's and Dementia. Journal of the Alzheimer's Association*, 2009, 5(2): 93-104. Abstract available at http://www.alzheimersanddementia.org/article/S1552-5260(08)02984-1/abstract, accessed Mar 1, 2011)

Alzheimer's Disease Assessment Scale Cognition Component (ADAS-Cog). The Alzheimer's Disease Assessment Scale (ADAS-Cog) developed by Rosen, Mohs and Davis is a well-validated multi-item test battery administered by a psychometrician (technician trained to perform tests used in psychological evaluation). The ADAS-Cog is a reliable instrument for measuring changes in memory and cognition. It evaluates 11 items, including aspects of memory, attention, praxis, reason and language and takes about 30 minutes.

The worst possible score is 70. Higher scores reflect poorer performance, and positive numerical changes from baseline score during clinical trials represent a worsening in cognitive ability. Elderly, normal adults may score as low as 0 or 1 unit, but individuals without dementia may score higher.

The ADAS-Cog score is reported to deteriorate at a rate of about 2 to 10 units per year for untreated patients with mild to moderate dementia. The ADAS-Cog is a useful tool in diagnosing dementia and in assessing the efficacy of therapeutic agents.

Alzheimer's Disease Centers of the NIA. The National Institutes of Aging Division of the National Institutes of Health has created 30 federally funded Alzheimer's Disease Centers that are located throughout the country. The centers specialize in Alzheimer's disease research.

Each center specializes in one particular area of expertise, and all the centers work together, sharing data and coordinating their efforts. Listing of centers is available on the NIA website at http://www.nia.nih.gov/Alzheimers/ResearchInformation/ResearchCenters/, accessed Jan 2, 2011.

Alzheimer's disease, clinical course. Alzheimer's disease (AD) is a chronic, progressive neurodegenerative disorder characterized by impairment of memory, thinking, behavior, and emotion. AD is the most common cause of dementia, and it is the fourth leading cause of death in the United States. One of the most prominent symptoms of AD is that patients forget things that they have just said or done, although they remember events from the past clearly. Other common symptoms include confusion, poor judgment, agitation, withdrawal, and hallucinations. In its early stages, AD is characterized by progressive loss of memory and orientation with preservation of motor, sensory, and linguistic abilities. It eventually evolves into global impairment that affects multiple cognitive functions.

Alzheimer's disease has a mean life expectancy of 8–10 years after onset of symptoms, with a range of 1–25 years. Three distinct stages occur in this disease, with the last stage ending in death, usually from secondary causes. Symptoms in the three stages may overlap, and individual symptoms and their severity may vary from patient to patient. Although the clinical signs of AD are generally predictable, there are no definitive clinical signs or laboratory tests available to diagnose AD. The customary clinical practice is to exclude other causes of dementia and give the patient a diagnosis of probable Alzheimer's disease. A definitive diagnosis can only be made by brain biopsy or autopsy.

The gross pathology of the brain in Alzheimer's disease is characterized by diffuse atrophy, particularly in the areas of the brain known as the cortex and hippocampus. Over time, patients with AD experience a progressive loss of nerve cells in both the gray matter of the brain and in the hippocampus, which governs memory. Pathological changes seen at autopsy include premature, severe diffuse atrophy of brain tissue, particularly in the frontal lobes. Neuropathological hallmarks of the brain tissue in AD include senile (neuritic) plaques, neurofibrillary tangles, and neuronal loss throughout the cerebral cortex. Additional pathology includes granulovacuolar changes and accumulation of lipofuscin. Loss of cholinergic neurons leads to deficiencies of the neurotransmitter acetylcholine. These features are also found to a lesser extent in the normal aging population.

There are three distinct types of Alzheimer's disease: 1) a sporadic disorder that accounts for about 75 percent of all cases; typically develops in patients older than 65, with chances of developing it increasing with age; 2) a familial disorder that accounts for about 25 percent of all cases; most familial disorders are late-onset, developing in individuals older than 65; less than 5 percent of all instances of Alzheimer's disease are early-onset familial with the mean age of onset usually before age 65; early onset familial Alzheimer's disease (EOFAD) can be further divided into subsets depending on the causative gene; 3) a disorder that accompanies Down Syndrome and represents less than 1 percent of all cases of Alzheimer's disease. Alzheimer's disease is also known as senile dementia/Alzheimer's type, diffuse brain atrophy and primary degenerative dementia. *See also* Dementia of the Alzheimer's Type; Diagnostic criteria for Alzheimer's disease; Epidemiology; Etiology of Alzheimer's disease; Reisberg's seven stages of Alzheimer's disease; Stages of Alzheimer's disease; Symptoms.

Alzheimer's Disease Clinical Trials Database. The Alzheimer's Disease Clinical Trials Database is a joint effort of the Food and Drug Administration and the National Institute on Aging, which lists about 5,000 clinical studies primarily sponsored by the National Institutes of Health. Here you can find comprehensive trial information, learn how to sign up for specific trials, receive updates and get information on drug development. (Clinical Trial Information, http://www.nia.nih.gov/Alzheimers/ResearchInformation/ClinicalTrials/, accessed Mar 2, 2011)

Alzheimer's Disease Cooperative Study (ADCS). The Alzheimer's Disease Cooperative Study (ADCS), established by the National Institute of Aging (NIA) in 1991, is a national consortium of 83 ADCS medical research centers and clinics in the United States and Canada co-ordinated by the University of California, San Diego (UCSD). The ADCS consortium was first organized under a cooperative agreement between the National Institutes of Health (NIA) and UCSD. During its first decade, the ADCS established a network of leading researchers who have carried out 13 clinical trials [involving 2,500 participants] for promising new therapies. Previous studies have investigated the use of vitamin E, selegiline, and estrogen therapy. Current projects include clinical trials involving the effects of a cholesterol-lowering statin drug, antioxidant therapy, valproic acid therapy, and a high dose vitamin regimen. The ADCS is also developing evaluation tools for Alzheimer's disease prevention research. Since 2007, Paul Aisen, M.D., has served as the director of the ADCS.

Alzheimer's Disease Cooperative Study–Clinical Global Impression of Change (ADCS-CGIC). Introduced by the National Institute on Aging's Alzheimer's Disease Cooperative Study in 1996, the ADCS-CGIC is a neuropsychiatric evaluation tool for assessing the efficacy of treatment. The ADCS-CGIC consists of three parts, including a semi-structured baseline interview administered to both the patient and an informant with knowledge of the patient's condition, a follow-up interview after treatment, administered to both the patient and informant, and a clinician's rating interview based on his impressions of the interviews, administered before and after treatment.

The ADCS-CGIC evaluates 15 parameters related to cognition, behavior, social skills and daily functioning. The global rating is based on the second interview and is graded by a 7-point scale: 1 = very much improved, 2 = much improved, 3 = minimally improved, 4 = no change, 5 = mild worsening, 6 = moderate worsening, 7 = marked worsening. (Schneider, L.S., Jason Olin, et al. "Validity and Reliability of the Alzheimer's Disease Cooperative Study-Clinical Global Impression of Change," *Alzheimer Disease: From Molecular Biology to Therapy*, edited by R. Becker and E. Giacobine. Boston: Birkhäuser Publishing, 1996, 425–429)

Alzheimer's Disease Demonstration Grants to States (ADDGS) Program. Administered through the Administration of Aging Division of the U.S. Department of Health and Human Services, The Alzheimer's Disease Demonstration Grants to States (ADDGS) Program is an award of more than $8 million in grants. The awards were given to 25 states in 2000 and 2001 to develop effective models of intervention to serve persons with Alzheimer's disease and their families and caregivers. The goal of this program is to expand the availability of diagnostic and support services for individuals with Alzheimer's disease and their families and caregivers. The program also aims to improve the responsiveness of home and community-based care for individuals with Alzheimer's disease. The primary focus of the program is areas that are hard-to-serve, including rural areas. Detailed information about the state programs, including family education and outreach information in several languages can be found at www.nia.nih.gov, accessed Feb 4, 2011.

Alzheimer's Disease Education and Referral (ADEAR) Center. The Alzheimer's Disease Education and Referral (ADEAR) Center operated by the National Institute of Aging provides information to health professions and the public on Alzheimer's disease and other conditions of memory impairment. (800) 438-4380, http://www.alzheimers.org, accessed Dec 10, 2010.

Alzheimer's Disease International. Alzheimer's Disease International is a worldwide confederation of Alzheimer's disease associations. The international groups provide advice, training, educational support, advocacy, informational brochures and helplines and access to the World Report. (http://www.alz.co.uk/, accessed Mar 1, 2011)

Alzheimer's Disease Neuroimaging Initiative (ADNI). In 2003 a group of scientists from the National Institutes of Health, the Food and Drug Administration, the pharmaceutical and medical-imaging industries, universities, non-profit groups and research centers joined in a collaborative effort to find the biological markers that show the progression of Alzheimer's disease in the human brain. The project, which was christened the Alzheimer's Disease Neuroimaging Initiative, located at the University of

California, Davis, is an initiative aimed at improved methods which will lead to uniform standards for acquiring longitudinal, multi-site MRI and PET data on patients with AD, MCI, as compared to normal elderly controls. Its goals are to acquire a generally accessible data repository that describes longitudinal changes in brain structure and metabolism.

In parallel, the initiative will acquire clinical cognitive and biomarker data for validation of imaging surrogates and develop optimal methods to determine treatment effects in trials involving these patients. In addition, members of the group will test a series of hypotheses based on the clinical and biomarker data as outlined in the statistical analysis section of the protocol. For information on clinical trials in this program, see http://alzheimer.ucdavis.edu/research/projects.php.

Alzheimer's Disease Research Program. The Alzheimer's Disease Research (ADR) Program, which began in 1985, currently funds 22 outstanding biomedical researchers in the United States, Canada, and Europe. Alzheimer's Disease Research invites applications for both Standard Awards and Pilot Project Awards. For further information and to access the program's resources, see http://www.ahaf.org/alzheimers/, accessed Feb 22, 2011.

Alzheimer's Project *see* HBO Alzheimer's Project

Ambulation. Ambulation refers to the ability to walk without assistance. Patients with intact ambulation are said to be ambulatory.

American Association of Homes and Services for the Aging. The American Association of Homes and Services for the Aging is a non-profit organization that sponsors the Continuing Care Accreditation Commission, a group that inspects and certifies care facilities for the elderly. This agency also aids individuals in locating housing, adult day care, companion services and assisted living or nursing home care. Financial assistance that is available depends on the type of service, your local community and the type of insurance that you have. (800) 272-3900, http://www.aahsa.org/, accessed Mar 1, 2011.

American Health Assistance Foundation. The American Health Assistance Foundation (AHAF) is a non-profit charitable organization dedicated to funding research on Alzheimer's disease, providing educational resources about Alzheimer's disease to the public. 16825 Shady Grove Road, Suite 140, Rockville, Maryland 20850, (800) 437-2423, http://www.ahaf.org.

American Journal of Alzheimer's Disease. The *American Journal of Alzheimer's Disease* is a medical publication dedicated to the management and treatment of patients with Alzheimer's disease. Subscription information, information on receiving a free trial copy, and a cumulative subject index of past articles can be found at http://aja.sagepub.com/.

Amino acids. Amino acids are chemical molecules, or building blocks, that link into molecular chains to form protein. Some amino acids also have the ability to act as neurotransmitters that aid in the communication of nervous system signals. Amino acids are made of nitrogen and carbon units bonded together to form various shapes and sizes with specific properties. Some amino acids also contain sulfur. Humans possess about 20 different types of naturally occurring amino acids, which are supplied by animal or plant proteins. The most important of these are glutamate and its derivative gamma-aminobutyric acid (GABA).

Some amino acids are altered slightly before they can be used as neurotransmitters. For instance, the amino acid tyrosine, which is found in cheese, is converted into at least two neurotransmitters, dopamine and norepinephrine. Tryptophan, an amino acid found in high concentrations in milk and turkey, is converted into the neurotransmitter serotonin. When a large amount of tyrosine is consumed, tryptophan absorption is inhibited since tyrosine and tryptophan compete for absorption sites in the gut.

Used as therapy the amino acid 5-hydroxytryptophan has been used in doses of 800 mg daily to raise serotonin levels in patients with Alzheimer's disease, and up to 4 grams of tyrosine have been used to raise dopamine levels. Both of these therapies are reported to offer some benefits for patients with Alzheimer's disease.

Ampakines. Ampakines are a class of drug compounds that were developed for their possible role as therapeutic agents in Alzheimer's disease, schizophrenia and other neurological disorders. Ampakines modulate synaptic responses on neurotransmitter receptors, and their benefits are thought to compensate for deficiencies of certain neurotransmitters such as glutamate. Ampakines exert their action by binding to α-amino-3-hydroxy-5-methyl-4-isoxazolepropionic acid (AMPA)-type glutamate receptors, which mediate synaptic transmission in the central nervous system.

Specific effects include increased alertness and attention span and improvements in memory and learning. Some researchers suspect that ampakines can also change information encoding and organization in the brain. Four ampakine subtypes have been developed including: the pyrrolidine derivative racetam drugs such as piracetam and aniracetam; the CX series of drugs, such as CX-516, which include benzoylpiperidine and benzoylpyrrolidine compounds; the benzothiazide derivatives such as cyclothiazide and IDRA-21; and the biarylpropylsulfonamides such as LY-392,098, LY-404,187, LY-451,646 and LY-503,430. Several of the ampakines are under current investigation as therapies in Alzheimer's disease.

Ampalex *see* CX 516

Amvid. Amvid is a copyrighted diagnostic imaging technique approved by the FDA in 2011 for use in patients with suspected Alzheimer's disease. This procedure can detect plaque build-up in the brain and provide early warning of the first signs of the disease. However, the approval is contingent on training for radiologists who must interpret the brain scans, which will be marketed by a company called Avid Radiopharmaceuticals. The test will be offered under the brand name Amvid. (American Council on Science and Health, Jan 24, 2011, Press Release http://www.acsh.org/factsfears/newsid.2276/news_detail.asp, accessed Feb 4, 2011)

AMY 117. AMY 117 is a protein found in the areas of the brain affected by Alzheimer's disease. AMY 117 forms plaques that resemble beta amyloid so closely that it can only be differentiated with sophisticated techniques.

Amygdaloid nucleus (amygdala). The amygdaloid nucleus (amygdala) of the brain's limbic system is an almond-shaped area situated partly anterior and partly superior to the tip of the inferior horn of the lateral ventricle. Destruction of the amygdaloid nucleus and its surrounding area in patients with aggressive behavior results in a decrease in aggressiveness, emotional instability and restlessness. Neurons in the amygdala as well as the neocortex, the entorhinal area, hippocampus, nucleus basalis, anterior thalamus, and several brain stem monoaminergic nuclei show signs of neurodegeneration in Alzheimer's disease.

Amyloid. Amyloid is a type of protein primarily composed of amyloid beta-peptide that is encoded within the larger beta amyloid precursor protein gene on chromosome 21 from which it is derived.

Amyloid angiopathy. Amyloid angiopathy is a cerebrovascular condition that almost invariably accompanies Alzheimer's disease. In this condition, the same amyloid protein deposits found in senile plaques also form deposits in the blood vessels serving the brain, reducing blood flow and inducing clot formation. Studies indicate that APOE gene polymorphism is a risk factor, influencing hemorrhage in cerebral amyloid angiopathy.

Amyloid beta (β) peptide (Abeta). Amyloid beta peptides are harmless fragments derived from the proteolytic process (enzyme degradation) of amyloid precursor protein (APP).

Amyloid beta (β) peptide antibody. Amyloid beta (β) peptide antibodies are naturally occurring antibodies that target and destroy beta amyloid protein. Amyloid beta peptide is produced by normal cells and can be detected in the plasma and cerebrospinal fluid. In studies, mice immunized with amyloid beta vaccines (to stimulate production of amyloid beta antibodies) or administered antibody to amyloid beta, showed dramatically reduced plaque deposits, neuritic dystrophy and reactive gliosis by astrocytes.

Amyloid Beta Protein. Amyloid beta protein, which is also known as β-amyloid, A beta, Aβ or beta amyloid protein (BAP), is a generic name for a class of sticky proteins found in the brains of patients with Alzheimer's disease. Amyloid beta protein consists of 38 to 43 amino acids. Several genes influence the type or specific amino acid sequence of beta amyloid protein that is formed. The longer forms, particularly those that end in 42 amino acids, have an increased propensity to aggregate into polymers and plaque deposits. These forms are also most likely to produce neuronal damage.

Amyloid beta protein in blood vessels is produced by smooth muscle cells. Derived from amyloid precursor protein (APP), amyloid beta protein has a molecular weight of 4 kD. A peptide protein, it is comprised of 11–15 amino acids of the transmembrane domain and 28 amino acids of the extracellular domain of APP.

Amyloid beta protein forms plaques on the outsides of brain cells. These plaques are found outside nerve cells surrounded by the debris of dying neurons. These plaques grow so dense that they trigger an inflammatory reaction from immune system cells located in the brain. This immune response destroys brain cells.

Amyloid beta protein is a subunit protein or fragment derived from its precursor, amyloid precursor protein (βAPP), by a mechanism known as proteolytic processing. More precisely, beta amyloid is formed by nerve cells when the enzymes beta and gamma secretase cause APP to split into uneven fragments. The slightly longer variant is directly toxic to nerve cells. Among other things, BAP appears to stimulate the release of oxygen free radicals, triggering a destructive biochemical cascade in the brain.

β-amyloid is produced by all cell types and is not unique to neurons. In fact, Aβ is produced and secreted as a soluble peptide protein during normal cell metabolism. The amyloid beta protein deposits seen in Alzheimer's disease are identical to the amyloid beta protein produced in the brain cells of normal individuals. Amyloid beta protein may have either neurotrophic or neurotoxic effects depending on neuronal age, protein concentration, and the presence of fetal or adult neurons. Neurotrophic effects may reside in the first 28 residues of Aβ since there is evidence of neurite outgrowth and neuronal survival in these forms. However, there is much evidence for the neurotoxic effects of Aβ. Aβ causes increases in intracellular calcium, induces apoptosis, activates

microglia, enhances oxidative damage and enhances the vulnerability of neurons to excitotoxicity and hypoglycemic damage. Neurotoxicity appears to be dependent on the length and aggregation of the amyloid beta fragment, with some fragments influencing hydrogen peroxide accumulation in cells, resulting in free radical-induced lipid peroxidation and cell death.

Amyloid beta protein tends to aggregate and form diffuse deposits as well as amyloid cores in the brain of patients with Alzheimer's disease. Senile neuritic plaques in Alzheimer's disease consist of beta amyloid cores surrounded by activated microglia, fibrillary astrocytes and dystrophic neuritis (neurites and axonal terminals). The type of amyloid beta protein seen in senile neuritic plaques exerts neurotoxic effects, causing neuronal degeneration. Deposits of amyloid beta protein are thought to be an early and obligatory event, preceding the development of tau-positive paired helical filaments, the substances that make up neurofibrillary tangles. However, amyloid beta protein deposits are also seen in normal aging, suggesting that it is the maturation or density of plaque deposits, or shifts in the pathways that produce or remove Aβ, that are critical to Alzheimer's disease development.

High levels of beta amyloid are also associated with reduced levels of the neurotransmitter acetylcholine and are suspected of disrupting channels that carry the elements sodium, potassium and calcium. These elements serve the brain as ions, producing electric charges that must fire regularly in order for signals to pass from one nerve cell to another. If the channels that carry ions are damaged, the resulting imbalance can interfere with nerve function and signal transmission.

Although it was once thought to be metabolically inert, beta amyloid is now known to damage neuronal processes, place them at risk for injury and stimulate cell death by apoptosis in response to excitotoxins. In non-neuronal cells, amyloid beta can also affect signal transduction processes.

Amyloid hypothesis. The notion that Alzheimer's disease is directly caused by increased beta amyloid protein formation is known as the amyloid hypothesis.

Amyloid plaques. Amyloid plaques are deposits or aggregates of beta amyloid protein found on the nerve cells of patients with Alzheimer's disease. Amyloid plaque may occur as diffuse deposits or in the amyloid core of senile neuritic plaque formations. *See* Senile neuritic plaques.

Amyloid Precursor Protein (APP). Amyloid precursor protein (APP) is the parent protein from which beta amyloid protein is derived. By a splicing or proteolytic process, APP is broken down into fragments. Depending on which secretase enzymes initiate the process, beta amyloid protein may be a harmless peptide chain or a longer form with more amino acids and more

propensity to damage neurons and form plaque. Recent studies indicate that a defect in APP rather than beta amyloid protein may be the underlying cause of Alzheimer's disease.

Amyloidosis. Amyloidosis is the generic term used to describe a number of diseases, including Alzheimer's disease, that have abnormal deposits of amyloid fibrils and plaques in specific organs. These abnormal plaque deposits eventually lead to organ failure. In systemic amyloidosis there is widespread distribution of amyloid deposits in several different organs of the body.

AN-1792 vaccine. AN-1792 is a synthetic form of the 42 amino acid beta amyloid protein. AN-1792 was formulated into a vaccine intended to reduce symptoms in Alzheimer's disease by preventing or reversing amyloid plaque formation, neuritic dystrophy, synaptic loss and gliosis.

AN-1792 was developed by Ireland's Elan Corporation at its San Francisco branch, in conjunction with Wyeth Ayerst Laboratories in New Jersey. Clinical trials were suspended in 2002 because of brain inflammation occurring in four test subjects. (Fact Sheet on AN-1792, Alzheimer's Disease Association, http://www.alzdsw.org/pdf_docuents/factsheets/an-1792.pdf, accessed Jan 2, 2011)

Anavex Life Science Corporation. Anavex Life Sciences Corporation is a publicly traded specialty pharmaceutical company engaged in the discovery and development of novel drug candidates for the treatment of neurological diseases and cancer. The Anavex proprietary SIGMACEPTOR Discovery Platform involves the rational design of drug compounds targeted to specific receptors involved in the modulation of multiple cellular biochemical signaling pathways. The SIGMACEPTOR-N program involves the development of novel drug candidates

BETA-AMYLOID PRECURSOR PROTEIN (bAPP)

CELL

ALPHA-GAMMA SECRETASE ENZYME

BETA-GAMMA SECRETASE ENZYME

P3 FRAGMENT (HARMLESS)

40-AMINO ACID BETA AMYLOID (HARMLESS)

TOXIC 42-AMINO ACID BETA AMYLOID

TOXIC BETA-AMYLOID BUILDS UP OUTSIDE OF THE CELLS

THE Microglia AND OTHER CELLS REACT TO THE TOXINS, FORMING PLAQUES WHICH DAMAGE THE DENDRITES OF THE NEURONS.

MICROGLIA

Amyloid Plaque Formation (illustration by Marvin G. Miller).

that target neurological and neurodegenerative diseases (Alzheimer's disease, epilepsy, depression, pain). The company's lead drug candidates exhibit high affinity for sigma receptors, which have been extensively documented as potentially valuable drug targets and have demonstrated anti-amnesic and neuroprotective properties. (http://www.anavex.com, accessed Feb 16, 2011)

ANAVEX 2-73. ANAVEX 2-73, developed by Anavex Life Sciences Corporation, is an experimental drug that will be evaluated in phase I clinical trials in early 2011. ANAVEX 2-73 is the first of a new class of oral, disease-modifying drugs being studied to potentially treat Alzheimer's disease itself, versus treating its symptoms. ANAVEX 2-73's mode of action produces a unique sigma-1 receptor agonism as well as muscarinic and cholinergic effects. ANAVEX 2-73 also modulates endoplasmic reticulum stress, causing it to trigger a series of intracellular effects thought to modify ion channel signaling at the mitochondrial level. On March 15, 2011, Anavex Life Science Corporation received approval from the German regulatory health authority, BfArM, to begin Phase I clinical trials of ANAVEX-2-73. The trial, which includes testing in healthy human volunteers, will begin immediately and will assess the safety, maximally tolerated dose, pharmacokinetics and pharmacodynamics of ANAVEX 2-73. The Phase I clinical trial of ANAVEX 2-73 will be carried out in collaboration with ABX-CRO and the University of Dresden in Germany. (Anavex Life Sciences Corporation press release, March 15, 2011, http://anavex.com/press_release_2011_03_15, accessed March 18, 2011)

Angiography. Angiography is an imaging technique used to detect blood vessel abnormalities. Cerebral angiography is used to detect and diagnose space-occupying lesions such as tumors, hematomas, or abscesses. Cerebral angiography is performed under general anesthesia, with the patient in the supine position using contrast dye. Cerebral angiography is an invasive technique with a morbidity of 0.5 to 2.5 percent. (Snell, Richard, M.D. *Clinical Neuranatomy for Medical Students*, Third Edition. Boston: Little, Brown and Company, 1992)

Animal models. Animal models are experimental studies conducted on animals, which are used to determine the etiology or underlying causes, of diseases and to assess treatment or to evaluate the safety of therapies. In animal model studies, animals (usually mice or rats) are subjected to certain factors, including environmental agents, to determine if disease symptoms develop under similar conditions to those seen in humans with the disease. In animal treatment models, animals are subjected to drugs and other therapies to determine if symptoms of disease are reversed and to assess the therapies for potential signs of toxicity.

Anomia. Anomia is a condition characterized by problems with names. Patients with anomia frequently confuse the names of relatives, for example, substituting daughter for mother or father for husband. Anomia also refers to the inability to recall the correct word (on the tip of the tongue).

Anorexia. Anorexia is a prolonged loss of appetite. A common symptom of Alzheimer's disease, anorexia may lead to nutrient deficiencies and wasting syndrome.

Anosmia. Anosmia is an inability to smell. There are several causes, some due to neuropathology, such as tumors of the base of the frontal lobe or pituitary area, arteriosclerosis, cerebrovascular disease, meningitis, hydrocephalus, and post-traumatic brain syndrome. *See* Odor identification test.

Anthocyanins. Anthocyanins are potent antioxidants found in fruit, vegetables and red wines. In many countries anthocyanin products are used as medications. In 2001, researchers at Michigan State University identified the presence of three anthocyanins and plant chemicals known as bioflavinoids in tart cherries. These compounds inhibit Cyclooxygenase 1 and 2 enzymes and prevent inflammation in the body. Their actions are similar to those of ibuprofen. Twenty cherries contain 25 mg of anthocyanins, an amount sufficient to inhibit the enzymes responsible for inflammation. Anthocyanin compounds in blueberries have been shown to reduce cognitive symptoms in patients with dementia. (Ilkay, Jasmine. "Blueberry buzz: Research investigates supplements' effects in multiple health conditions," *Today's Dietician*, 2010, 7 (12): 18, http://www.todaysdietitian.com/newarchives/06 2810p18.shtml, accessed Dec 14, 2010)

Antibodies. Antibodies are proteins known as immunoglobulins produced by the immune system to help protect against infectious agents. Antibodies are produced when individuals are exposed to infectious agents or given vaccines that contain specially treated forms of infectious agents. Serum and cerebrospinal fluid from some Alzheimer's disease patients contain an antibody that specifically recognizes amoeboid microglial cells. Studies suggest that microglial antibodies may be indicative of an ongoing degenerative process. Their presence may have diagnostic potential even in the early stages of Alzheimer's disease.

Anti-inflammatory drugs. Anti-inflammatory drugs, including non-steroidal anti-inflammatory drugs (NSAIDs) and steroids, are often used to treat the inflammatory process associated with Alzheimer's disease. Studies indicate that non-steroidal anti-inflammatory agents offer therapeutic value in Alzheimer's disease by preventing the production of amyloid beta protein. However, corticosteroids used long-term may actually cause memory loss and, unlike NSAIDs, do not appear to affect prostglandins, substances that appear to be related to the development of Alzheimer's disease.

Although researchers once suspected that anti-inflammatory drugs worked by inhibiting cyclooxygenase (COX) enzymes, it is now known that certain anti-inflammatory agents, particularly ibuprofen, reduce levels of amyloid-beta 42, a protein incriminated in the formation of plaque deposits. Indomethacin and sulindac are also effective in reducing levels of amyloid-beta 42 when high doses are used. (Greenwell, Ivy. "New light on how ibuprofen protects against Alzheimer's disease," *Life Extension*, February, 2002, 23)

Antioxidant therapy. Antioxidant vitamins and minerals function to prevent damage associated with free radicals, ions that lack coupling molecules. Free radicals are responsible for oxidative cell death associated with amyloid beta protein, hydrogen peroxide, and the excitatory amino acid glutamate. Many antioxidants, particularly vitamins E and C, have been shown to protect neurons from this damage. A placebo-controlled clinical trial of vitamin E (at a high dose of 2000 IU daily), the drug selegiline, or both, found that treatment with either compound delayed disease progression in patients with moderately severe Alzheimer's disease. Combinations of different antioxidants have been the subject of several clinical trials conducted by the National Center for Complementary and Alternative Medicine (http://nccam.nih.gov/health/alzheimer/). The most promising results have been seen with the antioxidant know as grapeseed oil extract.

Apathy. Apathy is a lack of feeling or emotion characterized by withdrawal and an inability to react with feeling to one's environment. Apathy is a common symptom in Alzheimer's disease and may be confused with depression. An apathetic person lacks emotions, motivation, interest, and enthusiasm while a depressed person is generally very sad, tearful, and hopeless.

Aphasia. Aphasia is a condition of an inability to use language. Aphasia is caused by destruction of the cells of the brain in areas that govern language. The two most common types of aphasia are Broca's aphasia and Wernicke's aphasia. Most neurological patients have some intact communication function. In tests used to evaluate aphasia, certain areas of dysfunction are diagnostic for certain conditions. Auditory receptive aphasia is associated with lesions at Wernicke's area of the temporal lobe, whereas visual receptive aphasia (alexia) indicates a lesion at the parietal-occipital area. Expressive speaking aphasia is associated with a lesion at Broca's area of the frontal lobe, whereas expressive writing aphasia (agraphia) is located with a lesion at the posterior frontal area. Global aphasia, which involves both expressive and receptive aphasias, indicates extensive lesions of Broca's area, Wernicke's area, the parietal-occipital area, and the posterior frontal area.

Aphasia-agnosia-apraxia syndrome *see* Pick's disease

Apoaequorin. Apoaequorin is a calcium-binding protein, derived from the *Aequorea victoria* jellyfish, and was patented in 2007 as the dietary supplement Prevage by Quincy Bioscience, a Madison, Wisconsin, research-based biotechnology company. In July 2010 scientists from Quincy attended the Alzheimer's Association International Conference on Alzheimer's Disease (ICAD) and shared information from the Madison Memory Study, a randomized controlled trial, which shows the jellyfish protein apoaequorin improves cognitive function in individuals with memory concerns. In this study, thirty-five generally healthy adults reporting memory concerns prior to the start of the trial showed a 14 percent improvement in cognitive scores after using apoaequorin for 60 days. Calcium-binding proteins are essential for maintaining intracellular calcium levels, and imbalances associated with age-related cognitive decline.

Apolipoprotein A (APOA). Apolipoprotein A (APOA) is a protein normally found in the body. Apolipoprotein A is produced in the small intestine and liver and helps prevent coronary heart disease because of its ability to clear cholesterol from the body. APOA is also thought to help reduce levels of beta amyloid. According to a study funded by the U.S. Public Health Service, increasing APOA levels may help prevent or delay the dementia associated with Alzheimer's' disease. Some foods, including fruits, soybeans, coconut oils, and some wines and teas can stimulate cells to produce more APOA.

Apolipoprotein E (APOE). Apolipoprotein E (APOE) is a naturally occurring protein found in the body. APOE is produced primarily by the liver, but is also produced by cells in the brain and adrenal glands and by macrophage cells in the circulation. In the brain, APOE is produced and secreted by astrocytes in the hippocampus. Research suggests that APOE is involved in cholinergic synaptic remodeling following injury to neurons in the entorhinal cortex. As both a free and a bound protein, APOE circulates between the cells of the brain and also within some neurons, suggesting multiple metabolic functions.

The APOE gene on chromosome 19 is associated with the development of Alzheimer's disease. APOE has three allelic variants, APOE2, APOE3, and APOE4. Everyone inherits one allele for APOE from each of their parents re-

sulting in five common genotypes — 2/3, 3/3, 2/4, 3/4 and 4/4. The APOE 4 allele is strongly associated with Alzheimer's disease and may represent an important risk factor for the disease.

Overall, APOE4 may account for more than 60 percent of all cases of late onset Alzheimer's disease. People who carry it do not necessarily develop Alzheimer's disease, but if they do, their brains appear more riddled with plaques and tangles than the brains of Alzheimer's patients with slightly different versions of the APOE gene. APOE4 also appears to have a broad impact on the well-being of nerve cells. People who are homozygous for APOE4, meaning they carry two identical alleles or copies of APOE4 have more difficulty recovering from strokes and traumatic head injuries, and they're more likely to sustain brain damage during cardiovascular surgery.

Allele 4 of the APOE gene has a dose-related effect on risk and the age of onset for late-onset familial Alzheimer's diseases as well as sporadic cases of the early onset form, whereas allele 2 appears to offer protection. The alleles apolipoprotein E 2, 3, and 4 all have different binding strengths. The APOE4 allele appears to promote the binding of amyloid beta protein, facilitating the formation of plaque deposits. An immunoreactive form of APOE has been found in the neurons containing neurofibrillary tangles in patients with Alzheimer's disease. Studies are being conducted to see what role APOE has in the abnormal phosphorylation of tau protein.

Patients with alleles e4/e4 have a 95 percent chance of developing Alzheimer's disease by 80 years of age, and patients with the rare e2/e2 rarely develop Alzheimer's disease. Although the presence of the APOE4 allele may be associated with cognitive decline in older persons, the APOE genotype alone is not considered useful in predicting whether an individual will develop Alzheimer's disease.

In one study, both the magnitude and the extent of brain activation during memory-activation tasks in regions affected by Alzheimer's disease, including the left hippocampal, parietal, and prefrontal regions, were greater among the carriers of the APOE4 allele than among carriers of the APOE3 allele. During periods of recall, individuals with the APOE4 allele had a greater average increase in signal intensity in the hippocampal region and a greater number of activated regions throughout the brain. Longitudinal assessment after two years indicated that the degree of baseline activation correlated with degree of decline in memory.

APOE is found in the cytoplasm of neurons. It regulates neurite outgrowth and sprouting of dorsal root ganglia neurons in vitro. It also appears to be involved in mobilization and redistribution of cholesterol in repair, growth, and maintenance of myelin and neuronal membranes during development or following injury. APOE, along with the more benign amyloid P and glycosaminoglycans may act as chaperones that mediate β-pleated amyloid formation from amyloid beta protein. APOE is found in senile plaques, vascular amyloid deposits and neurofibrillary tangles (NFTs). APOE is also present in hippocampal neurons in Alzheimer's disease even in the absence of NFTs. The APOE domain exhibits an isoform-specific association in that the E4 isoform segregates with a higher risk of the disease. Peptides derived from the receptor binding domain of apolipoprotein E have also been found to be toxic to neurons.

Recent studies indicate that patients with E4 are more likely to respond to drug treatment designed to reduce beta-amyloid formation than patients without E4. Results of the Nun Study show that individuals without the E4 allele are more likely to maintain high levels of cognitive function in old age. (Bookheimer, Susan, et al. "Patterns of Brain Activation in People at Risk for Alzheimer's Disease," *New England Journal of Medicine*; 343 (7): 450. Sabbagh, Marwan, et al. "β-Amyloid and Treatment Opportunities for Alzheimer's Disease," *Alzheimer's Disease Review*, 3:1–19 1998)

Apolipoprotein E Genotype. The apolipoprotein E gene on chromosome 19 is linked to Alzheimer's disease. Specifically, the apolipoprotein E 4 allele has been found to increase the risk for Alzheimer's disease in genetically diverse populations in Asia, the Americas and Europe. However, the risk is lower in Africans and African-Americans.

Aolipoprotein E plays a role in the transport and redistribution of lipids and is implicated in the growth and repair of injured neurons in the nervous system. Everyone inherits one allele for APOE from each of their parents resulting in five common genotypes — 2/3, 3/3, 2/4, 3/4 and 4/4. Two common polymorphisms of this gene exist, resulting in three isoforms, APOE e2, e3, and e4. The APOE4 allele is over-represented in Alzheimer's disease. APOE4 homozygotes (patients having both 2 copies of e4) have a 95 percent chance of developing Alzheimer's disease by age 80. These individuals may have a reduced ability to suppress amyloid fibril formation and an increased susceptibility for amyloid beta protein production. Besides its association with Alzheimer's disease, the epsilon 4 allele of apolipoprotein E is associated with higher lipid concentrations and higher risk of cardiovascular disease.

Several studies suggest that the APOE 4 allele is also present in greater frequency in persons with Lewy body disease, dementia pugilistica, and Pick's disease. Although the frequency of Alzheimer's disease is relatively similar in most populations, the allele frequencies vary significantly in different racial and ethnic groups. In some populations, the APOE 2 allele may increase risk for Alzheimer's disease.

Because Alzheimer's disease develops in the absence of the APOE 4 allele and because many people with this allele do not develop Alzheimer's disease, genetic testing for this allele is not recommended for use as a predictive genetic test. Testing for the APOE genotype would be helpful, however, in diagnosing early-onset dementia when diagnosis is uncertain. (Farrer, Lindsay, Ph.D. "Statement on Use of Apolipoprotein E Testing for Alzheimer Disease," American College of Medical Genetics, Bethesda, MD 1995)

Apolipoprotein J *see* Clusterin

Apolipoproteins. Lipoproteins are lipid substances normally present in the body. High density lipoproteins (HDLs) can be divided into subtypes apolipoprotein A, B, C and E. The major apolipoprotein, apolipoprotein A-1, sets the plasma level of HDL and appears to confer protection against the development of atherosclerosis. Higher levels of Apolipoprotein A-1 are associated with a low tendency toward developing congestive heart disease. All of the apolipoprotein subtypes have distinct roles and contribute to the body's total lipoprotein level.

Apoptosis. Apoptosis is a term referring to programmed cell death. All of the body's cells, including neurons or brain cells, have a certain life span. Apoptosis may be disrupted in two major ways, each of which is associated with different types of disease. Inappropriate activation of apoptosis leads to disorders such as the wide array of neurodegenerative conditions associated with pathological cell loss. Inappropriate apoptosis or extended cell survival leads to diseases associated with excessive accumulation of cells. Examples include cancer, chronic inflammatory conditions and autoimmune diseases.

An increasing body of indirect evidence suggests that neuronal cell apoptosis may be triggered by amyloid β deposits and other neurotoxic abnormal protein structures or aggregates such as those seen in Alzheimer's disease. Proteolytic enzymes called caspases are critical to the control of apoptosis. Researchers are currently working on developing therapeutic agents that inhibit capases, reducing accelerated apoptosis in neurodegenerative diseases.

Apoptosis-Related Gene 3 (ALG-3). The Apotosis-Related Gene 3 (ALG-3) codes for a partial complementary DNA that is homologous to the familial Alzheimer's gene STM2 and rescues cells from normal pathways of apoptosis.

Appearance. Appearance is often relevant to the diagnosis of mental disorders. Patients with Alzheimer's are often poorly groomed and sometimes dirty. It is not unusual for patients with Alzheimer's to adapt unusual modes of dress such as many layers of clothing or to wear clothing inappropriate for the season or temperature.

Apraxia. Apraxia is a condition characterized by the inability to perform an action, even though the muscles required are perfectly capable of performing the action in a different context. An apraxic patient might be unable to touch her nose with her index finger when asked to do so by an examiner, even if the examiner performed the motion. However, the same patient could perform the movement if her nose itched. Apraxia often accompanies certain forms of aphasia and is caused by damage or injury to areas of the brain associated with motor skills

and cortical motor integration. Apraxia is derived from the Greek word for lack of action.

Arachnoid mater. The arachnoid mater is a delicate impermeable membrane that covers the spinal cord and lies between the pia mater internally and the dura mater externally. The arachnoid mater is separated from the pia mater by a wide space known as the subarachnoid space, which is filled with cerebrospinal fluid.

Archicortex. The archicortex refers to the area of the cerebral cortex that covers the hippocampal formation.

Aricept *see* Donepezil hydrochloride

Arnold Pick's disease *see* Pick's disease

Art therapy. Art therapy is a form of therapy in which patients are encouraged to draw, color, or paint as a creative outlet. Art therapy is included as an activity in many nursing homes and adult day care programs.

Ashwaganda (Withania somnifera). Ashwaganda (Withania somnifera), which is commonly known as winter cherry, is an herbal preparation that is reported to offer benefits for patients with Alzheimer's disease. Ashwaganda reduces inflammation, reduces free radical damage, and enhances the effect of the neurotransmitter acetylcholine. Inflammation, free radical damage, and low acetylcholine levels are all considered contributing factors for the development of Alzheimer's disease. Ashwaganda contains bioflavonoid antioxidant compounds and other active ingredients of the withanolide class. These phytochemicals are thought to account for ashwaganda's many medicinal roles. Researchers from the Paul Flechsig Institute for Brain Research, University of Leipzig, Germany, and researchers in India have discovered that ashwaganda increases acetylcholine receptor activity in the brain and it is this that partly explains its cognition and memory enhancing effects in humans.

In addition, other researchers have discovered that ashwaganda stimulates the growth of axons and dendrites in human nerve cells. This may help in repairing damaged neuronal circuits (brain pathways) in the aging brain, while helping prevent the loss of other neurons and synapses. Ashwaganda also has mild sedative properties, enhances mood, and it is reported to improve sleep and behavior in those suffering from Alzheimer's disease or other forms of dementia.

Aspirin in Alzheimer's disease. The use of the analgesic compound in Alzheimer's disease has been evaluated because of its effects on reducing inflammation. While a positive effect was found on cardiac status, there was a slight increase of cerebral hemorrhage, which the researchers felt should not preclude its use. (Thoonsen, Hanneke, et al. "Aspirin in Alzheimer's disease: Increased risk of intracerebral hemorrhage: Cause for concern?" *Stroke*, 2010, 41: 2690-2692)

Assisted living. Assisted living, which is also known as residential care, is a housing option for older adults who are able to live alone but need some assistance with personal care. In many assisted living communities, residents may opt to have one or more meals provided by the facility. If the need for care increases, some assisted living facilities require that the resident transfer to a nursing home. Check with your local Area Agency on Aging to see if there are any subsidized assisted living facilities in your area.

Assisted-living costs. Costs for assisted living residences range from less than $1,000 monthly to more than $3,000 monthly, depending on the services and accommodations offered. The facility's charges reflect the number of services to which the resident has access, such as meals, help administering medications and laundry services. In addition to basic charges, there may be extra charges for some services. The cost may also vary according to the size of the room or apartment provided.

In some states, funds are available for those who cannot afford assisted living. In those states, the service components of assisted living may be paid by Medicaid if the state has applied for and been approved under a home and community-based waiver. The waiver is for persons who are determined to be eligible for nursing home care. The resident may then use Supplemental Security Income (SSI) to pay for the room and board costs. (American Associations of Homes and Services for the Aging)

Assisted-living facility. In assisted living facilities, residents live in private apartments, usually with kitchenettes and bathrooms in complexes that have staff available to help residents eat, bathe and dress. In some facilities, meals, housekeeping, laundry and transportation are provided. Although medical care is not provided, the staff will often supervise medications. Assisted living facilities do not have to follow the stringent guidelines required by long-term care facilities. Some facilities charge extra for minor assistance and as needs increase, a home health aide may be necessary. Furthermore, facilities in many states can evict residents with little notice as their level of care increases.

Up to one-half of all patients in assisted living facilities are reported to have dementia. One-quarter of all assisted living facilities in the U.S. offer special wings or pods for individuals with Alzheimer's disease and other forms of dementia. The annual cost of a private room in an assisted living facility is about $27,000, less than two-thirds the cost of a nursing home. Long-term care insurance policies generally help pay for assisted living. It is important when selecting an assisted-living facility to find out what provisions they have for patients who may eventually require full-term care and to know what safeguards the facility has in place to protect patients who may be inclined to wander from the facilities.

Astrocytes (Astroglial cells). A type of neuroglial cell found in the brain, astrocytes produce proteins that promote neuronal growth or survival and growth factors that stimulate the growth of microglial cells. Microglia, in turn, produce mitogens that activate astrocytes. Astrocytes also offer protection to neurons under attack by inflammatory cells.

With branching processes that extend in all directions, astrocytes may be fibrous or protoplasmic. Fibrous astrocytes are primarily found in the white matter, where their processes travel between nerve fibers. Protoplasmic astrocytes are primarily found in the gray matter, where their processes pass between the nerve cell bodies.

Many of the terminal processes of astrocytes link to blood vessels, netting capillaries into clusters and forming the glial limiting membranes

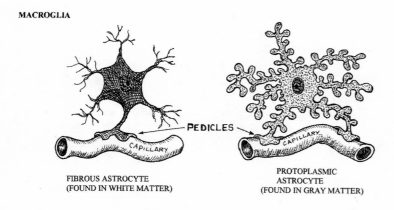

MACROGLIA

PEDICLES

CAPILLARY

FIBROUS ASTROCYTE
(FOUND IN WHITE MATTER)

PROTOPLASMIC
ASTROCYTE
(FOUND IN GRAY MATTER)

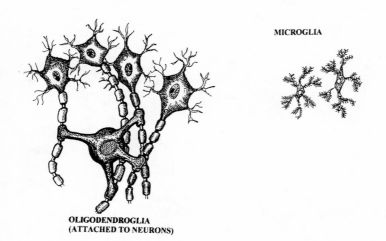

MICROGLIA

OLIGODENDROGLIA
(ATTACHED TO NEURONS)

Astrocytes and Microglial Cells (illustration by Marvin G. Miller).

of the central nervous system. Astrocytic processes are also found near the initial segment of most axons.

Astrocytes form a supporting framework for nerve cells and nerve fibers. By covering the synaptic contacts between neurons they may play a role in insulating axon terminals and preventing them from influencing other neurons. Astrocytes may also form barriers for neurotransmitters, and they are known to act as immune system scavengers, engulfing and destroying damaged neurons. Astrocytes store glycogen within their cytoplasm. In response to norepinephrine, the glycogen can be broken down into glucose and released to surrounding neurons.

At home assisted living. A brainchild of Sunrise Assisted Living, an industry founder 20 years ago, at home assisted living provides the services of assisted living in a person's own home. Special services include emergency response buttons and devices that store medications and remind patients to take their medications at the right time. If the patient does not comply, an alarm is sounded at the main Sunrise offices.

Ataxia. Ataxia is a disturbance of voluntary movement frequently seen in cerebellar disease. In individuals with ataxia, the muscles contract irregularly and weakly. Tremor may occur during fine movements such as writing and shaving. Muscle groups fail to work together and there is decomposition of movement. When asked to touch the tip of his nose with index finger, the patient fails to make contact.

Atherosclerosis. Atherosclerosis is an inflammatory condition causing plaque deposits within blood vessels. When these lesions block blood flow to the brain they may cause symptoms of dementia. While plaque build-up is regularly seen in the normal elderly population, it is an increased density or accumulation of plaque that leads to disease. Atherosclerosis is caused by a combination of cholesterol and immune system changes that result in inflammation.

Atrophy. Atrophy is a condition of increased cell destruction that results in shrinkage of tissue. Cerebral atrophy is typically seen in patients with Alzheimer's disease and it is also seen in the normal elderly population. However, in Alzheimer's disease, cerebral atrophy is associated with neurofibrillary tangles and senile plaques.

Atypical antipsychotic medications. Atypical antipsychotic medications are a class of drugs that include quatrain, olanzapine and risperdone. These drugs have been studied for their effects in Alzheimer's disease patients with psychosis and found to cause untoward side effects, including an increased risk of mortality. (Osterweil, Neil. "Atypical antipsychotics get poor grade for Alzheimer's psychoses," *Med Page Today*. Available at http://www.medpageto day.com/Neurology/AlzheimersDisease/4273, accessed Jan 12, 2011). *See also* Quetiapine fumarate

Autoimmune encephalopathy. Encephalopathy refers to any diffuse disease of the brain that alters brain function or structure. Encephalopathy has many causes, including infections, toxins, and autoimmunity. An increasing number of cases of autoimmune encephalopathy have been reported in recent years, and in some cases autoimmune encephalopathy causes a rapidly progressive form of dementia.

Some cases of autoimmune encephalopathy, such as Hashimoto's encephalopathy, are caused by thyroid autoantibodies, and some cases are paraneoplastic, which means that they have an association with cancer (and the immune system's response to the cancer, usually small lung cell cancer; ovarian, breast or testicular cancer; thymoma; or Hodgkin's lymphoma). Paraneoplastic neurological disorders (PNDs) often present as a rapidly progressive limbic encephalopathy. When the central nervous system is involved, there may be cerebellar syndromes, retinal degeneration, depression, personality changes, memory impairment or amnesia.

A number of autoimmune disorders may cause encephalopathy and rapidly progressive dementia. These disorders include connective tissue disorders, vasculitis and granulamatous conditions, including primary angiitis of the central nervous system (PACNS); polyarteritis nodosa (PAN); sarcoidosis, systemic lupus erythematosus (SLE); Sjogren's syndrome; celiac disease; Behcet's disease; and hypereosinophilic syndrome. Because autoantibodies directed against amyloid beta protein and neuronal components have been found in the circulation of some individuals with Alzheimer's disease, a number of researchers are investigating the possibility of Alzheimer's disease being an autoimmune disorder initiated by an erratic autoimmune response, perhaps as a result of molecular mimicry related to a latent viral infection. (Geschwind, Michael, Aissa Haman, and Bruce Miller. "Rapidly progressive dementia," *Neurologic Clinics*, August 2007, 25(3), available online at PubMedCentral, http://www.ncbi.nlm.nih. gov/pmc/articles/PMC2706263, accessed Sept 22, 2010. D'Andrea, MR. "Add Alzheimer's disease to the list of autoimmune diseases," *Medical Hypotheses*, 2005, 64 (3): 458-63, abstract available at http://www.ncbi.nlm.nih.gov/pubmed/ 15617848, accessed Mar 1, 2011). *See also* Encephalopathy; Hashimoto's encephalopathy

Autonomic nervous system. The autonomic nervous system refers to the part of the nervous system concerned with the innervation of involuntary structures, such as the heart, smooth muscles, and glands. The autonomic system has two major components: the sympathetic and the parasympathetic systems.

Autopsy. Autopsy is a procedure performed after death in which all of the internal organs of the body are examined to determine the cause of death. A brain autopsy is the final confirmation of an Alzheimer's disease diagnosis. If other forms or causes of dementia are also present, an autopsy will reveal this. A brain autopsy involves removal and examination of brain tissue for the characteristic structures, senile plaques and neurofibrillary tangles typically associated with Alzheimer's disease. Arrangements for autopsy should be made no less than 30 days prior to death. The cost of the autopsy may be reduced if the brain is donated for research.

Brain autopsy in Alzheimer's disease consists of an examination of the tissue. A microscopic count of the number of silver-staining (argyrophilic) plaques and neurofibrillary tangles is performed and compared to the number normally seen for the patient's age group. The National Institutes of Health has established minimal criteria for the pathologic diagnosis of Alzheimer's disease. For patients less than 50 years old, more than 2 neorcortical plaques plus more than 2 neurofibrillary tangles/any 20X magnified field are diagnostic for Alzheimer's disease, whereas in patients older than 75 years, more than 15 neocortical plaques are diagnostic.

Avlosulfon *see* Dapsone

Axon. Axons are long processes or neurites that arise from the central cell body of neurons or nerve cells. Axons are the main way by which neurons transmit or pass on information to other neurons. Axons generally arise from a small conical elevation on the cell body called the axon hillock. Occasionally, however, axons may arise from the proximal part of a dendrite. Axons have smooth surfaces and, although their diameter varies among different neurons, individual axons have uniform diameters.

Axons tend to branch away from the cell body, forming collateral branches along their length. Near the point at which they terminate, axons generally form profuse branches with enlarged distal ends called terminals. Axons may be very short, particularly in the nervous system or they may be long, for instance when extending from a peripheral receptor in the toe to the spinal cord. The initial segment arising from the axon hillock is the most excitable part of the axon and it is the site at which an action potential originates (*see* Excitation of nerve cells).

Axona. Axona is an FDA-approved medical food available by prescription that targets metabolic deficiencies associated with Alzheimer's disease. It has been shown in a Phase 2 clinical trial to improve cognition and memory in patients with mild to moderate disease. Medical foods were defined in 1988 as a special category of products intended for the specific dietary management of a disease or condition that has distinctive nutritional requirements, established by medical evaluation.

Axona can be taken safely alone or with other commonly prescribed Alzheimer's disease medications (acetylcholinesterase inhibitors and NMDA receptor antagonists), as no significant interactions have been observed. The most common adverse events observed in clinical trials were diarrhea, flatulence, and dyspepsia.

Ayurveda. Ayurveda is an ancient medical tradition with roots in India. Ayurveda uses herbs to treat dementia. For instance, winter cherry or ashwaganda (*Withania somnifera*) demonstrates antioxidant and anti-inflammatory properties in laboratory studies and it enhances the tolerance of stress in animals. Brahmi (*Herpestis monniera*) improves motor skills as well as the ability to learn and retain information. These herbs are used in Ayurvedic medicine to reduce symptoms in patients with Alzheimer's disease.

Babinski's sign. Normally, in response to stroking the sole of the foot, the big toe flexes and the other toes fan out. This is known as Babinski's sign. Absence of Babinski's sign is indicative of upper motor neuron lesions.

BACE1 enzyme. The BACE1 enzyme has been implicated as the enzyme responsible for the destructive plaques found in the brains of Alzheimer's disease patients. BACE1 begins the process that cleaves or snips amyloid precursor protein, forming beta amyloid protein fragments that aggregate to form plaques. Therapies that inhibit BACE1 are being studied for their role as treatment agents in Alzheimer's disease. ("Scientists Zero In on Enzyme at Work in Alzheimer's Disease," *NIA News*, Feb 26, 2001. Cole, Sarah, and Robert Vassar, "The Alzheimer's disease β-secretase enzyme, BACE1," *Molecular Degeneration*, 2007, 2(22), http://www.molecular neurodegeneration.com/content/2/1/22, accessed Mar 1, 2010)

Balanced Budget Refinement Act. The Balanced Budget Refinement Act of 1999 requires Medicare to pay for skilled nursing care following hospitalization. In October 2001 the amount of Medicare payments for skilled nursing facilities increased by 2.1 percent following guidelines proposed by the Balanced Budget Act. Payment increased again in 2002, which brought it to its full payment rate.

Baltimore Longitudinal Study of Aging (BLSA). The Baltimore Longitudinal Study of Aging (BLSA), which started in 1958, is America's longest running scientific study of human aging. Information on data and publications can be found at http://www.grc.nia.nih.gov/branches/blsa/blsa.htm, accessed Feb 1, 2011.

Baptist. Baptist is a term used to describe scientists who adhere to the theory that the formation of beta amyloid plaque deposits is the underlying disease mechanism in Alzheimer's disease. The debate between the Baptists and Tauists has subsided in recent years with the realization that both plaques and tangles may be the result rather than the cause of cellular changes in Alzheimer's disease.

Basal forebrain. The basal forebrain is a loosely used term that refers to the area at and near the inferior surface of the telencephalon, between the hypothalamus and the orbital cortex. Rich in cholinergic neurons, the basal forebrain reaches the surface of the brain in the anterior perforated substance, extending superiorly into the septal area.

Basal ganglia. The basal ganglia are a group of nuclei that form part of each cerebral hemisphere. Internally located, they are only visible in surgical sections of the hemispheres. The major basal ganglia are the caudate and lenticular nuclei.

Basal nuclei. The term basal nuclei refers to a collection of masses of gray matter located within each cerebral hemisphere. The three main basal nuclei include the corpus striatum, the amygdaloid nucleus and the claustrum.

Bazelon Center and Fund. Founded in 1972, the Bazelon Center for Mental Health Law is a nonprofit national legal advocacy organization for people with mental disabilities. The Center works to protect patients' rights and promote their access to needed services. The Fund, established in 1905, works with decision makers in the public and private sectors, using litigation, policy analysis, coalition building and technical support for local advocates to advance and protect the rights of adults and children with mental illness or developmental disabilities who rely on public services and to ensure their equal access to health and mental health care, education, housing, and employment. Bazelon Center for Mental Health Law, 1101 Fifteenth Street, NW, Suite 1212, Washington, DC 20005-5002, (202) 467-5730, www.bazelon.org, accessed Mar 1, 2011.

Beck Anxiety Inventory (BAI). The Beck Anxiety Inventory (BAI) is a 21-item self-administered evaluation tool that measures symptoms associated with anxiety. Initially used on cancer patients, it can be used in any disorder in which emotional symptoms occur.

Beck Depression Index (BDI). The Beck Depression Index (BDI) is a widely used evaluation tool that measures the severity of depression by evaluating 21 symptoms. A short form of the BDI (BDI-SF) consisting of 13 items is also used.

Behavioral and Social Research Program (BSR). The federal government's Behavioral and Social Research Program (BSR) division of the National Institute on Aging supports behavioral and social research and training on aging processes. It focuses on how people change over the adult life course and on the societal impact of the changing age-composition of the population. BSR fosters research that reaches across disciplinary boundaries, at multiple levels from the genetic to comparisons across national boundaries, and at stages from basic through translational. The BSR also supports numerous activities related to Alzheimer's disease including research on reducing the burden of care for caregivers and multidisciplinary studies on the design and effectiveness of special care units. (http://www.nia.nih.gov/ResearchInformation/ExtramuralPrograms/BehavioralAndSocialResearch/, accessed Jan 1, 2011)

Behavioral Pathology in Alzheimer's disease (BEHAVE-AD). The Behavioral Pathology in Alzheimer's disease (BEHAVE-AD) test is an evaluation tool used to evaluate emotional changes such as agitation in patients with Alzheimer's disease. This test, which provides a global rating of non-cognitive symptoms, is designed for use in assessing the efficacy of prospective clinical drugs.

Behavioral Rating Scale for Dementia. The Behavioral Rating Scale for Dementia is a questionnaire given to a patient informant by a trained interviewer. The questions focus on behavioral changes observed within the previous month. This assessment tool offers insight into the psychopathology of patients with dementia, including an evaluation of mood disorders, agitation, aggression, and psychotic symptoms.

Benton Visual Retention Test. The Benton Visual Retention Test is a neuropsychological test used to test memory and recall. Patients are shown pictures and later asked to recall what they saw. The test cutoff score is 6 or less. The Benton test assesses visual perception, visual memory and visuoconstructive abilities. There are three forms of the test, each consisting of 10 designs.

Berg, Leonard (1927–2007). Leonard Berg, a neurologist and former member of the U.S. Congress Advisory Panel on Alzheimer's Disease, was the first director of Washington University's Alzheimer's Disease Research Center in St. Louis. During the 1980s, Berg helped developed a series of tests to assess a patient's level of dementia by evaluating their abilities in language, memory, and everyday tasks. With these parameters, a numerical scale was established, with a 0 corresponding to no symptoms and a 3 representing severe symptoms. The tool developed into the Clinical Dementia Rating Scale, and has gained wide acceptance in Alzheimer's disease research.

Beta (β) Amyloid precursor protein (βAPP). Beta (β) Amyloid precursor protein (βAPP) is a transmembrane glycoprotein isoform or subtype of amyloid precursor protein (APP). βAPP can be between 695 and 770 amino acids long. βAPP is found on the cell surface of neurons where it matures. Its expression is stimulated by endogenous factors such as cytokines, growth factors, estrogens, head trauma and excitotoxicity. Increases in βAPP occur at the same time as neuronal differentiation. The cloning of the gene mutation coding for βAPP on chromosome 21 led to an understanding of the role of genes in conferring susceptibility to Alzheimer's disease. Beta APP may exist in different isoforms derived from alternative mRNA gene splicing. The gene products of Beta APP are expressed in different tissues, with the highest concentrations occurring in the brain.

Although the precise biological role of βAPP remains unclear, scientists have found that many kinds of cells and tissues produce βAPP. βAPP runs through the outer cell membrane, with a short piece jutting into the cell and a longer piece extending into the extracellular space (outside of the cell). Beta APP can be broken down or proteolyzed in two different ways resulting in extracellular secreted C-terminal truncated molecules or the beta-amyloid peptide product. The β-amyloid peptide is snipped out of the section of βAPP that spans the cell membrane.

Beta (β) amyloid protein (BAP). Beta amyloid protein (BAP) is a short 40–42 amino acid fragment of the transmembrane protein, β Amyloid precursor protein (β APP). It is the primary component of the senile plaques seen in the brain of patients with Alzheimer's disease and is thought to contribute to neuronal death. *See also* Amyloid beta protein; Senile neuritic plaque

Beta secretase (BACE). Beta secretase is an enzyme found in nerve cells that is essential for the production of beta amyloid protein. Beta amyloid protein is the primary constituent of the plaques responsible for neuronal death in the brains of individuals with Alzheimer's disease. Along with gamma secretase, beta secretase splices its precursor protein into uneven fragments, one of which results in a toxic version of beta amyloid protein. Inside nerve cells, beta secretase competes with an enzyme known as alpha secretase, an enzyme that may offer protection against Alzheimer's disease. Therapies including vaccines designed to inhibit beta secretase are currently being developed. *See also* BACE 1 enzyme

Beta-2 microglobulin. Beta 2 microglobulin is a precursor protein that breaks down into Abeta 2 M, a peptide increased in the amyloid disorder chronic hemodialysis arthropathy. Increased serum levels of beta-2 microglobulin result from reduced clearance by the kidneys. Alterations to beta-2 microglobulin may facilitate protein aggregation and fibril formation in neurons.

Binswanger's disease. Binswanger's disease is a rare form of vascular dementia distinct from Alzheimer's disease associated with stroke-related cerebral lesions in the brain. The trademark of this disease is damage to blood vessels in the white matter of the brain, particularly in the regions of the pons, basal ganglia and thalamus. These changes are discernible with magnetic resonance imaging (MRI) studies.

Patients with Binswanger's disease experience loss of memory and cognition and often show signs of hypertension, stroke, blood abnormalities, disease of the large blood vessels in the neck and disease of the heart valves. Other common symptoms include urinary incontinence, difficulty walking, Parkinsonian-like tremors, and tremors. However, not all patients have these symptoms, and symptoms are often transient. Sometimes, symptoms resolve and patients return to their pre–Binswanger selves. Symptoms generally occur after age 60. While treatment revolves around reducing blood pressure, there are reports of aspirin showing favorable results.

Bleomycin hydrolase. The gene for the enzyme bleomycin hydrolyase has been found to have an association with late onset Alzheimer's disease independent of that of the APOE 4 gene. This enzyme is suspected of playing a role in the formation of amyloid deposits in the brains of Alzheimer's patients.

Blessed, G. Blessed and his associates were the first to make the observation that most cases of dementia are caused by Alzheimer's disease. This initial observation was published in the *British Journal of Psychiatry* in 1968.

Blessed Dementia Rating Scale. The Blessed Dementia Rating Scale is a neuropsychiatric evaluation tool employing informant-based ratings of daily living skills in patients with dementia.

Blessed Test. The Blessed Test is a quick test of cognitive ability. The test assesses activities of daily living and evaluates memory, concentration and orientation.

Blood brain barrier. The blood brain barrier is a membrane separating the blood and the central nervous system. The strength of the barrier varies in different regions of the brain, and its permeability to various substances is variable and dependent on the size of the molecules. The barrier is almost impermeable to plasma proteins and other large organic molecules, whereas gas molecules, glucose, certain minerals, and water pass through freely.

Normally, the blood brain barrier protects us from potentially harmful substances. Certain drugs, however, especially lipid-soluble substances, are more readily able to enter the brain.

Blood tests for Alzheimer's disease. There are currently no blood tests available to diagnose Alzheimer's disease. A test is available to measure a specific protein (AD7c) in cerebrospinal fluid and urine that can help diagnose Alzheimer's disease. In addition, researchers at the Florida division of the Scripps Institute have isolated a protein in the blood of patients with Alzheimer's disease that may eventually be used as a diagnostic marker. ("Blood test for Alzheimer's disease?" *Science Daily*, Jan 7, 2011, http://www.science daily.com/releases/2011/01/110106071159.htm, accessed Mar 1, 2011). *See also* AD7c

Blueberries. Blueberries have long been found to improve memory. In the 1990s researchers from the Department of Agriculture at Tufts University tested the effects of blueberry supplementation on older animals. The data were so impressive that the researchers commented that treating Alzheimer's disease with diet was very possible. Other animal studies confirmed these results, and various universities began studying the bioactive phytochemicals in blueberries as well as the cognitive effects of blueberries in humans. Studies show that the phytochemical compound pterostilbene is primarily responsible for the cognitive improvement seen with blueberries. Similar to resveratrol, pterostilbene is a potent antioxidant that helps protect the heart and cardiovascular system. In addition, pterostilbene offers protection against diabetes. Researchers also found that the anthocyanins in blueberries increase levels of brain neutrophic factor which are necessary for proper cell signaling. (Sanchez, Ralph. "Blueberry polyphenols protect the brain from the degenerative processes associated with brain aging and Alzheimer's disease," *The Alzheimer's Solution. Com,* Feb 3, 2011, http://www.thealzheimerssolution.com/blue berry-polyphenols-protect-the-brain-from-the-degenerative-processes-associated-with-brain-aging-and-alzheimers-disease/, accessed Mar 17, 2011)

Board-and-care homes. In some communities, board-and-care homes provide another housing option for patients with dementia, especially those in the early stages who can no longer live independently. These homes are typically large homes that have been converted to provide accommodations for up to 20 residents. Residents generally share bathrooms, kitchens, living rooms and porches. Most of these facilities retain staff trained to help with personal care and meal preparation. In some facilities, meals are provided. If the need for healthcare increases, residents may be required to transfer to a nursing home.

Boston Naming Test (BNT). The Boston Naming Test, or BNT, is a psychological test used to measure language function, including naming ability. Developed by Kaplan, Goodglass, and Weintraub in 1983, the BNT is a confrontation-naming task, which presents line drawings of objects or actions and requires that the subject provide a word corresponding to each of the pictures.

Bovine spongiform encephalopathy (BSE). Bovine spongiform encephalopathy, a new variant of Creutzfeldt-Jakob disease commonly known as mad cow disease, is a disorder associated with the consumption of meat infected with prions. Gerald Wells and John Wilesmith of the Central Veterinary Laboratory in Weybridge, England, first recognized BSE in 1986, although there are early reports of its existence dated from 1980. The brains of animals affected by BSE are characteristic of prion disease. The brain tissue is riddled with holes, leading to severe neuronal loss, necrosis of the cerebral cortex, and ataxia. BSE has been traced to animal feed supplemented with meat and bone offal from contaminated dead sheep that might have been suffering from another type of prion spongiform encephalopathy, sheep and goat scrapie.

Braak and Braak Staging *see* Neuropathological staging of Alzheimer's disease

Brain. The brain is a central nervous system organ that lies in the cranial cavity. It is continuous with the spinal cord. Similar to the spinal cord, the brain is surrounded by three meninges, the dura mater, the arachnoid mater, and the pia mater.

Brain anatomy. The human brain contains three basic components: the hindbrain or rhombencephalon at the top of the spinal cord, the midbrain or mesencephalon and the forebrain or prosencephalon. Human brain development begins at about 14 days after conception. Cell division continues until about the eighth week when the three basic components of the brain

appear. The first weeks and months of fetal development are associated with rapid nerve cell development and differentiation. Cells with specialized functions migrate to specific areas of the brain. This migration affects how neurons differentiate into specialized cells.

Brain derived neurotrophic factor (BDNF). Brain derived neurotrophic factor is a growth factor encoded by the BDNF gene on chromosome 11. Neurotrophic factors are cytokines that influence nerve growth in the brain and peripheral nervous system. BDNF helps existing neurons survive and form new synapses and it helps regenerate new neurons. Polymorphisms to the BDNF gene can interfere with neuronal survival and neurogeneration. Drugs such as the ampakines are being investigated for their role in upregulating BDNF. In his book *Power Up Your Brain* (2011, Hay House) the neurologist David Perlmutter, M.D., explains ways to increase the body's production of BDNF. These include fasting, exercise, and calorie restriction. *See also* Val66Met polymorphism

Brain exercise. Numerous research studies have proven the concept of brain plasticity and have described ways in which the brain can increase its neural circuits. In his book, *The Better Brain* (Riverhead, 2004) the neurologist David Perlmutter describes the use of flashcards that help in recalling pictures and numbers. A number of software programs, including Brain Builder, are also recommended. Performing crossword puzzles and word games are also reported to offer benefits.

Brain imaging. Brain imaging is traditionally divided into 1) structural imaging (computed tomography or CT scan) and magnetic resonance imaging (MRI), techniques which reflect the anatomy of the brain; 2) functional imaging (single-photon emission tomography or SPECT and positron emission tomography or PET, techniques which assess cerebral function in relative or absolute terms. Sometimes, structural and functional imaging are combined into innovative techniques such as functional MRI.

Brain in Alzheimer's disease. Gross examination of the brain in Alzheimer's disease shows a variable degree of cortical atrophy (shrinkage

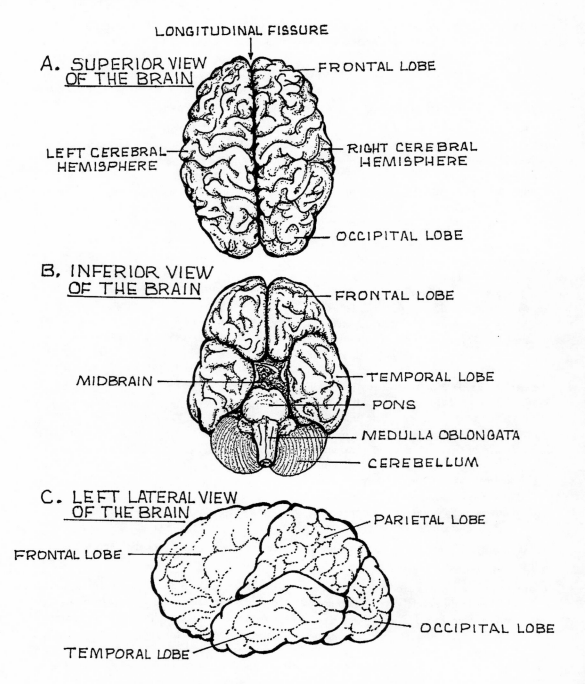

LONGITUDINAL FISSURE

A. SUPERIOR VIEW OF THE BRAIN

FRONTAL LOBE

LEFT CEREBRAL HEMISPHERE

RIGHT CEREBRAL HEMISPHERE

OCCIPITAL LOBE

B. INFERIOR VIEW OF THE BRAIN

FRONTAL LOBE

MIDBRAIN

TEMPORAL LOBE

PONS

MEDULLA OBLONGATA

CEREBELLUM

C. LEFT LATERAL VIEW OF THE BRAIN

PARIETAL LOBE

FRONTAL LOBE

OCCIPITAL LOBE

TEMPORAL LOBE

The adult brain (illustration by Marvin G. Miller).

of the cerebral cortex). There is a characteristic widening of the cerebral folds or sulci that is most pronounced in the frontal, temporal, and parietal lobes. When atrophy is significant, there is a compensatory enlargement of the ventricles secondary to loss of tissue or parenchyma.

Microscopic examination of the brain in Alzheimer's disease reveals nerofibrillary tangles, senile plaques, activated microglial cells, neuropil threads and amyloid angiopathy (deposits of beta amyloid protein in the blood vessels of the brain). A loss of neurons and synapses is prominent in specific areas, primarily the entorhinal and hippocampal areas, and in the neocortex. Tangles may not be involved in the cell loss of the neocortex. Synaptic loss can be measured in the cortex and hippocampal areas and occurs between and within areas of neuritic plaque.

All of these changes may be seen in patients without dementia although to a lesser degree and the distribution of these changes is markedly different. However, the diagnosis of Alzheimer's disease is based on a clinical correlation between the patient's neurologic or mental status and the frequency of plaques and tangles in the brain.

Brain injuries. Traumatic brain injury and Alzheimer's disease share similar clinical and pathological features that suggest common neurodegenerative mechanisms, including increases in amyloid precursor protein (APP), amyloid beta protein and tau protein. A dramatic increase in APP occurs in the first and third days after traumatic brain injury. It is suspected that injury-induced alterations in APP expression and processing may result in increased deposits of amyloid beta and initiation of Alzheimer's disease pathogenesis. *See also* Dementia pugilistica and Head injuries.

Brain plasticity. During the brain's development, as neurons mature each neuron sends out multiple branches (axons, which send information out; and dendrites, which take information in). During childhood the number of synapses (connections between neurons) increases. With age, weakened and ineffective synapses die and strong connections are reinforced and strengthened. By adulthood, most weak connections have been pruned away and the number of synapses per neuron declines to about half the amount seen in children. In the mid–1990s, researchers learned that even in advanced age, the brain continues to change and grow. Neuronal changes occur in the area of the synapses, and the number

Size of brain in man compared to that of the rhinoceros (illustration by Marvin G. Miller).

of synapses between neurons can increase as a consequence of numerous factors, including psychoactive drugs, hormones, vitamins, maturation, aging, diet, disease, and stress. Plasticity also encompasses the concept that learning tasks associated with certain areas of the brain such as playing musical instruments can increase synaptic connections in neighboring brain regions, improving math skills. ("Brain Plasticity, What Is It?" University of Washington, Seattle, at http://faculty.washington.edu/chudler/plast.html, accessed Dec 30, 2010. Kolb, Bryan, Robbin Gibb, and Terry Robinson. "Brain Plasticity and Behavior," *Current Directions in Psychological Science,* Feb 2003, 12 (3), http://www.psy.cmu.edu/~rakison/plasticity%20and%20the%20brain.pdf, accessed Mar 1, 2011)

Brain tumors. Brain tumors are frequently associated with organic brain syndromes. Gener-

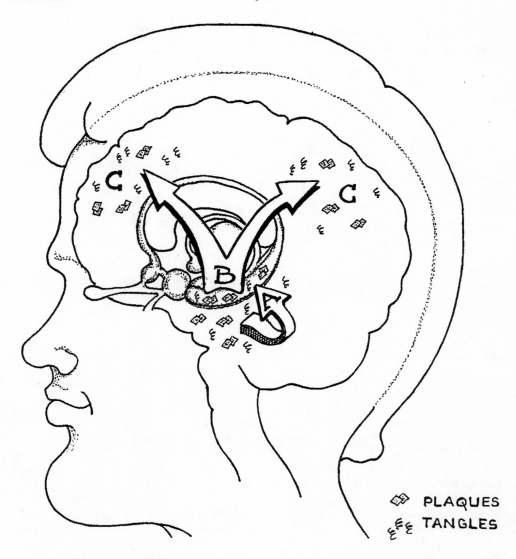

⟨⟩ PLAQUES
ƐƐƐ TANGLES

The brain in Alzheimer's disease (illustration by Marvin G. Miller).

ally, when brain tumors are present, there are also major focal findings and signs of increased intracranial pressure. However, brain tumors, especially those in the "silent" area of the brain, may present exclusively as a change of personality and intellectual decline. Subtle focal findings can usually be demonstrated on the neurologic examination, but they are occasionally lacking and require imaging tests for diagnosis. Symptoms may mimic those of Alzheimer's disease. (De-Kosky, S. "Over-expression of amyloid precursor protein after traumatic brain injury in rats and in human head-injured patients." [University of Pittsburgh] 2001)

Brainstem. The brainstem is a collective term referring to the medulla oblongata, the pons and the midbrain. The brainstem is the part of the brain that remains after the cerebral hemispheres and the cerebellum are removed. The brainstem plays a major role in cranial nerve function and is essential for conveying information to and from the cerebrum.

Brainstem Auditory Evoked Responses (BAER). Measurement of brainstem auditory evoked responses (BAER) is helpful in diagnosing demyelinating disease, posterior fossa tumors, cerebellar pontine angle tumors, stroke and

NORMAL CELLS

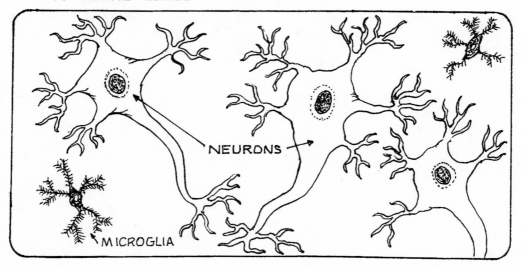

NEUROFIBRILLARY TANGLES AND AMYLOID PLAQUES

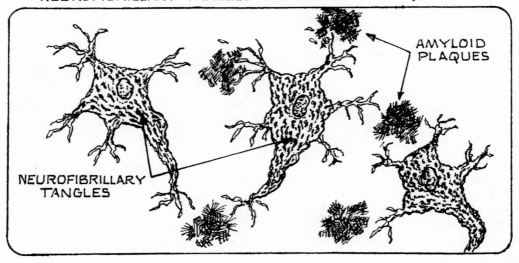

Brain cells in normal and Alzheimer's disease brain (illustration by Marvin G. Miller).

conduction hearing loss. Patients are subjected to sounds such as clicks and tone pips which act as stimuli.

Brainstem evoked potentials. The measurement of evoked potentials is noninvasive with no risk to the patient. Evoked potentials are minute voltage changes that occur in response to a brief sensory stimuli. Evoked potentials are measured from scalp electrodes and are time-related to sensory stimuli. In the test, a stimulus is repeated several times after periods of rest. A computerized instrument that averages the results measures each transient evoked response. Evoked potential studies reflect neural activity of the peripheral and central nervous systems. The Brief Cognitive Rating Scale consists of measures derived from and designed to be optimally concordant with the GDS. This tool is useful in the further guiding of staging assignments and predicting further deterioration.

Bright light therapy. In a number of studies, bright light therapy, particularly blue light, has been used to eliminate agitation, particularly sundowning, in patients with Alzheimer's disease. Bright light therapy is currently being evaluated by researchers at Harvard University and at the Centre de sant Elisabeth-Bruyere Health Centre in Ottawa, Ontario, Canada, through an ongoing grant from the National Institutes of Aging (http://www.nia.nih.gov/Alzheimers/Pub lications/ADProgress2008/rapid/ongoing1.htm, accessed Feb 23, 2011. Satlin, Andrew, M.D., et al. "Bright light treatment of behavioral and sleep disturbance in Alzheimer's disease patients," *American Journal of Psychiatry*, 1992 149: 1028–1032. "Bright light therapy and Alzheimer's disease," *Sleep Review*, Jan/Feb 2003, http://www.sleepreviewmag.com/issues/articles/2003-01_01.asp, accessed Jan 3, 2011)

Broca's aphasia. Individuals who sustain damage to the region of the brain known as Broca's area have difficulty producing language, a condition known as Broca's aphasia. This condition is also called nonfluent, motor, or expressive aphasia.

Broca's area. Broca's area refers to the left inferior frontal region of the brain. Damage to Broca's area causes an inability to use language (aphasia). Individuals who have damage in this area produce few written or spoken words. They tend to leave out all but the most meaningful words in a sentence and to speak or write in a telegraphic matter. Despite their difficulties in producing words, Broca's aphasics have relative little difficulty comprehending language because the affected area of the brain contains the motor programs for the generation of language.

Buschke-Fuld Selective Reminding Test. The Buschke-Fuld Selective Reminding test is a verbal memory task used to evaluate learning and memory. This test is included in neuropsychological evaluations.

Busipirone (Buspar). Busipirone (Buspar) is a partial 5-hydroxytryptamine (serotonin) agonist, which has anti-anxiety activity and few adverse side effects. Studies of busipirone used in patients with Alzheimer's disease showed an overall reduction of agitated behaviors, although the intensity of these effects varied among subjects.

CADASIL (Cerebral Autosomal Dominant Arteriopathy with Subcortical Infarcts and Leukoencephalopathy). CADASIL is the first known genetic form of vascular dementia with an identified gene. Mutations of the Notch3 gene located on chromosome 19 are responsible for CADASIL. CADASIL is a hereditary cause of stroke, dementia, and migraine with aura and mood disorders. Symptoms of this disorder emerge from the mid-twenties to around 45 years of age. Affected individuals usually die by age 65. The most common symptom is stroke. Patients exhibit cerebral non-atherosclerotic, non-amyloid angiopathy (disease of the blood vessels feeding the brain). The small arteries that innervate the white matter of the brain are primarily affected. Individuals with CADASIL rarely have the usual risk factors for stroke such as hypertension. Migraine headaches with aura are one of the earliest symptoms and occur in about ⅓ of patients with this disorder.

The second most common feature is a slowly progressing form of dementia, which causes frontal-like symptoms and memory impairment. Dementia commonly occurs after a history of recurrent stroke. Other accompanying symptoms include gait disturbances, pyramidal signs, and sphincter incontinence. These symptoms are all related to vascular dementia. Patients may also exhibit mood disorders, including severe depression, often with alternating manic episodes. Melancholia may also be present.

MRI studies reveal diffuse white matter cerebral lesions. These lesions typically occur two decades before the onset of disease although patients may suffer migraines with aura. CADASIL should be considered in affected individuals who have migraine with aura in mid–adulthood, when aura is atypical or prolonged, and when there is a family history of stroke, dementia, or depression. The prevalence of this order is unknown but it's suspected that many previously reported cases of vascular dementia were caused by CADASIL.

Vascular disorders can also cause cognitive dysfunction and psychiatric symptoms often associated with focal motor signs and seizures. An elevated erythrocyte sedimentation laboratory test often suggests that the disorder may have an autoimmune origin.

Caffeine. Caffeine is reported to reduce risk of Alzheimer's disease. A 2009 study published in the *Journal of Alzheimer's Disease* reports that drinking five medium-sized cups of coffee a day could lower risk for both Alzheimer's and Parkinson's disease. Side effects of caffeine include sleep problems, anxiety, restlessness, upset stomach and quickened heartbeat. Long-term use of caffeine may result in tolerance and psychological dependence.

The study followed mice that were bred to develop Alzheimer's. After two months of drinking water with 500 mg of caffeine added — the equivalent of five 8 oz. cups of coffee or two venti hot coffees from Starbucks — the mice performed much better on memory and thinking tests compared to mice that were given only water. In fact, the memories of the caffeinated mice were on par with mice that didn't have dementia at all. In addition, the caffeine supplemented mice had a 50 percent reduction of beta amyloid, a protein often found in Alzheimer's patients. (Sears, Al. "Can coffee combat Alzheimer's disease?" *Healthier Talk*, http://www.healthiertalk.com/can-coffee-combat-alzheimers-0841, accessed Dec 11, 2010)

Calcium. Many facets of brain metabolism are dependent on the mineral calcium. Amyloid beta protein, which is increased in patients with Alzheimer's disease, disturbs calcium metabolism and increases the calcium concentrations of neurons. This may activate enzymes and cause the production of the abnormal phosphorus metabolism that leads to neurofibrillary tangles and directly damages the mitochondria of neurons.

The abnormal calcium regulatory system in Alzheimer's disease may cause too much calcium to build up in brain cells, which leads to neuronal cell death.

Calcium channel blockers. Calcium channel blockers are drugs that block the entry of calcium into cells, thereby reducing activities that require calcium such as neurotransmission. Generally used for certain heart conditions, calcium channel blockers are being studied for their potential role in treating Alzheimer's disease especially when mutations to calcium signaling mechanisms are present. ("Calcium may hold the key for understanding Alzheimer's disease," *Science Daily*, July 21, 2008, http://www.sciencedaily.com/releases/2008/07/080717220948.htm, accessed Sept 13, 2010)

California Verbal Learning Tests. The California Verbal Learning Tests are psychological tests used to measure verbal memory. Patients are subjected to a verbal list of words, which they are asked to remember. Patients are later tested to see how many words they recall at different times after hearing the words.

Cambridge Examination for Mental Disorders of the Elderly (CAMDEX). The Cambridge Examination for Mental Disorders of the Elderly (CAMDEX) is a standardized instrument or evaluation tool used to help determine the date of onset of dementia. Three questions are used to help determine the age of onset.

Cambridge Neuropsychological Test Automated Battery (CANTAB). The Cambridge Neuropsychological Test Automated Battery (CANTAB) is a neuropsychological evaluation tool used to assess cognitive deficits in humans with neurodegenerative disease or brain damage. It consists of 13 interrelated computerized tests of memory, attention and executive function, administered via a touch sensitive personal computer screen. The tests are language and largely culture free and have shown to be highly sensitive in the early detection and routine screening of Alzheimer's disease.

Canadian Study of Health and Aging (CSHA). The Canadian Study of Health and Aging (CSHA) is a multicenter epidemiologic study of dementia and other health problems in elderly people in Canada conducted between 1992 and 1997. In the first phase of the study, 14,206 subjects 65 years old or older were randomly selected from throughout Canada, and 10,263 subjects agreed to participate. Subjects were interviewed and assessed with the Modified Mini-Mental State Examination. In the second phase of the study, this cohort was reevaluated. The data from this study is widely used in epidemiological studies of Alzheimer's disease.

Carbamazepine (Tegretol). The anticonvulsant carbamazepine (Tegretol) is sometimes used to treat symptoms of agitation in Alzheimer's disease patients.

Caregiver Bill of Rights. Caregivers have the right to receive adequate training in caregiver skills along with accurate, understandable information about the needs of the patients they are caring for. Caregivers have the right to appreciation and emotional support for their decision to accept the challenge of providing care. Caregivers have a right to protect their assets and financial future without severing their relationship with the patients under their care. Caregivers have a right to receive respite care during emergencies and so that they may attend to their own personal needs. Caregivers have a right to provide care at home for as long as they are able and find care alternatives when they are no longer able to provide care. Caregivers have the right to temporarily alter their premises to provide safe housing for those under their care.

Caregiver training. Caregiver training is provided free of charge by the Alzheimer's Association and through local community services. Research shows that caregivers who are given training are better able to provide home care for longer periods of time. Caregiver training also provides information for helpful community services that can help with home care when caregivers must be away, such as respite care assistance programs.

Caregivers. About 80 to 90 percent of the 5 million Americans with Alzheimer's disease are cared for at home by family caregivers, and this number is expected to grow. Potential stressors associated with this care include managing behavioral disturbances, attending to physical needs, and providing constant vigilance. The effects of these stressors can be catastrophic. Family caregiving has been associated with increased levels of depression and anxiety, poorer self-reported physical health, compromised immune function, and increased mortality.

According to the 2010 Alzheimer's Disease Facts and Figures, in 2009 nearly 11 million family and other unpaid caregivers provided an estimated 12.5 billion hours of care to persons with AD and other dementias; this care is valued at nearly $144 billion. Medicare payments for services to beneficiaries aged 65 years and older with AD and other dementias are three times higher than for beneficiaries without these conditions.

Total payments for 2010 for health care and long-term care services for people aged 65 and older with AD and other dementias are expected to be $172 billion (not including the contributions of unpaid caregivers). (Alzheimer's Association. "Alzheimer's Disease Facts and Figures," *Alzheimer's & Dementia: The Journal of the Alzheimer's Association*, March 2010, 6(2): 158–194)

As the disease progresses, caregivers often find themselves cut off from social activities. Feelings of resentment may arise, especially after the patient's behavior deteriorates. Studies show that caregivers who work full-time may end up using an average of three weeks vacation time to help with the special needs of those in their care, and one-fifth of caregivers will quit their jobs to provide this care. Caregivers can take advantage of programs such as support groups, adult day care, and respite care. Sometimes, local agencies will provide weekly nursing services to help with the burden of caring for a patient with dementia at home.

High levels of burden experienced by caregivers are associated with increasing distress, poor physical health, and greater use of healthcare, which can have a negative impact for Alzheimer's disease patients. Caregivers of Alzheimer's patients are reported to experience more depression than other caregivers. It is also reported that caregivers who are more burdened or stressed are more likely to place patients in institutions at earlier stages of dementia. In one report, a high percentage of spousal caregivers scored high on evaluations for depression. Behavioral problems in dementia patients are reported as being closely linked to stress in the caregiver.

Patients with mild to moderate Alzheimer's disease require, on average, 3 to 3.5 hours of caregiver time daily while severely demented patients may require 8 hours or more of caregiver time daily. In one study, 50 percent of caregivers who received intensive caregiver training were still managing patients in the home after 4 years, whereas only 8 percent of caregivers who had no training were still providing home caregiving.

Researchers have examined a number of psychosocial interventions aimed at alleviating distress associated with dementia caregiving. In many cases respite care and home care services are available through government, local, and medical support services. Resources for Enhancing Alzheimer's Caregiver Health (REACH) has developed a number of intervention strategies to help caregivers. *See* REACH and resources for caregivers in the Resource section.

Carnitine *see* Acetyl L-Carnitine

Casein kinase-1 (CK-1). Casein kinase-1 (CK-1) is an enzyme found in high concentrations in patients with Alzheimer's disease. Researchers from the National Institutes of Health found a high level of CK-1 in the nerve cells inside cellular sacs called vacuoles. These vacuoles had previously been associated with brain changes known as granulovacuolar degeneration.

The research, led by Dr. Jeffrey Kuret of Ohio State University, suggests that CK-1 may be involved in the process by which tau protein is phosphorylated and found in the plaques, tangles and granuovacuolar degeneration seen in the brains of patients with Alzheimer's disease. Not only does this discovery offer insight into the disease process, it suggests that this enzyme can perhaps be used as a diagnostic marker for Alzheimer's disease and therapies that inhibit CK-1 have potential therapeutic applications. (Rockefeller Center Newswire, "New therapeutic target for Alzheimer's could lead to drugs without side effects," Feb 26, 2007, http://newswire.rockefeller.edu/index.php?page=engine&id=612, accessed Feb 7, 2011)

Caspases. Caspases are proteolytic enzymes that help control apoptosis, the programmed death of cells. Caspases function to reorganize dying cells by facilitating safe clearance by immune system cells known as phagocytes. Although apoptosis plays a critical role in molding the central nervous system into its final appearance and function, inappropriate activation of this pathway in the aging brain may contribute to neurodegeneration. In Alzheimer's disease, an overwhelming body of evidence supports the activation of apoptosis in general, and caspases specifically, as an early event that may not only contribute to neurodegeneration but also promote the underlying pathology associated with this disease. Therefore, caspase inhibitors may provide an effective strategy for treating Alzheimer's disease. Researchers are currently working on caspase inhibitors, drugs with the potential of blocking caspase activity as therapies for Alzheimer's disease.

Catecholamines. Catecholamines are neurotransmitters that structurally have one amine group. Derived from the amino acid tyrosine, catecholamines include norepinephrine and dopamine. Neurons that produce catecholamines are primarily found in the brainstem and forebrain. Despite their restricted origins, catecholamines have far-reaching effects. Terminals for catecholamines are found in glands, smooth muscle and widespread areas of the brain.

Cathepsin D inhibitors. The precursor protein Beta APP can result in several different isoforms depending on how it is spliced. In Alzheimer's, beta APP is spliced to form increased amounts of beta amyloid peptide fragments ending in the amino acid 42. These peptides accumulate and represent the main components of senile plaques. The acid protease cathepsin D has similar properties to the beta secretase enzyme that facilitates the increased production of beta amyloid fragments. Research is directed toward drug therapy to block cathepsin D in an effort to simultaneously block beta secretase activity.

Causes of Alzheimer's disease. There are several schools of thought regarding the causes of Alzheimer's disease. While it is widely accepted that increased production of beta amyloid protein leads to Alzheimer's disease, alterations in tau protein and amyloid precursor protein, decreased permeability of the blood brain barrier, altered brain glucose metabolism, genetic mutations, defects in the cholinergic system, and the binding of toxic metals to amyloid beta protein are also suspected of playing a causative role. Many researchers today suspect that Alzheimer's is caused by a combination of genetic and environmental factors and that these variations account for the many variations or subtypes of Alzheimer's disease that exist. *See also* Environmental contributions to Alzheimer's disease

Cells. Cells are the basic building blocks of human tissue. The brain is primarily composed of central nervous system cells known as neurons and immune system cells known as microglia.

Centella asiatica. *Centella asiatica*, the herb commonly known as gotu kola, has long had the reputation of improving memory. In Ayurvedic and traditional Chinese medicine, gotu kola has long been used to boost memory, stall memory loss and support healthy blood vessels. Gotu kola appears to enhance blood flow and increase the tone of blood vessels. For Alzheimer's disease, 200 mg of the freeze-dried herb or 400–500 mg of the crude herb are used three times daily. (Duke, James A. *The Green Pharmacy.* Emmaus, PA: [Rodale Press,] 1997)

Center for Mental Health Services (CMHS). The Center for Mental Health Services (CMHS) is a service of the federal government that focuses on the diagnosis and treatment of mental illness.

Centers for Medicare & Medicaid Services (CMS). Formerly known as the Health Care Financing Administration, the Centers for Medicare & Medicaid Services (CMS) regulate government health insurance. With the name change, there is an increased emphasis on responsiveness to the people served by these programs. CMS provides health insurance for more than 74 million Americans through Medicare, Medicaid, and SCHIP. Individuals under these plans receive their benefits through a fee-for-service delivery system or through managed care plans. The CMS also provides technical assistance to the Public Health Service and other agencies to coordinate delivery and funding of the Department of Health and Human Services' maternal and child health care programs. Information on their programs is available at http://www.cms.gov/ and http://www.medicare.gov.

Central Nervous System (CNS). The central nervous system (CNS) consists of the brain and the spinal cord. The CNS is an intricate system linking the brain and the body's network of nerves. While generally shielded from the blood and lymphatic systems, the CNS is intimately linked to the immune and endocrine systems, with each of these systems influencing functions in the other systems. The interior of the central nervous system is organized into gray and white matter.

Central sulcus. The surface or outer regions of the cerebral cortex are thrown into folds or gyri, which are separated from one another by fissures

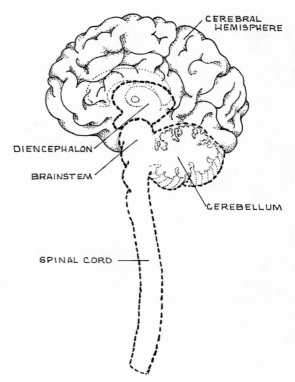

Central nervous system (illustration by Marvin G. Miller).

known as sulci. The sulci conveniently are used to divide the hemispheres of the brain into distinct sections or lobes. The central sulcus indents the hemisphere near its midpoint. The gyrus that lies in front of the central sulcus contains the motor cells that initiate movement for the opposite side of the body.

Centrophenoxine. Centrophenoxine is a compound composed of the natural substances dimethylaminoethanol (DMAE), which is found in fatty fish, particularly sardines, and parachlorphenoxylacetic acid (PCPA), which is a type of plant growth hormone. Centrophenoxine is widely used in Europe and Asia as a neuroenergizer, and it is officially used in disorders related to brain injuries, memory disturbances, barbiturate intoxication, alcoholism and cognitive decline. Animal studies show that centrophenoxine helps remove lipofusicin deposits and improves learning compared to age-related controls. Centrophenoxine has a protective action against Alzheimer's disease because of its ability to improve choline levels as well as reduce lipofuscin deposits. A human clinical trial involving 76 healthy, elderly subjects suffering from significant intellectual deterioration found that centrophenoxine increased storage of new, long-term memory information, while increasing vigilance and alertness. ("ENews articles about centrophenoxine," *Antiaging Systems Newsletter*, Sept 2010, http://www.antoagomg-systems.com/ENEWS-407/centrophenoxine.htm)

CERE-110. CERE-100, manufactured by Ceregene, is an investigational gene therapy product designed to deliver nerve growth factor (NGF) to the brain for the treatment of Alzheimer's disease. CERE-110 is currently in clinical trials.

Cerebellar ataxia. Cerebellar ataxia is a gait disturbance detected during neuropsychological testing. The gait is staggering, unsteady, and wide-based with exaggerated difficulty on the turns. The patient cannot stand steadily with feet together, whether eyes are open or closed. Cerebellar ataxia is caused by damage, degeneration or loss of nerve cells in the part of the brain that controls muscle coordination (cerebellum). Causes include autoimmune disease, head injuries, stroke, viral infections including chickenpox, cerebral palsy, transient ischemic attack, tumor, paraneoplastic (cancer-related) syndromes, and toxic reactions.

Cerebellum. The cerebellum is a highly developed area of the hindbrain associated with thinking, speaking, memory and emotions. The cerebellum lies within the posterior or rear cranial fossa posterior to the pons and the medulla oblongata. The cerebellum consists of two hemispheres connected by a median portion known as the vermis. The cerebellum is connected to the midbrain, pons, and medulla by processes known as peduncles.

Afferent nerve fibers enter the cerebellum through all three pairs of cerebellar peduncles and terminate as mossy fibers in the cerebellar cortex. The large Purkinje cells of the cerebellum link the cortex to the intracerebellar nuclei.

The main function of the cerebellum is to coordinate all reflex and voluntary muscular activity. It regulates muscle tone, maintains normal body posture and permits voluntary movement.

The cortex of the cerebellum does not vary between regions, either in its microscopic appearance or in its functions. The cerebellar hemispheres are linked by nervous pathways to their respective sides of the body. Thus, a lesion affecting the left cerebellar hemisphere would cause symptoms, such as gait impairment, in the left side of the body. Signs of cerebellar dysfunction include hypotonia, alteration of gait, ataxia, dysdiadochokinesis, nystagmus, dysarthia and disturbances of reflexes.

Cerebral atrophy. Cerebral atrophy is the shrinking of brain tissue due to neuronal damage or degeneration.

Cerebral blood flow studies. Cerebral blood flow, or blood flow within the brain, can be measured by the injection or inhalation of radioactive krypton or xenon. Normal cerebral blood flow is 50 to 60 ml/100 grams of brain per minute. Patients with Alzheimer's disease experience reduced blood flow velocity (BFV) values in their middle cerebral artery, which can be further demonstrated on MRI. The greatest reductions in blood flow were related to the greatest amounts of cerebral atrophy.

Cerebral circulation. The brain is supplied with arterial blood from two internal carotid arteries and two verterbral arteries, which unite anteriorly to form the basilar artery. The most important factor in moving blood through the brain is the arterial blood pressure. Arterial blood pressure is reduced or inhibited by raised intracranial pressure, increased blood viscosity or thickness and narrowing of the blood vessels. Cerebral blood flow, however, generally remains constant despite changes in the general blood pressure unless the arterial blood pressure becomes very low.

Cerebral cortex. The cerebral cortex refers to the surface layer of gray matter cushioning the cerebrum. The cerebral cortex is primarily involved in the coordination of sensory and motor information.

Representing approximately 80 percent of the human brain, the cerebral cortex refers to the expanded or surface portion of the cerebral hemispheres. The cerebral cortex consists of a sheet of neurons and their interconnections, which extend to about 2.5 square feet in area.

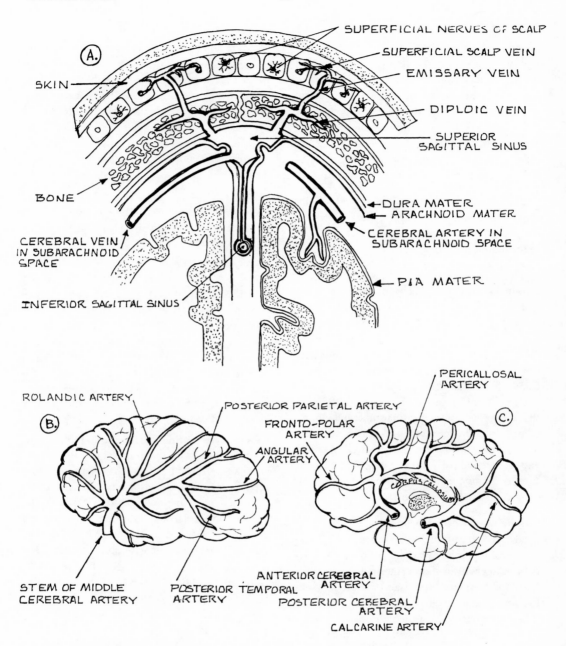

A. CORONAL SECTION OF BRAIN   B. LATERAL VIEW
C. MEDIAL VIEW

Cerebral blood vessels (illustration by Marvin G. Miller).

This thin layer contains about 30 billion neurons, interconnected by 100,000 km of axons and dendrites. One of the most striking changes in evolution is the tremendous increase in the size of the cerebral hemispheres and the even greater increase in the area of cerebral cortex on their surfaces.

The cortex is composed of gray matter, which is thrown into folds, or gyri, separated by closely set transverse fissures known as sulci. Only about

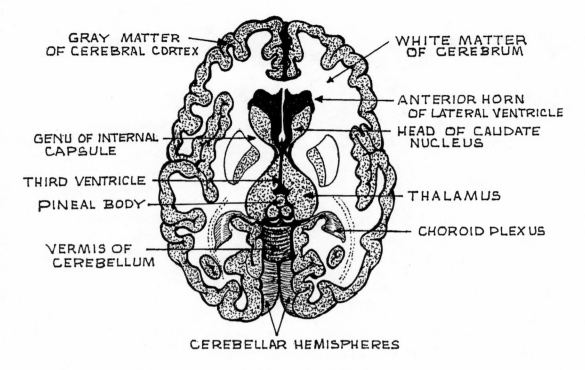

GRAY MATTER OF CEREBRAL CORTEX

WHITE MATTER OF CEREBRUM

ANTERIOR HORN OF LATERAL VENTRICLE

GENU OF INTERNAL CAPSULE

HEAD OF CAUDATE NUCLEUS

THIRD VENTRICLE

PINEAL BODY

THALAMUS

CHOROID PLEXUS

VERMIS OF CEREBELLUM

CEREBELLAR HEMISPHERES

Gray and white matter of the brain (illustration by Marvin G. Miller).

one-third of the cortex lies exposed. The remaining two-thirds form the walls of the sulci. The cortex is thickest over the crest of a fold and thinnest in the depth of a sulcus.

The neurons which form the cerebral cortex are located immediately below the bones of the skull, arching from just behind the forehead and over the top and sides, back to where the back of the head meets the neck. Like all gray matter, the cerebral cortex consists of a mixture of nerve cells, nerve fibers, neuroglia, and blood vessels. The nerve cells present include: pyramidal cells, stellate cells, fusiform cells, horizontal cells of Cajal and cells of Martinotti. These cells vary in size and the types of neurites or processes they contain.

The cerebral cortex can also be divided into layers that differ in the type of cells they are primarily composed of. The most superficial layer is known as the molecular or plexiform layer. This layer contains large numbers of synapses between neurons.

The cerebral cortex is the most complex region of the brain. It has many specialized regions and lobes that control particular functions, such as word association and reflection. For instance, widespread lesions of the frontal lobe might cause symptoms and signs indicative of loss of attention span or changes in social behavior. Widespread degeneration of the cerebral cortex causes symptoms of dementia. Basic aspects of perception, movement and adaptive response to the outside world also depend on the cerebral cortex.

The cerebral cortex in Alzheimer's disease, studied by electron microscopy, reveals innumerable, non-compacted deposits of beta amyloid protein containing few or no surrounding dystrophic neurites or glial cells. With recent studies indicating that certain neurons in the cerebral cortex involved with higher learning are capable of regeneration, therapies designed to stimulate neurogenesis are under investigation. *See* Neocortex

Cerebral hemispheres. The cerebral hemispheres that divide the cerebrum in the forebrain are separated by a deep midline sagittal fissure known as the longitudinal cerebral fissure. The fissure contains the fold of the dura mater, the

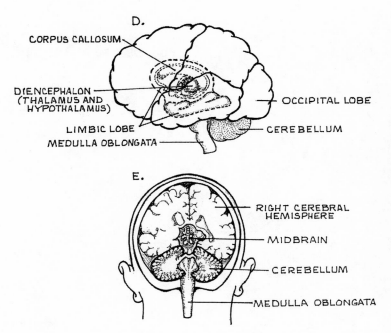

D.

CORPUS CALLOSUM

DIENCEPHALON
(THALAMUS AND
HYPOTHALAMUS)

OCCIPITAL LOBE

LIMBIC LOBE

MEDULLA OBLONGATA

CEREBELLUM

E.

RIGHT CEREBRAL
HEMISPHERE

MIDBRAIN

CEREBELLUM

MEDULLA OBLONGATA

Hemispheres and lobes of the brain (illustration by Marvin G. Miller).

falx cerebri and the anterior cerebral arteries. In the depths of the fissure, the corpus callosum connects the hemispheres across the midline. A second horizontal fold of dura mater called the tentorium cerebelli separates the cerebral hemispheres from the cerebellum.

In order to provide maximal surface area for the cerebral cortex, the surface of each hemisphere is thrown into folds or gyri, which are separated from each other by fissures known as sulci. The hemispheres are further divided into lobes, which have names corresponding to the cranial bones under which they lie. The primary lobes are the frontal, parietal, temporal and occipital lobes. The gyri that lie anterior to the central sulcus in each hemisphere initiate movement in the opposite side of the body.

Cerebral ischemia. Impairment of blood flow to the brain results in a lack of oxygen causing a condition of cerebral ischemia. Neuronal function ceases after about one minute of oxygen deprivation, and permanent changes occur after about 4 minutes of ischemia.

Cerebral thrombosis. Cerebral thrombosis refers to the presence or formation of a blood clot in vessels supplying the cerebrum, which may result in a cerebral accident or stroke.

Cerebrolysin. Cerebrolysin (Ebewe Pharmaceutical) is a neurotrophic and neuroprotective agent produced from purified brain proteins by standardized enzymatic breakdown. Although Cerebrolysin has not yet received FDA approval in the United States, it is an approved drug in other parts of the world.

Cerebrolysin contains biologically active peptides, which exert nerve growth factor–like activity on neurons from dorsal root ganglia. Cerebrolysin is an injectable protein-based solution that contains small-molecule biologically active neuropeptides. Neuropeptides are small protein-like molecules used by neurons to communicate with each other. They work as neuronal signaling molecules and influence the brain's activity in a number of specific ways. They are, therefore, involved in particular brain functions like learning and memory. Neuropeptides penetrate through the blood-brain barrier and act directly on neurons. Worldwide, its efficacy has been tested in 80 randomized controlled clinical trials involving over 5,000 patients. These studies have produced consistently excellent results. The studies have highlighted significant symptomatic improvements in patients with mild to moderate Alzheimer's disease who have received Cerebrolysin either via intra-muscular injections or via intravenous infusions for 5 days a week. ("Cerebrolysin," Antiaging Systems International, http://www.antiaging-systems.com/ENEWS-408/cerebrolysin-alzheimers-disease.htm, accessed Mar 1, 2011)

Cerebrospinal fluid (CSF). Cerebrospinal fluid (CSF) is a normally clear, colorless fluid that surrounds the brain and spinal cord. CSF is withdrawn during lumbar punctures and evaluated when certain conditions such as encephalitis or subarachnoid bleeding are suspected. Cerebrospinal fluid can also be tested for abnormal proteins present in various diseases including Alzheimer's disease to help with diagnosis.

Cerebrovascular disease. Cerebrovascular disease, which is also known as vascular disease, refers to the dysfunction of any of the blood vessels supplying the cerebrum. The severity of the condition is largely dependent on the size of the affected blood vessel. Infarcts to large vessels may result in ischemia (decreased blood supply to brain) whereas infarcts to small capillaries lead to microinfarcts, which, over time, may cause tissue injury. Affected vessels may be narrowed or they may be prone to spasm.

Infarcts or injuries to the cerebrovascular system cause neurodegenerative changes that may be confused with Alzheimer's disease. Chronic cerebrovascular disease, however, is commonly associated with an increased magnetic resonance imaging (MRI) signal in the periventricular white matter. This pattern often follows the general distribution of the deep border zone territory seen in the small vessels, particularly microangiopathy of hypertension, lipohyalinosis, and amyloid angiopathy.

Patients with Alzheimer's disease may have co-existing cerebrovascular disease. Several postmortem studies of suspected Alzheimer's patients show that co-existing vascular lesions are common. Furthermore, while neuroimaging studies, such as MRI, are more sensitive for detecting Alzheimer's disease, the neuropathological exam, including psychometric testing, is more sensitive than neuroimaging for detecting cerebrovascular disease. Because many treatments are able to reverse symptoms associated with cerebrovascular disease, it is important to determine if cerebrovascular disease is present. (Chui, Helen, et al. "Differentiating Alzheimer Disease and Vascular Dementia: Reframing the Question," *Alzheimer Disease: From Molecular Biology to Therapy.* Edited by R. Becker and E. Giacobine. Boston: Birkhäuser Publishing, 13–17 [1996])

Cerebrovascular system. The cerebrovascular system refers to the cerebrum and the blood vessels that support it.

Cerebrum. The cerebrum or telencephalon, along with the diencephalons, makes up the forebrain. The cerebrum can be divided into left and right sides, which are known as the cerebral hemispheres.

Certificate in Dementia Care. Certificates in dementia care are awarded to caregivers who take 32 hours of coursework through the Alzheimer's Learning Institute of the Alzheimer's Association or through certified programs at community colleges. The course must be completed within 18 months and is available to professional caregivers including RNs, LPNs, CNAs, personal care providers, social workers, activity directors, activity assistants, administrators, and special care coordinators. Typical course classes cover special concerns of teamwork in a dementia care environment, interpreting behavior, successful communication, sexuality and intimacy, assess-

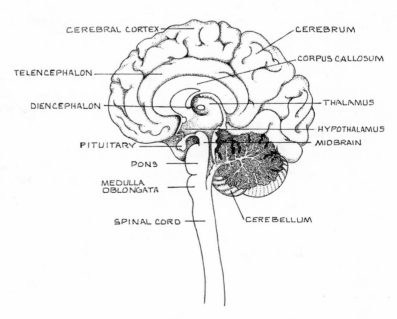

Midsagittal section of the brain (illustration by Marvin G. Miller).

ment and documentation, activities, and disease progression.

Chelation therapy. In chelation therapy, chelating agents, such as ethylenediaminetetraacetic acid (EDTA) are used to remove excess or harmful metals from the body. Garry F. Gordon, M.D., co-founder of the American College of Advancement in Medicine, reports that chelation therapy can benefit memory in patients with Alzheimer's-like dementia by improving blood flow to the brain. For senile dementia, Dr. Charles Farr, co-founder of the American Board of Chelation, recommends using 10 to 15 chelation therapies alternating with intravenous hydrogen peroxide.

Some researchers report that the binding of transition metals to amyloid peptide, rather than the peptide itself, is the cause of neurotoxicity in Alzheimer's disease. In June 2001, Ashley Bush at Massachusetts General and fellow researchers described how the copper/zinc chelator clioquinol cut Abeta deposits in the brain by half in mice without any apparent effects. This approach follows the concept that chelating copper and zinc should be able to break up plaques since these metals are shown to potentiate Abeta aggregation and toxicity. While these findings are undergoing further studies, they add support to chelation therapy. For more information on Dr. Richard Casdorph's protocol for treating Alzheimer's disease with chelation, visit the consumer health website at http://www.consumer health.org/articles/display.cfm?ID=19990303214 451, accessed Mar 1, 2011. *See also* Desferrioxamine

Chlamydia pneumoniae. In one study, *Chlamydia pneumoniae,* a bacterium that generally causes respiratory infections, has been found in the parts of the brain affected by late-onset Alzheimer's disease but not in unaffected parts. The presence of the bacterium may have been the result of Alzheimer's disease or it may be a causative agent. More studies are being undertaken to clarify the role of this bacterium although studies to date have not confirmed a positive association. For more information on current research studies, read the online report "Neurological diseases and Chlamydia pneumoniae," August 2004, http://www.chlamydiae.com/re stricted/docs/infections/chp_alzheimers.asp, accessed Feb 2, 2011.

Chlorpromazine (Thorazine). Chlorpromazine (Thorazine) is a major tranquilizer used for the manifestations of psychotic disorders.

Cholesterol. Cholesterol is a lipid compound produced in the liver with lesser amounts provided by diet. Studies show that very high cholesterol levels are associated with an increased risk for Alzheimer's disease. However, lipids are a structural component of neuronal membranes and low cholesterol levels are also associated with symptoms of dementia. *See also* High Density Lipoprotein (HDL)

Choline. The amino acid choline is one of the building blocks of both acetylcholine and lecithin. Lecithin contains the amino acids choline and inositol. Researchers have tried using choline and lecithin supplements as well as choline-rich foods to increase acetylcholine levels in individuals with Alzheimer's disease. Although preliminary reports were encouraging, recent studies have failed to prove conclusively that supplemental choline results in significant memory improvement. Still, many herbal products sold as memory aids contain significant amounts of choline. Foods that contain choline include brazil nuts, horehound, ginseng, eggs, English pea, mung beans, fava beans, fenugreek, and dandelion. (Duke, James A. *The Green Pharmacy.* Emmaus, PA: Rodale Press. 1997)

Cholinergic basal forebrain. The cholinergic basal forebrain is the area in which cholinergic neurons are concentrated. *See* Basal forebrain.

Cholinergic hypothesis. The cholinergic hypothesis refers to the theory that the destruction of cholinergic neurons is the primary mechanism leading to Alzheimer's disease.

Cholinergic neuronal pathways. Neurons at the basal forebrain provide most of the cholinergic innervation to the cortex. These neurons are preferentially affected by neurofibrillary tangles, which are responsible for the cholinergic neurotransmitter deficits. Drugs known as cholinesterase inhibitors, such as donepezil, are used to correct these deficits and increase cholinesterase levels.

Cholinergic system. The cholinergic system refers to the neurons in the brain that use acetylcholine to communicate. There are two main clusters of cells in the cholinergic system: cholinergic cells in the pedunculo-pontine region of the brainstem, which innervates the thalamus and basal ganglia, and cholinergic cells in the basal forebrain, which innervates regions of the cortex with cholinergic prominence. While patients with Alzheimer's disease experience a loss of cholinergic neurons in the basal forebrain, the cholinergic neurons found in the brainstem are not affected. The basal forebrain's cortical cholinergic system mediates attentional processes. Researchers at Ohio State University have postulated that dysfunctions in the excitability of these cholinergic neurons underlie the impaired attentional processing that contributes to the cognitive deficits seen in Alzheimer's disease.

The cholinergic system plays a role in emotion and non-cognitive behavior and may be involved in neuropsychiatric symptoms in Alzheimer's disease. Presynaptic neurons in the basal forebrain that produce the neurotransmitter acetylcholine in their axons transmit impulses to postsynaptic neurons. Deficits in acetylcholine or its failure to bind to receptors disrupt cholinergic activity in the brain. The amount of acetylcholine available for neurotransmission depends on the enzymes choline acetyltransferase and acetylcholinesterase (AChE).

Choline acetyltransferase catalyzes the synthesis of acetylcholine by transferring an acetyl group from acetyl-coenzyme A and combining it with choline. The newly synthesized acetylcholine molecules are then stored in specialized vesicles in the endings of presynaptic cholinergic neurons in the brain. In response to an incoming nerve impulse, calcium-activated movement of the vesicles releases their contents into the synaptic cleft. Here, most of the acetylcholine molecules rapidly bind to post-synaptic membrane receptors on neurons. Any remaining acetylcholine is quickly inactivated by the enzyme acetylcholinesterase. After the nerve impulse is transmitted, the receptor sites are vacated and used acetylcholine is also inactivated or hydrolyzed by acetylcholinesterase.

The cholinergic neurons in the basal forebrain and the brainstem act via two distinct mechanisms: the muscarinic and nicotinic systems.

Cholinesterase. Cholinesterase is an enzyme present in the brain, plasma and skeletal muscles that regulates levels of acetylcholine. There are two types of cholinesterase, acetylcholinesterase (AChE) and butyrylcholinesterase (BuChE), which is also known as pseudocholinesterase.

Both cholinesterase enzymes have multiple functions. AChE is involved in the development of certain pathways in the brain and inhibits dopamine release in the substantia nigra. BuChE has primary effects on butyrylcholine, although, like AChE, it hydrolyzes the neurotransmitter acetylcholine. Since both enzymes have multiple effects, the long-term effects and safety of cholinesterase inhibitors depend on how these other enzyme systems are affected.

Cholinesterase inhibitors *see* Acetylcholinesterase inhibitors

Chorea. Chorea is a disorder characterized by quick, jerky, irregular movements, including swift grimaces and sudden movements of the head or limbs.

Choroid plexus. The choroids plexuses are the areas of the brain found within the lateral, third, and fourth ventricles that produce cerebrospinal fluid.

Chromosomes. The entire genetic component of a human being is packed into 23 pairs of chromosomes. Chromosomes are H-shaped structures located inside the cell nucleus. Each chromosome contains the DNA for thousands of different genes. Genes are short pieces of DNA that tell the body's cells what proteins to produce and how to act or appear. Chromosomes 1, 14, 19 and 21 are associated with genetic mutations that are responsible for certain disease states, including Alzheimer's disease.

Chromosome 1. A mutation to the presenilin-2 gene on chromosome 1 is responsible for approximately 1 percent of all cases of Alzheimer's disease. The age of onset for this mutation is the late 40s to early 50s.

Chromosome 10. Researchers have found a susceptibility locus for Alzheimer's disease on chromosome 10 independent of the apolipoprotein E gene.

Chromosome 14. A mutation to the presenilin-1 gene on chromosome 14 is responsible for approximately 4 percent of all cases of Alzheimer's disease. The age of onset for this mutation is 28 years to 50 years.

Chromosome 19. A mutation to the Apolipoprotein E4 (APOE4) gene on chromosome 19 is the genetic mutation responsible for most cases of Alzheimer's disease. The APOE4 allele is associated with both early and late-onset Alzheimer's disease.

Chromosome 21. A mutation to the amyloid precursor protein (APP) gene on chromosome 21 is responsible for less than 1 percent of all cases of Alzheimer's disease. The age of onset for this mutation is 45 years to 65 years.

Circadian rhythm. Circadian rhythm refers to the normal peak and flow of the body's hormones and other chemicals in relationship to the time of day. Thyroid hormones, for instance, normally are released at their highest concentrations during the night. Disruption of circadian rhythm is related to a number of different illnesses. Researchers at Harvard University, through a grant from the National Institute on Aging, have conducted studies to see if disruption of circadian rhythm contributes to the development of Alzheimer's disease. David Harper, PhD, research fellow in the Department of Geriatric Psychiatry at Harvard's McLean Hospital, and his colleagues monitored two key features of the circadian system — the rise and fall of core body temperature and the waxing and waning of spontaneous motor activity — in 38 dementia patients with Alzheimer's disease or another form of dementia, fronto-temporal degeneration.

They found that body temperature reached its peak much later in the 24-hour day in the Alzheimer patients than it did in controls. People with fronto-temporal degeneration exhibited a much different pattern. Their activity levels reached a peak earlier in the day than in controls while their body temperature rhythm appeared normal. Intriguingly, fronto-temporal dementia patients were able to attain a stage of quiescence, or subdued activity, though it did not necessarily happen at night as it does in controls. This more restful state eluded Alzheimer's patients.

Alzheimer's effects on memory and cognition are notorious but the accompanying sleep disturbances were found to be among the most devastating aspects of Alzheimer's disease and other forms of dementia, including fronto-temporal degeneration. ("Circadian rhythms hold key to new Alzheimer's symptoms," McClean Hospital press release, April 2001, http://www.mclean.harvard.edu/PublicAffairs/20010412_Alzheimer Study.htm, accessed Feb 2, 2011)

Circumscribed brain atrophy *see* Pick's disease

Citicoline. Citicoline (Cognizin) is a substance sold as a dietary supplement currently being investigated as a therapeutic agent in Alzheimer's disease. Citicoline affects the cholinergic system and increases the production of nerve growth factor. Citicoline has proven beneficial in the past for treating head injury and stroke. Citicoline, from Kyowa Hakko USA, is a precursor of phosphatidylcholine, a type of phospholipid that is a component of cell membranes, according to information on it from Healthy Origins. It is believed that citicoline stabilizes the neuronal membranes. When absorbed by the body, citicoline breaks down into cytidine and choline.

Cleveland Scale for Activities of Daily Living. The Cleveland Scale for Activities of Daily Living is a global assessment tool used for documenting functional deficits such as the ability to bathe, dress and eat. This evaluation tool is helpful in determining disease staging and projecting the expected rate of disease progression in individuals with Alzheimer's disease. This tool can also be used to measure response to various therapeutic interventions.

Clinical Dementia Rating Scale (CDRS). The Clinical Dementia Rating Scale (CDRS) is an evaluation tool used to distinguish normal brain aging from progressive Alzheimer's disease by dividing Alzheimer's disease into 5 distinct stages. The CDRS also includes additional semistructured evaluation tools, such as a "sum of boxes," for further guiding staging assignments. One study has found that the CDRS was more sensitive and reliable than psychometric measures for tracking dementia progression relevant for clinical trials or responses to therapy.

Clinical Global Impression (CGI). Clinical Global Impression (CGI) is a neuropsychiatric evaluation tool. While it has been used to assess the efficacy of therapy in clinical trials, this tool has shown little sensitivity for evaluating treatments for Alzheimer's disease. This tool is a measurement of overall cognitive ability.

Clinical Global Impression of Change scale (CGIC). Clinical Global Impression of Change is a neuropsychiatric evaluation tool given at different times in order to determine alterations in mental status in response to treatment modalities. Patients and informants familiar with their condition are interviewed to assess changes in cognitive function over time. The unstructured format of the CGIC makes it less reliable than other evaluation tools. To address past concerns related to this tool, the National Institute on Aging's Alzheimer's Disease Cooperative Study combines the CGIC with other measures when conducting clinical trials.

Clinical trials. The purpose of clinical trials is to improve the understanding of certain conditions and to evaluate the benefits and risks of new therapeutic agents. Patients participating in a clinical trial for neurological conditions continue to receive medical care, routine laboratory tests and other diagnostic tests from their primary physicians. The patient's primary physician and the sponsoring agency simultaneously evaluate test results. For a listing of organizations that recruit for clinical trials, see the resource section.

According to one study, patients who participate in clinical trials are less likely to need nursing home placement than patients at a similar stage of disease who do not participate in trials. This may be due to the benefits of increased interaction and attention that patients in clinical trials experience. Alternately, it could be because the caregivers of Alzheimer's disease patients who encourage participation in clinical trials may be more involved and concerned with the individuals' care. Patients in clinical trials also have earlier access to drug therapies.

Clinical trials are conducted in phases. The trials at each phase have a different purpose and help scientists evaluate the safety as well as efficacy of a given drug.

- In Phase I trials, researchers test an experimental drug or treatment in a small group of people (20–80) for the first time to evaluate its safety, determine a safe dosage range, and identify side effects.
- In Phase II trials, the experimental study drug or treatment is given to a larger group of people (100–300) to see if it is effective and to further evaluate its safety.
- In Phase III trials, the experimental study drug or treatment is given to large groups of people (1,000–3,000) to confirm its effectiveness, monitor side effects, compare it to commonly used treatments, and collect information that will allow the experimental drug or treatment to be used safely.
- In Phase IV trials, post marketing studies delineate additional information including the drug's risks, benefits, and optimal use.

Every clinical trial in the U.S. must be approved and monitored by an Institutional Review Board (IRB) to make sure the risks are as low as possible and are worth any potential benefits. An IRB is an independent committee of physicians, statisticians, community advocates, and others that ensures that a clinical trial is ethical and the rights of study participants are protected. All institutions that conduct or support biomedical research involving people must, by federal regulation, have an IRB that initially approves and periodically reviews the research. (Albert, S.M., et al. "Participation in clinical trials and long-term outcomes in Alzheimer's disease," *Neurology* 49, 1997: 38–43. "Alzheimer's disease clinical trials," Wikipedia, http://en.wikipedia.org/wiki/Alzheimer's_disease_clinical_research, modified Jan 15, 2011, accessed Feb 10, 2011). *See also* the Resource section for more clinical trial information.

Clinician Interview Based Impression of Change (CIBI). The Clinician Interview Based Impression of Change (CIBI) is a tool used in evaluating mental status. The CIBI is a clinician's or physician's assessment of global change over time in response to therapy.

Clinician Interview Based Impression of Change with Caregiver Input (CIBIC Plus). The Clinician Interview Based Impression of Change with Caregiver Input (CIBIC Plus) is an assessment tool based on both an evaluation by a physician and input given by the patient's primary caretaker. Because mental status may vary from day to day, with alternating periods of lucidity, input from a caregiver offers a wider view of one's impairment and insight into daily living skills.

The CIBIC Plus is scored as a seven point categorical rating, ranging from a score of 1, indicating "markedly improved," to a score of 4, indicating "no change," to a score of 7, indicating "markedly worse."

Clioquinol. Clioquinol is a drug long used as an antiamoebic agent. It was withdrawn in 1971 because of its likely association with cases of subacute myelo-optic neuropathy mostly occurring in Japan. Researchers at Massachusetts General have shown that clioquinol is an effective chelator for zinc and copper. In studies with mice, clioquinol was shown to reduce Abeta production in half. Researchers at Harvard University and the University of Melbourne are currently studying clioquinol in clinical trials for its use as a therapy in Alzheimer's disease and Huntington's disease.

Clock Draw Test. The clock draw test is a neuropsychological evaluation tool best used in combination with other cognitive assessment tools. There are variations of the test, but its main focus is asking the patient to draw the face of a clock with all the numbers. The patient is then asked to draw the hands set at a certain time. The test assesses cognitive or visuospatial impairment.

Clozapine. Clozapine is an anti-psychotic medication occasionally used to manage symptoms in Alzheimer's disease. Side effects include sedation, ataxia, falls, delirium and bone marrow suppression, making this drug an unlikely first choice for patients with dementia.

Clusterin (apolipoprotein J). Clusterin or apolipoprotein J is a multifunctional protein present in the brain, which is associated with aggregated amyloid beta peptide in the senile and diffuse plaques of Alzheimer's disease. Clusterin is reported to enhance the oxidative stress caused by amyloid beta. Enhanced neurotoxicity has been observed in the highly aggregated amyloid deposits.

In 2010, Simon Lovestone, lead researcher from the Institute of Psychiatry at King's College London, used a technique called proteomics to analyze clusterin. They conducted two "discovery phase" studies in 95 patients and found that clusterin, a protein associated with apoptosis, or programmed cell death, was linked to early signs of Alzheimer's disease. The protein appears to increase atrophy in the hippocampal region of the brain. After the initial study, the researchers then evaluated clusterin levels in almost 700 people, including 464 with Alzheimer's disease, and found a link between higher levels of the protein and severity of disease, rapid progression of the condition, and atrophy in the enthorhinal cortex, which plays a role in memory. Lovestone's research suggests that abnormal accumulations of clusterin appear up to ten years before symptoms of Alzheimer's disease are exhibited. (Thambisetty M., et al. "Association of plasma clusterin concentration with severity, pathology, and progression in Alzheimer disease," *Archives of General Psychiatry,* 2010, 67(7): 739–748)

Cochrane Dementia Group registry of clinical trials. The Cochrane Collaboration is a nonprofit organization named after Archie Cochrane, a British physician who alerted other physicians that there was a need for ready access to evidence from randomized controlled clinical trials. The Cochrane Collaboration developed into an international organization which conducts systematic reviews of randomized controlled trials in all areas of health, including clinical trials related to dementia. Reviews of studies involving dementia are listed in the Cochrane Dementia Group registry of clinical trials.

Coenzyme Q-10 (Co-Q-10). Coenzyme Q-10 (Co-Q-10) is a substance known to enhance the bio-availability of other nutrients. A potent antioxidant, CoQ-10 has free-radical scavenging properties and helps transport electrons into cell mitochondria where they are used for energy production. Idebenone is a form of CoQ-10 with increased blood-brain barrier penetration. Studies show that deficiencies of Co-Q-10 can cause symptoms of dementia. Low Co-Q-10 levels are caused in malabsorption, including malabsorption caused by the use of statin cholesterol-lowering medications and individuals with hyperthyroidism and gluten sensitivity. Co-Q-10 is currently being evaluated in clinical trials for its effects in Alzheimer's disease.

Coexisting illness. Coexisting illnesses are illnesses that exist in addition to the patient's primary disorder. Patients with Alzheimer's disease frequently have coexisting illnesses, such as hypertension or diabetes. The effects of therapy on both disorders need to be considered. Certain drugs used to treat coexisting illnesses may have adverse effects on cognition. Drugs that are likely to be offenders include anticholinergics, antihypertensives, antidepressants, antianxiolytics and antipsychotics. Even over-the-counter medications, such as cough and cold preparations, have the potential to impair memory. If a new medication is introduced or its dosage is increased and new dementing symptoms appear, consideration should be given to stopping the drug to see if it is responsible for the change in symptoms.

Cognex *see* Tacrine hydrochloride

Cognision System. The Cognision System patented by Neuronetrix, Inc., is a diagnostic tool used to measure brainwaves as cognitive markers for Alzheimer's disease. This system is currently being evaluated by researchers at the University of Kentucky Sanders-Brown Center on Aging and the Duke University Medical Center. Testing will include 200 people recruited from four to six sites in the United States. Brainwaves or event-related potentials (ERPs) will be measured from subjects' scalps while they listen to a series of auditory stimuli or "beeps." These ERPs will be used to train a computer to distinguish subjects with AD from healthy volunteers. This clinical trial builds on an earlier pilot study in which the portable COGNISION System was tested at the UK College of Medicine for data quality, ease-of-use, and patient tolerance. (Neuronetrix Press Release, Jul 2, 2010, http://www.marketwire.com/press-release/Neuronetrix-Announces-Clinical-Trial-Collaboration-With-Premier-Research-Institutes-1285105.htm, accessed Jan 5, 2011)

Cognitive ability. Cognitive ability refers to the intact function of thought processes, such as learning, comprehension, memory, reasoning and judgment. Cognitive ability also refers to one's ability to logically deal with problems and to communicate.

Cognitive assessment. Cognitive ability is assessed by a number of different neuropsychological tests, including tests for verbal recall, visuospatial ability, praxis and orientation. These tests measure judgment, reason, logic and general intelligence. Because ethnic and cultural dif-

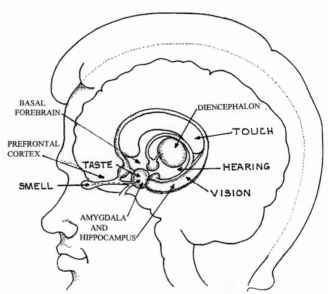

STIMULUS RECEIVED BY THE CEREBRAL CORTEX IS RELAYED BY THE AMYGDALA AND HIPPOCAMPUS TO THE DIENCEPHALON. THE INFORMATION IS NEXT TRANSMITTED TO THE PREFRONTAL CORTEX AND THE BASAL FOREBRAIN. WHERE IT IS TRANSMITTED BACK TO THE SAME SENSORY AREA THAT FIRST RECEIVED THE INFORMATION. SOME MEMORY MAY BE STORED IN THE CEREBRAL CORTEX DURING THIS PROCESS.

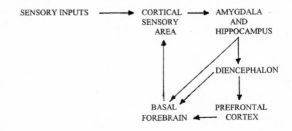

Learning/thought process (illustration by Marvin G. Miller).

ferences can affect some of these test results, a wide panel of tests offer a more accurate representation of cognitive ability. *See also* Neuropsychological tests.

Cognitive impairment. Cognitive impairment refers to a reduction in the ability to extract, process, retain, and retrieve thoughts. Cognitive impairment results from dysfunction or loss of the neurons responsible for cognition. Cognitive impairment may be temporary or transient as a result of injury, the side effects of medications or delirium or it may be permanent as in most forms of dementia.

Cognitive reserve. Cognitive reserve is the overall ability to withstand the declines of aging and disease. Epidemiologic evidence suggests that individuals with higher IQ, education, occupational attainment, or participation in leisure activities, or who are bilingual, have a reduced risk of developing Alzheimer's disease. The concept of cognitive reserve proposes that individual differences in how tasks are processed provide differential reserve against brain pathology. This is seen in two ways. In neural reserve, preexisting brain networks that are more efficient or have greater capacity may be less susceptible to disruption. In neural compensation, alternate networks may compensate for pathology's disruption of preexisting networks. Imaging studies have begun to identify the neural substrate of CR. Because CR may modulate the clinical expression of AD pathology, it is an important consideration in studies of "preclinical" AD and treatment studies. There is also the possibility that directly enhancing CR may help forestall the diagnosis of AD. Cognitive reserve explains why, on autopsy, Alzheimer's patients with the most severe pathology do not necessarily have the most severe symptoms.

Cohen-Mansfield Agitation Inventory (CMAI). The Cohen-Mansfield Agitation Inventory (CMAI) is an evaluation tool used to measure emotional behavior and neuropsychiatric manifestations in patients with Alzheimer's disease.

Columbia University Scale for Psychopathology in Alzheimer's disease (CUSPAD). The Columbia University Scale for Psychopathology in Alzheimer's disease (CUSPAD) is an evalua-

tion tool used to assess emotional behavior and neuropsychiatric manifestations in patients diagnosed with Alzheimer's disease.

Combativeness. Combativeness is a form of aggressive behavior in which those affected are inclined to initiate fights, both physical and verbal. Patients with Alzheimer's disease may become combative if they are confused and feel threatened.

Combination therapy. A disease as complex as Alzheimer's disease is unlikely to respond satisfactorily to one single drug therapy. A combination of drugs is generally used. The drugs most often used are: acetylcholinesterase inhibitors, inhibitors of beta-amyloid formation or deposition, neuronal growth factors, anti-inflammatory agents, estrogens, and neuroprotective agents including antioxidants.

Preliminary research findings presented at the annual meeting of the American Geriatrics Society in May 2001 suggest that a combination of the cholinesterase inhibitors donepezil and rivastigmine may be effective in improving cognitive function among patients with Alzheimer's disease. The study, which was conducted by J.R. Shua-Hain, M.D. and colleagues at Meridian Hospitals Corporation of New Jersey, involved reducing the dose of donepezil from 10 mg to 5 mg daily and adding an initial dose of 1.5 mg rivastigmine once daily. After three days with no side effects, rivastigmine was increased to 1.5 mg twice daily. Improvement was seen mostly in improved linguistic skills and functional performance.

Commissures. Commissures are nerve fibers of different diameters found in the white matter of the brain. Commissures are supported by neuroglial cells. The corpus callosum is the largest commissure of the brain, connecting the two cerebral hemispheres.

Communication. People with dementia eventually lose their language abilities and their ability to communicate. When first losing language skills, patients may rely more on other senses such as touch and sight. It is important that patients with dementia continue to have regular checkups for hearing and vision and that hearing aids and spectacles are of the right prescription. Caregivers should speak clearly and slowly and make eye contact, making sure they have the patient's attention before speaking. While patients may no longer understand language, they will still understand hugs, smiles and expressions of gratitude and appreciation. Cueing and memory aids can be used to help patients with impaired language skills.

Competence. Competence refers to one's ability to act in a specific capacity. For instance, individuals with Alzheimer's disease lose their mental competence.

Complement. Complement is an immune system chemical released during the immune response. There are several different types of complement, which are released in a cascade, initiated by the release of complement 1, or C1. According to one hypothesis, inflammation in Alzheimer's disease is triggered by the activation of C1. Activation of the complement system is a powerful immune system effector mechanism. It can initiate the production of other pro-inflammatory factors such as tumor necrosis factor (TNF) and contribute to neurodegeneration in Alzheimer's disease.

Computed axial tomography (CAT scan). Computed axial tomography is a CT scan performed on a specific axial plane; used as a synonym for CT scan.

Computed tomography (CT scan). Computed tomography is a diagnostic imaging technique introduced in 1980 used to determine structural anatomy. Computed tomography relies on the same principles as conventional x-rays. CT enabled clinicians to exclude intracranial lesions or tumors as a cause of dementia, and is the procedure of choice for visualizing the characteristic structural changes of Alzheimer's disease, such as increased ventricular size and the presence of cortical atrophy. Brain CT scans, particular views of the medial temporal lobe, are able to differentiate changes in the normal aging brain from those seen in Alzheimer's disease. This accuracy increases when a functional imaging technique such as SPECT is combined with CT.

In CT, structures in the brain are distinguished from one another by their ability to absorb x-rays. The x-ray tube emits a narrow beam of radiation as it passes in a series of scanning movements through a 180-degree arc surrounding the patient's head. The resulting x-ray images are fed to a computer which processes the information and displays it on a terminal screen. The sensitivity of the CT head scan is so precise that the gray matter of the cerebral cortex, white matter, internal capsule, corpus callosum, ventricles and subarachnoid spaces can all be recognized. By using a contrast dye, changes in blood flow can also be examined.

When it was introduced CT caused a rise in diagnostic accuracy of Alzheimer's disease from 43 percent to 70 percent. Before probable diagnoses were confirmed in postmortem examination. CT replaced invasive methods of pneumoencephalography and cerebral angiography, a procedure used sparingly in the elderly because of its associated morbidity. However, single CT scans, whether analyzed qualitatively or quantitatively, cannot distinguish Alzheimer's disease from normal elderly adults because of the overlap seen in brain atrophy in both groups. In Alzheimer's disease, CT reveals enlargement of the ventricular system and cortical sulci, but this is usually not significantly different from that in age matched controls. Serial quantitative CT scans of lateral ventricular volume, however, have been shown to demonstrate a distinct difference in patients with Alzheimer's disease when compared to normal elderly subjects. The real utility of CT in Alzheimer's disease lies in the exclusion of other treatable disorders.

Confrontations. Patients with Alzheimer's often become involved in confrontations with their caregivers. Caregivers are reminded not to draw attention to failure and to avoid confrontation by staying calm. Conflict causes unnecessary stress for both the patient and the caregiver. Patients with dementia invariably forget things or deny that they have done something wrong. Often, they accuse others of taking their possessions when they have hidden their possessions and forgotten where they put them. They may become defensive, making the situation worse. Caregivers are reminded that it is the fault of the disease, not the person. Experts suggest that caregivers nip confrontations in the bud by distracting the patient, giving them tasks to do such as folding towels or dusting furniture. Another suggestion is changing the scenery by taking the patient for a walk or car ride.

Confusion Assessment Method Diagnostic Algorithm (CAM). The Confusion Assessment Method Diagnostic Algorithm (CAM) is an evaluation tool used to measure confusion. CAM includes 4 features: acute onset and fluctuating course, inattention, disorganized thinking, and altered level of consciousness.

Consortium to Establish a Registry for Alzheimer's Disease (CERAD). CERAD is a standardized clinical and neuropsychological evaluation tool consisting of the verbal fluency test, Boston Naming Test, Mini-Mental Status Examination, ten-item word recall, constructional praxis, and delayed recall of praxis items. Testing usually takes 20–30 minutes and is useful in assessing and tracking cognitive decline.

CERAD was established in 1986 in an effort to develop standard methods to evaluate persons with Alzheimer's disease and to gather clinical, neuropsychological and neuropathological information about this disorder. CERAD also evaluates informant-based ratings of emotional and behavioral status collected by 30 Alzheimer's disease research centers in the United States. This information is analyzed for the purpose of standardizing and testing the reliability of commonly used brief assessment instruments so that it can provide accurate tools for use in epidemiologic surveys, dementia registries, and research protocols, including clinical trials, for Alzheimer's disease.

CERAD's clinical assessment protocol was designed to provide clinicians with the minimum information necessary to make a confident diagnosis of Alzheimer's disease. Tools used in this protocol include interviewing procedures for both patients and informants, a general physical and neurological examination including a structured assessment for extrapyramidal dysfunction, and brief cognitive scales. Global dementia severity can then be staged according to the Clinical Dementia Rating. Diagnosis is aided by the use of the NINCDS/ADRDA criteria.

CERAD neuropsychological measures are able to effectively distinguish cases with mild probable Alzheimer's disease from patients without dementia and education-matched control subjects. (Morris, John C. "Clinical and Neuropathological Findings From CERAD." *Alzheimer Disease: From Molecular Biology to Therapy,* edited by R. Becker and E. Giacobini. Boston: Birkhauser, 1996. 7–12)

Constructional praxis. Constructional praxis is a neurospsychological assessment tool. Patients are given tasks such as building with blocks. This test evaluates cognitive function by evaluating all aspects of motor planning, including the ability to perform tasks in logical steps that lead to completion.

Continuing Care Accreditation Commission (CCAC). The Continuing Care Accreditation Commission (CCAC), founded in 1985, is the nation's only accrediting body for continuing care retirement communities. Sponsored by the American Association of Homes & Services for the Aging (AAHSA), CCAC is an independent entity that accredits only those organizations that pass its inspections (http://www.carf.org/aging/, accessed Feb 1, 2011).

Continuing Care Retirement Communities. Continuing care retirement communities (CCRCs), which originated in the 1980s, are communities that offer several different types of care in one area or community. This allows residents the ability to move to units, including rooms in a nursing home, if the need arises. A CCRC may offer residents the use of apartments, small homes, or structured "life-care" facilities. Fees are based on the amount of care that residents require, with complete or life-care being the most expensive. Ninety-four percent of CCRCs are managed by nonprofit groups. The entrance fee in 2004 began at $38,000 for a one-bedroom apartment, although the rates may be as high as $400,000 at more luxurious communities. There are also monthly fees, averaging $2,000, for a two-bedroom unit, which can rise each year.

Advantages include the nursing care that is provided and the flexibility of being able to move to units providing full care if the need arises. Because all housing units are in the same general location, spouses remain nearby if one of them needs to enter a nursing home in the CCRC.

Disadvantages include the forfeiting of entry fees if the arrangement does not prove satisfactory. It is important to inquire about all of the facility's policies in advance. And while early communities occasionally went bankrupt, state laws ensure that CCRCs keep larger cash reserves. Still it is a good idea to ask the facility for its latest audit report or check with the state insurance commission, which generally regulates CCRCs. It is also important to check on the availability of the type of housing you initially need and to find out the policy regarding admission to the nursing home if the need should arise and the facility is full. (http://www.medicare.gov/LongTermCare/Static/CCRC.asp, accessed Jan 2, 2011)

Continuum of care. Continuum of care refers to the care services available to individuals throughout the course of their care. Changes to care can be made as disease symptoms progress or improve, but the course of care is still continuous.

Copper. Copper is a mineral found in inverse relation to zinc in the body. Results of the Nun Study show an association between high serum copper levels and Alzheimer's disease development. (Tully, C.L. et al. "Serum Zinc, Senile Plaques, and Neurofibrillary Tangles: Findings from the Nun Study." *Neuroreport*, 1995:6 (16), 2105–2108.) However, more recent research suggests that copper may play a role in inhibiting the development of beta amyloid plaques. Researchers at the University of Keele in the UK reported in 2009 that copper (Cu(II)) prevents the deposition of Aβ42 in β-sheets while in their most recent research they show that Cu(II) abolishes the β-sheet structure of preformed amyloid fibrils of Aβ42. A similar finding was made by the group of Jiang for the other form of beta amyloid, Aβ40, and together these observations strongly suggest that copper prevents both the formation and the accumulation of plaques in the brain. How this applies to Alzheimer's disease is still under investigation and currently a matter of debate ("Protective role for copper in Alzheimer's disease," *Science News*, Oct 13, 2009, http://www.sciencedaily.com/releases/2009/10/091008133457.htm, accessed Dec 20, 2010). Another recent study from researchers at the University of Michigan in Ann Arbor shows that copper from copper pipes and copper supplements may be more harmful in people older than 50 years although copper is essential for the health of younger people (Brewer, George. "The risks of copper toxicity contributing to cognitive decline in the aging population and in Alzheimer's disease," *Journal of the American College of Nutrition*, Vol. 28, No. 3, 238–242, abstract available at http://www.jacn.org/cgi/content/abstract/28/3/238, accessed Dec 12, 2010).

Cornell Scale for Depression. The Cornell Scale for Depression is a neuropsychological evaluation test which has proven to be sensitive, reliable and valid for assessing depression in patients with Alzheimer's disease.

Corpus callosum. The corpus callosum is the largest commissure or fiber bundle of the brain, connecting the two cerebral hemispheres. The corpus callosum is further divided into the rostrum, the genu, the body and the spenium. Most fibers within the corpus callosum interconnect symmetrical areas of the cerebral cortex. Because it transfers information from one hemisphere to another, the corpus callosum is essential for learned discrimination, sensory experience and memory.

Cortex. The cortex, or neomammalian area of the brain, the most developed of the brain's areas, is responsible for the brain's lower functions and associations, abstract thinking, and planning abilities.

Cortical basal (corticobasal) degeneration (CBD). CBD is a progressive neurological disorder characterized by nerve cell loss and atrophy of multiple areas of the brain including the cerebral cortex and the basal ganglia. Corticobasal degeneration progresses gradually. Initial symptoms, which typically begin at or around age 60, may first appear on one side of the body (unilateral), but eventually affect both sides as the disease progresses. Symptoms are similar to those found in Parkinson's disease, such as poor coordination, akinesia (an absence of movements), rigidity (a resistance to imposed movement), disequilibrium (impaired balance); and limb dystonia (abnormal muscle postures). Other symptoms such as cognitive and visual-spatial impairments, apraxia, hesitant and halting speech, muscular jerks, and dysphagia (difficulty swallowing) may also occur. An individual with corticobasal degeneration eventually becomes unable to walk.

Corticosteroid therapy *see* Prednisone

Cost of care. The cost of Alzheimer's disease is tremendous with expenditures for medical care, long-term care, home care, and lost productivity amounting to approximately $100 billion annually. Most of these costs are borne by family caregivers. The Alzheimer's Association reported in 2000 that the annual cost of nursing home care is approximately $42,000, not counting lost wages. With variations in different parts of the country, the cost may exceed $70,000 annually. More information can be found at http://www.alz.org/living_with_alzheimers_financial_matters.asp, accessed Jan 5, 2011.

Cranial nerves. Twelve pairs of cranial nerves extend from the lower surface of the brain through openings or foramina in the skull to the periphery of the body.

Cranium. The cranium, or skull, is the bony outer covering housing the brain.

Creutzfeldt-Jakob disease (CJD). Creutzfeldt-Jakob disease (CJD), a neurological disorder caused by an infectious agent known as a prion, results in a type of dementia that may be confused with Alzheimer's disease. Its onset is subacute rather than chronic. It causes other neurologic abnormalities besides organic brain syndrome, such as myoclonic jerks (muscle twitches), extrapyramidal findings, and visual disturbances. The hallmark of CJD is a spongiform change of the gray matter with slight involvement of the white matter. When examined by electron microscopy, the brain tissue in CJD appears vacuolated. The vacuoles contain vesicles and membranous debris.

Creutzfeldt-Jakob disease (CJD) is classified as a form of spongiform encephalopathy. The first cases of Creutzfeldt-Jakob disease were reported in 1920 by Drs. Hans Gerhard Creutzfeldt and Alfons Jakob. CJD appears to be more prevalent in Sephardic Jews and in families from Chile and Slovakia, and it generally presents as a type of dementia between the fifth and seventh

decades of life. Either injection of human pituitary-derived growth hormone (commonly given to children with growth disorders in the 1970s and 1980s) or grafting tissue surrounding the human brain can transmit this disease to humans. CJD can also be transmitted by corneal transplantation, the implantation of dura mater, and contaminated brain electrodes and surgical instruments.

CJD can occur in multiple forms including sporadic, iatrogenic, or familial. Sporadic CJD is a rare, poorly understood disorder whereas iatrogenic forms occur as a result of contamination with infected tissue. Familial CJD stems from a genetic mutation in the prion protein gene. New variant CJD (nvCJD) was recognized in 1996 in the United Kingdom, where the deaths of 48 from nvCJD patients had been documented by 2000. Cases of nvCJD have also been reported in the United States as a result of eating elk contaminated with wasting disease. *See also* Prions

Critically attained threshold of cerebral hypoperfusion (CATCH). The critically attained threshold of cerebral hypoperfusion (CATCH) hypothesis points to reduced cerebral blood flow as a contributing factor for the develop of both early and late-onset forms of Alzheimer's disease. This viewpoint is supported by the fact that chronic cerebral hypoperfusion (reduced blood flow) can affect metabolic, anatomic and cognitive function adversely. In addition, therapies aimed at improving or increasing cerebral blood flow often show benefits in patients with Alzheimer's disease. According to this theory, advanced aging in patients with vascular risk factors can result in the CATCH syndrome. This, in turn, triggers defects in the brain's blood circulation that impair neuronal cell function. According to this theory, this results in a cascade of events that ultimately lead to the development of Alzheimer's disease. (de la Torre, J.C. "Critically attained threshold of cerebral hypoperfusion: the CATCH hypothesis of Alzheimer's pathogenesis," *The Neurobiology of Aging*, Aug 2000: 21 (2), 331)

Crystallin, Alpha B. Alpha beta crystalline is a heat shock protein whose expression is elevated in Alzheimer's disease that is associated with increased neurotoxicity. The major component of the plaque aggregate in the brain of individuals with Alzheimer's disease is a 39–42 long peptide termed beta-amyloid (Abeta). Except for Abeta, plaques contain several other components which co-precipitate together with Abeta. One such component is alphaB-crystallin. Instead of preventing the cell from the neurotoxicity of Abeta, alphaB-crystallin induces an increased neurotoxicity. Heat shock proteins are produced in response to stress and by infectious agents. Normally, heat shock proteins play a valuable role in chaperoning toxins from the body. However, increased amounts can cause immune system changes that lead to inflammation.

Cueing. Cueing or priming refers to prompts, hints, and other information used to help patients with dementia remember words or tasks. Cueing can involve the use of pictures, lists or simple one-word reminders. Studies show that patients with Alzheimer's disease retain their ability to read even in severe disease. Leaving lists and other written reminders is a good cueing tool.

Curcumin (Curcuma longa). The herb curcumin is the most common type of the spice turmeric grown in India. Curcumin is used in curry, prepared mustard, and as a food preservative. As a dietary supplement curcumin is found in a capsule form. A potent antioxidant, curcumin has anti-inflammatory properties and has long been used to treat arthritis. Researchers have found that curcumin works by inhibiting several different pro-inflammatory chemicals including lipooxyenase, COX-2, leukotrienes, prostaglandins, nitric oxide, interferon-inducible protein, tumor necrosis factor (TNF) and interleukin-12 (IL-12). Because of its ability to relieve pain, researchers included it in their Alzheimer's Disease Anti-Inflammatory Prevention Trial (ADAPT), which involved more than 2,500 patients.

In the ADAPT trial, patients were given either of two non-steroidal anti-inflammatory (NSAID) medications (200 mg celocoxib or 220 mg naproxen twice daily) or a placebo. While the NSAIDs reduced symptoms in 30 percent of test subjects, side effects brought a halt to the NSAIDs. Instead, the researchers substituted curcumin. The results exceeded those of the NSAIDs. Symptoms improved and plaque was reduced by 43 to 50 percent in the brain of test subjects. The researchers concluded that curcumin showed promise. While more trials are needed before curcumin can be considered the gold standard, the recommended dose is 450–600 mg daily. To increase absorption, curcumin should be taken with a healthy fat such as coconut oil or olive oil. (Chainani-Wu, N. "Safety and anti-inflammatory activity of curcumin: a component of turmeric (Curcuma lona)," *Journal of Alternative and Complementary Medicine*, Feb 2003, 9(1): 161–8)

CX516 (Ampalex). CX516 (Ampalex) is an investigative drug produced by Cortex Pharmaceuticals that regulates receptors on which the excitotoxins glutamate and aspartame accumulate. Because these compounds are powerful nerve toxins, CX516 shows promise in that it reduces their concentrations. CX516 functions as a novel AMPA receptor mediator. It facilitates the function of a subtype of glutamate receptor by increasing the amount of current flow that takes place when glutamate binds to the AMPA receptor. CX516 is also used for the treatment of schizophrenia, and is reported to improve memory performance in healthy elderly subjects. Clinical trials for Ampalex in Alzheimer's disease have been proved disappointing due mainly to low potency and short half-life. (http://clinical-trials.gov/ct2/show/NCT00001662)

CX1632. CX1632 (compound S47445) is a high impact ampakine developed by Cortex Pharmaceuticals in collaboration with Les Laboratoires Servier (Servier), France's largest privately owned pharmaceutical company. Servier can develop and distribute S47445 in Europe, Asia, the Middle East and certain South American countries as a treatment for neurodegenerative diseases and anxiety disorders. Cortex retains the rights to develop and distribute S47445 in North America, most of South America, Australia and New Zealand. In November 2010, Servier announced that it will be initiating Phase I trials of CX1632 for Alzheimer's disease. ("First joint Cortex-Servier high-impact AMPAKINE compound moves into phase I clinical studies," *Business Wire*, Nov 10, 2010, http://www.businesswire.com/news/home/20101110005659/en/Joint-Cortex-

Servier-High-Impact-AMPAKINE-Compound-Moves-Phase, accessed Mar 3, 2011)

Cyclooxygenase (COX)-2. Cyclooxygenase-2 (COX-2) is an enzyme released during the inflammatory response. In neuronal activities, it helps the body produce chemicals known as prostglandins. Prostglandins are oxygenated unsaturated cyclic fatty acids that have a variety of hormone-like actions, such as muscle relaxation. Prostglandins also increase levels of the excitotoxin glutamate, which is a powerful neurotoxin.

COX-2 is upregulated or over-expressed in the Alzheimer's disease brain. Studies indicate that COX-2 overstatement causes neuronal cell cycle dysregulation in a murine model of Alzheimer's disease neuropathology. Preliminary evidence utilizing this model suggests that neuronal over-expression of COX-2 increases beta-amyloid peptide neurodegeneration, increases the susceptibility of excitotoxic lesions, and is associated with an age-dependent accumulation of brain microglia. Drugs designed to inhibit the action of cyclooxygenase may offer therapeutic benefits in patients with Alzheimer's disease. Inhibition of neuronal COX-2 by drug therapy may control microglial responses, demonstrating a neuron-to-glia interaction that may be mediated by oxidants generated by COX.

Cyclooxygenase 2 (COX-2) inhibitor. Cyclooxygenase (COX-2) inhibitors are anti-inflammatory drugs that inhibit the production of COX-2, a natural substance activated by inflammatory stimuli. Selective COX-2 inhibitors are currently undergoing clinical trials. Studies at the University of Michigan of Ann Arbor have detected the presence of natural COX inhibitors in tart cherries. Because COX-2 is a key player in neuroinflammation and has been implicated in the development of neurodegenerative diseases and worsening of damage from such insults as traumatic brain injury and stroke, several studies have focused on the use of COX-2 inhibitors as therapies for Alzheimer's disease. However, to date, the cardiovascular adverse effects associated with this class of drugs have prohibited their use in neurodegenerative diseases.

Cyclooxygenases. Cyclooxygenases are enzymes that convert acids in the body into prostglandins.

The most important of these compounds are cyclooxygenase 1 (COX-1) and cyclooxygenase 2 (COX-2).

Cytochrome-c oxidase. Cytochrome-c oxidase is an enzyme necessary for proper functioning of cell mitochondria. Deficiencies of cytochrome oxidase (complex IV) activity in the cerebral cortex and platelets have been reported in patients with Alzheimer's disease. Alzheimer's disease has specifically been linked to mitochondrial anomalies affecting cytochrome-c oxidase, and these anomalies may contribute to the abnormal production of free radicals. Free radicals are known to damage neurons. Free radicals are a normal part of aging and also occur in oxidative stress. Studies show that oxidative stress is increased in Alzheimer's disease patients.

Cytokines. Cytokines are immune system chemicals, such as the interferons, interleukins and various growth factors that modulate the immune response. In response to an immune system threat, glial cells in the brain come to the rescue and release cytokines, which work to modulate the immune response. As chemical messengers, cytokines in the brain contribute to the inflammation and tissue injury seen in many of the neurodegenerative disorders. Specifically, beta amyloid inflames surrounding microglial cells within the nervous system. These cells release inflammatory cytokines, nitric oxide, and other neurotoxins that can destroy nearby neurons. The cytokine transforming growth factor-β (TGF-beta) is suspected of contributing to the development of Alzheimer's disease.

Cytoskeletal abnormalities. Cytoskeletal abnormalities are seen in affected neurons in individuals with Alzheimer's disease. The most common cytoskeletal alteration is neurofibrillary tangles. Other fibrillar cytoskeletal abnormalities involve axons and terminals (dystrophic neuritis) and dendrites (Neuropil threads). The cytoskeleton is essential for maintaining cell structure and intracellular trafficking of proteins and organelles, including transport along axons. Cytoskeleton disturbances ultimately cause cell death.

D'Adamio, Luciano, M.D., Ph.D. Dr. Luciano D'Adamio is a Professor of Immunology at Albert Einstein College of Medicine in New York

City. While working as a principal investigator at the Laboratory of Cellular and Molecular Immunology Division of the National Institute of Allergy & Infectious Diseases in Bethesda, Maryland, Dr. D'Adamio isolated the Familial Alzheimer's Disease (FAD) Presenilin-2 (PS-2) gene and proved that the PS-2 gene could inhibit apoptosis of autoreactive cells in the thymus by cell membrane death receptors. At Albert Einstein, Luciano continues his research involving the processing of Amyloid βPP, the third FAD gene known to date. Dr. D'Adamio is also actively researching the Alzheimer's disease-like conditions Familial British Dementia and Familial Danish Dementia and their association with genetic mutations of BR12.

Dapsone (Avlosulfon). Dapsone (Avlosulfon), produced by Immune Network, Incorporated, is an anti-infective agent used to treat leprosy. Because dapsone-treated leprosy patients have a lower prevalence of Alzheimer's disease than the general population, dapsone has been investigated for its use as a therapeutic agent in Alzheimer's disease.

Deep Brain Stimulation (DBS). Deep brain stimulation is an invasive therapy commonly used in Parkinson's disease in which electrodes are implanted in brain tissue. Researchers in Toronto, Canada, are conducting a small trial of 6 patients to see if DBS offers benefits in Alzheimer's disease. The Phase I trial for safety took place between 2005 and 2008 and showed that three of the subjects showed significant improvement. The researchers are not planning a Phase II, multi-centered trial. In the Phase I trial, scientists implanted electrodes in the brain's hippocampus, which plays a role in long-term memory. The electrical conductor acts as a pacemaker-like device in the head just beneath the skin. It is connected to a battery pack in the chest. The patients were all discharged from the hospital within 2–3 days of the surgery. For more information about participating in the next phase of the trial, see http://www.uhn.on.ca/Focus_of_Care/KNC/Functional_Neurosurgery/research.asp, accessed Mar 22, 2011.

Dehydroepiandrosterone (DHEA) sulfate. Dehydroepiandrosterone (DHEA) sulfate is a naturally occurring hormone that declines with aging. In one study, 50 healthy subjects and 24 Alzheimer's patients were evaluated for levels of DHEA and cortisol. The ratio of DHEA sulfate to cortisol was significantly lower in the patients with Alzheimer's disease, particularly the female patients in the study. (Schwartz, A. "Biological role of dehydroepiandrosterone." *Gerontologist*, 1992: 32 (3), 425. Carlson, Linda E. and Barbara B. Sherwin. "Relationships among cortisol (CRT) dehydroepiandrosterone-sulfate (DHEAS), and memory in a longitudinal study of healthy elderly men and women." *Neurobiology of Aging:* 20 (3), 315–324.) Several small studies using 100 mg DHEA sulfate daily have shown no significant cognitive improvement in subjects with Alzheimer's disease. However, further studies are warranted. (Mayo Clinic Evidence, http://www.mayoclinic.com/health/dhea/NS_patient-dhea/DSECTION=evidence, accessed Jan 3, 2011)

DeKosky, Steven T., M.D. Dr. Steven T. DeKosky formerly director of the Division of Geriatrics and Neuropsychiatry at the University of Pittsburgh served as director of the Alzheimer's Disease Research Center from 1994 to 2008 and. He is currently the dean of the University of Virginia School of Medicine. Considered an international expert on the translational aspects of Alzheimer's disease, his clinical research includes differential diagnosis, neuroimaging, genetic risks of Alzheimer's disease and trials of new medications. His basic research centers on structural and neurochemical changes in human brains in dementia.

Delirium. Delirium is an acute condition characterized by a reduced ability to maintain attention to external stimuli and confusion or disorganized thinking, as indicated by rambling, irrelevant, or incoherent speech. The essential features of delirium include global cognitive impairment, abnormal psychomotor activity and a disturbance of the sleep-wake cycle.

Delirium is one of the most frequent forms of psychopathology seen in hospitalized elderly persons. The elderly are uniquely prone to developing delirium. Delirium can be precipitated by many different illnesses and by therapeutic amounts of many different medications. Certain acute and life-threatening illnesses such as myo-cardial infarction or pneumonia may initially present as delirium. The DSM-IV-TR 2000 criteria for delirium include:

1. disturbance of consciousness (e.g., reduced clarity of awareness of the environment with reduced ability to focus, sustain, or shift attention)
2. change in cognition (e.g., changes in memory deficit, disorientation, language disturbance), or the development of a perceptual disturbance that is not better accounted for by a preexisting, established, or evolving dementia
3. disturbance develops over a short period of time, usually hours to days, and tends to fluctuate during the course of the day
4. evidence from the history, physical examination, or laboratory results that the disturbance is caused by the direct physiological consequences of a general medical condition.

Delirium differs from dementia in the onset and duration of cognitive impairment and level of consciousness. The onset of cognitive impairment in delirium is typically hours or days, and it lasts days to weeks. Furthermore, patients with delirium shows signs of either diminished alertness (hypo-alertness) or intensified alertness (hyper-alertness). Patients with delirium show limited ability to extract, process and retain and recall information. The level of consciousness in delirium tends to fluctuate. (American Psychiatric Association, *Diagnostic and Statistical Manual of Mental Disorders* Fourth Edition, Text Revision DSM-IV-TR, Arlington, VA: American Psychiatric Association, 2000: 143)

Delusions. Delusions are false beliefs regarding the self, or persons or objects outside the self that persist despite facts to the contrary; from the word delude, which means to mislead the mind or its judgment.

Dementia. Dementia is a chronic brain disorder characterized by multiple cognitive deficits including a decline of memory and disorientation in comparison with previous normal cognitive function. For a diagnosis of dementia the cognitive deficits must be sufficiently severe to impair occupational or social functioning. A diagnosis of dementia is also based on a history of decline in performance and by abnormalities noted during clinical examination and neuropsychological testing and the cognitive deficits must not exclusively occur during the course of delirium. The criteria established by the NINCDS-ADRDA state that confirmation of dementia should be based on memory impairment, which is often the only early symptom. Other symptoms that may occur include aphasia (deterioration of language function), apraxia, agnosia, and disturbances in executive functioning. The term dementia is used to describe a number of different physical disorders of the brain arising from different causes. Dementia is not a disease, but rather a cluster of symptoms that are caused by various diseases or conditions.

Dementia is usually progressive, irreversible and ultimately fatal. Alzheimer's disease is the most common cause of dementia, accounting for about 60 percent of the irreversible cases. Dementia can also result from a number of different degenerative diseases, vascular disorders, traumas, infectious agents, toxic compounds, space-occupying lesions, substance abuse, nutrient deficiencies, and other disorders.

Degenerative disorders that can cause dementia include Alzheimer's disease, Pick's disease, Huntington's disease, progressive supranuclear palsy, some cases of Parkinson's disease, cerebellar degenerations, some cases of amyotrophic lateral sclerosis (ALS), Parkinson-ALS dementia complex of Guam and other island areas, and rare genetic and metabolic diseases (Hallervorden-Spatz, Kufs', Wilson's, late-onset metachromatic leukodystrophy, adrenoleukodystrophy).

Vascular dementia can be caused by multi-infarct dementia, cortical micro-infarcts, lacunar dementia, Binswanger disease, hydrocephalus, and cerebral embolic disease.

Anoxic dementia, which is caused by a lack of oxygen to the brain, can result from cardiac arrest, severe cardiac failure, and carbon monoxide poisoning. Traumatic dementia can occur as a result of dementia pugilistica (boxer's dementia) and head injuries (both open and closed).

Infectious dementia can occur a result of acquired immune deficiency syndrome (AIDS), opportunistic infections, Creutzfeldt-Jakob disease (subacute spongiform encephalopathy), progressive multifocal leukoencephalopathy, post-encephalitis dementia, herpes encephalitis, bacterial meningitis or encephalitis, brain abscess, parasitic encephalitis, neurosyphilis, and fungal meningitis or encephalitis.

Autoimmune disorders that may cause dementia include Behcet's syndrome, systemic lupus erythematosus (SLE), vasculitis, Hashimoto's encephalopathy, and some cases of multiple sclerosis (MS).

Space-occupying lesions that can cause dementia include chronic or acute subdural hematoma, primary brain tumors and metastatic tumors, including carcinoma, leukemia, lymphoma and sarcoma.

Toxic forms of dementia include alcoholic dementia, carbon monoxide poisoning, metallic dementia (caused by lead, mercury, arsenic, manganese, etc.) and organic poisons, including solvents and insecticides. A number of drugs may cause dementia when used in high doses, including sedatives, hypnotics, anti-anxiety medications, anti-hypertensives, anti-arrhythmics, anticonvulsants such as phenobarbital, anti-psychotics, digitalis and derivatives and drugs with anticholinergic side effects.

Psychiatric disorders that may progress to dementia include depression, anxiety, psychosis and sensory deprivation.

Nutrient deficiencies that may cause dementia include pellagra (vitamin B6 deficiency), thiamine deficiency (Wernicke-Korsakoff syndrome), cobalmin deficiency (vitamin B12 deficiency and pernicious anemia), folate deficiency, and Marchiafava-Bignami disease.

Other disorders that may cause dementia include myxedema coma, epilepsy, post-traumatic stress disorder, some cases of Whipple disease, heat stroke, hyperthyroidism, hypothyroidism, hypoglycemia, hypernatremia (high blood sodium), hyponatremia (low blood sodium), hyperlipidemia (high blood lipids), hypercapnia (excess carbon dioxide), kidney failure, liver failure, Cushing syndrome, Addison's disease and hypopituitarism. (Katzman, R. et al. "Accuracy of Diagnosis and Consequences of Misdiagnosis of Disorders Causing Dementia." Washington, DC: Office of Technology Assessment, U.S. Congress, 1986)

Dementia of the Alzheimer's type. Dementia of the Alzheimer's type is recognized when symptoms of dementia occur gradually and progressively and other causes of dementia including delirium have been ruled out. In early onset subtypes, symptoms occur before age 65, whereas in late onset conditions, the onset of dementia occurs after age 65. Dementia of the Alzheimer's type is also subdivided into conditions with and without behavioral disturbances. The prevalence at age 65 is 0.6 percent in males and 0.8 percent in females. At age 90, the prevalence rises to 21 percent in males and 25 percent in females.

The disease course is slowly progressive with an average loss of 3–4 points annually on standard assessment test such as the Mini-Mental State Exam. Over time, personality changes, including increased irritability, may occur. In the later stages, individuals may develop gait and motor disturbances and become bedridden. The average duration of the illness from onset of symptoms to death is 8–10 years although there is wide variability. (American Psychiatric Association, Diagnostic and Statistical Manual of Mental Disorders Fourth Edition, Text Revision DSM-IV-TR, Arlington, VA: American Psychiatric Association, 2000: 154–60)

Dementia pugilistica (DP). Dementia pugilistica (DP) is a neurological disorder also known as Punch Drunk, Traumatic Boxer's Encephalopathy, chronic traumatic brain injury associated with boxing (CTBI-B) or Boxer's Syndrome because of its association with brain injuries sustained during head injuries and concussions associated with sports. Symptoms and signs of DP develop progressively over a long latent period that can span decades, with the average time of onset being about 12–16 years after the start of a career in boxing. The condition is thought to affect around 15–20 percent of professional boxers. The incidence in football players is currently being evaluated. Researchers at the University of Pennsylvania's Center for Neurodegenerative Disease Research conducted a study comparing the brains of patients with DP to the brains of Alzheimer's disease patients. In their report, published in the June 2001 issue of the international neurology journal *Acta Neuropathologica*, the researchers wrote that their findings suggest that brain injury can cause DP by activating mechanisms similar to the ones that cause tau lesions in Alzheimer's disease. This suggests that head injury can increase susceptibility to Alzheimer's disease in later life. Symptoms of DP are similar to those of dementia, including declining mental ability, problems with memory, gait disturbances, language disturbances, as well as Parkinson's-like symptoms. Patients with DP may also exhibit inappropriate or explosive behavior and may display evidence of pathological jealousy or paranoid behavior. Individuals with DP may be treated with drugs used for Alzheimer's disease and Parkinson's disease.

Dementia Trialists' Collaboration. The Dementia Trialists' Collaboration evaluates data from clinical trials and determines the benefits or pitfalls of the therapies studied in the trials. Reviewers randomly select trials for inclusion and then evaluate individual patient data.

Dendrite. Dendrites are short processes arising from the cell body of neurons that receive information and conduct it toward the cell body. Dendrites, which may be referred to as neurites or nerve fibers, are necessary for learning.

The diameter of dendrites tapers the further away they extend from the cell body. Dendrites often branch profusely, causing large numbers of small projections called dendritic spines. Having cytoplasm similar to that of the cell body, dendrites are often considered extensions of the cell body, allowing for the reception of axons from other neurons. Dendrites conduct the nerve impulse toward the cell body.

Dentate nucleus. Masses of gray matter are embedded in the white matter of the cerebellum. The largest of these areas is known as the dentate nucleus.

Deoxyribonucleic acid (DNA). Deoxyribonucleic acid (DNA) is a chain of nucleotides (cytosine, guanine, adenine or thymine) linked with ribose sugar molecules. DNA forms the base of genetic material. Specific patterns of nucleotides (the composition of the molecules and how they are strung together) represent particular genes. Alterations to or mutations in DNA on specific genes such as the lipoprotein genes are found to influence the development of Alzheimer's dis-

ease. Treatment interventions, including diet, are under investigation that can influence the way certain genes are expressed.

Depression. Depression may be confused with dementia in that many of the symptoms are the same, including loss of interest in hobbies and community activities, apathy, weight loss, and sleep disorders. In some cases, depression coexists with dementia. Depression is more likely to occur in mild to moderate Alzheimer's disease as opposed to severe Alzheimer's disease. This may be because severely affected patients are unable to communicate their symptoms. Other symptoms of depression include dysphoric mood, loss of appetite, fatigue, irritability, insomnia and agitation.

Major depression with dementia that sometimes occurs in the elderly may be an early sign of Alzheimer's disease, preceding diagnosis by two years or less. Some experts believe that disease progression may even be delayed by treating such patients with both an antidepressant and a more specific therapeutic agent such as donepezil. Apathy may sometimes be confused with depression. Apathy is more commonly seen than depression in Alzheimer's disease. Apathy is characterized by a lack of emotions, motivations and interest rather than sadness, which is a symptom of depression.

Caregivers should be alert for symptoms of melancholia or depression including crying, complaining or suicidal ideation. Depression may contribute to impaired activities of daily living, and a sudden impairment of activities of daily living may suggest coexisting depression. Patients exhibiting symptoms of depression should be considered for a trial of antidepressants even if they do not meet the full diagnostic criteria for major depression because depression in patients with advanced Alzheimer's disease may present with atypical symptoms, including mood swings, impatience, and aggression.

Treatment of depression in elderly patients with Alzheimer's disease is usually initiated with selective serotonin reuptake inhibitors (SSRIs), such as fluoxetine or sertraline. These drugs may have cognitive-enhancing effects and are considered to be the treatment of choice for depression in Alzheimer's disease. Although these drugs have a low incidence of side effects, they should be started at low dosages and increased slowly. Older medications, such as the tricyclic antidepressants (amitriptyline, nortriptyline, imipramine, desipramine) often cause anticholinergic side effects that may impair cognition or cause urinary retention, constipation and orthostatic hypotension. Thus, they are usually contraindicated in Alzheimer's disease. (Evans, Rebecca, M.D., and Martin Farlow, M.D. "Drug Therapies for Alzheimer's Disease," *Home Healthcare Consultant*, 2000)

Desferrioxamine (Desferoxamine). Desferrioxamine is an iron chelating agent used to reduce toxic accumulations of iron and aluminum in the brains of Alzheimer's disease patients. Originally used to treat dementia in dialysis patients caused by aluminum toxicity, desferrioxiamine has been shown to improve cognitive function in some patients with Alzheimer's disease. While studies performed in the early 1990s showed promise, little research in this area has been completed aside from research on animal models with stroke symptoms. (Hanson, Leah R., et al. "Intranasal desferoxamine provides increased brain exposure and significant protection in rat ischemic stroke," *Journal of Pharmacology*, Sept 2009, 330 (3): 679–686, http://jpet.aspetjournals.org/content/330/3/679.full, accessed Sept 5, 2010)

DHA *see* Docosahexaenoic acid

Diabetes *see* Insulin

Diagnostic and Statistical Manual of Mental Disorders, 4th Edition, revised (DSM-IV-R). The *Diagnostic and Statistical Manual of Mental Disorders*, 4th Edition, revised (DSM-IVR) in 2000 is the current edition of the official diagnostic manual of the American Psychiatric Association. *See* DSM IV Diagnostic criteria for Alzheimer's dementia.

Diagnostic criteria for Alzheimer's disease. There are no simple blood or imaging tests that are routinely used to diagnose Alzheimer's disease. However, advances in positron emission tomography (PET) testing are enabling physicians to diagnose Alzheimer's disease accurately and at earlier stages. In addition, in 2010 two new tests were approved to help in the early di-

agnosis of Alzheimer's disease: PET scan assisted with an injected radioactive dye that binds to plaque; and a diagnostic test to measure tau and amyloid protein in cerebrospinal fluid.

The essential elements supporting diagnosis and that suggest a need for these new tests include an acquired decline in cognitive functions, an impairment of daily living activities, and a progressive disease course combined with imaging tests that show the characteristic brain changes seen in Alzheimer's disease.

General diagnostic criteria include: a progressive decline in cognitive function not associated with other causes with an onset between age 28 and 90 years. Diagnosis may be supported by one of the following criteria: loss of motor skills, diminished activities of daily living and altered patterns of behavior, family history of dementia, and imaging tests that support a diagnosis consistent with cerebral atrophy.

The American Academy of Neurology guidelines for a diagnosis of Alzheimer's disease include: a careful clinical history which includes the onset of symptoms and their progression, a mental status examination such as the Mini-Mental Status Examination (MMSE), a neurological examination, neuroimaging tests such as CT or MRI (to see if there is evidence of silent stroke, tumors, subdural hematoma), and basic laboratory tests to rule out other causes of dementia, such as vitamin B12 deficiency or thyroid dysfunction.

When symptoms alone are being considered, observation over time is often required before diagnosis of Alzheimer's disease can be certain. A significant association with the e4 allele of the apolipoprotein E gene supports the diagnosis of Alzheimer's disease in patients with dementia. However, this test is neither fully specific nor sensitive. The clinical diagnosis of Alzheimer's disease (prior to autopsy confirmation) is reported to be correct about 80–90 percent of the time. While tests for AD7c and amyloid beta 42 are available, they are best performed on spinal fluid and their use as diagnostic markers has not been established.

A definitive diagnosis can only be made at autopsy. Characteristic brain changes are seen postmortem, including neuronal cell death, brain shrinkage, microscopic Aβ-amyloid neuritic plaque deposits and intraneuronal neurofibrillary tangles. The plaque deposits stain positive with Aβ-amyloid antibodies and negative for prion antibodies. The numbers of plaques and tangles exceed those found in age-matched controls without dementia.

Cultural variables, including languages, social customs, traditions and the quality and quantity of education must all be taken into consideration when tests for cognitive ability are evaluated. Existing test batteries yield high false-negative results among educated individuals and false-positive results among the very elderly and illiterate. One study, the Age-Associated Dementia project, conducted by the World Health Organization (WHO), indicated that the following criteria are reliable for diagnosing Alzheimer's disease: the DSM-III-R, IVD10 and NINCDS-ADRDA.

The diagnosis of probable Alzheimer's disease is supported by deficits in two or more areas of cognition, progressive worsening of memory, no disturbances of consciousness, onset between the ages of 40 and 90 (most commonly after age 65), absence of other systemic disorders, and associated symptoms of depression, insomnia, incontinence, delusions, verbal outbursts, sexual disorders and weight loss. Features that make a diagnosis of Alzheimer's unlikely include sudden, apoleptic onset, and focal neurology findings such as sensory loss, incoordination and visual field deficits, seizures, and gait disturbances early in the course of the illness.

Early diagnosis is important because research indicates that current medication and care options are effective in people with mild to moderate symptoms. While there is currently no cure for Alzheimer's disease, medication can improve certain cognitive functions, including memory and thought. Early reports from clinical trials suggest that vaccines may be effective in breaking down amyloid deposits and reversing damage. (McAuliffe, Kathleen. "Early diagnosis for Alzheimer's disease," *Discover*, Jan/Feb 2011: 32). *See also* Diagnostic and Statistical Manual of Mental Disorders, 4th Edition, revised (DSM-IV-R); Differential diagnosis; Laboratory tests; Metabolic causes of dementia; NINCDS-ADRDA criteria for Alzheimer's disease; Positron emission tomography (PET) scan.

Dick, Malcolm Boyne, Ph.D. Dr. Malcolm Boyne Dick is a doctor of cognitive psychology and an expert in the treatment, diagnosis and possible preventative measures associated with Alzheimer's disease. Dr. Dick maintains an office at the Institute for Brain Aging and Dementia at the University of California at Irvine. His area of expertise is the inhibition of proteins that regulate apoptosis in Alzheimer's disease.

Diencephalon. The diencephalon, the central part of the forebrain, consists of a dorsal thalamus and a ventral hypothalamus as well as an epithalamus and subthalamus. Accounting for only about 2 percent of the weight of the brain, the diencephalon is very important for many of the body's primary functions. The diencephalon consists of the third ventricle and the structures that form its boundaries. The inferior surface of the dienchephalon is the only area exposed to the surface in the intact brain.

Diet and nutrition. Foods high in citrulline, such as watermelon, have been found to inhibit nitric oxide production, reducing free radical formation, and offering protection against Alzheimer's disease. Diets high in antioxidants, including red wine, blueberries and fish, have also been shown to have a protective effect. Dietary factors and other conditions that lead to increased blood lipid levels have been shown to increase the risk of developing Alzheimer's disease.

Dietary restriction. Dietary restriction refers to reduced calorie intake with maintained nutrition. In many studies dietary restriction has been found to extend the life span of rodents and prevent the neuronal degeneration characteristically seen in Alzheimer's disease. Specifically, it increases resistance of neurons, preventing dysfunction and degeneration and improves behavioral outcome in experimental models of Alzheimer's disease and other age-related neurodegenerative disorders. ("Neuroprotective strategies for Alzheimer's disease," *Life Extension*, Medical Updates, January 2002: 73. Excerpted from *Experimental Gerontology*, 2000: 35 (4), 489–502)

Dietary supplements used for the treatment of Alzheimer's disease. Dietary supplements are widely used in Alzheimer's disease to reduce free radical formation and improve antioxidant status. Studies have demonstrated benefits using vitamin E, alpha lipoic acid, acetyl-l-carnitine, and acanthocyanin bioflavonoids. ("Alpha lipoic acid and other treatments for Alzheimer's disease," *The Natural Path,* http://www.the-natural-path.com/alpha-lipoic-acid.html, accessed Jan 2, 2011)

Differential diagnosis. Dementia can occur from other causes besides Alzheimer's disease. The differential diagnosis of dementia should emphasize potentially treatable disorders that may cause, or exacerbate, dementia. Differential diagnosis is based on the knowledge of the salient features of Alzheimer's disease and a recognition of conditions that can mimic this disease.

Although reversible disorders are uncommon, their importance justifies a thorough evaluation of each patient. Before a diagnosis of Alzheimer's disease can be made other causes of dementia must be ruled out, especially treatable forms of cognitive decline such as cerebrovascular events, nutritional disorders, neoplastic disorders, genetic disorders, depression, chronic drug intoxication, chronic central nervous system infection, infectious processes, thyroid disease including Hashimoto's encephalopathy, toxic conditions, vitamin deficiencies (especially B12 and thiamine), and normal pressure hydrocephalus.

Other degenerative disorders associated with dementia such as fronto-temporal dementia, Picks disease, Parkinson's disease, diffuse Lewy body disease, Creutzfeldt-Jakob disease, and CADASIL may also be confused with Alzheimer's disease. Computerized topography and magnetic resonance imaging studies are valuable for identifying other causes of dementia, such as neoplasms or brain tumors, normal pressure hydrocephalus, and cerebral vascular disease.

Prior to arriving at a diagnosis of Alzheimer's disease, doctors should conduct a diagnostic work-up that either rules out these other disorders or shows that one or more of these conditions may be contributing to the dementia. The history should include the nature of the patient's symptoms, their onset, progression and any interference with work or family life. It should also include questioning of prior conditions, current medications, and psychiatric problems. The physical examination should include an evaluation for major relevant medical conditions, including stroke, cancer, hypertension nutritional disorders, and thyroid disorders. *See* Metabolic causes of dementia.

Diffuse Lewy body dementia (DLBD). Diffuse Lewy body dementia (DLBD) is a neurological condition clinically and pathologically distinct from Alzheimer's disease. DLBD is associated with a more profound and more generalized cholinergic deficit than Alzheimer's disease. In addition to parkinsonian symptoms, patients may experience delusions and visual hallucinations. The disease course tends to be more rapid than what is typically seen in Alzheimer's disease. Many subjects progress from symptom onset to death within 3 to 4 years. In clinical trials, the anticholinergic medication rivastigmine caused a reduction of parkinsonian symptoms and an increase in cognitive function as measured by neuropsychiatric testing. (Fallow, M.D., Martin. "Therapeutic Advances for Alzheimer's Disease and Other Dementias." *Medical Education Collaborative,* 2001)

Digital Subtraction Angiography (DSA). Digital subtraction angiography (DSA) is a computer-assisted imaging procedure used to visualize the blood vessels within and supplying the brain as well as other vascular abnormalities. The image produced by DSI is enhanced by the elimination of surrounding and interfering structures. DSA is used to diagnose arteriosclerotic disease, vascular lesions and tumors and other space occupying lesions.

Dignity. Caregivers are reminded of the importance of treating Alzheimer's disease patients with respect and dignity. Patients with Alzheimer's disease still have feelings and they often become frustrated as they begin to struggle with everyday tasks. Maintaining dignity is important for Alzheimer's disease patients. (Kolata, Gina. "Alzheimer's patients present human dignity," Health Section, *New York Times,* 1997, http://www.nytimes.com/1997/01/01/us/alzheimer-patients-present-a-lesson-on-human-dignity.html, accessed Feb 4, 2011. Warchol, Kim. "Preserving the dignity of a person with Alzheimer's disease," *Crisis Prevention,* 2010, http://www.crisiprevention.com/Resources/Article-Library/

Dementia-Care-Specialists-Articles/Preserving-the-Dignity-of-a-Person-with-Alzheimers, accessed Mar 1, 2011)

Dimebon *see* Latrepiridine

Disability Assessment for Dementia (DAD). The Disability Assessment for Dementia (DAD) is a global assessment tool used for documenting functional deficits such as the ability to bathe, dress and eat. The DAD is useful in predicting the individual disease course and expected disease progression in patients with Alzheimer's disease.

Disorientation. Patients with dementia frequently become disoriented to person, place and time. *See also* Orientation.

Distraction. Distraction refers to divergence of attention, inability to pay attention, or mental derangement. Patients in any of the stages of Alzheimer's disease may experience distraction.

Do not resuscitate (DNR) orders. As part of an advanced directive or a living will, do not resuscitate (DNR) orders are care directives prohibiting caregivers from using life-prolonging measures, such as cardiopulmonary resuscitation (CPR), to patients who would not survive without them. According to the Department of Medicine at West Virginia University in Charleston, only about 15 percent of hospitalized patients survive and are discharged after CPR. And as many as half of CPR patients suffer fractured ribs, fractured sternum, aspiration pneumonia, hemorrhage, or pulmonary edema. Patients are presumed to consent to CPR unless they have a signed DNR order, a living will, or a medical power of attorney indicating that the patient would not wish to receive CPR.

While laws may vary by state, in general, a DNR order may be written by any attending physician who shares primary responsibility for the patient. Informed consent of the patient or his surrogate is required. DNR orders may be written for a child, if a parent and two physicians agree. If the patient is incapacitated and there is no appointed surrogate, a physician may write a DNR order with the concurrence of a second examining physician.

A patient or surrogate may revoke a DNR order by a written or verbal request to any healthcare provider. The healthcare provider must immediately notify the attending physician, who must immediately cancel the order. When patients are transferred to other facilities, such as to a hospital from a nursing home, the DNR order should accompany the patient and will remain in effect until new orders are issued. DNR orders do not apply to patients who experience a cardiac or respiratory arrest as a result of a trauma situation.

A physician may ethically cancel CPR or refuse to initiate it when it is not medically appropriate, will likely not be successful or if it will likely harm the patient with no likely benefit. However, if the patient or family reasonably requests that the physician perform CPR, he may be legally challenged if he declines to initiate or continue CPR.

Docosahexaenoic acid (DHA). Docosahexaenoic acid (DHA) is an omega-3 essential fatty acid. DHA is the primary structural fatty acid in the gray matter of the brain and retina of the eye. DHA is important for mental and visual function. The average diet is low in DHA due to low consumption of red meats, animal organ meats, and eggs, as well as high consumption of refined carbohydrates. This results in an imbalance of omega-6 oils relative to omega-3 oils. Because of its importance as a neurotrophin, DHA is added to infant formula in England. In the United States, DHA is available as a dietary supplement. The ideal ration of omega-6 to omega-3 oils is 2:1, whereas the typical American diet provides a ratio of more than 10:1 omega-6 to omega-3 oils. The key omega-3 oils for brain nutrition are eicosapentaenoic acid (EPA) and DHA. Research indicates that DHA can help prevent the formation of beta amyloid plaque. Animal studies showed that mice on a DHA-rich diet developed only about 30 percent of plaque compared to mice given no or very little dietary DHA. Good sources of DHA and EPA include salmon, sardines and tuna.

For many years infant formula in Europe has been supplemented with DHA. This policy has recently been instituted in the United States. Infant formula manufacturers in the U.S. currently offer formulas containing docosahexaenoic acid (DHA) and the omega-3 oil arachidonic acid

(ARA). Formulas containing DHA and ARA have been shown to provide visual and mental development similar to that of the breastfed infant. The decision to supplement formulas with these nutritional long-chain polyunsaturated fatty acids (LCPUFAs) was made following years of research studying the clinical effects of both DHA and ARA in infants. The use of LCPUFAs in infant formulas has been reviewed and supported by the U.S. Food and Drug Administration, the European Food Safety Authority, the Food and Agriculture Organization and World Health Organization, the Codex Alimentarius Commission, the Agence Francaise De Securite Sanitaire Des Aliments, the American Dietetic Association and the Dietitians of Canada, the European Society for Paediatric Gastroenterology and Nutrition, the World Association of Perinatal Medicine and Child Health Foundation, the Commission of European Communities and the National Academy of Sciences. (Infant Feeding and Nutrition website, March 2010, http://www.infantformula.org/news-room/press-releases-and-statements/infant-formula-and-dha/ara, accessed Mar 4, 2011). *See also* Omega-3 fatty acids

Donepezil hydrochloride. The cholinesterase inhibitor donepezil hydrochloride (Aricept or E2020) is the drug most commonly used in the treatment of Alzheimer's disease in the United States. Approved by the FDA in 1996 for treatment of mild to moderate Alzheimer's disease, donepezil inhibits the breakdown of the chemical acetylcholine without causing the changes in liver enzymes seen with tacrine hydrochloride. Aricept is used in the management of patients with mild to moderate symptoms of Alzheimer's disease, although it does not stop or slow down the disease's progression. The usual dosage is 5 mg to 10 mg taken once daily. In 2010, a recommendation was made to change the dose to 23 mg daily although the dosage increase can increase the risk of side effects.

Side effects, which include diarrhea, vomiting, muscle cramps, nausea, fatigue, insomnia and anorexia, are generally mild and decline with continued use of the drug. Less common side effects include abnormal dreams, constipation, dizziness, drowsiness, fainting, frequent urination, weight loss, headache, joint pain, stiffness or swelling, mental depression and unusual bleeding or bruising.

Rare side effects include black, tarry stools, bloating, bloody or cloudy urine, blurred vision, burning, prickling or tingling sensations, cataracts, chills, clumsiness or unsteadiness, confusion, cough, decreased or painful urination, dryness of mouth, eye irritation, fever, flushing of skin, changes in blood pressure, hives, hot flashes, increased sexual desire, increased heart rate, urinary incontinence, agitation, abnormal crying, aggression, delusions, irritability, nervousness, nasal congestion, pain in chest, upper stomach or throat, shortness of breath, sneezing, and tremor.

Symptoms of overdose include convulsions, increased sweating, increased watering of mouth, increased muscle weakness, low blood pressure, severe nausea and vomiting, slow heartbeat and troubled breathing.

Dopamine. Dopamine is a catecholamine neurotransmitter derived from the amino acid tyrosine. The neurons that produce dopamine are known as dopaminergic neurons. Dopaminergic neurons are primarily located in the compact part of the substantia nigra and in the adjacent ventral tegmental area as well as the hypothalamus, the retina and the olfactory bulb. Dopamine is instrumental for movement and it is also involved in motivation and cognition. Deficiencies of dopamine are part of the underlying pathology in Parkinson's disease. Dopamine is widespread in the brain as well as the rest of the nervous system. This neurotransmitter plays a critical role in the control of movement, and it stimulates the heart, the circulation, the rate of metabolism, and serves to mobilize many of the body's energy reserves. It helps to modulate brain activity, control coordination and movement, and regulate the flow of information to different areas of the brain. Dopamine levels in the brain of patients with Alzheimer's disease are low due to a deficiency of dopamine D2 receptors. Therapies aimed at increasing dopamine in Alzheimer's disease are being investigated.

Doppler imaging. Doppler imaging is an enhanced noninvasive diagnostic test in which a Doppler ultrasonic probe is employed. Doppler imaging is used to diagnose abnormalities of carotid blood flow, ulcerative plaques and carotid artery occlusive disease.

Down Syndrome. Less than 1 percent of all cases of Alzheimer's disease are associated with Down Syndrome, which is also known as trisomy 21. However, essentially all patients with Down Syndrome develop the neuropathological hallmarks of Alzheimer's disease (neurofibrillary tangles and plaque deposits) after age 35. If they are carefully tested, more than half of these individuals show clinical evidence of cognitive decline. The incidence of Alzheimer's disease in the Down Syndrome population is estimated to be three to five times greater than in the general population. It is recommended that individuals with Down Syndrome be tested at age 30 to provide a baseline assessment of psychological performance. If the tests show deterioration, further tests must be done to rule out diseases that present similar symptoms.

The presumed explanation for this association is the lifelong over-expression of the amyloid precursor protein (APP) gene on chromosome 21 and the resultant overproduction of Aβ-amyloid, particularly Aβ42, in the brains of persons who are trisomic, having an extra copy for this gene. Neuropathological studies have shown that amyloid beta deposition occurs in Down Syndrome at a very young age (20–30 years). However, research in this area is lacking because of a paucity in obtaining brain tissue from patients with both disorders. The co-existence of Alzheimer's disease is responsible for the sharp decline in survival of Down Syndrome patients older than 45 years.

Driving. As soon as Alzheimer's disease is diagnosed, the patient should be prevented from driving. A Swedish study reported that over half of elderly people involved in fatal accidents had some degree of neurological impairment. Even in the early stages of Alzheimer's disease patients may lose their way home and experience other problems when driving. Judgmental deficits associated with dementia, visual field defects after stroke or other brain injury or delayed reflexes contribute to increased likelihood of collisions or loss of control.

Drug interactions. Many drugs, including over-the-counter, herbal, and prescription preparations, are known to interfere with the metabolism of other drugs. It is important to advise the patient's doctor of all medications, even herbs, administered to patients with Alzheimer's disease.

Drug therapy. Drug therapy refers to the use of oral or intravenous medications to help control or alleviate symptoms of disease. Drugs that are currently approved or being evaluated for Alzheimer's disease can be found at http://www.therubins.com/aging/alzheim5.htm, accessed Mar 2, 2010. *See also* Treatment in Alzheimer's disease

Drug toxicity. Many toxic drug metabolites produce a reversible delirium and rarely dementia. Older persons may be more susceptible than younger persons to drug side effects on cognition. This is due to many factors, including altered drug kinetics and the use of multiple medications. A typical presentation is the rapid worsening of dementia following the administration of a new drug or following the reinstitution of a previous medication that the patient has not taken for some time. Psychotropic medications, including neuroleptics, amphetamines and related sympathomimetic amines, sedative-hypnotics, and cardiovascular medications, especially antihypertensives, are common offending agents.

DSM IV diagnostic criteria for Alzheimer's dementia. The following diagnostic criteria are listed in the *Diagnostic and Statistical Manual of Mental Disorders* published by the American Psychiatric Association:

A. The development of multiple cognitive deficits manifested by both
   1. memory impairment (impaired ability to learn new information or to recall previously learned information)
   2. one (or more) of the following cognitive disturbances: aphasia (language disturbance) or apraxia (impaired ability to carry out motor activities despite intact motor function)
   3. amnesia (failure to recognize or identify objects despite intact sensory function)

4. disturbance in executive functioning (such as planning, organizing, sequencing, abstracting)

B. The cognitive deficits in Criteria A1 and A2 each cause significant impairment in social or occupational functioning and represent a significant decline from a previous level of functioning.

C. The course is characterized by gradual onset and continuing cognitive decline.

D. The cognitive deficits in Criteria A1 and A2 are not due to any of the following:
   1. other central nervous system conditions that cause progressive deficits in memory and cognition (e.g. cerebrovascular disease, Parkinson's disease, Huntington's disease, subdural hematoma, normal-pressure hydrocephalus, brain tumor)
   2. systemic conditions known to cause dementia (e.g., hypothyroidism, vitamin B12 deficiency, niacin deficiency, hypercalcemia (high blood calcium level), neurosyphilis, HIV infection)

E. The deficits do not occur exclusively during the course of a delirium.

F. The disturbance is not better accounted for by another Axis I disorder (e.g., Major Depressive Disorder, Schizophrenia) (Diagnosvtic and Statistical Manual of Mental Disorders IV TR-Text Revision, Washington, DC: American Psychiatric Press, 2000.)

Dura mater. The dura mater is a thick, dense, strong, inelastic fibrous membrane that encloses the spinal cord and the brain. Adhering firmly to the inner surface of the skull, the dura mater is often described as consisting of an outer layer, the cranial dura mater, and an inner layer known as the meningeal dura. The dura mater extends along each nerve root of the spinal cord and becomes continuous with the connective tissue surrounding each spinal nerve. The inner surface of the dura mater is in contact with the arachnoid mater of the brain. No space exists on either side of the dura under normal circumstances since one side is attached to the skull and the other side adheres to the arachnoid.

Durable power of attorney. A durable power of attorney is a legal document that allows an individual (the principal) an opportunity to authorize an agent to make legal decisions in the event the person is no longer able to make those decisions.

Durable power of attorney for health care. A durable power of attorney for health care is a legal document that allows an individual to appoint an agent to make all decisions regarding health care, including choices regarding health care providers, medical treatment and end-of-life issues.

Dysarthria. Dysarthria occurs in cerebellar disease as a result of loss of voluntary movement affecting the muscles of the larynx. In dysarthria, speech is jerky and the syllables are often separated from one another or slurred. Speech may also be explosive.

Dysdiadochokinesis. Dysdiadochokinesis, a sign of cerebellar disease, is the inability to perform alternating movements regularly and rapidly. On the side where cerebellar lesions occur, the movements are slow, jerky and incomplete.

Dysphasia. Dysphasia is the inability to find the right word or the loss of the power to use or understand language as a result of injury or disease affecting the brain.

Early onset familial Alzheimer's disease (EOFAD). Early onset familial Alzheimer's disease (EOFAD) refers to conditions of Alzheimer's disease occurring in families in which multiple cases of Alzheimer's disease occur with the mean age of onset occurring before age 65. Age of onset is usually in the 40s or early 50s although onset in the late 20s and early 60s has been reported. EOFAD represents about 5 to 10 percent of all cases of Alzheimer's disease. Prevalence in the general population has been reported to be 41.2 per 100,000 persons. Sixty-one percent of patients with EOFAD have been found to have a positive family history, and 13 percent met stringent criteria for autosomal dominant inheritance occurring in three generations. EOFAD causes symptoms identical to those seen in other forms of Alzheimer's disease. The distinguishing characteristics are age of onset and family history. Only about 120 families worldwide are currently known to carry the mutations for EOFAD.

At least three subtypes of EOFAD have been

identified based on the causative genes on chromosomes 14, 21 and 1. Because patients with apparent EOFAD have been reported to have no involvement with these three genes, it is suspected that other genetic associations exist. The most common responsible mutations are in the presenilin 1 gene on chromosome 14. Mutations to this gene account for 30 to 50 percent of all EOFAD.

AD1 represents 10–15 percent of all EOFAD. It is associated with the gene symbol APP on chromosomal locus 21q21.3-q22. The normal gene product is amyloid precursor protein. Three different mutations at codon 717 of the APP gene have been reported.

AD3 represents 20–70 percent of all EOFAD. It is associated with the gene symbol PSEN1 or PS-1 found on chromosomal locus 14q24. The normal gene product is presenilin 1. Typically, PS-1 mutations are found in patients with age of onset between 30 and 50.

AD4 is a rare form of EOFAD. It is associated with the gene symbol PSEN2 or PS-2 on chromosomal locus 1q31-q42. The normal gene product is presenilin 2. Typically, PS-2 mutations are found in patients with age of onset between 50 and 70. Both PS-1 and PS-2 mutations show overproduction of the longer forms of amyloid beta protein and increased serum levels of A_42. Testing for the responsible gene mutations is not necessary for diagnosis because the disease occurs so early it identifies itself. However, detecting the presence of an autosomal dominant Alzheimer's disease gene can be informative for other family members. (Bird, Thomas, M.D., University of Washington Medical Center, Seattle, 1996. *Alzheimer Overview,* July 2000 revision, National Institutes of Health)

Echoencephalography (ECHO) scan. An echoencephalogram (ECHO) is a simple diagnostic test that uses pulsating ultrasonic waves to indicate deviation of the midline structures of the brain. A probe with a transducer and ultrasonic beam is placed over the midaxis, which is on the temporal bones of the skull. The bones of the skull act as reflectors, helping project images of the spaces between the ventricles. If the ECHO shifts because of an abnormal focus, this suggests a space-occupying lesion. ECHO scans

have largely been replaced by computed axial tomography (CAT) scans.

Echolalia. Echolalia is a condition characterized by repetition of anything spoken to the person, as if echoing the person who is speaking to them. Echolalia is commonly seen in Pick's disease.

Eden alternative. The Eden alternative refers to a concept used in nursing homes, which emphasizes the placement of pets, plants, and other homelike amenities in patient rooms to help patients adapt and not feel displaced.

Efferent nerve fibers. Efferent nerve fibers carry nerve impulses away from the nervous system. Efferent fibers transmit impulses to muscles and glands.

Efficacy of treatment. Efficacy of treatment refers to the power of a particular treatment to produce its intended effects. The efficacy of a given treatment is evaluated in clinical trials.

EGb 761. EGb 761 is an extract of the herb *Ginkgo biloba* used in Europe to alleviate symptoms of cognitive dysfunction. In clinical trials, EGb 761 has been proven to be safe and appears capable of stabilizing, and, in a substantial number of cases, improving the cognitive performance and the social functioning of patients with dementia for 6 months to 1 year. These changes were measured by the ADAS-Cog. While modest, these changes were of sufficient magnitude to be recognized by the caregivers of patients who participated in the studies. (Le Bars, P. et al. "A placebo-controlled, double-blind, randomized trial of an extract of Ginkgo biloba for dementia. North American Egb Study Group." *JAMA,* Oct. 1997: 278 (3), 70)

Eldepryl *see* Selegiline

Elder Books. Elder Books, in Forest Knolls, California, is a publishing company dedicated to publishing practical hands-on guidebooks for family and professional caregivers of persons with Alzheimer's disease. Elder Books also offers a workshop, Activities in Action, designed to help caregivers enhance quality of life for Alzheimer's patients through the use of simple, stimulating activities. http://www.elderbooks.com.

Elder law attorneys. Elder law attorneys are lawyers who specialize in laws pertaining to the elderly and the protection of their assets. The Alzheimer's Association provides guidance in finding elder law attorneys in your area.

Eldercare Locator. The Eldercare Locator division of the Administration on Aging provides help locating needed resources for the elderly. The service can be reached at (800) 677-1116 (a 24-hour hotline in English and Spanish) or http://www.eldercare.gov/ELDERCARE.NET/ Public/Resources/Topic/Alzheimer_Disease.aspx, accessed Feb 1, 2011.

Electroencephalogram (EEG). An electroencephalogram (EEG) is a diagnostic technique used to measure changes in brain wave activity. While not as specific as MRI for diagnosing Alzheimer's disease, EEG is helpful in ruling out other causes of dementia. The EEGs of patients with severe dementia may reveal significant abnormalities whereas mild cases of dementia show only slight abnormalities. Generally, in the later stages of Alzheimer's disease, there is progressive slowing of the EEG tracing with decreased alpha and beta activity although there is increased activity of the delta and theta waves. Some researchers also report that Alzheimer's patients exhibit dominant occipital alpha wave activity, increases of theta power, and decreased EEG coherence. The type of EEG modality may also affect the results. Computerized quantitative EEG appears to be more sensitive than traditional EEG tracing procedures that are manually calculated.

According to current theory, a normal EEG pattern in an individual with severe dementia is likely to be indicative of Alzheimer's disease since most other conditions that result in dementia, including delirium, show abnormal EEG patterns even when there are only mild clinical symptoms. The EEG pattern is also useful in ruling out Creutzfeldt-Jakob disease and epilepsy because they both cause characteristic changes easily seen on an EEG. In Huntington's disease, there is low-amplitude background activity. In cerebrovascular dementia, 75 percent of individuals have been found to have focal abnormalities, including lateralized slow, sharp, or spike waves,

whereas in frontal lobe dementia, the EEG is generally normal.

Encephalitis. Encephalitis is a condition of brain inflammation. Encephalitis may be caused by bacterial or viral infections, toxins or autoimmunity.

Encephalopathy. Encephalopathy is a condition marked by brain inflammation resulting from exposure to environmental substances including infectious agents and organic solvents. Toxic encephalopathy may cause transient symptoms such as the reversible symptoms of acute ethyl alcohol (ethanol) poisoning or permanent residual cognitive impairment which occurs after an overwhelming acute exposure capable of causing coma or death. Long-term toxin exposure resulting in encephalopathy differs from Alzheimer's disease in that there is an absence of naming problems (anomia) and lack of progression to dementia. Symptoms, which can vary in severity, include progressive loss of memory and cognitive ability, subtle personality changes, inability to concentrate, lethargy, and progressive loss of consciousness. Other neurological symptoms may include myoclonus (involuntary twitching of a muscle or group of muscles), nystagmus (rapid, involuntary eye movement), tremor, muscle atrophy and weakness, dementia, seizures, and loss of ability to swallow or speak. *See also* Autoimmune encephalopathy; Hashimoto's encephalopathy

End of life care. End of life care refers to the final services of care provided by physicians, nursing homes, hospices, hospitals and other care providers. These providers are required to follow individual state guidelines and regulations defined by legislative enactments, case law and organizational policies and protocols. Adherence to these guidelines is monitored through risk managers and legal counsel.

Specifically, policies for end of life care focus on advance care planning directives such as health care proxies, do-not-resuscitate orders and living wills. Ethically, patients or their legal representatives have a right to ask for effective pain relief and palliative care, and legally, they have a right to choose or refuse treatment with full knowledge of the benefits or risks.

End of life decisions *see* Advance directives

Endoplasmic reticulum associated binding protein (ERAB). Endoplasmic reticulum associated binding protein (ERAB) is a protein present in the areas of the brain affected by Alzheimer's disease. ERAB appears to combine with beta amyloid, which in turn attracts new beta amyloid from outside the cells. High concentrations of ERAB are also suspected of enhancing the nerve-destructive power of beta amyloid.

Entorhinal cortex. The entorhinal region of the cerebral cortex links the hippocampus to the rest of the brain. In Alzheimer's disease, the entorhinal cortex is the first brain structure to suffer neuronal damage. Damage in this region is evident long before an individual develops perceptible memory loss. As the damage eventually spreads to the hippocampus, the memory deficit becomes more pronounced.

Environmental contributions to Alzheimer's disease. The Alzheimer's Association recognizes aging as the most significant environmental factor contributing to Alzheimer's disease. Environmental factors that contribute to Alzheimer's disease have been the subject of numerous studies. Factors found to influence Alzheimer's disease development advanced by authors at the Challenging Views of Alzheimer's Disease meeting held in Cincinnati on July 28 and 29, 2001, included diet, aluminum, and viruses. The idea that these factors are as important as genetic factors in the etiology of Alzheimer's disease (AD) was advanced by the authors. Diet, dietary fat, and to a lesser extent, total energy (caloric intake) were also documented as contributing factors, while fish consumption was found to be a significant risk reduction factor.

An acid-forming diet, such as one high in dietary fat or total energy, can lead to increased serum and brain concentrations of aluminum and transition metal ions, which are implicated in oxidative stress potentially leading to the neurological damage characteristic of AD. Many of the risk factors for AD, such as cholesterol and fat, and risk reduction factors, such as whole grain cereals and vegetables, are shared with ischemic heart disease. Aluminum may cause neurological damage and a number of studies have linked aluminum to an increased risk for developing AD. The evidence for viral agents playing a role in AD is the strong association between the presence of HSV1 in the brain and carriage of an apoE-l4 allele in the case of AD patients but not of controls; statistical analysis shows the association is causal. Diet, aluminum, and viral infections may increase the prevalence of AD by eliciting inflammation, which may cause the neurological damage that results in AD. *See also* Anthocyanins; Diet and nutrition; Exercise

Environmental factors. Environmental factors are causes of disease that originate outside of the body. External factors include contaminated food, chemical toxins, head injuries, atmospheric particles and pollutants, infectious agents, and stress.

For years scientists have suspected that the environment plays a role in neurodegenerative diseases, including Alzheimer's disease. The fact that identical twins may not both develop Alzheimer's disease is proof that more than genes play a role. Scientists are currently studying the environmental toxins that are related to the chronic death of neurons, the cells that serve as information transmitters and processors in the brain.

According to current theory, the effects of environmental agents may take years to show up. This latent period makes establishing causal relationships difficult. The body's nervous system also has an amazing ability to heal. After a stroke, for example, surviving neurons sprout and establish new connections in an effort to keep the brain in balance. With age, however, this compensatory mechanism declines and the effects of environmental agents become more severe.

In addition, the association between the HLA 2 allele and early onset Alzheimer's disease suggests immune system involvement. This is further supported by the presence of immune system chemicals known as cytokines in the brains of patients with Alzheimer's disease. The immune system initiates an immune response and produces these chemicals in response to environmental factors. Furthermore, several studies show a decreased prevalence of Alzheimer's disease among patients taking anti-inflammatory drugs on a long term basis.

Although no environmental factors responsible for the development of Alzheimer's disease have been convincingly identified, certain environmental factors are associated with disease development. These factors include low education, head trauma, smoking, arterial disease, diabetes and menopause. Results from the Nun study also indicate that a number of environmental factors, including emotional distress, low verbal skills, low anti-oxidant levels, abnormal zinc metabolism, elevated homocysteine levels and high copper levels may also contribute to the development of Alzheimer's disease. And some, but not all, studies on people exposed to intense electromagnetic fields have reported a higher incidence of Alzheimer's disease. Some researchers believe that magnetic fields may interfere with the concentration of calcium inside cells or cause increased production of beta amyloid.

Gary Oberg, M.D., past president of the American Academy of Environmental Medicine, warns that "Toxins such as chemicals in food and tap water, carbon monoxide, dies, fumes, solvents, aerosol sprays, and industrial chemicals can cause symptoms of brain dysfunction which may lead to an inaccurate diagnosis of Alzheimer's disease or senile dementia." (Oberg, M.D., Gary "Causes of Alzheimer's Disease and Other Forms of Senile Dementia," in *Alternative medicine: the definitive guide* by Larry Trivieri, John W. Anderson, and Burton Goldberg Group, Berkeley, CA: Celestial Arts, 2002.) *See also* Nun's study

Enzymes. Enzymes are bodily proteins that function to catalyze specific bodily processes.

Ependyma. Ependyma are neuroglial cells that line the cavities of the brain and the central canal of the spinal cord. Ependyma form a single layer of cells with microvilli and hair-like protrusions known as cilia which aid in the movement of cerebrospinal fluid.

Ependymomas. Ependymomas are brain tumors that originate in the ependymal cells lining the fourth ventricle of the brain. Ependymomas may invade the cerebellum and produce the symptoms and signs of cerebellar deficiency. Tumors in this region may also compress the vital nuclear centers situated beneath the floor of the ventricle, causing cardiac (heart) irregularities.

Epidemiology. Epidemiology refers to the incidence of disease in different populations. Worldwide, approximately twenty million people are suffering from Alzheimer's disease. According to the Alzheimer's Association, an estimated 5.3 million Americans are currently living with Alzheimer's disease. The number of Americans aged 65 and over with Alzheimer's is estimated to reach 7.7 million in 2030. By 2050, between 11 million and 16 million Americans over 65 are expected to have Alzheimer's disease.

Prevalence estimates suggest that Alzheimer's disease affects about 10 percent of persons over the age of 65, making it one of the most common chronic diseases in older persons. Other than age, there are no well-documented risk factors for Alzheimer's disease. Persons with lower educational attainment may be at greater risk, as they are more susceptible to many other common chronic diseases.

Nearly all patients who inherit Down Syndrome develop Alzheimer's disease if they live into their 40s. Women under the age of 35, but not older mothers, who give birth to children with Down Syndrome are also at much higher risk for developing Alzheimer's disease.

Alzheimer's disease is rare in West Africa, although African Americans have four times the risk as white Americans. Hispanics are twice as likely to develop Alzheimer's disease as whites. Alzheimer's disease occurs less in the Native American Crees and Cherokees and in Asians than in the general American population. While Alzheimer's disease occurs less often in Japan, a study of Japanese men indicated that their risk is increased if they move to America.

Researchers at the University of Pittsburgh also report that certain villages in rural India boast the lowest reported prevalence of Alzheimer's disease in the world. This population is also reported to have a low frequency of the apolipoprotein E4 gene variant. Other proposed causes for the low rates of Alzheimer's disease in India and Nigeria include better vascular health, indicated by lower blood pressure, cholesterol and body weight.

Eptastigmine (MF-201). Eptastigmine (MF-201) is a long-acting cholinesterase inhibitor that was evaluated for use as a therapeutic agent in

Alzheimer's disease. The study has been discontinued.

Ergoloid mesylate (Hydergine). Ergoloid mesylate (Hydergine) is one of the first drugs approved by the Food and Drug Administration (FDA) for use in treating dementia. Although Hydergine was once popular in treating Alzheimer's disease because it increases oxygen flow to the brain, it has fallen out of favor. Studies have been conflicting on its benefits.

Estrogen. Animal models have shown that chronic estrogen deficiency affects behavior and cognitive function. This deficiency has been associated with decreased cholinergic activity and is improved with estrogen replacement. Estrogen is thought to modulate multiple neurotransmitters within the brain, increasing the survival of cholinergic neurons and increasing levels of choline acetyltransferase. Estrogen has also been shown to stimulate neurite growth and synapse formation and improve regional blood flow in the brain. Estrogen may also play a role in modulating gene expression.

Estrogen replacement therapy. At least ten controlled trials conducted between 1952 and 2000 have assessed estrogen's role on cognitive function. Most trials did not control for related variables such as depression and education. Eight studies showed that estrogen improved cognitive function in at least one test parameter. In the first long-term study of its kind, researchers at the NIA have found that estrogen replacement therapy improves blood flow to the brain. Overall, the women in the study using estrogen scored higher on memory tests. However, the largest published trials (Polo-Canola, 1998 and Aleve's de Mores, 2001) did not show improvement in any cognitive parameter studied. Although more trials are in progress, several epidemiological studies suggest that the use of estrogen in postmenopausal women for a period not exceeding five years before age 65 may delay the onset or risk of Alzheimer's disease. Studies also indicate that estrogen replacement therapy started after age 65 does not protect against Alzheimer's disease and may increase risk.

Although early studies have shown conflicting results, further studies have suggested that the time in a woman's life at which the therapy is applied may be critical. Based on the results of a number of studies, several researchers have postulated that hormone therapy during a critical midlife period or "window of opportunity" in a woman's life could provide protection. (Green, Robert M.D. "Is the concept of a neuroprotective drug viable for dementia?" *Medscape*, September 9, 2001. "Study suggests ERT stimulates blood flow to key memory centers in the brain," NIA News, June 27, 2000. "Understanding the role of estrogen in Alzheimer's disease prevention," Stanford University Longevity Center, 2010, http://longevity.stanford.edu/node/908, accessed Mar 3, 2011)

Ethics committees. Most hospitals and nursing home facilities have ethics committees composed of physicians, social workers and nurses to determine if the care and treatment of a particular patient is being administered in accordance with ethical guidelines.

Ethnicity. Ethnicity refers to the risk of developing disease for different ethnic groups. The most significant new information coming from the 2010 Alzheimer's Association report: African Americans and Hispanics are at higher risk for developing Alzheimer's. African Americans are about twice as likely to have Alzheimer's as whites, and Hispanics are about 1.5 times more likely than whites to develop the disease. Although there appears to be no known genetic factor to explain these differences, the report examines the impact of health conditions like high blood pressure and diabetes, conditions that are prevalent in the African American and Hispanic communities and how these conditions also increase Alzheimer risk. Another interesting aspect explored is the fact that although African Americans and Hispanics have a higher rate of Alzheimer's than whites, they are less likely than whites to have a diagnosis. *See also* Epidemiology

Etiology of Alzheimer's disease. The etiology, or causes, of Alzheimer's disease include genetic and environmental factors. Like heart disease, Alzheimer's disease is related to a number of different causes. For instance, the genes associated with early-onset Alzheimer's disease cause changes that lead to the formation of beta amyloid protein plaque deposits in the brain. However, it is clear that genes in and of themselves are not enough to cause most instances of Alzheimer's disease. A number or researchers, for example, believe that elevated cholesterol levels contribute to both heart disease and Alzheimer's disease. Researchers at New York University's Nathan Kline Institute have shown how mice on high-fat diets have an increased rate of beta amyloid production in their brains. Other environmental causes include head injuries and heavy metals. ("2010 Alzheimer's Disease Association fact and figures," http://www.alz.org/alzheimers_disease_facts_and_figures.asp, accessed 3/1/2011). *See also* Environmental contributions to Alzheimer's disease

Excitation of nerve cells. When nerve cells are excited or stimulated by electrical, mechanical or chemical means, the cell membrane changes, allowing more sodium ions to enter or diffuse into the cell cytoplasm. This caused the cell membrane to become depolarized, resulting in a brief action potential which allows potassium ions rather than sodium ions to enter the cell. This action potential is conducted along neurites as nerve impulses. Nerve impulses are followed by brief non-excitable states known as refractory periods. The greater the excitatory stimulus, the stronger the impulse.

Excitotoxicity. Excitotoxicity refers to the toxic over-activation of glutamate receptors in neurons in the brain. Excitotoxicity is an important mechanism leading to neuronal cell death in many disease states, including Alzheimer's disease. There is some evidence that glial cells, particularly oligodendrocytes, are also damaged by excitotoxins, including excess glutamate.

Excitotoxins. Excitotoxins are chemical neurotransmitters, such as glutamate, that stimulate neurons. Excitotoxins primarily work by opening calcium channels on certain types of receptors. When excitotoxins are introduced at high concentrations or for extended periods of time, excess calcium enters the cells. This initiates a cascade of cell destruction mediated by free radical production and the release of an enzyme known as phospholipase C. This enzyme breaks down some of the fatty acids that make up the protective cell membrane. This releases an amino acid called arachidonic acid, which further

injures the cells and causes the production of two other enzymes, lipoxygenase and cyclo-oxygenase. Some of the chemical reactions produced by these processes result in rapid cell death.

Two excitotoxins that have been linked to the development of Alzheimer's disease include monosodium glutamate and aspartame. According to Dr. Russell Blaylock, Alzheimer's disease is a classic case of excitotoxin damage. One reason is that beta amyloid protein makes glutamate receptors more receptive to the effects of excitotoxin-induced neuronal cell death. (Blaylock, Russell L. M.D. *Excitotoxins: The Taste That Kills.* Sante Fe, NM: Health Press, 1994. 133–190)

Exelon *see* Rivastigmine

Exercise. Several studies conducted by the Society for Neuroscience indicate that exercise benefits the brain, particularly the hippocampus. In one study, adult mice with access to running wheels doubled the number of new brain cells produced in the hippocampus. In another study, voluntary physical activity alone was enough to cause neuronal growth, which was evidenced by improved performance on memory and learning tasks. Overall, the studies suggest that an active lifestyle helps maintain brain function and that specialized exercise regimens may help repair damaged or aged brains.

Although there is no proven way to prevent Alzheimer's disease, a new study provides some of the strongest evidence yet that regular exercise can protect the brain and even improve cognitive performance in older adults showing signs of mental decline. In this study, researchers at the University of Washington School of Medicine and Veterans Affairs Puget Sound Health Care System tested the effects of aerobic training in a clinical trial with 33 women and men diagnosed with mild cognitive impairment, often a prelude to Alzheimer's disease. Twenty-three of the volunteers, selected randomly, began an intense program of aerobic exercise, spending 45 to 60 minutes on a treadmill or stationary bike four days a week. The remaining 10, the study's control group, spent the same amount of time performing non-aerobic stretching and balance exercises. After six months, the aerobic exercisers showed significant gains in mental agility, while the non-aerobic group showed continuing decline in tests of thinking speed, fluency with words and ability to multi-task. (Rojas-Burke, Joe. "Alzheimer's research: Aerobic exercise can protect brain, improve mental agility," *The Oregonian* Jan 11, 2011, updated Jan 24, http://www.oregonlive.com/health/index.ssf/2010/01/aerobic_training_boosts_aging.html, accessed 2/5. 2011)

Exocytosis. Exocytosis refers to the process in which the neurotransmitter necessary for nerve impulses is discharged in to the synaptic cleft.

Fahr's disease. Fahr's disease is a neurodegenerative disease of unknown etiology that is usually slowly progressive although it can cause a rapidly progressive form of dementia. Fahr's disease is characterized by basal ganglia calcification that typically presents with a movement and neuropsychiatric disorder.

Falx cerebelli. The falx cerebelli of the brain is a small triangular process of dura mater, received into the posterior cerebellar notch. Its base is attached, above, to the under and back part of the tentorium.

Falx cerebri. The falx cerebri is a sickle-shaped fold of the dura mater situated in the midline between the two cerebral hemispheres. The falx cerebri is a strong, arched process which descends vertically in the longitudinal fissure between the cerebral hemispheres. It is narrow in front, where it is attached to the crista galli of the ethmoide, and broad behind, where it is connected with the upper surface of the tentorium cerebelli. Its upper margin is convex, and attached to the bioregion of the inner surface of the skull it contains the superior sagittal sinus. Its lower margin is free and concave, and contains the inferior sagittal sinus. The falx cerebri helps to limit movement of the brain within the skull.

Familial Alzheimer's disease (FAD). Approximately 4–8 percent of all cases of Alzheimer's disease are familial. Although one third of people with Alzheimer's disease have an affected relative, only a small percent of these people have familial Alzheimer's disease (FAD). Symptoms of FAD are identical to those seen in sporadic cases. However, patients with FAD have a family history or a genetic makeup consistent with FAD, which is entirely inherited. FAD may occur as early-onset or late-onset varieties. *See* Early-onset familial Alzheimer's disease and Late-onset familial Alzheimer's disease. (Munoz, David. "Causes of Alzheimer's Disease." *Canadian Medical Association Journal*; 2000 162; 65–72)

Familial fatal insomnia. Familial fatal insomnia is a prion disease that starts with protracted insomnia which progresses to dementia, with sufferers unable to differentiate reality from dreams. Death typically occurs between seven and 15 months after the onset of symptoms.

Fast-Functional Assessment Staging (FAST) *see* Reisberg's seven stages of Alzheimer's disease

Feeding problems. Patients in the early stages of dementia may no longer be able to choose nutritional food. It's important to ensure that patients living alone have nutrient rich meals available. In the later stages of dementia, patients may lose interest in eating and become difficult to feed, often refusing or spitting out food. While it is important to encourage dementia patients to maintain skills such as feeding themselves, this may necessitate having someone sit with them and ensure that they are eating. On occasion patients may have to be spoon-fed.

Studies indicate that tube feedings do not prolong life and frequently cause discomfort and medical complications. Alternatives to tube feeding include changing the consistency of food to pureed or liquid forms, adding thickening agents if aspiration is a problem, employing favorite foods and abandoning dietary restrictions that may no longer be necessary.

Financial burden. The financial burden of Alzheimer's disease is impressive. In 1991, the estimated cost of caring for an individual with Alzheimer's disease was $47,000 annually. The combined direct and indirect cost including medical care, loss of productivity, resource loss and family care for all patients with Alzheimer's disease in the United States are estimated at $172 billion per year. As the population ages, the number of people with Alzheimer's is expected to increase dramatically. ("Facts and figures on Alzheimer's disease," Alzheimer's Disease Association, 2010, http://www.alz.org/documents_

custom/report_alzfactsfigures2010.pdf, accessed March 2, 2011)

Financial capacity. Financial capacity is significantly impaired in the earliest stages of Alzheimer's disease. Patients with mild Alzheimer's disease demonstrate deficits in more complex financial decisions and show impairment in most financial activities. Patients with moderate Alzheimer's disease show severe impairment in all financial abilities and activities. Researchers at the Department of Neurology at the University of Alabama at Birmingham have developed a Financial Capacity Instrument to be used as a tool for assessing domain-level financial activities and task-specific financial abilities in patients with dementia. It is important that patients with Alzheimer's disease be relieved of managing financial activities when they are no longer capable of doing so. Information and video regarding financial capacity available at *Dementia Weekly,* http://www.alzheimersweekly.com/content/money-management-and-dementia, accessed Jan 12, 2011.

Financing long-term care. Long-term care, whether it is provided by a nursing home or a home care agency, may be paid for through personal funds, private insurance, public assistance or a combination of these. Typically, long-term nursing home residents pay for the first months or years of care with their personal funds or with long-term care insurance. When these funds are depleted, the Medicaid program pays for lifetime nursing home care. For patients requiring short nursing home care, Medicare and other insurance programs usually cover the costs. For patients younger than 65, Social Security may cover the first two years of care and then Medicaid kicks in. Medicare does not typically pay for nursing home care, other than for temporary care following hospitalization.

Folic acid deficiency. Folic acid or folate is a B vitamin. Folic acid deficiencies can lead to deficiencies of vitamin B 12, causing symptoms of dementia. While folate can correct vitamin B 12 deficiencies in blood levels, the changes in the brain are not necessarily corrected. For this reason folic acid and vitamin B 12 should be taken together. Furthermore, high amounts of folate in the absence of adequate B12 can provoke or worsen neurological conditions.

A recent long-range Swedish study (Kungsholmen Project) of persons 75 years old and older, which was published in the May 8, 2001, issue of *Neurology,* suggests that more than half of those in this age group have low levels of vitamin B12 and folic acid, and that low levels of either of these two vitamins are related to an increased risk of developing Alzheimer's disease.

Food and Drug Administration (FDA). The Food and Drug Administration (FDA) is the department of the federal government that conducts research and develops standards on the composition, quality and safety of drugs, cosmetics, foods, and food additives. The FDA is responsible for evaluating and regulating clinical trials on the experimental drugs and biological products intended for therapies in Alzheimer's disease.

Forebrain *see* prosencephalon

Fourth ventricle. The fourth ventricle, situated in the posterior cranial fossa, refers to the cavity of the hindbrain. Lined with ependymal cells, the fourth ventricle houses portions of the choroid plexus, and consequently, is filled with cerebrospinal fluid.

Free radicals. Free radicals are unstable chemical molecules that bind to other molecules in a process known as oxidation. Oxidation is a normal bodily process that enables us to utilize energy from food. Oxidation generates free radicals naturally. Free radicals are highly reactive compounds that take electrons from other molecules in an effort to stabilize themselves. In doing so, they produce more free radicals. Brain cells of Alzheimer's disease patients are suspected of being more susceptible to the effects of oxidative stress and subsequent cell death related to increased monoamine oxidase (MAO) activity.

When the body experiences prolonged exposure to free radicals due to oxidative stress, it can no longer neutralize them. Free radicals cause damage by affecting DNA and triggering other harmful processes. Free radicals play a role in many serious disorders including coronary artery disease and cancer. Many researchers think that free radicals released when beta amyloid breaks into protein contribute to the development of Alzheimer's disease. In response to oxidation the immune system initiates an inflammatory response. During this process, harmful chemical molecules and chemicals are released. In particular cyclooxygenase is released, which increases levels of the excitotoxin glutamate.

Neurons, the nervous system cells that make up the bulk of brain tissue, are extremely sensitive to attacks by destructive free radicals. Furthermore, lesions typically seen in the brains of Alzheimer's disease patients are associated with attacks by free radicals with consequences including damage to DNA, protein oxidation, lipid peroxidation, advanced glycosylation end products, and metal accumulation (iron, copper, zinc and aluminum). These metals have catalytic activity that perpetuate the production of free radicals.

Furthermore, beta amyloid is aggregated and produces more free radicals when it is in the presence of free radicals. Beta amyloid toxicity is eliminated by free radical scavengers known as antioxidants. Also, apoplipoprotein E is subject to attack by free radicals, and the resulting peroxidation is associated with Alzheimer's disease. Antioxidants are nutrient substance such as vitamin E that neutralize free radicals.

Friends Life Care at Home. Based in Blue Bell, Pennsylvania, the Quaker non-profit organization Friends Life Care at Home provides the lifetime care services of a continuing care community within the person's own home. Financing this care can be arranged through an insurance plan. Members sign up while they are still healthy and are guaranteed future care, including subsidized meals delivered to their door, daily visits by a registered nurse if needed, and home health care, including assistance with bathing, provided by a nurse's aide. Because care is provided at home, the fees are much less than those of other facilities. For its most comprehensive plan, the initial fee is $21,150, and there is a $350 monthly payment. Additional services are planned in the Maryland and Washington, D.C., areas. http://www.friendslifecare.org, accessed Sept 28, 2011.

Frontal cortex. The frontal area of the cortex is the area where memories are permanently stored after they are processed in the hippocampus. Individuals with Alzheimer's disease as well as the normal elderly experience age-related withering of this region. This explains why elderly people who do not have Alzheimer's disease may also show signs of short-term memory loss.

Frontal lobe. The frontal lobe refers to the front or central area of each cerebral hemisphere. The frontal lobe is nearly completely devoid of granular layers and is characterized by the prominence of its pyramidal nerve cells.

The frontal lobe may be divided into front (anterior) and back (posterior) sections with their own specialized functions. The posterior region, known as the motor area, primary motor, area or Brodmann's area, produces isolated movements in the opposite side of the body when stimulated. The primary auditory area, the taste area and the sensory speech area of Wernicke can be found within the motor regions of the frontal lobe.

Frontotemporal lobe dementia (FTD). Frontotemporal lobe dementia (FTD) is a disorder accounting for nearly 20 percent of all cases of dementia. Frontotemporal dementia describes a clinical syndrome associated with shrinking of the frontal and temporal anterior lobes of the brain. Originally known as Pick's disease, the name and classification of FTD has been a topic of discussion for over a century. The current designation of the syndrome groups together Pick's disease, primary progressive aphasia, and semantic dementia as FTD. Like Alzheimer's disease, FTD is also associated with deposits of tau protein, and some cases of frontotemporal dementia are familial. One of the genes associated with frontotemporal dementia lies on chromosome 17, home of the tau gene. In recent years, twenty different mutations to these gene have been described. Semantic dementia is a rare form of FTD.

Errors in the tau gene may interfere with the way tau protein binds to the tubular backbone of cells or they may cause an imbalance in the types of tau protein produced. Both of these situations would cause a buildup of excess free tau, the protein that accumulates in the neurofibrillary tangles seen in both frontotemporal dementia and Alzheimer's disease. Twenty-five percent of patients with FTD are reported to have a pathologic accumulation of hyperphosphorylated protein in their brain cells.

Another similarity to Alzheimer's disease is the presence of reactive glial cells. However, the pattern in frontotemporal lobe dementia is different as is the neuronal outcome. Unlike the brain in Alzheimer's disease, the brain in frontotemporal dementia is characterized by altered apoptosis and cell death in astrocytes and possibly microglia.

Most cases of FTD are diagnosed in individuals in their 40s through 60s and there is a strong familial component. Early symptoms in FTD are changes in personality and behavior. Memory is generally unaffected in the early stages of the diseases. Although it is difficult to diagnose FTD, it is important to differentiate it from Alzheimer's disease because cholinesterase inhibitors do not help in FTD and may make symptoms worse. As it is defined today, the symptoms of FTD fall into two clinical patterns that involve either (1) changes in behavior, or (2) problems with language. The first type features behavior that can be either impulsive (disinhibited) or bored and listless (apathetic) and includes inappropriate social behavior; lack of social tact; lack of empathy; distractibility; loss of insight into the behaviors of oneself and others; an increased interest in sex; changes in food preferences; agitation or, conversely, blunted emotions; neglect of personal hygiene; repetitive or compulsive behavior; and decreased energy and motivation. The second type primarily features symptoms of language disturbance, including difficulty making or understanding speech, often in conjunction with the behavioral type's symptoms. Spatial skills and memory remain intact. (Frontotemporal lobe dementia information sheet, National Institute of Neurological Disorders and Stroke [NINDS], http://www.ninds.nih.gov/disorders/picks/picks.htm, accessed Feb 23, 2011)

Functional loss. Functional loss in Alzheimer's disease can be assessed by a number of evaluation tools such as the Instrumental Activities of Daily Living (IADL). A characteristic pattern of progressive functional losses has been described as existing at 16 successive levels in Alzheimer's disease. Clinicians can use knowledge of these levels to help diagnose and stage Alzheimer's disease, identify any excess functional disabilities that may be adding to morbidity but which may be capable of being corrected, help in tracking the disease course in Alzheimer's disease.

Gait alterations. Gait refers to a person's manner of walking. Normally, gait or movement is performed voluntarily with precision and economy of effort. In disorders affecting the cerebellum, alterations of gait may occur. The head is often rotated and flexed and the shoulder on the side of the lesion is lower than that of the normal side. The patient assumes a wide base when standing and appears stiff-legged to compensate for the loss of muscle tone. When walking, the individual may lurch and stagger toward the affected side. In later stages of Alzheimer's disease, patients often have "reduced gait," meaning that their ability to lift their feet as they walk has diminished. Gait evaluation is part of the neurological examination.

Galantamine hydrobromide. Galantamine hydrobromide (Nivalin, Razadyne, Razadyne ER, Reminyl, Reminyl, and Lycoremine) is an acetylcholinesterase inhibitor approved for use in Alzheimer's disease. Galantamine has a dual mode of action in that it is able to modulate the nicotinic receptor and strengthen the ability of some neurons to receive chemical message. Galantamine is effective for treating patients with Alzheimer's disease who also have cerebrovascular disease or probable vascular disease. Galantamine is reported to improve all major cognitive and non-cognitive measures in Alzheimer's disease as well as cerebrovascular disease, including vascular dementia. According to Dr. Gary Small, a medical advisor to Jansen Pharmaceuticals, the developer of galantamine, clinical trials lasting one year showed that Reminyl can delay the emergence of debilitating behavioral disturbances associated with Alzheimer's disease, including agitation, aggression, delusions, hallucinations, and the lack of inhibition for at least five months. However, several other studies have shown a higher than expected mortality rate from patients with mild to moderate disease using this drug. (Loy, C. and L. Schnieder. "Galantamine for Alzheimer's and mild cognitive improvement," *Cochrane Database Reviews,* 2006, http://www2.cochrane.org/reviews/en/ab001747.html, accessed Mar 1, 2011)

Gamma-aminobutyric acid (GABA). Gamma-aminobutyric acid is an amino acid that acts as a neurotransmitter. GABA is the major transmitter for brief, point-to-point, inhibitory synaptic events in the central nervous system. Previous research has shown that levels of GABA fall as Alzheimer's disease progresses. Researchers at the University of Nevada Las Vegas are studying the reasons for this in order to see if therapies aimed at increasing GABA could help in Alzheimer's disease. (Leake, Eric. "What's GABA got to do with it?" *UNLV Magazine*, Fall 2006, http://magazine.unlv.edu/Issues/Fall06/23gaba.html, accessed Nov 6, 2010)

Gamma secretase. Gamma secretase is an enzyme directly responsible for the increased production of beta amyloid protein found in the brain of patients with Alzheimer's disease. The genes presenilin 1 and presenilin 2 exert tight control over gamma secretase. Individuals with early onset Alzheimer's disease frequently have mutations to these genes, and these mutations are associated with increased production of beta amyloid protein by gamma secretase and an enhanced penchant for making the more toxic version of beta amyloid protein. One aim of therapy, including vaccine therapy, is the inhibition of gamma secretase.

Gamma secretase inhibitors. Gamma secretase inhibitors are substances that inhibit gamma secretase, an enzyme that contributes to the development of beta amyloid protein. Researchers at the Washington University School of Medicine have discovered that these compounds also prevent certain immune system cells from being produced. These findings were presented in the June 19, 2001, issue of the *Proceedings of the National Academy of Sciences*. Several different gamma secretase inhibitors are currently being studied for their role as a therapeutic agent in Alzheimer's disease. Non-steroidal anti-inflammatory drugs (NSAIDs) inhibit the production of gamma-secretase, which in turn reduces beta-amyloid production. (Eriksen, Jason L., et al. "NSAIDs and enantiomers of flurbiprofen target γ-secretase and lower Aβ42 in vivo," *The Journal of Clinical Investigation*, August 1, 2003, 112 (3): 440–449, http://www.ncbi.nlm.nih.gov/pmc/articles/PMC166298/?tool=pmcentrez, accessed Mar 2, 2011)

Gammagard. Gammagard is an intravenous immunoglobulin (IVIG) therapy developed by Baxter International currently under investigation by the Scripps Research Institute and ModGene for Alzheimer's disease. *See also* Intravenous immunoglobulin (IVIG) therapy

Ganglia. Ganglia are fusiform swellings of nerve fibers. Each individual ganglion is surrounded by a layer of connective tissue that is continuous with the cell body.

GAP Study *see* Intravenous immunoglobulin (IVIG) therapy

Gene therapies in Alzheimer's disease. Several genetic polymorphisms or variants such as Val66 Met have been found to influence the disease course or symptoms in Alzheimer's disease. Genes related to dopamine, serotonin and brain derived neurotrophic factor (BDNF) are considered as candidate genes for Alzheimer's disease. Therapies aimed at influencing gene expression are the subject or continued research for the treatment of Alzheimer's disease.

Genes. Genes are the basic units of heredity. Genes are sections of DNA coding for a particular trait.

Genes in Alzheimer's disease. Scientists have identified four genetic mutations associated with familial forms of Alzheimer's disease. Analysis of the biochemical effects of these genes indicates that they all influence the breakdown of β-amyloid precursor protein (APP), causing the accumulation of beta amyloid protein deposits. All of these mutations enhance the proteolytic processing of β-APP, causing overproduction and accumulation of the neurotoxic derivative, amyloid-β-peptide. Some cases of early-onset AD, called familial AD (FAD), are inherited. FAD is caused by a number of different gene mutations on chromosomes 21, 14, and 1, and each of these mutations causes abnormal proteins to be formed. Mutations on chromosome 21 cause the formation of abnormal amyloid precursor protein (APP). A mutation on chromosome 14 causes abnormal presenilin 1 to be made, and a mutation on chromosome 1 leads to abnormal presenilin 2.

Even if only one of these mutated genes is inherited from a parent, the person will almost always develop early-onset AD. This inheritance pattern is referred to as "autosomal dominant" inheritance. In other words, offspring in the same generation have a 50/50 chance of developing FAD if one of their parents had it.

1. the β-amyloid precursor protein (APP) gene on chromosome 21; mutations in this gene account for less than 1 percent of Alzheimer's disease; onset of symptoms in people with this gene occurs between ages 45 to 65. Several point mutations in this gene are sufficient to cause early-onset autosomal dominant familial Alzheimer's disease. Some mutations increase the production of β-amyloid, while others favor the formation of long (42 amino acid) forms of β-amyloid, which aggregate more readily than the shorter (40 amino acid) forms.
2. the presenilin-1 gene on chromosome 14; accounts for approximately 4 percent of cases; onset ranges from age 28 to 50.
3. the presenilin-2 gene on chromosome 1; accounts for about 1 percent of cases; onset in the late 40s and 50s.
4. the APOE4 gene on chromosome 19; unlike the other three genes which occur only in early onset Alzheimer's disease, the APOE4 gene occurs in both early onset and late onset Alzheimer's disease. The APOE4 gene is known to reduce the clearance of amyloid beta protein, resulting in an accumulation of this neurotoxin protein. The APOE 4 gene is not as damaging as the early onset mutations. Many people who inherit this gene will never develop the disease even in their 90s. There may be other genes not yet identified that cause an increased risk of developing Alzheimer's disease, and there may be other genes that offer protection against disease development.

Most cases of Alzheimer's are of the late-onset form, developing after age 60. Scientists studying the genetics of AD have found that the mutations seen in early-onset AD are not involved in this form of the disease. Although a specific gene has not been identified as the cause of late-onset AD, the APOE4 does appear to increase a person's risk of developing the disease. APOE contains the instructions needed to make a protein that helps carry cholesterol in the bloodstream. APOE comes in several different forms, or alleles. Three forms — APOE ε2, APOE ε3, and APOE ε4 — occur most frequently.

APOE ε2 is relatively rare and may provide some protection against the disease. If AD does occur in a person with this allele, it develops later in life than it would in someone with the APOE ε4 gene.

APOE ε3 is the most common allele. Researchers think it plays a neutral role in AD — neither decreasing nor increasing risk.

APOE ε4 occurs in about 40 percent of all people who develop late-onset AD and is present in about 25 to 30 percent of the population. People with AD are more likely to have an APOE ε4 allele than people who do not develop AD. However, many people with AD do not have an APOE ε4 allele.

Early in 2007, fourteen teams of international researchers announced that variations of a gene called SORL1, which appear to increase the production of amyloid-beta plaques inside the brain, are also associated with an increased rate of late-onset AD. In 2008, researchers at Harvard Medical School and Massachusetts General Hospital identified four new genes that may increase the risk of the late-onset AD. One of the four appears to influence the age of Alzheimer's onset. A second gene causes a movement disorder called spinocerebellar ataxia; a third is involved in the innate immune system (part of the body's defense against bacteria and viruses); and a fourth gene produces a brain protein. (Alzheimer's Disease Genetics Fact Sheet, National Institute on Aging, Nov 2008, National Institute on Aging and the HBO Alzheimer's Disease Project, http://www.nia.nih.gov/Alzheimers/Publications/geneticsfs.htm, accessed Jan 3, 2011. "Significance of the APOE4 gene," *Preventive Health*, http://www.pcrm.org/health/Preventive_Medicine/alzheimers.html, accessed Jan 4, 2011). *See also* International Genomics of Alzheimer's Project

Genetic counseling. Genetic counseling refers to the process of providing individuals and families with information on the nature, inheritance and implications of genetic disorders to help them make informed medical and personal decisions.

First-degree relatives of individuals with sporadic Alzheimer's disease have about a 20 percent lifetime risk of developing Alzheimer's disease. Presumably, when several family members have Alzheimer's disease, the risk is further increased. Early-onset familial Alzheimer's disease is inherited in an autosomal dominant manner. Offspring of individuals with the early-onset form of the disease have a 50 percent chance of inheriting this gene, making their risk of developing early-onset Alzheimer's disease 50 percent.

Genetic mapping. Genetic mapping refers to a study of all of the genes in the human body and their properties.

Genetic mutations. Genetic mutations are changes occurring in the DNA of genes. Three specific genetic mutations have been discovered in patients with Alzheimer's disease. These are mutations in the amyloid precursor protein gene, influencing how it is spliced, and two mutations termed presenilin 1 (PS1) and presenilin 2 (PS2). Although these mutations are clearly associated with Alzheimer's disease, they occur very infrequently. In early-onset familial Alzheimer's disease, approximately 40 missense mutations and one exon deletion of presenilin 1 cosegregate, and the majority of these mutations occur within or adjacent to predicted transmembrane domains. Two mutations in the presenilin 2 gene on chromosome 1 have been reported to cause autosomal dominant Alzheimer's disease in two pedigrees. Nearly 30 percent of cases of early onset Alzheimer's disease are linked to the presenilin 1 gene on chromosome 14q.

Missense mutations in either amyloid precursor protein (APP) or presenilin genes promote the formation of more toxic forms of Aß peptide. It's thought that these peptide forms are central to the development of Alzheimer's disease. These mutations link Alzheimer's disease to changes in the processing of APP.

Another form of genetic mutation that is considered an early predisposing factor for Alzheimer's disease is trisomy of the 21st chromosome, which results in Down Syndrome. Although the relationship between Alzheimer's disease and Down Syndrome is not clearly understood, it is known that amyloid precursor protein is encoded in the long arm of chromosome 21.

Genetic testing. Currently, outside of research trials, tests are only available for presenilin-1, a gene associated with early-onset Alzheimer's disease. A significant association with the e4 allele of apolipoprotein E, a polymorphism associated with both early-onset and late-onset Alzheimer's disease, supports the diagnosis of Alzheimer's disease in patients with dementia, but this test is neither fully specific nor sensitive.

Results of testing at-risk asymptomatic (having no clinical symptoms) adults can only be interpreted after an affected family member's disease-causing mutation has been identified. Testing of asymptomatic at-risk individuals with equivocal symptoms is predictive rather than diagnostic testing. The National Society of Genetic Counselors does not recommend testing children at risk for adult onset disorders in the absence of symptoms because it removes their choice in knowing this, raises the possibility of stigmatization within the family and other social settings, and could have serious educational or career implications.

Several recent studies indicate that genetic testing for Apolipoprotein E may be appropriate for patients suspected of having Alzheimer's disease because patients with the APOE4 allele may respond better to certain therapies, such as protease inhibitors. However, the National Institute on Aging warns that ApoE testing raises ethical, legal, and social questions. Confidentiality laws protect information gathered for research purposes. However, the information may not remain confidential if it becomes part of a person's medical records. Thereafter, employers, insurance companies, and other health care organizations could obtain genetic test results and use them to discriminate against job-seekers, employees, and people seeking insurance coverage.

Genetics of Alzheimer's disease. Most cases of Alzheimer's disease are caused by a complex interaction of genes that confer susceptibility in combination with environmental factors, including infections and head injuries. Alzheimer's disease occurring in patients younger than 60 is associated with three distinct gene mutations. A common polymorphism in another gene, the apolipoprotein E gene, confers susceptibility in patients with both early-onset and late-onset Alzheimer's disease. Most incidences of Alzheimer's disease are late-onset, occurring in patients older than 60. In older patients, genes appear to cause susceptibility to Alzheimer's disease, but one can have the associated gene without ever developing Alzheimer's disease. *See also* Genes in Alzheimer's disease for a list of the genes associated with Alzheimer's disease.

Geriatric Depression Scale. The Geriatric Depression Scale is a neuropsychiatric evaluation tool developed by Yesavage in 1983. This tool is primarily used to diagnose depression in the elderly.

Gerontology. Gerontology is the scientific field dealing with the study of the aging population and their special problems. Gerontologists are physicians who specialize in the treatment of age-related disorders.

Gerstmann-Straussler-Scheinker Disease. Gerstmann-Straussler-Scheinker disease or syndrome is a condition caused by transmissible spongiform encephalopathies or prions. This disease characteristically causes a lack of muscle coordination and a destruction of brain tissue.

Ginkgo biloba. Ginkgo biloba is an herb used for a wide variety of conditions associated with aging, including memory loss and poor circulation. For centuries, extracts from the leaves of the ginkgo biloba tree have been used in Chinese herbal medicine for a variety of medical conditions including dizziness, inflammation, memory impairment and reduced blood flow to the brain. Because of its antioxidant properties, ginkgo biloba is reported to prevent damage caused by free radicals.

Having properties of a blood thinner or anticoagulant, gingko is thought to improve blood flow to the brain by dilating blood vessels. A daily dose of 240 milligrams of a standardized gingko biloba extract is approved for use in Alzheimer's disease in Germany. The two primary ingredients in ginkgo include glycosides and terpenes. Studies indicate that ginkgo biloba may slightly improve the memory of persons with

Alzheimer's disease, although it's unclear if the improvement is significant.

Side effects include allergic skin reactions and headaches. In large doses exceeding 240 milligrams daily, ginkgo may cause diarrhea, irritability and restlessness. Because of its anticoagulant properties, ginkgo should not be taken in conjunction with anticoagulant medications, such as coumadin, and it should not be used by individuals taking aspirin, vitamin E or other non-steroidal anti-inflammatory drugs. Ginkgo is also reported to be potentially harmful if taken with tricyclic antidepressant medications, including amitriptyline (Elavil).

Extracts of ginkgo biloba leaf, particularly EGb 761, have also been found to have a profound inhibitory influence on monoamine oxidase-B. Ginkgo biloba is also known to be involved in the reduction of inflammation, reduction of oxidative stress, membrane protection, and neuro-transmission modulation. In a study published in the *Journal of the American Medical Association*, conducted by Le Bars and co-workers, 202 subjects were given ginkgo biloba and evaluated for 52 weeks. In the treatment group, a substantial number of patients either stabilized or demonstrated improvement in cognitive performance as measured by psychometric testing.

The National Institute on Aging and the

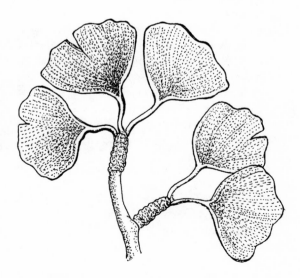

Ginkgo biloba leaves (illustration by Marvin G. Miller).

Office of Alternative Medicine, both at the National Institutes of Health, are currently funding studies on ginkgo biloba involving 3,000 individuals. To date, all trials have shown positive results. (Duke, James A. *The Green Pharmacy.* [Emmaus, PA:] Rodale Press, 1997. Perlmutter, David. "Functional therapeutics in neurodegenerative disease," Physicians Committee for Responsible Medicine. 2000). *See also* EGb 761

Glial cells. The primary cells of the brain are neurons and immune system cells known as glial cells (glia). There are approximately 100 billion neurons in the human brain and several times that many glial cells. Glial (from the word "glue") cells make up approximately 90 percent of the brain's cells. Glia beneficially modulate the function and viability of neurons.

The brain's glial cells include astrocytes, microglia, and oligodendrocytes. Glial cells act as caretakers, providing support, guidance, protection and nourishment for neurons. Schwann cells, a type of glial cell found in peripheral nerves, help to form the protective myelin sheath that covers axons. In neurodegenerative diseases, altered glial function, including reactivity, is seen. Generalized reactive astrocytosis is observed throughout pathologically affected regions of the brain in Alzheimer's disease.

During fetal development, neurons use the supporting framework of glial cells to help them migrate to other areas of the brain. After neuronal development and migration, glial cells remain although they may change their shape and molecular properties. At birth, there are about half as many glial cells as neurons. There are two distinct types of functional glial cells. One type controls the metabolism and function of neurons and the other type coats the neuronal axons with a fatty protective covering known as myelin.

Glial fibrillary acid protein (GFAP). GFAB is a cytoskeleton protein produced by nervous system cells known as astrocytes. Damage to GFAP caused by genetic mutations is thought to contribute to neuronal damage in Alzheimer's disease.

Glial fibrillary acid protein (GFAP) antibodies. GFAP antibodies are autoantibodies targeting the nervous system protein GFAB. GFAP antibodies, which are associated with several different nervous system diseases, including Alzheimer's disease, may be induced by exposure to toxic levels of lead. GFAP autoantibodies are seen in patients suffering from senile dementias and in healthy, aging people. Because of the suspected involvement of environmental pollutants such as lead in the development of neurological diseases, some researchers postulate that metal-induced alterations in neural proteins leads to production of neural antibodies, which, in turn, causes progressive degeneration of the nervous system. (Waterman, Stacey, et al, New York University Institute of Environmental Medicine, Nelson Institute of Environmental Medicine, Tuxedo, New York. "Lead Alters the Immunogenicity of Two Neural Proteins. A Potential Mechanism for the Progression of Lead-induced Neurotoxicity." *Environmental Health Perspectives*, 102(12) [1994,]: 1052–1056)

Gliosis. Proliferation of glial cells in an effort to replace damaged or destroyed neurons. In reactive gliosis, astrocytes fill in the spaces previously occupied by neurons.

Global assessments. Global assessments, such as the Global Deterioration Scale and the Clinical Dementia Rating, are procedures that outline the characteristic cognitive, functional, and behavioral course of individual cases of Alzheimer's disease. Global outlines are useful in providing clinicians a rapid and comprehensive overview of the disease course and in identifying features that occur out of sequence or prematurely.

Global assessments are also valuable in identifying generally benign, normal aged subjective forgetfulness as opposed to features consistent with incipient Alzheimer's disease. These assessments can also project the final stages of the disease process in individuals with incipient Alzheimer's disease. (Reisberg, Barry, et al. "Report of an IPA Special Meeting Work Group Under the co-sponsorship of Alzheimer's Disease International, the European Federation of Neurological Societies, the World Health Organization, and the World Psychiatric Association." International Psychogeriatric Association, 2000)

Global Deterioration Scale (GDS). The Global Deterioration Scale (GDS) is an evaluation tool

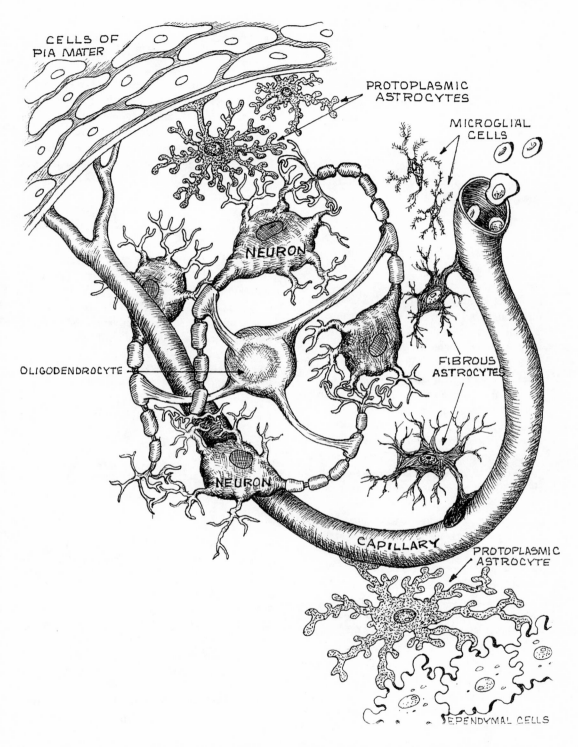

Glial cells of the brain (illustration by Marvin G. Miller). *Five functions of the glial cells:* **1.** Surround and transport neurons. **2.** Supply oxygen and nutrients to neurons. **3.** Insulate one neuron from another. **4.** Destroy and remove dead and injured neurons. **5.** Remove neurotransmitters from synapse clefts.

used to distinguish normal brain aging from progressive Alzheimer's disease by dividing Alzheimer's disease into 7 distinct stages. The GDS as a staging procedure is considered as reliable as conventional psychometric testing such as the MMSE for long-term longitudinal tracking of the course of Alzheimer's disease. The GDS also has a semi-structured component available for further guiding staging assignments. These measures include the Brief Cognitive Rating Scale and a number of assessments for documenting functional deficits such as activities of daily living.

Glutamate. Glutamate is an amino acid that acts as an excitatory neurotransmitter. Having excitatory properties, glutamate induces activity, or "firing," of neurons. Normally, glutamate helps send signals along nerve neuronal pathways and promotes learning, memory, and other cognitive functions. Glutamate also controls the flow of calcium ions into neurons through the methyl-D-aspartate-regulated channel.

Glutamate is the major neurotransmitter for brief, point-to-point excitatory synaptic events in the central nervous system, similar to the action of acetylcholine in the peripheral nervous system. In the presence of excess glutamate, however, too much calcium is able to enter neurons. According to one theory, glutamate would therefore cause the generation of free radicals that could be neurotoxic, causing the neurodegeneration seen in Alzheimer's disease.

The damage or neurotoxicity caused by glutamate starts with an excess of glutamate in the spaces between neurons, where it binds to and overstimulates receptors for N-methyl-D-aspartate (NMDA). A protein receptor, NMDA normally resides on cell surfaces. When NMDA receptors become overexcited, a cascade of events is initiated that eventually results in nerve cell death. Stroke, trauma and various forms of dementia are related to glutamate–NMDA excitotoxicity. Drugs such as memantine, which block NMDA receptors, have long been used in Europe for the treatment of neurodegenerative disorders. Since 2003, memantine has been an approved therapy for Alzheimer's disease in the United States.

Glutathione. Glutathione is a naturally-occurring antioxidant, which is also sold as a dietary supplement. Glutathione specifically works on cerebral mitochondria, maintaining both vitamins E and C in their reduced state and removing potentially damaging peroxides. It also inhibits the production of nitric oxide and protects against liver damage. Low levels of glutathione are associated with chronic illness and premature death. Patients with Parkinson's disease have been found to have profoundly decreased brain levels of glutathione, and the use of glutathione as a therapy for this disorder is currently under investigation. The body's production of glutathione may be increased by the use of vitamins C and E, silymarin (milk thistle), alpha lipoic acid, L-cysteine, N-acetyl-cysteine (NAC), L-methionine, L-glutamine, reducing xenobiotic challenges and by reducing drug challenges such as acetaminophen that induce cytochrome P450 enzymes. Because free radical damage from oxidative stress is associated with the development of Alzheimer's disease, and glutathione is essential for removing toxins that cause oxidative stress, it is important to increase the body's level of glutathione.

Glyceryl-phosphorylcholine (GPC). Glyceryl-phosphorylcholine is an orthomolecular compound (found naturally in the brain). As a supplement, GPC is used as a drug (generic name choline alphosecrate) in Europe and Japan to correct cognitive impairment associated with degenerative brain disease. In 1993 it was reported that a multicentre, randomized, controlled study compared the efficacy of l-alpha-glyceryl-phosphorylcholine (alpha GPC) and ST200 (acetyl-l-carnitine) among 126 patients with probable senile dementia of Alzheimer's type (SDAT) of mild to moderate degree. Efficacy was evaluated by means of behavioral scales and psychometric tests. The results showed significant improvements in most neuropsychological parameters in the alpha GPC recipients. Improvements also occurred in the ST200 recipients but to a lesser extent. Tolerability was good in both groups. These positive findings require replication in larger, double-blind, longitudinal studies coupling clinical and biological determinations (article abstract available at http://www.ncbi.nlm.nih.gov/pubmed/8477148, accessed Mar 5, 2011). In the United States, GPC is available as a dietary supplement, which is believed to prevent and ameliorate dementia and memory and learning loss by increasing levels of choline, which, in turn, increases production of acetylcholine and phosphatidycholine. In a double-blind, placebo-controlled study of 261 patients with mild-to-moderate Alzheimer's disease, patients receiving 1200 mg of GPC showed substantial improvement in cognitive function. Other human trials of GPC have been equally impressive. GPC has also been used in people with symptoms caused by stroke or transient ischemic attack. (Smithee, Alan. "Feed Your Brain," *Life Extension*, Jan 2011: 59–64)

Glycosaminoglycans (GAGs). Glycosaminoglycans (GAGs), formerly known as mucopolysaccharides, are congestive mucinous sugar polymer components such as hyaluronic acid. Glycosaminoglycans are found in the senile neuritic plaques that riddle the brains of patients with Alzheimer's disease. GAGs are thought to be critical for the assembly of components that make up senile plaques. Researchers are working on a compound that protects glycosaminoglycans from proteolysis. The sulfated GAGs resulting from proteolysis have an affinity for beta amyloid. Preventing proteolysis would effectively reduce the formation of the fibrils that ultimately lead to neuronal cell death.

Goldsmith, Harry S., M.D. Dr. Harry Goldsmith is a pioneer in the use of omentum implantation as a therapy for Alzheimer's disease and stroke. Currently at the University of Nevada, Dr. Goldsmith has been perfecting this treatment since the 1960s. One of his patients was featured on the Channel 2 nightly news in Southern California in 2000. (Goldsmith, Harry. "Omental transposition to the brain for Alzheimer's disease," *Annals of the New York Academies of Medicine* Dec 17, 2006, http://onlinelibrary.wiley.com/doi/10.1111/j.1749-6632.1997.tb4 8483.x/full, accessed Jan 10, 2011). *See also* Omentum

Gotu kola *see* Centella asiatica

Granulovacuolar degeneration. Granulovacuolar degeneration, one of the characteristic brain changes seen in Alzheimer's disease, refers to the formation of small (5 μm in diameter), clear holes or vacuoles. These are seen in the cytoplasm of neurons in postmortem brain biopsies. Each granuovacuolar degeneration contains an argyrophilic granule. Hirano bodies are elongated, glassy, eosinophilic bodies consisting of paracrystalline arrays of beaded filaments. The chemical compound actin is the major constituent of Hirano bodies. Both granulovacuolar degeneration and Hirano bodies are commonly seen in the pyramidal cells of the Hippocampus in patients with Alzheimer's diseases and other neurodegenerative disorders. Their significance is unclear.

Gray matter. The gray matter that makes up the interior of the central nervous system consists of nerve cells and the proximal or end portions of their processes embedded in neuroglia. The gray matter consists of a mixture of nerve cells including their dendrites, neuroglia and blood vessels. The nerve cells are multipolar and the neuroglia forms an intricate network around neurons. The abundance of blood vessels causes the characteristic pink-gray color of gray matter.

On cross-section of the spinal cord, the gray matter is seen as an H-shaped pillar with anterior and posterior gray columns, or horns, united by a thin gray commissure containing the small central canal. The amount of gray matter present in the spinal cord at any level is related to the amount of muscle innervated at that level.

Specific areas of gray matter are often called nuclei, particularly if the contained cell bodies are functionally related. An area where gray matter forms a surface covering on some part of the central nervous system is referred to as a cortex.

Green tea. Green tea has been found to help improve memory in studies conducted by researchers at Newcastle University in the United Kingdom. Results of laboratory tests by a team from the university's Medicinal Plant Research Centre found that both green and black tea inhibit the activity of certain enzymes in the brain which are associated with memory. Both teas inhibited the activity of the enzyme acetylcholinesterase (AChE), which breaks down the chemical messenger or neurotransmitter acetylcholine. Alzheimer's is characterized by a drop in acetylcholine. Green tea and black tea also hinder the activity of the enzyme butyrylcholinesterase (BuChE), which has been discovered in protein deposits which are found on the brains of patients with Alzheimer's.

However, green tea shows greater potency because of its increased ability to inhibit beta-secretase enzymes. Digested tea also produces more active phytochemicals than undigested tea. The findings, which are published in the academic journal, *Phytomedicine,* may lead to the development of a new treatment of Alzheimer's disease. ("Protective properties of green tea uncovered," *Science Daily,* Jan 6, 2011, http://www.sciencedaily.com/releases/2011/01/110105194844.htm, accessed Jan 30, 2011)

Grooved Pegboard Test. The grooved pegboard test is a psychological test used to measure visuomotor coordination.

Guarana (*Paullinia cupana*). Extracts of the caffeine-rich plant compound guarana are being studied for their use as a therapy in Alzheimer's disease. Guarana has some of the highest concentrations of caffeine in any plant with amounts ranging from 6 to 7 percent caffeine by weight compared to 2 percent caffeine in coffee. This herb has antioxidant properties and is reported to reduce production of beta amyloid protein. The side effects of guarana are generally the same as the side effects of caffeine. They include sleep problems, anxiety, restlessness, upset stomach and quickened heartbeat. Long-term use of caffeine may result in tolerance and psychological dependence. *See also* Caffeine

Haldol *see* Haloperidol

Hallervorden-Spatz disease. Hallervorden-Spatz disease is a rare, inherited neurological movement disorder characterized by progressive nervous system degeneration. Symptoms may develop as early as childhood and include slow writhing, distorting muscle contractions of the limbs, face or trunk, involuntary muscle spasms, muscle rigidity, ataxia, confusion, disorientation, seizures, stupor, and dementia. Other less common symptoms include painful muscle spasms, speech difficulties, mental retardation, facial grimacing, and visual impairment. Symptoms vary among those with this disorder, and death usually occurs within 10 years from the onset of symptoms.

Hallucination. Hallucination refers to the perception of something (visual image, tactile feeling, or auditory sound) with no external cause, usually arising from a central nervous system disorder or in response to drugs.

Haloperidol (Haldol). Haloperidol (Haldol) is a major tranquilizer indicated for the management of psychotic disorders and severe behavior problems, including combativeness. Haldol is contraindicated and not recommended for patients with severe toxic central nervous system depression, Parkinson's disease or who are in comatose states. Side effects include a syndrome characterized by potentially irreversible, involuntary, dyskinetic movements and a potentially fatal symptom complex sometimes referred to as Neuroleptic Malignant Syndrome (NMS). Symptoms of NMS include hyperexia (fever), muscle rigidity, altered mental status including catatonic signs, and evidence of autonomic instability (irregular pulse or blood pressure, tachycardia, increased sweating and renal failure). Haldol decanoate is a long-acting form of haloperidol.

Harry, Jean, Ph.D. Jean Harry is head of the neurotoxicology group at the National Institutes of Environmental Health Sciences. Her work focuses on the intricate role between neurons and glial cells and the role of this relationship as well as the role of environmental toxins in causing neurodegenerative disease.

Hashimoto's encephalopathy. Hashimoto's encephalopathy is a form of encephalopathy caused by an autoimmune process. In this disorder, which occurs more often in women than men, the thyroid autoantibodies responsible for Hashimoto's thyroiditis (autoimmune hypothyroidism) and Graves' disease (autoimmune hyperthyroidism) attack brain cells. Symptoms of this disease include dementia, myoclonus (erratic or jerking muscle contractions), ataxia (inability to coordinate muscles), epileptic seizures, disturbances of consciousness, headaches, and personality change or psychotic phenomena.

According to researchers, it is unclear whether the cerebral manifestation of Hashimoto's thyroiditis represents an autoimmune reaction against a shared antigen or if cerebral autoimmune vasculitis co-exists with the thyroiditis. Test results suggest the presence of a chronic inflammatory process. Unlike other causes of dementia, Hashimoto's encephalopathy responds to steroid treatment. It is important to differentiate Hashimoto's encephalopathy from Alzheimer's disease since with treatment, Hashimoto's encephalopathy is a reversible condition, although patients may still experience impaired cognitive abilities in longstanding untreated disease. Hashimoto's encephalopathy is suspected when thyroid autoantibodies in serum are raised and blood tests reveal clinical or subclinical hypothyroidism or hyperthyroidism. In doubtful cases, fine needle biopsy of the thyroid gland reveals characteristic cellular changes. (Seipelt, M. et al. "Hashimoto's encephalitis as a differential diagnosis of Creutzfeldt-Jakob disease." *J Neurol Neurosurg Psychiatry,* 1999, 66: 172–176)

HBO Alzheimer's Project. The Alzheimer's Project is an informative website and television series with the latest information on Alzheimer's disease. This multi-platform series takes a close look at groundbreaking discoveries made by the country's leading scientists, as well as the effects of this debilitating and fatal disease both on those with Alzheimer's and on their families. The Alzheimer's Project features a four-part documentary series, 15 short supplemental films, a robust website, and a nationwide community-based information and outreach campaign. A book published by Public Affairs Books was developed by the producers as a companion to the project. All films stream free of charge on hbo.com and are offered for free on multiple platforms by participating television service programs. (http://www.hbo.com/alzheimers/index.html, accessed Mar 1, 2011)

Head injuries. Blows to the head due to falls or injuries may injure the scalp, the skull and the brain. Severe blows to the head may even change the shape of the skull at the point of impact or cause the skull to be fractured. A severe, localized blow will produce local indentation and splintering of bone. Repeated blows, such as occur in boxing, result in a series of fractures.

Brain injuries can occur as a result of displacement and distortion of the neuronal tissues at the moment of impact. Floating in cerebrospinal fluid, the brain is capable of a certain amount of movement, although movement is limited by cerebral veins and other structures. Blows on the front or back of the head are more likely to cause displacement of the brain as well as stretching and distortion of the brainstem. Blows to the side of the head produce less cerebral displacement although they may cause considerable rotation of the brain. Brain lacerations are very likely to occur when the brain is forcibly thrown against the sharp edges of the skull bones.

A sudden severe blow to the head, for instance, as a result of an automobile accident, can cause brain damage at both the point of impact and at the pole of the brain opposite the point of impact where the brain is thrown against the skull wall. This is referred to as a contrecoup injury. In head injuries, cranial nerves and blood vessels may be damaged, reducing blood flow to the brain and causing intracranial hemorrhage. Individuals with a history of traumatic injury and the APOE4 genotype have demonstrated an increased risk for developing Alzheimer's disease.

An analysis of head injuries among World War II veterans links serious head injury in adulthood with Alzheimer's disease in early life. Researchers at Duke University in a study funded by the NIA looked at military records of male Navy and Marine veterans who were hospitalized during their period of service with a diagnosis of head injury or an unrelated condition. ("New Study Links Head Injury, Severity of Injury with Alzheimer's Disease," *NIA News,* October 23, 2000). *See also* Brain injuries; Dementia pugilistica.

Health Care Financing Administration (HFCA). The Health Care Financing Administration, an agency that manages government health insurance, is now known as the Centers for Medicare & Medicaid Services (CMS). *See* Centers for Medicare & Medicaid Services.

Health care proxy. A health care proxy is an individual that a patient or his or her representatives has legally appointed to make health care decisions for them in the event they are unable to make their own decisions.

Health Insurance Portability and Accountability Act of 1996 (HIPAA). The Health Insurance Portability and Accountability Act implements the civil monetary penalties, which can be assessed for Medicare fraud. This act has several stages that include provisions for medical privacy as well as a right for patients to see their own medical results with the exception of psychology notes. In addition, patients have the right to information about the diagnosis, prognosis and treatment options for their medical conditions. Information on the rights of patients and consumer health information can be found at the Department of Health and Human Services website at http://www.hhs.gov/ocr/privacy/hipaa/understanding/index.html, accessed Mar 1, 2011.

Health maintenance organization (HMO). Health maintenance organizations (HMOs) are insurance groups that offer lower cost health care by using a select group of health care providers [exclusively]. Patients may only consult these providers, usually for a small fee or co-payment.

Heavy metals. Heavy metals refer to 23 metals high in molecular weight such as antimony, arsenic, bismuth, lead, cadmium, and mercury. Exposure to these metals can cause cognitive impairment and symptoms that are indistinguishable from those that occur in Alzheimer's disease, ("Heavy Metal Toxicity," *Life Extension,* http://www.lef.org/protocols/prtcl-156.shtml, accessed Jan 3, 2011)

Helping Our Mobile Elderly (H.O.M.E.). Helping Our Mobile Elderly (H.O.M.E.) is a model project providing residential care in a small home-like settings for women with memory loss due to Alzheimer's disease and other brain disorders. H.O.M.E., which is an independent non-profit organization licensed by the State of California, has demonstrated its ability to provide life-enhancing care with minimal physical or chemical restraints and few acute hospitalizations. The Alzheimer's Association has featured H.O.M.E.'s philosophy in a new document called "Key Elements of Dementia Care." California Older Adult Task Force and UCLA information on H.O.M.E, and other services for individuals with Alzheimer's disease in California available at www01.smgov.net/hsd/senior/Documents/QuickRefGuide.pdf, accessed Mar 6, 2011.

Herbal therapy. In several major studies, herbal therapy has proven effective in reducing symptoms of Alzheimer's disease. The herbs most commonly used are ginkgo biloba, guarana (*Paullinia cupana*), gotu kola (*Centella asiatica*), huperzine, and rosemary (*Rosmarinus officinalis*). Other herbs reported to have benefits include Asian ginseng (*Panax ginseng*), American ginseng (*Panax quinquefolium*), Nicotine (*nicotiana tobaccum*), Snowdrop (*Galanthus nivalus*), Sage (*Salvia officianalis*), Lemon balm (*Melissa officinalis*), Bitter Melon, Cat's Claw and Peony (*Paeonia suffruticosa*).

Herpes viruses. Studies show that a high proportion of the brains of Alzheimer's disease patients and of age-matched healthy people contain latent Herpes Simplex Virus 1 (HSV 1). Researchers in Bristol, UK, have shown that the combination of HSV1 in the brain along with the apolipoprotein E 4 allele is a strong risk factor for developing Alzheimer's disease. Dr. David Perlmutter and others have also conducted research that supports this.

Individuals who die of Alzheimer's disease have been found to have a very high gene penetration of apolipoprotein E4 and a chronic infection with herpes simplex Type 1 (cold sores). These findings suggest that the virus harbored in the brain tissue reactivates periodically, causing more damage, and eventually Alzheimer's disease in carriers of the apolipoprotein E4 allele. (Itzhaki, R.F., G.K. Wilcock and W Lin. "Herpes Viruses, Alzheimer's Disease and Herpes Simplex Encephalitis," Molecular Neurobiology Lab. UMIST, Manchester M 60, Grenchay Hospital, Bristol BS16 1LE, UK. Itzhaki, R.F., et al. "Herpes simplex virus type 1 in brain and risk of Alzheimer's disease," *Lancet* 349, 241–244)

In 2008 the Canadian researchers Luc Letenneur and Karine Peres demonstrated a dramatic increase in HSV-1 antibodies (showing evidence of past infection) in patients with Alzheimer's disease compared to age-matched control subjects. That same year, Ruth Itzhaki, Ph.D., from the University of Manchester conducted a comprehensive review of HSV-1 in Alzheimer's disease and published her landmark article, "Herpes simplex virus type 1 in Alzheimer's disease: The enemy within," in which Itzhaki revealed that HSV 1 infects the brains of 90 percent of adults and that the virus can be found in the brains of individuals with Alzheimer's disease. In light of the fact that therapies used to reduce beta amyloid plaque often cause a worsening of symptoms, Itzhaki and her colleagues, propose that the virus is a major cause of the plaques in Alzheimer's disease and that anti-viral therapies may be more effective. As Itzhaki explains it, in Alzheimer's disease, beta amyloid plaque is produced as a response to the virus and serves as a biomarker of disease, rather than its cause. (Perlmutter, David. "Alzheimer's and herpes simplex virus: A link?" *Huffington Post*, Jan 31, 2011, http://www.huffingtonpost.com/dr-david-perlmutter-md/alzheimers-herpes-could-be-a-cause_b814047.html, accessed Mar 11, 2011)

In 2010 the Harvard researcher Stephanie Soscia and her team published the results of their research, which indicates that beta amyloid plaque in Alzheimer's disease patients is an antimicrobial peptide, that is, a protein produced in response to the infectious agent Herpes Simplex. (Soscia, Stephanie J., et al. "The Alzheimer's disease-associated amyloid β-protein is an antimicrobial peptide," *PLoS One (Public Library of Science Open Access)*, published online March 3, 2010 http://www.ncbi.nlm.nih.gov/pmc/articles/PMC2831066/, accessed Mar 11, 2011)

High Density Lipoprotein (HDL). High Density Lipoprotein (HDL), which is also known as "good" cholesterol reduces the risk for Alzheimer's disease in older individuals. In December 2010, researchers at the University of Pennsylvania reported that a cohort study involving more than 1,000 people over age 65 discovered that those in the highest quartile of HDL-C had a 60 percent reduction in their risk of developing Alzheimer's disease. This confirms previous research showing that elevated levels of total cholesterol and low levels of HDL are risk factors for Alzheimer's disease. (Smith, Michael. "High HDL linked to lower risk of Alzheimer's disease," *Med Page Today*, December 2010, http://www.medpagetoday.com/Neurology/AlzheimersDisease/23891, accessed Feb 1, 2011)

Hindbrain *see* Rhombencephalon

Hippocampus. The hippocampus refers to a specific region of the brain's mesial temporal lobe memory system. Alzheimer's disease is characterized by the death of nerve cells in this key memory center of the brain. The region primarily affected in Alzheimer's disease encompasses two paired structures symmetrically set on both sides of the brain: the seahorse-shaped hippocampus, which seems to be resting on the enthorhinal cortex, a cortical region which links the hippocampus to the rest of the brain. New memories reside in this region temporarily before they are eventually filed in the frontal cortex. If the circuitry in this region is damaged, these memories are lost. Alzheimer's disease wipes out new memories as well as the ability to learn.

Anatomically, the hippocampus is a curved elevation of gray matter that extends throughout the entire length of the floor of the inferior horn of the lateral ventricles. The hippocampus is part of the limbic system, a cluster of nuclei in the lower region of the forebrain. The hippocampus interacts with the cerebral cortex in determining emotions and processing memories. The hippocampus is responsible for modulation and storage of newly acquired data. It is affected in the earliest stages of Alzheimer's disease, with cell destruction accelerating proportionately to disease progression.

Damage to the hippocampus results in changes in autonomic and endocrine functions as well as behavior, memory and learning. However, there is not one precise general function related to neuronal damage in the hippocampus. The hippocampus is a major part of the medial temporal lobe. When parts of the medial temporal lobe are surgically removed, patients exhibit problems learning new information although they may be able to learn new tasks.

Several researchers have reported that a linear loss of volume of specific hippocampal brain regions correlates with the clinical changes seen in Alzheimer's disease. These volume changes are accompanied by changes in the percentages of neurons with neurofibrillary changes and with neuronal loss. In magnetic resonance imaging (MRI) studies, bilateral volumetric hippocampal atrophy has been found to be a highly sensitive indicator of early Alzheimer's disease. In one study, this measurement afforded a greater than 95 percent accuracy rating in correctly classifying Alzheimer's disease although researchers concluded that differentiation from other causes of temporal lobe pathology may be limited.

Hirano bodies. Hirano bodies are elongated, glassy, eosinophilic (studied microscopically in tissue sections, they stain red with eosin dye) bodies consisting of crystalline arrays of beaded filaments, primarily composed of actin. Hirano bodies are found most commonly in the hippocampal pyramidal cells of patients with Alzheimer's disease and other neurodegenerative disorders. They are of unknown significance. Hirano bodies were first described by Hirano in Sommer's sector of the hippocampus in Guam amyotrophic lateral sclerosis (ALS)-parkinsonism-dementia complex. As an age-related change, Hirano bodies begin to appear during the second decade and occur in small numbers up to the sixth decade at which time they markedly increase. Their concentrations are much higher in individuals with Alzheimer's disease.

Histology. Histology is the study of tissue cells. Histological changes seen in the brains of individuals with Alzheimer's disease include neuronal loss in the nucleus basalis of Meynert, hippocampus, and association cortex; neuronal degeneration, dendritic pruning, synaptic loss, presence of neurofibrillary tangles containing paired helical filaments, and the presence of senile plaques. Additional histological changes include granulovacuolar changes and accumulation of lipofuscin granules.

HLA 2. HLA are human leukocyte antigen markers for immune system genes found on the short arm of chromosome 6. Although HLA antigens are commonly associated with autoimmune disease development, the HLA 2 allele is associated with an earlier age of onset in individuals who develop Alzheimer's disease. This association also suggests that inflammation, a common immune system effect, may play a role in autoimmune disease development.

Hoarding. Hoarding refers to collecting and putting things away in a guarded manner. Alzheimer's disease patients may fear that others are stealing their possessions. This causes them to hoard certain items, although they are likely to forget where they have hidden these items.

Home and Community Based Programs. The goal of home and community based care is for people to be able to live as independently as possible for as long as possible. Home and community based programs include: adult day care services, clinical drug trials, driving assessment programs, transportation services, attorneys, free legal services and insurance counseling, meal programs, assisted living and residential care facilities, in-home agencies, and short-term respite care facilities. These programs are generally sponsored by a combination of local and federal government agencies. Information on local programs is available through the Alzheimer's Association or community based social service departments.

Home based care *see* **Friends Life Care at Home**

Home care. Of the 4 million Americans affected with Alzheimer's disease, it is estimated that 80 percent of these individuals are living at home and are being cared for by family caregivers. However, home care may also be provided by licensed home care agencies. Generally, Medicare will pay for some homecare services, including nursing care and physical therapy. Home care services also may assist with housekeeping, shopping, and other household chores that are too difficult for patients with dementia. These services may also be paid for or partially subsidized by local, county, or state programs or by private insurance.

Home Care Accreditation Program. Established in 1988, the Joint Commission's Home Care Accreditation Program accredits organizations that offer a variety of services in the patient's or client's home. Inspectors conduct surveys before the service provider receives accreditation. The length of the survey and its costs are dependent on the type of services provided, the volume of services provided and the organizational structure of the service provided.

Home Health Care. Home health care services are medical services provided by hospitals and home care agencies. Services include phlebotomy for laboratory testing, assistance with wound care, intravenous medications, and assistance with bathing. Home health care agencies can also provide respite care for patients with dementia if their caretaker is away.

Insurance companies generally pay for the services provided by home health care. Medicare and Medicaid cutbacks have reduced the amount of home care that they will provide, but in most instances they will provide limited home health care for patients with dementia who are able to live at home. Health care, which is generally provided by nurse's aides, includes assistance with bathing, laundry, and meal preparation. If private agencies provide home care, there may be a minimum requirement of three to four hours, which may be more time than is needed. *See also* Medicare HMOs

Homocysteine. The amino acid homocysteine, which is associated with low levels of B vitamins, has been found to be elevated in patients with both heart disease and Alzheimer's disease. In Alzheimer's disease, homocysteine is toxic to the brain. In ADCS clinical trials, researchers evaluated the effects of homocysteine reduction related to high dose supplements of folate, vitamin B6, and vitamin B12. Results indicate that patients with mild to moderate dementia and elevated plasma homocysteine levels respond well to vitamin substitution when assessed with the MMSE exam. However, patients with severe dementia and normal plasma homocysteine levels showed no signs of improvement. The study concluded that plasma homocysteine may be the best marker for detecting treatable vitamin deficiencies in patients with dementia. Boston University researchers have found that people with elevated homocysteine levels may have nearly double the risk of developing Alzheimer's disease. ("High homocysteine levels may double risk of dementia, Alzheimer's disease, new report suggests," Feb 13, 2002, NIH Press Release, http://www.nih.gov/news/pr/feb2002/nia-13.htm, accessed Mar 1, 2011)

Hormone replacement therapy (HRT) *see* Clinical trials; Estrogen; Estrogen replacement therapy

Horsebalm *see* Monarda

Huntington's chorea. Huntington's chorea, or disease, a form of severe dementia, is a condition characterized by quick, jerky, irregular movements. Patients with this disorder experience degeneration of the neurons that produce the neurotransmitters GABA, acetylcholine and P-substance. This results in an overactivity of the dopamine-secreting neurons of the substantia nigra region of the brain. Huntington's disease is caused by a dominant gene located on chromosome 4. A strong association between affective disorder and Huntington's disease suggests that affective disorder may be an early manifestation of Huntington's disease.

Huperzine-A. Huperzine-A is a natural herbal extract derived from Chinese club moss (*Huperzia serrata*), which has long been used to treat fever and increase alertness. *Huperzia* is also an alternate name used for some of the *Lycopodium* club mosses. Studies indicate that huperzine, like the prescription drug tacrine, inhibits the breakdown of the neurotransmitter acetylcholine. People with Alzheimer's disease generally have low levels of acetylcholine. By preserving levels of acetylcholine, huperzine-A promotes connectivity in the brain's neural circuits. With the success of pre-clinical trials, huperzine-A is currently being evaluated in clinical trials, which were actively recruiting subjects in January 2011. The primary aim of this multicenter, randomized, double-blind, double-dummy, placebo- and active-controlled therapeutic trial is to determine whether treatment with huperzine-A sustained-release tablets can improve cognitive function in individuals with AD.

A total of 390 participants will be randomly assigned to three groups of equal size. This will allow a comparison of huperzine-A sustained-release tablets 400μg once a day, huperzine-A tablets 200μg twice a day, and placebo. Information is available at the Clinical Trials website, http://clinicaltrials.gov/ct2/show/NCT01282619, accessed Mar 14, 2011.

HWA285 *see* Propentofylline

Hydergine *see* Ergoloid mesylate

Hydrocephalus. Hydrocephalus is a condition characterized by an abnormal increase in the volume of cerebrospinal fluid within the skull. Hydrocephalus generally develops as a result of a blockage of the foramina in the roof of the fourth ventricle in the brain. Hydrocephalus may occur as a congenital defect or it may be caused by adhesions that develop during meningitis. Hydrocephalus may occur due to displacement of the medulla oblongata by a tumor.

In normal pressure hydrocephalus, patients show signs of gait disturbance, dementia and incontinence. The onset usually occurs over several months, although the onset may be acute. Compared to Alzheimer's disease, the dementia is mild and the gait is severe, although in some cases the dementia may be more pronounced. Brain scans typically demonstrate hydrocephalus with enlargement of ventricles out of proportion to sulci. Other clinical signs include motor signs preceding cognitive dysfunction, short duration of dementia prior to surgery, and known causes such as traumatic or spontaneous subarachnoid hemorrhage, meningitis or partial obstruction.

Hydrogen peroxide. Theories supporting the claim that beta amyloid protein is the major culprit in Alzheimer's disease lend themselves to the hypothesis that beta amyloid increases production of hydrogen peroxide within neurons. According to this theory, hydrogen peroxide contributes to free radical oxidative damage and neuronal cell death.

Hypertension. Chronic hypertension, a condition of high blood pressure, increases the risk for mental impairment, including reduced short-term memory and attention, Alzheimer's disease, and dementia. Studies indicate, however, that controlling blood pressure may ward off memory impairment. Treating hypertension can reduce the risk of dementia in elderly patients with elevated systolic pressure.

Hypothalamus. The hypothalamus located in the forebrain forms the lower part of the lateral wall and floor of the third ventricle. The hypothalamus has a controlling influence on the autonomic nervous system and appears to integrate the autonomic and neuroendocrine systems. The hypothalamus is regarded as a higher nervous center for the control of lower autonomic centers in the brainstem and spinal cord. Nerve cells in the hypothalamus produce and release many releasing factors that control or inhibit many of the body's hormones. The hypothalamus also helps control emotions and behaviors by processing information received from other areas of the body.

Ibuprofen. Ibuprofen is a non-steroidal anti-inflammatory drug. Several studies show that the use of ibuprofen may protect against Alzheimer's disease, specifically by inhibiting the formation of beta amyloid protein 42. Research shows that taking as little as 800 mg of ibuprofen daily reduces the risk of contracting Alzheimer's disease without serious side effects. In one study, anti-inflammatory drugs slashed the incidence of Alzheimer's disease by 75 percent. In another study, ibuprofen was shown to have a neuroprotective effect after regular use for 5 years. (Greenwell, Ivy. "New light on how ibuprofen protects against Alzheimer's disease," *Life Extension*, February 2002, 23. "Ibuprofen linked to reduced risk of Alzheimer's disease," 2*Science Daily*, May 6, 2008, http://www.sciencedaily.com/releases/2008/05/080505162913.htm, accessed Feb 10, 2011)

Idebenone. Idebenone is a form of Co-Q-10 with increased blood-brain barrier penetration. Idebenone has been reported to protect cell mitochondria and increase levels of nerve growth factor (NGF) in the body, suggesting its value as an alternative therapy for Alzheimer's disease. In dementia, including Alzheimer's disease, it is known that learning and memory are impaired by the loss of neurons in an area of the brain called the magnocellular cholinergic neuronal system.

Nerve Growth Factor (NGF) cannot cross the blood-brain barrier and in scientific experiments, it has only been able to be utilized when it is injected directly into the brain. However, animal experiments have shown that oral use of idebenone tablets induce an increase in NGF and improve choline-acetyltransferase activity. ("Idebenone, a drug with a myriad of anti-aging benefits," *Anti-Aging Systems* report, http://www.antiaging-systems.com/ARTICLE-544/idebenone-antiaging-benefits.htm, accessed Mar 2, 1011)

Imaging studies. Imaging studies are diagnostic tests that involve the process of producing an image of the body's parts by radiographic (X-ray) or related techniques. In Alzheimer's disease, imaging tests are used to detect abnormalities in various areas of brain matter. In 2010 researchers demonstrated that changes seen on PET scan were able to accurately diagnose Alzheimer's disease. *See also* Activation imaging; Amvid; Computed tomography (CT scan); Magnetic resonance imaging (MRI); Positron emission tomography (PET) scan

Immobility. In the late stages of Alzheimer's disease, many patients become immobile, apparently forgetting how to move. Immobility may weaken muscles to the point where patients become entirely wheelchair bound or bedridden. Bedsores may also become a problem in bedridden patients. Frequent washing of bed linens and moving the patients every two hours during the day can help prevent bedsores. Lotions to soothe dry skin also offer benefits. Patients should be encouraged to move and exercises can be administered to the legs and arms to help maintain flexibility. One study reported that 62 percent of patients with mild to moderate dementia reported having joint pain yet few patients with severe dementia receive pain medication although there is no evidence that they are not experiencing pain. (DeNoon, Daniel. "Pain a problem in Alzheimer's disease," Alzheimer's Disease Health Center at WebMD, http://www.webmd.com/alzheimers/news/20060922/pain-problem-in-alzheimers-disease, accessed Jan 3, 2011)

Immune system. The immune system is a constellation of organs and blood cells that work together to protect us from disease. Immune system organs include the bone marrow, lymph glands, spleen, appendix, tonsils, and adenoids. The key players of the immune system are white blood cells, primarily lymphocytes and macrophages. Immune system cells travel to locations in the body where they perceive a foreign threat, usually an infectious agent or an allergen. Here they release factors that result in inflammation. Immune system cells also produce antibodies to fight the foreign agent during a subsequent attack.

Inanition. Inanition is a condition of exhaustion caused by a lack of food and water. Inanition may eventually lead to death in patients with Alzheimer's disease.

Incidence. The incidence of Alzheimer's disease is estimated at 0.5 percent per year at age 65 and 8 percent per year after the age of 85. Alzheimer's disease is estimated to affect 5.3 million people in the United States. From 2000 to 2006, Alzheimer's disease deaths increased 46.1 percent, while other selected causes of death decreased. ("Alzheimer's disease 2010 facts and figures," Alzheimer's Association 2010 report, http://www.alz.org/alzheimers_disease_facts_and_figures.asp, accessed Mar 3, 2011)

Incontinence. Incontinence, which may be urinary or fecal, refers to the inability of the body to control evacuative functions. Incontinence is commonly seen in the later stages of Alzheimer's disease. Incontinence is one of the main reasons patients are moved into nursing home settings. When the patient first shows signs of incontinence the doctor should be notified so he can check for evidence of urinary tract infection. Urinary incontinence may be controlled for some time by limiting liquid intake in the evening and reminding the patient to use the bathroom.

Independence. Patients with dementia are encouraged to remain independent for as long as possible. This helps maintain self-respect and decreases the burden for the caregiver. Patients who are able to still shop and perform other tasks away from their home should always carry proper identification, including information about where they live. Patients should be encouraged to eat with proper utensils and write their name so that these skills are not readily lost. Patients should not be discouraged from keeping pets since pets can provide companionship and purpose. If the patient cannot look after his or her pet, caregivers should make arrangements so that the person can still see the pet on a regular basis.

Indiana Alzheimer's Disease National Cell Repository (NCRAD). The Indiana Alzheimer's Disease National Cell Repository sponsored by the federal government gathers family history information and genetic material from families with histories of Alzheimer's disease. This information is available to researchers worldwide. (http://ncrad.iu.edu/forResearchers/sampleTransfer.asp, assessed Jan 3, 2011)

Indole-3-proprionic acid (IPA). Indole-3-proprionic acid (IPA), which has been patented as the compound OXIGON, is a highly potent, naturally occurring antioxidant similar to melatonin. Research indicates that IPA has the ability to inhibit the action of the enzymes that contribute to beta amyloid plaque deposits in Alzheimer's disease. ADCS clinical trials are currently evaluating the safety and tolerability of IPA in patients with Alzheimer's disease. ("OXIGON neutralizes Alzheimer's disease plaques," *Alzheimer's Weekly*, 2008, http://alzheimersweekly.com/content/oxigon-neutralizes-alzheimers-plaques, accessed Mar 3, 2011)

Infection related dementia. Dementia can result from infection with a number of different infectious agents including the retrovirushuman immunodeficiency virus (HIV), which causes acquired immune deficiency syndrome (AIDS). Bacterial and viral forms of meningitis, especially

cryptococcal meningitis, can present as dementia, although onset is sudden and there are almost always other associated signs and symptoms such as severe headache. Syphilis, resulting from the infectious agent *Treponema pallidium*, also causes a form of dementia as it forms brain abscesses. Creutzfeldt-Jakob disease also causes a form of dementia related to a slow virus known as a prion. *See also* Acquired immune deficiency syndrome related dementia and Cretuzfeldt-Jakob disease.

Inflammation. Inflammation is a process initiated by the immune system. In a reaction known as the inflammatory response, white blood cells, particularly microglial cells, cluster or aggregate at the point of injury or threat by foreign organisms. Activation of microglial cells is necessary

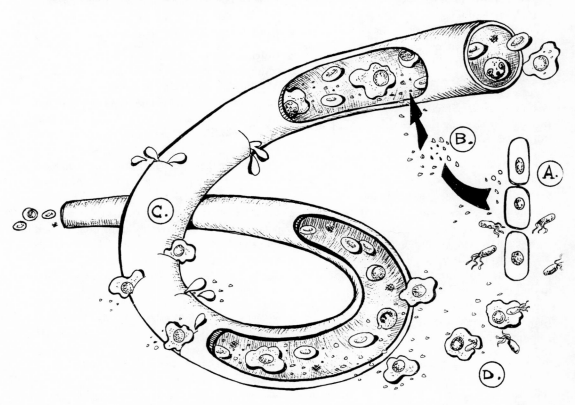

Inflammation Response (illustration by Marvin G. Miller).

A. Bacteria or other irritants invade and damage tissue. B. Chemicals, such as histamines and cytokines, are released by tissue cells and enter blood vessels. C. The blood vessel wall becomes more elastic and permeable, allowing fluid and activated macrocytes to enter the affected area. D. Phagocytes cells attack the bacteria; serum complement and other protein molecules enter the affected area. E. Secondary inflammatory reaction follows, including heat, swelling and pain.

for chronic inflammation. In addition, during the immune response, immune system cells release neurotoxic chemicals such as cytokines and complement. Cytokines regulate the severity of the inflammation. Complement cascades into a number of compounds that sustain the inflammatory process.

Studies of the brain in patients with Alzheimer's disease show evidence of inflammation within or adjacent to neuritic plaques. Multiple cytokines have been detected in these lesions, and there is also evidence of other immune system chemicals known as complement, indicating activation of the complement cascade. Research is currently underway regarding the beneficial effects of anti-inflammatory medications.

In one study of identical twins, it was found that the only significant difference in pairs where one twin developed Alzheimer's disease was the use of anti-inflammatory medications by the twin who was not afflicted. Since identical twins have identical genes, this shows that more than genes are at stake in the development of Alzheimer's disease.

Other evidence for the role of inflammation in the pathogenesis (disease process) of Alzheimer's disease include the presence of activated microglial cells and reactive astrocytes. These cells are known to produce cytokines and complement. The white matter of patients with Alzheimer's disease has been found to contain a high concentration of activated microglial cells, especially in relation to plaque and its amyloid and also in the neuropil between plaque deposits. *See* Anti-inflammatory drugs

Informant Questionnaire on Cognitive Decline in the Elderly (IQCODE). The Informant Questionnaire on Cognitive Decline in the Elderly (IQCODE) is a neuropsychiatric evaluation tool. It consists of a questionnaire administered to a proxy or informant and measures the fall from higher to lower intellectual level.

Inheritance, genetic. Two-thirds of people with Alzheimer's disease do not have a family history of it. One-third of Alzheimer's disease patients have a close relative (parent or sibling) with the disorder. Having a family history of Alzheimer's does not include grandparents with the disease or parents if they developed Alzheimer's disease

after age 65. Patients without a family history have the same risk factors, depending on their age, as the general population. People with a family history may have an increased risk of inheriting Alzheimer's disease but this is difficult to prove unless there are other blood relatives who are affected. Even in these patients, the risk of inheriting familial Alzheimer's disease is low and reported to be less than one percent. *See also* Genes in Alzheimer's disease

Instrumental Activities of Daily Living (IADL). The Instrumental Activities of Daily Living (IADL) is a global assessment tool used for documenting functional deficits such as the ability to bathe, dress and eat. By assessing how individuals with Alzheimer's disease are able to manage activities of daily living, evaluators can determine the disease stage and predict one's individual disease course. In conjunction with a carefully documented history, the IADL can be useful in documenting the presence of functional deterioration.

Insulin. Insulin is a hormone produced by the islet cells of the pancreas. Insulin regulates blood glucose (sugar) levels. Patients with insulin dependent diabetes are unable to produce sufficient insulin. There are many studies examining the relationship between diabetes and Alzheimer's disease. While there is no consensus of agreement, it is known that increased insulin is a characteristic finding in the early stages of Alzheimer's disease. When this results in a normal or slightly increased blood sugar, memory is enhanced because glucose utilization in the hippocampal formation and increased formation of acetyl coenzyme A is promoted. This results in increased formation of the neurotransmitter acetylcholine, which is deficient in Alzheimer's disease. However, a chronic severe high blood sugar can impair memory. This is seen in the later stages of Alzheimer's disease, when reduced insulin levels are common. While changes in insulin levels and blood glucose levels appear to be a part of the mechanism in dementia, overall, most studies show a low incidence of diabetes in patients with Alzheimer's disease. (Michel, Jean-Pierre, et al. "Diabetes and Dementia: A Retrospective Neuropathologic Study of Old Diabetics Compared to Non-Diabetic Controls." *Alz-*

heimer Disease: From Molecular Biology to Therapy, edited by R. Becker and E. Giacobine. Boston: Birkhäuser Publishing, 1996, 3–46)

Integrins. Integrins are a family of extracellular matrix (ECM) receptors that adhere to ECM proteins such as fibronectin and laminin. Researchers at the Utah School of Medicine in Salt Lake City, Utah, injected human integrin genes into adenoviruses and infected dorsal root ganglion neurons of adult rats with this virus to cause gene mutations. The mutated cells experienced cell growth and pronounced improvement. Researchers are currently repeating their studies in other types of central nervous system neurons to see if there are therapeutic applications for Alzheimer's disease. It is thought that the production of antibodies that target integrins cause disruptions in the normal signaling pathways. These disruptions are thought to contribute to beta amyloid formation.

Interleukin 1 (IL-1). Interleukin 1 (IL-1) is an inflammatory cytokine produced during the immune response. Microglia in the brain produce IL-1 during their response to beta amyloid deposits. IL-1 initiates a cascade of cell destruction and upregulates expression and processing of βAPP. Over-expression of IL-1 in Alzheimer's disease sets in motion a self-propagating cascade of cellular events known as the cytokine cycle, which correlates with formation of neuritic beta amyloid plaques and with progression of neurofibrillary tangles. Other consequences include the production of S-100 beta, a protein which induces intraneuronal free calcium concentrations, which are neurotoxic.

Studies in Italy suggest that there is either a linkage dysequilibrium with an unknown locus relevant to Alzheimer's disease on chromosome 2q or that IL-1 polymorphisms contribute to neurodegenerative processes in the pathology of Alzheimer's disease.

Internal capsule. The internal capsule is a compact band of white matter composed of ascending and descending nerve fibers that connect the cerebral cortex to the brainstem and spinal cord. The internal capsule is often involved in vascular brain disorders. Even small hemorrhages may cause clots that destroy immediate neural tissue and compress or destroy surrounding nerve fibers. Further information on white matter changes in Alzheimer's disease can be found at http://www.ncbi.nlm.nih.gov/pmc/articles/PMC1737921/pdf/v072p00742.pdf, accessed Mar 1, 2011.

International Classification of Diseases, 10th revision (ICD-10). While the criteria of the National Institute of Neurological and Communicative Disorders and Stroke and the DSM-IV-TR are generally used to diagnose Alzheimer's disease in the United States, the International Classification of Diseases, 10th revision (ICD-10) is generally used in Europe, and it is sometimes also used in the United States to define subcategories of vascular dementia and other types of dementia.

International Genomics of Alzheimer's Project. The International Genomics of Alzheimer's Project, a collaboration formed to discover and map the genes that contribute to Alzheimer's disease, was announced as part of the World Alzheimer Report 2010 on Feb 1, 2011. (*Applied Clinical Trials Newswire*, Feb 1, 2011, http://applied clinicaltrialsonline.findpharma.com/appliedclin icaltrials/Phase+News/First-International-Col laboration-on-the-Genetics-/ArticleNewsFeed/ Article/detail/705646?ref=25, accessed Mar 1, 2011)

Interview for Deterioration in Daily Living Activities in Dementia (IDDD). The Interview for Deterioration in Daily Living Activities in Dementia (IDDD) is a global assessment tool used for documenting functional deficits such as the ability to bathe, dress and eat. It is a useful tool in predicting one's individual disease course and expected rate of disease progression for patients with Alzheimer's disease.

Intracranial area of the brain. The intracranial area of the brain is the area situated or occurring within the cranium.

Intravenous immunoglobulin intravenous gammaglobulin (IVIG) therapy. Intravenous immunoglobulin therapy is an FDA-approved purified immunoglobulin fraction from normal human donor blood widely used in the treatment of autoimmune disorders. The use of IVIG in treating Alzheimer's disease is based on the hypothesis that IVIG contains naturally occurring autoantibodies (nAbs-Abeta) that specifically recognize and block the toxic effects of Abeta.

The Gammaglobulin Alzheimer's Partnership (GAP) Study is evaluating the effectiveness, safety, and tolerability of IVIG for Alzheimer's. The purpose of the study is to determine if IVIG may help slow the progression of Alzheimer's disease symptoms.

In April 2010, Baxter International released the results from its Phase II clinical trial, demonstrating that their Gammagard IVIG product could help stop the loss of brain cells in Alzheimer's patients. IVIG for Alzheimer's disease is currently under investigation.

Iron deposits. Redox-active iron deposits have been found in the senile plaques and neurofibrillary tangles seen in the brain of patients with Alzheimer's disease. Iron has long been known to catalyze free radical formation, and free radical oxidation is also linked to the development of Alzheimer's disease. Increased levels of the iron binding protein melanotransferrin seen in Alzheimer's disease patients indicate that iron metabolism in the brains of these patients may be impaired.

Researchers at the University of Tennessee in Knoxville have shown that iron interacts with oxygen to produce free radicals. These radicals oxidatively modify proteins and make them more susceptible to proteolysis; damage DNA; and peroxidize lipids. Beta-amyloid production is also increased in the presence of iron. (Joshi, Jayant et al. "Iron and Aluminum Homeostasis in Neural Disorders." *Environmental Health Perspectives* 102, Supplement 3, September 1994.)

Desferrioxamine, an iron-chelating agent, as well as anti-inflammatory drugs and estrogens, have been found to have antioxidant effects, reducing iron concentrations and offering a therapeutic role in the prevention of Alzheimer's disease. *See also* Desferrioxamine

Ischemia. Ischemia is a condition of localized tissue anemia caused by a lack of cerebral blood circulation due to obstruction or impairment of the inflow of arterial blood. Ischemia also is caused by the narrowing of arteries by spasm or disease.

Ischemia Scores. Ischemia scores (Rosen Modification) are used to evaluate if cognitive impairment is related to ischemia or dementia. In Alzheimer's disease, Ischemia Scores are less than 4, with higher scores relating to ischemia.

Joint Commission on Accreditation of Healthcare Organizations (JCAHO). The Joint Commission is a private, nonprofit organization dedicated to improving the quality of care in organized healthcare settings. JCAHO evaluates, accredits, consults, and sets standards for long-term care facilities, home care agencies, hospices, hospitals, and other healthcare delivery systems. Accreditation surveys assess the organization's compliance with applicable safety and other standards and provide guidance for the organization to improve its future delivery of care.

Journal of Alzheimer's Disease. The international medical publication *Journal of Alzheimer's Disease* is a peer-reviewed journal published by IOS press. Its goals are to facilitate progress in understanding the etiology, pathogenesis, epidemiology, genetics, behavior, treatment, and psychology of Alzheimer's disease. The journal publishes research reports, reviews, short communications, book reviews and letters to the editor. For more information see http://www.j-alz.com, accessed Jan 4, 2011.

Judgment. In neuropsychological exams, judgment is tested by a series of questions designed to show how well the patient perceives the circumstances of the situation described. Questions include asking the patient what he or she would do if he or she lost their credit cards. Judgment is poor in organic brain disease, mental retardation, and psychotic states.

Ketoglutarate dehydrogenase enzyme complex (KGDHC). The ketoglutarate dehydrogenase enzyme complex (KGDHC) is a mechanism involved in normal metabolism. Abnormal oxidative processes, including a reduction in activity of the ketoglutarate dehydrogenase enzyme complex, are seen in the brains of Alzheimer's disease patients. The decline in KGDHC activity correlates with the degree of dementia. The deficiency occurs in brains from Alzheimer's disease patients of undefined etiology, and in fibroblasts from both sporadic and familial cases. To further assess the nature of the abnormality of KGDHC in Alzheimer's disease, KGDHC activities, and immunoreactivities, researchers analyzed KGDHC in brains from patients with the Swedish APP670/671 mutation. This gene defect causes overproduction of amyloid β peptide. KGDHC activities were reduced by 55 to 57 percent compared with control values in the mutation-bearing cases in the medial temporal and superior frontal cortices. The immunochemical levels of KGDHC subunits E1k (-51 percent) and E2k (-76 percent) declined, whereas E3 concentrations were unchanged. The results suggest that mitochondrial dysfunction is a part of the pathophysiological process in AD even when the primary pathogenic cause is nonmitochondrial. (Gibson, G., et al. "α-ketoglutarate dehydrogenase in Alzheimer brains bearing the APP670/671 mutation," *Annals of Neurology,* 1998, 44(4): 676–681)

Khachaturian, Zaven, Ph.D. One of the leading experts on Alzheimer's disease, Dr. Zaven Khachaturian serves as president of Prevent Alzheimer's Disease 2020 Inc. (PAD 2020), as editor-in-chief of *Alzheimer's & Dementia: The Journal of the Alzheimer's Association,* as senior science advisor to the Alzheimer's Association, and as senior science advisor to Cleveland Clinic Lou Ruvo Center for Brain Health. In addition, he is the former director of the Alzheimer's Association's Ronald & Nancy Reagan Research Institute. Khachaturian is widely regarded as the architect of many successful and international scientific programs in neurobiology and Alzheimer's disease which were launched from the National Institute on Aging, National Institutes on Health, as well as Khachaturian, Radebaugh & Associates, Inc., an international consulting group focused on the conceptualization, development, and management of large scale research programs in Alzheimer's disease. In addition, Khachaturian is credited with creating the Virtual Center concept and has championed, along with other past and present members of the Alzheimer's Commission, to bring Virginia's Comprehensive Virtual Center on Alzheimer's Disease and Related Disorders to reality.

Kinases. Kinases are protein enzymes involved in many of the body's processes. Kinases are enzymes responsible for the phosphorylation (addition of phosphorus molecules) of hydryoxyl side chains on proteins. Protein kinases accomplish this by catalyzing the transfer of phosphate ions from adenosine triphosphates, ATP, the body's energy source derived from food. In Alzheimer's disease, disturbances to the balance of kinase and phosphatase activities may lead to the inappropriate hyperphosphorylation of various proteins, including tau protein. Specifically, altered activity of kinases, particularly cyclin-dependent kinase 5 (cdk5) are thought to be responsible for the aberrant phosphorylation of microtubule-associated proteins. Studies show that a particular kinase, phospho-JNK/SAPK, is significantly increased in patients with Alzheimer's disease compared to control cases. These findings suggest that JNK/SAPK dysregulation, probably resulting from oxidative stress, plays an important role in the increased phosphorylation of cytoskeletal proteins found in AD. Therapy geared toward reducing the activity of these kinases would reduce this process. This is one of the primary focuses in Alzheimer's disease research.

Korean ginseng. The herb Korean ginseng has been reported to improve cognitive function in healthy persons when used at a dose of 100 mg taken twice daily. It has also been used with good results for Alzheimer's patients in a study conducted at the University of Seoul in South Korea, which had participants using 4.5 grams daily. According to the authors of the study, the repeated measures analysis of variance revealed that at four weeks, the ginseng group showed an improvement in ADAS-cog score compared with the control group, after adjusting the baseline values. At 12 weeks, the ginseng group showed improvements in both ADAS-cog and MMSE scores, after adjusting the baseline values. (Baumgartner, Becki. "Korean ginseng benefits for Alzheimer's disease," *Luminearth,* Jan 4, 2010, http://www.luminearth.com/2010/01/04/korean-ginseng-benefits-for-alzheimers-disease/, accessed Nov 2, 2010)

Korsakoff's syndrome (Korsakoff's psychosis). Korsakoff's syndrome is a form of dementia caused by thiamine (vitamin B1) deficiency. Thiamine deficiency is caused by alcoholism, malnutrition or malabsorption of nutrients. It may also be precipitated by administration of carbohydrates to patients with marginal thiamine stores. Korsakoff's syndrome presents with an anterograde amnesia in which the patient is unable to learn new information. Classically, this condition develops in the wake of an acute Wernicke's encephalopathy (inflammation in Wernicke's region of the brain) with confusion, ophthalmoplegia (visual disturbance) and ataxia. However, many patients with Korsakoff's syndrome do not present with Wernicke's encephalopathy.

Patients with Korsakoff's psychosis may have relatively intact intelligence but an inability to form new memories. They typically make up answers as they go along, concealing to some extent the memory loss.

Kunitz protease inhibitor (KPI) domain. Amyloid precursor protein (APP) has several different isoforms it can take. Certain of these isoforms contain a Kunitz protease inhibitor (KPI) domain. This molecule regulates the clotting cascade, a biological mechanism that leads to normal blood clotting. Isoforms with the KPI domain may primarily function to regulated clotting within the brain. Normal processing of APP includes cleavage of a peptide bond in the middle of the amyloid beta sequence. This prevents the potential formation of insoluble aggregates of amyloid beta protein.

The development of amyloid deposits in Alzheimer's disease is thought to arise from abnormal processing of the APP molecule in such a way that increased amounts of amyloid beta protein are formed. Tissue cultures of neurons show that amyloid beta protein has both toxic and trophic effects.

Laboratory tests. There are no laboratory tests routinely used to diagnose Alzheimer's disease. A test for the apolipoprotein E4 allele can be used to suggest Alzheimer's disease in cases of early-onset dementia, although the presence of the E4 allele is not evidence of Alzheimer's disease.

Laboratory tests are helpful, however, in ruling out other causes of dementia. The most frequently ordered tests include: vitamin B12 level to rule out B12 deficiency, T4 or TSH levels to rule out hypothyroidism, RPR and FTA to rule out syphilis, and a thyroglobulin antibody titer to rule out Hashimoto's encephalopathy.

In addition, chemical profiles are also frequently ordered to role out chronic metabolic disturbances, including diabetes and dehydration. A ceruloplasmin level may be used to rule out Wilson's disease and a drug screen may be performed to rule out drug toxicity. A complete blood count (CBC) is used to rule out chronic infections and anemia, and a heavy metal screen can be performed to rule out lead, mercury, arsenic and copper poisoning. Also, an HIV test is often used to rule out HIV encephalopathy. A sedimentation rate and an autoantibody panel may be performed to rule out inflammatory and autoimmune conditions. In 2011, tests to measure certain proteins in the cerebrospinal fluid and urine of patients with Alzheimer's disease were approved to help in the diagnosis of Alzheimer's disease. *See also* AD7c

Laisure, Linda. Linda Laisure is the founder and director of H.O.M.E. (Helping Our Mobile Elderly), a model project providing residential care in a small home-like setting. A specialist in gerontology with a certificate from the University of California at Los Angeles, Laisure has presented at the American Society on Aging Conference for the past 10 years and was speaker at the National Conference on Residential Care in 1992.

Language. Language refers to the ability of the brain to elaborate sounds used for communication and to produce mental images of sounds as part of the thinking process. Sounds are trapped in the back of the brain near the primary auditory cortex. The frontal speech area of the brain elicits these sounds and articulates them into speech. As the link between human thought and communication, language is dependent on memory.

Both normal aging and dementia are associated with many language changes, including both linguistic knowledge and performance. In diagnosing dementia, language changes associated with aging, such as a reduction in naming ability, must be considered. Studies show a significant decline in naming ability for the general population at about age 70. Age-related language problems have been found to be caused by a reduction of retrieval skills rather than a loss of knowledge. In several studies, cueing or priming resulted in an improved performance.

A number of studies indicate that patients with Alzheimer's disease have a mixture of lexical, semantic and pragmatic language problems. While these changes are seen in all stages of the disease, the degree of language impairment appears to correlate with the severity of dementia. The major language impairments in Alzheimer's disease include: difficulties with naming, auditory and written comprehension, speech and no change in syntax, repetition abilities or articulation. Naming deficits are considered one of the earliest signs of Alzheimer's disease with nouns being particularly affected. (Melvod, Jais et al. "Language During Aging and Dementia." *Clinical Neurology of Aging, Second Edition.* New York: Oxford University Press, 1994, 329–343)

Late-onset familial Alzheimer's disease (LOFAD). Late-onset familial Alzheimer's disease (LOFAD) is a complex disorder that may involve multiple susceptibility genes. Many families have multiple affected members, most or all of who experience the onset of dementia after the age of 60–65 years. Disease duration is typically 8–10 years, but ranges from 2 to 25 years. Although no one gene is responsible for this disorder, several genetic associations have been made.

A well-documented association of LOFAD with the e4 allele of Apolipoprotein E chromosomal locus 19q13 has been made. APOE e4 appears to affect the age of onset by shifting the onset age toward an earlier age. Two common polymorphisms of this gene exist, resulting in three isoforms APOE e2, 23, and e4. The most common isoform in the general population is APOE3. In clinical series, the APOE4 allele is over-represented in LOFAD.

There is also evidence that a region on chromosome 12 may contain a susceptibility gene for LOFAD and an association with the alpha2 macroglobulin gene has been made.

The usefulness of APOE testing remains unclear since the e4 allele may be found in individuals with no signs of dementia. Presence of an e4 allele in an individual with dementia increases the probability that Alzheimer's disease

is the cause. However, a three-generation family history with close attention to the history of individuals with dementia is sufficient to support a diagnosis of LOFAD.

Late-stage Alzheimer's disease. The late-stage of Alzheimer's disease refers to the terminal or final stage of Alzheimer's disease, which can last for several months up to a year or longer. In this stage, symptoms are severe, and patients can no longer care for themselves in a life-sustaining manner. For family caregivers, the terminal phases of dementing illness can be challenging. In this stage, the patient has few or no verbal abilities, may not recognize family members or caregivers, may become incontinent and usually non-ambulatory (unable to walk without assistance), and may demonstrate agitated behavior. It is recommended that patients make advance directives before they reach this stage.

Lateral sulcus. The lateral sulcus of the cerebral hemisphere is a deep cleft found mainly on the inferior and lateral surfaces of the brain.

Latrepiridine. Latrepiridine is an orally-administered antihistamine that has been shown to inhibit brain cell death in preclinical studies of Alzheimer's disease and Huntington's disease, making it a potential treatment for these and other neurodegenerative diseases. Several clinical trials, however, failed to show any benefits for patients with Alzheimer's disease. However, because data from Russian trials and trials in other countries did not correlate well, one trial is still ongoing and was recruiting new subjects as of September 2010. Researchers caution that it is important to wait for these results before deciding if latrepiridine has value in Alzheimer's disease. (http://alzres.com/content/2/5/25, accessed Oct 30, 2010)

Lawton and Brody Scale for Instrumental Activities of Daily Living (IADL). The IADL, designed by M. P. Lawton and E. M. Brody, describes activities of daily living that are impaired in neurodegenerative diseases. An assessment of IADL can be performed periodically to evaluate disease progression or response to treatment. Activities included in the IADL include the ability to use the telephone, shop independently, prepare and serve adequate meals, maintain housekeeping skills, do personal laundry, travel independently, take appropriate medications and handle finances.

Lead. The element lead (Pb) is a heavy metal. Similar to the heavy metal mercury, lead is a potent neurotoxin that accumulates both in soft tissues and bones. In 2008 Nasser Zawia and his colleagues at the University of Rhode Island discovered a link between excess exposure to lead in early life and the development of Alzheimer's disease in later life. More studies are needed to confirm these findings although lead is already known to have a negative effect on cognitive function.

Lewy bodies. Lewy bodies are inclusions found within the cytoplasm of neurons. Lewy bodies are more frequently seen as a spheroid with a dense central core and a less dense surrounding area, although in nerve cell processes they may be elongated. Lewy bodies are primarily seen in idiopathic Parkinsonism and less frequently in postencephalitic Parkinsonism, Hallervorden-Spatz disease, progressive supranuclear palsy, and with aging and Alzheimer's disease. Large numbers in the cerebral cortex represent diffuse Lewy body dementia.

Lewy body dementia. Lewy body dementia is the second most common form of degenerative dementia, accounting for up to 25 percent of cases of dementia in the elderly population. Lewy body dementia is being diagnosed more frequently and is characterized by fluctuating cognitive impairment, alterations of alertness or attention span, spontaneous Parkinsonism and recurrent visual hallucinations. Variations or subtypes of this disease exist, with variations in symptom severity. Patients with Lewy body dementia show a reduction in pre-synaptic cholinergic transmission from the basal forebrain as well as deficits in cholinergic transmission from brain stem nuclei.

Accurate diagnosis of this condition is important as the management of psychosis and behavioral disturbances is complicated by the sensitivity to neuroleptic medications exhibited by patients with this disorder. Evidence indicates that patients with this disorder also respond well to cholinergic enhancers. Neuroimaging findings show a preservation of medial temporal lobe structures although there is a similarity to Alzheimer's disease in the distribution pattern of white matter observed on MRI. On SPECT exam, patients with Lewy body dementia exhibit a greater degree of occipital hypoperfusion when compared to patients with Alzheimer's disease. Lewy body disease may overlap with both Alzheimer's disease and with the dementia associated with Parkinson's disease. (Barber, R., et al. "Dementia with Lewy bodies: Diagnosis and management." *International Journal of Geriatric Psychiatry*, Dec 2001, S12–S18)

Lewy body variant of Alzheimer's disease. Although Lewy bodies are regarded as hallmarks of Parkinson's disease, these neuronal inclusions are also seen in the brains of individuals with clinical and pathological features of Alzheimer's disease. These cases are said to be Lewy body variants of Alzheimer's disease. There is considerable overlap of symptoms in diffuse Lewy body dementia and Alzheimer's disease although Lewy body dementia patients do not have the characteristic senile plaques and neurofibrillary tangles seen in Alzheimer's disease.

Life prolonging interventions. Life prolonging interventions are treatments such as cardiopulmonary resuscitation (CPR) that, if withheld, would likely result in death.

Life sustaining treatment. Life sustaining treatment is treatment that slows the dying process and includes feeding, hydration, and medications.

Limbic system. The limbic system includes a group of structures within the brain associated with emotion, behavior, drive and memory. Anatomically, the limbic structures include the subcallosal, the cingulated, and the parahippocampal gyri, the hippocampal formation, the amygdaloid nucleus, the mammillary bodies and the anterior thalamic nucleus.

Lipid peroxidation. Lipid peroxidation is a free radical-related process that occurs as a part of the body's normal metabolism. Lipid peroxidation causes the familiar brown spots that occur on the skin as a result of aging. Lipid peroxidation associated with inflammation may cause cellular damage as a result of oxidative stress. The accumulation of products of lipid peroxidation, including lipid hydroperoxides and aldehydes, has been reported in the brains of patients with Alzheimer's disease.

Lipofuscin. Lipofuscin is a yellowish-brown pigment found in various parts of the body. The amount of lipofuscin within the body increases with age. Lipofuscin granules are present in the cytoplasm of neurons, possibly as a harmless metabolic by-product.

Liver function. Several studies suggest that impaired liver function can contribute to Alzheimer's disease by interfering with the body's natural detoxification functions. In particular, liver disease can interfere with the normal metabolism of drugs, chemicals and xenobiotics. In addition, researchers at the Scripps Research Institute and Mod Gene LLC have found three genes, including presenilin, in mice that protect against the development of amyloid plaque accumulations. For each of these three genes, lower gene expression in the liver protected the mouse brain. In another animal study, scientists at Case Western found a gene product called Presenilin2, which is found in the liver but not in the brain. Higher expression of Presenilin2 in the liver correlated with greater accumulation of beta amyloid in the brain and development of Alzheimer's-like pathology. Further studies are needed to see how the animal results translate to humans.

Living trust. A living trust is a legal document allowing an individual (the grantor or trustor) to create a trust and appoint someone else as trustee (usually a trusted individual or a bank representative). The trustee has authority to carefully invest and manage the grantor's assets.

Living will. A living will is a legal document that expresses an individual's decision on the use of artificial life support systems.

Lobar distribution. Lobar distribution refers to cellular differences such as atrophy seen in the lobes of the brain. Abnormalities of lobar distribution are commonly associated with and helpful in diagnosing neurodegenerative disorders. For instance, studies of lobar distribution in Alzheimer's disease are characterized by temporoparietal predominance whereas loss of deep nuclear structures such as selective early loss of caudate mass or signal abnormality in the striatum are seen in Huntington's chorea or Creutzfeldt-Jakob disease.

Lobar sclerosis *see* Pick's disease

Logical Memory Delayed Recall. A section of the Wechsler memory scale test, the measurement of logical memory delayed recall is used to assess dementia.

Long-term care. Long-term refers to the care needed for patients suffering from a chronic condition or illness that limits their ability to carry out basic self-care tasks. Long-term care often involves the most intimate aspects of living including feeding and personal care. According to the Family Caregiver Alliance (FCA), an estimated 12.8 million Americans of all ages need long-term care. Approximately 57 percent of these people are aged 65 and older. The most severely disabled population, those who need substantial help carrying out 3 or more self-care tasks, comprise approximately 5.1 million Americans. Many long-term care options exist, including nursing homes, senior services, homecare, live-in help, senior housing with services, subsidized senior housing, assisted living residential care, and board-and-care homes.

Most people who need long-term care live at home or in community settings, not in institutions. About 2.4 million Americans live in institutions such as nursing homes. The General Accounting Office reports that public and private spending on long-term care services in 1993 was estimated to exceed $108 billion. About $70 billion of this money was paid by federal and state government funds, primarily Medicaid. Most of the remaining $38 billion was paid by individuals and their families. It's estimated that the number of older people requiring long-term care may as much as double over the next 25 years. (GAO/HEHS-95-26, November 7, 1994. *Long-Term Care: Diverse, Growing Population Includes Millions of Americans of All Ages*, U.S. General Accounting Office)

Long-term care insurance. Long-term care insurance is private insurance taken out before it is needed that may pay for some or all of nursing home care costs, depending on the particular coverage. Typically, there is a limit on the fees paid daily and the duration of the coverage. For instance, a policy may pay up to $160 daily for five years. Some long-term care insurance policies also cover home care services. For most people, long-term care coverage is only affordable if the policy is purchased when they are in their fifties or sixties. By age 70, the cost for a new policy is generally prohibitive. Many companies sell long-term policies but these companies may not be in business when they are needed. Make sure there are provisions for this possibility. Local agencies dedicated to the needs of the aging population can help provide assistance and advice for older adults seeking insurance.

In general long-term care insurance is appropriate for people who have significant financial assets that they would like to protect. Typically, policies have a waiting period of 6 months before they will pay for nursing home care. If a family expects to use up all their financial resources during this period, they will then qualify for Medicaid. In this case, long-term insurance would not be helpful.

Low dose naltrexone. Low doses of the opioid antagonist naltrexone are used off-label in patients with Alzheimer's disease. Low doses of naltrexone work to increase production of beta endorphins. According to the neurologist Bernard Bihari, M.D., increases in beta endorphins modulate the immune system and help prevent further progression of neurodegenerative disorders. (Moore, E., and S. Wilkinson, *The Promise of Low Dose Naltrexone Therapy: Potential Benefits in Cancer, Autoimmune, Neurological and Infectious Disorders.* Jefferson, NC: McFarland, 2008. The Low Dose Naltrexone Homepage, http://www.lowdosenaltrexone.org/index.htm#What_diseases_has_it_been_useful_for, accessed Feb 12, 2011)

Lumbar puncture. Lumbar puncture (spinal tap) is a medical procedure used to withdraw a sample of cerebrospinal fluid for laboratory testing or to inject drugs, including anesthetic agents. To rule out other causes of dementia a lumbar puncture may be performed to look for signs of chronic meningitis, syphilis multiple sclerosis, and other inflammatory diseases.

Lynch, Gary, PhD. Gary Lynch is a neuroscientist at the University of California, Irvine. Since the early 1970s, Lynch has been studying memory, neurotransmitters, long-term potentiation, ampakines (which he discovered), and their role in upregulating brain-derived neurotrophic factor (BDNF), as well as the potential therapeutic application of ampakines in Alzheimer's disease and Huntington's disease.

M266. M266 is a synthetic monoclonal antibody, which binds to Abeta, drawing it out of the brain and reducing plaque formation. Researchers at Eli Lilly and Company in Indianapolis are currently evaluating M266 for its role as a therapy in Alzheimer's disease.

Mad cow disease *see* Bovine spongiform encephalopathy

Magnesium. The mineral magnesium is essential for many of the body's metabolic processes, including more than 300 different enzyme reactions. Low magnesium levels are associated with neurodegenerative conditions, perhaps because of the resulting free radical production.

Magnesium levels in the brain can be extremely low even when plasma or blood levels of magnesium are normal. This can happen when the brain is exposed to toxic metals since there is competition for entry into brain cells. Magnesium is depleted within the hippocampus of patients with Alzheimer's disease. Some researchers say it is the low levels of magnesium, rather than the high levels of aluminum, that are responsible for dementia. Normally, magnesium is transported throughout the body, linked to the protein albumin. It's thought that the type of albumin that serves this purpose has more of an affinity for aluminum.

Magnesium deficiency occurs in alcoholism, chronic diarrhea, malabsorption syndromes, chronic use of diuretics, diabetes, and in a high percent of patients undergoing heart surgery. Magnesium is currently being evaluated as a therapy for dementia. (Guosong Liu. "Magnesium deficiency and brain health," 2010, Nutritional Magnesium Association Website, http://www.nutritionalmagnesium.org/articles/brain-health/45-blog-4.html, accessed Jan 2, 2011)

Magnetic resonance imaging (MRI). Magnetic resonance imaging (MRI) is a diagnostic technique that uses the magnetic properties of the hydrogen nucleus excited by radio-frequency radiation. In this procedure, radiation is transmitted by a coil surrounding the head. The excited hydrogen nuclei emit a signal that is detected as induced electric currents in a receiver coil. MRI is used to demonstrate atrophy or deterioration of brain cells. MRI in older patients with normal cognition may show medial temporal atrophy and thus indicate the possibility of future decline, whereas cerebral atrophy is seen after a substantial proportion of neural cells have died. Coronal T1-weighted spin echo sequences from MRI of the brain are used in the diagnostic protocol set up by CERAD. This MRI assessment protocol is used to rate atrophy (both focal and global), white matter abnormalities, and areas of cerebral infarction or hemorrhage.

MRI can easily distinguish gray and white matter because gray matter contains more hydrogen in the form of water than white matter. Because MRI provides better differentiation between gray and white matter, it can provide more information than computed tomography. Providing better anatomical resolution, MRI has shown that atrophy of the hippocampus is a hallmark of Alzheimer's disease and can be seen in the very early stages of the disease. Longitudinal studies have shown that dilation of the peri-hippocampal fissure can predict the diagnosis of Alzheimer's disease with over 90 percent accuracy.

MRI studies of the entorhinal cortex, the banks of the superior temporal cortex, and the anterior cingulate indicate that these areas show reduced volume changes before the hippocampal area. Researchers in Boston found that they could identify people who would develop Alzheimer's disease over time based on measurements of these brain regions with 93 percent accuracy.

Visual ratings of MRI scans of the entorhinal cortex are particularly useful for differentiating Alzheimer's disease from normal aging. Subcortical white-matter lesions (leukoariois) are related to age whereas lesions around the ventricular system appear to be associated with cognitive decline and are found in Alzheimer's disease. MRI reveals the same atrophic changes as seen on CT scans but it can better image focal enlargement of the temporal horns of the lateral ventricles, correlating with hippocampal atrophy. This atrophy is best seen in the coronal plane. In

studies, a more extensive smooth halo of periventricular hyperintensity was noted in 50 percent of patients with Alzheimer's disease compared with controls. Although there are few specific findings in Alzheimer's disease, the absence of white matter abnormality, hydrocephalus, mass lesion, or metabolic disorder in a demented patient strongly indicates Alzheimer's or Parkinson's disease.

Functional MRI (fMRI) is a similar technique that creates real-time images of active brain regions by measuring oxygen metabolism. In a normal elderly person doing a memory task, a computer enhanced image shows that the memory centers of the brain are activated. In a person with Alzheimer's disease, the pattern is disturbed. The memory centers of the hippocampus and entorhinal cortex fire weakly and at the wrong time. Functional MRI (fMRI) provides a safe non-invasive *in vivo* means to investigate alterations in brain function related to the earliest symptoms of AD, possibly before development of significant irreversible structural damage occurs. Another technique in fMRI — based on imaging of the endogenous blood-oxygen level-dependent (BOLD) contrast has proved to be helpful in investigating brain function during complex cognitive processes such as memory formation in humans. Studies of BOLD fMRI in conjunction with several other related studies have confirmed the central role of the medial temporal lobe (MTL) structures (the hippocampus and neighboring parahippocampal cortices) in encoding new events into long-term memory. Typically, fMRI experiments compare the BOLD signal during one cognitive condition (e.g., encoding novel information) to a control task (e.g., viewing familiar information) or to a passive baseline condition (e.g., simple visual fixation). Changes on fMRI in subjects with mild cognitive impairment and Alzheimer's disease differ from those seen with normal aging. fMRI is being evaluated in clinical trials in individuals with early Alzheimer's disease.

Structural MRI (sMRI) is an imaging technique that measures brain morphometry. sMRI is able to capture gray matter atrophy related to the loss of neurons, synapses, and dendritic dearborization that occurs on a microscopic level in Alzheimer's disease; white matter atrophy related to the loss of structural integrity of white matter tracts, which presumably result from demyelination and dying back of axonal processes, and the expansion of cerebrospinal fluid spaces. sMRI indirectly reflects neurofibrillary tangles, which is related to cognitive function. The value of sMRI is that it provides a non-invasive measure of neuronal loss. (Vemuri, Prashanthi, and Clifford Jack, Jr. "Role of structural MRI in Alzheimer's disease," *Alzheimer's Research & Therapy*, 2010, 2(23), http://alzres.com/content/2/24/23, accessed Dec 20, 2010)

Magnetic resonance spectroscopy (MRS). Magnetic resonance spectroscopy (MRS) is an advanced imaging technique capable of measuring changes in brain metabolism. MRS produces spectra of relatively weak magnetic signals from nuclei of phosphorus, carbon, or hydrogen not associated with water. These spectra provide information about chemical compounds and the energy state within specific regions of the brain. MRS has the ability to measure the concentrations of various neurotransmitters and brain metabolites and metabolite fluxes through brain compartments. Alterations of cerebral metabolites can help in the diagnosis and response to therapy in many different neurological disorders, including Alzheimer's disease.

Malnutrition. Malnutrition is a condition of nutrient deficiency caused by poor diet, the inability to properly absorb nutrients (malabsorption syndromes such as celiac disease, gluten sensitivity, Crohn's disease, and hyperthyroidism), chronic diarrhea, or the chronic use of diuretics or laxatives. Specific nutrient deficiencies, such as vitamin B1 and B12 and magnesium deficiencies may contribute to the development of neurodegenerative disorders.

Malnutrition may also occur in patients with Alzheimer's disease due to improper or poorly supervised diets. Malnutrition may cause a worsening of dementia and contribute to death.

Managed care. Managed care refers to health care provisions and guidelines established by insurance providers, including the federal government, which are based on patient diagnosis. As of 2000, 31 states had Medicaid managed care plans for at least some individuals in the public

mental health system. However, the term "managed care" has different meanings for medical providers and insurance companies.

The American Medical Association defines managed care as "those processes or techniques used by any entity that delivers, administers and/or assumes risk for health care services in order to control or influence the quality, accessibility, utilization or costs and prices or outcomes of such services provided to a defined enrollee population."

The Health Insurance Association of America (HIAA) defines managed care as "systems that integrate the financing and delivery of appropriate health care services to covered individuals through the use of four elements: arrangements with selected providers to furnish a defined set of health care services to members; explicit standards for choosing those providers; formal programs for ongoing quality assurance and utilization review; and significant financial incentives for members to use the plan's providers and procedures." However, the HIAA's qualifications of incentives to use the plan's providers and procedures may prohibit those insured from using providers outside of the plan.

Managed care is designed to achieve cost efficiency while protecting medical consumers. The expansion of managed care to people on federal medical assistance (Medicaid) has been controversial. According to a report by the Milbank Memorial Fund, positive effects include: increased access, decreased use of inappropriate inpatient care, an expanded array of services, more flexibility in service delivery, more consistency in clinical decision making, more focused, goal-directed treatment and increased emphasis on accountability and outcomes.

Problems include: an incentive in a risk-based contract to under-treat, particularly to underserved, people with serious disorders, an undue focus on acute care and neglect of rehabilitation and other services associated with significant long-term payoff in improved functioning, potential difficulties created by Medicaid managed care contracts in serving the non–Medicaid population, frequent billing difficulties, initial payment difficulties, difficulties ensuring, quality and consistent outcomes across regions. ("Effective Public Management of Mental Health Care:

Views from States on Medicaid Reforms That Enhance Service Integration and Accountability." New York, Milbank Memorial Fund in conjunction with the Bazelon Center for Mental Health Law, [2000])

Manchester and Oxford Universities Scale for the Psychopathological Assessment of Dementia (MOUSEPAD). The Manchester and Oxford Universities Scale for the Psychopathological Assessment of Dementia (MOUSEPAD) is an evaluation tool used to assess emotional changes and neuropsychiatric manifestations in patients diagnosed with dementia.

Massage therapy and physical therapy. The loss of communication skills causes frustration in Alzheimer's disease patients. Massage and physical therapy are forms of touch therapy that can cross these communication barriers. In one study, patients who received hand massages and were spoken to in a calm manner had a reduction in pulse rate and in inappropriate behavior. Some nursing homes now provide massage. Healthcare professionals speculate that massage or touch therapy may offer benefits because of its relaxing effects and because it provides a form of nonverbal social communication and a moderate form of exercise. (University of Maryland Medical Center, 2010, http://www.umm.edu/altmed/articles/alzheimers-disease-000005.htm, accessed Mar 1, 2011)

Medicaid. Medicaid is a joint federal and state program that helps older people and those with disabilities pay for medical expenses that they can no longer afford. Medicaid will help pay for nursing home care and for some community services, usually limited home health, hospice, and personal care, with the amount of services determined by the state in which you live.

Most nursing homes participate in the Medicaid program. Medicaid typically pays 60 percent of all nursing home bills nationwide. In a few states, Medicaid may also pay for other long-term care options, including assisted living care, board-and-care homes, and some community-based services. To qualify for Medicaid, most people must contribute a substantial amount of their income, for instance, a social security check, before the state will pay for the balance.

Widowed and single people must spend down their assets, owning no more than about $2,000 before their coverage starts. To do this, most people must sell their homes unless they can establish that they will eventually be able to move back home. For individuals with living spouses, many assets, including the residence and some income, are exempt. A resident's spouse is allowed to keep their home, car, clothing and generally up to $80,000 in assets such as stocks, bonds, pension and annuity income, and savings and bank accounts. The exact amounts vary by states.

Penalties for divesting assets in an attempt to qualify for Medicaid are high, and residents may be disqualified for Medicaid benefits if they are found to have divested assets. Some attorneys specialize in arranging assets advantageously to help people qualify for Medicaid. Medicaid is careful in only allowing admission to nursing homes that are appropriate for dementia patients. The nursing home's social worker will help prospective residents determine if they are eligible. Nursing home coverage as well as other care services that allow families to postpone long-term care services are available through Medicaid Waivers. For information on coordinating Medicaid and Medicare services and on Medicaid waivers that allow for day care, short-term care, and respite services while eligible long-term is postponed, *see also* Nursing Home — Medicaid alternatives to long-term care; Program for All-Inclusive Care for the Elderly (PACE)

Medical ethics. Medical ethics is a branch of medicine that focuses on the ethical ramifications of patient care, ensuring that treatment is in the patient's best interest. Most healthcare providers have medical ethics boards that review patient care directives.

Medical problems. Individuals with Alzheimer's disease are at increased risk for developing certain other medical problems. They suffer from an increased incidence of neurologic complications, infections, hip fractures and malnutrition. These patients have also been shown to have an increased risk for stroke, myoclonus, urinary tract infections and aspiration pneumonia.

Medicare. Medicare is the federal government's health insurance plan for the elderly. Medicare underwrites health insurance for persons 65 and older and some persons with disability. Medicare also covers limited nursing home care, limited home health and hospice care. Medicare will only cover nursing home care under certain circumstances, including short-term stays following hospitalization. Medicare may also cover home or inpatient hospice care during the last 6 months of life. If the resident qualifies, Medicare covers the bill of nursing home care for the first 20 days. After that, residents are required to make a co-payment of about $96 daily for a maximum of about 100 days. Many supplemental Medicare plans will cover this co-payment. When coverage runs out, the resident may use Medicaid or private payment. However, not all nursing homes are Medicare certified although they may be Medicaid certified. If you plan on using short-term Medicare coverage, make sure the nursing home you select is Medicare certified.

A 2010 report from the Alzheimer's Association placed Medicare expenditures for Alzheimer's care at $88 billion annually and projected an increase of more than 600 percent, to $627 billion a year, by 2050. Between 2010 and 2050 the number of Americans with Alzheimer's disease is expected to swell from an estimated 5.1 million to an estimated 13.5 million (Alzheimer's Association, "Alzheimer's Disease to Cost United States $20 Trillion Over Next 40 Years," www.alz.org/documents_custom/FINAL _Trajectory_Report_Release-EMB_5-11-10.pdf, accessed Jan. 6, 2012).). For information on coordinating Medicaid and Medicare services and on Medicaid waivers that allow for day care, short-term care, and respite services while eligible long-term is postponed, *see also* Nursing Home — Medicaid alternatives to long-term care; Program for All-Inclusive Care for the Elderly

Medicare HMOs. Medicare HMOs, which are also known as social HMOs or SHMOs, are federally funded programs that provide home-care aides, home medical supplies, and other home-based medical services. Medicare HMOs can also arrange to send Alzheimer patients to adult day care. The idea behind SHMOs is that it is far less expensive to care for patients in their own home than in a nursing home. The services that they provide make this possible. Four SHMOs located in various parts of the country serve approximately 80,000 Medicare recipients. *See also* SCAN Health Plan of Mountain View and Long Beach, California

Medicare Payment Advisory Commission (MedPAC). The Medicare Payment Advisory Commission (MedPAC) was established in 1997 by the merger of the Physician Payment Review Commission and the Prospective Payment Assessment Commission. Created by congressional mandate, MedPAC's 15 members review payment policies and make congressional recommendations by March 1 of each year. They also evaluate current Medicare policies and send a report of their findings to Congress each June. MedPAC holds regular meetings that are open to the public.

Medications that may cause or worsen cognitive impairment. Medications that may cause or worsen cognitive impairment include: antiarrhythmic agents for the treatment of heart rhythm disturbances, antibiotics, anticholinergic agents, anticonvulsants, antidepressants, antiemetics, antihistamines/decongestants, antihypertensive agents, antimanic agents, antineoplastic agents, antiparkinsonian agents, corticosteroids, histamine H2-receptor antagonists, immunosuppressive agents, muscle relaxants, narcotic analgesics, radiocontrast agents, sedatives, and overdoses of nonsteroidal anti-inflammatory agents. (Sloane, Philip. "Advances in the Treatment of Alzheimer's Disease." *American Family Physician*, November 1, 1998). *See also* Treatment of Alzheimer's disease

Meditation. In numerous studies meditation has been shown to improve cognition. Using magnetic resonance imaging tests, researchers have previously found that the area of the brain associated with memory is stimulated by even short periods of meditation. In a study published in 2010, psychologists studying the effects of a meditation technique known as "mindfulness" found that meditation-trained participants showed a significant improvement in their critical cognitive skills (and performed significantly higher in cognitive tests than a control group) after only four days of training for only 20 minutes each day.

In a related study, Dharma Singh Khalsa and his team at the Alzheimer's Research and Prevention Foundation in Tucson, Arizona, conducted an 8-week trial in which participants engaged in a type of meditation called Kirtan Kriya, a variation of the Kundalini yoga tradition. The researchers found that meditation increased cerebral blood flow in the frontal lobe and parietal lobes, both areas involved in retrieving memories; improvement was seen in tests used to evaluate general memory, attention, and cognition.

In addition, David Perlmutter, M.D., in his book *Power Up Your Brain: The Neuroscience of Enlightenment* (Hay House, 2011) explains how meditation is a powerful stress reduction technique. Chronic stress, including post–traumatic stress, is very harmful to the brain. Animal studies show that chronically stressed rats lose their ability to break out of repetitive behavior patterns and they become less creative and cunning. Chronic stress in humans leads to a stagnant wiring of neural networks in which the same behavior is repeated with hopes for a different outcome. Stress prevents the learning of new behaviors that encourage brain plasticity, and meditation reduces the effects of stress.

Medulla oblongata. The medulla oblongata or myelencephalon, a cone-shaped tissue, situated in the hindbrain, connects the pons superiorly and the spinal cord inferiorly. A median fissure is present on the front or anterior surface flanked by swellings known as pyramids. Olives, arising from olivary nuclei, are situated behind the pyramids. Posterior to the olives are the inferior cerebellar peduncles, which connect the medulla to the cerebellum.

Mega, Michael, M.D., Ph.D. Dr. Michael Mega is an expert on Alzheimer's disease and memory disorders at the Providence Brain Institute at the Providence St. Vincent's Medical Center in Portland, Oregon. He is also the former director of the Memory Disorder and Alzheimer's Disease Clinic at the University of California, Los Angeles. Dr. Mega's focus is on cognitive neurology: disorders of memory, language, visuospatial processing and problem solving. In addition to working with patients who have already been diagnosed with early dementia, Dr. Mega sees people who are worried that their memory is worse than others their age.

Melancholia. Melancholia is a mental condition characterized by extreme depression, bodily complaints, and often hallucinations and delusions.

Melanin. The pigment melanin is found in various parts of the body. Melanin granules are scattered throughout the cytoplasm of certain neurons, particularly those found in the substantia nigra region of the midbrain. Their presence is thought to be related to ability of these cells whose neurotransmitter is dopamine to produce compounds known as catecholamines.

Melatonin. Melatonin is a natural-occurring hormone involved in regulation of sleeping and waking. It is also sold as a dietary supplement. Melatonin, a potent antioxidant which is secreted by the pineal gland, had free-radical scavenging properties, and it has been demonstrated to increase gene expression for antioxidant enzymes. Levels of melatonin are high in children and decline with aging. Levels are low in Alzheimer's disease. Researchers in Malaysia have evaluated the use of melatonin for sleep disturbances in Alzheimer's disease and found that it has a beneficial effect. (Srinivasan,V., et al. "Melatonin in Alzheimer's disease and other neurodegenerative disorders," *Behavioral and Brain Functions*, 2006, http://www.behavioralandbrainfunctions.com/content/2/1/15, accessed Jan 2, 2011)

MEM 1003. MEM 1003 is a novel calcium channel blocker created by Eric Kandel as a potential therapy for Alzheimer's disease. MEM 1003, which is now being developed by Roche Pharmaceuticals, failed Phase II clinical trials for Alzheimer's disease in 2009 and its status as an investigational drug is now uncertain.

Memantine. Memantine, a N-methyl-d-aspartate (NMDA) receptor antagonist, is a synthetic drug reported to improve functioning in patients with advanced Alzheimer's disease. Derived from the anti-influenza drug amantadine, memantine blocks the overstimulation of the NMDA receptor caused by the excitotoxin glutamate. Memantine blocks the NMDA receptor, protecting neurons from excessive stimulation by the neurotransmitter glutamate without upsetting glutamate's normal role in brain function.

First synthesized by the Eli Lilly Company in the United States, memantine has been used as a therapeutic agent for Alzheimer's and other degenerative diseases in Europe since 1980. In the United States, memantine was first approved for use in Alzheimer's disease in 2003. Memantine is marketed under the brands Axura and Akatinol by Merz; Namenda by Forest; Ebixa and Abixa by Lundbeck; and Memox by Unipharm.

Side effects, although rare, are related to the ability of memantine to indiscriminately shut down normal signaling systems, including those required for mental functioning. Other side effects observed in patients with dementia treated with memantine include vertigo, restlessness, hyperexcitation and fatigue. Parkinsonian patients using 30mg/day of memantine have experienced nervous energy, emotional agitation, confusion, dizziness and stomach upset. The effects appear to be increased in patients with AIDS dementia and in patients taking antidepressant medications. ("Needless brain wasting," *Life Extension*, July 2001, 65–68). *See also* Glutamate

Memorial Delirium Assessment Scale (MDAS). The Memorial Delirium Assessment Scale (MDAS) is a neuropsychiatric evaluation tool which measures awareness, disorientation, short-term memory impairment, impaired digit span, shift attention, disorganized thinking, perceptual disturbance, delusions, psychometric activity and disorder of arousal. The MDAS is used to aid in the diagnosis of delirium.

Memory. Memory is the process or power of recalling or reproducing what has been learned or retained, especially through associative mechanisms. Memory also refers to the store of things learned in the past either through activity or experience and recalled through repetition or recognition. Memory can be subdivided into immediate, short-term, recent and remote memory.

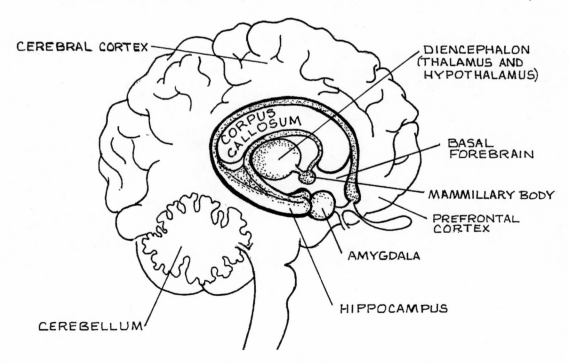

The Memory Center of the Brain (illustration by Marvin G. Miller). • The Cerebral Cortex is involved in conscious thought and language. • The Basal Forebrain is important in memory and learning and consists of numerous neurons containing acetylcholine. • The Hippocampus is essential for memory storage.

Serially subtracting numbers from a list is a function of immediate memory. Short-term memory can be tested by showing or reciting a list of three objects and having the person repeat this list 15 minutes later. Recent memory refers to recall of events occurring in past days or weeks or months. Remote memory refers to recall of events occurring many years in the past. In patients with dementia, recent memory is usually more severely impaired than remote memory.

Memory aids. Memory aids are techniques and tools used to help patients with short-term memory impairment although they are not as helpful in the later stages of dementia. Message boards, large clocks, lists and instruction sheets can be used to remind patients of mealtimes and other activities. Caregivers are encouraged to keep familiar objects in their usual places, make sure clocks and watches are accessible and show the correct time, indicate dates on calendars, use message boards, leave notes when they are away indicating when they will return, and display photographs of family members and close friends that are clearly labeled. Research suggests that gently encouraging patients to use their brain may help them as long as they are not overwhelmed or pushed. Michelle Bourgeois, a speech pathology professor at Ohio State University, is an expert at communicating with people who have dementia. As she explained, the patient still has memories but can't access them. She encourages caregivers to use memory flashcards because individuals with Alzheimer's disease retain the ability to read. Adding words (with large print) to photos helps the patient identify family members. Many patients ask questions repeatedly. Writing answers to those questions on a notepad can help calm patients. Bourgeois has taught thousands of caregivers her methods, and they in turn have taught others. Bourgeois has the goal of improving communication between caregivers and Alzheimer's patients. (Wicker, Christine. "Unlocking the silent prison," *Parade Magazine,* Nov 21, 2010)

Memory impairment. Memory impairment refers to the diminished ability to process, reproduce, or recall what has been learned and retained.

Meninges of the brain. Three meninges or membranes surround the brain: the dura mater, the arachnoid mater, and the pia mater.

Meningitis. Meningitis is a condition caused by inflammation of the meninges of the brain, causing headache over the entire head and back of the neck. Meningitis is usually of a bacterial or viral origin.

Mercury. Studies of brain tissue from Alzheimer's disease patients show high concentrations of mercury. Patients with amalgam dental fillings, which are primarily made of mercury, are reported to have a higher incidence of Alzheimer's disease. Amalgam fillings also contain silver, tin, copper and zinc. ("Mercury linked to Alzheimer's disease," *Business Wire,* 2010, http://www.businesswire.com/news/home/20101115005878/en/Mercury-Linked-Alzheimer's-Disease, accessed Jan 1, 2011. Sullivan, Kip. "Evidence implicating dental amalgam in Alzheimer's disease,"

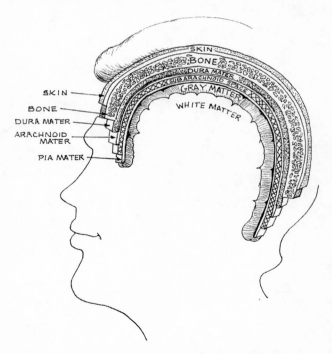

Protective layers of the brain (dura mater, pia mater, arachnoid mater) (illustration by Marvin G. Miller).

2009, http://www.hbci.com/~wenonah/hydro/amalgam.htm, accessed Jan 14, 2011)

Mesencephalon. The mesencephalon or midbrain is a narrow part of the brain about 0.8 inches long connecting the forebrain to the pons and cerebellum of the hindbrain. The narrow cavity of the midbrain consists of a cerebral aqueduct, which connects the third and fourth ventricles. The tectum refers to the part of the midbrain that lies posterior to the cerebral aqueduct.

Mesial temporal lobe. The mesial temporal lobe refers to the area of the temporal lobe situated in, near, or directed toward the median plane of the body, compared to the distal part, which is furthest away from the body.

Metabolic causes of dementia. A number of different medical conditions are well-known for causing organic brain syndrome. One of the most common causes is untreated hypothyroidism that has progressed to myxedema or total thyroid failure. However, the autoantibodies responsible for autoimmune hypothyroidism (Hashimoto's thyroiditis) may target brain rather than thyroid tissue, causing dementia in the absence of thyroid dysfunction.

Similar cases are seen with disorders of calcium metabolism, especially hypercalcemia, and also with electrolyte imbalance. Chronic liver and renal diseases are frequently associated with an organic brain syndrome. However, it would be unusual for organic brain syndrome to emerge in these conditions without evidence of the primary disorder. Repeated episodes of hypoglycemia can also cause dementia, although in this case, the history is usually clearly episodic rather than gradual or sporadic.

Pernicious anemia, which can be diagnosed by a decreased vitamin B 12 level, can cause an organic brain syndrome even without hematologic or other neurologic findings. Korsakoff's syndrome, due to thiamine (vitamin B1) deficiency, presents with a type of amnesia in which the patient is unable to learn new information. Vascular dementia is caused by any of the syndromes resulting from brain damage due to diminished oxygen reserves, including ischemia, anoxia, or hypoxia. CADASIL is another cause of vascular dementia. *See* Vascular dementia

Metabolism. Metabolism is the process of building up and breaking down of chemical foods within the body. Digestion is an example of metabolism. The products of metabolism are known as metabolites. For instance, drugs known as phenothiazines are metabolized by the body, forming hundreds of different chemical metabolites. Changes in metabolism of the brain have been seen in many neurological disorders including stroke, alcoholism and Alzheimer's disease.

Metalloproteinases. Matrix metalloproteinases are enzymes that facilitate the binding of metals such as copper and aluminum to proteins, including amyloid beta protein. High levels of matrix metalloproteinases are known to increase the risk of developing Alzheimer's disease. Therapies that inhibit metalloproteinases are currently being evaluated. (Stromrud, E., et al. "Alterations of matrix metalloproteinases in the healthy elderly with increased risk of prodromal Alzheimer's disease," *Alzheimer's Research & Therapy*, 2010, 2:20 doi:10.1186/alzrt44, http://alzres.com/content/2/3/20, accessed Feb 2, 2011)

Metals *see* Minerals

Methionine. Researchers at Temple University reported in 2010 that diets rich in methionine contribute to the development of Alzheimer's disease. The amino acid methionine is found in red meats, fish, beans, eggs, garlic, lentils, onions, yogurt and seeds. These researchers reported that patients in the early to moderate stages of Alzheimer's disease could have their cognitive impairment slowed or even reversed by switching to a healthier diet. ("Healthy diet could slow or reverse early effects of Alzheimer's disease," Temple University June 8, 2010, press release, http://www.temple.edu/newsroom/2009_2010/06/stories/Healthy_diet.htm, accessed Nov 1, 2010)

Metrifonate. Currently under consideration by the FDA as a treatment for Alzheimer's disease, metrifonate has a 30 year record of safety and tolerability. Introduced in the 1960s, it was originally used as treatment for schistosomiasis. Although it is not a cholinesterase inhibitor, it is gradually converted in the body to a phosphate compound that acts as a long-inhibitor of both cholinesterase enzymes. Metrifonate produces a stable inhibition of acetylcholinesterase that is longer-lasting than that observed with either Tacrine hydrochloride or donepezil hydrochloride.

In one study involving 4 different randomized, 12-week long, placebo-controlled trials at 120 ambulatory clinics, metrifonate given at doses of 30 to 80 mg daily was found to safely improve the cognitive performance of patients with mild to moderate Alzheimer's disease, not only relative to placebo, but, at doses of 60 to 80 mg daily, also relative to baseline performance levels. This is the first such finding for an acetylcholinesterase inhibitor. Metrifonate also stands out in that is has been demonstrated to have the capacity to improve not only cognition, but also psychiatric and behavioral disturbances, the ability to conduct activities of daily living, and global functioning of patients with mild to moderate Alzheimer's disease. Side effects were primarily of a gastrointestinal nature and included diarrhea and nausea. (Farlow, Martin R., M.D., and Pamela A. Cyrus, M.D. "Metrifonate Improves the Cognitive Deficits of Patients with Alzheimer's Disease Relative to Placebo Treatment and to Baseline Performance *The Annals of Long-Term Care* 2000)

Microglial cells. Microglia are the smallest of the neuroglial cells. They are found scattered throughout the central nervous system. The brain's micloglial cells are immune system cells that become activated by neurotoxins and other injuries, causing inflammation and initiating an immune response that, according to some researchers, results in the destruction of neurons. Jean Harry and Jau-Shyong Hong, researchers at the National Institutes of Environmental Health Sciences (NIEHS) are currently studying reactive gliosis in experiments conducted with in vitro (outside of the body) cell cultures. Hong's experiments have supported the theory that overactive microglia kill neurons, and that, in contrast, cells known as astroglia produce proteins that promote neuronal growth or survival. On exposure to amyloid beta peptide fragments, microglia exhibit scavenger cell activity, engulfing exposed neurons.

Harry suspects that specific patterns of neurodegeneration may be due to signaling interactions that occur between the brain's neural and glial cells. Her work focuses on the effects of environmental chemicals on this interaction. ("Environmental Toxins and the Brain," NIEHS News, 1996; *Environmental Health Perspectives* 104 (8), 5)

Although microglial cells in the brain do have a role in the development of Alzheimer's disease, Tony Wyss-Coray and colleagues at the Gladstone Institute of Neurological Disease at the University of California, San Francisco, found that in the presence of increased Transforming Growth Factor Beta-1 (TGF-b1), microglia clear away beta amyloid. Their study, which was published in the May 2000 issue of *Nature Medicine*, reports that the molecules produced by TGF-b1 have a potential role in the treatment of Alzheimer's disease. (Franzen, Harald. "Molecule Helps Brain Cells Clear Alzheimer's Plaques," *Scientific American*, Medicine, May 1, 2000)

Microtubule-associated protein tau (MAPT). Microtubule-associated protein tau includes a number of different proteins that bind the microtubule structure of neurons and stabilize their polymerized structure. In Alzheimer's disease, a hyperphosphorylated form of tau protein is responsible for the defective microtubules that lead to neuronal degeneration.

Midbrain *see* mesencephalon

Milbank Memorial Fund. The Milbank Memorial Fund is an endowed national foundation that has contributed to innovation in health and social policy since 1905. The Fund supports nonpartisan analysis, study, research and communication on significant issues in health policy. 645 Madison Avenue, New York, NY 10022, (212) 355-8400, www.milbank.org, accessed Mar 1, 2011.

Mild cognitive impairment (MCI). Mild cognitive impairment (MCI) is a condition characterized by isolated lapses in short-term memory, memory complaints and poor performance on memory tasks, normal function in other cognitive domains, and normal basic activities of daily living. Once thought to be manifestation of the normal aging process, mild cognitive impairment is associated with an increased likelihood of ultimately progressing to Alzheimer's disease.

Dr. John Morris and other researchers at the Washington University School of Medicine in St. Louis, Missouri, report that the key here is repeated lapses in memory. A temporary period of mild cognitive impairment can occur as a result of taking too much of certain medicines, a blow to the head or the lassitudes of depression. But when repeated problems of short-term memory occur, this is likely to be an early stage of Alzheimer's disease. In this early stage, magnetic resonance scans of the brain reveal that the hippocampus is somewhat smaller than normal or it may even be shrunken in appearance.

Research at the Mayo Clinic in Rochester indicates that patients with MCI progress to Alzheimer's disease at a rate of 10 to 15 percent each year, while normal control subjects progress at a rate of 1 to 2 percent each year. Mayo Clinic researchers describe MCI as a state that may be transition between normal cognitive abilities and clearly recognizable Alzheimer's disease. In psychometric screening, patients with MCI may show only slight deviations from normal. Generally they have scores of 24 or higher (out of 30) on the Mini-Mental Status Exam.

Treatment of MCI is considered not only critical not only for alleviating early deficits in memory, but also for prevention to more severe cognitive decline. Drugs under development include PDE4 inhibitors and ampakines.

Patients with greater cognitive impairment, positive tests for the apolipoprotein E 4 allele, and hippocampus atrophy on MRI are predictors of a more rapid disease progression. (Waldemar, Gunhild, M.D. "New Perspectives in Dementia." XVII World Congress of Neurology, June 17, 2001)

Minerals. Minerals are chemical elements or compounds that result from the inorganic processes of nature. A number of minerals are involved in the normal metabolic functions of the brain, and a number of mineral imbalances have been suspected of contributing to the development of Alzheimer's disease.

While early studies suggested that an increased ingestion of aluminum was responsible for the development of Alzheimer's disease, this has turned out to be untrue. However, metabolic changes that lead to accumulations of aluminum

in the brain may play a role. Because nerve cells grow but do not regenerate, the brain is the organ best suited for the accumulation of metabolic errors over an extended period of time. Researchers at the University of Tennessee in Knoxville have proposed that imbalances in both aluminum and iron contribute to but do not initiate Alzheimer's disease. (Joshi, Jayant G., et al. "Iron and Aluminum Homeostasis in Neural Disorders." *Environmental Health Perspectives 102*, Supplement 3, September 1994)

Results of the Nun's Study indicate that alterations in the normal balance of copper and zinc are also associated with the development of Alzheimer's disease. Researchers have found that high levels of zinc, copper, iron, magnesium and chromium in cerebrospinal fluid are inversely related to beta amyloid 42. (Strozyk, D., et al. "Zinc and copper modulate Alzheimer A_ levels in human cerebrospinal fluid," *Neurobiology of Aging*, July 2009, 30(7), full-text article available through NIH Author Public Access at http://www.ncbi.nlm.nih.gov/pmc/articles/PMC27098 21/?tool=pmcentrez, accessed Jan 4, 2011)

Mini Mental Status Examination (MMSE). The Mini Mental Status Examination (MMSE) is the most widely used evaluation tool used to measure the severity of dementia. Patients with mild dementia have a score of 22–30, with moderate dementia a score of 11–21 and severe dementia 0–10. Patients with dementia generally have scores below 30.

The MMSE includes assessments of orientation, memory, attention and calculation, language, ability to follow commands, reading comprehension, ability to write a sentence, and ability to copy a drawing.

Some researchers have suggested using a cutoff score of 23 or less for the presence of dementia in individuals with at least 8 years of education. It's been noted that education, occupation, and cultural and background factors can strongly influence MMSE scores. In one study, normal farmers were found to score an average of more than 2 points lower on the MMSE than normal white-collar workers. The MMSE also permits considerable flexibility in administration, and the mode of administration has also been found to influence the score.

Mitochondria. Mitochondria are cellular component found in the cell cytoplasm that have recently been found to have their own DNA. Mitochondria also produce enzymes essential for energy metabolism. Mitochondrial dysfunction is related to a number of different diseases. In Alzheimer's disease, mitochondrial dysfunction is related to the toxic effects of excitatory neurotransmitters, primarily glutamate. These excitatory neurotransmitters stimulate specific neuronal receptors, which, when altered by defective mitochondrial energy production, cause a self-perpetuating cascade of events that ultimately result in neuronal cell death.

Normally, with adequate mitochondrial energy production, a normal transmembrane potential exists. This transmembrane potential has a profound effect on the activity of the NMDA receptor for the excitatory neurotransmitter glutamate. Normally, this receptor is blocked by magnesium ions. However, when mitochondrial activity is depressed, alterations in the transmembrane potential reduce this magnesium block. This allows glutamate to react with the NMDA receptor, causing an influx of calcium in the neuron. It is the influx of calcium into the cell that ultimately initiates the cascade of events leading to neuronal cell destruction.

Mitochondrial DNA polymorphisms. Polymorphisms to mitochondrial DNA are linked to many diseases, including Alzheimer's disease. The mitochondrial dysfunction caused by these polymorphisms leads to excessive free-radical production and oxidative tissue damage, which is confined to the brain.

Mixed forms of dementia. Mixed forms of dementia are conditions in which more than one form of dementia is present. Examples include Lewy body dementia or vascular dementia occurring in individuals with co-existing Alzheimer's disease.

Modified Mini-Mental State Examination. The Modified Mini-Mental State Examination is a screening test for cognitive impairment on which scores range from 0 to 100 with lower scores indicating greater impairment. Scores of less than 78 suggest cognitive impairment.

Modified Scales of Psychological Development (M-OSPD). The Modified Scales of Psychological Development (M-OSPD) is an evaluation tool used to diagnose dementia. Developed in 1994, the M-OSPD assesses dementia severity in ranges where the MMSE scores are low or at bottom.

Molecular genetics. Molecular genetics refers to the study of the structure and function of particular genes. The molecular genetics of Alzheimer's disease involves mutations of several different genes, particularly those influencing amyloid precursor protein and its processing, immune system genes, neurotransmission, the immune system, neurotrophic factors, and signal transduction.

Monarda. *Monarda* includes various species of the herb commonly referred to as horsebalm. Horsebalm is rich in carvacrol, a compound found by Austrian scientists to help inhibit the breakdown of acetylcholine. Horsebalm also contains the compound thymol, which also prevents the breakdown of acetylcholine. Of importance, horsebalm has the ability to cross the blood-brain barrier. Normally, this barrier acts as a protective mechanism, preventing toxic drugs from directly injuring brain tissue. In the case of horsebalm, this ability is a benefit because of the possibility that it could directly influence acetylcholine levels in the brain when added to shampoo. (Duke, James A. *The Green Pharmacy.* Emmaus, PA: Rodale Press, [2000] 1997)

Monoamine oxidase (MAO). The naturally occurring enzyme monoamine oxidase (MAO) catalyzes the oxidation of dopamine to an aldehyde compound, dihydroxyphenylacetaldehyde, with formation of hydrogen peroxide. Without sufficient glutathione peroxidase enzymes to break down this substance, excess hydrogen peroxidate combines with ferrous iron forming ferric iron and the highly reactive hydroxyl radical which is responsible for free radical damage to the body. Inhibiting MAO with drugs such as Selegiline may offer benefits in many of the neurodegenerative disorders including Alzheimer's disease.

Monoamine oxidase inhibitor (MAO inhibitor). Monoamine oxidase inhibitors are drugs that inhibit the production of monoamine oxidase, which reduces free radical production. Selegeline, a potent inhibitor of a type of MAO known as MAO_B, delays the need for dopamine replacement therapy in patients with Parkinson's disease. Selegeline is also being evaluated for its ability to improve cognitive defects in Alzheimer's disease. Extracts of ginkgo biloba have also been found to inhibit MAO. (Perlmutter, David. "Functional therapeutics in neurodegenerative disease," Physicians Committee for Responsible Medicine, 2010)

Monoclonal Antibody Therapy. Monoclonal antibodies are laboratory produced protein antibodies that have a single, selected specificity. Monoclonal antibodies are capable of reacting with and destroying certain antigens or proteins in the body that are associated with disease. Monoclonal antibodies are currently being used to treat a variety of cancers and autoimmune disease. They are also being evaluated for their role in the treatment of Alzheimer's disease.

Monosodium glutamate (MSG). Monosodium glutamate is a flavor enhancer added to many foods. Monosodium glutamate, like the artificial sweetener aspartame, is also an excitotoxin capable of destroying neurons in the hypothalamus. In 1968, Dr. Olney of Washington University in St. Louis, Missouri, found that MSG causes widespread destruction of neurons in the hypothalamus and other areas of the brain adjacent to the ventricular system. He found the damage to be most severe in the brain of the newborn. As a result, MSG was voluntarily removed from baby foods in 1969. Both glutamate and aspartame can cause neurons to become extremely excited. If given in large enough doses, they can cause these cells to degenerate and die, generally within two hours. (Blaylock, M.D., Russell L. *Excitotoxins, the Taste That Kills*. Sante Fe, NM: Health Press, 1994, 33–57)

Mood. Mood is a conscious state of mind or predominant emotion, including feelings such as well-being, mania and depression.

Morrison-Bogorad, Marcelle. Marcelle Morrison-Bogorad is the former Director of Neurosciences at the U.S. National Institute of Aging in Bethesda, Maryland. She was appointed in 1996 and retired from this position in 2010.

Mortality. According to the National Center for Health statistics, there were 22,725 deaths attributed to Alzheimer's disease in 1998, making Alzheimer's disease the 9th cause of death rank among Americans ages 65 years and older. (National Vital Statistics Reports, Vol. 48, No. 11, U.S. Department of Health and Human Services, Hyattsville, MD). In 1998, Alzheimer's disease was ranked 12th for all causes of death. In 1999, the number jumped, moving into the 9th place for all causes of death, due mainly to the inclusion of death formerly classified as "presenile dementia." The 44,507 deaths from Alzheimer's disease in 1999 surpassed the totals for other major causes of death, including motor vehicle accidents and breast cancer. ("Mortality declines for several leading causes of death, 1999," Press Release of U.S. Department of Health and Human Services, June 26, 2001.) In March 2010, Alzheimer's disease was listed as the sixth leading cause of death in the United States (http://www.alz.org/alzheimers_disease_facts_and_figures.asp, accessed March 1, 2011).

Dementia is known to shorten life expectancy; previous estimates of median survival after the onset of dementia have ranged from 8 to 10 years. According to a 2001 report published by The Clinical Progression of Dementia Study Group, previous studies may not consider patients with rapidly progressive illness who were not yet officially diagnosed with dementia. After adjustment for length bias, the median survival for dementia was reported to be 3.1 years for subjects with probable Alzheimer's disease, 3.5 years for subjects with possible Alzheimer's disease, and 3.3 years for subjects with vascular dementia. Overall, a younger age at the onset of dementia was associated with longer survival. The level of education was not associated with survival. (Wolfson, Ph.D., Christina, et al. "A Reevaluation of the Duration of Survival after the Onset of Dementia." *The New England Journal of Medicine*, 344 (15), April 12, 2001, 1111–1116)

Motor fibers. Motor nerve fibers are efferent nerve fibers that transmit impulses from the central nervous system to muscles, causing them to contract. Their cells of origin lie in the anterior gray horn of the spinal cord.

Multi-infarct dementia (MID) *see* Vascular dementia

Multiple Sclerosis (MS). Multiple sclerosis is an inflammatory disease characterized by destruction of the protective myelin sheath that covers nerve axons. The inflammatory reaction in MS primarily occurs within the white matter of the central nervous system. Approximately 1 million individuals are affected worldwide, with about 300,000 of them living in the United States. Women with MS outnumber men by 2:1 and symptoms usually commence in early adulthood. Paralysis, sensory disturbances, uncoordination, and visual impairment are common features. The exact cause of MS is unknown although current theories suggest that an inflammatory venous malformation may be responsible.

Muscarinic agonists. Muscarinic agonists are a class of drugs (e.g., xanomeline and talsaclidine) investigated as therapies for Alzheimer's disease in the early to mid 1990s. Preclinical studies suggested a reduction in beta amyloid in cerebrospinal fluid, suggesting that subtype selective agonists might be effective in slowing down the disease processes and preventing neuron loss. Although the first generation drugs validated this therapeutic approach, unacceptable adverse events and side effects were seen including muscarinic effects such as sweating, salivation, diarrhea, and fainting, which ultimately led to their abandonment as potential therapies for Alzheimer's disease.

Muscarinic receptors. Acetylcholine reacts with post-synaptic muscarinic receptors in the hippocampus and temporal cortex. Muscarinic receptors are not affected in Alzheimer's disease.

Music therapy. For centuries, music has been used as a form of therapy. On August 1, 1991, the U.S. Senate Special Committee on Aging met with music therapists, doctors, musicians, nursing home residents and family members of Alzheimer's patients to hear testimony on the benefits of music therapy for the elderly. Dr. Oliver Sacks, a renowned neurologist, stated that music is a lifeline for Alzheimer's patients, because meaningful music does for them what their damaged brains can no longer do — organize and make incoming stimuli comprehensible, allowing them to "hold themselves and their worlds together."

As Dr. Sacks explained, Alzheimer's disease patients do not lose their personalities or their minds, just their access to them. Music helps sort through this confusion. Music therapy is used to improve physical, psychological, cognitive and social functioning and is reported to cause significant increases in levels of melatonin, norepinephrine and epinephrine in Alzheimer's disease patients. ("Music therapy in Alzheimer's disease," from the Music Therapy Association, 2006, http://www.musictherapy.org/factsheets/MT%20Alzheimers%202006.pdf, accessed Mar 1, 2011)

Mutations. Mutations are changes that occur in genes. Genes are composed of proteins, and proteins are composed of amino acids. A difference in one amino acid or a rearrangement of the amino acid sequence causes a gene mutation. Mutations are permanent and can be passed on from generation to generation. Some mutations alter specific attributes or characteristics, which can cause disease or disease susceptibility. Mutations in the presenilin genes are involved in the etiology of the majority of cases of familial early-onset Alzheimer's disease. Mutations in Alzheimer's disease are generally dominant, meaning that they predominate over their partner allele.

Mycoplasma fermentans. Mycoplasma is an infectious agent distinct from bacteria and viruses. *Mycoplasma fermentans* is thought to occur as a mutated form of the *brucellosis* bacteria. While most people harbor traces of this infectious agent, it is usually innocuous. However, according to the Consumer Health Organization of Canada, one out of 300,000 people with mycoplasma develop Alzheimer's disease depending on their genetic predisposition. (Scott, Donald, *Consumer Health Organization of Canada Newsletter*, 2000, June; vol. 23)

Myelencephalon *see* Medulla oblongata

Myelin basic protein (MBP). Myelin basic protein is the primary constituent of the protective myelin sheath that covers nerve axons. Myelin basic protein is also expressed within the nervous system in locations outside of the myelin sheath and it may be found in the thymus and other lymphoid tissues. In patients with multiple sclerosis, myelin basic protein is one of the major targets of the inflammatory immune response.

Myelin basic protein (MBP) antibodies. MBP antibodies are autoantibodies that destroy the protective myelin covering of nerve axons, interfering with the proper transmission of nerve impulses. Toxic concentrations of lead are associated with the development of MBP antibodies. MBP antibodies are seen in multiple sclerosis, amyotrophic lateral sclerosis (ALS) and Alzheimer's disease. Although Alzheimer's disease primarily affects neurons, there is secondary involvement of myelin.

Myelin sheath. The myelin sheath is a protective segmented, discontinuous layer or covering found on nerve axons, which is essential for the normal transmission of nerve impulses. The myelin sheath is destroyed or demyelinated in both multiple sclerosis and Alzheimer's disease.

Myelinated nerve fibers. Myelinated nerve fibers are processes surrounded by myelin sheaths. The myelin sheath is not formed by the neuron but by supporting cells (oligodendrocytes in the central nervous system and Schwann cells in the peripheral nervous system).

Myoclonus. Myoclonus is a condition of uncontrolled muscle twitches.

Myo-Inositol. Myo-inositol is a naturally occurring isomer of the amino acid inositol that is derived from glucose. In 1993 proton spectroscopy studies showed that the frontal and parietal white matter of the brains of patients with Alzheimer's had elevated levels of the protein myo-inositol, with increases of 22 percent compared to normal subjects. The elevation of myo-inositol in patients with mild to moderate AD suggests that abnormalities in the inositol polyphosphate messenger pathway occur early in the natural history of AD. This finding may not be sufficiently sensitive for diagnosing early Alzheimer's, but it may be a useful marker for assessing response to new therapies.

N-acetylcysteine (NAC). The supplement N-acetylcysteine (NAC) has been reported to prevent apoptotic death in nerve cells and protect mitochondria proteins (cell components responsible for energy production) from free radical damage in aged mice, slowing age-related memory loss. The antioxidant properties are related to significant increases in glutathione and the probable action on mitochondrial bioenergetic ability in the synaptic terminals may explain these effects. NAC has also been reported to inhibit the production of nitric oxide. (*Brain Research*, 2000, vol 855(1); 100–106)

Namenda *see* Memantine

Naproxen. Naproxen is a non-steroidal anti-inflammatory agent (Aleve, Anaprox, Naprosyn), which inhibits prostaglandin production. Naproxen is currently being evaluated for its use in treating Alzheimer's disease.

National Alzheimer's Coordinating Center (NACC). The National Alzheimer's Coordinating Center at the University of Washington in Seattle is a coordinating agency sponsored by the National Institute on Aging. The Center facilitates collaborative research among the 30 Alzheimer's Disease Centers, evaluating data and making it available to researchers and the public.

National Center on Caregiver Division. Initiated by a grant from the Archstone Foundation and managed by the Family Caregiver Alliance, the National Center on Caregiver Division, established in July 2001, is an organization dedicated to empowering caregivers. Its objectives are to develop and disseminate information about best practices for caregiving at the state and national levels, to provide assistance to policy makers, to deliver high quality consumer information to caregivers, and to provide quality information for media researching caregiver issues. For more information, see the Family Caregiver Alliance under Caregivers in the Resource Section.

National Citizens' Coalition for Nursing Home Reform (NCCNHR). The National Citizens' Coalition for Nursing Home Reform is a national advocacy group that works to define and improve the quality of long-term care. Their web site offers links to a number of affiliated state advocacy groups. The NCCNHR was formed because of public concern about substandard care in nursing homes. NCCNHR provides information and leadership on federal and state regulatory and legislative policy development and models and strategies to improve care and life for residents of nursing homes and other long term care facilities. (http://www.nccnhr.org/, accessed Jan 4, 2011)

National Institute of Allergy and Infectious Disease (NIAID). The Clinical Immunology Division of the National Institute of Allergy and Infectious Diseases division of the National Institutes of Health is conducting research in the area of vaccines for Alzheimer's disease. (http://www.niaid.nih.gov/, accessed Feb 1, 2011)

National Institute of Mental Health (NIMH). The National Institute of Mental Health (NIMH) is the division of the National Institutes of Health dedicated to mental disorders. The NIMH conducts and supports research to learn more about the causes, prevention, and treatment of mental and emotional illnesses, including multiple aspects of Alzheimer's disease. (http://www.nimh.nih.gov/, accessed Feb 1. 2011)

National Institute of Neurological and Communicative Disorders and Stroke (NINDS). NINDS is the Federal Government's principal agency for research on the causes, prevention, detection and treatment of neurological diseases and stroke. The NINDS also studies Alzheimer's disease and works on research geared toward developing new medications for Alzheimer's disease and other neurological disorders. (http://www.ninds.nih.gov/, accessed Feb 1, 2011)

National Institute on Aging (NIA). The National Institute on Aging (NIA) is a branch of the National Institutes of Health. The NIA is the federal government's principal agency for conduction and support of biomedical, social and behavioral research on the aging process. The NIA maintains an Office of Biological Resources and Resource Development dedicated to research in diseases that target the elderly population. The NIA also supports the NIA Aging Cell Repository located at the Cornell Institute for Medical Research in Camden, New Jersey. The repository maintains skin fibroblast cultures from documented Alzheimer's cases and from individuals who are at high risk. The repository also has prepared DNA from many of the cell lines, including the Characterized Alzheimer's Disease mutation DNA panel. The NIA also supports a Geriatrics Program that supports research and research training directed at the pathology and treatment of age-related diseases. (http://www.nia.nih.gov/, accessed Feb 1, 2011)

National Institutes of Health (NIH). The National Institutes of Health is a constellation of federally sponsored agencies dedicated to advances in the prevention, diagnosis and treatment of diseases. (http://www.nih.gov/, accessed Feb 1, 2011)

National Library of Medicine (NLM). The National Library of Medicine (NLM) is the world's largest research library in a single scientific and professional field. The NLM's database includes references to more than 9 million medical articles published in 3900 biomedical journals. The NLM can be accessed free on the Internet. (www.nlm.nih.gov/, accessed Feb 1, 2011)

National Senior Citizens Law Center (NSCLC). The National Senior Citizens Law Center (NSCLC) advocates nationwide to promote the independence of low-income elderly individuals, as well as persons with disabilities, with particular emphasis on women and racial and ethnic minorities. As a national support center, the NSCLC advocates through litigation, legislative and agency representation and assistance to attorneys and paralegals in field programs.

Nefiracetam. Nefiracetam is a chemical compound that enhances the activity of nicotinic acetylcholine receptors by interacting with a protein kinase C pathway, which accelerates acetylcholine turnover and release. Clinical trials of nefiracetam for Alzheimer's disease have been discontinued.

Neocortex. The cerebral cortex does not have a uniform structure. Almost all the cortex that can be seen from the outside of the brain is composed of neocortex. The prefix "neo" refers to the common notion that the neocortex first appeared late in vertebrate evolution. The neocortex accounts for more than 90 percent of the total cortical area in man. The remainder is made up of paleocortex and archicortex. The two principal neuronal cell types in the neocortex are stellate cells and pyramidal cells.

Neomammalian brain *see* Cortex

Neostigmine. Neostigmine is a drug used to inhibit the action of the enzyme acetylcholinesterase. This potentiates the activity of the neurotransmitter acetylcholine.

NEOTROFIN. NEOTROFIN (experimental name AIT-082) is an experimental drug containing leptiprimin potassium, which is under development by NeoTherapeutics, Inc. A hypoxanthine analog, NEOTROFIN is capable of stimulating nerve growth factor, causing neuronal regeneration. This drug is currently undergoing evaluation in clinical trials. NEOTROFIN acts at the site of heme oxygenase to generate carbon monoxide and by activation of guanylyl cyclase induces a cascade of biochemical reactions through the second messenger system leading to the production of mRNA for neurotrophins. In a press release from Jan 11, 2011, NeoTherapeutics announced that NEOTROFIN produced a statistically significant positive effect on memory function in healthy elderly volunteers after seven days of treatment. This double-blinded, placebo-controlled, Phase Ib study demonstrated that NEOTROFIN was well tolerated and produced no serious adverse events when doses up to 2,000 mg were administered once daily for seven days. *See* Neurotrophins

Nerve cell *see* Neuron

Nerve fibers. Nerve fibers are the processes (axons and dendrites) that project from the body of nerve cells. Bundles of nerve fibers in the central nervous system are known as nerve tracts.

Nerve growth factor (NGF). Nerve growth factor (NGF) is a chemical substance normally produced by the body that helps promote nerve growth and offers protection from damage. Therapies that are able to increase levels of NGF are being studied for their role in the treatment of Alzheimer's disease. Levels of NGF are increased by idebenone, a form of coenzyme–Q-10 that readily crosses the blood brain barrier. By increasing levels of NGF, vulnerable cholinergic neurons may be preserved. Cerebrolysin is another agent showing promise. Produced from purified brain proteins, cerebrolysin mimics one of the natural nerve growth factors. In one study, more than 60 percent of subjects treated with cerebrolysin reported improved memory and concentration. *See also* Cerebrolysin

Nerve impulses. The nerve impulse begins at one spot on either a dendrite or axon. The axon acts as a semi-permeable membrane, keeping sodium ions on the outside of the cell body and chloride and potassium ions on the inside. This produces a net positive charge on the outside of the axon and a net negative charge on the inside. When a site on the axon is stimulated, sodium rushes into the interior of the nerve fiber, depolarizing the axon. This is called the axon potential. The rushing of sodium into the interior of the nerve fiber continues down the axon until it reaches the end of the fiber. While there is an electric current generated, the impulse serves as a chemical message. A gap or synapse must be bridged in order for this chemical message to reach the next neuron down the line.

Nervous system. The nervous system, together with the endocrine or glandular system, controls the functions of the body. The nervous system is composed of specialized cells which receive sensory stimuli and transmit them to effector organs. The nervous system is divided into two major components, the central nervous system and the peripheral nervous system.

Neural thread protein (NTP). Neural thread proteins are protein molecules, such as myelin basic protein, that are produced by brain cells. Nymox Pharmaceutical Corporation has developed a test called AlzheimAlert to measure concentrations of neural thread protein (NTP) in urine. This protein is found in higher amounts in the urine of patients with Alzheimer's disease. However, this protein may be increased in other conditions. Nymox offers this test through its Clinical Reference Laboratory in Maywood, New Jersey.

Neurites. Neurites are the nerve fiber processes, both axons and dendrites, that extend from the cell body of neurons. Neurites are responsible for both receiving and transmitting information.

Neuritic plaque *see* Senile plaque

Neurodegenerative disease. Neurodegenerative diseases affect the gray matter of the brain. Neurodegenerative diseases are characterized princi-

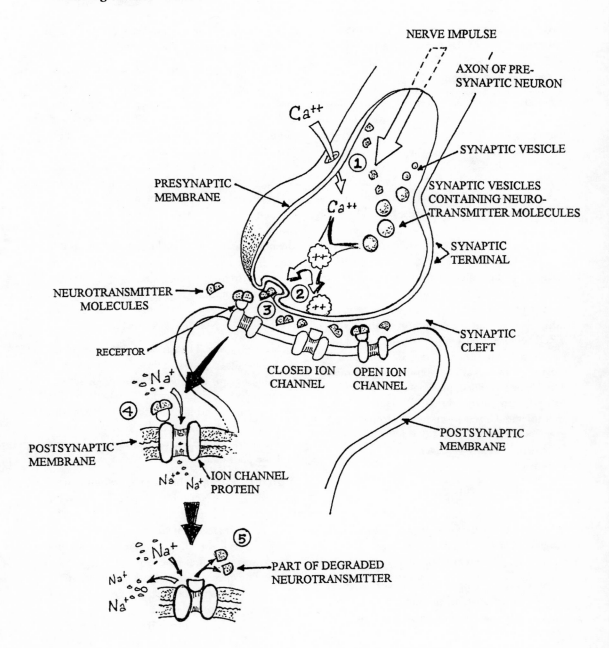

Transmission of nerve impulses (illustration by Marvin G. Miller).

1. Nerve impulses trigger an influx of calcium ions; calcium causes synaptic vesicles to fuse with the pre-synaptic membrane. 2. The synaptic vesicle releases neurotransmitter molecules into the synaptic gap; these molecules bind to receptors on the post-synaptic membrane of neurons specific for this neurotransmitter. 3. When the neurotransmitter binds to its receptor, the ion channel opens, allowing ions to enter. This changes the voltage of the post-synaptic membrane and transmits the impulse. 4. The neurotransmitter molecules are broken down by enzymes and the ion channel closes.

pally by the progressive loss of neurons with associated changes in white matter tracts. In these disorders, the pattern of neuronal loss is selective, affecting one or more groups of neurons, while leaving others intact. Also, neurodegenerative diseases appear to emerge without any clear inciting event in patients who have shown no previous indications of neurologic deficits. Neuropathologic findings differ greatly. In some disorders, there are intracellular abnormalities with some degree of specificity such as the neu-

rofibrillary tangles seen in Alzheimer's disease. In other disorders, there may only be loss of the affected neurons. Generally, neurodegenerative diseases are grouped according to the anatomic regions of the brain that are primarily affected.

The major neurodegenerative diseases affecting the cerebral cortex are Alzheimer's disease and Pick's disease. Their principal clinical manifestation is dementia, a condition characterized by progressive loss of cognitive function independent of the state of dementia. Gross examination of the brain shows a variable degree of cortical atrophy or shrinkage with widening of the cerebral sulci that is most pronounced in the frontal, temporal and parietal lobes. With significant atrophy, there may be an compensatory enlargement of the ventricles due to loss of tissue cells.

Neurofibrillary tangles (NFTs). Neurofibrillary tangles (NFTs) are one of the characteristic brain findings seen in individuals with Alzheimer's disease. In Alzheimer's disease, NFT clusters are found inside neurons in the hippocampus and neocortex. NFTs resemble pairs of threads wound around each other in a helix. Thus, the tangles are known as paired helical filaments or PHFs.

These tangles consist of an abnormal (containing too much phosphorus/protein molecule) form of a protein called tau. Normally, tau is significant because it binds to a protein named tubulin, which in turn forms structures known as microtubules. Microtubules are important in that they run through cells, imparting support and shape. Microtubules also provide routes that allow

TANGLED TUBULES

TAU PARTICLES

NEUROFIBRILLARY TANGLES (TAU TANGLES)

Neurofibrillary tangles in the neuron cell (illustration by Marvin G. Miller). *Top:* Microtubules provide structural support and routes of transport for nutrients and other elements needed by the neuron; *middle:* Microtubules are constructed of a protein called tubulin. The protein tau binds readily to the tubulin in the microtubules; *bottom:* During Alzheimer's disease, either the tau produced is altered or the tubulin-tau binding process changes. As a result the microtubules become distorted and twisted due to the faulty binding process. This distortion of the tubules disrupts the neurons' ability to function and transport material properly.

for the flow of nutrients through nerve cells. The abnormal tau isolated from the brain of patients with Alzheimer's disease causes a breakdown of microtubule assembly. Thus, while neurons are degenerating because of their damaged microtubule systems, the abnormal tau continues to accumulate and form PHFs.

NFTs represent the damaged remains of the microtubule support structures. NFTs are bundles of protein filaments, including mutated forms of tau protein, that cluster or aggregate in the neuronal cell cytoplasm. These bundles encircle or displace the cell nucleus, giving the cell an elongated "flame" shape. In some cells, the fibers form a basket weave pattern that surrounds the cell nucleus, causing the nucleus to take on a rounded contour (globose tangles).

Neurofibrillary tangles are visible microscopically, appearing as basophilic fibrillary structures with H&E staining. They are dramatically demonstrated with silver staining. NFTs are commonly found in cortical neurons, especially in the entorhinal cortex, as well as in other sites such as the pyramidal cells of the hippocampus, the amygdala, the basal forebrain and the raphe nuclei. NFTs are very insoluble and difficult to break down or proteolyze.

Neurofibrillary tangles consist of aberrantly phosyphorylated fibrillary forms of the protein tau. Structurally, NFTs are composed predominantly of paired helical filaments (PHFs) along with some straight filaments that appear to have the same composition as the helical filaments. Other antigens besides tau that have been found in paired helical filaments include microtubule associated protein (MAP2), ubiquitin and amyloid beta peptide. PHFs are also found in the dystrophic neurites that form the outer portions of neuritic plaques and in axons coursing through the gray matter of the brain.

The presence of NFTs signifies the failure of the neuron to properly maintain its cytoskeleton, which is required to support the complex branching shape of its numerous processes. Although plaques are occasionally seen in the brain of normal elderly people, neurofibrillary tangles are not seen in normal aging. Patients with Alzheimer's disease have an increased number of NFTs and their architectural distribution promotes and defines the stages of the disease. The development of NFTs contributes to the death of neurons which characterizes the brain in Alzheimer's disease.

The areas of the brain preferentially affected by NFTs, such as the hippocampus, determine the specific symptoms. For example, NFTs frequently destroy areas of the hippocampus that are involved in processing experiences before storing this information as permanent memories. Symptoms of impaired short-term memory seen in the early stages of Alzheimer disease are a direct result. This also explains why memories from earlier times remain intact.

Neurofibrillary tangles have also been associated with other neurologic disorders including postencephalitic Parkinson's disease, progressive supranuclear palsy, dementia pugilistica (type of dementia resulting from repeated head blows), subacute sclerosing disorders, amyotrophic lateral sclerosis (ALS)/Parkinsonism dementia complex of Guam, panencephalitis and early onset epilepsy.

While there is debate as to which comes first, the NFTs or the plaques, dementia in Alzheimer's disease is generally thought to be better correlated with NFT pathology than with plaque deposits.

A compound capable of increasing tau phosphatase activity would inhibit the hyperphosphorylation of tau protein and prevent the formation of NFTs. Studies are being conducted to develop such compounds. Another therapeutic approach would be the use of compounds capable of breaking the abnormal phosphate bounds. (Bouras, Constantin, et al. "Regional Distribution of Neuropathological Changes in Alzheimer's Disease." *Alzheimer Disease: From Molecular Biology to Therapy*, Edited by R. Becker and E. Giacobine. Boston: Birkhäuser Publishing, 1996, 25–29)

Neurofilament inclusion body disease (NIBD). NIBD is a recently described pathologic condition that can cause rapidly progressive dementia. Symptoms are similar to those of frontotemporal dementia and cortical basal degeneration. Duration is usually two to four years. Brain MRI and pathology show frontal, temporal and caudate atrophy. The hallmark of the disease is the presence of intracytoplasmic neuronal inclusions in brain cells that stain strongly with antibodies to neurofilament proteins and ubiquitin, but not tau or alpha-synuclein. (Geschwind, Michael, Aissa Haman, and Bruce Miller. "Rapidly progressive dementia," *Neurologic Clinics* August 2007, 25(3), available online at PubMedCentral July 6, 2009, http://www.ncbi.nlm.nih.gov/pmc/articles/PMC2706263, accessed Sept 22, 2010)

Neurogenesis. Neurogenesis refers to the regeneration of neurons. For years, researchers thought that human neurons could not regenerate. In 1998, researchers discovered that certain hippocampal neurons have the ability to regenerate and did so when exposed to hippocampal dependent learning tasks.

Neuroglia. Neuroglia refers to the specialized non-excitable cells that make up the central nervous tissue. Neuroglia are generally smaller than neurons and outnumber them by 5–10 times. Comprising about half of the total volume of the brain and spinal cord, neuroglia form the supporting framework or scaffolding of neurons. Neuroglial cells include: astrocytes, oligodendrocytes, microglia, and ependyma.

Neuroleptic medications. Neuroleptic agents, such as thioridazine, haloperidol, and loxapine, are sometimes beneficial in reducing symptoms of anxiety and agitation in patients with Alzheimer's disease. The more potent neuroleptics are generally reserved for the acutely and uncontrollably agitated patient. It is important in using these drugs to be aware of side effects such as increased confusion and extrapyramidal signs.

Neurological disorder. Neurological disorders refer to conditions associated with disturbance in the structure or function of the nervous system resulting from developmental abnormalities, disease, injury or toxins.

Neurologist. A neurologist is a physician who specializes in the field of neurology. Neurologists diagnose and treat patients with neurodegenerative diseases and with disorders caused by nervous system injury or trauma.

Neurology. Neurology is the scientific study of the nervous system, including the brain, especially in respect to its structure, functions and abnormalities.

Neuroma. Neuromas are tumors or masses growing from a nerve and usually consist of nerve fibers. Neuromas may also occur as masses of nerve tissue in an amputation stump, resulting from the abnormal regrowth of severed nerves.

Neuromodulator. Neuromodulators are substances, generally polypeptide chemicals that potentiate or inhibit the transmission of a nerve impulse but are not the actual means of transmission.

Neuromuscular junction. The area where nerve fibers meet muscle fibers is known as the neuromuscular junction. In smooth muscle, a single neuron can exert control over a large number of muscle fibers.

Neuron destruction. Central nervous system neurons destroyed by trauma or disease ordinarily do not regenerate. The first reaction of a neuron to injury is loss of function. Whether the cell recovers or dies depends on the severity and duration of the damage. Typically, the injured nerve cell becomes swollen and the nucleus becomes distorted. Immune system cells known as phagocytes engulf and remove cells that are injured beyond repair. In Alzheimer's disease, several different mechanisms contribute to neuronal destruction.

Neuronal degeneration. Many neurons degenerate during fetal development probably due to their failure to establish adequate functional connections. After birth, a continuous number of neurons gradually degenerate and die. By old age, most individuals have lost about 20 percent of the neurons they were born with. This may account for some of the loss of central nervous system efficiency typically seen in the elderly.

Neurons. The brain is composed of two basic cell types, neurons and glial cells. There are about 100 billion neurons in the human brain and several times that many glial cells. Neurons contain cell bodies or perikaryons and extensions or processes (axons and nerve fibers). Located in the brain, spinal cord and ganglia, neurons vary in size from 4 microns to 100 microns in diameter. Their length varies from several millimeters to several feet. Neurons can transmit nerve signals to and from the brain at a rate of 200 mph.

The nerve cell body of neurons consists of a

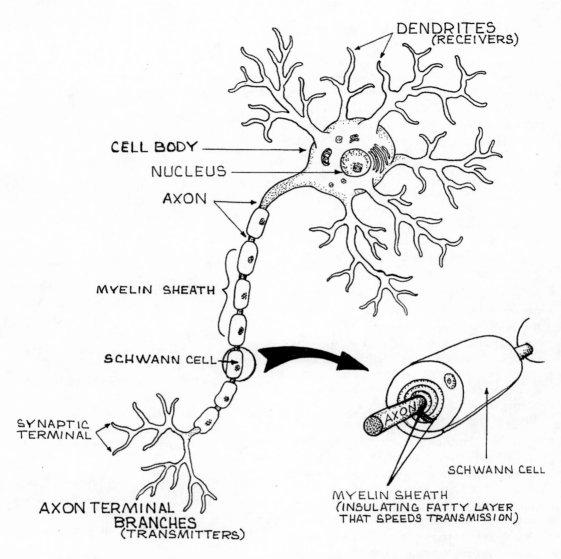

Neurons with processes (axons and dendrites) (illustration by Marvin G. Miller).

mass or microtubule of cytoplasm surrounding a centrally located large cell nucleus. The region in the granular cytoplasm next to the axon is called the axon hillock. Nissl substance, a compound found in the cytoplasm is responsible for producing protein and distributing it to the axon and dendrites. In damaged or fatigued neurons, Nissl substance clusters to the periphery or edge of the cell membrane. Neurofibrils are numerous parallel fibrils that run through the cytoplasm and aid in cell transport. The neurofibrils may form bundles of microfilaments. The external membrane of the cell body is composed of loosely arranged protein layers situated between

a fatty lipid layer. The lipid layer allows carbohydrates and minerals to enter the cell as needed. The permeability of the membrane to potassium ions is much greater than it is for sodium ions.

Each neuron evolves as a round cell body, or soma, that migrates to specific locations during development. Here, neurons grow projections known as axons and dendrites. Each neuron has one axon and about 100,000 dendrites. Neurons send out axons and dendrites in all directions through which they can communicate with other axons and dendrites. These connections intertwine, but do not touch, to form an interconnected tangle with 100 trillion constantly changing connections. The space or gap between these projections is known as a synaptic cleft or synapse. A single neuron may communicate across 100,000 different synapses.

Neurons may be unipolar, bipolar, or multipolar depending on the number of neurites arising from the cell body. Neurons may also be classified as pseudopolare (spelling cells or interneurons). Pseudopolare cells form all the neural wiring within the central nervous system. These cells have two axons, one which communicates with the spinal cord, the other which communicates with skin or muscle cells. Unipolar neurons have a single process or neuron, whereas bipolar neurons have projections at each end, and multipolar neurons have one axon and many dendrites. Most vertebrate neurons are multipolar. By size, neurons may be classified into Golgi type 1 neurons with axons up to 1 meter or longer in length, and Golgi type II neurons with short axons that terminate near the cell body.

Not all neurons fire or produce action. Some neurons are inhibitory — they stop other neurons from firing. Still others modulate and modify the action of the primary neurons. Everything in the brain is very carefully regulated, right down to the subcellular level. Some single brain cells may connect to thousands of other neurons. However, for neurons to function, they must be able to transport materials between the cell body and synapses. For this transport, an intact microtubule system is essential.

Thus, neurons may also be classified according to their connections. Sensory neurons are either directly sensitive to various stimuli, such as temperature and touch, or they are capable of receiving director connection from non-neuronal receptor cells. Motor neurons act directly on muscles or glands, and interneurons connect other neurons. The central nervous system is almost entirely composed of interneurons.

In Alzheimer's disease, neurons in specific areas, such as the hippocampus and neocortex, become dysfunctional. Specifically, the microtubule system of these neurons is disrupted and replaced by neurofibrillary tangles with characteristic paired helical filaments. This injury eventually leads to cell death, leaving behind neuronal fragments known as "tombstones" or "ghost cells." Although it has long been thought that human neurons cannot regenerate, studies indicate that hippocampal neurons from a section of the brain known as the dentate gyrus are able to do so. (Gibbs, W. Wayne. "Dogma Overturned, Upending a long-held theory, a study finds that humans can grow new brain neurons throughout life — even into old age." *Scientific American: Science and the Citizen* Online. November 1998). *See also* Brain plasticity

Neuropathological staging of Alzheimer's disease. In 1992, H. Braak and E. Braak described a system in which the neuropathological changes in Alzheimer's disease occur in progressive stages, based on the alterations found in the hippocampus. For instance in stage I and II of the Braak and Braak staging, abnormal tau protein phosphorylation is increased long before there is any clinical evidence of disease. (Braak, H. and Braak, E. "Neuropathological staging of Alzheimer-related changes." *Acta Neuropath.* 1992, 82: 239–259)

Neuropathology. Neuropathology refers to pathology or disease occurring in the central nervous system. While some of the neuropathological changes seen in Alzheimer's disease also occur in the normal non-demented elderly population, the density and distribution of the principal lesions found in Alzheimer's disease are significantly different.

Neuropathy. Neuropathy is an abnormal and usually degenerative state of the nervous system, including its nerves. The term neuropathy is also used to refer to a systemic condition, such as muscular atrophy, that stems from a neuropathy.

Neuropeptides. Neuropeptides are chemicals composed of amino acids which have the ability to act as neurotransmitters. Produced in the central nervous system, neuropeptides, such as somatostatin and substance P, control many bodily functions such as muscle relaxation and blood pressure. Most neurons that contain neuropeptides also contain classical neurotransmitters such as acetylcholine.

Neuropraxia. Neuropraxia is the term used to describe a transient or temporary injury to peripherally nerves. The resulting paralysis is incomplete and recovery is rapid. The most common cause of neuropraxia is pressure.

Neuroprotective agents. Neuroprotective agents are subjects designed to preserve the function of neurons. Neuroprotective agents such as nerve growth factor and vitamin E are currently being studied for their protective roles. Neuroprotective agents are considered the Alzheimer's disease therapy of the future. In contrast to drugs that prevent the pathways that lead to neurodegenerative changes, neuroprotective agents are designed to protect neurons from this assault.

Neuropsychiatric inventory (NPI). The Neuropsychiatric Inventory or NPI is a caregiver-based inventory that evaluates twelve symptoms commonly seen in patients with Alzheimer's disease, including delusion, hallucinations, agitation, depression, dysphoria, euphoria or elation, anxiety, apathy, irritability and disinhibition, night-time behavior disturbances, eating disturbances and abnormal motor or movement behavior. The NPI is commonly used to evaluate response to drug therapy, with favorable results causing a four point increase in the score.

Neuropsychologic symptoms in Alzheimer's disease. Neuropsychologic symptoms in Alzheimer's disease include symptoms of memory loss and impairment of judgment, language, learning, abstract thinking, and visual-spatial coordination skills.

Neuropsychological evaluation. A neuropsychological evaluation is the first step used to help diagnose patients having symptoms of cognitive impairment. A battery of tests is used to assess a number of cognitive domains in diagnosing, screening, and following patients with mild cognitive impairment, Alzheimer's disease, frontotemporal lobe dementia, and Lewy body dementia, among other brain disorders.

The first of these cognitive domains evaluated is premorbid intellectual functioning (symptoms can occur prior to the onset of any brain dysfunction), which is evaluated from several pieces of information: level of education, level of occupational functioning, and certain cognitive skills that can be relatively resistant to aging effects, such as vocabulary or basic reading of words. Intellectual functioning is also evaluated, which includes how the individual processes, classifies, and integrates information. The level of functioning on those skills provides an idea of where that patient or individual should be, given no symptomatology. Other parameters evaluated include: attention/concentration, memory functioning, language functioning, executive functioning, visual perception, motor functioning, and personality functioning.

Neuropsychological tests. Neuropsychological tests refer to a wide array of procedures used to objectively assess neuropsychological or neurobehavioral performance, including cognitive, adaptive and emotional behaviors. These tests are used as part of the neuropsychological evaluation. Neuropsychological tests include full-scale verbal and performance parameters of intelligence quotient (IQ). Tests are used to measure various parameters, including verbal and nonverbal memory, remote memory, mood, affect, visuomotor coordination, visuospatial planning and organization, cognitive function, language function, attention and spontaneous speech. Tests are usually conducted over a period of 6 to 10 hours. A clinical neuropsychologist administers and evaluates the tests. Progressive dementing processes such as Alzheimer's disease and multi-infarct dementia are associated with marked worsening of performances on serial neuropsychological assessments. Neuropsychological tests are used to assist in diagnosing the presence or absence of organic brain lesion, assist in determining if the brain dysfunction is localized (focal) or diffuse, describe the effects of an identified lesion on cognition and behavior and assist in planning treatment.

Neuroscience and Neuropsychology of Aging (NNA) Program of the NIA. The Neuroscience and Neuropsychology of Aging (NNA) Program, which is sponsored by the National Institute on Aging, supports extramural research and training to further the understanding of the aging of the nervous system. In addition, this program supports basic and clinical research on normal aging and diseases of the aging brain, including cerebrovascular aging. An important component of this program is the support of basic, clinical and epidemiological studies of Alzheimer's disease and related dementia of aging.

Neurotoxin. Neurotoxins are substances with the ability to injure or destroy neurons or brain cells. In Alzheimer's disease amyloid β protein is known to exert neurotoxic effects. Biological neurotoxins include a diverse family of bacterial, animal and plant derived chemicals.

Neurotransmitters. Neurotransmitters are chemical messenger molecules that allow individual neurons to communicate with one another and also with muscles and other cells. While there are some instances in which neurons are directly connected or coupled, allowing ionic currents to flow between neurons, in most cases neurons communicate with each other by releasing neurotransmitters, typically at specialized sites known as synapses.

Neurotransmitters, which are sometimes called neuromodulators or neurohormones, excite or inhibit the cellular functions of neurons during synaptic communication. Neurotransmitters are necessary for transmitting impulses at the presynaptic axon to the postsynaptic axon. Once stimulation or inhibition has taken place, the neurotransmitter is broken down by an enzyme or it is taken up by the presynaptic axon terminal. For example, the neurotransmitter acetylcholine is broken down by the enzyme acetylcholinesterase. Mitochondria within the presynaptic vesicles provide energy for the synthesis of new transmitter substance, which is stored in prepackaged aliquots.

Most neurons produce and release only one type of neurotransmitter at their nerve endings. However, a few neurons release an excitor neurotransmitter, such as glutamate, at one synapse, and a neuropeptide at another synapse. Different neurons may produce and release different neurotransmitters. For example, acetylcholine is widely used by neurons in the central and peripheral nervous system, whereas dopamine is produced by neurons in a part of the brain known as the substantia nigra. While the list of neurotransmitters is likely to grow, current neurotransmitters include acetylcholine, norepinephrine, epinephrine, dopamine, glycine, serotonin, gamma-aminobutyroic acid (GABA), enkephalins, substance P, and glutamic acid.

Neurotransmitters are released from their nerve endings during the nerve impulse. Once in the synaptic cleft they achieve their potential by briefly raising or lowering the resting potential of the post-synaptic membrane. Many drug therapies revolve around changing the concentrations of neurotransmitters. For instance, the benzodiazepine drugs such as diazepam (Valium) bind to GABA receptors and increase the effects of GABA released at nerve synapses. While l-dopa is beneficial in restoring levels of dopamine in patients with Parkinson's disease, attempts to raise the acetylcholine level in patients with Alzheimer's disease have not been as successful since multiple transmitter systems are affected. For example, cortical somatostatin-containing interneurons are affected as much as cholinergic neurons.

While deficiencies of acetylcholine are one of the best known chemical aberrations seen in Alzheimer's disease, other neurotransmitters not related to the cholinergic system, including serotonin, GABA, somatostatin, and norepinephrine, are also reduced in Alzheimer's disease. These deficiencies may also contribute to cognitive dysfunction.

Neurotrophic factors. Neurotrophic factors are endogenous cytokine proteins, such as nerve growth factor, that promote nerve cell growth and survival.

Neurotrophins. Neurotrophins are substances, such as the essential fatty acid docosahexaenoic acid (DHA), which provide nutrition to nerves.

Niacinamide (Vitamin B3, Nicotinamide). Niacinamide is a B vitamin present in red meat. Humans with a diet low in nicotinamide, choline or methyl donors early in life and low N-methyl-nicotinamide enzyme activity may be prone to Alzheimer's as their brain and its structures may have impaired development. One prediction, proposed in a 2005 article in *Medical Hypotheses*, is that a diet rich in these micronutrients while young will improve brain development and reduce the risk of Alzheimer's disease. In 2006, researchers at the University of California at Irvine conducted animal studies giving very high doses of niacinamide to mice with Alzheimer's disease and deemed the mice completely cured. As a result, the Irvine team began a clinical trial for safety using 1500 mg niacinamide twice a day or a placebo to patients with diagnosed stages I-IV Alzheimer's disease from 50–95 years old. The trial was expected to be completed in 2011. A similar trial is being conducted in the UK.

To prevent deficiencies of other B vitamins, vitamin B complex is also recommended. (Williams, A.C., and D.B. Ramsden. "Nicotinamide homeostasis: A xenobiotic pathway that is key to development and degenerative diseases," *Medical Hypotheses*, 2005, 65 (2): 353–62)

Nicotinamide adenine dinucleotide (NADH). The naturally occurring substance nicotinamide adenine dinucleotide (NADH), which is also sold as a dietary supplement, has been reported to improve cognitive function in patients with Alzheimer's disease when administered at a dose of 5 mg given twice daily. (Perlmutter, David. "Functional therapeutics in neurodegenerative disease," Physicians Committee for Responsible Medicine, 2000)

Nicotine. Nicotine is a basic drug that acts on receptors in the cholinergic system in the brain that are depleted. Some studies suggest that nicotine may protect nerve cells and help prevent the formation of beta amyloid protein. Unlike the chemicals released in cigarette smoke, nicotine itself does not cause cancer. However, in high doses it acts like a poison and has long been used as an insecticide. Researchers are investigating nicotine-like drugs that may protect nerve cells without causing side effects.

Nicotinic acetylcholine receptor. The nicotinic receptor is one of the two main categories of receptors that the body has for acetylcholine. The nicotinic acetylcholine receptor is a specialized ion channel that plays an important role in learning, memory, stress response and survival. Ion channels function as portholes in cell membranes, regulating the flow of current to cells. These channels are influenced by both the neurotransmitter acetylcholine and exogenous sources of nicotine. These channels, in turn, regulate neuronal activity in a region of the brain known as the hippocampus. Research in this area indicates that nicotinic ligands, substances that bind to the nicotinic receptor, may be useful in preventing neurological disorders such as Alzheimer's disease, depression, epilepsy, and Parkinson's disease. It's known that individuals with

Alzheimer's disease have fewer nicotinic receptors in their cerebral cortex. ("A New Side of the Nicotinic Receptor." *Environmental Health Perspectives.* 1998; 106 (4): Forum)

NINCDS-ADRDA criteria for Alzheimer's disease. The National Institute of Neurological and Communicative Disorders and Stroke (NINCDS) and the Alzheimer's Disease and Related Disorders Association (ADRDA) have established criteria to aid in the diagnosis of patients with Alzheimer's disease. The NINCDS-ADRDA criteria require unmistakable deterioration in at least two cognitive domains relative to the patient's previous level of function. This is determined by a history of intellectual decline and must be documented by formal mental status testing. The NINCDS-ADRDA criteria for dementia do not require that the loss of cognitive function be severe enough to interfere with impaired social and occupational functioning as dictated by some other criteria.

The terms benign senescent forgetfulness and age-associated memory impairment have been proposed to refer to some persons with evidence of cognitive impairment who do not meet present clinical criteria for dementia. (Bennett, David, and Jacob Fox. "Alzheimer's disease and other dementias," *Neurology for the Non-Neurologist*, Third Edition, 1994, [edited by William J. Weiner.] Philadelphia: J.B. Lippincott, 195–196)

Nitric oxide (NO). Nitric oxide (NO) is a gaseous neurotransmitter which acts as the primary vasodilator (dilates or relaxes blood vessels) in the brain. Nitric oxide is formed when the amino acid L-arginine is oxidized to citrulline by the action of the enzyme nitric oxide synthase. Although nitric oxide is a free radical due to its unpaired electron, it does not appear to cause any damage by itself, with the exception of damage to mitochondrial complex I. However, when combined with the superoxide anion, the potent oxidant peroxynitrite is formed. Peroxynitrite has been implicated in neuronal cell damage, including DNA strand breaks, DNA deamination, and damage to mitochondrial complexes.

In the hippocampus, NO and another gaseous neurotransmitter, carbon monoxide, serve as retrograde messengers that produce activity-dependent presynaptic enhancement during long-term potentiation. Long-term potentiation, which can last hours or days, refers to prolonged changes in a target neuron resulting from intense but brief trains of stimuli delivered to a presynaptic neuron.

Nitric oxide synthase. Nitric oxide synthase is an enzyme used in the production of nitric oxide. Nitric oxide synthase is heavily concentrated in the hippocampus. Neuronal nitric oxide synthase is activated by a calcium-dependent mechanism, but it can also be stimulated by the cytokine IL-1 beta. Elevated levels of nitric oxide synthase can result in excess amounts of nitric oxide, which may contribute to the pathogenesis of Alzheimer's disease. Therapies, such as arginine analogues, intended to inhibit nitric oxide synthase are currently being researched.

NMDA (N-methyl-d-aspartate) receptor. The NMDA receptor is the most common of the three types of glutamate receptors found on neuron membranes in the brain. A component of the excitatory pathway, the NMDA (N-methyl-d-aspartate) receptor is stimulated by the excitatory neurotransmitter glutamate. Enhanced NMDA receptor sensitivity to glutamate can result from an altered electrochemical gradient caused by dysfunctional mitochondria, which occurs in Alzheimer's disease and is thought to be due to decreased mitochondrial energy production. The net result is excess glutamate, a neurotransmitter, which is thought to be toxic to neurons.

Some researchers explain that the excitotoxins aspartame and monosodium glutamate can cause excess stimulation of the NMDA receptor. It is postulated that excess excitation of the NMDA receptor destroys it, rendering this transduction system ineffective. The NR receptor is also known to weaken with age.

Protective agents that inhibit the release of glutamate or the stimulation of the NMDA receptor include the anticonvulsant medications gabapentin, lamotrigene, muscarinic receptor antagonists, GABA receptor antagonists, alpha 2-receptor antagonists, diphenylhydantoin, carbamazepine, the NMDA antagonists remacemide and memantine, and Huperzine A. *See also* Excitotoxins

Noncognitive behavioral abnormalities. The original patient described by Dr. Alois Alzheimer in 1907 was remarkable for both her progressive cognitive impairment and for a number of non-cognitive behavioral abnormalities. The presence of these non-cognitive behavioral symptoms has become as much a part of the symptomatology of Alzheimer's disease as the cognitive decline and often precipitate institutionalization. These non-cognitive symptoms include apathy, hyperexcitability, delusions, hallucinations, depression, agitation, and hostility. A number of studies consistently suggest that the presence of psychotic symptoms in Alzheimer's disease is associated with an accelerated deterioration of cognitive function.

Although antipsychotic drugs were once used to treat these symptoms, studies have found that at recommended doses they are only modestly helpful when compared to placebos. At higher doses, these drugs cause increased sedation which has been found to result in unsteady gait and a higher incidence of falls.

Nonsteroidal anti-inflammatory drugs (NSAIDs). Non-steroidal anti-inflammatory drugs (NSAIDs) are compounds distinct from steroids that effectively inhibit the inflammatory process. NSAIDs inhibit cyclooxygenases and thus inhibit synthesis of prostaglandin signals for IL-1 production, although they have little effect on complement. Nevertheless, evidence indicates that low doses of NSAIDs may suffice to achieve a neuroprotective effect that appears to require sustained exposure, most likely for several years before the onset of dementia, to produce effects. Short-term incidence studies suggest that NSAIDs can prevent incident Alzheimer's disease if exposure pre-dates disease onset by several years.

Norepinephrine (Noradrenaline). Norepinephrine is a catecholamine neurotransmitter derived from the amino acid tyrosine. Neurons containing norepinephrine as their neurotransmitter are called noradrenergic neurons. Noradrenergic neurons are found only in the pons and medulla. All areas of the cerebral cortex appear to receive some noradrenergic innervation. The actions of norepinephrine are nearly silent during sleep and become activated during wakefulness, becoming most active in situations that are startling or call for watchfulness. Thus, the primary role of norepinephrine appears to be one of maintaining attention and vigilance.

Normal pressure hydrocephalus (NPH). Normal pressure hydrocephalus (NPH) is a clinical syndrome characterized by the gradual onset of a cluster of gradually worsening symptoms, including gait apraxia, dementia and incontinence. First described by Solomon Hakin in 1964, NPH may also present with more overt psychiatric symptoms such as mania or depression. Other neurological features such as speech impairment may also develop. Diagnosis is made with computed tomography imaging or magnetic resonance imaging. These studies commonly show increased ventricular size and a reduction of both white matter in the areas surrounding the ventricles and gray matter in the cortical regions. Even in the absence of these changes, patients with the classical symptoms of NPH should be evaluated further. An abnormal cerebrospinal fluid absorption pathway is suspected of being the underlying cause of NPH because when the volume of spinal fluid is reduced, patients often improve.

Alzheimer's disease, Binswanger's disease and NPH may all cause dementia and dilated cerebral ventricles. Imaging studies may fail to distinguish if the dilation is from cerebral atrophy (Alzheimer's or Binswanger's) or from NPH. Patients with NPH, however, generally exhibit gait disturbances and incontinence before cognitive impairment. NPH may be precipitated by subarachnoid hemorrhage, infection, central nervous system trauma and neoplasm.

Novartis Foundation for Gerontology. The Novartis Foundation for Gerontology is dedicated to promoting healthy aging. The Alzheimer's disease center funded by this organization provides educational support related to Alzheimer's disease. The Novartis website, Health and Age, contains information on healthy aging (http://www.healthandage.com/, accessed Feb 2, 2011).

Nucleus basalis of Meynert. The nucleus basalis of Meynert is the area of the neocortex rich in cells that produce acetylcholine. It is one of the earliest areas of the brain affected in Alzheimer's disease.

Nun study. The Nun Study of 2,500 Catholic nuns (School Sisters of Notre Dame) living in convents throughout the Midwest has provided researchers with insight into the many factors that contribute to the development of Alzheimer's disease. In a number of published reports and one popular book, DH Snowdon and his colleagues from the Sanders-Brown Center on Aging of the College of Medicine at the University of Kentucky in Lexington described their findings.

From the Nun Study, Snowdon et al. showed that the presence of cerebral infarcts, even if small and scarce, raised the risk of dementia as much as 20 times for those with brain lesions similar to those seen in Alzheimer's disease. Infarcts unrelated to Alzheimer's disease-type lesions were found to be associated with few cogniztive effects. Other factors related to the development of Alzheimer's disease included low serum folate levels, high copper levels, greater functional dependence on others, increased weight loss in old age and a lower number of positive emotions. This study suggests that careful monitoring and treatment of hypertension and other vascular risk factors along with a healthy diet and exercise plan could potentially reduce the incidence of dementia.

Of interest, researchers also showed that the nuns who retained the highest levels of cognitive ability throughout their life were least likely to have the APOE4 allele. *See* also Writing study. (Snowdon, David. *Aging with Grace: What the Nun Study Teaches Us About Leading Longer, Healthier and More Meaningful Lives.* New York: Bantam Publishing, 2001. Snowdon, David. "The Nun Study: What Is It?" 2000, http://www.alzheimermonterrey.com/estudios/estudios/Estudio-Monjas-I.pdf, accessed Jan 2, 2011)

Nursing home accreditations. Federal and state nursing home inspections are a matter of public record. When evaluating nursing homes, request their most recent state survey, although if it is more than 6 months old, circumstances may have changed since the report. Government inspections, including Medicaid and Medicare inspections, occur at least annually and are designed to

insure that minimum federal and state requirements are met regarding the building, sanitation,
safety features, adequate staffing and administration. Another report worth viewing is the
"quality indicators" report, which is available for
all Medicare and Medicaid certified nursing
homes. This report lists all problems experienced
by residents at the facility, including weight loss,
dehydration, skin breakdown, falls, fractures and
behavioral problems. Scores for each nursing
home are compared or ranked to those of other
homes in the state.

All nursing homes are licensed by the state in
which they are located. Homes that receive Medicaid or Medicare reimbursement must also be
certified by the state agency responsible for nursing home regulation. See resource section for a
listing of state licensure and certification programs for assistance in helping choose a nursing
home.

**Nursing home — Medicaid alternatives to
long-term care.** Medicaid offers waivers to help
people postpone long-term care. The purpose of
Medicaid Long-Term Care Waiver programs is
to avoid or delay unnecessary and costly nursing
home placement and enhance quality of life by
providing alternative, less restrictive long-term
care options for seniors who qualify for Medicaid
skilled nursing home care. These options include
care in the home, or in a community setting such
as an assisted living facility or adult day care center. For a detailed list of waivers provided by
Elder Care, see http://www.oppaga.state.fl.us/
profiles/5023/, accessed Mar 4, 2011.

Nursing home costs. Before making any
arrangements for nursing home care, it is important to completely understand all the financial arrangements of the home you have selected.
Nursing homes charge a basic daily or monthly
rate.

Besides the daily or monthly fee, the nursing
home may charge extra for physician's fees, medications, laundry, special feeding, frequent linen
changes, or special supplies such as wheelchairs
and walkers and physical therapy.

Many residents or their families pay for nursing home care out of their private funds. Long-
term care insurance policies can be used to help
defray these costs. Others whose finances are de-

pleted rely on Medicaid to cover the costs of their
nursing home care. To find out whether a resident is financially eligible for Medicaid, call the
Department of Social Services in your area. For
information regarding Medicare, call the Social
Security Administration. However, Medicare
pays for very little nursing home care, and it
never pays for long-term nursing home care.
Veterans of the United States armed forces
should also check with the Veterans Administration to see if they are eligible for nursing care
benefits.

Nursing homes generally ask for financial dis-
closure to help determine the appropriate payment mechanism. Admissions personnel will assist families in determining what information is
necessary and what forms need to be filed to ex-
pedite placement. Because some nursing homes
have waiting lists, it is a good idea to complete
paperwork in advance in the event that an emergency placement becomes necessary. (American
Association of Homes and Services for the
Aging)

Nursing home facilities. Most nursing homes
in the United States are owned and operated by
for-profit corporations. Others are owned and
operated by not-for-profit organizations, including churches and fraternal groups. In addition,
a small number of facilities are operated by government agencies or the Veteran's Administration.

Nursing home options. Nursing homes have
changed in recent years, both in the multi-tiered
levels of care that they provide and in their individual philosophies. Resident-Centered care
facilities are moving away from the institutionalized settings of the past and offering individ-
ualized holistic care. No two nursing homes are
alike today. It is important to explore all of the
nursing homes in your area before deciding on
which one is most suitable for your family member. The one closest to home may not be the best
when it comes to personalized care and activities
that encourage residents to maintain their skills.

Several factors must be considered when
choosing a nursing home, including inspection
reports (*See* Nursing home accreditations) and
the type of insurance plans they are accredited
to accept. The environment must also be care-

fully observed. Odor is a key indicator of quality. The facility should be clean, odor-free, spacious, and quiet with a pleasant atmosphere. The building should be well-lighted with ample windows so that residents do not feel contained. The building must be safe so that residents cannot escape from the grounds, but there should be adequate escape routes in the event of a fire. If there are multiple stories, see if there are adequate elevators that function properly.

The staff should be clean and well-groomed, and the turnover rate should be low. Nurses should be trained in geriatric care and at least some of the staff should have advanced training in caring for Alzheimer's disease patients. During your visit, observe the residents to see if they are involved in activities or given opportunities for socialization. See what policy the nursing home has if you intend to arrange occasional home visits or want to have a pet visit.

Check to see if staffing is adequate. One national advocacy organization recommends that the ratio of licensed practical nurses (LPNs) to patients be 1:15 on days, 1:25 on evenings and 1:35 on the night shift. There should also be a sufficient number of nurses' aides (1:5 on days, 1:10 on evenings, and 1:15 on nights) and registered nurses (RNs) working in supervisory capacities. The nursing home you select should pay their workers salaries equivalent or higher than other nursing homes in the area.

Find out if there are hidden charges (*see* Nursing home costs) and ask if the facility provides services such as barber and beauty shops, religious services, or routine dental care. Find out in an advance deposit is required and the terms for its refund. Find out how long the current owner of the facility has operated it. Facilities with long-term ownership offer greater stability.

Find out if all residents have roommates, and, if so, find out the guidelines used when roommates do not get along. Find out if there are resident and family councils established to help solve problems as they arise. Ask if food can be brought in from the outside and find out what happens if the resident has special food needs. Find out if physical restraints are used, and, if so, find out what circumstances mandate their use. Find out how often patients are bathed. Ask if side-rails are routinely used on beds. Their use

is generally not recommended because they are associated with a higher rate of injuries. Find out what areas patients are allowed to wander in and inquire if they have ever had problems with patients wandering away from the facility. Find out if there are night call lights or lights that can be pulled in case of an emergency. Find out when visiting hours are and see if additional visits can be arranged as new residents become accustomed to their new facility.

When you select a nursing home, find out how much clothing you'll need to bring and how much closet space is allocated for patients. Find out how the facility would like you to label the residents' personal items. Find out if there are any limitations on what you can bring to make rooms more home-like. And be sure to let staff members know what name the resident prefers to use and any special needs they may have.

Look for a nursing home with a philosophy similar to that of Beatitudes in Phoenix, which was singled out in a *New York Times* article for its willingness to let patients be allowed to bathe and dine when they wanted if doing so kept the patient from becoming combative or agitated. (Belluck, Pam. "Giving Alzheimer's patients their way, even chocolate," *The New York Times*, Dec 31, 2010, http://www.nytimes.com/2011/01/01/health/01care.html?ref=thevanishingmind, accessed Jan 31, 2011)

Nursing home violations. Nursing home violations include reported incidents (that violate rules and standards) as well as deficiencies found on inspections. In 2007, the Department of Health and Human Services reported that 94 percent of nursing homes were cited for violations of federal health and safety standards. For-profit nursing homes were found more likely to have problems than other types of nursing homes. In evaluating nursing homes, it is important to find out what violations have been reported and how the facility responded. (Memorandum Report "Trends in nursing home deficiencies and complaints," OEI-02-08-00140, Sept 18, 2008. Pear, Robert. "Violations reported at 94 percent of nursing homes," *The New York Times*, Sept 29, 2008)

Nutrient deficiencies. Studies show that brain thiamine (vitamin B1) levels are decreased in patients with Alzheimer's disease, and 25 percent of Alzheimer's disease patients have lower levels of vitamin B12. Deficiencies in both of these nutrients can contribute to symptoms of dementia. Studies also show that 50 percent of institutionalized patients suffer from protein malnutrition. (Folstein, M. "Nutrition and Alzheimer's Disease." *Nutrition Reviews*, 1997, vol 55 (1): 23–25.) David Perlmutter, M.D., writes that an imbalance and deficiency of essential fatty acids contribute to symptoms in Alzheimer's disease. ("Brain doctor links nutrition and Alzheimer's prevention," 2009, http://www.cbn.com/700 club/guests/bios/david_perlmutter_090804.aspx, accessed Feb 10, 2011)

Nystagmus. Nystagmus refers to loss of voluntary movement of the ocular muscles. A sign of cerebellar disease, nystagmus is characterized by rhythmical oscillation of the eyes.

Occipital lobe. The occipital lobe of the cerebrum is bound anteriorly by the parietal and temporal lobes on both the lateral and medial surfaces of each hemisphere.

Odor Identification Test. Studies funded by the NIA and the NIMH suggest that a simple odor identification test may help doctors predict which individuals with mild cognitive impairment will go on to develop Alzheimer's disease. Study participants were exposed to a 15 to 20 minute scratch and sniff test using distinct smells such as methanol, peanuts and soap. After smelling the odor, participants were asked to pick what it was from 4 alternative choices. None of the participants who scored well on the test developed Alzheimer's within 20 months. However, 19 of 47 subjects who had difficulty identifying the odors, although they reported having no trouble identifying odors, went on to develop Alzheimer's disease during the follow up period. ("Odor Identification Test May Help Predict Alzheimer's Disease." NIA NEWS, August 28, 2000)

Olanzopine (Zyprexa). Olanzoprine (Zypexa) is an atypical antipsychotic medication, which effectively reduces symptoms of psychosis and aggression in patients with Alzheimer's disease while posing a very low risk for side effects. In one study, following a double-blind, 6-week ex-

posure to 1 mg-10 mg olanzapine daily, patients improved significantly on the primary efficacy measured by psychometric tests used to determine Agitation/Aggression, Delusions and Hallucinations. Symptoms which emerged during treatment included sleepiness, accidental injury and rash. Measures of agitation and psychosis improved significantly at 5 mg daily versus placebo. Results were less apparent at 10 mg/daily and not evident at 15 mg daily. (Street, J.S. et al. "Long-term efficacy of olanzapine in the control of psychotic and behavioral symptoms in nursing home patients with Alzheimer's dementia." *International Journal of Geriatric Psychiatry*, 2001, December; 16 (1): 62–70)

Older Americans Act (OAA). The Older Americans Act (OAA) offers a form of federal assistance that pays for some supportive services including home health care. Congress passed the OAA in 1965 in response to concern by policymakers about a lack of community social services for older persons. The original legislation established authority for grants to states for community planning and social services, research and development projects, and personnel training in the field of aging. The law also established the Administration on Aging (AoA) to administer the newly created grant programs and to serve as the federal focal point on matters concerning older persons.

Although older individuals may receive services under many other federal programs, today the OAA is considered to be the major vehicle for the organization and delivery of social and nutrition services to this group and their caregivers. It authorizes a wide array of service programs through a national network of 56 state agencies on aging, 629 area agencies on aging, nearly 20,000 service providers, 244 tribal organizations, and two Native Hawaiian organizations representing 400 tribes.

The OAA also includes community service employment for low-income older Americans; training, research, and demonstration activities in the field of aging; and vulnerable elder rights protection activities. The links below offer an unofficial compilation of the OAA, an outline of changes made to the OAA at the most recent reauthorization (2006), a set of frequently asked questions (FAQs) about the OAA and other related sources of information anddata. Programs established by the Act are often a combination of federal and State Units on Aging initiatives. This results in a wide variation of programs and services from state to state although the AoA awards state grants to ensure that all states comply with the Act. The Act is a plan ensuring community-based services, supportive services and centers, long-term care ombudsman programs and services for the special needs of Alzheimer's disease patients.

A primary purpose of the Act is to encourage and assist state and area agencies on aging to develop greater capacity and foster the development and implementation of comprehensive and coordinated systems to serve the elderly. The Act defines three essential services, including information and assistance, transportation and case management. The Act also mandates nutrition programs, including congregate and home-delivered nutrition services and programs for minorities, including American Indians, Alaska natives and Native Hawaiians. ("Older Americans Act," Administration on Aging, http://www.aoa.gov/aoaroot/aoa_programs/oaa/index.aspx, updated Dec 27, 2010, accessed Jan 3, 2011)

Oligodendrocytes. Oligodendrocytes are neuroglial cells frequently found in rows along myelinated nerve fibers and cell bodies. With small cell bodies and only a few delicate processes, oligodendrocytes are responsible for the formation of the myelin sheath of nerve fibers in the central nervous system. Age-related alteration in oligodendrocytes may contribute to dysfunctional axon connections leading to cognitive deficits even in the absence of neuron loss. Age-related alterations include changes, such as the presence of inclusion bodies, in their internal structure and also their processes.

Olmstead Decision, American with Disabilities Act. In July 1999, the Supreme Court issued the Olmstead Decision, which interpreted Title II of the Americans with Disabilities Act and its implementing regulating, requiring states to administer their services, programs and activities "in the most integrated setting appropriate to the needs of qualified individuals with disabilities" with no exclusion based on age. Unfortu-

nately, the older population has not taken advantage of the opportunities the Olmstead Act presents to them to improve access to community based care preventing premature institutionalization and in some cases allowing frail elders living in nursing homes to go back to the community they love.

In 2004, only a few states were in compliance with the Act, especially as it pertains to elders with physical and mental disabilities. However, because the Olmstead decision interpreted Title II of the Americans with Disabilities Act (ADA) and its implementing regulation, elders and caregivers of elderly individuals have assumed the Olmstead decision applies to younger individuals with disabilities and therefore have not pushed to reform the poorly integrated network of services to older disabled individuals.

The Olmstead decision never intended to exclude elders from the freedom and options provided by Act. The fact that a great many elders are dealing with physical, mental and emotional disabilities make them eligible to be covered under the mandates of the Olmstead Act. This important information has not reached elders nor their caregivers and care managers who continue to ask for more funding, not realizing that the Olmstead law is on their side. Particularly, the Olmstead Act is there in the case of frail elders already residing in nursing homes but able to function outside if appropriate services are given to him or her. (Hernandez, Gema. "Promises to keep: The Olmstead Act also applies to elders," 2004, http://communitiesforlife.com/indge26.html, accessed Mar 1, 2011)

Ombudsman. An ombudsman is a consumer advocate who investigates nursing home complaints and attempts to resolve problems. Your local ombudsman may also be able to help you in your selection of a good nursing home. A list of contact information by state for the ombudsman program can be found in the resource section.

Omega-3 fatty acids. A good balance of omega-3 and omega-6 essential fatty acids is critical for a well-functioning brain. With changes in food processing and the widespread use of trans-fatty acids and saturated fats, the consumption of these essential oils has gotten severely out of balance, with most people deficient in omega-3 oils. Omega-6 oils are found in cooking oils, nuts, and most seeds and cereals. Omega-3 fatty acids are found in cold water fatty fish, deep green vegetables such as purlane, and some seeds and grains. In the body omega-3 fatty acids are broken down into eicosaentanoic acid (EPA) and docosahexaneoic acid (DHA). Low levels of DHA in adults are associated with depressed cognitive function, depression, moodiness, irritability, slow response time, and Alzheimer's disease. Balance can be restored by cutting out saturated fats found in meat and full dairy products and trans-fatty acids, found in commercial bread, crackers, frozen waffles, cookies and processed snack foods; and fried foods. Increasing consumption of foods rich in omega-3 oils such as fatty fish, flaxseed, walnuts and pumpkin seeds and DHA-rich eggs can help as can dietary supplements containing DHA. Low levels of omega-3 oils are considered a risk factor for Alzheimer's disease. *See also* Docosahexaneoic acid (DHA)

Omentum. The omentum is a pocket of fat and blood vessels that lies like a blanket covering the intestines. Dr. Harry Goldsmith, a researcher at the University of Nevada, has found that the omentum can be used to provoke new blood vessel growth in areas of the body lacking blood flow. Besides promoting angiogenesis or new blood vessel growth, omentum also increases choline acetyltransferase, the enzyme necessary for the synthesis of acetylcholine in the brain.

In the late 1970s, Goldsmith successfully implanted omentum into stroke patients. In studies he conducted in 1993, Goldsmith implanted omentum into a man who had Alzheimer's disease for nine years. A single photon/positron emission computed tomography can (SPECT) showed that blood flow had increased dramatically after the operation, and the man's personal physician reported that his patient was remarkably improved. Among the areas of improvement noted were judgment, confusion, naming, and gait. Although the patient died of other causes two years later, an autopsy showed that in the area where the omentum had been placed, the number of senile plaques was greatly reduced.

In the procedure used by Dr. Goldsmith, the omentum is brought up through the neck and placed over the brain. The omentum remains attached to its original blood supply. According to Goldsmith, keeping the omentum attached to its blood supply prevents problems associated with transposing only a piece of it onto the brain.

Besides its ability to stimulate blood vessels, the omentum contains numerous nerves and neurochemicals that help nerves grow, such as fibroblast growth factor (FGF). FGF has been shown to provoke the growth of new brain cells in areas of the brain affected by Alzheimer's disease. The omentum also appears to maintain dopamine, serotonin and norepinephrine when implanted into the brain. ("An Exiting New Treatment for Alzheimer's Disease." *Life Extension*, August, 2000, 63–65)

Omnibus Reconciliation Act (OBRA) regulations. The Omnibus Reconciliation Act (OBRA) provides regulations with clear recommendations for the treatment of behavioral, cognitive, and affective symptoms in elderly patients with Alzheimer's disease. These regulations help in determining the specific symptoms likely to respond to specific pharmaceutical therapies. These regulations also set guidelines for the amount of time a specific drug should be given before its efficacy can be determined. In long-term care settings, treatment is monitored to ensure that it conforms to OBRA regulations. Provisions of the act, including eligible benefits, are available on the Social Security website at http://www.ssa.gov/OP_Home/comp2/F099-509.html, accessed Feb 8, 2011.

Opiod peptides. Opiod peptides are naturally occurring as well as synthetic chemicals of the opiod family. Duke University's Jau-Shyong Hong and the NIEHS's Jean Harry are currently researching the effects of opiod peptides on neurodegeneration caused by microglia. In a different study, researchers demonstrated that chronic exposure to morphine inhibited neuronal growth in the adult hippocampus. (Eisch, A., et al. "Opiates inhibit neurogenesis in the adult rat hippocampus." Proceedings of the National Academy of Sciences, June 6, 2000). *See also* Low dose naltrexone

Organic brain syndrome. Organic brain syndrome is a term commonly used for patients with impaired memories.

Organic solvents. Organic solvents refers to a class of chemicals such as naptha, toluene, xylene, chloroform and hexane used in industries such as painting and cleaning. Organic solvents can cause transient symptoms such as inebriation, dizziness, headache and nausea. Used chronically, organic solvents may cause symptoms of encephalopathy, including poor attention, mood changes, memory problems and delirium.

Orientation. Patients being assessed for mental status are generally evaluated for orientation of time, place and purpose. To be considered disoriented for time, the patient should be off by more than one day of the week and more than several days off the current date. Misidentifying the relationship of relatives is a sign of disorientation to place. For instance, patients with Alzheimer's disease may mistakenly say that their doctor is their son.

OXIGON *see* Indole-3-proprionic acid (IPA)

P97. P97 is a valosin containing protein known as melanotransferrin that was first isolated by Korean researchers. P97, which binds iron, is found in higher concentration in the blood of people with Alzheimer's disease than in normal people, according to the results of one study (available in full-text at http://www.nature.com/npp/journal/v25/n1/full/1395638a.html, accessed Mar 1, 2011).

   If other studies confirm this finding, this test could be used as a diagnostic tool for Alzheimer's disease and as a diagnostic marker for assessing a favorable response to therapy. Research suggests that P97 is cleaved by capase-6 and is involved in protein degradation.

   In 2009, biOasis Technologies Inc. (South Surrey, BC, Canada) announced that a major step in the application of its p97 test for diagnosis of Alzheimer's disease was achieved by the signing of an agreement with UK-based Fleet Bioprocessing Ltd. (Fleet; Hartley Whitney, UK). (Moyer, Paula. "New blood test may help diagnose Alzheimer's disease, eventual goal: treatment before symptoms develop," *WebMD Health*, May 17, 2000. "Agreement Will Hasten Development of Alzheimer's Disease Diagnostic Test" LabMedica International Press Release, 2009, http://www.labmedica.com/immunology/articles/294726920/agreement_will_hasten_development_of_alzheimers_disease_diagnostic_test.html, accessed Jan 3, 2011)

Pacing. Patients with Alzheimer's disease often pace or wander aimlessly, especially in the evening hours. Experts recommend that pacing should be allowed as it is a reflection of the body's natural reaction to dealing with stress and agitation. Pacing is often triggered by an internal stimulus such as pain, hunger or boredom or some environmental distraction such as noise or temperature.

Paclitaxel (Taxol). Paclitaxel (Taxol), a drug used in the treatment of ovarian and breast cancer, may slow nerve degeneration and is under investigation as a therapeutic agent for Alzheimer's disease and other neurodegenerative disorders characterized by altered microtubule networks. Paclitaxel has the ability to bundle the microtubule protein, possibly protecting it from the aberrant phosphorylation seen in Alzheimer's disease.

Pain. While Alzheimer's disease is not generally associated with pain, patients with this disorder may not be able to convey the pain they experience for other reasons. Caregivers must be alert for signs such as holding one's head or favoring one leg or arm, and they must be on the alert for falls and other injuries.

Paleocortex. The paleocortex refers to the surface cortex covering some restricted parts of the base of the telencephalon. The paleocortex is thought to be of ancient origin compared to the neocortex.

Paleomammalian brain. The paleomammalian brain refers to the region of the brain descending upward from the reptilian brain. The paleomammalian brain, which includes the limbic system, promotes survival and refines and coordinates movement. This area is also associated with the development of the apparatuses for memory and emotions that stem from the body's internal regulatory system.

Palliative care. Palliative care, also known as comfort care, focuses on quality of life for individuals with a progressive disease. The goal of palliative care, rather than offering a cure, is to provide comfort, control of pain, and a reduction of symptoms associated with one's illness. It includes the management of psychological, social and spiritual challenges that affect the patient. Palliative care is also used to support the family of a person with a progressive life-limiting disease.

Paranoia. Paranoia refers to psychosis characterized by systematized delusions of persecution or grandeur usually without hallucinations; a tendency on the part of an individual or group toward excessive or irrational suspiciousness and distrustfulness of others.

Parasympathetic nervous system. The parasympathetic functions of the autonomic nervous system are involved with conserving and restoring energy. Parasympathetic nerves slow the heart rate, increase peristalsis in the intestine, and increase glandular activity.

Parietal lobe. The parietal lobe found in each cerebral hemisphere occupies the area posterior to the central sulcus and superior to the lateral sulcus. The cortical areas of the parietal lobe can be divided into several distinct somesthetic areas and the outer layer of Baillarger. The cortical areas of the parietal lobe receive sensations from the pharyngeal region including the tongue and jaws, the face, fingers, hands, arm, trunk, thigh, and enable one to recognize objects placed in hand without the aid of vision.

Parkinson's disease (Parkinsonism). Parkinson's disease is a disorder associated with neuronal degeneration in the substantia nigra and other areas of the brain. This results in a reduction of the neurotransmitter dopamine, which leads to hypersensitivity of the dopamine receptors in the post-synaptic neurons in the corpus striatum. Signs and symptoms of this disorder include tremor, postural disturbances, cogwheel rigidity and bradykinesis, marked by difficulty in initiating and performing new movements. Consequently, movements are slow, the face is expressionless, and the voice is slurred and unmodulated.

Parkinson's disease (Parkinsonism) is the most common disease involving the basal ganglia. The symptoms are variable in relative severity and onset and usually include tremor, rigidity and difficulty moving. The tremor is a resting tremor, characteristically involving the hands in a "pill-rolling" movement, which diminishes during voluntary movement and increases during emotional stress. The rigidity is caused by increased tone in all muscles, although strength is nearly normal and reflexes are not particularly affected. The rigidity may be uniform throughout the range of movements imposed by an examiner and are often referred to as plastic or lead-pipe rigidity. Alternately, the rigidity may be interrupted by a series of brief relaxations referred to as cog-wheel rigidity.

Rigidity in Parkinsonism is quite distinct from spasticity. Patients with spasticity exhibit muscle tone that is increased selectively in the extensors of the leg and the flexors of the arm and can be overcome by force.

Difficulty in movement (bradykinesia or slow movement and hypokinesia or few movements) shows up as decreased blinking, an expressionless face, and the absence of the arm movements normally associated with walking. Parkinson gait is characterized by stooped posture, with the hips and knees slightly flexed. Steps are short and often shuffling, with decreased arm swings. Patients often turn around stiffly.

The underlying defect in Parkinsonism is damage to the dopaminergic neurons (neurons that secrete the neurotransmitter dopamine) in the basal ganglia of the substantia nigra. While it has long been suspected that environmental agents were responsible for this damage, in recent years, pesticides have been pinpointed as the major culprit. The decreased dopamine levels caused by this damage cause the symptoms of Parkinsonism.

Alzheimer's disease and Parkinson's disease are distinct neurological disorders, but up to one-third of Alzheimer's patients develop Parkinson's and some Parkinson's patients develop signs of Alzheimer's disease. To study the connection, researchers from the University of California San Diego's departments of neurosciences and pathology in collaboration with researchers from the Gladstone Institute of Neurological Diseases at the University of California San Francisco have developed strains of mice with the same protein abnormalities seen in these two disorders. In Alzheimer's disease, amyloid precursor protein (APP) accumulates in brain cells, whereas alpha-synuclein (SYN) is known to accumulate in patients with Parkinson's disease.

When both proteins were increased in the studies with mice, symptoms of both Alzheimer's disease and Parkinson's disease intensified. In addition, increased levels of the breakdown product of APP, amyloid beta, enhanced the accumulation of SYN in brain cells. Drugs aimed at preventing the accumulation of these proteins could offer improvement for both disorders. (Nolte, John. *The Human Brain: An Introduction to its Functional Anatomy*, Third Edition, 1993. St. Louis: Mosby Year Book. "Alzheimer's and Parkinson's Proteins Create a Destructive Team." Sept 26, 2001, *Science Daily Magazine*)

Pathology. Pathology refers to the study of the essential nature of diseases, especially the structural and functional cellular changes that contribute to disease development. The pathology of Alzheimer's disease involves the destruction of neurons in certain areas of the brain, a loss of synaptic connections and an alteration in the neurotransmitters that allow neurons to communicate with one another and process information.

Peripheral nervous system. The peripheral nervous system consists of the cranial and spinal nerves and their associated ganglia. The nerve fibers, or axons, of the peripheral nervous system conduct information to and from the central nervous system. Although they are surrounded by fibrous sheaths, nerve fibers have little protection and are commonly damaged by trauma.

Perlmutter, David, M.D., F.A.C.N. Dr. David Perlmutter is a practicing neurologist as well as a world-renowned Alzheimer's disease researcher. He has proposed a model of Alzheimer's disease that involves genetics, environmental agents, nutrition, lifestyle and infection. Dr. Perlmutter theorizes that many exposures can initiate an upregulation of the immune system. This immune response releases inflammatory cytokines which, in turn, upregulate the expression of the immune

inducible form of nitric oxide synthase. This sets forth a destructive cascade of metabolic steps that eventually result in neuronal cell death.

Environmental agents responsible for this cascade include enteric bacteria, toxic metals, pesticides, food and environmental antigens, medications, physiological stress responses mediated through the pituitary-thyroid-adrenal axis, and chronic infection. Perlmutter's research suggests that Alzheimer's disease is primarily related to nutrient deficiencies, which can be caused by many over-the-counter and prescription medications as well as environmental agents. Dr. Perlmutter has been successful in reversing symptoms in Alzheimer's disease with a comprehensive integrationist medical approach. (Perlmutter, David. "Nutritional supplementation and Alzheimer's disease," 2010, http://www.needs.com/product/NDNL-0404-01/l_Vitamin_B12, accessed Mar 1, 2011. Perlmutter, David, and Carol Colman. *The Better Brain Book: The Best Tools for Improving Memory and Sharpness and Preventing Aging of the Brain*, New York: Riverhead Publishing, 2004. Perlmutter, David, and Alberto Villoldo. *Power Up Your Brain: The Neuroscience of Enlightenment*, New York: Hay House, 2011)

Personality changes. Personality changes are often seen in Alzheimer's disease. According to researchers at the University Memory and Aging Center in Cleveland, in some cases, personality changes occur before any cognitive changes become apparent. Personality changes range from apathy and indifference to marked agitation and include irritability, suspiciousness, aggressiveness, fearful behavior, drastically inappropriate behavior, heightened anger, hostility, mood swings, childish impulsiveness, paranoia, and overt sexuality or promiscuousness.

Phenserine. Phenserine, a phenylcarbamate of physostigmine, is a reversible acetyl-selective cholinesterase inhibitor currently being evaluated in clinical trials for Alzheimer's disease. In studies of rats with lesions of the forebrain cholinergic system, an injection of phenserine were found to significantly decrease the levels of secreted beta-amyloid precursor protein in the rats' cerebrospinal fluid. In a 2008 Swedish study of 20 patients with Alzheimer's disease, improvement was observed compared to a control group treated with donepezil (http://www.ncbi.nlm.nih.gov/pubmed/18300284, accessed Feb 2, 2011). In the United States, the biopharmaceutical company Axonyx first developed phenserine as a next-generation acetylcholinesterase (AChE) inhibitor indicated for the treatment of Alzheimer's disease. In 2006 phenserine was licensed to QR Pharma, a startup biotechnology company, after Axonyx merged with TorreyPines Therapeutics. In May 2009, QR Pharma decided to stop the production of phenserine, after it failed in Phase III of its development. The drug, its patents, and the material stored in a number of locations were withdrawn. Studies using phenserine with other compounds as well as stem cells are under current investigation (http://www.drugdevelopment-technology.com/projects/phenserine/, accessed Feb 2, 2011).

Phosphatidylserine. Phosphatidylserine is a naturally occurring lipid substance that promotes cell health and boosts the activity of acetylcholine and other brain chemicals. Phosphatidylserine is essential to help brain neurons support and maintain memory function and neuroplasticity (ability to replace damaged neurons and make new ones). Phosphatidylserine is available as a prescription drug widely used in Europe and as a dietary supplement in Japan to correct cognitive impairment associated with degenerative brain disease. Sold as a health food supplement in the United States, it can be found in many preparations designed to improve memory naturally. Phosphatidylserine enhances both neuronal and mitochondrial stability and activity. In addition, it reduces mitochondrial free-radical production and it is essential for the construction of new brain cell membranes.

Researcher Tomas Crook and his team at Stanford University School of Medicine evaluated a group of 149 patients with age-associated memory impairment who were given 100 mg of phosphatidylserine or a placebo twice daily. Actual improvement based on psychometric testing was seen in a majority of phosphatidyl treated patients, specifically those who had scored above the range of cognitive performance associated with dementing disorders such as Alzheimer's disease, but who were performing in the low

normal range for persons of the same age. These patients were also better able to concentrate, recall telephone numbers, memorize paragraphs, and find misplaced objects compared to the placebo group. The recommended dose for individuals with moderate symptoms is 100 mg taken twice daily and 100 mg taken three times daily for individuals with severe symptoms. (Perlmutter, David, and Carol Colman. *The Better Brain Book: The Best Tools for Improving Memory and Sharpness and Preventing Aging of the Brain*, New York: Riverhead Publishing, 2004: 118–9, 200, 205)

Phosphodiesterase-4 (PDE4). The different forms or subtypes of the naturally occurring enzyme phosphodiesterase were initially isolated from rat brains by Uzunov and Weiss in 1972. Phosphodiesterase-4 (PDE4), which is present in immune cells regulating inflammation, is an enzyme that degrades the important intracellular signaling molecule cyclic AMP (cAMP). cAMP is critically involved in long-term potentiation, a process widely believed to underlie memory formation. Because researchers had observed reduced cAMP signaling in the hippocampus of a mouse model of Alzheimer's disease, they reasoned that PDE4 inhibition might work to prevent memory defects.

To test this hypothesis, the researchers selected rolipram, a selective PDE4 inhibitor approved for the treatment of depression in Japan and Europe. In a preclinical trial using double transgenic mice (amyloid precursor protein and presenilin-1) as a model for Alzheimer's disease, rolipram administration improved dendritic architecture, long term potentiation and contextual learning. Most importantly, the benefits of a course of rolipram treatment extended for several months after cessation of the drug regimen, suggesting a protective/adaptive mechanism. (Columbia Technology Ventures, 2008, http://www.ibridgenetwork.org/columbia/ir_1584, accessed Jan 1, 2011)

Phosphodiesterase (PDE4) inhibitors. Phosphodiesterase is a naturally occurring enzyme that degrades the important intracellular signaling molecule cyclic AMP (cAMP). cAMP is critically involved in long-term potentiation, a process widely believed to underlie memory formation. Soon after the phosphodiesterase enzymes were discovered, therapies designed to target these enzymes were developed.

Several lines of evidence indicate that targeting PDE4 with selective inhibitors may offer novel strategies in the treatment of age-related memory impairment and Alzheimer's disease. The rationale for such an approach stems from preclinical studies indicating that PDE4 inhibitors can counteract deficits in long-term memory caused by pharmacological agents, aging, or overexpression of mutant forms of human amyloid precursor proteins. In addition to their pro-cognitive and pro-synaptic plasticity properties, PDE4 inhibitors are potent neuroprotective, neuroregenerative, and anti-inflammatory agents. Based on the fact that Alzheimer's disease is a progressive neurodegenerative disorder that is characterized by cognitive impairment, and that neuroinflammation is now recognized as a prominent feature in Alzheimer's pathology, researchers have concluded that targeting PDE4 with selective inhibitors may offer a novel therapy aimed at slowing progression, prevention, and, eventually, therapy of Alzheimer's disease. Therapies that inhibit PDE4 are under investigation for Alzheimer's disease.

PDE4 inhibitors include the drugs mesembrine, an herbal alkaloid derived from *Sceletium tortuosum*; rolipram, which is used to treat depression in Japan and is the subject of research for disorders of memory impairment; idululast, a neuroprotective and bronchodilator non-selective PDE4 inhibitor drug (inhibits PDE4 as well as other PDE enzymes) used in the treatment of asthma and stroke; piclamist, which has greater inhibitor potency than rolipram; luteolin, a compound derived from peanuts with PDE4 inhibitory and IGF-1 properties; drotaverine, used for renal colic and cervical dilation; and roflumilast, which is used in the treatment of chronic obstructive pulmonary disorders. *See also* Phosphodiesterase-4 (PDE4).

Phosphorylation. Phosphorylation is a process in which phosphorus molecules in the form of phosphate ions bind to other molecules. In Alzheimer's disease, aberrant or abnormal phosphorylation of tau protein leads to a cascade of events resulting in the death of brain cells known as neurons. This abnormal tau protein contains 5 to 9 moles of phosphate for each mole of protein, whereas normal tau contains 2 to 3 moles of phosphate for each mole of protein.

This increased phosphorylation is known as hyperphosphorylation. Before the microtubule structure is permanently damaged, neuronal plasticity occurs. In neuronal plasticity, the rigid neuron structure becomes flexible and dendritic processes are impaired.

One of the causes of aberrant phosphorylation of tau protein is a defect in the normal activity of enzymes known as kinases. Changes in the activity of kinases are thought to be due to altered patterns of apoptosis, which are under genetic regulation.

Physostigmine. Physostigmine is a carbamate compound similar to the cholinesterase inhibitor rivastigmine. Physostigmine is reported to be useful in reducing delusions and agitation.

Physostigmine salicylate (Synapton). Physostigmine salicylate available in the sustained-release compound Synapton is a cholinesterase inhibitor investigated for the treatment of Alzheimer's disease. Cholinesterase inhibitors delay the intrasynaptic degradation of the neurotransmitter acetylcholine, thereby increasing its effects. Small but reliable improvement in memory performance has been noted after administration of physostigmine salicylate although the side effects of this drug, which include nausea, vomiting, diarrhea, flushing, sweating and bradycardia, limit its use. There is evidence, however, that long-term use retards the deterioration in cognitive function over time even in patients who fail to improve during short-term trials of the drug. FDA evaluation of this drug for Alzheimer's disease has been discontinued. (Tariot, Pierre, M.D., et al. "Treating Alzheimer's Disease, Pharmacologic options now and in the near future." *Postgraduate Medicine*, vol 101 (6), June 1997)

Phytochemicals. Phytochemicals, which are also known as nutraceuticals, are naturally occurring chemicals found in plants that have medicinal properties. As alternative therapies used for Alzheimer's disease, numerous phytochemicals, particularly the bioflavinoid anthocyanins and omega-3 oils, have been shown beneficial because of their anti-inflammatory and antioxidant properties. For more information on phytochemicals under investigation, see http://nccam.nih.gov/news/newsletter/2010_may/natural product.htm, accessed Mar 4, 2011.

Pia mater. The pia mater is a vascular membrane that closely covers the spinal cord. The pia mater extends along each nerve root and becomes continuous with the connective tissue surrounding each spinal nerve.

Pick's complex. Pick's complex is a term proposed by some doctors to describe disorders of frontotemporal lobe dementia as well as corticobasal degeneration and progressive supranuclear palsy. (Frontotemporal Lobe Dementia Information Page, National Institute of Neurological Disorders and Stroke, Jan 2011, http://www.ninds.nih.gov/disorders/picks/picks.htm, accessed Feb 23, 2011)

Pick's disease. Pick's disease, which is more commonly known as frontotemporal lobe dementia (FTD), is a neurodegenerative disorder of the cerebral cortex that results in a dementia characterized by progressive impairment of intellect and judgment and transitory aphasia. Pick's disease results from disease-related changes in brain tissue, including shrinking of the brain tissues and the presence of abnormal bodies (Pick bodies) in the nerve cells of the affected areas of the brain. Pick's disease is also known as aphasia-agnosia-apraxia syndrome, Arnold Pick's disease, cerebral atrophy, circumscribed brain atrophy, lobar sclerosis and presenile dementia.

Pick's disease affects about 1 out of every 100,000 people. It affects both sexes although it is more common in women. It may occur as early as 20 years old, but usually begins between the ages of 40 and 60 years. The average age of onset is 54 years. Pick's disease is suspected of being a dominant hereditary disorder. Risk factors include having a personal or family history of Pick's disease or senile dementia.

Movement and coordination difficulties may be one of the earliest symptoms. Other symptoms include mood and personality changes, loss of initiative, flat affect, impaired judgment, excessive manual exploration of the environment, withdrawal from social interaction, decreased ability to function in self-care, repetition of anything spoken to the person (echolalia), incomprehensible speech, aphasia, inability to comprehend speech, poor enunciation, decreased reading and writing abilities, loss of cognitive skills, weakness, increased muscle tone, urinary incontinence, and progressive dementia.

Diagnosis is based on neurologic exam and testing to rule out other conditions. Temporal and frontal lobe signs are most common, with resulting behavioral and language changes. An electroencephalogram shows nonspecific changes in electrical activity, although a head CT scan shows atrophy (loss of tissue mass) of affected areas of the brain.

Far less common than Alzheimer's disease, Pick's disease results in distinct brain changes. The brain in Pick's disease invariably exhibits a pronounced, although frequently asymmetric atrophy of the frontal and temporal lobes with conspicuous sparing of the posterior two-thirds of the superior temporal gyrus. Only rarely is there involvement of either the parietal or occipital lobe.

Brain atrophy can be severe, reducing the gyri to a thin wafer, which can be observed on gross examination as a "knife-edge" appearance. This pattern of lobar atrophy is often prominent enough to distinguish Pick's disease from Alzheimer's disease from a gross or direct observation of the brain. Besides the localized cortical atrophy, the caudate and putamen also show signs of atrophy.

When examined microscopically, neuronal loss is most severe in the outer three layers of the cortex and may be severe enough to superficially resemble another disorder, laminar necrosis. Some of the surviving neurons, called Pick cells, exhibit characteristic swelling. These cells may also contain Pick bodies, which are cytoplasmic, round to oval, filamentous inclusions that stain weakly with eosin but dramatically with silver stains. Structurally, they are composed of neurofilaments, endoplasmic reticulum, and paired helical filaments similar to those seen in Alzheimer's disease. Unlike the neurofibrillary tangles of Alzheimer's disease, however, Pick bodies do not survive the death of their host neuron and do not remain as markers of disease.

Although there is no cure for Pick's disease, treatment, similar to that used in Alzheimer's disease, is used in an effort to improve cognitive function and reduce further deterioration. Behavior modification may also be used to help control unacceptable behavior. *See also* Frontotemporal dementia

Pillaging. Pillaging, or stealing, is commonly seen in patients with Alzheimer's disease. Some patients with Alzheimer's disease become inordinately fond of hiding their possessions, and sometimes they confuse their own possessions with those of others. In nursing homes, this may be a problem as patients will sometimes wander into the rooms of others to pillage items. The problems of pillaging can be managed by supervision, understanding, keeping valuables locked up, and gentle admonitions.

Plaque. Plaque refers to deposits of protein and other substances that interfere with normal cell function. Plaque deposits in the brain are one of the characteristic signs of Alzheimer's disease. Studies show that plaque formation tends to begin 10 to 15 years before any cognitive signs of dementia appear. *See* Senile neuritic plaque

Platelet activation studies. Platelets, or thrombocytes, are blood components distinct from blood cells that are involved in the clotting process. Derived from the megakaryocyte cell line, platelets are normally found in the blood. Studies have shown that blood platelets are abnormally highly activated in Alzheimer's diseases. Clues to this mechanism may enable researchers to find out why the neurons in Alzheimer's disease become abnormal.

Blood platelets secrete both amyloid precursor protein (APP) and beta amyloid protein, components of the cortical plaques associated with Alzheimer's disease. While platelets are normally activated at a rate of about 0.5 percent, Alzheimer's disease patients show rates 30 to 50 percent higher than the baseline rate. Researchers at the University of Miami who made this discovery report that a test for platelet activation can serve as a diagnostic marker when combined with other parameters such as clinical symptoms and genetic studies. These studies were confirmed by French researchers who found that increased platelet activation in Alzheimer's disease is related to increased lipid peroxidation and insufficient vitamin D.

Some researchers think that platelet abnormalities contribute to thrombosis or clot formation, causing ministrokes and other cerebrovascular abnormalities that may be connected to Alzheimer's disease. In 2010 German researchers reported that significantly higher baseline expression of both platelet activation biomarkers, activated glycoprotein IIb-IIIa complex, and P-selectin, were observed in patients with AD with fast cognitive decline compared with AD patients with slow cognitive decline during a one-year follow-up period. These results also confirm that platelet activation could be a putative prognostic biomarker for the rate of cognitive decline and a potential new treatment target in AD patients. (Sevush, S. and L. Horstmann. "Platelet Activation Observed in Alzheimer's Patients." *Medical Tribune, Family Physician Edition*, June 1998, 18l39 (12): 31. Ciabattoni, G. et al. "Determinants of platelet activation in Alzheimer's disease," *Neurobiology of Aging*, Mar 2007, 28 (3): 336–42, abstract available at http://www.ncbi.nlm.nih.gov/pubmed/16442186, accessed Mar 4, 2011. Stellos, K., et al. "Predictive value of platelet activation for the rate of cognitive decline in Alzheimer's disease patients," *Journal of Cerebral Blood Flow and Metabolism*, Nov 2010, 30 (11): 1817–20)

Pons. The pons, or bridge, a section of the hindbrain, is situated on the anterior or front surface of the cerebellum, inferior to the midbrain and superior to the medulla oblongata. The anterior of the pons is covered by transverse fibers that connect the two cerebellar hemispheres.

Porteus Mazes. The Porteus Mazes Test is a mental status evaluation tool used to measure planning ability. While memory deficit is usually the first prominent complaint in Alzheimer's disease, attention, planning and abstract reasoning are also affected.

Positron emission tomography (PET) scan. Positron emission tomography (PET) is an imaging technique that provides a direct measure of the brain's metabolic activities. Specifically, PET identifies changes in cell metabolism, particularly the utilization of glucose and oxygen. PET scans have the advantage of providing numerical values for regional cerebral metabolic rates, making them useful in differentiating Alzheimer's disease from vascular dementia, multiple infarct dementia, Pick's disease, Huntington's disease, and depression. Patterns of impairment characteristically seen in Alzheimer's disease include temporoparietal and frontal hypometabolism with relative sparing of the visual and sensorimotor cortex. These changes are often asymmetric.

Glucose metabolism is determined by using 18-F-fluorodeoxyglucose (FDG-PET). In Alzheimer's disease, FDG-PET shows decreased accumulation in the neocortical association areas, but sparing of the basal ganglia, thalamus, cerebellum, and the primary sensory and motor cortex. The classic pattern is biparietal temporal hypometabolism. The extent of this reduced glucose metabolism correlates well with the severity of the cognitive impairment. PET studies performed in middle-aged persons with normal cognition who have the APOE4 allele have identified parietal, temporal and prefrontal deficits in glucose metabolism. PET scans of people with Alzheimer's disease show less baseline neural activity than those of age-matched controls. PET has also elucidated blood-brain barrier integrity, dopamine metabolism, and specific receptors in brains of Alzheimer's disease patients.

Besides assessing glucose metabolism, some PET techniques involve using the isotype O15 in cases of suspected dementia. With this technique, patients with Alzheimer's disease exhibit diminished oxygen consumption in the frontotemporal-parietal lobes. In severe disease the frontal lobes are primarily affected.

However, PET scans cannot differentiate familial from sporadic Alzheimer's disease. Some studies indicate that reductions in mean PET measures of regional brain metabolism are more severe in patients who have more severe dementia. Cognitive defects have also been demonstrated to be associated with specific metabolic deficits, making PET an excellent tool for correlating brain metabolism with cognitive deficits. For instance, patients scoring low on tests such as visual recall that reflect right neocortical function exhibited functional asymmetry with altered metabolism in the right hemisphere.

A consortium of PET centers worldwide has provided their brain imaging and autopsy data from 138 dementia patients. Autopsy confirma-

tion of Alzheimer's disease was obtained in 70 percent of the cases. PET had a sensitivity of 94 percent and specificity of 78 percent for detecting the presence of neurodegenerative disease. The sensitivity of PET for detecting Alzheimer's disease was 94 percent, and specificity was 73 percent, demonstrating the good correlations between PET imaging and brain autopsy.

In a related study of 129 cognitive impaired subjects, PET scan accurately identified 87 percent of subjects with mild to moderate dementia and 96 percent of subjects with severe dementia. In another study, PET scan was shown capable of identifying patients with mild cognitive impairment who went on to develop Alzheimer's disease. These patients showed greater metabolic reduction in the posterior association cortex on the initial PET scan compared with those subjects who did not progress to a diagnosis of probably Alzheimer's disease. (Edward, Coleman, M.D., R. "Positron Emission Tomography in the Evaluation of Dementia." presented at the 48th Annual Meeting of the Society of Nuclear Medicine, June 23, 2001)

In January 2001, researchers at the University of California–Los Angeles announced that they have developed a variation of PET testing which is presumably more capable of accurately diagnosing Alzheimer's disease in its early stages. This test combines PET imaging with the injection of a chemical tracer and identifies the specific lesions seen in Alzheimer's disease.

In 2010, researchers developed a PET technique in which injections of radioactive dye bound to plaque accumulations in the brain, which could then be measured. Researchers at Avid Radiopharmaceuticals in Philadelphia used this technique to identify 34 of 35 Alzheimer's patients. These findings were later confirmed at autopsy. Because Alzheimer's disease is reported to be misdiagnosed in as many as 20 percent of patients, this diagnostic tool, which was approved in 2011 as a confirmatory test for Alzheimer's disease, is a huge advance. (McAuliffe, Kathleen. "Early diagnosis for Alzheimer's disease," *Discover* Jan/Feb 2011: 32)

Postsynaptic vesicles. Depolarization of the presynaptic endings of neuronal processes causes a release of neurotransmitter into the synaptic cleft. Some of the neurotransmitter molecules then bind to receptors in waiting or postsynaptic vesicles. Transmitter-receptor binding causes some change in the postsynaptic neuron, such as rapid opening of an ion channel or a slower cascade of biochemical events that culminates in an electrical or similar charge.

Preclinical phase of Alzheimer's disease. The preclinical phase of Alzheimer's disease refers to the time frame when pathological changes can be seen in brain tissue although there are no symptoms of cognitive impairment. Depression may be a hallmark of the preclinical phase.

Prednisone. Prednisone is a synthetic glucocorticoid steroid used as an anti-inflammatory agent. Prednisone suppresses both the acute phase inflammatory response and the complement cascade. In pilot studies involving 138 patients, prednisone showed no improvement over a 16-month period. Compared to the placebo group, patients on prednisone showed moderate to severe problems. (*Nia News*. Alzheimer's disease research update, February 8, 2000)

Prenatal genetic testing. It is possible to perform prenatal diagnosis of early-onset familial Alzheimer's disease by analyzing fetal DNA extracted from cells obtained by chorionic villus sampling at about 10–12 weeks gestation or amniocentesis at 16–18 weeks gestation. These samples can be tested for mutations in the presenilin 1 (PSEN 1) gene for those families in which a disease-causing mutation has been identified in an affected family member.

Presenile dementia. Presenile dementia occurs to dementia occurring in individuals younger than 50 years of age. *See also* Early-onset familial Alzheimer's disease and Pick's disease.

Presenilin genes. The genes for presenilin are associated with Alzheimer's disease. Chromosome 14 linkage has been reported in a number of autosomal dominant early-onset pedigrees of familial Alzheimer's disease. The chromosome 14 gene called S182, AD2, or presenilin 1 (PS-1), encodes a predicted membrane-spanning protein whose function and possible interactions with β APP are unclear. According to one current theory, mutations to PS-1 may affect Golgi or mem-

brane traffic permitting β APP to enhance production of amyloid beta protein. Over 30 different mis-sense mutations and one deletion mutation in the coding region of 10 axons of the PS-1 gene have been identified in over forty families. PS-1 is reported to have more than 40 sites of mutations, with most mutations leading to amino acid substitutions. Two exon deletion and two truncation mutations have also been reported.

The presenilin 2 (PS-2 or STM2 gene), on chromosome 1, codes for a membrane protein with amino acids similar to that of PS-1. PS-2 is also linked to familial Alzheimer's disease. While PS-1 mutations are associated with early onset FAD (ages 30–50), PS-2 mutations are association with familial forms of Alzheimer's disease occurring in individuals aged 50–70 years. Two sites of PS-2 mutations have been identified.

Presenilin therapy. Presenilin is a protein containing two aspartate amino acids aligned in strategic positions suggesting that they could act as protease enzymes capable of splitting other proteins. Both gamma and beta secretase promote formation of beta amyloid protein, whereas alpha secretase promotes binding of a harmless peptide fragment.

Recent studies suggest that presenilins may either have gamma secretase activity or they may be part of a group of proteins that is complexed together to influence gamma secretase cleavage of amyloid precursor protein. Presenilin may also be involved in trafficking amyloid precursor protein, thereby promoting its splicing into beta amyloid protein. In addition, the protein nicastrin has been found to bind to presenilin. This protein appears to facilitate the formation of beta amyloid protein. In studies where PS-1 has been activated or removed, levels of secreted beta amyloid protein are markedly reduced. Therapies designed to reduce presenilin are being evaluated for their role in reducing Abeta production.

Presynaptic vesicles. Presynaptic vesicles, which are found near the ending of neuronal processes, contained pre-packaged amounts of neurotransmitter. Depolarization of the presynaptic ending causes some of the presynaptic vesicles to merge with the presynaptic membrane and dump their contents into the synaptic cleft. Neurotransmitter molecules then diffuse across the synaptic cleft.

Prevagen *see* Apoaequorin

Prevalence. Alzheimer's disease is the most common cause of dementia in North America and Europe. Prevalence increases with increasing age. An estimated 5.3 million Americans have AD; approximately 200,000 persons under age 65 with AD comprise the younger-onset AD population. Every 70 seconds, someone in America develops AD; by 2050 this is expected to increase to every 33 seconds. Over the coming decades, the baby boom population is projected to add 10 million people to these numbers. In 2050, the incidence of AD is expected to approach nearly a million people per year, with a total estimated prevalence of 11–16 million people. Dramatic increases in the numbers of "oldest old" (aged 85 years and older) across all racial and ethnic groups will also significantly affect the numbers of people living with AD ("Alzheimer's Association: 2010 Alzheimer's Disease Facts and Figures," *Alzheimer's & Dementia: The Journal of the Alzheimer's Association*, March 2010, 6 (2): 158–194).

Approximately 10 percent of all persons over the age of 70 years have significant memory loss and more than half of these individuals have Alzheimer's disease. The prevalence of dementia in individuals over the age of 85 years is estimated to be 30 to 50 percent with approximately 20 percent of individuals older than 80 having Alzheimer's disease.

Studies have shown that the prevalence of Alzheimer's disease doubles every five years, with 3 percent of 65 to 74 year olds affected. Approximately 47 percent of those aged 85 and older may become affected. According to the United Nations Department of International Economics and Social Affairs, more than 7 million people in North America and Europe have been diagnosed with dementia.

Prevent Alzheimer's Disease by 2020 (PAD 2020). PAD 2020 is an initiative started in 2008, which has as its mission the development of a global strategy to prevent AD within the next decade through international collaborative studies. Dr. Zaven Khachaturian is the president of PAD 2020. One of the first steps of this strategy will be to recruit large cohorts of asymptomatic and presymptomatic individuals to participate in studies of potential interventions. Interventions will include the effects of preventive measures as well as therapies. PAD 2020 has developed a collaboration with the supercomputing center at the University of Nevada, Las Vegas, to develop strategies and models to make sense of the huge amounts of data that will be collected in preventive studies.

Primary Progressive Aphasia. Primary progressive aphasia (PPA) is a form of dementia that can occur before the age of 65. Individuals with PPA have impaired language functions, including difficulty with speaking, reading, writing, speaking and understanding speech.

Principal. Principal refers to the patient or individual signing the power of attorney to authorize another individual to legally make his or her decisions.

Prions. Prions are infectious agents composed of nude (without any type of nuclear or cytoplasmic membrane) polypeptide proteins devoid of genetic material. Capable of multiplying rapidly, prions can cause neurodegenerative disorders in humans and domestic animals. Distinct from viruses, bacteria, fungi and parasites, prions do not use the nucleic acid template DNA-RNA for reproduction, a mechanism ordinarily common to all living things. Infected prions can damage brain tissue through a process of vacillation, making neurons appear like sponges with pitted holes, thus the diseases they cause are known as spongiform encephalopathy.

To prevent the possible dissemination of human prion infections like Creutzfeldt-Jakob disease (CJD), the FDA has implemented guidelines for blood banks. Blood banks now permanently defer donors who have been diagnosed with CJD, donors who have received a dura mater transplant or human pituitary-derived growth hormone, donors who have traveled in the United Kingdom between 1980 and 1996, and donors who have injected bovine insulin since 1980.

Extremely hardy prions can survive the pressurized steam of autoclaves, filtration, extreme heat, radiation, formaldehyde and decades of freezing.

Program for All-Inclusive Care for the Elderly (PACE). The PACE program is a federal health insurance program initiated in 1994 that serves the frail elderly and features a comprehensive service that integrates Medicare and Medicaid financing. States that elect to cover PACE services as a State Plan option must enter into a program agreement with a PACE provider and the Department of Health and Human Services (http://www.vcu.edu/vcoa/ageaction/agefall07.pdf, accessed Mar 1, 2011).

Progressive Deterioration Scale (PDS). The Progressive Deterioration Scale (PDS) is an evaluation tool that measures quality of life changes. The PDS is helpful in evaluating responses to therapy.

Progressive supranuclear palsy (PSP). Progressive supranuclear palsy (PSP) is a rare brain disorder causing symptoms similar to those of Parkinson's disease that causes serious and permanent problems with control of gait and balance. The most obvious manifestations are an inability to aim the eyes properly and blurry vision. These optical changes occur because of lesions in the area of the brain that coordinate eye movements. Patients also show alterations of mood and behavior, including depression, apathy and progressive mild dementia, changes in pupil sizes, deep facial lines, facial jerks and spasms and forgetfulness. Symptoms can vary, and this disease may be confused with Parkinson's disease, Alzheimer's disease and prion diseases.

Many areas of the brain are affected in PSP, including the part of the brainstem where cells that control eye movement are located. Also affected is an area of the brain that controls steadiness when walking. The frontal lobes of the brain are also affected, leading to personality changes. The cause of the damage to the brain cells is unknown. The key to diagnosis is the identification of early gait disturbances and difficulty with eye movement. ("Progressive supranuclear palsy," Pub Med Health, 2010, http://www.ncbi.nlm.nih.gov/pubmedhealth/PMH0001772/, accessed Feb 3, 2011)

Propentofylline. Propentofylline is a medication with nerve-protective properties that was thought to enhance metabolism in the brain. The drug has been investigated as agent HWA285 for its ability to improve symptoms and slow Alzheimer's disease progression. With disappointing clinical trial results, the investigation of this drug as a treatment for Alzheimer's disease has been discontinued. (Frampton, M., R.J. Harvey, and V. Kirchner. "Propentofylline for dementia," *Cochrane Database Syst Rev.* 2003 (2): CD002853)

Prosencephalon. The prosencephalon or forebrain is the third major section of the brain at the furthest or highest point from the spinal cord. The prosencephalon consists of the diencephalons (between brain), which is the central part of the forebrain, and the telencephalon, or cerebrum.

Prostate apoptosis response-4 (Par-4) protein. Prostate apoptosis response-4 (Par-4) protein is a protein compound found in the areas of the brain affected by Alzheimer's disease. PAR-4 is a receptor for the coagulation factors thrombin and prothrombin. Par-4 is suspected of causing nerve cells to self-destruct. Consequently, thrombin and thrombin receptors such as PAR-4 represent novel therapeutic targets for treating neurodegenerative diseases.

Protein kinases *see* Kinases

Pseudodementia. Pseudodementia is a rare syndrome of depression with impaired cognition in which treatment of the depression relieves the cognitive deficit.

Psychologist, clinical. Clinical psychologists are scientists with doctoral degrees in the field of psychology who have been trained to treat patients with psychological disorders.

Psychology. Psychology is the scientific study of the mind and behavior.

Psychosis. Psychosis is a general term for a state of mind or mental disorder characterized by defective or lost contact with reality including unfounded fears. Psychotic patients may have personality changes, hallucinations, delusions, or other severe thought processes.

Psychotropic agent. Psychotropic agents are medications designed to change psychological behavior. The mode of these agents varies, and specific agents are selected on the basis of clinical symptoms. For instance, patients showing signs of apathy and depression are likely to be prescribed antidepressant medications.

Pupil Dilation Test. Pupil dilation using an acetylcholine receptor test is used to measure the cholinergic neuronal system in an effort to help diagnose Alzheimer's disease. In this test, a single drop of 0.01 percent solution of tropicamide (an acetylcholine receptor antagonist) is placed in one eye and a drop of water in the other. Hypersensitivity to antagonists of acetylcholine neurotransmission is measured by an increase in pupil size. This test has been reported to distinguish Alzheimer's disease with an accuracy rate of 95 percent.

Puromycin-sensitive aminopeptidase (PSA/ NPEPPS). Puromycin-sensitive aminopeptidase is the most abundant brain enzyme found in humans. Stanislav Karsten, principal researcher, and his team at LA BioMed, a nonprofit independent research institute, in conjunction with the UCLA Alzheimer's Disease Research Center, have discovered that increasing levels of this enzyme slows the accumulation of tau proteins in the brain. Tau proteins are toxic to nerve cells and lead to the neurofibrillary tangles characteristic of Alzheimer's disease. In animal studies, researchers were able to safely increase levels of PSA/NPEPPS two- to three-fold, which removed neuronal tau proteins. This restored neuronal density and slowed disease progression. ("Increasing brain enzyme may slow Alzheimer's disease progression," Feb 16, 2011, Public Release, Eureka Alert at http://www.eurekalert.org/pub_releases/2011-02/labr-ibe021511.php, accessed Feb 17, 2011)

Pyrroquinolone quinone (PQQ). Pyrroquinolone quinone is a potent antioxidant that defends the body's cells against mitochondrial decay. Mitochondria, which possess their own DNA, are cellular energy sources that influence human longevity. In studies, 20 mg of PQQ in combination with CoQ10 can significantly preserve and enhance memory, attention, and cognition in aging humans and stimulate the growth of new functional mitochondria. As an essential micronutrient, PQQ is not synthesized in the body although it can be derived from all plant species and human milk. Researchers at the University of California, Davis, have conducted studies of PQQ's influence on cell signaling pathways involved in the formation of new mitochondria and discovered that PQQ activates genes involved in cellular energy metabolism, development, and function. In pre-clinical models, PQQ has been shown to optimize central nervous system function, reverse cognitive impairment caused by chronic oxidative stress and improve performance on memory tests. (Chowanadisai, W., et al. "Pyrroloquinoline quinone Stimulates mitochondrial biogenesis through cAMP response element-binding protein phosphorylation and increased PGC-1 expression," *Journal of Biological Chemistry*, 2009, 285 (1): 142–152, http://cortopassilab.ucdavis.edu/papers/Pyrroloquinoline.pdf, accessed March 20, 2011)

Quetiapine fumarate (Seroquel). Quetiapine fumarate is an atypical anti-psychotic medication that has been studied for use in patients with dementia. In one study using flexible doses of quetiapine, 15 percent of subjects withdrew over 1 year because of adverse experiences or co-existing illnesses. Side effects were mild and typically transient. Thirty percent of subjects experienced sedation, 15 percent developed orthostatic hypotension (low blood pressure on rising), and 12 percent experienced dizziness. Encouraging behavioral effects were observed in patients with dementia. However, in 2008 a black box warning was added to this classification of drugs indicating that they are associated with a substantially higher mortality rate (4.5 percent) in geriatric patients with dementia-related psychosis receiving atypical antipsychotic agents (e.g., quetiapine, aripiprazole, olanzapine, risperidone) compared with those receiving placebo (2.6 percent). Most fatalities resulted from cardiac-related events (e.g., heart failure, sudden death) or infections (mostly pneumonia). Atypical antipsychotics are *not* approved for the treatment of dementia-related psychosis. In 2011, New Jersey Attorney General Paula Dow fined AstraZeneca $68.5 million for deceptively marketing quetiapine as effective in reducing agitation in individuals with dementia when it has been found to worsen cognitive functioning in elderly patients with dementia. This is the largest-ever, multi-state, consumer protection-based pharmaceutical settlement. (Tariot, Pierre N., M.D., et al. "Pharmacologic therapy for behavioral symptoms of Alzheimer's disease," *Clinics in Geriatric Medicine*, [2001], volume 17 (2): 359–376. "FDA Review of Seroquel," 2008, http://www.fda.gov/Safety/MedWatch/SafetyInformation/Safety-RelatedDrugLabelingChanges/ucm123259.htm, accessed Feb 10, 2011. "Seroquel suit settled for $68.5M," *Alzheimer's Weekly*, March 13–20, 2011)

Radionuclide Brain Scan. A radionuclide scan or brain scan is a diagnostic procedure in which a small amount of a radioisotope is administered intravenously to measure the tissue uptake of the isotope. A brain scan is used to detect the presence of a space-occupying intracranial lesion. The scan cannot determine if the lesion is due to a tumor, hematoma, abscess or vascular malformation. Before having this procedure, patients should be apprised that the scan is performed by using a large overhanging machine, which emits a ticking sound as the machine moves. Other than the intravenous administration of the radioisotope, the procedure is painless.

Rapid eye movement (REM). Rapid eye movement (REM) is a mentally active period during which dreaming occurs. Rapid eye movement during this period is a reflection of increased brain activity. REM accounts for about 25 percent of the sleep cycle. The non–REM portion can be divided into 4 different stages. In each stage, brain waves become progressively larger and slower, and sleep becomes deeper. After reaching the deepest period, stage 4, the pattern reverses and sleep becomes lighter until REM sleep, the most active period, occurs. This cycle typically occurs about once every 90 minutes in humans.

Rapidly progressive dementia. Rapidly progressive dementias (RPDs) are neurological conditions that develop subacutely over the course of weeks to months, or, rarely, acutely over days. In contrast to most conditions of dementia, which take years to progress, RPDs can quickly be fatal. Researchers at the University of California, San Francisco, in reviewing data from 2001 through 2006 from their dementia center determined that 54 percent of RPD cases were caused by prion disease (37 percent probable or definite sporadic; 15 percent genetic, and 2 percent acquired); 28 percent undetermined (often leukoencephalopathies or encephalopathies of unknown etiology; neurofilament inclusion body disease; Fahr's disease, corticobasal degeneration); and 18 percent with non-prion treatable conditions. Of the 18 percent of treatable RPD conditions, 26 percent were neurodegenerative; 15 percent autoimmune; 11 percent infectious; 11 percent psychiatric; and 9 percent miscellaneous. Alzheimer's disease is rarely rapid, although unusual presentations of Alzheimer's disease in conjunction with angiopathy have been mistaken for Creutzfeldt-Jakob disease. (Geschwind, Michael, Aissa Haman, and Bruce Miller. "Rapidly Progressive Dementia," Neurologic Clinics, August 2007, 25(3), available online at PubMed Central, July 6, 2009, http://www.ncbi.nlm.nih.gov/pmc/articles/PMC2706263, accessed Sept 22, 2010). *See also* Autoimmune encephalopathy; Creutzfeldt-Jakob disease

REACH *see* Resources for Enhancing Alzheimer's Caregiver Health

Receptor. Receptors are protein molecules found on the surface or nucleus of cells that react with substances, including hormones, neurotransmitters and drugs, and cause reciprocal physiological actions. Free nerve endings can also act as receptors, reacting to sensations such as pain, touch, pressure, cold and heat. Some drugs work by blocking biochemical reactions that occur at the receptor level. For instance, acetylcholinesterase inhibitors work by blocking this enzyme from reacting with its intended cell receptor.

Recombinant DNA technology. Recombinant DNA technology refers to the artificial rearrangement of DNA. In this process segments of DNA from one organism are incorporated into the genetic makeup of another organism. Using these techniques, researchers can study the actions and functions of specific genes and attempt to create therapies that alter gene expression.

Reflex disturbances. In cerebellar disease, movement of the tendon reflexes is extended.

Because of loss of influence on the stretch reflexes, the movement consists of a series of flexion and extension movements with the leg moving like a pendulum. Reflex testing is a well-known, sensitive indicator of nervous system integrity. Reflex changes occur in the later stages of Alzheimer's disease and other cerebral degenerative diseases.

Some researchers have noted that the overt occurrence of a continuous sucking, licking or grasping in cerebral degenerative diseases. Signs of dysfunction of the plantar extensor reflex differentiates Alzheimer's disease patients. Those with these overt reflexes may have deficiencies in basic activities of daily living but are not yet incontinent as opposed to permanently incontinent Alzheimer's disease patients who are deficient in activities of daily living, but are still ambulatory. It appears that these neurologic reflexes emerge at a certain stage of Alzheimer's disease just as they disappear in certain stages in the course of infancy. Reflex testing has the advantage of not being influenced by education and cultural factors. (Reisberg, Barry, et al. "Report of an IPA Special Meeting Work Group Under the Co-sponsorship of Alzheimer's Disease International, the European Federation of Neurological Societies, the World Health Organization, and the World Psychiatric Association." International Psychogeriatric Association, 2000)

Reisberg's seven stages of Alzheimer's disease. Reisberg's seven stages of Alzheimer's disease (also known as FAST-Functional Assessment Staging Scale) is a very helpful tool that breaks down each stage of the disease into specific activities of daily living (ADLs). This step-wise progression is based on a system developed by Barry Reisberg, M.D., clinical director of the New York University School of Medicine's Silberstein Aging and Dementia Research Center. The stages include:

Stage 1: No impairment (normal ADL) characterized by no memory problems or evidence of symptoms.

Stage 2: Very mild cognitive decline (may be normal age-related changes or earliest signs of Alzheimer's disease). The person may feel as if he or she is having memory lapses — forgetting familiar words or the location of everyday objects. But no symptoms can be detected during a medical examination or by friends, family or co-workers.

Stage 3: Mild cognitive decline (early-stage Alzheimer's can be diagnosed in some, but not all, individuals with these symptoms). Friends, family or co-workers begin to notice difficulties. During a detailed medical interview, doctors may be able to detect problems in memory or concentration. Common stage 3 difficulties include inability to choose the right word (on tip of one's tongue); difficulty remembering names when meeting new people; losing or misplacing objects; difficulty following what's going on in the workplace and in social settings; and difficulty with planning and organization.

Stage 4: Moderate cognitive decline (mild or early-stage Alzheimer's disease). A careful medical interview should be able to detect clear-cut problems in several areas such as forgetfulness of recent events or communication; inability to perform challenging mental arithmetic such as counting backward by multiple numbers; difficulty with performing complex tasks such as paying bills; mood changes, especially when flustered or overwhelmed.

Stage 5: Moderately severe cognitive decline (moderate or mid-stage Alzheimer's disease). This stage is characterized by noticeable gaps in memory and thinking; help is needed with daily activities. Individuals in this stage may be unable to recall their address, phone numbers or educational background, and they may be uncertain of the date or where they are. They also may have trouble with less challenging mathematical tasks such as counting backward using every fourth number. In addition, while they may remember significant details about themselves and their family, they may need help choosing appropriate clothing.

Stage 6: Severe cognitive decline (moderately severe or mid-stage Alzheimer's disease). This stage is characterized by a worsening of memory, changes in personality and the need for extensive help with daily activities. At this stage, individuals may forget recent activities and surroundings; understand their name but not their personal history; distinguish familiar from unfamiliar faces but not recognize individual caretakers or individuals close to them; need help dressing properly such as not putting pants over a nightgown; experience major changes in sleep patterns — sleeping during the day and becoming restless at night. Additionally, they may need help with toileting; have difficulty controlling bladder or bowels; experience major personality and behavioral changes including suspiciousness and delusions or compulsive behaving; and individuals may develop a tendency to pace, wander or become lost.

Stage 7: Very severe cognitive decline (severe or late-stage Alzheimer's disease). In the final stage of Alzheimer's disease, individuals lose the ability to respond to their environment, to converse, and, eventually, to control movement although they may still say words or phrases. At this stage, individuals need help with much of their daily personal care, including eating or using the toilet. They may also lose the ability to smile, to sit without support and to hold their heads up. Reflexes become abnormal. Muscles grow rigid. Swallowing may become impaired.

Remacemide. The drug Remacemide is a NMDA antagonist. By inhibiting the neurotransmission of glutamate in the brain, remacemide offers protection against neuronal destruction. Excess glutamate is thought to be toxic to neurons, and elevated levels of glutamate have been associated with various neurodegenerative disorders, including Alzheimer's disease and Huntington's disease.

Reminyl *see* Galantamine hydrobromide

Repetitive behavior. Patients with Alzheimer's disease exhibit repetitive behavior, often repeating the same questions, pacing, and performing repetitive activities, such as cleaning the same item.

Reptilian brain. The reptilian brain refers to the base of the brain where the necessary command centers for living, including sleep and waking, respiration and temperature regulation, are located.

Research. The Alzheimer's Association supports many types of research on Alzheimer's disease. All patients with Alzheimer's disease should be allowed to enroll in research efforts particularly when there is a potential benefit or therapeutic

value for the individual. Regardless of the particular program, patients should have access to an available proxy, such as a family member or caregiver, who can decide if the research protocol is in the patient's best interest. All research projects have Institutional Review Boards that oversee the projects and evaluate potential risks.

Resident-Centered Care. Nursing home philosophy, advocates decision-making by residents, rather than having the staff make all decisions. In Resident-Centered care, the staff focuses on the individual needs of the patients and offers holistic care for those who are terminally ill.

Resources for Enhancing Alzheimer's Caregiver's Health (REACH). REACH is a unique, 5-year program sponsored by the National Institute on Aging and the National Institute for Nursing Research. REACH grew out of a National Institutes of Health (NIH) initiative that acknowledged the well-documented burdens associated with caring for dementia patients, as well as the emergence in the literature of promising dementia caregiver interventions.

In 1995, NIH funded six intervention sites and a coordinating center to develop interventions for family caregivers of individuals with moderated degrees of impairment. Each site investigated a different intervention, although there were some items common to all groups, and all of the sites included substantial minority participation. The following caregiver interventions were investigated: (1) home-based behavioral skills training and problem solving, (2) telephone-based system offering voice mail support and advice, (3) training in behavior and stress management provided through a primary care setting, (4) home-based, family-focused multisystem intervention with computer-telephone integration, (5) group-based coping skills training and enhanced support, and (6) home-based environmental and behavioral skills training.

Respite care. Respite care refers to temporary home-care. Respite care can be provided by volunteers through some local Alzheimer's Associations and as a paid service by home-care nursing services. Respite care may be covered by Medicaid for individuals with Alzheimer's disease eligible for nursing home care who are cared for in the home. *See also* Nursing Home — Medicaid alternatives to long-term care; Program for All-Inclusive Care for the Elderly (PACE).

Resveratrol. Resveratrol is a plant chemical known as a flavinoid found in red wine and grape juice. Because of its antioxidant properties, resveratrol is suspected of offering therapeutic benefits in Alzheimer's disease. Clinical studies show that individuals who drink a small glass of red wine daily have a reduced incidence of Alzheimer's disease. Furthermore, a prospective analysis of risk factors for AD in the Canadian population determined that wine consumption was the most protective variable against AD by reducing the risk of AD by 50 percent. Because of these studies, researchers at Albert Einstein College of Medicine in the Bronx, New York, have conducted a study to show the effects of resveratrol on beta amyloid using cell cultures. The results indicate that resveratrol reduces Aβ accumulation in cell cultures but does not inhibit Aβ production, since it has no effect on the Aβ-producing enzymes β- and γ-secretases, However, resveratrol promotes instead the proteolytic clearance of Aβ. (Vingtdeux, Valérie, et al. "Therapeutic potential of resveratrol in Alzheimer's disease," *BMC Neuroscience,* 2008, 9 (Suppl 2): S6doi:10.1186/1471-2202-9-S2-S6, http://www.biomedcentral.com/1471-2202/9/S2/S6, accessed Mar 5, 2011)

Retention and immediate recall. The cognitive skill of retention and immediate recall can be tested by giving the patient a list of words, including dates, addresses, and objects. The patient should repeat the words at the time the examiner recites them to verify that the words have been heard. Three to 5 minutes later the patient should be asked to repeat the words. If the answers are wrong, the examiner attempts to determine if the subject is aware that he or she is wrong or if they are attempting to contrive answers.

Normally, subjects recall the words correctly. Poor recent memory is characteristic of organic brain disease. Poor remote memory is seen in psychiatric and severe emotional disorders.

Rey-Osterreith complex figure. The Rey-Osterreith complex figure is used as a psychological profile test to measure visuo-spatial planning and organization and nonverbal memory.

Rhombencephalon. The rhombencephalon, or hindbrain, is the first major division or section of the brain found in ascending order from the spinal cord. The rhombencephalon consists of three major sections: the myencephalon or medulla oblongata, the metencephalon or pons, and the cerebellum.

Rifamycin (rifampicin). The antibiotic rifampicin, which is widely used is the treatment of tuberculosis and leprosy, has been found to prevent the aggregation and neurotoxicity of amyloid beta protein in test tube studies. This inhibitory activity is attributed to the naphthohydroquinone structure, which acts as a free radical scavenger. Researchers at McMaster University in Canada are investigating the use of rifampicin in conjunction with the antibiotic doxycycline in a clinical trial for Alzheimer's disease (http://clinicaltrials.gov/ct2/show/NCT 00715858, accessed Mar 15, 2011).

Risk factors. Multiple studies have been conducted to help determine which patient groups may be at highest risk for developing Alzheimer's disease. Risk factors are not causes of disease but factors that make people more susceptible to developing a certain disease. This does not mean they will develop the disease. Knowing what factors confer risk can enable these populations to seek preventative measures. The most reproducible risk factors for Alzheimer's disease include: increasing age, family history of dementia in a first degree relative before age 65, Down syndrome in a first degree relative and the APOE-e4 allele. Approximately 50 percent of all patients with a first degree relative with Alzheimer's disease will develop this disorder if followed into the 80th decade. This represents a 2–4 fold increase compared to age-matched controls.

Some researchers also consider the female gender a risk factor since women are 2 to 3 times more likely than men to develop Alzheimer's disease, with a lifetime risk of 1 in 3 women at age 65. Studies indicate that 50–70 percent of all women older than 80 years are affected.

A history of head trauma has been associated with an increased risk of developing Alzheimer's disease. Head circumference and brain size have been inversely associated with Alzheimer's disease. Smaller brain size has also been associated with an earlier disease onset. Low intelligence and limited education have also been associated with an increased risk of Alzheimer's disease. More recent research shows that elevated homocysteine levels, lack of exercise, low levels of omega-3 oils, particularly DHA, high homocysteine levels, low vitamin B levels, and high body mass indexes all pose risk for Alzheimer's disease. (Perlmutter, David. "Alzheimer's disease prevention: reducing your risk," *Huffington Post*, Feb 17, 2011, http://www.huffingtonpost.com/dr-david-perlmutter-md/alzheimers-prevention-reduci_b_822619.html, accessed Mar 7, 2011). *See also* Nun studies; Writing studies

Risperidone (Risperdal). Risperidone (Risperdal) is one of the newer atypical anti-psychotic medications used to treat verbal or physical aggression and wandering. Risperidone appears to significantly decrease symptoms of psychosis and aggression while posing a very low risk for severe side effects.

Two large, multicenter trials have been completed in nursing home patients with fairly severe dementia. The first trial, using doses ranging from 0.5 mg to 2mg daily, showed beneficial effects on both psychosis and aggression. The second study used doses of 1.1 mg to 1.2 mg daily and compared risperidone to haloperidol. While effects were comparable, the tolerability of risperidone appeared to be better with low risk of dose-related Parkinsonism and sedation. However, atypical antipsychotics are no longer recommended for psychosis in patients with dementia because of higher mortality. *See also* Atypical antipsychotics

Rivastigmine. Rivastagmine (Exelon), a drug commonly used for the treatment of mild to moderate Alzheimer's disease, is a carbamate compound that acts as a cholinesterase inhibitor, with selective action in the cortex and hippocampus. Formerly known as ENA 713, rivastigmine is an intermediate-acting inhibitor. Its effects are reversible after an intermediate length of time, and as the disease progresses and the brain's concentration of acetylcholine diminishes, the drug is less effective. The daily dose is generally 3 mg to 12 mg taken twice daily in divided doses taken in the morning and evening.

Side effects, which may be significant, include nausea, vomiting, loss of appetite and weight loss. Less common side effects include high blood pressure, runny nose, slow heartbeat and fainting. Rare side effects include aggression, irritability, nervousness, seizures, trembling and difficulty urinating.

Rivastigmine may also increase the effects of neuromuscular blocking agents used in surgery to relax muscles. Rivastigmine may also cause some people to become dizzy, clumsy, or unsteady. This drug should not be stopped abruptly. Stopping or decreasing the dose by a large amount may cause mental or behavioral changes.

An overdose of rivastigmine, from either pills or using more than one patch simultaneously, may lead to seizures or shock. Some signs of an overdose include large pupils, irregular breathing, fast or weak pulse, severe nausea and vomiting, increasing muscle weakness, greatly increased sweating and greatly increased watering of the mouth.

Rofecoxib (Vioxx). Rofecoxib (Vioxx) is a drug approved by the FDA for relief of the signs of osteoarthritis. A selective COX-2 inhibitor, rofecoxib is undergoing clinical trials for its use in Alzheimer's disease.

Rolipram *see* Phosphophodiesterase (PDE4) inhibitors

Rosemary (*Rosmarinus officinalis*). The herb rosemary contains a number of different antioxidants, most notably, rosmarinic acid, which are known to help reduce free radicals. Rosemary also contains several compounds that are reported to inhibit the breakdown of acetylcholine. Rosemary has long been used as a memory booster. Rosemary can be drunk as a tea. Alternately, it can be used as an essential oil added to bathwater, but not directly to skin. (Duke, James A. *The Green Pharmacy*. [Emmaus, PA:] Rodale Press, Emmaus, PA, 1997)

Routines. Caregivers are reminded of the importance routines play in reducing the decisions patients with Alzheimer's disease must make. Routines provide security for patients with dementia. Daily routines which keep the patient active help them sleep at night and regular toileting may reduce the chance of accidents. Keeping keys and other possessions in one place, even wearing them on a safety pin over clothing, can prevent confusion and frustration.

S-adenosylmethionine (SAMe). S-adenosylmethionine (SAMe) is a naturally occurring compound available as a dietary supplement that increases the body's levels of serotonin, melatonin, and dopamine. Clinical studies indicate that patients with Alzheimer's disease and depression have decreased levels of SAMe in their brain tissues. Although there are reports of improvement in Alzheimer's disease using SAMe, more studies are needed to determine the safety and effectiveness of this supplement for dementia patients.

Safe Return Program. Safe Return is the only nationwide identity program for people with Alzheimer's disease who wander. Sponsored by the Alzheimer's Association, the program includes identification products like wallet cards and clothing tags, a national photo/information database, wandering behavior education, training for families and caregivers, and a 24-hour toll free emergency crisis line.

To register, a person with dementia or their caregiver fills out a form, supplies a photo, and chooses the type of ID product the registrant will wear or carry. If a person is later reported missing, Safe Return immediately alerts local law enforcement agencies and helps in distributing and faxing photo flyers to law enforcement personnel and hospitals. Since 1993, the program has helped to locate and return more than 2,700 registrants to their families. Details can be obtained through the national Alzheimer's Association office or through local Alzheimer's Association chapters. *See also* Resource Section.

Safety. Caregivers are reminded to keep the home and surroundings as safe as possible. As dementia progresses, loss of physical coordination and memory increases the chances of injury. Common hazards include loose or worn carpets and throw rugs, polished floors, loose stair railings and clutter. Patients who have a tendency to wander must be properly supervised regardless if they live at home or in an assisted living facility. Patients with a tendency to pace should be encouraged to take supervised walks.

Physical activity may also help patients sleep better at night.

St. George-Hyslop, Peter, M.D., D.Sc. Since 2003, Dr. Peter St George-Hyslop has been a professor in the Department of Medicine, Division of Neurology and has served as the director of the Center for Research in Neurodegenerative Disease at the University of Toronto. The recipient of numerous medical awards, including an Award for Medical Research from the Metropolitan Life Foundation, he is a member of the American Society for Clinical Investigation where he is well known for his research into Alzheimer's disease. In 2004 he was awarded the Oon Prize in Medicine from the University of Cambridge; in 2007 he was elected as a foreign member to the Institute of Medicine of the National Academies; and in 2009 he was elected Fellow of the Academy of Medical Sciences in the United Kingdom.

Sandoz Clinical Assessment-Geriatric (SCAG). The SCAG is a neuropsychological assessment tool which has been largely replaced by the cognitive testing sections of the Alzheimer's Disease Assessment Scale (ADAS-Cog). The SCAG is reported to have limited utility because of its lack of sensitivity and its limited scope. Evaluations are best made in patients with either mild or severe dementia and only one or two categories of symptoms. SCAG does not encompass behavioral disorders, altered mood states and impaired cognitive function.

SCAN Health Plan of Mountain View and Long Beach, California. The SCAN Health Plan, a model social HMO, provides half the cost of adult day care and medical services for Alzheimer's patients who are able to live at home. The adult day care center charges $40 a day and SCAN pays half of this and also provides medical supplies costing $100/month. Caseworkers regularly visit the home to help with household problems. The SCAN plan includes a mobile van with a brain fitness gym. The brain gym consists of more than 20 brain training games, each scientifically designed to target one or more of the five major cognitive functions of memory, language, attention, visual spatial skills and executive function. The *HAPPYneuron Vital* online brain gym is specially designed with seniors in mind, including large buttons for visual ease, easier games, no time pressure and other hints and tips to encourage the game play activity.

Delivered through the SCAN Van's wi-fi network to the on-board computers, the brain gym offers seniors the opportunity to educate themselves about the importance of brain stimulation in maintaining a vital and healthy brain with age.

Secretase enzymes. Secretase enzymes are naturally occurring chemicals that act as proteases (break down protein molecules). Both beta and gamma secretase cleave amyloid precursor protein (APP) in a way that results in the neurotoxic form of amyloid beta protein. Alpha secretase cleaves APP in a way that results in harmless amyloid beta peptides. Drugs are currently being studied that would inhibit beta or gamma secretase or cause increased production of alpha secretase.

Selective Serotonin Reuptake Inhibitors (SSRI's) Selective Serotonin Reuptake Inhibitors, SSRIs, are a class of drugs, such as fluoxetine (Prozac), that are commonly used as antidepressants. SSRIs are psychoactive drugs and may impair judgment, thinking, and motor skills.

Selegiline hydrochloride (Eldepryl, Atapryl). Selegiline, a drug commonly known as l-deprenyl, is sold under the brand names Atapryl and Eldepryl. Primarily used for the treatment of Parkinson's disease, selegiline is an inhibitor of the enzyme monoamine oxidase (MAO) type B. In addition, it also increases dopamine activity in the brain. In the central nervous system MAO compounds are used in the catabolism of catecholamines and serotonin. Because elevated levels of MAO-B are also found in patients with Alzheimer's disease, long-term inhibition with selegiline may have anti-neurotoxic properties.

Side effects include vitamin K deficiency, which has been associated with a necrotizing form of enterocolitis. At least 3–5 weeks should elapse between the discontinuation of fluoxetine (Prozac) and the initiation of MAO inhibitors such as selegiline. Selegiline should not be used in patients undergoing therapy with opiod narcotics, including meperidine (Demerol). Severe agitation, hallucinations, and death have oc-

curred with concomitant administration of selegiline and meperidine.

Selegiline has been studied in clinical trials for its benefits in Alzheimer's disease. The study showed that mental deterioration from Alzheimer's disease was slowed by an average of 7 months by either selegiline or high doses (2,000 I.U. daily) of vitamin E. The researchers concluded that selegiline or alpha-tocopherol slowed the progression of AD in patients with moderate impairment. This study adds to evidence that neuronal loss in AD is mediated by inflammation (involving free radicals) and that anti-inflammatory drugs may delay the onset and progression of AD. (http://www.therubins.com/aging/alzheim2.htm, accessed Mar 2, 2011)

Semagacestat. Semagacestat is a gamma secretase inhibitor that was under development by the Eli Lilly Company as a therapy for Alzheimer's disease. Its development was halted in August 2010. The decision was made after researchers analyzed the preliminary results of the second Phase III clinical trial of the drug, which indicated that semagacestat failed to slow disease progression. The drug, in fact, worsened cognition and the ability to perform day-to-day activities. ("Semagacestat," Drug Development Technology, 2010, http://www.drugdevelopment-technology.com/projects/semagacestat/, accessed Mar 2, 2011)

Senile dementia / Alzheimer's type (SDAT). Before sophisticated imaging techniques became available, there were few diagnostic tools to aid in the diagnosis of Alzheimer's disease. When patients died and were autopsied, many were found to have other forms of dementia besides Alzheimer's disease. Because of this, patients suspected of having Alzheimer's disease were given the diagnosis of senile dementia/Alzheimer's type. With modern imaging techniques and the ability to rule out other causes of dementia, however, a diagnosis of Alzheimer's disease is generally more than 90 percent accurate, and this term is not used as often as it was in the past. *See* Alzheimer's disease

Senile (neuritic) plaque. Senile or neuritic plaques are neurotoxic protein deposits found in excess amounts in the brains of patients with Alzheimer's disease. Senile neuritic plaques are complex extracellular (located in the spaces outside of cells) lesions composed of a central deposit or core of beta amyloid protein surrounded by activated microglia, fibrillary astrocytes, and dystrophic neurites (dendrites and axonal terminals). Microscopically viewed, neuritic plaques are focal, spherical collections of dilated, tortuous, silver-staining neuritic processes known as dystrophic neurites surrounding a central amyloid core. Often, a clear halo surrounds these components. Neuritic plaques range from 20 to 200 μm in diameter.

Dystrophic neurites are swollen, distorted neuronal processes. Complex sugar polymer components known as glycosaminoglycans are critical for the formation of plaque, acting as the glue for the assembly of these deposits. Senile plaques are often surrounded by microglial cells and reactive astrocytes.

The amyloid core consists of β-amyloid, a predominantly 42kDa protein derived from its precursor amyloid precursor protein by a mechanism known as proteolytic processing. β-amyloid is produced by all cell types and is not unique to neurons. Other components of senile plaque include al-1-antichymotrypsin, glycosaminoglycans and apolipoprotein E.

In Alzheimer's disease, plaques can be found in the hippocampus and amygdala as well as in the neocortex. Similar to the invasions of NFTs, there is usually relative sparing of primary motory and sensory cortices. In some patients there are also diffuse plaques that lack the surrounding neuritic reaction. Diffuse plaques are found in superficial portions of the cerebral cortex as well as in basal ganglia and cerebellar cortex. When diffuse plaques are found in the cerebral cortex, they usually appear to be centered on small vessels or on clusters of neurons. These lesions, which generally occur along with senile plaques, are thought to possibly represent an earlier disease stage.

In the fifth decade of life, many individuals begin to develop senile plaque deposits in their cerebral cortex. By the eighth decade of life, approximately 75 percent of the population is affected by these plaques. The density of these plaques does not increase with age, suggesting that plaque forms quickly. Initially, plaques begin as innocuous deposits of non-aggregated, beta amyloid protein free of neurotoxic effects. However, in some individuals these deposits transform into the neurotoxic senile plaques associated with Alzheimer's disease. It is suspected that a certain enzyme, butyrcholinesterase, plays an essential role in this maturation process.

The distribution and chemical composition of senile neuritic plaques and neurofibrillary tangles are similar in normal elderly people and those with Alzheimer's disease. After a certain density of these lesions is reached, symptoms of Alzheimer's disease develop. Among people with Alzheimer's disease, this level varies depending on genetic and environmental risk factors, as well as co-morbid brain pathology.

In postmortem examination, the plaques should stain positively with A-amyloid antibodies and negative for prion antibodies. The numbers of plaques and tangles must exceed those found in age-matched controls for a diagnosis of Alzheimer's disease.

Senility. Senility refers to the physical and mental bodily changes or infirmities associated with aging.

Senior Medicare Patrol Project. The United States Department of Health and Human Services, through the Administration on Aging, has created 52 Senior Medicare Patrol Project Grants. Senior volunteers undergo several days of training reviewing health care benefit statements and outlining the steps seniors can take to protect themselves. Volunteers work in local senior centers and other places to assist seniors with questions about their benefits and billing problems. In 2010 funding for this project was doubled under the Centers for Medicare and Medicaid Services. The primary purpose of the program is to educate seniors about ways to prevent fraud.

Sentinel Event Alert. A sentinel event alert refers to a medication, condition, or flaw in nursing care that leads to the injury or death of patients. Sentinel event alerts are monitored by accreditation agencies including the Joint Commission on Accreditation of Hospitals to determine the cause of the alert and how it can be corrected.

Sequencing. Sequencing refers to the human behavior of doing things in a logical, predictable order.

Serotonin. Serotonin, or 5-hydroxytryptamine, is a monoamine (having one amine group in its structure) neurotransmitter derived from the amino acid tryptophan. Neurons that produce serotonin are primarily found in the region of the brainstem known as the Raphe nuclei. The actions of serotonin are widespread, with firing rates fluctuating between sleep and wakefulness. Serotonin is involved in arousal, mood and pain control. Studies of postmortem brain tissue from Alzheimer's disease patients show a distinct deficit of serotonin. In several small studies, drugs such as Trazodone, which are known to increase serotonin level, were found to be effective in reducing agitation.

Seven Minute Screen. The Seven Minute Screen, developed by researchers at the University of Vermont, is a test used to help identify patients who should be evaluated for Alzheimer's disease. The Seven Minute Screen, which takes an average of seven minutes and 42 seconds to complete, consists of four sets of questions that focus on orientation, memory, visuospatial skills and expressive language. These are the areas must likely to reveal deficiencies related to Alzheimer's disease.

The test may be administered by a nurse practitioner, physician assistant, or other trained office personnel. Orientation is tested by asking the subject to identify the present month, date, year, day of the week and time of day. The degree of error is graded. A one day error in date is scored as one, while a one month error is scored as 5.

To test memory, subjects are asked identify 16 items drawn on four cards. They are given clues or hints from the tester. After successful identification, the card is hidden and the subject is asked to recall the item after being given the clue. The subject is then distracted by being asked to state the months of the year backwards. The subject is then asked to recall the 16 items.

Visuospatial skills are tested by showing the subject two-dimensional visual images such as a clock with different times. To test expressive language or verbal fluency, the subject is asked to name as many animals as possible within one minute.

In studies, individuals with Alzheimer's disease had significantly worse scores on each of the four tests, and 92 percent of individuals with Alzheimer's disease were correctly identified. (Solomon, P.R., W.W. Pendlebury. "Recognition of Alzheimer's disease: the 7 minute screen." *Family Medicine*, 1998, vol 30, 265–271)

Severe Impairment Battery. The Severe Impairment Battery developed by Saxton in 1990 is an evaluation tool for assessing dementia. This series of tests is found to be reliable in gauging the severity of dementia in patients with low scores on the Mini Mental Status Examination.

Sexuality. Patients with dementia are still sexual beings although they may no longer remember how to arouse their partners or remember what behavior is appropriate. In many cases Alzheimer's patients become uninhibited sexually. At the same time their physical condition and indifference to grooming may make sexual activity despairing for the caregiver spouse. Other patients may lose complete interest in sex.

S47447 *see* **CX1632**

Shadowing. Shadowing refers to following, mimicking, and interrupting behaviors that people with dementia may experience.

Single-nucleotide polymorphisms (SNPs). Single-nucleotide polymorphisms are common, single base-pair variations of DNA.

Single photon/positron emission computed tomography (SPECT). Single photon/positron emission computed tomography (SPECT) is an imaging technique capable of assessing function in relative or absolute terms. SPECT studies of the brain involve the administration of compounds that are normally distributed in the brain according to cerebral blood flow. Thus, a relative measure of cerebral activity can be assessed in different regions of the brain. SPECT usually measures blood flow but it can also image muscarinic and dopamine receptors. In Alzheimer's disease, temporoparietal hypoperfusion is usually seen, with frontal lobe blood flow sometimes also being diminished. When present in sufficient magnitude, temporal lobe dementia is generally present. SPECT is also used to assess the response to drug therapy.

SIRT1. SIRT1 is an enzyme that helps de-acetylate (remove acetyl groups) harmful phosphorylated (p) tau protein. SIRT1 is encoded by the SIRT1 gene. The SIRT1 enzyme is reduced in Alzheimer's disease, and this contributes to accumulations of p-tau protein. In a process of acetylation, excess p-tau protein is produced and contributes to neurodegeneration. Researchers at the Gladstone Institute of Neurological Disease in San Francisco, California, are investigating the role of SIRT1 in acetylation of tau protein. Other research on SIRT1 includes its role in reducing harmful heat shock proteins capable of damaging neurons. ("New study may lead to new strategies for treatment of Alzheimer's," *Elements for Health* website, Sept 27, 2010, http://www.elements4health.com/new-study-may-lead-to-new-strategies-for-treatment-of-alzheimers.html, accessed Dec 30, 2010)

Skilled nursing care. Skilled nursing care is a level of care that includes ongoing medical or nursing services.

Sleep disturbances. Sleep disturbances typically seen in dementia include increased difficulty falling asleep, frequent awakenings, and decreased total sleep time. Studies indicate that there is a rough relationship between the severity of dementia and the magnitude of the sleep disorder. Management of sleep disturbances includes an avoidance of caffeine and other stimulants, an adherence to a regular sleep-wake cycle, and enhanced activity or exercise during the day. Benzodiazepine medications, such as diazepam (Valium) and lorazepam (Ativan) are widely used but are associated with significant side effects. Antidepressant medications, particularly Trazodone (Desyrel), are also commonly used because of the association between sleep disorders and depression.

In one study, changes in sleep structure, especially REM sleep, and in EEG activation were studied in relation to the cholinergic deficit seen in Alzheimer's disease. Only REM sleep was reduced when compared to control subjects. REM is associated with EEG slowing, and Alzheimer's disease patients showed increased EEG activation. Research suggests that bioactive milk peptides may be as effective as benzodiazepines and have the advantage of contributing to daytime wakefulness without the side effects associated with benzodiazepines and other tranquilizers (http://www.aseanfood.info/Articles/11024008.pdf, accessed Mar 14, 2011).

Smoking. The effects of cigarette smoking on Alzheimer's disease are unclear, although one recent study found that the risk of dementia is significantly increased in smokers. Factors that cause increased risk of heart disease, including smoking, have also been found to cause an increased risk for developing Alzheimer's disease. The specific effects of nicotine from smoking, however, remain unclear although researchers suspect that free radical production and the depletion of antioxidants caused by smoking contribute to brain inflammation.

Social HMOs (SHMOs) *see* Medicare HMOs

Social Security benefits. People under the age of 65 of who have Alzheimer's disease may qualify for Social Security disability payments (SSDI). After 24 months on SSI, they would then be covered by Medicare.

Spearman's rank order correlation coefficient. Spearman's rank order correlation coefficient is a system used to evaluate results of paired word testing.

Special care units (SCUs). Special care units (SCUs) are designated areas in residential care facilities or nursing homes that care specifically for the special needs of patients with Alzheimer's disease.

SPECT *see* Single photon/positron emission computed tomography scan

Spinal cord. The spinal cord is a grayish-white structure extending along the back of the body from the foramen magnum in the middle portion of the skull to the lower border of the first lumbar vertebra, a region in the lower back. The spinal cord is situated within the verterbral canal of the vertebral column. It is surrounded by three meninges, or protective layers: the dura mater, the arachnoid mater and the pia mater. The spinal cord is further protected by cerebrospinal fluid which surrounds the spinal cord in an area known as the subarachnoid space.

The spinal cord is — for the most part — cylin-

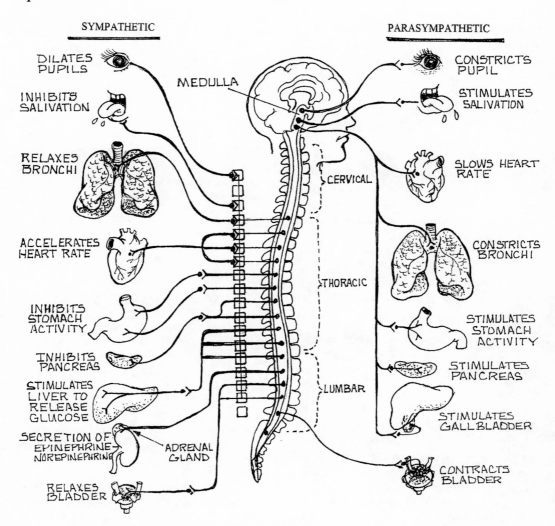

SYMPATHETIC　　　　　　　　　　　PARASYMPATHETIC

DILATES PUPILS

INHIBITS SALIVATION

RELAXES BRONCHI

MEDULLA

ACCELERATES HEART RATE

INHIBITS STOMACH ACTIVITY

INHIBITS PANCREAS

STIMULATES LIVER TO RELEASE GLUCOSE

SECRETION OF EPINEPHRINE-NOREPINEPHRINE

ADRENAL GLAND

RELAXES BLADDER

CONSTRICTS PUPIL

STIMULATES SALIVATION

SLOWS HEART RATE

CERVICAL

CONSTRICTS BRONCHI

THORACIC

STIMULATES STOMACH ACTIVITY

STIMULATES PANCREAS

LUMBAR

STIMULATES GALLBLADDER

CONTRACTS BLADDER

Spinal cord and central nervous system (illustration by Marvin G. Miller).

drical. However, there are fusiform enlargements in the cervical region of the neck and at the lumbosacral region of the lower back. The entire length of the spinal cord is attached to pairs of spinal nerves by motor roots anteriorly and sensory roots posteriorly.

The spinal cord is composed of an inner core of gray matter surrounded by an outer covering of white matter. The gray matter is composed of columns or horns united by a thin gray commissure containing the central canal. The white matter consists of anterior (front), lateral (side) and posterior (rear) columns of tissue.

Spinal nerves. Thirty-one pairs of spinal nerves extend from the spinal cord through spaces be-

tween the vertebrae of the spine. The spinal nerves are named after the regions of the vertebral column with which they are associated: cervical, thoracic, lumbar, sacral and coccygeal.

Sporadic Alzheimer's disease. Sporadic Alzheimer's disease, as opposed to the familial type, is the primary category of Alzheimer's disease, representing approximately 75 percent of all cases. Patients with sporadic Alzheimer's disease have a negative family history for this disease. Onset in sporadic Alzheimer's disease can occur at any time during adulthood but typically occurs in individuals older than 65 years.

Stages of Alzheimer's disease. While the predominant symptoms of Alzheimer's disease vary from patient to patient, certain characteristic behavioral changes occur over a time frame that can be generally broken down into three stages. However some of these symptoms may appear in any of the stages. Furthermore, in all stages, short lucid periods can occur. The typical clinical duration of Alzheimer's disease is 8–10 years with a range of 1 to 25 years.

1. Early Stage (2 to 4 years)—characterized by short term memory loss that may be subtle with patient attempting to cover up by using lists and notes; declining interest in environment, people, and present affairs; vague uncertainty and hesitancy in initiating actions, particularly those involving new situations; difficulty in making decisions; shows signs of depression and aggression; poor work performance by the end of this stage with patients often being dismissed from their jobs. In the early stage, patients may exhibit difficulties with language, become disoriented in time, and become lost in familiar places. They may also lack initiative and motivation and lose interest in hobbies and activities. At this stage the dementia is often overlooked and may be incorrectly diagnosed as old age. Because onset is gradual, it is difficult to sometimes determine exactly when the disease process began.

2. Middle Stage (2 to 12 years)—characterized by progressive memory loss, hesitation in responding to questions; signs of memory loss such as difficulty following simple instructions or doing simple calculations; can no longer manage to live alone without problems; is unable to cook, clean or shop; may experience hallucinations and episodic bouts of irritability and unprovoked aggression; evasiveness, anxiety, and agitated movement including night activity due to disturbances of the sleep-wakefulness cycle; misplaces bills, documents, keys; loses way home in familiar surroundings; forgets to pay bills, lets household chores slip and newspapers pile up; neglects to dispose of garbage; forgets to take medications; loses possessions and then claims they were stolen; neglects personal hygiene (bathing, shaving, dressing), adopts a bizarre mode of dress such as many inappropriate layers of

clothing; loses social graces, which may result in social isolation for the patient and his family. Diagnosis is often made in this stage, with the person having increasing difficulty in coping with day-to-day living.

3. Final Stage (up to a year)—characterized by marked loss of weight due to disinterest in eating or inability to hold utensils; patients in this stage typically become totally dependent and inactive and often require 24-hour nursing care; unable to communicate verbally or in writing; no recognition of family and close friends; incontinence of urine and feces; possibility of major seizures; infantile gestures such as grasping; snout and sucking reflexes are readily elicited; inability to stand and walk, becomes bedridden or confined to a wheelchair; increasing degrees of physical disability; death is usually caused by aspiration pneumonia, inanition or malnutrition. *See also* Reisberg's seven stages of Alzheimer's disease

State policies on mental health care. Policies regarding provisions for mental health care, including long-term care and day care, are determined by individual states. As of 2001, 31 states had elected to participate in at least some Medicaid-sponsored managed care programs. States that have sought to move away from public bureaucracies have favored using for-profit-out-of-state vendors, hoping the influences of corporate business can improve outdated systems. States with these contracts report success both in holding down costs and in expanding access while securing consumer satisfaction. Still other states have created their own managed care systems or modified public programs, combining them with existing county-based systems or community mental health boards.

Cost control is always an issue although it may arise in different contexts. Some states feel that efficiency of a particular program and integration of state and local systems make one program more attractive than another. States have been motivated to shift to managed care so that they may exert more control over the providers and managers of control. With a government contract in hand, state officials can require accountability, demand or improve performance and become eligible for incentives and participation in innovative programs.

Each state makes its own decision regarding the specific populations that will be covered in a Medicaid managed care arrangement.

Statins. Statins refer to a class of cholesterol-lowering drugs. Studies indicate that cholesterol plays a role in Alzheimer's disease development. In ADCS clinical trials, patients with mild or moderate Alzheimer's disease taking statins are being studied and compared to patients of similar age and disease progression who are not taking statin medications. While lowering cholesterol levels lowers the risk for Alzheimer's disease, statins deplete the co-enzyme CoQ10. Deficiencies of CoQ10 increase inflammation and increase cardiovascular risk, which, in turn, increases risk for stroke and Alzheimer's disease. The recommendation is for people on statins to take higher amounts of CoQ10. In Europe, CoQ10 is routinely added to statin medications.

Stem cells. Stem cells are early primitive embryonic cells that differentiate to form all of the cell types in the human body, depending on the body's needs. The process of differentiation allows some cells to become brain cells, whereas others become blood or liver cells. In embryos less than 4 days old, the stem cells are called totipotent stem cells because they have total potential to form all of the cells needed to sustain life. Implanted into a woman's uterus, these cells could form a complete human being.

After 4 or 5 days, the cells are pluripotent. They still have the potential to differentiate into virtually every cell in the body, but they can no longer form an entire human being. As the cells continue to divide into more cells, they become multipotent. Multipotent stem cells can form many, but not all, types of cells.

Stem cells are found in both embryos, infants, children and adults. While embryonic stem cells offer a wealth of possibilities, most adult stem cells are multipotent and can form only a limited number of cell types. There are other disadvantages to using adult stem cells, including the fact that they are hard to identify and take a long time to grow in tissue cultures.

When transplanted into the human body, stem cells are able to form whatever cell type is needed. In other words, stem cells can differentiate and form new brain cells or new kidney cells. In experiments, stem cells have been shown to work just like this. However, because stem cells are immortal and do not have a programmed cell death, many researchers think that they are more likely to eventually become cancerous. If stem cells prove to be safe and effective, they may one day be used to treat neurodegenerative diseases such as Alzheimer's disease. Now that neurons in the human adult brain are known to regenerate, stem cell therapy seems a likely therapy. The feasibility of neuron grafting

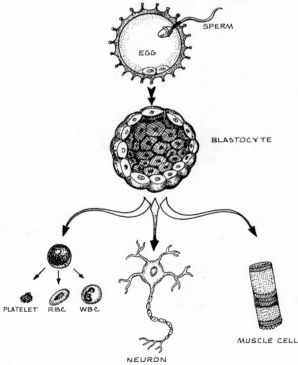

Stem cell differentiation (illustration by Marvin G. Miller). The origin of the stem cell is thought to arise from either the fertilized egg, or the inner cell mass of the blastocyte (hollow sphere of cells created following several divisions of the egg cell). Stem cells differentiate into many unique types of cells including blood, tissue, nerve, and muscle cells.

in general is currently being explored in animal models.

Stress. Stress is a physical, chemical or emotional factor that causes bodily or mental tension, which, when chronic, is known to contribute to the development of many inflammatory and autoimmune diseases. Although stress is inevitable and accompanies any change, it is one's reaction to stress that can cause problems. Both aging and stress are chronic negative regulators of neurogenesis (regeneration of neurons) in humans. One of the major effects of stress is impaired hippocampal-dependent learning. Stress also causes immune system changes that may promote inflammation, which is thought to be a factor in the development of Alzheimer's disease. Stress reduction techniques such as yoga and massage are being investigated for their ability to reduce the risk of developing Alzheimer's disease and improve symptoms in patients with Alzheimer's disease. In addition, the National Center for Complementary and Alternative Medicine division of the National Institutes of Health is evaluating stress reduction techniques for caregivers.

Stroke. Stroke or cerebral accident is a condition of sudden diminution or loss of consciousness, sensation, or voluntary movement caused by rupture or obstruction (such as due to a blood clot) of an artery of the brain. *See also* Vascular dementia

Stroop Color Interference Test. The Stroop Color Interference Test is a mental status evaluation tool used to measure attention to a complex set.

Subarachnoid space. The subarachnoid space, which completely surrounds the brain, is the interval or space between the arachnoid mater and pia mater. The space is filled with cerebrospinal fluid and contains the large blood vessels of the brain.

Subdural hemorrhage. Subdural hemorrhage refers to intracranial bleeding resulting from tearing of the superior cerebral veins of the brain. The cause is usually a blow to the front or back of the head. This results in excessive front-back displacement of the brain within the skull. When the vein is torn, even under low pressure, blood begins to accumulate in the potential space between the dura and the arachnoid spaces. Clots can form (subdural haematoma). Subdural clots can increase rapidly causing acute symptoms.

Subsidized senior housing. Many federal and state programs are set up to pay for a portion of the cost of housing for older and disabled adults with low and moderate incomes. In subsidized senior housing, residents live in their own apartments within a senior housing complex. Some of these facilities provide assistance with shopping, laundry, and transportation needs. Individuals may hire a home health care agency to help with their medical needs. In some communities, resources are available to help with the cost of home health care. Other communities offer services such as Meals-On-Wheels to help the elderly and disabled.

Substance P. Substance P, a neuropeptide found in the axons of some neurons, is associated with pain and temperature. Substance P is released from terminals of electrically stimulated primary sensory neurons by a mechanism that depends on the presence of calcium. Substance P is destroyed by a neutral metallopeptidase enzyme known as substance P degrading enzyme.

Substantia nigra. The midbrain can be divided into two halves called the cerebral peduncles. Each of these is divided into an anterior portion known as the crus cerebri and an anterior portion known as the tegmentum. The crus cerebri and the tegmentum are separated by a pigmented band of gray matter known as the substantia nigra. The substantia nigra is a large motor nucleus composed of medium-size neurons with many processes. These neurons contain inclusion granules of melanin pigment within their cytoplasm. The substantia nigra is associated with muscle tone and has connections extending to the cerebral cortex, the spinal cord, the hypothalamus and the basal nuclei.

Sundowning. Sundowning is a term used to describe the restlessness and agitation dementia patients experience during the late afternoon or evening hours.

Sunrise Assisted Living's "At Home" Assisted Living Program. Sunrise Assisted Living was founded in 1981 by Paul and Terry Klaasen in response to their difficulties finding suitable care for Terry's mother. They modeled Sunrise after senior homes Paul had remembered seeing in Holland. At Sunrise, seniors live in a comfortable residential environment with all the services they need.

Support group. Support groups are organizations dedicated to the education and support of patients, their families and caregivers. Whether local groups or Internet resources, support groups play an invaluable role. The Alzheimer's Association supports local chapters in most areas of the country. There are no costs and most groups meet once a month. The purpose of support groups is for patients, family members, and caregivers to share with one another in a confidential setting.

Suspiciousness. Patients with Alzheimer's disease often become suspicious when they are confused. Frequently, they misplace possessions and accuse others of stealing them. This behavior is more common in the early stages of Alzheimer's disease.

Sympathetic nervous system. The sympathetic role of the autonomic nervous system prepares the body to handle emergencies. It accelerates the heart rate, causes constriction of peripheral blood vessels and raises the blood pressure. The sympathetic nervous system also elicits a redistribution of blood flow, causing blood to leave the skin and intestines and move to the brain, heart and skeletal muscles.

Symptoms. The most common initial symptom of Alzheimer's disease is memory impairment. Important tasks are left undone and possessions may be misplaced. The major symptoms in Alzheimer's disease include: (1) problems with intellect, such as impaired memory, judgment and abstract thinking (2) orientation problems, including not knowing what day or time it is or who they are (3) problems with language and communication, and (4) changes in personality including anxiety, irritability, and agitation. Other symptoms commonly seen include mood disturbances, depression, social withdrawal, lack of initiative, altered perception, hallucinations, wandering, verbal and physical aggression, apathy, altered sleep patterns and vegetative behaviors such as lack of appetite.

The onset of symptoms may be almost imperceptible but will typically progress, becoming serious within a few years' time. After the memory disorder becomes apparent, disorders of cognition, such as the inability to balance a checkbook, will emerge. Other common symptoms include confusion in following directions, getting lost while driving a car, and frightening lapses of memory such as leaving on a gas stove, may also occur.

In the later stages of the disease, the patient with Alzheimer's disease experiences difficulty communicating. Reading and writing also become impaired and activities of daily living, such as bathing and dressing, are usually neglected. Agitation, hallucinations, delusions, and violent outbursts may occur at any time during the course of the illness. Previous personality traits are often exaggerated or they may be completely obscured by new behavior patterns. A general physical decline is not seen until the latest stages of the illness. *See also* Diagnosis; Reisberg's seven stages of Alzheimer's disease; Warning signs

Synapse. The nervous system consists of large numbers of neurons that are linked together to form functional conducting pathways. Where two neurons or a neuron and a skeletal muscle cell come into close proximity and communicate with one another, their communication occurs over a gap or bridge known as a synapse. Axons and dendrites communicate with one another by sending chemical messengers across synapses. The synaptic cleft or synapse refers to the space or gap between the neurons' axons and dendrites where functional communication occurs. Under physiological conditions, communication takes place in one direction only.

Synapses may be either chemical or electrical. Most synapses are chemical, in which a chemical substance known as a neurotransmitter passes across the narrow space between cells and attaches to a protein receptor. Chemical synapses may excite (stimulate) or inhibit other cells. Electrical synapses are ordinary gap junctions between two neurons which permit the spread of activity between one neuron and another, ensur-

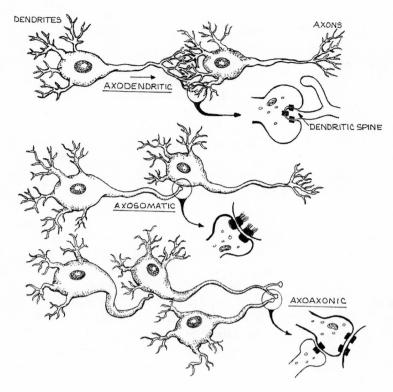

Chemical synapses (illustration by Marvin G. Miller).

Neurons that fail to receive synaptic signals from their target cells undergo cell death. As the brain matures, the synaptic connections are modified by use. In the absence of proper stimulation, the number of synaptic connections are reduced and neurons die. With enriched experiences and stimulation, neural synapses sprout new branches and connections. Surviving neurons fire quick responses across synapses. The more firing (such as repetition in learning) across a specific connection, the stronger the connection.

Synaptic density. Measurements of synaptic density are used to measure the synaptic loss seen in Alzheimer's disease.

ing that a group of neurons performing together will function as a group.

The surfaces of the terminal axon expansion and the neuron are referred to, respectively, as pre-synaptic and post-synaptic membranes. On the pre-synaptic side, the presynaptic terminal contains many small vesicles that contain the neurotransmitter. The vesicles fuse with the pre-synaptic membrane and discharge the neurotransmitter in the synaptic cleft by a process of exocytosis.

Synaptic loss is commonly seen in the hippocampus and neocortex of patients with Alzheimer's disease. This loss, which can be measured by measuring synaptic density, correlates with disease severity. The immediate cause of dementia in Alzheimer's disease is a loss of these synapses, which results in cerebral disconnections and the inability to process thoughts.

Synaptic connections. Axons connect to other axons through chemical messages sent through synaptic connections. These connections are necessary for the survival of individual neurons.

Synaptic spines. Synaptic spines are extensions of the surface of a neuron that form receptive sites for synaptic contact with afferent nerves.

Synaptic strengths. The strength of a particular synapse. Synaptic strength, which varies among the many synapses, regulates the effectiveness of a particular connection.

Synaptic vesicles. Synaptic vesicles are small sacs located at the ends of nerve cell axons that store neurotransmitters. During activity the vesicles release their contents at the synapse, and the neurotransmitter stimulates receptors on other cells.

Synapton *see* Physostigmine salicylate

Synaptophysin. The compound synaptophysin can be measured to evaluate synaptic density. Levels of synaptophysin correlate well with cognitive function.

Tacrine hydrochloride (THA). Tacrine hydrochloride or THA (brand name Cognex) is a drug known as a reversible cholinesterase inhibitor commonly used in the treatment of Alzheimer's disease. The first cholinesterase inhibitor to receive FDA approval for treatment of mild to moderate Alzheimer's disease, tacrine is given in daily doses ranging from 10 mg to 640 mg. Because the drug is short-acting, it is usually given 4 times daily. Tacrine works by blocking the enzyme acetylcholinesterase, an enzyme that breaks down acetylcholine, therefore prolonging the period of time that neurons are exposed to acetylcholine.

Although widespread degeneration of multiple neuronal systems eventually occurs in patients with Alzheimer's disease, early changes in this disease selectively involve neuronal pathways that project from the basal forebrain to the cerebral cortex and hippocampus. These changes result in deficiencies of cortical acetylcholine that ultimately account for some of the symptoms associated with mild to moderate dementia. Tacrine acts by elevating acetylcholine concentrations in the cerebral cortex by slowing the degradation of acetylcholine released in cholinergic neurons that are still intact. While it does not improve function in damaged neurons, tacrine helps preserve functional neurons. However, there is no evidence that tacrine alters the course of the underlying disease process in Alzheimer's disease.

Presumably, tacrine elevates acetylcholine concentrations in the cerebral cortex by slowing the degradation of acetylcholine that is released by still intact cholinergic neurons. While tacrine does not alter the course of the underlying dementing process, it can reduce mild symptoms. As the disease progresses and fewer cholinergic neurons remain functionally intact, the effects of tacrine may diminish.

Side effects include elevation of liver enzymes, nausea, vomiting, diarrhea, indigestion, myalgia (muscle pain), and anorexia. The major disadvantage of tacrine is that patients must be closely monitored for liver damage. Also, because elevated levels of acetylcholine can exacerbate bladder outflow problems, aggravate obstructive pulmonary disease and increase the risk of gastric acidity and gastrointestinal bleeding, patients must be under close medical supervision. Cimetidine (Tagamet) may cause higher blood levels of tacrine, which may increase the chance of side effects. Tacrine may cause higher blood levels of theophylline, which may increase the chance of side effects from this drug.

According to the results of one study, tacrine has no effect on women with the APOE4 gene although it did help those who carried the APOE2 or APOE3 alleles. Because both cigarette smoking and tacrine have effects on liver function, smokers have lower rates of tacrine absorption. Tacrine should be prescribed carefully in patients with a history of abnormal liver function tests.

A report published by the Dementia Trialists' Collaboration in JAMA (JAMA, Nov. 28, 1998; 280(20): 1777–1782) found that cholinesterase inhibition with tacrine appears to reduce deterioration in cognitive performance during the first 3 months and increase the odds of global clinical improvement. Effects observed on measures of behavioral disturbance were of questionable significance, and functional autonomy was not significantly affected.

In one clinical trial, more than 80 percent of patients without the APOE4 allele responded well to tacrine. Of the patients with the APOE4 gene, 60 percent of patients were unchanged or worse after 30 weeks. The results of this study indicate that patients not carrying APOE4 respond better to tacrine than those carrying APOE4. The results indicate that there is a genotype-dependent difference in the way individuals with Alzheimer's disease respond to cholinesterase inhibitors and that the APOE4 genotype influences the function and integrity of the cholinergic system. (Poirer, Judes, Isabelle Aubert, et al. "Apolipoprotein E4 and Cholinergic Activity in Alzheimer's Disease," *Alzheimer Disease: From Molecular Biology to Therapy*, edited by R. Becker and E. Giacobini. Boston: Birkhäuser Publishing, 1996, 55–60.)

In 1991, the Life Extension Foundation sued the United States Food and Drug Administration (FDA) because the FDA failed to approve Tacrine (THA) to treat Alzheimer's disease. While the lawsuit was dismissed on technical grounds, it forced the FDA to finally approve THA seven years after it was shown in a *New England Journal of Medicine* report to slow the progression of Alzheimer's disease.

Tau protein. Tau protein is a normal brain constituent. Specifically, tau is a microtubule-associated protein that is involved in microtubule assemble and stabilization. In adult human brain, six tau isoforms are produced from a single gene by alternative mRNA splicing. These isoforms differ from each other by variations in their amino acid structures. Some forms of tau are helpful in that they provide stability to the neuronal cytoskeleton. Tau mutations can form phosphorylated forms of tau that are harmful.

Tau isolated from the brains of patients with Alzheimer's disease contains higher concentrations of the amino acids serine and heroine phosphate than tau in normal brains. This "hyperphosphorylation" of tau may lead to the abnormal conformation characteristic of Alzheimer's disease. Conformational changes in tau are among the first detectable changes in the neurons of the hippocampus in the brains of Alzheimer's disease patients. Studies suggest that an accumulation of phosphorylated tau protein is responsible for neurodegeneration in Alzheimer's disease.

One of the pathologic hallmarks of Alzheimer's disease is the presence of neurofibrillary tangles, intraneuronal deposits of paired helical filaments (as well as fewer straight filaments) made of hyperphosphorylated tau and ubiquitin. Both of these elements are increased in the spinal fluid of patients with Alzheimer's disease. Besides Alzheimer's disease, other conditions, such as the frontotemporal dementias, are associated with abnormal deposits of tau.

Although tau protein is elevated in the spinal fluid of patients with Alzheimer's disease, measurements of its concentration are not routinely performed because their diagnostic significance remains unclear. Tau is also increased in conditions associated with rapid destruction to the central nervous system, such as acute strokes, trauma and encephalitis. Tau is also elevated in the spinal fluid of 20 to 40 percent of patients with frontal lobe dementia and a number of patients with vascular dementia. (Check, William, Ph.D. "Puzzling out a role for Alzheimer's tests." *CAP Today*, In the News, publication of the College of American Pathologists, June 1998)

Taub Institute for Research on Alzheimer's Disease and the Aging Brain. The Taub Institute is a research center funded by the National Institute on Aging located at Columbia University Medical Center in New York City. The Institute conducts research on Alzheimer's disease and other conditions such as Parkinson's Disease that are associated with aging (http://www.cumc.columbia.edu/dept/taub/, accessed Feb 22, 2011).

Tauists. Scientists who adhere to the theory that tau protein formation is responsible for the development of Alzheimer's disease.

Taxol *see* Paclitaxel

Tela choroidea. The tela choroidea is a two-layered fold of pia mater. On either side of the midline the tela choroidea projects downward through the roof of the third ventricle to form the choroids plexuses of the third ventricle.

Telencephalon *see* Cerebrum

Telomerase. Telomerase is a specialized form of reverse transcriptase, an enzyme which facilitates messenger RNA. Telomerase has been proposed to possess anti-aging properties. Specifically, its catalytic subunit is active in neurons throughout the brain during development, but is absent from neurons in the adult brain. This subunit of telomerase also exhibits neuroprotective properties in experimental models of neurodegenerative disorders. That suggests that inducing telomerase in neurons may protect against age-related neurodegeneration. ("Neuroprotective strategies for Alzheimer's disease." *Life Extension*, Medical Updates, January 2002, 73, excerpted from Experimental Gerontology, 2000, 35(4), 489–502)

Temporal lobe. The temporal lobe of each cerebral hemisphere occupies the area inferior the lateral sulcus. The lateral surface of the temporal lobe can be further divided into three gyri or folds, the superior, the middle and the inferior temporal gyri.

Tentorium cerebelli. The tentorium cerebelli of the brain is an arched lamina, elevated in the middle, and sloping downward toward the circumference. It covers the superior surface of the cerebellum and supports the occipital lobes of the brain. Its anterior border is free and concave and bounds a large oval opening, the incisura tontorii, for the transmission of the cerebral peduncles.

Terminal illness. Terminal illnesses refer to disorders for which there is no cure. Terminal disorders eventually lead to death.

Testosterone. Testosterone, like estrogen, has recently been found to be beneficial in reducing the amount of plaque formation by altering the mechanism in which beta peptides are produced from A beta precursor protein (beta APP). Increasing evidence indicates that testosterone increases the secretion of the non-amyloidogenic APP fragment, spAPP alpha, and decreases the secretion of A beta peptides from nerve cells. This result raises the possibility that testosterone supplementation in elderly men may be protective in the treatment of Alzheimer's disease. (Proceedings of the National Academy of Sciences of the United States of America, 2000; vol 97 (3): 1202–1205; Hammond, J., et al. "Testosterone-mediated Neuroprotection through the Androgen Receptor in Human Primary Neurons." Journal of Neurochemistry, June 2001, 77(5): 1319–1326)

Texas Functional Living Scale (TFLS). The Texas Functional Living Scale (TFLS) is a new performance-based measure of functional abilities with an emphasis on instrumental activities of daily living skills. Introduced by researchers at the University of Texas Southwestern Medical Center in Dallas, the procedure is brief and weighted toward the ability to perform cognitive tasks, rather than informant-based.

Thal, Leon, M.D. (1944–2007). Dr. Leon Thal was chair of the Department of Neurosciences at the University of California San Diego School of Medicine and principal investigator of the Alzheimer's Disease Cooperative Study (ADCS) consortium until his untimely death in a plane crash at age 62. One of the world's leading experts on the development of new therapies for Alzheimer's disease, Thal was also the director of the UC San Diego Shiley-Marcos Alzheimer's Disease Research Center, and was director of the multi-center Alzheimer's Disease Cooperative Study (ADCS) since it was first established in 1991. He was also on staff at the Veterans Affairs San Diego Healthcare System.

Thalamus. The thalamus is a large egg-shaped mass of gray matter that forms the dorsal portion of the forebrain. The anterior end of the thalamus forms the posterior boundary of the interventricular foramen.

Think Gum. Think Gum is an FDA approved dietary supplement (sugar-free, candy-coated gum) reported to improve memory. Its active ingredients include the herbs vinpocetine, bacopa, ginkgo biloba, guarana, rosemary and peppermint. All six herbal additives are reported to work together to improve cognitive function in healthy individuals (http://thinkgum.com/about.html, accessed Nov 10, 2010).

Third ventricle. The third ventricle, an area of the brain derived from the forebrain vesicle, is a narrow cleft that separates the two thalami.

Thyroid disease. Thyroid diseases have long been associated with Alzheimer's disease. The autoimmune hyperthyroid disorder, Graves' disease, is reported to occur more often in patients with a family history of Alzheimer's disease. (Riddha Arem, M.D., *The Thyroid Solution*, New York, 1999) While the reasons for this relationship are unclear, both disorders are associated with deficiencies of B vitamins, increased levels of glycosaminoglycan, and a suspected causative relationship with the excitotoxins monosodium glutamate and aspartame. Many patients with Graves' disease go on to develop autoimmune hypothyroidism or Hashimoto's thyroiditis, which is also associated with Alzheimer's disease.

Acquired cerebellar ataxia has been described in patients with hypothyroidism and is typically reversible by thyroid hormone replacement therapy. The cerebellar dysfunction is attributed to metabolic and physiological effects related to thyroid hormone deficiency. Even when thyroid function is corrected, patients with thyroid auto-antibodies may develop Hashimoto's encephalopathy or Hashimoto's associated ataxia, conditions in which thyroid antibodies attack neurons rather than thyroid cells. (Selim, M., and D. Drachman, "Ataxia associated with Hashimoto's disease" progressive non-familial adult onset cerebellar degeneration with autoimmune thyroiditis." *J Neurol Neurosurg Psychiatry*, Jul 2001; 7 (1): 81–87)

Hyperthyroidism is rarely associated with dementia. One elderly patient with dementia, who was diagnosed with possible Alzheimer's disease on the basis of SPECT, was found to have Graves' disease. When therapy with beta blockers and anti-thyroid drugs was instituted, his memory improved and his initial uptake defect in the temporoparietal region also responded to therapy. (T. Fukui, et al. "Hyperthyroid dementia: clinicoradiological findings and response to treatment." *Journal of Neurological Science*, Feb 2001; 184(1): 81–88)

One earlier study involving medical record reviews determined that for hypothyroidism, there was a slight positive association for Alzheimer's disease, whereas patients with Graves' disease had a negative association for Graves' disease. (Yoshimasu, F., et al. "The association between Alzheimer's disease and thyroid disease in Rochester, Minnesota." *Neurology*, Nov 1991; 41(11): 1745–1747)

Timeframe *see* Alzheimer's disease, clinical course; Stages of Alzheimer's disease

Touch therapy. Alzheimer's disease patients have the need for touch, love and companionship. Touch can convey care, compassion, and reassurance. Because touch is so important, some institutions use touch therapy as part of their healing philosophy. In touch therapy, caregivers touch patients in their course of administering therapy.

Toxins. Toxins are environmental substances, including drugs, chemicals and infectious agents, capable of causing harm to the body. During fetal development, toxins can affect the migration of neurons, disrupting normal brain function.

Toxins can also injure brain cells and disrupt the brain's chemical messengers after birth. Scientists theorize that environmental exposures have a latent effect on the brain, causing a noticeable degeneration years later. Many toxins are considered risk factors for Alzheimer's disease, including numerous industrial chemicals, pesticides, drugs, and heavy metals. *See also* Risk factors

Trailmaking Test, Parts A and B. The Trailmaking test (TMT) is a mental status evaluation tool used to measure attention. Part A consists of encircled numbers from 1 to 25, randomly spread across a sheet of paper. The object of the test is for the subject to connect the numbers in order, beginning with 1 and ending with 25, in as little time as possible. Part B is more complex because it requires the subject to connect numbers and letters in an alternating pattern (1-A-2-B-3-C, etc.) in as little time as possible. Because Part B requires more thought processing and attention on behalf of the subject, it takes longer to complete the test; however, if a test subject works on Part B for more than two or three minutes, they typically become frustrated, and the frustration may influence performance on other tests.

Transcutaneous electrical nerve stimulation (TENS). Transcutaneous electrical nerve stimulation (TENS) is a well-known treatment that uses low-level electrical pulses to suppress chronic pain. Several studies utilizing this therapy have demonstrated improvement in memory and functioning in Alzheimer's patients. An experimental surgical technique being tested on animals employs small plastic implants in the brain that release a powerful nerve growth factor that may prevent neuronal destruction.

Transforming Growth Factor Beta-1 (TGF-β1). Transforming growth factor beta-1 (TGF-β1) is a cytokine suspected of playing a central role in the development of Alzheimer's disease. Released during the immune response, TGF-β1 regulates beta amyloid precursor protein synthesis and processing, plaque formation, astroglial and microglial response, and neuronal cell death. Its role in influencing amyloid beta protein production has long been thought to directly contribute to the pathological changes in Alzheimer's disease. However, researchers at the Gladstone Institute of Neurological Disease in San Francisco have found that increased levels of TGF-β1 cause the production of molecules that destroy beta amyloid. Mice genetically engineered to produce increased levels of both beta amyloid and TGF-β1 were found to have 75 percent fewer plaques and 60 percent lower beta-amyloid levels. (Franzen, Harald. "Molecule Helps Brain Cells Clear Alzheimer's Plaques." *Scientific American*, Medicine, May 1, 2000)

Traumatic head injury. Traumatic head injuries are listed as a risk factor for Alzheimer's disease. *See* Brain injuries and Head injuries.

Treatment in Alzheimer's disease. Treatment options in Alzheimer's disease are diverse. Neurologists such as Harvard University's Dr. Kenneth Kosik report that controlling symptoms will likely require more than one drug therapy. Approved drugs include the cholinesterase inhibitors, which are used for mild symptoms. These medications include Razadyne (galantamine), Exelon (rivastigmine), and Aricept (donepezil). Another drug, Cognex (tacrine), was the first approved cholinesterase inhibitor, but is rarely prescribed today due to safety concerns. The drug Namenda (memantine), an N-methyl D-aspartate (NMDA) antagonist, is prescribed to treat moderate to severe Alzheimer's disease.

In general, there are four therapeutic approaches to treating Alzheimer's disease: (1) the relief of behavioral symptoms associated with dementia, including depression, agitation and psychosis (2) the relief of cognitive dysfunction in an effort to improve memory, language, praxis, attention and orientation (3) to slow the rate of progression of the illness, in an effort to preserve quality of life and independence, and 4) to delay the time of onset of illness. The targets of treatment include: (1) decreasing amyloid beta production by affecting the processing of β APP (2) preventing or reducing amyloid beta aggregation and plaque maturation or improving clearance of amyloid beta through microglia or alphalipoprotein E or J (3) inhibiting neurotoxic effects of amyloid beta by restoring calcium homeostasis, reducing oxidative damage with antioxidants or decreasing inflammation with anti-inflammatory drugs, and (4) decreasing cellular response to injury.

Therapeutic agents used to treat behavioral symptoms include antipsychotics such as haloperidol, lithium and thioridazine, anticonvulsants, antidepressants, anti-anxiety meds such as buspirone, anti-parkinson drugs such as selegiline, beta adrenergic blocking agents and minor tranquilizers such as the benzodiazepines (diazepam, lorazepam, etc.)

Cholinesterase inhibitors such as tacrine and cholinergic receptor agents such as arecoline and pilocarpine are used in an effort to improve cognitive function. To restore the precursor compounds of acetylcholine, compounds such as choline and lecithin are sometimes prescribed.

Nerve growth factor is prescribed experimentally in an effort to enhance or stimulate neuronal sprouting. Animal studies suggest that NGF administration may promote neuronal survival even when damage is present. Anti-inflammatory agents are sometimes prescribed because of evidence that these drugs may prevent Alzheimer's disease.

To delay the onset of illness, treatment may target single components of the complex biological mechanism that leads to senile plaque formation. In particular, treatment may focus on preventing, removing, and decreasing aggregates of beta amyloid with the use of vaccines, cholinesterase inhibitors, secretase enzyme inhibitors, and drugs that affect APP secretion. Drugs that increase alpha secretase directly or indirectly, changing the pathway and reducing production of beta amyloid protein, are also promising.

However, patients may still need drugs that prevent the formation of tangles that disrupt nerve cells from within. Different therapies may also be used to reduce the associated free radical toxicity, inflammation and cell membrane damage. In addition, tranquilizers and antidepressants are often employed to reduce the anxiety and restlessness associated with Alzheimer's disease. Other therapies commonly employed include nutrient supplements to correct calcium, copper and zinc imbalances, antioxidant vitamins, non-steroidal inflammatory drugs, cholesterol-lowering drugs and estrogens. (Husain Mustafa M., et al. "Present and prospective clinical therapeutic regimens for Alzheimer's disease," *Neuropsychiatric Disease and Treatment*, August 2008, 4(4): 765–777, http://www.ncbi.nlm.nih.gov/pmc/articles/PMC2536544/, accessed Mar 2, 2011. "Alzheimer's disease medication fact sheet," NIA, http://www.nia.nih.gov/Alzheimers/Publications/medicationsfs.htm, accessed Mar 11, 2011)

Triune brain. Proposed by Paul MacLean in 1967, the triune brain is a model of brain development based on the theory that the human brain developed by keeping areas found to be useful in our predecessors and adding new structures by chance mutations designed to aid in the survival of the fittest.

Trophic factors. Trophic factors are chemical signals that regulate cells away from their origin. Trophic factors found in neurotransmitters control axonal connections. Where axonal connections are made and how long they are sustained determines whether a given neuron lives or dies.

Tumor necrosis factor (TNF). Tumor necrosis factor (TNF) is an immune system chemical known as a cytokine that contributes to inflammation in various autoimmune diseases. Many autoimmune diseases including rheumatoid arthritis, Crohn's disease, psoriasis, uveitis and other complications in Behcet's disease, and ankylosing spondylitis, are routinely treated with TNF inhibitors, which are also called biologics. In these autoimmune disorders, TNF inhibitors suppress the activity of B-lymphocytes related to inflammation. Persistent, chronic inflammation causes a number of complications including amyloidsosis. In amyloidosis, excess deposits of amyloid protein infiltrate and damage various organs. In Alzheimer's disease, amyloid deposits are found in the brain.

TNF is a critical component of the brain's immune system network. Normally, TNF works to regulate the transmission of neural impulses. It's suspected that in Alzheimer's disease, increased levels of TNF interfere with signal regulation. A previous study has demonstrated that excess levels of TNF-alpha are found in the cerebrospinal fluid of patients with Alzheimer's disease. ("Reversal of Alzheimer's symptoms within minutes in human study," *Science Daily*, 2008, www.sciencedaily.com/releases/2008/01/080109091102.htm, accessed Jan 11, 2011)

Tumor necrosis factor (TNF) inhibitor. TNF inhibitors are drugs that block the production of tumor necrosis factor by white blood cells, thereby reducing inflammation. A recent study shows that the incidence of Alzheimer's disease is lower in patients with rheumatoid arthritis who had been treated with TNF inhibitors, particularly TNF-alpha inhibitors. Investigators at Dartmouth University Medical School recently discovered that people with rheumatoid arthritis using infliximab, etanercept and adalimumab

had a 55 percent lower risk of developing Alzheimer's disease. This confirms a prior University of California, Los Angeles, study showing that this class of drugs reversed symptoms of dementia quickly when administered via perispinal injections. ("Anti-TNF therapies for rheumatoid arthritis could reduce Alzheimer's risk," Press Release, American College of Rheumatology, Nov 2010)

Turmeric *see* Curcumin

Ubiquinone *see* Coenzyme-Q-10

Ultrasonography. Ultrasonography is a non-invasive imaging technique based on the principle that body tissues have a property called acoustic impedance. Sound waves entering tissue can be either transmitted through the tissue or reflected. Changes in tissue density caused by changes in density result in different properties of acoustic impedance. Ultrasonography is helpful in measuring changes in brain density.

Vaccines for Alzheimer's disease. Developing a vaccine against amyloid-beta accumulation in the brain, one of the hallmarks of Alzheimer's disease, is considered as important as finding therapeutic interventions. However, with the failure of several clinical vaccine trials, finding a safe, effective vaccine has proven challenging. Although several animal studies suggested efficacy, test subjects experienced dangerous autoimmune inflammation of the brain during human clinical trials. In 2010, researchers at the University of California Irvine published the results of animal studies using a vaccine that targeted a non-human protein similar to beta amyloid but different enough to not cause side effects. The research was presented at Neuroscience 2010, the annual meeting of the Society for Neuroscience and the world's largest source of emerging news about brain science and health. Research on this vaccine is ongoing.

At Stanford University, Dr. Wyss-Coray and his team reported in 2010 that they are investigating the use of antibodies to A-beta, a breakdown product of amyloid beta protein. According to this line of research, the smaller aggregations (oligomers) of A-beta molecules are most toxic to neurons. Antibodies to A-beta have been found in both Alzheimer's patients and normal controls, with lower levels seen in Alzheimer's disease, suggesting that these antibodies offer protection. ("Stanford Alzheimer's research pinpoints antibodies that may prevent disease," *Business Wire*, July 6, 2009, http://www.businesswire.com/news/home/20090706005014/en/Stanford-Alzheimer's-Research-Pinpoints-Antibodies-Prevent-Disease, accessed Mar 2, 2011)

Researchers in Tel Aviv are working on a nasally-delivered vaccine that may offer protection against Alzheimer's disease and stroke. Research suggests that this vaccine could help reduce symptoms in individuals with Alzheimer's disease symptoms. This investigational vaccine works by activating white blood cells known as macrophages, which, in turn, work to clear up beta amyloid plaque. ("An Alzheimer's vaccine in a nasal spray." Feb 28, 2011, Press Release, American Friends Tel Aviv University, http://www.aftau.org/site/News2?page=NewsArticle&id=14055, accessed Mar 19, 2011)

Valproic acid (Valproate). The anticonvulsant medication valproic acid (Depakene, Depakote) is being evaluated in ADCS clinical trials for its ability to reduce agitation and psychosis in Alzheimer's disease patients in the later disease stages. The drug is also being evaluated for its neuroprotective effects. In trials, the drug has been found to help prevent clinical disease progression, including agitation and psychosis, if it is administered to patients in the early stages of Alzheimer's disease. (Hitti, Miranda. "Valproic acid may treat Alzheimer's: Epilepsy drug shows promise when given early enough in tests on mice," Alzheimer's Disease Health Center at WebMD, http://www.webmd.com/alzheimers/news/20081027/valproic-acid-may-treat-alzheimers, accessed Mar 16, 2011)

Val66Met polymorphism. Val66Met is a single nucleotide polymorphism in the brain derived neurotrophic factor (BDNF) gene on chromosome 11 where adenine and guanine alleles vary, resulting in a variation between valine and methionine at codon 66. This polymorphism is being investigated for its role in the development of Alzheimer's disease and in schizophrenia and related psychoses. In one study the difference in subjects with this polymorphism appeared to be associated with different symptoms in males than

in females. The gene variants of this polymorphism were significantly associated with psychotic symptoms in male, but not in female patients with Alzheimer's disease. The results suggests that this polymorphism did not cause susceptibility to Alzheimer's disease but that it might present a risk factor for psychosis in Alzheimer's disease. (Pivac, N., et al. "Brain derived neurotrophic factor Vl66Met polymorphism and psychotic symptoms in Alzheimer's disease," *Progress in Neuro-Psychopharmacology & Biological Psychiatry*, Oct 31, 2010, abstract available at http://www.ncbi.nlm.nih.gov/pubmed/21044653, accessed Mar 1, 2011)

Vascular dementia. Vascular dementia, which was formerly known as multi-infarct dementia, is a term used to describe a wide range of disorders characterized by marked loss of intellectual abilities resulting from some abnormality to blood flow in the brain. Vascular dementia includes all dementia syndromes resulting from failure of the brain to receive adequate oxygen, causing ischemic, anoxic or hypoxic brain damage. Other types of vascular dementia include conditions resulting from stroke, cerebrovascular disease, Binswanger's disease, CADASIL and hypertension. Next to Alzheimer's disease, vascular dementia is the second most common form of dementia in the elderly. Many patients with Alzheimer's disease have been found to have co-existing vascular dementia. High levels of low-density lipoproteins (LDL) are significantly associated with the development of both vascular dementia and stroke.

Other common risk factors for vascular dementia are high blood pressure, heart disease, and diabetes. Because specific areas of the brain control specific functions and any part of the brain can be affected, patients with vascular dementia do not have a consistent pattern or symptoms.

There is no absolute way of differentiating vascular dementia from Alzheimer's disease although protein marker ratios present in cerebrospinal fluid make a diagnosis of Alzheimer's disease more likely. Still, the problem remains that a significant number of patients, particularly elderly patients, have elements of both disorders, making complete differentiation sometimes impossible. However, because infarcts may affect any part of the brain, symptoms do not follow a pattern as they do in Alzheimer's disease. On average, patients with vascular dementia live several years less than Alzheimer's disease patients due to their propensity for heart attacks and severe strokes.

In vascular dementia, the patient characteristically shows a stepwise deterioration in neurologic function with a background of risk factors for cerebrovascular disease, particularly hypertension. Multi-infarct dementia is usually accompanied by other focal signs in addition to mental decline. Minor focal abnormalities might be found in the neurologic examination and imaging procedures, particularly MRI, may show signs of numerous small infarcts.

The history in Alzheimer's disease is generally that of a gradual progressive dementia with a normal general neurologic examination and an imaging procedure that shows evidence of cerebral atrophy. The medical history is generally negative.

Ventricles of the brain. The brain's ventricles or cavities include the lateral ventricles, the third ventricle, and the fourth ventricle.

Veterans Affairs. The Department of Veterans Affairs provides healthcare benefits to military service veterans and their families.

Vinpocetine. Vinpocetine is a derivative of the periwinkle plant approved in Europe and Japan to correct cognitive impairment inflicted by degenerative brain disease, including Alzheimer's disease. Vinpocetine is available as a dietary supplement in the United States. Vinpocetine is reported to offer benefits to individuals with cognitive problems who have elevated homocysteine levels, a history of heart disease, or vascular dementia. Vinpocetine helps improve blood flow, which helps nourish and oxygenate brain cells. It is contraindicated in patients using the blood thinner Coumadin. In his practice, the neurologist David Perlmutter, M.D., uses vinpocetine for vascular dementia and often sees vast improvement quickly. (Perlmutter, David. *The Better Brain Book*. New York: Riverhead, 2004: 119–121)

Vitamin B deficiency. Specific vitamin B deficiencies, including B1 (thiamine), B3 (niacin in the form of niacinamide), B6 (pyridoxine), folic acid, and B12 (cobalamin), are associated with increased inflammation, which is reflected in elevated homocysteine and C-reactive protein levels. This, in turn, increases risk for developing Alzheimer's disease. Many medications, including estrogens, aspirin, trimethoprim, antacids, metformin, antihypertensives, anticonvulsants, and drugs used for asthma, can deplete vitamin B and increase the risk for Alzheimer's disease. Recommendations are for 50 mg of B1, B3, and 800 mcg folic acid, and 1000 mcg of vitamin B12. (Perlmutter, David. *The Better Brain Book*. New York: Riverhead, 2004: 47–54)

Vitamin B12 deficiency. Deficiencies of vitamin B12 (cobalamin) can cause a dementia that looks exactly like Alzheimer's disease. Other symptoms of B12 deficiency include memory loss, confusion, delusion, fatigue, loss of balance, decreased reflexes, numbing and tingling in the arms and legs, tinnitus and noise-induced hearing loss. Alzheimer's disease itself is characterized by brain deficiencies of both vitamin B12 and the methylating factor, S-adenosylmethionine (SAMe). Vitamin B12 deficiency in patients with Alzheimer's disease has been reported to cause two distinct personality changes — irritability and disturbed behavior.

In the body, vitamin B12 is methylated (combined with methyl groups) to form methylcobalamin. Methylcobalamin protects neurons from the damaging effects of glutamate, nitric oxide, low blood sugar and low oxygen. Glutamate and nitric oxide toxicity are features of both Alzheimer's and Parkinson's diseases. The proper synthesis of myelin is also dependent on adequate stores of vitamin B12. Vitamin B12 also plays an important role in reducing homocysteine levels in the body. High levels of homocysteine are associated with heart disease, cancer, DNA damage, and memory impairment.

Although the body's daily requirements for vitamin B12 are minimal (6 mcg), blood levels are diminished by H. Pylori infections, many drugs, including estrogens and blood pressure medications, over-cooking meat, and other factors. However, many people older than age 60 cannot extract vitamin B12 from food because their stomachs no longer secrete adequate gastric acid, making supplements often necessary. (Feinstein, Alice. *Prevention's Healing with Vitamins.* Emmaus, PA: Rodale Press, 1996; Mitchell, Terri. "Vitamin B12: Surprising New Findings." *Life Extension*; Dec 2000 6 (12): 21–28)

Vitamin D. Vitamin D has been studied for its role in cognitive disturbances, but no conclusions have been made. Because vitamin D receptors are present in both fetal and adult brains, indicating that vitamin D plays a role in normal brain function, a number of researchers have proposed that vitamin D may be involved in neuroprotection, control of proinflammatory cytokine-induced cognitive dysfunction and synthesis of calcium-binding proteins as well as the neurotransmitter acetylcholine. However, the observational studies conducted in humans are still inconclusive, given the various tests of the cognitive functions that have been used, the performance of the studies either in patients or in healthy subjects, and different designs and/or confounding factors. It is recommended that the role of the vitamin D receptor in the pathophysiology of cognitive decline, incidence of Alzheimer's disease or vascular dementia and/or cognitive decline with respect to previous plasma 25OHD concentration, and the effect on cognition of vitamin D supplementation should be explored in further studies. The vitamin D council reports that in a cross-sectional study, vitamin-D-sufficient Alzheimer patients had significantly higher Mini-Mental State Examination scores as compared to vitamin-D-insufficient ones, indicating a relationship between vitamin D status and cognition in patients. (Vitamin D research studies from the Vitamin D Council, http://www.vitamindcouncil.org/research.shtml, accessed Feb 4, 2011)

Vitamin E therapy. A potent antioxidant, vitamin E, at doses as low as 100 nM, has been found to protect neurons in the brain against free radical damage associated with amyloid beta protein, hydrogen peroxide and the excitatory amino acid glutamate. Vitamin E prevents the oxidative damage induced by beta-amyloid in cell culture and delays memory deficits in animal models. Because of its antioxidant properties, vitamin E is reported to reduce the cell damage normally associated with aging.

Vitamin E also has been shown to induce the activation of the redox-sensitive transcription factor NF-kappa B, which is involved in control of nerve cell survival. In ADCS clinical trials, vitamin E therapy is being evaluated to see if it can help prevent progression to Alzheimer's disease in patients with mild cognitive impairment. A recent report showed that both high doses of vitamin E (2,000 I.U. daily) and the drug selegiline slowed mental deterioration by 7 months in patients ongoing clinical trials.

A placebo-controlled clinical trial of vitamin E in patients with moderately advanced Alzheimer's disease was conducted by the Alzheimer's Disease Cooperative Study. Subjects in the vitamin E group were treated with 2000 IU (1342 alpha-tocopherol equivalents) of vitamin E daily. The results indicated that vitamin E may slow functional deterioration leading to nursing home placement. A new clinical trial is planned that will examine whether vitamin E can delay or prevent a clinical diagnosis of Alzheimer's disease in elderly patients with mild cognitive impairment.

In a study of 341 Alzheimer's disease patients using 2000 IU of vitamin E in conjunction with 10 mg of selegeline, over a two-year period, progression of the disease was reduced in subjects using either of these compounds as compared to groups receiving placebos or both compounds. (Perlmutter, David. *The Better Brain Book.* New York: Riverhead, 2004: 113–114, 178, 187–8)

Vitamins. Vitamins are nutrient substances essential for many metabolic functions. Deficiencies of vitamin and mineral nutrients are known to cause numerous disorders. As an example, deficiencies of B vitamins have long been associated with neurological disorders.

According to a number of researchers, a diet rich in antioxidant vitamins can help prevent the development of Alzheimer's disease. Studies conducted by researchers at the National Institute on Aging report that blueberries, green tea and other foods containing antioxidant phytochemicals may protect the body against damage from oxidative stress. Oxidative stress is one of the biological processes implicated in aging, inflammation and the development of neurodegenerative diseases. In one study, animals receiving blueberry and strawberry extracts scored the highest in tests of balance and coordination. The animals also showed signs of the presence of vitamin E, a key antioxidant, in their brains.

Two large clinical trials involving 600 people over 4 years suggest that vitamins C and E may prevent the onset of Alzheimer's disease, improve cognitive skills in healthy individuals and decrease the symptoms of dementia. A total of 91 people in the study developed Alzheimer's disease, but none of the subjects who took vitamins C and E supplements developed dementia.

Preliminary studies suggest that patients with Alzheimer's disease may have significantly lower levels of vitamin A, its precursor beta-carotene, folic acid and vitamin B12 than normal individuals. Numerous studies in the last decade have shown that vitamins can improve cognition. In *The Better Brain Book* (Riverhead, 2004), the neurologist David Perlmutter, M.D., has excellent information on the use of vitamins for dementia. A recent study conducted by researchers at the University of Oxford shows that vitamin B supplements can reduce brain shrinkage, a phenomenon that occurs with normal aging that is accelerated in Alzheimer's disease.

The researchers used an advanced magnetic resonance imaging (MRI) technique to study brain shrinkage in 168 volunteers over the age of 70 with diagnosed mild cognitive impairment (MCI). Over a period of two years, half were given a daily tablet containing high doses of the B vitamins folic acid, B6 and B12. The rest received a "dummy" placebo pill with no active ingredients. At the end of the trial the effects of the vitamin treatment were found to be dramatic, and most pronounced in participants who started out with the highest rates of brain shrinkage. On average, taking B vitamins slowed the rate of brain atrophy by 30 percent, and in many cases reductions as high as 53 percent were seen. (Alleyne, Richard. "Vitamin B is revolutionary new weapon against Alzheimer's disease," *The Telegraph (UK) Health News*, Sept 9. 2010, http://www.telegraph.co.uk/health/healthnews/7989889/Vitamin-B-is-revolutionary-new-weapon-against-Alzheimers-Disease.html, accessed Jan 3, 2011). *See also* Niacinamide

Wandering. Wandering is a common symptom in Alzheimer's disease. Many patients set out on a mission, rushing from their homes in the middle of the night, although they are unable to say where they are going. Dressed inappropriately for the elements, these patients are at risk for injury. Most medical experts agree that wandering, like other behaviors associated with Alzheimer's disease, has a purpose, such as expressing an urgent need such as loneliness, restlessness or boredom. In addition, certain stimuli, such as the presence of coats or boots or the picture of someone who has passed away, act as triggers.

While haloperidol has traditionally been used to treat wandering, haloperidol has very severe side effects that impair motor control and coordination. *See also* Safe Return Program

Warning signs. The Alzheimer's Association has developed a list of warning signs, including several common symptoms of Alzheimer's disease. Individuals who exhibit several of these symptoms should see a physician for further evaluation.

1. Memory loss that affects job skills
2. Difficulty performing familiar tasks
3. Problems with language
4. Disorientation to time and place (getting lost)
5. Poor or decreased judgment
6. Problems with abstract thinking
7. Misplacing things
8. Changes in mood or behavior
9. Changes in personality
10. Loss of initiative

Wechsler Adult Intelligence Scale (WAIS). The Wechsler Adult Intelligence Scale is a test used to measure various parameters of intelligence in adults. In Alzheimer's patients, the WAIS test initially shows memory impairment, which persists over a plateau phase during which language and cognitive functions typically do not change for the first 9–35 months after diagnosis.

Wechsler Memory Scale. The Wechsler Memory Scale is an evaluation tool used to measure verbal and visual recent memory.

Wellness recommendations. Individuals with Alzheimer's disease benefit from wellness recommendations, including exercise, a nutrient rich diet, social activity, and maintaining a familiar routine and environment. Regular walking has been reported to improve cognitive function. Many of the risk factors for heart disease such as high cholesterol are also risk factors for Alzheimer's disease. Therefore, according to some researchers, reducing risk factors for heart disease may also reduce the risk of Alzheimer's disease. For instance, the anti-inflammatory drug aspirin, which also has anticoagulant properties, appears to lower the risk of both heart disease and Alzheimer's disease. (Stewart, W., et al." Risk of Alzheimer's disease and Duration of NSAID Use." *Neurology*, March, 1997; 48(3): 626–632)

Wernicke's aphasia. Individuals who sustain damage to Wernicke's area develop a condition known as Wernicke's aphasia, which is characterized by an inability to comprehend language. Language can be produced but not understood. Wernicke's aphasia is also known as fluent, sensory, or receptive aphasia.

Wernicke's area. Wernicke's area refers to the inferior parietal regions of the brain, specifically the posterior part of the superior temporal gyrus of the brain that controls the formulation of language. Damage to Wernicke's area causes a type of aphasia in which its victims have difficulty comprehending whether their own speech makes sense. Wernicke's aphasics can produce but not understand language because this area of the brain contains the mechanisms for the formulation of language. Wernicke's area, like Broca's area, is a region in which stimulation on the dominant side causes the patient to cease speaking, make linguistic errors or be unable to find appropriate words.

Wernicke's encephalopathy. Wernicke's encephalopathy is a condition caused by inflammation of Wernicke's area of the brain causing aphasia.

White matter. The white matter of the central nervous system consists of nerve fibers and blood vessels embedded in neuroglia. In the spinal cord, white matter surrounds the gray matter, and its white color is associated with the high proportion of myelinated nerve fibers and axons. Subdivisions of white matter go by a variety of names including fasciculus, funiculus, lemniscus

and peduncle. In the spinal cord, the white matter contains long descending tracts leading from the brainstem and cerebrum and long ascending tracts that lead to the brainstem, cerebellum, and cerebrum.

Wisconsin Card Sort Test. The Wisconsin Card Sort Test is a psychological test used to measure attention and executive function.

Wise, Brad, M.D. Dr. Brad Wise is the chief of the Neurobiology Branch of the National Institutes on Aging and also the program director of Fundamental Neuroscience, Neurodegeneration, Neuroplasticity, Bioenergetics, and Glia in Bethesda, Maryland.

World Alzheimer's Day. World Alzheimer's day is celebrated worldwide on September 21 each year. This day is set aside to promote awareness of Alzheimer's disease.

Writing studies. Writing studies are part of the Nun Study, one of the first long-term studies of a well controlled population sponsored by the National Institute of Aging. In the writing studies, researchers reviewed the autobiographical writing of nuns written at an average age of 22. The autobiographies were examined for linguistic ability as a measure of cognitive function in early life. One component of linguistic ability, idea density, defined as the average number of ideas for each 10 written words, is associated with educational level, vocabulary, and general knowledge. A second measure, grammatical complexity, is linked with worked memory, test performance and writing skills. Approximately 58 years after these writings, the nuns were tested for cognitive ability.

Study results indicated that low idea density in early life was strongly linked with low cognitive test scores and later development of Alzheimer's disease. The nuns with low idea density scores were 30 times more likely to do poorly on a the MMSE exam, a standard measure of cognitive function when compared to those nuns with more complex writing ability. At autopsy, 90 percent of the nuns with low writing scores in early life were found to have neurofibrillary tangles in their brain tissue. ("Landmark Study Links Cognitive Ability of Youth With Alzheimer's Disease in Later Life." Press Release of

U.S. Department of Health and Human Services, Feb 20, 1996)

Xanomeline. Xanomeline, administered via a skin patch, is a selective M1 muscarinic receptor agonist. Xanomeline was evaluated as a therapeutic agent for Alzheimer's disease but adverse effects led to a discontinuation of clinical trials.

Xenobiotics. Xenobiotics are environmental agents capable of causing biologic effects. Significant abnormalities in the metabolism of xenobiotics have been demonstrated in patients with Alzheimer's disease. Specifically, the detoxification process is impaired and involves decreased activity of phase II sulfation by the liver. Research, which was conducted at the University of Birmingham, showed that individuals with Alzheimer's disease have reduced sulfoxidation of the probe drug *S*-carboxymethyl-l-cysteine; in addition, they form less of the sulfate conjugate of acetaminophen as well as lower activity of the enzyme thiolmethyltransferase. In contrast, the capacity to oxidize debrisoquin and to acetylate sulfamethazine was normal. These findings suggest that a major risk factor for the development of AD is a skewed capacity for xenobiotic metabolism especially of compounds containing sulfur.

Zinc. Zinc is a trace mineral normally found in the body. Ashley Bush, a researcher at Harvard Medical School, first noticed that the addition of zinc to amyloid protein in vitro (in a test tube) caused strands of amyloid protein to clump together. Chelating, a process that removes minerals, has been found to reverse the process in studies of postmortem brain tissue. Subsequent studies show that zinc tends to accumulate in areas of the brain most prone to the damage typically seen in Alzheimer's disease. Zinc is suspected of aggregating beta amyloid deposits and also of pulling copper into the deposits. Together, the metals generate free radicals that are suspected of causing oxidative damage to nearby tissue. Current research is being done to develop chelating agents that can effectively remove zinc and copper deposits.

Several reports indicate that zinc levels that are abnormal, either too high or too low, seem to increase production of amyloid beta protein. It has also been reported that altered zinc metabolism and a subsequent imbalance in copper levels contribute to beta amyloid deposits. In the Nun Study, high levels of serum copper were found to correlate with the development of Alzheimer's disease.

Zyprexa *see* Olanzapine

Long Term and Day Care Treatment Centers, by State

The following is a list of nursing homes in the United States that accommodate individuals with Alzheimer's disease. It is important to visit nursing home facilities before choosing one, and it is essential to compare the quality scores of several facilities using the tools available on the Medicare website at http://www.medicare.gov/NHCompare/Include/DataSection/Questions/ ProximitySearch.asp as well as other nursing home evaluation agencies listed in Resources. Also check the encyclopedia section of this book under **Nursing home options**

Abbreviations used in this section of the book:

HRF— Health-Related Facility
ICF— Intermediate Care Facility
ICF/MR— Intermediate Care Facility for Mentally Retarded
HIS— Integrated Health Services

MR— Mentally Retarded
RCF— Residential Care Facility
SCF— Skilled Care Facility
SNF— Skilled Nursing Facility

ALABAMA

Alexander City

Bill Nichols State Veterans Home
1784 Elkahatchee Rd., Alexander City, AL 35010, (256) 329-0868; Fax: (256) 329-1101; Facility Type: Skilled care; Alzheimer's; Certified Beds: 120; Certified: Veterans, Owner: Government/State Local License: Current state

Ashville

Healthcare Inc.
PO Box 130, Ashville, AL 35953, (205) 594-5148; Facility Type: Skilled care; ICF; ICF/MR; Alzheimer's; Certified Beds: 53; Certified: Medicaid; Medicare Owner: Private; License: Current state

Bessemer

Beverly Healthcare Center
820 Golf Course Rd., Bessemer, AL 35023, (205)

425-5241; Facility Type: Skilled care; ICF; ICF/MR; Alzheimer's; Certified Beds: 180; Certified: Medicaid; Medicare; Veterans; Owner: Beverly Enterprises Inc.; License: Current state; this facility is affiliated with Beverly Healthcare Meadowood, an independent living facility that also accepts Alzheimer's patients

Oak Trace Care and Rehabilitation Center
325 Selma Rd., Bessemer, AL 35020, (205) 428-9383; Facility Type: Skilled care; ICF; Alzheimer's; Certified Beds: 79; Certified: Medicaid; Medicare; Owner: Private; License: Current state

Birmingham

Estes Nursing Home–Northway
1424 N 25th St., Birmingham, AL 35234; Facility Type: Skilled care; Alzheimer's; Certified Beds: 113; Certified: Medicaid; Medicare; Owner: Northport Health Services Inc.; License: n/a

Fairview Health and Rehabilitation Center
1028 Bessemer Rd., Birmingham, AL 35228, (205) 923-1777; Facility Type: Skilled care; ICF; Alz-

heimer's; Certified Beds: 165; Certified: Medicaid; Medicare; Veterans; Owner: Mariner Post Acute Network; License: Current state

Lakeview Nursing Home Inc.
8017 2nd Ave. S, Birmingham, AL 35206, (205) 836-4231; Facility Type: Skilled care; Alzheimer's; Certified Beds: 54; Certified: Medicare; Owner: Nonprofit corp.; License: Current state

Mountainview Health Care Center
507 44th Street Southwest, PO Box 28665, Birmingham, AL 35228, (205) 428-3292; Facility Type: Skilled care; Alzheimer's; Certified Beds: 86; Certified: Medicaid; Medicare; Owner: Private; License: Current state

Saint Martins in the Pines, Irondale
4941 Montevallo Rd., Birmingham, AL 35210, (205) 956-1831; Facility Type: Skilled care; Alzheimer's; Certified Beds: 138; Alzheimer's 18; Domiciliary 106; Certified: Medicaid; Medicare; Owner: Nonprofit/Religious organization; License: Current state; this facility, founded by Episcopalian ministry, is being extensively renovated in 2011 and will include residential cottages

Centre

Cherokee County Nursing Home
877 Cedar Bluff Rd., Centre, AL 35960, (256) 927-5778; Facility Type: Skilled care; ICF; ICF/MR; Alzheimer's; Certified Beds: 153; Certified: Medicaid; Medicare; Owner: Government/State/Local; License: Current state

Cherokee Village Assisted Living
201 Hospital Ave., Centre, AL 35960, (256) 927-4307; specialty care; accepts patients with early onset Alzheimer's disease; Certified Beds: 36, 16 residential; Owner: Healthcare Authority

Cullman

Cullman Health Care Center
1607 Main Ave. NE, Cullman, AL 35056, (256) 734-8745; Facility Type: Skilled care; Alzheimer's; Certified Beds: 95; Certified: Medicaid; Medicare; Owner: USA Healthcare; License: n/a

Daphne

Mercy Medical
PO Box 1090, Daphne, AL 36526, (334) 626-2694; Facility Type: Skilled care; Alzheimer's; Certified Beds: 90; Alzheimer's 16; Certified: Medicare; Veterans; Owner: Nonprofit/Religious Organization; License: Current state

Elmore

SunBridge Care & Rehabilitation for Elmore
Mt Hebron Rd., Box 7, Elmore, AL 36025, (334) 567-8484; Facility Type: Skilled care; ICF/MR; Alzheimer's; Certified Beds: 124; Certified: Medicaid; Medicare; Veterans; Owner: Sun Healthcare Group, Inc.; License: Current state

Fairhope

Beverly Healthcare
108 S Church St., Fairhope, AL 36523, (334) 928-2153; Facility Type: Skilled care; Alzheimer's; Certified Beds: 131; Certified: Medicaid; Medicare; Veterans; Owner: Beverly Enterprises, Inc.; License: Current state

Florence

Florence Comprehensive Care Center
2107 Cloyd Blvd., Florence, AL 35630, (256) 766-5771; Facility Type: Skilled care; Alzheimer's; Certified Beds: 147; Certified: Medicaid; Medicare; Owner: Beverly Enterprises Inc.; License: Current state

Glenwood Healthcare Inc.
211 Ana Dr., Florence, AL 35630, (256) 766-8963; Facility Type: Skilled care; Alzheimer's; Certified Beds: 125; Certified: Medicaid; Medicare; Owner: Private

Guin

Southern Care, LLC
251 Sunset Pl., Guin, AL 35563, (205) 468-3331; Facility Type: Skilled care; ICF; Alzheimer's; Certified Beds: 71; Certified: Medicaid; Medicare; Owner: Private; License: Current state

Guntersville

Barfield Health Care
22444 Hwy 431, Guntersville, AL 35976, (256) 582-3112; Facility Type: Skilled care; ICF; Alzheimer's; Certified Beds: 113; Certified: Medicaid; Medicare; Owner: Private; License: Current state

Marshall Manor Nursing Home
3120 North St., Guntersville, AL 35976, (256) 582-6561; Facility Type: Skilled care; Alzheimer's; Assisted Living: Certified Beds: 91; Certified: Medicaid; Medicare; Owner: Private; License: Current state

Hanceville

Hanceville Nursing and Rehabilitation Center
420 Main St NE, Hanceville, AL 35077, (256) 352-6481; Facility Type: Skilled care; Alzheimer's; Certified Beds: 208; Certified: Medicaid, Medicare; Owner: Private; License: Current state

Hartford

Hartford Healthcare
PO Box 190, 217 Toro Rd., Hartford, AL 36344, (334) 588-3842; Facility Type: Skilled care; Alzheimer's; Certified Beds: 86; Certified: Medicaid, Medicare; Owner: Diversicare Management Services Inc.; License: n/a

Huntsville

Big Springs Specialty Care Center
500 St Clair Ave. SW, Huntsville, AL 35801, (256) 539-5111; Facility Type: Skilled care; ICF; ICF/MR; Alzheimer's; Certified Beds: 145; Certified: Medicaid; Medicare; Owner: Vencor Inc.; License: Current state

Whitesburg Gardens Healthcare
105 Teakwood Dr., Huntsville, AL 35811, (256) 851-5000; Facility Type: Skilled care; ICF; ICF/MR; Alzheimer's; Certified Beds: 159; ICF; Certified: Medicaid; Medicare; Veterans; Owner: Vencor, Inc.; License: Current state

Windsor House
4411 McAllister Dr., Huntsville, AL 35805, (256) 837-8585; Facility Type: Skilled care; ICF; Alzheimer's; Certified Beds: 117; ICF; ACLF; Certified: Medicaid; Medicare; Owner: Diversicare Management Services Inc.; License: Current state

Jasper

Ridgeview Health Care Center
907 11th St. NE, Jasper, AL 35501, (205) 221-9111; Facility Type: Skilled care; Alzheimer's; Certified Beds: 122; Certified: Medicaid; Medicare; Owner: Proprietary/Public corp.; License: Current state

Shadecrest Health Care Center
331 West 25th Street, Jasper, AL 35502, (205) 384-9086; Facility Type: Skilled care; Alzheimer's; Certified Beds: 107; Certified: Medicaid; Medicare; Owner: Private; License: Current State

Killen

Lauderdale Christian Nursing Home
2019 County Road 394, Killen, AL 35645, (256) 757-2103; Facility Type: Skilled care; ICF; Alzheimer's; Certified Beds: 58; Certified: Medicaid; Medicare; Owner: Nonprofit corp; License: Current state

Luverne

Luverne Nursing Facility
142 W 3rd St., Luverne, AL 36049, (334) 335-6528; Facility Type: Skilled care; ICF; ICF/MR; Alzheimer's; Certified Beds: 151; Certified: Medicaid;

Medicare; Owner: Northport Health Services Inc.; License: n/a

Marion

Perry County Nursing Home
PO Box 149, Marion, AL 36756, (334) 683-9696; Facility Type: Skilled care; ICF; ICF/MR; Alzheimer's; Certified Beds: 61; Certified: Medicaid; Medicare; Owner: Vaughan Healthcare; License: Current state

Southland Nursing Home
500 Shivers Terrace, Marion, AL 36756, (334) 683-6141; Facility Type: Skilled care; Alzheimer's; ICF; Independent and Assisted Living; Certified Beds: 91; Certified: Medicaid; Medicare; License: Current state; Rated in 2010 as one of the Best Nursing Homes by *U.S. News*

Mobile

Cogburn Health and Rehabilitation, Inc.
148 Tuscaloosa St., Mobile, AL 36607, (251) 471-5431; Facility Type: Skilled care; Alzheimer's; Certified Beds: 164; Certified: Medicaid; Medicare; Owner: Private; License: Current state

Crowne Health Care of Mobile
954 Navco Rd., Mobile, AL 36605, (251) 473-8684; Facility Type: Skilled care; Alzheimer's (secured unit and secured courtyard); Certified Beds: 174; Certified: Medicaid; Medicare; Veterans; Owner: Crowne Investments; License: Current state

Lynwood Nursing Home
4164 Halls Mill Rd., Mobile, AL 36693, (334) 661-5404; Facility Type: Skilled care; ICF; ICF/MR; Alzheimer's; Certified Beds: 127; Certified: Medicaid; Medicare; Owner: Diversicare Management Services; License: Current state

Mobile Nursing and Rehabilitation Center
7020 Bruns Dr., Mobile, AL 36695, (334) 639-1588; Facility Type: Skilled care; Alzheimer's; Certified Beds: 120; Certified: Medicaid; Medicare; Veterans; Owner: Beverly Enterprises Inc.; License: Current state

Twin Oaks Nursing Home
857 Crawford Ln., Mobile, AL 36617, (334) 476-3420; Facility Type: Skilled care; ICF; ICF/MR; Alzheimer's; Certified Beds: 131; Certified: Medicaid; Medicare; Owner: Ball Healthcare; License: Current state

Montgomery

Capitol Hill Healthcare Center
520 S Hull St., Montgomery, AL 36104, (334) 834-2920; Facility Type: Skilled care; Alzheimer's; Cer-

tified Beds: 284; Certified: Medicaid; Medicare; Owner: Capitol Hill Healthcare & Rehabilitation Center; License: Current state

Crowne Health Care of Montgomery

1837 Upper Wetumpka Rd., Montgomery, AL 36107, (334) 264-8416; Facility Type: Skilled care; ICF; ICF/MR; Alzheimer's; Certified Beds: 185; Certified: Medicaid; Medicare; Veterans; Owner: Crowne Investments Inc.; License: Current state

Golden LivingCenter–Montgomery

2020 North Country Club Dr., Montgomery, AL 36106, (334) 263-1643; Facility Type: Skilled care; Alzheimer's; Certified Beds: 138; Certified: Medicaid; Medicare; Owner: Private: License: Current state

Hillview Terrace

100 Perry Hill Rd., Montgomery, AL 36109, (334) 272-0171; Facility Type: Skilled care; Alzheimer's; ICF; Assisted and Independent Living; Certified Beds: 143; Certified: Medicaid; Medicare; Owner: Private; License: Current state

Muscle Shoals

Cypress Cove Care and Rehabilitation Center

200 Alabama Ave., Muscle Shoals, AL 35661, (256) 381-4330; Facility Type: Skilled care; ICF; Alzheimer's; Certified Beds: 90; Certified: Medicaid; Medicare; Owner: Private; License: Current state

Northport

Forest Manor, Inc.

2215 32nd St., Northport, AL 35476, (205) 339-5400; Facility Type; Skilled care; Alzheimer's; Certified Beds: 182; Certified: Medicaid; Medicare; Owner: Private; License: Current state

Glen Haven Health and Rehabilitation, LLC

2201 32nd St., Northport, AL 35476, (205) 339-5700; Facility Type: Skilled care; ICF; ICF/MR; Alzheimer's; Certified Beds: 200; Domiciliary care; Certified: Medicaid; Medicare; Owner: Northport Health Services Inc.; License: Current state

Hunter Creek Health and Rehabilitation

600 34th St., Northport, AL 35473, (205) 339-5900; Facility Type: Skilled care; ICF/MR; Alzheimer's; Certified Beds: 78; Certified: Medicaid; Medicare; Veterans; Owner: Northport Health Services Inc.; License: Current state

Park Manor Health and Rehabilitation Center, LLC

2201 McFarland Blvd. East, Northport, AL 35476, (205) 339-5300; Facility Type: Skilled care; Alzheimer's; Certified Beds: 152; Certified: Medicaid; Medicare; Owner: Private; License: Current state

Opelika

Arbor Springs Health and Rehab Center, LTD

1/2 Pepperell Pkwy., Opelika, AL 36801, (334) 749-1471; Facility Type: Skilled care; ICF; Alzheimer's; Certified Beds: 224; Alzheimer's; SNF/ICF; Certified: Medicaid; Medicare; Owner: Proprietary/Public Corp.; License: Current state

Opp

Opp Health and Rehabilitation

115 Paulk Ave., Box 730, Opp, AL 35467, (334) 493-4558; Facility Type: Skilled care; Alzheimer's; Certified Beds: 197; Certified: Medicaid; Medicare; Owner: Northport Health Services Inc.; License: Current state

Piedmont

Piedmont Health Care Center

30 Roundtree Dr., Piedmont, AL 36272, (256) 447-8258; Facility Type: Skilled care; ICF; ICF/MR; Alzheimer's; Certified Beds: 91; Certified: Medicaid; Medicare; Owner: Government/State/Local; License: Current state

Selma

Park Place Nursing and Rehabilitation Center, LLC

100 Park Place, Selma, AL 36701, (334) 872-3471; Facility Type: Skilled care; Alzheimer's; Certified Beds: 103; Certified: Medicaid; Medicare; Owner: private: License: Current state

Warren Manor Health & Rehabilitation Center

11 Bell Rd., Selma, AL 36701, (334) 874-7425; Facility Type: Skilled care; ICF; ICF/MR; Alzheimer's; Certified Beds: 176; Certified: Medicaid; Medicare; Owner: Mariner Post Acute Network; License: Current state

Tuscumbia

Cottage of the Shoals Care & Rehabilitation Center

500 John Aldridge Dr., Tuscumbia, AL 35674, (256) 383-4541; Facility Type: Skilled care; ICF; ICF/MR; Alzheimer's; Certified Beds: 103; Certified: Medicaid; Medicare; Owner: Mariner Post Acute Network; License: Current state

Keller Landing Care and Rehabilitation Center

813 Keller Ln., Tuscumbia AL 35674, (256) 383-1535; Facility Type: Skilled care; ICF; ICF/MR; Alzheimer's; Certified Beds: 109; Certified: Medicaid; Medicare; Owner: Mariner Post Acute Network; License: Current state

Tuskegee

Magnolia Haven Nursing Home
603 Wright St., Tuskegee, AL 36083, (334) 727-4960; Facility Type: Skilled care; ICF; ICF/MR; Alzheimer's; Certified Beds: 77; Certified: Medicaid; Medicare; Veterans; Owner: Ball Healthcare; License: Current state

Salem Nursing and Rehabilitation Center of Tuskegee
PO Drawer 830599, Tuskegee, AL 36083, (334) 727-1945; Facility Type: Skilled care; ICF; ICF/MR; Alzheimer's; Certified Beds: 125; Certified: Medicaid; Medicare; Veterans; Owner: Ball Healthcare; License: Current state

ALASKA

Anchorage

Prestige Care & Rehab Center of Anchorage
9100 Centennial Dr., Anchorage, AK 99504, (907) 333-8100; Facility Type: Skilled care; Alzheimer's; Certified Beds: 90; Certified: Medicaid; Medicare; Owner: Private, For-Profit; License: Current state

Providence Extended Care Center
4900 Eagle St., Anchorage, AK 99503, (907) 562-2281; Facility Type: Skilled care; Alzheimer's; Certified Beds: 190; Certified: Medicaid; Medicare; Owner: Nonprofit, Religious; License: Current state

Fairbanks

Denali Center
1510 19th Ave., Fairbanks, AK 99701, (907) 458-5100; Facility Type: Skilled care; Alzheimer's; Certified Beds: 90; Certified: Medicaid; Medicare; Owner: Nonprofit; License: Current state; Voted by *U.S. News* in 2010 as one of the best nursing homes

Palmer

Palmer Pioneers' Home
250 E Fireweed, Palmer, AK 99645, (907) 745-4242; Facility Type: Skilled care; Alzheimer's; Certified Beds: 30; Alzheimer's 16; Certified: n/a; Owner: State/Local Government; License: Current state

Petersburg

Petersburg Medical Center Long Term Care
PO Box 589, Petersburg, AK 99833, (907) 772-4291; Facility Type: Skilled care; ICF; Alzheimer's; Certified Beds: Skilled care 20; Certified: Medicaid; Medicare; Veterans; Owner: Government/State/Local; License: Current state

ARIZONA

Apache Junction

Apache Junction Health Center
2012 West Southern Ave., Apache Junction, AZ 85120, (480) 983-0700; Facility Type: Skilled care; Alzheimer's; Adult Day Care; Certified Beds: 190; Certified: Medicaid; Medicare; Owner: Private, For-Profit; License: Current state

Avondale

Estrella Care and Rehabilitation Center
350 E. La Canada, Avondale, AZ 85323, (623) 932-2282; Facility Type: Skilled care; Alzheimer's; Assisted Living; Certified Beds: 161; Certified: Medicaid; Medicare; Owner: Private, For-Profit; License: Current state

Bullhead City

The Legacy Rehab & Care Center
2812 Silver Creek Rd., Bullhead City, AZ 86442, (928) 763-1404; Facility Type: Skilled care; Alzheimer's; Certified Beds: 120; Certified: Medicaid; Medicare; Owner: Private, For-Profit; License: Current state

The River Gardens Rehab & Care Center
2150 Silver Creek Rd., Bullhead City, AZ 86442, (928) 763-8700; Facility Type: Skilled care; Alzheimer's; Assisted Living; Certified Beds: 90; Certified: Medicaid; Medicare; Owner: Private, For-Profit; License: Current state

Camp Verde

Verde Vista Care and Rehab, Inc.
86 W. Salt Mine Rd., Camp Verde, AZ 86322, (928)

567-5253; Facility Type: Skilled care; Alzheimer's; Assisted Living; Respite care, Hospice; Certified Beds: 118; Certified: Medicaid; Medicare; Owner: Private, For-Profit; License: Current state

Chandler

Archstone Care Center
1980 W. Pecos Rd., Chandler, AZ 85224, (480) 821-1268; Facility Type: Skilled care; Alzheimer's; Certified Beds: 120; Certified: Medicaid; Medicare; Owner: Private, For-Profit; License: Current state

Desert Cove Nursing Center
1750 W. Frye Rd., Chandler, AZ 85224, (480) 899-0641; Facility Type: Skilled care; Alzheimer's; Certified Beds: 90; Certified: Medicaid; Medicare; Owner: Private, For-Profit; License: Current state

Cottonwood

Red Rock Care and Rehab, Inc.
197 S. Willard St., Cottonwood, AZ 86326, (928) 634-5548; Facility Type: Skilled care; Alzheimer's; Certified Beds: 80; Certified: Medicaid; Medicare; Owner: Private, For-Profit; License: Current state

Flagstaff

Ponderosa Pines Care and Rehab, Inc.
800 W. University Ave., Flagstaff, AZ 86001, (928) 779-6931; Facility Type: Skilled care; Alzheimer's; Certified Beds: 80; Certified: Medicaid; Medicare; Owner: Private, For-Profit; License: Current state

Fountain Hills

Fountain View Village
16455 East Avenue of the Fountains, Fountain Hills, AZ 85268, (480) 836-4800; Facility Type: Skilled care; Alzheimer's; Certified Beds: 64; Certified: Medicaid; Medicare; Owner: Private, For-Profit; License: Current state

Globe

Copper Mountain Inn
1100 Monroe St., Globe, AZ 85501, (928) 425-5721; Facility Type: Skilled care; Alzheimer's; Certified Beds: 114; Certified: Medicaid; Medicare; Owner: Private, For-Profit; License: Current state

Heritage Healthcare Center
1300 S South Street, Globe, AZ 85501, (928) 425-3118; Facility Type: Skilled care; Alzheimer's; Certified Beds: 96; Certified: Medicaid; Medicare; Owner: Private, For-Profit; License: Current state

Green Valley

La Hacienda at La Posada
700 S. La Posada Circle, Green Valley, AZ 85614,

(520) 648-8380; Facility Type: Skilled care; Alzheimer's; Assisted Living; Certified Beds: 60; Certified: Medicaid; Medicare; Veterans; Owner: Private, For-Profit; License: Current state

Santa Rita Nursing & Rehabilitation Center
150 N. La Canada Dr., Green Valley, AZ 85614, (520) 625-0178; Facility Type: Skilled care; Alzheimer's; Certified Beds: 115; Certified: Medicaid; Medicare; Veterans; Owner: Private, For-Profit; License: Current state

Kingman

Desert Highlands Care Center
1081 Kathleen Ave., Kingman, AZ 86401, (928) 753-5580; Facility Type: Skilled care; Alzheimer's; Assisted Living; Certified Beds: 120; Certified: Medicaid; Medicare; Owner: Nonprofit; License: Current state

Gardens Care Center
3131 Western Ave., Kingman, AZ 86401, (928) 718-0718; Facility Type: Skilled care; Alzheimer's; Certified Beds: 128; Certified: Medicaid; Medicare; Owner: Private, For-Profit; License: Current state

The Lingenfelter Center
1099 Sunrise Ave., Kingman, AZ 86401, (928) 718-0718 Facility Type: Skilled care; Alzheimer's; Assisted Living; Certified Beds: 88; Certified: Medicaid; Medicare; Owner: Private, For-Profit; License: Current state

Lake Havasu City

Havasu Nursing Center
3576 Kearsage Dr., Lake Havasu City, AZ 86406, (928) 453-1500; Facility Type: Skilled care; Alzheimer's; Certified Beds: 118; Certified: Medicaid; Medicare; Owner: Private, For-Profit; License: Current state

Lake Hills Inn
2781 Osborn Dr., Lake Havasu City, AZ 86406, (928) 505-5552; Facility Type: Skilled care; Alzheimer's; Certified Beds: 104; Certified: Medicaid; Medicare; Owner: Private, For-Profit; License: Current state

Mesa

Chula Vista Care Center
60 S. 58th St., Mesa, AZ 85206, (480) 832-3903; Facility Type: Skilled care; Alzheimer's; Certified Beds: 100; Certified: Medicaid; Medicare; Owner: Private, For-Profit; License: Current state

Citadel Care Center
5121 E Broadway Rd., Mesa, AZ 85206, (480) 832-5555; Facility Type: Skilled care; Alzheimer's; Certified Beds: 128; Certified: Medicaid; Medicare; Owner: Private, For-Profit; License: Current state

East Mesa Emiritus Healthcare Center
51 S. 48th St., Mesa, AZ 85206, (480) 832-8333; Facility Type: Skilled care; Alzheimer's; Certified Beds: 222; Certified: Medicaid; Medicare; Owner: Private, For-Profit; License: Current state

Good Samaritan Society–Mesa Good Shepherd
5848 E. University Dr., Mesa, AZ 85205, (480) 981-0098; Facility Type: Skilled care; Alzheimer's; Certified Beds: 80; Certified: Medicaid; Medicare; Owner: Private, For-Profit; License: Current state

Mesa Christian Health and Rehabilitation Center
255 W. Brown Rd., Mesa, AZ 85201, (480) 833-3988; Facility Type: Skilled care; Alzheimer's; Certified Beds: 191; Certified: Medicaid; Medicare; Owner: Private, For-Profit; License: Current state

Mi Casa Nursing Center
330 S. Pinnule Cr., Mesa, AZ 85206, (480) 981-0687; Facility Type: Skilled care; Alzheimer's; Certified Beds: 180; Certified: Medicaid; Medicare; Owner: Private, For-Profit; License: Current state

Springdale West
3130 E. Broadway Rd., Mesa, AZ 85204, (480) 924-7777; Facility Type: Skilled care; Alzheimer's; Assisted Living; Certified Beds: 204; Certified: Medicaid; Medicare; Owner: Private, For-Profit; License: Current state

Payson

Payson Care Center
107 E. Lone Pine Dr., Payson, AZ 85541, (928) 474-6896; Facility Type: Skilled care; Alzheimer's; Certified Beds: 163; Certified: Medicaid; Medicare; Veterans; Owner: Private, For-Profit; License: Current state

Rim Country Health & Retirement Community
807 W. Longhorn Rd., Payson, AZ 85541, (928) 474-1120; Facility Type: Skilled care; Alzheimer's; Certified Beds: 109; Certified: Medicaid; Medicare; Owner: Private, For-Profit; License: Current state

Peoria

Forum at Desert Harbor
13840 N. Desert Harbor Dr., Peoria, AZ 85381, (623) 972-0995; Facility Type: Skilled care; Alzheimer's; Assisted Living; Certified Beds: 57; Certified: Medicaid; Medicare; Owner: Private, For-Profit Corp.; License: Current state

Freedom Plaza Care Center
13714 N. Plaza Del Rio Blvd., Peoria, AZ 85381, (623) 815-6100; Facility Type: Skilled care; Alzheimer's; Short-Term Care; Certified Beds: 111; Certified: Medicaid; Medicare; Owner: Private, For-Profit, Individual; License: Current state

Good Samaritan Society–Peoria Good Shepherd
10323 W. Olive Ave., Peoria, AZ 85345, (623) 875-0100; Facility Type: Skilled care; Alzheimer's; Certified Beds: 157; Certified: Medicaid; Medicare; Owner: Private, For-Profit; License: Current state

Immanuel Campus of Care
11301 N. 99th Ave., Peoria, AZ 85345, (623) 977-8373; Facility Type: Skilled care; Alzheimer's; Certified Beds: 228; Certified: Medicaid; Medicare; Owner: Private, Nonprofit; License: Current state

Plaza Del Rio Care Center
13215 N. 94th Dr., Peoria, AZ 85381, (623) 933-7722; Facility Type: Skilled care; Alzheimer's; Certified Beds: 128; Certified: Medicaid; Medicare; Owner: Private, For-Profit; License: Current state

Sun Grove Village Care Center
20625 N. Lake Pleasant Rd., Peoria, AZ 85382, (623) 566-0642; Assisted Living; Hospice; Facility Type: Skilled care; Alzheimer's; Certified Beds: 128; Certified: Medicaid; Medicare; Owner: Private, For-Profit; License: Current state

Phoenix

Arizona State Veteran Home — Phoenix
4141 N. 3rd St., Phoenix, AZ 85012, (602) 248-1550; Facility Type: Skilled care; Alzheimer's; Certified Beds: 200; Certified: Medicaid; Medicare; Veterans; Owner: Government/State; License: Current state

Beatitudes Campus
1712 W. Glendale Ave., Phoenix, AZ 85021, (602) 995-2611; Facility Type: Skilled care; Alzheimer's; Certified Beds: 146; Certified: Medicaid; Medicare; Owner: Private, For-Profit; License: Current state

Capri at the Pointe Rehab
1501 E. Orangewood Ave., Phoenix, AZ 85020, (602) 944-1574; Facility Type: Skilled care; Alzheimer's; Certified Beds: 133; Certified: Medicaid; Medicare; Owner: Private, For-Profit; License: Current state

Coronado Healthcare Center
11411 N. 19th Ave., Phoenix, AZ 85029, (602) 256-7500; Facility Type: Skilled care; Alzheimer's; Short-term Care; Certified: Medicaid; Medicare; Owner: Private, For-Profit; License: Current state

Desert Haven Care Center
2645 E. Thomas Rd., Phoenix, AZ 85016, (602) 956-8000; Facility Type: Skilled care; Alzheimer's; Certified Beds: 115; Certified: Medicaid; Medicare; Owner: Private, For-Profit; License: Current state

La Estancia Nursing & Rehabilitation Center
15810 S. 42nd St., Phoenix, AZ 85048, (480) 759-0358; Facility Type: Skilled care; Alzheimer's; Assisted

Living; Certified Beds: 192; Certified: Medicaid; Medicare; Owner: Private, For-Profit Partnership; License: Current state

Grace Healthcare of Phoenix
4202 N. 20th Ave., Phoenix, AZ 85015, (602) 264-3824; Facility Type: Skilled care; Alzheimer's; Short-term and Respite Care; Certified Beds: 100; Certified: Medicaid; Medicare; Owner: Private, For-Profit; License: Current state

Life Care Center at South Mountain
8008 S. Jesse Owens Pkwy., Phoenix, AZ 85040, (602) 243-2780; Facility Type: Skilled care; Alzheimer's; Certified Beds: 124; Certified: Medicaid; Medicare; Veterans; Owner: Private, For-Profit; License: Current state

Life Care Center of Paradise Valley
4065 E. Bell Rd., Phoenix, AZ 85032, (602) 867-0212; Facility Type: Skilled care; Alzheimer's; Assisted Living; Independent Living; Certified Beds: 210; Certified: Medicaid; Medicare; Owner: Private, For-Profit; License: Current state

Maravilla Care Center
8825 S. 7th St., Phoenix, AZ 85042, (602) 243-6121; Facility Type: Skilled care; Alzheimer's; Certified Beds: 194; Certified: Medicaid; Medicare; Owner: Private, For-Profit; License: Current state

North Mountain Medical and Rehabilitation Center
9155 N. Third St., Phoenix, AZ 85020, (602) 944-1666; Facility Type: Skilled care; Alzheimer's; Certified Beds: 155; Certified: Medicaid; Medicare; Veterans; Owner: Private, For-Profit; License: Current state

Phoenix Mountain Nursing Center
13232 N. Tatum Blvd., Phoenix, AZ 85032, (602) 996-5200; Facility Type: Skilled care; Alzheimer's; Certified Beds: 130; Certified: Medicaid; Medicare; Owner: Private, For-Profit; License: Current state

Ridgecrest Healthcare
16640 N. 38th St., Phoenix, AZ 85032, (602) 482-6671; Facility Type: Skilled care; Alzheimer's; Hospice; Respite Care; Certified Beds: 100; Certified: Medicaid; Medicare; Owner: Private, For-Profit; License: Current state

Suncrest Healthcare Center LLC
2211 E. Southern Ave., Phoenix, AZ 85040, (602) 305-7134; Facility Type: Skilled care; Alzheimer's; Assisted Living; Certified Beds: 115; Certified: Medicaid; Medicare; Veterans; Owner: Private, For-Profit; License: Current state

Prescott

Las Fuentes Care Center
1045 Scott Dr., Prescott, AZ 86301, (928) 778-9603;

Facility Type: Skilled care; Alzheimer's; Independent and Assisted Living; Certified Beds: 128; Certified: Medicaid; Medicare; Owner: Private, For-Profit; License: Current state

Good Samaritan Society — Prescott Village
1030 Scott Dr., Prescott, AZ 86301, (928) 778-2450; Facility Type: Skilled care; Alzheimer's; Respite and Short-Term Care; Certified Beds: 80; Certified: Medicaid; Medicare; Owner: Private, Nonprofit, Church-Related; License: Current state

Mountain View Manor
1045 Sandretto Dr., Prescott, AZ 86305, (928) 778-4837; Facility Type: Skilled care; Alzheimer's; Certified Beds: 116; Certified: Medicaid; Medicare; Owner: Private, For-Profit; License: Current state

Sacaton

Caring House
PO Box 2187, 519 S. Ocitillio St., Sacaton, AZ 85247, (520) 562-7400; Facility Type: Skilled care; Alzheimer's; Certified Beds: 100; Certified: Medicaid; Medicare; Owner: Private, For-Profit; License: Current state

Safford

Sunset Hills Care & Rehab, Inc.
1933 Peppertree Dr., Safford, AZ 85546, (928) 428-4910; Facility Type: Skilled care; Alzheimer's; Certified Beds: 128; Certified: Medicaid; Medicare; Owner: Private, For-Profit; License: Current state

Scottsdale

Avalon Care Center — Shadow Mountain
11150 N. 92nd St., Scottsdale, AZ 85260, (480) 860-1766; Facility Type: Skilled care; Alzheimer's; Certified Beds: 120; Certified: Medicaid; Medicare; Veterans; Owner: Private, For-Profit; License: Current state

Life Care Center of Scottsdale
9494 E. Becker Ln., Scottsdale, AZ 85260, (480) 860-6396; Facility Type: Skilled care; Alzheimer's; Certified Beds: 132; Certified: Medicaid; Medicare; Owner: Private, For-Profit; License: Current state

Osborn Health and Rehabilitation
3333 N. Civic Center Plaza, Scottsdale, AZ 85251, (480) 994-1333; Facility Type: Skilled care; Alzheimer's; Certified Beds: 130; Certified: Medicaid; Medicare; Veterans; Owner: Private, For-Profit; License: Current state

Plaza Healthcare
1475 N. Granite Reef Rd., Scottsdale, AZ 85257, (480) 990-1904; Facility Type: Skilled care; Alzheimer's; Certified Beds: 179; Certified: Medicaid;

Medicare; Owner: Private, For-Profit; License: Current state

Scottsdale Heritage Court
3339 N. Drinkwater Blvd., Scottsdale, AZ 85251, (480) 949-5400; Facility Type: Skilled care; Alzheimer's; Certified Beds: 130; Certified: Medicaid; Medicare; Veterans; Owner: Private, For-Profit; License: Current state

Scottsdale Nursing and Rehab Center
3293 N. Drinkwater Blvd., Scottsdale, AZ 85251, (480) 947-7443; Facility Type: Skilled care; Alzheimer's; Certified Beds: 90; Certified: Medicaid; Medicare; Veterans; Owner: Private, For-Profit; License: Current state

Scottsdale Village Square
2620 N. 68th St., Scottsdale, AZ 85257, (480) 946-6571; Facility Type: Skilled care; Alzheimer's; Assisted Living: Respite and Short-Term Care; Certified Beds: 132; Certified: Medicaid; Medicare; Owner: Private, For-Profit; License: Current state

Sells

Archie Hendricks Senior Skilled Nursing Facility
HCO 1 Box 9100, Federal Route 15 Milepost 9, Sells, AZ 85634, (520) 361-1800; Facility Type: Skilled care; Alzheimer's; Certified Beds: 57; Certified: Medicaid; Owner: Government/Federal; License: Current state

Show Low

Tall Pines Care and Rehab, Inc.
2401 E. Hunt St., Show Low, AZ 85901, (928) 537-5333; Facility Type: Skilled care; Alzheimer's; Certified Beds: 100; Certified: Medicaid; Medicare; Owner: Private, For-Profit; License: Current state

Sierra Vista

Hacienda Rehabilitation and Care Center
660 S. Coronado Dr., Sierra Vista, AZ 85635, (520) 459-4900; Facility Type: Skilled care; Alzheimer's; Certified Beds: 100; Certified: Medicaid; Medicare; Owner: Private, For-Profit; License: Current state

Life Care Center of Sierra Vista
2305 E. Wilcox Dr., Sierra Vista, AZ 85635, (520) 458-1050; Facility Type: Skilled care; Alzheimer's; Certified Beds: 152; Certified: Medicaid; Medicare; Owner: Private, For-Profit; License: Current state

Sun City

Banner Boswell Rehabilitation Center
10601 W. Santa Fe Dr., Sun City, AZ 85351, (623) 974-7000; Facility Type: Skilled care; Alzheimer's; Assisted Living; Certified Beds: 71; Certified: Medicaid; Medicare; Owner: Private, Nonprofit; License: Current state

Brighton Gardens of Sun City
17225 N. Boswell Rd., Sun City, AZ 85373, (623) 933-2222; Facility Type: Skilled care; Alzheimer's; Certified Beds: 56; Certified: Medicaid; Medicare; Owner: Private, For-Profit; License: Current state

Sun City Health and Rehabilitation Center
9940 W. Union Hills Dr., Sun City, AZ 85373, (623) 933-0022; Facility Type: Skilled care; Alzheimer's; Certified Beds: 118; Certified: Medicaid; Medicare; Owner: Private, For-Profit; License: Current state

Trillium Specialty Hospital — West Valley
13818 N. Thunderbird Blvd., Sun City, AZ 85351, (623) 977-1325; Facility Type: Skilled care; Alzheimer's; Certified Beds: 120; Certified: Medicaid; Medicare; Owner: Private, For-Profit; License: Current state

Surprise

Baptist Village — Sun Ridge
12215 W. Bell Rd., Surprise, AZ 85374, (623) 583-5482; Facility Type: Skilled care; Alzheimer's; Certified Beds: 58; Certified: Medicaid; Medicare; Owner: Private, Nonprofit; License: Current state

Tempe

Westchester Care Center
6100 S. Rural Rd., Tempe, AZ 85283, (480) 831-8660; Facility Type: Skilled care; Alzheimer's; Certified Beds: 111; Certified: Medicaid; Medicare; Owner: Private, Nonprofit; License: Current state

Tucson

Avalon Health and Rehabilitation Center — Tucson
1400 N. Wilmot Rd., 3rd Floor, Tucson, AZ 85712, (520) 546-3800; Facility Type: Skilled care; Alzheimer's; Certified Beds: 42; Certified: Medicaid; Medicare; Owner: Private, For-Profit; License: Current state

Catalina Health Care Center
2611 N. Warren Ave., Tucson, AZ 85719, (520) 795-9574; Facility Type: Skilled care; Alzheimer's; Certified Beds: 102; Certified: Medicaid; Medicare; Owner: Private, For-Profit; License: Current state

La Colina Care Center
2900 E. Milber St., Tucson, AZ 85714, (520) 294-0005; Facility Type: Skilled care; Alzheimer's; Short-term Care; Certified Beds: 240; Certified: Medicaid; Medicare; Owner: Private, For-Profit; License: Current state

Desert Life Rehabilitation and Care Center
1919 W. Medical St., Tucson, AZ 85704, (520) 297-8311; Facility Type: Skilled care; Alzheimer's; Short-Term Care; Hospice; Certified Beds: 240; Certified: Medicaid; Medicare; Owner: Private, For-Profit; License: Current state

Devon Gables Health Care Center
6150 E. Grant Rd., Tucson, AZ 85712, (520) 296-6181; Facility Type: Skilled care; Alzheimer's; Certified Beds: 312; Certified: Medicaid; Medicare; Owner: Private, For-Profit; License: Current state

Life Care Center of Tucson
6211 N. La Cholla Blvd., Tucson, AZ 85741, (520) 575-0900; Facility Type: Skilled care; Alzheimer's; Certified Beds: 162; Certified: Medicaid; Medicare; Owner: Private, For-Profit; License: Current state

Mountain View Care Center
1313 W. Magee Rd., Tucson, AZ 85704, (520) 797-2600; Facility Type: Skilled care; Alzheimer's; Certified Beds: 120; Certified: Medicaid; Medicare; Owner: Private, For-Profit; License: Current state

Park Avenue Health and Rehabilitation Center
2001 N. Park Ave., Tucson, AZ 85719, (520) 882-6151; Facility Type: Skilled care; Alzheimer's; Certified Beds: 200; Certified: Medicaid; Medicare; Owner: Private, For-Profit; License: Current state

Posado Del Sol Health Care Center
2250 N. Craycroft Rd., Tucson, AZ 85712, (520) 733-8700; Facility Type: Skilled care; Alzheimer's; Certified Beds: 156; Certified: Medicaid; Medicare; Owner: Government/County; License: Current state

Santa Rosa Care Center
1650 N. Santa Rosa Ave., Tucson, AZ 85712, (520) 795-1610; Facility Type: Skilled care; Alzheimer's; Certified Beds: 144; Certified: Medicaid; Medicare; Owner: Private, For-Profit; License: Current state

Youngtown

Cook Health Care
11527 W. Peoria Ave., Youngtown, AZ 85363, (623) 933-4683; Facility Type: Skilled care; Alzheimer's; Certified Beds: 128; Certified: Medicaid; Medicare; Owner: Private, For-Profit; License: Current state

Sunview Health and Rehabilitation Center
12207 N. 113th Ave., Youngtown, AZ 85363, (623) 977-6532; Facility Type: Skilled care; Alzheimer's; Certified Beds: 127; Certified: Medicaid; Medicare; Owner: Private, For-Profit; License: Current state

Yuma

Life Care Center of Yuma
2450 S. 19th Ave., Yuma, AZ 85364, (928) 344-0425; Facility Type: Skilled care; Alzheimer's; Assisted Living; Certified Beds: 128; Certified: Medicaid; Medicare; Owner: Private, For-Profit; License: Current state

La Mesa Healthcare Center
2470 S. Arizona Ave., Yuma, AZ 85364, (928) 344-8541; Facility Type: Skilled care; Alzheimer's; Assisted Living; Certified Beds: 128; Certified: Medicaid; Medicare; Owner: Private, For-Profit; License: Current state

Palm View Rehabilitation and Care Center
2222 South Avenue A, Yuma, AZ 85364, (928) 783-8831; Facility Type: Skilled care; Alzheimer's; Respite Care; Certified Beds: 143; Certified: Medicaid; Medicare; Owner: Private, Nonprofit; License: Current state

Yuma Nursing Center
1850 W. 25th St., Yuma, AZ 85364, (928) 726-6700; Facility Type: Skilled care; Alzheimer's; Certified Beds: 120; Certified: Medicaid; Medicare; Owner: Private, For-Profit; License: Current state

ARKANSAS

Ash Flat

Ash Flat Convalescent Center
66 Ozborne St., Ash Flat, AR 72513, (870) 994-2341; Facility Type: Skilled care; Alzheimer's; Certified Beds: 105; Certified: Medicaid; Medicare; Veterans; Owner: Diversicare Management Services Inc.; License: Current state

Eaglecrest Nursing and Rehab Center
916 Highway 62/412, Ash Flat, AR 72513, (870) 994-3040; Facility Type: Skilled care; Alzheimer's; Certified Beds: 90; Certified: Medicaid; Medicare; Veterans; Owner: Private, For-Profit; License: Current state

Blytheville

Heritage Square Nursing and Rehabilitation Center — Blytheville
710 N Ruddle, Blytheville, AR 72315, (870) 763-3654; Facility Type: Skilled care; Alzheimer's; Certified Beds: 86; Certified: Medicaid; Owner: Proprietary/Public corp.; License: Current state

Camden

Longmeadow Nursing Center — Camden
365 Alpha St., Camden, AR 71701, (870) 836-9337;

Facility Type: Skilled care; Alzheimer's; Assisted Living; Certified Beds: 69; Certified: Medicaid; Medicare; Owner: Private, For-Profit; License: Current state

Ouachita Nursing and Rehabilitation Center
1411 Country Club Rd., Camden, AR 71701, (870) 836-4111; Facility Type: Skilled care; Alzheimer's; Certified Beds: 142; Certified: Medicaid; Medicare; Owner: Private, For-Profit; License: Current state

Pine Hills Health and Rehabilitation, LLC
900 Magnolia Rd., Camden, AR 71701, (870) 836-6833; Facility Type: Skilled care; Alzheimer's; Certified Beds: 120; Certified: Medicaid; Medicare; Owner: Private, For-Profit; License: Current state

Silver Oaks Health and Rehabilitation Center
1875 Old Wire Rd., Camden, AR 71701, (870) 836-6831; Facility Type: Skilled care; ICF; ICF/MR; Alzheimer's; Certified Beds: 106; Certified: Medicaid; Medicare; Veterans; Owner: Nonprofit Corp.; License: Current state

Danville

Mitchell's Nursing Home Inc.
501 W 10th St., Danville, AR 72833, (501) 495-2914; Facility Type: Skilled care; ICF; Alzheimer's; Certified Beds: 105; Certified: Medicaid; Owner: Private, For-Profit; License: Current state

England

England Manor Nursing Home Inc.
516 NE 4th, England, AR 72046, (501) 842-2771; Facility Type: Skilled care; ICF; Alzheimer's; Certified Beds: 70; Certified: Medicaid; Owner: Proprietary/Public corp.; License: Current state

Eureka Springs

Brighton Ridge Nursing Center
235 Huntsville Rd., Eureka Springs, AR 72632, (501) 253-7038; Facility Type: Skilled care; Alzheimer's; Certified Beds: 100; Certified: Medicaid; Medicare; Owner: Diversicare Management Services Inc.; License: Current state

Fayetteville

Butterfield Trail Village
1923 E. Joyce Blvd., Fayetteville, AR 72703, (479) 442-7220; Facility Type: Skilled care; Alzheimer's; Certified Beds: 70; Certified: Medicare; Owner: Private, For-Profit; License: Current state

Fayetteville City Hospital and Geriatric Center
221 S. School St., Fayetteville, AR 72701, (479) 442-5100; Facility Type: Skilled care; Alzheimer's; Certified Beds: 140; Certified: Medicaid; Medicare; Owner: Private, Nonprofit; License: Current state

Fayetteville Health & Rehabilitation
3100 Old Missouri Rd., Fayetteville, AR 72701, (501) 521-4353; Facility Type: Skilled care; ICF; Alzheimer's; Certified Beds: 140; Certified: Medicaid; Medicare; Owner: Private; License: Current state

Fayetteville Veterans Home
1125 N. College, Fayetteville, AR 72703, (479) 444-7001; Facility Type: Skilled care; Alzheimer's; Certified Beds: 108; Certified: Medicaid; Medicare; Veterans; Owner: Government/State; License: Current state

Katherine's Place at Weddington
4405 W. Persimmon St., Fayetteville, AR 72704, (479) 444-6108; Facility Type: Skilled care; Alzheimer's; Assisted Living by Americare; Certified Beds: 109; Certified: Medicaid; Owner: Private, For-Profit; License: Current state

North Hills Life Care and Rehabilitation
27 E Appleby Rd., Fayetteville, AR 72701, (479) 444-9000; Facility Type: Skilled care; Alzheimer's; Certified Beds: 92; Certified: Medicaid; Medicare; Owner: Private, For-Profit; License: Current state

Fordyce

St. John's Place of Arkansas, LLC
1400 Hwy 79/167 Bypass, Fordyce, AR 71742, (870) 352-2104; Facility Type: Skilled care; Alzheimer's; Beds: Skilled care 126; Certified: Medicaid; Owner: Private; License: Current state

Heber Springs

Seven Springs Health and Rehabilitation, LLC
1040 Weddingford Rd., Heber Springs, AR 72543, (501) 362-8137; Facility Type: Skilled care; Alzheimer's; Assisted Living; Certified Beds: 140; Certified: Medicaid; Medicare; Veterans; Owner: Private, For-Profit; License: Current state

Southridge Village Nursing and Rehab Center
400 Southridge Pkwy., Heber Springs, AR 72543, (501) 362-3185; Facility Type: Skilled care; Alzheimer's; Independent Living; Certified Beds: 122; Certified: Medicaid; Medicare; Owner: Private, For-Profit; License: Current state

Jonesboro

Craighead Nursing Center
5101 Harrisburg Rd., Jonesboro, AR 72404, (870) 933-4535; Facility Type: Skilled care; ICF; Alzheimer's; Certified Beds: 110; Certified: Medicaid; Owner: Government/State/Local; License: Current state

Jonesboro Healthcare Center
800 Southwest Dr., Jonesboro, AR 72401, (870) 935-7550; Facility Type: Skilled care; Alzheimer's; Certified Beds: 113; Certified: Medicaid; Medicare; Owner: Private, For-Profit; License: Current state

Ridgecrest Health and Rehabilitation
3016 N. Church St., Jonesboro, AR 72401, (870) 932-3271; Facility Type: Skilled care; Alzheimer's; Certified Beds: 83; Certified: Medicaid; Medicare; Owner: Private, For-Profit; License: Current state

St. Bernard's Medical Center
225 E. Jackson Ave., Jonesboro, AR 72401, (870) 972-4100; Facility Type: Skilled care; Alzheimer's; Certified Beds: 27; Certified: Medicare; Owner: Private, Nonprofit; License: Current state

St. Elizabeth's Place
3010 Middlefield Dr., Jonesboro, AR 72401, (870) 802-0090; Facility Type: Skilled care; Alzheimer's; Certified Beds: 110; Certified: Medicaid; Medicare; Owner: Private, For-Profit; License: Current state

Skilcare Nursing Center
2911 Browns Ln., Jonesboro, AR 72401, (870) 935-8330; Facility Type: Skilled care; Alzheimer's; Certified Beds: 152; Certified: Medicaid; Medicare; Owner: Private, For-Profit; License: Current state

Little Rock

Abington Place Health and Rehab Center
1516 S. Cumberland St., Little Rock, AR 72202, (501) 374-7565; Facility Type: Skilled care; Alzheimer's; Assisted Living; Independent Living; Certified Beds: 120; Certified: Medicaid; Medicare; Owner: Private, For-Profit; License: Current state

All-American Care of Little Rock
2600 Barrow Rd., Little Rock, AR 72204, (501) 224-4173; Facility Type: Skilled care; ICF; Alzheimer's; Certified Beds: 139 Certified: Medicaid; Medicare; Owner: Private; License: Current state

Briarwood Nursing and Rehabilitation Center, Inc.
516 S. Rodney Parham Rd., Little Rock, AR 72205, (501) 224-9000; Facility Type: Skilled care; Alzheimer's; Assisted Living; Independent Living; Certified Beds: 90; Certified: Medicaid; Medicare; Owner: Private, For-Profit; License: Current state

Brookside Health and Rehabilitation Center
800 Brookside Dr., Little Rock, AR 72205, (501) 224-3940; Facility Type: Skilled care; Alzheimer's; Assisted Living; Short-Term Care; Certified Beds: 143; Certified: Medicaid; Medicare; Owner: Private, For-Profit; License: Current state

Chenal Heights Nursing and Rehabilitation
#3 Chenal Heights Dr., Little Rock, AR 72223, (501) 830-2273; Facility Type: Skilled care; Alzheimer's; Assisted Living; Certified Beds: 120; Certified: Medicaid; Medicare; Owner: Private, For-Profit; License: Current state

Chenal Rehabilitation and Healthcare Center
3115 Bowman Rd., Little Rock, AR 72211, (501) 228-4848; Facility Type: Skilled care; Alzheimer's; Certified Beds: 70; Certified: Medicaid; Medicare; Veterans; Owner: Private, For-Profit; License: Current state

Madison Health and Rehabilitation, LLC
2821 W Dixon Rd., Little Rock, AR 72206, (501) 888-4200; Facility Type: Skilled care; ICF; Alzheimer's; Certified Beds: 140; Certified: Medicaid; Owner: Private, For-Profit; License: Current state

Nursing and Rehabilitation Center at Good Shepherd
3001 Aldersgate Rd., Little Rock, AR 72205, (501) 217-9774; Facility Type: Skilled care; Alzheimer's; Certified Beds: 120; Certified: Medicaid; Medicare; Owner: Private, For-Profit; License: Current state

Pleasant Valley Nursing and Rehabilitation
12111 Hinson Rd., Little Rock, AR 72212, (501) 225-8888; Facility Type: Skilled care; Alzheimer's; Certified Beds: 97; Certified: Medicaid; Medicare; Owner: Private, Nonprofit; License: Current state

Woodland Hills Healthcare and Rehabilitation
8701 Riley Dr., Little Rock, AR 72205, (501) 224-2700; Facility Type: Skilled care; Alzheimer's; Certified Beds: 196; Certified: Medicaid; Medicare; Owner: Private, For-Profit; License: Current state

Malvern

Arbor Oaks Healthcare and Rehabilitation Center
105 Russelville Rd., Malvern, AR 72104, (501) 332-5251; Facility Type: Skilled care; ICF; Alzheimer's; Certified Beds: 104; Certified: Medicaid; Medicare; Owner: Private, For-Profit; License: Current state

Longmeadow Nursing Center — Malvern
912 Section Line Rd., Malvern, AR 72104, (501) 332-6934; Facility Type: Skilled care; Alzheimer's; Assisted Living; Certified Beds: 69; Certified: Medicaid; Medicare; Owner: Private, For-Profit; License: Current state

Malvern Nursing and Rehabilitation
829 Cloud Rd., Malvern, AR 72104, (501) 337-9581; Facility Type: Skilled care; Alzheimer's; Certified Beds: 95; Certified: Medicaid; Medicare; Owner: Private, For-Profit; License: Current state

Mountain Home

Auburn Hills Nursing & Rehabilitation Center
3545 Hwy 5 N, Mountain Home, AR 72653, (870)

425-6931; Facility Type: Skilled care; Alzheimer's; Certified Beds: 105; Certified: Medicaid; Owner: Proprietary/Public corp.; License: n/a

Care Manor
804 Burnett Dr., Mountain Home, AR 72653, (870) 424-5030; Facility Type: Skilled care; Alzheimer's; Certified Beds: 104; Certified: Medicaid; Medicare; Owner: Private, For-Profit; License: Current state

Good Samaritan Society — Mountain Home
300 Good Samaritan Dr., Mountain Home, AR 72653, (870) 425-2494; Facility Type: Skilled care; Alzheimer's; Certified Beds: 70; Certified: Medicaid; Medicare; Veterans; Owner: Private, Nonprofit; License: Current state

Hiram Shaddox Geriatric Center
620 Hospital Dr., Mountain Home, AR 72653, (870) 425-6203; Facility Type: Skilled care; Alzheimer's; Certified Beds: 81; Certified: Medicaid; Medicare; Owner: Private, For-Profit; License: Current state

Pine Lane Therapy and Living Center, Inc.
1100 Pine Tree Ln., Mountain Home, AR 72653, (870) 425-6316; Facility Type: Skilled care; Alzheimer's; Certified Beds: 105; Certified: Medicaid; Medicare; Owner: Private, For-Profit; License: Current state

Pine Bluff

Arkansas Convalescent Center
6301 S Hazel, Pine Bluff, AR 71603, (870) 534-8153; Facility Type: Skilled care; Alzheimer's; Certified Beds: 103; Certified: Medicaid; Medicare; Owner: Proprietary/Public corp.; License: Current state

Davis East
6811 S. Hazel St., Pine Bluff, AR 71603, (870) 535-1155; Facility Type: Skilled care; Alzheimer's; Certified Beds: 126; Certified: Medicaid; Medicare; Owner: Private, Nonprofit; License: Current state

Davis Life Care Center
6810 S. Hazel Pine Bluff, AR 71603, (870) 541-0342; Facility Type: Skilled care; Alzheimer's; Certified Beds: 177; Certified: Medicaid; Medicare; Owner: Private, Nonprofit; License: Current state

Jefferson Regional Medical Center
1600 W. 40th Ave., Pine Bluff, AR 71603, (870) 541-7100; Facility Type: Skilled care; Alzheimer's; Certified Beds: 25; Certified: Medicare; Owner: Private, Nonprofit; License: Current state

Trinity Village Medical Center
6400 Trinity Dr., Pine Bluff, AR 71603, (870) 879-3117; Facility Type: Skilled care; Alzheimer's; Certified Beds: 80; Certified: Medicaid; Owner: Private, Nonprofit; License: Current state

Prescott

Hillcrest Care and Rehab
1421 W. Second Street North, Prescott, AR 71857, (870) 887-3811; Facility Type: Skilled care; Alzheimer's; Certified Beds: 90; Certified: Medicaid; Medicare; Owner: Private, For-Profit; License: Current state

Prescott Manor Nursing Center
700 Manor Dr., Prescott, AR 71857, (870) 887-6639; Facility Type: Skilled care; ICF; ICF/MR; Alzheimer's; Assisted Living; Certified Beds: 111; Certified: Medicaid; Medicare; Owner: Private, For-Profit; License: Current state

Rogers

Ashley Health and Rehabilitation
2600 N. 22nd St., Rogers, AR 72756, (479) 899-6778; Facility Type: Skilled care; Alzheimer's; Certified Beds: 111; Certified: Medicaid; Medicare; Owner: Private, For-Profit; License: Current state

Heritage Park Nursing Center
1513 S. Dixieland Rd., Rogers, AR 72756, (479) 636-5841; Facility Type: Skilled care; Alzheimer's; Certified Beds: 110; Certified: Medicaid; Medicare; Owner: Private, For-Profit; License: Current state

Innisfree Nursing and Rehabilitation
301 S. 24th St., Rogers, AR 72758, (479) 636-5545; Facility Type: Skilled care; Alzheimer's; Certified Beds: 80; Certified: Medicaid; Medicare; Owner: Private, For-Profit; License: Current state

Jamestown Health and Rehab
2001 Hampton Pl., Rogers, AR 72758, (479) 986-9945; Facility Type: Skilled care; Alzheimer's; Assisted Living; Certified Beds: 140; Certified: Medicaid; Owner: Private, For-Profit; License: Current state

New Hope Health and Rehabilitation, LLC
1149 W. New Hope Rd., Rogers, AR 72758, (479) 636-6290; Facility Type: Skilled care; Alzheimer's; Certified Beds: 140; Certified: Medicaid; Medicare; Owner: Private, For-Profit; License: Current state

Stamps

Homestead Manor
826 North St., Stamps, AR 71860, (870) 533-4444; Facility Type: Skilled care; ICF; ICF/MR; Alzheimer's; Certified Beds: 104; Certified: Medicaid; Medicare; Owner: Rose Care Inc.; License: Current stat

Yellville

Marion County Nursing Home
Hwy 14 N, Yellville, AR 72687, (870) 449-4201; Facility Type: Skilled care; Alzheimer's; Certified Beds: 105; Certified: Medicaid; Owner: Nonprofit/Religious organization; License: Current state

CALIFORNIA

Alameda

Alameda Healthcare & Wellness Center
430 Willow St., Alameda, CA 94501, (510) 523-8857;
Facility Type: Skilled care; Alzheimer's; Certified
Beds: 166; Certified: Medicaid; Medicare; Owner:
Private, For-Profit; License: Current state

Bay View Nursing & Rehabilitation Center
516 Willow St., Alameda, CA 94501, (510) 521-5600;
Facility Type: Skilled care; ICF; Alzheimer's; Certified
Beds: 180; Certified: Medicaid; Medicare; Medi-Cal;
Owner: Vencor Inc.; License: Current state

Crown Bay Nursing & Rehabilitation Center
508 Westline Dr., Alameda, CA 94501, (510) 521-
5765; Facility Type: Skilled care; Alzheimer's; Certified Beds: 151; Certified: Medicaid; Medicare; Owner:
Private, For-Profit; License: Current state

Alta Loma

Rancho Mesa Care Center
9333 La Mesa Dr., Alta Loma, CA 91701, (909) 987-
2501; Facility Type: Skilled care; ICF/MR; Alzheimer's; Certified Beds: 59; Certified: Medicaid;
Medical; Owner: Private; License: n/a

Anaheim

Anaheim Crest Nursing Center
3067 W. Orange Ave., Anaheim, CA 92804, (714)
827-2440; Facility Type: Skilled care; Alzheimer's;
Certified Beds: 83; Certified: Medicaid; Veterans;
Owner: Private, For-Profit; License: Current state

Anaheim Healthcare Center, LLC
501 S. Beach Blvd., Anaheim, CA 92804, (714) 816-
0540; Facility Type: Skilled care; Alzheimer's; Certified Beds: 250; Certified: Medicaid; Medicare;
Owner: Private: Cal-Quality Care Org.; License:
Current state

Anaheim Terrace Care Center
141 S. Knott Ave., Anaheim, CA 92804, (714) 821-
7310; Facility Type: Skilled care; Alzheimer's; Certified Beds: 99; Certified: Medicaid; Medicare; Owner:
Private, For-Profit; License: Current state

Buena Vista Care Center
1440 S. Euclid Ave., Anaheim, CA 92802, (714) 535-
7264; Facility Type: Skilled care; Alzheimer's; Certified Beds: 99; Certified: Medicaid; Medicare; Owner:
Private, For-Profit; License: Current state

Harbor Villa Care Center
861 S. Harbor Blvd., Anaheim, CA 92805, (714) 635-
8131; Facility Type: Skilled care; Alzheimer's; Certified
Beds: 99; Certified: Medicaid; Medicare; Veterans;
Owner: Private, For-Profit; License: Current state

Leisure Court Nursing Center
1135 Leisure Ct., Anaheim, CA 92801, (714) 772-
1353; Facility Type: Skilled care; Alzheimer's; Certified Beds: 115; Certified: Medicare; Medi-Cal; Owner:
Proprietary/Public corp.; License: Current state

Park Anaheim Healthcare Center
3435 W. Ball Rd., Anaheim, CA 92804, (714) 827-
5880; Facility Type: Skilled care; Alzheimer's; Assisted
Living; Certified Beds: 115; Certified: Medicaid;
Medicare; Veterans; Owner: Private, For-Profit; License: Current state

Walnut ManorCare Center
1401 W. Ball Rd., Anaheim, CA 92802, (714) 776-
7150; Facility Type: Skilled care; Alzheimer's; Certified Beds: 138; Certified: Medicaid; Medicare; Owner:
Private, For-Profit; License: Current state

West Anaheim Extended Care
645 S. Beach Blvd., Anaheim, CA 92804, (714) 821-
1993; Facility Type: Skilled care; Alzheimer's; Certified Beds: 166; Certified: Medicaid; Medicare; Owner:
Private, For-Profit; License: Current state

**Windsor Gardens Convalescent Center of
Anaheim**
3415 W. Ball Rd., Anaheim, CA 92804, (714) 826-
8950; Facility Type: Skilled care; Alzheimer's; Certified Beds: 154; Certified: Medicaid; Medicare; Owner:
Private, Cal-Quality Care Org.; License: Current state

Bakersfield

Bakersfield Healthcare Center
730 34th St., Bakersfield, CA 93301, (661) 327-7687;
Facility Type: Skilled care; Alzheimer's; Certified
Beds: 150; Certified: Medicaid; Medicare; Owner:
Private, For-Profit; License: Current state

Corinthian Gardens Health Care Center
1611 Height St., Bakersfield, CA 93305, (661) 872-
2324; Facility Type: Skilled care; Alzheimer's; Certified Beds: 237; Certified: Medicaid; Medicare;
Owner: Private, For-Profit; License: Current state

Evergreen Health Care Center Inc.
6212 Tudor Way, Bakersfield, CA 93306, (661) 871-
3133; Facility Type: Skilled care; Alzheimer's; Beds:
Skilled care 99; Certified: Medicare; Medi-Cal;
Owner: Evergreen Healthcare Management LLC; License: Current state

Parkview Healthcare Center
329 N. Real Rd., Bakersfield, CA 93309, (661) 327-
7107; Facility Type: Skilled care; Alzheimer's; Certified Beds: 184; Certified: Medicaid; Medicare;
Owner: Private, For-Profit; License: Current state

The Rehabilitation Center of Bakersfield
2211 Mount Vernon Avenue, Bakersfield, CA 93306,
(661) 872-2121; Facility Type: Skilled care; Alzheimer's; Certified Beds: 184; Certified: Medicaid;

Medicare; Owner: Private, For-Profit; License: Current state

Berkeley

Ashby Care
Center 2270 Ashby Ave., Berkeley, CA 94705, (510) 841-9494; Facility Type: Skilled care; ICF; Alzheimer's; Certified Beds: 31; Certified: Medicare; Medi-Cal; Owner: Proprietary/Public corp.; License: Current state

Elmwood Care Center
2829 Shattuck Ave., Berkeley, CA 94705, (510) 665-2800; Facility Type: Skilled care; Alzheimer's; Certified Beds: 74; Certified: Medicaid; Medicare; Owner: Private, For-Profit; License: Current state

Burbank

Alameda Care Center
925 W Alameda Ave., Burbank, CA 91506, (818) 843-1771; Facility Type: Skilled care; Alzheimer's; Certified Beds: 89; Alzheimer's 89; Certified: Medicare; Medi-Cal; Veterans; Owner: Beverly Enterprises Inc.; License: Current state

Burbank Healthcare & Rehab
1041 S. Main St., Burbank, CA 91506, (818) 843-2330; Facility Type: Skilled care; Alzheimer's; Certified Beds: 188; Certified: Medicaid; Medicare; Owner: Private, For-Profit; License: Current state

Canoga Park

Canyon Oaks Nursing & Rehabilitation Center
22029 Saticoy St., Canoga Park, CA 91303, (818) 887-7050; Facility Type: Skilled care; Alzheimer's; Certified Beds: 185; Certified: Medicare; Medi-Cal; Owner: Private; License: Current state

Holiday ManorCare Center
20554 Roscoe Blvd., Canoga Park, CA 91306, (818) 341-9800; Facility Type: Skilled care; Alzheimer's; Hospice; Certified Beds: 94; Certified: Medicaid; Medicare; Owner: Private, For-Profit; License: Current state

Topanga Terrace
22125 Roscoe Blvd., Canoga Park, CA 91304, (818) 883-7292; Facility Type: Skilled care; Alzheimer's; Certified Beds: 112; Certified: Medicaid; Medicare; Owner: Private, For-Profit; License: Current state

West Hills Health & Rehab Center
7940 Topanga Canyon Blvd., Canoga Park, CA 91304, (818) 347-3800; Facility Type: Skilled care; Alzheimer's; Certified Beds: 145; Certified: Medicaid; Medicare; Owner: Private, For-Profit; License: Current state

Carmichael

American River Care Center
3900 Garfield Ave., Carmichael, CA 95608, (916) 481-6455; Facility Type: Skilled care; Alzheimer's; Certified Beds: 99; Certified: Medicaid; Medicare; Owner: Private, For-Profit; License: Current state

Carmichael Care & Rehabilitation Center
8336 Fair Oaks Blvd., Carmichael, CA 955608, (916) 944-3100; Facility Type: Skilled care; ICF; ICF/MR; Alzheimer's; Certified Beds: 126; ICF; Alzheimer's; Certified: Medicare; Medi-Cal; Veterans; Owner: Sun Healthcare Group Inc.; License: Current state

Eskaton Village Care Center
3847 Walnut Ave., Carmichael, CA 95608, (916) 974-2060; Facility Type: Skilled care; Alzheimer's; Certified Beds: 35; Certified: Medicaid; Medicare; Medi-Cal; Owner: Eskaton; License: Current state

Mission Carmichael Healthcare Center
3630 Mission Ave., Carmichael, CA 95608, (916) 488-1580; Facility Type: Skilled care; Alzheimer's; Certified Beds: 126; Certified: Medicaid; Medicare; Owner: Private, For-Profit; License: Current state

Whitney Oaks Care Center
3529 Walnut Ave., Carmichael, CA 95608, (916) 488-8601; Facility Type: Skilled care; Alzheimer's; Certified Beds: 126; Certified: Medicaid; Medicare; Owner: Private, For-Profit; License: Current state

Windsor El Camino Care Center
2540 Carmichael Way, Carmichael, CA 95608, (916) 482-0465; Facility Type: Skilled care; Alzheimer's; Certified Beds: 178; Certified: Medicaid; Medicare; Owner: Private, For-Profit; License: Current state

Claremont

Claremont ManorCare Center
621 Bonita Ave., Claremont, CA 91711, (909) 626-3490; Facility Type: Skilled care; Alzheimer's; Certified Beds: 59; Certified: Medicaid; Medicare; Owner: Private, For-Profit; License: Current state

Pilgrim Place Health Services Center
721 W Harrison Ave., Claremont, CA 91711, (909) 399-5536; Facility Type: Skilled care; Alzheimer's; Certified Beds: 68; Certified: Medicaid; Medicare; Medi-Cal; Owner: Nonprofit corp.; License: Current state

Compton

Villa Maria Elena Healthcare
2309 N. Santa Fe Ave., Compton, CA 90222, (310) 639-8111; Facility Type: Skilled care; Alzheimer's; Certified Beds: 99; Certified: Medicaid; Medicare; Owner: Private, For-Profit; License: Current state

Downey

Downey Care Center
13007 S. Paramount Blvd., Downey, CA 90242, (562) 923-9301; Facility Type: Skilled care; Alzheimer's; Certified Beds: 99; Certified: Medicaid; Medicare; Owner: Private, For-Profit; License: Current state

Downey Community Health Center
8425 Iowa St., Downey, CA 90241, (562) 862-6506; Facility Type: Skilled care; Alzheimer's; Certified Beds: 198; Certified: Medicaid; Medicare; Owner: Private, For-Profit; License: Current state

Lakewood Park Health Center
12023 S Lakewood Blvd., Downey, CA 90242, (562) 869-0978; Facility Type: Skilled care; ICF; Alzheimer's; Assisted Living; Independent Living; Certified Beds 290; Certified: Medicaid; Medicare; Medi-Cal; Owner: Proprietary/Public corp.; License: Current state

El Cajon

Chase Care Center, Inc.
1201 S. Irabge Ave., El Cajon, CA 92020, (619) 441-1988; Facility Type: Skilled care; Alzheimer's; Certified Beds: 240; Certified: Medicaid; Medicare; Owner: Private, For-Profit; License: Current state

Cottonwood Canyon Healthcare Center
1391 Madison Ave., El Cajon, CA 92021, (619) 444-1107; Facility Type: Skilled care; Alzheimer's; assisted Living' Certified Beds: 96; Certified: Medicaid; Medicare; Owner: Private, For-Profit; License: Current state

Country Hills Health Center
1580 Broadway, El Cajon, CA 92021, (619) 441-8745; Facility Type: Skilled care; Alzheimer's; Certified Beds: 305; Certified: Medicare; Medi-Cal; Veterans; Owner: Proprietary/Public corp.; License: Current state

Eldorado Care Center, LLC
510 E. Washington Ave., El Cajon, CA 92020, (619) 440-1211; Facility Type: Skilled care; Alzheimer's; Certified Beds: 256; Certified: Medicaid; Medicare; Owner: Private, For-Profit; License: Current state

Magnolia Special Care Center
635 S. Magnolia, El Cajon, CA 92020, (619) 442-8826; Facility Type: Skilled care; Alzheimer's; Certified Beds: 99; Certified: Medicaid; Medicare; Owner: Private, For-Profit; License: Current state

Parkside Special Care Centre
444 W Lexington Ave., El Cajon, CA 92020, (619) 442-7744; Facility Type: Skilled care; Alzheimer's; Certified Beds: 52; Certified: Medi-Cal; Owner: Kennon S. Shea & Assoc.; License: Current state

Villa Las Palmas Healthcare Center
622 S. Anza St., El Cajon, CA 92020, (619) 442-0544; Facility Type: Skilled care; Alzheimer's; Certified Beds: 151; Certified: Medicaid; Medicare; Owner: Private, For-Profit; License: Current state

El Monte

Alliance Nursing & Rehabilitation Center
3825 N Durfee Ave., El Monte, CA 91732, (626) 444-2535; Facility Type: Skilled care; Alzheimer's; Certified Beds: 135; Certified: Medicaid; Medicare; Owner: Private, For-Profit; License: Current state

El Monte Convalescent Hospital
4096 Easy St., El Monte, CA 91731, (626) 442-1500; Facility Type: Skilled care; Alzheimer's; Assisted Living; Certified Beds: 99; Certified: Medicaid; Medicare; Owner: Private, For-Profit; License: Current state

Elmcrest Care Center
3111 Santa Anita Ave., El Monte, CA 91733, (626) 443-0218; Facility Type: Skilled care; Alzheimer's; Certified Beds: 96; Certified: Medicaid; Medicare; Veterans; Owner: Private, For-Profit; License: Current state

Fidelity Health Care
11210 Lower Azusa Rd., El Monte, CA 91731, (626) 442-6863; Facility Type: Skilled care; Alzheimer's; Certified Beds: 91; Certified: Medicaid; Medicare; Owner: Private, For-Profit; License: Current state

Ramona Care Center
11900 Ramona Blvd., El Monte, CA 91732, (626) 442-5721; Facility Type: Skilled care; Alzheimer's; Certified Beds: 148; Alzheimer's; Certified: Medicare; Medi-Cal; Owner: Proprietary/Public corp.; License: Current state

Elk Grove

Windsor Elk Grove Care & Rehabilitation Center
9461 Batey Ave., Elk Grove, CA 95624, (916) 685-9525; Facility Type: Skilled care; ICF; Alzheimer's; Certified Beds: 136; Certified: Medicare; Medi-Cal; Veterans; Owner: Sun Healthcare Group Inc.; License: Current state

Escondido

Escondido Care Center
421 E. Mission Ave., Escondido, CA 92025, (760) 747-0430; Facility Type: Skilled care; Alzheimer's; Certified Beds: 180; Certified: Medicaid; Medicare; Owner: Private, For-Profit; License: Current state

Life Care Center of Escondido
1980 Felicita Rd., Escondido, CA 92025, (760) 741-6109; Facility Type: Skilled care; Alzheimer's; Certified Beds: 120; Certified: Medicare; Medi-Cal;

Owner: Life Care Centers of America; License: Current state

Palomar Continuing Care Center D/P SNF
1817 Avenue Del Diablo, Escondido, CA 92029, (760) 739-2000; Facility Type: Skilled care; Alzheimer's; Certified Beds: 96; Certified: Medicaid; Medicare; Owner: Government/Health District; License: Current state

Las Villas Del Norte Health Center
1335 Las Villas Way, Escondido, CA 92026, (760) 741-1046; Facility Type: Skilled care; Alzheimer's; Assisted Living; Certified Beds: 46; Certified: Medicaid; Medicare; Owner: Private, For-Profit; License: Current state

Fresno

Alzheimer's Living Center at Elim
668 E. Bullard, Fresno, CA 93710, (559) 320-2281; Facility Type: Skilled care; Alzheimer's; Certified Beds: 99; Certified: Medicaid; Medicare; Veterans; Owner: Private, For-Profit; License: Current state

California Home for the Aged
6720 E. Kings Canyon, Fresno, CA 93727, (559) 251-8414

Golden LivingCenter–Fresno
2715 Fresno St., Fresno, CA 93721, (559) 486-4433; Facility Type: Skilled care; Alzheimer's; Certified Beds: 235; Certified: Medicaid; Medicare; Owner: Private, For-Profit; License: Current state

Horizon Health & Rehabilitation Center
3034 E Herndon, Fresno, CA 93705, (559) 237-0883; Facility Type: Skilled care; ICF; Alzheimer's; Certified Beds: 180 Certified: Medicaid; Medicare; Medi-Cal; Veterans; Owner: Proprietary/Public corp.; License: Current state

Pacific Gardens Nursing & Rehabilitation Center
577 S. Peach Ave., Fresno, CA 93727, (209) 251-8463; Facility Type: Skilled care; Alzheimer's; Certified Beds: 180; Certified: Medicaid; Medicare; Owner: Private, For-Profit; License: Current state

Gardena

Las Flores Convalescent Hospital
14165 Purche Ave., Gardena, CA 90249, (310) 323-4570; Facility Type: Skilled care; Alzheimer's; Certified Beds: 99; Certified: Medicaid; Medicare; Owner: Private, For-Profit; License: Current state

Gardena Convalescent Center
14819 S. Vermont, Gardena, CA 90247, (310) 532-9460; Facility Type: Skilled care; Alzheimer's; Respite Care; Short-term care; Certified Beds: 74; Certified:

Medicaid; Medicare; Owner: Private, For-Profit; License: Current state

Greenfield Care Center of Gardena
16530 S Broadway, Gardena, CA 90248, (310) 329-7581; Facility Type: Skilled care; Alzheimer's; Certified Beds: 50; Certified: Medicare; Medi-Cal; Owner: Private; License: Current state

Rosecrans Care Center
1140 W. Rosecrans Ave., Gardena, CA 90247, (310) 323-3194; Facility Type: Skilled care; Alzheimer's; Certified Beds: 99; Certified: Medicaid; Medicare; Owner: Private, For-Profit; License: Current state

Hawthorne

Hawthorne Convalescent Center
11630 S. Greenvillea Ave., Hawthorne, CA 90250, (310) 679-9732; Facility Type: Skilled care; Alzheimer's; Respite Care; Certified Beds: 99; Certified: Medicaid; Medicare; Owner: Private, For-Profit; License: Current state

Windsor Gardens of Hawthorne
13922 Cerise Ave., Hawthorne, CA 90250, (310) 675-3304; Facility Type: Skilled care; Alzheimer's; Certified Beds: 99; Alzheimer's; Certified: Medicare; Medi-Cal; Owner: Proprietary/Public corp.; License: Current state

Hayward

Bay Point Healthcare Center
442 Sunset Blvd., Hayward, CA 94541, (510) 582-8311; Facility Type: Skilled care; Alzheimer's; Certified Beds: 99; Certified: Medicaid; Medicare; Owner: Private, For-Profit; License: Current state

Bethesda Home
22427 Montgomery St., Hayward, CA 94541, (510) 538-8300; Facility Type: Skilled care; Alzheimer's; Certified Beds: 40; Certified: Medicare; Medi-Cal; Owner: Proprietary/Public corp/Church Related; License: Current state

Driftwood Health Care
19700 Hesperian Blvd., Hayward, CA 94541, (510) 785-2880; Facility Type: Skilled care; Alzheimer's; Certified Beds: 88; Certified: Medicaid; Medicare; Owner: Private, For-Profit; License: Current state

Hayward Convalescent Hospital
1832 B St., Hayward, CA 94541, (510) 538-3866; Facility Type: Skilled care; Alzheimer's; Assisted Living Certified Beds: 99; Certified: Medicaid; Medicare; Owner: Private, For-Profit; License: Current state

Hayward Hills Health Care Center
1768 'B' Street, Hayward, CA 94541, (510) 538-4424; Facility Type: Skilled care; Alzheimer's; Certified

Beds: 74; Certified: Medicaid; Medicare; Owner: Private, For-Profit; License: Current state

Morton Bakar Center
494 Blossom Way, Hayward, CA 94541, (510) 582-7676; Facility Type: Skilled care; Alzheimer's; Certified Beds: 97; Certified: Medicaid; Medicare; Owner: Private, For-Profit; License: Current state

St. Francis Extended Care
718 Bartlett Ave., Hayward, CA 94541, (510) 785-3630; Facility Type: Skilled care; Alzheimer's; Certified Beds: 62; Certified: Medicaid; Medicare; Owner: Private, For-Profit; License: Current state

La Mesa

Arbor Hills Nursing Center
7800 Parkway Dr., La Mesa, CA 91942, (619) 460-2330; Facility Type: Skilled care; Alzheimer's; Certified Beds: 106; Certified: Medicare; Medi-Cal; Owner: Private; License: Current state

California Special Care Center
8787 Center Dr., La Mesa, CA 91942, (619) 460-4444; Facility Type: Skilled care; Alzheimer's; Certified Beds: 90; Certified: Medicaid; Medicare; Veterans; Owner: Private, For-Profit; License: Current state

Community Convalescent Hospital of La Mesa
8665 La Mesa Blvd., La Mesa, CA 91941, (619) 465-0702; Facility Type: Skilled care; Alzheimer's; Certified Beds: 119; Certified: Medicaid; Medicare; Owner: Private, For-Profit; License: Current state

Country Villa La Mesa Healthcare Center
5696 Lake Murray Blvd., La Mesa, CA 91942, (619) 460-7871; Facility Type: Skilled care; Alzheimer's; Certified Beds: 99; Certified: Medicaid; Medicare; Owner: Private, Nonprofit; License: Current state

La Mesa Healthcare Center
3780 Massachusetts Ave., La Mesa, CA 91941, (619) 465-1313; Facility Type: Skilled care; Alzheimer's; Assisted Living; Certified Beds: 90; Certified: Medicaid; Medicare; Owner: Private, For-Profit; License: Current state

Long Beach

Alamitos Belmont Rehabilitation Hospital
3901 E. Fourth St., Long Beach, CA 90814, (562) 434-8421; Facility Type: Skilled care; Alzheimer's; Certified Beds: 94; Certified: Medicaid; Medicare; Owner: Private, For-Profit; License: Current state

Atlantic Memorial Healthcare Center
2750 Atlantic Ave., Long Beach, CA 90806, (562) 424-8101; Facility Type: Skilled care; Alzheimer's; Certified Beds: 109; Certified: Medicaid; Medicare; Owner: Private, For-Profit; License: Current state

Catered Manor Nursing Center
4010 Virginia Rd., Long Beach, CA 90807, (562) 426-0394; Facility Type: Skilled care; Alzheimer's; Certified Beds: 83; Certified: Medicaid; Medicare; Owner: Private, For-Profit; License: Current state

Colonial Care Center
1913 E 5th St., Long Beach, CA 90802, (562) 432-5751; Facility Type: Skilled care; Alzheimer's; Certified Beds: 196; Certified: Medicaid; Medicare; Medi-Cal; Owner: Private; License: Current state

Edgewater Convalescent Hospital
2625 E. Fourth St., Long Beach, CA 90814, (562) 434-0974; Facility Type: Skilled care; Alzheimer's; Certified Beds: 81; Certified: Medicaid; Medicare; Owner: Private, For-Profit; License: Current state

Hillcrest Care Center
3401 Cedar Ave., Long Beach, CA 90807, (562) 426-4461; Facility Type: Skilled care; Alzheimer's; Certified Beds: 154; Certified: Medicaid; Medicare; Owner: Private, For-Profit; License: Current state

Intercommunity Care Center
2626 Grand Ave., Long Beach, CA 90815, (562) 427-8915; Facility Type: Skilled care; Alzheimer's; Certified Beds: 147; Certified: Medicaid; Medicare; Owner: Private, For-Profit; License: Current state

Long Beach Care Center, Inc.
2615 Grand Ave., Long Beach, CA 90815, (562) 426-6141; Facility Type: Skilled care; Alzheimer's; Certified Beds: 163; Certified: Medicaid; Medicare; Owner: Private, For-Profit; License: Current state

Royal Care Skilled Nursing Center
2725 Pacific Ave., Long Beach, CA 90806, (562) 427-7493; Facility Type: Skilled care; Alzheimer's; Certified Beds: 98 Certified: Medicaid; Medicare; Medi-Cal; Owner: Covenant Care Corporation; License: Current state

Windsor Convalescent Center of North Long Beach
260 E Market St., Long Beach, CA 90805, (562) 428-4681; Facility Type: Skilled care; Alzheimer's; Certified Beds: 120; Certified: Medicaid; Medicare; Medi-Cal; Owner: Covenant Care Corporation; License: Current state

Los Angeles

Alcott Rehabilitation Hospital
3551 W. Olympic Blvd., Los Angeles, CA 90019, (213) 737-2000; Facility Type: Skilled care; Alzheimer's; Certified Beds: 121; Certified: Medicaid; Medicare; Veterans; Owner: Private, For-Profit; License: Current state

Alden Terrace Convalescent Hospital
1240 S Hoover St., Los Angeles, CA 90006, (213)

382-8461; Facility Type: Skilled care; Alzheimer's; Assisted Living; Respite Care; Certified Beds: 210; Certified: Medicare; Medi-Cal; Veterans; Owner: Proprietary/Public corp.; License: Current state

Alexandria Care Center
1515 N. Alexandria Ave., Los Angeles, CA 90027, (213) 660-1800; Facility Type: Skilled care; Alzheimer's; Certified Beds: 177; Certified: Medicaid; Medicare; Owner: Private, For-Profit; License: Current state

Amberwood Convalescent Hospital
6071 York Blvd., Los Angeles, CA 90042, (323) 254-3407; Facility Type: Skilled care; ICF; Alzheimer's; Certified Beds: 107; Certified: Medicare; Medi-Cal; Owner: Proprietary/Public corp.; License: Current state

Brier Oak on Sunset
5154 Sunset Blvd., Los Angeles, CA 90027, (323) 663-3951; Facility Type: Skilled care; Alzheimer's; Respite Care; Short-term Care; Certified Beds: 159; Certified: Medicaid; Medicare; Owner: Private, For-Profit; License: Current state

Country Villa Mar Vista Nursing Center
2966 Marcasel Ave., Los Angeles, CA 90066, (310) 397-2372; Facility Type: Skilled care; Alzheimer's; Certified Beds: 68; Certified: Medicare; Owner: Country Villa Healthcare Corporation; License: Current state

Fountain View Subacute and Nursing Center
5310 Fountain Ave., Los Angeles, CA 90029, (323) 461-9961; Facility Type: Skilled care; Alzheimer's; Respite Care; Short-term Care; Certified Beds: 99; Certified: Medicaid; Medicare; Owner: Private, For-Profit; License: Current state

Grand Park Convalescent Hospital
2312 W. 8th St., Los Angeles, CA 90057, (213) 382-7315; Facility Type: Skilled care; Alzheimer's; Certified Beds: 151; Certified: Medicaid; Medicare; Owner: Private, For-Profit; License: Current state

Keiro Nursing Home II
2221 Lincoln Park Ave., Los Angeles, CA 90031, (323) 276-5700; Facility Type: Skilled care; Alzheimer's; Certified Beds: 300; Certified: Medicaid; Medicare; Owner: Private, Nonprofit; License: Current state

Kennedy Care Center
619 N Fairfax Ave., Los Angeles, CA 90036, (323) 651-0043; Facility Type: Skilled care; ICF; ICF/MR; Alzheimer's; Certified Beds: 97; Certified: Medicare; Medi-Cal; Owner: Proprietary/Public corp.; License: Current state

Longwood Manor Convalescent Hospital
4853 W. Washington Blvd., Los Angeles, CA 90016, (323) 935-1157; Facility Type: Skilled care; Alzheimer's; Certified Beds: 199; Certified: Medicaid;

Medicare; Veterans; Owner: Private, For-Profit; License: Current state

Saint John of God Retirement & Care Center
2648 S. St. Andrew's Place, Los Angeles, CA 90018, (323) 731-0641; Facility Type: Skilled care; ICF; Alzheimer's; Certified Beds: 131; Certified: Medicare; Medi-Cal; Owner: Nonprofit corp.; License: Current state

Sharon Care Center
8167 W 3rd St., Los Angeles, CA 90048, (323) 655-2023; Facility Type: Skilled care; Alzheimer's; Certified Beds: 86; Certified: Medicare; Medi-Cal; Owner: Fountain View Inc.; License: Current state

Windsor Gardens Convalescent Hospital
915 Crenshaw Blvd., Los Angeles, CA 90019, (323) 937-5466; Facility Type: Skilled care; Alzheimer's; Certified Beds: 98; Certified: Medicare; Medi-Cal; Owner: Proprietary/Public corp.; License: Current state

Merced

Country Villa Merced Nursing & Rehabilitation Center
510 W 26th St., Merced, CA 95340, (209) 723-2911; Facility Type: Skilled care; Alzheimer's; Certified 79; Alzheimer's; Certified: Medicaid; Medicare; Medi-Cal; Owner: Health Care Management; License: Current state

Franciscan Convalescent Hospital
3169 M St., Merced, CA 95340, (209) 722-6231; Facility Type: Skilled care; Alzheimer's; Certified Beds: 71; Certified: Medicaid; Medicare; Owner: Private, For-Profit; License: Current state

Modesto

Acacia Park Nursing & Rehabilitation Center
1611 Scenic Dr., Modesto, CA 95355, (209) 523-5667; Facility Type: Skilled care; Alzheimer's (wanderer alert, no locked ward); Assisted Living; Certified Beds: 99; Certified: Medicaid; Medicare; Owner: Private, For-Profit; License: Current state

Country Villa Modesto Nursing & Rehabilitation Center
159 E Orangeburg Ave., Modesto, CA 95350, (209) 526-2811; Facility Type: Skilled care; Alzheimer's; Certified Beds: 99; Certified: Medicaid; Medicare; Medi-Cal; Owner: Health Care Management; License: Current state

Crestwood Manor 112
1400 Celeste Dr., Modesto, CA 95355, (209) 526-8050; Facility Type: Skilled care; Alzheimer's; Assisted Living; Certified Beds: 194; Certified: Medicaid; Owner: Private, For-Profit; License: Current state

English Oaks Convalescent & Rehabilitation Hospital
2633 W. Rumble Rd., Modesto, CA 95350, (209) 577-1001; Facility Type: Skilled care; Alzheimer's; Certified Beds: 180; Certified: Medicaid; Medicare; Owner: Private, For-Profit; License: Current state

Monterey

Carmel Hills Care Center
23795 W. R. Holman Highway, Monterey, CA 93940, (831) 624-1875; Facility Type: Skilled care; Alzheimer's; Certified Beds: 99; Certified: Medicaid; Medicare; Owner: Private, For-Profit; License: Current state

Monterey Pines Skilled Nursing Facility
1501 Skyline Dr., Monterey, CA 93940, (831) 373-3716; Facility Type: Skilled care; Alzheimer's; Memory Care; Respite Care; Certified Beds: 99; Certified: Medicaid; Medicare; Owner: Private, For-Profit; License: Current state

Windsor Monterey Care Center
1575 Skyline Dr., Monterey, CA 93940, (831) 373-2731; Facility Type: Skilled care; Alzheimer's; Certified Beds: 78; Certified: Medicaid; Medicare; Owner: Private, For-Profit; License: Current state

North Hollywood

All Saint Healthcare Subacute
11810 Saticoy St., N. Hollywood, CA 91605, (818) 982-4600; Facility Type: Skilled care; Alzheimer's; Assisted Living; Certified Beds: 128; Certified: Medicaid; Medicare; Owner: Private, For-Profit; License: Current state

Chandler Convalescent Hospital
5335 Laurel Canyon Blvd., N. Hollywood, CA 91607, (818) 985-1814; Facility Type: Skilled care; Alzheimer's; Certified Beds: 201; Certified: Medicaid; Medicare; Owner: Private, For-Profit; License: Current state;

Valley Manor Convalescent Hospital
6120 N. Vineland Ave., N. Hollywood, CA 91606, (818) 763-6275; Facility Type: Skilled care; Alzheimer's; Certified Beds: 72; Certified: Medicaid; Medicare; Veterans; Owner: Private, For-Profit; License: Current state

Oakland

ABSMC Summit Campus D/P SNF
3100 Summit St., Oakland, CA 94609, (510) 655-4000; Facility Type: Skilled care; Alzheimer's; Certified Beds: 71; Certified: Medicare; Medi-Cal; Owner: Private; License: Current state

Excell Health Care
3025 High St., Oakland, CA 94619, (510) 261-5200;

Facility Type: Skilled care; Alzheimer's; Respite Care; Certified Beds: 99; Certified: Medicaid; Medicare; Owner: Private, For-Profit; License: Current state

Garfield Neurobehavioral Center
1451 28th Ave., Oakland, CA 94601, (510) 261-9191; Facility Type: Skilled care; Alzheimer's; Certified Beds: 96; Certified: Medicaid; Medicare; Owner: Private, For-Profit; License: Current state

Mercy Retirement & Care Center
3431 Foothill Blvd., Oakland, CA 94601, (510) 534-8540; Facility Type: Skilled care; Alzheimer's; Certified Beds: 59; Certified: Medicare; Medi-Cal; Owner: Nonprofit corp.; License: Current state

Saint Paul's Tower
100 Bay Pl., Oakland CA 94610, (510) 835-4700; Facility Type: Skilled care; ICF; ICF/MR; Alzheimer's; Certified Beds: 43; Certified: Medicare; Owner: Nonprofit/Religious organization; License: Current state

Paramount

Paramount Convalescent Hospital
8558 E Rosecrans Ave., Paramount, CA 90723, (562) 634-6877; Facility Type: Skilled care; Alzheimer's; Certified Beds: 59; Certified: Medicaid; Medicare; Medi-Cal; Owner: Sun Mar Healthcare; License: Current state

Paramount Meadows
7039 Alondra Blvd., Paramount, CA 90723, (562) 531-0990; Facility Type: Skilled care; ICF; ICF/MR; Alzheimer's; Respite Care; Certified Beds: 104 Certified: Medicaid; Medicare; Medi-Cal; Owner: Proprietary/Public corp.; License: Current state

La Paz at Paramount
8835 Vans St., Paramount, CA 90723, (562) 633-5111; Facility Type: Skilled care; Alzheimer's; Certified Beds: 173; Certified: Medicaid; Medicare; Owner: Private, For-Profit; License: Current state

Pasadena

Brighton Convalescent Center
1836 N. Fair Oaks, Pasadena, CA 91103, (626) 798-9124; Facility Type: Skilled care; Alzheimer's; Certified Beds: 99; Certified: Medicaid; Medicare; Owner: Private, For-Profit; License: Current state

Camellia Gardens Care Center
1920 N. Fair Oaks Ave., Pasadena, CA 91103, (626) 798-6777; Facility Type: Skilled care; Alzheimer's; Certified Beds: 80; Certified: Medicaid; Medicare; Owner: Private, For-Profit; License: Current state

Eisenhower Nursing & Convalescent Hospital
1470 N Fair Oaks Ave., Pasadena, CA 91103; (626) 798-9133; Facility Type: Skilled care; Alzheimer's; Certified Beds: 71; Certified: Medicaid; Medicare;

Medi-Cal; Owner: Proprietary/Public corp.; License: Current state

Marlinda Imperial Convalescent Hospital
150 Bellefontaine, Pasadena, CA 91105, (626) 796-1103; Facility Type: Skilled care; Alzheimer's; Certified Beds: 130; Certified: Medicaid; Medicare; Owner: Private, For-Profit; License: Current state

Monte Vista Grove Homes
2889 San Pasqual Ave., Pasadena, CA 91107, (626) 796-6135; Facility Type: Skilled care; ICF; Alzheimer's; Certified Beds: 40; Certified: Medicare; Owner: Nonprofit corp.; License: Current state

Pomona

Chino Valley Health Care Center
2351 S. Towne Ave., Pomona, CA 91766, (909) 628-1245; Facility Type: Skilled care; Alzheimer's; Certified Beds: 102; Certified: Medicaid; Medicare; Owner: Private, For-Profit; License: Current state

Country Villa Park Avenue Nursing and Health Center
1550 N. Park Ave., Pomona, CA 91768, (909) 623-0791; Facility Type: Skilled care; Alzheimer's; Certified Beds: 231; Certified: Medicaid; Medicare; Owner: Private, For-Profit; License: Current state

Inland Valley Care and Rehabilitation Center
250 W. Artresia St., Pomona, CA 91768, (909) 623-7100; Facility Type: Skilled care; Alzheimer's; Certified Beds: 241; Certified: Medicaid; Medicare; Owner: Private, For-Profit; License: Current state

Lanterman Developmental Center D/P SNF
3530 Pomona Blvd., Pomona, CA 91767, (909) 595-1221; Facility Type: Skilled care; Alzheimer's; Certified Beds: 275; Certified: Medicaid; Medicare; Owner: Private, For-Profit; License: Current state

Pomona Vista Alzheimer's Center
651 N Main St., Pomona, CA 91768, (909) 623-2481; Facility Type: Skilled care; ICF; ICF/MR; Alzheimer's; Certified Beds: 59; Certified: Medicaid; Medicare; Medi-Cal; Owner: Proprietary/Public corp.; License: Current state

Reseda

Grancell Village
7150 Tampa Ave., Reseda, CA 91335, (818) 774-3307; Facility Type: Skilled care; ICF; Alzheimer's; Certified Beds: 105 Certified: Medicare; Medi-Cal; Owner: Jewish Home for the Aging; License: Current state

Joyce Eisenberg Keefer Medical Center D/P SNF
7150 Tampa Avenue, Reseda, CA 91335, (818) 774-3000; Facility Type: Skilled care; Alzheimer's; Certified Beds: 239; Certified: Medicaid; Medicare; Owner: Private, For-Profit; License: Current state

Los Angeles Jewish Home for the Aging–Eisenberg Village
18855 Victory Blvd., Reseda, CA 91335, (818) 774-3000; Facility Type: Skilled care; Alzheimer's; Certified Beds: 166 Certified: Medicaid; Medicare; Medi-Cal; Owner: Jewish Home for the Aging; License: Current state

Woodland Care Center
7120 Corbin Ave., Reseda, CA 91335, (818) 881-4540; Facility Type: Skilled care; Alzheimer's; Respite Care; Certified Beds: 157; Certified: Medicaid; Medicare; Owner: Private, For-Profit; License: Current state

Sacramento

Arden Rehab & Health Center
3400 Alta Arden Expressway, Sacramento, CA 95825, (916) 481-5500; Facility Type: Skilled care; Alzheimer's; Certified Beds: 177; Certified: Medicaid; Medicare; Owner: Private, For-Profit; License: Current state

Asbury Park Nursing & Rehabilitation Center
2257 Fair Oaks Blvd., Sacramento, CA 95825, (916) 649-2000; Facility Type: Skilled care; Alzheimer's; Certified 110; Alzheimer's; Certified: Medicare; Medi-Cal; Owner: Private; License: Current state

Briarwood Health Care
5901 Lemon Hill Ave., Sacramento, CA 95824, (916) 383-2741; Facility Type: Skilled care; ICF; ICF/MR; Alzheimer's; Certified Beds: 49 Certified: Medicaid; Medicare; Medi-Cal; Veterans; Owner: Proprietary/Public corp.; License: Current state

Eskaton Care Center–Greenhaven
455 Florin Rd., Sacramento, CA 95831, (916) 393-2550; Facility Type: Skilled care; Alzheimer's; Beds: Skilled care 110; Certified: Medicaid; Medicare; Medi-Cal; Owner: Eskaton; License: Current state

Gramercy Court
2200 Gramercy Dr., Sacramento, CA 95825, (916) 482-2200; Facility Type: Skilled care; Alzheimer's; Respite Care; Certified Beds: 120; Certified: Medicaid; Medicare; Owner: Private, For-Profit; License: Current state

Norwood Pines Alzheimers Center
500 Jessie Ave., Sacramento, CA 95838, (916) 922-7177; Facility Type: Skilled care; Alzheimer's; Certified Beds: 161; Certified: Medicaid; Medicare; Owner: Private, For-Profit; License: Current state

Saylor Lane Health Care Center
3500 Folsom Blvd., Sacramento, CA 95816, (916) 457-6521; Facility Type: Skilled care; Alzheimer's; Beds: Skilled care 42; Alzheimer's; Certified: Medicare; Owner: Proprietary/Public corp.; License: Current state

San Bernardino

Community Hospital of San Bernardino DP SNF
1805 Medical Center Dr., San Bernardino, CA 92411, (909) 887-6333; Facility Type: Skilled care; Alzheimer's; Certified Beds: 161; Certified: Medicaid; Medicare; Owner: Private, For-Profit; License: Current state

Country Villa Hacienda Healthcare
1311 E. Date St., San Bernardino, CA 92404, (909) 882-3316; Facility Type: Skilled care; Alzheimer's; Certified Beds: 99; Certified: Medicaid; Medicare; Owner: Private, For-Profit; License: Current state

Hillcrest Care
4280 Cypress Dr., San Bernardino, CA 92403, (909) 882-2965; Facility Type: Skilled care; Alzheimer's; Certified Beds: 59; Certified: Medi-Cal; Owner: Proprietary/Public corp.; License: Current state

Valley Healthcare Center
1680 N. Waterman Ave., San Bernardino, CA 92404, (909) 886-5291; Facility Type: Skilled care; Alzheimer's; Certified Beds: 109; Certified: Medicaid; Medicare; Owner: Private, For-Profit; License: Current state

San Diego

Balboa Nursing & Rehabilitation
3520 Fourth Ave., San Diego, CA 92103, (619) 291-5270; Facility Type: Skilled care; Alzheimer's; Certified Beds: 130; Certified: Medicaid; Medicare; Owner: Private, For-Profit; License: Current state

Brighton Place San Diego
1350 N. Euclid Ave., San Diego, CA 92105, (619) 263-2166; Facility Type: Skilled care; Alzheimer's; Certified Beds: 161; Certified: Medicaid; Medicare; Owner: Private, For-Profit; License: Current state

Care with Dignity Convalescent Hospital
8060 Frost St., San Diego, CA 92123, (858) 278-4750; Facility Type: Skilled care; Alzheimer's; Certified Beds: 99; Certified: Medicare; Owner: Proprietary/Public corp.; License: Current state

Golden Hill Subacute & Rehab Center
1201 34th St., San Diego, CA 92102, (619) 232-2946; Facility Type: Skilled care; Alzheimer's; Certified Beds: 99; Certified: Medicaid; Medicare; Owner: Private, For-Profit; License: Current state

Point Loma Convalescent Hospital
3202 Duke St, San Diego, CA 92110, (619) 224-4141; Facility Type: Skilled care; Alzheimer's; Certified Beds: 133; Certified: Medicaid; Medicare; Owner: Private, For-Profit; License: Current state

Reo Vista Healthcare Center
6061 Banbury St., San Diego, CA 92139, (619) 475-2211; Facility Type: Skilled care; Alzheimer's; Certified Beds: 162; Certified: Medicaid; Medicare; Owner: Private, For-Profit; License: Current state

San Diego Healthcare Center
2828 Meadowlark Dr., San Diego, CA 92123, (858) 277-6460; Facility Type: Skilled care; Alzheimer's; Beds: Skilled care 305; Certified: Medicare; Medi-Cal; Veterans; Owner: Pleasant Care Corp.; License: Current state

San Francisco

California Pacific Medical Center–California East Campus
3698 California St., San Francisco, CA 94118, (415) 600-6000; Facility Type: Skilled care; Alzheimer's; Adult Daycare; Certified Beds: 101; Certified: Medicaid; Medicare; Owner: Private, For-Profit; License: Current state

Central Gardens
1355 Ellis St., San Francisco, CA 94115, (415) 567-2967; Facility Type: Skilled care; Alzheimer's; Certified Beds: 92; Certified: Medicaid; Medicare; Owner: Private, For-Profit; License: Current state

Golden Gate Care Center
2707 Pine St., San Francisco, CA 94115, (415) 563-7600; Facility Type: Skilled care; Alzheimer's; Certified Beds: 120; Certified: Medicare; Medi-Cal; Owner: Vencor Inc.; License: Current state

Grove Street Extended Care and Living Center
1477 Grove St., San Francisco, CA 94117, (415) 563-0565; Facility Type: Skilled care; Alzheimer's; Certified Beds: 168; Certified: Medicaid; Medicare; Owner: Private, Nonprofit; License: Current state

Jewish Home D/P SNF
302 Silver Ave., San Francisco, CA 94112, (415) 334-2500; Facility Type: Skilled care; Alzheimer's; Certified Beds: 478; Certified: Medicaid; Medicare; Owner: Private, For-Profit; License: Current state

Laguna Honda Hospital & Rehabilitation Center D/P SNF
375 Laguna Honda Blvd., San Francisco, CA 94116, (415) 759-2300; Facility Type: Skilled care; Alzheimer's; Certified Beds: 810; Certified: Medicaid; Medicare; Owner: Government/City, County; License: Current state

Nineteenth Avenue Healthcare Center
2043 19th Ave., San Francisco, CA 94116, (415) 661-8787; Facility Type: Skilled care; Alzheimer's; Certified Beds: 140; Certified: Medicaid; Medicare; Owner: Private, For-Profit; License: Current state

The Tunnell Center for Rehabilitation & Healthcare
1359 Pine St., San Francisco, CA 94109, (415) 673-8405; Facility Type: Skilled care; Alzheimer's; Certi-

fied Beds: 180; Certified: Medicaid; Medicare; Owner: Private, For-Profit; License: Current state

San Jacinto

The Bradley Gardens
980 W 7th St., San Jacinto, CA 92582, (909) 654-9347; Facility Type: Skilled care; ICF; Alzheimer's; Certified Beds: 45 Certified: Medicare; Medi-Cal; Owner: Private; License: Current state

Emanuel Convalescent Hospital
180 N Jackson Ave., San Jose, CA 95116, (408) 259-8700; Facility Type: Skilled care; Alzheimer's; Beds: Skilled care 181; ICF 17; Certified: Medicare; Medi-Cal; Owner: Nonprofit corp.; License: Current state

San Jose Care & Guidance Center
401 Ridge Vista Ave., San Jose, CA 95127, (408) 923-7232; Facility Type: Skilled care; Alzheimer's; Beds: Skilled care 108; Certified: Medi-Cal; Owner: Beverly Enterprises Inc.; License: Current state

San Leandro

Alameda County Medical Center D/P SNF
15400 Foothill Blvd., San Leandro, CA 94578, (510) 895-4279; Facility Type: Skilled care; Alzheimer's; Certified Beds: 109; Certified: Medicaid; Medicare; Owner: Private, For-Profit; License: Current state

All Saints Subacute and Rehabilitation Center
1652 Mono Ave., San Leandro, CA 94578, (510) 357-5351; Facility Type: Skilled care; Alzheimer's; Certified Beds: 86; Vent program; Certified: Medicaid; Medicare; Medi-Cal; Veterans; Owner: Private; License: Current state

Kaiser Permanente Post Acute
1440 168th Ave., San Leandro, CA 94578, (510) 481-8575; Facility Type: Skilled care; Alzheimer's; Certified Beds: 176; Certified: Medicare; Owner: Private, For-Profit; License: Current state

Santa Ana

Country Villa Plaza Convalescent Center
1209 Hemlock Way., Santa Ana, CA 92707, (714) 546-1966; Facility Type: Skilled care; Alzheimer's; Certified Beds: 142; Certified: Medicaid; Medicare; Medi-Cal; Owner: Private, For-Profit; License: Current state

French Park Care Center
600 E Washington Ave., Santa Ana, CA 92701, (714) 973-1656; Facility Type: Skilled care; Alzheimer's; Certified Beds: 202; Certified: Medicare; Medi-Cal; Owner: Sun Mar Healthcare; License: Current state

Royale Health Care Center
1030 W. Warner Ave., Santa Ana, CA 92707, (714) 546-6450; Facility Type: Skilled care; Alzheimer's;

Certified Beds: 255; Certified: Medicaid; Medicare; Owner: Private, For-Profit; License: Current state

Santa Monica

Arbor View Rehabilitation & Wellness Center
1338 20th St., Santa Monica, CA 90404, (310) 255-2800; Facility Type: Skilled care; Alzheimer's; Certified Beds: 144; Certified: Medicaid; Medicare; Owner: Private, For-Profit; License: Current state

Berkley East Convalescent Hospital
2021 Arizona Ave., Santa Monica, CA 90404, (310) 829-5377; Facility Type: Skilled care; Alzheimer's; Certified Beds: 207; Certified: Medicaid; Medicare; Owner: Private, For-Profit; License: Current state

Goldstar Rehabilitation & NSG Center of Santa Monica
1340 15th St., Santa Monica, CA 90404, (310) 451-9706; Facility Type: Skilled care; Alzheimer's; Certified Beds: 227; Certified: Medicaid; Medicare; Owner: Private, For-Profit; License: Current state

Santa Monica Convalescent Center II
2250 29th St., Santa Monica, CA 90405, (310) 450-7694; Facility Type: Skilled care; Alzheimer's; Certified Beds: 44; Certified: Medicare; Medi-Cal; Owner: Private; License: Current state

Spring Valley

Brighton Place Spring Valley
9009 Campo Rd., Spring Valley, CA 91977, (619) 460-2711; Facility Type: Skilled care; Alzheimer's; Certified Beds: 75; Certified: Medicaid; Medicare; Owner: Private, For-Profit; License: Current state

Mount Miguel Covenant Village Health Facility
325 Kempton St., Spring Valley, CA 91977, (619) 479-4790; Facility Type: Skilled care; Alzheimer's; Certified Beds: 90; Certified: Medicare; Medi-Cal; Owner: Covenant Retirement Communities Inc.; License: Current state

Presidio Health Care Center
8625 La Mar St., Spring Valley, CA 91977, (619) 461-3222; Facility Type: Skilled care; Alzheimer's; Certified Beds: 50; Certified: Medicare; Medi-Cal; Owner: Proprietary/Public corp.; License: n/a

Sunland

High Valley Lodge
7912 Topley Ln., Sunland, CA 91040, (818) 352-3158; Facility Type: Skilled care; ICF/MR; Alzheimer's; Certified Beds: 50; Certified: Medicaid; Medicare; Medi-Cal; Owner: Private; License: Current state

New Vista Nursing & Rehabilitation Center
8647 Fenwick St., Sunland, CA 91040, (818) 352-

1421; Facility Type: Skilled care; Alzheimer's; Certified Beds: 121; Alzheimer's; SNF/ICF; Certified: Medicaid; Medicare; Medi-Cal; Veterans; Owner: Private; License: Current state

Sunnyvale

Cedar Crest Nursing & Rehabilitation Center
797 E Fremont Ave., Sunnyvale, CA 9408, (408) 738-4880; Facility Type: Skilled care; ICF; Alzheimer's; Certified Beds: 99 Certified: Medicaid; Medicare; Medi-Cal; Veterans; Owner: Beverly Enterprises Inc.; License: Current state

Idylwood Care Center
1002 W. Fremont Ave., Sunnyvale, CA 94087, (408) 739-2383; Facility Type: Skilled care; Alzheimer's; Certified Beds: 185; Certified: Medicare; Medi-Cal; Owner: Nonprofit; License: Current state

Torrance

Bay Crest Care Center
3750 Garnet St., Torrance, CA 90503, (310) 371-2431; Facility Type: Skilled care; Alzheimer's; Certified Beds: 80; Certified: Medicare; Medi-Cal; Owner: Private; License: Current state

Driftwood Healthcare Center
4109 Emerald St., Torrance, CA 90503, (310) 371-4628; Facility Type: Skilled care; Alzheimer's; Certified Beds: 99; Certified: Medicare; Medi-Cal; Owner: For-Profit; License: Current state

Harbor Convalescent Hospital
21521 S Vermont Ave., Torrance, CA 90502, (310) 320-0961; Facility Type: Skilled care; ICF; ICF/MR; Alzheimer's; Certified Beds: 127; Certified: Medicare; Medi-Cal; Owner: Proprietary/Public corp.; License: Current state

Heritage Rehabilitation Center
21414 S. Vermont Ave., Torrance, CA 90502, (310) 320-8714; Facility Type: Skilled care; Alzheimer's; Certified Beds: 161; Certified: Medicare; Medi-Cal; Owner: Private, For-Profit; License: Current state

Sunnyside Nursing Center
22617 S. Vermont Ave., Torrance, CA 90502, (310) 320-4130; Facility Type: Skilled care; Alzheimer's; Certified Beds: 299; Certified: Medicare; Medi-Cal; Owner: Private, For-Profit; License: Current state

Van Nuys

Berkley Valley Convalescent Hospital
6600 Sepulveda Blvd., Van Nuys, CA 91411, (818) 786-0020; Facility Type: Skilled care; Alzheimer's; Certified Beds: 125; Certified: Medicare; Medi-Cal; Owner: Private, For-Profit; License: Current state

California Healthcare & Rehabilitation
6700 Sepulveda Blvd., Van Nuys, CA 91411, (818) 988-2501; Facility Type: Skilled care; Alzheimer's; Certified Beds: 201; Certified: Medicare; Medi-Cal; Owner: Private, For-Profit; License: Current state

Lake Balboa Care Center
16955 Vanowen St., Van Nuys, CA 91406, (818) 343-0700; Facility Type: Skilled care; Alzheimer's; Certified Beds: 50; Certified: Medicaid; Medicare; Medi-Cal; Veterans; Owner: Care Center Consultants Inc.; License: Current state

Windsor Terrace Health Care
7447 Sepulveda Blvd., Van Nuys, CA 91405, (818) 787-3400; Facility Type: Skilled care; Alzheimer's; Certified Beds: 133; Certified: Medicare; Medi-Cal; Owner: Private, For-Profit; License: Current state

West Covina

Clara Baldwin Stocker Home
527 S Valinda Ave., West Covina, CA 91790, (626) 962-7151; Facility Type: Skilled care; Alzheimer's; Certified Beds: 48; Certified: Medicaid; Medicare; Owner: Nonprofit corp.; License: Current state

Country Villa West Covina Healthcare Center
850 S. Sunkist Ave., West Covina, CA 91790, (626) 962-3368; Facility Type: Skilled care; Alzheimer's; Certified Beds: 75; Certified: Medicaid; Medicare; Owner: Private, For-Profit; License: Current state

COLORADO

Alamosa

Evergreen Nursing Home
1991 Carroll St., Alamosa, CO 81101, (719) 589-4951; Facility Type: Skilled care; Alzheimer's; Certified Beds: 60; Certified: Medicaid; Medicare; Owner: Private; License: Current state

San Luis Care Center
240 Craft Dr., Alamosa, CO 81101, (719) 589-9081; Facility Type: Skilled care; Alzheimer's; Certified Beds: 70; Certified: Medicaid; Medicare; Owner: Private, For-Profit; License: Current state

Arvada

Arvada Care & Rehabilitation Center
6121 W 60th Ave., Arvada, CO 80003, (303) 420-

4550; Facility Type: Skilled care; Alzheimer's; Certified Beds: 54; Certified: Medicaid; Medicare; Owner: Nonprofit corp.; License: Current state

Exempla/Colorado Lutheran Home
7991 W 71 Ave., Arvada, CO 80004, (303) 403-3100; Facility Type: Skilled care; Alzheimer's; Certified Beds: 120; Certified: Medicaid; Medicare; Owner: Nonprofit corp.; License: Current state

Aurora

Aurora Care Center
10201 E 3rd Ave., Aurora, CO 80010, (303) 364-3364; Facility Type: Skilled care; ICF; Alzheimer's; Certified Beds: 108; Certified: Medicaid; Medicare; Veterans; Owner: Proprietary/Public corp.; License: Current state

Beth Israel at Shalom Park
14800 E. Belleview Dr., Aurora, CO 80015, (303) 680-5000; Facility Type: Skilled care; Alzheimer's; Certified Beds: 135; Certified: Medicaid; Medicare; Owner: Private, Nonprofit; License: Current state

Camelia Health Care Center
500 Geneva St., Aurora, CO 80010, (303) 364-9311; Facility Type: Skilled care; ICF; ICF/MR; Alzheimer's Certified Beds: 132; Certified: Medicaid; Medicare Owner: Mariner Post Acute Network; License: Current state

Cherry Creek Nursing Center
14699 E Hampden Ave., Aurora, CO 80014, (303) 693-0111; Facility Type: Skilled care; ICF; Alzheimer's; Certified Beds: 218Certified: Medicaid; Medicare; Veterans; Owner: Proprietary/Public corp.; License: Current state

Colorado State Veterans Home at Fitzsimmons
1919 Quentin St., Aurora, CO 80045, (720) 857-6400; Facility Type: Skilled care; Alzheimer's; Certified Beds: 180; Certified: Medicaid; Medicare; Veterans; Owner: Government/State; License: Current state

Garden Terrace Alzheimers Center of Excellence
1600 S Potomac St., Aurora, CO 80012, (303) 750-8418; Facility Type: Alzheimer's; Certified Beds: 120; Certified: Medicare; Owner: Proprietary/Public corp.; License: Current state

Boulder

Boulder Manor Progressive Care Center
4685 Baseline Rd., Boulder, CO 80303, (303) 494-0535; Facility Type: Skilled care; ICF; ICF/MR; Alzheimer's; Certified Beds: 165; Certified: Medicaid; Medicare; Owner: Mariner Post Acute Network; License: Current state

Frasier Meadows Manor Health Care Center
4950 Thunderbird Dr., Boulder, CO 80303, (303) 499-8412; Facility Type: Skilled care; ICF; Alz-

heimer's; Certified Beds: 108; Retirement; Certified: Medicaid; Medicare; Owner: Nonprofit corp.; License: Current state

ManorCare Health Services–Boulder
2800 Palo Pkwy., Boulder, CO 80301, (303) 440-9100; Facility Type: Skilled care; Alzheimer's; Certified Beds: 150; Certified: Medicaid; Medicare; Owner: Private, For-Profit; License: Current state

Mesa Vista of Boulder
2121 Mesa Dr., Boulder, CO 80304, (303) 442-4037; Facility Type: Skilled care; Alzheimer's; Certified Beds: 162; Certified: Medicaid; Medicare; Owner: Private, For-Profit; License: Current state

Brush

Eben Ezer Lutheran Care Center
122 Hospital Rd., Brush, CO 80723, (970) 842-2861; Facility Type: Skilled care; Alzheimer's; Certified Beds: 132; Certified: Medicaid; Medicare; Veterans; Owner: Nonprofit/Religious organization; License: Current state

Sunset Manor
2200 Edison St., Brush, CO 80723, (970) 842-2825; Facility Type: Skilled care; ICF; ICF/MR; Alzheimer's; Certified Beds: 85; Certified: Medicaid; Medicare; Owner: Mariner Post Acute Network; License: Current state

Canon City

Canon Lodge Care Center
905 Harding Ave., Canon City, CO 81212, (719) 275-4106; Facility Type: Skilled care; Alzheimer's; Certified Beds: 60; Certified: Medicaid; Medicare; Owner: Private, For-Profit; License: Current state

Centura Health Progressive Care Center
1338 Phay Ave., Canon City, CO 81212, (719) 285-2540; Facility Type: Skilled care; Alzheimer's; Certified Beds: 116; Certified: Medicaid; Medicare; Owner: Private, For-Profit; License: Current state

Hilderbrand Care Center
1401 Phay Ave., Canon City, CO 81212, (719) 275-8656; Facility Type: Skilled care; Alzheimer's; Certified Beds: 90; Certified: Medicaid; Medicare; Veterans; Owner: Proprietary/Public corp.; License: Current state

Skyline Ridge Nursing & Rehabilitation Center
515 Fairview St., Canon City, CO 81212, (719) 275-0665; Facility Type: Skilled care; Alzheimer's; Certified Beds: 85; Certified: Medicaid; Medicare; Owner: Private, For-Profit; License: Current state

Valley View Health Care Center, Inc.
2120 N. 10th St., Canon City, CO 81212, (719) 275-7569; Facility Type: Skilled care; Alzheimer's; Cer-

tified Beds: 60; Certified: Medicaid; Medicare; Owner: Private, For-Profit; License: Current state

Carbondale

Heritage Park Care Center
1200 Village Rd., Carbondale, CO 81623, (970) 963-1500; Facility Type: Skilled care; ICF; Alzheimer's; Certified Beds: 90; Certified: Medicaid; Medicare; Owner: Private; License: Current state

Castle Rock

Brookside Inn
1297 S. Perry St., Castle Rock, CO 80104, (303) 688-2500; Facility Type: Skilled care; Alzheimer's; Certified Beds: 120; Certified: Medicaid; Medicare; Owner: Private, For-Profit; License: Current state

Castle Rock Care Center
4001 Home St., Castle Rock, CO 80104, (303) 688-3174; Facility Type: Skilled care; Alzheimer's; Certified Beds: 91; Certified: Medicaid; Medicare; Owner: Nonprofit corp.; License: Current state

Colorado Springs

Aspen Living Center
1795 Monterey Rd., Colorado Springs, CO 80910, (719) 471-7850; Facility Type: Skilled care; Alzheimer's; Certified Beds: 112; Certified: Medicaid; Medicare; Owner: Private, For-Profit; License: Current state

Cedarwood Health Care Center Inc.
924 W Kiowa St., Colorado Springs, CO 80905, (719) 636-5221; Facility Type: Skilled care; ICF; Alzheimer's; Certified Beds: 83Certified: Medicaid; Medicare; Owner: Mariner Post Acute Network; License: Current state

Centura Health Center at Centennial
3490 Centennial Blvd., Colorado Springs, CO 80907, (719) 685-8888; Facility Type: Skilled care; Alzheimer's; Certified Beds: 80; Certified: Medicare; Owner: Private, For-Profit; License: Current state

Centura Health Namasté Alzheimer Center
2 Penrose Blvd., Colorado Springs, CO, 80906, (719) 776-8398; http://www.centuraseniors.org; Facility Type: Alzheimer's (residential and day care); Certified Beds: 64; Certified: Medicare; Namasté Alzheimer Center is a long-term residential treatment center. Modeled after the pod system, patients are primarily housed in nursing units occupied by patients with similar levels of cognitive function. As an innovative form of therapy, clinical massage students spend part of their internships at Namasté. Residents and adults in the day care program participate in art and music therapy and those who are able have access to exercise equipment.

Cheyenne Mountain Care & Rehabilitation Center
835 Tenderfoot Hill Rd., Colorado Springs, CO 80906, (719) 576-8380; Facility Type: Skilled care; Alzheimer's; Certified Beds: 159; Certified: Medicaid; Medicare; Owner: Private, For-Profit; License: Current state

Colonial Columns Health Care Center
1340 E Fillmore St., Colorado Springs, CO 80907, (719) 473-1105; Facility Type: Skilled care; Alzheimer's; Hospice; Certified Beds: 80; Certified: Medicaid; Medicare; Owner: Mariner Post Acute Network; License: Current state

Garden of the Gods Care Center
104 Lois Ln., Colorado Springs, CO 80904, (719) 635-2569; Facility Type: Skilled care; Alzheimer's; Certified Beds: 52; Certified: Medicaid; Medicare; Owner: Nonprofit corp.; License: n/a

Laurel ManorCare Center
920 S Chelton Rd., Colorado Springs, CO 80910, (719) 473-7780; Facility Type: Skilled care; ICF; Alzheimer's; Certified Beds 98; Certified: Medicaid; Medicare; Veterans; Owner: Nonprofit/Religious organization; License: Current state

Life Care Center of Colorado Springs
2490 International Cir., Colorado Springs, CO 80910, (719) 630-8888; Facility Type: Skilled care; Alzheimer's; Certified Beds: 120; Certified: Medicaid; Medicare; Owner: Private, For-Profit; License: Current state

Mount St. Francis Nursing Center
7550 Assisi Heights, Colorado Springs, CO 80919, (719) 598-1336; Facility Type: Skilled care; Alzheimer's; Certified Beds: 108; Certified: Medicaid; Medicare; Owner: Private, Nonprofit, Catholic; License: Current state

Mountain View Care Center
2612 W Cucharras St., Colorado Springs, CO 80904, (719) 632-7474; Facility Type: Skilled care; ICF/MR; Alzheimer's; Certified Beds: 68; Certified: Medicaid; Medicare; Owner: Nonprofit corp.; License: Current state

Pikes Peak Care & Rehabilitation Center
2719 N Union Blvd., Colorado Springs, CO 80909, (719) 636-1676; Facility Type: Skilled care; Alzheimer's; Certified Beds: 210; Certified: Medicaid; Medicare; Owner: For-Profit; License: Current state

Springs Village Care Center
110 W Van Buren, Colorado Springs, CO 80907, (719) 475-8686; Facility Type: Skilled care; ICF; Alzheimer's; Certified Beds: 91; Certified: Medicaid; Medicare; Owner: For-Profit; License: Current state

Terrace Gardens Health Care Center
2438 Fountain Blvd., Colorado Springs, CO 80910,

(719) 473-8000; Facility Type: Skilled care; ICF; ICF/MR; Alzheimer's; Certified Beds: 108Certified: Medicaid; Medicare; Veterans; Owner: Mariner Post Acute Network; License: Current state

Union Printers Home — LTC
101 S. Union Blvd., Colorado Springs, CO 80910, (719) 634-3711; Facility Type: Skilled care; Alzheimer's; Certified Beds: 108; Certified: Medicaid; Medicare; Owner: Private, Nonprofit, Retired Printers; License: Current state

Commerce City

Woodbridge Park Nursing & Rehabilitation
7150 Poplar St., Commerce City, CO 80022, (303) 289-7110; Facility Type: Skilled care; Alzheimer's; Certified Beds: 95; Certified: Medicaid; Medicare; Owner: For-Profit; License: Current state

Woodbridge Terrace Nursing & Rehabilitation
5230 E 66th Way, Commerce City, CO 80022, (303) 289-1848; Facility Type: Skilled care; Alzheimer's; Certified Beds: 105Certified: Medicaid; Medicare; Veterans; Owner: Nonprofit corp.; License: Current state

Cortez

Vista Grande Inn
680 E. Hospital Dr., Cortez, CO 81321, (970) 564-1122; Facility Type: Skilled care; Alzheimer's; Certified Beds: 101; Certified: Medicaid; Medicare; Owner: For-Profit; License: Current state

Craig

Sandrock Ridge Care & Rehabilitation
943 W 8th Dr., Craig, CO 81625, (970) 824-4432; Facility Type: Skilled care; ICF; Alzheimer's; Certified Beds: 58; Certified: Medicaid; Medicare; Owner: Mariner Post Acute Network; License: Current state

Cripple Creek

Cripple Creek Rehabilitation & Wellness Center
700 N. A St., Cripple Creek, CO 80813, (719) 689-2931; Facility Type: Skilled care; Alzheimer's; Certified Beds: 138; Certified: Medicaid; Medicare; Owner: Government/Hospital District.; License: Current state

Denver

Autumn Heights Health Care Center
3131 S. Federal Blvd., Denver, CO 80236, (303) 761-0260; Facility Type: Skilled care; Alzheimer's; Certified Beds: 178; Certified: Medicaid; Medicare; Owner: For-Profit; License: Current state

Berkley ManorCare Center
735 S. Locust St., Denver, CO 80224, (303) 320-4377; Facility Type: Skilled care; Alzheimer's; Certified Beds: 118; Certified: Medicaid; Medicare; Owner: For-Profit; License: Current state

Briarwood Health Care Center
1440 Vine St., Denver, CO 80206, (303) 399-0350; Facility Type: Skilled care; Alzheimer's; Certified Beds: 201; Certified: Medicaid; Medicare; Owner: Life Care Centers of America; License: Current state

Brookshire House
4660 E Asbury Cir., Denver, CO 80222, (303) 756-1546; Facility Type: Skilled care; ICF; Alzheimer's; Certified Beds: 67; Certified: Medicaid; Medicare; Owner: Raintree Healthcare Corporation; License: Current state

Clermont Park Skilled Nursing
2480 S. Clermont St., Denver, CO 80222, (303) 758-4528; Facility Type: Skilled care; Alzheimer's; Certified Beds: 94; Certified: Medicaid; Medicare; Owner: For-Profit; License: Current state

Hallmark Nursing Center
3701 W. Radcliffe Ave., Denver, CO 80236, (303) 794-6484; Facility Type: Skilled care; Alzheimer's; Certified Beds: 143; Certified: Medicaid; Medicare; Owner: For-Profit; License: Current state

Highline Rehabilitation and Care Community Center
6060 E Iliff Ave., Denver, CO 80222, (303) 759-4221; Facility Type: Skilled care; ICF; Alzheimer's; Certified Beds: 120; Certified: Medicaid; Medicare; Owner: Vencor Inc.; License: Current state

Holly Heights Nursing Home, Inc.
6000 E. Iliff Ave., Denver, CO 80222, (303) 757-5441; Facility Type: Skilled care; Alzheimer's; Certified Beds: 133; Certified: Medicaid; Medicare; Owner: For-Profit; License: Current state

Jewell Care Center of Denver
4450 E Jewell Ave., Denver, CO 80222, (303) 757-7438; Facility Type: Skilled care; ICF; ICF/MR; Alzheimer's; Certified Beds: 106; Certified: Medicaid; Medicare; Owner: Mariner Post Acute Network; License: Current state

Juniper Village — The Spearly Center
2205 W. 29th Ave., Denver, CO 80211, (303) 458-1112; Facility Type: Skilled care; Alzheimer's; Certified Beds: 135; Certified: Medicaid; Medicare; Owner: For-Profit; License: Current state

ManorCare Nursing Center
290 S Monaco Pkwy., Denver, CO 80224, (303) 355-2525; Facility Type: Skilled care; ICF; Alzheimer's; Certified Beds: 160 Certified: Medicare; Owner: Proprietary/Public corp.; License: Current state

Rowan Community

4601 E Asbury Cir., Denver, CO 80222, (303) 757-1228; Facility Type: Skilled care; ICF; Alzheimer's; Certified Beds: 66; Certified: Medicaid; Medicare; Owner: Proprietary/Public corp.; License: Current state

Uptown Health Care Center Inc.

745 E 18th Ave., Denver, CO 80203, (303) 860-0500; Facility Type: Skilled care; ICF; Alzheimer's; Hospice; Certified Beds: 79 Certified: Medicaid; Medicare; Owner: Proprietary/Public corp.; License: Current state

Eckert

Horizons Health Care & Retirement Community

1141 Hwy 65, Eckert, CO 81418, (970) 835-3113; Facility Type: Skilled care; ICF; Alzheimer's; Certified Beds: 79; Certified: Medicaid; Medicare; Veterans; Owner: Volunteers of America National Services; License: Current state

Englewood

Cherry Hills Health Care Center

3575 S. Washington St., Englewood, CO 80110, (303) 789-2265; Facility Type: Skilled care; Alzheimer's; Certified Beds: 86; Certified: Medicaid; Medicare; Owner: For-Profit; License: Current state

Julia Temple Center

3401 S Lafayette St., Englewood, CO 80110, (303) 761-0075; Facility Type: Skilled care; ICF; Alzheimer's; Certified Beds: 128; Certified: Medicaid; Medicare; Owner: Nonprofit/Religious organization; License: Current state

Pearl Street Health & Rehabilitation Center

3636 S. Pearl St., Englewood, CO 80110, (303) 761-1640; Facility Type: Skilled care; Alzheimer's; Certified Beds: 81; Certified: Medicaid; Medicare; Owner: For-Profit; License: Current state

Florence

Bruce McCandless Colorado State Veterans Nursing Home

903 Moore Dr., Florence, CO 81226, (719) 784-6331; Facility Type: Skilled care; Alzheimer's; Certified Beds: 105; Certified: Medicaid; Veterans; Owner: Nonprofit corp.; License: Current state

Fort Collins

Golden Peaks Care & Rehabilitation Center

1005 E Elizabeth St., Fort Collins, CO 80524, (970) 482-2525; Facility Type: Skilled care; Alzheimer's; Beds: Skilled care 60; Alzheimer's; SNF/ICF; Cer-

tified: Medicaid; Medicare; Owner: Sun Healthcare Group Inc.; License: Current state

Lemay Avenue Health & Rehabilitation

4824 S. Lemay Ave., Fort Collins, CO 80525, (970) 482-158; Facility Type: Skilled care; Alzheimer's; Certified Beds: 130; Certified: Medicaid; Medicare; Owner: For-Profit; License: Current state

Rehabilitation and Nursing Center of the Rockies

1020 Patton St., Fort Collins, CO 80524, (970) 484-6133; Facility Type: Skilled care; Alzheimer's; Certified Beds: 96; Certified: Medicaid; Medicare; Veterans; Owner: Mariner Post Acute Network; License: Current state

Spring Creek Health Care Center

1000 E. Stuart St., Fort Collins, CO 80525, (970) 482-5712; Facility Type: Skilled care; Alzheimer's; Certified Beds: 138; Certified: Medicaid; Medicare; Owner: For-Profit; License: Current state

Fort Morgan

Valley View Villa

815 Fremont Ave., Fort Morgan, CO 80701, (970) 867-8261; Facility Type: Skilled care; Alzheimer's; Certified Beds: 120; Certified: Medicaid; Medicare; Owner: Life Care Centers of America; License: Current state

Fruita

Family Health West Nursing Home

228 N Cherry, Fruita, CO 81521, (970) 858-9871; Facility Type: Skilled care; Alzheimer's; Certified Beds: 120; Certified: Medicaid; Medicare; Owner: Nonprofit corp.; License: Current state

Grand Junction

Eagle Ridge at Grand Valley

2425 Teller Ave., Grand Junction, CO 81501, (970) 243-3381; Facility Type: Skilled care; ICF; Alzheimer's; Certified Beds: 45; Certified: Medicaid; Medicare; Owner: Proprietary/ Public corp.; License: Current state

Grand Junction Regional Center

2800 Riverside Pkwy., Grand Junction, CO 81501, (970) 255-5711; Facility Type: Skilled care; Alzheimer's; Certified Beds: 32; Certified: Medicaid; Owner: Government, State; License: Current state

Larchwood Inns

2845 N. 15th St., Grand Junction, CO 81506, (970) 245-0022; Facility Type: Skilled care; Alzheimer's; Certified Beds: 130; Certified: Medicaid; Medicare; Owner: For-Profit; License: Current state

LaVilla Grande Care Center
2501 Little Bookcliff Dr., Grand Junction, CO 81501, (970) 245-1211; Facility Type: Skilled care; Alzheimer's; Certified Beds: 96; Certified: Medicaid; Medicare; Veterans; Owner: Private, For-Profit; License: Current state

Greeley

Centennial Health Care Center
1637 29th Avenue Pl., Greeley, CO 80634, (970) 356-8181; Facility Type: Skilled care; Alzheimer's; Certified Beds: 118; Certified: Medicaid; Medicare; Owner: For-Profit; License: Current state

Fairacres Manor Inc.
1700 18th Ave., Greeley, CO 80631, (970) 353-3370; Facility Type: Skilled care; Alzheimer's; Certified Beds: 116; Certified: Medicaid; Medicare; Owner: Private; License: Current state

Good Samaritan Society — Bonell Community
708 22nd St., Greeley, CO 80631, (970) 352-6082; Facility Type: Skilled care; Alzheimer's; Certified Beds: 210; Certified: Medicaid; Medicare; Veterans; Owner: Nonprofit corp.; License: Current state

Life Care Center of Greeley
4800 W 25th St., Greeley, CO 80634, (970) 330-6400; Facility Type: Skilled care; Alzheimer's; Certified Beds: 119; Certified: Medicaid; Medicare; Owner: For-Profit; License: Current state

Holly

Holly Nursing Care Center
320 N 8th St., Holly, CO 81047, (719) 537-6555; Facility Type: Skilled care; Alzheimer's; Certified Beds: 45; Certified: Medicaid; Medicare; Owner: Proprietary/Public corp.; License: Current state

Lakewood

Azura of Lakewood
7395 W. Eastman Pl., Lakewood, CO 80227, (303) 730-8000; Facility Type: Skilled care; Alzheimer's; Certified Beds: 96; Certified: Medicare; Owner: For-Profit; License: Current state

Bethany Healthplex
5301 W 1st Ave., Lakewood, CO 80226, (303) 238-8333; Facility Type: Skilled care; ICF; Alzheimer's; Certified Beds: 170; Certified: Medicaid; Medicare; Owner: Private; License: Current state

Cambridge Care Center Inc.
1685 Eaton St., Lakewood, CO 80214, (303) 232-4405; Facility Type: Skilled care; ICF; Alzheimer's; Certified Beds: 100; Alzheimer's; Certified: Medicaid; Medicare; Owner: Private; License: Current state

Evergreen Terrace Care Center
1625 Simms St., Lakewood, CO 80215, (303) 238-8161; Facility Type: Alzheimer's; Beds: Certified 57; Certified: Medicaid; Owner: Private; License: Current state

Glen Ayr Health Center
1655 Eaton St., Lakewood, CO 80214, (303) 238-5363; Facility Type: Skilled care; ICF; Alzheimer's; Certified Beds: 75; Certified: Medicaid; Medicare; Owner: Private; License: Current state

Harmony Pointe Nursing Center
1655 Yarrow St., Lakewood, CO 80215, (303) 238-1275; Facility Type: Skilled care; ICF; Alzheimer's; Certified Beds: 110; Certified: Medicaid; Medicare; Owner: Solomon Health Services LLC; License: Current state

Sierra Healthcare Community
1432 Depew St., Lakewood, CO 80214, (303) 238-1375; Facility Type: Skilled care; ICF; Alzheimer's; Certified Beds: 83; Certified: Medicaid; Medicare; Owner: Proprietary/Public corp.; License: Current state

Villa ManorCare Center
7950 W. Mississippi Ave., Lakewood, CO 80226, (303) 986-4511; Facility Type: Skilled care; Alzheimer's; Certified Beds: 240; Certified: Medicaid; Medicare; Owner: For-Profit; License: Current state

Las Animas

Bent County Memorial Nursing Home
810 3rd St., Las Animas, CO 81054-1002, (719) 456-1340; Facility Type: Skilled care; ICF; Alzheimer's; Certified Beds: 60; Certified: Medicaid; Medicare; Veterans; Owner: Nonprofit corp.; License: Current state

Littleton

Cherrelynn Healthcare Center
5555 S. Elati St., Littleton, CO 80120, (303) 798-8686; Facility Type: Skilled care; Alzheimer's; Certified Beds: 200; Certified: Medicaid; Medicare; Owner: For-Profit; License: Current state

Life Care Center of Littleton
1500 W. Mineral Ave., Littleton, CO 80120, (303) 795-7300; Facility Type: Skilled care; Alzheimer's; Certified Beds: 120; Certified: Medicaid; Medicare; Owner: For-Profit; License: Current state

Orchard Park Health Care Center
6005 S. Holly St., Littleton, CO 80121, (303) 773-1000; Facility Type: Skilled care; Alzheimer's; Certified Beds: 120; Certified: Medicaid; Medicare; Owner: For-Profit; License: Current state

Longmont

Applewood Living Center
1800 Stroh Pl., Longmont, CO 80501, (303) 776-6081; Facility Type: Skilled care; Alzheimer's; Certified Beds: 120; Certified: Medicaid; Medicare; Owner: For-Profit; License: Current state

Life Care Center of Longmont
2451 Pratt St., Longmont, CO 80501, (303) 776-5000; Facility Type: Skilled care; Alzheimer's; Certified Beds: 187; Certified: Medicaid; Medicare; Owner: Life Care Centers of America; License: Current state

The Peaks Care Center
1440 Coffman St., Longmont, CO 80501, (303) 776-2814; Facility Type: Skilled care; ICF; Alzheimer's; Certified Beds: 105; Certified: Medicaid; Medicare; Owner: Private; License: Current state

Mancos

The Valley Inn
211 Third Ave., Mancos, CO 81328, (970) 533-9031; Facility Type: Skilled care; Alzheimer's; Certified Beds: 110; Alzheimer's; Certified: Medicaid; Medicare; Veterans; Owner: Private; License: Current state

Monte Vista

Colorado State Veterans Center — Homelake
3749 Sherman Ave., Monte Vista, CO 81144, (719) 852-5118; Facility Type: Skilled care; Alzheimer's; Certified Beds: 60; Certified: Medicaid; Medicare; Veterans; Owner: Government, State; License: Current state

Juniper Village at Monte Vista
2277 East Dr., Monte Vista, CO 81144, (719) 852-5138; Facility Type: Skilled care; ICF; Alzheimer's; Certified Beds: 60; Certified: Medicaid; Medicare; Owner: Proprietary/Public corp.; License: Current state

Montrose

San Juan Living Center
1043 Ridge St., Montrose, CO 81401, (970) 249-9638; Facility Type: Skilled care; Alzheimer's; Certified Beds: 104; Certified: Medicaid; Medicare; Owner: Mariner Post Acute Network; License: n/a

Morrison

SunBridge Bear Creek Care & Rehabilitation
150 Spring St., Morrison, CO 80465, (303) 697-8181; Facility Type: Skilled care; Alzheimer's; Beds: Skilled care 163; Alzheimer's; Medicare; Certified: Medicaid; Medicare; Veterans; Owner: Sun Healthcare Group Inc.; License: Current state

Valley ManorCare Center
1401 S. Cascade, Montrose, CO 81401, (970) 249-9634; Facility Type: Skilled care; Alzheimer's; Certified Beds: 107; Certified: Medicaid; Medicare; Owner: Nonprofit, Church-related; License: Current state

Palisade

Palisade Living Center
151 E 3rd St., Palisade, CO 81526, (970) 464-7500; Facility Type: Skilled care; Alzheimer's; Certified Beds: 91; Certified: Medicaid; Medicare; Veterans; Owner: Proprietary/Public corp.; License: Current state

Pueblo

Belmont Lodge Health Care Center
1601 Constitution Rd., Pueblo, CO 81001, (719) 562-7200; Facility Type: Skilled care; Alzheimer's; Certified Beds: 120; Certified: Medicaid; Medicare; Owner: For-Profit; License: Current state

Centura Health Pavilion at Villa Pueblo
855 Hunter Dr., Pueblos, CO 81001, (719) 545-5911; Facility Type: Skilled care; Alzheimer's; Certified Beds: 60; Certified: Medicaid; Medicare; Owner: Nonprofit; License: Current state

Life Care Center of Pueblo
2118 Chatalet Ln., Pueblo, CO 81005, (719) 564-2000; Facility Type: Skilled care; Alzheimer's; Certified Beds: 187; Certified: Medicaid; Medicare; Owner: For-Profit; License: Current state

Minnequa Midecenter Inc.
2701 California St., Pueblo, CO 81004, (719) 561-1300; Facility Type: Skilled care; Alzheimer's; Certified Beds: 115; Ins; Private; Medicaid; Certified: Medicaid; Medicare; Veterans; Owner: Mariner Post Acute Network; License: Current state

Pueblo Care & Rehabilitation Center
2611 Jones Ave., Pueblo, CO 81004, (719) 564-1735; Facility Type: Skilled care; Alzheimer's; Certified Beds: 146; Certified: Medicaid; Medicare; Owner: For-Profit; License: Current state

University Park Care Center
945 Desert Flower Blvd., Pueblo, CO 81001, (719) 545-5321; Facility Type: Skilled care; Alzheimer's; Certified Beds: 180; Certified: Medicaid; Medicare; Owner: Proprietary/Public corp.; License: Current state

Westwind Special Care Center
1610 Scranton Ave., Pueblo, CO 81004, (719) 564-5161; Facility Type: Skilled care; Alzheimer's; Certified Beds: 81; Certified: Medicaid; Medicare; Owner: Private; License: Current state

Rocky Ford

Pioneer Health Care Center
900 S 12th St., Rocky Ford, CO 81067, (719) 254-3314; Facility Type: Skilled care; Alzheimer's; Certified Beds: 91; Certified: Medicaid; Medicare; Veterans; Owner: Nonprofit corp.; License: Current state

Salida

Columbine ManorCare Center
530 W 16th St., Salida, CO 81201, (719) 539-6112; Facility Type: Skilled care; Alzheimer's; Certified Beds: 112; Certified: Medicaid; Medicare; Owner: Life Care Centers of America; License: Current state

Springfield

Southeast Colorado Hospital & Long Term Care Center
373 E 10th Ave., Springfield, CO 81073, (719) 523-4501; Facility Type: ICF; Alzheimer's; Certified Beds: 56; Certified: Medicaid; Owner: Government/State/Local; License: Current state

Thornton

Alpine Living Center
501 E. Thornton Pkwy., Thornton, CO 80229, (303) 452-6101; Facility Type: Skilled care; Alzheimer's; Certified Beds: 126; Certified: Medicaid; Medicare; Owner: For-Profit; License: Current state

Elms Haven Care Center
12080 Bellaire Way., Thornton, CO 80501, (303) 450-2700; Facility Type: Skilled care; Alzheimer's; Certified Beds: 242; Certified: Medicaid; Medicare; Owner: Peak Medical Corporation

The Villas at Sunny Acres
2501 E 104th Ave., Thornton, CO 80233, (303) 452-4181; Facility Type: Skilled care; Alzheimer's; Certified Beds: 160; Certified: Medicaid; Medicare; Owner: For-Profit; License: Current state

Trinidad

Trinidad State Nursing Home
409 Benedicta Ave., Trinidad, CO 81082, (719) 846-9291; Facility Type: Skilled care; ICF; Alzheimer's; Certified Beds: 119; Certified: Medicaid; Owner: Government/State/Local; License: Current state

Walsenburg

Colorado State Veterans Nursing Home–Walsenburg
23500 US Hwy 160, Walsenburg, CO, 81089, (719) 738-5100; Facility Type: Skilled care; Alzheimer's;

Certified Beds: 120; Certified: Medicaid; Veterans; Owner: Nonprofit corp.; License: Current state

Walsenburg Care Center
135 W. 7th St., Walsenburg, CO 81089, (719) 738-2750; Facility Type: Skilled care; Alzheimer's; Certified Beds: 42; Certified: Medicaid; Medicare; Owner: Nonprofit; License: Current state

Westminster

Creek Care Center
7481 Knox Pl., Westminster, CO 80030, (303) 427-7101; Facility Type: Skilled care; ICF; Alzheimer's; Certified Beds: 113; Certified: Medicaid; Medicare; Owner: Proprietary/Public corp.; License: Current state

Life Care Center of Westminster
7751 Zenobia Ct., Westminster, CO 80030, (303) 412-9121; Facility Type: Skilled care; Alzheimer's; Certified Beds: 120; Certified: Medicaid; Medicare; Owner: For-Profit; License: Current state

Park Forest Care Center Inc.
7045 Stuart St., Westminster, CO 80030, (303) 427-7045; Facility Type: ICF; ICF/MR; Alzheimer's; Certified Beds: 103; Certified: Medicaid; Veterans; Owner: Proprietary/Public corp.; License: Current state

The Village Care & Rehabilitation Center
9221 Wadsworth Pkwy., Westminster, CO 80021, (303) 403-2900; Facility Type: Skilled care; Alzheimer's; Certified Beds: 60; Certified: Medicaid; Medicare; Owner: For-Profit; License: Current state

Wheat Ridge

Christopher House
6270 W. 38th Ave., Wheat Ridge, CO 80033, (303) 421-2272; Facility Type: Skilled care; Alzheimer's; Certified Beds: 72; Certified: Medicaid; Medicare; Owner: For-Profit; License: Current state

Mountain Vista Health Center
4800 Tabor St., Wheat Ridge, CO 80033, (303) 421-4161; Facility Type: Skilled care; Alzheimer's; Certified Beds: 168; Certified: Medicaid; Medicare; Owner: Nonprofit corp.; License: Current state

Wheat Ridge ManorCare Center
2920 Fenton St., Wheat Ridge, CO 80214, (303) 238-0481; Facility Type: Skilled care; ICF; Alzheimer's; Certified Beds: 78; Certified: Medicaid; Medicare; Owner: Proprietary/Public corp.; License: Current state

Windsor

Windsor Health Care Center
710 3rd St., Windsor, CO 80550, (970) 686-7474;

Facility Type: Skilled care; Alzheimer's; Certified Beds: 112; Certified: Medicaid; Medicare; Veterans;

Owner: Proprietary/Public corp.; License: Current state

CONNECTICUT

Avon

Apple Rehab Avon
220 Scoville Rd., Avon, CT 06001, (860) 673-3265; Facility Type: Skilled care; Alzheimer's; Certified Beds: 60; Certified: Medicaid; Medicare; Owner: For-Profit; License: Current state

Avon Health Center
652 W Avon Rd., Avon, CT 06001, (860) 673-2521; Facility Type: Skilled care; Alzheimer's; Certified Beds: 120 Certified: Medicaid; Medicare; Owner: Private; License: Current state

Bloomfield

Alexandria Manor
55 Tunxis Ave., Bloomfield, CT 06002, (860) 242-0703; Facility Type: Skilled care; Alzheimer's; Certified Beds: 120; Certified: Medicaid; Medicare; Owner: For-Profit; License: Current state

Bloomfield Health Care Center
355 Park Ave., Bloomfield, CT 06002, (860) 242-8595; Facility Type: Skilled care; ICF; ICF/MR; Alzheimer's; Certified Beds: 120; Certified: Medicaid; Medicare; Veterans; Owner: Private; License: Current state

Wintobury Care Center, LLC
140 Park Ave., Bloomfield, CT 06002, (860) 243-9591; Facility Type: Skilled care; Alzheimer's; Certified Beds: 150; Certified: Medicaid; Medicare; Owner: For-Profit; License: Current state

Bridgeport

Astoria Park
725 Park Ave., Bridgeport, CT 06604, (203) 366-3653; Facility Type: Skilled care; Alzheimer's; Certified Beds: 135; Certified: Medicaid; Medicare; Owner: For-Profit; License: Current state

Bridgeport Health Care Center Inc.
600 Bond St., Bridgeport, CT 06610, (203) 384-6400; Facility Type: Skilled care; Alzheimer's; Certified Beds: 300; Certified: Medicaid; Medicare; Veterans; Owner: Private; License: Current state

Bridgeport Manor
540 Bond St., Bridgeport, CT 06610, (203) 384-6500; Facility Type: Skilled care; Alzheimer's; Certified Beds: 240; Certified: Medicaid; Medicare; Owner: For-Profit; License: Current state

The Springs at Watermark 3030 Park
3030 Park Ave., Bridgeport, CT 06604, (203) 374-5611; Facility Type: Skilled care; ICF; Alzheimer's; Certified Beds: 22; Certified: Medicare; Owner: For-profit organization

Bristol

Ingraham Manor
400 N. Main St., Bristol, CT 06010, (860) 584-3400; Facility Type: Skilled care; ICF; Alzheimer's; Certified Beds: 128; Certified: Medicare; Owner: For-Profit organization

The Pines at Bristol for Nursing & Rehabilitation
61 Bellevue Ave., Bristol, CT 06010, (860) 589-1682; Facility Type: Skilled care; ICF; Alzheimer's; Certified 132; Certified: Medicaid; Medicare; Owner: Eden Park Management Inc.; License: Current state

Sheriden Woods Health Care Center
321 Stonecrest Dr., Bristol, CT 06010, (860) 583-1827; Facility Type: Skilled care; Alzheimer's; Certified Beds: 146; Certified: Medicaid; Medicare; Veterans; Owner: Proprietary/Public corp.; License: Current state

Colchester

Apple Rehab Colchester
36 Broadway, Colchester, CT 06415, (860) 537-4606; Facility Type: Skilled care; ICF; Alzheimer's; Assisted Living; Independent Living; Certified Beds: 60; Certified: Medicare; Owner: For-Profit organization

Harrington Court
59 Harrington Ct., Colchester, CT 06415, (860) 537-2339; Facility Type: Skilled care; ICF; ICF/MR; Alzheimer's' Certified Beds: 130 30; Certified: Medicaid; Medicare; Owner: Proprietary/Public corp.; License: Current state

Danbury

Danbury Health Care Center
107 Osborne St., Danbury, CT 06810, (203) 792-8102; Facility Type: Skilled care; ICF; Alzheimer's; Certified Beds: 180; Certified: Medicare; Owner: For-Profit organization

Filosa Convalescent Home Inc.
13 Hakim St., Danbury, CT 06810, (203) 744-3366; Facility Type: Skilled care; Alzheimer's; Certified Beds: 64; Short-term rehab; Certified: Medicaid; Medicare; Owner: Proprietary/ Public corp.; License: Current state

Pope John Paul II Center for Health
Care 33 Lincoln Ave., Danbury, CT 06810, (203) 797-8300; Facility Type: Skilled care; ICF; Alzheimer's; Certified Beds: 141; Certified: Medicaid; Medicare; Owner: Nonprofit/Religious organization; License: Current state

Durham

Twin Maples Home
809R New Haven Rd., Durham, CT 06422, (860) 349-1041; Facility Type: ICF; Alzheimer's; Certified Beds: 44; Certified: Medicaid; Veterans; Owner: Proprietary/Public corp.; License: Current state

Greenwich

Greenwich Woods Health Care Center
1165 King St., Greenwich, CT 06831, (203) 531-1335; Facility Type: Skilled care; ICF; Alzheimer's; Certified Beds: 217; Certified: Medicare; Owner: For-Profit organization

Nathaniel Witherell
70 Parsonage Rd., Greenwich, CT 06836, (203) 869-4130; Facility Type: Skilled care; Alzheimer's; Certified Beds: 202; Certified: Medicaid; Medicare; Owner: Government/City; License: Current state

Hamden

Arden House Rehabilitation & Nursing Center
850 Mix Ave., Hamden, CT 06514, (203) 281-3500; Facility Type: Skilled care; ICF; Alzheimer's; Certified Beds: 360; Certified: Medicaid; Medicare; Owner: For-Profit organization

Hamden Health Care Center
1270 Sherman Ln., Hamden, CT 06514, (203) 281-7555; Facility Type: Skilled care; Alzheimer's; Certified Beds: 153; Certified: Medicaid; Medicare; Owner: Proprietary/Public corp.; License: Current state

Whitney Manor Convalescent Center
2798 Whitney Ave., Hamden, CT 06518, (203) 288-6230; Facility Type: Skilled care; ICF; Alzheimer's; Certified Beds: 150; Certified: Medicaid; Medicare; Owner: For-Profit organization

Hartford

Avery Nursing Home
705 New Britain Ave., Hartford CT 06106, (860) 527-9126; Facility Type: Skilled care; ICF; Alzheimer's; Certified Beds: 199; Certified: Medicaid; Medicare; Owner: For-Profit organization

Chelsea Place Care Center
25 Lorraine St., Hartford, CT 06105, (860) 233-8241; Facility Type: Skilled care; ICF; Alzheimer's; Certified Beds: 234; Certified: Medicaid; Medicare; Owner: For-Profit organization

Ellis Manor
210 George St., Hartford, CT 06114, (860) 296-9166; Facility Type: Skilled care; ICF; ICF/MR; Alzheimer's; Certified Beds: 105; Certified: Medicaid; Medicare; Owner: Affinity health Care Group; License: Current state

Middletown

Apple Rehab Middletown
600 Highland Ave., Middletown, CT 06457, (860) 347-3315; Facility Type: Skilled care; ICF; Alzheimer's; Certified Beds: 150; Certified: Medicaid; Medicare; Owner: For-Profit organization

Wadsworth Glen Health Care & Rehabilitation Center
30 Boston Rd., Middletown, CT 06457, (860) 346-9299; Facility Type: Skilled care; ICF; Alzheimer's; Certified Beds: 102; Certified: Medicaid; Medicare; Owner: Proprietary/Public corp.; License: Current state

Water's Edge Center for Health & Rehab
111 Church St., Middletown, CT 06457, (860) 347-7286; Facility Type: Skilled care; Alzheimer's; Certified Beds: 150; Certified: Medicaid; Medicare; Owner: Private; License: Current state

New Canaan

Waveny Care Center
3 Farm Rd., New Canaan, CT 06840, (203) 594-5200; Facility Type: Skilled care; Alzheimer's; Certified Beds: 76; Certified: Medicaid; Medicare; Owner: Private; License: Current state

Norwich

Norwichtown & Care Center
93 W. Town St., Norwich, CT 06360, (860) 889-2614; Facility Type: Skilled care; Alzheimer's; Certified Beds: 120; Certified: Medicaid; Medicare; Owner: Private; License: Current state

Regency Heights of Norwich, LLC
60 Crouch Ave., Norwich, CT 06360, (860) 889-2631; Facility Type: Skilled care; Alzheimer's; Certified Beds: 120; Certified: Medicaid; Medicare; Owner: Private; License: Current state

Old Saybrook

Apple Rehab Saybrook
1775 Boston Post Rd., Old Saybrook, CT 06475, (860) 399-6216; Facility Type: Skilled care; Alzheimer's; Certified Beds: 120; Certified: Medicaid; Medicare; Owner: Proprietary/Public corp.; License: Current state

Gladeview Health Care Center
60 Boston Post Rd., Old Saybrook, CT 06475, (860) 388-6696; Facility Type: Skilled care; Alzheimer's; Certified Beds: 132; Certified: Medicaid; Medicare; Owner: Private; License: Current state

Rocky Hill

Apple Rehab Rocky Hill
45 Elm St., Rocky Hill, CT 06067, (860) 529-8661; Facility Type: Skilled care; Alzheimer's; Certified Beds: 120; Certified: Medicaid; Medicare; Owner: Apple Health Care; License: Current state

Maple View Manor
856 Maple St., Rocky Hill, CT 06067, (860) 563-2861; Facility Type: Skilled care; Alzheimer's; Certified Beds: 120; Certified: Medicaid; Medicare; Owner: Private; License: Current state

Rocky Hill Skilled Nursing and Rehabilitation
60 West St., Rocky Hill, CT 06067, (860) 529-2521; Facility Type: Skilled care; Alzheimer's; Certified Beds: 120; Alzheimer's; SNF/ICF; Certified: Medicaid; Medicare; Veterans; Owner: Private; License: Current state

Simsbury

Governor's House Rehabilitation & Nursing Center
36 Firetown Rd., Simsbury, CT 06070, (860) 658-1018; Facility Type: Skilled care; ICF; Alzheimer's; Certified Beds: 73; Certified: Medicaid; Medicare; Owner: Harborside Healthcare; License: Current state

McLean Health Center
75 Great Pond Rd., Simsbury, CT 06070, (860) 658-3700; Facility Type: Skilled care; Alzheimer's; Certified Beds: 154; Certified: Medicaid; Medicare; Owner: Private; License: Current state

South Windsor

South Windsor Nursing & Rehabilitation Center
1060 Main St., South Windsor, CT 06074, (860) 289-7771; Facility Type: Skilled care; Alzheimer's; Certified Beds: 120; Certified: Medicaid; Medicare; Owner: Nonprofit/Religious organization; License: Current state

Stamford

Courtland Gardens Health Center
53 Courtland Ave., Stamford, CT 06902, (203) 353-6118; Facility Type: Skilled care; ICF; Alzheimer's; Certified Beds: 156; Certified: Medicaid; Medicare; Owner: Vencor Inc.; License: Current state

Long Ridge of Stamford
710 Long Ridge Rd., Stamford, CT 06902, (203) 329-4026; Facility Type: Skilled care; Alzheimer's; Certified Beds: 120; Certified: Medicaid; Medicare; Owner: Private; License: Current state

St. Camillus Rehabilitation & Nursing Center
494 Elm St., Stamford, CT 06902, (203) 325-0200; Facility Type: Skilled care; Alzheimer's; Certified Beds: 124; Certified: Medicaid; Medicare; Owner: Private; License: Current state

Smith House Health Care Center, SNF
88 Rockrommon Rd., Stamford, CT 06903, (203) 322-3428; Facility Type: Skilled care; Alzheimer's; Certified Beds: 128; Certified: Medicaid; Medicare; Owner: Government/State/Local; License: Current state

Torrington

Litchfield Woods Health Care Center
255 Roberts St., Torrington, CT 06790, (860) 489-5801; Facility Type: Skilled care; Alzheimer's; Certified Beds: 160; Certified: Medicaid; Medicare; Owner: Private; License: Current state

Torrington Health & Rehabilitation Center
225 Wyoming Ave., Torrington, CT 06790, (860) 482-8563; Facility Type: Skilled care; Alzheimer's; Certified Beds: 126; Certified: Medicaid; Medicare; Owner: Private; License: Current state

Valerie Manor
1360 Torringford St., Torrington CT 06790, (860) 489-1008; Facility Type: Skilled care; Alzheimer's; Certified Beds: 151; Certified: Medicaid; Medicare; Owner: Private; License: Current state

Wolcott Hall Nursing Center
215 Forrest St., Torrington, CT 06790, (860) 482-8554; Facility Type: Skilled care; ICF/MR; Alzheimer's; Respite Care; Hospice; Certified Beds: 87; Certified: Medicaid; Medicare; Owner: Apple Health Care; License: Current state

Vernon

Vernon Manor Health Care Center
180 Regan Rd., Vernon, CT 06066, (860) 871-0385; Facility Type: Skilled care; Alzheimer's; Certified Beds: 120; Sub-acute; Hospice; Certified: Medicaid; Medicare; Owner: Proprietary/Public corp.; License: Current state

Wallingford

Masonicare Health Center
22 Masonic Ave., PO Box 70, Wallingford, CT 06492, (203) 679-5900; Facility Type: Skilled care; Alzheimer's; Certified Beds: 151; Certified: Medicaid; Medicare; Owner: Private; License: Current state

Regency House of Wallingford
181 E Main St., Wallingford, CT 06492, (203) 265-1661; Facility Type: Skilled care; Alzheimer's; Certified Beds: 130 Certified: Medicaid; Medicare; Owner: Proprietary/Public corp.; License: n/a

Village Green of Wallingford Rehab & Health Center
55 Kondracki Ln., Wallingford, CT 06492, (203) 265-6771; Facility Type: Skilled care; Alzheimer's; Certified Beds: 180; Certified: Medicaid; Medicare; Owner: Private, Nonprofit; License: Current state

Waterbury

Abbott Terrace Health Center
44 Abbott Terrace, Waterbury, CT 06702, (203) 755-4870; Facility Type: Skilled care; Alzheimer's; Certified Beds: 205; Certified: Medicaid; Medicare; Owner: Private, Nonprofit; License: Current state

Bucks Hill Nursing & Rehabilitation Center
2817 N. Main St., Waterbury, CT 06704, (203) 757-0731; Facility Type: Skilled care; Alzheimer's; Certified Beds: 90; Certified: Medicaid; Medicare; Owner: Private, Nonprofit; License: Current state

Cheshire House Health Care Facility & Rehabilitation Center
3396 E Main St., Waterbury, CT 06705, (203) 754-2161; Facility Type: Skilled care; Alzheimer's; Certified Beds: 60; Certified: Medicaid; Medicare; Owner: Private; License: Current state

Paradigm Healthcare Center at Waterbury, LLC
177 Whitewood Rd., Waterbury, CT 06708, (203) 757-9491; Facility Type: Skilled care; ICF; Alzheimer's; Certified Beds: 120; Certified: Medicaid; Medicare; Veterans; Owner: Proprietary/Public corp.; License: Current state

West Hartford

Bishops Corner Skilled Nursing & Rehabilitation
2432 Albany Ave., West Hartford, CT 06117, (860) 236-3557; Facility Type: Skilled care; Alzheimer's; Certified Beds: 130; Certified: Medicaid; Medicare; Owner: Private, Nonprofit; License: Current state

Hebrew Home & Hospital Inc.
1 Abrahams Blvd., West Hartford, CT 06117, (860) 523-3800; Facility Type: Skilled care; Alzheimer's; Certified Beds: 287; Certified: Medicaid; Medicare; Owner: Nonprofit corp.; License: Current state

St. Mary Home
2021 Albany Ave., West Hartford, CT 06117, (860) 570-8200; Facility Type: Skilled care; Alzheimer's; Certified Beds: 256; Certified: Medicaid; Medicare; Owner: Private, Nonprofit; License: Current state

West Hartford Health & Rehabilitation Center
130 Loomis Dr., West Hartford, CT 06107, (860) 521-8700; Facility Type: Skilled care; ICF; Alzheimer's; Certified Beds: 160; Certified: Medicaid; Medicare; Owner: Proprietary/Public corp.; License: Current state

Wilton

Lourdes Health Care Center, Inc.
345 Belden Hill Rd., Wilton, CT 06897, (203) 762-3318; Facility Type: Skilled care; ICF; Alzheimer's; Certified Beds: 40; Certified: Medicaid; Medicare; Owner: Proprietary/Public corp.; License: Current state

Wilton Meadows Health Care Center
439 Danbury Rd., Rte. 7, Wilton, CT 06987, (203) 834-0199; Facility Type: Skilled care; ICF; Alzheimer's; Certified Beds: 148; Certified: Medicaid; Medicare; Owner: Private; License: Current state

Windsor

Kimberly Hall–North
1 Emerson Dr., Windsor, CT 06095, (860) 688-6443; Facility Type: Skilled care; ICF; Alzheimer's; Certified Beds: 150; Certified: Medicaid; Medicare; Owner: Proprietary/Public corp.; License: Current state

Kimberly Hall–South Center
1 Emerson Dr., Windsor, CT 06095, (860) 688-6443; Facility Type: Skilled care; ICF; Alzheimer's; Certified Beds: 180; Certified: Medicaid; Medicare; Owner: Proprietary/Public corp.; License: Current state

Windsor Rehabilitation & Healthcare Center
581 Poquonock Ave., Windsor, CT 06095, (860) 688-7211; Facility Type: Skilled care; Alzheimer's; Certified Beds: 120; Alzheimer's 30; Hospice; Certified: Medicaid; Medicare; Veterans; Owner: Vencor Inc.; License: Current state

DELAWARE

Dover

Capitol Healthcare Services
1225 Walker Rd., Dover, DE 19904, (302) 734-1199; Facility Type: Skilled care; ICF; ICF/MR; Alzheimer's; Certified Beds: 120; Certified: Medicaid; Medicare; Veterans; Owner: Private; License: Current state

Courtland Manor Nursing & Convalescent Home
889 S Little Creek Rd., Dover, DE 19901, (302) 674-0566; Facility Type: Skilled care; ICF; Alzheimer's; Certified Beds: 70; Certified: Medicaid; Medicare; Veterans; Owner: Private; License: Current state

Silver Lake Center
1080 Silver Lake Blvd., Dover, DE 19904, (302) 734-5990; Facility Type: Skilled care; ICF; Alzheimer's; Certified Beds: 120; Certified: Medicaid; Medicare; Owner: Proprietary/Public corp.; License: Current state

Westminster Village Health Care
1175 McKee Rd., Dover, DE 19904, (302) 674-8030; Facility Type: Skilled care; ICF; Alzheimer's; Certified Beds: 61; Certified: Medicaid; Medicare; Veterans; Owner: Nonprofit corp.; License: Current state

Georgetown

Harrison House of Georgetown
110 W North St., Georgetown, DE 19947, (302) 856-4574; Facility Type: Skilled care; ICF; ICF/ MR; Alzheimer's; Certified Beds: 109; Certified: Medicaid; Medicare; Veterans; Owner: Proprietary/Public corp.; License: Current state

Hockessin

Regal Heights Healthcare & Rehab Center
6525 Lancaster Pike, Hockessin, DE 19707, (302) 998-0181; Facility Type: Skilled care; ICF; Alzheimer's; Certified Beds: 172; Certified: Medicaid; Medicare; Owner: Proprietary/Public corp.; License: Current state

Saint Francis Care Center at Brackenville
100 S Claire Dr., Hockessin, DE 19707, (302) 234-5420; Facility Type: Skilled care; ICF; Alzheimer's; Certified Beds: 104; Certified: Medicaid; Medicare; Veterans; Owner: Catholic Health Initiatives; License: n/a

Milford

Delaware Veteran's Home
100 Delaware Veterans Dr., Milford, DE 19963, (302) 424-6000; Facility Type: Skilled care; ICF; Alzheimer's; Certified Beds: 120; Certified: Medicaid; Medicare; Veterans; Owner: Government/state.; License: Current state

Milford Center — Genesis ElderCare Network
700 Marvel Rd., Milford, DE 19963, (302) 422-3303; Facility Type: Skilled care; ICF; Alzheimer's; Certified Beds: 136; Residential care; Certified: Medicaid; Medicare; Owner: Genesis ElderCare; License: Current state

Wilmington

Brandywine Nursing & Rehabilitation Center
505 Greenbank Rd., Wilmington, DE 19808, (302) 998-0101; Facility Type: Skilled care; ICF; Alzheimer's; Certified Beds: 169; Certified: Medicaid; Medicare; Owner: Nonprofit; License: Current state

Hillside Center
810 S Broom St., Wilmington, DE 19805, (302) 652-1181; Facility Type: Skilled care; ICF; Alzheimer's; Certified Beds: 106; Certified: Medicaid; Medicare; Veterans; Owner: Genesis ElderCare; License: Current state

ManorCare Health Services–Pike Creek
5651 Limestone Rd., Wilmington, DE 19808, (302) 239-8583; Facility Type: Skilled care; ICF; Alzheimer's; Certified Beds: 167; Certified: Medicaid; Medicare; Owner: For-Profit; License: Current state

ManorCare Health Services–Wilmington
700 Foulk Rd., Wilmington, DE 19803, (302) 364-0181; Facility Type: ICF; Alzheimer's; Certified Beds: 138; Certified: Medicare; Medicaid; Owner: Private, For-Profit; License: Current state license

Milton & Hattie Kutz Home
704 River Rd., Wilmington, DE 19809, (302) 764-7000; Facility Type: Skilled care; ICF; Alzheimer's; Certified Beds: 90; Certified: Medicaid; Medicare; Owner: Nonprofit corp.; License: Current state

Parkview Nursing & Rehab
2801 W 6th St., Wilmington, DE 19805, (302) 655-6135; Facility Type: Skilled care; ICF; Alzheimer's; Certified Beds: 150; Certified: Medicaid; Medicare; Veterans; Owner: Nonprofit, Genesis Eldercare; License: Current state

DISTRICT OF COLUMBIA

Washington

Capitol Hill Nursing Center
700 Constitution Ave. NE, Washington, DC 20002, (202) 546-5700; Facility Type: Skilled care; Alzheimer's; Certified Beds: 117; Certified: Medicaid; Medicare; Owner: Private, For-Profit; License: Current state

Carolyn Boone Lewis Healthcare Center
1380 Southern Ave SE, Washington, DC 20032, (202) 279-5880; Facility Type: Skilled care; Alzheimer's; Certified Beds: 183; Certified: Medicaid; Medicare; Owner: Private, For-Profit; License: Current state

Carrol Manor Nursing & Rehabilitation
725 Buchanan St. NE, Washington, DC 20017, (202) 269-7221; Facility Type: Skilled care; Alzheimer's; Certified Beds: 192; Certified: Medicaid; Medicare; Owner: Private, For-Profit; License: Current state

Deanwood Rehabilitation & Wellness Center
5000 Burroughs Ave. NE, Washington, DC 20019, (202) 399-7504; Facility Type: Skilled care; Alzheimer's; Memory Care; Certified Beds: 296; Certified: Medicaid; Medicare; Owner: Private, For-Profit; License: Current state

J B Johnson Nursing Center
901 First St. NW, Washington, DC 20001, (202) 535-2055; Facility Type: Skilled care; Alzheimer's; Certified Beds: 230; Certified: Medicaid; Medicare; Veterans; Owner: Government/City; License: Current state

Rock Creek Manor Nursing Center
2131 O St. NW, Washington, DC 20037, (202) 785-2577; Facility Type: Skilled care; Alzheimer's; Certified Beds: 180; Certified: Medicaid; Medicare; Owner: Private, For-Profit; License: Current state

Stoddard Baptist Nursing Home
1818 Newton St. NW, Washington, DC 20010, (202) 328-7400; Facility Type: Skilled care; Alzheimer's; Certified Beds: 164; Certified: Medicaid; Medicare; Owner: Private, For-Profit; License: Current state

Washington Center for Aging Services
2601 18th St., NE Washington, DC 20018, (202) 541-6200; Facility Type: Skilled care; ICF; Alzheimer's; Certified Beds: 259; Certified: Medicaid; Medicare; Owner: Government/State/Local; License: Current state

The Washington Home
3720 Upton St., NW Washington, DC 20016, (202) 966-3720; Facility Type: Skilled care; Alzheimer's; Respite; Hospice; Certified Beds: 188 Certified: Medicaid; Medicare; Owner: Genesis ElderCare; License: Current state

---

FLORIDA

Altamonte Springs

Consulate Healthcare at West Altamonte
1099 W. Town Pkwy., Altamonte Springs, FL 32714, (407) 865-8000; Facility Type: Skilled care; Alzheimer's; Certified Beds: 116; Certified: Medicaid; Medicare; Owner: Private, For-Profit; License: Current state

Life Care Center of Altamonte Springs
989 Orienta Ave., Altamonte Springs, FL 32701, (407) 831-3446; Facility Type: Skilled care; ICF; Alzheimer's; Certified Beds: 240; Certified: Medicaid; Medicare; Veterans; Owner: Proprietary/Public corp.; License: Current state

Atlantic Beach

Fleet Landing
1 Fleet Landing Blvd., Atlantic Beach, FL 32233, (904) 246-9900; Facility Type: Skilled care; ICF; Alzheimer's; Certified Beds: 80; Certified: Medicare; Veterans; Owner: Nonprofit corp.; License: Current state

Avon Park

The Oaks at Avon
1010 US 27 N, Avon Park, FL 33825, (863) 453-5200; Facility Type: Skilled care; Alzheimer's; Certified Beds: 104; Certified: Medicaid; Medicare; Owner: Proprietary/Public corp.; License: Current state

Royal Care of Avon Park
1213 W. Stratford Rd., Avon Park, FL 33825, (863) 453-6674; Facility Type: Skilled care; Alzheimer's; Certified Beds: 90; Certified: Medicaid; Medicare; Owner: Private, For-Profit; License: Current state

Boca Raton

Avante at Boca Raton Inc.
1130 NW 15th St., Boca Raton, FL 33486, (561) 394-6282; Facility Type: Skilled care; ICF; Alzheimer's; Assisted Living; Certified Beds: 144; Certified: Medicaid; Medicare; Owner: Avante Group; License: Current state

Boca Raton Rehabilitation Center
755 Meadows Rd., Boca Raton, FL 33486, (561) 391-

5200; Facility Type: Skilled care; Alzheimer's; Certified Beds: 120; Certified: Medicaid; Medicare; Owner: Private, For-Profit; License: Current state

Heartland Health Care Center of Boca Raton
722 Boca Del Mar Dr., Boca Raton, FL 33433, (561) 362-9644; Facility Type: Skilled care; ICF; Alzheimer's; Certified Beds: 120; Certified: Medicare; Owner: HCR ManorCare; License: Current state

ManorCare Health Services
375 NW 51st St., Boca Raton, FL 33431, (561) 997-8111; Facility Type: Skilled care; Alzheimer's; Certified Beds: 180; Certified: Medicaid; Medicare; Owner: Private, For-Profit; License: Current state

Menorah House
9945 Central Park Blvd., North Boca Raton, FL 33428, (561) 483-0498; Facility Type: Skilled care; Alzheimer's; Certified Beds: 120; Certified: Medicaid; Medicare; Owner: Private, For-Profit; License: Current state

Regents Park Nursing & Rehabilitation Center
6363 Verde Trail, Boca Raton, FL 33433, (561) 483-9282; Facility Type: Skilled care; Alzheimer's; Certified Beds: 180; Certified: Medicaid; Medicare; Owner: Private, For-Profit; License: Current state

Whitehall Boca Raton
7300 Del Prado, South Boca Raton, FL 33433, (561) 392-3000; Facility Type: Skilled care; Alzheimer's; Certified Beds: 154; Certified: Medicaid; Medicare; Owner: Private, For-Profit; License: Current state

Boynton Beach

Barrington Terrace of Boynton Beach
1425 S. Congress Ave., Boynton Beach, FL 33426, (561) 369-7919; Facility Type: Skilled care; Alzheimer's; Certified Beds: 29; Certified: Medicare; Owner: Private, For-Profit; License: Current state

Boulevard Rehabilitation Center
2839 S Seacrest Blvd., Boynton Beach, FL 33435, (561) 732-2464; Facility Type: Skilled care; Alzheimer's; Certified Beds: 167; Certified: Medicaid; Medicare; Owner: Private, For-Profit; License: Current state

Boynton Beach Rehabilitation Center
9600 Lawrence Rd., Boynton Beach, FL 33436, (561) 740-4100; Facility Type: Skilled care; Alzheimer's; Certified Beds: 168; Certified: Medicaid; Medicare; Owner: Private, For-Profit; License: Current state

Heartland Health Care Center of Boynton
3600 Old Boynton Rd., Boynton Beach, FL 33436, (561) 736-9992; Facility Type: Skilled care; Alzheimer's; Certified Beds: 120; Certified: Medicaid; Medicare; Owner: HCR ManorCare; License: Current state

Bradenton

Braden River Care Center
2010 Manatee Ave. E., Bradenton, FL 34208, (941) 747-3706; Facility Type: Skilled care; Alzheimer's; Certified Beds: 208; Certified: Medicaid; Medicare; Owner: Private, For-Profit; License: Current state

Casa Mora Rehabilitation & Extended Care
1902 59th St., W Bradenton, FL 34209, (941) 761-1000; Facility Type: Skilled care; ICF; Alzheimer's; Certified Beds: 240; Certified: Medicaid; Medicare; Owner: Proprietary/Public corp.; License: Current state

Heritage Park Care & Rehabilitation Center
2302 59th St., W., Bradenton, FL 34209, (941) 792-8480; Facility Type: Skilled care; Alzheimer's; Certified Beds: 120; Certified: Medicaid; Medicare; Owner: Private, For-Profit; License: Current state

The Nursing Center at Freedom Village
6410 21st Ave. W., Bradenton, FL 34209, (941) 798-8300; Facility Type: Skilled care; Alzheimer's; Certified Beds: 120; Certified: Medicaid; Medicare; Owner: Private, For-Profit; License: Current state

Riverfront Nursing & Rehabilitation Center
105 15th St. E., Bradenton, FL 34208, (941) 747-8681; Facility Type: Skilled care; Alzheimer's; Certified Beds: 110; Certified: Medicaid; Medicare; Owner: Private, For-Profit; License: Current state

Brooksville

Brooksville Healthcare Center
114 Chatman Blvd., Brooksville, FL 34601, (352) 796-6701; Facility Type: Skilled care; ICF; Alzheimer's; Certified Beds: 180; Certified: Medicaid; Medicare; Veterans; Owner: Private; License: Current state

Heartland of Brooksville
575 Lamar Ave., Brooksville, FL 34601, (352) 799-2226; Facility Type: Skilled care; Alzheimer's; Certified Beds: 120; Certified: Medicaid; Medicare; Owner: Private, For-Profit; License: Current state

Spring Hill Health & Rehabilitation Center
12170 Cortez Blvd., Brooksville, FL 34613, (352) 597-5100; Facility Type: Skilled care; Alzheimer's; Certified Beds: 120; Certified: Medicaid; Medicare; Owner: Private, For-Profit; License: Current state

Clearwater

Advanced Rehabilitation & Health Center
401 Fairwood Ave., Clearwater, FL 33759, (727) 210-2600; Facility Type: Skilled care; Alzheimer's; Certified Beds: 120; Certified: Medicaid; Medicare; Owner: Private, For-Profit; License: Current state

Belleair Health Care Center
1150 Ponce de Leon Blvd., Clearwater, FL 33756,

(727) 585-5491; Facility Type: Skilled care; Alzheimer's; Certified Beds: 120; Certified: Medicaid; Medicare; Owner: Private, For-Profit; License: Current state

Comprehensive Healthcare of Clearwater
2055 Palmetto St., Clearwater, FL 33758, (727) 461-6613; Facility Type: Skilled care; Alzheimer's; Certified Beds: 150; Certified: Medicaid; Medicare; Owner: Private, For-Profit; License: Current state

Highland Pines Rehabilitation Center
1111 S. Highland Ave., Clearwater, FL 33756, (727) 446-0581; Facility Type: Skilled care; Alzheimer's; Certified Beds: 120; Certified: Medicaid; Medicare; Owner: Private, Nonprofit; License: Current state

Sunset Point Care & Rehabilitation Center
1980 Sunset Point Rd., Clearwater, FL 33765, (727) 443-1588; Facility Type: Skilled care; Alzheimer's; Certified Beds: 120; Certified: Medicaid; Medicare; Owner: Private, For-Profit; License: Current state

Westchester Gardens Rehabilitation & Care Center
3301 McMullen Booth Rd., Clearwater, FL 33761, (727) 785-8335; Facility Type: Skilled care; ICF; Alzheimer's; Certified Beds: 120; Certified: Medicaid; Medicare; Owner: Private; License: Current state

Dade City

Heritage Park
37135 Coleman Ave., Dade City, FL 33525, (352) 567-8615; Facility Type: Skilled care; Alzheimer's; Certified Beds: 120; Certified: Medicaid; Medicare; Owner: Private, For-Profit; License: Current state

Royal Oak Nursing Center
37300 Royal Oak Ln., Dade City, FL 33525, (352) 567-3122; Facility Type: Skilled care; Alzheimer's; Certified Beds: 120; Certified: Medicaid; Medicare; Owner: Private, For-Profit; License: Current state

Daytona Beach

Coastal Health & Rehabilitation Center
820 N Clyde Morris Blvd., Daytona Beach, FL 32117, (904) 274-5020; Facility Type: Skilled care; ICF; Alzheimer's; Certified Beds: 120; Certified: Medicaid; Medicare; Owner: Private; License: Current state

Daytona Beach Health & Rehabilitation Center
1055 3rd St., Daytona Beach, FL 32117, (386) 252-3686; Facility Type: Skilled care; Alzheimer's; Certified Beds: 180; Certified: Medicaid; Medicare; Owner: Private, For-Profit; License: Current state

Good Samaritan Society — Daytona
325 S Segrave St., Daytona Beach, FL 32114, (904) 253-6791; Facility Type: Skilled care; ICF; Alzheimer's; Certified Beds: 120; Certified: Medicaid; Medicare; Owner: Nonprofit/Religious org.; License: Current state

The Health Center of Daytona Beach
550 National Healthcare Dr., Daytona Beach, FL 32114, (386) 257-6362; Facility Type: Skilled care; Alzheimer's; Certified Beds: 70; Certified: Medicaid; Medicare; Owner: Private, For-Profit; License: Current state

Indigo Manor
595 Williamson Blvd., Daytona Beach, FL 32114, (904) 257-4400; Facility Type: Skilled care; ICF; Alzheimer's; Certified Beds: 173; Certified: Medicaid; Medicare; Veterans; Owner: Private; License: Current state

Manor on the Green
324 Wilder Blvd., Daytona Beach, FL 32114, (386) 252-2600; Facility Type: Skilled care; Alzheimer's; Certified Beds: 120; Certified: Medicaid; Medicare; Owner: Private, For-Profit; License: Current state

DeLand

Ridgecrest Nursing & Rehabilitation Center
1200 N Stone St., DeLand, FL 32720, (904) 734-6200; Facility Type: Skilled care; Alzheimer's; Certified Beds: 160; Certified: Medicaid; Medicare; Owner: Private; License: Current state

University Center West
545 W Euclid Ave., DeLand, FL 32720, (904) 734-9085; Facility Type: Skilled care; ICF; Alzheimer's; Certified Beds: 60; Certified: Medicaid; Medicare; Veterans; Owner: Genesis ElderCare; License: Current state

Delray Beach

Abbey Delray
2105 SW 11th Ct., Delray Beach, FL 33445, (561) 454-1136; Facility Type: Skilled care; Alzheimer's; Certified Beds: 100; Certified: Medicaid; Medicare; Owner: Private, Nonprofit; License: Current state

Abbey Delray South
1717 Homewood Blvd., Delray Beach, FL 33445, (561) 454-5200; Facility Type: Skilled care; Alzheimer's; Certified Beds: 90; Certified: Medicaid; Medicare; Owner: Private, Nonprofit; License: Current state

Harbour's Edge Health Center
401 E Linton Blvd., Delray Beach, FL 33483, (561) 272-7979; Facility Type: Skilled care; Alzheimer's; Certified Beds: 54; Certified: Medicare; Owner: Nonprofit corp.; License: Current state

Lake View Care Center at Delray
5430 Linton Blvd., Delray Beach, FL 33484, (561) 495-3188; Facility Type: Skilled care; Alzheimer's;

Certified Beds: 120; Certified: Medicaid; Medicare; Owner: Private, For-Profit; License: Current state

ManorCare Health Services
16200 Jog Rd., Delray Beach, FL 33446, (561) 638-0000; Facility Type: Skilled care; Alzheimer's; Certified Beds: 120; Certified: Medicaid; Medicare; Owner: Private, For-Profit; License: Current state

Dunedin

Edinborough Healthcare Center
1061 Virginia St., Dunedin, FL 34698, (727) 733-4189; Facility Type: Skilled care; ICF; Alzheimer's; Certified Beds: 93; Certified: Medicaid; Medicare; Veterans; Owner: Proprietary/Public corp.; License: Current state

ManorCare Health Services Dunedin
870 Patricia Ave., Dunedin, FL 34698, (727) 734-8861; Facility Type: Skilled care; Alzheimer's; Certified Beds: 120; Certified: Medicaid; Medicare; Owner: Private, For-Profit; License: Current state

Fort Lauderdale

Fort Lauderdale Health & Rehabilitation Center
2000 E. Commercial Blvd., Fort Lauderdale, FL 33308, (954) 771-2300; Facility Type: Skilled care; Alzheimer's; Certified Beds: 155; Certified: Medicaid; Medicare; Owner: Private, For-Profit; License: Current state

Harbor Beach Nursing & Rehabilitation Center
1615 S Miami Rd., Fort Lauderdale, FL 33316, (954) 523-5673; Facility Type: Skilled care; Alzheimer's; Certified Beds: 59; Certified: Medicaid; Medicare; Owner: Proprietary/Public corp.; License: Current state

Manor Oaks Nursing & Rehabilitation Center National Health Care Center of Fort Lauderdale
2121 E Commercial Blvd., Fort Lauderdale, FL 33308, (954) 771-8400; Facility Type: Skilled care; ICF; Alzheimer's; Certified Beds: 116; Certified: Medicaid; Medicare; Owner: Proprietary/Public corp.; License: n/a

Manor Pines Convalescent Center
1701 NE 26th St., Fort Lauderdale, FL 33305, (954) 566-8353; Facility Type: Skilled care; Alzheimer's; Certified Beds: 206; Certified: Medicaid; Medicare; Owner: Private, For-Profit; License: Current state

Fort Myers

Consulate Health Care of North Fort Myers
991 Pondella Rd., Fort Myers, FL 33903, (239) 995-8809; Facility Type: Skilled care; Alzheimer's; Cer-

tified Beds: 120; Certified: Medicaid; Medicare; Owner: Private, For-Profit; License: Current state

Healthpark Care Center, Inc.
16131 Roserush Ct., Fort Myers, FL 33908, (239) 433-4647; Facility Type: Skilled care; Alzheimer's; Certified Beds: 116; Certified: Medicaid; Medicare; Owner: Government/Hospital District; License: Current state

Heritage Park Rehabilitation & Healthcare Center
2826 Cleveland Ave., Fort Myers, FL 33901, (941) 334-1091; Facility Type: Skilled care; Alzheimer's; Certified Beds: 116; Certified: Medicaid; Medicare; Veterans; Owner: Beverly Enterprises Inc.; License: Current state

Page Rehabilitation & Healthcare Center
2310 N Airport Rd., Fort Myers, FL 33907, (941) 277-5000; Facility Type: Skilled care; Alzheimer's; Certified Beds: 190 Certified: Medicaid; Medicare; Owner: Nonprofit corp.; License: Current state

Shell Point Nursing Pavilion
15000 Shell Point Blvd., Fort Myers, FL 33908, (941) 415-5430; Facility Type: Skilled care; Alzheimer's; Assisted Living; Certified Beds: 219; Certified: Medicare; Owner: Nonprofit/Religious org.; License: Current state

Fort Pierce

Fort Pierce Healthcare
611 S 13th St., Fort Pierce, FL 34950, (561) 464-5262; Facility Type: Skilled care; ICF; Alzheimer's; Certified Beds: 171; Certified: Medicaid; Medicare; Veterans; Owner: Beverly Enterprises Inc.; License: Current state

Laurell Pointe Health & Rehabilitation
703 29th St., Fort Pierce, FL 34947, (772) 466-3322; Facility Type: Skilled care; Alzheimer's; Certified Beds: 107; Certified: Medicaid; Medicare; Owner: Private, For-Profit; License: Current state

Gainesville

Gainesville Health Care Center
1311 SW 16th St., Gainesville, FL 32608, (352) 376-8821; Facility Type: Skilled care; Alzheimer's; Certified Beds: 180; Certified: Medicaid; Medicare; Owner: Private, For-Profit; License: Current state

North Florida Rehabilitation & Specialty Care
6700 NW 10th Pl., Gainesville, FL 32605, (352) 331-3111; Facility Type: Skilled care; Alzheimer's; Certified Beds: 120; Certified: Medicaid; Medicare; Owner: Private, For-Profit; License: Current state

Park Meadows Health & Rehabilitation Center
3250 SW 41st Pl., Gainesville, FL 32608, (352) 378-

1558; Facility Type: Skilled care; ICF; Alzheimer's; Certified Beds: 154; Certified: Medicaid; Medicare; Veterans; Owner: Proprietary/Public corp.; License: Current state

Inverness

Arbor Trail Rehab & Skilled Nursing Center
611 E Turner Camp Rd., Inverness, FL 34453, (352) 637-1130; Facility Type: Skilled care; ICF; Alzheimer's; Certified Beds: 116; Certified: Medicaid; Medicare; Owner: Mariner Post Acute Network; License: Current state

Avante at Inverness Inc.
304 S Citrus Ave., Inverness, FL 34452, (352) 726-3141; Facility Type: Skilled care; Alzheimer's; Certified Beds: 104; Certified: Medicaid; Medicare; Owner: Proprietary/Public corp.; License: Current state

Jacksonville

All Saints Catholic Nursing Home & Rehabilitation Center
5888 Blanding Blvd., Jacksonville, FL 32244, (904) 772-1220; Facility Type: Skilled care; Alzheimer's; Certified Beds: 120; Certified: Medicaid; Medicare; Owner: Private, Nonprofit; License: Current state

Cathedral Gerontology Center, Inc.
333 E Ashley St., Jacksonville, FL 32202, (904) 798-5300; Facility Type: Skilled care; Alzheimer's; Certified Beds: 120; Certified: Medicaid; Medicare; Owner: Private, Nonprofit; License: Current state

Cedar Hills Healthcare Center
2061 Hyde Park Rd., Jacksonville, FL 32210, (904) 786-7331; Facility Type: Skilled care; Alzheimer's; Certified Beds: 180; Certified: Medicaid; Medicare; Owner: Private, For-Profit; License: Current state

Harts Harbor Health Care Center
11565 Harts Rd., Jacksonville, FL 32218, (904) 751-1834; Facility Type: Skilled care; Alzheimer's; Certified Beds: 180; Certified: Medicaid; Medicare; Owner: Private, For-Profit; License: Current state

Heartland Health Care Center of South Jacksonville
3648 University Blvd., S Jacksonville, FL 32216, (904) 733-7440; Facility Type: Skilled care; ICF; Alzheimer's; Certified Beds: 117; Certified: Medicaid; Medicare; Owner: HCR ManorCare; License: Current state

Lanier Manor
12740 Lanier Rd., Jacksonville, FL 32226, (904) 757-0600; Facility Type: Skilled care; ICF; Alzheimer's; Certified Beds: 120; Certified: Medicaid; Medicare; Veterans; Owner: Private; License: Current state

The Riverwood Center
2802 Parental Home Rd., Jacksonville, FL 32216,

(904) 721-0088; Facility Type: Skilled care; ICF; Alzheimer's; Certified Beds: 240; Certified: Medicaid; Medicare; Veterans; Owner: Genesis ElderCare; License: Current state

Taylor Care Center
6535 Chester Ave., Jacksonville, FL 32217, (904) 731-8230; Facility Type: Skilled care; ICF; Alzheimer's; Certified Beds: 120; ICF; Alzheimer's; SNF/ICF; Certified: Medicaid; Medicare; Owner: Nonprofit corp.; License: Current state

Kissimmee

Consulate Health Care of Kissimmee
2511 John Young Pkwy., North Kissimmee, FL 34741, (407) 931-3336; Facility Type: Skilled care; Alzheimer's; Certified Beds: 120; Certified: Medicaid; Medicare; Owner: Private, For-Profit; License: Current state

Oaks of Kissimmee
320 N Mitchell St., Kissimmee, FL 34741, (407) 847-7200; Facility Type: Skilled care; ICF; Alzheimer's; Certified Beds: 59; Certified: Medicaid; Medicare; Owner: Proprietary/Public corp.; License: Current state

The Palms at Park Place
221 Park Place Blvd., Kissimmee, FL 34741, (407) 935-0200; Facility Type: Skilled care; Alzheimer's; Certified Beds: 120; Certified: Medicaid; Medicare; Owner: Private, For-Profit; License: Current state

Lake City

Baya Pointe Nursing & Rehabilitation Center
587 SE Ermine Ave., Lake City, FL 32025, (386) 752-7800; Facility Type: Skilled care; Alzheimer's; Certified Beds: 90; Certified: Medicaid; Medicare; Owner: Private, For-Profit; License: Current state

Health Center of Lake City
920 McFarlane Ave., Lake City, FL 32025, (904) 758-4777; Facility Type: Skilled care; ICF; Alzheimer's; Certified Beds: 120; Certified: Medicaid; Medicare; Veterans; Owner: Proprietary/Public corp.; License: Current state

Lake Wales

Dove Healthcare at Lake Wales
730 N Scenic Hwy., Lake Wales, FL 33853, (863) 676-1512; Facility Type: Skilled care; ICF; Alzheimer's; Certified Beds: 100; Certified: Medicaid; Medicare; Veterans; Owner: Private; License: Current state

The Groves Center
512 S 11th St., Lake Wales, FL 33853, (863) 676-8502; Facility Type: Skilled care; ICF; Alzheimer's;

Certified Beds: 120; Certified: Medicaid; Medicare; Veterans; Owner: Nonprofit/Religious org.; License: Current state

Lake Worth

American-Finnish Nursing Home
1800 South Dr., Lake Worth, FL 33461, (561) 588-4333; Facility Type: Skilled care; Alzheimer's; Certified Beds: 60; Certified: Medicaid; Medicare; Owner: Private, Nonprofit; License: Current state

Avante at Lake Worth
2501 North A St., Lake Worth, FL 33460, (561) 585-9301; Facility Type: Skilled care; ICF; ICF/ MR; Alzheimer's; Certified Beds: 138; Certified: Medicaid; Medicare; Owner: Avante Group; License: Current state

Oasis Health & Rehabilitation Center
1201 12th Ave S., Lake Worth, FL 33460, (561) 586-7404; Facility Type: Skilled care; Alzheimer's; Certified Beds: 120; Certified: Medicaid; Medicare; Owner: Private, For-Profit; License: Current state

Terraces of Lake Worth Rehabilitation & Health Center
1711 6th Ave., S Lake Worth, FL 33460, (561) 585-2997; Facility Type: Skilled care; ICF; Alzheimer's; Certified Beds: 90; Certified: Medicaid; Medicare; Owner: Proprietary/Public corp.; License: Current state

Lakeland

Consulate Health Care of Lakeland
5245 Socrum Loop Rd., N Lakeland, FL 33809, (863) 859-1446; Facility Type: Skilled care; ICF; Alzheimer's; Certified Beds: 120; Certified: Medicaid; Medicare; Owner: Private, For-Profit; License: Current state

Highlands Lake Center
4240 Lakeland Highlands Rd., Lakeland, FL 33813, (863) 646-8699; Facility Type: Skilled care; ICF; Alzheimer's; Certified Beds: 179; Certified: Medicaid; Medicare; Owner: Private; License: Current state

Lakeland Hills Center
610 E Bella Vista Dr., Lakeland, FL 33805, (863) 688-8591; Facility Type: Skilled care; ICF; Alzheimer's; Certified Beds: 117 Certified: Medicaid; Medicare; Veterans; Owner: Genesis ElderCare; License: Current state

Oakbridge Healthcare Center
3110 Oakbridge Blvd. E., Lakeland, FL 33803, (863) 648-4800; Facility Type: Skilled care; Alzheimer's; Certified Beds: 120; Certified: Medicaid; Medicare; Owner: Private, For-Profit; License: Current state

Valencia Hills Health & Rehabilitation Center
1350 Sleepy Hill Rd., Lakeland, FL 33810, (863) 858-

4402; Facility Type: Skilled care; Alzheimer's; Certified Beds: 300; Certified: Medicaid; Medicare; Owner: Private, For-Profit; License: Current state

Largo

Largo Rehabilitation & Spa
9035 Bryan Dairy Rd., Largo, FL 33777, (727) 395-9619; Facility Type: Skilled care; Alzheimer's; Assisted Living; CCRC; Certified Beds: 158; Certified: Medicaid; Medicare; Owner: Private, For-Profit; License: Current state

Oak Manor Healthcare & Rehabilitation Center
3500 Oak Manor Ln., Largo, FL 34641, (727) 581-9427; Facility Type: Skilled care; Alzheimer's; Certified Beds: 180; Certified: Medicaid; Medicare; Owner: Private, For-Profit; License: Current state

Sabal Palms Health Care Center
499 Alternate Keene Rd., Largo, FL 33771, (727) 586-4211; Facility Type: Skilled care; ICF; Alzheimer's; Certified Beds: 244; Certified: Medicaid; Medicare; Owner: Private; License: Current state

Tierra Pines Center
7380 Ulmerton Rd., Largo, FL 33771, (727) 535-9833; Facility Type: Skilled care; Alzheimer's; Certified Beds: 120; Certified: Medicaid; Medicare; Owner: Private, For-Profit; License: Current state

Live Oak

Good Samaritan Center
10676 Marvin Jones Blvd., Live Oak, FL 32060, (386) 658-5550; Facility Type: Skilled care; Alzheimer's; Certified Beds: 161; Certified: Medicaid; Medicare; Owner: Private, For-Profit; License: Current state

Suwannee Health Care Center
1620 E Helvenston St., Live Oak, FL 32060, (904) 362-7860; Facility Type: Skilled care; ICF; ICF/MR; Alzheimer's; Certified Beds: 180; Certified: Medicaid; Medicare; Veterans; Owner: Beverly Enterprises Inc.; License: Current state

Melbourne

Atlantic Shores Nursing & Rehabilitation
4251 Stack Blvd., Melbourne, FL 32901, (321) 953-2219; Facility Type: Skilled care; Alzheimer's; Certified Beds: 120; Certified: Medicaid; Medicare; Owner: Private, For-Profit; License: Current state

Carnegie Gardens Nursing Center
1415 S Hickory St., Melbourne, FL 32901, (321) 723-1321; Facility Type: Skilled care; ICF; Alzheimer's; Certified Beds: 138; Certified: Medicaid; Medicare; Owner: Proprietary/Public corp.; License: Current state

Consulate Health Care of Melbourne
3033 Sarno Rd., Melbourne, FL 32934, (321) 255-9200; Facility Type: Skilled care; Alzheimer's; Certified Beds: 120; Certified: Medicaid; Medicare; Owner: Private, For-Profit; License: Current state

Miami

Coral Reef Nursing & Rehabilitation Center
9869 SW 152 St., Miami, FL 33157, (305) 255-3220; Facility Type: Skilled care; ICF; Alzheimer's; Certified Beds: 180 Certified: Medicaid; Medicare; Owner: n/a; License: Current state

Florida Club Care Center
220 Sierra Dr., Miami, FL 33179, (305) 653-8427; Facility Type: Skilled care; ICF; Alzheimer's; Certified Beds: 180; Certified: Medicaid; Medicare; Owner: Proprietary/Public corp.; License: Current state

Harmony Health Care Center
9820 N. Kendall Dr., Miami, FL 33176, (305) 271-6311; Facility Type: Skilled care; Alzheimer's; Certified Beds: 203; Certified: Medicaid; Medicare; Owner: Private, For-Profit; License: Current state

Hialeah Shores
8785 NW 32nd Ave., Miami, FL 33147, (305) 691-5711; Facility Type: Skilled care; ICF; ICF/ MR; Alzheimer's; Certified Beds: 106; Certified: Medicaid; Medicare; Owner: Private; License: Current state

Jackson Memorial Longterm Care Center
2500 NW 22nd Ave., Miami, FL 33142, (786) 466-3000; Facility Type: Skilled care; Alzheimer's; Certified Beds: 180; Certified: Medicaid; Medicare; Veterans; Owner: Government/County; License: Current state

Miami Jewish Home & Hospital for the Aged, Inc.
5200 NE 2nd Ave., Miami, FL 33137, (305) 751-8626; Facility Type: Skilled care; Alzheimer's; Certified Beds: 462; Certified: Medicaid; Medicare; Owner: Nonprofit/Religious org.; License: Current state

Palace at Kendall Nursing & Rehabilitation Center
11215 SW 84th St., Miami, FL 33173, (305) 271-2225; Facility Type: Skilled care; Alzheimer's; Certified Beds: 180; Certified: Medicaid; Medicare; Owner: Private, For-Profit; License: Current state

St. Anne's Nursing Center, Residence, Inc.
11855 Quail Roost Dr., Miami, FL 33177, (305) 252-4000; Facility Type: Skilled care; Alzheimer's; Certified Beds: 220; Certified: Medicaid; Medicare; Owner: Private, Nonprofit; License: Current state

Unity Health & Rehabilitation Center
1404 NW 22nd St., Miami, FL 33142, (305) 325-1050; Facility Type: Skilled care; Alzheimer's; Certified Beds: 291; Certified: Medicaid; Medicare; Owner: Private, For-Profit; License: Current state

Monticello

Brynwood Center
Rte. 1 Box 21 Monticello, FL 32344, (850) 997-1800; Facility Type: Skilled care; ICF; Alzheimer's; Certified Beds: 97; Certified: Medicaid; Medicare; Owner: Nonprofit corp.; License: Current state

Cross Landings Health & Rehabilitation Center
1780 N. Jefferson St., Monticello, FL 32344, (850) 997-2313; Facility Type: Skilled care; Alzheimer's; Certified Beds: 60; Certified: Medicaid; Medicare; Owner: Private, For-Profit; License: Current state

Naples

The Chateau at Moorings Park
130 Moorings Park Dr., Naples, FL 34105, (239) 643-9133; Facility Type: Skilled care; Alzheimer's; Certified Beds: 106; Certified: Medicaid; Medicare; Owner: Private, Nonprofit; License: Current state

Imperial Health Care Center
900 Imperial Golf Course Blvd., Naples, FL 34110, (239) 591-4800; Facility Type: Skilled care; Alzheimer's; Certified Beds: 113; Certified: Medicaid; Medicare; Owner: Private, For-Profit; License: Current state

Lakeside Pavillion Care & Rehabilitation Center
2900 12th St., N Naples, FL 34103, (941) 261-2554; Facility Type: Skilled care; ICF; ICF/MR; Alzheimer's; Certified Beds: 120; Certified: Medicaid; Medicare; Owner: Proprietary/Public corp.; License: Current state

Premier Place at the Glenview
100 Glenview Pl., Naples, FL 34108, (941) 591-0011; Facility Type: Skilled care; ICF; Alzheimer's; Certified Beds: 35 Certified: Medicare; Owner: Nonprofit corp.; License: Current state

North Miami

Berkshire Manor
1255 NE 135th St., North Miami, FL 33161, (305) 891-6850; Facility Type: Skilled care; Alzheimer's; Certified Beds: 256; Certified: Medicaid; Medicare; Owner: Private, For-Profit; License: Current state

Claridge House Nursing & Rehabilitation Center
13900 NE 3rd Ct., North Miami, FL 33161, (305) 893-2288; Facility Type: Skilled care; Alzheimer's; Certified Beds: 240; Certified: Medicaid; Medicare; Owner: Private, For-Profit; License: Current state

Villa Marie Nursing Center
1050 NE 125th St., North Miami, FL 33161, (305) 891-8850; Facility Type: Skilled care; ICF; Alzheimer's; Certified Beds: 212; Certified: Medicaid; Medicare; Owner: Nonprofit corp.; License: Current state

North Miami Beach

Aventura Plaza Nursing & Rehabilitation Center
1800 NE 168th Street, North Miami Beach, FL 33162, (305) 947-3445; Facility Type: Skilled care; Alzheimer's; Alzheimer's Treatment Program; Kosher cuisine; Certified Beds: 86; Certified: Medicaid; Medicare; Owner: Private, Nonprofit; License: Current state

Hampton Court Nursing & Rehabilitation
16100 NW Second Ave., North Miami Beach, FL 33169, (305) 354-8800; Facility Type: Skilled care; ICF; Alzheimer's; Hospice; Certified Beds: 120 Certified: Medicaid; Medicare; Owner: Private; License: Current state

Palm Garden of Aventura
21251 E Dixie Hwy., North Miami Beach, FL 33180, (305) 935-4827; Facility Type: Skilled care; Alzheimer's; Certified Beds: 120; Certified: Medicaid; Medicare; Owner: Private, Nonprofit; License: Current state

Ocala

Hawthorne Health & Rehabilitation of Ocala
4100 SW 33rd Ave., Ocala, FL 34474, (352) 237-7776; Facility Type: Skilled care; Alzheimer's; Certified Beds: 120; Certified: Medicaid; Medicare; Owner: Private, Nonprofit; License: Current state

Marion House Health Care Center
3930 E. Silver Springs Blvd., Ocala, FL 34470, (352) 236-2626; Facility Type: Skilled care; Alzheimer's; Certified Beds: 120; Certified: Medicaid; Medicare; Owner: Private, For-Profit; License: Current state

Palm Garden of Ocala
3400 SW 27th Ave., Ocala, FL 34474, (352) 854-6262; Facility Type: Skilled care; Alzheimer's; Certified Beds: 180; Certified: Medicaid; Medicare; Owner: Private; License: Current state

Timberridge Nursing & Rehabilitation Center
9848 SW 110th St., Ocala, FL 34481, (352) 854-8200; Facility Type: Skilled care; Alzheimer's; Certified Beds: 180; Certified: Medicaid; Medicare; Owner: Private, For-Profit; License: Current state

Orlando

Adventist Care Centers — Courtland, Inc.
730 Courtland St., Orlando, FL 32804, (407) 975-3800; Facility Type: Skilled care; Alzheimer's; Certified Beds: 120; Certified: Medicaid; Medicare; Owner: Private, Nonprofit, Church-related; License: Current state

Commons at Orlando Lutheran Towers
210 Lake Ave., Orlando, FL 32801, (407) 872-7088; Facility Type: Skilled care; Alzheimer's; Certified Beds: 135; Certified: Medicaid; Medicare; Owner: Private, Nonprofit; License: Current state

Courtlands of Orlando Rehabilitation & Health Center
1900 Mercy Dr., Orlando, FL 32808, (407) 299-5404; Facility Type: Skilled care; Alzheimer's; Certified Beds: 120; Certified: Medicaid; Medicare; Owner: Private, Nonprofit; License: Current state

Guardian Care Convalescent Center
2500 W Church St., Orlando, FL 32805, (407) 295-5371; Facility Type: Skilled care; ICF; Alzheimer's; Certified Beds: 120; Certified: Medicaid; Medicare; Veterans; Owner: Nonprofit corp.; License: Current state

The Health Center of Windermere
4875 Cason Cove Dr., Orlando, FL 32811, (407) 420-2090; Facility Type: Skilled care; Alzheimer's; Certified Beds: 120; Certified: Medicaid; Medicare; Owner: Private, Nonprofit; License: Current state

Orlando Health & Rehabilitation Center
830 W 29th St., Orlando, FL 32805, (407) 843-3230; Facility Type: Skilled care; Alzheimer's; Certified Beds: 420; Certified: Medicaid; Medicare; Owner: Private, Nonprofit; License: Current state

Westminster Towers
70 W Lucerne Cir., Orlando, FL 32801, (407) 841-1310; Facility Type: Skilled care; Alzheimer's; Certified Beds: 120; Certified: Medicaid; Medicare; Owner: Nonprofit/Religious org.; License: Current state

Panama City

Bay Center
1336 St. Andrews Blvd., Panama City, FL 32405, (850) 763-3911; Facility Type: Skilled care; Alzheimer's; Certified Beds: 160; Certified: Medicaid; Medicare; Owner: Private, Nonprofit; License: Current state

Clifford Chester Sims State Veterans Home
4419 Tram Rd., Panama City, FL 32404, (850) 747-5401; Facility Type: Skilled care; Alzheimer's; Certified Beds: 120; Certified: Medicaid; Medicare; Veterans; Owner: Government/State; License: Current state

GlenCove Nursing Pavilion
1027 E Business Hwy 98, Panama City, FL 32401, (850) 872-1438; Facility Type: Skilled care; ICF; Alz-

heimer's; Certified Beds: 115; Certified: Medicaid; Medicare; Owner: Proprietary/Public corp.; License: Current state

St. Andrews Bay Skilled Nursing & Rehabilitation
2100 Jenks Ave., Panama City, FL 32405, (850) 763-0446; Facility Type: Skilled care; Alzheimer's; Certified Beds: 120; Certified: Medicaid; Medicare; Owner: Private, Nonprofit; License: Current state

Pensacola

Baptist Manor
10095 Hillview Rd., Pensacola, FL 32514, (850) 479-4000; Facility Type: Skilled care; Alzheimer's; Certified Beds: 170; Certified: Medicaid; Medicare; Owner: Private, Nonprofit; License: Current state

Bayside Manor
4343 Langley Ave., Pensacola, FL 32504, (850) 477-4550; Facility Type: Skilled care; Alzheimer's; Certified Beds: 120; Certified: Medicaid; Medicare; Owner: Private, For-Profit; License: Current state

The Health Center of Pensacola
8475 University Pkwy Pensacola, FL 32514, (850) 474-1252; Facility Type: Skilled care; ICF; Alzheimer's; Certified Beds: 180; Certified: Medicaid; Medicare; Veterans; Owner: Proprietary/Public corp.; License: Current state

Rosewood Manor
3107 North H St., Pensacola, FL 32501, (850) 435-8400; Facility Type: Skilled care; Alzheimer's; Certified Beds: 155; Certified: Medicaid; Medicare; Owner: Private; License: Current state

Southern Oaks Rehabilitation & Nursing Center
600 W. Gregory St., Pensacola, FL 32501, (850) 437-3131; Facility Type: Skilled care; Alzheimer's; Certified Beds: 210; Certified: Medicaid; Medicare; Owner: Private, For-Profit; License: Current state

Specialty Care of Pensacola
6984 Pine Forest Rd., Pensacola, FL 32526, (850) 944-9997; Facility Type: Skilled care; Alzheimer's; Certified Beds: 120; Certified: Medicaid; Medicare; Owner: Private, Nonprofit; License: Current state

Plantation

Covenant Village Care Center
9211 W. Broward Blvd., Plantation, FL 33324, (954) 370-8982; Facility Type: Skilled care; Alzheimer's; Certified Beds: 60; Certified: Medicaid; Medicare; Owner: Private, Nonprofit; License: Current state

ManorCare Health Services
6931 W Sunrise Blvd., Plantation, FL 33313, (954) 583-6200; Facility Type: Skilled care; Alzheimer's; Certified Beds: 120; Certified: Medicaid; Medicare; Owner: HCR ManorCare; License: Current state

Plantation Nursing & Rehabilitation Center
4250 NW 5th St., Plantation, FL 33317, (954) 587-3296; Facility Type: Skilled care; Alzheimer's; Certified Beds: 152; Certified: Medicaid; Medicare; Owner: Private, For-Profit; License: Current state

Pompano Beach

Deerfield Beach Health & Rehabilitation Center
401 E. Sample Rd., Pompano Beach, FL 33064, (954) 941-4100; Facility Type: Skilled care; Alzheimer's; Certified Beds: 194; Certified: Medicaid; Medicare; Owner: Private, Nonprofit; License: Current state

John Knox Village Health Center
830 Lakeside St., St., Pompano Beach, FL 33060, (954) 783-4001; Facility Type: Skilled care; ICF; Alzheimer's; Certified Beds: 177; Certified: Medicaid; Medicare; Owner: Nonprofit corp.; License: Current state

Pompano Beach Health & Rehabilitation Center
51 W. Sample Rd., Pompano Beach, FL 33064, (954) 942-5530; Facility Type: Skilled care; Alzheimer's; Certified Beds: 127; Certified: Medicaid; Medicare; Owner: Private, Nonprofit; License: Current state

Seaview Nursing & Rehabilitation Center
2401 NE 2nd St., Pompano Beach, FL 33062, (954) 943-5100; Facility Type: Skilled care; Alzheimer's; Certified Beds: 83; Certified: Medicaid; Medicare; Owner: Private, Nonprofit; License: Current state

Port St. Joe

Bridge at Bay St. Joe
220 Ninth St., Port St. Joe, FL 32456, (850) 229-8244; Facility Type: Skilled care; Alzheimer's; Certified Beds: 120; Certified: Medicaid; Medicare; Owner: Private, Nonprofit; License: Current state

Saint Petersburg

Abbey Rehabilitation & Nursing Center
7101 Dr. Martin Luther King Jr. St. N., St. Petersburg, FL 33702, (727) 527-7231; Facility Type: Skilled care; Alzheimer's; Certified Beds: 152; Certified: Medicaid; Medicare; Owner: Private, Nonprofit; License: Current state

Apollo Health & Rehabilitation Center
1000 24th St. N., St. Petersburg, FL 33713, (727) 323-4711; Facility Type: Skilled care; Alzheimer's; Certified Beds: 99; Certified: Medicaid; Medicare; Owner: Private, Nonprofit; License: Current state

Bayside Rehabilitation & Health Center
811 Jackson St. N, St. Petersburg, FL 33705, (727) 896-3651; Facility Type: Skilled care; ICF; ICF/MR; Alzheimer's; Certified Beds: 92; Certified: Medicaid; Medicare; Veterans; Owner: Integrated Health Services Inc.; License: Current state

Baywood Nursing Center
2000 17th Ave. S., St. Petersburg, FL 33712, (727) 821-3544; Facility Type: Skilled care; Alzheimer's; Certified Beds: 59; Certified: Medicaid; Medicare; Owner: Private, Nonprofit; License: Current state

Bon Secours — Maria Manor Nursing & Rehabilitation Center
10300 4th St. N, St. Petersburg, FL 33716, (727) 576-1025; Facility Type: Skilled care; Alzheimer's; Certified Beds: 274; Certified: Medicaid; Medicare; Owner: Nonprofit/Religious org.; License: Current state

Carrington Place Nursing & Rehabilitation Center
10501 Roosevelt Blvd. N., St. Petersburg, FL 33716, (727) 577-3800; Facility Type: Skilled care; Alzheimer's; Certified Beds: 120; Certified: Medicaid; Medicare; Owner: Private, Nonprofit; License: Current state

Egret Cove Center
550 62nd St. S., St. Petersburg, FL 33707, (727) 347-6151; Facility Type: Skilled care; Alzheimer's; Certified Beds: 120; Certified: Medicaid; Medicare; Owner: Private, Nonprofit; License: Current state

Jacaranda Manor
4250 66th St. N., St. Petersburg, FL 33709, (727) 546-2405; Facility Type: Skilled care; Alzheimer's; Certified Beds: 299; Certified: Medicaid; Medicare; Owner: Private, Nonprofit; License: Current state

Rehabilitation Center of St. Petersburg
435 42nd Ave. S., St. Petersburg, FL 33705, (727) 822-1871; Facility Type: Skilled care; Alzheimer's; Certified Beds: 159; Certified: Medicaid; Medicare; Owner: Private, For-Profit; License: Current state

South Heritage Health & Rehabilitation Center
718 Lakeview Ave. S, St. Petersburg, FL 33705, (727) 894-5125; Facility Type: Skilled care; ICF; Alzheimer's; Certified Beds: 69; Certified: Medicaid; Medicare; Medi-Cal; Owner: ExtendiCare Health Services Inc.; License: Current state

Sanford

Healthcare & Rehabilitation of Sanford
950 Mellonville Ave., Sanford, FL 32771, (407) 322-8566; Facility Type: Skilled care; Alzheimer's; Certified Beds: 159; Certified: Medicaid; Medicare; Owner: Private, For-Profit; License: Current state

Sarasota

Bay Village of Sarasota
8400 Vamo Rd., Sarasota, FL 34231, (941) 966-5611; Facility Type: Skilled care; Alzheimer's; Respite Care; Short-term care; Certified Beds: 99; Certified: Medicaid; Medicare; Owner: Private, Nonprofit; License: Current state

Beneva Lakes Healthcare & Rehabilitation Center
741 S. Beneva Rd., Sarasota, FL 34232, (941) 957-0310; Facility Type: Skilled care; Alzheimer's; Certified Beds: 120; Certified: Medicaid; Medicare; Owner: Private, For-Profit; License: Current state

Consulate Health Care of Sarasota
4783 Fruitville Rd., Sarasota, FL 34232, (941) 378-8000; Facility Type: Skilled care; Alzheimer's; Certified Beds: 91; Certified: Medicaid; Medicare; Owner: Private, For-Profit; License: Current state

Heartland Health Care & Rehabilitation Center
5401 Sawyer Rd., Sarasota, FL 34233, (941) 925-3427; Facility Type: Skilled care; Alzheimer's; Certified Beds: 140; Certified: Medicaid; Medicare; Owner: Private, For-Profit; License: Current state

ManorCare Health Services Sarasota
5511 Swift Rd., Sarasota, FL 34231, (941) 921-7462; Facility Type: Skilled care; Alzheimer's; Certified Beds: 178; Certified: Medicaid; Medicare; Owner: Private, For-Profit; License: Current state

Pines of Sarasota
1501 N. Orange Ave., Sarasota, FL 34236, (941) 365-0250; Facility Type: Skilled care; Alzheimer's; Certified Beds: 204; Certified: Medicaid; Medicare; Owner: Private, For-Profit; License: Current state

Tarpon Point Nursing & Rehabilitation Center
5157 Park Club Dr., Sarasota, FL 34235, (941) 377-0022; Facility Type: Skilled care; ICF; Alzheimer's; Certified Beds: 120; Certified: Medicaid; Medicare; Owner: Private; License: Current state

Sun City Center

Palm Garden of Sun City
3850 Upper Creek Dr., Sun City Center, FL 33573, (813) 633-2875; Facility Type: Skilled care; Alzheimer's; Certified Beds: 120; Certified: Medicaid; Medicare; Owner: Private, For-Profit; License: Current state

Plaza West
912 American Eagle Blvd., Sun City Center, FL 33573, (813) 633-3066; Facility Type: Skilled care; ICF; Alzheimer's; Certified Beds: 113; Certified: Medicaid; Medicare; Owner: Private; License: Current state

Sun Terrace Health Care Center
105 Trinity Lakes Dr., Sun City Center, FL 33573,

(813) 634-3324; Facility Type: Skilled care; ICF; Alzheimer's; Certified Beds: 109; Certified: Medicaid; Medicare; Veterans; Owner: Private; License: Current state

Tampa

Canterbury Towers, Inc.
3501 Bayshore Blvd., Tampa, FL 33629, (813) 837-1083; Facility Type: Skilled care; Alzheimer's; Certified Beds: 60; Certified: Medicaid; Medicare; Owner: Private, For-Profit; License: Current state

Carrollwood Care Center
15002 Hutchinson Rd., Tampa, FL 33625, (813) 960-1969; Facility Type: Skilled care; Alzheimer's; Certified Beds: 120; Certified: Medicaid; Medicare; Owner: Private, Nonprofit; License: Current state

Excel Rehabilitation & Health Center
2811 Campus Hill Dr., Tampa, FL 33612, (813) 979-9400; Facility Type: Skilled care; Alzheimer's; Certified Beds: 120; Certified: Medicaid; Medicare; Owner: Private, For-Profit; License: Current state

Fletcher Health & Rehabilitation Center
518 W Fletcher Ave., Tampa, FL 33612, (813) 265-1600; Facility Type: Skilled care; Alzheimer's; Certified Beds: 120; Certified: Medicaid; Medicare; Owner: Proprietary/Public corp.; License: Current state

Health Care Center of Tampa
1818 E. Fletcher Ave., Tampa, FL 33612, (813) 971-2383; Facility Type: Skilled care; Alzheimer's; Certified Beds: 244; Certified: Medicaid; Medicare; Owner: Private, For-Profit; License: Current state

The Home Association
1203 E 22nd Ave., Tampa, FL 33605, (813) 229-6901; Facility Type: Skilled care; Alzheimer's; Certified Beds: 96; Certified: Medicaid; Medicare; Owner: Private, For-Profit; License: Current state

John Knox Village Medical Center
4100 E. Fletcher Ave., Tampa, FL 33613, (813) 632-2455; Facility Type: Skilled care; Alzheimer's; Certified Beds: 163; Certified: Medicaid; Medicare; Owner: Private, Nonprofit; License: Current state

Lakeshore Villas Healthcare Center
16002 Lakeshore Villa Dr., Tampa, FL 33613, (813) 968-5093; Facility Type: Skilled care; Alzheimer's; Certified Beds: 179; Certified: Medicaid; Medicare; Owner: Private, Nonprofit; License: Current state

The Nursing Center at University Village
12250 N 22nd St., Tampa, FL 33612, (813) 975-5001; Facility Type: Skilled care; ICF; Alzheimer's; Certified Beds: 120; Certified: Medicaid; Medicare; Veterans; Owner: Proprietary/ Public corp.; License: Current state

Palm Garden of Tampa
3612 138th Ave., Tampa, FL 33613, (813) 972-8775; Facility Type: Skilled care; ICF; Alzheimer's; Certified Beds: 120; Certified: Medicaid; Medicare; Owner: Proprietary/Public corp.; License: Current state

Rehabilitation & Healthcare Center of Tampa
4411 N. Habana Ave., Tampa, FL 33614, (813) 872-2771; Facility Type: Skilled care; Alzheimer's; Certified Beds: 1574; Certified: Medicaid; Medicare; Owner: Private, Nonprofit; License: Current state

South Tampa Health & Rehabilitation Center
4610 S Manhattan Ave, Tampa, FL 33611, (813) 839-5311; Facility Type: Skilled care; Alzheimer's; Certified Beds: 179; Certified: Medicaid; Medicare; Owner: Private, Nonprofit; License: Current state

Whispering Oaks
1514 E. Chelsea St., Tampa, FL 33610, (813) 238-6406; Facility Type: Skilled care; Alzheimer's; Certified Beds: 236; Certified: Medicaid; Medicare; Owner: Private, Nonprofit; License: Current state

Venice

Heritage Health Care Center — Venice
1026 Albee Farm Rd., Venice, FL 34292, (941) 484-0425; Facility Type: Skilled care; ICF; Alzheimer's; Certified Beds: 120; Certified: Medicaid; Medicare; Owner: Proprietary/Public corp.; License: Current state

ManorCare Health Services
1450 E. Venice Ave., Venice, FL 34292, (941) 486-8088; Facility Type: Skilled care; Alzheimer's; Certified Beds: 129; Certified: Medicaid; Medicare; Owner: Private, For-Profit; License: Current state

Village on the Isle
910 Tamiami Trail S., Venice, FL 34285, (941) 486-5420; Facility Type: Skilled care; Alzheimer's; Certified Beds: 60; Certified: Medicaid; Medicare; Owner: Private, Nonprofit; License: Current state

West Palm Beach

Consulate Health Care of West Palm Beach
1626 Davis Rd., West Palm Beach, FL 33406, (561) 439-8897; Facility Type: Skilled care; Alzheimer's; Certified Beds: 120; Certified: Medicaid; Medicare; Owner: Private, For-Profit; License: Current state

Darcy Hall of Life Care
2170 Palm Beach Lakes Blvd., West Palm Beach, FL 33409, (561) 683-3333; Facility Type: Skilled care; Alzheimer's; Certified Beds: 220; Certified: Medicaid; Medicare; Owner: Private, For-Profit; License: Current state

Edward J. Healey Nursing & Rehabilitation Center
1200 45th Street, West Palm Beach, FL 33407, (561)

842-6111; Facility Type: Skilled care; Alzheimer's; Certified Beds: 198; Certified: Medicaid; Medicare; Veterans; Owner: Government/County; License: Current state

The Joseph L Morse Geriatric Center Inc.
4847 Fred Gladstone Dr., West Palm Beach, FL 33417, (561) 471-5111; Facility Type: Skilled care; Alzheimer's; Certified Beds: 280; Certified: Medicaid; Medicare; Owner: Nonprofit corp.; License: Current state

Lourdes-Noreen McKeen Residence for Geriatric Care
315 S. Flagler Dr., West Palm Beach, FL 33401, (561) 655-8544; Facility Type: Skilled care; Alzheimer's; Certified Beds: 132; Certified: Medicaid; Medicare; Owner: Private, Nonprofit, Church-related; License: Current state

Palm Garden of West Palm Beach
300 Executive Center Dr., West Palm Beach, FL 33401, (561) 471-5566; Facility Type: Skilled care; ICF; Alzheimer's; Certified Beds: 176; Certified: Medicaid; Medicare; Owner: Proprietary/ Public corp.; License: Current state

Renaissance Health & Rehabilitation
5065 Wallis Rd., West Palm Beach, FL 33415, (561) 689-1799; Facility Type: Skilled care; Alzheimer's; Certified Beds: 120; Certified: Medicaid; Medicare; Owner: Private, Nonprofit; License: Current state

Winter Haven

Brandywyne Health Care Center
1801 N. Lake Mariam Dr., Winter Haven, FL 33884, (863) 293-1989; Facility Type: Skilled care; Alzheimer's; Certified Beds: 115; Certified: Medicaid; Medicare; Owner: Private, For-Profit; License: Current state

Life Care Center of Winter Haven
1510 Cypress Gardens Blvd., Winter Haven, FL 33884, (863) 318-8646; Facility Type: Skilled care; Alzheimer's; Certified Beds: 177; Certified: Medicaid; Medicare; Owner: Private, For-Profit; License: Current state

Spring Lake Rehabilitation Center
1540 6th St. NW, Winter Haven, FL 33881, (863) 294-3055; Facility Type: Skilled care; ICF; Alzheimer's; Certified Beds: 120; Certified: Medicaid; Medicare; Medi-Cal; Owner: Private; License: Current state

Winter Haven Health & Rehabilitation Center
202 Ave. ONE, Winter Haven, FL 33881, (863) 293-3103; Facility Type: Skilled care; Alzheimer's; Certified Beds: 144; Certified: Medicaid; Medicare; Veterans; Owner: Proprietary/ Public corp.; License: Current state

Winter Park

ManorCare Nursing & Rehabilitation Center
2075 Loch Lomond Dr., Winter Park, FL 32792, (407) 628-5418; Facility Type: Skilled care; Alzheimer's; Certified Beds: 117; Certified: Medicaid; Medicare; Owner: Private, For-Profit; License: Current state

Mary Lee DePugh Nursing Home
550 W Morse Blvd., Winter Park, FL 32789, (407) 644-6634; Facility Type: Skilled care; ICF; Alzheimer's; Certified Beds: 40; Certified: Medicaid; Medicare; Veterans; Owner: Nonprofit/Religious org.; License: Current state

Mayflower Healthcare Center
1620 Mayflower Ct., Winter Park, FL 32792, (407) 672-1620; Facility Type: Skilled care; Alzheimer's; Certified Beds: 60; Certified: Medicaid; Medicare; Owner: Private, Nonprofit; License: Current state

Regents Park of Winter Park
558 N. Semoran Blvd., Winter Park, FL 32792, (407) 679-1515; Facility Type: Skilled care; Alzheimer's; Certified Beds: 120; Certified: Medicaid; Medicare; Owner: Private, Nonprofit; License: Current state

Winter Park Towers
1111 S. Lakemont Ave., Winter Park, FL 32792, (407) 647-4083; Facility Type: Skilled care; Alzheimer's; Certified Beds: 159; Certified: Medicaid; Medicare; Owner: Private, Nonprofit, Church-related; License: Current state

Zephyrhills

Heartland of Zephyrhills
38220 Henry Dr., Zephyrhills, FL 33540, (813) 788-7114; Facility Type: Skilled care; Alzheimer's; Certified Beds: 120; Certified: Medicaid; Medicare; Owner: Private, For-Profit; License: Current state

Zephyr Haven Health & Rehab Center, Inc.
38250 Ave. A, Zephyrhills, FL 33541, (813) 782-5508; Facility Type: Skilled care; Alzheimer's; Certified Beds: 120; Certified: Medicaid; Medicare; Veterans; Owner: Nonprofit/Religious org.; License: Current state

GEORGIA

Albany

Albany Health Care Inc.
223 Third Ave., Albany, GA 31701, (912) 435-0741; Facility Type: Skilled care; ICF; Alzheimer's; Assisted Living; Micro-Community; Certified Beds: 252; Certified: Medicaid; Medicare; Owner: Proprietary/public corp.; License: Current state

Palmyra Nursing Home
1904 Palmyra Rd., Albany, GA 31702, (229) 883-0500; Facility Type: Skilled care; Alzheimer's; Certified Beds: 250; Certified: Medicaid; Medicare; Owner: Private, For-Profit; License: Current state

Alma

Twin Oaks Convalescent Center Inc.
301 S Baker St., Alma, GA 31510, (912) 632-7293; Facility Type: Skilled care; ICF; Alzheimer's; Certified Beds: 88; Certified: Medicaid; Medicare; Veterans; Owner: Nonprofit/Religious organization; License: Current state

Atlanta

A.G. Rhodes Home Inc.
350 Boulevard SE, Atlanta, GA 30312, (404) 688-6731; Facility Type: Skilled care; ICF; Alzheimer's; Certified Beds: 138; Certified: Medicaid; Medicare; Owner: Nonprofit corp.; License: Current state

A.G. Rhodes Home, Wesley Woods
1819 Clifton Rd., NE, Atlanta, GA 30329, (404) 315-0900; Facility Type: Skilled care; Alzheimer's; Certified Beds: 150; Certified: Medicaid; Medicare; Owner: Private, Nonprofit; License: Current state

Budd Terrace Intermediate Care Home
1833 Clifton Rd., NE Atlanta, GA 30329, (404) 728-6500; Facility Type: ICF; Alzheimer's; Certified Beds: 250; Certified: Medicaid; Medicare; Owner: Nonprofit corp.; License: Current state

Crestview Health & Rehabilitation Center
2800 Springdale Rd., Atlanta, GA 30315, (404) 616-8100; Facility Type: Skilled care; Alzheimer's; Located within a hospital; Certified Beds: 388; Certified: Medicaid; Medicare; Owner: Government/County; License: Current state

Fountainview Center for Alzheimer's Disease
2631 N Druid Hills Rd., NE Atlanta, GA 30329, (404) 325-7994; Facility Type: ICF; Alzheimer's; Certified Beds: 120; Certified: Medicaid; Medicare Owner: Private; License: Current state

Golden LivingCenter — Northside
5470 Meridian Mark Rd., Atlanta, GA 30342, (404) 256-5131; Facility Type: Skilled care; ICF; Alzheimer's; Certified Beds: 240; Certified: Medicaid; Veterans; Owner: Beverly Enterprises Inc.; License: Current state

Northeast Atlanta Health & Rehabilitation Center
1500 S. Johnson Ferry Rd., Atlanta, GA 30319, (404) 252-2002; Facility Type: Skilled care; Alzheimer's; Certified Beds: 165; Certified: Medicaid; Medicare; Owner: Private, For-Profit; License: Current state

Nurse Care of Buckhead
2920 Pharr Ct., S., Atlanta, GA 30305, (404) 261-9043; Facility Type: Skilled care; ICF; ICF/MR: Alzheimer's; Certified Beds: 220; Certified: Medicaid; Medicare; Veterans; Owner: Private; License: Current state

Signature Healthcare of Buckhead
54 Peachtree Park Dr., Atlanta, GA 30309, (404) 351-6041; Facility Type: Skilled care; ICF; ICF/MR; Alzheimer's; Certified Beds: 179; Certified: Medicaid; Medicare; Owner: Private; License: Current state

The William Bremen Jewish Home
3150 Howell Mill Rd. NW, Atlanta, GA 30327, (404) 351-8410; Facility Type: Skilled care; Alzheimer's; Certified Beds: 96; Certified: Medicaid; Medicare; Owner: Private, For-Profit; License: Current state

Augusta

Amara Health Care & Rehabilitation
2021 Scott Rd., Augusta, GA 30906, (706) 793-1057; Facility Type: Skilled care; ICF; ICF/MR; Alzheimer's; Certified Beds: 213; Certified: Medicaid; Medicare; Veterans; Owner: Proprietary/Public corp.; License: Current state

Golden LivingCenter–Windermere
3618 J. Dewey Gray Cr, Augusta, GA 30909, (706) 860-7572; Facility Type: Skilled care; Alzheimer's; Certified Beds: 120; Certified: Medicaid; Medicare; Owner: Private, For-Profit; License: Current state

Unihealth Post Acute Care–Augusta Hills
2122 Cumming Rd., Augusta, GA 30914, (706) 737-8258; Facility Type: Skilled care; ICF; ICF/MR; Alzheimer's; Respite Care Certified Beds: 126; Certified: Medicaid; Medicare; Owner: Nonprofit corp.; License: Current state

Byromville

Pinehill Nursing Center
712 Patterson St., Byromville, GA 31007, (912) 433-5711; Facility Type: Skilled care; ICF; Alzheimer's; Certified Beds: 102; Certified: Medicaid; Medicare; Owner: Proprietary/Public corp.; License: Current state

Calhoun

Calhoun Health Care Center Inc.
1387 Hwy. 41 N, Calhoun, GA 30701, (706) 629-1289; Facility Type: Skilled care; ICF; ICF/MR; Alzheimer's; Certified Beds: 106; Certified: Medicaid; Medicare; Owner: Proprietary/Public corp.; License: Current state

Gordon Health & Rehabilitation
1280 Mauldin Rd., NE, Calhoun GA 30703, (706) 625-0044; Facility Type: Skilled care; Alzheimer's; Certified Beds: 117; Certified: Medicaid; Medicare; Owner: Private, For-Profit; License: Current state

Carrollton

Carrollton Manor, Inc.
2455 Oak Grove Church Road, Carrollton, GA 30117, (770) 834-1737; Facility Type: Skilled care; Alzheimer's; Certified Beds: 100; Certified: Medicaid; Medicare; Owner: Private, For-Profit; License: Current state

Carrollton Nursing & Rehabilitation Center
2327 N Hwy. 27, Carrollton, GA 30117, (770) 834-4404; Facility Type: Skilled care; ICF; ICF/ MR; Alzheimer's; Certified Beds: 159; Certified: Medicaid; Medicare; Owner: Integrated Health Services Inc.; License: n/a

The Oaks of Carrollton
921 Old Newnan Rd., Carrollton, GA 30117, (770) 834-3501; Facility Type: Skilled care; Alzheimer's; Certified Beds: 42; Certified: Medicaid; Medicare; Owner: Private, For-Profit; License: Current state

Chatsworth

Chatsworth Health Care Center
102 Hospital Dr., Chatsworth, GA 30705, (706) 695-8313; Facility Type: Skilled care; ICF; Alzheimer's; Certified Beds: 120; Certified: Medicaid; Medicare; Veterans; Owner: n/a; License: n/a

Cleveland

Friendship Health & Rehabilitation
161 Friendship Rd., Cleveland, GA 30528, (706) 865-3131; Facility Type: Skilled care; Alzheimer's; Certified Beds: 89; Certified: Medicaid; Medicare; Owner: Private, For-Profit; License: Current state

Gateway Community Living Center
3201 Westmoreland Rd., Cleveland, GA 30528, (706) 865-5686; Facility Type: Skilled care; Alzheimer's; Certified Beds: 60; Alzheimer's; Certified: Medicaid; Medicare; Owner: Community Eldercare Services LLC; License: Current state

Columbus

Azalea Trace Nursing Center
910 Talbotton Rd., Columbus, GA 31995, (706) 323-9513; Facility Type: Skilled care; ICF; ICF/MR; Alzheimer's; Certified Beds: 100; Certified: Medicaid; Medicare; Owner: Nonprofit corp.; License: Current state

Fountain City Care & Rehabilitation
5131 Warm Springs Rd., Columbus, GA 31908, (706) 561-1371; Facility Type: Skilled care; ICF; Alzheimer's; Certified Beds: 210; Certified: Medicaid; Medicare; Owner: Sun Healthcare Group Inc.; License: Current state

Magnolia Manor of Columbus Nursing Center–West
2000 Warm Springs Rd., Columbus, GA 31908, (706) 324-2252; Facility Type: Skilled care; ICF; Alzheimer's; Certified Beds: 166; Certified: Medicaid; Medicare; Owner: Oak & Pine Manor Nursing Home Inc.; License: Current state

Muscogee Manor & Rehabilitation Center
7150 Manor Rd., Columbus, GA 31907, (706) 561-3218; Facility Type: Skilled care; ICF; Alzheimer's; Certified Beds: 242; Certified: Medicaid; Medicare; Veterans; Owner: Government/City/County; License: Current state

Commerce

Hill Haven Nursing Home
880 Ridgeway Rd., Commerce, GA 30529, (706) 336-8000; Facility Type: Skilled care; Alzheimer's; Certified Beds: 70; Certified: Medicaid; Medicare; Owner: Private, For-Profit; License: Current state

Restoration Healthcare of Commerce
100 Medical Center Dr., Commerce, GA 30529, (706) 335-1104; Facility Type: Skilled care; Alzheimer's; Certified Beds: 167; Certified: Medicaid; Medicare; Owner: Private, For-Profit; License: Current state

Dahlonega

Gold City Community Living Center
222 Moore's Dr., Dahlonega, GA 30533, (706) 864-3045; Facility Type: Skilled care; ICF; ICF/ MR; Alzheimer's; Certified Beds: 102; Certified: Medicaid; Medicare; Owner: Community Eldercare Services LLC

Dalton

Quinton Memorial Health Care & Rehabilitation Center
1114 Burleyson Rd., Dalton GA 30720, (706) 226-4642; Facility Type: Skilled care; Alzheimer's; Cer-

tified Beds: 120; Certified: Medicaid; Medicare; Owner: Private, For-Profit; License: Current state

Ridgewood Manor Health & Rehabilitation
1110 Burleyson Rd., Dalton, GA 30720, (706) 226-1021; Facility Type: Skilled care; ICF; Alzheimer's; Certified Beds: 102; Certified: Medicaid; Medicare; Owner: Proprietary/Public corp.; License: n/a

Decatur

Georgia Regional Hospital, LTC Unit
3073 Panthersville Rd., SNF Bldg. #17, Decatur, GA 30034, (404) 212-4780; Facility Type: Skilled care; Alzheimer's; Certified Beds: 77; Certified: Medicaid; Medicare; Veterans; Owner: Government/State; License: Current state

Golden LivingCenter — Glenwood
4115 Glenwood Rd., Decatur, GA 30032, (404) 284-6414; Facility Type: Skilled care; Alzheimer's; Certified Beds: 225; Certified: Medicaid; Medicare; Owner: Private, For-Profit; License: Current state

ManorCare Rehabilitation Center — Decatur
2722 N Decatur Rd., Decatur, GA 30033, (404) 296-5440; Facility Type: Skilled care; Alzheimer's; Certified Beds: 104; Rehabilitation; Certified: Medicaid; Medicare; Medi-Cal; Owner: HCR ManorCare; License: Current state

East Point

Bonterra Nursing Center
2801 Felton Dr., East Point, GA 30344, (404) 767-7591; Facility Type: Skilled care; ICF; Alzheimer's; Certified Beds: 118; Certified: Medicaid; Medicare; Owner: Integrated Health Services Inc.; License: Current state

Eastman

Heart of Georgia Nursing Home
815 Legion Dr., Eastman, GA 31023, (912) 374-5571; Facility Type: Skilled care; ICF; ICF/MR; Alzheimer's; Micro-Community; Certified Beds: 100; Certified: Medicaid; Medicare; Owner: Integrated Health Services Inc.; License: Current state

Middle Georgia Nursing Home
556 Chester Hwy., Eastman GA 31023, (478) 374-4733; Facility Type: Skilled care; Alzheimer's; Certified Beds: 225; Certified: Medicaid; Medicare; Owner: Private, For-Profit; License: Current state

Elberton

Heritage Healthcare at Spring Valley
651 Rhodes Dr., Elberton, GA 30635, (706) 283-3880; Facility Type: Skilled care; ICF; Alzheimer's;

Certified Beds: 60; Certified: Medicaid; Medicare; Owner: Private; License: Current state

Nancy Hart Nursing Center
2117 Dr. Ward Rd., Elberton, GA 30635, (706) 283-3335; Facility Type: Skilled care; Alzheimer's; Certified Beds: 67; Certified: Medicaid; Medicare; Owner: Private, For-Profit; License: Current state

Fairburn

Fairburn Health Care
178 W Campbellton St., Fairburn, GA 30213, (770) 964-1320; Facility Type: Skilled care; ICF; Alzheimer's; Certified 120; Certified: Medicaid; Medicare; Veterans; Owner: Proprietary/Public corp.; License: Current state

Unihealth Post Acute Care–Fairburn
7560 Butner Rd., Fairburn, GA 30213, (770) 306-7878; Facility Type: Skilled care; ICF; Alzheimer's; Certified Beds: 82; Certified: Medicaid; Medicare; Veterans; Owner: Proprietary/Public corp.; License: Current state

Fort Valley

Fort Valley Healthcare Center
604 Bluebird Blvd., Fort Valley, GA 31030, (478) 825-2031; Facility Type: Skilled care; Alzheimer's; Certified Beds: 75; Certified: Medicaid; Medicare; Owner: Private, For-Profit; License: Current state

Franklin

Heritage Health Care of Franklin
360 S. River Rd., Franklin, GA 30217, (706) 675-6674; Facility Type: Skilled care; ICF; ICF/MR; Alzheimer's; Certified Beds: 78; Certified: Medicaid; Owner: Proprietary/Public corp.; License: n/a

Gainesville

The Bell Minor Home
2200 Old Hamilton Pl., NE, Gainesville, GA 30507, (770) 532-2066; Facility Type: Skilled care; Alzheimer's; Certified Beds: 104; Certified: Medicaid; Medicare; Owner: Private, For-Profit; License: Current state

New Horizons North
2020 Beverly Rd., NE, Gainesville, GA 30501, (770) 219-8600; Facility Type: Skilled care; Alzheimer's; Certified Beds: 271; Certified: Medicaid; Medicare; Owner: Private, Nonprofit; License: Current state

The Oaks at Limestone
2560 Flintridge Rd., Gainesville, GA 30501, (770) 536-3391; Facility Type: Skilled care; Alzheimer's; Certified Beds: 104; Certified: Medicaid; Medicare; Owner: Private, For-Profit; License: Current state

Greensboro

Boswell-Parker Nursing Center
1201 Siloam Rd., Greensboro, GA 30642, (706) 453-7331; Facility Type: Skilled care; ICF; ICF/MR; Alzheimer's; Certified Beds: 29; SNF/ICF; Certified: Medicaid; Medicare; Owner: Government/State/Local; License: Current state

Jasper

Grandview Health Care Center
618 Gennett Dr., Grandview, GA 30143, (706) 692-6323; Facility Type: Skilled care; Alzheimer's; Certified Beds: 60; Certified: Medicaid; Medicare; Owner: Private, For-Profit; License: Current state

Heritage Healthcare of Jasper
1350 E Church St., Jasper, GA 30143, (706) 692-2441; Facility Type: Skilled care; ICF; ICF/MR; Alzheimer's; Certified Beds: 60; Certified: Medicaid; Owner: Proprietary/Public corp.; License: Current state

Jesup

Altamaha Healthcare Center
1311 W. Cherry St., Jesup, GA 31545, (912) 427-7792; Facility Type: Skilled care; Alzheimer's; Certified Beds: 62; Certified: Medicaid; Medicare; Owner: Private, For-Profit; License: Current state

Golden LivingCenter–Jesup
1090 W Orange St., Jesup, GA 31545, (912) 427-6858; Facility Type: Skilled care; ICF; Alzheimer's; Certified Beds: 90; Certified: Medicaid; Medicare; Owner: For-Profit; License: Current state

Jesup Healthcare
3100 Savannah Hwy., Jesup, GA 31545, (912) 427-6873; Facility Type: Skilled care; Alzheimer's; Certified Beds: 72; Certified: Medicaid; Medicare; Owner: Private, For-Profit; License: Current state

Jonesboro

Arrowhead Healthcare
239 Arrowhead Blvd., Jonesboro, GA 30236, (770) 478-3013; Facility Type: Skilled care; ICF; Alzheimer's; Certified Beds: 116; Certified: Medicaid; Medicare; Owner: Proprietary/Public corp.; License: Current state

Jonesboro Nursing & Rehabilitation Center
2650 Highway 138 SE, Jonesboro, GA 30236, (770) 473-4436; Facility Type: Skilled care; Alzheimer's; Certified Beds: 129; Certified: Medicaid; Medicare; Owner: Private, For-Profit; License: Current state

Keysville

Keysville Nursing & Rehabilitation Center
1005 Hwy. 88 N, Keysville, GA 30816, (706) 547-2591; Facility Type: Skilled care; ICF; Alzheimer's; Certified Beds: 64; Certified: Medicaid; Medicare; Veterans; Owner: Proprietary/Public corp.; License: Current state

LaGrange

Florence Hand Home
200 Medical Dr., LaGrange, GA 30240, (706) 845-3256; Facility Type: Skilled care; ICF; ICF/MR; Alzheimer's; Certified Beds: 150; Certified: Medicaid; Medicare; Owner: n/a; License: Current state

LaGrange Nursing & Rehab Center
2111 W. Point Rd., LaGrange, GA 30240, (706) 812-9293; Facility Type: Skilled care; Alzheimer's; Certified Beds: 138; Certified: Medicaid; Medicare; Owner: Private, For-Profit; License: Current state

Lithonia

Traditions Health & Rehabilitation
2816 Evans Mill Rd., Lithonia, GA 30058, (770) 482-2961; Facility Type: Skilled care; ICF; Alzheimer's; Certified Beds: 182; Certified: Medicaid; Medicare; Veterans; Owner: Proprietary/Public corp.; License: Current state

Macon

Bel-Arbor Health Care
3468 Napier Ave., Macon, GA 31204, (912) 477-4464; Facility Type: Skilled care; ICF; Alzheimer's; Certified Beds: 131; Certified: Medicaid; Medicare; Owner: Proprietary/Public corp.; License: Current state

Bolingreen Nursing Center
529 Bolingreen Dr., Macon, GA 31210, (912) 477-1720; Facility Type: ICF; ICF/MR; Alzheimer's; Certified Beds: 121; Certified: Medicaid; Medicare; Owner: Nonprofit/Religious organization; License: n/a

Eastview Nursing Center
3020 Jeffersonville Rd., Macon, GA 31217, (478) 746-3547; Facility Type: Skilled care; Alzheimer's; Certified Beds: 92; Certified: Medicaid; Medicare; Owner: Private, For-Profit; License: Current state

Goodwill Nursing Home, Inc.
4373 Houston Ave., Macon, GA 31206, (478) 784-1500; Facility Type: Skilled care; Alzheimer's; Certified Beds: 172; Certified: Medicaid; Medicare; Owner: Private, For-Profit; License: Current state

Heritage Healthcare of Macon
2255 Anthony Rd., Macon, GA 31203, (478) 784-7900; Facility Type: Skilled care; Alzheimer's; Certified Beds: 228; Certified: Medicaid; Medicare; Owner: Private, For-Profit; License: Current state

The Oaks at Peake
6190 Peake Rd., Macon, GA 31220, (478) 471-7474;
Facility Type: Skilled care; Alzheimer's; Certified
Beds: 122; Certified: Medicaid; Medicare; Owner:
Private, For-Profit; License: Current state

Marietta

A.G. Rhodes Home Inc.–Cobb
900 Wylie Rd., Marietta, GA 30067, (770) 427-8727;
Facility Type: Skilled care; ICF; Alzheimer's; Certified
Beds: 130; Certified: Medicaid; Medicare; Veterans;
Owner: Nonprofit corp.; License: Current state

Golden LivingXenter–Kennestone
613 Roselane St., Marietta, GA 30064, (770) 792-
9800; Facility Type: Skilled care; Alzheimer's; Certified Beds: 137; Certified: Medicaid; Medicare;
Owner: Private, For-Profit; License: Current state

ManorCare Rehabilitation Center — Marietta
4360 Johnson Ferry Pl., Marietta, GA 30068, (770)
971-5870; Facility Type: Skilled care; ICF; Alzheimer's; Certified Beds: 117; Certified: Medicare; Veterans; Owner: HCR ManorCare; License: Current
state

Marietta Health & Rehabilitation Center
50 Saine Dr., SW Marietta, GA 30060, (770) 429-
8600; Facility Type: Skilled care; ICF; Alzheimer's;
Certified Beds: 119; Certified: Medicaid; Medicare;
Owner: Sun Healthcare Group Inc.; License: n/a

Monroe

Park Place Nursing Facility
1865 Bold Springs Rd., Monroe, GA 30656, (770)
267-8677; Facility Type: Skilled care; ICF; ICF/MR:
Alzheimer's; Certified Beds: 107; Certified: Medicaid;
Owner: n/a; License: n/a

Walton Regional Nursing Home
330 Alcovy St., Monroe, GA 30655, (770) 267-8461;
Facility Type: Skilled care; Alzheimer's; Certified
Beds: 58; Certified: Medicaid; Medicare; Owner: Private, For-Profit; License: Current state

Moultrie

Heritage Healthcare at Magnolia Manor
2015 First Ave. SE, Moultrie, GA 31768, (229) 985-
4320; Facility Type: Skilled care; Alzheimer's; Certified Beds: 68; Certified: Medicaid; Medicare;
Owner: Private, For-Profit; License: Current state

Unihealth Magnolia Manor South
3003 Veterans Pkwy., Moultrie GA 31788, (229) 985-
3422; Facility Type: Skilled care; Alzheimer's; Certified Beds: 100; Certified: Medicaid; Medicare;
Owner: Private, For-Profit; License: Current state

Nashville

Berrien Nursing Center
405 Laurel St., Nashville, GA 31639, (912) 686-7471;
Facility Type: Skilled care; ICF; ICF/MR: Alz-
heimer's; Certified Beds: 108; Certified: Medicaid;
Medicare; Owner: Proprietary/Public corp.; License:
Current state

Ocilla

Osceola Nursing Home
209 W. Hudson St., Ocilla, GA 31774, (229) 468-
9431; Facility Type: Skilled care; Alzheimer's; Certified Beds: 83; Certified: Medicaid; Medicare;
Owner: Private, For-Profit; License: Current state

Palemon Gaskin Memorial Nursing Home
201 W Dismuke Ave., Ocilla, GA 31774, (912) 468-
3890; Facility Type: Skilled care; ICF; Alzheimer's;
Certified Beds: 30; Certified: Medicaid; Owner: Gov-
ernment/State/ Local; License: Current state

Peachtree City

Southland Nursing Home
151 Wisdom Rd., Peachtree City, GA 30269, (770)
631-9000; Facility Type: Skilled care; Alzheimer's;
Certified Beds: 155; Certified: Medicaid; Medicare;
Owner: Proprietary/Public corp.; License: Current
state

Powder Springs

**Powder Springs Nursing & Rehabilitation
  Center**
3460 Powder Springs Rd., Powder Springs, GA 30127,
(770) 439-9199; Facility Type: Skilled care; ICF;
ICF/MR; Alzheimer's; Certified Beds: 208; Certified:
Medicaid; Medicare; Veterans; Owner: Private; License: Current state

Pulaski

Orchard Health & Rehabilitation
1321 Pulaski School Rd., Pulaski, GA 30451, (912)
685-5072; Facility Type: Skilled care; ICF; ICF/MR:
Alzheimer's; Certified Beds: 89; SNF/ICF; Certified:
Medicaid; Medicare; Veterans; Owner: Taylor & Bird
Inc.; License: Current state

Richmond Hill

Bryan County Health & Rehabilitation Center
127 Carter St., Richmond Hill, GA, 31324; (912) 756-
6131; Facility Type: Skilled care; ICF; Alzheimer's;
Certified Beds: 100; Certified: Medicaid; Medicare;
Owner: n/a; License: Current state

Rome

Chulio Hills Health & Rehab
1170 Chulio Rd., Rome, GA 30161, (706) 235-1132; Facility Type: Skilled care; Alzheimer's; Certified Beds: 100; Certified: Medicaid; Medicare; Owner: Private, For-Profit; License: Current state

Etowah Landing Care & Rehabilitation Center
809 S. Broad St., Rome, GA 30161, (706) 235-1337; Facility Type: Skilled care; Alzheimer's; Certified Beds: 100; Certified: Medicaid; Medicare; Owner: Private, For-Profit; License: Current state

Fifth Avenue Health Care Center
505 N 5th Ave., Rome, GA 30165, (706) 291-0521; Facility Type: Skilled care; ICF; Alzheimer's; Certified Beds: 100; Certified: Medicaid; Medicare; Veterans; Owner: Proprietary/Public corp.; License: Current state

Golden LivingCenter–Rome
1345 Redmond Rd., Rome, GA 30165, (706) 234-8281; Facility Type: Skilled care; Alzheimer's; Certified Beds: 100; Certified: Medicaid; Medicare; Owner: Private, For-Profit; License: Current state

Winthrop Health & Rehabilitation
12 Chateau Dr., Rome, GA 30161, (706) 235-1422; Facility Type: Skilled care; Alzheimer's; Certified Beds: 100; Certified: Medicaid; Medicare; Owner: Private, For-Profit; License: Current state

Savannah

Azalealand Nursing Home Inc.
2040 Colonial Dr., Savannah, GA 31406, (912) 354-2752; Facility Type: Skilled care; ICF; Alzheimer's; Certified Beds: 107; Certified: Medicare; Owner: n/a

Heritage Healthcare of Savannah
12825 White Bluff Rd., Savannah GA 31419, (912) 927-9416; Facility Type: Skilled care; Alzheimer's; Certified Beds: 120; Certified: Medicaid; Medicare; Owner: Private, For-Profit; License: Current state

Riverview Health & Rehabilitation Center
6711 Laroche Ave., Savannah, GA 31406, (912) 354-8225; Facility Type: Skilled care; Alzheimer's; Certified Beds: 204; Certified: Medicaid; Medicare; Owner: Private, Nonprofit; License: Current state

Savannah Rehab & Nursing Center
815 E. 63rd St., Savannah, GA 31405, (912) 352-8615; Facility Type: Skilled care; Alzheimer's; Certified Beds: 120; Certified: Medicaid; Medicare; Owner: Private, For-Profit; License: Current state

Savannah Square Health Care
1 Savannah Square Dr., Savannah, GA 31406, (912) 927-7550; Facility Type: Skilled care; ICF; ICF/MR; Alzheimer's; Certified Beds: 40; Certified: Medicare; Owner: Private; License: Current state

Snellville

New London Health Center
2020 McGee Rd., Snellville, GA 30078, (770) 978-7250; Facility Type: Skilled care; Alzheimer's; Certified Beds: 144; Certified: Medicaid; Medicare; Owner: Private, For-Profit; License: Current state

Parkwood Nursing & Rehabilitation Center
3000 Lenora Church Rd., Snellville, GA 30078, (770) 972-2040; Facility Type: Skilled care; ICF; ICF/MR; Alzheimer's; Certified Beds: 167; Certified: Medicaid; Veterans; Owner: Health Management Resources Inc.; License: Current state

Statesboro

Eagle Health & Rehabilitation
405 S College St., Statesboro, GA 30458, (912) 764-6108; Facility Type: Skilled care; ICF; ICF/MR; Alzheimer's; Certified Beds: 99; Certified: Medicaid; Owner: Taylor & Bird Inc.; License: Current state

Heritage Inn Health & Rehabilitation
307 Jones Mill Rd., Statesboro, GA 30458, (912) 764-9011; Facility Type: Skilled care; Alzheimer's; Certified Beds: 92; Certified: Medicaid; Medicare; Owner: Private, Nonprofit; License: Current state

Stone Mountain

Park Springs Health Center
500 Springhouse Cr., Stone Mountain, GA 30087, (678) 684-3800; Facility Type: Skilled care; Alzheimer's; Certified Beds: 42; Certified: Medicaid; Medicare; Owner: Private, For-Profit; License: Current state

Rosemont at Stone Mountain
5160 Spring View Ave., Stone Mountain, GA 30083, (770) 498-4144; Facility Type: Skilled care; ICF; Alzheimer's; Certified Beds: 149; Certified: Medicaid; Medicare; Veterans; Owner: Private; License: Current state

Swainsboro

Emanuel County Nursing Home
117 Kite Rd., Swainsboro, GA 30401, (478) 289-1334; Facility Type: Skilled care; Alzheimer's; Facility located within a hospital; Certified Beds: 49; Certified: Medicaid; Medicare; Owner: Private, For-Profit; License: Current state

Unihealth Post-Acute Care — Swainsboro
PO Box 1758 Swainsboro, GA 30401, (912) 237-7022; Facility Type: Skilled care; ICF/MR; Alzheimer's; Certified Beds: 103; Certified: Medicaid; Medicare; Veterans; Owner: Taylor & Bird Inc.; License: Current state

Sylvester

Sylvester Health Care Inc.
PO Box 406 Sylvester, GA 31791, (912) 776-5541; Facility Type: Skilled care; ICF; Alzheimer's; Certified Beds: 117; ICF; Certified: Medicaid; Medicare; Owner: Proprietary/Public corp.; License: Current state

Thomasville

Camellia Gardens of Life Care
804 S. Broad St., Box 1959, Thomasville, GA 31792, (229) 226-0076; Facility Type: Skilled care; Alzheimer's; Certified Beds: 83; Certified: Medicaid; Medicare; Owner: Private, For-Profit; License: Current state

Glenn-Mor Nursing Home
10629 US Hwy. 19 S, Thomasville, GA 31792, (912) 226-8942; Facility Type: Skilled care; ICF; ICF/MR; Alzheimer's; Certified Beds: 64; Certified: Medicaid; Medicare; Veterans; Owner: Nonprofit corp.; License: Current state

Rose Haven Nursing Facility
400 S. Peachtree Blvd., Thomasville, GA 31799, (229) 227-2871; Facility Type: Skilled care; Alzheimer's; Certified Beds: 21; Certified: Medicaid; Medicare; Owner: Government/State; License: Current state

Toomsboro

Heritage Healthcare of Toomsboro
210 Main St., Toomsboro, GA 31090, (912) 933-5395; Facility Type: Skilled care; ICF; ICF/MR; Alzheimer's; Certified Beds: 62; Certified: Medicaid; Medicare; Veterans; Owner: UHS Pruitt Corporation; License: Current state;

Tucker

Golden LivingCenter — Briarwood
3888 Lavista Rd., Tucker, GA 30084, (770) 938-5740; Facility Type: Skilled care; Alzheimer's; Certified Beds: 100; Certified: Medicaid; Medicare; Owner: Private, For-Profit; License: Current state

Grace Healthcare of Tucker
2165 Idlewood Rd., Tucker, GA 30084, (770) 934-3172; Facility Type: Skilled care; Alzheimer's; Certified Beds: 136; Certified: Medicaid; Medicare; Owner: Private, For-Profit; License: Current state

Meadowbrook Nursing Home Inc.
4608 Lawrenceville Hwy., Tucker, GA 30084, (770) 491-9444; Facility Type: Skilled care; ICF; Alzheimer's; Certified Beds: 144; Certified: Medicaid; Medicare; Owner: Private; License: Current state

Tybee Island

Oceanside Nursing Home
PO Box 2509, Tybee Island, GA 31328, (912) 786-4511; Facility Type: Skilled care; ICF; ICF/MR; Alzheimer's; Certified Beds: 85; Certified: Medicaid; Medicare; Owner: n/a; License: Current state

Savannah Beach Nursing & Rehab Center
90 Van Horne St., Tybee Island, GA 31328, (912) 786-4511; Facility Type: Skilled care; Alzheimer's; Certified Beds: 50; Certified: Medicaid; Medicare; Owner: Private, For-Profit; License: Current state

Union City

Christian City Convalescent Center
7300 Lester Rd., Union City, GA 30291, (770) 964-3301; Facility Type: Skilled care; ICF' Alzheimer's; Certified Beds: 200; Certified: Medicaid; Medicare; Veterans; Owner: Nonprofit corp.; License: Current state

Valdosta

Heritage Healthcare at Crestwood
415 Pendleton Pl., Valdosta, GA 31602, (229) 242-6868; Facility Type: Skilled care; Alzheimer's; Certified Beds: 79; Certified: Medicaid; Medicare; Owner: Private, For-Profit; License: Current state

Heritage Healthcare at Holly Hill
413 Pendleton Pl., Valdosta, GA 31602, (912) 244-6968; Facility Type: Skilled care; ICF; Alzheimer's; Certified Beds: 100; Certified: Medicaid; Medicare; Owner: Proprietary/Public corp.; License: Current state

Heritage Healthcare at Lakehaven
410 E. Northside Dr., Valdosta, GA 31602, (229) 242-7368; Facility Type: Skilled care; Alzheimer's; Certified Beds: 90; Certified: Medicaid; Medicare; Owner: Private, For-Profit; License: Current state

Heritage Healthcare of Valdosta
2501 N. Ashley St., Valdosta, GA 31602, (229) 244-7368; Facility Type: Skilled care; Alzheimer's; Certified Beds: 98; Certified: Medicaid; Medicare; Owner: Private, For-Profit; License: Current state

Waverly Hall

Oak View Home
119 Oak View St., Waverly Hall, GA 31831, (706) 582-2117; Facility Type: Skilled care; ICF; ICF/MR; Alzheimer's; Certified Beds: 100; Alzheimer's; Certified: Medicaid; Medicare; Owner: Golden Age Properties; License: Current state

Wrightsville

Wrightsville Manor Inc.
608 W Court St., Wrightsville, GA 31096, (912)

864-2286; Facility Type: Skilled care; ICF; Alzheimer's; Certified Beds: 94; Certified: Medicaid; Medicare; Veterans; Owner: Private; License: Current state

HAWAII

Hilo

Hale Anuenue Restorative Care
1333 Waianuenue Ave., Hilo, HI 96720, (808) 961-6644; Facility Type: Skilled care; Alzheimer's; Certified Beds: 120; Certified: Medicaid; Medicare; Owner: Private, For-Profit; License: Current state

Hilo Medical Center
1190 Waianuenue Ave., Hilo, HI 96720, (808) 974-4700; Facility Type: Skilled care; Alzheimer's; Certified Beds: 134; Certified: Medicaid; Medicare; Owner: Government/State; License: Current state

Life Care Center of Hilo
944 W Kawailani St., Hilo, HI 96720, (808) 959-9151; Facility type: Skilled care, Alzheimer's; Certified Beds: 252; Certified: Medicaid, Medicare; Owner: Private; License: state; Activities: Arts & Crafts; Dances; Pet therapy; Group exercise; Outings; Support Groups; Other: Alzheimer's secured unit

Yukio Okutsu State Veterans Home
1180 Waianuenue Ave., Hilo, HI 96720, (808) 961-1500; Facility Type: Skilled care; Alzheimer's; Certified Beds: 95; Certified: Medicaid; Medicare; Veterans; Owner: Government/State; License: Current state

Honolulu

Avalon Care Center — Honolulu, LLC
1930 Kameameha IV Rd., Honolulu, HI 96819, (808) 847-4834; Facility Type: Skilled care; Alzheimer's; Certified Beds: 108; Certified: Medicaid; Medicare; Owner: Private, For-Profit; License: Current state

Convalescent Center of Honolulu
1900 Bachelot St., Honolulu, HI 96817, (808) 531-5302; Facility Type: Skilled care; Alzheimer's; Certified Beds: 162; Certified: Medicaid; Medicare; Owner: Private, For-Profit; License: Current state

Hale Nani Rehabilitation & Nursing Center
1677 Pensacola St., Honolulu, HI 96822, (808) 537-3371; Facility type: Skilled care, Alzheimer's; Certified Beds: 288; Certified: Medicaid, Medicare; Owner: Proprietary/Public; License: state; Activities: Arts & Crafts; Dances; Pet therapy; Group exercise; Outings; Support Groups

Hawaii Medical Center East
2230 Liliha St., Honolulu, HI 96817, (808) 547-6011; Facility Type: Skilled care; Alzheimer's; Certified Beds: 52; Certified: Medicaid; Medicare; Owner: Private, For-Profit; License: Current state

Island Nursing Home
1205 Alexander St., Honolulu, HI 96826, (808) 946-5027; Facility type: Skilled care, Alzheimer's; Certified Beds: 42; Certified: Medicaid, Medicare; Owner: Private; License: state; Activities: Arts & Crafts; Dances; Pet therapy; Group exercise; Outings; Support Groups

Kuakini Geriatric Care
347 N. Kuakini St., Honolulu, HI 96817, (808) 547-9357; Facility Type: Skilled care; Alzheimer's; Certified Beds: 187; Certified: Medicaid; Medicare; Owner: Private, Nonprofit; License: Current state

Leahi Hospital
3675 Kilauea Ave., Honolulu, HI 96816, (808) 733-8000; Facility Type: Skilled care; Alzheimer's; Certified Beds: 144; Certified: Medicaid; Medicare; Veterans; Owner: Government/State; License: Current state

Maluhia
1027 Hala Dr., Honolulu, HI 96817, (808) 832-3000; Facility Type: Skilled care; Alzheimer's; Certified Beds: 158; Certified: Medicaid; Medicare; Veterans; Owner: Private, Government/State; License: Current state

Kailua Kona

Life Care Center of Kona
78-6957 Kamehameha III Rd., Kailua Kona, HI 96740, (808) 322-2790; Facility type: Skilled care, Alzheimer's; Certified Beds: 94; Certified: Medicaid, Medicare; Owner: Lenox Healthcare; License: state; Activities: Arts & Crafts; Dances; Pet therapy; Group exercise; Outings; Support Groups; Other: Alzheimer's secured unit

Kaneohe

Aloha Nursing & Rehabilitation Center
45-545 Kamehameha Hwy., Kaneohe, HI 96744, (808) 247-2220; Facility type: Skilled care, Alzheimer's; Certified Beds: 104; Certified: Medicaid, Medicare, Veterans; Owner: Private; License: state;

Activities: Arts & Crafts; Dances; Pet therapy; Group exercise; Outings; Support Groups; Other: Adult day care

Ann Pearl Nursing Facility
45-181 Waikalua Rd., Kaneohe, HI 96744, (808) 247-8558; Facility Type: Skilled care; Alzheimer's; Certified Beds: 104; Certified: Medicaid; Medicare; Owner: Private, For-Profit; License: Current state

Harry & Jeanette Weinberg Care Center
45-090 Namoku St., Kaneohe, HI 96744, (808) 247-1670; Facility type: Skilled care, Alzheimer's; Certified Beds: 44; Certified: Medicaid, Medicare, Veterans; Owner: Private; Nonprofit; License: state; Activities: Arts & Crafts; Dances; Pet therapy; Group exercise; Outings; Support Groups; Other: Home health care

Kapaau (North Kohala)

Kohala Hospital
PO Box 10, Kapaau (North Kohala), HI 96775, (808) 889-6211; Facility type: Skilled care, Alzheimer's; Beds: 24; Certified: Medicaid, Medicare, Veterans; Owner: State & Local Gov.; License: state; Activities: Arts & Crafts; Dances; Pet therapy; Group exercise; Outings; Support Groups

Kaunakakai

Molokai General Hospital
280 Puali St., Kaunakakai, HI 96748, (808) 553-331; Facility type: Skilled care, Alzheimer's; Certified Beds: 2; Certified: Medicaid, Medicare, Veterans; Owner: Private; License: state; Activities: Arts & Crafts; Dances; Pet therapy; Group exercise; Outings; Support Groups; Other: Alzheimer's secured unit

---

IDAHO

Boise

Capitol Care Center
8211 Ustick Rd., Boise, ID 83704, (208) 375-3800; Facility type: Skilled care, Alzheimer's; Certified Beds: 148; Certified: Medicaid, Medicare; Owner: Peak Medical Corporation; License: state; Activities: Arts & Crafts; Dances; Pet therapy; Group exercise; Outings; Support Groups; Other: Alzheimer's secured unit

Good Samaritan Society — Boise Village
3115 Sycamore Dr., Boise, ID 83703, (208) 343-7726; Facility type: Skilled care, Alzheimer's; Certified Beds: 127; Certified: Medicaid, Medicare, Veterans; Owner: The Evangelical Lutheran Good Samaritan Society; License: state; Activities: Arts & Crafts; Dances; Pet therapy; Group exercise; Outings

Idaho State Veterans Home — Boise
320 Collins Rd., Boise, ID 83702, (208) 334-5000; Facility type: Skilled care, Alzheimer's; Certified Beds: 131; Certified: Medicaid, Medicare; Owner: Peak Medical Corporation; License: state; Activities: Arts & Crafts; Dances; Pet therapy; Group exercise; Outings; Support Groups; Other: Alzheimer's secured unit

Life Care Center of Boise
808 N Curtis, Boise, ID 83706, (208) 376-5274; Facility type: Skilled care, Alzheimer's; Certified Beds: 153; Certified: Medicaid, Medicare, Veterans; Owner: Life Care Centers of America; License: state; Activities: Arts & Crafts; Dances; Pet therapy; Group exercise; Outings; Support Groups; Other: Alzheimer's secured unit

Life Care Center of Treasure Valley
502 N. Kimball Pl., Boise, ID 83704, (208) 377-1900; Facility Type: Skilled care; Alzheimer's; Certified Beds: 120; Certified: Medicaid; Medicare; Owner: Private, For-Profit; License: Current state

Coeur D'Alene

Ivy Court
2200 Ironwood Pl., Coeur D'Alene, ID 83814, (208) 667-6486; Facility Type: Skilled care; Alzheimer's; Certified Beds: 125; Certified: Medicaid; Medicare; Owner: Private, For-Profit; License: Current state

LaCrosse Health & Rehabilitation Center
210 La Crosse St., Coeur D'Alene, ID 83814, (208) 664-2185; Facility type: Skilled care, Alzheimer's; Certified Beds: 130; Certified: Medicaid, Medicare, Veterans; Owner: ExtendiCare Health Services; License: state; Activities: Arts & Crafts; Dances; Pet therapy; Group exercise; Outings; Support Groups; Other: Alzheimer's secured unit

Pinewood Care Center
2514 N 7th St., Coeur D'Alene, ID 83814, (208) 664-8128; Facility type: Skilled care, Alzheimer's; Certified Beds: 117; Certified: Medicaid, Medicare; Owner: Centennial Healthcare; License: state; Activities: Arts & Crafts; Dances; Pet therapy; Group exercise; Outings; Support Groups; Other: Alzheimer's secured unit, Adult day care

Emmett

Cherry Ridge at Emmett Care & Rehab Center
501 W. Idaho Blvd., Emmett, ID 83617, (208) 365-3597; Facility Type: Skilled care; Alzheimer's;

Certified Beds: 40; Certified: Medicaid; Medicare; Owner: Private, For-Profit; License: Current state

Emmett Care & Rehabilitation
714 N Butte Ave., Emmett, ID 83617, (208) 365-4425; Facility type: Skilled care, Alzheimer's; Certified Beds: 74; Certified: Medicaid, Medicare, Veterans; Owner: Vencor, Inc.; License: state; Activities: Arts & Crafts; Dances; Pet therapy; Group exercise; Outings; Support Groups; Other: Alzheimer's secured unit, Adult day care, Home health care

Gooding

Bennett Hills Care & Rehabilitation Center
1220 Montana St., Gooding, ID 83330, (208) 934-5601; Facility type: Skilled care, Alzheimer's; Certified Beds: 80; Certified: Medicaid, Medicare, Veterans; Owner: Proprietary/Public; License: state; Activities: Arts & Crafts; Dances; Pet therapy; Group exercise; Outings; Support Groups; Other: Alzheimer's secured unit, Adult day care

Hailey

Blaine Manor
PO Box 927, Hailey, ID 83333, (208) 788-7180; Facility Type: Skilled care; Alzheimer's; Certified Beds: 25; Certified: Medicaid; Medicare; Owner: Government/County; License: Current state

Idaho Falls

Eastern Idaho Regional Medical Center — TCU
PO Box 2077, Idaho Falls, ID 83403, (208) 529-7690; Facility is a transitional care unit located within a hospital; Facility Type: Skilled care; Alzheimer's; Certified Beds: 16; Certified: Medicaid; Medicare; Owner: Private, For-Profit; License: Current state

Good Samaritan Center Idaho Falls Village
840 E Elva St., Idaho Falls, ID 83401, (208) 523-4795; Facility type: Skilled care, Alzheimer's; Certified Beds: 113; Certified: Medicaid, Medicare; Owner: Evangelical Lutheran Good Samaritan Society; License: state; Activities: Arts & Crafts; Dances; Pet therapy; Group exercise; Outings; Support Groups; Other: Alzheimer's secured unit, Adult day care, Home health care

Idaho Falls Care & Rehabilitation Center
3111 Channing Way, Idaho Falls, ID 83404, (208) 529-0067; Facility Type: Skilled care; Alzheimer's; Certified Beds: 108; Certified: Medicaid; Medicare; Owner: Private, For-Profit; License: Current state

Life Care Center of Idaho Falls
2725 E 17th St., Idaho Falls, ID 83406, (208) 529-4567; Facility type: Skilled care, Alzheimer's; Certified Beds: 109; Certified: Medicaid, Medicare; Owner: Life Care Centers of America; License: state;

Activities: Arts & Crafts; Dances; Pet therapy; Group exercise; Outings; Support Groups; Other: Alzheimer's secured unit, Adult day care, Adult day care

Kellogg

Mountain Valley Rehabilitation Center
601 W Cameron, Kellogg, ID 83837, (208) 784-1283; Facility type: Skilled care, Alzheimer's; Certified Beds: 68; Certified: Medicaid, Medicare; Owner: Vencor, Inc.; License: state; Activities: Arts & Crafts; Dances; Pet therapy; Group exercise; Outings; Support Groups; Other: Adult day care

Lewiston

Idaho State Veterans Home — Lewiston
821 21st Ave., Lewiston, ID 83501, (208) 799-3422; Facility Type: Skilled care; Alzheimer's; Certified Beds: 66; Certified: Medicaid; Medicare; Veterans; Owner: Government/State; License: Current state

Lewiston Rehabilitation & Care Center
3315 8th St., Lewiston, ID 83501, (208) 743-9543; Facility Type: Skilled care; Alzheimer's; Certified Beds: 96; Certified: Medicaid; Medicare; Owner: Private, For-Profit; License: Current state

Life Care Center of Lewiston
325 Warner Dr., Lewiston, ID 83501, (208) 798-8500; Facility Type: Skilled care; Alzheimer's; Certified Beds: 121; Certified: Medicaid; Medicare; Owner: Private, For-Profit; License: Current state

The Orchards Rehabilitation & Care Center
1014 Burrell Ave., Lewiston, ID 83501, (208) 743-4558; Facility type: Skilled care, Alzheimer's; Certified Beds: 127; Certified: Medicaid, Medicare, Veterans; Owner: Proprietary/Public; License: state; Activities: Arts & Crafts; Dances; Pet therapy; Group exercise; Outings; Support Groups; Other: Alzheimer's secured unit

Royal Plaza Retirement & Care Center, LLC
2870 Juniper Dr., Lewiston, ID 83501, (208) 746-2855; Facility Type: Skilled care; Alzheimer's; Certified Beds: 56; Certified: Medicaid; Medicare; Owner: Private, For-Profit; License: Current state

Moscow

Aspen Park Healthcare
420 Rowe St, Moscow, ID 83843, (208) 882-4576; Facility Type: Skilled care; Alzheimer's; Certified Beds: 70; Certified: Medicaid; Medicare; Owner: Private, For-Profit; License: Current state

Good Samaritan Society — Moscow Village
640 N Eisenhower St., Moscow, ID 83843, (208) 882-6560; Facility type: Skilled care, Alzheimer's; Certified Beds: 64; Certified: Medicaid, Medicare,

Veterans, Medi-Cal; Owner: Evangelical Lutheran Good Samaritan Society; License: state; Activities: Arts & Crafts; Dances; Pet therapy; Group exercise; Outings; Support Groups; Other: Alzheimer's secured unit, Home health care

Nampa

Karcher Estates
1127 Caldwell Blvd., Nampa, ID 83651, (208) 465-4935; Facility Type: Skilled care; Alzheimer's; Certified Beds: 66; Certified: Medicaid; Medicare; Owner: Private, For-Profit; License: Current state

Nampa Care Center
404 N Horton St., Nampa, ID 83651, (208) 466-9292; Facility type: Skilled care, Alzheimer's; Certified Beds: 100; Certified: Medicaid, Medicare, Veterans; Owner: Private; License: state; Activities: Arts & Crafts; Dances; Pet therapy; Group exercise; Outings; Support Groups; Other: Alzheimer's secured unit, Adult day care

Trinity Mission Health & Rehab of Holly
2105 12th Avenue Rd., Moscow, ID 83686, (208) 467-5721; Facility Type: Skilled care; Alzheimer's; Certified Beds: 120; Certified: Medicaid; Medicare; Owner: Private, For-Profit; License: Current state

Trinity Mission Health & Rehab of Midland
46 N Midland Blvd., Nampa, ID 83651, (208) 466-7803; Facility type: Skilled care, Alzheimer's; Certified Beds: 112; Certified: Medicaid, Medicare, Veterans; Owner: Private; License: state; Activities: Arts & Crafts; Dances; Pet therapy; Group exercise; Outings; Support Groups; Other: Alzheimer's secured unit, Adult day care

Pocatello

Hillcrest Haven Convalescent Center
1071 Renee Ave., Pocatello, ID 83201, (208) 233-1411; Facility Type: Skilled care; Alzheimer's; Certified Beds: 113; Certified: Medicaid; Medicare; Owner: Private, For-Profit; License: Current state

Idaho State Veterans Home — Pocatello
1957 Alvin Ricken Dr., Pocatello, ID 83201, (208) 236-6340; Facility type: Skilled care, Alzheimer's; Certified Beds: 66; Certified: Medicaid, Medicare, Veterans; Owner: State & Local Gov.; License: state; Activities: Arts & Crafts; Dances; Pet therapy; Group exercise; Outings; Support Groups; Other: Alzheimer's secured unit

Pocatello Care & Rehab Center
527 Memorial Dr., Pocatello, ID 83201, (208) 478-3333; Facility Type: Skilled care; Alzheimer's; Certified Beds: 88; Certified: Medicaid; Medicare; Owner: Private, For-Profit; License: Current state

Quinn Meadows Rehabilitation & Care Center
1033 W. Quinn Rd., Pocatello, ID 83202, (208) 637-8888; Facility Type: Skilled care; Alzheimer's; Certified Beds: 41; Certified: Medicaid; Medicare; Owner: Private, For-Profit; License: Current state

Safe Haven Care Center of Pocatello
1200 Hospital Way, Pocatello, ID 83201, (208) 232-2570; Facility Type: Skilled care; Alzheimer's; Located within a hospital; Certified Beds: 84; Certified: Medicaid; Medicare; Owner: Private, For-Profit; License: Current state

Saint Maries

Valley Vista Care Center of St. Maries
820 Elm St., Saint Maries, ID 83861, (208) 245-4576; Facility type: Skilled care, Alzheimer's; Certified Beds: 74; Certified: Medicaid, Medicare, Veterans; Owner: Nonprofit; License: state; Activities: Arts & Crafts; Dances; Pet therapy; Group exercise; Outings; Support Groups; Other: Alzheimer's secured unit

Sandpoint

Life Care Center of Sandpoint
1125 N. Division St., Sandpoint, ID 83864, (208) 265-9299; Facility Type: Skilled care; Alzheimer's; Certified Beds: 124; Certified: Medicaid; Medicare; Owner: Private, For-Profit; License: Current state

Valley Vista Care Center of Sandpoint
220 S. Division St., Sandpoint, ID 83864, (208) 265-4514; Facility Type: Skilled care; Alzheimer's; Certified Beds: 73; Certified: Medicaid; Medicare; Owner: Private, For-Profit; License: Current state

Silverton

Good Samaritan Center — Silver Wood Village
7th St., Box 358, Silverton, ID 83867, (208) 556-1147; Facility type: Skilled care, Alzheimer's; Certified Beds: 50; Certified: Medicaid, Medicare, Veterans; Owner: Evangelical Lutheran Good Samaritan Society; License: state; Activities: Arts & Crafts; Dances; Pet therapy; Group exercise; Outings; Support Groups; Other: Alzheimer's secured unit

Twin Falls

Bridgeview Estates
1828 Bridgeview Blvd., Twin Falls, ID 83301, (208) 736-3933; Facility Type: Skilled care; Alzheimer's; Certified Beds: 116; Certified: Medicaid; Medicare; Owner: Private, For-Profit; License: Current state

River Ridge Care & Rehabilitation Center
640 Filer Ave. W, Twin Falls, ID 83301, (208) 734-8645; Facility type: Skilled care, Alzheimer's; Certified

Beds: 158; Certified: Medicaid, Medicare, Veterans; Owner: Sun Healthcare; License: state; Activities: Arts & Crafts; Dances; Pet therapy; Group exercise; Outings; Support Groups; Other: Alzheimer's secured unit, Adult day care

Twin Falls Care & Rehabilitation Center
674 Eastland Dr., Twin Falls, ID 83301, (208) 734-4264; Facility Type: Skilled care; Alzheimer's; Certified Beds: 116; Certified: Medicaid; Medicare; Owner: Private, For-Profit; License: Current state

ILLINOIS

Aledo

Aledo Rehab & Health Care Center
304 SW 12th St., Aledo, IL 61231, (309) 582-5376; Facility type: Skilled care, Alzheimer's; Certified Beds: 80; Certified: Medicaid, Medicare, Veterans; Owner: For-Profit; License: state; Activities: Arts & Crafts; Dances; Pet therapy; Group exercise; Outings; Support Groups; Other: Alzheimer's secured unit, Adult day care

Mercer County Nursing Home
309 NW 9th Ave., Aledo, IL 61231, (309) 582-5361; Facility Type: Skilled care; Alzheimer's; Certified Beds: 92; Certified: Medicaid; Medicare; Owner: Private, For-Profit; License: Current state

Arlington Heights

Lutheran Home for the Aged
800 W Oakton St., Arlington Heights, IL 60004, (847) 253-3710; Facility type: Skilled care, Alzheimer's; Certified Beds: 310; Certified: Medicaid, Medicare; Owner: Nonprofit, Church-related; License: state; Activities: Arts & Crafts; Dances; Pet therapy; Group exercise; Support Groups; Other: Alzheimer's secured unit, Adult day care

Belvidere

Home Bridge Center
1701 W. 5th Ave., Belvidere, IL 61008, (815) 547-5451; Facility Type: Skilled care; Alzheimer's; Certified Beds: 80; Certified: Medicaid; Medicare; Owner: Private, For-Profit; License: Current state

Maple Crest Care Centre
4452 Squaw Prairie Rd., Belvidere, IL 61008, (815) 547-6377; Facility Type: Skilled care; Alzheimer's; Certified Beds: 86; Certified: Medicaid; Medicare; Owner: Private, For-Profit; License: Current state

Northwoods Health Care Center
2250 Pearl St., Belvidere, IL 61008, (815) 544-0358; Facility type: Skilled care, Alzheimer's; Certified Beds: 113; Certified: Medicaid, Medicare; Owner: Private; License: state; Activities: Arts & Crafts; Dances; Pet therapy; Group exercise; Support Groups; Other: Alzheimer's secured unit

Berwyn

Courtyard Healthcare Center Fairfax Nursing Home Inc.
3601 S Harlem Ave., Berwyn, IL 60402, (708) 749-4160; Facility type: Skilled care, Alzheimer's; Certified Beds: 145; Certified: Medicaid, Medicare, Veterans; Owner: Private; License: state; Activities: Arts & Crafts; Dances; Pet therapy; Group exercise; Support Groups; Other: Alzheimer's secured unit

MacNeal Memorial Hospital
3249 S. Oak Park Ave., Berwyn, IL 60402, (708) 783-9100; Facility Type: Skilled care; Alzheimer's; Certified Beds: 40; Certified: Medicare; Owner: Private, For-Profit; License: Current state

Pershing Convalescent Home
3900 S. Oak Park Ave., Berwyn, IL 60402, (708) 484-7543; Facility Type: Skilled care; Alzheimer's; Certified Beds: 51; Certified: Medicaid; Medicare; Owner: Private, For-Profit; License: Current state

Bloomingdale

Alden Valley Ridge Rehabilitation & Healthcare Center
275 E. Army Trail Rd., Bloomingdale, IL 60108, (630) 893-9616; Facility Type: Skilled care; Alzheimer's; Certified Beds: 207; Certified: Medicaid; Medicare; Owner: Private, For-Profit; License: Current state

Lexington Health Care Center, Bloomingdale
165 S. Bloomingdale Rd., Bloomingdale, IL 60108, (630) 980-8700; Facility Type: Skilled care; Alzheimer's; Certified Beds: 166; Certified: Medicaid; Medicare; Owner: Private, For-Profit; License: Current state

West Suburban Nursing & Rehabilitation Center
311 Edgewater Dr., Bloomingdale, IL 60108, (630) 894-7400; Facility Type: Skilled care; ICF; Alzheimer's; Certified Beds: 259; Alzheimer's 60; Certified: Medicaid, Medicare; Owner: Private; License: Current state

Bolingbrook

Meadowbrook Manor — Bolingbrook
431 W Remington Blvd., Bolingbrook, IL 60440,

(630) 759-1112; Facility type: Skilled care, Alzheimer's; Certified Beds: 298; Certified: Medicaid, Medicare, Veterans; Owner: Private; License: state; Activities: Arts & Crafts; Dances; Pet therapy; Group exercise; Support Groups; Other: Alzheimer's secured unit

Buffalo Grove

Claremont Rehabilitation & Living Center
150 N Weiland Rd., Buffalo Grove, IL 60089, (847) 465-0200; Facility type: Skilled care, Alzheimer's; Certified Beds: 200; Certified: Medicaid, Medicare; Owner: Private; License: state; Activities: Arts & Crafts; Dances; Pet therapy; Group exercise; Support Groups; Other: Alzheimer's secured unit

Byron

The Neighbors Rehabilitation Center
PO Box 585, Byron, IL 61010, (815) 235-2511; Facility type: Skilled care, Alzheimer's; Certified Beds: 101 0; Certified: Medicaid, Medicare, Veterans; Owner: Proprietary/Public; License: state; Activities: Arts & Crafts; Dances; Pet therapy; Group exercise; Support Groups; Other: Alzheimer's secured unit, Adult day care

Carlinville

Carlinville Rehabilitation & Healthcare Center
751 N. Oak St., Carlinville, IL 62626, (217) 854-2511; Facility Type: Skilled care; Alzheimer's; Certified Beds: 98; Certified: Medicaid; Medicare; Owner: Private, For-Profit; License: Current state

Friendship Home
826 N. High St., Carlinville, IL 62626, (217) 854-9606; Facility Type: Skilled care; Alzheimer's; Certified Beds: 49; Certified: Medicaid; Medicare; Owner: Private, For-Profit; License: Current state

Heritage Manor Carlinville
1200 University Ave., Carlinville, IL 62626, (217) 854-4433; Facility Type: Skilled care; Alzheimer's; Certified Beds: 108; Certified: Medicaid; Medicare; Owner: Private, For-Profit; License: Current state

Champaign

Heartland of Champaign
309 E. Springfield, Champaign, IL 61820, (217) 352-5135; Facility Type: Skilled care; Alzheimer's; Certified Beds: 102; Certified: Medicaid; Medicare; Owner: Private, For-Profit; License: Current state

Helia Healthcare of Champaign
1915 S. Mattis St., Champaign, IL 61821, (217) 352-0516; Facility Type: Skilled care; Alzheimer's; Certified Beds: 118; Certified: Medicaid; Medicare; Owner: Private, For-Profit; License: Current state

Heritage Nursing Center
1315B Curt Dr., Champaign, IL 61820, (217) 352-5707; Facility Type: Skilled care; Alzheimer's; Certified Beds: 60; Certified: Medicaid; Medicare; Owner: Private, For-Profit; License: Current state

Chenoa

Meadows Mennonite Home
RR 1, Chenoa, IL 61726, (309) 747-2702; Facility type: Skilled care, Alzheimer's; Certified Beds: 130; Certified: Medicaid; Owner: Nonprofit/Religious; License: state; Activities: Arts & Crafts; Dances; Pet therapy; Group exercise; Support Groups; Other: Alzheimer's secured unit

Chicago

Alden-Lincoln Rehabilitation & Health Care Center Inc.
504 W Wellington St., Chicago, IL 60657, (773) 281-6200; Facility type: Skilled care, Alzheimer's; Certified Beds: 96; Certified: Medicaid, Medicare; Owner: Nonprofit/Religious; License: state; Activities: Arts & Crafts; Dances; Pet therapy; Group exercise; Support Groups; Other: Alzheimer's secured unit, Home health care

Alden Northmoor Rehabilitation & Healthcare Center
5831 N. Northwest Hwy., Chicago, IL 60631, (773) 775-8080; Facility Type: Skilled care; Alzheimer's; Certified Beds: 198; Certified: Medicaid; Medicare; Owner: Private, For-Profit; License: Current state

Alden Nursing Center–Lakeland
820 W Lawrence Ave., Chicago, IL 60640, (773) 769-2570; Facility type: Skilled care, Alzheimer's; Certified Beds: 300; Certified: Medicaid, Medicare, Veterans; Owner: Nonprofit/Religious; License: state; Activities: Arts & Crafts; Dances; Pet therapy; Group exercise; Support Groups; Other: Alzheimer's secured unit

Alden Princeton Rehabilitation & Healthcare Center
255 W. 69th St., Chicago, IL 60621, (773) 224-5900; Facility Type: Skilled care; Alzheimer's; Certified Beds: 225; Certified: Medicaid; Medicare; Owner: Private, For-Profit; License: Current state

Alden Wentworth Rehabilitation & Healthcare Center
201 W. 69th St., Chicago, IL 60621, (773) 487-1200; Facility Type: Skilled care; Alzheimer's; Pathways Program; Certified Beds: 300; Certified: Medicaid; Medicare; Owner: Private, For-Profit; License: Current state

All American Nursing Home
5448 N. Broadway St., Chicago, IL 60640, (773)

334-2224; Facility Type: Skilled care; Alzheimer's; Certified Beds: 144; Certified: Medicaid; Medicare; Owner: Private, For-Profit; License: Current state

All Faith Pavilion

3500 S. Giles Ave., Chicago, IL 60653, (312) 326-2000; Facility Type: Skilled care; Alzheimer's; Certified Beds: 231; Certified: Medicaid; Medicare; Owner: Private, For-Profit; License: Current state

Ambassador Nursing & Rehabilitation Center

4900 N. Bernard, Chicago, IL 60625, (773) 583-7130; Facility Type: Skilled care; Alzheimer's; Certified Beds: 190; Certified: Medicaid; Medicare; Owner: Private, For-Profit; License: Current state

Arbour Health Care Center

1512 W. Fargo, Chicago, IL 60626, (773) 465-7751; Facility Type: Skilled care; Alzheimer's; Certified Beds: 99; Certified: Medicaid; Medicare; Owner: Private, For-Profit; License: Current state

Astoria Place Living & Rehabilitation

6300 N California Ave., Chicago, IL 60659, (773) 973-1900; Facility type: Skilled care, Alzheimer's; Beds: 164; Certified: Medicaid, Medicare; Owner: Nonprofit/Religious; License: state; Activities: Arts & Crafts; Dances; Pet therapy; Group exercise; Support Groups; Other: Alzheimer's secured unit

Atrium Healthcare Center

1425 W. Estes Ave., Chicago, IL 60626, (773) 973-4780; Facility Type: Skilled care; Alzheimer's; Certified Beds: 160; Certified: Medicaid; Medicare; Owner: Private, For-Profit; License: Current state

Balmoral Home

2055 W Balmoral Ave., Chicago, IL 60625, (773) 561-8661; Facility type: Skilled care, Alzheimer's; Certified Beds: 213; Certified: Medicaid, Medicare, Veterans; Owner: Proprietary/Public; License: state; Activities: Arts & Crafts; Dances; Pet therapy; Group exercise; Support Groups

Birchwood Plaza

1426 W. Birchwood, Chicago, IL 60626, (773) 274-4405; Facility Type: Skilled care; Alzheimer's; Certified Beds: 200; Certified: Medicaid; Medicare; Owner: Private, For-Profit; License: Current state

Birchwood Plaza Nursing Home

1426 W Birchwood Ave., Chicago, IL 60626, (773) 274-4405; Facility type: Skilled care, Alzheimer's; Certified Beds: 200; Certified: Medicaid, Medicare, Veterans; Owner: Proprietary/Public; License: state; Activities: Arts & Crafts; Dances; Pet therapy; Group exercise; Support Groups; Other: Adult day care

Brightview Care Center Inc.

4538 N Beacon, Chicago, IL 60640, (773) 275-7200; Facility type: Skilled care, Alzheimer's; Certified Beds: 143; Certified: Medicaid, Medicare; Owner: Proprietary/Public; License: state; Activities: Arts & Crafts; Dances; Pet therapy; Group exercise; Support Groups; Other: Alzheimer's secured unit

Bronzeville Park Nursing & Living Center

3400 S. Indiana, Chicago, IL 60616, (312) 842-5000; Facility Type: Skilled care; Alzheimer's; Certified Beds: 302; Certified: Medicaid; Medicare; Owner: Private, For-Profit; License: Current state

Buckingham Pavilion

2625 W. Touhy Ave., Chicago, IL 60645, (773) 973-5333; Facility Type: Skilled care; Alzheimer's; Certified Beds: 247; Certified: Medicaid; Medicare; Owner: Private, For-Profit; License: Current state

California Gardens Nursing & Rehabilitation Center

2829 S. California Blvd, Chicago, IL 60608, (773) 847-8061; Facility Type: Skilled care; Alzheimer's; Certified Beds: 297; Certified: Medicaid; Medicare; Owner: Private, For-Profit; License: Current state

The Carlton at the Lake

725 W. Montrose Ave., Chicago, IL 60613, (773) 929-1700; Facility Type: Skilled care; Alzheimer's; Certified Beds: 244; Certified: Medicaid; Medicare; Owner: Private, For-Profit; License: Current state

Center Home Hispanic Elderly

1401 N. California, Chicago, IL 60622, (773) 782-8700; Facility Type: Skilled care; Alzheimer's; Certified Beds: 156; Certified: Medicaid; Medicare; Owner: Private, For-Profit; License: Current state

Clark Manor Convalescent Center

7433 N. Clark St., Chicago, IL 60626, (773) 338-8778; Facility Type: Skilled care; Alzheimer's; Certified Beds: 267; Certified: Medicaid; Medicare; Owner: Private, For-Profit; License: Current state

Community Care

4314 S. Wabash Ave., Chicago, IL 60653, (773) 538-8300; Facility Type: Skilled care; Alzheimer's; Certified Beds: 204; Certified: Medicaid; Medicare; Owner: Private, For-Profit; License: Current state

Fairmont Care Centre

5061 N. Pulaski Rd., Chicago, IL 60630, (773) 604-8112; Facility Type: Skilled care; Alzheimer's; Certified Beds: 176; Certified: Medicaid; Medicare; Owner: Private, For-Profit; License: Current state

Glencrest Nursing Rehabilitation Center Ltd.

2451 W Touhy Ave., Chicago, IL 60645, (773) 338-6800; Facility type: Skilled care, Alzheimer's; Certified Beds: 312; Certified: Medicaid, Medicare, Veterans; Owner: Health & Home Care Management; License: state; Activities: Arts & Crafts; Dances; Pet therapy; Group exercise; Support Groups; Other: Home health care

Harmony Nursing & Rehabilitation Center

3919 W Foster Ave., Chicago, IL 60625, (773) 588-

9500; Facility type: Skilled care, Alzheimer's; Certified Beds: 180; Certified: Medicaid, Medicare, Veterans; Owner: Itex Corp; License: state; Activities: Arts & Crafts; Dances; Pet therapy; Group exercise; Support Groups; Other: Alzheimer's secured unit

Heritage Nursing Home Inc.

5888 N Ridge Ave., Chicago, IL 60660, (773) 769-2626; Facility type: Skilled care, Alzheimer's; Certified Beds: 128; Certified: Medicaid, Medicare; Owner: Health & Home Care Management; License: state; Activities: Arts & Crafts; Dances; Pet therapy; Group exercise; Support Groups; Other: Alzheimer's secured unit; Home health care

The Imperial Grove Pavilion

1366 W. Fullerton Ave., Chicago, IL 60614, (773) 248-9300; Facility Type: Skilled care; Alzheimer's; Certified Beds: 248; Certified: Medicaid; Medicare; Owner: Private, For-Profit; License: Current state

Kenwood Healthcare Center

6125 S. Kenwood, Chicago, IL 60637, (773) 752-6000; Facility Type: Skilled care; Alzheimer's; Certified Beds: 318; Certified: Medicaid; Medicare; Owner: Private, For-Profit; License: Current state

Lake Shore Healthcare & Rehabilitation Center

7200 N. Sheridan Rd., Chicago, IL 60626, (773) 973-7200; Facility Type: Skilled care; Alzheimer's; Certified Beds: 313; Certified: Medicaid; Medicare; Owner: Private, For-Profit; License: Current state

Margaret Manor

1121 N. Orleans, Chicago, IL 60610, (312) 943-4300; Facility Type: Skilled care; Alzheimer's; Certified Beds: 135; Certified: Medicaid; Owner: Private, For-Profit; License: Current state

Methodist Home

1415 W Foster Ave., Chicago, IL 60640, (773) 769-5500; Facility type: Skilled care, Alzheimer's; Certified Beds: 126; Certified: Medicaid, Medicare; Owner: Nonprofit/Religious; License: state; Activities: Arts & Crafts; Dances; Pet therapy; Group exercise; Support Groups; Alzheimer's secured unit

Mid-America Care Center

4920 N Kenmore Ave., Chicago, IL 60640, (773) 769-2700; Facility type: Skilled care, Alzheimer's; Certified Beds: 310; Certified: Medicaid, Medicare; Owner: Proprietary/Public License: state; Activities: Arts & Crafts; Dances; Pet therapy; Group exercise; Support Groups; Other: Alzheimer's secured unit; Adult day care

Montgomery Place

5550 S Shore Dr., Chicago, IL 60637, (773) 753-4100; Facility type: Skilled care, Alzheimer's; Certified Beds: 20; Certified: Medicaid, Medicare, Veterans; Owner: Nonprofit; License: state; Activities: Arts & Crafts; Dances; Pet therapy; Group exercise; Support

Groups; Other: Alzheimer's secured unit; Home health care

Peterson Park Care Center

6141 N Pulaski Rd., Chicago, IL 60646, (773) 478-2000; Facility type: Skilled care, Alzheimer's; Certified Beds: 188; Certified: Medicaid, Veterans; Owner: Nonprofit/Religious; License: state; Activities: Arts & Crafts; Dances; Pet therapy; Group exercise; Support Groups

Presidential Pavilion

8001 S. Western Ave., Chicago, IL 60620, (773) 436-6600; Facility Type: Skilled care; Alzheimer's; Certified Beds: 328; Certified: Medicaid; Medicare; Owner: Private, For-Profit; License: Current state

Rainbow Beach Care Center

7325 S. Exchange, Chicago, IL 60649, (773) 731-7300; Facility Type: Skilled care; Alzheimer's; Certified Beds: 211; Certified: Medicaid; Owner: Private, For-Profit; License: Current state

The Renaissance at 87th Street

2940 W. 87th St., Chicago, IL 60652, (773) 434-8787; Facility Type: Skilled care; Alzheimer's; Certified Beds: 210; Certified: Medicaid; Medicare; Owner: Private, For-Profit; License: Current state

The Renaissance at Midway

4437 S. Cicero St., Chicago, IL 60632, (773) 884-0484; Facility Type: Skilled care; Alzheimer's; Certified Beds: 249; Certified: Medicaid; Medicare; Owner: Private, For-Profit; License: Current state

The Renaissance at South Shore

2425 E. 71st St., Chicago, IL 60649, (773) 721-5000; Facility Type: Skilled care; Alzheimer's; Certified Beds: 248; Certified: Medicaid; Medicare; Owner: Private, For-Profit; License: Current state

Renaissance Park South

10935 S. Halsted St., Chicago, IL 60628, (773) 928-2000; Facility Type: Skilled care; Alzheimer's; Certified Beds: 300; Certified: Medicaid; Medicare; Owner: Private, For-Profit; License: Current state

Resurrection Life Center

7370 W. Talcott Ave., Chicago, IL 60631, (773) 594-7400; Facility Type: Skilled care; Alzheimer's; Certified Beds: 147; Certified: Medicaid; Medicare; Owner: Private, Nonprofit; License: Current state

Sacred Heart Home

1550 S. Albany, Chicago, IL 60623, (773) 277-6868; Facility Type: Skilled care; Alzheimer's; Certified Beds: 172; Certified: Medicaid; Medicare; Owner: Private, Nonprofit; License: Current state

St. Agnes Healthcare & Rehabilitation Center

1725 S. Wabash, Chicago, IL 60616, (312) 922-2777; Facility Type: Skilled care; Alzheimer's; Certified Beds: 197; Certified: Medicaid; Medicare; Owner: Private, For-Profit; License: Current state

Sherwin Manor Nursing Center, LLC
7350 N. Sheridan Rd., Chicago, IL 60626, (773) 274-1000; Facility Type: Skilled care; Alzheimer's; Certified Beds: 219; Certified: Medicaid; Medicare; Owner: Private, For-Profit; License: Current state

South Shore Nursing & Rehabilitation Center
2649 E. 75th St., Chicago, IL 60649, (773) 356-9300; Facility Type: Skilled care; Alzheimer's; Certified Beds: 240; Certified: Medicaid; Medicare; Owner: Private, For-Profit; License: Current state

Warren Barr Pavilion
66 W Oak St., Chicago, IL 60610, (312) 337-5400; Facility type: Skilled care, Alzheimer's; Certified Beds: 271; Certified: Medicaid, Medicare, Veterans; Owner: Health & Home Care Management; License: state; Activities: Arts & Crafts; Dances; Pet therapy; Group exercise; Support Groups; Other: Alzheimer's secured unit; Home health care, Adult day care

Waterfront Terrace
7750 S Shore Dr., Chicago, IL 60649, (773) 731-4200; Facility type: Skilled care, Alzheimer's; Certified Beds: 118; Certified: Medicaid, Veterans; Owner: Proprietary/Public License: state; Activities: Arts & Crafts; Dances; Pet therapy; Group exercise; Support Groups; Alzheimer's secured unit

Chicago Heights

Prairie Manor Nursing & Rehabilitation Center
345 Dixie Hwy., Chicago Heights, IL 60411, (708) 754-7601; Facility Type: Skilled care; Alzheimer's; Certified Beds: 248; Certified: Medicaid; Medicare; Owner: Private, For-Profit; License: Current state

Riviera Manor Inc.
490 W 16th Pl., Chicago Heights, IL 60411, (708) 481-4444; Facility type: Skilled care, Alzheimer's; Certified Beds: 200; Certified: Medicaid, Medicare, Veterans; Owner: Nonprofit/Religious; License: state; Activities: Arts & Crafts; Dances; Pet therapy; Group exercise; Support Groups

Chicago Ridge

Chicago Ridge Nursing Center
10602 Southwest Hwy., Chicago Ridge, IL 60415, (708) 448-1540; Facility Type: Skilled care; Alzheimer's; Certified Beds: 231; Certified: Medicaid; Medicare; Owner: Private, For-Profit; License: Current state

Lexington of Chicago Ridge
10300 Southwest Hwy., Chicago Ridge, IL 60415, (708) 425-1100; Facility type: Skilled care, Alzheimer's; Certified Beds: 203; Certified: Medicaid, Medicare; Owner: Nonprofit/Religious; License: state; Activities: Arts & Crafts; Dances; Pet therapy; Group exercise; Support Groups; Other: Alzheimer's secured unit, Home health care

Danforth

Prairieview Lutheran Home
PO Box 4, Danforth, IL 60930, (815) 269-2970; Facility type: Skilled care, Alzheimer's; Certified Beds: 90; Certified: Medicaid, Medicare; Owner: Nonprofit/Religious; License: state; Activities: Arts & Crafts; Dances; Pet therapy; Group exercise; Support Groups; Other: Alzheimer's secured unit

Deerfield

The Whitehall North
300 Waukegan Rd., Deerfield, IL 60015, (847) 945-4600; Facility type: Skilled care, Alzheimer's; Certified Beds: 190; Certified: Medicare; Owner: Nonprofit/Religious; License: state; Activities: Arts & Crafts; Dances; Pet therapy; Group exercise; Support Groups; Other: Alzheimer's secured unit

Des Plaines

Alden Des Plaines Rehabilitation & Healthcare
1221 E. Golf Rd., Des Plaines, IL 60016, (847) 768-1300; Facility Type: Skilled care; Alzheimer's; Certified Beds: 110; Certified: Medicaid; Medicare; Owner: Private, For-Profit; License: Current state

Ballard Nursing Center
9300 Ballard Rd., Des Plaines, IL 60016, (847) 294-2300; Facility type: Skilled care, Alzheimer's; Certified Beds: 231; Certified: Medicaid, Medicare; Owner: Nonprofit/Religious; License: state; Activities: Arts & Crafts; Dances; Pet therapy; Group exercise; Support Groups; Other: Alzheimer's secured unit, Adult day care

Holy Family Nursing & Rehabilitation Center
2380 Dempster St., Des Plaines, IL 60016, (847) 296-3335; Facility Type: Skilled care; Alzheimer's; Certified Beds: 247; Certified: Medicaid; Medicare; Owner: Private, For-Profit; License: Current state

Lee Manor
1301 Lee St., Des Plaines, IL 60018, (847) 635-4000; Facility type: Skilled care, Alzheimer's; Certified Beds: 260; Certified: Medicaid, Medicare; Owner: Private; License: state; Activities: Arts & Crafts; Dances; Pet therapy; Group exercise; Support Groups; Other: Alzheimer's secured unit

Oakton Pavillion
1660 Oakton Pl., Des Plaines, IL 60018, (847) 299-5588; Facility Type: Skilled care; Alzheimer's; Certified Beds: 294; Certified: Medicaid; Medicare; Owner: Private, For-Profit; License: Current state

Dixon

Dixon Health Care Center
141 North Ct, Dixon, IL 61021, (815) 288-1477; Fa-

cility type: Skilled care, Alzheimer's; Certified Beds: 97; Certified: Medicaid, Medicare; Owner: Proprietary/Public; License: state; Activities: Arts & Crafts; Dances; Pet therapy; Group exercise; Support Groups; Other: Alzheimer's secured unit

Heritage Square
620 N. Ottawa Ave., Dixon, IL 61021, (815) 288-2251; Facility Type: Skilled care; Alzheimer's; Certified Beds: 27; Certified: Medicaid; Medicare; Owner: Private, For-Profit; License: Current state

Downer's Grove

Fairview Baptist Home
250 Village Dr., Downers Grove, IL 60516, (630) 769-6200; Facility type: Skilled care, Alzheimer's; Certified Beds: 50; Certified: Medicaid, Medicare; Owner: Nonprofit/Religious; License: state; Activities: Arts & Crafts; Dances; Pet therapy; Group exercise; Support Groups; Other: Alzheimer's secured unit, Home health care; Affiliations: Baptist Church

Providence Downer's Grove
3450 Saratoga Ave., Downers Grove, IL 60515, (630) 969-2900; Facility type: Skilled care, Alzheimer's; Certified Beds: 145; Certified: Medicaid, Medicare; Owner: Nonprofit/Religious; License: state; Activities: Arts & Crafts; Dances; Pet therapy; Group exercise; Support Groups; Other: Alzheimer's secured unit, Home health care

East Moline

East Moline Nursing & Rehabilitation
430 S. 30th Ave., East Moline, IL 61244, (309) 755-3466; Facility Type: Skilled care; Alzheimer's; Certified Beds: 120; Certified: Medicaid; Medicare; Owner: Private, For-Profit; License: Current state

Forest Hill Health Rehabilitation
4747 11th St., East Moline, IL 61244, (309) 796-0922; Facility type: Skilled care, Alzheimer's; Certified Beds: 137; Certified: Medicaid, Medicare; Owner: Proprietary/Public; License: state; Activities: Arts & Crafts; Dances; Pet therapy; Group exercise; Support Groups; Other: Alzheimer's secured unit, Home health care

Hope Creek Care Center
4343 Kennedy Dr., East Moline, IL 61244, (309) 796-6600; Facility Type: Skilled care; Alzheimer's; Certified Beds: 245; Certified: Medicaid; Medicare; Owner: Private, Government/County; License: Current state

Edwardsville

Edwardsville Nursing & Rehabilitation Center
401 St. Mary Dr., Edwardsville, IL 62025, (618) 692-1330; Facility Type: Skilled care; Alzheimer's; Certified Beds: 120; Certified: Medicaid; Medicare; Owner: Private, For-Profit; License: Current state

Rosewood Care Center of Edwardsville
6277 Center Grove Rd., Edwardsville, IL 62025, (618) 659-0605; Facility Type: Skilled care; Alzheimer's; Certified Beds: 78; Certified: Medicaid; Medicare; Owner: Private, For-Profit; License: Current state

University Nursing & Rehabilitation
University Dr., Edwardsville, IL 62025, (618) 656-1081; Facility Type: Skilled care; Alzheimer's; Certified Beds: 118; Certified: Medicaid; Medicare; Owner: Private, For-Profit; License: Current state

Effingham

Effingham Rehabilitation & Healthcare Center
1610 N. Lakewood, Effingham, IL 62401, (217) 347-7781; Facility Type: Skilled care; Alzheimer's; Certified Beds: 62; Certified: Medicaid; Medicare; Owner: Private, For-Profit; License: Current state

Evergreen Nursing & Rehabilitation Center
1115 N. Wenthee, Effingham, IL 62401, (217) 347-7121; Facility Type: Skilled care; Alzheimer's; Certified Beds: 120; Certified: Medicaid; Medicare; Owner: Private, For-Profit; License: Current state

Lakeland Healthcare Center
800 W Temple St., Effingham, IL 62401, (217) 342-2171; Facility type: Skilled care, Alzheimer's; Certified Beds: 140; Certified: Medicaid, Medicare; Owner: Nonprofit/Religious; License: state; Activities: Arts & Crafts; Dances; Pet therapy; Group exercise; Support Groups; Other: Alzheimer's secured unit

St. Anthony's Memorial Hospital
503 N. Maple St., Effingham, IL 62401, (217) 342-2121; Facility Type: Skilled care; Alzheimer's; Certified Beds: 13; Certified: Medicaid; Medicare; Owner: Nonprofit, Church-related; License: Current state

Eldorado

Fountainview
1001 A Jefferson St., Eldorado, IL 62930, (618) 273-3353; Facility Type: Skilled care; Alzheimer's; Certified Beds: 111; Certified: Medicaid; Medicare; Owner: Private, For-Profit; License: Current state

Elgin

Apostolic Christian Resthaven
2750 W. Highland Ave., Elgin, IL 60123, (847) 741-4543; Facility Type: Skilled care; Alzheimer's; Certified Beds: 350Certified: Medicaid; Medicare; Owner: Private, Nonprofit, Church-related; License: Current state

Asta Care Center of Elgin
134 N. Mclean Blvd., Elgin, IL 60121, (847) 742-8822; Facility Type: Skilled care; Alzheimer's;

Certified Beds: 102; Certified: Medicaid; Medicare; Owner: Private, For-Profit; License: Current state

Heritage Manor — Elgin
355 Raymond St., Elgin, IL 60120, (847) 697-6636; Facility Type: Skilled care; Alzheimer's; Certified Beds: 94; Certified: Medicaid; Medicare; Owner: Private, For-Profit; License: Current state

ManorCare of Elgin
180 S State St., Elgin, IL 60123, (847) 742-3310; Facility type: Skilled care, Alzheimer's; Certified Beds: 88; Certified: Medicaid, Medicare; Owner: HCR ManorCare; License: state; Activities: Arts & Crafts; Dances; Pet therapy; Group exercise; Support Groups; Other: Alzheimer's secured unit, Adult day care

Maplewood Care
50 N Jane Dr., Elgin, IL 60123, (847) 697-3750; Facility type: Skilled care, Alzheimer's; Certified Beds: 203; Certified: Medicaid, Medicare; Owner: Proprietary/Public; License: state; Activities: Arts & Crafts; Dances; Pet therapy; Group exercise; Support Groups

Rosewood Care Center of Elgin
2355 Royal Blvd., Elgin, IL 60123, (847) 888-9585; Facility Type: Skilled care; Alzheimer's; Certified Beds: 89; Certified: Medicaid; Medicare; Owner: Private, For-Profit; License: Current state

Elk Grove Village

ManorCare at Elk Grove Village
1920 Nerge Rd., Elk Grove Village, IL 60007, (847) 301-0550; Facility type: Skilled care, Alzheimer's; Certified Beds: 190; Certified: Medicaid, Medicare; Owner: HCR ManorCare; License: state; Activities: Arts & Crafts; Dances; Pet therapy; Group exercise; Support Groups; Other: Alzheimer's secured unit, Adult day care

Elmhurst

Elm Brook Health Care & Rehabilitation Center
127 W Diversey Ave., Elmhurst, IL 60126, (630) 530-5225; Facility type: Skilled care, Alzheimer's; Certified Beds: 180; Certified: Medicaid, Medicare, Veterans; Owner: Proprietary/Public; License: state; Activities: Arts & Crafts; Dances; Pet therapy; Group exercise; Support Groups

Elmhurst Extended Care Center Inc.
200 E Lake St., Elmhurst, IL 60126, (630) 834-4337; Facility type: Skilled care, Alzheimer's; Certified Beds: 39; Certified: Medicaid, Medicare; Owner: Proprietary/Public; License: state; Activities: Arts & Crafts; Dances; Pet therapy; Group exercise; Support Groups; Other: Alzheimer's secured unit

Elmhurst Memorial Hospital
200 Berteau Ave., Elmhurst, IL 60126, (630) 833-

1400; Facility Type: Skilled care; Alzheimer's; Located within a hospital; Certified Beds: 38; Certified: Medicaid; Medicare; Owner: Private, Nonprofit; License: Current state

Lexington of Elmhurst
420 W. Butterfield Rd., Elmhurst, IL 60126, (630) 832-2300; Facility Type: Skilled care; Alzheimer's; Certified Beds: 145; Certified: Medicaid; Medicare; Owner: Private, For-Profit; License: Current state

Eureka

Apostolic Christian Home of Eureka
610 W Cruger Ave., Eureka, IL 61530, (309) 467-2311; Facility type: Skilled care, Alzheimer's; Certified Beds: 105; Certified: Medicaid, Medicare, Veterans; Owner: Nonprofit/Religious; License: state; Activities: Arts & Crafts; Dances; Pet therapy; Group exercise; Support Groups, Alzheimer's secured unit, Home health care

Maple Lawn Health Center
700 N. Main St., Eureka, IL 61530, (309) 467-2337; Facility Type: Skilled care; Alzheimer's; Certified Beds: 89; Certified: Medicaid; Medicare; Owner: Private, For-Profit; License: Current state

Evanston

Albany Care
901 Maple Ave., Evanston, IL 60202, (847) 475-4000; Facility Type: Skilled care; Alzheimer's; Certified Beds: 417; Certified: Medicaid; Owner: Private, For-Profit; License: Current state

Alden Estates of Evanston
2520 Gross Point Rd., Evanston, IL 60201, (847) 328-6000; Facility Type: Skilled care; Alzheimer's; Certified Beds: 52; Certified: Medicaid; Medicare; Owner: Private, For-Profit; License: Current state

Dobson Plaza
120 Dodge Ave., Evanston, IL 60202, (847) 869-7744; Facility type: Skilled care, Alzheimer's; Assisted Living; Certified Beds: 97; Certified: Medicaid, Medicare; Owner: Nonprofit/Religious; License: state; Activities: Arts & Crafts; Dances; Pet therapy; Group exercise; Support Groups, Alzheimer's secured unit, Adult day care

Evanston Nursing & Rehabilitation Center
1300 Oak Ave, Evanston, IL 60201, (847) 869-1300; Facility Type: Skilled care; Alzheimer's; Certified Beds: 57; Certified: Medicaid; Medicare; Owner: Private, For-Profit; License: Current state

Greenwood Care
1406 Chicago Ave., Evanston, IL 60202, (847) 328-6503; Facility Type: Skilled care; Alzheimer's; Certified Beds: 145; Certified: Medicaid; Medicare; Owner: Private, For-Profit; License: Current state

Grove of Evanston
500 Asbury St., Evanston, IL 60202, (847) 316-3320; Facility Type: Skilled care; Alzheimer's; Certified Beds: 124; Certified: Medicaid; Medicare; Owner: Private, Nonprofit; License: Current state

Mather Pavilion
820 Foster St., Evanston, IL 60201, (847) 492-7700; Facility type: Skilled care, Alzheimer's; Certified Beds: 13; Certified: Medicare; Owner: Nonprofit Proprietary/Public; License: state; Activities: Arts & Crafts; Dances; Pet therapy; Group exercise; Support Groups, Alzheimer's secured unit

Westminster Place
3200 Grant St., Evanston, IL 60201, (847) 492-4800; Facility Type: Skilled care; Alzheimer's; Certified Beds: 105; Certified: Medicaid; Medicare; Owner: Private, Nonprofit; License: Current state

Freeport

F H N Freeport Memorial Hospital
1045 W. Stevenson, Freeport, IL 61032, (815) 599-6000; Facility Type: Skilled care; Alzheimer's; Located within a Hospital; Certified Beds: 43; Certified: Medicaid; Medicare; Owner: Private, Nonprofit; License: Current state

Freeport Rehabilitation & Health Center
900 S. Kiwanis Dr., Freeport, IL 61032, (815) 235-6196; Facility Type: Skilled care; Alzheimer's; Certified Beds: 143; Certified: Medicaid; Medicare; Owner: Private, Nonprofit; License: Current state

Manor Court of Freeport
2170 W. Navajo Dr., Freeport, IL 61032, (815) 233-2400; Facility Type: Skilled care; Alzheimer's; Certified Beds: 45; Certified: Medicaid; Medicare; Owner: Private, Nonprofit; License: Current state

Provena St. Joseph Center
659 E. Jefferson St., Freeport, IL 61032, (815) 232-6181; Facility Type: Skilled care; Alzheimer's; Certified Beds: 120; Certified: Medicaid; Medicare; Owner: Private, Nonprofit, Church-related; License: Current state

Stephenson Nursing Center
2946 S Walnut Rd., Freeport, IL 61032, (815) 235-6173; Facility type: Skilled care, Alzheimer's; Certified Beds: 162; Certified: Medicaid, Medicare; Owner: Government/County; License: state; Activities: Arts & Crafts; Dances; Pet therapy; Group exercise; Support Groups, Alzheimer's secured unit, Adult day care

Geneva

Provena Geneva Care Center
1101 E State St., Geneva, IL 60134, (630) 232-7544; Facility type: Skilled care, Alzheimer's; Beds: 107; Certified: Medicaid; Owner: Proprietary/Public; License: state; Activities: Arts & Crafts; Dances; Pet therapy; Group exercise; Support Groups, Alzheimer's secured unit

Glen Carbon

Eden Village Care Center
400 S Station Rd., Glen Carbon, IL 62034, (618) 288-5014; Facility type: Skilled care, Alzheimer's; Certified Beds: 138; Certified: Medicaid, Medicare; Owner: Nonprofit/Religious; License: state; Activities: Arts & Crafts; Dances; Pet therapy; Group exercise; Support Groups, Alzheimer's secured unit

Meridian Village Care Center
27 Auerbach Pl., Glen Carbon, IL 62034, (618) 288-3700; Facility Type: Skilled care; Alzheimer's; Certified Beds: 64; Certified: Medicaid; Medicare; Owner: Private, Nonprofit, Church-related; License: Current state

Glenview

Abington of Glenview
3901 Glenview Rd., Glenview, IL 60025, (847) 729-0000; Facility type: Skilled care, Alzheimer's; Certified Beds: 100; Certified: Medicare; Owner: Nonprofit/Religious; License: state; Activities: Arts & Crafts; Dances; Pet therapy; Group exercise; Support Groups, Alzheimer's secured unit

Glenview Terrace Nursing Center
1511 Greenwood Rd., Glenview, IL 60025, (847) 729-9090; Facility type: Skilled care, Alzheimer's; Certified Beds: 314; Certified: Medicaid, Medicare; Owner: Private; License: state; Activities: Arts & Crafts; Dances; Pet therapy; Group exercise; Support Groups, Alzheimer's secured unit

Maryhaven Nursing & Rehabilitation
1700 E. Lake Ave., Glenview, IL 60025, (847) 729-1300; Facility Type: Skilled care; Alzheimer's; Certified Beds: 135; Certified: Medicaid; Medicare; Owner: Nonprofit, Church-related; License: Current state

Hinsdale

ManorCare of Hinsdale
600 W. Ogden Ave., Hinsdale, IL 60521, (630) 325-9630; Facility Type: Skilled care; Alzheimer's; Certified Beds: 202; Certified: Medicaid; Medicare; Owner: Private, For-Profit; License: Current state

Itasca

The Arbor of Itasca
535 S Elm St., Itasca, IL 60143, (630) 773-9416; Facility type: Skilled care, Alzheimer's; Hospice; Certified Beds: 144; Certified: Medicaid, Medicare;

Owner: Private; License: state; Activities: Arts & Crafts; Dances; Pet therapy; Group exercise; Support Groups, Alzheimer's secured unit

Jacksonville

Care Center of Jacksonville
1320 Tendick, PO Box 1115, Jacksonville, IL 62650, (217) 243-6405; Facility Type: Skilled care; Alzheimer's; Respite care; Certified Beds: 93; Certified: Medicaid; Owner: Private, For-Profit; License: Current state

Heritage Health
873 Grove St., Jacksonville, IL 62650, (217) 479-3400; Facility type: Skilled care, Alzheimer's; Certified Beds: 185; Certified: Medicaid, Medicare; Owner: Private; License: state; Activities: Arts & Crafts; Dances; Pet therapy; Group exercise; Support Groups, Alzheimer's secured unit

Jacksonville Convalescent Center
1517 W. Walnut St. Jacksonville, IL 62650, (217) 243-6451; Facility Type: Skilled care; Alzheimer's; Certified Beds: 88; Certified: Medicaid; Medicare; Owner: Private, For-Profit; License: Current state

North Church Nursing & Rehabilitation
1021 N. Church St., Jacksonville, IL 62650, (217) 245-4174; Facility Type: Skilled care; Alzheimer's; Certified Beds: 113; Certified: Medicaid; Medicare; Owner: Private, For-Profit; License: Current state

Prairie Village Healthcare Center
1024 W. Walnut, Jacksonville, IL 62650, (217) 245-5175; Facility Type: Skilled care; Alzheimer's; Certified Beds: 126; Certified: Medicaid; Medicare; Owner: Private, For-Profit; License: Current state

Joliet

Deerbrook Care Centre
306 N Larkin Ave., Joliet, IL 60435, (815) 744-5560; Facility type: Skilled care, Alzheimer's; Certified Beds: 214; Certified: Medicaid, Medicare; Owner: Private; License: state; Activities: Arts & Crafts; Dances; Pet therapy; Group exercise; Support Groups, Alzheimer's secured unit

Fairview Care Center of Joliet
222 N. Hammes, Joliet, IL 60435, (815) 725-0443; Facility Type: Skilled care; Alzheimer's; Certified Beds: 203; Certified: Medicaid; Medicare; Owner: Private, For-Profit; License: Current state

Hillcrest Nursing & Rehabilitation Center
777 Draper, Joliet, IL 60432, (815) 727-4794; Facility Type: Skilled care; Alzheimer's; Adult Day Care; Assisted Living; Certified Beds: 168; Certified: Medicaid; Medicare; Owner: Private, For-Profit; License: Current state

Joliet Terrace
2230 McDonough, Joliet, IL 60436, (815) 729-3801; Facility Type: Skilled care; Alzheimer's; Certified Beds: 120; Certified: Medicaid; Owner: Private, For-Profit; License: Current state

Our Lady of Angels Retirement Home
1201 Wyoming Ave., Joliet, IL 60435, (815) 725-6631; Facility Type: Skilled care; Alzheimer's; Certified Beds: 87; Certified: Medicaid; Medicare; Owner: Private, Nonprofit, Church-related; License: Current state

Provena Villa Franciscan
210 N Springfield Ave., Joliet, IL 60435, (815) 725-3400; Facility type: Skilled care, Alzheimer's; Certified Beds: 176; Certified: Medicaid, Medicare; Owner: Nonprofit; License: state; Activities: Arts & Crafts; Dances; Pet therapy; Group exercise; Support Groups, Alzheimer's secured unit

Rosewood Care Center of Joliet
3401 Hennepin Dr., Joliet, IL 60435, (815) 436-5900; Facility Type: Skilled care; Alzheimer's; Certified Beds: 78; Certified: Medicaid; Medicare; Owner: Private, For-Profit; License: Current state

Salem Village
1314 Rowell Ave., Joliet, IL 60433, (815) 727-5451; Facility type: Skilled care, Alzheimer's; Certified Beds: 266; Certified: Medicaid, Medicare; Owner: Nonprofit; License: state; Activities: Arts & Crafts; Dances; Pet therapy; Group exercise; Support Groups, Alzheimer's secured unit, Adult day care

Sunny Hill Nursing Home of Will County
421 Doris Ave., Joliet, IL 60433, (815) 727-8710; Facility Type: Skilled care; Alzheimer's; Certified Beds: 300; Certified: Medicaid; Medicare; Owner: Private, Government/County; License: Current state

Kankakee

ManorCare at Kankakee
900 W River Pl., Kankakee, IL 60901, (815) 933-1711; Facility type: Skilled care, Alzheimer's; Certified Beds: 107; Certified: Medicaid, Medicare, Veterans; Owner: HCR ManorCare; License: state; Activities: Arts & Crafts; Dances; Pet therapy; Group exercise; Support Groups, Alzheimer's secured unit

Miller Health Care Center
1601 Butterfield Tr., Kankakee, IL 60901, (815) 936-6500; Facility Type: Skilled care; Alzheimer's; Certified Beds: 120; Certified: Medicaid; Medicare; Owner: Private, Nonprofit; License: Current state

Provena Heritage Village
901 N. Entrance Ave., Kankakee, IL 60901, (815) 939-4506; Facility Type: Skilled care; Alzheimer's; Certified Beds: 51; Certified: Medicaid; Medicare; Owner: Nonprofit, Church-related; License: Current state

La Grange

Lexington of La Grange
4735 Willow Springs Rd. La Grange, IL 60525, (630) 327-5814; Facility Type: Skilled care; Alzheimer's; Certified Beds: 109; Certified: Medicaid; Medicare; Owner: Private, For-Profit; License: Current state

Meadowbrook Manor — La Grange
339 S 9th Ave., La Grange, IL 60525, (708) 354-4660; Facility type: Skilled care, Alzheimer's; Certified Beds: 197; Certified: Medicaid, Medicare, Veterans; Owner: Sun Healthcare; License: state; Activities: Arts & Crafts; Dances; Pet therapy; Group exercise; Support Groups, Alzheimer's secured unit

Lake Bluff

Claridge Healthcare Center
700 Jenkisson Ave., Lake Bluff, IL 60044, (847) 295-3900; Facility type: Skilled care, Alzheimer's; Certified Beds: 231; Certified: Medicaid, Medicare, Veterans; Owner: Proprietary/Public; License: state; Activities: Arts & Crafts; Dances; Pet therapy; Group exercise; Support Groups, Alzheimer's secured unit

Lawrenceville

The United Methodist Village
1616 Cedar St., Lawrenceville, IL 62439, (618) 943-3347; Facility type: Skilled care, Alzheimer's; Certified Beds: 163; Certified: Medicaid, Medicare, Veterans; Owner: Proprietary/Public; License: state; Activities: Arts & Crafts; Dances; Pet therapy; Group exercise; Support Groups, Alzheimer's secured unit

United Methodist Village, North Campus
2101 James St., Lawrenceville, IL 62439, (618) 943-3444; Facility Type: Skilled care; Alzheimer's; Certified Beds: 98; Certified: Medicaid; Medicare; Owner: Nonprofit, Church-related; License: Current state

Lemont

Franciscan Village
1270 Franciscan Dr., Lemont, IL 60439, (630) 243-3406; Facility Type: Skilled care; Alzheimer's; Certified Beds: 67; Certified: Medicaid; Medicare; Owner: Private, For-Profit; License: Current state

Lemont Nursing & Rehabilitation Center
12450 Walker Rd., Lemont, IL 60439, (630) 243-0400; Facility type: Skilled care, Alzheimer's; Certified Beds: 158; Certified: Medicaid, Medicare, Veterans; Owner: Genesis ElderCare; License: state; Activities: Arts & Crafts; Dances; Pet therapy; Group exercise; Support Groups, Alzheimer's secured unit

LeRoy

Leroy Manor
PO Box 149, LeRoy, IL 61752, (309) 962-5000; Fa-

cility type: Skilled care, Alzheimer's; Certified Beds: 96; Certified: Medicaid, Medicare, Veterans; Owner: Proprietary/Public; License: state; Activities: Arts & Crafts; Dances; Pet therapy; Group exercise; Support Groups, Alzheimer's secured unit

Libertyville

Libertyville Manor Extended Care
610 Peterson Rd., Libertyville, IL 60048, (847) 367-6100; Facility Type: Skilled care; Alzheimer's; Certified Beds: 31; Certified: Medicare; Owner: Private, For-Profit; License: Current state

ManorCare of Libertyville
1500 S. Milwaukee Ave., Libertyville, IL 60048, (847) 816-3200; Facility Type: Skilled care; Alzheimer's; Certified Beds: 150; Certified: Medicaid; Medicare; Owner: Private, For-Profit; License: Current state

Winchester House
1125 N Milwaukee Ave., Libertyville, IL 60048, (847) 362-4340; Facility type: Skilled care, Alzheimer's; Certified Beds: 360; Certified: Medicaid, Medicare, Veterans; Owner: Government/County; License: state; Activities: Arts & Crafts; Dances; Pet therapy; Group exercise; Support Groups, Alzheimer's secured unit

Lincoln

Christian Nursing Home
1507 7th St., Lincoln, IL 62656, (217) 732-2189; Facility Type: Skilled care; Alzheimer's; Certified Beds: 112; Certified: Medicaid; Medicare; Owner: Nonprofit, Church-related; License: Current state

Maple Ridge Care Centre
2202 N Kickapoo St., Lincoln, IL 62656, (217) 735-1538; Facility type: Skilled care, Alzheimer's; Certified Beds: 126; Certified: Medicaid, Medicare, Veterans; Owner: Proprietary/Public; License: state; Activities: Arts & Crafts; Dances; Pet therapy; Group exercise; Support Groups, Alzheimer's secured unit

St. Clara's Manor
200 Fifth St., Lincoln, IL 62656, (217) 735-1507; Facility Type: Skilled care; Alzheimer's; Certified Beds: 140; Certified: Medicaid; Medicare; Owner: Private, Nonprofit; License: Current state

Lindenhurst

Village at Victory Lakes
1055 E Grand Ave., Lindenhurst, IL 60046, (847) 356-5900; Facility type: Skilled care, Alzheimer's; Certified Beds: 120; Certified: Medicare, Veterans; Owner: Proprietary/Public; License: state; Activities:

Arts & Crafts; Dances; Pet therapy; Group exercise; Support Groups, Alzheimer's secured unit

Mattoon

Douglas Rehabilitation & Care Center
3516 Powell Ln, Mattoon, IL 61938, (217) 234-6401; Facility Type: Skilled care; Alzheimer's; Certified Beds: 79; Certified: Medicaid; Medicare; Owner: Private, For-Profit; License: Current state

Mattoon Healthcare & Rehabilitation Center
2121 S. Ninth, Mattoon, IL 61938, (217) 235-7138; Facility Type: Skilled care; Alzheimer's; Certified Beds: 148; Certified: Medicaid; Medicare; Owner: Private, For-Profit; License: Current state

Odd Fellow & Rebekah Home
201 Lafayette Ave. E, Mattoon, IL 61938, (217) 235-5449; Facility type: Skilled care, Alzheimer's; Certified Beds: 162; Certified: Medicaid, Veterans; Owner: Proprietary/Public; License: state; Activities: Arts & Crafts; Dances; Pet therapy; Group exercise; Support Groups, Alzheimer's secured unit

Palm Terrace of Mattoon
1000 Palm Ave., Mattoon, IL 61938, (217) 234-7403; Facility type: Skilled care, Alzheimer's; Certified Beds: 178; Certified: Medicare, Veterans; Owner: Proprietary/Public; License: state; Activities: Arts & Crafts; Dances; Pet therapy; Group exercise; Support Groups, Alzheimer's secured unit

Moline

Heartland Health Care Center
833 16th Ave., Moline, IL 61265, (309) 764-6744; Facility type: Skilled care, Alzheimer's; Certified Beds: 149; Certified: Medicaid, Medicare, Veterans; Owner: HCR ManorCare; License: state; Activities: Arts & Crafts; Dances; Pet therapy; Group exercise; Support Groups

Rosewood Care Center of Moline
7300 34th Ave., Moline, IL 61265, (309) 792-5940; Facility Type: Skilled care; Alzheimer's; Certified Beds: 86; Certified: Medicaid; Medicare; Owner: Private, For-Profit; License: Current state

Morton Grove

Bethany Terrace Nursing Care
8425 N Waukegan Rd., Morton Grove, IL 60053, (847) 965-8100; Facility type: Skilled care, Alzheimer's; Certified Beds: 163; Certified: Medicaid, Medicare; Owner: Nonprofit/Religious; License: state; Activities: Arts & Crafts; Dances; Pet therapy; Group exercise; Support Groups, Alzheimer's secured unit

Mount Carmel

Oakview Heights
1320 W 9th St., Mount Carmel, IL 62863, (618) 263-4337; Facility type: Skilled care, Alzheimer's; Certified Beds: 90; Certified: Medicaid, Medicare, Veterans; Owner: Nonprofit/Religious; License: state; Activities: Arts & Crafts; Dances; Pet therapy; Group exercise; Support Groups, Alzheimer's secured unit

Murphysboro

Rehabilitation & Care Center of Jackson County
1441 N 14th St., Murphysboro, IL 62966; (618) 684-2136; Facility type: Skilled care, Alzheimer's; Certified Beds: 178; Certified: Medicaid, Medicare, Veterans; Owner: Government/County; License: state; Activities: Arts & Crafts; Dances; Pet therapy; Group exercise; Support Groups, Alzheimer's secured unit

Nashville

Friendship Manor Nashville
485 S Friendship Dr., Nashville, IL 62263, (618) 327-3041; Facility type: Skilled care, Alzheimer's; Certified Beds: 230; Certified: Medicaid, Medicare, Veterans; Owner: Proprietary/Public; License: state; Activities: Arts & Crafts; Dances; Pet therapy; Group exercise; Support Groups, Alzheimer's secured unit

Oak Lawn

Concord Nursing & Rehabilitation Center
9401 S. Ridgeland Ave., Oak Lawn, IL 60453, (708) 599-6700; Facility Type: Skilled care; Alzheimer's; Certified Beds: 134; Certified: Medicaid; Medicare; Owner: Private, For-Profit; License: Current state

ManorCare at Oak Lawn–East
9401 S. Kostner Ave., Oak Lawn, IL 60453, (708) 423-7882; Facility Type: Skilled care; Alzheimer's; Certified Beds: 122; Certified: Medicaid; Medicare; Owner: Private, For-Profit; License: Current state

ManorCare at Oak Lawn–West
6300 W 95th St., Oak Lawn, IL 60453, (708) 599-8800; Facility type: Skilled care, Alzheimer's; Certified Beds: 191; Certified: Medicaid, Medicare, Veterans; Owner: HCR ManorCare; License: state; Activities: Arts & Crafts; Dances; Pet therapy; Group exercise; Support Groups, Alzheimer's secured unit, Adult day care

Olney

Burgin Nursing Manor
900-928 E Scott St., Olney, IL 62450, (618) 393-2914; Facility type: Skilled care, Alzheimer's; Certified Beds: 156; Certified: Medicaid, Medicare, Veterans;

Owner: HCR ManorCare; License: state; Activities: Arts & Crafts; Dances; Pet therapy; Group exercise; Support Groups, Alzheimer's secured unit, Adult day care

Richland Care & Rehabilitation
410 E. Mack, Olney, IL 62450, (618) 395-7421; Facility Type: Skilled care; Alzheimer's; Certified Beds: 118; Certified: Medicaid; Medicare; Owner: Private, For-Profit; License: Current state

Ottawa

La Salle County Nursing Home
1380 N. 27th Rd., Ottawa, IL 61350, (815) 433-0476; Facility Type: Skilled care; Alzheimer's; Certified Beds: 99; Certified: Medicaid; Medicare; Owner: Private, government/County; License: Current state

Ottawa Pavilion
800 E. Center St., Ottawa, IL 61350, (815) 434-7144; Facility Type: Skilled care; Alzheimer's; Certified Beds: 119; Certified: Medicaid; Medicare; Owner: Private, For-Profit; License: Current state

Pleasant View Luther Home
505 College Ave., Ottawa, IL 61350, (815) 434-1130; Facility type: Skilled care, Alzheimer's; Certified Beds: 112; Certified: Medicaid, Medicare; Owner: Nonprofit/Religious; License: state; Activities: Arts & Crafts; Dances; Pet therapy; Group exercise; Support Groups, Alzheimer's secured unit

Palos Heights

ManorCare at Palos Heights–East
7850 W College Dr., Palos Heights, IL 60463, (708) 361-6990; Facility type: Skilled care, Alzheimer's; Certified Beds: 174; Certified: Medicaid, Medicare; Owner: HCR ManorCare; License: state; Activities: Arts & Crafts; Dances; Pet therapy; Group exercise; Support Groups, Alzheimer's secured unit, Adult day care

ManorCare at Palos Heights–West
11860 Southwest Hwy., Palos Heights, IL 60463, (708) 361-4555; Facility Type: Skilled care; Alzheimer's; Certified Beds: 130; Certified: Medicaid; Medicare; Owner: Private, For-Profit; License: Current state

Park Ridge

Resurrection Nursing & Rehabilitation Center
1001 N. Greenwood Ave., Park Ridge, IL 60068, (847) 692-5600; Facility Type: Skilled care; Alzheimer's; Certified Beds: 298; Certified: Medicaid; Medicare; Owner: Private, Nonprofit; License: Current state

Saint Matthew Lutheran Home
1601 N Western Ave., Park Ridge, IL 60068, (847)

825-5531; Facility type: Skilled care, Alzheimer's; Certified Beds: 82; Certified: Medicaid, Medicare; Owner: Nonprofit/Religious; License: state; Activities: Arts & Crafts; Dances; Pet therapy; Group exercise; Support Groups, Alzheimer's secured unit

Pekin

Pekin Manor
1520 El Camino Dr., Pekin, IL 61554, (309) 353-1099; Facility type: Skilled care, Alzheimer's; Beds: 180; Certified: Medicaid, Medicare; Owner: Nonprofit/Religious; License: state; Activities: Arts & Crafts; Dances; Pet therapy; Group exercise; Support Groups, Alzheimer's secured unit, Adult day care

Timbercreek Rehabilitation & Healthcare Center
2220 State St., Pekin, IL 61554, (309) 347-1110; Facility Type: Skilled care; Alzheimer's; Certified Beds: 202; Certified: Medicaid; Medicare; Owner: Private, For-Profit; License: Current state

Peoria

Apostolic Christian Skylines
7023 NE Skyline Dr., Peoria, IL 61614, (309) 691-2816; Facility type: Skilled care, Alzheimer's; Certified Beds: 57; Certified: Medicaid; Owner: Nonprofit/Religious; License: state; Activities: Arts & Crafts; Dances; Pet therapy; Group exercise; Support Groups, Alzheimer's secured unit

Bel-Wood Nursing Home
6701 W. Plank Rd., Peoria, IL 61604, (309) 697-4541; Facility Type: Skilled care; Alzheimer's; Certified Beds: 300; Certified: Medicaid; Medicare; Owner: Government/County; License: Current state

Heartland of Peoria
5600 Glen Elm Dr., Peoria, IL 61614, (309) 693-8777; Facility Type: Skilled care; Alzheimer's; Certified Beds: 144; Certified: Medicaid; Medicare; Owner: Private, For-Profit; License: Current state

Rosewood Care Center Inc.–Peoria
1500 W Northmoor Rd., Peoria, IL 61614, (309) 691-2200; Facility type: Skilled care, Alzheimer's; Certified Beds: 70; Certified: Medicaid, Medicare; Owner: Proprietary/Public; License: state; Activities: Arts & Crafts; Dances; Pet therapy; Group exercise; Support Groups

Sharon Health Care Pines Inc.
3614 N Rochelle Ln., Peoria, IL 61604, (309) 688-0350; Facility type: Skilled care, Alzheimer's; Certified Beds: 98; Certified: Medicaid, Medicare; Owner: Nonprofit/Religious; License: state; Activities: Arts & Crafts; Dances; Pet therapy; Group exercise; Support Groups, Alzheimer's secured unit

Quincy

Good Samaritan Home Inc.
2130 Harrison St., Quincy, IL 62301, (217) 223-8717; Facility type: Skilled care, Alzheimer's; Certified Beds: 178; Certified: Medicaid, Medicare; Owner: Non-profit/Religious; License: state; Activities: Arts & Crafts; Dances; Pet therapy; Group exercise; Support Groups, Alzheimer's secured unit

Sunset Home
418 Washington St., Quincy, IL 62301, (217) 223-2636; Facility Type: Skilled care; Alzheimer's; Certified Beds: 182; Certified: Medicaid, Medicare; Owner: Nonprofit, Church-related; License: Current state

Sycamore
720 Sycamore St., Quincy, IL 62301, (217) 222-1480; Facility type: Skilled care, Alzheimer's; Certified Beds: 205; Certified: Medicaid, Medicare; Owner: Non-profit/Religious; License: state; Activities: Arts & Crafts; Dances; Pet therapy; Group exercise; Support Groups, Alzheimer's secured unit

Richton Park

Glenshire Nursing & Rehabilitation Center
22660 S Cicero Ave., Richton Park, IL 60471, (708) 747-6120; Facility type: Skilled care, Alzheimer's; Certified Beds: 294; Certified: Medicaid, Medicare, Veterans; Owner: Nonprofit/Religious; License: state; Activities: Arts & Crafts; Dances; Pet therapy; Group exercise; Support Groups, Alzheimer's secured unit, Home health care

Riverwoods

Brentwood North Nursing, Rehabilitation & Specialized Health Care Center
3705 Deerfield Rd., Riverwoods, IL 60015, (847) 459-1200; Facility type: Skilled care, Alzheimer's; Certified Beds: 240; Certified: Medicare; Owner: Nonprofit/Religious; License: state; Activities: Arts & Crafts; Dances; Pet therapy; Group exercise; Support Groups, Alzheimer's secured unit, Home health care

Rock Island

Rock Island Nursing & Rehabilitation Center
2545 24th St., Rock Island, IL 61201, (309) 788-0458; Facility Type: Skilled care; Alzheimer's; Certified Beds: 177; Certified: Medicaid; Medicare; Owner: Nonprofit, Church-related; License: Current state

St. Anthony's Nursing & Rehabilitation Center
767 30th St., Rock Island, IL 61201, (309) 788-7631; Facility type: Skilled care, Alzheimer's; Certified Beds: 134; Certified: Medicaid, Medicare; Owner: Non-profit/Religious; License: state; Activities: Arts & Crafts; Dances; Pet therapy; Group exercise; Support Groups

Rockford

Alden Alma Nelson Manor
550 S. Mulford Ave., Rockford, IL 61108, (815) 484-1002; Facility Type: Skilled care; Alzheimer's; Certified Beds: 268; Certified: Medicaid; Medicare; Owner: Nonprofit, Church-related; License: Current state

P.A. Peterson Center for Health
1311 Parkview Ave., Rockford, IL 61107; (815) 399-8832; Facility type: Skilled care, Alzheimer's; Certified Beds: 129; Certified: Medicare; Owner: Nonprofit/Religious; License: state; Activities: Arts & Crafts; Dances; Pet therapy; Group exercise; Support Groups, Alzheimer's secured unit, Home health care

Riverbluff Nursing Home
4401 N Main St., Rockford, IL 61103, (815) 877-8061; Facility type: Skilled care, Alzheimer's; Certified Beds: 304; Certified: Medicaid, Medicare; Owner: State & Local Gov.; License: state; Activities: Arts & Crafts; Dances; Pet therapy; Group exercise; Support Groups, Alzheimer's secured unit, Home health care

Willows Health Center
4054 Albright Ln., Rockford, IL 61103, (815) 654-2534; Facility type: Skilled care, Alzheimer's; Certified Beds: 42; Certified: Medicaid; Owner: Nonprofit/Religious; License: state; Activities: Arts & Crafts; Dances; Pet therapy; Group exercise; Support Groups, Alzheimer's secured unit, Adult day care

Rolling Meadows

ManorCare at Rolling Meadows
4225 Kirchoff Rd., Rolling Meadows, IL 60008, (847) 387-2400; Facility type: Skilled care, Alzheimer's; Certified Beds: 155; Certified: Medicaid, Medicare; Owner: Nonprofit/Religious; License: state; Activities: Arts & Crafts; Dances; Pet therapy; Group exercise; Support Groups, Alzheimer's secured unit

Saint Elmo

Friendship Manor of Saint Elmo
221 E Cumberland Rd., Saint Elmo, IL 62458, (618) 829-5581; Facility type: Skilled care, Alzheimer's; Certified Beds: 60; Certified: Medicaid, Medicare; Owner: Proprietary/Public; License: state; Activities: Arts & Crafts; Dances; Pet therapy; Group exercise; Support Groups, Alzheimer's secured unit, Adult day care

Savoy

Champaign-Urbana Rehabilitation Center
302 W Burwash, Savoy, IL 61874, (217) 383-3090;
Facility type: Skilled care, Alzheimer's; Certified Beds:
213; Certified: Medicaid, Medicare; Owner: Non-
profit/Religious; License: state; Activities: Arts &
Crafts; Dances; Pet therapy; Group exercise; Support
Groups, Alzheimer's secured unit, Adult day care

Schaumburg

Friendship Village of Schaumburg
350 W Schaumburg Rd., Schaumburg, IL 60194,
(847) 884-5000; Facility type: Skilled care, Alzheimer's; Certified Beds: 250; Certified: Medicaid,
Medicare; Owner: Nonprofit/Religious; License:
state; Activities: Arts & Crafts; Dances; Pet therapy;
Group exercise; Support Groups, Alzheimer's secured
unit, Home health care

Lexington of Schaumburg
675 S Roselle Rd., Schaumburg, IL 60193, (847) 352-
5500; Facility type: Skilled care, Alzheimer's; Certified
Beds: 214; Certified: Medicaid, Medicare; Owner:
Nonprofit/Religious; License: state; Activities: Arts
& Crafts; Dances; Pet therapy; Group exercise; Support Groups, Alzheimer's secured unit, Home health
care

South Holland

ManorCare Health Services–South Holland
2145 E 170th St., South Holland, IL 60473, (708)
895-3255; Facility type: Skilled care, Alzheimer's;
Certified Beds: 200; Certified: Medicaid, Medicare;
Owner: HCR ManorCare; License: state; Activities:
Arts & Crafts; Dances; Pet therapy; Group exercise;
Support Groups, Alzheimer's secured unit, Adult day
care

Providence South Holland
16300 Wausau Ave., South Holland, IL 60473, (708)
596-5500; Facility type: Skilled care, Alzheimer's;
Certified Beds: 171; Certified: Medicare; Owner: Non-
profit/Religious; License: state; Activities: Arts &
Crafts; Dances; Pet therapy; Group exercise; Support
Groups, Alzheimer's secured unit

Windmill Nursing Pavilion
16000 S. Wabash, South Holland, IL 60473, (708)
339-0600; Facility Type: Skilled care; Alzheimer's;
Certified Beds: 182; Certified: Medicaid; Medicare;
Owner: Nonprofit, Church-related; License: Current
state

Springfield

Capitol Care Center
555 W. Carpenter, Springfield, IL 62702, (217) 525-
1880; Facility Type: Skilled care; Alzheimer's; Certified Beds: 251; Certified: Medicaid; Medicare; Owner:
Nonprofit, Church-related; License: Current state

Lewis Memorial Christian Village
3400 W Washington, Springfield, IL 62707, (217)
787-9600; Facility type: Skilled care, Alzheimer's;
Certified Beds: 155; Certified: Medicare; Owner:
Nonprofit/Religious; License: state; Activities: Arts
& Crafts; Dances; Pet therapy; Group exercise; Support Groups, Alzheimer's secured unit

Springfield Care Center
525 S Martin Luther Kind Dr., Springfield, IL 62803,
(217) 789-1680; Facility type: Skilled care, Alzheimer's; Certified Beds: 55; Certified: Medicaid;
Owner: Proprietary/Public: state; Activities: Arts &
Crafts; Dances; Pet therapy; Group exercise; Support
Groups, Alzheimer's secured unit

Swansea

Rosewood Care Center of Swansea
100 Rosewood Village Dr., Swansea, IL 62220, (618)
236-1391; Facility Type: Skilled care; Alzheimer's;
Certified Beds: 58; Certified: Medicaid; Medicare;
Owner: Nonprofit, Church-related; License: Current
state

Swansea Rehabilitation & Health Care
1405 N. Second St., Swansea, IL 62226, (618) 233-
6625; Facility Type: Skilled care; Alzheimer's; Certified Beds: 94; Certified: Medicaid; Medicare; Owner:
Nonprofit, Church-related; License: Current state

Urbana

Champaign County Nursing Home
701 E Main St., Urbana, IL 61801, (217) 384-3784;
Facility type: Skilled care, Alzheimer's; Certified Beds:
243; Certified: Medicaid, Medicare, Veterans/ Public:
Owner: Government/County; Licensed: state; Activities: Arts & Crafts; Dances; Pet therapy; Group exercise; Support Groups, Alzheimer's secured unit,
Adult day care

Clark-Lindsey Village
101 W Windsor Rd., Urbana, IL 61802, (217) 344-
2144; Facility type: Skilled care, Alzheimer's; certified
Beds: 25; Certified: Medicare, Veterans; Owner: State
& Local Gov.; Licensed: state; Activities: Arts &
Crafts; Dances; Pet therapy; Group exercise; Support
Groups, Alzheimer's secured unit, Home health care

Waterloo

Canterbury Manor Nursing Center
718 N. Market St., Waterloo, IL 62298, (618) 939-
8565; Facility Type: Skilled care; Alzheimer's; Certified Beds: 74; Certified: Medicaid; Medicare;
Owner: For-Profit; License: Current state

Oak Hill
623 Hamacher St., Waterloo, IL 62298, (618) 939-

3488; Facility Type: Skilled care; Alzheimer's; Certified Beds: 131; Certified: Medicaid; Medicare; Owner: Government/county; License: Current state

Watseka

The Iroquois Residents Home
200 Fairman Ave., Watseka, IL 60970, (815) 432-7768; Facility Type: Skilled care; Alzheimer's; Certified Beds: 35; Certified: Medicaid; Medicare; Owner: Nonprofit, Church-related; License: Current state

Watseka Rehabilitation & Health Care Center
715 E Raymond Watseka, IL 60970, (815) 432-5476; Facility type: Skilled care, Alzheimer's; Beds: 120; Certified: Medicaid, Medicare, Veterans; Owner: State & Local Gov.; Licensed: state; Activities: Arts & Crafts; Dances; Pet therapy; Group exercise; Support Groups, Alzheimer's secured unit

Wheaton

Du Page Convalescent Center
400 N County Farm Rd., Wheaton, IL 60187; (630) 665-6400; Facility type: Skilled care, Alzheimer's; Certified Beds: 508; Certified: Medicaid, Medicare, Veterans; Owner: State & Local Gov.; Licensed: state; Activities: Arts & Crafts; Dances; Pet therapy; Group exercise; Support Groups, Alzheimer's secured unit

Wheaton Care Center
1325 Manchester Rd., Wheaton, IL 60187, (630) 668-2500; Facility Type: Skilled care; Alzheimer's; Certified Beds: 123; Certified: Medicaid; Medicare; Owner: For-Profit; License: Current state

Wynscape
2180 Manchester Rd., Wheaton, IL 60187, (630) 665-4330; Facility Type: Skilled care; Alzheimer's; Certified Beds: 127; Certified: Medicaid; Medicare; Owner: Nonprofit; License: Current state

White Hall

White Hall Nursing & Rehabilitation Center
620 W Bridgeport, White Hall, IL 62092, (217) 374-2144; Facility type: Skilled care, Alzheimer's; Certified Beds: 119; Certified: Medicaid, Medicare, Veterans; Owner: Crescent Health Services; Licensed: state; Activities: Arts & Crafts; Dances; Pet therapy; Group exercise; Support Groups

Willowbrook

Chateau Center
7050 Madison St., Willowbrook, IL 60521, (630) 323-6380; Facility type: Skilled care, Alzheimer's; Certified Beds: 150; Certified: Medicaid, Medicare, Veterans; Owner: Genesis Elder Care; Licensed: state; Activities: Arts & Crafts; Dances; Pet therapy; Group exercise; Support Groups, Alzheimer's secured unit

Wilmette

ManorCare of Wilmette
432 Poplar Dr., Wilmette, IL 60091, (847) 256-5000; Facility type: Skilled care, Alzheimer's; Certified Beds: 80; Certified: Medicaid, Medicare; Owner: HCR ManorCare; Licensed: state; Activities: Arts & Crafts; Dances; Pet therapy; Group exercise; Support Groups, Alzheimer's secured unit

Wilmington

The Embassy Care Center
555 Kahler Rd., Wilmington, IL 60481, (815) 476-2200; Facility type: Skilled care, Alzheimer's; Certified Beds: 169; Certified: Medicaid, Medicare, Veterans; Owner: Proprietary/Public; Licensed: state; Activities: Arts & Crafts; Dances; Pet therapy; Group exercise; Support Groups, Alzheimer's secured unit

INDIANA

Alexandria

Alexandria Care Center
1912 S Park Ave., Alexandria, IN 46001; (765) 724-4478; Facility type: Skilled care, Alzheimer's; Certified Beds: 70; Certified: Medicaid; Owner: Private; License: state; Activities: Arts & Crafts; Dances; Pet therapy; Group exercise; Outings; Support Groups; Other: Alzheimer's secured unit

Anderson

Community Northview Care Center
1235 W. Cross St., Anderson, IN 46011, (765) 298-2540; Facility Type: Skilled care; Alzheimer's; Certified Beds: 101; Certified: Medicaid; Medicare; Owner: For-Profit; License: Current state

Edgewater Woods
1809 N. Madison Ave., Anderson, IN 46011, (765) 644-0903; Facility Type: Skilled care; Alzheimer's; Certified Beds: 125; Certified: Medicaid; Medicare; Veterans Owner: Government/County; License: Current state

ManorCare Health Services
1345 N Madison Ave., Anderson, IN 46011, (765) 644-2888; Facility type: Skilled care, Alzheimer's; Certified Beds: 216; Certified: Medicaid, Medicare; Owner: HCR ManorCare; License: state; Activities:

Arts & Crafts; Dances; Pet therapy; Group exercise; Outings; Support Groups; Other: Alzheimer's secured unit

Angola

Lakeland Skilled Nursing & Rehabilitation
500 N. Williams St., Angola, IN 46703, (260) 665-2161; Facility Type: Skilled care; Alzheimer's; Certified Beds: 75; Certified: Medicaid; Medicare; Owner: For-Profit; License: Current state

Northern Lakes Nursing & Rehabilitation Center
516 N Williams St., Angola, IN 46703, (219) 665-9467; Facility type: Skilled care, Alzheimer's; Certified Beds: 99; Certified: Medicaid, Medicare; Owner: Crescent Health Care Services; License: state; Activities: Arts & Crafts; Dances; Pet therapy; Group exercise; Outings; Support Groups; Other: Alzheimer's secured unit

Avon

Avon Health & Rehabilitation Center
4171 Forest Pointe Circle, Avon, IN 45123, (317) 745-5184; Facility type: Skilled care, Alzheimer's; Certified Beds: 77; Certified: Medicaid, Medicare; Owner: Proprietary/Public; License: state; Activities: Arts & Crafts; Dances; Pet therapy; Group exercise; Outings; Support Groups; Other: Alzheimer's secured unit

ManorCare Health Services — Prestwick
445 S County Rd. 525 East, Avon, IN 46123, (317) 745-2522; Facility Type: Skilled care; Alzheimer's; Certified Beds: 140; Certified: Medicaid; Medicare; Owner: For-Profit; License: Current state

Berne

Chalet Village Health & Rehabilitation Center
1065 Parkway St., Berne, IN 46711, (260) 589-2127; Facility Type: Skilled care; Alzheimer's; Certified Beds: 80; Certified: Medicaid; Medicare; Owner: For-Profit; License: Current state

Swiss Village Inc.
1350 W Main St., Berne, IN 46711, (219) 589-3173; Facility type: Skilled care, Alzheimer's; Certified Beds: 128; Certified: Medicaid; Owner: Nonprofit, Church-related; License: state; Activities: Arts & Crafts; Dances; Pet therapy; Group exercise; Outings; Support Groups; Other: Alzheimer's secured unit

Bloomington

Bell Trace Health & Living Center
725 Bell Trace Cir., Bloomington, IN 47408, (812) 323-2858; Facility Type: Skilled care; Alzheimer's; Certified Beds: 80; Certified: Medicaid; Medicare; Owner: For-Profit; License: Current state

Garden Villa
1100 S Curry Pike, Bloomington, IN 47403, (812) 339-1657; Facility type: Skilled care, Alzheimer's; Certified Beds: 224; Certified: Medicaid, Medicare, Veterans; Owner: Nonprofit; License: state; Activities: Arts & Crafts; Dances; Pet therapy; Group exercise; Outings; Support Groups; Other: Alzheimer's secured unit, Home health care

Golden LivingCenter–Bloomington
155 E. Burks Dr., , Bloomington, IN 47401, (812) 332-4437; Facility type: Skilled care, Alzheimer's; Certified Beds: 160; Certified: Medicaid, Medicare, Veterans; Owner: Beverly Enterprises; License: state; Activities: Arts & Crafts; Dances; Pet therapy; Group exercise; Outings; Support Groups; Other: Alzheimer's secured unit

Exceptional Living Center Holly Hill Health Care Facility
501 S Murphy Ave., Brazil, IN 47834, (812) 446-2636; Facility type: Skilled care, Alzheimer's; Certified Beds: 105; Certified: Medicaid, Medicare; Owner: Nonprofit; License: state; Activities: Arts & Crafts; Dances; Pet therapy; Group exercise; Outings; Support Groups; Other: Alzheimer's secured unit

Carmel

ManorCare Health Services–Summer Trace
12999 N. Pennsylvania St., Carmel, IN 46032, (317) 848-2448; Facility Type: Skilled care; Alzheimer's; Certified Beds: 104; Certified: Medicaid; Medicare; Owner: For-Profit; License: Current state

McGivney Health Care Center
2907 E 136th St., Carmel, IN 46033, (317) 846-0265; Facility type: Skilled care, Alzheimer's; Certified Beds: 37; Certified: Medicaid; Owner: Nonprofit; License: state; Activities: Arts & Crafts; Dances; Pet therapy; Group exercise; Outings; Support Groups; Other: Adult day care

Riverview Hospital
118 Medical Dr., Carmel, IN 46032, (317) 844-4211; Facility type: Skilled care, Alzheimer's; Certified Beds: 188; Certified: Medicaid, Medicare; Owner: Nonprofit; License: state; Activities: Arts & Crafts; Dances; Pet therapy; Group exercise; Outings; Support Groups; Other: Alzheimer's secured unit

Columbus

Columbus Health & Rehabilitation Center
2100 Midway St., Columbus, IN 47201, (812) 372-8447; Facility type: Skilled care, Alzheimer's; Certified Beds: 212; Certified: Medicaid, Medicare, Veterans; Owner: Private; License: state; Activities: Arts & Crafts; Dances; Pet therapy; Group exercise; Outings; Support Groups; Other: Alzheimer's secured unit, Adult day care, Home health care

Silver Oaks Health Campus
2011 Chapa Dr., Columbus, IN 47203, (812) 373-0787; Facility Type: Skilled care; Alzheimer's; Certified Beds: 80; Certified: Medicaid; Medicare; Owner: For-Profit; License: Current state

Willow Crossing Health & Rehabilitation Center
3550 Central Ave., Columbus, IN 47203, (812) 379-9669; Facility Type: Skilled care; Alzheimer's; Certified Beds: 80; Certified: Medicaid; Medicare; Owner: For-Profit; License: Current state

Crown Point

Chicagoland Christian Village
6685 E. 117th Ave., Crown Point, IN 46307, (219) 662-0642; Facility Type: Skilled care; Alzheimer's; Certified Beds: 146; Certified: Medicaid; Medicare; Owner: Nonprofit; License: Current state

Saint Anthony Home Inc.
203 Franciscan Dr., Crown Point, IN 46307, (219) 757-6281; Facility type: Skilled care, Alzheimer's; Certified Beds: 184; Certified: Medicaid, Medicare; Owner: Private; License: state; Activities: Arts & Crafts; Dances; Pet therapy; Group exercise; Outings; Support Groups; Other: Alzheimer's secured unit, Adult day care, Home health care

Wittenberg Lutheran Village
1200 E Luther Dr., Crown Point, IN 46307, (219) 663-3860; Facility type: Skilled care, Alzheimer's; Certified Beds: 155; Certified: Medicaid, Medicare; Owner: Private; License: state; Activities: Arts & Crafts; Dances; Pet therapy; Group exercise; Outings; Support Groups; Other: Alzheimer's secured unit

Decatur

Woodcrest Nursing Center
1300 Mercer Ave., Decatur, IN 46733, (219) 724-3311; Facility type: Skilled care, Alzheimer's; Certified Beds: 143; Certified: Medicaid, Medicare, Veterans; Owner: Government/County; License: state; Activities: Arts & Crafts; Dances; Pet therapy; Group exercise; Outings; Support Groups; Other: Alzheimer's secured unit

Demotte

Autumn Hills Health & Rehabilitation Center
10352 N 600 E. County Line Rd., Demotte, IN 46310, (219) 345-5211; Facility type: Skilled care, Alzheimer's; Certified Beds: 93; Certified: Medicaid, Medicare; Owner: Private; License: state; Activities: Arts & Crafts; Dances; Pet therapy; Group exercise; Outings; Support Groups; Other: Alzheimer's secured unit

East Chicago

Lake County Nursing & Rehabilitation Center
5025 McCook Ave., East Chicago, IN 46312, (219) 397-0380; Facility Type: Skilled care; Alzheimer's; Certified Beds: 117; Certified: Medicaid; Medicare; Owner: Nonprofit; License: Current state

Elkhart

East Lake Nursing & Rehabilitation Center
1900 Jeanwood Dr., Elkhart, IN 46514, (574) 264-1133; Facility Type: Skilled care; Alzheimer's; Certified Beds: 160; Certified: Medicaid; Medicare; Veterans; Owner: Government/County; License: Current state

Golden LivingCenter–Elkhart
1001 W. Hively Ave., Elkhart, IN 46517, (574) 294-7641; Facility Type: Skilled care; Alzheimer's; Certified Beds: 175; Certified: Medicaid; Medicare; Owner: For-Profit; License: Current state

Riverside Village
1400 W Franklin St., Elkhart, IN 46516, (574) 522-2020; Facility Type: Skilled care; Alzheimer's; Certified Beds: 197 Certified: Medicaid; Medicare; Veterans; Owner: Government/County; License: Current state

Valley View Health Care Center
333 W. Mishawaka Rd., Elkhart, IN 46517, (574) 293-1550; Facility Type: Skilled care; Alzheimer's; Certified Beds: 126; Certified: Medicaid; Medicare; Owner: For-Profit; License: Current state

Woodland Manor
343 S Nappanee St., Elkhart, IN 46514, (219) 295-0096; Facility type: Skilled care, Alzheimer's; Certified Beds: 80; Certified: Medicaid, Medicare, Veterans; Owner: Private; License: state; Activities: Arts & Crafts; Dances; Pet therapy; Group exercise; Outings; Support Groups; Other: Alzheimer's secured unit, Adult day care

Elwood

Community Parkview Care Center
2300 Parkview Ln., Elwood, IN 46036, (765) 552-9884; Facility type: Skilled care, Alzheimer's; Certified Beds: 92; Certified: Medicaid, Medicare; Owner: Private; License: state; Activities: Arts & Crafts; Dances; Pet therapy; Group exercise; Outings; Support Groups; Other: Alzheimer's secured unit, Adult day care

Evansville

Bethel Manor
6015 Kratzville Rd., Evansville, IN 47710, (812) 425-8182; Facility type: Skilled care, Alzheimer's; Certified Beds: 63; Certified: Medicaid; Owner: Nonprofit/Re-

ligious; License: state; Activities: Arts & Crafts; Dances; Pet therapy; Group exercise; Outings; Support Groups; Other: Alzheimer's secured unit, Adult day care

Columbia Healthcare Center
621 W. Columbia St., Evansville, IN 47710, (812) 428-5678; Facility Type: Skilled care; Alzheimer's; Certified Beds: 186; Certified: Medicaid; Medicare; Veterans; Owner: Government/County; License: Current state

Golden LivingCenter — Woodbridge
816 N 1st Ave., Evansville, IN 47710, (812) 426-2841; Facility type: Skilled care, Alzheimer's; Certified Beds: 67; Certified: Medicaid, Medicare; Owner: Beverly Enterprises; License: state; Activities: Arts & Crafts; Dances; Pet therapy; Group exercise; Outings; Support Groups; Other: Alzheimer's secured unit, Adult day care

Good Samaritan Home Inc.
601 N Boeke Rd., Evansville, IN 47728, (812) 476-4912; Facility type: Skilled care, Alzheimer's; Certified Beds: 212; Certified: Medicaid; Owner: Nonprofit/Religious; License: state; Activities: Arts & Crafts; Dances; Pet therapy; Group exercise; Outings; Support Groups; Other: Alzheimer's secured unit, Adult day care

Heritage Center
1201 W. Buena Vista Rd., Evansville IN 47710, (812) 429-0700; Facility Type: Skilled care; Alzheimer's; Certified Beds: 172; Certified: Medicaid; Medicare; Owner: For-Profit; License: Current state

North Park Nursing Center
650 Fairway Dr., Evansville, IN 47710, (812) 425-5243; Facility Type: Skilled care; Alzheimer's; Certified Beds: 120; Certified: Medicaid; Medicare; Owner: Government/County; License: Current state

Fort Wayne

Bethlehem Woods Nursing & Rehabilitation Center
4430 Elsdale Dr., Fort Wayne, IN 46835, (260) 485-8157; Facility Type: Skilled care; Alzheimer's; Certified Beds: 126; Certified: Medicaid; Medicare; Veterans; Owner: Government/County; License: Current state

Byron Health Center
12101 Lima Rd., Fort Wayne, IN 46818, (219) 637-3166; Facility type: Skilled care, Alzheimer's; Certified Beds: 191; Certified: Medicaid, Medicare; Owner: For-Profit; License: state; Activities: Arts & Crafts; Dances; Pet therapy; Group exercise; Outings; Support Groups; Other: Alzheimer's secured unit

Canterbury Nursing & Rehabilitation Center
2827 Northgate Blvd., Fort Wayne, IN 46835, (219) 485-9691; Facility type: Skilled care, Alzheimer's; Certified Beds: 120; Certified: Medicaid, Medicare; Owner: ExtendiCare; License: state; Activities: Arts & Crafts; Dances; Pet therapy; Group exercise; Outings; Support Groups; Other: Alzheimer's secured unit, Adult day care

Coventry Meadows
7843 W. Jefferson Blvd., Fort Wayne, IN 46804, (260) 432-4848; Facility Type: Skilled care; Alzheimer's; Certified Beds: 150; Certified: Medicaid; Medicare; Veterans; Owner: Government/County; License: Current state

Golden Years Homestead Inc.
8300 Maysville Rd., Fort Wayne, IN 46815, (219) 749-9655; Facility type: Skilled care, Alzheimer's; Certified Beds: 106; Certified: Medicaid; Owner: Nonprofit/Religious; License: state; Activities: Arts & Crafts; Dances; Pet therapy; Group exercise; Outings; Support Groups; Other: Alzheimer's secured unit

Heritage Park
2001 Hobson Rd., Fort Wayne, IN 46805, (219) 484-9557; Facility type: Skilled care, Alzheimer's; Certified Beds: 180; Certified: Medicaid, Medicare, Veterans; Owner: Government/County; License: state; Activities: Arts & Crafts; Dances; Pet therapy; Group exercise; Outings; Support Groups; Other: Alzheimer's secured unit

Kingston Care Center of Fort Way
1070 W Jefferson St., Fort Wayne, IN 46131, (317) 736-7185; Facility type: Skilled care, Alzheimer's; Certified Beds: 120; Owner: Covenant Care; License: state; Activities: Arts & Crafts; Dances; Pet therapy; Group exercise; Outings; Support Groups; Other: Alzheimer's secured unit

Lutheran Life Villages
6701 S. Anthony Blvd., Fort Wayne, IN 46816, (260) 447-1591; Facility Type: Skilled care; Alzheimer's; Certified Beds: 262; Certified: Medicaid; Medicare; Owner: Nonprofit; License: Current state

Regency Place of Fort Wayne
6006 Brandy Chase Cove, Fort Wayne, IN 46815, (219) 486-3001; Facility type: Skilled care, Alzheimer's; Certified Beds: 160; Certified: Medicaid, Medicare, Veterans; Owner: Vencor; License: state; Activities: Arts & Crafts; Dances; Pet therapy; Group exercise; Outings; Support Groups; Other: Alzheimer's secured unit

Saint Anne Home
1900 Randallia Dr., Fort Wayne, IN 46805, (260) 484-5555; Facility Type: Skilled care; Alzheimer's; Certified Beds: 166; Certified: Medicaid; Medicare; Owner: Nonprofit, Church-related; License: Current state

University Park Nursing Center

1400 Medical Park Dr., Fort Wayne, IN 46825, (219) 484-1558; Facility type: Skilled care, Alzheimer's; Certified Beds: 104; Certified: Medicaid, Medicare; Owner: Covenant Care; License: state; Activities: Arts & Crafts; Dances; Pet therapy; Group exercise; Outings; Support Groups; Other: Alzheimer's secured unit

Waters of Summit County

2940 N Clinton St., Fort Wayne, IN 46805, (219) 484-0602; Facility type: Skilled care, Alzheimer's; Certified Beds: 88; Certified: Medicaid, Medicare, Veterans; Owner: Beverly Enterprises; License: state; Activities: Arts & Crafts; Dances; Pet therapy; Group exercise; Outings; Support Groups; Other: Alzheimer's secured unit, Adult day care, Home health care

Goshen

Courtyard Healthcare Center

2400 College Ave., Goshen, IN 46526, (574) 533-0351; Facility Type: Skilled care; Alzheimer's; Certified Beds: 138; Certified: Medicaid; Medicare; Owner: Nonprofit; License: Current state

Greencroft Healthcare

Care 1904 S 15th St., Goshen, IN 46527, (219) 537-4000; Facility type: Skilled care, Alzheimer's; Certified Beds: 240; Certified: Medicare; Owner: Nonprofit; License: state; Activities: Arts & Crafts; Dances; Pet therapy; Group exercise; Outings; Support Groups; Other: Alzheimer's secured unit

Maples at Waterford Crossing Health Campus

1332 Waterford, Goshen, IN 46526, (574) 534-3920; Facility Type: Skilled care; Alzheimer's; Certified Beds: 89; Certified: Medicaid; Medicare; Owner: For-Profit; License: Current state

Greenfield

Golden LivingCenter–Brandywine

745 N. Swope St., Greenfield, IN 46140, (317) 462-9221; Facility Type: Skilled care; Alzheimer's; Certified Beds: 128; Certified: Medicaid; Medicare; Owner: For-Profit; License: Current state

Regency Place of Greenfield

200 Green Meadows Dr., Greenfield, IN 46140, (317) 462-3311; Facility type: Skilled care, Alzheimer's; Certified Beds: 197; Certified: Medicaid, Medicare, Veterans; Owner: Vencor; License: state; Activities: Arts & Crafts; Dances; Pet therapy; Group exercise; Outings; Support Groups; Other: Alzheimer's secured unit, Adult day care

Springfield Health Campus

628 N. Meridian Rd., Greenfield, IN 46140, (317) 462-7067; Facility Type: Skilled care; Alzheimer's; Certified Beds: 60; Certified: Medicaid; Medicare; Owner: For-Profit; License: Current state

Greenwood

Greenwood Health & Living Community LLC

937 Fry Rd., Greenwood, IN 46142, (317) 881-3535; Facility Type: Skilled care; Alzheimer's; Certified Beds: 121; Certified: Medicaid; Medicare; Owner: For-Profit; License: Current state

Greenwood Village South

295 Village Ln. Greenwood, IN 46143, (317) 859-4444; Facility Type: Skilled care; Alzheimer's; Certified Beds: 137; Certified: Medicaid; Medicare; Owner: For-Profit; License: Current state

Regency Place of Greenwood

377 Westridge Blvd., Greenwood, IN 46142, (317) 888-4948; Facility type: Skilled care, Alzheimer's; Certified Beds: 206; Certified: Medicaid, Medicare, Veterans; Owner: Vencor; License: state; Activities: Arts & Crafts; Dances; Pet therapy; Group exercise; Outings; Support Groups; Other: Alzheimer's secured unit, Home health care

Hanover

Hanover Nursing Center

410 W La Grange Rd., Hanover, IN 47243, (812) 866-2625; Facility type: Skilled care, Alzheimer's; Certified Beds: 130; Certified: Medicaid, Medicare; Owner: Nonprofit; License: state; Activities: Arts & Crafts; Dances; Pet therapy; Group exercise; Outings; Support Groups; Other: Alzheimer's secured unit, Adult day care

Thornton Terrace Health Center

188 Thornton Rd., Hanover, IN 47243, (812) 866-8396; Facility Type: Skilled care; Alzheimer's; Certified Beds: 55; Certified: Medicaid; Medicare; Owner: For-Profit; License: Current state

Huntington

Heritage of Huntington

1180 W 500 N. Huntington, IN 46750, (260) 355-2750; Facility Type: Skilled care; Alzheimer's; Certified Beds: 60; Certified: Medicaid; Medicare; Owner: Nonprofit, Church-related; License: Current state

Miller's Merry Manor

1500 Grant St., Huntington, IN 46750, (219) 356-5713; Facility type: Skilled care, Alzheimer's; Certified Beds: 85; Certified: Medicaid, Medicare; Owner: Private; License: state; Activities: Arts & Crafts; Dances; Pet therapy; Group exercise; Outings; Support Groups; Other: Alzheimer's secured unit, Adult day care

Norwood Health & Rehabilitation Center
3720 N Norwood Rd., Huntington, IN 46750, (260) 356-1252; Facility Type: Skilled care; Alzheimer's; Certified Beds: 88; Certified: Medicaid; Medicare; Owner: For-Profit; License: Current state

Indianapolis

American Village
2026 E 54th St., Indianapolis, IN 46220, (317) 253-6950; Facility type: Skilled care, Alzheimer's; Certified Beds: 150; Certified: Medicaid, Medicare; Owner: Government/County; License: state; Activities: Arts & Crafts; Dances; Pet therapy; Group exercise; Outings; Support Groups; Other: Alzheimer's secured unit, Home health care, Hospice

Bethany Village Nursing Home
3518 S. Shelby St., Indianapolis, IN 46227, (317) 783-4042; Facility Type: Skilled care; Alzheimer's; Certified Beds: 100; Certified: Medicaid; Medicare; Owner: Government/County; License: Current state

Community Nursing & Rehabilitation Center
5600 E 16th St., Indianapolis, IN 46218, (317) 356-0911; Facility type: Skilled care, Alzheimer's; Certified Beds: 115; Certified: Medicaid, Medicare; Owner: Government/County; License: state; Activities: Arts & Crafts; Dances; Pet therapy; Group exercise; Outings; Support Groups

Eagle Valley Meadows
3017 Valley Farms Rd., Indianapolis, IN 46214, (317) 293-2555; Facility Type: Skilled care; Alzheimer's; Certified Beds: 115; Certified: Medicaid; Medicare; Owner: Government/County; License: Current state

Forest Creek Village
525 E Thompson Rd., Indianapolis, IN 46227, (317) 787-8253; Facility type: Skilled care, Alzheimer's; Certified Beds: 128; Certified: Medicaid, Medicare; Owner: Government/County; License: state; Activities: Arts & Crafts; Dances; Pet therapy; Group exercise; Outings; Support Groups; Other: Alzheimer's secured unit

Hooverwood
7001 Hoover Rd., Indianapolis, IN 46260, (317) 251-2261; Facility type: Skilled care, Alzheimer's; Beds: 188; Certified: Medicaid, Medicare; Owner: Nonprofit; License: state; Activities: Arts & Crafts; Dances; Pet therapy; Group exercise; Outings; Support Groups; Other: Alzheimer's secured unit, Adult day care

Lakeview Manor Inc.
45 Beachway Dr., Indianapolis, IN 46224, (317) 243-3721; Facility type: Skilled care, Alzheimer's; Certified Beds: 184; Certified: Medicaid, Medicare; Owner: Nonprofit; License: state; Activities: Arts & Crafts; Dances; Pet therapy; Group exercise; Outings; Support Groups; Other: Alzheimer's secured unit, Adult day care

Marquette
8140 Township Line Rd., Indianapolis, IN 46260, (317) 875-9700; Facility type: Skilled care, Alzheimer's; Certified Beds: 102; Certified: Medicare; Owner: Nonprofit; License: state; Activities: Arts & Crafts; Dances; Pet therapy; Group exercise; Outings; Support Groups; Other: Home health care, Adult day care

North Capitol Nursing & Rehabilitation Center
2010 N. Capitol Ave., Indianapolis, IN 46202, (317) 924-5821; Facility Type: Skilled care; Alzheimer's; Certified Beds: 123; Certified: Medicaid; Medicare; Owner: Government/County; License: Current state

Rosewalk Village at Indianapolis
1302 N. Lesley Ave., Indianapolis, IN 46219, (317) 353-8061; Facility Type: Skilled care; Alzheimer's; Certified Beds: 182; Certified: Medicaid; Medicare; Owner: Government/County; License: Current state

Spring Mill Meadow
2140 W 86th St., Indianapolis, IN 46260, (317) 872-7211; Facility Type: Skilled care; Alzheimer's; Certified Beds: 142; Certified: Medicaid; Medicare; Owner: Government/County; License: Current state

Wellington Manor HealthCare Center
1924 Wellesley Blvd., Indianapolis, IN 46219, (317) 353-6270; Facility type: Skilled care, Alzheimer's; Certified Beds: 112; Certified: Medicaid, Medicare; Owner: Proprietary/Public; License: state; Activities: Arts & Crafts; Dances; Pet therapy; Group exercise; Outings; Support Groups; Other: Alzheimer's secured unit

Lafayette

Regency Place of Lafayette
300 Windy Hill Dr., Lafayette, IN 47905, (765) 477-7791; Facility Type: Skilled care; Alzheimer's; Certified Beds: 160; Certified: Medicaid; Medicare; Owner: For-Profit; License: Current state

Rosewalk Village Healthcare Center
1903 Union St., Lafayette, IN 47904, (765) 447-9431; Facility type: Skilled care, Alzheimer's; Certified Beds: 155; Certified: Medicaid, Medicare, Veterans; Owner: Government/County; License: state; Activities: Arts & Crafts; Dances; Pet therapy; Group exercise; Outings; Support Groups; Other: Adult day care

Saint Mary Health Care
2201 Cason St., Lafayette, IN 47904, (765) 47-4102; Facility type: Skilled care, Alzheimer's; Certified Beds: 101; Certified: Medicaid, Medicare; Owner: Proprietary/Public; License: state; Activities: Arts & Crafts; Dances; Pet therapy; Group exercise; Outings; Support Groups

Lebanon

Hickory Creek at Lebanon
1585 Perry Worth Rd., Lebanon, IN 46052, (765) 482-6391; Facility Type: Skilled care; Alzheimer's; Certified Beds: 64; Certified: Medicaid; Medicare; Owner: Nonprofit; License: Current state

Homewood Health Campus
2494 N. Lebanon St. Lebanon, IN 46052, (765) 482-2076; Facility Type: Skilled care; Alzheimer's; Certified Beds: 68; Certified: Medicaid; Medicare; Owner: For-Profit; License: Current state

Parkwood Health Care Center
1001 N Grant St., Lebanon, IN 46052, (765) 482-6400; Facility type: Skilled care, Alzheimer's; Certified Beds: 138; Certified: Medicaid, Medicare; Owner: Vencor; License: state; Activities: Arts & Crafts; Dances; Pet therapy; Group exercise; Outings; Support Groups; Other: Alzheimer's secured unit

Marion

Merry Manor — Marion
505 Bradner Ave., Marion, IN 46952, (765) 662-3981; Facility type: Skilled care, Alzheimer's; Certified Beds: 176; Certified: Medicaid, Medicare, Veterans; Owner: Proprietary/Public; License: state; Activities: Arts & Crafts; Dances; Pet therapy; Group exercise; Outings; Support Groups; Other: Alzheimer's secured unit, Adult day care, Home health care, Assisted living

Park Villa, LTC
221 N. Washington St., Marion, IN 46952, (765) 664-4573; Facility Type: Skilled care; Alzheimer's; Certified Beds: 65; Certified: Medicaid; Medicare; Owner: For-Profit; License: Current state

Wesleyan Health Care Center
729 W 35th St., Marion, IN 46953, (765) 674-3371; Facility type: Skilled care, Alzheimer's; Certified Beds: 169; Certified: Medicaid, Medicare, Medi-Cal; Owner: Proprietary/Public; License: state; Activities: Arts & Crafts; Dances; Pet therapy; Group exercise; Outings; Support Groups; Other: Alzheimer's secured unit

Markle

Markle Health & Rehabilitation
170 N Tracy St., Markle, IN 46770, (219) 758-2131; Facility type: Skilled care, Alzheimer's; Certified Beds: 100; Certified: Medicaid, Medicare; Owner: Government/County; License: state; Activities: Arts & Crafts; Dances; Pet therapy; Group exercise; Outings; Support Groups; Other: Alzheimer's secured unit, Adult day care

Martinsville

Grandview Convalescent Center
1959 E Columbus St., Martinsville, IN 46151, (765) 342-7114; Facility type: Skilled care, Alzheimer's; Certified Beds: 82; Certified: Medicaid, Medicare, Veterans; Owner: Private; License: state; Activities: Arts & Crafts; Dances; Pet therapy; Group exercise; Outings; Support Groups; Other: Alzheimer's secured unit, Adult day care, Home health care

The Waters of Martinsville
2055 Heritage Dr., Martinsville, IN 46151, (765) 342-3305; Facility Type: Skilled care; Alzheimer's; Certified Beds: 103; Certified: Medicaid; Medicare; Owner: For-Profit; License: Current state

Michigan City

Arbors at Michigan City
1101 E Coolspring Ave., Michigan City, IN 46360, (219) 874-5211; Facility type: Skilled care, Alzheimer's; Certified Beds: 180; Certified: Medicaid, Medicare; Owner: Integrated Health Services; License: state; Activities: Arts & Crafts; Dances; Pet therapy; Group exercise; Outings; Support Groups; Other: Alzheimer's secured unit

Life Care Center of Michigan City
802 US Highway 20 East, Michigan City, IN 46360, (219) 872-7251; Facility Type: Skilled care; Alzheimer's; Certified Beds: 120; Certified: Medicaid; Medicare; Owner: For-Profit; License: Current state

Middletown

Middletown Nursing & Rehabilitation Center
131 S 10th St., Middletown, IN 47356, (765) 354-2223; Facility Type: Skilled care; Alzheimer's; Certified Beds: 45; Certified: Medicaid; Medicare; Owner: For-Profit; License: Current state

Millers Merry Manor
981 Beechwood Rd., Middletown, IN 47356, (765) 354-2278; Facility type: Skilled care, Alzheimer's; Certified Beds: 60; Certified: Medicaid, Medicare; Owner: Miller's Health Care Systems; License: state; Activities: Arts & Crafts; Dances; Pet therapy; Group exercise; Outings; Support Groups; Other: Alzheimer's secured unit

Milan

Milan Health Care Center
301 W Carr St., Milan, IN 47031, (812) 654-2231; Facility type: Skilled care, Alzheimer's; Beds: 68; Certified: Medicaid; Owner: Proprietary/Public; License: state; Activities: Arts & Crafts; Dances; Pet therapy; Group exercise; Outings; Support Groups; Other: Alzheimer's secured unit

Ripley Crossing
1200 Whitlatch Way, Milan, IN 47031, (812) 654-2231; Facility Type: Skilled care; Alzheimer's; Certified Beds: 100; Certified: Medicaid; Medicare; Owner: For-Profit; License: Current state

Muncie

Bethel Pointe Health & Rehabilitation
3400 W Community Dr., Muncie, IN 47304, (765) 289-2273; Facility type: Skilled care, Alzheimer's; Certified Beds: 101; Certified: Medicaid, Medicare; Owner: Proprietary/Public; License: state; Activities: Arts & Crafts; Dances; Pet therapy; Group exercise; Outings; Support Groups

Golden LivingCenter–Muncie
2701 Lyn-Mar Dr., Muncie, IN 47302, (765) 286-5979; Facility type: Skilled care, Alzheimer's; Certified Beds: 117; Certified: Medicaid, Medicare; Owner: Proprietary/Public; License: state; Activities: Arts & Crafts; Dances; Pet therapy; Group exercise; Outings; Support Groups

Liberty Village
4600 E. Jackson St., Muncie, IN 47303, (765) 282-1416; Facility Type: Skilled care; Alzheimer's; Certified Beds: 104; Certified: Medicaid; Medicare; Owner: For-Profit; License: Current state

Muncie Health & Rehabilitation Center
4301 N Walnut St., Muncie, IN 47303, (765) 282-0053; Facility Type: Skilled care; Alzheimer's; Certified Beds: 185; Certified: Medicaid; Medicare; Owner: For-Profit; License: Current state

New Castle

Glen Oaks Health Campus
601 W. County Rd. 200 South, New Castle, IN 47362, (765) 529-5796; Facility Type: Skilled care; Alzheimer's; Certified Beds: 68; Certified: Medicaid; Medicare; Owner: For-Profit; License: Current state

Heritage House of New Castle
1023 N 20th St., New Castle, IN 47362, (765) 529-9694; Facility Type: Skilled care; Alzheimer's; Certified Beds: 95; Certified: Medicaid; Medicare; Owner: For-Profit; License: Current state

Stonebrook Rehabilitation Center & Suites
990 N 16th St., New Castle, IN 47362, (765) 529-0230; Facility type: Skilled care, Alzheimer's; Certified Beds: 152; Certified: Medicaid, Medicare; Owner: Government County; License: state; Activities: Arts & Crafts; Dances; Pet therapy; Group exercise; Outings; Support Groups; Other: Alzheimer's secured unit, Adult day care

New Harmony

New Harmonie Healthcare Center
251 Hwy., 66, New Harmony, IN 47631, (812) 682-4104; Facility type: Skilled care, Alzheimer's; Certified Beds: 96; Certified: Medicaid, Medicare; Owner: Centennial Healthcare; License: state; Activities: Arts & Crafts; Dances; Pet therapy; Group exercise; Outings; Support Groups; Other: Alzheimer's secured unit, Adult day care

Oakland City

Good Samaritan Home Inc.
210 N Givson St., Oakland City, IN 47660, (812) 749-4774; Facility type: Skilled care, Alzheimer's; Certified Beds: 110; Certified: Medicaid, Veterans; Owner: Government/County; License: state; Activities: Arts & Crafts; Dances; Pet therapy; Group exercise; Outings; Support Groups; Other: Alzheimer's secured unit

Osgood

Manderley Health Care Center
806 S Buckeye St., Osgood, IN 47037, (812) 689-4143; Facility type: Skilled care, Alzheimer's; Certified Beds: 71; Certified: Medicaid, Medicare; Owner: Proprietary/Public; License: state; Activities: Arts & Crafts; Dances; Pet therapy; Group exercise; Outings; Support Groups; Other: Alzheimer's secured unit

Petersburg

Amber ManorCare Center
801 E. Illinois St., Petersburg, IN 47567, (812) 354-3001; Facility type: Skilled care, Alzheimer's; Certified Beds: 64; Certified: Medicaid, Medicare; Owner: Private, For-Profit; License: state; Activities: Arts & Crafts; Dances; Pet therapy; Group exercise; Outings; Support Groups; Other: Alzheimer's secured unit, Home

Golden LivingCenter–Petersburg
309 W Pike Ave., Petersburg, IN 47567, (812) 354-8833; Facility type: Skilled care, Alzheimer's; Certified Beds: 86; Certified: Medicaid, Medicare, Veterans; Owner: Centennial Healthcare; License: state; Activities: Arts & Crafts; Dances; Pet therapy; Group exercise; Outings; Support Groups; Other: Alzheimer's secured unit, Home health care

Rensselaer

Rensselaer Care Center
1309 E Grace St., Rensselaer, IN 47978, (219) 866-4181; Facility type: Skilled care, Alzheimer's; Certified Beds: 157; Certified: Medicaid, Medicare; Owner: Life Care Centers of America; License: state; Activities: Arts & Crafts; Dances; Pet therapy; Group exercise; Outings; Support Groups; Other: Alzheimer's secured unit, Adult day care

Richmond

Arbor Trace Health & Living, Inc.
3701 Hodgin Rd., Richmond, IN 47374, (765) 962-

8175; Facility Type: Skilled care; Alzheimer's; Certified Beds: 86; Certified: Medicaid; Medicare; Owner: For-Profit; License: Current state

Golden LivingCenter–Golden Rule
2330 Straight Line Pike, Richmond, IN 47374, (765) 966-7681; Facility Type: Skilled care; Alzheimer's; Certified Beds: 170; Certified: Medicaid; Medicare; Owner: For-Profit; License: Current state

Golden LivingCenter–Richmond
1042 Oak Dr., Richmond, IN 47374, (765) 966-7788; Facility Type: Skilled care; Alzheimer's; Certified Beds: 122; Certified: Medicaid; Medicare; Owner: For-Profit; License: Current state

Rosegate Village
2050 Chester Blvd., Richmond, IN 47374, (765) 935-4440; Facility Type: Skilled care; Alzheimer's; Certified Beds: 110; Certified: Medicaid; Medicare; Owner: For-Profit; License: Current state

Shelbyville

Ashford Place Health Center
2200 North Riley Hwy, Shelbyville, IN 46176, (317) 398-8422; Facility Type: Skilled care; Alzheimer's; Certified Beds: 68; Certified: Medicaid; Medicare; Owner: For-Profit; License: Current state

Heritage House Convalescent Center
2309 S Miller St., Shelbyville, IN 46176, (317) 398-9781; Facility type: Skilled care, Alzheimer's; Certified Beds: 141; Owner: Nonprofit; License: state; Activities: Arts & Crafts; Dances; Pet therapy; Group exercise; Outings; Support Groups; Other: Alzheimer's secured unit

South Bend

Cardinal Nursing & Rehabilitation Center
1121 E. LaSalle Ave., South Bend, IN 46617, (574) 287-6501; Facility Type: Skilled care; Alzheimer's; Certified Beds: 158; Certified: Medicaid; Medicare; Owner: Government/County; License: Current state

Healthwin Specialized Care Facility
20531 Darden Rd., South Bend, IN 46637, (219) 272-0100; Facility type: Skilled care, Alzheimer's; Certified Beds: 143; Certified: Medicaid, Medicare; Owner: Nonprofit; License: state; Activities: Arts & Crafts; Dances; Pet therapy; Group exercise; Outings; Support Groups; Other: Alzheimer's secured unit

Ironwood Health & Rehabilitation Center
1950 E Ridgedale Rd., South Bend, IN 46614, (219) 291-6722; Facility type: Skilled care, Alzheimer's; Certified Beds: 198; Certified: Medicaid, Medicare, Veterans; Owner: Nonprofit; License: state; Activities: Arts & Crafts; Dances; Pet therapy; Group exercise; Outings; Support Groups; Other: Alzheimer's secured unit

Regency Place of South Bend
52654 N. Ironwood Rd., South Bend, IN 46635, (574) 277-8710; Facility Type: Skilled care; Alzheimer's; Certified Beds: 150; Certified: Medicaid; Medicare; Owner: For-Profit; License: Current state

Sanctuary at Holy Cross — Indiana
17475 Dugdale Dr., South Bend, IN 46635, (574) 271-3990; Facility Type: Skilled care; Alzheimer's; Certified Beds: 120; Certified: Medicaid; Medicare; Owner: Nonprofit; License: Current state

Sanctuary at Saint Joseph's
4600 W Washington Ave., South Bend, IN 46619, (219) 282-1294; Facility type: Skilled care, Alzheimer's; Certified Beds: 177; Certified: Medicaid, Medicare; Owner: Nonprofit/ Religious; License: state; Activities: Arts & Crafts; Dances; Pet therapy; Group exercise; Outings; Support Groups; Other: Alzheimer's secured unit

Spencer

Owen Valley Health Campus
920 W Hwy. 46, Spencer, IN 47460, (812) 829-2331; Facility Type: Skilled care; Alzheimer's; Certified Beds: 113; Certified: Medicaid; Medicare; Owner: For-Profit; License: Current state

Residence at McCormick's Creek
210 State Highway 43, Spencer, IN 47460, (812) 829-3444; Facility Type: Skilled care; Alzheimer's; Certified Beds: 87; Certified: Medicaid; Medicare; Owner: For-Profit; License: Current state

Terre Haute

Cobblestone Crossings Health Campus
1850 E. Howard Wayne Dr., Terre Haute, IN 47802, (812) 232-0406; Facility Type: Skilled care; Alzheimer's; Certified Beds: 60; Certified: Medicaid; Medicare; Owner: For-Profit; License: Current state

Meadows Manor Convalescent & Rehabilitation Center
3300 Poplar St., Terre Haute, IN 47803, (812) 235-6281; Facility Type: Skilled care; Alzheimer's; Certified Beds: 95; Certified: Medicaid; Medicare; Owner: For-Profit; License: Current state

Meadows Manor North Retirement & Convalescent Center
3150 N. Seventh St., Terre Haute, IN 47804, (812) 466-5217; Facility Type: Skilled care; Alzheimer's; Certified Beds: 104; Certified: Medicaid; Medicare; Owner: For-Profit; License: Current state

Royal Oaks Health Care & Rehabilitation Center
3500 Maple Ave., Terre Haute, IN 47804, (812) 238-1555; Facility type: Skilled care, Alzheimer's; Certified Beds: 207; Certified: Medicaid, Medicare, Veterans;

Owner: Nonprofit/ Religious; License: state; Activities: Arts & Crafts; Dances; Pet therapy; Group exercise; Outings; Support Groups; Other: Alzheimer's secured unit, Adult day care

Westridge Health Care
120 W Margaret Dr., Terre Haute, IN 47802, (812) 232-3311; Facility type: Skilled care, Alzheimer's; Certified Beds: 66; Certified: Medicaid, Medicare; Owner: Nonprofit/ Religious; License: state; Activities: Arts & Crafts; Dances; Pet therapy; Group exercise; Outings; Support Groups

Valparaiso

Golden LivingCenter–Valparaiso
251 Sturdy Rd., Valparaiso, IN 46383, (219) 462-6158; Facility Type: Skilled care; Alzheimer's; Certified Beds: 85; Certified: Medicaid; Medicare; Owner: For-Profit; License: Current state

Life Care Center of Valparaiso
3405 N. Campbell Rd., Valparaiso, IN 46385, (219) 462-1023; Facility Type: Skilled care; Alzheimer's; Certified Beds: 110; Certified: Medicaid; Medicare; Owner: For-Profit; License: Current state

Valparaiso Care & Rehabilitation Center
606 Wall St., Valparaiso, IN 46383, (219) 464-4976; Facility type: Skilled care, Alzheimer's; Certified Beds: 168; Certified: Medicaid, Medicare, Veterans; Owner: Government/County; License: state; Activities: Arts & Crafts; Dances; Pet therapy; Group exercise; Outings; Support Groups; Other: Alzheimer's secured unit

Wabash

Autumn Ridge Rehabilitation Center
600 Washington St., Wabash, IN 46992, (219) 563-8402; Facility type: Skilled care, Alzheimer's; Certified Beds: 94; Certified: Medicaid, Medicare, Veterans; Owner: Government/County; License: state; Activities: Arts & Crafts; Dances; Pet therapy; Group exercise; Outings; Support Groups; Other: Alzheimer's secured unit, Adult day care

Miller's Merry Manor
1900 N. Alber St., Wabash IN 46992, (260) 563-

7427; Facility Type: Skilled care; Alzheimer's; Certified Beds: 84; Certified: Medicaid; Medicare; Owner: For-Profit; License: Current state

Wabash Skilled Care Center
710 N East St., Wabash, IN 46992, (260) 569-2291; Facility Type: Skilled care; Alzheimer's; Certified Beds: 25; Certified: Medicaid; Medicare; Owner: Government/County; License: Current state

West Lafayette

Cumberland Pointe Health Center
1051 Cumberland Ave., West Lafayette, IN 47906, (765) 463-2571; Facility Type: Skilled care; Alzheimer's; Certified Beds: 72; Certified: Medicaid; Medicare; Owner: For-Profit; License: Current state

Heritage Healthcare
3401 Soldiers Home Rd., West Lafayette, IN 47906, (765) 463-1541; Facility Type: Skilled care; Alzheimer's; Certified Beds: 127; Certified: Medicaid; Medicare; Owner: For-Profit; License: Current state

Indiana Veterans Home
3851 N River Rd., West Lafayette, IN 47906, (765) 463-1502; Facility type: Skilled care, Alzheimer's; Certified Beds: 197; Certified: Medicaid, Veterans; Owner: Nonprofit; License: state; Activities: Arts & Crafts; Dances; Pet therapy; Group exercise; Outings; Support Groups; Other: Alzheimer's secured unit

Westminster Village–West Lafayette
2741 N. Salisbury St., West Lafayette, IN 47906, (765) 463-7546; Facility Type: Skilled care; Alzheimer's; Certified Beds: 58; Certified: Medicaid; Medicare; Owner: Nonprofit; License: Current state

Westfield

Maple Park Village
776 N Union St., Westfield, IN 46074, (317) 896-2515; Facility type: Skilled care, Alzheimer's; Certified Beds: 112; Certified: Medicaid, Medicare, Veterans; Owner: Government/County; License: state; Activities: Arts & Crafts; Dances; Pet therapy; Group exercise; Outings; Support Groups; Other: Alzheimer's secured unit

IOWA

Algona

Algona ManorCare Center
2221 E. McGregor St., Algona, IA 50511, (515) 295-3505; Facility Type: Skilled care; Alzheimer's;

Certified Beds: 60; Certified: Medicaid; Medicare; Owner: For-Profit; License: Current state

Good Samaritan Society–Algona
412 W Kennedy St., Algona, IA 50511, (515) 295-2414; Facility type: Skilled care, Alzheimer's; Certified Beds: 90; Certified: Medicaid, Veterans; Owner: Evangelical Lutheran Good Samaritan Society; Li-

cense: state; Activities: Arts & Crafts; Dances; Pet therapy; Group exercise; Outings; Support Groups; Other: Alzheimer's secured unit

Altoona

Altoona Nursing & Rehabilitation Center
200 7th Ave., SW, Altoona, IA 50009, (515) 967-4267; Facility type: Skilled care, Alzheimer's; Certified Beds: 106; Certified: Medicaid, Medicare Veterans; Owner: Mariner Post Acute Network; License: state; Activities: Arts & Crafts; Dances; Pet therapy; Group exercise; Outings; Support Groups; Other: Alzheimer's secured unit

Audubon

Friendship Home
714 N Division St., Audubon, IA 50025, (712) 563-2651; Facility type: Skilled care, Alzheimer's; Certified Beds: 67; Certified: Medicaid, Medicare; Owner: Nonprofit/Religious; License: state; Activities: Arts & Crafts; Dances; Pet therapy; Group exercise; Outings; Support Groups

Bloomfield

Bloomfield Care Center
800 N Davis St., Bloomfield, IA 52537, (515) 664-2699; Facility type: Skilled care, Alzheimer's; Certified Beds: 91; Certified: Medicaid, Medicare; Owner: Private; License: state; Activities: Arts & Crafts; Dances; Pet therapy; Group exercise; Outings; Support Groups; Other: Adult day care

Davis County Hospital
509 N. Madison St., Bloomfield, IA 52537, (641) 664-2145; Facility Type: Skilled care; Alzheimer's; Certified Beds: 32; Certified: Medicaid; Medicare; Owner: Government/County; License: Current state

Britt

Westview Care Center
445 8th Ave., SW, Britt, IA 50423, (515) 843-3835; Facility type: Skilled care, Alzheimer's; Certified Beds: 71; Certified: Medicaid; Owner: Nonprofit; License: state; Activities: Arts & Crafts; Dances; Pet therapy; Group exercise; Outings; Support Groups; Other: Alzheimer's secured unit

Cedar Falls

Cedar Falls Health Care Center
1728 W. 8th St., Cedar Falls, IA 50613, (319) 277-2437; Facility Type: Skilled care; Alzheimer's; Certified Beds: 100; Certified: Medicaid; Medicare; Owner: For-Profit; License: Current state

Cedar Falls Lutheran Home
7511 University Ave., Cedar Falls, IA 50613, (319)

268-0401; Facility Type: Skilled care; Alzheimer's; Certified Beds: 135; Certified: Medicaid; Medicare; Owner: Nonprofit; License: Current state

Martin Health Center
420 E. 11th St. Cedar Falls, IA 50613, (319) 277-2141; Facility Type: Skilled care; Alzheimer's; Certified Beds: 100; Certified: Medicaid; Medicare; Owner: Nonprofit; License: Current state

Windsor Nursing & Rehabilitation Center
2305 Crescent Dr., IA 50613, (319) 268-0489; Facility Type: Skilled care; Alzheimer's; Certified Beds: 100; Certified: Medicaid; Medicare; Owner: Nonprofit; License: Current state

Clarinda

Goldenrod ManorCare Center
225 W. Laperla Dr., Clarinda, IA 51632, (712) 542-5621; Facility Type: Skilled care; Alzheimer's; Certified Beds: 49; Certified: Medicaid; Medicare; Owner: For-Profit; License: Current state

Mental Health Institute
1800 N 16th St., Clarinda, IA 51632, (712) 542-2161; Facility Type: Skilled care; Alzheimer's; Assisted Living; Independent Living; Certified Beds: 63; Certified: Medicaid; Medicare; Owner: Government/State; License: Current state

Westridge Quality Care & Rehabilitation
600 Manor Dr., Clarinda, IA 51632, (712) 542-5161; Facility type: Skilled care, Alzheimer's; Certified Beds: 70; Certified: Medicaid, Medicare, Veterans; Owner: Nonprofit; License: state; Activities: Arts & Crafts; Dances; Pet therapy; Group exercise; Outings; Support Groups; Other: Alzheimer's secured unit

Clarion

Careage of Clarion
110 13th Ave., SW, Clarion, IA 50525, (515) 532-2893; Facility type: Skilled care, Alzheimer's; Certified Beds: 76; Certified: Medicaid, Medicare, Veterans; Owner: USA Healthcare; License: state; Activities: Arts & Crafts; Dances; Pet therapy; Group exercise; Outings; Support Groups; Other: Alzheimer's secured unit

Council Bluffs

Bethany Lutheran Home
7 Elliott St., Council Bluffs, IA 51503, (712) 328-9500; Facility type: Skilled care, Alzheimer's; Certified Beds: 121; Certified: Medicaid, Medicare, Veterans; Owner: Nonprofit/Religious; License: state; Activities: Arts & Crafts; Dances; Pet therapy; Group exercise; Outings; Support Groups; Other: Alzheimer's secured unit, Independent living

Midlands Living Center, LLC
2452 N Broadway, Council Bluffs, IA 51503, (712) 323-7135; Facility type: Skilled care, Alzheimer's; Certified Beds: 100; Certified: Medicaid, Medicare, Veterans; Owner: USA Healthcare; License: state; Activities: Arts & Crafts; Dances; Pet therapy; Group exercise; Outings; Support Groups

Regency Rehabilitation & Skilled Nursing
1600 McPherson, Council Bluffs, IA 51501, (712) 322-9285; Facility Type: Skilled care; Alzheimer's; Certified Beds: 160; Certified: Medicaid; Medicare; Owner: For-Profit; License: Current state

Risen Son Christian Village
3000 Risen Sons Blvd., Council Bluffs, IA 51503, (712) 323-7135; Facility type: Skilled care, Alzheimer's; Certified Beds: 102; Certified: Medicaid; Owner: Christian Homes, Inc.; License: state; Activities: Arts & Crafts; Dances; Pet therapy; Group exercise; Outings; Support Groups; Other: Alzheimer's secured unit

Cresco

Cresco Care Center
701 Vernon Rd. SW, Cresco, IA 52136, (563) 547-3580; Facility Type: Skilled care; Alzheimer's; Certified Beds: 63; Certified: Medicaid; Medicare; Owner: For-Profit; License: Current state

Evans Memorial Home
1010 N. Elm St., Cresco, IA 52136, (563) 547-2364; Facility Type: Skilled care; Alzheimer's; Certified Beds: 52; Certified: Medicaid; Medicare; Owner: Nonprofit; License: Current state

Patty Elwood Center
21668 80th St., Cresco, IA 52136, (319) 547-2398; Facility type: Skilled care, Alzheimer's; Certified Beds: 24; Certified: Medicaid, Medicare, Veterans; Owner: Nonprofit; License: state; Activities: Arts & Crafts; Dances; Pet therapy; Group exercise; Outings; Support Groups; Other: Alzheimer's secured unit, Adult day care

Davenport

Davenport Lutheran Home
1130 W 53rd St., Davenport, IA 52806, (319) 391-5342; Facility type: Skilled care, Alzheimer's; Certified Beds: 98; Certified: Medicaid; Owner: Lutheran Home for the Aged Society; License: state; Activities: Arts & Crafts; Dances; Pet therapy; Group exercise; Outings; Support Groups; Other: Alzheimer's secured unit; Home health care

Good Samaritan Society–Davenport
700 Waverly Rd., Davenport, IA 52804, (319) 324-1651; Facility type: Skilled care, Alzheimer's; Certified Beds: 190; Certified: Medicaid, Medicare; Owner: Evangelical Lutheran Good Samaritan Society; License: state; Activities: Arts & Crafts; Dances; Pet therapy; Group exercise; Outings; Support Groups; Other: Alzheimer's secured unit

Kahl Home for the Aged & Infirm
1101 W 9th St., Davenport, IA 52804, (319) 324-1621; Facility type: Skilled care, Alzheimer's; Certified Beds: 135; Certified: Medicaid, Medicare; Owner: Carmelite Sisters for the Aged & Infirm; License: state; Activities: Arts & Crafts; Dances; Pet therapy; Group exercise; Outings; Support Groups

ManorCare Health Services
815 E Locust St., Davenport, IA 52803, (319) 324-3276; Facility type: Skilled care, Alzheimer's; Certified Beds: 105; Certified: Medicaid, Medicare, Veterans; Owner: HCR ManorCare; License: state; Activities: Arts & Crafts; Dances; Pet therapy; Group exercise; Outings; Support Groups; Other: Alzheimer's secured unit

ManorCare Health Services–Utica Ridge
3800 Commerce Blvd., Davenport, IA 52807, (563) 334-2000; Facility Type: Skilled care; Alzheimer's; Certified Beds: 120; Certified: Medicaid; Medicare; Owner: For-Profit; License: Current state

Ridgecrest Village
4130 Northwest Blvd., Davenport, IA 52806, (563) 391-3430; Facility Type: Skilled care; Alzheimer's; Certified Beds: 137; Certified: Medicaid; Medicare; Owner: Nonprofit; License: Current state

Des Moines

Fleur Heights Center for Wellness & Rehabilitation
4911 SW 19th St., Des Moines, IA 50315, (515) 285-2559; Facility Type: Skilled care; Alzheimer's; Certified Beds: 120; Certified: Medicaid; Medicare; Owner: For-Profit; License: Current state

Genesis Senior Living Center
5608 SW Ninth St., Des Moines, IA 50315, (515) 285-3070; Facility Type: Skilled care; Alzheimer's; Certified Beds: 80; Certified: Medicaid; Medicare; Owner: For-Profit; License: Current state

Iowa Jewish Senior Life Center
900 Polk Blvd., Des Moines, IA 50312, (515) 255-5433; Facility Type: Skilled care; Alzheimer's; Certified Beds: 72; Certified: Medicaid; Medicare; Owner: For-Profit; License: Current state

Ramsey Village
1611 27th St., Des Moines, IA 50310, (515) 274-3612; Facility type: Skilled care, Alzheimer's; Certified Beds: 72; Certified: Medicaid; Owner: Nonprofit; License: state; Activities: Arts & Crafts; Dances; Pet therapy; Group exercise; Outings

Trinity Center at Luther Park
1555 Hull Ave., Des Moines, IA 50316, (515) 262-5639; Facility Type: Skilled care; Alzheimer's; Certified Beds: 120; Certified: Medicaid; Medicare; Owner: For-Profit; License: Current state

University Park Nursing & Rehabilitation Center
233 University Ave., Des Moines, IA 50314, (515) 284-1280; Facility type: Skilled care, Alzheimer's; Certified Beds: 108; Certified: Medicaid, Medicare, Veterans; Owner: Proprietary/Public; License: state; Activities: Arts & Crafts; Dances; Pet therapy; Group exercise; Outings; Support Groups

Dubuque

Bethany Home
1005 Lincoln Ave., Dubuque, IA 52001, (563) 556-5233; Facility Type: Skilled care; Alzheimer's; Certified Beds: 54; Certified: Medicaid; Medicare; Owner: Government/City, County; License: Current state

Dubuque Nursing & Rehab Center
2935 Kaufmann Ave., Dubuque, IA 52001, (563) 556-0673; Facility Type: Skilled care; Alzheimer's; Certified Beds: 98; Certified: Medicaid; Medicare; Owner: Nonprofit; License: Current state

Luther Manor
3131 Hillcrest Rd., Dubuque, IA 52001, (319) 588-1413; Facility type: Skilled care, Alzheimer's; Certified Beds: 103; Certified: Medicaid; Owner: HCR Manor-Care; License: state; Activities: Arts & Crafts; Dances; Pet therapy; Group exercise; Outings; Support Groups; Other: Adult day care

ManorCare Health Services
901 W. Third St, Dubuque, IA 52001, (563) 556-1161; Facility Type: Skilled care; Alzheimer's; Certified Beds: 99; Certified: Medicaid; Medicare; Owner: For-Profit; License: Current state

Stonehill Care Center
3485 Windsor Ave., Dubuque, IA 52001, (319) 557-7180; Facility type: Skilled care, Alzheimer's; Certified Beds: 177; Certified: Medicaid, Veterans; Owner: HCR ManorCare; License: state; Activities: Arts & Crafts; Dances; Pet therapy; Group exercise; Outings; Support Groups; Other: Alzheimer's secured unit, Adult day care

Sunnycrest Manor
2375 Roosevelt St., Dubuque, IA 52001, (563) 583-1781; Facility Type: Skilled care; Alzheimer's; Certified Beds: 77; Certified: Medicaid; Medicare; Owner: Government/County; License: Current state

Eldora

Eldora Nursing & Rehabilitation Center
1510 22nd St., Eldora, IA 50627, (515) 858-3491; Facility type: Skilled care, Alzheimer's; Certified Beds: 49; Certified: Medicaid, Medicare; Owner: Care Initiatives; License: state; Activities: Arts & Crafts; Dances; Pet therapy; Group exercise; Outings; Support Groups; Other: Alzheimer's secured unit

Valley View Nursing & Rehab Center
2313 15th Ave., Eldora, IA 50627, (641) 858-5422; Facility Type: Skilled care; Alzheimer's; Certified Beds: 72; Certified: Medicaid; Medicare; Owner: Nonprofit; License: Current state

Emmetsburg

Emmetsburg Care Center
2405 21st St., Emmetsburg, IA 50536, (712) 852-4266; Facility Type: Skilled care; Alzheimer's; Certified Beds: 52; Certified: Medicaid; Medicare; Owner: For-Profit; License: Current state

Lakeside Lutheran Home
301 N Lawler St., Emmetsburg, IA 50536, (712) 852-4060; Facility type: Skilled care, Alzheimer's; Certified Beds: 60; Certified: Medicaid, Veterans; Owner: Nonprofit/Religious; License: state; Activities: Arts & Crafts; Dances; Pet therapy; Group exercise; Outings; Support Groups; Other: Alzheimer's secured unit

Palo Alto County Hospital
3201 First St., Emmetsburg, IA 50536, (712) 852-5520; Facility Type: Skilled care; Alzheimer's; Certified Beds: 22; Certified: Medicaid; Medicare; Owner: Government/County; License: Current state

Estherville

Good Samaritan Society–Estherville
1646 5th Ave., N, Estherville, IA 51334, (712) 362-3522; Facility type: Skilled care, Alzheimer's; Certified Beds: 100; Certified: Medicaid, Medicare, Veterans; Owner: Evangelical Lutheran Good Samaritan Society; License: state; Activities: Arts & Crafts; Dances; Pet therapy; Group exercise; Outings; Support Groups; Other: Alzheimer's secured unit

Rosewood Manor
2001 First Ave. N., Estherville, IA 51334, (712) 362-3594; Facility Type: Skilled care; Alzheimer's; Certified Beds: 60; Certified: Medicaid; Medicare; Owner: For-Profit; License: Current state

Fort Dodge

Careage of Fort Dodge
728 14th Ave. N., Fort Dodge, IA 50501, (515) 576-7226; Facility Type: Skilled care; Alzheimer's; Certified Beds: 65; Certified: Medicaid; Medicare; Owner: For-Profit; License: Current state

Fort Dodge Villa Care Center
2721 10th Ave. N., Fort Dodge, IA 50501, (515) 576-

7525; Facility Type: Skilled care; Alzheimer's; Certified Beds: 107; Certified: Medicaid; Medicare; Owner: For-Profit; License: Current state

Friendship Haven
420 S Kenon Rd., Fort Dodge, IA 50501, (515) 573-2121; Facility type: Skilled care, Alzheimer's; Certified Beds: 155; Certified: Medicaid, Medicare, Veterans; Owner: Nonprofit/Religious; License: state; Activities: Arts & Crafts; Dances; Pet therapy; Group exercise; Outings; Support Groups; Other: Alzheimer's secured unit, Adult day care, Home health care

Marian Home
2400 Sixth Ave. N., Fort Dodge, IA 50501, (515) 576-1138; Facility Type: Skilled care; Alzheimer's; Certified Beds: 97; Certified: Medicaid; Medicare; Owner: Nonprofit, Church-related; License: Current state

Grinnell

Friendship ManorCare Centre
415 W Sixth Ave., Grinnell, IA 50112, (641) 236-6511; Facility Type: Skilled care; Alzheimer's; Certified Beds: 75; Certified: Medicaid; Medicare; Owner: For-Profit; License: Current state

Mayflower Health Care Center
616 Broad St., Grinnell, IA 50112, (515) 236-6151; Facility type: Skilled care, Alzheimer's; Certified Beds: 60; Certified: Medicaid; Owner: Nonprofit; License: state; Activities: Arts & Crafts; Dances; Pet therapy; Group exercise; Outings; Support Groups; Other: Alzheimer's secured unit

St. Francis Manor
2021 Fourth Ave., Grinnell, IA 50112, (641) 236-7592; Facility Type: Skilled care; Alzheimer's; Certified Beds: 78; Certified: Medicaid; Medicare; Owner: Nonprofit; License: Current state

Holstein

Good Samaritan Society–Holstein
505 W 2nd St., Holstein, IA 51025, (712) 368-4304; Facility type: Skilled care, Alzheimer's; Certified Beds: 60; Certified: Medicaid, Medicare, Veterans; Owner: Nonprofit; License: state; Activities: Arts & Crafts; Dances; Pet therapy; Group exercise; Outings; Support Groups; Other: Alzheimer's secured unit; Adult day care, Home health care

Hubbard

Hubbard Care Center
403 S State St., Hubbard, IA 50122, (515) 864-3264; Facility type: Skilled care, Alzheimer's; Certified Beds: 60; Certified: Medicaid, Medicare; Owner: Nonprofit; License: state; Activities: Arts & Crafts; Dances; Pet therapy; Group exercise; Outings; Support Groups; Other: Alzheimer's secured unit, Adult day care

Indianola

Good Samaritan Society–Indianola
708 S Jefferson St., Box 319, Indianola, IA 50125, (515) 961-2596; Facility type: Skilled care, Alzheimer's; Certified Beds: 131; Certified: Medicaid, Medicare, Veterans; Owner: Evangelical Lutheran Good Samaritan Society; License: state; Activities: Arts & Crafts; Dances; Pet therapy; Group exercise; Outings; Support Groups; Other: Alzheimer's secured unit

The Village
1203 N. E St., Indianola, IA 50125, (515) 961-7458; Facility Type: Skilled care; Alzheimer's; Certified Beds: 54; Certified: Medicaid; Medicare; Owner: Nonprofit; License: Current state

Westview of Indianola Care Center
1900 W. Third Place, Indianola, IA 50125, (515) 961-3189; Facility Type: Skilled care; Alzheimer's; Certified Beds: 78; Certified: Medicaid; Medicare; Owner: For-Profit; License: Current state

Iowa City

Greenwood Manor
605 Greenwood Dr., Iowa City, IA 52240, (319) 338-7912; Facility Type: Skilled care; Alzheimer's; Certified Beds: 72; Certified: Medicaid; Medicare; Owner: Nonprofit; License: Current state

Iowa City Rehabilitation & Healthcare
3661 Rochester Ave., Iowa City, IA 52245, (319) 351-7460; Facility Type: Skilled care; Alzheimer's; Certified Beds: 89 Certified: Medicaid; Medicare; Owner: Nonprofit; License: Current state

Oaknoll Retirement Residence
701 Oaknoll Dr., Iowa City, IA 52246, (319) 351-1720; Facility type: Skilled care, Alzheimer's; Certified Beds: 48; Certified: Medicaid, Medicare; Owner: Nonprofit; License: state; Activities: Arts & Crafts; Dances; Pet therapy; Group exercise; Outings; Support Groups; Other: Alzheimer's secured unit

Johnston

Bishop Drumm Care Center
5837 Winwood Dr., Johnston, IA 50131, (515) 270-1100; Facility type: Skilled care, Alzheimer's; Certified Beds: 150; Certified: Medicaid, Medicare; Owner: Catholic Health Initiatives; License: state; Activities: Arts & Crafts; Dances; Pet therapy; Group exercise; Outings; Support Groups; Other: Alzheimer's secured unit

Kalona

Pleasantview Home
PO Box 309, Kalona, IA 52247, (319) 656-2421; Facility type: Skilled care, Alzheimer's; Certified Beds:

80; Certified: Medicaid; Owner: Nonprofit; License: state; Activities: Arts & Crafts; Dances; Pet therapy; Group exercise; Outings; Support Groups; Other: Alzheimer's secured unit

Keosauqua

Good Samaritan Society–Van Buren
RR 1 Box 48B, Keosqaua, IA 52565, (319) 293-3761; Facility type: Skilled care, Alzheimer's; Certified Beds: 75; Certified: Medicaid, Medicare; Owner: Evangelical Lutheran Good Samaritan Society; License: state; Activities: Arts & Crafts; Dances; Pet therapy; Group exercise; Outings; Support Groups; Other: Alzheimer's secured unit, Home health care, Adult day care

Madrid

Madrid Home for the Aging
613 W North St., Madrid, IA 50156, (515) 795-3007; Facility type: Skilled care, Alzheimer's; Certified Beds: 155; Certified: Medicaid, Medicare, Veterans; Owner: Nonprofit/Religious; License: state; Activities: Arts & Crafts; Dances; Pet therapy; Group exercise; Outings; Support Groups; Other: Alzheimer's secured unit

Marshalltown

Grandview Heights, Inc.
910 E. Olive, Marshalltown, IA 50158, (641) 752-4581; Facility Type: Skilled care; Alzheimer's; Certified Beds: 115 Certified: Medicaid; Medicare; Owner: Nonprofit; License: Current state

Iowa Veterans Homes
1301 Summit St., Marshalltown, IA 50158, (515) 753-4325; Facility type: Skilled care, Alzheimer's; Certified Beds: 702; Certified: Medicaid, Medicare, Veterans; Owner: State & Local Gov.; License: state; Activities: Arts & Crafts; Dances; Pet therapy; Group exercise; Outings; Support Groups; Other: Alzheimer's secured unit

Southridge Nursing & Rehabilitation Center
309 W. Merle Hibbs Blvd., Marshalltown, IA 50158, (641) 752-4553; Facility Type: Skilled care; Alzheimer's; Certified Beds: 82; Certified: Medicaid; Medicare; Owner: Nonprofit; License: Current state

Villa Del Sol
2401 S. Second St., Marshalltown, IA 50158, (641) 752-1553; Facility Type: Skilled care; Alzheimer's; Certified Beds: 110; Certified: Medicaid; Medicare; Owner: Nonprofit; License: Current state

Monticello

Monticello Nursing & Rehabilitation Center
500 Pine Haven Dr., Monticello, IA 52310, (319)

465-5415; Facility type: Skilled care, Alzheimer's; Certified Beds: 115; Certified: Medicaid; Owner: Proprietary/Public; License: state; Activities: Arts & Crafts; Dances; Pet therapy; Group exercise; Outings; Support Groups; Other: Alzheimer's secured unit

Newton

Careage of Newton
2130 W. 18th St. South, Newton, IA 50208, (641) 791-1127; Facility Type: Skilled care; Alzheimer's; Certified Beds: 53; Certified: Medicaid; Medicare; Owner: Nonprofit; License: Current state

Heritage ManorCare Center
1743 S. Eighth Ave. East, Newton, IA 50208, (641) 792-5680; Facility Type: Skilled care; Alzheimer's; Certified Beds: 62; Certified: Medicaid; Medicare; Owner: Nonprofit; License: Current state

Newton Healthcare Center
200 S 8th Ave., E, Newton, IA 50208, (515) 792-7440; Facility type: Skilled care, Alzheimer's; Certified Beds: 91; Certified: Medicaid; Owner: USA Healthcare; License: state; Activities: Arts & Crafts; Dances; Pet therapy; Group exercise; Outings; Support Groups; Other: Alzheimer's secured unit

Wesley Park Centre
500 First St. North, Newton, IA 50208, (641) 791-5000; Facility Type: Skilled care; Alzheimer's; Certified Beds: 66; Certified: Medicaid; Medicare; Owner: Nonprofit; License: Current state

Oelwein

Grandview Healthcare Center
800 5th St., SE, Oelwein, IA 50662, (319) 283-1908; Facility type: Skilled care, Alzheimer's; Certified Beds: 93; Certified: Medicaid; Owner: Nonprofit; License: state; Activities: Arts & Crafts; Dances; Pet therapy; Group exercise; Outings; Support Groups; Other: Alzheimer's secured unit, Adult day care

Mercy Hospital of the Franciscan Sisters
201 Eighth Ave. SE, Oelwein, IA 50662, (319) 283-6000; Facility Type: Skilled care; Alzheimer's; Certified Beds: 39; Certified: Medicaid; Medicare; Owner: Nonprofit, Church-related; License: Current state

Oelwein Health Care Center
600 Seventh St. SE, Oelwein, IA 50662, (319) 283-2794; Facility Type: Skilled care; Alzheimer's; Certified Beds: 61; Certified: Medicaid; Medicare; Owner: Nonprofit; License: Current state

Ottumwa

Good Samaritan Society–Ottumwa
2035 Chester Ave., W, Ottumwa, IA 52501, (515)

682-8041; Facility type: Skilled care, Alzheimer's; Certified Beds: 146; Certified: Medicaid, Medicare; Owner: Evangelical Lutheran Good Samaritan Society; License: state; Activities: Arts & Crafts; Dances; Pet therapy; Group exercise; Outings; Support Groups; Other: Alzheimer's secured unit, Home health care

Ridgewood Nursing & Rehabilitation Center
1977 Albia Rd., Ottumwa, IA 52501, (641) 683-3111; Facility Type: Skilled care; Alzheimer's; Certified Beds: 70; Certified: Medicaid; Medicare; Owner: Nonprofit; License: Current state

Vista Woods Care Center
Three Pennsylvania Place, Ottumwa, IA 52501, (641) 683-3372; Facility Type: Skilled care; Alzheimer's; Certified Beds: 60; Certified: Medicaid; Medicare; Owner: Nonprofit; License: Current state

Pleasantville

Pleasant Care Living Center
909 N State St., Pleasantville, IA 50225; (515) 848-5718; Facility type: Skilled care, Alzheimer's; Certified Beds: 53; Certified: Medicaid, Medicare, Veterans; Owner: Proprietary/Public; License: state; Activities: Arts & Crafts; Dances; Pet therapy; Group exercise; Outings; Support Groups; Other: Alzheimer's secured unit

Postville

Good Samaritan Society–Postville
400 Hardin Dr., Postville, IA 52162, (319) 864-7425; Facility type: Skilled care, Alzheimer's; Certified Beds: 68; Certified: Medicaid, Medicare; Owner: Nonprofit; License: state; Activities: Arts & Crafts; Dances; Pet therapy; Group exercise; Outings; Support Groups; Other: Alzheimer's secured unit

Red Oak

Good Samaritan Society–Red Oak
201 Alix Ave., Red Oak, IA 51566, (712) 623-3170; Facility type: Skilled care, Alzheimer's; Certified Beds: 88; Certified: Medicaid, Medicare; Owner: Evangelical Lutheran Good Samaritan Society; License: state; Activities: Arts & Crafts; Dances; Pet therapy; Group exercise; Support Groups; Other: Alzheimer's secured unit

Red Oak Rehabilitation & Care Center
1600 Summit St., Red Oak, IA 51566, (712) 623-5156; Facility Type: Skilled care; Alzheimer's; Certified Beds: 58; Certified: Medicaid; Medicare; Owner: Nonprofit; License: Current state

Remsen

Happy Siesta Nursing Home
423 Roosevelt St., Remsen, IA 51050, (712) 786-1117;

Facility type: Skilled care, Alzheimer's; Certified Beds: 78; Certified: Medicaid; Owner: Proprietary/Public; License: state; Activities: Arts & Crafts; Dances; Pet therapy; Group exercise; Outings; Support Groups; Other: Alzheimer's secured unit

Story City

Bethany Manor
212 Lafayette St., Story City, IA 50248, (515) 733-4325; Facility type: Skilled care, Alzheimer's; Certified Beds: 180; Certified: Medicaid; Owner: Proprietary/Public; License: state; Activities: Arts & Crafts; Dances; Pet therapy; Group exercise; Outings

Stratford

Stratford Nursing & Rehabilitation Center
1200 Hwy. 175 E, Stratford, IA 50249, (515) 838-2795; Facility type: Skilled care, Alzheimer's; Certified Beds: 66; Certified: Medicaid, Medicare; Owner: Care Initiatives; License: state; Activities: Arts & Crafts; Dances; Pet therapy; Group exercise; Outings; Support Groups; Other: Alzheimer's secured unit

Strawberry Point

Strawberry Point Lutheran Home
313 Elkader St., Strawberry Point, IA 52076, (319) 933-6037; Facility type: Skilled care, Alzheimer's; Certified Beds: 58; Certified: Medicaid, Medicare, Veterans; Owner: Nonprofit/Religious; License: state; Activities: Arts & Crafts; Dances; Pet therapy; Group exercise; Outings; Support Groups; Other: Alzheimer's secured unit

Urbandale

Deerfield Retirement Community, Inc.
13731 Hickman Rd., Urbandale, IA 50323, (515) 267-0438; Facility Type: Skilled care; Alzheimer's; Certified Beds: 30; Certified: Medicaid; Medicare; Owner: Nonprofit; License: Current state

Karen Acres Care Center
3605 Elm Dr., Urbandale, IA 50322, (515) 276-4969; Facility Type: Skilled care; Alzheimer's; Certified Beds: 38; Certified: Medicaid; Medicare; Owner: For-Profit; License: Current state

Urbandale Healthcare Center
4614 84th St., Urbandale, IA 50322, (515) 270-6838; Facility type: Skilled care, Alzheimer's; Certified Beds: 180; Certified: Medicaid, Medicare, Veterans; Owner: Proprietary/Public; License: state; Activities: Arts & Crafts; Dances; Pet therapy; Group exercise; Outings; Support Groups; Other: Alzheimer's secured unit, Home health care

Villisca

Good Samaritan Society — Villisca
202 Central Ave., Villisca, IA 50864, (712) 826-9592;
Facility type: Skilled care, Alzheimer's; Certified Beds:
50; Certified: Medicaid, Medicare, Veterans; Owner:
The Evangelical Lutheran Good Samaritan Society;
License: state; Activities: Arts & Crafts; Dances; Pet
therapy; Group exercise; Outings; Support Groups;
Other: Alzheimer's secured unit, Home health care

Waterloo

Country View
1410 W Dunkerton Rd., Waterloo, IA 50703, (319)
291-2509; Facility type: Skilled care, Alzheimer's;
Certified Beds: 134; Certified: Medicaid, Medicare,
Veterans; Owner: State & Local Gov.; License: state;
Activities: Arts & Crafts; Dances; Pet therapy; Group
exercise; Outings; Support Groups; Other: Alzheimer's secured unit

Friendship Village Retirement
600 Park Ln., Waterloo, IA 50702, (319) 291-8100;

Facility Type: Skilled care; Alzheimer's; Certified
Beds: 67; Certified: Medicaid; Medicare; Owner:
Nonprofit; License: Current state

ManorCare Health Service
201 W Ridgeway Ave., Waterloo, IA 50701, (319) 234-
7777; Facility type: Skilled care, Alzheimer's; Certified
Beds: 97; Certified: Medicaid, Medicare, Veterans;
Owner: State & Local Gov.; License: state; Activities:
Arts & Crafts; Dances; Pet therapy; Group exercise;
Outings; Support Groups; Other: Alzheimer's secured
unit

Parkview Nursing & Rehabilitation Center
310 Upland Dr., Waterloo, IA 50701, (319) 234-4423;
Facility Type: Skilled care; Alzheimer's; Certified
Beds: 135; Certified: Medicaid; Medicare; Owner:
Nonprofit; License: Current state

Ravenwood Nursing & Rehabilitation Center
2651 St. Francis Dr., Waterloo, IA 50702, (319) 232-
6808; Facility Type: Skilled care; Alzheimer's; Certified Beds: 196; Certified: Medicaid; Medicare;
Owner: Nonprofit; License: Current state

KANSAS

Abilene

Memorial Hospital TCU (Village Manor)
705 N Brady St., Abilene, KS 67410, (785) 263-1431;
Facility Type: Skilled care; ICF; Alzheimer's; Certified
Beds: 75; Certified: Medicare; Owner: Government/
County; License: Current state

Arkansas City

Arkansas City Presbyterian Manor
1711 N 4th St., Arkansas City, KS 67005, (620) 442-
8700; Facility Type: Skilled care; Alzheimer's; Certified Beds: 50; Certified: Medicaid; Medicare;
Owner: Nonprofit; License: Current state

Medicoladges Arkansas City
203 E. Osage Ave., Arkansas City, KS 67005, (316)
442-9300; Facility Type: Skilled care; Alzheimer's;
Beds: ICF 55; Certified: Medicaid; Owner: Medicalodges Inc.; License: n/a

Cherryvale

Cherryvale Nursing & Rehabilitation Center
1001 W Main St., Cherryvale, KS 67335, (316) 336-
2102; Facility Type: Skilled care; ICF; Alzheimer's;
Certified Beds: 59; Certified: Medicaid; Medicare;
Owner: Pioneer Health Care Services Inc.; License:
Current state

Cottonwood Falls

Golden LivingCenter–Chase County
612 Walnut St. Cottonwood Falls, KS 66845, (316)
273-6369; Facility Type: Skilled care; ICF; ICF/MR;
Alzheimer's; Certified Beds: 51; Certified: Medicaid;
Medicare; Veterans; Owner: Beverly Enterprises Inc.;
License: Current state

Council Grove

Council Grove Healthcare Center
400 Sunset Dr., Council Grove, KS 66846, (316)
767-5172; Facility Type: Skilled care; ICF; Alzheimer's; Certified Beds: 80; Certified: Medicaid;
Medicare; Owner: Lenox Healthcare Inc.; License:
Current state

Dodge City

Good Samaritan Society–Dodge City
501 W Beeson Rd., Dodge City, KS 67801, (316) 227-
7512; Facility Type: Skilled care; ICF; Alzheimer's;
Certified Beds: 60; Certified: Medicaid; Medicare;
Owner: The Evangelical Lutheran Good Samaritan
Society; License: Current state

Manor of the Plains
200 Campus Dr., Dodge City, KS 67801, (620) 225-
1928; Facility Type: Skilled care; Alzheimer's; Certified Beds: 58; Certified: Medicaid; Medicare;
Owner: Nonprofit; License: Current state

Trinity Manor
510 W Frontview St., Dodge City, KS 67801, (316) 227-8551; Facility Type: Skilled care; ICF; Alzheimer's; Certified Beds: 59; Alzheimer's 23; Certified: Medicaid; Medicare; Owner: Nonprofit/Religious organization; License: Current state

Douglass

Medicalodges Douglass
619 S Hwy., 77 Douglass, KS 67039, (316) 747-2157; Facility Type: Skilled care; ICF; Alzheimer's; Certified Beds: 42; Certified: Medicaid; Medicare; Owner: Medicalodges Inc.; License: Current state

El Dorado

Golden LivingCenter–El Dorado
900 Country Club Ln., El Dorado, KS 67042, (316) 321-4444; Facility Type: Skilled care; Alzheimer's; Certified Beds: 55; Certified: Medicaid; Medicare; Owner: Nonprofit; License: Current state

Lakepoint Nursing & Rehabilitation Center of El Dorado
1313 S High St., El Dorado, KS 67042, (316) 321-4140; Facility Type: Skilled care; ICF; Alzheimer's; Certified Beds: 107; Certified: Medicaid; Medicare; Veterans; Owner: Proprietary/Public corp.; License: Current state

Emporia

Emporia Presbyterian Manor
2300 Industrial Rd., Emporia, KS 66801, (620) 343-2613; Facility Type: Skilled care; Alzheimer's; Certified Beds: 60; Certified: Medicaid; Medicare; Owner: Nonprofit; License: Current state

Flint Hills Care Center
1620 Wheeler St., Emporia, KS 66801, (620) 342-3280; Facility Type: Skilled care; Alzheimer's; Certified Beds: 72; Certified: Medicaid; Medicare; Owner: For-Profit; License: Current state

Holiday Resort
2700 W 30th St., Emporia, KS 66801, (620) 343-9285; Facility Type: Skilled care; Alzheimer's; Certified Beds: 120; Certified: Medicaid; Medicare; Owner: For-Profit; License: Current state

Eudora

Medicalodges Eudora
1415 Maple Eudora, KS 66025, (785) 542-2176; Facility Type: ICF; Alzheimer's; Certified Beds: 74; Certified: Medicaid; Owner: Proprietary/Public corp.; License: Current state

Fort Scott

Fort Scott Manor
736 Heylman St., Fort Scott, KS 66701, (316) 223-3120; Facility Type: Skilled care; ICF; Alzheimer's; Certified Beds: 52; Certified: Medicaid; Medicare; Owner: Proprietary/Public corp.; License: Current state

Medicalodges Fort Scott
915 S Horton Ave., Fort Scott, KS 66701, (316) 223-0210; Facility Type: Skilled care; ICF; Alzheimer's; Certified Beds: 61; Certified: Medicaid; Medicare; Owner: Medicalodges Inc.; License: Current state

Garden City

Garden Valley Retirement Village
1505 E Spruce St., Garden City, KS 67846, (316) 275-9651; Facility Type: Skilled care; ICF; Alzheimer's; Certified Beds: 115; Certified: Medicaid; Medicare; Owner: Nonprofit corp.; License: Current state

The Homestead Health & Rehabilitation Center
2308 N 3rd Garden City, KS 67846, (316) 276-7643; Facility Type: Skilled care; ICF; Alzheimer's; Certified Beds: 60; Certified: Medicaid; Medicare; Owner: For-Profit; License: Current state

Goodland

Good Samaritan Society–Sherman County
208 W 2nd St., Goodland, KS 67735, (785) 899-7517; Facility Type: Skilled care; ICF; Alzheimer's; Certified Beds: 60; Certified: Medicaid; Medicare; Owner: Nonprofit/Religious organization; License: Current state

Great Bend

Cherry Village
1401 Cherry Ln., Great Bend, KS 67530, (316) 792-2165; Facility Type: ICF; Alzheimer's; Certified Beds: 46; Certified: Medicaid; Owner: Nonprofit corp.; License: Current state

Great Bend Health & Rehab Center
1560 K 96 Hwy., Great Bend, KS 67530, (620) 792-2448; Facility Type: Skilled care; Alzheimer's; Certified Beds: 136; Certified: Medicaid; Medicare; Owner: For-Profit; License: Current state

Hays

Good Samaritan Society–Hays
2700 Canal Blvd. Hays, KS 67601, (785) 625-7331; Facility Type: Skilled care; Alzheimer's; Certified Beds: 75; Certified: Medicaid; Medicare; Owner: Nonprofit; License: Current state

St. John's of Hays
2401 Canterbury, Hays, KS 67601, (785) 628-3241; Facility Type: Skilled care; Alzheimer's; Certified

Beds: 60; Certified: Medicaid; Medicare; Owner: Nonprofit; License: Current state

Haysville

Haysville Healthcare Center
215 N Lamar Ave., Haysville, KS 67060, (316) 524-3211; Facility Type: Skilled care; ICF; Alzheimer's; Certified Beds: 119; Certified: Medicaid; Medicare; Veterans; Owner: Proprietary/Public corp.; License: Current state

Horton

Tri-County Manor Living Center
1890 Euclid Ave., Horton, KS 66439, (785) 486-2697; Facility Type: ICF; Alzheimer's; Certified Beds: 59; Certified: Medicaid; Owner: Nonprofit corp.; License: Current state

Hugoton

Stephens County Hospital, LTCU
6th & Polk, Box 758, Hugoton, KS 67951, (316) 544-2023; Facility Type: ICF; Alzheimer's; Certified Beds: 58; Certified: Medicaid; Owner: Government/State/Local; License: Current state

Humboldt

Pinecrest Nursing Home
1020 Pine St., Humboldt, KS 66748, (316) 473-2393; Facility Type: Skilled care; ICF; Alzheimer's; Certified Beds: 48; Certified: Medicaid; Medicare; Owner: Nonprofit corp.; License: Current state

Hutchinson

Golden Plains Health Care Center
1202 E 23rd Ave, Hutchinson, KS 67502, (620) 669-9393; Facility Type: Skilled care; Alzheimer's; Certified Beds: 107; Certified: Medicaid; Medicare; Owner: Nonprofit; License: Current state

Good Samaritan Society–Hutchinson Village
810 E 30th Ave., Hutchinson, KS 67502, (620) 663-1189; Facility Type: Skilled care; Alzheimer's; Certified Beds: 90; Certified: Medicaid; Medicare; Owner: Nonprofit; License: Current state

Hutchinson Care Center LLC
2301 N Severance St., Hutchinson, KS 67502, (620) 662-0597; Facility Type: Skilled care; Alzheimer's; Certified Beds: 60; Certified: Medicaid; Medicare; Owner: For-Profit; License: Current state

Ray E. Dillon Living Center
1901 E 23rd Ave., Hutchinson, KS 67502, (620) 665-2170; Facility Type: Skilled care; Alzheimer's; Certified Beds: 60; Certified: Medicaid; Medicare; Owner: For-Profit; License: Current state

Wesley Towers
700 Monterey Pl., Hutchinson, KS 67502, (316) 663-9175; Facility Type: Skilled care; ICF; Alzheimer's; Certified Beds: 130; Certified: Medicaid; Medicare; Owner: Nonprofit/Religious organization; License: Current state

Independence

The Regal Estate of Glenwood
1000 Mulberry St., Independence, KS 67301, (316) 331-8420; Facility Type: Skilled care; ICF; Alzheimer's; Certified Beds: 55; Certified: Medicaid; Medicare; Owner: Lenox Healthcare Inc.; License: Current state

Windsor Place of Independence LLC
614 S 8th St., Independence, KS 67301, (620) 331-2577; Facility Type: Skilled care; Alzheimer's; Certified Beds: 43; Certified: Medicaid; Medicare; Owner: For-Profit; License: Current state

Junction City

Valley View Senior Life
1417 W Ash St., Junction City, KS 66441, (785) 762-2162; Facility Type: Skilled care; Alzheimer's; Certified Beds: 103; Certified: Medicaid; Medicare; Owner: Nonprofit; License: Current state

Kansas City

Kansas City Presbyterian Manor
7850 Freeman Ave., Kansas City, KS 66112, (913) 334-3666; Facility Type: Skilled care; ICF; Alzheimer's; Certified Beds: 161; Certified: Medicaid; Medicare; Owner: Nonprofit corp.; License: Current state

Medicalodges Post Acute Center
6500 Greeley Ave., Kansas City, KS 66104, (913) 334-0200; Facility Type: ICF; Alzheimer's; Certified Beds: 123; Certified: Medicaid; Owner: Medicalodges Inc.; License: Current state

Providence Place
8909 Parallel Pkwy., Kansas City, KS 66112, (913) 596-4200; Facility Type: Skilled care; Alzheimer's; Certified Beds: 90; Certified: Medicaid; Medicare; Owner: Nonprofit; License: Current state

Kingman

The Wheatlands Health Care Center
750 W Washington St., Kingman, KS 67068, (316) 532-5801; Facility Type: ICF; Alzheimer's; Certified Beds: 54; Certified: Medicaid; Owner: Nonprofit corp.; License: Current state

Larned

Larned Healthcare Center
1114 W 11th St., Larned, KS 67550, (316) 285-6914;

Facility Type: Skilled care; ICF; Alzheimer's; Certified Beds: 80; Certified: Medicaid; Medicare; Owner: Proprietary/Public corp.; License: Current state

Lawrence

Brandon Woods at Alvamar
1501 Inverness Dr., Lawrence, KS 66047, (785) 843-4571; Facility Type: Skilled care; Alzheimer's; Certified Beds: 140; Certified: Medicaid; Medicare; Owner: Proprietary/Public corp.; License: Current state

Lawrence Presbyterian Manor
1429 Kasold Dr. Lawrence, KS 66049, (785) 841-4262; Facility Type: Skilled care; Alzheimer's; Certified Beds: 50; Certified: Medicaid; Medicare; Owner: Nonprofit; License: Current state

Pioneer Ridge Retirement Community
4851 Harvard, Lawrence, KS 66049, (785) 749-2000; Facility Type: Skilled care; Alzheimer's; Certified Beds: 76; Certified: Medicaid; Medicare; Owner: For-Profit; License: Current state

Liberal

Good Samaritan Society–Liberal
2160 Zinnia Ln., Liberal, KS 67901, (316) 624-3832; Facility Type: Skilled care; ICF; Alzheimer's; Certified Beds: 70; Certified: Medicaid; Medicare; Owner: The Evangelical Lutheran Good Samaritan Society; License: Current state

Southwest Medical Center SNF
315 W 15th St., Liberal, KS 67905, (620) 629-6567; Facility Type: Skilled care; Alzheimer's; Certified Beds: 18; Certified: Medicaid; Medicare; Owner: Government/County; License: Current state

Wheatridge Park Care Center
1501 S Holly Dr., Liberal, KS 67901, (620) 624-0130; Facility Type: Skilled care; Alzheimer's; Certified Beds: 55; Certified: Medicaid; Medicare; Owner: For-Profit; License: Current state

Lincoln

Lincoln Park Manor
922 N 5th St., Lincoln, KS 67455, (785) 524-4428; Facility Type: ICF; Alzheimer's; Certified Beds: 40; Certified: Medicaid; Medicare; Owner: Proprietary/Public corp.; License: Current state

Logan

Logan Manor Community Health Services
108 S Adams Logan, KS 67646, (785) 689-4201; Facility Type: ICF; Alzheimer's; Certified Beds: 36; Alzheimer's; Certified: Medicaid; Owner: Government/County.; License: Current state

Lyons

Good Samaritan Society–Lyons
1311 S Douglass Ave., Lyons, KS 67554, (316) 257-5163; Facility Type: Skilled care; Alzheimer's; Certified Beds: 50; Certified: Medicaid; Medicare; Owner: The Evangelical Lutheran Good Samaritan Society

Manhattan

Meadowlark Hills
2121 Meadowlark Rd., Manhattan, KS 66502, (785) 537-4610; Facility Type: Skilled care; Alzheimer's; Certified Beds: 133; Certified: Medicaid; Medicare; Owner: Nonprofit corp.; License: Current state

Stoneybrook Retirement Community
2025 Little Kitten Ave., Manhattan, KS 66503, (785) 776-0065; Facility Type: Skilled care; Alzheimer's; Certified Beds: 70; Certified: Medicaid; Medicare; Owner: For-Profit; License: Current state

Via Christi Village Manhattan, Inc.
2800 Willow Grove Rd., Manhattan, KS 66502, (785) 539-7671; Facility Type: Skilled care; Alzheimer's; Certified Beds: 96; Certified: Medicaid; Medicare; Owner: Nonprofit; License: Current state

McPherson

The Cedars Inc.
1021 Cedars Dr., McPherson, KS 67460, (316) 241-0919; Facility Type: Skilled care; Alzheimer's; Certified Beds: 105; Certified: Medicaid; Owner: Nonprofit/Religious organization; License: Current state

McPherson Care Center, LLC
1601 N Main St., McPherson, KS 67460, (316) 241-5360; Facility Type: ICF; Alzheimer's; Certified Beds: 50; Certified: Medicaid; Owner: Proprietary/Public corp.; License: n/a

Merriam

Trinity Lutheran Manor
9700 W 62nd St., Merriam, KS 66203, (913) 384-0800; Facility Type: Skilled care; ICF; Alzheimer's; Certified Beds: 120; Certified: Medicaid; Medicare; Owner: Nonprofit/Religious org.; License: Current state

Minneapolis

Good Samaritan Society–Minneapolis
815 N Rothsay Minneapolis, KS 67467, (785) 392-2162; Facility Type: Skilled care; ICF; Alzheimer's; Certified Beds: 68; Certified: Medicaid; Medicare; Owner: The Evangelical Lutheran Good Samaritan Society; License: Current state

Ottawa County Health Center, LTCU
215 E 8th St., Minneapolis, KS 67467, (785) 392-2122; Facility Type: Skilled care; Alzheimer's; Certified Beds: 27; Certified: Medicaid; Medicare; Owner: Government/City/County; License: Current state

Newton

Asbury Park
200 SW 14th, Newton, KS 67114, (316) 283-4770; Facility Type: Skilled care; Alzheimer's; Certified Beds: 99; Certified: Medicaid; Medicare; Owner: Nonprofit, Church-related; License: Current state

Kansas Christian Home
1035 SE 3rd St., Newton, KS 67114, (316) 283-6600; Facility Type: Skilled care; Alzheimer's; Certified Beds: 92; Certified: Medicaid; Medicare; Owner: Nonprofit; License: Current state

Newton Presbyterian Manor
1200 E 7th St., Newton, KS 67114, (316) 283-5400; Facility Type: Skilled care; ICF; Alzheimer's; Certified Beds: 60; Certified: Medicaid; Medicare; Veterans; Owner: Nonprofit corp.; License: Current state

Onaga

Deseret Nursing & Rehabilitation at Onaga
500 Western St., Onaga, KS 66521, (785) 889-4227; Facility Type: Skilled care; ICF; Alzheimer's; Certified Beds: 46; Certified: Medicaid; Medicare; Owner: For-Profit; License: Current state

Osawatomie

Life Care Center of Osawatomie
1615 Parker Ave., Osawatomie, KS 66064, (913) 755-4165; Facility Type: Skilled care; ICF; Alzheimer's; Certified Beds: 110; Certified: Medicaid; Medicare; Veterans; Owner: Life Care Centers of America; License: current state

Oskaloosa

Hickory Pointe Care & Rehabilitation Center
700 Cherokee Oskaloosa, KS 66066, (785) 863-2108; Facility Type: Skilled care; ICF; Alzheimer's; Certified Beds: 60; Certified: Medicaid; Medicare; Owner: Proprietary/Public corp.; License: Current state

Oswego

Deseret Nursing & Rehabilitation at Oswego
1104 Ohio St., Oswego, KS 67356, (620) 795-4429; Facility Type: Skilled care; Alzheimer's; Certified Beds: 40; Certified: Medicaid; Medicare; Owner: Nonprofit; License: Current state

Overland Park

Delmar Gardens of Overland Park
12100 W 109th St., Overland Park, KS 66210, (913) 469-4210; Facility Type: Skilled care; Alzheimer's; Certified Beds: 120; Certified: Medicaid; Medicare; Owner: Nonprofit; License: Current state

Garden Terrace at Overland Park
7541 Switzer St., Overland Park, KS 66214, (913) 631-2273; Facility Type: Skilled care; Alzheimer's; Certified Beds: 163; Certified: Medicaid; Medicare; Owner: Nonprofit; License: Current state

Indian Creek Healthcare Center
6515 W 103rd St., Overland Park, KS 66212, (913) 642-5545; Facility Type: Skilled care; Alzheimer's; Certified Beds: 120; Certified: Medicaid; Medicare; Owner: For-Profit; License: Current state

ManorCare Health Services–Overland Park
5211 W 103rd St., Overland Park, KS 66207, (913) 383-2569; Facility Type: Skilled care; Alzheimer's; Certified Beds: 223; Certified: Medicaid; Medicare; Owner: Nonprofit; License: Current state

Overland Park Nursing & Rehabilitation Center, Inc.
6501 W 75th St. Overland Park, KS 66204, (913) 383-9866; Facility Type: Skilled care; Alzheimer's; Certified Beds: 102; Certified: Medicaid; Medicare; Owner: Nonprofit, Church-related; License: Current state

Villa St. Joseph
11901 Rosewood, Overland Park, KS 66209, (913) 345-1745; Facility Type: Skilled care; Alzheimer's; Certified Beds: 116; Certified: Medicaid; Medicare; Owner: Nonprofit; License: Current state

Parsons

Elmhaven East
1400 S 15th St., Parsons, KS 67357, (620) 421-1430; Facility Type: Skilled care; Alzheimer's; Certified Beds: 58; Certified: Medicaid; Medicare; Owner: Nonprofit; License: Current state

Elmhaven West Nursing Home
1315 S 15th St., Parsons, KS 67357, (620) 421-1320; Facility Type: Skilled care; Alzheimer's; Certified Beds: 50; Certified: Medicaid; Medicare; Owner: Nonprofit; License: Current state

Good Samaritan Society–Parsons
809 Leawood Ave., Parsons, KS 67357, (316) 421-1110; Facility Type: ICF; Alzheimer's; Certified Beds: 56; Certified: Medicaid; Medicare; Owner: The Evangelical Lutheran Good Samaritan Society; License: Current state

Parsons Presbyterian Manor
3501 Dirr Ave., Parsons, KS 67357, (620) 421-1450;

Facility Type: Skilled care; Alzheimer's; Certified Beds: 43; Certified: Medicaid; Medicare; Owner: Nonprofit; License: Current state

Peabody

Legacy Park
407 N Locust St., Peabody, KS 66866, (316) 983-2152; Facility Type: ICF; Alzheimer's; Certified Beds: 55.; Certified: Medicaid; Veterans; Owner: Nonprofit corp.; License: Current state

Westview Manor of Peabody
500 Peabody, Peabody, KS 66866, (620) 983-2165; Facility Type: Skilled care; Alzheimer's; Certified Beds: 52; Certified: Medicaid; Medicare; Owner: Nonprofit; License: Current state

Richmond

Richmond Healthcare & Rehabilitation Center
340 E South St., Richmond, KS 66080, (785) 835-6135; Facility Type: ICF; Alzheimer's; Certified Beds: 60; Certified: Medicaid; Owner: Government/State/Local; License: Current state

Russell

Wheatland Nursing & Rehabilitation Center
320 S Lincoln St., Box 913 Russell, KS 67665, (785) 483-536; Facility Type: Skilled care; ICF; Alzheimer's; Beds: Skilled care 55; Certified: Medicaid; Medicare; Veterans; Owner: Americare Systems Inc.; License: Current state

Salina

Russell Regional Hospital, LTCU
200 S. Main St., Russell, KS 67665, (785) 483-3131; Facility Type: Skilled care; Alzheimer's; Certified Beds: 29; Certified: Medicaid; Medicare; Owner: Nonprofit; License: Current state

Salina Presbyterian Manor
2601 E Crawford St., Salina, KS 67401, (785) 825-1366; Facility Type: Skilled care; ICF; Alzheimer's; Certified Beds: 59; Certified: Medicaid; Medicare; Owner: Nonprofit/Religious org.; License: Current state

Smith Center

Deseret Nursing & Rehabilitation at Smith Center
117 W 1st St., Smith Center, KS 66967, (785) 282-6696; Facility Type: Skilled care; ICF; Alzheimer's; Certified Beds: 40; Certified: Medicaid; Medicare; Medi-Cal; Veterans; Owner: Private; License: Current state

Smith County Memorial Hospital, LTCU
614 S Main St., Smith Center, KS 66967, (785) 282-6845; Facility Type: Skilled care; Alzheimer's; Certified Beds: 29; Certified: Medicaid; Medicare; Owner: Government/County; License: Current state

Spring Hill

Golden LivingCenter–Spring Hill
251 E Wilson St., Spring Hill, KS 66083, (913) 592-3100; Facility Type: Skilled care; ICF; Alzheimer's; Beds: Skilled care 6; ICF 50; Certified: Medicaid; Medicare; Owner: Proprietary/Public corp.; License: Current state

Topeka

Aldersgate Village Health Unit
3220 SW Albright Dr., Topeka, KS 66614, (785) 478-9440; Facility Type: Skilled care; Alzheimer's; Certified Beds: 209; Certified: Medicaid; Medicare; Owner: Nonprofit/Religious org.; License: Current state

Brewster Health Center
1001 SW 29th St., Topeka, KS 66611, (785) 267-1666; Facility Type: Skilled care; Alzheimer's; Certified Beds: 79; Certified: Medicaid; Medicare; Owner: Nonprofit/Religious org.; License: Current state

Lexington Park Nursing & Post Acute Center
1031 Fleming Ct., Topeka, KS 66604, (785) 440-0500; Facility Type: Skilled care; Alzheimer's; Certified Beds: 90; Certified: Medicaid; Medicare; Owner: Nonprofit; License: Current state

McCrite Plaza Health Center
1610 SW 37th St., Topeka, KS 66611, (785) 267-2960; Facility Type: Skilled care; Alzheimer's; Certified Beds: 100; Certified: Medicaid; Medicare; Owner: Private; License: Current state

Plaza West Regional Health Center
1570 SW Westport Dr., Topeka, KS 66604, (785) 271-6700; Facility Type: Skilled care; Alzheimer's; Certified Beds: 151; Certified: Medicaid; Medicare; Owner: Nonprofit; License: Current state

Rolling Hills Health Center
2400 SW Urish Rd., Topeka, KS 66614, (785) 273-5001; Facility Type: Skilled care; ICF; ICF/MR; Alzheimer's; Certified Beds: 102; Certified: Medicaid; Medicare; Veterans; Owner: Proprietary/Public corp.; License: Current state

Topeka Community Health Center
1821 SE 21st St., Topeka, KS 66607, (785) 234-0018; Facility Type: Skilled care; ICF; Alzheimer's; Certified Beds: 82; Certified: Medicaid; Medicare; Owner: Integrated Health Services Inc.; License: Current state

Topeka Presbyterian Manor
4712 SW 6th Ave., Topeka, KS 66606, (785) 272-

6510; Facility Type: Skilled care; ICF; Alzheimer's; Certified Beds: 120; Certified: Medicaid; Medicare; Owner: Nonprofit corp.; License: Current state

Victoria

Saint John Rest Home
701 7th St., Victoria, KS 67671, (785) 735-2208; Facility Type: ICF; Alzheimer's; Certified Beds: 70; Certified: Medicaid; Owner: Nonprofit/Religious org.; License: Current state

Wellington

Deseret Nursing & Rehabilitation at Wellington
1600 W 8th St., Wellington, KS 67152, (316) 326-2232; Facility Type: Skilled care; ICF; Alzheimer's; Certified Beds: 44; Certified: Medicaid; Medicare; Owner: Nonprofit corp.; License: Current state

Golden LivingCenter–Wellington
102 W Botkin St., Wellington, KS 67152, (620) 326-7437; Facility Type: Skilled care; ICF; Alzheimer's; Certified Beds: 55; Certified: Medicaid; Medicare; Owner: License: Current state

Sumner Regional Medical Center, SNF
1323 N A St., Wellington, KS 67152, (620) 326-7451; Facility Type: Skilled care; ICF; Alzheimer's; Certified Beds: 13; Certified: Medicaid; Medicare; Owner: Government/Health District.; License: Current state

Wichita

College Hill Nursing & Rehabilitation Center
5005 E 21st St. N, Wichita, KS 67208, (316) 685-9291; Facility Type: Skilled care; ICF; Alzheimer's; Certified Beds: 96; Certified: Medicaid; Medicare; Owner: For-profit; License: Current state

Deseret Nursing & Rehabilitation at Wichita
1600 S. Woodlawn, Wichita, KS 67218, (316) 691-9999; Facility Type: Skilled care; Alzheimer's; Certified Beds: 93; Certified: Medicaid; Medicare; Owner: Nonprofit; License: Current state

Kansas Masonic Home
401 S Seneca St., Wichita, KS 67213, (316) 269-7500; Facility Type: Skilled care; Alzheimer's; Certified Beds: 120; Certified: Medicaid; Medicare; Owner: Nonprofit; License: Current state

Lakepoint Retirement & Rehab Center of Wichita
1315 N West St., Wichita, KS 67203, (316) 943-1294; Facility Type: Skilled care; ICF; Alzheimer's; Certified Beds: 110; Certified: Medicaid; Owner: Private; License: Current state

Life Care Center of Wichita
622 N Edgemoor St., Wichita, KS 67208, (316) 686-5100; Facility Type: Skilled care; ICF; Alzheimer's; Certified Beds: 120; Certified: Medicaid; Medicare; Owner: Life Care Centers of America; License: Current state

ManorCare Health Services–Wichita
7101 E 21st St. N, Wichita, KS 67206, (316) 684-8018; Facility Type: Skilled care; Alzheimer's; Certified Beds: 119; Certified: Medicaid; Medicare; Owner: Nonprofit; License: Current state

Meridian Nursing & Rehabilitation Center
1555 N Meridian St., Wichita, KS 67203, (316) 942-8471; Facility Type: Skilled care; Alzheimer's; Certified Beds: 106; Certified: Medicaid; Medicare; Owner: Nonprofit; License: Current state

Sandpiper Bay Health Care Center
5808 W 8th St. N., Wichita, KS 67212, (316) 945-3606; Facility Type: Skilled care; Alzheimer's; Certified Beds: 145; Certified: Medicaid; Medicare; Owner: Nonprofit; License: Current state

Wichita Nursing Center
2840 S Hillside St., Wichita, KS 67216, (316) 652-9940; Facility Type: Skilled care; Alzheimer's; Certified Beds: 70; Certified: Medicaid; Medicare; Owner: Nonprofit; License: Current state

Winfield

Cumbernauld Village
716 Tweed St., Winfield, KS 67156, (620) 221-4141; Facility Type: Skilled care; Alzheimer's; Certified Beds: 42; Certified: Medicaid; Medicare; Owner: Nonprofit; License: Current state

Good Samaritan Society–Winfield
1320 Wheat Rd., Winfield, KS 67156, (316) 221-4660; Facility Type: Skilled care; Alzheimer's; Certified Beds: 70; Certified: Medicaid; Medicare; Owner: Nonprofit corp.; License: Current state

Winfield Rest Haven II, LLC
1611 Ritchie, Winfield, KS 67156, (620) 221-9290; Facility Type: Skilled care; Alzheimer's; Certified Beds: 50; Certified: Medicaid; Medicare; Owner: Nonprofit; License: Current state

KENTUCKY

Ashland

Boyd Nursing & Rehabilitation Center
12800 Princeland Ave., Ashland, KY 41102, (606) 928-2963; Facility Type: Skilled care; Alzheimer's; Certified Beds: 60; Certified: Medicaid; Medicare; Owner: Nonprofit; License: Current state

King's Daughters Medical Center
2201 Lexington Ave., Ashland, KY 41101, (606) 327-4000; Facility Type: Skilled care; Alzheimer's; Certified Beds: 10; Certified: Medicaid; Medicare; Owner: Nonprofit corp.; License: Current state

Kingsbrook Lifecare Center
2500 State Route 5, Ashland, KY 41102, (606) 324-1414; Facility Type: Skilled care; Alzheimer's; Certified Beds: 147; Certified: Medicaid; Medicare; Owner: Nonprofit; License: Current state

Woodland Oaks Health Care Facility
1820 Oakview Rd., Ashland, KY 41105, (606) 325-5200; Facility Type: Skilled care; ICF; ICF/MR; Alzheimer's; Certified Beds: 110; Personal care 10; Certified: Medicaid; Medicare; Owner: n/a; License: Current state

Barbourville

Barbourville Health & Rehabilitation Center
117 Shelby Str., PO Box 1090, Barbourville, KY 40906, (606) 546-5136; Facility Type: Skilled care; ICF; Alzheimer's; Certified Beds: 119; Certified: Medicaid; Owner: Proprietary/Public corp.; License: Current state

Knox County Hospital
80 Hospital Dr., Barbourville, KY 40906, (606) 546-4175; Facility Type: Skilled care; Alzheimer's; Located within a Hospital; Certified Beds: 16; Certified: Medicaid; Medicare; Owner: Nonprofit; License: Current state

Beattyville

Lee County Constant Care Inc.
249 E Main St., Beattyville, KY 41311, (606) 464-3611; Facility Type: Skilled care; ICF; Alzheimer's; Certified Beds: 124; Certified: Medicaid; Medicare; Owner: Nonprofit corp.; License: Current state

Bowling Green

Britthaven of Bowling Green
5079 Scottsville Rd., Bowling Green, KY 42104, (270) 782-1125; Facility Type: Skilled care; Alzheimer's; Certified Beds: 128; Certified: Medicaid; Medicare; Owner: For-Profit; License: Current state

Colonial ManorCare & Rehabilitation Center
2365 Nashville Rd., Bowling Green, KY 42101, (270) 842-1641; Facility Type: Skilled care; Alzheimer's; Certified Beds: 48; Certified: Medicaid; Medicare; Owner: For-Profit; License: Current state

Magnolia Village Care & Rehabilitation Center
1381 Campbell Ln., Bowling Green, KY 42104, (270) 843-0587; Facility Type: Skilled care; Alzheimer's; Certified Beds: 60; Certified: n/a; Owner: n/a; License: Current state

Medco Center of Bowling Green
1561 Newton Ave., Bowling Green, KY 42104, (270) 842-1611; Facility Type: Skilled care; Alzheimer's; Certified Beds: 66; Certified: Medicaid; Medicare; Owner: For-Profit; License: Current state

Rosewood Healthcare Center
550 High St., Bowling Green, KY 42101, (270) 843-3296; Facility Type: Skilled care; Alzheimer's; Certified Beds: 176; Certified: Medicaid; Medicare; Owner: For-Profit; License: Current state

Columbia

Summit Manor
400 Bomar Heights Columbia, KY 42728, (270) 384-2153; Facility Type: Skilled care; ICF; ICF/ MR; Alzheimer's; Certified Beds: 104; Certified: Medicaid; Medicare; Owner: EPI Corp.; License: Current state

Corbin

Christian Health Center
116 S. Commonwealth Ave., PO Box 1304, Corbin, KY 40702, (606) 258-2500; Facility Type: Skilled care; Alzheimer's; Certified Beds: 104; Certified: Medicaid; Medicare; Owner: Nonprofit, Church-related; License: Current state

Corbin Nursing Home
270 Bacon Creek Rd., PO Box 1190, Corbin, KY 40702, (606) 528-8822; Facility Type: Skilled care; Alzheimer's; Certified Beds: 100; Certified: Medicaid; Medicare; Owner: For-Profit; License: Current state

The Heritage
192 Bacon Creek Rd., PO Box 1530, Corbin, KY 40702, (606) 526-1900; Facility Type: Skilled care; Alzheimer's; Certified Beds: 85; Certified: Medicaid; Medicare; Owner: For-Profit; License: Current state

Hillcrest Nursing Home
1245 American Greeting Rd., Corbin, KY 40702; (606) 528-8917; Facility Type: Skilled care; ICF; Alzheimer's; Certified Beds: 120; Certified: Medicaid; Medicare; Owner: Proprietary/ Public corp.; License: Current state

Dawson Springs

Dawson Pointe, LLC
213 Water St., Dawson Springs, KY 42408, (270)

797-2025; Facility Type: Skilled care; Alzheimer's; Certified Beds: 59; Certified: Medicaid; Medicare; Owner: For-Profit; License: Current state

Tradewater Pointe
100 W. Ramsey St., Dawson Springs, KY 42408, (270) 797-8131; Facility Type: Skilled care; ICF; Alzheimer's; Certified Beds: 60; Certified: Medicaid; Medicare; Veterans; Owner: Proprietary/Public corp.; License: Current state

Florence

Bridge Point Care & Rehabilitation Center
7300 Woodspoint Dr., Florence, KY 41042, (859) 371-5731; Facility Type: Skilled care; Alzheimer's; Certified Beds: 151; Certified: Medicaid; Medicare; Owner: For-Profit; License: Current state

Florence Park Care Center
6975 Burlington Pike Florence, KY 41042, (606) 525-0007; Facility Type: Skilled care; ICF; Alzheimer's; Adult Day Care; Certified Beds: 150; Certified: Medicaid; Medicare; Owner: Proprietary/Public corp.; License: Current state

St. Luke Hospital West
7380 Turfway Rd., Florence, KY 41042, (859) 212-4302; Facility Type: Skilled care; Alzheimer's; Certified Beds: 16; Certified: Medicaid; Medicare; Owner: Nonprofit; License: Current state

Greenville

Belle Meade Home
521 Greene Dr., Greenville, KY 42345, (270) 338-1523; Facility Type: Skilled care; ICF; Alzheimer's; Certified Beds: 60; Certified: Medicaid; Owner: Private; License: current state

Maple Manor Health Care Center
515 Greene Dr., Greenville, KY 42345, (270) 338-5400; Facility Type: Skilled care; Alzheimer's; Certified Beds: 97; Certified: Medicaid; Medicare; Owner: For-Profit; License: Current state

Muhlenberg Community Hospital
440 Hopkinsville St., Greenville, KY 42345, (270) 338-8431; Facility Type: Skilled care; Alzheimer's; Certified Beds: 45; Certified: Medicaid; Medicare; Owner: For-Profit; License: Current state

Lexington

Bluegrass Care & Rehabilitation Center
3576 Pimlico Pkwy., Lexington, KY 40517, (859) 272-0608; Facility Type: Skilled care; Alzheimer's; Certified Beds: 124; Certified: Medicaid; Medicare; Owner: For-Profit; License: Current state

Cambridge Place
2020 Cambridge Dr., Lexington, KY 40504, (606)

252-6747; Facility Type: Skilled care; ICF; ICF/MR; Alzheimer's; Certified Beds: 118; Certified: Medicaid; Medicare; Owner: Proprietary/Public corp.; License: Current state

Homestead Nursing Center
1608 Versailles Rd., Lexington, KY 40504, (859) 252-0871; Facility Type: Skilled care; Alzheimer's; Certified Beds: 136; Certified: Medicaid; Medicare; Owner: For-Profit; License: Current state

Mayfair Manor
3300 Tates Creek Rd., Lexington, KY 40502, (606) 266-2126; Facility Type: Skilled care; ICF; Alzheimer's; Certified Beds: 61; Certified: Medicaid; Medicare; Owner: Proprietary/Public corp.; License: Current state

Northpoint Lexington Healthcare Center
1500 Trent Blvd., Lexington, KY 40515, (859) 272-2273; Facility Type: Skilled care; Alzheimer's; Certified Beds: 150; Certified: Medicaid; Medicare; Owner: For-Profit; License: Current state

Richmond Place Rehabilitation & Health Center
2770 Palumbo Dr., Lexington, KY 40509, (606) 263-2410; Facility Type: Skilled care; ICF; Alzheimer's; Certified Beds: 90; Certified: Medicaid; Medicare; Owner: Nonprofit/Religious org.; License: Current state

Louisville

Bashford East Health Care
3535 Bardstown Rd., Louisville, KY 40218, (502) 459-1400; Facility Type: Skilled care; Alzheimer's; Certified Beds: 122; Certified: Medicaid; Medicare; Owner: For-Profit; License: Current state

Britthaven of South Louisville
9600 Lambord Blvd., Louisville, KY 40272, (502) 935-7284; Facility Type: Skilled care; Alzheimer's; Certified Beds: 128; Certified: Medicaid; Medicare; Owner: For-Profit; License: Current state

Christian Health Center
920 S. 4th St., Louisville, KY 40203, (502) 583-6533; Facility Type: Skilled care; Alzheimer's; Certified Beds: 122; Certified: Medicaid; Medicare; Owner: Nonprofit; License: Current state

Christopher East Health Care Center
4200 Browns Ln., Louisville, KY 40220, (502) 459-8900; Facility Type: Skilled care; Alzheimer's; Certified Beds: 178; Certified: Medicaid; Medicare; Owner: For-Profit; License: Current state

Episcopal Church Home
7504 Westport Rd., Louisville, KY 40222, (502) 736-7800; Facility Type: Skilled care; Alzheimer's; Certified Beds: 139; Certified: Medicaid; Medicare; Owner: For-Profit; License: Current state

Franciscan Health Care Center
3625 Fern Valley Rd., Louisville, KY 40219, (502) 964-3381; Facility Type: Skilled care; Alzheimer's; Certified Beds: 135; Certified: Medicaid; Medicare; Owner: For-Profit; License: Current state

Golden LivingCenter–Camelot
1101 Lyndon Ln., Louisville, KY 40222, (502) 425-0331; Facility Type: Skilled care; Alzheimer's; Certified Beds: 155; Certified: Medicaid; Medicare; Owner: For-Profit; License: Current state

Golden LivingCenter–Hillcreek
3116 Breckinridge Ln., Louisville, KY 40220, (502) 459-9120; Facility Type: Skilled care; Alzheimer's; Certified Beds: 172; Certified: Medicaid; Medicare; Owner: For-Profit; License: Current state

Highlands Nursing & Rehabilitation Center
1705 Stevens Ave., Louisville, KY 40205, (502) 451-7330; Facility Type: Skilled care; Alzheimer's; Certified Beds: 154; Certified: Medicaid; Medicare; Owner: For-Profit; License: Current state

Hurstbourne Care Center at Stony Brook
2200 Stony Brook Dr., Louisville, KY 40220, (502) 495-6240; Facility Type: Skilled care; ICF; Alzheimer's; Certified Beds: 132; Certified: Medicaid; Medicare; Owner: Centennial HealthCare Corp.; License: Current state

James S. Taylor Memorial Home
1015 W Magazine St., Louisville, KY 40203, (502) 589-0727; Facility Type: Skilled care; Alzheimer's; Certified Beds: 122; Certified: Medicaid; Medicare; Owner: For-Profit; License: Current state

Little Sisters of the Poor
15 Audubon Plaza Dr., Louisville, KY 40217, (502) 636-2300; Facility Type: Skilled care; Alzheimer's; Certified Beds: 35; Certified: Medicaid; Medicare; Owner: Nonprofit; License: Current state

Nazareth Home
2000 Newburg Rd., Louisville, KY 40205, (502) 459-9681; Facility Type: Skilled care; ICF; Alzheimer's; Certified Beds: 118; Certified: Medicaid; Medicare; Owner: Nonprofit/Religious org.; License: Current state

Northfield Center for Health & Rehabilitation
6000 Hunting Rd., Louisville, KY 40222, (502) 426-1425; Facility Type: Skilled care; Alzheimer's; Certified Beds: 120; Certified: Medicaid; Medicare; Owner: For-Profit; License: Current state

Oaklawn Nursing & Rehabilitation Center
300 Shelby Station Dr., Louisville, KY 40245, (502) 254-0009; Facility Type: Skilled care; Alzheimer's; Certified Beds: 128; Certified: Medicaid; Medicare; Owner: For-Profit; License: Current state

Parkway Medical Center
1155 Eastern Pkwy., Louisville, KY 40217, (502) 636-5241; Facility Type: Skilled care; Alzheimer's; Certified Beds: 252; Certified: Medicaid; Medicare; Owner: For-Profit; License: Current state

Regis Woods Care & Rehabilitation Center
4604 Lowe Rd., Louisville, KY 40220, (502) 451-1401; Facility Type: Skilled care; Alzheimer's; Certified Beds: 186; Certified: Medicaid; Medicare; Owner: For-Profit; License: Current state

Sacred Heart Village
2120 Payne St., Louisville, KY 40206, (502) 895-9425; Facility Type: Skilled care; Alzheimer's; Certified Beds: 125; Certified: Medicaid; Medicare; Owner: Nonprofit; License: Current state

Springhurst Health & Rehabilitation Center
3001 Hurstbourne Pkwy Louisville, KY 40241, (502) 426-5531; Facility Type: Skilled care; ICF; ICF/MR; Alzheimer's; Certified Beds: 90; Certified: Medicaid; Medicare; Owner: Nonprofit/Religious organization; License: Current state

Summerfield Health & Rehabilitation Center
1877 Farnsley Rd., Louisville, KY 40216, (502) 448-8622; Facility Type: Skilled care; Alzheimer's; Certified Beds: 168; Certified: Medicaid; Medicare; Owner: For-Profit; License: Current state

Wesley Manor Nursing Center & Retirement Community
5012 E Manslick Rd., Louisville, KY 40219, (502) 969-3277; Facility Type: Skilled care; ICF; Alzheimer's; Certified Beds: 68; Certified: Medicaid; Medicare; Owner: Nonprofit corp. License: n/a

Owensboro

Bon Harbor Nursing & Rehabilitation Center
2420 W. 3rd St., Owensboro, KY 42301, (270) 685-3141; Facility Type: Skilled care; Alzheimer's; Certified Beds: 132; Certified: Medicaid; Medicare; Owner: For-Profit; License: Current state

Hermitage Care & Rehabilitation Center
1614 Parrish Ave. West, Owensboro, KY 42301, (270) 684-4559; Facility Type: Skilled care; Alzheimer's; Certified Beds: 72; Certified: Medicaid; Medicare; Owner: For-Profit; License: Current state

Hillcrest Health Care Center
3740 Old Hartford Rd., Owensboro, KY 42303, (270) 684-7259; Facility Type: Skilled care; ICF; Alzheimer's; Certified Beds: 156; Certified: Medicaid; Medicare; Veterans; Owner: Vencor Inc.; License: Current state

Owensboro Place Care & Rehabilitation Center
1205 Leitchfield Rd., Owensboro, KY 42303, (270) 684-0464; Facility Type: Skilled care; Alzheimer's; Certified Beds: 145; Certified: Medicaid; Medicare; Owner: For-Profit; License: Current state

The Transitional Care Center of Owensboro
811 E. Parrish Ave., Owensboro, KY 42303, (270) 688-3300; Facility Type: Skilled care; Alzheimer's; Certified Beds: 30; Certified: Medicaid; Medicare; Owner: Nonprofit; License: Current state

Wellington Parc of Owensboro
2885 New Hartford Rd., Owensboro, KY 42303, (270) 685-2374; Facility Type: Skilled care; Alzheimer's; Certified Beds: 80; Certified: Medicaid; Medicare; Veterans; Owner: Private; License: Current state

South Shore

South Shore Nursing & Rehabilitation Center
PO Box 489 South Shore, KY 41175, (606) 932-3127; Facility Type: Skilled care; ICF; ICF/MR; Alzheimer's; Certified Beds: 60; Certified: Medicaid; Medicare; Owner: Proprietary/Public corp.; License: Current state

South Williamson

Williamson Appalachian Regional Hospital– Skilled Nursing Facility
260 Hospital Dr., South Williamson, KY 42503, (606) 237-1725; Facility Type: Skilled care; Alzheimer's; Certified Beds: 35; Certified: Medicaid; Medicare; Owner: Nonprofit corp.; License: Current state

Williamstown

Grant Manor Inc.
201 Kimberly Ln., Williamstown, KY 41097, (606) 824-7803; Facility Type: Skilled care; ICF; ICF/MR; Alzheimer's; Certified Beds: 95; Certified: Medicaid; Medicare; Owner: Proprietary/Public corp.; License: Current state

LOUISIANA

Baker

Northridge Care Center
3612 Baker Blvd., Baker, LA 70714, (225) 778-0573; Facility Type: Skilled care; ICF; Alzheimer's; Certified Beds: 132; Certified: Medicaid; Medicare; Veterans; Owner: Nonprofit corp.; License: Current state

Baton Rouge

Acadian Nursing & Rehabilitation Center
4005 North Blvd., Baton Rouge, LA 70806, (225) 387-5934; Facility Type: Skilled care; Alzheimer's; Certified Beds: 184; Certified: Medicaid; Medicare; Owner: For-Profit; License: Current state

Baton Rouge Health Care Center
5550 Thomas Rd., Baton Rouge, LA 70811, (225) 774-2141; Facility Type: Skilled care; ICF; Alzheimer's; Certified Beds: 145; Certified: Medicaid; Medicare; Veterans; Owner: Private, Nonprofit; License: Current state

Baton Rouge Heritage House II
1335 Wooddale Blvd. Baton Rouge, LA 70806, (225) 924-2851; Facility Type: Skilled care; Alzheimer's; Certified Beds: 132; Certified: Medicaid; Medicare; Owner: For-Profit; License: Current state

Capitol House Nursing & Rehab Center
11546 Florida Blvd., Baton Rouge, LA 70815, (225) 275-0474; Facility Type: Skilled care; Alzheimer's; Certified Beds: 132; Certified: Medicaid; Medicare; Owner: For-Profit; License: Current state

Flannery Oaks Guest House
1642 N. Flannery Rd., Baton Rouge, LA 70815, (225) 275-6393; Facility Type: Skilled care; Alzheimer's; Certified Beds: 163; Certified: Medicaid; Medicare; Owner: For-Profit; License: Current state

Guest House of Baton Rouge
10145 Florida Blvd., Baton Rouge, LA 70815, (225) 272-0111; Facility Type: Skilled care; ICF; Alzheimer's; Beds: Skilled care 144; SNF/ICF; Certified: Medicaid; Owner: Nonprofit corp.; License: Current state

Heritage Manor of Baton Rouge
9301 Oxford Place Dr., Baton Rouge, LA 70809, (225) 291-8474; Facility Type: Skilled care; Alzheimer's; Certified Beds: 176; Certified: Medicaid; Medicare; Owner: For-Profit; License: Current state

Jefferson Manor Nursing & Rehab
9919 Jefferson Hwy., Baton Rouge, LA 70809, (225) 293-1434; Facility Type: Skilled care; Alzheimer's; Certified Beds: 122; Certified: Medicaid; Medicare; Owner: For-Profit; License: Current state

Lakewood Quarters Rehabilitation & Nursing Center
8225 Summa Ave., Baton Rouge, LA 70809, (225) 766-0130; Facility Type: Skilled care; Alzheimer's; Certified Beds: 172; Certified: Medicaid; Medicare; Owner: For-Profit; License: Current state

Old Jefferson Community Care Center
8340 Baringer Foreman Rd., Baton Rouge, LA 70817, (225) 753-3203; Facility Type: Skilled care; Alzheimer's; Certified Beds: 136; Certified: Medicaid; Medicare; Owner: Nonprofit; License: Current state

Regency Place Nursing & Rehabilitation Center
14333 Old Hammond Hwy., Baton Rouge, LA 70816, (225) 272-1401; Facility Type: Skilled care; Alzheimer's; Certified Beds: 120; Certified: Medicaid; Medicare; Owner: For-Profit; License: Current state

Saint Clare Manor
7435 Bishop Ott Dr., Baton Rouge, LA 70806, (225) 216-3604; Facility Type: Skilled care; ICF; Alzheimer's; Certified Beds: 216; Certified: Medicaid; Owner: Nonprofit/Religious org.; License: Current state

Sherwood Manor Nursing & Rehabilitation Center
2828 Westfork, Baton Rouge, LA 70816, (225) 291-7049; Facility Type: Skilled care; Alzheimer's; Certified Beds: 176; Certified: Medicaid; Medicare; Owner: For-Profit; License: Current state

Sterling Place
3888 North Blvd., Baton Rouge, LA 70806, (225) 344-3551; Facility Type: Skilled care; Alzheimer's; Certified Beds: 160; Certified: Medicaid; Medicare; Owner: For-Profit; License: Current state

Bernice

Bernice Nursing & Rehabilitation Center
101 Reeves St., Bernice, LA 71222, (318) 285-7600; Facility Type: Skilled care; ICF; Alzheimer's; Certified Beds: 126; Certified: Medicaid; Owner: Private; License: Current state

Bossier City

Colonial Oaks Care Center, LLC
4921 Medical Dr., Bossier City, LA 71112, (318) 742-5420; Facility Type: Skilled care; Alzheimer's; Certified Beds: 120; Certified: Medicaid; Medicare; Owner: For-Profit; License: Current state

Cypress Point Nursing & Rehabilitation Center
2901 Douglas St., Bossier City, LA 71111, (318) 747-2700; Facility Type: Skilled care; Alzheimer's; Certified Beds: 104; Certified: Medicaid; Medicare; Owner: For-Profit; License: Current state

Garden Court Health & Rehabilitation Center
4405 Airline Dr., Bossier City, LA 71111, (318) 747-5440; Facility Type: Skilled care; ICF; Alzheimer's; Certified Beds: 77; Certified: Medicare; Owner: Proprietary/Public corp.; License: Current state

Northwest Louisiana War Veterans Home
3130 Arthur Ray Teague Pkwy., Baton Rouge, LA 71112, (318) 741-2763; Facility Type: Skilled care; Alzheimer's; Certified Beds: 20; Certified: Medicaid; Medicare; Veterans; Owner: Government/State; License: Current state

Pilgrim Manor Guest Care Services
1524 Doctors Dr., Bossier City, LA 71111, (318) 742-

1623; Facility Type: Skilled care; Alzheimer's; Certified Beds: 153; Certified: Medicaid; Medicare; Owner: For-Profit; License: Current state

Columbia

Haven Nursing Center Inc.
7726 Hwy. 165 S, Columbia, LA 71418, (318) 649-9800; Facility Type: Skilled care; ICF; Alzheimer's; Certified Beds: 120; Certified: Medicaid; Medicare; Owner: Private; License: Current state

Denham Springs

Golden Age Nursing Home
26739 Hwy., 1032 Denham Springs, LA 70726, (225) 665-5544; Facility Type: Skilled care; ICF; Alzheimer's; Certified Beds: 175; Certified: Medicaid; Owner: Private; License: Current state

Harvest Manor Nursing Home
9171 Cockerham Rd., Denham Springs, LA 70726, (225) 665-8946; Facility Type: Skilled care; Alzheimer's; Certified Beds: 171; Certified: Medicaid; Medicare; Owner: For-Profit; License: Current state

DeRidder

DeRidder Rehabilitation & Retirement Center
1420 Blankenship Dr., DeRidder, LA 70634, (337) 463-9022; Facility Type: Skilled care; ICF; Alzheimer's; Certified Beds: 90; Certified: Medicaid; Medicare; Veterans; Owner: Proprietary/Public corp.; License: Current state

Westwood Manor Nursing Home, Inc.
714 High School Dr., DeRidder, LA 70634, (337) 463-6293; Facility Type: Skilled care; Alzheimer's; Certified Beds: 112; Certified: Medicaid; Medicare; Owner: For-Profit; License: Current state

Donaldsonville

The DeVille House Nursing Home
401 Vatican House Donaldsonville, LA 70346, (225) 473-8614; Facility Type: Skilled care; ICF; Alzheimer's; Certified Beds: 141; Certified: Medicaid; Medicare; Veterans; Owner: Nonprofit corp.; License: Current state

Ferriday

Camelot Leisure Living
6818 Hwy., 84 Ferriday, LA 71334, (318) 757-2181; Facility Type: Skilled care; ICF; Alzheimer's; Certified Beds: 91; Certified: Medicaid; Owner: Private; License: Current state

Heritage Manor Health & Rehabilitation Center
110 Serio Blvd., Ferriday, LA 71334, (318) 757-8671;

Facility Type: Skilled care; Alzheimer's; Certified Beds: 120; Certified: Medicaid; Medicare; Owner: For-Profit; License: Current state

Hammond

Belle Maison Nursing Home
15704 Medical Arts Plaza, Hammond, LA 70403, (985) 542-0110; Facility Type: Skilled care; Alzheimer's; Certified Beds: 179; Certified: Medicaid; Medicare; Owner: For-Profit; License: Current state

Hammond Nursing Home
501 Old Covington Hwy., Hammond, LA 70403, (985) 542-1200; Facility Type: Skilled care; Alzheimer's; Certified Beds: 120; Certified: Medicaid; Medicare; Owner: For-Profit; License: Current state

Heritage Healthcare–Hammond
800 S. Oak St., Hammond, LA 70401, (985) 345-7210; Facility Type: Skilled care; Alzheimer's; Certified Beds: 176; Certified: Medicaid; Medicare; Owner: For-Profit; License: Current state

Landmark Nursing Center–Hammond
1300 Derek Dr., Hammond, LA 70401, (504) 542-8570; Facility Type: Skilled care; ICF; Alzheimer's; Certified Beds: 150; Certified: Medicaid; Owner: Private; License: Current state

Harvey

Maison De Ville Nursing Home of Harvey
2233 8th St., Harvey, LA 70058, (504) 362-9522; Facility Type: Skilled care; ICF; Alzheimer's; Certified Beds: 100; Certified: Medicaid; Owner: Private; License: Current state

West Jefferson Health Care Center
1020 Manhattan Blvd. Harvey, LA 70058, (504) 362-2020; Facility Type: Skilled care; Alzheimer's; Certified Beds: 104; Certified: Medicaid; Medicare; Owner: For-Profit; License: Current state

Houma

Chateau Terrebonne Health Care
1386 W. Tunnel Blvd., Houma, LA 70360, (985) 872-4553; Facility Type: Skilled care; Alzheimer's; Certified Beds: 198; Certified: Medicaid; Medicare; Owner: For-Profit; License: Current state

Heritage Manor of Houma
1701 Polk St., Houma, LA 70360, (985) 851-2307; Facility Type: Skilled care; Alzheimer's; Certified Beds: 120; Certified: Medicaid; Medicare; Owner: For-Profit; License: Current state

Maison De Ville of Houma
107 S Hollywood Dr., Houma, LA 70360, (504) 876-3250; Facility Type: ICF; Alzheimer's; Certified Beds: 200; Certified: Medicaid; Owner: Private; License: Current state

The Oaks of Houma
400 Monarch Dr., Houma, LA 70364, (985) 876-5692; Facility Type: Skilled care; Alzheimer's; Certified Beds: 120; Certified: Medicaid; Medicare; Owner: For-Profit; License: Current state

Terrebonne General Medical Center SNF
8166 Main St., Houma, LA 70360, (985) 873-4141; Facility Type: Skilled care; Alzheimer's; Certified Beds: 16; Certified: Medicaid; Medicare; Owner: Government/Hospital district; License: Current state

Jackson

Louisiana War Veterans Home
4739 Hwy. 10, Jackson, LA 70748, (225) 634-5265; Facility Type: ICF; Alzheimer's; Certified Beds: 86; Certified: Veterans; Owner: Government/State/Local; License: Current state

Villa Feliciana Chronic Disease
5002 Highway 19, Jackson, LA 70748, (225) 634-4000; Facility Type: Skilled care; Alzheimer's; Certified Beds: 297; Certified: Medicaid; Medicare; Veterans; Owner: Government/State; License: Current state

Jefferson

Jefferson Health Care Center
2200 Jefferson Hwy., Jefferson, LA 70121, (504) 837-3144; Facility Type: ICF; Alzheimer's; Certified Beds: 276; Certified: Medicaid; Medicare; Veterans; Owner: Proprietary/Public corp.; License: Current state

Kaplan

Kaplan Healthcare Center
1300 W. Eighth St., Kaplan, LA 70548, (337) 643-7302; Facility Type: Skilled care; Alzheimer's; Certified Beds: 120; Certified: Medicaid; Medicare; Owner: For-Profit; License: Current state

Vermilion Health Care Center
14008 Cheneau, Kaplan, LA 70548, (337) 643-1949; Facility Type: Skilled care; ICF; ICF/MR; Alzheimer's; Certified Beds: 120; Certified: Medicaid; Owner: Private; License: Current state

Lacombe

Lacombe Nursing Centre
28119 Hwy. 190, Davis Ave., Lacombe, LA 70445, (504) 882-5417; Facility Type: Skilled care; ICF; Alzheimer's; Certified Beds: 98; Certified: Medicaid; Medicare; Owner: Private; License: Current state

Lafayette

Amelia Manor Nursing Home Inc.
903 Center St., Lafayette, LA 70501, (337) 234-7331; Facility Type: Skilled care; ICF; Alzheimer's; Certified Beds: 151; Certified: Medicaid; Medicare; Veterans; Owner: Proprietary/Public corp.; License: Current state

Courtyard Manor Nurse Care & Assisted Living
306 Sydney Martin Rd., Lafayette, LA 70507, (337) 237-3940; Facility Type: Skilled care; Alzheimer's; Certified Beds: 92; Certified: Medicaid; Medicare; Owner: For-Profit; License: Current state

Magnolia Estates
1511 Dulles Dr., Lafayette, LA 70506, (337) 216-0950; Facility Type: Skilled care; Alzheimer's; Certified Beds: 160; Certified: Medicaid; Medicare; Owner: For-Profit; License: Current state

Maison De Lafayette
2707 Kaliste Saloom Rd., Lafayette, LA 70508, (337) 981-2258; Facility Type: Skilled care; Alzheimer's; Certified Beds: 189; Certified: Medicaid; Medicare; Owner: For-Profit; License: Current state

River Oaks Retirement Manor
2500 E Simcoe St., Lafayette, LA 70501, (337) 233-7115; Facility Type: Skilled care; ICF; Alzheimer's; Certified Beds: 100; Certified: Medicaid; Owner: Proprietary/Public corp.; License: Current state

Lake Charles

Grand Cove Nursing & Rehabilitation Center
1525 W McNeese St., Lake Charles, LA 70605, (337) 474-6000; Facility Type: Skilled care; Alzheimer's; Certified Beds: 109; Certified: Medicaid; Medicare; Owner: For-Profit; License: Current state

Lake Charles Care Center
2701 Ernest St., Lake Charles, LA 70601, (337) 439-0336; Facility Type: Skilled care; Alzheimer's; Certified Beds: 182; Certified: Medicaid; Medicare; Owner: For-Profit; License: Current state

Landmark of Lake Charles
2335 Oak Park Blvd., Lake Charles, LA 70601, (337) 478-2920; Facility Type: Skilled care; Alzheimer's; Certified Beds: 177; Certified: Medicaid; Medicare; Owner: For-Profit; License: Current state

Rosewood Nursing Center
534 15th St., Lake Charles, LA 70601, (337) 439-8338; Facility Type: Skilled care; Alzheimer's; Certified Beds: 150; Certified: Medicaid; Medicare; Owner: For-Profit; License: Current state

St. Martin De Porres Multi-Care Center
200 Teal St., Lake Charles, LA 70615, (337) 439-5761; Facility Type: Skilled care; Alzheimer's; Certified Beds: 250; Certified: Medicaid; Medicare; Owner: For-Profit; License: Current state

Mandeville

Heritage Manor of Mandeville
1820 W. Causeway Approach, Mandeville, LA 70471, (985) 626-4798; Facility Type: Skilled care; Alzheimer's; Certified Beds: 145; Certified: Medicaid; Medicare; Owner: For-Profit; License: Current state

Pontchartrain Health Care Centre
PO Box 338 Mandeville, LA 70470, (504) 626-8581; Facility Type: Skilled care; ICF; Alzheimer's; Certified Beds: 182 Certified: Medicaid; Medicare; Veterans; Owner: Private; License: Current state

Metairie

Colonial Oaks Living Center
4312 Ithaca St., Metairie, LA 70006, (504) 887-6414; Facility Type: Skilled care; Alzheimer's; Certified Beds: 110; Certified: Medicaid; Medicare; Owner: For-Profit; License: Current state

East Jefferson Hospital SNF
4200 Houma Blvd., Metairie, LA 70002, (504) 454-4699; Facility Type: Skilled care; Alzheimer's; Certified Beds: 49; Certified: Medicaid; Medicare; Owner: Government/Hospital District; License: Current state

Metairie Health Care Center
6401 Riverside Dr., Metairie, LA 70003, (504) 885-8611; Facility Type: Skilled care; Alzheimer's; Certified Beds: 202; Certified: Medicaid; Medicare; Owner: For-Profit; License: Current state

Saint Anthony Nursing Home Inc.
6001 Airline Dr., Metairie, LA 70003, (504) 733-8448; Facility Type: ICF; Alzheimer's; Certified Beds: 124; Certified: Medicaid; Owner: Proprietary/ Public corp.; License: Current state

Monroe

Avalon Place
4385 Old Sterlington Rd., Monroe, LA 71203, (318) 322-2000; Facility Type: Skilled care; Alzheimer's; Certified Beds: 115; Certified: Medicaid; Medicare; Owner: For-Profit; License: Current state

Christus St. Joseph Home
2301 Sterlington Rd., Monroe, LA 71203, (318) 323-3426; Facility Type: Skilled care; Alzheimer's; Certified Beds: 130; Certified: Medicaid; Medicare; Owner: Nonprofit; License: Current state

Mary Goss Nursing Home
3300 White St., Monroe, LA 71203, (318) 323-9013; Facility Type: Skilled care; Alzheimer's; Certified Beds: 91; Certified: Medicaid; Medicare; Owner: For-Profit; License: Current state

Northeast LA War Veterans Home
6700 Highway 155 N., Monroe, LA 71211, (318) 362-

4206; Facility Type: Skilled care; Alzheimer's; Certified Beds: 202; Certified: Medicaid; Medicare; Owner: Government/State; License: Current state

Oaks (The)
1000 McKeen Pl., Monroe, LA 71201, (318) 387-5300; Facility Type: Skilled care; Alzheimer's; Certified Beds: 156; Certified: Medicaid; Medicare; Owner: For-Profit; License: Current state

Riverside Nursing Home
3001 S Grand St., Monroe, LA 71201, (318) 388-3200; Facility Type: Skilled care; ICF; Alzheimer's; Certified Beds: 167; Certified: Medicaid; Owner: Proprietary/Public corp.; License: n/a

Southern Acres Care Center
4600 Reddix Ln., Monroe, LA 71202, (318) 322-3100; Facility Type: Skilled care; Alzheimer's; Certified Beds: 74; Certified: Medicaid; Medicare; Owner: For-Profit; License: Current state

Napoleonville

Heritage Manor of Napoleonville
252 Hwy. 402, Napoleonville, LA 70390, (504) 369-6011; Facility Type: Skilled care; ICF; ICF/ MR; Alzheimer's; Certified Beds: 130; Certified: Medicaid; Veterans; Owner: Private; License: Current state

Natchitoches

Courtyard of Natchitoches
708 Keyser Ave, Natchitoches, LA 71457, (318) 214-4361; Facility Type: Skilled care; Alzheimer's; Certified Beds: 108; Certified: Medicaid; Medicare; Veterans; Owner: Government/Hospital district; License: Current state

Natchitoches Community Care Center
720 Keyser Ave., Natchitoches, LA 71457, (318) 352-8296; Facility Type: Skilled care; ICF; Alzheimer's; Certified Beds: 120; Certified: Medicaid; Medicare; Owner: Private; License: Current state

Natchitoches Nursing & Rehabilitation Center, LLC
750 Keyser Ave., Natchitoches, LA 71457, (318) 352-8779; Facility Type: Skilled care; Alzheimer's; Certified Beds: 198; Certified: Medicaid; Medicare; Owner: For-Profit; License: Current state

New Iberia

Belle Teche Nursing & Rehabilitation Center
1306 W Admiral Doyle Dr., New Iberia, LA 70560, (337) 364-5472; Facility Type: Skilled care; Alzheimer's; Certified Beds: 150; Certified: Medicaid; Medicare; Owner: For-Profit; License: Current state

Consolata Home
2319 E Main St., New Iberia, LA 70560, (337) 365-8226; Facility Type: ICF; Alzheimer's; Certified Beds: 114; Certified: Medicaid; Owner: Nonprofit/Religious org. License: Current state

New Iberia Manor North
1803 Jane St., New Iberia, LA 70562, (337) 365-2466; Facility Type: Skilled care; Alzheimer's; Certified Beds: 121; Certified: Medicaid; Medicare; Owner: For-Profit; License: Current state

New Iberia Manor South
600 Bayard St., New Iberia, LA 70560, (337) 365-3441; Facility Type: Skilled care; Alzheimer's; Certified Beds: 100; Certified: Medicaid; Medicare; Owner: For-Profit; License: Current state

New Orleans

Chateau De Notre Dame
2832 Burdette St., New Orleans, LA 70125, (504) 866-2741; Facility Type: Skilled care; Alzheimer's; Certified Beds: 171; Certified: Medicaid; Medicare; Owner: Nonprofit, Church-related; License: Current state

Covenant Nursing Home
5919 Magazine St., New Orleans, LA 70115, (504) 897-6216; Facility Type: ICF; Alzheimer's; Certified Beds: 96; Certified: Medicaid; Owner: Nonprofit/Religious org.; License: Current state

Fern Crest Manor Living Center
14500 Hayne Blvd., New Orleans, LA 70128, (504) 246-1426; Facility Type: Skilled care; ICF; Alzheimer's; Certified Beds: 200; Certified: Medicaid; Medicare; Owner: Private; License: Current state

Good Samaritan Society–New Orleans
6400 Hayne Blvd., New Orleans, LA 70126, (504) 246-7900; Facility Type: Skilled care; ICF; Alzheimer's; Beds: Skilled care; ICF 200; SNF/ICF; Certified: Medicaid; Owner: Nonprofit corp.; License: Current state

Jo Ellen Smith Convalescent Center
4502 General Meyers Ave., New Orleans, LA 70131, (504) 361-7923; Facility Type: Skilled care; Alzheimer's; Certified Beds: 180; Certified: Medicaid; Medicare; Owner: For-Profit; License: Current state

John J. Hainkel Jr. Home & Rehabilitation Center
612 Henry Clay Ave., New Orleans, LA 70118, (504) 896-1315; Facility Type: Skilled care; Alzheimer's; Certified Beds: 142; Certified: Medicaid; Medicare; Veterans; Owner: Government/State; License: Current state

LaFon Nursing Facility of the Holy Family
6900 Chef Menteur Hwy., New Orleans, LA 70126, (504) 241-6285; Facility Type: Skilled care; Alzheimer's; Certified Beds: 155; Certified: Medicaid; Medicare; Owner: Nonprofit; License: Current state

Our Lady of Wisdom Healthcare Center
5600 General DeGaulle Dr., New Orleans, LA 70131, (504) 304-5406; Facility Type: Skilled care; Alzheimer's; Certified Beds: 138; Certified: Medicaid; Medicare; Owner: Nonprofit, Church-related; License: Current state

St. Charles Health Center
1539 Delachaise St., New Orleans, LA 70115, (504) 895-3953; Facility Type: Skilled care; Alzheimer's; Certified Beds: 116; Certified: Medicaid; Medicare; Owner: For-Profit; License: Current state

Willow Wood at Woldenberg Village
3701 Behrman Pl., New Orleans, LA 70114, (504) 367-5640; Facility Type: Skilled care; Alzheimer's; Certified Beds: 116; Certified: Medicaid; Medicare; Owner: Nonprofit; License: Current state

Woodland Village Nursing & Rehabilitation Center
5301 Tullis Dr., New Orleans, LA 70131, (504) 394-5807; Facility Type: Skilled care; Alzheimer's; Certified Beds: 186; Certified: Medicaid; Medicare; Owner: For-Profit; License: Current state

New Roads

Lakeview Manor Nursing Home
400 Hospital Rd., New Roads, LA 70760, (225) 638-4404; Facility Type: Skilled care; Alzheimer's; Certified Beds: 120; Certified: Medicaid; Medicare; Owner: For-Profit; License: Current state

Pointe Coupee Parish Nursing Home
2202-A Hospital Rd., New Roads, LA 70760, (225) 638-4431; Facility Type: ICF; Alzheimer's; Certified Beds: 120; Certified: Medicaid; Owner: Government/State/Local; License: Current state

Oberlin

Saint Francis Nursing & Rehabilitation Center
417 Industrial Park Dr., Oberlin, LA 70655, (337) 639-2934; Facility Type: Skilled care; ICF; Alzheimer's; Certified Beds: 100; Certified: Medicaid; Veterans; Owner: Private; License: Current state

Opelousas

Heritage Manor of Opelousas
7941 I-49 South Service Rd., Opelousas, LA 70570, (337) 942-7588; Facility Type: Skilled care; ICF; Alzheimer's; Certified Beds: 109; Certified: Medicaid; Medicare; Owner: Proprietary/Public corp.; License: Current state

Our Lady of Prompt Succor Nursing Facility
954 E Prudhomme Ln, Opelousas, LA 70570, (337) 948-3634; Facility Type: Skilled care; Alzheimer's; Certified Beds: 120; Certified: Medicaid; Medicare; Owner: Nonprofit; License: Current state

Senior Village Nursing & Rehabilitation Center
315 Harry Guilbeau Rd., Opelousas, LA 70570, (337) 948-4486; Facility Type: Skilled care; Alzheimer's; Certified Beds: 176; Certified: Medicaid; Medicare; Owner: For-Profit; License: Current state

Rayville

Colonial Manor Nursing & Rehabilitation Center, LLC
114 Whatley St., Rayville, LA 71269, (318) 728-3251; Facility Type: Skilled care; ICF; Alzheimer's; Certified Beds: 134; Certified: Medicaid; Medicare; Owner: Private; License: Current state

Rayville Nursing & Rehabilitation Center, Inc.
294 Hwy. 3048, Rayville LA 71269, (318) 728-2089; Facility Type: Skilled care; Alzheimer's; Certified Beds: 149; Certified: Medicaid; Medicare; Owner: For-Profit; License: Current state

Ruston

Alpine Care Center, LLC
4396 Hwy. 80 E., Ruston, LA 71270, (318) 255-6492; Facility Type: Skilled care; Alzheimer's; Certified Beds: 159; Certified: Medicaid; Medicare; Owner: For-Profit; License: Current state

Princeton Place–Ruston
1405 White St., Ruston, LA 71270, (318) 255-4400; Facility Type: Skilled care; ICF; Alzheimer's; Certified Beds: 123; Certified: Medicaid; Medicare; Veterans; Owner: Nonprofit corp.; License: Current state

Ruston Nursing & Rehabilitation Center, LLC
3720 Hwy. 80 E., Ruston, LA 71270, (318) 255-5001; Facility Type: Skilled care; Alzheimer's; Certified Beds: 157; Certified: Medicaid; Medicare; Owner: For-Profit; License: Current state

Saint Bernard

Poydras Manor Nursing Facility
Rte. 1 Box 132 Saint Bernard, LA 70085, (504) 682-0012; Facility Type: Skilled care; ICF; ICF/MR; Alzheimer's; Certified Beds: 36; Certified: Medicaid; Owner: Private; License: Current state

Shreveport

Booker T. Washington Nursing Center
7605 Line Ave., Shreveport, LA 71106, (318) 219-2608; Facility Type: Skilled care; Alzheimer's; Certified Beds: 80; Certified: Medicaid; Medicare; Owner: For-Profit; License: Current state

Bradford Guest Care, LLC
3050 Baird Rd., Shreveport, LA 71118, (318) 688-1010; Facility Type: ICF; Alzheimer's; Certified Beds: 146;

Certified: Medicaid; Medicare; Owner: Gamble Guest Care Corp.; License: Current state

Garden Park Nursing Home
9111 Lynnwood, Shreveport, LA 71106, (318) 688-0961; Facility Type: Skilled care; ICF; ICF/MR; Alzheimer's; Certified Beds: 160; Certified: Medicaid; Medicare; Veterans; Owner: Central Management Co.; License: Current state

Guest Care at Spring Lake, LLC (The)
8622 Line Ave., Shreveport, LA 71106, (318) 868-4126; Facility Type: Skilled care; Alzheimer's; Certified Beds: 160; Certified: Medicaid; Medicare; Owner: For-Profit; License: Current state

Guest Home (The)
9225 Normandie Dr., Shreveport, LA 71118, (318) 686-0515; Facility Type: Skilled care; Alzheimer's; Certified Beds: 177; Certified: Medicaid; Medicare; Owner: For-Profit; License: Current state

Heritage Manor South
9712 Mansfield Rd., Shreveport, LA 71118, (318) 687-2080; Facility Type: Skilled care; Alzheimer's; Certified Beds: 169; Certified: Medicaid; Medicare; Owner: For-Profit; License: Current state

Live Oak
600 E Flournoy Lucas Rd., Shreveport, LA 71115, (318) 797-1900; Facility Type: Skilled care; ICF; Alzheimer's; Certified Beds: 130; Certified: Medicaid; Owner: Nonprofit/Religious org.; License: Current state

Magnolia Manor Nursing Home Inc.
1411 Claiborne Ave., Shreveport, LA 71103, (318) 861-2526; Facility Type: Skilled care; ICF; Alzheimer's; Certified Beds: 98; Certified: Medicaid; Medicare;

Owner: Central Management Co.; License: Current state

Nursecare Nursing & Rehabilitation Center
1736 Irving Pl, Shreveport, LA 71101, (318) 221-1983; Facility Type: Skilled care; Alzheimer's; Certified Beds: 227; Certified: Medicaid; Medicare; Owner: For-Profit; License: Current state

Pierremont Healthcare Center
725 Mitchell Ln., Shreveport, LA 71106, (318) 868-2789; Facility Type: Skilled care; Alzheimer's; Certified Beds: 196; Certified: Medicaid; Medicare; Owner: For-Profit; License: Current state

Simmesport

Bayou Chateau Nursing Center
1632 Rte. 1, Simmesport, LA 71369, (318) 941-2294; Facility Type: Skilled care; ICF; ICF/MR; Alzheimer's; Certified Beds: 104; Certified: Medicaid; Veterans; Owner: Proprietary/ Public corp.; License: Current state

Wisner

Mary Anna Nursing Home Inc.
125 Turner St., Wisner, LA 71378, (318) 724-7244; Facility Type: Skilled care; ICF; Alzheimer's; Certified Beds: 81; Certified: Medicaid; Owner: Private; License: Current state

Plantation Oaks Nursing & Rehabilitation Center
110 Maple St., Wisner, LA 71378, (318) 724-7493; Facility Type: Skilled care; Alzheimer's; Certified Beds: 76; Certified: Medicaid; Medicare; Owner: For-Profit; License: Current state

MAINE

Augusta

Maine General Rehab & Nursing at Glenridge
40 Glenridge, Augusta, ME 04330, (207) 626-2600; Facility Type: Skilled care; ICF; Alzheimer's; Certified Beds: 125; Certified: Medicaid; Medicare; Owner: Nonprofit; License: Current state

Maine General Rehab & Nursing at Graybirch
37 Graybirch Dr., Augusta, ME 04330, (207) 622-6226; Facility Type: Skilled care; ICF; Alzheimer's; Certified Beds: 77; Certified: Medicaid; Medicare; Owner: Private; License: Current state

Maine Veterans Home
310 Cony Rd., Augusta, ME 04330, (207) 622-2454;

Facility Type: Skilled care; ICF; Alzheimer's; Certified Beds: 120; Certified: Medicaid; Medicare; Veterans; Owner: Nonprofit corp.; License: Current state

Bangor

Eastside Rehabilitation & Living Center
516 Mt. Hope Ave., Bangor, ME 04401, (207) 947-6131; Facility Type: Skilled care; ICF; ICF/ MR; Alzheimer's; Certified Beds: 67; Certified: Medicaid; Medicare; Owner: Vencor Inc.; License: n/a

Maine Veteran's Home–Bangor
44 Hogan Rd., Bangor, ME 04401, (207) 942-2333; Facility Type: Skilled care; ICF; Alzheimer's; Certified Beds: 120; Certified: Medicaid; Medicare; Veterans; Owner: Non-Profit; License: Current state

Ross Manor
758 Broadway, Bangor, ME 04401, (207) 941-8400; Facility Type: Skilled care; ICF; Alzheimer's; Certified Beds: 83; Certified: Medicaid; Medicare; Owner: Private; License: Current state

Westgate Manor
750 Union St., Bangor, ME 04401, (207) 942-7336; Facility Type: Skilled care; ICF; Alzheimer's; Certified Beds: 65; Certified: Medicaid; Medicare; Veterans; Owner: Vencor Inc.; License: Current state

Biddeford

Saint Andre Health Care Facility
407 Pool St., Biddeford, ME 04005, (207) 282-5171; Facility Type: Skilled care; ICF; Alzheimer's; Certified Beds: 96; Certified: Medicaid; Medicare; Owner: Nonprofit/Religious organization; License: Current state

Brewer

Brewer Rehabilitation & Living Center
74 Parkway S. Brewer, ME 04412, (207) 989-7300; Facility Type: Skilled care; ICF; ICF/MR; Alzheimer's; Certified Beds: 111; Certified: Medicaid; Medicare; Owner: Vencor Inc.; License: Current state

Caribou

Caribou Rehabilitation and Nursing Center
10 Bernadette St., Caribou, ME 04736, (207) 498-3102; Facility Type: ICF; Alzheimer's; Certified Beds: 68; Certified: Medicaid; Medicare; Veterans; Owner: Private; License: Current state

Deer Isle

Island Nursing Home Inc.
587 Deer Isle Rd., Deer Isle, ME 04627, (207) 348-2351; Facility Type: Skilled care; ICF; Alzheimer's; Certified Beds: 38; Certified: Medicaid; Medicare; Veterans; Owner: Nonprofit corp.; License: Current state

Ellsworth

Courtland Rehabilitation & Living Center
42 Bucksport Rd., Ellsworth, ME 04605, (207) 667-9036; Facility Type: Skilled care; ICF; Alzheimer's; Certified Beds: 54; Certified: Medicaid; Medicare; Owner: North Country Associates; License: Current state

Falmouth

Sedgewood Commons
22 Northbrook Dr., Falmouth, ME 04105, (207) 781-5775; Facility Type: Skilled care; ICF; Alzheimer's; Certified Beds: 65; Certified: Medicaid; Medicare; Owner: Private; License: Current state

Freeport

Hawthorne House
6 Old County Rd., Freeport, ME 04032, (207) 865-4782; Facility Type: Skilled care; ICF; Alzheimer's; Certified Beds: 81; Certified: Medicaid; Medicare; Veterans; Owner: First Atlantic Corp.; License: Current state

Kennebunk

Kennebunk Nursing & Rehabilitation Center
158 Ross Rd., Kennebunk, ME 04043, (207) 985-7141; Facility Type: Skilled care; ICF; Alzheimer's; Certified Beds: 78; Certified: Medicaid; Medicare; Owner: Vencor Inc.; License: Current state

Lewiston

Montello Manor
540 College St., Lewiston, ME 04240, (207) 783-2039; Facility Type: Skilled care; ICF; Alzheimer's; Certified Beds: 57; Alzheimer's; Certified: Medicaid; Medicare; Owner: Proprietary/Public corp.; License: Current state

Saint Mary's d'Youville Pavilion
102 Campus Ave., Lewiston, ME 04240, (207) 777-4200; Facility Type: Skilled care; ICF; Alzheimer's; Certified Beds: 280; Certified: Medicaid; Medicare; Owner: Nonprofit/Religious org.; License: Current state

Portland

Barron Center
1145 Brighton Ave., Portland, ME 04102, (207) 774-2623; Facility Type: Skilled care; ICF; Alzheimer's; Certified Beds: 219; Certified: Medicaid; Medicare; Owner: Government/State/ Local; License: Current state

Seaside Rehabilitation & Healthcare Center
850 Baxter Blvd., Portland, ME 04103, (207) 774-7878; Facility Type: Skilled care; ICF; Alzheimer's; Certified Beds: 124; Certified: Medicaid; Medicare; Owner: First Atlantic Corp.; License: Current state

Skowhegan

Cedar Ridge Center
23 Cedar Ridge Dr., Skowhegan, ME 04976, (207) 474-9686; Facility Type: Skilled care; ICF; Alzheimer's; Certified Beds: 75; Certified: Medicaid; Medicare; Veterans; Owner: Private; License: Current state

Van Buren

Borderview Manor Inc.
208 State St., Van Buren, ME 04785, (207) 868-5211;
Facility Type: Skilled care; ICF; Alzheimer's; Certified
Beds: 55; Certified: Medicaid; Owner: Proprietary/
Public corp.; License: Current state

Waterville

Mount Saint Joseph Nursing Home
Highwood St., Waterville, ME 04901, (207) 873-
0705; Facility Type: Skilled care; ICF; Alzheimer's;
Certified Beds: 111; Certified: Medicaid; Medicare;
Owner: Nonprofit/Religious org.; License: Current
state

Oak Grove Center
27 Cool St., Waterville, ME 04901, (207) 873-0721;
Facility Type: Skilled care; ICF; Alzheimer's; Certified
Beds: 90; Certified: Medicaid; Medicare; Veterans;
Owner: Proprietary/Public corp.; License: Current
state

Westbrook

Springbrook Center
300 Spring St., Westbrook, ME 04092, (207) 856-
1230; Facility Type: Skilled care; ICF; Alzheimer's;

Certified Beds: 100; Alzheimer's; Dementia unit 23;
Certified: Medicaid; Medicare; Owner: Private; License: Current state

Winthrop

Heritage Rehabilitation & Living Center
457 Old Lewiston Rd., Winthrop, ME 04364, (207)
377-9965; Facility Type: Skilled care; ICF; ICF/MR;
Alzheimer's; Certified Beds: 28; Residential; Certified:
Medicaid; Medicare; Owner: Proprietary/Public
corp.; License: Current state

Yarmouth

Brentwood Rehabilitation & Nursing Center
370 Portland St., Yarmouth, ME 04096, (207) 846-
9021; Facility Type: Skilled care; ICF; Alzheimer's;
Certified Beds: 78; Certified: Medicaid; Medicare;
Owner: Proprietary/Public corp.; License: Current
state

Coastal Manor
PO Box 429., Yarmouth, ME 04096, (207) 846-5013;
Facility Type: Skilled care; ICF; Alzheimer's; Certified
Beds: 39; Certified: Medicaid; Medicare; Owner: Pri-
vate; License: Current state

MARYLAND

Adelphi

Heartland Health Care Center–Adelphi
1801 Metzerott Rd., Adelphi, MD 20783, (301) 434-
0500; Facility Type: Skilled care; ICF; Alzheimer's;
Certified Beds: 142; Certified: Medicaid; Medicare;
Veterans; Owner: HCR ManorCare; License: Current state

Baltimore

Alice Manor Nursing Home
2095 Rockrose Ave., Baltimore, MD 21211, (410) 889-
9700; Facility Type: Skilled care; ICF; ICF/MR; Alzheimer's; Certified Beds: 105; Certified: Medicaid;
Medicare; Owner: Proprietary/Public corp.; License:
Current state

Augsburg Lutheran Home
6811 Campfield Rd., MD 21207, (410) 486-4573; Facility Type: Skilled care; ICF; Alzheimer's; Certified
Beds: 123; Certified: Medicaid; Medicare; Owner:
Nonprofit, church related; License: Current state

Caton Manor
3330 Wilkens Ave., Baltimore, MD 21229, (410) 525-

1544; Facility Type: Skilled care; ICF; ICF/MR; Alz-
heimer's; Certified Beds: 140; Certified: Medicaid;
Medicare; Veterans; Owner: Proprietary/Public corp.;
License: Current state

Courtland Gardens Nursing & Rehab Center
7920 Scotts Level Rd., Baltimore, MD 21208, (410)
521-3600; Facility Type: Skilled care; ICF; Alzheimer's; Certified Beds: 145; Certified: Medicaid;
Medicare; Owner: Private, For-Profit License: Current state

Fayette Health & Rehabilitation Center
1217 W. Fayette St., Baltimore, MD 21223, (410) 727-
3947; Facility Type: Skilled care; ICF; Alzheimer's;
Certified Beds: 198; Certified: Medicaid; Medicare;
Owner: Private, For-Profit, License: Current state

Frankford Nursing & Rehabilitation Center
5009 Frankford Ave., Baltimore, MD 21206, (410)
325-4000; Facility Type: Skilled care; ICF; Alzheimer's; Memory care; short-term and respite care;
Certified Beds: 238; Certified: Medicaid; Medicare;
Owner: Private, For-Profit, License: Current state

Future Care & Charles Village
2327 N. Charles St., Baltimore, MD 21218, (410)
889-8500; Facility Type: Skilled care; ICF; Alzheimer's; Certified Beds: 109; Certified: Medicaid; Medi-

care; Owner: Private, For-Profit, License: Current state

Harborside Nursing & Rehab Center
501 W. Franklin St., Baltimore, MD 21201, (410) 837-4990; Facility Type: Skilled care; ICF; Alzheimer's; Certified Beds: 270; Certified: Medicaid; Medicare; Owner: Nonprofit; License: Current state

Keswick Multicare Center
700 W. 40th St., Baltimore, MD 21211, (410) 235-8860; Facility Type: Skilled care; ICF; Alzheimer's; Certified Beds: 242; Certified: Medicaid; Medicare; Owner: Nonprofit; License: Current state

Levindale Hebrew Geriatric Center & Hospital
2434 W Belvedere Ave., Baltimore, MD 21215, (410) 466-8700; Facility Type: Skilled care; ICF; Alzheimer's; Certified Beds: 192; Certified: Medicaid; Medicare; Owner: Nonprofit/Religious org.; License: Current state

Riverview Rehabilitation & Health Center
1 Eastern Blvd., Baltimore, MD 21221, (410) 574-1400; Facility Type: Skilled care; ICF; Alzheimer's; Certified Beds: 238; Certified: Medicaid; Medicare; Owner: For-Profit; License: Current state

St. Elizabeth Rehabilitation and Nursing CE
3320 Benson Ave., Baltimore, MD 21227, (410) 644-7100 Facility Type: Skilled care; ICF; Alzheimer's; Certified Beds: 162; Certified: Medicaid; Medicare; Owner: Nonprofit; Church-related; License: Current state

Bel Air

Bel Air Health & Rehabilitation Center
410 E McPhail Rd., Bel Air, MD 21014, (410) 879-1120; Facility Type: Skilled care; ICF; Alzheimer's; Certified Beds: 155; Certified: Medicaid; Medicare; Veterans; Owner: Proprietary/Public corp.; License: Current state

Bethesda

Bethesda Health & Rehabilitation Center
5721 Grosvenor Ln., Bethesda, MD 30814, (301) 530-1600; Facility Type: Skilled care; ICF; Alzheimer's; Certified Beds: 200; Certified: Medicaid; Medicare; Veterans; Owner: Proprietary/Public corp.; License: Current state

Carriage Hill Bethesda
5215 Cedar Ln., Bethesda, MD 20814, (301) 897-5500; Facility Type: Skilled care; ICF; Alzheimer's; Certified Beds: 108; Certified: Medicare; Owner: For-Profit; License: Current state

Brooklyn Park

Hammonds Lane Center
613 Hammonds Ln., Brooklyn Park, MD 21225, (410) 636-3400; Facility Type: Skilled care; ICF; Alzheimer's; Certified Beds: 129; Certified: Medicaid; Medicare; Owner: Proprietary/Public corp.; License: Current state

Cambridge

Chesapeake Woods Center
525 Glenburn Ave., Cambridge, MD 21613, (410) 221-1400; Facility Type: Skilled care; Alzheimer's; Certified Beds: 98; SNF/ICF; Certified: Medicaid; Medicare; Owner: Proprietary/Public corp.; License: Current state

Signature Healthcare at Mallard Bay
520 Glenburn Ave., Cambridge MD 21613, (410) 228-9191; Facility Type: Skilled care; ICF; Alzheimer's; Certified Beds: 160; Certified: Medicaid; Medicare; Owner: For-Profit; License: Current state

Catonsville

Catonsville Commons
16 Fusting Ave., Catonsville, MD 21228, (410) 747-1800; Facility Type: Skilled care; ICF; ICF/ MR; Alzheimer's; Certified Beds: 143; Certified: Medicaid; Medicare; Veterans; Owner: Genesis Eldercare; License: Current state

Chestertown

Chester River Manor
200 Morgnec Rd., Chestertown, MD 21620, (410) 778-4550; Facility Type: Skilled care; ICF; Alzheimer's; Certified Beds: 98; Certified: Medicaid; Medicare; Veterans; Owner: Nonprofit corp.; License: Current state

Clinton

Future Care Pineview Nursing
9106 Pineview Ln., Clinton, MD 20735, (410) 880-4353; Facility Type: Skilled care; ICF; Alzheimer's; Certified Beds: 192; Certified: Medicaid; Medicare; Owner: Proprietary/Public corp.; License: n/a

Cumberland

Mid-Atlantic of Cumberland, LLC
730 Furnace St., Cumberland, MD 21502, (301) 777-5941; Facility Type: Skilled care; ICF; Alzheimer's; Certified Beds: 192; Certified: Medicaid; Medicare; Owner: Government/State/Local; License: Current state

Frederick

Golden LivingCenter Frederick
30 North Pl., Frederick, MD 21701, (301) 695-6618;

Facility Type: Skilled care; ICF; ICF/MR; Certified Beds: 120; Certified: Medicaid; Medicare; Veterans; Owner: Beverly Enterprises Inc. License: Current state

Hagerstown

Golden LivingCenter–Hagerstown
750 Dual Hwy., Hagerstown, MD 21740, (301) 797-4020; Facility Type: Skilled care; ICF; Alzheimer's; Certified Beds: 140; Certified: Medicaid; Medicare; Owner: For-Profit; License: Current state

NMS Healthcare of Hagerstown, LLC
14014 Marsh Pike Hagerstown, MD 21742, (301) 739-9360; Facility Type: Skilled care; ICF; ICF/ MR; Certified Beds: 186; Certified: Medicaid; Medicare; Veterans; Owner: Private; License: n/a

Western MD Hospital Center
1500 Pennsylvania Ave., Hagerstown, MD 21742, (301) 745-4200 Facility Type: Skilled care; ICF; Alzheimer's; Certified Beds: 63; Certified: Medicaid; Medicare; Veterans; Owner: Government, State; License: Current state

Hyattsville

Heartland Health Care Center–Hyattsville
6500 Riggs Rd., Hyattsville, MD 20783, (301) 559-0300; Facility Type: Skilled care; ICF; Alzheimer's; Certified Beds: 160; Certified: Medicaid; Medicare; Medi-Cal; Veterans; Owner: Proprietary/Public corp.; License: Current state

Laurel

Cherry Lane
9001 Cherry Ln., Laurel, MD 20708, (410) 792-8275; Facility Type: Skilled care; ICF/MR; Alzheimer's; Certified Beds: 155; Certified: Medicaid; Medicare; Owner: Government/State/Local; License: Current state

Manchester

Longview Nursing Home
3332 Main St., Manchester, MD 21102, (410) 239-7139; Facility Type: Skilled care; Alzheimer's; Certified Beds: 109; Certified: Medicaid; Medicare; Owner: Private; License: Current state

Oakland

Oakland Nursing and Rehabilitation Center
706 E Alder St., Oakland, MD 21550, (301) 334-2319; Facility Type: Skilled care; ICF; Alzheimer's; Certified Beds: 112; Certified: Medicaid; Medicare; Veterans; Owner: Proprietary/Public corp.; License: Current state

Rockville

Collingswood Nursing & Rehabilitation Center
299 Hurley Ave., Rockville, MD 20850, (301) 762-8900; Facility Type: Skilled care; ICF; Alzheimer's; Certified Beds: 160; Certified: Medicaid; Medicare; Veterans; Owner: Private; License: Current state

Potomac Valley Nursing & Wellness Center
1235 Potomac Valley Rd., Rockville, MD 20850, (301) 762-0700; Facility Type: Skilled care; Alzheimer's; Certified Beds: 175; Certified: Medicaid; Medicare; Owner: Private; License: Current state

Salisbury

Salisbury Center
200 Civic Ave., Salisbury, MD 21801, (410) 749-1466; Facility Type: Skilled care; ICF; ICF/MR; Alzheimer's; Certified Beds: 305; Certified: Medicaid; Medicare; Owner: Proprietary/Public corp. License: Current state

Silver Spring

Fairland Nursing & Rehabilitation Center
2101 Fairland Rd., Silver Spring, MD 20904, (301) 384-6161; Facility Type: Skilled care; ICF; Alzheimer's; Certified Beds: 92; Certified: Medicaid; Medicare; Owner: Nonprofit/Religious org.; License: Current state

ManorCare Health Services–Silver Spring
2501 Musgrove Rd., Silver Spring, MD 20904, (301) 890-5552; Facility Type: Skilled care; ICF; ICF/MR; Alzheimer's; Certified Beds: 129; Certified: Medicaid; Medicare; Owner: Proprietary/Public corp.; License: Current state

Sykesville

Fairhaven, Inc.
7200 Third Ave., Sykesville, MD 21784, (410) 795-8800; Facility Type: Skilled care; ICF; Alzheimer's; Certified Beds: 79; Certified: Medicare; Owner: Nonprofit corp.; License: Current state

Transitions Healthcare at Sykesville
7309 Second Ave., Sykesville, MD 21784, (410) 795-1100; Facility Type: Skilled care; ICF; Alzheimer's; Certified Beds: 118; Certified: Medicaid; Medicare; Veterans; Owner: Continuum Care Corporation; License: Current state

Towson

ManorCare Health Services–Ruxton
7001 Charles St., Towson, MD 21204, (410) 821-9600; Facility Type: Skilled care; ICF; Alzheimer's; Certified Beds: 232; Certified: Medicaid; Medicare;

Owner: Proprietary/Public corp.; License: Current state

Multi-Medical Center
7700 York Rd., Towson, MD 21204, (410) 821-5500; Facility Type: Skilled care; ICF; Alzheimer's; Certified Beds: 118; Certified: Medicaid; Medicare; Veterans; Owner: Proprietary/Public corp.; License: Current state

Wheaton

Randolph Hills Nursing Center
4011 Randolph Rd., Wheaton, MD 20902, (301) 933-

2500; Facility Type: Skilled care; ICF; Alzheimer's; Certified Beds: 112; Certified: Medicaid; Medicare; Veterans; Owner: Private; License: Current state

Williamsport

Homewood at Williamsport Maryland
16505 Virginia Ave., Williamsport, MD 21795, (301) 582-1628; Facility Type: Skilled care; ICF; Alzheimer's; Certified Beds: 120; Certified: Medicaid; Medicare; Owner: Nonprofit/Religious org.; License: Current state

MASSACHUSETTS

Abington

Colony House Nursing & Rehabilitation Center
277 Washington St., Abington, MA 02351, (781) 871-0200; Facility Type: Skilled care; ICF; Alzheimer's; Certified Beds: 92; Certified: Medicaid; Medicare; Veterans; Owner: Vencor Inc.; License: Current state

Amherst

Center for Extended Care at Amherst
150 University Dr., Amherst, MA 01002, (413) 256-8185; Facility Type: Skilled care; ICF; Alzheimer's; Certified Beds: 134; Certified: Medicaid; Medicare; Owner: Private; License: Current state

Andover

Academy Manor
89 Morton St., Andover, MA 01810, (978) 475-0944; Facility Type: Skilled care; ICF; Alzheimer's; Certified Beds: 174; Certified: Medicaid; Medicare; Veterans; Owner: Genesis ElderCare; License: Current state

Wingate at Andover Rehab & Skilled Nursing Residence
80 Andover St., Andover, MA 01810, (978) 470-3434; Facility Type: Skilled care; ICF; Alzheimer's; Certified Beds: 135; Certified: Medicaid; Medicare; Owner: For-Profit; License: Current state

Athol

Quabbin Valley Health Care
821 Daniel Shays Hwy., Athol, MA 01331, (978) 249-3717; Facility Type: Skilled care; ICF; Alzheimer's; Certified Beds: 142; Certified: Medicaid; Medicare; Veterans; Owner: Proprietary/Public corp.; License: Current state

Bedford

Carleton-Willard Village Retirement &Nursing Center
100 Old Billerica Rd., Bedford, MA 01730, (781) 275-8700; Facility Type: Skilled care; ICF; Alzheimer's; Certified Beds: 100; Certified: Medicaid; Medicare; Owner: Nonprofit corp.; License: Current state

Boston

Armenian Nursing & Rehabilitation Center
431 Pond St., Boston, MA 02130, (617) 522-2600; Facility Type: Skilled care; ICF; Alzheimer's; Certified Beds: 83; Certified: Medicaid; Medicare; Owner: Nonprofit; License: Current state

Benjamin Health Care Center
120 Fisher Ave., Boston, MA 02120, (617) 825-3905; Facility Type: Skilled care; ICF; ICF/MR; Alzheimer's; Certified Beds: 96; Certified: Medicaid; Medicare; Veterans; Owner: Nonprofit corp.; License: Current state

Don Orione Nursing Home
111 Orient Ave., Boston, MA 02128, (617) 569-2100; Facility Type: Skilled care; ICF; Alzheimer's; Certified Beds: 190; Certified: Medicaid; Medicare; Owner: Nonprofit; Church-related; License: Current state

German Center for Extended Care
2222 Centre St., Boston MA 02132; (617) 325-1230; Facility Type: Skilled care; ICF; Alzheimer's; Certified Beds: 133; Certified: Medicaid; Medicare; Owner: Nonprofit; License: Current state

Marian Manor
130 Dorchester Ave., Boston, MA 02127, (617) 268-3333; Facility Type: Skilled care; ICF; Alzheimer's; Certified Beds: 355; Certified: Medicaid; Medicare; Owner: Nonprofit; License: Current state

Sherrill House, Inc.
135 S. Huntington Ave., Boston, MA 02130, (617)

731-2400; Facility Type: Skilled care; ICF; Alzheimer's; Certified Beds: 196; Certified: Medicaid; Medicare; Owner: Nonprofit; License: Current state

Spaulding Nursing & Therapy Center–North End
70 Fulton St., Boston, MA 02109, (617) 726-9701; Facility Type: Skilled care; ICF; Alzheimer's; Certified Beds: 140; Certified: Medicaid; Medicare; Owner: Nonprofit; License: Current state

Braintree

Braintree Manor Rehabilitation & Nursing Center
1102 Washington St., Braintree, MA 02184, (781) 848-3100; Facility Type: Skilled care; ICF; Alzheimer's; Certified Beds: 177; Certified: Medicaid; Medicare; Veterans; Owner: Proprietary/ Public corp.; License: Current state

Royal Rehabilitation & Nursing Center
95 Commercial St., Braintree, MA 02184, (781) 848-0596; Facility Type: Skilled care; ICF; Alzheimer's; Certified Beds: 204 Certified: Medicaid; Medicare; Veterans; Owner: Private; License: Current state

Brockton

Guardian Center
888 N Main St., Brockton, MA 02301, (508) 587-6556; Facility Type: Skilled care; ICF; Alzheimer's; Certified Beds: care 123; Certified: Medicaid; Owner: Proprietary/Public corp.; License: Current state

Cambridge

Cambridge Rehabilitation & Nursing Center
8 Dana St., Cambridge, MA 02138, (617) 864-4267; Facility Type: Skilled care; ICF; Alzheimer's; Certified Beds: 83; Certified: Medicaid; Medicare; Owner: For-Profit; License: Current state

Sancta Maria Nursing Facility
799 Concord Ave., Cambridge, MA 02138, (617) 868-2200; Facility Type: Skilled care; ICF; Alzheimer's; Certified Beds: 141; Certified: Medicaid; Medicare; Owner: Nonprofit; License: Current state

Chelsea

Chelsea Jewish Nursing Home
17 Lafayette Ave., Chelsea, MA 02150, (617) 884-6766; Facility Type: Skilled care; ICF; Alzheimer's; Certified Beds: 123; Certified: Medicaid; Medicare; Owner: Nonprofit/Religious org.; License: Current state

Eastpointe Nursing Care Center
255 Central Ave., Chelsea, MA 02150, (617) 884-

5700; Facility Type: Skilled care; ICF; Alzheimer's; Certified Beds: 195; Certified: Medicaid; Medicare; Owner: For-Profit; License: Current state

Soldiers' Home in Massachusetts
91 Crest Ave., Chelsea, MA 02150, (617) 884-5660; Facility Type: Skilled care; Alzheimer's; Certified Beds: 88; Certified: Medicaid; Veterans; Owner: Government/State/Local; License: n/a

Danvers

Cedarglen Care & Rehabilitation Center
44 Summer St., Danvers, MA 01923, (978) 774-6955; Facility Type: Skilled care; ICF; Alzheimer's; Certified Beds: 100; Certified: Medicaid; Medicare; Owner: For-Profit; License: Current state

Hunt Nursing & Retirement Center
90 Lindall St., Danvers, MA 01923, (978) 777-3740; Facility Type: Skilled care; ICF; Alzheimer's; Certified Beds: 120; Certified: Medicaid; Medicare; Owner: Nonprofit corp.; License: Current state

Radius Healthcare–Danvers
56 Liberty St. Danvers, MA 01923, (978) 777-2700; Facility Type: Skilled care; ICF; Alzheimer's; Certified Beds: 159; Certified: Medicaid; Medicare; Owner: For-Profit; License: Current state

East Longmeadow

East Longmeadow Skilled Nursing Center
305 Maple St., East Longmeadow, MA 01028, (413) 525-6361; Facility Type: Skilled care; ICF; Alzheimer's; Certified Beds: 119; Certified: Medicaid; Medicare; Owner: Nonprofit corp.; License: Current state

Everett

Everett Nursing & Rehabilitation Center
289 Elm St., Everett, MA 02149, (617) 387-6560; Facility Type: Skilled care; ICF; Alzheimer's; Certified Beds: 183; Certified: Medicaid; Medicare; Veterans; Owner: Nonprofit/Religious org.; License: Current state

Fall River

Catholic Memorial Home
2446 Highland Ave., Fall River, MA 02720, (508) 679-0011; Facility Type: Skilled care; Alzheimer's; Certified Beds: 300; Certified: Medicaid; Medicare; Owner: Nonprofit/Religious org.; License: Current state

Kimwell
495 New Boston Rd., Fall River, MA 02720, (508) 679-0106; Facility Type: Skilled care; ICF; ICF/MR;

Alzheimer's; Certified Beds: 124; Certified: Medicaid; Medicare; Veterans; Owner: Centennial HealthCare Corp.; License: Current state

Falmouth

Falmouth Care & Rehabilitation Center
359 Jones Rd., Falmouth, MA 02540, (508) 457-9000; Facility Type: Skilled care; ICF; Alzheimer's; Certified Beds: 120; Alzheimer's; Certified: Medicaid; Medicare; Owner: Private; License: Current state

JML Care Center, Inc.
184 Ter Heun Dr., Falmouth, MA 02540, (508) 457-4621; Facility Type: Skilled care; Alzheimer's; Certified Beds: 132; Certified: Medicaid; Medicare; Owner: Nonprofit corp. License: Current state

Royal Nursing Center, LLC
545 Main St., Falmouth, MA 02540, (508) 548-3800; Facility Type: Skilled care; ICF; Alzheimer's; Certified Beds: 121; Certified: Medicaid; Owner: Proprietary/Public corp.; License: n/a

Fitchburg

The Highlands
335 Nichols Rd., Fitchburg, MA 01420, (978) 343-4411; Facility Type: Skilled care; ICF; Alzheimer's; Certified Beds: 168; Certified: Medicaid; Medicare; Owner: Nonprofit corp.; License: Current state

Framingham

Carlyle House
342 Winter St., Framingham, MA 01701, (508) 879-6100; Facility Type: Skilled care; Alzheimer's; Certified Beds: 55; Certified: Medicaid; Medicare; Owner: Private; License: Current state

Kathleen Daniel
485 Franklin St., Framingham, MA 01702, (508) 872-8801; Facility Type: Skilled care; ICF; Alzheimer's; Certified Beds: 124; Certified: Medicaid; Medicare; Veterans; Owner: Centennial HealthCare Corp.; License: Current state

Saint Patrick's Manor Inc.
863 Central St., Framingham, MA 01701, (508) 879-8000; Facility Type: Skilled care; ICF; Alzheimer's; Certified Beds: 333; Certified: Medicaid; Medicare; Owner: Nonprofit corp.; License: Current state

Great Barrington

Fairview Commons Nursing & Rehabilitation Center
Christian Rd., Great Barrington, MA 01230, (413) 528-2650; Facility Type: Skilled care; ICF; Alzheimer's; Certified Beds: 71; Certified: Medicaid;

Medicare; Owner: Proprietary/Public corp.; License: Current state

Greenfield

Charlene Manor Extended Care Facility
130 Colrain Rd., Greenfield, MA 01301, (413) 774-3724; Facility Type: Skilled care; ICF; Alzheimer's; Certified Beds: 123; Certified: Medicaid; Medicare; Veterans; Owner: Nonprofit corp.; License: Current state

Harwich

Epoch Senior Healthcare of Harwich
111 Headwaters Dr., Harwich, MA 02645, (508) 430-1717; Facility Type: Skilled care; Alzheimer's; Certified Beds: 135; Certified: Medicaid; Medicare; Veterans; Owner: Private; License: Current state

Haverhill

Baker Katz Nursing Home
194 Boardman St., Haverhill, MA 01830, (978) 373-5697; Facility Type: ICF; Alzheimer's; Certified Beds: 77; Certified: Medicaid; Owner: Proprietary/Public corp; License: Current state

The Oxford
689 Main St., Haverhill, MA 01830, (978) 373-1131; Facility Type: Skilled care; Alzheimer's; Certified Beds: 120; Certified: Medicaid; Medicare; Veterans; Owner: Proprietary/Public corp.; License: Current state

Holyoke

Holyoke Geriatric & Convalescent Center
45 Lower Westfield Rd., Holyoke, MA 01040, (413) 536-8110; Facility Type: Skilled care; ICF; Alzheimer's; Certified Beds: 120; Certified: Medicaid; Medicare; Owner: Nonprofit; License: Current State

Holyoke Rehabilitation Center
260 Easthampton Rd., Holyoke, MA 01040, (413) 538-9733; Facility Type: Skilled care; ICF; Alzheimer's; Certified Beds: 164; Certified: Medicaid; Medicare; Owner: For-Profit; License: Current state

Mount Saint Vincent Nursing Home
35 Holy Family Rd., Holyoke, MA 01040, (413) 532-3246; Facility Type: Skilled care; ICF; Alzheimer's; Certified Beds: 125; Certified: Medicaid; Medicare; Owner: Nonprofit/Religious org.; License: Current state

Lawrence

MI Nursing & Restorative Center
172 Lawrence St., Lawrence, MA 01841, (978) 685-6321; Facility Type: Skilled care; ICF; Alzheimer's;

Certified Beds: 250; Certified: Medicaid; Medicare; Owner: Nonprofit/Religious org.; License: Current state

Wood Mill Care & Rehabilitation Center
800 Essex St., Lawrence, MA 01841, (978) 686-2994; Facility Type: Skilled care; ICF; Alzheimer's; Certified Beds: 94; Certified: Medicaid; Medicare; Veterans; Owner: Private; License: Current state

Lowell

D'Youville Senior Care
981 Varnum Ave., Lowell, MA 01854, (978) 454-5681; Facility Type: Skilled care; Alzheimer's; Certified Beds: 208; Certified: Medicaid; Medicare; Owner: Nonprofit/Religious org.; License: Current state

Fairhaven Healthcare Center
476 Varnum Ave., Lowell, MA 01854, (978) 458-3388; Facility Type: Skilled care; ICF; Alzheimer's; Certified Beds: 169; Certified: Medicaid; Medicare; Owner: For-Profit; License: Current state

Lowell Health Care Center
19 Varnum St., Lowell, MA 01850, (978) 454-5644; Facility Type: Skilled care; ICF; Alzheimer's; Certified Beds: 160; Certified: Medicaid; Medicare; Owner: For-Profit; License: Current state

Wingate at Belvidere Rehabilitation & Skilled Nursing Residence
500 Wentworth Ave., Lowell, MA 01852, (978) 458-1271; Facility Type: Skilled care; ICF; Alzheimer's; Certified Beds: 115; Certified: Medicaid; Medicare; Owner: Proprietary/Public corp.; License: Current state

Malden

Golden LivingCenter–Dexter House
120 Main St., Malden, MA 02148, (781) 324-5600; Facility Type: Skilled care; ICF; ICF/MR; Alzheimer's; Certified Beds: 130; Certified: Medicaid; Medicare; Veterans; Owner: Beverly Enterprises Inc.; License: Current state

Marblehead

Devereux House Nursing Home
39 Lafayette St., Marblehead, MA 01945, (781) 631-6120; Facility Type: Skilled care; ICF; Alzheimer's; Certified Beds: 64; Certified: Medicaid; Medicare; Owner: Proprietary/Public corp.; License: Current state

Milford

Blaire House of Milford
20 Claflin St., Milford, MA 01757, (508) 473-1272;

Facility Type: Skilled care; Alzheimer's Certified Beds: 73; Certified: Medicaid; Medicare; Veterans; Owner: Proprietary/Public corp.; License: Current state

Natick

Mary Ann Morse Nursing & Rehabilitation Center
45 Union St., Natick, MA 01760, (508) 650-9003; Facility Type: Skilled care; Alzheimer's; Certified Beds: 123; Certified: Medicaid; Medicare; Owner: Nonprofit corp.; License: Current state

New Bedford

Brandon Woods of New Bedford
397 County St., New Bedford, MA 02740, (508) 997-9396; Facility Type: Skilled care; Alzheimer's; Certified Beds: 135; Certified: Medicaid; Medicare; Veterans; Owner: Private; License: Current state

Hathaway Manor Extended Care Facility
863 Hathaway Rd., New Bedford, MA 02740, (508) 996-6763; Facility Type: Skilled care; Alzheimer's; Certified Beds: 142; Certified: Medicaid; Medicare; Owner: Proprietary/Public corp.; License: Current state

North Andover

Prescott House Nursing Home
140 Prescott St., North Andover, MA 01845, (978) 685-8086; Facility Type: Skilled care; ICF; Alzheimer's; Certified Beds: 126; Certified: Medicaid; Medicare; Owner: Proprietary/Public corp.; License: Current state

Northampton

Northampton Rehabilitation & Nursing Center
737 Bridge Rd., Northampton, MA 01060, (413) 586-3300; Facility Type: Skilled care; ICF; Alzheimer's; Certified Beds: 166; Certified: Medicaid; Medicare; Veterans; Owner: Proprietary/Public corp.; License: Current state

Norwell

Norwell Knoll Nursing Home
329 Washington St., Norwell, MA 02061, (781) 659-4901; Facility Type: Skilled care; ICF; Alzheimer's; Certified Beds: 86; Certified: Medicaid; Medicare; Veterans; Owner: Proprietary/Public corp.; License: Current state

Norwood

Charlwell House Skilled Nursing Facility
305 Walpole St., Norwood, MA 02062, (781) 762-7700; Facility Type: Skilled care; ICF; Alzheimer's;

Certified Beds: 124; Certified: Medicaid; Medicare; Veterans; Owner: Proprietary/Public corp.; License: Current state

Peabody

Peabody Glen Nursing Center
199 Andover St., Peabody, MA 01960, (978) 531-0772; Facility Type: Skilled care; ICF; Alzheimer's; Certified Beds: 150; Certified: Medicaid; Medicare; Owner: Proprietary/Public corp.; License: Current state

Pittsfield

Hillcress Commons Nursing & Rehabilitation Center
169 Valentine Rd., Pittsfield, MA 01201, (413) 445-2300; Facility Type: Skilled care; Alzheimer's; Certified Beds: 265; Certified: Medicaid; Medicare; Veterans; Owner: Proprietary/ Public corp.; License: Current state

Rockland

Coyne Healthcare Center
56 Webster St., Rockland, MA 02370, (781) 871-0555; Facility Type: Skilled care; Alzheimer's; Certified Beds: 110; Certified: Medicaid; Medicare; Veterans; Owner: Proprietary/Public corp.; License: Current state

Saugus

Saugus Care and Rehabilitation Center
266 Lincoln Ave., Saugus, MA 01906, (781) 233-6830; Facility Type: Skilled care; Alzheimer's; Certified Beds: 80; Certified: Medicaid; Medicare; Owner: Harborside Healthcare; License: Current state

South Dartmouth

Brandon Woods of Dartmouth
567 Dartmouth St., South Dartmouth, MA 02748, (508) 997-7787; Facility Type: Skilled care; ICF; ICF/MR; Alzheimer's; Certified Beds: 118; Certified: Medicaid; Medicare; Veterans; Owner: Proprietary/ Public corp.; License: Current state

South Dennis

Eagle Pond Rehabilitation & Living Center
1 Love Ln., South Dennis, MA 02660, (508) 385-6034; Facility Type: Skilled care; ICF; Alzheimer's; Certified Beds: 128; Certified: Medicare; Owner: Proprietary/Public corp.; License: Current state

Springfield

Park View Rehabilitation & Nursing Center
1400 State St., Springfield, MA 01109, (413) 726-6145;

Facility Type: Skilled care; Alzheimer's; Certified Beds: 172; SNF/ ICF; Certified: Medicaid; Medicare; Owner: Proprietary/Public corp.; License: Current state

Wakefield

Wakefield Care & Rehabilitation Center
One Bathol St., Wakefield, MA 01880, (781) 245-7600; Facility Type: Skilled care; ICF; Alzheimer's; Certified Beds: 145; Certified: Medicaid; Medicare; Owner: Proprietary/Public corp.; License: Current state

Waltham

Meadow Green Nursing & Rehabilitation Center
45 Woburn St., Waltham, MA 02453, (781) 899-8600; Facility Type: Skilled care; Alzheimer's; Certified Beds: 123; Certified: Medicaid; Medicare; Owner: Proprietary/Public corp.; License: Current state

West Newton

Golden LivingCenter–West Newton
25 Armory St., West Newton, MA 02465, (617) 969-2300; Facility Type: Skilled care; ICF; Alzheimer's; Certified Beds: 123; Certified: Medicare; Owner: Nonprofit corp.; License: Current state

West Roxbury

Spaulding Nursing & Therapy Center–West Roxbury
1245 Centre St., West Roxbury, MA 02132, (617) 325-5400; Facility Type: Skilled care; ICF; Alzheimer's; Certified Beds: 81; Certified: Medicare; Owner: Nonprofit corp.; License: Current state

Westborough

Beaumont Rehabilitation & Skilled Nursing Center–Westborough
3 Lyman St., Westborough, MA 01581, (508) 366-9933; Facility Type: Skilled care; ICF; Alzheimer's; Certified Beds: 152; Certified: Medicaid; Medicare; Veterans; Owner: Private; License: Current state

Westford

Westford House
3 Park Dr., Westford, MA 01886, (978) 392-1144; Facility Type: Skilled care; ICF; Alzheimer's; Certified Beds: 123; Certified: Medicaid; Medicare; Veterans; Owner: Private; License: Current state

Williamstown

Sweet Brook Transitional Care & Living Centers
1561 Cold Spring Rd., Williamstown, MA 01267, (413) 458-8127; Facility Type: Skilled care; Alzheimer's; Certified Beds: 184; Alzheimer's; Certified: Medicaid; Medicare; Owner: Proprietary/Public corp.; License: Current state

Worcester

Autumn Village, LLC
25 Oriol Dr., Worcester, MA 01605, (508) 852-3330; Facility Type: Skilled care; ICF; Alzheimer's; Certified Beds: 160; Certified: Medicare; Owner: For-profit corp.; License: Current state

Beaumont at University Campus
378 Plantation St., Worcester, MA 01605, (508) 755-7300; Facility Type: Skilled care; ICF; Alzheimer's; Certified Beds: 164; Certified: Medicaid; Medicare; Owner: Private; License: Current state

Blaire House of Worcester
116 Houghton St., Worcester, MA 01604, (508) 791-5543; Facility Type: Skilled care; ICF; Alzheimer's; Certified Beds: 75; Certified: Medicaid; Medicare; Veterans; Owner: Proprietary/Public corp.; License: Current state

Christopher House of Worcester
10 Mary Scano Dr., Worcester, MA 01605, (508) 754-3800; Facility Type: Skilled care; ICF; Alzheimer's; Certified Beds: 156; Certified: Medicaid, Medicare; Owner: Nonprofit corp.; License: Current state

Jewish Healthcare Center
629 Salisbury St., Worcester, MA 01609, (508) 798-8653; Facility Type: Skilled care; ICF; Alzheimer's; Certified Beds: 141; Certified: Medicaid, Medicare; Owner: Nonprofit corp.; License: Current state

Neuro-Rehab Center Worcester
59 Acton St., Worcester, MA 01604, (508) 791-3147; Facility Type: Skilled care; ICF; Alzheimer's; Certified Beds: 173; Certified: Medicaid, Medicare; Owner: For-profit corp.; License: Current state

Parsons Hill Nursing & Rehabilitation Center
1350 Main St., Worcester, MA 01603, (508) 791-4200; Facility Type: Skilled care; ICF; Alzheimer's; Certified Beds: 162; Certified: Medicaid; Medicare; Owner: Proprietary/Public corp.; License: Current state

Saint Mary Health Care
39 Queen St., Worcester, MA 01610, (508) 753-4791; Facility Type: Skilled care; ICF; Alzheimer's; Certified Beds: 172; Alzheimer's; SNF/ICF; Respite care; Certified: Medicaid; Medicare; Owner: Nonprofit/Religious org.; License: Current state

MICHIGAN

Adrian

Lenawee Medical Care Facility
200 Sand Creek Hwy, Adrian, MI 49221, (517) 263-6794; Facility Type: Skilled care; ICF; Alzheimer's; Certified Beds: 126; Certified: Medicaid, Medicare, Veterans; Owner: Government/county.; License: Current state

Magnum Care of Adrian
130 Sand Creek Hwy., Adrian, MI 49221, (517) 263-6794; Facility Type: Skilled care; ICF; ICF/MR; Alzheimer's; Certified Beds: 120; Certified: Medicaid; Medicare; Veterans; Owner: Proprietary/Public corp.; License: Current state

Provincial House of Adrian
700 Lakeshire Tr., Adrian, MI 49221, (517) 263-0781 Facility Type: Skilled care; ICF; Alzheimer's; Certified Beds: 117; Certified: Medicaid, Medicare; Owner: Nonprofit corp.; License: Current state

Albion

Magnum Care of Albion
1000 W Erie St., Albion, MI 49224, (517) 629-5501; Facility Type: Skilled care; ICF/MR; Alzheimer's; Certified Beds: 80; Certified: Medicaid; Medicare; Owner: Beverly Enterprises Inc.; License: Current state

Alma

Michigan Masonic Home
1200 Wright Ave., Alma, MI 48801, (989) 463-3141; Facility Type: Skilled care; ICF; Alzheimer's; Certified Beds: 204; Certified: Medicaid; Medicare; Owner: Nonprofit corp.; License: Current state

Alpena

Tendercare Alpena
301 Long Rapids Rd., Alpena, MI 49707, (989) 356-2194; Facility Type: Skilled care; ICF; Alzheimer's; Certified Beds: 123; Certified: Medicaid, Medicare; Owner: For-profit corp.; License: Current state

Tendercare Green View
1234 Golf Course Rd., Alpena, MI 49707, (989) 356-1030; Facility Type: Skilled care; ICF; ICF/MR; Alzheimer's; Certified Beds: 56; Certified: Medicaid; Owner: Proprietary/Public corp.; License: Current state

Ann Arbor

Care & Rehabilitation Center at Glacier Hills
1200 Earhart Rd., Ann Arbor, MI 48105, (734) 769-0177; Facility Type: Skilled care; Alzheimer's; Certified Beds: 161; Certified: Medicaid; Medicare; Owner: Nonprofit corp.; License: n/a

Heartland Health Care Center–Ann Arbor
4701 E. Huron Dr., Ann Arbor, MI 48105, (734) 975-2600; Facility Type: Skilled care; ICF; Alzheimer's; Certified Beds: 180; Certified: Medicaid, Medicare; Owner: For-profit corp.; License: Current state

Whitehall Healthcare Center of Ann Arbor
3370 Morgan Rd., Ann Arbor, MI 48108, (734) 971-3230; Facility Type: Skilled care; ICF; Alzheimer's; Certified Beds: 102; Certified: Medicaid; Medicare; Owner: Centennial HealthCare Corp.; License: Current state

Bad Axe

Huron County Medical Care Facility
1116 S Van Dyke Rd., Bad Axe, MI 48413, (989) 269-6425; Facility Type: Skilled care; ICF; Alzheimer's; Certified Beds: 112; Certified: Medicaid; Medicare; Veterans; Owner: Government/State/Local; License: Current state

Battle Creek

Calhoun County Medical Care Facility
1150 E. Michigan Ave., Battle Creek, MI 49014, (269) 962-5458; Facility Type: Skilled care; ICF; Alzheimer's; Certified Beds: 120; Certified: Medicaid, Medicare; Veterans Owner: Government/county.; License: Current state

The Laurels of Bedford
270 N Bedford Rd., Battle Creek, MI 49017, (269) 968-2296; Facility Type: Skilled care; ICF; Alzheimer's; Certified Beds: 123; Certified: Medicaid; Medicare; Owner: Private; License: Current state

Manor of Battle Creek Nursing & Rehabilitation Center
675 Wagner Dr., Battle Creek, MI 49017, (616) 969-6244; Facility Type: Skilled care; ICF; Alzheimer's; Certified Beds: 99; Certified: Medicaid; Medicare; Veterans; Owner: Tendercare Inc.; License: Current state

Bloomfield Hills

Heartland Health Care Center–Georgian Bloomfield
2975 N Adams Rd., Bloomfield Hills, MI 48304, (248) 645-2900; Facility Type: Skilled care; ICF; ICF/MR; Alzheimer's; Certified Beds: 199; Certified: Medicare; License: n/a

Woodward Hills Nursing Center
39312 Woodward, Bloomfield Hills, MI 48304, (248) 644-5522; Facility Type: Skilled care; ICF; Alzheimer's; Certified Beds: 190; Certified: Medicaid, Medicare; Owner: For-profit corp.; License: Current state

Charlotte

Eaton County Medical Care Facility
530 W Beech St., Charlotte, MI 48813, (517) 543-2940; Facility Type: Skilled care; ICF; ICF/MR; Alzheimer's; Certified Beds: 142; Certified: Medicaid; Medicare; Owner: Government/State/Local; License: Current state

Cheboygan

Cheboygan Memorial Hospital LTCU
748 S. Main St., Cheboygan, MI 49721, (231) 627-5601; Facility Type: Skilled care; ICF; Alzheimer's; Located within a Hospital; Certified Beds: 50; Certified: Medicaid, Medicare; Owner: For-profit corp.; License: Current state

Tendercare Health Center of Cheboygan
824 S Huron St., Cheboygan, MI 49721, (231) 627-4347; Facility Type: Skilled care; ICF; Alzheimer's; Beds: Alzheimer's 42; SNF/ICF 70; Certified: Medicaid; Medicare; Veterans; Owner: For Profit corp.; License: Current state

Chelsea

Chelsea Retirement Community
805 W Middle St., Chelsea, MI 48118, (734) 475-8633; Facility Type: Skilled care; ICF; Alzheimer's; Certified Beds: 85; Certified: Medicaid; Medicare; Owner: Nonprofit corp.; License: Current state

Clawson

Cambridge North Health Care Center
535 N Main St., Clawson, MI 48017, (248) 435-5200; Facility Type: Skilled care; ICF; Alzheimer's; Certified Beds: 120; Certified: Medicaid; Medicare; Owner: Mariner Post Acute Network; License: Current state

Crystal Falls

Iron County Medical Care Facility
1523 W U.S. Highway 2, Crystal Falls, MI 49920, (906) 875-6671; Facility Type: Skilled care; ICF; Alzheimer's; Certified Beds: 200; Certified: Medicaid; Medicare; Veterans; Owner: Government/County; License: Current state

Detroit

Alpha Manor Nursing Home
722 E Grand Blvd., Detroit, MI 48207, (313) 923-

8080; Facility Type: ICF; Alzheimer's; Certified Beds: 80; Certified: Medicaid; Owner: Proprietary/Public corp.; License: Current state

Ambassador Nursing & Rehabilitation Center
8045 E. Jefferson Ave., Detroit, MI 48214, (313) 821-3525; Facility Type: Skilled care; ICF; Alzheimer's; Beds: Alzheimer's 176; SNF/ICF 70; Certified: Medicaid; Medicare; Veterans; Owner: For Profit corp.; License: Current state

Americare Convalescent Center of Detroit
19211 Anglin Rd., Detroit, MI 48234, (313) 893-9745; Facility Type: Skilled care; ICF; ICF/MR; Alzheimer's; Certified Beds: 133; Certified: Medicaid; Medicare; Owner: Private; License: Current state

Boulevard Temple Care Center, LLC
2567 W. Grand Blvd., Detroit, MI 48208, (313) 895-5340; Facility Type: Skilled care; ICF; Alzheimer's; Certified Beds: 124; Certified: Medicaid, Medicare; Owner: For-profit corp.; License: Current state

Elmwood Geriatric Village
1881 E. Grand Blvd., Detroit, MI 48211, (313) 922-1600; Facility Type: Skilled care; ICF; Alzheimer's; Certified Beds: 120; Certified: Medicaid, Medicare; Owner: For-profit corp.; License: Current state

Fairlane Senior Care & Rehabilitation Center
15750 Joy Rd., Detroit, MI 48228, (313) 273-6850; Facility Type: Skilled care; ICF; Alzheimer's; Certified Beds: 229; Certified: Medicaid; Medicare; Owner: Proprietary/Public corp.; License: Current state

Hartford Nursing & Rehabilitation Center
6700 W Outer Dr., Detroit MI 48235, (313) 836-1700; Facility Type: Skilled care; ICF; Alzheimer's; Certified Beds: 140; Certified: Medicaid, Medicare; Owner: For-profit corp.; License: Current state

Lakeshore Healthcare Skilled Nursing & Specialty Care
9146 Woodward, Detroit, MI 48202, (313) 875-1263; Facility Type: Skilled care; ICF; ICF/MR; Alzheimer's; Certified Beds: 110; Certified: Medicaid; Medicare; Owner: Private; License: Current state

Manor of Northwest Detroit Skilled Nursing & Rehabilitation
16181 Hubbell St., Detroit, MI 48235, (313) 273-8764; Facility Type: Skilled care; ICF; Alzheimer's; Certified Beds: 154; Certified: Medicaid, Medicare; Owner: For-profit corp.; License: Current state

New Light Nursing Home
9500 Grand River Ave., Detroit, MI 48204, (313) 491-7920; Facility Type: Skilled care; ICF; Alzheimer's; Certified Beds: 150; Certified: Medicaid, Medicare; Owner: Nonprofit, Church-related; License: Current state

Redford Geriatric Village
22811 W Seven Mile Rd., Detroit, MI 48219, (313)

534-1440; Facility Type: Skilled care; ICF; ICF/MR; Alzheimer's; Certified Beds: 106; Certified: Medicaid; Medicare; Owner: Private; License: n/a

Saint Francis Nursing Center
1533 Cadillac Blvd., Detroit, MI 48214, (313) 823-0435; Facility Type: Skilled care; Alzheimer's; Certified Beds: 81; Certified: Medicaid; Medicare; Owner: Private; License: Current state

St. John Senior Community
18300 E Warren Dr., Detroit, MI 48224, (313) 343-8000; Facility Type: Skilled care; ICF; Alzheimer's; Certified Beds: 180; Certified: Medicaid; Medicare; Owner: Non Profit corp.; License: Current state

Westwood Nursing Center
16588 Schaefer Detroit, MI 48235, (313) 345-5000; Facility Type: Skilled care; Alzheimer's; Certified Beds: 130; Certified: Medicaid; Medicare; Owner: Proprietary/Public corp.; License: Current state

East Lansing

Burcham Hills Retirement Center II
2700 Burcham Dr., East Lansing, MI 48823, (517) 351-8377; Facility Type: Skilled care; ICF; ICF/MR; Alzheimer's; Certified Beds: 133; Certified: Medicaid; Medicare; Owner: Nonprofit corp.; License: Current state

East Lansing Health Care Center
2815 Northwind Dr., East Lansing, MI 48823, (517) 332-0817; Facility Type: Skilled care; Alzheimer's; Certified Beds: 113; Certified: Medicaid; Medicare; Owner: Private, For-Profit; License: Current state

Whitehills Health Care Center
1843 N. Hagadorn Rd., East Lansing, MI 48823, (517) 332-5061; Facility Type: Skilled care; Alzheimer's; Certified Beds: 103; Certified: Medicaid; Medicare; Owner: Private corp.; License: Current state

Escanaba

Christian Park Village
2525 7th Ave. S, Escanaba, MI 49829, (906) 786-0408; Facility Type: Skilled care; Alzheimer's; Certified Beds: 59; Certified: Medicaid; Medicare; Owner: Proprietary/Public corp.; License: Current state

Farmington Hills

The Manor of Farmington Hills
21017 Middlebelt Rd., Farmington Hills, MI 48336, (248) 476-8300; Facility Type: Skilled care; ICF; Alzheimer's; Certified Beds: 106; Certified: Medicaid; Medicare; Owner: Centennial HealthCare Corp.; License: Current state

Flint

Heartland Health Care Center at Briarwood
3011 N Center Rd., Flint, MI 48506, (810) 736-0600;

Facility Type: Skilled care; Alzheimer's; Certified Beds: 106; Certified: Medicaid; Medicare; Owner: HCR ManorCare; License: Current state

Heritage Manor Healthcare Center
G-3201 Beecher Rd., Flint, MI 48532, (810) 732-9200; Facility Type: Skilled care; ICF/MR; Alzheimer's; Certified Beds: 180; Certified: Medicaid; Medicare; Owner: Mariner Post Acute Network; License: Current state

Frankfort

Maples Benzie Co Medical Center
210 Maple St., Frankfort, MI 49635, (231) 352-9674; Facility Type: Skilled care; Alzheimer's; Certified Beds: 62; Certified: Medicaid; Medicare; Veterans; Owner: Government/county; License: Current state

Paul Oliver Memorial Hospital–Long Term Care Unit
224 Park Ave., Frankfort, MI 49635, (231) 352-2200; Facility Type: Skilled care; Alzheimer's; Certified Beds: 39; Certified: Medicaid; Medicare; Owner: Nonprofit corp.; License: Current state

Fremont

Transitional Health Services of Fremont
4554 W 48th St., Fremont, MI 49412, (231) 924-3990; Facility Type: Skilled care; ICF; Alzheimer's; Certified Beds: 129; Certified: Medicaid; Medicare; Owner: Private; License: Current state

Grand Rapids

Christian Rest Home Association
1000 Edison Ave. NW, Grand Rapids, MI 49504, (616) 453-2475; Facility Type: Skilled care; ICF; Alzheimer's; Certified Beds: 149; Certified: Medicaid; Medicare; Owner: Nonprofit, Church-related; License: Current state

Clark Retirement Community
1551 Franklin Street, SE, Grand Rapids, MI 49506, (616) 452-1568; Facility Type: Skilled care; ICF; Alzheimer's; Certified Beds: 111; Certified: Medicaid; Medicare; Owner: Nonprofit; License: Current state

Heartland Health Care Center–Grand Rapids
2320 E Beltline SE, Grand Rapids, MI 49546, (616) 949-3000; Facility Type: Skilled care; ICF; ICF/MR; Alzheimer's; Certified Beds: 198; Certified: Medicaid; Medicare; Owner: HCR ManorCare; License: Current state

Holland Home–Fulton Manor
1450 E Fulton Ave., Grand Rapids, MI 49503, (616) 643-2600; Facility Type: Skilled care; Alzheimer's; Certified Beds: 82; Certified: Medicaid; Medicare; Owner: Nonprofit corp.; License: Current state

Michigan Christian Home
1845 Boston Blvd. S.E., Grand Rapids MI 49506, (616) 245-9179; Facility Type: Skilled care; ICF; Alzheimer's; Certified Beds: 29; Certified: Medicaid; Medicare; Owner: Nonprofit; License: Current state

Pilgrim Manor
2000 Leonard N.E., Grand Rapids, MI 49505, (616) 458-1133; Facility Type: Skilled care; ICF; Alzheimer's; Certified Beds: 55; Certified: Medicaid; Medicare; Owner: Nonprofit; Church-related; License: Current state

Porter Hills Health Center
3600 E Fulton St., Grand Rapids, MI 49506, (616) 949-4971; Facility Type: Skilled care; ICF; Alzheimer's; Certified Beds: 81; Certified: Medicaid; Medicare; Owner: Nonprofit/Religious org.; License: Current state

Sanctuary at St. Mary's
1050 Four Mile N.W., Grand Rapids, MI 49504, (616) 784-0646; Facility Type: Skilled care; ICF; Alzheimer's; Certified Beds: 187; Certified: Medicaid; Medicare; Owner: Nonprofit; License: Current state

Spectrum Health, Nursing & Rehab Center–Fuller Avenue
750 Fuller Ave, NE MC 160, Grand Rapids, MI 49503, (616) 486-2411; Facility Type: Skilled care; ICF; Alzheimer's; Certified Beds: 278; Certified: Medicaid; Medicare; Owner: Nonprofit; License: Current state

Holland

Heartland of Holland
493 W 32nd St., Holland, MI 49423, (616) 396-1438; Facility Type: Skilled care; ICF; ICF/MR; Alzheimer's; Certified Beds: 103; Certified: Medicaid; Medicare; Owner: HCR ManorCare; License: Current state

The Inn at Freedom Village
145 Columbia Ave., Holland, MI 49423, (616) 820-7679; Facility Type: Skilled care; ICF; Alzheimer's; Certified Beds: 39; Certified: Medicare; Owner: n/a License: Current state

Howell

Howell Care Center
3003 W Grand River Ave., Howell, MI 48843, (517) 546-4210; Facility Type: Skilled care; ICF; ICF/MR; Alzheimer's; Certified Beds: 149; Certified: Medicaid; Medicare; Owner: Integrated Health Services Inc.; License: Current state

Ishpeming

Marquette County Medical Care Facility
200 Saginaw, Ishpeming, MI 49849, (906) 485-1061;

Facility Type: Skilled care; Alzheimer's; Certified Beds: 140; Certified: Medicaid; Medicare; Owner: Government/State/Local; License: Current state

Jackson

Faith Haven Senior Care Center
6531 W Michigan Ave., Jackson, MI 49201, (517) 750-3822; Facility Type: Skilled care; ICF; ICF/MR; Alzheimer's; Certified Beds: 83; Certified: Medicaid; Medicare; Owner: For-profit; License: Current state

Kalamazoo

Alamo Nursing Home, Inc.
8290 W. C Ave., Kalamazoo, MI 49009, (269) 343-2587; Facility Type: Skilled care; ICF; Alzheimer's; Certified Beds: 100; Certified: Medicaid; Medicare; Owner: For profit; License: Current state

Borgess Gardens
3057 Gull Rd Kalamazoo, MI 49048, (269) 382-2392; Facility Type: Skilled care; ICF; Alzheimer's; Certified Beds: 121; Certified: Medicaid; Medicare; Owner: Nonprofit; License: Current state

Harold and Grace Upjohn Community
2400 Portage St., Kalamazoo, MI 49001, (269) 381-4290; Facility Type: Skilled care; ICF; Alzheimer's; Certified Beds: 118; Certified: Medicaid; Medicare; Owner: Nonprofit; License: Current state

Heartland Health Care Center–Kalamazoo
3625 W Michigan Ave., Kalamazoo, MI 49006, (269) 375-4550; Facility Type: Skilled care; ICF; ICF/MR; Alzheimer's; Certified Beds: 172; Certified: Medicaid; Medicare; Owner: HCR ManorCare; License: Current state

Tendercare Kalamazoo
1701 S 11th St. Kalamazoo, MI 49009, (269) 375-2020; Facility Type: Skilled care; ICF; Alzheimer's; Certified Beds: 117; Certified: Medicaid; Medicare; Owner: For profit; License: Current state

Tendercare of Westwood
2575 N Drake Rd. Kalamazoo, MI 49007, (269) 342-0206; Facility Type: Skilled care; ICF; Alzheimer's; Certified Beds: 117; Certified: Medicaid; Medicare; Owner: For profit; License: Current state

Lansing

The Pines Healthcare Center
707 Armstrong, Lansing, MI 48911, (517) 393-5680; Facility Type: Skilled care; ICF; Alzheimer's; Certified Beds: 145; Certified: Medicaid; Medicare; Owner: For profit; License: Current state

Tendercare West
731 Starkweather Dr., Lansing, MI 48917, (517) 323-

9133; Facility Type: Skilled care; ICF; Alzheimer's; Certified Beds: 117; Certified: Medicaid; Medicare; Owner: For profit; License: Current state

Livonia

Autumnwood of Livonia
14900 Middlebelt Rd., Livonia, MI 48154, (734) 425-4200; Facility Type: Skilled care; ICF; Alzheimer's; Certified Beds: 142; Certified: Medicaid; Medicare; Owner: Proprietary/Public corp.; License: Current state

Camelot Hall Convalescent Center
35100 Ann Arbor Trail, Livonia, MI 48150, (734) 522-1444; Facility Type: Skilled care; Alzheimer's; Certified Beds: 142; Certified: Medicaid; Medicare; Veterans; Owner: For-profit; License: Current state

Heartland Health Care Center–University
28550 Five Mile Rd., Livonia, MI 48154, (734) 427-8270; Facility Type: Skilled care; Alzheimer's; Certified Beds: 172; Certified: Medicaid; Medicare; Owner: HCR ManorCare; License: n/a

Midland

Britanny Manor
3615 E Ashman St., Midland MI 48640, (989) 631-0460; Facility Type: Skilled care; ICF; Alzheimer's; Certified Beds: 153; Certified: Medicaid; Medicare; Owner: For profit; License: Current state

Midmichigan Stratford Village
2121 Rockwell Dr., Midland, MI 48642, (989) 633-5350; Facility Type: Skilled care; ICF; Alzheimer's; Certified Beds: 80; Certified: Medicaid; Medicare; Owner: Nonprofit; License: Current state

Tendercare Midland
4900 Hedgewood Dr., Midland, MI 48640, (989) 631-9670; Facility Type: Skilled care; ICF; Alzheimer's; Certified Beds: 120; Certified: Medicaid; Medicare; Owner: For profit; License: Current state

Monroe

Lutheran Home–Monroe
1236 S Monroe St., Monroe, MI 48161, (734) 241-9533; Facility Type: Skilled care; ICF; Alzheimer's; Certified Beds: 102; Certified: Medicaid; Medicare; Owner: For-profit corp.; License: Current state

Mount Clemens

Martha T. Berry Medical Care Facility
43533 Elizabeth Rd. Mount Clemens, MI 48043, (586) 469-5265; Facility Type: Skilled care; ICF; Alzheimer's; Certified Beds: 217; Certified: Medicaid; Medicare; Veterans Owner: Government/county; License: Current state

Mount Pleasant

Isabella County Medical Care Facility
1222 North Dr., Mount Pleasant, MI 48858, (989) 772-2957; Facility Type: Skilled care; ICF; ICF/MR; Alzheimer's; Certified Beds: 100; Certified: Medicaid; Medicare; Owner: Government/State/Local; License: Current state

The Laurels of Mt. Pleasant
400 S Crapo St., Mount Pleasant, MI 48858, (989) 773-5918; Facility Type: Skilled care; ICF; Alzheimer's; Certified Beds: 112; Certified: Medicaid; Medicare; Veterans; Owner: Proprietary/Public corp.; License: Current state

Muskegon

Brookhaven Medical Care Facility
1890 Apple Ave. Muskegon, MI 49442, (231) 724-3500; Facility Type: Skilled care; ICF; Alzheimer's; Certified Beds: 205; Certified: Medicaid; Medicare; Veterans; Owner: Government/county; License: Current state

Heartland Health Care Center–Knollview
1061 W Hackley, Muskegon, MI 49441, (231) 755-2255; Facility Type: Skilled care; ICF; Alzheimer's; Certified Beds: 107; Certified: Medicaid; Medicare; Owner: For profit; License: Current state

Sanctuary at McAuley
1380 E Sherman Blvd., Muskegon, MI 49444, (231) 672-2578; Facility Type: Skilled care; ICF; ICF/MR; Alzheimer's; Beds: Skilled care 50; Alzheimer's 48; Certified: Medicaid; Medicare; Owner: Nonprofit/Religious org.; License: Current state

Sanctuary at the Park
570 S Harvey St., Muskegon, MI 49442, (231) 672-2202; Facility Type: Skilled care; ICF; Alzheimer's; Certified Beds: 99; Certified: Medicaid; Medicare; Owner: Nonprofit; License: Current state

Pontiac

Golden Oaks Medical Care Facility
1200 N Telegraph Rd., Bldg. 32 East, Pontiac, MI 48341, (248) 858-1415; Facility Type: Skilled care; ICF; Alzheimer's; Certified Beds: 120; Certified: Medicaid; Medicare; Veterans; Owner: Government/county; License: Current state

Powers

Pinecrest Medical Care Facility
15995 Main St., Powers, MI 49874, (906) 497-5244; Facility Type: Skilled care; ICF; Alzheimer's; Certified Beds: 160; Certified: Medicaid; Medicare; Veterans; Owner: Government/State/Local; License: Current state

Riverview

Rivergate Terrace
14141 Pennsylvania, Riverview, MI 48193, (734) 284-8000; Facility Type: Skilled care; ICF; Alzheimer's; Certified Beds: 290; Certified: Medicaid; Medicare; Owner: For-profit corp.; License: Current state

Saginaw

Healthsource Saginaw, Inc
3340 Hospital Rd., Saginaw, MI 48608, (989) 790-7700; Facility Type: Skilled care; ICF; Alzheimer's; Certified Beds: 213; Certified: Medicaid; Medicare; Owner: Nonprofit; License: Current state

Heartland Health Care Center–Saginaw
2901 Galaxy Dr., Saginaw, MI 48601, (989) 777-5110; Facility Type: Skilled care; Alzheimer's; Certified Beds: 103; Certified: Medicaid; Medicare; Owner: HCR ManorCare; License: n/a

Hoyt Nursing & Rehab Centre
1202 Weiss St., Saginaw, MI 48602, (989) 754-1419; Facility Type: Skilled care; ICF; Alzheimer's; Certified Beds: 128; Certified: Medicaid; Medicare; Owner: For profit; License: Current state

Luther Manor Nursing Home
3161 Davenport St. Saginaw, MI 48602, (989) 799-1902; Facility Type: Skilled care; ICF; Alzheimer's; Certified Beds: 98; Certified: Medicaid; Medicare; Owner: Nonprofit, Church-related; License: Current state

St. Francis Home
915 N River Rd., Saginaw, MI 48603, (989) 781-3150; Facility Type: Skilled care; ICF; Alzheimer's; Certified Beds: 100; Certified: Medicaid; Medicare; Owner: Nonprofit; License: Current state

Saint Clair Shores

Saint Mary's Nursing & Rehabilitation Center
22601 E Nine Mile Rd., Saint Clair Shores, MI 48080, (586) 772-4300; Facility Type: Skilled care; ICF; Alzheimer's; Certified Beds: 107; Certified: Medicaid; Medicare; Owner: For-profit corp.; License: n/a

Saint Johns

Hazel I. Findlay Country Manor
1101 S Scott Rd., Saint Johns, MI 48879, (989) 224-8936; Facility Type: ICF; Alzheimer's; Certified Beds: 157; Alzheimer's; Assisted living 22; Certified: Medicaid; Owner: Nonprofit corp.; License: Current state

Southfield

Evergreen Health & Living Center
19933 W. Thirteen Mile Rd., Southfield, MI 48076,

(248) 203-9000; Facility Type: Skilled care; ICF; Alzheimer's; Certified Beds: 151; Certified: Medicaid; Medicare; Owner: For profit; License: Current state

Lahser Hills Care Centre
25300 Lahser Rd., Southfield, MI 48034, (248) 354-3222; Facility Type: Skilled care; ICF; Alzheimer's; Certified Beds: 143; Certified: Medicaid; Medicare; Owner: For profit; License: Current state

Medilodge of Southfield, Inc.
26715 Greenfield Rd., Southfield, MI 48076, (248) 557-0050; Facility Type: Skilled care; ICF; Alzheimer's; Certified Beds: 220; Certified: Medicaid; Medicare; Owner: Nonprofit; License: Current state

Tawas City

Iosco County Medical Care Facility
1201 Harris Ave., Tawas City, MI 48763, (989) 362-4424; Facility Type: Skilled care; Alzheimer's; Certified Beds: 83; Certified: Medicaid; Medicare; Owner: Government/State/Local; License: Current state

Taylor

Medilodge of Taylor, Inc.
23600 Northline Rd., Taylor, MI 48180, (734) 287-8580; Facility Type: Skilled care; Alzheimer's; Certified Beds: 142; Certified: Medicaid; Medicare; Owner: Private; License: Current state

Traverse City

Grand Traverse Pavilions
1000 Pavilions Cr., Traverse City, MI 49684, (231) 932-3163; Facility Type: Skilled care; Alzheimer's; Certified Beds: 221 Certified: Medicaid; Medicare; Owner: Government/State/Local; License: Current state

Tendercare Health Center–Birchwood
2950 Lafranier Rd., Traverse City, MI 49686, (231) 947-0506; Facility Type: Skilled care; ICF; ICF/MR; Alzheimer's; Certified Beds: 135; Certified: Medicaid; Medicare; Veterans; Owner: Tendercare Inc.; License: Current state

Warren

Warren Woods Health & Rehabilitation Center
11535 E Ten Mile Rd., Warren, MI 48089, (586) 759-0700; Facility Type: Skilled care; ICF; ICF/MR; Alzheimer's; Certified Beds: 185; Certified: Medicaid; Medicare; Owner: For-profit corp.; License: Current state

Wayne

Manor of Wayne; Skilled Nursing & Rehabilitation
4429 Venoy Rd., Wayne, MI 48184, (734) 326-6424; Facility Type: Skilled care; ICF; ICF/MR; Alzheimer's; Certified Beds: 99; Certified: Medicaid; Owner: Proprietary/Public corp.; License: Current state

Transitional Health Services of Wayne
34330 Van Born Rd., Wayne, MI 48184, (734) 721-0740; Facility Type: Skilled care; ICF; Alzheimer's; Certified Beds: 49; Certified: Medicaid; Medicare; Owner: Proprietary/Public corp.; License: Current state

Westland

Hope Healthcare Center
38410 Cherry Hill Rd., Westland, MI 48185, (734) 326-1200; Facility Type: Skilled care; ICF; Alzheimer's; Certified Beds: 142; Certified: Medicaid; Medicare; Veterans; Owner: Mariner Post Acute Network; License: Current state

Woodhaven

Applewood Nursing Center, Inc.
18500 Vanhorn Rd., Woodhaven, MI 48183, (734) 676-7575; Facility Type: Skilled care; ICF/MR; Alzheimer's; Certified Beds 150; Certified: Medicaid; Medicare; Owner: Proprietary/Public corp.; License: Current state

Zeeland

Providence Christian Healthcare & Rehabilitation Center
285 N State St., Zeeland, MI 49464, (616) 772-4641; Facility Type: Skilled care; Alzheimer's; Certified Beds: 153; Certified: Medicaid; Medicare; Owner: Nonprofit/Religious org.; License: Current state

MINNESOTA

Alexandria

Bethany Home Inc.
1020 Lark St., Alexandria, MN 56398, (320) 762-1567; Facility Type: Skilled care; Alzheimer's; Certified Beds: 92; Certified: Medicaid; Medicare; Veterans; Owner: Nonprofit corp.; License: Current state

Baudette

Lakewood Care Center
600 Maine Avenue South, Baudette, MN 56623, (218) 634-3488; Facility Type: Skilled care; ICF; Alzheimer's; Certified Beds: 44; Certified: Medicaid; Medicare; Owner: Nonprofit/Religious org.; License: Current state

Belle Plaine

The Lutheran Home
611 W Main St., Belle Plaine, MN 56011, (952) 873-2215; Facility Type: Skilled care; ICF; ICF/ MR; Alzheimer's; Certified Beds: 97; Certified: Medicaid; Medicare; Veterans; Owner: The Lutheran Home Association; License: Current state

Bloomington

Martin Luther Care Center
1401 E 100th St., Bloomington, MN 55425, (952) 888-7751; Facility Type: Skilled care; Alzheimer's; Certified Beds: 137; Certified: Medicaid; Medicare; Owner: Nonprofit corp.; License: Current state

Canby

Sylvan Court
112 St. Olaf Ave. S, Canby, MN 56620, (507) 223-7277; Facility Type: Skilled care; Alzheimer's; Certified Beds: 75; Certified: Medicaid; Medicare; Veterans; Owner: Nonprofit corp.; License: Current state

Cannon Falls

Angels Care Center
300 N Dow St., Cannon Falls, MN 55009, (507) 263-4658; Facility Type: Skilled care; ICF/MR; Alzheimer's; Certified Beds: 89; Certified: Medicaid; Medicare; Veterans; Owner: Nonprofit/Religious org.; License: Current state

Chaska

Auburn Manor
501 Oak St., Chaska, MN 55318, (952) 448-9303; Facility Type: Skilled care; Alzheimer's; Certified Beds: 63; Assisted living; Certified: Medicaid; Medicare; Owner: Nonprofit/Religious org.; License: Current state

Crystal

Crystal Care Center
3245 Vera Cruz Ave. N, Crystal, MN 55422, (763) 535-6260; Facility Type: Skilled care; Alzheimer's; Certified Beds: 138; Certified: Medicaid; Medicare; Veterans; Owner: Nonprofit/Religious org.; License: Current state

Detroit Lakes

Emmanuel Nursing Home
1415 Madison Ave., Detroit Lakes, MN 56501, (218) 847-4486; Facility Type: Skilled care; Alzheimer's; Certified Beds: 130; Certified: Medicaid; Medicare; Veterans; Owner: Nonprofit corp.; License: Current state

Duluth

Bayshore Health Center
1601 St. Louis Ave., Duluth, MN 55802, (218) 727-8651; Facility Type: Skilled care; Alzheimer's; Certified Beds: 160; Certified: Medicaid; Medicare; Owner: Proprietary/Public corp.; License: Current state

Faribault

Saint Lucas Care Center
500 SE 1st St., Faribault, MN 55021, (507) 332-5100; Facility Type: Skilled care; Alzheimer's; Certified Beds: 109; Certified: Medicaid; Medicare; Owner: Nonprofit corp.; License: Current state

Fergus Falls

Pioneer Care Center
1006 S Sheridan St., Fergus Falls, MN 56537, (218) 739-7700; Facility Type: Skilled care; Alzheimer's; Certified Beds: 105; Certified: Medicaid; Medicare; Owner: Nonprofit corp.; License: Current state

Frazee

Frazee Care Center
311 W Maple Ave., Frazee, MN 56544, (218) 334-4501; Facility Type: Skilled care; Alzheimer's; Certified Beds: 84 Certified: Medicaid; Medicare; Veterans; Owner: Proprietary/ Public corp.; License: Current state

Golden Valley

Trevilla of Golden Valley
7505 Country Club Dr., Golden Valley, MN 55427,

(763) 545-0416; Facility Type: Skilled care; ICF; Alzheimer's; Certified Beds: 175; Certified: Medicaid; Medicare; Owner: ExtendiCare Health Services Inc.; License: n/a

Grand Rapids

Grand Village
923 Hale Lake Point, Grand Rapids, MN 55744, (218) 326-0543; Facility Type: Skilled care; Alzheimer's; Certified Beds: 133; Certified: Medicaid; Medicare; Owner: Government/State/ Local; License: Current state

Hopkins

Augastana Chapel View Care Center
615 Minnetonka Mills Rd., Hopkins, MN 55343, (952) 938-2761; Facility Type: Skilled care; ICF; ICF/MR; Alzheimer's; Certified Beds: 118; Certified: Medicaid; Medicare; Owner: Nonprofit corp.; License: Current state

Golden LivingCenter–Hopkins
725 Second Ave. South, Hopkins, MN 55343, (952) 935-3338; Facility Type: Skilled care; ICF; ICF/MR; Alzheimer's; Certified Beds: 138; Certified: Medicaid; Medicare; Owner: For-profit corp.; License: Current state

Janesville

Janesville Nursing Home
102 E North St., Janesville, MN 56048, (507) 231-5113; Facility Type: Skilled care; Alzheimer's; Certified Beds: 45; Certified: Medicaid; Medicare; Owner: Government/State/Local; License: Current state

Le Sueur

Minnesota Valley Health Center
621 S 4th St., Le Sueur, MN 56058, (507) 665-3375; Facility Type: Skilled care; Alzheimer's; Certified Beds: 80; Certified: Medicaid; Medicare; Owner: Nonprofit corp.; License: Current state

McIntosh

McIntosh Manor
600 NE Riverside Ave., McIntosh, MN 56556, (218) 563-2715; Facility Type: Skilled care; Alzheimer's; Certified Beds: 45; Certified: Medicaid; Medicare; Veterans; Owner: Proprietary/ Public corp.; License: Current state

Melrose

Centracare Health System–Melrose Pine Villa CC
525 W. Main St., Melrose, MN 56352, (320) 256-4231; Facility Type: Skilled care; ICF; ICF/MR; Alzheimer's; Certified Beds: 75; Certified: Medicaid; Medicare; Owner: Nonprofit; License: Current state

Minneapolis

Andrew Residence
1215 S. 9th St. Minneapolis, MN 55404, (612) 333-0111; Facility Type: Skilled care; ICF; ICF/MR; Alzheimer's; Certified Beds: 212; Certified: Medicaid; Medicare; Owner: For profit corp.; License: Current state

Augustana Health Care Center of Minneapolis
1007 E 14th St., Minneapolis, MN 55404, (612) 238-5101; Facility Type: Skilled care; Alzheimer's; Certified Beds: 289; Geriatric behavioral; Certified: Medicaid; Medicare; Owner: Nonprofit/Religious org.; License: Current state

Benedictine Health Center of Minneapolis
618 E. 17th St. Minneapolis, MN 55404, (612) 879-2800; Facility Type: Skilled care; ICF; ICF/MR; Alzheimer's; Certified Beds: 110; Certified: Medicaid; Medicare; Owner: Nonprofit corp.; License: Current state

Bryn Mawr Healthcare Center
275 Penn Ave. N., Minneapolis, MN 55405, (612) 377-4723; Facility Type: Skilled care; ICF; ICF/MR; Alzheimer's; Certified Beds: 112; Certified: Medicaid; Medicare; Owner: For profit corp.; License: Current state

Catholic Eldercare on Main
817 Main St, NE, Minneapolis, MN 55413, (612) 379-1370; Facility Type: Skilled care; ICF; ICF/MR; Alzheimer's; Certified Beds: 150; Certified: Medicaid; Medicare; Owner: For-profit corp.; License: Current state

Good Samaritan Society–University Specialty Care
22 27th Ave. SE, Minneapolis, MN 55414, (612) 332-4262; Facility Type: Skilled care; Alzheimer's; Certified Beds: 194; Certified: Medicaid; Medicare; Veterans; Owner: The Evangelical Lutheran Good Samaritan Society; License: Current state

Mount Olivet Careview Home
5517 Lyndale Ave. S, Minneapolis, MN 55419, (612) 827-5677; Facility Type: Skilled care; Alzheimer's; Certified Beds: 153; Certified: Medicaid; Medicare; Owner: Nonprofit corp.; License: Current state

Providence Place
3720 23rd Ave S, Minneapolis, MN 55407, (612) 724-5495; Facility Type: Skilled care; ICF; ICF/MR; Alzheimer's; Certified Beds: 210; Certified: Medicaid; Medicare; Owner: For-profit corp.; License: Current state

Redeemer Residence, Inc.
625 W. 31st, Minneapolis, MN 55408, (612) 827-2555; Facility Type: Skilled care; ICF; ICF/MR; Alzheimer's; Certified Beds: 141; Certified: Medicaid; Medicare; Owner: For-profit corp.; License: Current state

Walker Methodist Health Center
3737 Bryant Ave. S., Minneapolis, MN 55409, (612) 827-8383; Facility Type: Skilled care; ICF; ICF/MR; Alzheimer's; Certified Beds: 348; Certified: Medicaid; Medicare; Owner: For-profit corp.; License: Current state

Moorhead

Eventide Lutheran Home
1405 S. 7th St., Moorhead, MN 56560, (218) 233-7508; Facility Type: Skilled care; Alzheimer's; Certified Beds: 195; Certified: Medicaid; Medicare; Owner: Nonprofit corp.; License: Current state

New Hope

North Ridge Care Center
5430 Boone Ave. N, New Hope, MN 55428, (763) 592-3000; Facility Type: Skilled care; Alzheimer's; Certified Beds: 397; Certified: Medicaid; Medicare; Owner: Nonprofit corp.; License: n/a

Onamia

Mille Lacs Health System
200 N Elm St., Onamia, MN 56359, (320) 532-3154; Facility Type: Skilled care; ICF; Alzheimer's; Certified Beds: 57; Certified: Medicaid; Medicare; Veterans; Owner: Nonprofit corp.; License: Current state

Plymouth

Mission Nursing Home
3401 E Medicine Lake Blvd., Plymouth, MN 55441, (763) 559-3123; Facility Type: Skilled care; ICF; Alzheimer's; Certified Beds: 104; Certified: Medicaid; Medicare; Owner: Nonprofit corp.; License: Current state

Red Wing

Red Wing Health Center
1412 W 4th St., Red Wing, MN 55066, (651) 385-4800; Facility Type: Skilled care; Alzheimer's; Certified Beds: 145; Certified: Medicaid; Medicare; Veterans; Owner: Private; License: Current state

Richfield

Richfield Health Center
7727 Portland Ave. S, Richfield, MN 55423, (612)
861-1691; Facility Type: Skilled care; Alzheimer's; Certified Beds: 118; Certified: Medicaid; Medicare; Owner: ExtendiCare Health Services Inc.; License: Current state

Roseville

Golden LivingCenter–Lake Ridge
2727 N Victoria, Roseville, MN 55113, (651) 483-5431; Facility Type: Skilled care; Alzheimer's; Certified Beds: 175; Certified: Medicare; Owner: Private; License: Current state

Saint Cloud

Talahi Care Center
1717 Michigan Ave. SE, Saint Cloud, MN 56304, (320) 251-9120; Facility Type: Skilled care; Alzheimer's; Certified Beds: 77; Certified: Medicaid; Medicare; Veterans; Owner: Proprietary/Public corp.; License: Current state

Saint Louis Park

Golden LivingCenter–Saint Louis Park Plaza
3201 Virginia Ave. S, Saint Louis Park, MN 55426, (952) 935-0333; Facility Type: Skilled care; Alzheimer's; Certified Beds: 208; Certified: Medicaid; Medicare; Owner: Proprietary/Pubic corp.; License: Current state

Saint Paul

Bethel Care Center
420 Marshall Ave., St. Paul, MN 55102, (651) 224-2368; Facility Type: Skilled care; ICF; Alzheimer's; Certified Beds: 131; Certified: Medicaid; Medicare; Owner: For profit corp.; License: Current state

Cerenity Care Center on Humboldt
512 Humboldt Ave., Saint Paul, MN 55107, (651) 227-8091; Facility Type: Skilled care; Alzheimer's; Certified Beds: 125; Certified: Medicaid; Medicare; Owner: Nonprofit corp.; License: Current state

Episcopal Church Home of Minnesota
1879 Ferona Ave, St. Paul, MN 55104, (651) 646-4061; Facility Type: Skilled care; ICF; Alzheimer's; Certified Beds: 131; Certified: Medicaid; Medicare; Owner: Nonprofit corp.; License: Current state

Galtier Health Center
445 Galtier Ave., St. Paul, MN 55103, (651) 224-1848; Facility Type: Skilled care; ICF; Alzheimer's; Certified Beds: 120; Certified: Medicaid; Medicare; Owner: For profit corp.; License: Current state

Lyngblomsten Care Center
1415 Almond Ave., St. Paul, MN 55108, (651) 646-2941; Facility Type: Skilled care; ICF; Alzheimer's;

Certified Beds: 237; Certified: Medicaid; Medicare; Owner: Nonprofit corp.; License: Current state

Saint Anthony Park Home
2237 Commonwealth Ave., Saint Paul, MN 55108, (651) 632-3500; Facility Type: Skilled care; Alzheimer's; Certified Beds: 84; Certified: Medicaid; Medicare; Owner: Proprietary/ Public corp.; License: Current state

St. Mary's Home
1925 Norfolk Ave, St. Paul, MN 55116, (651) 696-8400; Facility Type: Skilled care; ICF; Alzheimer's; Certified Beds: 100; Certified: Medicaid; Medicare; Owner: Nonprofit corp.; License: Current state

Slayton

Golden LivingCenter–Slayton
2957 Redwood Ave. S, Slayton, MN 56172, (507) 836-6135; Facility Type: Skilled care; Alzheimer's; Certified Beds: 55; Certified: Medicaid; Medicare; Owner: Beverly Enterprises Inc.; License: Current state

Wabasha

Saint Elizabeth Medical Center
1200 5th Grant Blvd. W, Wabasha, MN 44981, (651) 565-4531; Facility Type: Skilled care; Alzheimer's; Certified Beds: 100; Certified: Medicaid; Medicare; Veterans; Owner: Nonprofit/Religious org.; License: Current state

Wayzata

Golden LivingCenter–Hillcrest of Wayzata
15409 Wayzata Blvd., Wayzata, MN 55391, (952) 473-5466; Facility Type: Skilled care; ICF; Alzheimer's; Certified Beds: 134; Certified: Medicare; Owner: Beverly Enterprises Inc.; License: Current state

Winnebago

Parker Oaks Communities, Inc.
211 6th St., NW Winnebago, MN 56098, (507) 893-3171; Facility Type: Skilled care; Alzheimer's; Certified Beds: 55; Certified: Medicaid; Medicare; Owner: American Baptist Homes of the Midwest; License: Current state

MISSISSIPPI

Columbia

The Grove
11 Pecan Dr., Columbia, MS 39429, (601) 736-9557; Facility Type: Skilled care; ICF/MR; Alzheimer's; Certified Beds: 80; Certified: Medicaid; Medicare; Owner: Proprietary/Public corp.; License: Current state

De Kalb

Mississippi Care Center of Dekalb LLC
220 Willow Ave., De Kalb, MS 39328, (601) 743-5888; Facility Type: Skilled care; ICF; ICF/MR; Alzheimer's; Certified Beds: 60; Certified: Medicaid; Medicare; Owner: Proprietary/ Pubic corp.; License: Current state

Fulton

Daniel Health Care, Inc.
1905 S. Adams St., Fulton, MS 38843, (662) 862-2165; Facility Type: Skilled care; Alzheimer's; Certified Beds: 130; Certified: Medicaid; Medicare; Owner: Private; License: Current state

Gulfport

Driftwood Nursing Home
1500 Broad Ave., Gulfport, MS 39501, (228) 868-1314; Facility Type: Skilled care; ICF; Alzheimer's;

Certified Beds: 151; Certified: Medicaid; Veterans; Owner: Proprietary/Public corp.; License: Current state

Hattiesburg

Hattiesburg Health & Rehabilitation Center
514 Bay St., Hattiesburg, MS 39401, (601) 544-4230; Facility Type: Skilled care; Alzheimer's; Certified Beds: 184; Certified: Medicaid; Owner: Proprietary/ Public corp.; License: Current state

Jackson

Compere's Nursing Home
865 North St., Jackson, MS 39202, (601) 948-6531; Facility Type: Skilled care; ICF; Alzheimer's; Certified Beds: 60; Certified: Medicaid; Medicare; Owner: Private; License: Current state

Lakeland Nursing & Rehabilitation Center
3680 Lakeland Ln., Jackson, MS 39216, (601) 982-5505; Facility Type: Skilled care; ICF; Alzheimer's; Certified Beds: 105; Certified: Medicaid; Medicare; Veterans; Owner: Beverly Enterprises Inc.; License: Current state

Natchez

Adams County Nursing Center
587 John R Junkin Dr., Natchez, MS 39120, (601) 446-8426; Facility Type: Skilled care; ICF; ICF/MR; Alzheimer's; Certified Beds: 105 Alzheimer's 22;

SNF/ICF; Certified: Medicaid; Medicare; Veterans; Owner: Private; License: Current state

Quitman

Lakeside Living Center
191 Hwy. 511 E, Quitman, MS 39355, (601) 776-2141; Facility Type: Skilled care; ICF; Alzheimer's; Certified Beds: 120; Certified: Medicaid; Owner: Proprietary/Public corp.; License: n/a

Ruleville

Ruleville Nursing & Rehabilitation Center
800 Stansel Dr., Ruleville, MS 38771, (662) 756-4361; Facility Type: Skilled care; ICF; ICF/MR; Alzheimer's; Certified Beds: 109; Certified: Medicaid; Medicare; Owner: Beverly Enterprises Inc.; License: Current state

Southaven

Golden LivingCenter–Southaven
1730 Dorchester Dr., Southaven, MS 38671, (662) 393-0050; Facility Type: Skilled care; ICF; ICF/MR; Alzheimer's; Certified Beds: 140; Certified: Medicaid; Medicare; Veterans; Owner: Beverly Enterprises Inc.; License: Current state

West Point

Dugan Memorial Home
804 E Main St., West Point, MS 39773, (662) 494-3640; Facility Type: Skilled care; Alzheimer's; Certified Beds: 60; Certified: n/a; Owner: Nonprofit/Religious org.; License: Current state

Wiggins

Azalia Gardens Nursing Center
530 Hall St., Wiggins, MS 39577, (601) 928-5281; Facility Type: Skilled care; ICF; Alzheimer's; Certified Beds: 149; ICF; Certified: Medicaid; Veterans; Owner: Private; License: Current state

MISSOURI

Ash Grove

AshGrove Healthcare Facility
401 North Medical Drive, PO Box 427, Ash Grove, MO 65604, (417) 751-2575; Facility Type: Skilled care; ICF; ICF/MR; Alzheimer's; Certified Beds: 82; Certified: Medicaid; Medicare; Owner: Proprietary/Public corp.; License: Current state

Belleview

Belleview Valley Nursing Home
HCR 63, Box 1620, Belleview, MO 63623, (573) 697-5311; Facility Type: Skilled care; ICF; ICF/MR; Alzheimer's; Certified Beds: 109; Certified: Medicaid; Medicare; Owner: Proprietary/Public corp.; License: Current state

Bethany

Crestview Home Inc.
1313 S 25th St., PO Box 430, Bethany, MO 64424, (660) 425-3128; Facility Type: Skilled care; Alzheimer's; Certified Beds: 160; Certified: Medicaid; Owner: For-profit corp.; License: Current state

Birch Tree

Birch View Nursing Center
RR 2, Box 2215, Birch Tree, MO 65438, (573) 292-3212; Facility Type: Skilled care; Alzheimer's; Certified Beds: 90; Certified: Medicaid; Medicare; Owner: Americare Systems Inc.; License: Current state

Boonville

Riverdell Care Center
1121 11th St., Boonville, MO 65233, (660) 882-7600; Facility Type: Skilled care; ICF; ICF/MR; Alzheimer's; Certified Beds: 60; Alzheimer's; Certified: Medicaid; Medicare; Owner: Nonprofit corp.; License: Current state

Butler

Medicalodges Butler
103 E Nursery, Butler, MO 64730, (660) 679-3179; Facility Type: ICF; Alzheimer's; Certified Beds: 110; Certified: Medicaid; Medicare; Owner: Medicalodges Inc.; License: Current state

Cameron

Quail Run Health Care Center
1405 W Grand Ave., PO Box 525, Cameron, MO 64429, (816) 632-2151; Facility Type: Skilled care; ICF; ICF/ MR; Alzheimer's; Certified Beds: 84; Certified: Medicaid; Medicare; Veterans; Owner: Proprietary/Public corp.; License: Current state

Cape Girardeau

Heartland Care & Rehabilitation Center
2525 Boutin Dr., Cape Girardeau, MO 63701, (573)

334-5225; Facility Type: Skilled care; ICF; Alzheimer's; Certified Beds: 102; Certified: Medicaid; Medicare; Owner: Health Facilities Management Corp.; License: Current state

Cassville

Red Rose Health & Rehabilitation Center
812 Old Exeter Rd., Cassville, MO 65625, (417) 847-2184; Facility Type: Skilled care; ICF; Alzheimer's Certified Beds: 94; Certified: Medicaid; Medicare; Owner: Rose Care Inc.; License: Current state

Charleston

Charleston Manor Skilled Nursing by Americare
1220 E Marshall, Charleston, MO 63834, (573) 683-3721; Facility Type: Skilled care; ICF; Alzheimer's; Certified Beds: 120; Certified: Medicaid; Medicare; Veterans; Owner: Americare Systems Inc.; License: Current state

Chesterfield

Brooking Park
307 S Woods Mill Rd., Chesterfield, MO 63017, (314) 576-5545; Facility Type: Skilled care; Alzheimer's; Certified Beds: 37; Certified: n/a; Owner: Nonprofit/Religious org.; License: Current state

Columbia

Lenoir Health Care Center
3300 New Haven Rd., Columbia, MO 65201, (573) 876-5800; Facility Type: Skilled care; Alzheimer's; Certified Beds: 42; Certified: Medicaid; Medicare; Owner: Nonprofit/Religious org.; License: Current state

Crane

Ozark Mountain Regional Healthcare Center
509 Meadowlark Ave., Crane, MO 65633, (417) 723-5281; Facility Type: Skilled care; Alzheimer's; Certified Beds: 100; Certified: Medicaid; Medicare; Owner: For-profit corp.; License: Current state

De Soto

Baisch Nursing Center
3260 Baisch Dr., De Soto, MO 63020, (636) 586-2291; Facility Type: Skilled care; ICF; Alzheimer's; Certified Beds: 61; Certified: n/a; Owner: For-profit corp.; License: Current state

Dexter

Crowley Ridge Care Center
1204 N Outer Rd., PO Box 668, Dexter, MO 63841,

(573) 624-5557; Facility Type: Skilled care; ICF; Alzheimer's; Certified Beds: 90; Certified: Medicaid; Veterans; Owner: Proprietary/Public corp.; License: Current state

El Dorado Springs

Community Springs Healthcare Facility
400 E Hospital Rd., El Dorado Springs, MO 64744, (417) 876-2531; Facility Type: Skilled care; Alzheimer's; Certified Beds: 120; Certified: Medicaid; Medicare; Owner: Nonprofit corp.; License: Current state

Eureka

Marymount Manor
313 Augustine Rd., Eureka, MO 63025, (636) 938-6770; Facility Type: Skilled care; Alzheimer's; Certified Beds: 174; Certified: Medicaid; Medicare; Veterans; Owner: Private; License: Current state

Farmington

Camelot Nursing & Rehabilitation Center
705 Grand Canyon Dr., Farmington, MO 63640, (573) 756-8911; Facility Type: Skilled care; ICF; Alzheimer's; Certified Beds: 97; Certified: Medicaid; Medicare; Owner: For profit corp.; License: Current state

Presbyterian Manor of Farmington
500 Cayce, Farmington, MO 63640, (573) 756-6768; Facility Type: Skilled care; ICF; Alzheimer's; Certified Beds: 90; Certified: Medicaid; Medicare; Owner: Nonprofit corp.; License: Current state

St. Francis Manor
1180 Old Jackson Rd., Farmington, MO 63640, (573) 760-1700; Facility Type: Skilled care; ICF; Alzheimer's; Certified Beds: 118; Certified: Medicaid; Medicare; Owner: For profit corp.; License: Current state

Fenton

Cori Manor Healthcare & Rehabilitation Center
560 Corisande Hill Rd., Fenton, MO 63026, (636) 343-2282; Facility Type: Skilled care; ICF; ICF/MR; Alzheimer's; Certified Beds: 124; ICF; ICF/MR; Alzheimer's; SNF/ICF; Residential care 22; Certified: Medicaid; Medicare; Owner: Healthcare Corp.; License: Current state

Festus

Arbor Place of Festus, Inc.
12827 Highway TT, Festus, MO 63028, (636) 937-3150; Facility Type: Skilled care; Alzheimer's; Cer-

tified Beds: 77 Certified: Medicaid; Veterans; Owner: Private; License: Current state

Florissant

Crestwood Healthcare Center, LLC
11400 Mehl Ave., Florissant, MO 63033, (314) 741-3525; Facility Type: Skilled care; ICF; Alzheimer's; Certified Beds: 150; Certified: Medicaid; Medicare; Owner: For profit corp.; License: Current state

Crystal Creek Health & Rehabilitation Center
250 New Florissant Rd., South, Florissant, MO 63031, (314) 838-2211; Facility Type: Skilled care; ICF; Alzheimer's; Certified Beds: 158; Certified: Medicaid; Medicare; Owner: For profit corp.; License: Current state

ManorCare Health Services
1200 Graham Rd., Florissant, MO 63031, (314) 838-6555; Facility Type: Skilled care; ICF; Alzheimer's; Certified Beds: 98; Certified: Medicaid; Medicare; Owner: For profit corp.; License: Current state

The Pillars of North County Health & Rehab Center
13700 Old Halls Ferry Rd., Florissant, MO 63033, (314) 355-0760; Facility Type: Skilled care; ICF; Alzheimer's; Certified Beds: 120; Certified: Medicaid; Medicare; Owner: For profit corp.; License: Current state

St. Sophia Health & Rehab Center
936 Charbonier Rd., Florissant, MO 63031, (314) 831-4800; Facility Type: Skilled care; ICF; Alzheimer's; Certified Beds: 240; Certified: Medicaid; Medicare; Owner: For profit corp.; License: Current state

Gerald

Gerald Nursing & Rehabilitation
533 Canaan Rd., PO Box 180, Gerald, MO 63037, (573) 764-2135; Facility Type: Skilled care; Alzheimer's; Certified Beds: 60; Certified: Medicaid; Medicare; Owner: Proprietary/Public corp.; License: Current state

Grandview

Life Care Center of Grandview
6301 E. 125th St., Grandview MO 64030, (816) 765-7714; Facility Type: Skilled care; ICF; Alzheimer's; Certified Beds: 172; Certified: Medicaid; Medicare; Owner: For profit corp.; License: Current state

Hannibal

Beth Haven Nursing Home
2500 Pleasant St., Hannibal, MO 63401, (573) 221-6000; Facility Type: Skilled care; Alzheimer's; Cer-

tified Beds: 105; Certified: Medicaid; Medicare; Owner: Nonprofit corp.; License: n/a

Hermann

Frene Valley Health Center
1800 Wein St., PO Box 468, Hermann, MO 65041, (573) 486-3155; Facility Type: Skilled care; ICF; ICF/MR; Alzheimer's; Certified Beds: 118; Certified: Medicaid; Medicare; Owner: For-profit corp.; License: Current state

Jefferson City

Jefferson City Nursing & Rehabilitation Center, LLC
1221 Southgate Ln., Jefferson City, MO 65109, (573) 635-3131; Facility Type: Skilled care; Alzheimer's; Certified Beds: 120; Certified: Medicaid; Medicare; Owner: Private; License: Current state

Joplin

Joplin Health & Rehabilitation Center
2218 W 32nd St., Joplin, MO 64804, (417) 623-5264; Facility Type: Skilled care; Alzheimer's; Certified Beds: 120; Certified: Medicaid; Medicare; Owner: Proprietary/Public corp.; License: Current state

NYC Health Care, Joplin
2700 E 34th St., PO Box 2877, Joplin, MO 64803, (417) 781-1737; Facility Type: Skilled care; ICF; Alzheimer's; Certified Beds: 126; Certified: Medicaid; Medicare; Veterans; Owner: National Healthcare Company; License: Current state

Kansas City

Blue River Rehabilitation Center
10425 Chestnut Dr., Kansas City, MO 64137, (816) 763-4444; Facility Type: Skilled care; ICF; Alzheimer's; Certified Beds: 160; Certified: Medicaid; Medicare; Owner: For profit corp.; License: Current state

Bridgewood Healthcare Center
11515 Troost, Kansas City, MO 64131, (816) 943-0101; Facility Type: Skilled care; ICF; Alzheimer's; Certified Beds: 162; Certified: Medicaid; Medicare; Owner: For profit corp.; License: Current state

Corner Brook Place
12942 Wornall Rd., Kansas City, MO 64145, (816) 423-8500; Facility Type: Skilled care; ICF; Alzheimer's; Certified Beds: 180; Certified: Medicaid; Medicare; Owner: For profit corp.; License: Current state

Garden Valley Nursing & Rehabilitation Center
8575 N. Granby Ave., Kansas City, MO 64154, (816)

436-8575; Facility Type: Skilled care; ICF; Alzheimer's; Certified Beds: 156; Certified: Medicaid; Medicare; Owner: For profit corp.; License: Current state

Highland Nursing & Rehabilitation Center
904 E. 68th St., Kansas City, MO 64131, (816) 333-5485; Facility Type: Skilled care; Alzheimer's; Certified Beds: 162; Certified: Medicaid; Medicare; Veterans; Owner: Proprietary/Public corp.; License: Current state

New Mark Care Center
11221 N. Nashua Dr., Kansas City, MO 64155, (816) 734-4433; Facility Type: Skilled care; ICF; Alzheimer's; Certified Beds: 191; Certified: Medicaid; Medicare; Owner: For profit corp.; License: Current state

Plaza Manor
4330 Washington, Kansas City, MO 64111, (816) 753-6800; Facility Type: Skilled care; ICF; Alzheimer's; Certified Beds: 154; Certified: Medicaid; Medicare; Owner: For profit corp.; License: Current state

Swope Ridge Geriatric Center
5900 Swope Pkwy., Kansas City, MO 64130, (816) 333-2700; Facility Type: Skilled care; ICF; Alzheimer's; Certified Beds: 180; Certified: Medicaid; Medicare; Owner: Nonprofit corp.; License: Current state

Truman Medical Center Lakewood
7900 Lee's Summit Rd., Kansas City, MO 64139, (816) 404-7000; Facility Type: Skilled care; ICF; Alzheimer's; Certified Beds: 212; Certified: Medicaid; Medicare; Owner: Nonprofit corp.; License: Current state

Kimberling City

Tablerock Healthcare
276 Fountain Ln., Kimberling City, MO 65686, (417) 739-2481; Facility Type: Skilled care; ICF; Alzheimer's; Certified Beds: 120; Certified: Medicaid; Medicare; Owner: Lenox Healthcare Inc.; License: Current state

La Belle

La Belle ManorCare Center
1002 Central, La Belle, MO 63447, (660) 213-3234; Facility Type: Skilled care; Alzheimer's; Certified Beds: 94; RCF 8; Certified: Veterans; Owner: Proprietary/Public corp.; License: Current state

Lamar

Truman Healthcare & Rehabilitation
206 W. First St., Lamar, MO 64759, (417) 682-3315; Facility Type: Skilled care; Alzheimer's; Certified

Beds: 109; Certified: Medicaid; Medicare; Owner: Private; License: Current state

Lexington

Lexington Care Center
1221 S. Hwy 13, Lexington, MO 64067, (660) 259-4695; Facility Type: Skilled care; ICF; Alzheimer's; Certified Beds: 148; Certified: Medicaid; Medicare; Owner: For profit corp.; License: Current state

Liberty

Ashton Court Care/Rehabilitation Center
1200 W. College St., Liberty, MO 64068, (816) 781-3020; Facility Type: Skilled care; Alzheimer's; Certified Beds: 140; Certified: Medicaid; Medicare; Owner: Centennial HealthCare Corp.; License: Current state

Linn

Autumn Meadows
196 Highway CC, Linn, MO 65051, (573) 897-4726; Facility Type: Skilled care; ICF; Alzheimer's; Certified Beds: 132; Certified: Medicaid; Medicare; Owner: For profit corp.; License: Current state

Marble Hill

Woodland Hills–A Stonebridge Community
702 Highway 34 West, Marble Hill, MO 63764, (573) 238-2614; Facility Type: Skilled care; ICF; ICF/MR; Alzheimer's; Certified Beds: 98; Certified: Medicaid; Medicare; Owner: Private; License: Current state

Maryland Heights

NHC Healthcare–Maryland Heights
2920 Fee Rd., Maryland Heights, MO 63043, (314) 291-0121; Facility Type: Skilled care; Alzheimer's; Certified Beds: 220; Certified: Medicaid; Medicare; Owner: Proprietary/Public corp.; License: Current state

Maryville

Golden LivingCenter–Maryville
524 N. Laura, Maryville, MO 64468, (660) 582-7447; Facility Type: Skilled care; Alzheimer's; Certified Beds: 105; Certified: Medicaid; Medicare; Veterans; Owner: Proprietary/Public corp.; License: Current state

Memphis

Scotland County Care Center
Rte. 1, Box 52, Memphis, MO 63555, (660) 465-

7221; Facility Type: Skilled care; Alzheimer's; Certified Beds: 120; Certified: Medicaid; Owner: Government/State/Local; License: Current state

Moberly

Moberly Nursing & Rehabilitation
700 E Urbandale, Moberly, MO 65270, (660) 263-9060; Facility Type: Skilled care; Alzheimer's; Certified Beds: 101; Certified: Medicaid; Medicare; Owner: Private; License: Current state

Mountain Grove

Autumn Oaks Caring Center
1310 Hovis St., PO Box 804, Mountain Grove, MO 65711, (417) 926-5128; Facility Type: Skilled care; Alzheimer's; Certified Beds: 120; Certified: Medicaid; Medicare; Owner: Proprietary/Public corp.; License: Current state

Nevada

Moore-Few Care Center
901 S. Adams, Nevada, MO 64772, (417) 448-3841; Facility Type: Skilled care; ICF; Alzheimer's; Certified Beds: 108; Certified: Medicaid; Medicare; Owner: Government/State/Local; License: Current state

Ozark

Ozark Nursing & Care Center
1486 N Riverside Rd., Ozark, MO 65721, (417) 581-7126; Facility Type: Skilled care; Alzheimer's; Certified Beds: 120; Certified: Medicaid; Owner: Proprietary/Public corp.; License: Current state

Pacific

Pacific Care Center LLC
105 S. Sixth St., Pacific, MO 63069, (636) 271-4222; Facility Type: Skilled care; ICF; ICF/MR; Alzheimer's; Certified Beds: 118; Certified: Medicaid; Medicare; Owner: Proprietary/Public corp.; License: Current state

Perryville

Perry Oaks Nursing & Rehabilitation Center
430 N. West St., Perryville, MO 63775, (573) 547-1011; Facility Type: Skilled care; ICF; Alzheimer's; Certified Beds: 156; Certified: Medicaid; Medicare; Owner: Nonprofit corp.; License: Current state

Poplar Bluff

Oakdale Care Center
2702 Debbie Ln., PO Box 340, Poplar Bluff, MO 63902, (573) 686-5242; Facility Type: Skilled care;

ICF; ICF/MR; Alzheimer's; Certified Beds: 70; Certified: Medicaid; Medicare; Owner: Proprietary/Public corp.; License: Current state

Puxico

Puxico Nursing & Rehabilitation Center
540 N Hwy. 51, Puxico, MO 63960, (573) 222-3125; Facility Type: Skilled care; ICF; Alzheimer's; Certified Beds: 60; Certified: Medicaid; Medicare; Veterans; Owner: Proprietary/Public corp.; License: Current state

Saint James

Golden LivingCenter–Saint James
415 Sidney St., PO Box 69, Saint James, MO 65559, (573) 265-8921; Facility Type: Skilled care; Alzheimer's; Certified Beds: 90; Certified: Medicaid; Medicare; Owner: Proprietary/Public corp.; License: Current state

Saint Joseph

Carriage Square Health Care Center
4009 Gene Field Rd., Saint Joseph, MO 64506, (816) 364-1526; Facility Type: Skilled care; Alzheimer's; Certified Beds: 130; Certified: Medicaid; Medicare; Owner: Proprietary/Public corp.; License: Current state

Saint Louis

The Abbey Care Center
5303 Bermuda Rd., St. Louis, MO 63121, (314) 385-0910; Facility Type: Skilled care; ICF; Alzheimer's; Certified Beds: 126; Certified: Medicaid; Medicare; Owner: For profit corp.; License: Current state

Alexian Brothers Lansdowne Village
4624 Lansdowne Ave., Saint Louis, MO 63116, (314) 351-6888; Facility Type: Skilled care; ICF; Alzheimer's; Certified Beds: 145; Certified: Medicaid; Medicare; Owner: Nonprofit corp.— church related; License: Current state

Beauvais Manor Healthcare & Rehab Center
3625 Magnolia Ave., St. Louis, MO 63110, (314) 771-2990; Facility Type: Skilled care; ICF; Alzheimer's; Certified Beds: 184; Certified: Medicaid; Medicare; Owner: For profit corp.; License: Current state

Bethesda Dilworth
9645 Big Bend Blvd., Saint Louis, MO 63122, (314) 968-5460; Facility Type: Skilled care; ICF; Alzheimer's; Certified Beds: 314; Certified: Medicaid; Owner: Nonprofit corp.; License: Current state

Bethesda South Gate
5943 Telegraph Rd., Saint Louis, MO 63129, (314) 846-2000; Facility Type: Skilled care; Alzheimer's;

Certified Beds: 118; Alzheimer's; Certified: Medicaid; Medicare; Owner: Proprietary/Public corp.; License: Current state

Delhaven Manor
5460 Delmar Blvd., St. Louis, MO 63112, (314) 361-2902; Facility Type: Skilled care; ICF; Alzheimer's; Certified Beds: 156; Certified: Medicaid; Medicare; Owner: For profit corp.; License: Current state

Friendship Village Sunset Hills
12509 Village Circle Dr., Saint Louis, MO 63127, (314) 842-6840; Facility Type: Skilled care; Alzheimer's; Certified Beds: 19; Certified: Medicaid; Owner: Nonprofit corp.; License: Current state

Hillside Manor Healthcare & Rehab Center
1265 McLaran Ave., St. Louis, MO 63147, (314) 388-4121; Facility Type: Skilled care; ICF; Alzheimer's; Certified Beds: 208; Certified: Medicaid; Medicare; Owner: For profit corp.; License: Current state

Northview Village
2415 N. Kings Hwy., St. Louis, MO 63113, (314) 361-1300; Facility Type: Skilled care; ICF; Alzheimer's; Certified Beds: 310; Certified: Medicaid; Medicare; Owner: For profit corp.; License: Current state

Parkside Towers
4960 Laclede Ave., St. Louis, MO 63108, (314) 361-6240; Facility Type: Skilled care; ICF; Alzheimer's; Certified Beds: 168; Certified: Medicaid; Medicare; Owner: For profit corp.; License: Current state

Sunset Hills Health & Rehabilitation Center
10954 Kennerly Rd., Saint Louis, MO 63128, (314) 843-4242; Facility Type: Skilled care; Alzheimer's; Certified Beds: 166; Certified: Medicaid; Medicare; Owner: Proprietary/Public corp.; License: Current state

Willowbrooke Nursing & Rehabilitation Center
2600 Redman Rd., St. Louis, MO 63136, (314) 355-8585; Facility Type: Skilled care; ICF; Alzheimer's; Certified Beds: 120; Certified: Medicaid; Medicare; Owner: For profit corp.; License: Current state

Salisbury

Chariton Park Healthcare Center
902 Manor Dr., Salisbury, MO 65281, (660) 388-6486; Facility Type: Skilled care; ICF; ICF/MR; Alzheimer's; Certified Beds: 120; Certified: Medicaid; Medicare; Owner: Proprietary/Public corp.; License: Current state

Sikeston

Hunter Acres Caring Center
628 N. West St., Sikeston, MO 63801, (573) 471-7130; Facility Type: Skilled care; ICF; ICF/MR; Alzheimer's; Certified Beds: 120; Certified: Medicaid;

Medicare; Owner: Nonprofit corp.; License: Current state

Springfield

Christian Healthcare of Springfield West
3403 W. Mt. Vernon, Springfield, MO 65802, (417) 864-5600; Facility Type: Skilled care; Alzheimer's; Certified Beds: 172; SNF/ICF; Certified: Medicaid; Medicare; Owner: Proprietary/Public corp.; License: Current state

Jordan Creek Nursing & Rehabilitation
910 S. West Ave., Springfield, MO 65802, (417) 865-8741; Facility Type: Skilled care; Alzheimer's; Certified Beds: 120; Certified: Medicaid; Medicare; Owner: Nonprofit corp.; License: Current state

ManorCare Health Services
2915 S. Fremont, Springfield, MO 65804, (417) 883-4022; Facility Type: Skilled care; Alzheimer's; Certified Beds: 194; Certified: Medicaid; Medicare; Owner: Proprietary/Public corp.; License: Current state

Woodland Manor
1347 E. Valley Water Mill Rd., Springfield, MO 65803, (417) 833-1220; Facility Type: Skilled care; Alzheimer's; Certified Beds: 180; Certified: Medicaid; Medicare; Owner: Proprietary/ Public corp.; License: Current state

Town and Country

NHC Healthcare, Town & Country
13995 Clayton Rd., Town and Country, MO 63017, (636) 227-5070; Facility Type: Skilled care; Alzheimer's; Certified Beds: 282; Alzheimer's; SNF/ICF; Certified: Medicaid; Medicare; Owner: Proprietary/ Public corp.; License: Current state

Union

Sunset Health Care Center
400 W. Park Ave., Union, MO 63084, (636) 583-2252; Facility Type: Skilled care; ICF; Alzheimer's; Certified Beds: 120; Certified: Medicaid; Medicare; Veterans; Owner: Proprietary/ Public corp.; License: Current state

Vandalia

Tri-County Care Center
601 N. Galloway Rd., Vandalia, MO 63382, (573) 594-6467; Facility Type: Skilled care; Alzheimer's; Certified Beds: 90; Certified: Medicaid; Medicare; Owner: Government/State/Local; License: Current state

Warrensburg

Johnson County Care Center
122 E. Market St., Warrensburg, MO 64093, (660) 747-8181; Facility Type: ICF; Alzheimer's; Certified

Beds: 87; Certified: Medicaid; Owner: Leisure Care Corp.; License: Current state

Ridge Crest Nursing Center
706 S. Mitchell, Warrensburg, MO 64093, (660) 429-2177; Facility Type: Skilled care; Alzheimer's; Certified Beds: 120; Certified: Medicaid; Medicare; Veterans; Owner: Proprietary/ Public corp.; License: Current state

Washington

Cedarcrest Manor
324 W. 5th St., Washington, MO 63090, (636) 239-7848; Facility Type: Skilled care; ICF; ICF/ MR; Alzheimer's; Certified Beds: 177; Certified: Medicaid; Medicare; Owner: Private; License: Current state

Webb City

Webb City Health & Rehabilitation Center
2077 W Carl Junction Rd., Webb City, MO 64870, (417) 673-1933; Facility Type: Skilled care; ICF; ICF/MR; Alzheimer's; Certified Beds: 120; Certified: Medicaid; Medicare; Owner: Private; License: Current state

Willow Springs

Willow Care Nursing Home
2646 State Route 76, PO Box 309, Willow Springs, MO 65793, (417) 469-3152; Facility Type: Skilled care; Alzheimer's; Certified Beds: 120; Certified: Medicaid; Medicare; Owner: Nonprofit corp.; License: Current state

---

MONTANA

Big Sandy

Big Sandy Medical Center
166 Montana Ave E, Big Sandy, MT 59520, (406) 378-2188; Facility Type: Skilled care; ICF; ICF/MR; Alzheimer's; Certified Beds: 22; Certified: Medicaid; Medicare; Owner: Nonprofit; License: Current state

Billings

Eagle Cliff Manor
1415 Yellowstone River Rd., Billings, MT 59101, (406) 245-9330; Facility Type: Skilled care; ICF; Alzheimer's; Certified Beds: 129; Certified: Medicaid; Medicare; Owner: Proprietary/ Public corp.; License: Current state

Saint John's Lutheran Home
3940 Rimrock Rd., Billings, MT 59102, (406) 655-5600; Facility Type: Skilled care; ICF; Alzheimer's; Certified Beds: 186; Certified: Medicaid; Medicare; Owner: Nonprofit/Religious org.; License: Current state

Bozeman

Bozeman Health & Rehabilitation Center
321 N 5th Ave., Bozeman, MT 59715, (406) 587-4404; Facility Type: Skilled care; Alzheimer's; Certified Beds: 103; Certified: Medicaid; Medicare; Veterans; Owner: Private; License: Current state

Choteau

Teton Nursing Home
24 N. Main, Choteau, MT 59422, (406) 466-5338; Facility Type: Skilled care; ICF; Alzheimer's; Certified

Beds: 41; Certified: Medicaid; Medicare; Owner: Government/State/Local; License: Current state

Columbus

Beartooth Manor
350 W Pike Ave., Columbus, MT 59019, (406) 322-5342; Facility Type: Skilled care; Alzheimer's; Certified Beds: 82; Certified: Medicaid; Medicare; Veterans; Owner: Nonprofit corp.; License: Current state

Ennis

Madison Valley Manor
211 N Main St., Ennis, MT 59729, (406) 682-7271; Facility Type: Skilled care; ICF; Alzheimer's; Certified Beds: 40; Certified: Medicaid; Medicare; Veterans; Owner: Government/State/Local; License: Current state

Fort Benton

Missouri River Medical Center–Nursing Home
1501 Saint Charles St., Fort Benton, MT 59442, (406) 622-3331; Facility Type: Skilled care; ICF; ICF/MR; Alzheimer's; Certified Beds: 45; Certified: Medicaid; Medicare; Owner: Government/State/Local; License: Current state

Helena

Big Sky Care Center
2475 Winne Ave., Helena, MT 59601, (406) 442-1350; Facility Type: Skilled care; ICF; Alzheimer's; Certified Beds: 108; Certified: Medicaid; Medicare; Veterans; Owner: Proprietary/Public corp.; License: Current state

Rocky Mountain Care Center
30 S Rodney, Helena, MT 59601, (406) 443-5880;
Facility Type: Skilled care; ICF; ICF/MR; Alzheimer's; Certified Beds: 101; Certified: Medicaid; Medicare; Veterans; Owner: Private; License: Current state

Lewistown

Valle Vista Manor
402 Summitt Ave., Lewistown, MT 59457, (406) 538-8775; Facility Type: Skilled care; ICF; Alzheimer's; Certified Beds: 101; Certified: Medicaid; Medicare; Veterans; Owner: Private; License: Current state

Miles City

Friendship Villa Care Center
2300 Wilson, Miles City, MT 59301, (406) 232-2687; Facility Type: Skilled care; ICF; Alzheimer's; Certified Beds: 107; Certified: Medicaid; Medicare; Veterans; Owner: Proprietary/Public corp.; License: Current state

Holy Rosary Extended Care Unit
2600 Wilson, Miles City, MT 59301, (406) 233-2600; Facility Type: Skilled care; ICF; Alzheimer's; Certified Beds: 84; Certified: Medicaid; Medicare; Veterans; Owner: Nonprofit corp.; License: Current state

Missoula

Missoula Health & Rehabilitation Center
3018 Rattlesnake Dr., Missoula, MT 59802, (406) 549-0988; Facility Type: Skilled care; ICF; ICF/MR; Alzheimer's Certified Beds: 53; Certified: Medicaid; Medicare; Veterans; Owner: Proprietary/Pubic corp.; License: Current state

Village Health Care Center
2651 South Ave. W., Missoula, MT 59804, (406) 728-9162; Facility Type: Skilled care; Alzheimer's; Certified Beds: 193; Certified: Medicaid; Medicare; Veterans; Owner: Private; License: Current state

Red Lodge

Cedar Wood Villa
1 S Oaks, Red Lodge, MT 59068, (406) 446-2525; Facility Type: Skilled care; ICF; ICF/MR; Alzheimer's; Certified Beds: 76; Certified: Medicaid; Medicare; Veterans; Owner: Private; License: Current state

Sheridan

Tobacco Root Mountains Care Center
326 Madison St., Sheridan, MT 59749, (406) 842-5600; Facility Type: Skilled care; ICF; Alzheimer's; Certified Beds: 39; Certified: Medicaid; Owner: Government/State/Local; License: Current state

NEBRASKA

Alliance

Good Samaritan Society Village
1016 E 6th St., Alliance, NE 69301, (308) 762-5675; Facility Type: Skilled care; ICF; Alzheimer's; Certified Beds: 77 Certified: Medicaid; Owner: The Evangelical Lutheran Good Samaritan Society; License: Current state

Ashland

Ashland Care Center
1700 Furnas St., Ashland, NE 68003, (402) 944-7031; Facility Type: Skilled care; ICF; Alzheimer's; Certified Beds: 92; Certified: Medicaid; Medicare; Owner: Proprietary/Public corp.; License: Current state

Auburn

Good Samaritan Society–Auburn
1322 U Street, Auburn, NE 68305, (402) 274-4954;
Facility Type: Skilled care; ICF; ICF/MR; Alzheimer's; Certified Beds: 102; Certified: Medicaid; Medicare; Veterans; Owner: The Evangelical Lutheran Good Samaritan Society; License: Current state

Beatrice

Good Samaritan Society–Beatrice
1306 S 9th St., Beatrice, NE 68310, (402) 228-3304; Facility Type: Skilled care; Alzheimer's; Certified Beds: 87; Alzheimer's; Certified: Medicaid; Medicare; Veterans; Owner: The Evangelical Lutheran Good Samaritan Society; License: Current state

Callaway

Good Samaritan Society Callaway
600 Kimball St., Callaway, NE 68825, (308) 836-2267; Facility Type: Skilled care; ICF; ICF/MR; Alzheimer's; Beds: 43; Certified: Medicaid; Medicare; Owner: Nonprofit/Religious org.; License: Current state

Crete

Crete Manor
830 E 1st St., Crete, NE 68333, (402) 826-4325; Facility Type: Skilled care; ICF; ICF/MR; Alzheimer's; Certified Beds: 104; Certified: Medicaid; Medicare; Owner: Mariner Post Acute Network; License: Current state

David City

David Place
260 S 10th St., David City, NE 68632, (402) 367-3144; Facility Type: Skilled care; ICF; ICF/MR; Alzheimer's; Certified Beds: 86; Certified: Medicaid; Medicare; Veterans; Owner: Vetter Health Services Inc.; License: Current state

Edgar

Rose Brook Care Center
106 5th St., Edgar, NE 68935, (402) 224-5015; Facility Type: Skilled care; ICF; ICF/MR; Alzheimer's; Certified Beds: 47; Certified: Medicaid; Medicare; Veterans; Owner: Integrated Health Services Inc.; License: Current state

Gothenburg

Hilltop Estates
2520 Ave. M, Gothenburg, NE 69138, (308) 537-7138; Facility Type: Skilled care; ICF; Alzheimer's; Certified Beds: 64; Certified: Medicaid; Medicare; Veterans; Owner: Private; License: Current state

Hastings

Good Samaritan Society Hastings Village
926 East E St., Hastings, NE 68902, (402) 463-3181; Facility Type: Skilled care; ICF; Alzheimer's; Certified Beds: 204; Certified: Medicaid; Medicare; Owner: Nonprofit/Religious org.; License: Current state

Hebron

Blue Valley Lutheran Home
220 Park Ave., Hebron, NE 68470, (402) 768-3900; Facility Type: Skilled care; ICF; Alzheimer's; Certified Beds: 64; Certified: Medicaid; Owner: Nonprofit corp.; License: Current state

Kearney

Mount Carmel Home–Keens Memorial
412 W. 18th St., Kearney, NE 68847, (308) 237-2287; Facility Type: Skilled care; Alzheimer's; Certified Beds: 75; Alzheimer's 16; Certified: Medicaid; Medicare; Owner: Nonprofit/Religious org.; License: Current state

Lexington

Plum Creek Care Center
1505 N Adams St., Lexington, NE 68850, (308) 324-5531; Facility Type: Skilled care; Alzheimer's; Certified Beds: 66; Certified: Medicaid; Medicare; Owner: Proprietary/Public corp.; License: Current state

Lincoln

Holmes Lake Manor
6101 Normal Blvd., Lincoln, NE 68506, (402) 489-7175; Facility Type: Skilled care; ICF; Alzheimer's; Certified Beds: 26; Certified: Medicaid; Medicare; Owner: Private; License: Current state

Lancaster Manor
1001 South St., Lincoln, NE 68502, (402) 441-7101; Facility Type: Skilled care; ICF; Alzheimer's; Certified Beds: 293; Certified: Medicaid; Owner: Government/State/Local; License: Current state

Tabitha Nursing Home
4720 Randolph St., Lincoln, NE 68510, (402) 483-7671; Facility Type: Skilled care; ICF; Alzheimer's; Certified Beds: 205; Certified: Medicaid; Medicare; Owner: Nonprofit corp.; License: Current state

Ogallala

Indian Hills Manor
1720 N. Spruce, Ogallala, NE 69153, (308) 284-4068; Facility Type: Skilled care; ICF; ICF/MR; Alzheimer's; Certified Beds: 82; Certified: Medicaid; Medicare; Veterans; Owner: Proprietary/Public corp.; License: Current state

Omaha

Allegent Health Immanuel Fontenelle Home
6901 N 72nd St., Omaha, NE 68122, (402) 572-2970; Facility Type: Skilled care; ICF; Alzheimer's; Certified Beds: 165; Certified: Medicaid; Veterans; Owner: Nonprofit/Religious org.; License: Current state

Golden LivingCenter–Sorensen
4809 Redman Ave., Omaha, NE 68104, (402) 455-5025; Facility Type: Skilled care; ICF; ICF/MR; Alzheimer's; Certified Beds: 64; Certified: Medicaid; Medicare; Owner: Beverly Enterprises Inc.; License: Current state

Nebraska Skilled Nursing & Rehabilitation
7410 Mercy Rd., Omaha, NE 68124, (402) 397-1220; Facility Type: Skilled care; Alzheimer's; Certified Beds: 174; Certified: Medicaid; Medicare; Veterans; Owner: Proprietary/Public corp.; License: Current state

Papillion

Huntington Park Care Center
1507 Gold Coast Rd., Papillion, NE 68046, (402) 339-6010; Facility Type: ICF; Alzheimer's; Certified Beds: 111; Certified: Medicaid; Owner: Proprietary/ Public corp.; License: Current state

Pierce

Pierce Manor
515 E Main St., Pierce, NE 68767, (402) 329-6228; Facility Type: Skilled care; ICF; Alzheimer's; Certified Beds: 75; Certified: Medicaid; Owner: Mariner Post Acute Network; License: Current state

Plattsmouth

Golden LivingCenter–Plattsmouth
602 S. 18th St., Plattsmouth, NE 68048, (402) 296-2800; Facility Type: Skilled care; Alzheimer's; Certified Beds: 111; Certified: Medicaid; Medicare; Veterans; Owner: Proprietary/ Public corp.; License: Current state

Stanton

Stanton Health Center
301 17th St., Stanton, NE 68779, (402) 439-2111; Facility Type: Skilled care; ICF; Alzheimer's; Certified Beds: 70; Certified: Medicaid; Medicare; Owner: Government/State/ Local; License: Current state

Valentine

Good Samaritan Society–Valentine
601 W. 4th St., Valentine, NE 69201, (402) 376-1260; Facility Type: Skilled care; ICF; Alzheimer's; Certified Beds: 58; Certified: Medicaid; Medicare; Veterans; Owner: The Evangelical Lutheran Good Samaritan Society; License: Current state

Wauneta

Heritage of Wauneta
427 Legion St., Wauneta, NE 69045, (308) 394-5738; Facility Type: Skilled care; Alzheimer's; Certified Beds: 38; Certified: Medicaid; Owner: Proprietary/Public corp.; License: Current state

York

The Hearthstone
2600 N. Lincoln Ave., York, NE 68467, (402) 362-4333; Facility Type: Skilled care; Alzheimer's; Certified Beds: 129; Certified: Medicaid; Medicare; Veterans; Owner: Nonprofit corp.; License: Current state

NEVADA

Carson City

Mountain View Health & Rehabilitation
201 Koontz Ln., Carson City, NV 89701, (775) 883-3622; Facility Type: Skilled care; Alzheimer's; Certified Beds: 73; Certified: Medicaid; Medicare; Veterans; Owner: Integrated Health Services Inc.; License: Current state

Henderson

Delmar Gardens of Green Valley
100 Delmar Gardens Dr., Henderson, NV 89014, (702) 361-6111; Facility Type: Skilled care; Alzheimer's; Certified Beds: 202; Certified: n/a; Owner: Private; License: Current state

North Las Vegas

North Las Vegas Care Center
3215 E Cheyenne Ave., North Las Vegas, NV 89030, (702) 649-7800; Facility Type: Skilled care; ICF; Alzheimer's; Certified Beds: 182; Certified: Medicaid; Medicare; Veterans; Owner: Integrated Health Care Services Inc.; License: Current state

Reno

ManorCare Health Services
3101 Plumas, Reno, NV 89509, (775) 829-7220; Facility Type: Skilled care; ICF; Alzheimer's; Certified Beds: 145; Certified: Medicaid; Medicare; Owner: HCR ManorCare; License: Current state

Sparks

Renown Skilled Nursing
1835 Oddie Blvd., Sparks, NV 89431, (775) 982-5140; Facility Type: Skilled care; ICF; Alzheimer's; Certified Beds: 160; Certified: Medicaid; Medicare; Owner: Proprietary/Public corp.; License: Current state

Winnemucca

Harmony Manor HGH Skilled Nursing Facility
118 E Haskell St., Winnemucca, NV 89445, (775) 623-5222; Facility Type: Skilled care; Alzheimer's; Certified Beds: 30; Certified: Medicaid; Medicare; Owner: Government/State/Local; License: Current state

NEW HAMPSHIRE

Bedford

Bedford Hills Care & Rehabilitation Center
30 Colby Ct., Bedford, NH 03110, (603) 625-6462; Facility Type: Skilled care; Alzheimer's; Certified Beds: 147; Certified: Medicaid; Owner: Private; License: Current state

Concord

Havenwood
33 Christian Ave., Concord, NH 03301, (603) 224-5363; Facility Type: Skilled care; ICF; Alzheimer's; Certified Beds: 70; Certified: Medicaid; Medicare; Owner: Nonprofit/Religious org.; License: Current state

Exeter

Riverwoods at Exeter
7 Riverwoods Dr., Exeter, NH 03833, (603) 658-1521; Facility Type: Skilled care; ICF; Alzheimer's; Certified Beds: 62; Certified: Medicare; Owner: Nonprofit corp.; License: Current state

Goffstown

Hillsborough County Nursing Home
400 Mast Rd., Goffstown, NH 03045, (603) 627-5540; Facility Type: Skilled care; ICF; Alzheimer's; Certified Beds: 300; Certified: Medicaid; Medicare; Owner: Government/State/ Local; License: Current state

Hanover

Hanover Terrace Healthcare
49 Lyme Rd., Hanover, NH 03755, (603) 643-2854; Facility Type: Skilled care; ICF; Alzheimer's; Certified Beds: 100; Independent living; Certified: Medicaid; Medicare; Veterans; Owner: Proprietary/Public corp.; License: Current state

Laconia

Laconia Center Genesis Healthcare
175 Blueberry Ln., Laconia, NH 03246, (603) 524-3340; Facility Type: Skilled care; ICF; Alzheimer's; Certified Beds: 108; Certified: Medicaid; Medicare; Veterans; Owner: Private; License: Current state

Manchester

Hanover Hill Health Care Center
700 Hanover St., Manchester, NH 03104, (603) 627-3826; Facility Type: Skilled care; ICF; Alzheimer's; Certified Beds: 124; Certified: Medicaid; Medicare; Veterans; Owner: Private; License: Current state

IHS of Manchester
191 Hackett Hill Rd., Manchester, NH 03102, (603) 668-8161; Facility Type: Skilled care; ICF; Alzheimer's; Certified Beds: 68; Certified: Medicaid; Medicare; Veterans; Owner: Proprietary/Public corp.; License: Current state

Villa Crest Nursing & Retirement Community
1276 Hanover St., Manchester, NH 03104, (603) 622-3262; Facility Type: Skilled care; ICF; Alzheimer's; Certified Beds: 126; Certified: Medicaid; Medicare; Owner: Proprietary/Public corp.; License: Current state

North Conway

Mineral Springs of North Conway Care & Rehabilitation
1251 White Mountain Hwy., North Conway, NH 03860, (603) 356-7294; Facility Type: Skilled care; ICF; Alzheimer's; Certified Beds: 81; Certified: Medicaid; Veterans; Owner: Private; License: Current state

North Haverhill

Grafton County Nursing Home
3855 Dartmouth College Hwy., North Haverhill, NH 03774, (603) 787-6871; Facility Type: Skilled care; ICF; Alzheimer's; Certified Beds: 135; Certified: Medicaid; Medicare; Owner: Government/State/ Local; License: Current state

Ossipee

Mountain View Nursing Home
10 County Farm Rd., Ossipee, NH 03864, (603) 539-7511; Facility Type: ICF; Alzheimer's; Certified Beds: 103F; Certified: Medicaid; Medicare; Owner: Government/State/ Local; License: Current state

Peterborough

Harborside Healthcare–Pheasant Wood
50 Pheasant Rd., Peterborough, NH 03458, (603) 924-7267; Facility Type: Skilled care; ICF; ICF/ MR; Alzheimer's; Certified Beds: 99; Certified: Medicaid; Medicare; Veterans; Owner: Harborside Healthcare; License: Current state

West Stewartstown

Coos County Nursing Hospital
136 County Farm Rd., West Stewartstown, NH 03597, (603) 246-3321; Facility Type: ICF; Alzheimer's; Certified Beds: 97; Certified: Medicaid; Owner: Government/State/Local; License: Current state

NEW JERSEY

Atlantic City

Eastern Pines Convalescent Center
29 N. Vermont Ave., Atlantic City, NJ 08401, (609)
344-8911; Facility Type: Skilled care; Alzheimer's;
Certified Beds: 151; Certified: Medicaid; Medicare;
Owner: Private; License: Current state

Belleville

Clara Maass Medical Center
One Clara Maass Dr., Belleville, NJ 07109, (973)
450-2963; Facility Type: Skilled care; Alzheimer's;
Certified Beds: 20; Certified: Medicaid; Medicare;
Owner: Nonprofit corp.; License: Current state

Bloomfield

Job Haines Home for Aged People
250 Bloomfield Ave., Bloomfield, NJ 07003, (973)
743-0792; Facility Type: Skilled care; Alzheimer's;
Certified Beds: 40; Certified: Medicaid; Medicare;
Owner: Nonprofit corp.; License: Current state

Brick

Laurelton Village
475 Jack Martin Blvd., Brick, NJ 08724, (732) 458-
6600; Facility Type: Skilled care; ICF; Alzheimer's;
Certified Beds: 180; Certified: Medicaid; Medicare;
Owner: Proprietary/Public corp.; License: Current
state

Bridgewater

Green Knoll Care & Rehabilitation Center
875 Rte. 202-206 N., Bridgewater, NJ 08807, (908)
526-8600; Facility Type: Skilled care; ICF; Alzheimer's; Certified Beds: 176; Certified: Medicaid;
Medicare; Owner: Private; License: Current state

Camden

South Jersey Health Care Center
2 Cooper Plaza, Camden, NJ 08103, (856) 342-7600;
Facility Type: Skilled care; Alzheimer's; Certified
Beds: 120; Certified: Medicaid; Medicare; Veterans;
Owner: Sun Healthcare Group Inc. License: Current
state

Cape May Court House

Oceana Rehabilitation and Nursing Care
502 Rte. 9 N., Cape May Court House, NJ 08210,
(609) 465-7633; Facility Type: Skilled care; ICF; Alzheimer's; Certified Beds: 116; Certified: Medicaid;
Medicare; Veterans; Owner: Private; License: Current
state

Cedar Grove

Waterview Center
536 Ridge Rd., Cedar Grove, NJ 07009, (973) 239-
9300; Facility Type: Skilled care; Alzheimer's; Certified Beds: 190; Alzheimer's; SNF/ ICF 138; Certified:
Medicaid; Medicare; Owner: Genesis ElderCare; License: Current state

Cherry Hill

Silver Care Health Care Center
1417 Brace Rd., Cherry Hill, NJ 08034, (856) 795-
3131; Facility Type: Skilled care; ICF; Alzheimer's;
Certified Beds: 246; Certified: Medicaid; Medicare;
Owner: Private; License: Current state

Eatontown

Gateway Care Center
139 Grant Ave., Eatontown, NJ 07724, (732) 542-
4700; Facility Type: Skilled care; ICF; Alzheimer's;
Certified Beds: 178; Certified: Medicaid; Medicare;
Owner: Proprietary/Public corp.; License: Current
state

Edison

JFK Hartwyck at Edison Estates
10 Brunswick Ave., Edison, NJ 08817, (732) 985-
1500; Facility Type: Skilled care; Alzheimer's; Certified Beds: 280; Certified: Medicaid; Medicare;
Owner: Nonprofit corp.; License: Current state

Elizabeth

Elmora Hills Health & Rehabilitation Center
225 W. Jersey St., Elizabeth, NJ 07202, (908) 353-
1220; Facility Type: Skilled care; ICF; ICF/ MR; Alzheimer's; Certified Beds: 180; Certified: Medicaid;
Medicare; Owner: Nonprofit/Religious org.; License:
Current state

Hackensack

Regent Care Center
50 Polifly Rd., Hackensack, NJ 07601, (201) 646-
1166; Facility Type: Skilled care; Alzheimer's; Certified
Beds: 180; Certified: Medicaid; Medicare; Owner:
Proprietary/Public corp.; License: Current state

Hammonton

Greenbriar Health Care Center of Hammonton
43 N. White Horse Pike, Hammonton, NJ 08037,
(609) 567-3100; Facility Type: Skilled care; Alzheim-

er's; Certified Beds: 220; Certified: Medicaid; Medicare; Owner: Proprietary/Public corp.; License: Current state

Jersey City

Newport Nursing & Rehabilitation Center
198 Stevens Ave., Jersey City, NJ 07305, (201) 451-9000; Facility Type: Skilled care; ICF; Alzheimer's; Certified Beds: 183; Certified: Medicaid; Medicare; Owner: Nonprofit/Religious org.; License: Current state

Saint Ann's Home for the Aged
198 Old Bergen Rd., Jersey City, NJ 07305, (201) 433-0950; Facility Type: Skilled care; ICF/MR; Alzheimer's; Certified Beds: 120; Certified: Medicaid; Owner: Nonprofit corp.; License: Current state

Lakewood

Concord Healthcare & Rehabilitation Center
963 Ocean Ave., Lakewood, NJ 08701, (732) 367-7444; Facility Type: Skilled care; ICF; ICF/ MR; Alzheimer's; Certified Beds: 120; Certified: Medicaid; Medicare; Owner: Proprietary/ Public corp.; License: Current state

Leisure Park Health Center
1400 Rte. 70, Lakewood, NJ 08701, (732) 370-0444; Facility Type: Skilled care; ICF; Alzheimer's; Certified Beds: 60; Certified: Medicare; Owner: Proprietary/ Public corp.; License: Current state

Linwood

Linwood Care Center
New Rd. & Central Ave., Linwood, NJ 08221, (609) 927-6131; Facility Type: Skilled care; Alzheimer's; Certified Beds: 174; Certified: Medicaid; Medicare; Owner: Proprietary/Pubic corp.; License: Current state

Manahawkin

Southern Ocean Center
1361 Rte. 72 W., Manahawkin, NJ 08050, (609) 978-0600; Facility Type: Skilled care; ICF; Alzheimer's; Certified Beds: 136; Certified: Medicaid; Medicare; Owner: Proprietary/Pubic corp.; License: Current state

Mendham

Holly Manor Center
84 Cold Hill Rd., Mendham, NJ 07945, (973) 543-2500; Facility Type: Skilled care; Alzheimer's; Certified Beds: 124; Certified: Medicaid; Medicare; Owner: Genesis ElderCare; License: Current state

Monroe Township

Cranbury Center
292 Applegarth Rd., Monroe Township, NJ 08831, (609) 860-2500; Facility Type: Skilled care; ICF; Alzheimer's; Certified Beds: 154; Certified: Medicaid; Medicare; Owner: Proprietary/Pubic corp.; License: Current state

Morristown

Morris Hills Center
77 Madison Ave., Morristown, NJ 07960, (973) 540-9800; Facility Type: Skilled care; ICF; Alzheimer's; Certified Beds: 287; Certified: Medicaid; Medicare; Veterans; Owner: Proprietary/Public corp.; License: Current state

Neptune

King ManorCare & Rehabilitation Center
2303 W Bangs Ave., Neptune, NJ 07753, (732) 774-3500; Facility Type: Skilled care; Alzheimer's; Certified Beds: 120; Certified: Medicaid; Medicare; Owner: Proprietary/Public corp.; License: Current state

New Brunswick

Rose Mountain Care Center
Route 1 & 18, New Brunswick, NJ 08901, (732) 828-2400; Facility Type: Skilled care; Alzheimer's; Certified Beds: 112; Certified: Medicaid; Owner: Private; License: Current state

New Providence

ManorCare Health Services–New Providence
144 Gales Dr., New Providence, NJ 07974, (908) 464-8600; Facility Type: Skilled care; ICF; Alzheimer's; Certified Beds: 106; Certified: Medicaid; Medicare; Owner: HCR ManorCare; License: Current state

Newton

Barn Hill Care Center
249 High St., Newton NJ 07860, (973) 383-5600; Facility Type: Skilled care; Alzheimer's; Certified Beds: 154; Certified: Medicaid; Medicare; Owner: Private; License: Current state

North Bergen

Fritz Reuter Altenheim
3161 Kennedy Blvd., North Bergen, NJ 07047, (201) 867-3585; Facility Type: Skilled care; ICF; Alzheimer's; Beds: Skilled care 156; Certified: n/a; Owner: Nonprofit corp.; License: Current state

Hudson View Care & Rehabilitation Center
9020 Wall St., North Bergen, NJ 07047, (201) 861-4040; Facility Type: Skilled care; Alzheimer's; Certified Beds: 273; Certified: Medicaid; Medicare; Owner: Proprietary/Public corp.; License: Current state

Ocean Grove

Meridian Nursing and Rehabilitation at Ocean Grove
160 Main St., Ocean Grove, NJ 07756, (732) 775-0554; Facility Type: Skilled care; Alzheimer's; Certified Beds: 120; Long-term care; Certified: Medicaid; Medicare; Owner: Nonprofit/Religious org.; License: Current state

Passaic

Hamilton Plaza Nursing & Rehabilitation Center
56 Hamilton Ave., Passaic, NJ 07055, (973) 773-7070; Facility Type: Skilled care; ICF; ICF/MR; Alzheimer's; Certified Beds: 120; ICF; Certified: Medicaid; Medicare; Owner: Proprietary/Public corp.; License: Current state

Phillipsburg

Brakeley Park Center
290 Red School Ln., Phillipsburg, NJ 08865, (908) 859-2800; Facility Type: Skilled care; ICF; Alzheimer's; Certified Beds: 120; Certified: Medicaid; Medicare; Owner: Proprietary/Public corp.; License: Current state

Pleasantville

Our Lady's Residence
1100 Clematis Ave., Pleasantville, NJ 08232, (609) 646-2450; Facility Type: Skilled care; Alzheimer's; Certified Beds: 214; Certified: Medicaid; Medicare; Owner: Nonprofit/Religious org.; License: Current state

Red Bank

Chapin Hill at Red Bank
100 Chapin Ave., Red Bank, NJ 07701, (732) 741-8811; Facility Type: Skilled care; ICF; ICF/MR; Alzheimer's; Certified Beds: 130; Certified: Medicaid; Medicare; Owner: Private; License: Current state

Scotch Plains

Ashbrook Care & Rehabilitation Center
1610 Raritan Rd., Scotch Plains, NJ 07076, (908) 889-5500; Facility Type: Skilled care; ICF; Alzheimer's; Certified Beds: 120; Certified: Medicaid;

Medicare; Owner: Nonprofit/Religious org.; License: Current state

Sewell

Kennedy Health Care Center
535 Egg Harbor Rd., Sewell, NJ 08080, (856) 582-3170; Facility Type: Skilled care; ICF; Alzheimer's; Certified Beds: 130; Certified: Medicaid; Medicare; Owner: Nonprofit corp.; License: Current state

Somerset

Margaret McLaughlin McCarrick
15 Dellwood Ln., Somerset, NJ 08873, (732) 545-4200; Facility Type: Skilled care; Alzheimer's; Certified Beds: 120; Certified: Medicaid; Medicare; Owner: Nonprofit corp.; License: Current state

Toms River

Arbors Care Center
1750 Rte. 37 W., Toms River, NJ 08757, (732) 914-0090; Facility Type: Skilled care; ICF; ICF/MR; Alzheimer's; Certified Beds: 120; Certified: Medicaid; Medicare; Owner: Private; License: Current state

Green Acres Manor
1931 Lakewood Rd., Toms River, NJ 08755, (732) 286-2323; Facility Type: Skilled care; ICF; ICF/ MR; Alzheimer's; Certified Beds: 185; Certified: Medicaid; Medicare; Owner: Proprietary/ Public corp.; License: Current state

Trenton

The Millhouse
325 Jersey St., Trenton, NJ 08611, (609) 394-3400; Facility Type: Skilled care; ICF; Alzheimer's; Certified Beds: 131; Certified: Medicaid; Medicare; Veterans; Owner: Private; License: Current state

Water's Edge Healthcare & Rehabilitation
512 Union St., Trenton, NJ 08611, (609) 393-8622; Facility Type: Skilled care; Alzheimer's; Certified Beds: 215; Certified: Medicaid; Medicare; Owner: Proprietary/Public corp.; License: n/a

Voorhees

Kresson View Center
2601 Evesham Rd., Voorhees, NJ 08043, (856) 596-1113; Facility Type: Skilled care; ICF; ICF/MR; Alzheimer's; Certified Beds: 240; Certified: Medicaid; Medicare; Veterans; Owner: Genesis ElderCare; License: Current state

Watchung

McAuley Hall
1633 Hwy. 22, Watchung, NJ 07069, (908) 754-

3663; Facility Type: Skilled care; ICF; Alzheimer's; Certified Beds: 74; Certified: Medicaid; Medicare; Owner: Nonprofit/Religious org.; License: Current state

Wayne

The Atrium at Wayne
1120 Alps Rd., Wayne, NJ 07474, (973) 694-2100; Facility Type: Skilled care; ICF; ICF/MR; Alzheimer's; Certified Beds: 209; Certified: Medicaid; Owner: Proprietary/Public corp.; License: n/a

West Orange

Daughters of Israel Pleasant Valley Home
1155 Pleasant Valley Way, West Orange, NJ 07052, (973) 731-5100; Facility Type: Skilled care; Alzheimer's; Certified Beds: 303; Certified: Medicaid; Medicare; Owner: Nonprofit/Religious org.; License: Current state

Stratford ManorCare & Rehabilitation
787 Northfield Ave., West Orange, NJ 07052, (973) 731-4500; Facility Type: Skilled care; Alzheimer's; Certified Beds: 131; Certified: Medicare; Owner: Proprietary/Public corp.; License: Current state

Summit Ridge Center
20 Summit St., West Orange, NJ 07052, (973) 736-

2000; Facility Type: Skilled care; ICF; Alzheimer's; Certified Beds: 152; Certified: Medicaid; Medicare; Owner: Proprietary/ Public corp.; License: Current state

Whiting

Whiting Health Care Center
3000 Hilltop Rd., Whiting, NJ 08759, (732) 849-4400; Facility Type: Skilled care; Alzheimer's; Certified Beds: 200; Certified: Medicaid; Medicare; Owner: Proprietary/Public corp.; License: Current state

Woodstown

Friends Village at Woodstown
Friends Dr., Woodstown, NJ 08098, (856) 769-1500; Facility Type: Skilled care; ICF; Alzheimer's; Certified Beds: 60; Certified: Medicaid; Medicare; Owner: Nonprofit/Religious org.; License: Current state

Wyckoff

Christian Health Care Center
301 Sicomac Ave., Wyckoff, NJ 07481, (201) 848-5200; Facility Type: Skilled care; Alzheimer's; Certified Beds: 292; Certified: Medicaid; Owner: Nonprofit/Religious org.; License: Current state

---

NEW MEXICO

Alamogordo

Good Samaritan Society Betty Dare
3101 N. Florida Ave., Alamogordo, NM 88310, (575) 434-0033; Facility Type: Skilled care; ICF; Alzheimer's; Certified Beds: 90; Certified: Medicaid; Medicare; Owner: Nonprofit/Religious org.; License: Current state

Albuquerque

Montebello on Academy
10500 Academy Rd. NE, Albuquerque, NM 87111, (505) 294-9944; Facility Type: Skilled care; ICF; Alzheimer's; Certified Beds: 60; Assisted living 35; Certified: Medicare; Owner: Proprietary/Public corp.; License: Current state

Princeton Place
500 Louisiana Blvd. NE, Albuquerque, NM 87108, (505) 255-1717; Facility Type: Skilled care; ICF; Alzheimer's; Certified Beds: 119; Certified: Medicaid; Medicare; Veterans; Owner: Private; License: Current state

Saint Catherine Healthcare & Rehabilitation Center
5123 Juan Tabo Blvd., NE, Albuquerque, NM 87111, (505) 292-3333; Facility Type: Skilled care; ICF; Alzheimer's; Certified Beds: 178; Certified: Medicaid; Medicare; Veterans; Owner: Proprietary/Public corp.; License: Current state

Carlsbad

Northgate Unit of Lakeview Christian
1905 W. Pierce, Carlsbad, NM 88220, (575) 885-3161; Facility Type: Skilled care; ICF; Alzheimer's; Certified Beds: 112; Certified: Medicaid; Medicare; Veterans; Owner: Nonprofit corp.; License: Current state

Hobbs

Hobbs Health Care Center
5715 Lovington Hwy., Hobbs, NM 88240, (575) 392-6845; Facility Type: Skilled care; ICF; ICF/ MR; Alzheimer's; Certified Beds: 118; Certified: Medicaid; Medicare; Veterans; Owner: Proprietary/Public corp.; License: Current state

Las Cruces

Casa De Oro Care & Rehabilitation Center
1005 Lejan Hill Rd., Las Cruces, NM 88005, (575) 523-4573; Facility Type: Skilled care; ICF; ICF/ MR; Alzheimer's; Certified Beds: 158; Certified: Medicaid; Medicare; Owner: Proprietary/Public corp.; License: Current state

Rio Rancho

Rio Rancho Care & Rehabilitation Center
4210 Sabana Grande SE, Rio Rancho, NM 87124, (505) 892-6603; Facility Type: Skilled care; ICF; ICF/MR; Alzheimer's; Certified Beds: 120; Certified: Medicaid; Medicare; Veterans; Owner: Integrated Health Services Inc.; License: Current state

Roswell

Mission Arch Care & Rehabilitation Center
3200 Mission Arch Dr., Roswell, NM 88201, (575) 624-2583; Facility Type: Skilled care; ICF; Alzheimer's; Certified Beds: 120; Certified: Medicaid; Medicare; Veterans; Owner: Proprietary/Public corp.; License: Current state

Sante Fe

Casa Real Health Care Center
1650 Galisteo St., Santa Fe, NM 87505, (505) 984-8313; Facility Type: Skilled care; ICF; Alzheimer's; Certified Beds: 118; Certified: Medicaid; Medicare; Owner: Integrated Health Services Inc.; License: Current state

Santa Fe Care Center
635 Harkle Rd., Santa Fe, NM 87505, (505) 982-2574; Facility Type: Skilled care; ICF; Alzheimer's; Certified Beds: 120; Certified: Medicaid; Medicare; Veterans; Owner: Integrated Health Services Inc.; License: Current state

NEW YORK

Albany

Teresian House Nursing Home Co Inc.
200 Washington Ave. Ext., Albany, NY 12203, (518) 456-2000; Facility Type: Skilled care; Alzheimer's; Certified Beds: 302; Certified: Medicaid; Medicare; Owner: Nonprofit/Religious org.; License: Current state

Amityville

Broadlawn Manor Nursing & Rehabilitation Center
399 County Line Rd., Amityville, NY 11701, (631) 264-0222; Facility Type: Skilled care; ICF; Alzheimer's; Certified Beds: 320; Alzheimer's; Assisted living; Certified: Medicaid; Medicare; Owner: Nonprofit corp.; License: Current state

Arverne

Horizon Care Center
64-11 Beach Channel Dr., Arverne, NY 11692, (718) 945-0700; Facility Type: Skilled care; Alzheimer's; Certified Beds: 280; Certified: Medicaid; Medicare; Owner: Proprietary/Public corp.; License: Current state

Lawrence Nursing Care Center
350 Beach 54th St., Arverne, NY 11692, (718) 945-0400; Facility Type: Skilled care; Alzheimer's; Certified Beds: 200; Certified: Medicaid; Medicare; Owner: Proprietary/Public corp.; License: Current state

Batavia

Genesee County Nursing Home
278 Bank St., Batavia, NJ 14020, (585) 344-0584; Facility Type: Skilled care; ICF; Alzheimer's; Certified Beds: 160; Certified: Medicaid; Medicare; Owner: Government/State/Local; License: Current state

Bronx

Beth Abraham Health Services
612 Allerton Ave., Bronx, NY 10467, (718) 519-4029; Facility Type: Skilled care; Alzheimer's; Certified Beds: 520; Short-term rehab 120; Certified: Medicaid; Medicare; Owner: Nonprofit/Religious org.; License: Current state

Daughters of Jacob Nursing Home Co., Inc.
1160 Teller Ave., Bronx, NY 10456, (718) 293-1500; Facility Type: Skilled care; ICF; Alzheimer's; Certified Beds: 515; Certified: Medicaid; Medicare; Owner: Nonprofit corp.; License: Current state

Hudson Point at Riverdale Center for Nursing & Rehabilitation
3220 Henry Hudson Pkwy., Bronx, NY 10463, (718) 549-9400; Facility Type: Skilled care; Alzheimer's; Certified Beds: 167; Alzheimer's; Certified: Medicaid; Medicare; Owner: Nonprofit corp.; License: Current state

Kings Harbor Multicare Center
2000 E. Gun Hill Rd., Bronx, NY 10469, (718) 320-

0400; Facility Type: Skilled care; Alzheimer's; Certified Beds: 720; Certified: Medicaid; Medicare; Owner: Proprietary/Public corp.; License: Current state

Riverdale Nursing Home
641 W. 230th St., Bronx, NY 10463, (718) 796-4800; Facility Type: Skilled care; Alzheimer's; Certified Beds: 146; Certified: Medicaid; Medicare; Owner: Proprietary/Public corp.; License: n/a

Brooklyn

Brooklyn Center for Rehabilitation & Residential Health Care
1455 Coney Island Ave., Brooklyn, NY 11230, (718) 252-9800; Facility Type: Skilled care; Alzheimer's; Certified Beds: 215; Certified: Medicaid; Medicare; Owner: Nonprofit corp.; License: Current state

Center for Nursing & Rehabilitation Skilled Nursing Facility
520 Prospect Pl., Brooklyn, NY 11238, (718) 636-1000; Facility Type: Skilled care; Alzheimer's; Certified Beds: 320; Certified: Medicaid; Medicare; Owner: Nonprofit corp.; License: Current state

Four Seasons Nursing & Rehab
1555 Rockaway Pkwy Brooklyn, NY 11236, (718) 927-6300; Facility Type: Skilled care; Alzheimer's; Certified Beds: 270; Certified: Medicaid; Medicare; Owner: Private; License: Current state

Haym Salomon Home for the Aged
2430 Cropsey Ave., Brooklyn, NY 11214, (718) 373-1700; Facility Type: Skilled care; ICF; Alzheimer's; Certified Beds: 240; Certified: Medicaid; Medicare; Veterans; Owner: Private; License: Current state

Metropolitan Jewish Geriatric Center
4915 10th Ave., Brooklyn, NY 11219, (718) 851-3700; Facility Type: Skilled care; Alzheimer's; Certified Beds: 510; Certified: Medicaid; Medicare; Owner: Nonprofit corp.; License: Current state

Buffalo

Ridge View Manor, LLC
300 Dorrance Ave., Buffalo, NY 14220, (716) 566-552; Facility Type: Skilled care; ICF; Alzheimer's; Certified Beds: 120; Certified: Medicaid; Medicare; Veterans; Owner: Private; License: Current state

Canandaigua

MM Ewing Continuing Care Center
350 Parrish St., Canandaigua, NY 14424, (585) 396-6040; Facility Type: Skilled care; Alzheimer's; Certified Beds: 190Skilled care 130; Skilled care 40; Certified: Medicaid; Medicare; Owner: Nonprofit corp.; License: Current state

Cortlandt Manor

Cortlandt Healthcare LLC
110 Oregon Rd., Cortlandt Manor, NY 10567, (914) 739-9150; Facility Type: Skilled care; ICF; Alzheimer's; Certified Beds: 120; Certified: Medicaid; Medicare; Veterans; Owner: Proprietary/Public corp.; License: Current state

Endicott

Ideal Senior Living Center
601 High Ave., Endicott, NY 13760, (607) 786-7300; Facility Type: Skilled care; Alzheimer's; Certified Beds: 150; Certified: Medicaid; Medicare; Owner: Nonprofit corp.; License: Current state

Far Rockaway

Bezalel Rehabilitation & Nursing Center
29-38 Far Rockaway Blvd., Far Rockaway, NY 11691, (718) 471-2600; Facility Type: Skilled care; ICF; Alzheimer's; Certified Beds: 120; Certified: Medicaid; Medicare; Owner: Nonprofit corp.; License: Current state

Peninsula Center for Extended Care & Rehabilitation
50-15 Beach Channel Dr., Far Rockaway, NY 11691, (718) 734-2000; Facility Type: Skilled care; Alzheimer's; Certified Beds: 200; Certified: Medicaid; Medicare; Owner: Nonprofit corp.; License: Current state

Flushing

Flushing ManorCare Center
139-66 35th Ave., Flushing, NY 11354, (718) 961-5300; Facility Type: Skilled care; Alzheimer's; Certified Beds: 278; Certified: Medicaid; Medicare; Veterans; Owner: Proprietary/Public corp.; License: Current state

Jamaica

Highland Care Center, Inc.
91-31 175th St., Jamaica, NY 11432, (718) 657-6363; Facility Type: Skilled care; ICF; Alzheimer's; Certified Beds: 320; Certified: Medicaid; Medicare; Owner: Proprietary/Public corp.; License: Current state

Margaret Tietz Center for Nursing
164-11 Chapin Pkwy., Jamaica, NY 11432, (718) 298-7800; Facility Type: Skilled care; ICF; Alzheimer's; Certified Beds: 200; Certified: Medicaid; Medicare; Owner: Nonprofit corp.; License: Current state

Johnson City

Susquehanna Nursing & Health Related Center, LLC
282 Riverside Dr., Johnson City, NY 13790, (607)

729-9206; Facility Type: Skilled care; ICF; Alzheimer's; Certified Beds: 160; Certified: Medicaid; Medicare; Owner: Private; License: Current state

Long Beach

Komanoff Center for Geriatric & Rehabilitative Medicine
375 E. Bay Dr., Long Beach, NY 11561, (516) 897-1220; Facility Type: Skilled care; Alzheimer's; Certified Beds: 200; Certified: Medicaid; Medicare; Owner: Nonprofit corp.; License: Current state

Massapequa

Parkview Care & Rehabilitation Center, Inc.
5353 Merrick Rd., Massapequa, NY 11758, (516) 798-1800; Facility Type: Skilled care; Alzheimer's; Certified Beds: 169; Certified: Medicaid; Medicare; Owner: Proprietary/Public corp.; License: Current state

New York

Amsterdam Nursing Home Corp.
1060 Amsterdam Ave., New York, NY 10025, (212) 316-7700; Facility Type: Skilled care; Alzheimer's; Certified Beds: 409; Certified: Medicaid; Medicare; Owner: Nonprofit corp.; License: Current state

Cabrini Center for Nursing & Rehab SNF
542 E. Fifth St., New York, NY 10009, (212) 358-3000; Facility Type: Skilled care; Alzheimer's; Certified Beds: 240; Certified: Medicaid; Medicare; Owner: Nonprofit corp.; License: Current state

Dewitt Rehab & Healthcare Center
211 E. 79th St., New York, NY 10021, (212) 879-1600; Facility Type: Skilled care; Alzheimer's; Certified Beds: 499; Certified: Medicaid; Medicare; Owner: For profit corp.; License: Current state

Fort Tyron Rehab & Healthcare Facility LT HH CP
801 W. 190th St., New York, NY 10040, (212) 543-6400; Facility Type: Skilled care; Alzheimer's; Certified Beds: 205; Certified: Medicaid; Medicare; Owner: For profit corp.; License: Current state

Isabella Geriatric Center
515 Audubon Ave., New York, NY 10040, (212) 342-9200; Facility Type: Skilled care; ICF; Alzheimer's; Certified Beds: 705; Certified: Medicaid; Medicare; Owner: Nonprofit corp.; License: Current state

Jewish Home & Hospital for the Aged
120 W. 106th St., New York, NY 10025, (212) 870-5000; Facility Type: Skilled care; Alzheimer's; Certified Beds: 514; Certified: Medicaid; Medicare; Owner: Nonprofit corp.; License: Current state

Kateri Residence
150 Riverside Dr., New York, NY 10024, (646) 505-3500; Facility Type: Skilled care; Alzheimer's; Certified Beds: 520; Certified: Medicaid; Medicare; Owner: Nonprofit corp.; License: Current state

Mary Manning Walsh Nursing Home
1339 York Ave., New York, NY 10021, (646) 475-4800; Facility Type: Skilled care; Alzheimer's; Certified Beds: 362; Certified: Medicaid; Medicare; Owner: Nonprofit corp.; License: Current state

Northern Manhattan Rehab & Nursing Center
116 E. 125th St., New York, NY 10035, (212) 426-1284; Facility Type: Skilled care; Alzheimer's; Certified Beds: 320; Certified: Medicaid; Medicare; Owner: For profit corp.; License: Current state

Terrence Cardinal Cook Healthcare Center
1249 Fifth Ave., New York, NY 10029, (212) 360-3600; Facility Type: Skilled care; Alzheimer's; Certified Beds: 679; Certified: Medicaid; Medicare; Owner: Nonprofit corp.; License: Current state

Newark

Wayne Health Care
100 Sunset Dr., Newark, NY 14513, (315) 332-2700; Facility Type: Skilled care; Alzheimer's; Certified Beds: 182; Certified: Medicaid; Medicare; Owner: Nonprofit corp.; License: Current state

Niagara Falls

Schoellkopf Health Center
621 Tenth St., Niagara Falls, NY 14302, (716) 278-4578; Facility Type: Skilled care; ICF; ICF/MR; Alzheimer's; Certified Beds: 120; Certified: Medicaid; Medicare; Owner: Nonprofit corp.; License: Current state

North Tonawanda

North Gate Health Care Facility
7264 Nash Rd., North Tonawanda, NY 14120, (716) 694-7700; Facility Type: Skilled care; Alzheimer's; Certified Beds: 200; Certified: Medicaid; Medicare; Veterans; Owner: Private; License: Current state

Rochester

Blossom Health Care Center
989 Blossom Rd., Rochester, NY 14610, (585) 482-3500; Facility Type: Skilled care; Alzheimer's; Certified Beds: 80; Certified: Medicaid; Medicare; Veterans; Owner: Private; License: Current state

Episcopal Church Home
505 Mt. Hope Ave., Rochester, NY 14620, (585) 546-8400; Facility Type: Skilled care; Alzheimer's; Certified Beds: 182; Certified: Medicaid; Medicare; Owner: Nonprofit corp.; License: Current state

Jewish Home of Rochester
2021 Winton Rd. S, Rochester, NY 14618, (585) 427-7760; Facility Type: Skilled care; ICF; Alzheimer's; Certified Beds: 362; ICF; Certified: Medicaid; Medicare; Owner: Nonprofit corp.; License: Current state

Monroe Community Hospital
435 E. Henrietta Rd., Rochester, NY 14620, (585) 760-6500; Facility Type: Skilled care; ICF; Alzheimer's; Certified Beds: 566; Certified: Medicaid; Medicare; Owner: Government/State/ Local; License: Current state

Saint Ann's Home for the Aged
1500 Portland Ave., Rochester, NY 14621, (585) 697-6000; Facility Type: Skilled care; Alzheimer's; Certified Beds: 388; Certified: Medicaid; Medicare; Owner: Nonprofit corp.; License: Current state

Rome

Betsy Ross Health Related Facility
1 Elsie St., Rome, NY 13440, (315) 339-2220; Facility Type: Skilled care; ICF; Alzheimer's; Beds: Skilled care 120; ICF; Certified: Medicaid; Medicare; Owner: Private; License: Current state

Scarsdale

Sprain Brook Manor Nursing Home
77 Jackson Ave., Scarsdale, NY 10583, (914) 472-3200; Facility Type: Skilled care; Alzheimer's; Certified Beds: 121; Short-term rehab; Certified: Medicaid; Medicare; Owner: Private; License: Current state

Staten Island

Lily Pond Nursing Home
150 Lily Pond Ave., Staten Island, NY 10305, (718) 981-5300; Facility Type: Skilled care; ICF/MR; Alzheimer's; Certified Beds: Skilled care 35; Certified: Medicaid; Medicare; Owner: Private; License: Current state

Verrazano Nursing Home
100 Castleton Ave., Staten Island, NY 10301, (718) 273-1300; Facility Type: Skilled care; ICF/MR; Alzheimer's; Certified Beds: 120; Certified: Medicaid; Medicare; Owner: Private; License: Current state

Syracuse

James Square Health & Rehabilitation Center
918 James St., Syracuse, NY 13203, (315) 474-1561;

Facility Type: Skilled care; Alzheimer's; Certified Beds: 455; Alzheimer's; Certified: Medicaid; Medicare; Veterans; Owner: Private; License: Current state

Plaza Nursing Home Co. Inc.
614 S. Crouse Ave., Syracuse, NY 13210, (315) 474-4431; Facility Type: Skilled care; Alzheimer's; Certified Beds: 242; Wellness unit 12; Certified: Medicaid; Medicare; Veterans; Owner: Nonprofit corp.; License: Current state

Utica

Eden Park Nursing Home
1800 Butterfield Ave., Utica, NY 13501, (315) 797-3570; Facility Type: Skilled care; Alzheimer's; Certified Beds: 117; ICF; Respite care 1; Certified: Medicaid; Medicare; Owner: Private; License: Current state

Warsaw

Wyoming County Community Hospital
400 N Main St., Warsaw, NY 14569, (585) 786-2233; Facility Type: Skilled care; Alzheimer's; Certified Beds: care 160; Certified: Medicaid; Medicare; Owner: Government/State/Local; License: Current state

Watertown

Genesis Health Care of New York
218 Stone St., Watertown, NY 13601, (315) 782-7400; Facility Type: Skilled care; Alzheimer's; Certified Beds: 224; Certified: Medicaid; Medicare; Owner: Nonprofit corp.; License: Current state

West Islip

Our Lady of Consolation Geriatric Care Center
111 Beach Dr., West Islip, NY 11795, (631) 587-1600; Facility Type: Skilled care; Alzheimer's; Certified Beds: 450; Certified: Medicaid; Medicare; Owner: Nonprofit/Religious org.; License: Current state

Yonkers

Saint Joseph's Hospital
127 S Broadway, Yonkers, NY 10701, (914) 378-7358; Facility Type: Skilled care; Alzheimer's; Certified Beds: 200; Certified: Medicaid; Medicare; Owner: Nonprofit corp.; License: Current state

NORTH CAROLINA

Albemarle

Britthaven of Piedmont
33426 Old Salisbury Rd., Albemarle, NC 28002, (704) 983-1195; Facility Type: Skilled care; ICF; Alzheimer's; Certified Beds: 180; Certified: Medicaid; Medicare; Owner: License: Current state

Stanley Manor
625 Bethany Rd., Albemarle, NC 28001, (704) 982-0770; Facility Type: Skilled care; ICF; Alzheimer's; Certified Beds: 90; Certified: Medicaid; Medicare; Owner: License: Current state

Asheville

Aston Park Health Care Center
380 Brevard Rd., Asheville, NC 28806, (828) 253-4437; Facility Type: Skilled care; ICF; Alzheimer's; Certified Beds: 120; Certified: Medicaid; Medicare; Veterans; Owner: Nonprofit corp.; License: Current state

Rickman Nursing Care Center
213 Richmond Hill Dr., Asheville, NC 28806, (828) 254-9675; Facility Type: Skilled care; ICF; Alzheimer's; Certified Beds: 100; Certified: Medicaid; Medicare; Owner: Nonprofit/Religious org.; License: Current state

Black Mountain

Black Mountain Medical Treatment Center
932 Old US 70 Hwy., Black Mountain, NC 28711, (828) 259-6700; Facility Type: Skilled care; Alzheimer's; Certified Beds: 163; Certified: Medicaid; Veterans; Owner: Government/state.; License: Current state

Mountain Ridge Wellness Center
315 Old US Hwy 70 E., Black Mountain NC 28711, (828) 669-9991; Facility Type: Skilled care; Alzheimer's; Certified Beds: 100; Certified: Medicaid; Medicare; Owner: For profit corp.; License: Current state

Burlington

White Oak Manor–Burlington
323 Baldwin Rd., Burlington, NC 27217, (336) 229-5571; Facility Type: Skilled care; ICF; Alzheimer's; Certified Beds: 141 60; Certified: Medicaid; Medicare; Veterans; Owner: White Oak Manor Inc.; License: Current state

Candler

Pisgah Manor Health Care Center
95 Holcombe Cove Rd., Candler, NC 28715, (828) 667-9851; Facility Type: Skilled care; ICF; Alzheimer's; Certified Beds: 118; Certified: Medicaid; Medicare; Owner: Nonprofit/Religious org.; License: Current state

Charlotte

Brian Center Health & Retirement
5939 Reddman Rd., Charlotte, NC 28212, (704) 563-6862; Facility Type: Skilled care; ICF; Alzheimer's; Certified Beds: 120; Lodge assisted care; Certified: Medicaid; Medicare; Veterans; Owner: Private; License: Current state

Hunter Woods Nursing and Rehabilitation
620 Tom Hunter Rd., Charlotte, NC 28256, (704) 598-5136; Facility Type: Skilled care; ICF; ICF/MR; Alzheimer's; Certified Beds: 120; Certified: Medicaid; Medicare; Owner: Centennial HealthCare Corp.; License: Current state

Liberty Nursing and Rehabilitation Center of Mecklenburg City
3700 Shamrock Dr., Charlotte, NC 28215, (704) 940-8300; Facility Type: Skilled care; Alzheimer's; Certified Beds: 289; Certified: Medicaid; Medicare; Owner: Nonprofit corp.; License: Current state

Concord

Five Oaks Manor
413 Winecoff School Rd., Concord, NC 28027, (704) 788-2131; Facility Type: Skilled care; ICF; Alzheimer's; Certified Beds: 160; Certified: Medicaid; Medicare; Veterans; Owner: Private; License: Current state

Durham

Rose Manor Healthcare Center
4230 N. Roxboro Rd., Durham, NC 27704, (919) 477-9805; Facility Type: Skilled care; ICF; Alzheimer's; Certified Beds: 111; Certified: Medicaid; Medicare; Owner: Vencor Inc.; License: Current state

Unihealth Post-Acute Care–Carolina Point
5935 Mt. Sinai Rd., Durham, NC 27705, (919) 402-2450; Facility Type: Skilled care; ICF; Alzheimer's; Certified Beds: 138; Alzheimer's; Certified: Medicaid; Medicare; Owner: Proprietary/Public corp.; License: Current state

Elizabethtown

Poplar Heights Care & Rehabilitation
804 S. Popular St., Elizabethtown, NC 28337, (910) 862-8100; Facility Type: Skilled care; ICF; Alzheimer's; Certified Beds: 90; Certified: Medicaid; Medicare; Veterans; Owner: Sun Healthcare Group Inc.; License: Current state

Fayetteville

Highland House Rehabilitation and Healthcare
1700 Pamalee Dr., Fayetteville, NC 28301, (910) 488-2295; Facility Type: Skilled care; ICF; Alzheimer's; Certified Beds: 106; Certified: Medicaid; Medicare; Veterans; Owner: Private; License: Current state

Whispering Pines Nursing & Rehabilitation Center
523 Country Club Dr., Fayetteville, NC 28301, (910) 488-0711; Facility Type: Skilled care; ICF; Alzheimer's; Certified Beds: 86; Home for aged; Certified: Medicaid; Medicare; Owner: Private; License: Current state

Hendersonville

Brian Center Health & Rehabilitation–Hendersonville
1870 Pisgah Dr., Hendersonville, NC 28791, (828) 693-9796; Facility Type: Skilled care; ICF; Alzheimer's; Certified Beds: 140; Certified: Medicaid; Medicare; Veterans; Owner: Proprietary/Public corp.; License: Current state

Hickory

Lutheran Home Hickory
1265 21St. NE, Hickory, NC 28601, (828) 328-2006; Facility Type: Skilled care; ICF; Alzheimer's; Certified Beds: 104; Certified: Medicaid; Medicare; Owner: Nonprofit corp.; License: Current state

Lumberton

Wesley Pines Retirement Community
1000 Wesley Pines Rd., Lumberton, NC 28358, (910) 738-9691; Facility Type: Skilled care; ICF; Alzheimer's; Certified Beds: 62; Certified: Medicaid; Medicare; Veterans; Owner: Nonprofit/Religious org.; License: Current state

Woodhaven Nursing & Alzheimer Care Center
1150 Pine Run Dr., Lumberton, NC 28358, (910) 671-5703; Facility Type: Skilled care; ICF; Alzheimer's; Certified Beds: 115; Certified: Medicaid; Medicare; Owner: Nonprofit corp.; License: Current state

Monroe

Rehabilitation & Nursing Center of Monroe
1212 E. Sunset Dr., Monroe, NC 28112, (704) 283-8548; Facility Type: Skilled care; ICF; Alzheimer's; Certified Beds: 147; Certified: Medicaid; Medicare; Owner: Vencor Inc.; License: Current state

New Bern

Britthaven of New Bern
2600 Old Cherry Point Rd., New Bern, NC 28563, (252) 637-4730; Facility Type: Skilled care; ICF; Alzheimer's; Certified Beds: 105; Certified: Medicaid; Medicare; Veterans; Owner: Britthaven Inc.; License: Current state

Raleigh

Blue Ridge Health Care Center
3830 Blue Ridge Rd., Raleigh, NC 27612, (919) 781-4900; Skilled care; ICF; Alzheimer's; Certified Beds: 147; Certified: Medicaid; Medicare; Owner: For profit; License: Current state

City of Oaks Health & Rehab
3609 Bond St., Raleigh NC 27604, (919) 231-8113; Skilled care; ICF; Alzheimer's; Certified Beds: 180; Certified: Medicaid; Medicare; Owner: For profit; License: Current state

Raleigh Rehab & Healthcare Center
616 Wade Ave. Raleigh, NC 27605, (919) 828-6251; Facility Type: Skilled care; ICF; Alzheimer's; Certified Beds: 174; Certified: Medicaid; Medicare; Owner: For profit; License: Current state

Rex Rehab & Nursing Care Center
4420 Lake Boone Tr., Raleigh NC 27607, (919) 784-6600; Facility Type: Skilled care; ICF; Alzheimer's; Certified Beds: 120; Certified: Medicaid; Medicare; Owner: Nonprofit; License: Current state

Sunnybrook Healthcare & Rehabilitation
25 Sunnybrook Rd., Raleigh, NC 27610, (919) 231-6150; Facility Type: Skilled care; ICF; Alzheimer's; Certified Beds: 114; Alzheimer's; Certified: Medicaid; Medicare; Veterans; Owner: Vencor Inc.; License: Current state

Southern Pines

Penick Village
E. Rhode Island Ave., Southern Pines, NC 28388, (910) 692-0300; Facility Type: Skilled care; ICF; Alzheimer's; Certified Beds: 50; Certified: Medicaid; Medicare; Owner: Nonprofit corp.; License: Current state

Stokesdale

Countryside Manor
7700 US 158 E., Stokesdale, NC 27357, (336) 643-6301; Facility Type: Skilled care; ICF; Alzheimer's; Certified Beds: 60; Certified: Medicaid; Medicare; Veterans; Owner: Proprietary/Public corp.; License: Current state

Thomasville

Piedmont Crossing
100 Hedrick Dr., Thomasville, NC 27360, (336) 472-2017; Facility Type: Skilled care; ICF; Alz-

heimer's; Certified Beds: 54; Certified: Medicaid; Medicare; Veterans; Owner: Nonprofit/Religious org.; License: Current state

Wake Forest

Hillside Nursing Center of Wake Forest
968 E. Wait Ave., Wake Forest, NC 27587, (919) 556-4082; Facility Type: Skilled care; ICF; Alzheimer's; Certified Beds: 130; Certified: Medicaid; Medicare; Owner: Proprietary/Public corp.; License: Current state

Williamston

IHS of Williamston
119 Gatling St., Williamston, NC 27842, (252) 792-1616; Facility Type: Skilled care; ICF; Alzheimer's; Certified Beds: 154; Certified: Medicaid; Medicare; Owner: Proprietary/Public corp.; License: Current state

Wilmington

Liberty Commons Rehabilitation Center
121 Racine Dr., Wilmington, NC 28403, (910) 452-4070; Facility Type: Skilled care; ICF; Alzheimer's; Certified Beds: 100; Certified: Medicaid; Medicare; Owner: Private; License: Current state

Wilson

Avante at Wilson
1804 Forest Hills Rd., Wilson, NC 27893, (252) 237-8161; Facility Type: Skilled care; ICF; Alzheimer's;

Certified Beds: 110; Certified: Medicaid; Medicare; Veterans; Owner: Avante Group; License: n/a

Wilmed Nursing Care Center
1705 S. Tarboro St., Wilson, NC 27893, (252) 399-8998; Facility Type: Skilled care; ICF; Alzheimer's; Certified Beds: 90; Certified: Medicaid; Medicare; Owner: Nonprofit corp.; License: Current state

Winston-Salem

Salemtowne
2000 Salemtowne Dr., Winston-Salem, NC 27106, (336) 767-8130; Facility Type: Skilled care; ICF; Alzheimer's; Certified Beds: 33; Certified: n/a; Owner: Nonprofit/Religious org.; License: Current state

Yadkinville

Willowbrook Rehabilitation & Health Care Center
333 E. Lee St., Yadkinville, NC 27055, (336) 679-8028; Facility Type: Skilled care; ICF; Alzheimer's; Certified Beds: 76; Certified: Medicaid; Medicare; Veterans; Owner: Centennial HealthCare Corp.; License: Current state

Yanceyville

Brian Center Nursing Care–Yanceyville
1086 Main St. North, Yanceyville, NC 27379, (336) 694-5916; Facility Type: Skilled care; ICF; Alzheimer's; Certified Beds: 157; Certified: Medicaid; Medicare; Owner: Proprietary/Public corp.; License: Current state

---

NORTH DAKOTA

Aneta

Aneta Parkview Health Center
113 5th St. S, Aneta, ND 58212, (701) 326-4234; Facility Type: Skilled care; ICF; Alzheimer's; Certified Beds: 39; Certified: Medicaid; Medicare; Owner: Nonprofit corp.; License: Current state

Bismarck

Baptist Home Inc.
1100 E Boulevard Ave., Bismarck, ND 58501, (701) 223-3040; Facility Type: Skilled care; Alzheimer's; Certified Beds: 141; Certified: Medicaid; Medicare; Owner: Nonprofit corp.; License: Current state

Saint Vincent's Care Center
1021 N. 26th St., Bismarck, ND 58501, (701) 323-

1999; Facility Type: Skilled care; Alzheimer's; Certified Beds: 101; Certified: Medicaid; Medicare; Owner: Nonprofit/Religious org.; License: Current state

Dickinson

Saint Benedict's Health Center
851 4th Ave. E, Dickinson, ND 58601, (701) 456-7242; Facility Type: Skilled care; Alzheimer's; Certified Beds: 164; Certified: Medicaid; Medicare; Owner: Benedictine Health System; License: Current state

Ellendale

Prince of Peace Care Center
201 8th St., Ellendale, ND 58436, (701) 349-3312; Facility Type: Skilled care; Alzheimer's; Certified Beds: 53; Certified: Medicaid; Medicare; Veterans;

Owner: Nonprofit/Religious org.; License: Current state

Fargo

Bethany Home
201 S. University Dr., Fargo, ND 58103, (701) 239-3000; Facility Type: Skilled care; Alzheimer's; Certified Beds: 172; Certified: Medicaid; Medicare; Owner: Nonprofit corp.; License: Current state

Villa Maria
3102 S. University Dr., Fargo, ND 58103, (701) 293-7750; Facility Type: Skilled care; ICF; ICF/MR; Alzheimer's; Certified Beds: 140; Certified: Medicaid; Medicare; Owner: Nonprofit corp.; License: Current state

Garrison

Benedictine Living Center of Garrison
609 4th Ave. NE, Garrison, ND 58540, (701) 463-2226; Facility Type: Skilled care; Alzheimer's; Certified Beds: 42; Certified: Medicaid; Medicare; Veterans; Owner: Nonprofit/Religious org.; License: Current state

Minot

Trinity Homes
305 8th Ave. NE, Minot, ND 58701, (701) 857-5800; Facility Type: Skilled care; Alzheimer's; Certified Beds: 292; Certified: Medicaid; Medicare; Veterans; Owner: Nonprofit corp.; License: Current state

Mohall

North Central Good Samaritan Center
602 E. Main St., Mohall, ND 58761, (701) 756-6831;

Facility Type: Skilled care; Alzheimer's; Certified Beds: 61; Certified: Medicaid; Owner: The Evangelical Lutheran Good Samaritan Society; License: Current state

Parshall

Good Samaritan Society–Rock View at Parshall
307 3rd St., NE, Parshall, ND 58770, (701) 862-3138; Facility Type: Skilled care; ICF/MR; Alzheimer's; Certified Beds: 38; Certified: Medicaid; Medicare; Owner: Nonprofit org.; License: Current state

Wahpeton

Saint Catherine's Living Center
1307 N. 7th St., Wahpeton, ND 58075, (701) 642-6667; Facility Type: Skilled care; Alzheimer's; Certified Beds: 104; Certified: Medicaid; Medicare; Veterans; Owner: Benedictine Health System; License: Current state

Williston

Bethel Lutheran Home Inc.
1512 2nd Ave. West, Williston, ND 58801, (701) 572-6766; Facility Type: Skilled care; Alzheimer's; Certified Beds: 169; Certified: Medicaid; Medicare; Owner: Nonprofit corp.; License: Current state

Wishek

Wishek Home for the Aged
400 S. 4th St., Wishek, ND 58495, (701) 452-2333; Facility Type: Skilled care; Alzheimer's; Certified Beds: 74; Certified: Medicaid; Medicare; Owner: Nonprofit corp.; License: Current state

OHIO

Akron

Bath Manor Special Care Center
2330 Smith Road, Akron, OH 44333, (330) 836-1006; Facility type: Skilled care, Alzheimer's, Intermediate care; Certified Beds: 150; Certified: Medicaid, Medicare, Veterans; License: Current state

Bridgepark Center for Rehabilitation & Nursing Services
145 Olive St., Akron, OH 44310, (330) 762-0901; Facility Type: Skilled care; Alzheimer's, intermediate care, special nursing units, home health care; Certified Beds: 140; Certified: Medicaid; Medicare; Veterans;

Owner: Vencor Inc. (Proprietary/ Public); License: Current state

Healthaven Nursing Home
615 Latham Lane, Akron, OH 44319, (330) 644-3914; Facility Type: Skilled care; Alzheimer's, Intermediate care; Certified Beds: 56; Certified: Medicaid; Medicare; Veterans; Owner: Health Network of Ohio (Nonprofit); License: Current state

Lorantffy Care Center Incorporated
2631 Copley Road, Akron, Ohio 44321, (330) 666-1313; Facility Type: Skilled care, Alzheimer's; Beds: 130; Certified: Medicaid; Medicare; intermediate care; special nursing unit; retirement and life care community; Owner: Nonprofit/Religious; License: Current state

ManorCare Health Services–Akron
1211 W. Market Street, Akron, OH 44313, (330) 867-8530; Facility Type: Skilled care, Alzheimer's, Intermediate care; Certified Beds: 117; Certified: Medicaid, Medicare; Owner: HCR ManorCare; License: Current state

The Merriman of Akron
209 Merriman Rd., Akron, Ohio 44303, (330) 762-9341; Facility Type: Skilled care, Alzheimer's; Certified Beds: 60; Certified: Medicaid; Medicare; Owner: Nonprofit corporation; License: Current state

Ridgewood Place
3558 Ridgewood Rd., Akron, OH 44313, (330) 666-3776; Facility Type: Skilled care, Alzheimer's; Certified Beds: 123; Certified: Medicaid, Medicare; Veterans; Owner: Proprietary/Public; License: Current state

Alliance

Canterbury Villa of Alliance
1785 Freshley Ave., Alliance, OH 44601, (330) 821-4000; Facility Type: Skilled care; Alzheimer's, Intermediate care; Certified Beds: 92; Certified: Medicaid, Medicare; Owner: Integrated Health Services, Inc. (Proprietary/Public); License: Current state

McCrea Manor Nursing & Rehabilitation Center
2040 McCrea Street, Alliance, OH 44601, (330) 823-9005; Facility Type: Skilled care; Alzheimer's, Assisted Living; Certified Beds: 100; Certified: Medicaid; Medicare; Veterans; Owner: Proprietary/Public; License: Current state

Amherst

Golden Acres Lorain County Nursing Home
PO Box 190, Amherst, OH 44001, (440) 988-2322; Facility Type: Skilled care, Alzheimer's; Certified Beds: 79; Certified: Medicaid; Medicare; Owner: Government/State and Local

Andover

Andover Village Retirement Community
486 S. Main St., Andover, OH 44003, (440) 293-5416; Facility Type: Skilled care, Alzheimer's; Beds: 200; Certified: Medicaid; Medicare; Owner: Ohio Health Ventures; License: Current state

Ashland

Brethren Care Incorporated
2000 Center St., Ashland, OH 44805, (419) 289-1585; Facility Type: Skilled care, Alzheimer's; Certified Beds: 96; Certified: Medicaid; Owner: Nonprofit corporation; License: Current state

Kingston of Ashland
20 Amberwood Pkwy, Ashland, OH 44805, (419) 289-3859; Facility Type: Skilled care, Alzheimer's, Intermediate care; Certified Beds: 100; Certified: Medicaid; Medicare; Owner: Proprietary/Public; License: Current state

Ashtabula

Carrington Park
2217 West Ave., Ashtabula, OH 44004, (440) 964-8446; Facility Type: Skilled care; Alzheimer's; Certified Beds: 207; Certified: Medicaid; Medicare; Veterans; Owner: Strategic Nursing; License: Current state

Country Club Retirement Center
925 E. 26th St., Ashtabula, OH 44004, (440) 992-0022, Facility Type: Skilled care, Alzheimer's, Intermediate care; Certified Beds: 65; Certified: Medicaid, Medicare; Owner: Proprietary/Public; License: Current state

Park Haven Home
4533 Park Ave., Ashtabula, OH 44004, (440) 992-9441; Facility Type: Skilled care, Alzheimer's; Certified Beds: 50; Certified: Medicaid, Medicare; Owner: Private; License: Current state

Aurora

Ann Maria of Aurora Incorporated
889 N. Aurora Rd., Aurora, OH 44202, (330) 562-6171; Facility Type: Skilled care, Alzheimer's; Certified Beds: 98; Certified: Medicaid, Medicare; Owner: Proprietary; License: state

Aurora Manor Special Care Center
101 Bissell Rd., Aurora, OH 44202, (440) 424-4000; Facility Type: Skilled care, Alzheimer's, Intermediate care; Certified Beds: 100; Certified: Medicaid; Medicare; Veterans; License: Current state

Avon

Avon Oaks Nursing Home
37800 French Creek Rd., Avon, OH 44011, (440) 934-5204; Facility Type: Skilled care, Alzheimer's; Beds: 105; Certified: Medicaid; Medicare; Owner: Private: License: Current state

Good Samaritan Nursing Home
32900 Detroit Rd., Avon, OH 44011, (440) 937-6201; Facility Type: Skilled care, Alzheimer's; Certified Beds: 170; Certified: Medicaid, Medicare; License: state

Baltic

Baltic Country Manor
130 Buena Vista St., Baltic, OH 43804, (330) 897-

4311; Facility Type: Skilled care, Alzheimer's, Intermediate Care; Certified Beds: 99; Certified: Medicaid; Medicare, Veterans; Owner: Integrated Health Services; License: state

Barberton

ManorCare Health Services–Barberton
85 Third St. SE, Barberton, OH 44203, (330) 753-5005; Facility Type: Skilled care, Alzheimer's; Certified Beds: 120; Certified: Medicaid; Medicare; Veterans; Owner: HCR ManorCare; License: Current state

Batavia

Batavia Nursing Care Center
4000 Golden Age Dr., Batavia, OH 45103, (513) 732-6500; Facility Type: Skilled care; Alzheimer's, Special Nursing Unit, Intermediate Care; Certified Beds: 166; Certified: Medicaid, Medicare; Owner: Carrington Health Systems; License: state

Bay Village

Bradley Bay Health Center
605 Bradley Rd., Bay Village, OH 44140, (440) 871-3474; Facility Type: Skilled care, Alzheimer's; Certified Beds: 138; Certified: Medicaid; Medicare; Owner: Private; License: state

Beachwood

Beachwood Pointe Care Center
23900 Chagrin Blvd., Beachwood, OH 44122, (216) 464-1000; Facility Type: Skilled care, Alzheimer's, Certified Beds: 140; Certified: Medicaid, Medicare; Veterans; Owner: Proprietary; License: state

Harborside Healthcare–Beachwood
3800 Park E, Beachwood, OH 44122, (216) 831-4303; Facility Type: Skilled care, Alzheimer's; Certified Beds: 274; Certified: Medicaid; Medicare; Veterans; Owner: Harborside Healthcare; License: state

Menorah Park Center for Senior
27100 Cedar Rd., Beachwood, OH 44122, (216) 831-6500; Facility Type: Skilled care, Alzheimer's; Certified Beds: 360; Certified: Medicaid; Medicare; Owner: Nonprofit/Religious; License: Current state

Bellevue

Bellevue Care Center
1 Audrich Square, Bellevue, OH 44811, (419) 483-6225; Facility Type: Skilled care; Alzheimer's; Certified Beds: 69; Certified: Medicaid; Owner: Proprietary/Public; License: Current state

Berea

Aristocrat Berea
255 Front St., Berea, OH 44017, (440) 243-4000; Facility Type: Skilled care, Alzheimer's, Intermediate care; Certified Beds: 165; Certified: Medicaid; Medicare; Owner: CommuniCare Health Services; License: Current state

Bidwell

Scenic Hills Nursing Center
311 Buckridge Rd., Bidwell, OH 45614, (740) 446-7150; Facility Type: Skilled care, Alzheimer's; Certified Beds: 99, Certified: Medicaid; Medicare; Owner: Integrated Health Services; License: Current state

Bloomville

Ruffin Care Center of Bloomville
22 Clinton St., Bloomville, OH 44818, (419) 983-2021; Facility Type: Skilled care, Alzheimer's; Certified Beds: 30; Certified: Medicaid; Medicare; Veterans; Owner: St. Catherine's Health Care Management; License: Current state

Bluffton

Mennonite Memorial Home
410 W. Elm St., Bluffton, OH 45817, (419) 358-1015; Facility Type: Skilled care; Alzheimer's, Intermediate Care; Certified Beds: 92; Certified: Medicaid; Owner: Nonprofit; License: Current state

Bowling Green

Bowling Green Manor
1021 W. Poe Rd., Bowling Green, OH 43402, (419) 352-4694; Facility Type: Skilled care, Alzheimer's; Certified Beds: 100; Certified: Medicaid; Medicare; Owner: Private; License: Current state

Broadview Heights

Harborside Healthcare, Broadview Heights
2801 E. Royalton Rd., Broadview Heights, OH 44147, (440) 526-4770; Facility Type: Skilled care; Alzheimer's; Certified Beds: 159; Certified: Medicaid; Medicare; Owner: Harbor-side Healthcare; License: Current state

Bryan

Williams County Hillside Country Living
09-876 County Rd. 16, Bryan, OH 43506, (419) 636-4508; Facility Type: Skilled care; Alzheimer's; Certified Beds: 71; Certified: Medicaid, Medicare; Owner: Government/ state and local; License: Current state

Bucyrus

Altercare of Bucyrus
1929 Whetstone St., Bucyrus, OH 44820, (419) 562-7644; Facility Type: Skilled care; Alzheimer's; Certified Beds: 80; Certified: Medicaid, Medicare; Owner: Altercare; License: Current state

Cambridge

Cambridge Health & Rehabilitation Center
1471 Wills Creek Valley Dr., Cambridge, OH 43725, (740) 439-4437; Facility Type: Skilled care; Alzheimer's, Intermediate, Special Nursing care; Certified Beds: 144; Certified: Medicaid, Medicare, Veterans; Owner: Vencor; License: Current state

Canal Fulton

Chapel Hill Community
12200 Strausser St., NW, Canal Fulton, OH 44614, (330) 854-4177; Facility Type: Skilled care, Alzheimer's, Assisted living; Certified Beds: 125; Certified: Medicaid, Medicare, Veterans; Owner: United Church Homes; License: Current state

Canton

Bethany Nursing Home
626 34th St., NW, Canton, OH 44709, (330) 492-7171; Facility Type: Skilled care, Alzheimer's, Intermediate care; Certified Beds: 39; Certified: Medicaid, Medicare; Owner: Proprietary/Public; License: Current state

Canton Health Care Center
1223 Market Ave. N., Canton, OH 44714, (330) 454-2152; Facility Type: Skilled care, Alzheimer's, Intermediate care; Certified Beds: 116; Certified: Medicaid; Medicare; Owner: Essex Healthcare Corporation; License: Current state

ManorCare
5005 Higbee Ave., NW, Canton, OH 44718, (330) 492-7835; Facility Type: Skilled care, Alzheimer's; Certified Beds: 139; Certified: Medicaid, Medicare; Owner: HCR ManorCare; License: Current state

McKinley Health Care
800 Market Ave. N, Canton, OH 44702, (330) 456-1014; Facility Type: Skilled care, Alzheimer's, Adult Day care; Certified Beds: 176; Certified: Medicaid, Medicare; Owner: Proprietary/Public; License: Current state

Carlisle

Carlisle Manor Health Care
730 Hillcrest Dr., Carlisle, OH 45005, (937) 746-2662; Facility Type: Skilled care, Alzheimer's, Certified Beds: 48; Certified: Medicaid; Medicare; Veterans; Owner: Proprietary/Public; License: Current state

Carrollton

Carroll Health Care Center
648 Longhorn St., Carrollton, OH 44615, (330) 627-5501; Facility Type: Skilled care, Alzheimer's; Beds: 101; Certified: Medicaid, Medicare; Owner: Private; License: Current state

Morning View Care Center of Centerburg
4531 Columbus Rd., Centerburg, OH 43011, (740) 625-5401; Facility Type: Skilled care, Alzheimer's; Certified Beds: 76; Certified: Medicaid; Owner: Proprietary/Public; License: Current state

Centerville

The Franciscan at Saint Leonard Center
8100 Clyo Rd., Centerville, OH 45458, (937) 433-0480; Facility Type: Skilled care, Alzheimer's, Adult day care; Certified Beds: 120; Certified: Medicaid; Medicare; Owner: Nonprofit/Religious; License: Current state

Chardon

Heather Hill Inc.
12340 Bass Lake Rd., Chardon, OH 44024, (440) 285-4040; Facility Type: Skilled care, Alzheimer's, Adult day care; Certified Beds: 55; Certified: Medicaid, Medicare; Owner: Nonprofit; License: Current state

Chesterville

Morrow Manor Nursing Center
St Rte. 314, Chesterville, OH 43317, (419) 768-2401; Facility Type: Skilled care, Alzheimer's; Certified Beds: 46; Certified: Medicaid, Medicare, Veterans; License: Current state

Chillicothe

Westmoreland Place
230 Cherry St., Chillicothe, OH 45601, (740) 773-6470; Facility Type: Skilled care, Alzheimer's; Certified Beds: 150; Certified: Medicaid; Medicare; Veterans; Owner: Proprietary/Public; License: Current state

Cincinnati

The Anderson
8139 Beechmont Ave., Cincinnati, OH 45255, (513) 474-6200; Facility Type: Skilled care, Alzheimer's; Certified Beds: 100; Certified: Medicaid, Medicare; License: state

Bayley Place
990 Bayley Place Dr., Cincinnati, OH 45233, (513) 347-5500; Facility Type: Skilled care, Alzheimer's; Certified Beds: 110; Certified: Medicaid, Medicare; Veterans; Owner: Catholic Church; License: Current state

Hilltop Rehabilitation & Nursing Center
2586 LaFeuille Ave., Cincinnati, OH 45211, (513) 662-2444; Facility Type: Skilled care, Alzheimer's; Certified Beds: 199; Certified: Medicaid, Medicare, Veterans; Owner: CommuniCare Health Services; License: Current state

Ridge Pavilion
5501 Verulam, Cincinnati, OH 45213, (513) 631-1310; Facility Type: Skilled care; Alzheimer's; Certified Beds: 99; Certified: Medicaid; Medicare; Veterans; Owner: Private; License: Current state

Circleville

Pickway ManorCare Center
391 Clark Dr., Circleville, OH 43113, (740) 474-6036; Facility Type: Skilled care, Alzheimer's; Certified Beds: 99; Certified: Medicaid, Medicare, Veterans; License: Current state

Cleveland

Aristocrat West Nursing Home
4387 W. 150th St., Cleveland, OH 44135, (216) 252-7730; Facility Type: Skilled care, Alzheimer's; Certified Beds: 90; Certified: Medicaid, Medicare; Veterans; Owner: Private; License: Current state

Franklin Plaza Extended Care
3600 Franklin Blvd., Cleveland, OH 44113, (216) 651-1600; Facility Type: Skilled care, Alzheimer's; Certified Beds: 174; Certified: Medicaid; Medicare; Owner: DMD Management Incorporated

Kindred Hospital Cleveland Subacute Unit
11900 Fairhill Rd., Cleveland, OH 44120, (216) 983-8030; Facility Type: Skilled care; Alzheimer's; Certified Beds: 40; Certified; Medicaid, Medicare; Owner: Nonprofit; License: Current state

Sunset Nursing Home
1802 Crawford Rd., Cleveland, OH 44106, (216) 795-5710; Facility Type: Skilled care, Alzheimer's; Certified Beds: 50; Certified: Medicaid, Medicare; License: Current state

University Manor Health & Rehabilitation
2186 Ambleside Rd., Cleveland OH 44106, (216) 721-1400; Facility Type: Skilled care, Alzheimer's; Certified Beds: 208; Certified: Medicaid; Medicare; Veterans; Owner: Proprietary/Public; License: Current state

Westpark Health Care Center
4401 W. 150th St., Cleveland, OH 44135, (216) 252-7555; Facility Type: Skilled care; Alzheimer's; Certified Beds: 100; Certified: Medicaid; Medicare; Owner: Private; License: Current state

Columbiana

Saint Mary's Alzheimer's Center
1899 Garfield Rd., Columbiana, OH 44408, (330) 549-9259; Facility Type: Skilled care, Alzheimer's; Certified Beds: 108; Certified: Medicaid, Medicare; Owner: Windsor House Incorporated; License: Current state

Columbus

Broadview Health & Rehabilitation Center
5151 N Hamilton Rd., Columbus, OH 43232, (614) 337-1066; Facility Type: Skilled care, Alzheimer's; Certified Beds: 112; Certified: Medicaid, Medicare, Veterans; Owner: Private; License: Current state

Columbus Alzheimer Care Center
700 Jasonway Ave., Columbus, OH 43214, (614) 459-7050; Facility Type: Skilled care, Alzheimer's; Certified Beds: 100; Certified: Medicaid; Owner: Proprietary/Public; License: Current state

First Community Village Healthcare Center
1801 Riverside Dr., Columbus, OH 43212, (614) 486-5047; Facility Type: Skilled care; Alzheimer's; Certified Beds: 163; Certified: Medicaid; Medicare; Owner: Nonprofit; License: Current state

Health Center at Wesley Glen
5155 N High St., Columbus, OH 43214, (614) 888-7492; Facility Type: Skilled care, Alzheimer's, Beds: 81; Certified: Medicaid, Medicare, Veterans; Owner: Nonprofit; License: current state

Isabelle Ridgeway Care Center
1520 Hawthorne Ave., Columbus, OH 43203, (614) 252-4931; Facility Type: Skilled care; Alzheimer's, Adult day care, Home health care; Certified Beds: 99; Certified: Medicaid, Medicare; Owner: Nonprofit; License: Current state

Lutheran Village of Columbus Care Center
935 N. Cassady Ave., Columbus, OH 43219, (614) 252-4987; Facility Type: Skilled care, Alzheimer's; Beds: Certified 186; Certified: Medicaid, Medicare; Veterans; Owner: Nonprofit/Religious; License: Current state

Regency Manor Rehabilitation & Subacute Center
2000 Regency Manor Cir., Columbus, OH 43207, (614) 445-8261; Facility Type: Skilled care; Alzheimer's; Certified Beds: 275; Certified: Medicaid, Medicare; Owner: CommuniCare Health Services; License: Current state

Yorkland Park Care Center
1425 Yorkland Rd., Columbus, OH 43232, (614) 861-

6666; Facility Type: Skilled care, Alzheimer's; Certified Beds: 165; Certified: Medicaid, Medicare; Owner: Beverly Enterprises Incorporated; License: Current state

Cortland

Cortland Healthcare Center
369 N. High St., Cortland, OH 44410, (330) 638-4015; Facility Type: Skilled care; Alzheimer's, Adult Day Care; Certified Beds: 50; Certified: Medicaid; Owner: Genesis Elder Care; License: Current state

Cuyahoga Falls

Cuyahoga Falls Country Place
2728 Bailey Rd., Cuyahoga Falls, OH 44221, (330) 929-4231; Facility Type: Skilled care; Alzheimer's, Certified Beds: 107, Certified: Medicaid, Medicare, Veterans

Dayton

Bethany Lutheran Village
6451 Far Hills Ave., Dayton, OH 45459, (937) 436-6841; Facility Type: Skilled care, Alzheimer's; Certified Beds: 252; Certified: Medicaid, Medicare; Owner: Nonprofit/Religious; License: Current state

Carriage Inn of Dayton
5040 Philadelphia Dr., Dayton, OH 45415, (937) 278-0404; Facility Type: Skilled care, Alzheimer's; Certified Beds: 85; Certified: Medicaid; Medicare; Owner: Integrated Health Services Incorporated; License: Current state

The Maria-Joseph Center
4830 Salem Ave., Dayton, OH 45416, (937) 278-2692; Facility Type: Skilled care, Alzheimer's; Certified Beds: 305; Certified: Medicaid, Medicare; Owner: Catholic Health Initiatives; License: state

Wood Glen Alzheimer's Community
3800 Summit Glen Dr., Dayton, OH 45449, (937) 436-2273; Facility Type: Skilled care, Alzheimer's; Certified Beds: 148; Certified: Medicaid; Medicare; Owner: AdCare Health Systems Incorporated; License: Current state

Defiance

Leisure Oaks Convalescent Center
214 Harding St., Defiance, OH 43512, (419) 784-1014; Facility Type: Skilled care, Alzheimer's, Adult day care; Certified Beds: 99; Certified: Medicaid, Medicare, Veterans; Owner: Proprietary; License: state

Dover

Country Club Center
860 Iron Ave., Dover, OH 44622, (330) 343-5568;

Facility Type: Skilled care; Alzheimer's; Certified Beds: 72; Certified: Medicaid; Medicare; Owner: Proprietary/Public; License: Current state

Hennis Care Center
1720 Cross St., Dover, OH 44622, (330) 364-8849; Facility Type: Skilled care, Alzheimer's; Certified Beds: 137; Certified: Medicaid, Medicare; Owner: Private; License: state

East Liverpool

East Liverpool Convalescent Center
701 Armstrong Ln., East Liverpool, OH 43920, (330) 385-5212; Facility Type: Skilled care; Alzheimer's; Certified Beds: 24; Certified: Medicaid, Medicare, Veterans; Owner: Private

Nentwick Convalescent Home Incorporated
500 Selfridge St., East Liverpool, OH, 43920, (330) 385-5001; Facility Type: Skilled care, Alzheimer's; Certified Beds: 100; Certified: Medicaid; Medicare, Veterans; License: state

Eaton

Greenbriar Nursing Center
501 W. Lexington Rd., Eaton, OH 45320, (937) 456-9535; Facility Type: Skilled care, Alzheimer's; Certified Beds: 74; Certified: Medicaid, Medicare; Owner: Public; License: state

Elyria

Elyria United Methodist Village
807 West Ave., Elyria, OH 44035, (440) 284-9000; Facility Type: Skilled care; Alzheimer's, Adult day care; Certified Beds: 164; Certified: Medicaid; Medicare; Veterans; Owner: Religious; Activities

Euclid

BracView Manor Health Care Facility
20611 Euclid Ave., Euclid, OH 44117, (216) 486-9300; Facility Type: Skilled care; Alzheimer's; Certified Beds: 107; Certified: Medicaid; Medicare; Veterans; Owner: Public; License: Current state

Fairfield

Tri-County Extended Care Center
5200 Camelot Dr., Fairfield, OH 45014, (513) 829-8100; Facility Type: Skilled care, Alzheimer's; Certified Beds: 258; Certified: Medicaid; Medicare, Veterans; Owner: Private; License: Current state

Fairlawn

Arbors at Fairlawn
575 S. Cleveland-Massillon Rd., Fairlawn, OH

44333, (330) 666-5866; Facility Type: Skilled care; Alzheimer's, Assisted living; Certified Beds: 100; Certified: Medicaid, Medicare; Owner: ExtendiCare Health Services; License: Current state

Saint Edward Home
3131 Smith Rd., Fairlawn, OH 44313, (330) 666-1183; Facility Type: Skilled care, Alzheimer's; Certified Beds: 81; Certified: Medicaid; Owner: Proprietary; License: Current state

Findlay

Saint Catherine's Care Center of Findlay
8455 County Rd. 140, Findlay, OH 45840, (419) 422-3978; Facility Type: Skilled care; Alzheimer's; Certified Beds: 96; Certified: Medicaid, Medicare, Veterans; Owner: St. Catherine's Health Care; License: Current state

Fostoria

Good Shepherd Home
725 Columbus Ave., Fostoria, OH 44830, (419) 435-1801; Facility Type: Skilled care; Alzheimer's, assisted Living; Certified Beds: 112; Certified: Medicaid, Medicare, Veterans; Owner: Religious; License: Current state

Saint Catherine's Center of Fostoria
25 Christopher Dr., Fostoria, OH 44830, (419) 435-8112; Facility Type: Skilled care; Alzheimer's; Certified Beds: 91; Certified: Medicaid, Medicare; Owner: Saint Catherine's Health Care; License: state

Fowler

Meadowbrook Manor–Hartford
3090 Five Point-Hartford Rd., Fowler, OH 44418, (330) 772-5253; Facility Type: Skilled care, Alzheimer's; Certified Beds: 54; Certified: Medicaid, Medicare; Owner: Private; License: Current state

Frankfort

Valley View Alzheimer's Care Center
3363 Ragged Ridge Rd., Frankfort, OH 45628, (740) 998-2948; Facility Type: Skilled care, Alzheimer's; Certified Beds: 50; Certified: Medicaid; Medicare; Veterans; Owner: AdCare Health Systems; License: state

Franklin

Franklin Ridge
421 Mission Ln., Franklin, OH 45005, (937) 746-3943; Facility Type: Skilled care, Alzheimer's; Certified Beds: 99; Certified: Medicaid, Medicare, Veterans; Owner: Proprietary; License: state

Fremont

Bethesda Care Center
600 N. Brush St., Fremont, OH 43420, (419) 334-9521; Facility Type: Skilled care, Alzheimer's; Certified Beds: 99; Certified: Medicaid; Medicare; Veterans; Owner: Volunteers of America National Services; License: Current state

Fremont Center Genesis Eldercare
825 June St., Fremont, OH 43420, (419) 332-0357; Facility Type: Skilled care, Alzheimer's, Adult day care; Certified Beds: 60; Certified: Medicaid, Medicare; Owner: Genesis ElderCare; License: state

Garfield Heights

Jennings Hall
10204 Granger Rd., Garfield Heights, OH 44125, (216) 581-2900; Facility Type: Skilled care, Alzheimer's; Certified Beds: 174; Certified: Medicaid, Medicare; Owner: Religious; License: state

Geneva

Esther Marie Nursing Center
60 West St., Geneva, OH 44041, (440) 466-1181; Facility Type: Skilled care, Alzheimer's; Certified Beds: 66; Certified: Medicaid; Medicare; Owner: Proprietary/Public; License: Current state

Green Springs

Elmwood
430 N. Broadway St., Green Springs, OH 44836, (419) 639-2581; Facility Type: Skilled care, Alzheimer's, Assisted Living; Certified Beds: 31; Certified: Medicaid, Medicare, Veterans; Owner: Elmwood Centers; License: state

Greenfield

Long Term Care of Greenfield
850 Nellie St., Greenfield, OH 45123, (937) 981-2165; Facility Type: Skilled care, Alzheimer's; Certified Beds: 57; Certified: Medicaid, Medicare, Veterans; Owner: McQuen Management; License: state

Holgate

Holgate Quality Care Nursing & Rehabilitation Center
600 Joe E Brown Rd., Holgate, OH 43527, (419) 264-0700; Facility Type: Skilled care; Alzheimer's, Adult day care; Certified Beds: 50; Certified: Medicaid; Medicare; Owner: Genesis ElderCare; License: Current state

Kent

Kent Center
1290 Fairchild Ave., Kent, OH 44240, (330) 678-4912; Facility Type: Skilled care, Alzheimer's; Certified Beds: 92; Certified: Medicaid; Medicare; Owner: Genesis ElderCare; License: Current state

Kenton

Kenton Nursing & Rehabilitation Center
117 Jacob Parrott Blvd., Kenton, OH 43326, (419) 674-4197; Facility Type: Skilled care; Alzheimer's; Certified Beds: 115; Certified: Medicaid, Medicare; Owner: Proprietary/Public; License: Current state

Kettering

Lincoln Park Manor
694 Isaac Prugh Way, Kettering, OH 45429, (937) 297-4300; Facility Type: Skilled care, Alzheimer's, Assisted Living; Certified Beds: 60; Certified: Medicaid, Medicare, Veterans; Owner: Proprietary/Public, Osborne Management; License: Current state

The Oaks of West Kettering, Inc.
1150 W. Dorothy Ln., Kettering, OH 45409, (937) 293-1152; Facility Type: Skilled care, Alzheimer's; Certified Beds: 118; Certified: Medicaid, Medicare, Veterans; Owner: Aegis Consulting Services, Private; License: Current state

Walnut Creek Nursing Center
5070 Lamme Rd., Kettering, OH 45439, (937) 293-7703; Facility Type: Skilled care; Alzheimer's, Special Nursing Facility, Assisted Living; Certified Beds: 169; Certified: Medicaid; Medicare; Owner: Proprietary/Public, the Mariner Management Company; License: Current state

Kingsville

Ashtabula County Nursing Home
5740 Dibble Rd., Kingsville, OH 44048, (440) 224-2161; Facility Type: Skilled care; Alzheimer's, Adult day care; Certified Beds: 177; Certified: Medicaid; Medicare; Veterans; Owner: State and Local Gov.; License: Current state

Kirkersville

Pine Kirk Care Center
205 E. Main St., Kirkersville, OH 43033, (740) 927-3209; Facility Type: Skilled care; Alzheimer's; Certified Beds: 24; Certified: Medicaid; Medicare; Veterans; Owner: Proprietary/Public; License: Current state

Lancaster

Homestead Care & Rehabilitation
1900 E. Main St., Lancaster, OH 43130, (740) 653-8630; Facility Type: Skilled care, Alzheimer's; Certified Beds: 99; Certified: Medicaid; Medicare; Owner: Sun Healthcare Group; License: Current state

Lebanon

Cedars of Lebanon
102 E. Silver St., Lebanon, OH 45036, (513) 932-0300; Facility Type: Skilled care, Alzheimer's; Certified Beds: 45; Certified: Medicaid; Owner: Health Care Opportunities; License: Current state

Otterbein-Lebanon Retirement Community
585 N. State Rte. 741, Lebanon, OH 45036, (513) 933-5427; Facility Type: Skilled care; Alzheimer's, Adult day care; Certified Beds: 256; Certified: Medicaid; Medicare; Owner: Otterbein Homes; License: Current state

Lima

Lima Convalescent Home
1650 Allentown Rd., Lima, OH 45805, (419) 224-9741; http://www.limaconvalescenthome.com; Facility Type: Skilled care, Alzheimer's; Certified Beds: 84; Certified: Medicaid; Owner: Nonprofit; License: Current state

Lorain

Anchor Lodge Nursing Home, Inc.
3756 W. Erie Ave., Lorain, OH 44053, (440) 244-2019; Facility Type: Skilled care, Alzheimer's; Certified Beds: 114; Certified: Medicaid, Medicare; Owner: Proprietary/Public; License: Current state

Lake Pointe Health Care
3364 Kolbe Rd., Lorain, OH 44053, (440) 282-2244; Facility Type: Skilled care, Alzheimer's; Certified Beds: 182; Certified: Medicaid, Medicare; Owner: CommuniCare Health Services; License: Current state

Louisville

Green Meadows Health & Wellness Center
7770 Columbus Rd. NE, Louisville, OH 44641, (330) 875-1456; Facility Type: Skilled care; Alzheimer's; Certified Beds: 145; Certified: Medicaid; Medicare; Veterans; Owner: Government/ State and Local; License: Current state

Loveland

Loveland Health Care Center
501 N. 2nd St., Loveland, OH 45140, (513) 683-6000; Facility Type: Skilled care, Alzheimer's; Certified Beds: 99; Certified: Medicaid, Medicare; Owner: Private; License: Current state

Mansfield

Crystal Care Center of Mansfield
1159 Wyandotte Ave., Mansfield, OH 44906, (419) 747-2666; Facility Type: Skilled care; Alzheimer's; Certified Beds: 74; Certified: Medicaid, Medicare; Owner: Private; License: Current state

Mansfield Memorial Homes
50 Blymyer Ave., Mansfield, OH 44903, (419) 774-5100; Facility Type: Skilled care, Alzheimer's, Adult day care; Certified Beds: 99; Certified: Medicaid, Medicare; Owner: Nonprofit; License: Current state

Marietta

Harmar Place Rehabilitation & Extended Care
401 Harmar St., Marietta, OH 45750, (740) 376-5600; Facility Type: Skilled care, Alzheimer's; Certified Beds: 86; Certified: Medicaid, Medicare, Veterans; Owner: Extendicare; License: Current state; Activities: Arts & Crafts; Cards; Games; Exercise; Pet therapy; Other: Affiliated: O'Neill Senior Center

Marietta Center for Health & Rehabilitation
117 Bartlett St., Marietta, OH 45750, (740) 373-1867; Facility Type: Skilled care, Alzheimer's; Certified Beds: 150; Certified: Medicaid, Medicare, Veterans; Owner: Vencor Health Services; License: Current state

Marion

Community Healthcare Center
175 Community Dr., Marion, OH 43302, (740) 387-7537; Facility Type: Skilled care, Alzheimer's; Certified Beds: 110; Certified: Medicaid, Medicare; Owner: Vencor; License: Current state

Medina

Life Care Center of Medina
2400 Columbia Rd., Medina, OH 44256, (330) 483-3131; Facility Type: Skilled care, Alzheimer's, Assisted living; Certified Beds: 156; Certified: Medicaid, Medicare, Veterans; Owner: Life Care Centers of America; License: Current state

Medina Village Retirement Community, Ltc.
555 Springbrook Dr., Medina, OH 44256, (330) 725-3393; Facility Type: Skilled care, Alzheimer's; Certified Beds: 120; Certified: Medicaid, Medicare, Veterans; Owner: Home Health Care; License: Current state

Middleburg Heights

Century Oak Care Center
7250 Old Oak Blvd., Middleburg Heights, OH 44130, (440) 243-7888; Facility Type: Skilled care, Alzheimer's; Certified Beds: 116; Certified: Medicaid, Medicare; Owner: Proprietary/Public; License: Current state

Royal Oak Nursing & Rehabilitation
6973 Pearl Rd., Middleburg Heights, OH 44130, (440) 884-9191; Facility Type: Skilled care, Alzheimer's; Certified Beds: 99; Certified: Medicaid, Medicare; Owner: Private; License: Current state

Middletown

Liberty Retirement Community of Middletown, Inc.
4400 Vannest Ave., Middletown, OH 45042, (513) 422-5600; Facility Type: Skilled care, Alzheimer's; Certified Beds: 90; Certified: Medicaid, Medicare; Owner: Nonprofit; License: Current state

Residence at Kensington
751 Kensington St., Middletown, OH 45044, (513) 424-3511; Facility Type: Skilled care, Alzheimer's; Certified Beds: 109; Certified: Medicaid, Medicare; Owner: Envision Group; License: Current state; Activities: Arts & Crafts; Cards; Games; Pet therapy; Outings/Sightseeing; Support groups; Other: Alzheimer's secured unit

Millersburg

Majora Lane Care Center
105 Majora Ln., Millersburg, OH 44654, (330) 674-4444; Facility Type: Skilled care, Alzheimer's; Certified Beds: 80; Certified: Medicaid, Medicare; Owner: Proprietary/Public; License: Current state

Minerva

Minerva Eldercare Center
1035 E. Lincoln Way, Minerva, OH 44657, (330) 868-4147; Facility Type: Skilled care, Alzheimer's; Certified Beds: 34; Certified: Medicaid, Medicare, Veterans; License: Current state

Monroe

Mount Pleasant Retirement Village
225 Britton Ln., Monroe, OH 45050, (513) 539-7391; Facility Type: Skilled care, Alzheimer's, Adult day care; Certified Beds: 117; Certified: Medicaid, Medicare; Owner: Presbyterian Retirement Services; License: Current state

Mount Vernon

Country Club Center II
1350 Yauger Rd., Mount Vernon, OH 43050, (740) 397-2350; Facility Type: Skilled care, Alzheimer's; Adult day care; Certified Beds: 76; Certified: Medicaid; Owner: Proprietary/Public; License: Current state

Navarre

Altercare of Navarre
517 Park St. NW, Navarre, OH 44662, (330) 879-2765; Facility Type: Skilled care, Alzheimer's; Certified Beds: 131; Certified: Medicaid, Medicare; Owner: Altercare; License: Current state

Country Lawn Nursing Home
10608 Navarre Rd., SW, Navarre, OH 44662, (330) 767-3455; Facility Type: Skilled care, Alzheimer's; Certified Beds: 124; Certified: Medicaid, Medicare; Owner: Consolidated Healthcare Related; Altercare; License: Current state

New Carlisle

Belle Manor Nursing Home
197 N. Pike St., New Carlisle, OH 45344, (937) 845-3561; Facility Type: Skilled care, Alzheimer's; Certified Beds: 65; Certified: Medicaid; Medicare; Owner: Proprietary/Public; License: Current state

New Concord

Becket House at New Concord
1280 Friendship Dr., New Concord, OH 43762, (740) 826-7649; Facility Type: Skilled care, Alzheimer's; Certified Beds: 99; Certified: Medicaid; Owner: Zandex Health Care; License: Current state

New Lexington

SunBridge Care & Rehabilitation for New Lexington
920 S. Main St., New Lexington, OH 43764, (740) 342-5161; Facility Type: Skilled care, Alzheimer's; Certified Beds: 97; Certified: Medicaid, Medicare; Owner: Sun Healthcare Group; License: Current state

New London

The Rehabilitation & Nursing Center at Firelands
204 W. Main St., New London, OH 44851, (419) 929-1563; Facility Type: Skilled care, Alzheimer's, Home Health care; Beds: 50; Certified: Medicaid, Medicare; Owner: Integrated Health Services; License: state

Newark

Flint Ridge Nursing & Rehabilitation Center
1450 W. Main St., Newark, OH 43055, (740) 344-9465; Facility Type: Skilled care, Alzheimer's; Certified Beds: 101; Certified: Medicaid, Medicare, Veterans; Owner: Proprietary/Public; License: Current state

Newark Healthcare Center
75 McMillen Dr., Newark, OH 43055, (740) 344-

0357; Facility Type: Skilled care, Alzheimer's; Certified Beds: 271; Certified: Medicaid, Medicare, Veterans; Owner: Public; License: Current state

North Baltimore

Blakely Care Center
600 Sterling Dr., North Baltimore, OH 45872, (419) 257-2421; Facility Type: Skilled care, Alzheimer's; Certified Beds: 74; Certified: Medicaid, Medicare; Veterans; Owner: Proprietary/Public; License: Current state

North Canton

Saint Luke Lutheran Home for the Aging
220 Applegrove St., NE, North Canton, OH 44720, (330) 499-8341; Facility Type: Skilled care, Alzheimer's; Certified Beds: 202; Certified: Medicaid, Medicare; Owner: Lutheran Church; License: Current state

North Lima

The Assumption Village
9800 Market St., North Lima, OH 44452, (330) 549-0740; Facility Type: Skilled care; Alzheimer's, Assisted living; Certified Beds: 150; Certified: Medicaid, Medicare, Veterans; Owner: Catholic Church; License: Current state

Ivy Woods Manor
9625 Market St., North Lima, OH 44452, (330) 549-3939; Facility Type: Skilled care, Alzheimer's; Certified Beds: 91; Certified: Medicaid; Medicare; Veterans; Owner: Government/ State and Local; License: Current state

North Olmsted

ManorCare Health Services
23225 Lorain Rd., North Olmsted, OH 44070, (440) 779-6900; Facility Type: Skilled care, Alzheimer's; Certified Beds: 178; Certified: Medicaid, Medicare; Owner: HCR ManorCare; License: Current state

Olmsted Manor Skilled Nursing Center
27500 Mill Rd., North Olmsted, OH 44070, (440) 777-8444; Facility Type: Skilled care, Alzheimer's; Certified Beds: 74; Certified: Medicaid, Medicare; Owner: Private; License: Current state

Norwalk

Gaymont Nursing Center
66 Norwood Ave., Norwalk, OH 44857, (419) 668-8258; Facility type: Skilled care, Alzheimer's; Beds: 112; Certified: Medicaid, Medicare, Veterans; Owner: Public; License: Current state

Oak Harbor

Ottawa County Riverview Nursing Home
8180 W. State Rte. 163, Oak Harbor, OH 43449,
(419) 898-2851; Facility type: Skilled care, Alzheimer's; Certified Beds: 190; Certified: Medicaid, Medicare, Veterans; Owner: Private; License: Current state

Oberlin

Kendal at Oberlin
600 Kendal Dr., Oberlin, OH 44074, (440) 775-0094; Facility type: Skilled care, Alzheimer's; Certified Beds: 42; Certified: Medicaid, Medicare; Owner: Public; License: Current state

Ottawa

Putnam Acres Care Center
10170 Rd. 5 H RR 1, Ottawa, OH 45875, (419) 523-4092; Facility type: Skilled care, Alzheimer's; Certified Beds: 72; Certified: Medicaid, Medicare, Veterans; Owner: State and Local Gov.; License: Current state

Port Clinton

Edgewood Manor Nursing Center
1330 S. Fulton St., Port Clinton, OH 43452, (419) 734-5506; Facility type: Skilled care, Alzheimer's; Certified Beds: 99; Certified: Medicaid, Medicare; Owner: Covenant Care; License: Current state

Sandusky

Lutheran Memorial Home, Inc.
795 Bardshar Rd., Sandusky, OH 44870, (419) 625-4046; Facility type: Skilled care, Alzheimer's; Certified Beds: 76; Certified: Medicaid; Owner: Religious; License: Current state

Springfield

IOOF Home of Ohio
404 E. McCreight Ave., Springfield, OH 45503, (937) 399-8311; Facility type: Skilled care, Alzheimer's; Certified Beds: 76; Certified: Medicaid, Medicare; Owner: Nonprofit; License: Current state

Mercy St. John's Center
100 W. McCreight Ave., Springfield, OH 45504, (937) 399-9910; Facility type: Skilled care, Alzheimer's; Certified Beds: 89; Certified: Medicaid, Medicare, Veterans; Owner: Catholic Healthcare Partners; License: Current state

Stow

The Briarwood
3700 Englewood Dr., Stow, OH 44224, (330) 688-1828; Facility type: Skilled care, Alzheimer's, Assisted Living; Certified Beds: 50; Certified: Medicaid, Medicare; Owner: Proprietary; License: Current state

Maison Aine
2910 L'Ermitage Pl., Stow, OH 44224, (330) 668-1188; Facility type: Skilled care, Alzheimer's; Certified Beds: 150; Certified: Medicaid, Medicare; Owner: ExtendiCare Health Services; License: Current state

Sylvania

Goerlic Center
5320 Harroun Rd., Sylvania, OH 43560, (419) 824-1250; Facility type: Skilled care, Alzheimer's; Certified Beds: 60; Certified: Medicaid, Medicare; Owner: Nonprofit; License: Certified state

Toledo

Concord Care Center of Toledo, Inc.
3121 Glanzman Rd., Toledo, OH 43614, (419) 385-6616; Facility type: Skilled care, Alzheimer's; Certified Beds: 84; Certified: Medicaid, Medicare; Owner: Horizon Healthcare; License: Current state

Fairview Skilled Nursing and Rehabilitation
4420 South Ave., Toledo, OH 43615, (419) 531-4201; Facility type: Skilled care, Alzheimer's; Certified Beds: 110; Certified: Medicaid, Medicare; Owner: Covenant Care; License: Current state

Foundation Park Dementia Care Center
1621 S. Byrne Rd. Toledo, OH 43614, (419) 385-3958; Facility type: Skilled care, Alzheimer's; Certified Beds: 125; Certified: Medicaid, Medicare; Owner: Nursing Care Mgt; License: Current state

Upper Sandusky

Fairhaven Retirement & Health Care Community
850 S. Marseilles Ave., Upper Sandusky, OH 43351, (419) 294-4973; Facility type: Skilled care, Alzheimer's; Certified Beds: 150; Certified: Medicaid, Medicare, Veterans; Owner: Nonprofit; License: Current state

Urbana

Heartland of Urbana
741 E. Water St., Urbana, OH 43078, (937) 652-1381; Facility type: Skilled care, Alzheimer's; Certified Beds: 85; Certified: Medicaid, Medicare, Veterans; Owner: HCR ManorCare; License: Current state

McAuley Center
906 Scioto St., Urbana, OH 43078, (937) 653-5432; Facility type: Skilled care, Alzheimer's; Certified Beds: 129; Certified: Medicaid, Medicare, Veterans; Owner: Catholic Healthcare Partners; License: Current state

Wadsworth

Altercare of Wadsworth
147 Garfield St., Wadsworth, OH 44281, (330) 335-2555; Facility type: Skilled care, Alzheimer's; Certified Beds: 120; Certified: Medicaid, Medicare; Owner: Altercare; License: Current state

Warren

Community Skilled Health Care
1320 Mahoning Ave., NW, Warren, OH 44483, (330) 373-1160; Facility type: Skilled care, Alzheimer's; Certified Beds: 160; Certified: Medicaid, Medicare; Owner: Nonprofit; License: Current state

Gillette Nursing Home
3310 Elm Rd., NE, Warren, OH 44483, (330) 372-1960; Facility type: Skilled care, Alzheimer's; Certified Beds: 99 Certified: Medicaid, Medicare, Medi-Cal, Veterans: Owner: Private; License: Current state

Ridge Crest Care Center
1926 Ridge Ave., Warren, OH 44484, (330) 369-4672; Facility type: Skilled care, Alzheimer's; Certified Beds: 62; Certified: Medicaid, Medicare, Medi-Cal, Veterans; Owner: Integrated Health Services; License: Current state

Washington Court House

Court House Manor
250 Glenn Ave., Washington Court House, OH 43160, (740) 335-9290, Facility type: Skilled care, Alzheimer's; Certified Beds: 100; Certified: Medicaid, Medicare, Veterans; Owner: Proprietary/Public; License: Current state

Saint Catherine's Care Center
1771 Palmer Rd., Washington Court House, OH 43160, (740) 335-6391, Facility type: Skilled care, Alzheimer's; Certified Beds: 50; Certified: Medicaid, Medicare, Veterans; Owner: Carington Health Systems; Proprietary/Public; License: Current state

Xenia

Greene Oaks Health Center
164 Office Park Dr., Xenia, OH 45385, (937) 352-2800; Facility type: Skilled care, Alzheimer's; Certified Beds: 90; Certified: Medicaid, Medicare; Owner: Med Health System; Proprietary/Public; License: Current state

Youngstown

Dandridge Burgundi Manor
31 Maranatha Dr., Youngstown, OH 44505, (330) 746-5157; Facility type: Skilled care, Alzheimer's; Certified Beds: 62; Certified: Medicaid, Medicare; Owner: Proprietary/Public; License: Current state

Zanesville

Adams Lane Care Center
1856 Adams Ln., Zanesville, OH 43701, (740) 454-9769, Facility type: Skilled care, Alzheimer's; Certified Beds: 178; Certified: Medicaid, Medicare; Owner: Zandex; License: Current state

OKLAHOMA

Alva

Share Medical Center
730 Share Dr., Alva, OK 73717, (580) 327-2800; Facility type: Skilled care, Alzheimer's; Certified Beds: 80; Certified: Medicaid; Owner: Nonprofit, Quarum; License: Current state

Ardmore

Whispering Oaks
111 13th NW, Ardmore, OK 73401, (580) 223-4803; Facility type: Skilled care, Alzheimer's; Certified Beds: 76; Certified: Medicaid, Medicare; Owner: Private; License: state

Woodview Home
1630 3rd NE, Ardmore, OK 73401, (580) 226-5454; Facility type: Skilled care, Alzheimer's; Certified Beds: 68; Certified: Medicaid, Medicare, Veterans; Owner: Private; License: state

Arkoma

Medi-Home Inc. of Arkoma, Inc.
1008 Arkansas St., Arkoma, OK 74901, (918) 875-3107; Facility type: Skilled care, Alzheimer's; Beds: 60; Certified: Medicaid, Medicare, Veterans; Owner: Proprietary/Public; License: state

Bixby

Bixby Manor Nursing Home
76 W Rachel St., Bixby, OK 74008, (918) 366-4491; Facility type: Skilled care, Alzheimer's; Certified Beds: 102; Certified: Medicaid, Medicare; Owner: Private; License: state

Clinton

United Methodist Health Care Center, Inc.
2316 Modelle, Clinton, OK 73601, (580) 323-0912;

Facility type: Skilled care, Alzheimer's; Certified Beds: 101; Certified: Medicaid; Owner: Nonprofit; License: state

Cushing

Linwood Village Nursing & Retirement Apartments
533 S. Linwood, Cushing, OK 74023, (918) 225-2220; Facility type: Skilled care, Alzheimer's; Beds: 70; Certified: Medicaid, Medicare, Veterans; Owner: Proprietary/Public; License: state

Duncan

Wilkins Nursing Center
1205 S. 4th St., Duncan, OK 73533, (580) 252-3955; Facility type: Skilled care, Alzheimer's; Beds: 108; Certified: Medicaid; Owner: Proprietary/Public; License: state

Edmond

Edmond Health Care Center
39 E. 33rd St., Edmond, OK 73013, (405) 341-7715; Facility type: Skilled care, Alzheimer's; Certified Beds: 109; Certified: Medicaid, Medicare; Owner: Proprietary/Public; License: state

Elk City

Elk City Nursing Center
301 N. Garrett, Elk City, OK 73644, (580) 225-2811; Facility type: Skilled care, Alzheimer's; Certified Beds: 118; Certified: Medicaid, Medicare; Owner: Proprietary/Public; License: state

Enid

The Commons
301 S. Oakwood Rd., Enid, OK 73706, (580) 237-6164; Facility type: Skilled care, Alzheimer's; Certified Beds: 129; Certified: Medicaid; Owner: Nonprofit; License: state

Fairview

Fairview Fellowship Home for Senior Citizens, Inc.
605 E. State Rd., Fairview, OK 73737, (580) 227-3783; Facility type: Skilled care, Alzheimer's; Beds: 140; Certified: Medicaid; Owner: Nonprofit; License: state

Grove

Betty Ann Nursing Center
1400 S. Main St., Grove, OK 74344, (918) 786-2275; Facility type: Skilled care, Alzheimer's; Beds: 60; Certified: Medicaid; Owner: Private; License: state

Guymon

Dr. WF & Mada Dunaway Manor Nursing Home of Guymon
1401 N. Lelia, Guymon, OK 73942, (580) 338-3186; Facility type: Skilled care, Alzheimer's; Beds: 70; Certified: Medicaid; Owner: Proprietary/Public; License: state

Hollis

Colonial Manor II
120 W. Versa, Hollis, OK 73550, (580) 688-2828; Facility type: Skilled care, Alzheimer's; Certified Beds: 92; Certified: Medicaid, Medicare, Veterans; Owner: State & Local Gov.; License: state

Jay

Monroe Manor
226 E. Monroe St., Jay, OK 74346, (918) 253-4500; Facility type: Skilled care, Alzheimer's; Beds: 100; Certified: Medicaid; Owner: State & Local Gov.; License: state

Lawton

McMahon-Tomlinson Nursing Center
3126 Northwest Arlington, Lawton, OK 73505, (580) 357-3240; Facility type: Skilled care, Alzheimer's; Certified Beds: 135; Certified: Medicaid; Owner: Proprietary/Public; License: state

McAlester

Blevins Retirement & Care Center
1220 E. Electric Blvd., McAlester, OK 74501, (918) 423-9095; Facility type: Skilled care, Alzheimer's, Independent living; Certified Beds: 55; Certified: Medicaid, Medicare; Owner: Private; License: state

Heartland Care Center
615 E. Morris St., McAlester, OK 74501, (918) 426-4010; Facility type: Skilled care, Alzheimer's; Certified Beds: 63; Certified: Medicaid, Medicare; Owner: Heartland Care Group; License: state

Heritage Hills Nursing Center
411 North West St., McAlester, OK 74502, (918) 423-2920; Facility type: Skilled care, Alzheimer's; Certified Beds: 81; Certified: Medicaid, Medicare, Veterans; Owner: Private; License: state

Mitchell Manor Convalescent Home
315 W. Electric Ave., McAlester, OK 74501, (918) 423-4661; Facility type: Skilled care, Alzheimer's; Beds: 100; Certified: Medicaid, Veterans; Owner: Proprietary/Public; License: state

Muskogee

Brentwood Extended Care & Rehabilitation
841 N. 38th St., Muskogee, OK 74401, (918) 683-

8070; Facility type: Skilled care, Alzheimer's; Certified Beds: 90; Certified: Medicaid, Medicare; Owner: Private; License: state

Eastgate Village Retirement Center
3500 Haskell Blvd., Muskogee, OK 74403, (918) 682-3191; Facility type: Skilled care, Alzheimer's; Certified Beds: 110; Certified: Medicaid, Medicare, Veterans; Owner: Dale Scott Mgt; License: state

Newkirk

Newkirk Nursing Center
1351 W. Peckham Rd., Newkirk, OK 74647, (580) 362-3277; Facility type: Skilled care, Alzheimer's; Certified Beds: 43; Certified: Medicaid; Owner: Proprietary/Public; License: state

Okeene

Summit Healthcare
119 N. 6th, Okeene, OK 73763, (580) 822-4441; Facility type: Skilled care, Alzheimer's; Certified Beds: 48; Certified: Medicaid, Medicare, Veterans; Owner: Private; License: state

Oklahoma City

Central Oklahoma Christian Home
6312 N. Portland, Oklahoma City, OK 73112, (405) 946-6932; Facility type: Skilled care, Alzheimer's; Certified Beds: 62; Certified: Medicaid; Owner: Church of Christ; License: state

Skyview Nursing Center
2200 Coltrane Rd., Oklahoma City, OK 73121, (405) 427-1322; Facility type: Skilled care, Alzheimer's; Certified Beds: 60; Certified: Medicaid, Veterans; Owner: Private; License: state

Warr Acres Nursing Center
6501 N. MacArthur Blvd., Oklahoma City, OK 73132, (405) 721-5444; Facility type: Skilled care, Alzheimer's; Certified Beds: 103; Certified: Medicaid, Medicare; Owner: HCR ManorCare; License: state

Owasso

Evergreen Care Center
12600 E. 73rd St. N., Owasso, OK 74055, (918) 272-8007; Facility type: Skilled care, Alzheimer's; Certified Beds: 120; Certified: Medicaid; Owner: Baptist Church; License: state

Ponca City

Ponca City Nursing & Rehabilitation Center
1400 N. Waverly, Ponca City, OK 74601, (580) 762-6668; Facility type: Skilled care, Alzheimer's; Certified Beds: 157; Certified: Medicaid, Medicare; Owner: Private; License: state

Shawnee

Golden Rule Home
38801 Hardesty Rd., Shawnee, OK 74801, (405) 273-7106; Facility type: Skilled care, Alzheimer's; Hardesty Beds: 83; Certified: Medicaid; Owner: Church of God; License: state

Shawnee Colonial Estates Nursing Home
535 W. Federal, Shawnee, OK 74801, (405) 273-7661; Facility type: Skilled care, Alzheimer's; Beds: 170; Certified: Medicaid, Medicare; Owner: Proprietary/Public; License: state

Stroud

Stroud Health Care Center South
721 W. Olive, Stroud, OK 74079, (918) 968-2075; Facility type: Skilled care, Alzheimer's; Hardesty Beds: 58; Certified: Medicaid; Owner: Private; License: state

Sulphur

Callaway Nursing Home
1300 W. Lindsay, Sulphur, OK 73086, (580) 622-2416; Facility type: Skilled care, Alzheimer's; Hardesty Beds: 86; Certified: Medicaid, Veterans; Owner: Private; License: state

Tulsa

Ambassador Manor Nursing Center
1340 E. 61st St., Tulsa, OK 74136, (918) 743-8978; Facility type: Skilled care, Alzheimer's; Certified Beds: 171; Certified: Medicaid, Medicare, Veterans; Owner: Proprietary/Public; License: state

Vinita

Rosewood Terrace
1200 W. Canadian Ave., Vinita, OK 74301, (918) 256-8768; Facility type: Skilled care, Alzheimer's; Certified Beds: 146; Certified: Medicaid; Owner: Nonprofit; License: state

Wagoner

Wagoner Care Center
205 N. Lincoln, Wagoner, OK 74467, (918) 485-2203; Facility type: Skilled care, Alzheimer's; Beds: 150; Certified: Medicaid; Owner: Nonprofit; License: state

OREGON

Baker City

Trinity Saint Elizabeth Care Services, Inc.
3325 Pocahontas Rd., Baker City, OR 97814, (541) 523-4452; Facility type: Skilled care, Alzheimer's; Certified Beds: 120; Certified: Medicaid, Medicare; Owner: Catholic Health Initiatives; License: state

Beaverton

Maryville Nursing Home
14645 SW Farmington Rd., Beaverton, OR 97007, (503) 643-8626; Facility type: Skilled care, Alzheimer's; Certified Beds: 155; Certified: Medicaid, Medicare, Veterans; Owner: Nonprofit/Religious; License: state

Bend

Cascade View Nursing & Alzheimer's Care Center
119 SE Wilson Ave., Bend, OR 97702, (541) 382-7161; Facility type: Skilled care, Alzheimer's; Certified Beds: 87; Certified: Medicaid, Veterans; Owner: Sun River Living Centers; License: state

Coos Bay

Hearthside Care Center
2625 Koos Bay Blvd., Coos Bay, OR 97420, (541) 267-2161; Facility type: Skilled care, Alzheimer's; Certified Beds: 92; Certified: Medicaid, Medicare, Veterans; Owner: Genesis Healthcare; License: state

Corvallis

Corvallis Manor
160 NE Conifer Blvd., Corvallis, OR 97330, (541) 757-1651; Facility type: Skilled care, Alzheimer's; Certified Beds: 135; Certified: Medicaid, Medicare, Veterans; Owner: Private; License: state

Eugene

Eugene Rehabilitation & Specialty Care
2360 Chambers St., Eugene, OR 97405, (541) 687-1310; Facility type: Skilled care, Alzheimer's; Certified Beds: 123; Certified: Medicaid, Medicare, Veterans; Owner: Private; License: state

South Hills Health Care Center
1166 E. 28th Ave., Eugene, OR 97403, (541) 345-0534; Facility type: Skilled care, Alzheimer's; Beds: 110; Certified: Medicaid, Medicare; Owner: Private; License: state

Valley West Health Care Center
2300 Warren Ave., Eugene, OR 97405, (541) 686-2828; Facility type: Skilled care, Alzheimer's; Certified Beds: 121; Certified: Medicaid, Medicare; Owner: Life Care Centers of America; License: state

Florence

Siuslaw Care Center
1951 E. 21st St., Florence, OR 97439, (541) 997-8436; Facility type: Skilled care, Alzheimer's; Certified Beds: 72; Certified: Medicaid, Medicare, Veterans; Owner: Cascade Health Care; License: state

Grants Pass

Highland House Nursing & Rehabilitation Center
2201 NW Highland Ave., Grants Pass, OR 97526, (541) 474-1901; Facility type: Skilled care, Alzheimer's; Certified Beds: 174; Certified: Medicaid, Medicare, Medi-Cal, Veterans; Owner: State & Local Gov.; License: state

Royale Gardens Health & Rehabilitation Center
2075 NW Highland Ave., Grants Pass, OR 97526, (541) 476-8891; Facility type: Skilled care, Alzheimer's; Certified Beds: 191; Certified: Medicaid, Medicare; Owner: Private; License: state

Gresham

Village Health Care
3955 SE 182nd Ave., Gresham, OR 97030, (503) 665-0183; Facility type: Skilled care, Alzheimer's; Certified Beds: 106; Certified: Medicaid, Medicare, Veterans; Owner: Private; License: state

Hillsboro

Evergreen Hillsboro Health & Rehabilitation Center
1778 NE Cornell Rd., Hillsboro, OR 97124, (503) 648-6621; Facility type: Skilled care, Alzheimer's; Certified Beds: 78; Certified: Medicaid, Medicare; Owner: Evergreen Healthcare Management; License: state

Keizer

Avamere Court at Keizer
5210 River Rd. N., Keizer, OR 97303, (503) 393-3624; Facility type: Skilled care, Alzheimer's; Certified Beds: 69; Certified: Medicaid, Medicare; Owner: Private; License: state

Sherwood Park Nursing & Rehabilitation Center
4062 Arleta Ave. NE, Keizer, OR 97303, (503) 390-2271; Facility type: Skilled care, Alzheimer's; Certified Beds: 49; Certified: Medicaid, Medicare; Owner: Perception Health Care; License: state

Klamath Falls

Marquis Care at Plum Ridge
1401 Bryant Williams Dr., Klamath Falls, OR 97601, (541) 882-6691; Facility type: Skilled care, Alzheimer's; Certified Beds: 116; Certified: Medicaid, Medicare, Medi-Cal, Veterans; Owner: Proprietary/Public; License: state

La Grande

Vista Specialty Care
103 Adams Ave., La Grande, OR 97850, (541) 963-4184; Facility type: Skilled care, Alzheimer's; Certified Beds: 78; Certified: Medicaid, Medicare, Veterans; Owner: Evergreen Health Care; License: state

Lebanon

Villa Cascade Care Center
350 S 8th, Lebanon, OR 97355, (541) 259-1221; Facility type: Skilled care, Alzheimer's; Certified Beds: 117; Certified: Medicaid, Medicare; Owner: Marquis Quality Healthcare; License: state

Medford

Avamere at Three Fountains
835 Crater Lake Ave., Medford, OR 97504, (541) 773-7717; Facility type: Skilled care, Alzheimer's; Certified Beds: 80; Certified: Medicaid, Medicare, Veterans; Owner: Proprietary/Public; License: state

Hearthstone Manor
2901 E. Barnett Rd., Medford, OR 97504, (541) 779-4221; Facility type: Skilled care, Alzheimer's; Certified Beds: 151; Certified: Medicaid, Medicare; Owner: Nonprofit; License: state

Rogue Valley Manor
1200 Mira Mar Ave., Medford, OR 97504, (541) 857-7777; Facility type: Skilled care, Alzheimer's; Certified Beds: 68; Certified: Medicare; Payer mix: 100% Private pay; Owner: Nonprofit; License: state

Milton Freewater

Evergreen Milton Freewater Health & Rehabilitation Center
120 Elzora St., Milton Freewater, OR 97862, (541) 938-3318; Facility type: Skilled care, Alzheimer's, Assisted Living; Certified Beds: 129; Certified: Medicaid, Medicare, Veterans; Owner: Evergreen Healthcare; License: state

North Bend

Saint Catherine's Residence
3959 Sheridan Ave., North Bend, OR 97459, (541) 756-4151; Facility type: Skilled care, Alzheimer's; Certified Beds: 75; Certified: Medicaid, Medicare; Owner: Catholic Health Initiatives; License: state

Ontario

Presbyterian Community Care Center
1085 N. Oregon St., Ontario, OR 97914, (541) 889-9133; Facility type: Skilled care, Alzheimer's; Certified Beds: 96; Certified: Medicaid, Medicare; Owner: Nonprofit; License: state

Oregon City

Marquis Care at Oregon City
1680 Molalla Ave., Oregon City, OR 97045, (503) 655-2588; Facility type: Skilled care, Alzheimer's; Certified Beds: 102; Certified: Medicaid, Medicare; Owner: Marquis Quality Healthcare; License: state

Portland

Cherry Wood Rehabilitation at Mount Tabor
6040 SE Belmont St., Portland, OR 97215, (503) 231-7166; Facility type: Skilled care, Alzheimer's; Certified Beds: 175; Certified: Medicaid, Medicare, Veterans; Owner: Nonprofit/Religious; License: state

Glisan Care Center
9750 NE Glisan St., Portland, OR 97220, (503) 256-3920; Facility type: Skilled care, Alzheimer's; Certified Beds: 100; Certified: Medicaid, Medicare, Veterans; Owner: Prestige Care; License: state

Gracelen Terrace
10948 SE Boise, Portland, OR 97266, (503) 760-1727; Facility type: Skilled care, Alzheimer's; Certified Beds: 80; Certified: Medicaid; Owner: Private; License: state

Holladay Park Plaza
1300 NE 16th Ave., Portland, OR 97232, (503) 288-6671; Facility type: Skilled care, Alzheimer's; Certified Beds: 51; Owner: Nonprofit; License: state

Laurelhurst Village
3060 SE Stark St., Portland, OR 97214, (503) 535-4700; Facility type: Skilled care, Alzheimer's; Certified Beds: 109; Certified: Medicaid, Medicare; Owner: Catholic Health Initiatives; License: state

Redwood Extended Care Center
3540 SE Francis St., Portland, OR 97202, (503) 232-5767; Facility type: Skilled care, Alzheimer's; Certified Beds: 64; Certified: Medicaid, Medicare; Owner: Proprietary/Public; License: state

Robinson Home
6125 SW Boundary St., Portland, OR 97221, (503) 535-4300; Facility type: Skilled care, Alzheimer's; Certified Beds: 88; Certified: Medicaid, Medicare; Owner: Nonprofit; License: state

Rose City Nursing Home
34 NE 20th Ave., Portland, OR 97232, (503) 231-0276; Facility type: Skilled care, Alzheimer's; Certified Beds: 30; Certified: Medicaid; Owner: Private; License: state

Saint Jude Care Center
6003 SE 136th Ave., Portland, OR 97236, (503) 761-1155; Facility type: Skilled care, Alzheimer's; Certified Beds: 114; Certified: Medicaid, Veterans; Owner: Proprietary/Public; License: state

Prineville

Ochoco Care Center
950 N Elm St., Prineville, OR 97754, (541) 447-7667; Facility type: Skilled care, Alzheimer's; Certified Beds: 63; Certified: Medicaid, Medicare, Veterans; Owner: Sun River Living Centers; License: state

Roseburg

Umpqua Valley Nursing & Rehabilitation Center
525 W. Umpqua St., Roseburg, OR 97470, (541) 464-7100; Facility type: Skilled care, Alzheimer's; Certified Beds: 118; Certified: Medicaid, Medicare, Veterans; Owner: Catholic Health Initiatives; License: state

Scappoose

Columbia Care Center
33910 E. Columbia Ave., Scappoose, OR 97056, (503) 543-7131; Facility type: Skilled care, Alzheim-er's; Certified Beds: 40; Certified: Medicaid; Owner: Nonprofit; License: state

Sheridan

Sheridan Care Center
411 SE Sheridan Rd., Sheridan, OR 97378, (503) 843-2204; Facility type: Skilled care, Alzheimer's; Certified Beds: 61; Certified: Medicaid; Owner: Private; License: state

Sublimity

Marian Estates
390 SE Church St., Sublimity, OR 97385, (503) 769-3499; Facility type: Skilled care, Alzheimer's; Certified Beds: 214; Certified: Medicaid, Medicare; Owner: Proprietary/Public; License: state

West Linn

Rose Linn Care Center
2330 DeBok Rd., West Linn, OR 97068, (503) 655-0474; Facility type: Skilled care, Alzheimer's; Certified Beds: 71; Certified: Medicaid; Owner: Proprietary/Public; License: state

Wood Village

Village Manor
2060 NE 238th Dr., Wood Village, OR 97060, (503) 491-0553; Facility type: Skilled care, Alzheimer's; Certified Beds: 60; Certified: Medicaid, Veterans; Owner: Proprietary/Public; License: state

PENNSYLVANIA

Allentown

Cedarbrook Nursing Home
350 S. Cedarbrook Rd., Allentown, PA 18104, (610) 395-3727; Facility type: Skilled care, Alzheimer's; Certified Beds: 680; Certified: Medicaid, Medicare; Owner: State & Local Gov.; License: state

Luther Crest Nursing Facility
800 Hausman Rd., Allentown, PA 18104, (610) 398-8011; Facility type: Skilled care, Alzheimer's; Certified Beds: 60; Certified: Medicaid, Medicare; Owner: Lutheran Services Northeast; License: state

Phoebe Home, Inc.
1925 Turner St., Allentown, PA 18104, (610) 794-5300; Facility type: Skilled care, Alzheimer's; Certified Beds: 395; Certified: Medicaid, Medicare; Owner: Nonprofit; License: state

Allison Park

Concordia at Rebecca Residence
3746 Cedar Ridge Rd., Allison Park, PA 15101, (724) 444-0600; Facility type: Skilled care, Alzheimer's; Certified Beds: 60; Certified: Medicaid; Owner: Proprietary/Public; License: state

Altoona

Beverly Healthcare–Hillview
700 S. Cayuga Ave., Altoona, PA 16602, (814) 946-0471; Facility type: Skilled care, Alzheimer's; Certified Beds: 133; Certified: Medicaid, Medicare, Veterans; Owner: Beverly Enterprises; License: state

Ambler

Artman Community
250 N. Bethlehem Pike, Ambler, PA 19002, (215)

643-6333; Facility type: Skilled care, Alzheimer's; Beds: 100; Certified: Medicaid, Medicare; Owner: Nonprofit; License: state

Brighton at Ambler
32 S. Bethlehem Pike, Ambler, PA 19002, (215) 646-7050; Facility type: Skilled care, Alzheimer's; Certified Beds: 100; Certified: Medicaid; Owner: Proprietary/Public; License: state

Bellefonte

Centre Crest
502 E. Howard St., Bellefonte, PA 16823, (814) 355-6777; Facility type: Skilled care, Alzheimer's; Certified Beds: 240; Certified: Medicaid, Medicare; Owner: State & Local Gov.; License: state

Bethel Park

ManorCare Health Services–Bethel Park
60 Highland Rd., Bethel Park, PA 15102, (412) 831-6050; Facility type: Skilled care, Alzheimer's; Certified Beds: 160; Certified: Medicaid, Medicare; Owner: HCR ManorCare; License: state

Meadowcrest Nursing Center
1200 Braun Rd., Bethel Park, PA 15102, (412) 854-5500; Facility type: Skilled care, Alzheimer's; Certified Beds: 50; Certified: Medicaid, Medicare, Veterans; Owner: Extendicare Health Services; License: state

Bethlehem

Blough Health Care Center, Inc.
316 E. Market St., Bethlehem, PA 18018, (610) 868-4982; Facility type: Skilled care, Alzheimer's; Certified Beds: 50; Certified: Medicaid, Medicare; Owner: Proprietary/Public; License: state

Bradford

Bradford Nursing Pavilion
200 Pleasant St., Bradford, PA, 16701, (814) 362-8293; Facility type: Skilled care, Alzheimer's; Certified Beds: 95; Certified: Medicaid, Medicare; Owner: Proprietary/Public; License: state

Bristol

Silver Lake Center
905 Tower Rd., Bristol, PA 19007, (215) 785-3201; Facility type: Skilled care, Alzheimer's; Certified Beds: 174; Certified: Medicaid, Medicare, Veterans; Owner: Genesis ElderCare; License: state

Broomall

Broomall Presbyterian Village
146 Marple Rd., Broomall, PA 19008, (610) 356-0100;

Facility type: Skilled care, Alzheimer's; Certified Beds: 146; Certified: Medicaid, Medicare; Owner: Nonprofit; License: state

Bryn Mawr

Beaumont at Bryn Mawr
601 N. Ithan Ave., Bryn Mawr, PA 19010, (610) 526-7000; Facility type: Skilled care, Alzheimer's; Certified Beds: 46; Certified: Medicaid, Medicare; Owner: Proprietary/Public; License: state

Bryn Mawr Terrace Convalescent Center
773 E. Haverford Rd., Bryn Mawr, PA 19010, (610) 525-8300; Facility type: Skilled care, Alzheimer's; Certified Beds: 170; Certified: Medicare; Owner: Proprietary/Public; License: state

Carlisle

Chapel Pointe at Carlisle
770 S. Hanover St., Carlisle, PA 17013, (717) 249-1363; Facility type: Skilled care, Alzheimer's; Certified Beds: 59; Certified: Medicaid, Medicare; Owner: Nonprofit: state

Claremont Nursing & Rehabilitation Center
375 Claremont Rd., Carlisle, PA 17013, (717) 243-2031; Facility type: Skilled care, Alzheimer's; Certified Beds: 290; Certified: Medicaid, Medicare, Veterans; Owner: State & Local Gov.; License: state. Korean, Tagalog

Forest Park Health Center
700 Walnut Bottom Rd., Carlisle, PA 17013, (717) 243-1032; Facility type: Skilled care, Alzheimer's; Certified Beds: 1114; Certified: Medicaid, Medicare; Owner: Presbyterian Homes, Inc.; License: state

Chambersburg

Falling Spring Nursing & Rehabilitation Center
201 Franklin Farm Ln., Chambersburg, PA 17201, (717) 264-2715; Facility type: Skilled care, Alzheimer's; Certified Beds: 186; Certified: Medicaid, Medicare; Owner: State & Local Gov.; License: state

ManorCare Health Services
1070 Stouffer Ave., Chambersburg, PA 17201, (717) 263-0436; Facility type: Skilled care, Alzheimer's; Certified Beds: 210; Certified: Medicaid, Medicare; Owner: HCR ManorCare; License: state

Menno Haven
2075 Scotland Ave., Chambersburg, PA 17201, (717) 263-8545; Facility type: Skilled care, Alzheimer's; Certified Beds: 153; Certified: Medicaid, Medicare; Owner: Mennonite Church; License: state

The Shook Home
55 S. Second St., Chambersburg, PA 17201, (717) 264-6815; Facility type: Skilled care, Alzheimer's;

Certified Beds: 65; Certified: Medicaid, Medicare; Owner: Nonprofit; License: state

Coudersport

Sweden Valley Manor
1028 E. Second St., Coudersport, PA 16915, (814) 274-7610; Facility type: Skilled care, Alzheimer's; Certified Beds: 121; Certified: Medicaid, Medicare; Owner: Proprietary/Public; License: state

Darby

Saint Francis Country House
1412 Landsdowne Ave., Darby, PA 19023, (610) 461-6510; Facility type: Skilled care, Alzheimer's; Certified Beds: 273; Certified: Medicaid, Medicare; Owner: Nonprofit; License: state

Doylestown

Briarleaf Nursing & Convalescent Center
252 Belmont Ave., Doylestown, PA 18901, (215) 348-2983; Facility type: Skilled care, Alzheimer's; Certified Beds: 178; Certified: Medicare; Owner: Accord Health Services; License: state

Pine Run Health Center
777 Ferry Rd., Doylestown, PA 18901, (215) 340-5156; Facility type: Skilled care, Alzheimer's; Certified Beds: 127; Certified: Medicaid, Medicare; Owner: Constellation Senior Services; License: state

Easton

Easton Nursing Center
498 Washington St., Easton, PA 18042, (610) 258-2985; Facility type: Skilled care, Alzheimer's; Certified Beds: 181; Certified: Medicaid, Medicare, Veterans; Owner: Penn Med Consultants; License: state

Praxis Alzheimer's Facility
500 Washington St., Easton, PA 18042, (610) 253-3573; Facility type: Skilled care, Alzheimer's; Certified Beds: 115; Certified: Medicaid, Medicare; Owner: Penn Med Consultants; License: state

Elizabethtown

ManorCare Health Services–Elizabethtown
320 S. Market St., Elizabethtown, PA 17022, (717) 367-1377; Facility type: Skilled care, Alzheimer's, Assisted Living; Certified Beds: 73; Certified: Medicaid, Medicare; Owner: HCR ManorCare; License: state

Masonic Village at Elizabethtown
One Masonic Dr., Elizabethtown, PA 17022, (717) 367-1121; Facility type: Skilled care, Alzheimer's; Certified Beds: 453; Certified: Medicaid, Medicare; Owner: Nonprofit; License: state

Erie

Ball Pavilion
5416 E. Lake Rd., Erie, PA 16511, (814) 899-8600; Facility type: Skilled care, Alzheimer's; Certified Beds: 85; Certified: Medicaid, Medicare; Owner: Nonprofit; License: state

Saint Mary's Home of Erie
607 E. 26th St., Erie, PA 16504, (814) 459-0621; Facility type: Skilled care, Alzheimer's; Certified Beds: 139; Certified: Medicaid, Medicare; Owner: Nonprofit; License: state

Sarah A Reed Retirement Center
227 W. 22 St., Erie, PA 16502, (814) 878-2600; Facility type: Skilled care, Alzheimer's; Certified Beds: 106; Certified: Medicaid, Medicare; Owner: Nonprofit; License: state

Gettysburg

Shepherd's Choice
867 York Rd., Gettysburg, PA 17325, (717) 337-3238; Facility type: Skilled care, Alzheimer's; Certified Beds: 118; Certified: Medicaid, Medicare, Veterans; Owner: Affinity Health Services; License: state

Glenside

Edgehill Nursing & Rehabilitation Center
146 Edgehill Rd., Glenside, PA 19038, (215) 886-1043; Facility type: Skilled care, Alzheimer's; Certified Beds: 60; Certified: Medicaid, Medicare; Owner: AmCare; License: state

Greensburg

Saint Anne Home
685 Angela Dr., Greensburg, PA 15601, (724) 837-6070; Facility type: Skilled care, Alzheimer's; Certified Beds: 125; Certified: Medicaid, Medicare, Veterans; Owner: Nonprofit; License: state

Westmoreland Manor
2480 S. Grand Blvd., Greensburg, PA 15601, (724) 830-4010; Facility type: Skilled care, Alzheimer's; Certified Beds: 408; Certified: Medicaid, Medicare; Owner: State & Local Gov, Complete Care Services; License: state

Grove City

Grove Manor
435 N. Broad St., Grove City, PA 16127, (412) 458-7800; Facility type: Skilled care, Alzheimer's; Certified Beds: 59; Certified: Medicare; Owner: ExtendiCare; License: state

Trinity Living Center
400 Hillcrest Ave., Grove City, PA 16127, (724) 458-

9501; Facility type: Skilled care, Alzheimer's; Certified Beds: 109; Certified: Medicaid, Medicare, Veterans; Owner: Genesis ElderCare; License: state

Hanover

Hanover Hall
267 Frederick St., Hanover, PA 17331, (717) 637-8937; Facility type: Skilled care, Alzheimer's; Certified Beds: 152; Certified: Medicaid, Medicare, Veterans; Owner: Proprietary/Public; License: state

Homewood at Hanover PA
425 Westminister Ave., Hanover, PA 17331, (717) 637-4166; Facility type: Skilled care, Alzheimer's; Certified Beds: 120; Certified: Medicaid, Medicare; Owner: Nonprofit; License: state

Harrisburg

Blue Ridge East
3625 N. Progress Ave., Harrisburg, PA 17110, (717) 652-2345; Facility type: Skilled care, Alzheimer's; Certified Beds: 95; Certified: Medicaid, Medicare, Veterans; Owner: Beverly Enterprises; License: state

Dauphin Manor
1205 S. 28th St., Harrisburg, PA 17111, (717) 565-7000; Facility type: Skilled care, Alzheimer's; Certified Beds: 404; Certified: Medicaid, Medicare, Veterans; Owner: State & Local Gov.; License: state

Homeland Center
1901 N. Fifth St., Harrisburg, PA 17102, (717) 221-7900; Facility type: Skilled care, Alzheimer's; Certified Beds: 92; Certified: Medicaid, Medicare, Veterans; Owner: Nonprofit; License: state

Jewish Home of Greater Harrisburg
4000 Linglestown Rd., Harrisburg, PA 17112, (717) 657-0700; Facility type: Skilled care, Alzheimer's; Certified Beds: 138; Certified: Medicaid, Medicare; Owner: Nonprofit/Religious; License: state

Pavilion at Saint Luke
1000 Stacie Dr., Hazleton, PA 18201, (570) 453-5100; Facility type: Skilled care, Alzheimer's; Beds: 120; Certified: Medicaid, Medicare, Veterans; Owner: Nonprofit; License: state

Hollidaysburg

Hollidaysburg Veterans Home
PO Box 319, Hollidaysburg, PA 16648, (814) 696-5356; Facility type: Skilled care, Alzheimer's; Certified Beds: 347; Certified: Medicaid, Medicare, Veterans; Owner: State & Local Gov.; License: state

Honey Brook

Tel Hai Retirement Community
1200 Tel Hai Cir., Honey Brook, PA 19344, (610)

273-9333; Facility type: Skilled care, Alzheimer's; Certified Beds: 139; Certified: Medicaid, Medicare; Owner: Nonprofit; License: state

Indiana

Beacon Manor
1515 Wayne Ave., Indiana, PA 15701, (724) 349-5300; Facility type: Skilled care, Alzheimer's; Certified Beds: 121; Certified: Medicaid, Medicare; Owner: Proprietary/Public; License: state

Saint Andrew's Village
1155 Indian Springs Rd., Indiana, PA 15701, (724) 349-4870; Facility type: Skilled care, Alzheimer's; Certified Beds: 131; Certified: Medicaid, Medicare; Owner: Presbyterian Homes, Inc.; License: state

Johnstown

Laurel Wood Care Center
100 Woodmont Rd., Johnstown, PA 15905, (814) 255-1488; Facility type: Skilled care, Alzheimer's; Certified Beds: 120; Certified: Medicaid, Medicare, Veterans; Owner: Grane Healthcare; License: state

Kittanning

Armstrong County Health Center
265 S. McKean St., Kittanning, PA 16201, (724) 548-2222; Facility type: Skilled care, Alzheimer's; Certified Beds: 115; Certified: Medicaid, Medicare; Owner: State & Local Gov.; License: state; Activities: Arts & Crafts; Dances; Support groups; Pet therapy; Group exercise; Outings; Other: Alzheimer's secured unit

Kittanning Care Center
120 Kittanning Care Dr., Kittanning, PA 16201, (724) 545-2273; Facility type: Skilled care, Alzheimer's; Certified Beds: 120; Certified: Medicaid, Medicare; Owner: State & Local Gov.; License: state

Lancaster

Calvary Fellowship Homes
502 Elizabeth Dr., Lancaster, PA 17601, (717) 393-0711; Facility type: Skilled care, Alzheimer's; Certified Beds: 45; Certified: Medicaid, Medicare; Owner: Nonprofit; License: state

Conestoga View
900 E. King St., Lancaster, PA 17602, (717) 299-7850; Facility type: Skilled care, Alzheimer's; Certified Beds: 446; Certified: Medicaid, Medicare, Veterans; Owner: State & Local Gov.; License: state

Langhorne

Attleboro Nursing & Rehabilitation Center
300 E. Winchester Ave., Langhorne, PA 19047, (215)

757-3739; Facility type: Skilled care, Alzheimer's; Certified Beds: 179; Certified: Medicaid, Medicare; Owner: Private; License: state

Lansdale

Willowbrooke Court at Brittany
1001 Valley Forge Rd., Lansdale, PA 19446, (215) 855-9700; Facility type: Skilled care, Alzheimer's; Certified Beds: 92; Certified: Medicaid, Medicare; Owner: Acts Retirement Life Communities; License: state

Lititz

Moravian Manor
300 W. Lemon St. Lititz, PA 17543, (717) 626-0214; Facility type: Skilled care, Alzheimer's; Certified Beds: 127; Certified: Medicaid, Medicare, Veterans; Owner: Moravian Church; License: state

Mechanicsburg

Messiah Village
100 Mount Allen Rd., Mechanicsburg, PA 17055, (717) 697-4666; Facility type: Skilled care, Alzheimer's; Certified Beds: 184; Certified: Medicaid, Medicare; Owner: Brethren in Christ Church; License: state

New Castle

Haven Convalescent Home, Inc.
725 Paul St., New Castle, PA 16101, (724) 654-8833; Facility type: Skilled care, Alzheimer's; Certified Beds: 91; Certified: Medicaid; Owner: Proprietary/Public; License: state

Silver Oaks Nursing Center
715 Harbor St., New Castle, PA 16101, (724) 652-3863; Facility type: Skilled care, Alzheimer's; Certified Beds: 62; Certified: Medicaid, Medicare, Veterans; Owner: Penn Med Consultants; License: state

Newtown

Chandler Hall Health Services
99 Barclay St., Newtown, PA 18940, (215) 860-4000; Facility type: Skilled care, Alzheimer's; Certified Beds: 53; Certified: Medicaid, Medicare, Veterans; Owner: Nonprofit; License: state

Newtown Square

Dunwoody Village
3500 W. Chester Pike, Newtown Square, PA 19073, (215) 359-4401; Facility type: Skilled care, Alzheimer's; Certified Beds: 81; Certified: Medicare; Payer mix: 100% Private pay; Owner: Nonprofit; License: state

Oil City

Golden LivingCenter–Oil City
1293 Grandview Rd., Oil City, PA 16301, (814) 676-8208; Facility type: Skilled care, Alzheimer's; Certified Beds: 95; Certified: Medicaid, Medicare, Veterans; Owner: Beverly Enterprises; License: state

Olyphant

Lackawanna Health & Rehabilitation Center
108 Terrace Dr., Olyphant, PA 18447, (570) 489-8611; Facility type: Skilled care, Alzheimer's; Beds: 280; Certified: Medicaid, Medicare, Veterans; Owner: State & Local Gov.; License: state

Philadelphia

Ashton Hall Nursing & Rehabilitation Center
2109 Red Lion Rd., Philadelphia, PA 19115, (215) 673-7000; Facility type: Skilled care, Alzheimer's; Certified Beds: 148; Certified: Medicaid, Medicare, Veterans; Owner: Private; License: state

Care Pavilion of Walnut Park
63rd and Walnut Streets, Philadelphia, PA 19139, (215) 476-6264; Facility type: Skilled care, Alzheimer's; Certified Beds: 396; Certified: Medicaid, Medicare, Veterans; Owner: Genesis Elder Care; License: state

Cheltenham Nursing & Rehabilitation Center
600 W. Cheltenham Ave., Philadelphia, PA 19126, (215) 927-7300; Facility type: Skilled care, Alzheimer's; Certified Beds: 255; Certified: Medicaid, Medicare, Veterans; Owner: Nonprofit; License: state

Deer Meadows Retirement Community
8301 Roosevelt Blvd., Philadelphia, PA 19152, (215) 624-7575; Facility type: Skilled care, Alzheimer's; Certified Beds: 206; Certified: Medicaid, Medicare, Veterans; Owner: Baptist Church; License: state

Germantown Home
6950 Germantown Ave., Philadelphia, PA 19119, (215) 848-3306; Facility type: Skilled care, Alzheimer's; Certified Beds: 180; Certified: Medicaid, Medicare; Owner: Genesis Elder Care; License: state

Pittsburgh

Asbury Health Center
700 Bower Hill Rd., Pittsburgh, PA 15243, (412) 341-1030; Facility type: Skilled care, Alzheimer's; Certified Beds: 139; Certified: Medicaid, Medicare; Owner: United Methodist Church; License: state

Baptist Homes of Western Pennsylvania
489 Castle Shannon Blvd., Pittsburgh, PA 15234, (412) 563-6550; Facility type: Skilled care, Alzheim-

er's; Certified Beds: 126; Certified: Medicaid, Medicare; Owner: Baptist Church; License: state

Canterbury Place
310 Fisk St., Pittsburgh, PA 15201, (412) 622-9000; Facility type: Skilled care, Alzheimer's; Certified Beds: 59; Certified: Medicaid, Medicare; Owner: Nonprofit, Religious; License: state

Forbes Nursing Center
6655 Frankstown Ave., Pittsburgh, PA 15206, (412) 665-3232; Facility type: Skilled care, Alzheimer's; Certified Beds: 134; Certified: Medicaid, Medicare; Owner: Nonprofit; License: state

Golden LivingCenter–Mount Lebanon
350 Old Gilkeson Rd., Pittsburgh, PA 15228, (412) 257-4444; Facility type: Skilled care, Alzheimer's; Certified Beds: 121; Certified: Medicaid, Medicare, Veterans; Owner: Beverly Enterprises; License: state

Heartland Health Care Center (Pittsburgh)
550 S Negley Ave., Pittsburgh, PA 15232, (412) 665-2400; Facility type: Skilled care, Alzheimer's; Certified Beds: 224; Certified: Medicaid, Medicare; Owner: HCR ManorCare; License: state

Marian Manor Corp
2695 Winchester Dr., Pittsburgh, PA 15220, (412) 563-6866; Facility type: Skilled care, Alzheimer's; Certified Beds: 154; Certified: Medicaid, Medicare; Owner: Nonprofit, Religious; License: state

Vincentian Home
111 Perrymont Rd., Pittsburgh, PA 15237, (412) 366-5600; Facility type: Skilled care, Alzheimer's; Certified Beds: 180; Certified: Medicaid, Medicare; Owner: Nonprofit; License: state

Pottstown

ManorCare Health Services–Pottstown
724 N. Charlotte St., Pottstown, PA 19464, (610) 323-1837; Facility type: Skilled care, Alzheimer's; Beds: 170; Certified: Medicaid, Medicare; Owner: HCR ManorCare; License: state

Pottsville

Schuylkill Center
1000 Schuylkill Manor Rd., Pottsville, PA 17901, (570) 622-9666; Facility type: Skilled care, Alzheimer's; Certified Beds: 190; Certified: Medicaid, Medicare; Owner: Genesis ElderCare; License: state

Saxonburg

Saxony Health Center
223 Pittsburg St., Saxonburg, PA 16056, (724) 352-9445; Facility type: Skilled care, Alzheimer's; Certified Beds: 68; Certified: Medicaid, Medicare; Owner: Nonprofit/Religious; License: state

Schuylkill Haven

Schuylkill County Home–Rest Haven
401 University Dr., Schuylkill Haven, PA 17972, (570) 385-0331; Facility type: Skilled care, Alzheimer's; Certified Beds: 142; Certified: Medicaid, Medicare, Veterans; Owner: State & Local Gov.; License: state

Scranton

Allied Services Skilled Nursing Center
303 Smallacombe Dr., Scranton, PA 18501, (570) 348-1424; Facility type: Skilled care, Alzheimer's; Certified Beds: 371; Certified: Medicaid, Medicare, Veterans; Owner: Nonprofit; License: state

Linwood Nursing and Rehabilitation Center
100 Linwood Ave., Scranton, PA 18505, (570) 346-7381; Facility type: Skilled care, Alzheimer's; Certified Beds: 102; Certified: Medicaid, Medicare, Veterans; Owner: AmCare Management; License: state

Tremont

Tremont Health & Rehabilitation Center
44 Donaldson Rd., Tremont, PA 17981, (570) 695-3141; Facility type: Skilled care, Alzheimer's; Certified Beds: 180; Certified: Medicaid, Medicare, Veterans; Owner: ExtendiCare Health Services; License: state

Upper Saint Clair

Friendship Village of South Hills
1290 Boyce Rd., Upper Saint Clair, PA 15241, (724) 941-3100; Facility type: Skilled care, Alzheimer's; Certified Beds: 89; Certified: Medicaid, Medicare, Veterans; Owner: Life Care Services; License: state

Verona

Seneca Place
5360 Saltsburg Rd., Verona, PA 15147, (412) 798-8000; Facility type: Skilled care, Alzheimer's; Certified Beds: 178; Certified: Medicaid, Medicare; Owner: St., Margaret Health Systems; License: state

Warrington

Neshaminy Manor Home
1660 Easton Rd., Warrington, PA 18976, (215) 345-3810; Facility type: Skilled care, Alzheimer's; Certified Beds: 360; Certified: Medicaid, Medicare; Owner: Genesis ElderCare; License: state

Washington

Kade Nursing Home
1198 W. Wylie Ave., Washington, PA 15301, (724) 222-2148; Facility type: Skilled care, Alzheimer's;

Certified Beds: 74; Certified: Medicaid, Medicare, Veterans; Owner: Penn Med Consultants; License: state

Washington County Health Center
36 Old Hickory Ridge Rd., Washington, PA 15301, (724) 228-5010; Facility type: Skilled care, Alzheimer's; Certified Beds: 288; Certified: Medicaid, Medicare; Owner: State & Local Gov.; License: state

Waynesburg

Golden LivingCenter–Waynesburg
300 Center Ave., Waynesburg, PA 15370, (724) 852-2020; Facility type: Skilled care, Alzheimer's; Certified Beds: 111; Certified: Medicaid, Medicare, Veterans; Owner: Beverly Enterprises; License: state

West Chester

Barclay Friends
700 N. Franklin St., West Chester, PA 19380, (610) 696-5211; Facility type: Skilled care, Alzheimer's, Assisted Living; Certified Beds: 99; Certified: Medicaid, Medicare, Veterans; Owner: Kendal Corp; License: state

Pembrooke Health & Rehabilitation Residence
1130 W. Chester Pike, West Chester, PA 19380, (610) 692-3636; Facility type: Skilled care, Alzheimer's; Certified Beds: 180; Certified: Medicaid, Medicare; Owner: Sunrise Assisted Living, Brandywine Senior Care; License: state

Pocopson Home
1695 Lenape Rd., West Chester, PA 19382, (610) 793-1212; Facility type: Skilled care, Alzheimer's; Certified Beds: 275; Certified: Medicaid, Medicare, Veterans; Owner: State & Local Gov.; License: state

West Reading

ManorCare Health Care Services–West Reading North
425 Buttonwood St., West Reading, PA 19611, (610) 375-5166; Facility type: Skilled care, Alzheimer's; Certified Beds: 176; Certified: Medicaid, Medicare; Owner: HCR ManorCare; License: state

Wilkes-Barre

Little Flower Manor & St., Therese Residence of the Diocese of Scranton
200 S. Meade St., Wilkes Barre, PA 18702, (570) 823-6131; Facility type: Skilled care, Alzheimer's; Certified Beds: 133; Certified: Medicaid, Medicare; Owner: Nonprofit; License: state

Williamsport

ManorCare Health Services–Williamsport North
300 Leader Dr., Williamsport, PA 17701, (570) 323-8267; Facility type: Skilled care, Alzheimer's; Certified Beds: 152; Certified: Medicaid, Medicare, Veterans; Owner: HCR ManorCare; License: state

ManorCare Health Services–Williamsport South
101 Leader Dr., Williamsport, PA 17701, (570) 323-3758; Facility type: Skilled care, Alzheimer's; Certified Beds: 116; Certified: Medicaid, Medicare; Owner: HCR ManorCare; License: state

Worthington

Sugar Creek Rest & Meadow Lake Manor
120 Lakeside Dr., Worthington, PA 16262, (724) 445-3146; Facility type: Skilled care, Alzheimer's; Certified Beds: 114; Certified: Medicaid, Medicare, Veterans; Owner: Private; License: state

York

ManorCare Health Services–Kingston Court
2400 Kingston Ct, York, PA 17402, (717) 755-8811; Facility type: Skilled care, Alzheimer's; Certified Beds: 151; Certified: Medicaid, Medicare; Owner: HCR ManorCare; License: state

ManorCare Health Services–North
1770 Barley Rd., York, PA 17404, (717) 767-6530; Facility type: Skilled care, Alzheimer's; Certified Beds: 161; Certified: Medicaid, Medicare; Owner: HCR ManorCare; License: state

York County Nursing Home
118 Pleasant Acres Rd., York, PA 17402, (717) 840-7100; Facility type: Skilled care, Alzheimer's; Certified Beds: 375; Certified: Medicaid, Medicare; Owner: State & Local Gov.; License: state

Youngsville

Rouse-Warren County Home
701 Rouse Ave., Youngsville, PA 16371, (814) 563-7565; Facility type: Skilled care, Alzheimer's; Certified Beds: 176; Certified: Medicaid, Medicare, Veterans; Owner: State & Local Gov.; License: state

RHODE ISLAND

Bristol

Metacom Manor Health Center
1 Dawn Hill, Bristol, RI 08209, (401) 253-2300; Facility type: Skilled care, Alzheimer's; Certified Beds: 133; Certified: Medicaid, Medicare; Owner: Nonprofit; License: state

Silver Creek Manor
7 Creek Ln., Bristol, RI 02809, (401) 253-3000; Facility type: Skilled care, Alzheimer's; Certified Beds: 128; Certified: Medicaid, Medicare, Veterans; Owner: Private; License: state

Central Falls

Harris Health Care Center–North
60 Eben Brown Ln., Central Falls, RI 02863, (401) 722-6000; Facility type: Skilled care, Alzheimer's; Certified Beds: 33; Certified: Medicaid, Medicare, Veterans; Owner: Private; License: state

Coventry

Coventry Skilled Nursing & Rehabilitation
10 Woodland Dr., Coventry, RI 02816, (401) 826-2000; Facility type: Skilled care, Alzheimer's; Beds: 140; Certified: Medicaid, Medicare, Veterans; Owner: HealthCare Mgt; License: state

Healthcare Community
546 Main St., Coventry, RI 02816, (401) 821-6837; Facility type: Skilled care, Alzheimer's; Certified Beds: 190; Certified: Medicaid, Medicare; Owner: Health Concepts, LTD; License: state

East Providence

Harris Health Center
833 Broadway, East Providence, RI 02914, (401) 434-7404; Facility type: Skilled care, Alzheimer's; Certified Beds: 31; Certified: Medicaid, Medicare; Owner: Private; License: state

Hattie Ide Chaffe Home
200 Wampanoag Trail, East Providence, RI 02914, (401) 434-1520; Facility type: Skilled care, Alzheimer's; Beds: 60; Certified: Medicaid, Medicare; Owner: Nonprofit; License: state

Orchard View Manor Nursing & Rehabilitation Center
135 Tripps Ln., East Providence, RI 02915, (401) 438-2250; Facility type: Skilled care, Alzheimer's; Certified Beds: 166; Certified: Medicaid, Medicare, Veterans; Owner: Private; License: state

Waterview Villa, Inc.
1275 S. Broadway, East Providence, RI 02914, (401) 438-7020; Facility type: Skilled care, Alzheimer's; Beds: 130; Certified: Medicaid, Medicare; Owner: Proprietary/Public; License: state

Johnston

Briarcliffe Manor
49 Old Pocasset Rd., Johnston, RI 02919, (401) 944-2450; Facility type: Skilled care, Alzheimer's; Certified Beds: 122; Certified: Medicaid, Medicare; Owner: Medical Homes of RI, Inc.; License: state

Manville

The Holiday Retirement Home, Inc.
30 Sayles Hill Rd., Manville, RI 02838, (401) 765-1440; Facility type: Skilled care, Alzheimer's; Beds: 180; Certified: Medicaid, Medicare, Veterans; Owner: Proprietary/Public; License: state

Newport

Scalabrini Villa
860 N Quidesset Rd., North Kingstown, RI 02852, (401) 884-1802; Facility type: Nonprofit, Alzheimer's; Certified Beds: 120; Certified: Medicaid, Medicare; Owner: Nonprofit; License: state

Village House Nursing & Rehabilitation Center
70 Harrison Ave., Newport, RI 02840, (401) 849-5222; Facility type: Skilled care, Alzheimer's; Certified Beds: 95; Certified: Medicaid, Medicare; Owner: Health Concepts LTD; License: state

North Providence

Golden Crest Nursing Center
100 Smithfield Rd., North Providence, RI 02904, (401) 353-1710; Facility type: Skilled care, Alzheimer's; Certified Beds: 152; Certified: Medicaid, Medicare; Owner: Private; License: state

Hopkins Manor
610 Smithfield Rd., North Providence, RI 02904, (401) 353-6300; Facility type: Skilled care, Alzheimer's; Certified Beds: 200; Certified: Medicaid, Medicare; Owner: Health Mgt Systems; License: state

Providence

Bannister House, Inc.
135 Dodge St., Providence, RI 02907, (401) 521-9600; Facility type: Skilled care, Alzheimer's; Certified Beds: 95; Certified: Medicaid, Medicare, Veterans; Owner: The QAC Healthcare Group; License: state

Charlesgate Nursing Center
100 Randall St., Providence, RI 02904, (401) 861-5858; Facility type: Skilled care, Alzheimer's; Certified Beds: 140; Certified: Medicaid, Medicare; Owner: Davenport Assoc; License: state

Steere House Nursing & Rehabilitation Center
100 Borden St., Providence, RI 02903, (401) 454-7070; Facility type: Skilled care, Alzheimer's; Certified Beds: 120; Certified: Medicaid, Medicare; Owner: Nonprofit; License: state

Summit Commons Skilled Nursing & Rehabilitation Center
99 Hillside Ave., Providence, RI 02906, (401) 574-4800; Facility type: Skilled care, Alzheimer's; Certified Beds: 130; Certified: Medicaid, Medicare; Owner: Sterling HealthCare; License: state

Tockwotton Home
75 East St., Providence, RI 02903, (401) 272-5280; Facility type: Skilled care, Alzheimer's; Certified Beds: 42; Certified: Medicaid, Medicare; Owner: Nonprofit; License: state

Warren

Grace Barker Nursing Center
54 Barker Ave., Warren, RI 02885, (401) 245-9100; Facility type: Skilled care, Alzheimer's; Certified Beds: 86; Certified: Medicaid, Medicare, Veterans; Owner: Private; License: state

Warwick

Kent Regency Center
660 Commonwealth Ave., Warwick, RI 02886, (401) 739-4241; Facility type: Skilled care, Alzheimer's; Certified Beds: 153; Certified: Medicaid, Medicare; Owner: Genesis ElderCare; License: state

Westerly

Westerly Nursing Home, Inc.
79 Beach St., Westerly, RI 02891, (401) 596-4925; Facility type: Skilled care, Alzheimer's; Certified Beds: 66; Certified: Medicaid, Medicare, Veterans; Owner: Private; License: state

Woonsocket

Mount Saint Francis Health Center
4 St. Joseph St., Woonsocket, RI 02895, (401) 765-5844; Facility type: Skilled care, Alzheimer's; Certified Beds: 158; Certified: Medicaid, Medicare; Owner: Sterling Healthcare; License: state

Woonsocket Health Center
262 Poplar St., Woonsocket, RI 02895, (401) 765-2100; Facility type: Skilled care, Alzheimer's; Certified Beds: 150; Certified: Medicaid, Medicare, Veterans; Owner: Private; License: state

SOUTH CAROLINA

Abbeville

Abbeville Nursing Home, Inc.
83 Thompson Cir., Abbeville, SC 29620, (864) 366-5122; Facility type: Skilled care, Alzheimer's; Certified Beds: 94; Certified: Medicaid, Medicare, Veterans; Owner: Proprietary/Public; License: state

Aiken

Azalea Woods Rehabilitation & Nursing Center, LLC
123 DuPont Dr., Aiken, SC 29801, (803) 648-0434; Facility type: Skilled care, Alzheimer's; Certified Beds: 86; Certified: Medicaid, Medicare, Veterans; Owner: Beverly Enterprises; License: state

Pepper Hill Nursing & Rehabilitation Center, LLC
3525 Augustus Rd., Aiken, SC 29802, (803) 642-8376; Facility type: Skilled care, Alzheimer's; Certified Beds: 126; Certified: Medicaid, Medicare, Veterans; Owner: Private; License: state

Unihealth Post Acute Care–Aiken, LLC
830 Laurens St. N., Aiken, SC 29801, (803) 649-6264; Facility type: Skilled care, Alzheimer's; Certified Beds: 176; Certified: Medicaid, Medicare; Owner: State & Local Gov.; License: state

Bamberg

Unihealth Post-Acute Care of Bamberg
439 North St., Bamberg, SC 29003, (803) 245-7525; Facility type: Skilled care, Alzheimer's; Certified Beds: 88; Certified: Medicaid, Medicare, Veterans; Owner: State & Local Gov.; License: state

Charleston

Heartland of West Ashley Rehab & Nursing Center
1137 Sam Rittenberg Blvd., Charleston, SC 29407, (843) 763-0233; Facility type: Skilled care, Alzheimer's; Certified Beds: 99; Certified: Medicaid, Medicare, Veterans; Owner: HCR ManorCare; License: state

Columbia

Life Care Center of Columbia
2514 Faraway Dr., Columbia, SC 29223, (803) 865-1999; Facility type: Skilled care, Alzheimer's, Assisted living; Certified Beds: 179; Certified: Medicaid,

Medicare, Veterans; Owner: Life Care Centers of America; License: state

Unihealth Post-Acute Care–Columbia
2451 Forest Dr., Columbia, SC 29204, (803) 254-5960; Facility type: Skilled care, Alzheimer's; Certified Beds: 190; Certified: Medicaid, Medicare, Veterans; Owner: Mariner Post Acute Network; License: state

Dillon

The Pines Nursing & Convalescent Home
413 Lakeside Ct., Dillon, SC 29536, (843) 774-2741; Facility type: Skilled care, Alzheimer's; Certified Beds: 84; Certified: Medicaid, Medicare, Veterans; Owner: Beverly Enterprises; License: state

Fountain Inn

Fountain Inn Nursing Home
501 Gulliver St., Fountain Inn, SC 29644, (864) 862-2554; Facility type: Skilled care, Alzheimer's; Certified Beds: 44; Certified: Medicaid, Medicare; Owner: Cooke Mgt; License: state

Greenville

Glorified Health & Rehabilitation of Greenville, LLC
8 N. Texas Ave., Greenville, SC 29611, (864) 295-1331; Facility type: Skilled care, Alzheimer's; Certified Beds: 132; Certified: Medicaid, Medicare; Owner: Health Mgt Resources; License: state

Oakmont West Nursing Center
600 Sulphur Springs Rd., Greenville, SC 29611, (864) 246-2721; Facility type: Skilled care, Alzheimer's; Certified Beds: 125; Certified: Medicaid, Medicare, Veterans; Owner: HCR ManorCare; License: state

Rolling Green Village–Mildred L. Smith Health Center
1 Hoke Smith Blvd., Greenville, SC 29615, (864) 987-9800; Facility type: Skilled care, Alzheimer's, Assisted Living; Certified Beds: 44; Certified: Medicare; Owner: Life Care Services; License: state

Greer

Piedmont Nursing & Rehabilitation Center
401 Chandler Rd., Greer, SC 29651, (864) 879-1370; Facility type: Skilled care, Alzheimer's; Certified Beds: 132; Certified: Medicaid, Medicare; Owner: Health Mgt Resources; License: state

Hilton Head Island

Fraser Health Center
300 Woodhaven Dr., Hilton Head Island, SC 29928, (843) 842-3747; Facility type: Skilled care, Alz-heimer's; Certified Beds: 33; Certified: Medicare; Payer mix: 91% Private pay. Owner: Nonprofit; License: state

Life Care Center of Hilton Head
120 Lamotte Dr., Hilton Head Island, SC 29926, (843) 681-6006; Facility type: Skilled care, Alzheimer's; Certified Beds: 88; Certified: Medicaid, Medicare, Veterans; Owner: Life Care Centers of America; License: state

Lancaster

White Oak Manor
253 Craig Manor Rd., Lancaster, SC 29720, (803) 286-1464; Facility type: Skilled care, Alzheimer's; Certified Beds: 132; Certified: Medicaid, Medicare, Veterans; Owner: White Oak Manor, Inc.; License: state

Laurens

Martha Franks Baptist Retirement Center
One Martha Franks Dr., Laurens, SC 29360, (864) 984-4541; Facility type: Skilled care, Alzheimer's; Certified Beds: 88; Certified: Medicare; Owner: Baptist Church; License: state

NHC Health Care
301 Pinehaven St. Extension, Laurens, SC 29360, (864) 984-6584; Facility type: Skilled care, Alzheimer's; Certified Beds: 176; Certified: Medicaid, Medicare, Veterans; Owner: National Healthcare Company; License: state

Mount Pleasant

Mount Pleasant Manor
921 Bowman Rd., Mount Pleasant, SC 29464, (843) 884-8903; Facility type: Skilled care, Alzheimer's; Certified Beds: 132; Certified: Medicaid, Medicare, Veterans; Owner: Proprietary/Public; License: state

Sandpiper Rehabilitation & Nursing
1049 Anna Knapp Blvd., Mount Pleasant, SC 29464, (843) 881-3210; Facility type: Skilled care, Alzheimer's; Certified Beds: 176; Certified: Medicaid; Owner: Proprietary/Public; License: state

Myrtle Beach

Myrtle Beach Manor
9547 Hwy. 17 N., Myrtle Beach, SC 29572, (843) 449-5283; Facility type: Skilled care, Alzheimer's; Certified Beds: 104; Certified: Medicaid, Medicare; Owner: Marriott Senior Living Services; License: state

Newberry

J. F. Hawkins Nursing Home
1330 Kinard St., Newberry, SC 29108, (803) 276-

2601; Facility type: Skilled care, Alzheimer's; Certified Beds: 118; Certified: Medicaid, Medicare, Veterans; Owner: State & Local Gov.; License: state

North Charleston

Life Care Center of Charleston
2600 Elms Plantation Blvd., North Charleston, SC 29406, (843) 764-3500; Facility type: Skilled care, Alzheimer's; Certified Beds: 148; Certified: Medicaid, Medicare, Veterans; Owner: Private; License: state

Rock Hill

White Oak Manor–Rock Hill
1915 Ebenezer Rd., Rock Hill, SC 29732, (803) 366-8155; Facility type: Skilled care, Alzheimer's; Beds: 141; Certified: Medicaid, Medicare, Veterans; Owner: White Oak Manor, Inc.; License: state

Saluda

Saluda Nursing Center
581 Newberry Hwy., Saluda, SC 19138, (864) 445-2146; Facility type: Skilled care, Alzheimer's; Certified Beds: 176; Certified: Medicaid, Medicare; Owner: State & Local Gov.; License: state

Seneca

Seneca Health & Rehabilitation Center
140 Tokeena Rd., Seneca, SC 29678, (864) 882-1642; Facility type: Skilled care, Alzheimer's; Certified Beds:

132; Certified: Medicaid, Medicare, Veterans; Owner: Proprietary/Public; License: state

Sumter

Hopewell Healthcare Center
1761 Pinewood Rd., Sumter, SC 29154, (803) 481-8591; Facility type: Skilled care, Alzheimer's; Certified Beds: 96; Certified: Medicaid, Medicare; Owner: Proprietary/Public; License: state

NHC Health–Sumter
1018 N. Guignard Dr., Sumter, SC 29150, (803) 773-5567; Facility type: Skilled care, Alzheimer's; Certified Beds: 138; Certified: Medicaid, Medicare, Veterans; Owner: National Healthcare Co; License: state

White Rock

Lowman Home Nursing Home
201 Fortress Dr., White Rock, SC 29177, (803) 732-3000; Facility type: Skilled care, Alzheimer's; Certified Beds: 176; Certified: Medicaid, Medicare, Veterans; Owner: Nonprofit/ Religious; License: state

Woodruff

Woodruff Manor, LLC
1114 E. Georgia Rd., Woodruff, SC 29388, (864) 476-7092; Facility type: Skilled care, Alzheimer's; Certified Beds: 88; Certified: Medicaid, Medicare; Owner: Integrated Health Services; License: state

---

SOUTH DAKOTA

Aberdeen

Aberdeen Health & Rehabilitation
1700 N. Hwy. 281, Aberdeen, SD 57401, (605) 225-7315; Facility type: Skilled care, Alzheimer's; Certified Beds: 172; Certified: Medicaid, Medicare, Veterans; Owner: Benedictine Health System; License: state

ManorCare Health Services
400 8th Ave., NW, Aberdeen, SD 57401, (605) 225-2550; Facility type: Skilled care, Alzheimer's; Certified Beds: 99; Certified: Medicaid, Medicare; Owner: HCR ManorCare; License: state

Morningside Manor
101 Church St., Alcester, SD 57001, (605) 943-2011; Facility type: Skilled care, Alzheimer's; Certified Beds: 84; Certified: Medicaid, Medicare, Veterans; Owner: Nonprofit; License: state

Bristol

Sun Dial Manor
410 Second St., Bristol, SD 57219, (605) 492-3615; Facility type: Skilled care, Alzheimer's; Certified Beds: 37; Certified: Medicaid, Medicare; Owner: SunDial Manor; License: state

Britton

Wheatcrest Hills
1311 Vander Horck, Britton, SD 57430, (605) 448-2251; Facility type: Skilled care, Alzheimer's; Certified Beds: 63; Certified: Medicaid, Medicare; Owner: Private; License: state

Canton

Good Samaritan Society Canton
1022 North Dakota Ave., Canton, SD 57013, (605) 987-2696; Facility type: Skilled care, Alzheimer's;

Certified Beds: 78; Certified: Medicaid, Medicare; Owner: Evangelic Lutheran Good Samaritan Society; License: state

DeSmet

Good Samaritan Society DeSmet
411 Calumet Ave. NW, DeSmet, SD 57231, (605) 854-3327; Facility type: Skilled care, Alzheimer's, Assisted Living; Certified Beds: 72; Certified: Medicaid, Medicare, Veterans; Owner: Evangelical Lutheran Good Samaritan Society; License: state

Eureka

Avera Eureka Health Care Center
202 J Ave., Eureka, SD 57437, (605) 284-2145; Facility type: Skilled care, Alzheimer's; Certified Beds: 62; Certified: Medicaid, Medicare; Owner: Banner Health System; License: state

Gettysburg

Oahe Manor
700 E. Garfield, Gettysburg, SD 57442, (605) 765-2461; Facility type: Skilled care, Alzheimer's; Certified Beds: 60; Certified: Medicaid; Owner: Catholic Health Initiatives; License: state

Gregory

Avera Rosebud Country Care Center
300 Park St., Gregory, SD 57533, (605) 835-8296; Facility type: Skilled care, Alzheimer's; Certified Beds: 58; Certified: Medicaid, Medicare; Owner: Nonprofit; License: state

Highmore

Highmore Healthcare Center
410 8th St. SE, Highmore, SD 57345, (605) 852-2255; Facility type: Skilled care, Alzheimer's; Certified Beds: 46; Certified: Medicaid; Owner: Tealwood Care Centers; License: state

Irene

Sunset Manor
129 Clay St., Irene, SD 57037, (605) 263-3318; Facility type: Skilled care, Alzheimer's; Certified Beds: 68; Certified: Medicaid; Owner: Proprietary/Public; License: state

Lake Norden

Golden LivingCenter–Lake Norden
803 Park St., Lake Norden, SD 57248, (605) 785-3654; Facility type: Skilled care, Alzheimer's; Certified Beds: 63; Certified: Medicaid, Medicare, Veterans; Owner: Beverly Enterprises; License: state

Madison

Bethel Lutheran Home
1001 S. Egan Ave., Madison, SD 57042, (605) 256-4539; Facility type: Skilled care, Alzheimer's; Certified Beds: 59; Certified: Medicaid, Medicare; Owner: Nonprofit; License: state

Mobridge

Mobridge Care Center
1100 Fourth Ave. E., Mobridge, SD 57601, (605) 845-7201; Facility type: Skilled care, Alzheimer's; Certified Beds: 117; Certified: Medicaid, Medicare, Veterans; Owner: Beverly Enterprises; License: state

Pierre

Golden LivingCenter–Pierre
950 E. Park St., Pierre, SD 57501, (605) 224-8628; Facility type: Skilled care, Alzheimer's; Certified Beds: 72; Certified: Medicaid, Medicare, Veterans; Owner: Beverly Enterprises; License: state

Rapid City

Golden LivingCenter–Bella Vista
302 St. Cloud St., Rapid City, SD 57701, (605) 343-4738; Facility type: Skilled care, Alzheimer's; Certified Beds: 70; Certified: Medicaid, Medicare, Veterans; Owner: Beverly Enterprises; License: state

Golden LivingCenter–Meadowbrook
2500 Arrowhead Dr., Rapid City, SD 57702, (605) 348-0285; Facility type: Skilled care, Alzheimer's; Certified Beds: 68; Certified: Medicaid, Medicare, Veterans; Owner: Beverly Enterprises; License: state

Fountain Springs Health Care
2000 Wesleyan Blvd., Rapid City, SD 57702, (605) 343-3555; Facility type: Skilled care, Alzheimer's; Certified Beds: 90; Certified: Medicaid, Medicare, Veterans; Owner: Private; License: state

Redfield

Golden LivingCenter–Redfield
1015 Third St. E., Redfield, SD 57469, (605) 472-2288; Facility type: Skilled care, Alzheimer's; Certified Beds: 87; Certified: Medicaid, Medicare, Veterans; Owner: Beverly Enterprises; License: state

Salem

Golden LivingCenter–Salem
500 Colonial Dr., Salem SD 57058, (605) 425-2203; Facility type: Skilled care, Alzheimer's; Certified Beds: 63; Certified: Medicaid, Medicare, Veterans; Owner: Beverly Enterprises; License: state

Sioux Falls

Avera Prince of Peace
4500 Prince of Peace Pl., Sioux Falls, SD 57103, (605) 322-5613; Facility type: Skilled care, Alzheimer's; Certified Beds: 90; Certified: Medicaid, Medicare; Owner: Nonprofit; License: state

Bethany Lutheran Home
1901 S. Holly Ave., Sioux Falls, SD 57105, (605) 338-2351; Facility type: Skilled care, Alzheimer's; Certified Beds: 112; Certified: Medicaid, Medicare, Veterans; Owner: Nonprofit; License: state

Good Samaritan Society Sioux Falls Village
3901 S. Marion Rd., Sioux Falls, SD 57106, (605) 361-3311; Facility type: Skilled care, Alzheimer's; Certified Beds: 222; Certified: Medicaid, Medicare, Veterans;

Evangelical Lutheran Good Samaritan society: Nonprofit; License: state

Viborg

Pioneer Memorial Nursing Home
315 N. Washington, Viborg, SD 57070, (605) 326-5161; Facility type: Skilled care, Alzheimer's; Certified Beds: 52; Certified: Medicaid, Medicare, Veterans; Owner: Nonprofit; License: state

Winner

Winner Regional Healthcare Center
805 E. 8th St., Winner, SD 57580, (605) 842-7200; Facility type: Skilled care, Alzheimer's; Certified Beds: 81; Certified: Medicaid, Medicare, Veterans; Owner: Nonprofit; License: state

---

TENNESSEE

Algood

Masters Healthcare Center Inc.
278 Dry Valley Rd., Algood, TN 38501, (931) 537-6524; Facility type: Skilled care, Alzheimer's; Certified Beds: 175; Certified: Medicaid, Medicare; Owner: Vencor, Inc.; License: state

Ardmore

Ardmore on Main Care and Rehabilitation Center
25385 Main St., Ardmore, TN 38449, (931) 427-2143; Facility type: Skilled care, Alzheimer's; Certified Beds: 79; Certified: Medicaid, Medicare; Owner: Sun Healthcare; License: state

Bruceton

Life Care Center of Bruceton–Hollow Rock
105 Rowland Ave., Bruceton, TN 38317, (731) 586-2061; Facility type: Skilled care, Alzheimer's; Certified Beds: 130; Certified: Medicaid; Owner: Life Care Centers of America; License: state

Chattanooga

The Health Center at Standifer Place
2626 Walker Rd., Chattanooga, TN, 37421, (423) 490-1599; Facility type: Skilled care, Alzheimer's; Certified Beds: 474; Certified: Medicaid, Medicare; Owner: Non-Profit; License: state

Life Care Center of East Ridge
1500 Fincher Ave., East Ridge, TN 37412, (423) 894-1254; Facility type: Skilled care, Alzheimer's; Certified

Beds: 160; Certified: Medicaid, Medicare; Owner: Nonprofit; License: state

Life Care Center of Red Bank
1020 Runyan Dr., Chattanooga, TN 37405, (423) 877-1155; Facility type: Skilled care, Alzheimer's; Certified Beds: 178; Certified: Medicaid, Medicare; Owner: Non-Profit; License: state

NHC Health Care–Chattanooga
2700 Parkwood Ave., Chattanooga, TN 37404, (423) 624-1533; Facility type: Skilled care, Alzheimer's; Certified Beds: 207; Certified: Medicaid, Medicare; Owner: National Healthcare Co; License: state

Clarksville

Grace Healthcare of Clarksville
111 Ussery Rd., Clarksville, TN 37043, (931) 647-0269; Facility type: Skilled care, Alzheimer's; Certified Beds: 122; Certified: Medicaid, Medicare; Owner: Tennessee Health Mgt; License: state

Montgomery Care and Rehabilitation Center
198 Old Farmer Rd., Clarksville, TN 37043, (931) 358-2900; Facility type: Skilled care, Alzheimer's; Certified Beds: 120; Certified: Medicaid, Medicare; Owner: Tennessee Health Mgt; License: state

Spring Meadows Health Care Center
220 State Rt. 76, TN 37043, (931) 552-0181; Facility type: Skilled care, Alzheimer's; Certified Beds: 121; Certified: Medicaid, Medicare; Owner: Tennessee Health Mgt; License: state

Cleveland

Bradley Healthcare & Rehabilitation
2910 Peerless Rd., Cleveland, TN 37312, (423) 472-

7116; Facility type: Skilled care, Alzheimer's; Certified Beds: 213; Certified: Medicaid, Medicare; Owner: Nonprofit; License: state

Cleveland Care & Rehabilitation Center
2750 Executive Park Pl., Cleveland, TN 37312, (423) 476-4444; Facility type: Skilled care, Alzheimer's; Certified Beds: 100; Certified: Medicaid, Medicare, Veterans; Owner: Nonprofit; License: state

Columbia

Life Care Center of Columbia
841W. James Campbell Blvd., Columbia, TN 38401, (931) 388-5035; Facility type: Skilled care, Alzheimer's; Certified Beds: 123; Certified: Medicaid, Medicare; Owner: Life Care Centers of America; License: state

NHC–Healthcare, Hillview
2710 Trotwood Ave., Columbia, TN 38401, (931) 388-7182; Facility type: Skilled care, Alzheimer's; Certified Beds: 92; Certified: Medicaid, Medicare; Owner: National Healthcare Co; License: state

Signature Healthcare of Columbia
1410 Trotwood Ave., Columbia, TN 38401, (931) 388-6443; Facility type: Skilled care, Alzheimer's; Certified Beds: 181; Certified: Medicaid, Medicare; Owner: Tennessee Health Mgt; License: state

Cordova

Grace Healthcare of Cordova
955 Germantown Pkwy., Cordova, TN 38018, (901) 754-1393; Facility type: Skilled care, Alzheimer's; Certified Beds: 284; Certified: Medicaid, Medicare, Veterans; Owner: Vencor, Inc.; License: state

Memphis Jewish Home
36 Bazeberry Rd., Cordova, TN 38018, (901) 758-0036; Facility type: Skilled care, Alzheimer's; Certified Beds: 160; Certified: Medicaid, Medicare, Veterans; Owner: Nonprofit; License: state

Crossville

Life Care Center of Crossville
80 Justice St., Crossville, TN 38555, (931) 484-4782; Facility type: Skilled care, Alzheimer's; Certified Beds: 122; Certified: Medicaid, Medicare, Veterans; Owner: Private; License: state

Elizabethton

Pine Ridge Care & Rehabilitation Center
1200 Spruce Ln., Elizabethton, TN 37643, (423) 543-3202; Facility type: Skilled care, Alzheimer's; Certified Beds: 94; Certified: Medicaid, Medicare; Owner: Nonprofit; License: state

Etowah

Etowah Health Care Center
409 Grady Rd., PO Box 957, Etowah, TN 37331, (423) 263-1138; Facility type: Skilled care, Alzheimer's; Certified Beds: 120; Certified: Medicaid, Veterans; Owner: Nonprofit; License: state

Fayetteville

Donalson Assisted Living
1681 Winchester Hwy., Fayetteville, TN 37334, (931) 433-7156; Facility type: Skilled care, Alzheimer's; Beds: 350; Certified: Medicaid, Medicare; Owner: State & Local Gov., Lincoln Care Center; License: state; Activities: Arts & Crafts; Dances; Pet therapy; Group exercise; Outings; Support Groups

Lincoln Donalson Care Centers
501 Amana Ave., Fayetteville, TN 37334, (931) 433-6146; Facility type: Skilled care, Alzheimer's; Certified Beds: 270; Certified: Medicaid, Medicare; Owner: State & Local Gov.; License: state

Franklin

Claiborne & Hughes Health Center
200 Strahl St., Franklin, TN 37064, (615) 791-1103; Facility type: Skilled care, Alzheimer's; Certified Beds: 157; Certified: Medicaid, Medicare; Owner: Nonprofit; License: state

Hermitage

McKendree Village
4347 Lebanon Rd., Hermitage, TN 37076, (615) 889-6990; Facility type: Skilled care, Alzheimer's; Certified Beds: 300; Certified: Medicaid, Medicare; Owner: Nonprofit; License: state

Humboldt

Tennessee State Veterans Home
2865 Main St., Humboldt, TN 38343, (731) 784-8405; Facility type: Skilled care, Alzheimer's; Certified Beds: 140; Certified: Medicaid, Medicare, Veterans; Owner: State & Local Gov.; License: state

Jackson

SunBridge Care & Community Center
131 Cloverdale St., Jackson, TN 38301, (901) 423-8750; Facility type: Skilled care, Alzheimer's; Beds: 110; Certified: Medicaid; Owner: Sun Healthcare Group; License: state; Activities: Arts & Crafts; Dances; Pet therapy; Group exercise; Outings; Support Groups

Jellico

Beech Tree Manor
240 Hospital Ln., PO Box 300, Jellico, TN 37762,

(423) 784-6626; Facility type: Skilled care, Alzheimer's; Certified Beds: 110; Certified: Medicaid, Medicare; Owner: Generations Health Assoc; License: state

Knoxville

Little Creek Sanitarium
1810 Little Creek Ln., Knoxville, TN 37922, (423) 690-6727; Facility type: Skilled care, Alzheimer's; Beds: 40; Payer mix: 99% Private pay; Owner: Nonprofit; License: state; Activities: Arts & Crafts; Dances; Pet therapy; Group exercise; Outings; Support Groups; Other: Affiliations: Seventh Day Adventist Church

Summit View of Farragut, LLC
12823 Kingston Pike, Knoxville, TN 37923, (865) 966-0600; Facility type: Skilled care, Alzheimer's; Certified Beds: 113; Certified: Medicaid, Medicare, Veterans; Owner: Private; License: state

La Follette

St. Mary's Health & Rehab Center of Campbell County
200 Torry Rd., La Follette, TN 37766, (423) 907-1380; Facility type: Skilled care, Alzheimer's; Certified Beds: 98; Certified: Medicaid, Medicare, Medi-Cal, Veterans; Owner: State & Local Gov.; Managed by: Baptist Health System; License: state

Lebanon

Quality Care Health Center
932 Baddour Pkwy, Lebanon, TN 37087, (615) 444-1836; Facility type: Skilled care, Alzheimer's; Certified Beds: 290; Certified: Medicaid; Owner: Private; License: state

Lexington

Briarwood Community Living Center
PO Box 1067, Lexington, TN 38351, (731) 968-6629; Facility type: Skilled care, Alzheimer's; Certified Beds: 55; Certified: Medicaid, Medicare; Owner: Eldercare Services; License: state

Martin

Van Ayer Manor
640 Hannings Ln., Martin, TN 38237, (731) 587-3193; Facility type: Skilled care, Alzheimer's; Certified Beds: 95; Certified: Medicaid; Owner: American Health Foundation; License: state

Maryville

Maryville Healthcare & Rehabilitation
1012 Jamestown Way, Maryville, TN 37803, (865)

984-7400; Facility type: Skilled care, Alzheimer's; Certified Beds: 187; Certified: Medicaid, Medicare; Owner: Vencor, Inc.; License: state

McMinnville

NHC–Healthcare, McMinnville
928 Old Smithville Rd., McMinnville, TN 37110, (931) 473-8431; Facility type: Skilled care, Alzheimer's; Certified Beds: 150; Certified: Medicaid, Medicare, Veterans; Owner: National Healthcare Co; License: state

Raintree Manor
415 Pace St., McMinnville, TN 37110, (931) 668-2011; Facility type: Skilled care, Alzheimer's; Certified Beds: 140; Certified: Medicaid, Medicare; Owner: Proprietary/Public; License: state

Memphis

Allenbrooke Nursing & Rehabilitation Center
3933 Allenbrooke Cove, Memphis, TN 38118, (901) 795-2444; Facility type: Skilled care, Alzheimer's; Certified Beds: 180; Certified: Medicaid, Medicare, Veterans; Owner: Beverly Enterprises; License: state

Bright Glade Convalescent Center
5070 Sanderlin Ave., Memphis, TN 38117, (901) 682-5677; Facility type: Skilled care, Alzheimer's; Certified Beds: 81; Owner: Proprietary; License: state

Harbor View Nursing & Rehabilitation Center, Inc.
1513 N 2nd St., Memphis, TN 38107, (901) 272-2494; Facility type: Skilled care, Alzheimer's; Certified Beds: 98; Certified: Medicaid; Owner: Proprietary/Public; License: state

Kirby Pines Manor
3535 Kirby Rd., Memphis, TN 38115, (901) 365-0772; Facility type: Skilled care, Alzheimer's; Certified Beds: 30; Certified: Medicare; Owner: Retirement Communities of America; License: state

Midsouth Health & Rehabilitation Center
2380 James Rd., Memphis, TN 38127, (901) 358-1707; Facility type: Skilled care, Alzheimer's; Certified Beds: 155; Certified: Medicaid; Owner: Nonprofit; License: state

Saint Peter Villa DMHC
141 N McLean, Memphis, TN 38104, (901) 276-2021; Facility type: Skilled care, Alzheimer's; Certified Beds: 180; Certified: Medicaid, Medicare; Owner: Nonprofit; License: state

Nashville

Belcourt Terrace Nursing Home
1710 Belcourt Ave., Nashville, TN 37212, (615) 383-

3570; Facility type: Skilled care, Alzheimer's; Certified Beds: 49; Certified: Medicare; Owner: Nonprofit; License: state

Greenhills Health & Rehabilitation Center
3939 Hillsboro Cir., Nashville, TN 37215, (615) 297-2100; Facility type: Skilled care, Alzheimer's; Certified Beds: 150; Certified: Medicare; Owner: Mariner Post Acute Network; License: state

The Health Care Center at Richland Place
504 Elmington Ave., Nashville, TN 37205, (615) 269-4200; Facility type: Skilled care, Alzheimer's; Certified Beds: 107; Certified: Medicare; Owner: National Health Care Corp; License: state

Lakeshore Wedgewood
832 Wedgewood Ave., Nashville, TN 37203, (615) 383-4006; Facility type: Skilled care, Alzheimer's; Certified Beds: 23; Nonprofit; License: state

The Meadows
8044 Coley Davis Rd., Nashville, TN 37221, (615) 646-4466; Facility type: Skilled care, Alzheimer's; Certified Beds: 10; Owner: Nonprofit; License: state

Trevecca Health Care Center
329 Murfreesboro Rd., Nashville, TN 37210, (615) 244-6900; Facility type: Skilled care, Alzheimer's; Certified Beds: 240; Certified: Medicaid, Medicare; Owner: Private; License: state

Pulaski

Meadowbrook Nursing Center
1245 E College St., Pulaski, TN 38478, (931) 363-7548; Facility type: Skilled care, Alzheimer's; Certified Beds: 83; Certified: Medicaid; Owner: Nonprofit; License: state

NHC Health Care
993 E College, Pulaski, TN 38478, (931) 363-3572; Facility type: Skilled care, Alzheimer's; Certified Beds:

102; Certified: Medicaid, Medicare, Veterans; Owner: National Healthcare Co; License: state

Sneedville

Hancock Manor Nursing Home
1423 Main St., Sneedville, TN 37869, (423) 733-4783; Facility type: Skilled care, Alzheimer's; Certified Beds: 50; Certified: Medicaid; Owner: Nonprofit; License: state

Tiptonville

Reelfoot Manor
1034 Reelfoot Dr., Tiptonville, TN 38079, (731) 253-6681; Facility type: Skilled care, Alzheimer's; Certified Beds: 116; Certified: Medicaid, Medicare; Owner: Nonprofit; License: state

Westmoreland

Westmoreland Care & Rehab Center
1559 New Hwy., 52, Westmoreland, TN 37186, (615) 644-5111; Facility type: Skilled care, Alzheimer's; Certified Beds: 100; Certified: Medicaid, Medicare; Owner: Royal Care Inc.; License: state

Winchester

Golden LivingCenter–Mountain View
1360 Bypass Rd., Winchester, TN 37398, (931) 967-7082; Facility type: Skilled care, Alzheimer's; Certified Beds: 140; Certified: Medicaid, Medicare, Veterans; Owner: Beverly Enterprises; License: state

Willows at Winchester Care & Rehabilitation Center
32 Memorial Dr., Winchester, TN 37398, (931) 967-0200; Facility type: Skilled care, Alzheimer's; Certified Beds: 80; Certified: Medicaid; Owner: Sun Healthcare; License: state

TEXAS

Abilene

Abilene Convalescent Center
2630 Old Anson Rd., Abilene, TX 79603, (325) 673-5101; Facility type: Skilled care, Alzheimer's; Certified Beds: 114; Certified: Medicaid, Medicare; Owner: Pyramid Healthcare; License: state

Coronado Nursing Center LP
1751 N 15th St., Abilene, TX 79603, (325) 673-3531; Facility type: Skilled care, Alzheimer's; Beds: Certified

217; Certified: Medicaid, Medicare, Veterans; Owner: Fountain View, Inc.; License: state

Wind Crest Alzheimer's Care Center
6050 Hospital Dr., Abilene, TX 79606, (325) 692-1533; Facility type: Skilled care, Alzheimer's; Beds: Certified 120; Certified: Medicaid, Medicare, Veterans; Owner: Sears Methodist Retirement System; License: state

Alvarado

Alvarado LTC Partners Inc.
101 N Parkway, Alvarado, TX 76009, (817) 790-3304;

Facility type: Skilled care, Alzheimer's; Certified Beds: 115; Certified: Medicaid, Medicare, Veterans; Owner: Nonprofit; License: state

Amarillo

Heritage Convalescent Center
1009 Clyde St., Amarillo, TX 79106, (806) 352-5295; Facility type: Skilled care, Alzheimer's; Certified Beds: 116; Certified: Medicaid, Medicare, Veterans; Owner: Proprietary/Public. License: state

Plum Creek Health Care Center
5601 Plum Creek Dr., Amarillo, TX 79124, (806) 351-1000; Facility type: Skilled care, Alzheimer's; Certified Beds: 50; Certified: Medicaid, Medicare, Veterans; Owner: Private; License: state

Palo Duro Care Center
1931 Medipark Dr., Amarillo, TX 79106, (806) 352-5600; Facility type: Skilled care, Alzheimer's; Certified Beds: 99; Certified: Medicaid, Medicare, Veterans; Owner: Private; License: state

Texan Nursing & Rehab of Amarillo LLC
4033 W 51st Ave., Amarillo, TX 79109, (806) 355-4488; Facility type: Skilled care, Alzheimer's; Certified Beds: 150; Certified: Medicaid, Medicare, Veterans; Owner: Private; License: state

Arlington

Interlochen Health and Rehabilitation Center
2645 W Randol Mill Rd., Arlington, TX 76012, (817) 277-6789; Facility type: Skilled care, Alzheimer's; Certified Beds: 122; Certified: Medicaid, Medicare; Owner: Proprietary/Public; License: state

Arsansas Pass

Aransas Pass Nursing & Convalescent Center
1661 W Yoakum St., Aransas Pass, TX 78336, (361) 758-7686; Facility type: Skilled care, Alzheimer's; Beds: 170; Certified: Medicaid, Medicare; Owner: Nonprofit; License: state; Activities: Arts & Crafts; Dances; Pet therapy; Group exercise; Outings; Support Groups; Other: Alzheimer's secured unit

Austin

Buckner Villa Siesta Home
1110 Tom Adams Dr., Austin, TX 78753, (512) 836-1515; http://www.bucknervillas.citysearch.com; Facility type: Skilled care, Alzheimer's; Certified Beds: 28; Certified: Medicaid, Medicare, Veterans; Owner: Nonprofit; License: state

Gracy Woods Nursing Center
12021 Metric Blvd., Austin, TX 78758, (512) 228-3300; Facility type: Skilled care, Alzheimer's; Certified

Beds: 118; Certified: Medicaid; Owner: Nonprofit; License: state

Gracy Woods II Living Center
12042 Bittern Hollow, Austin, TX 78758, (512) 228-3350; Facility type: Skilled care, Alzheimer's; Certified Beds: 110; Certified: Medicaid; Owner: Nonprofit; License: state

Govalle Care Center
3101 Govalle Ave., Austin, TX 78702, (512) 926-7871; Facility type: Skilled care, Alzheimer's; Certified Beds: 83; Certified: Medicaid, Medicare; Owner: Care Centers Mgt; License: state

Ballinger

Runnels County Rehabilitation and Nursing Center I
1800 N Broadway Bronte Hwy., Ballinger, TX 76821, (325) 365-2538; Facility type: Skilled care, Alzheimer's; Certified Beds: 154; Certified: Medicaid, Medicare; Owner: Proprietary; License: state

Beaumont

Clairmont Beaumont LP
1020 S 23rd St., Beaumont, TX 77707, (409) 842-9700; Facility type: Skilled care, Alzheimer's; Certified Beds: 148; Certified: Medicaid, Medicare; Owner: Nonprofit; License: state

Big Spring

Parkview Nursing and Rehabilitation Center
3200 Parkway Dr., Big Spring, TX 79720, (915) 263-4041; Facility type: Skilled care, Alzheimer's; Certified Beds: 119; Certified: Medicaid, Medicare, Veterans; Owner: Fountain View, Inc.; License: state

Brownsville

Ebony Lake Healthcare Center
1001 Central Blvd., Brownsville, TX 78520, (956) 541-0917; Facility type: Skilled care, Alzheimer's; Certified Beds: 107; Certified: Medicaid, Medicare; Owner: Nonprofit; License: state

Valley Grande Manor
901 Wild Rose Ln., Brownsville, TX 78520, (956) 546-4568; Facility type: Skilled care, Alzheimer's; Certified Beds: 162; Certified: Medicaid, Medicare; Owner: Nonprofit; License: state

Columbus

River Oaks and Rehabilitation Center
300 North St., Columbus, TX 78934, (979) 732-2347; Facility type: Skilled care, Alzheimer's; Certified Beds: 137; Certified: Medicaid; Owner: Private; License: state

Corpus Christi

Alameda Oaks Nursing Center
1101 S Alameda St., Corpus Christi, TX 78404, (361) 882-2711; Facility type: Skilled care, Alzheimer's; Certified Beds: 146; Certified: Medicaid, Medicare; Owner: Life Care Centers of America; License: state

Harbor View Care Center
1314 3rd St., Corpus Christi, TX 78401, (361) 888-5511; Facility type: Skilled care, Alzheimer's; Certified Beds: 114; Certified: Medicaid, Medicare; Owner: Nonprofit; License: state

South Park Rehabilitation & Nursing Center
3115 McArdle, Corpus Christi, TX 78415, (361) 853-2577; Facility type: Skilled care, Alzheimer's; Beds: 190; Certified: Medicaid, Medicare; Owner: Proprietary/Public; License: state; Activities: Arts & Crafts; Dances; Pet therapy; Group exercise; Outings; Other: Alzheimer's secured unit

Sunnybrook Health Care Center
3050 Sunnybrook Dr., Corpus Christi, TX 78415, (361) 853-9981; Facility type: Skilled care, Alzheimer's; Certified Beds: 168; Certified: Medicaid; Owner: Proprietary/Public; License: state

Trisun Care Center–Westwood
801 Cantwell Ln., Corpus Christi, TX 78408, (361) 882-4284; Facility type: Skilled care, Alzheimer's; Certified Beds: 94; Certified: Medicaid, Medicare; Owner: Proprietary/Public; License: state

Dallas

C.C. Young Memorial Home–Young Health Center
4829 Lawther Dr., Dallas, TX 75214, (214) 841-8080; http://www.ccyoung.org; Facility type: Skilled care, Alzheimer's; Certified Beds: 88; Certified: Medicaid, Medicare, Veterans; Owner: Nonprofit; License: state

Dallas Nursing & Rehabilitation Center
11301 Dennis Rd., Dallas, TX 75229, (972) 247-4866; Facility type: Skilled care, Alzheimer's; Certified Beds: 180; Certified: Medicaid, Medicare, Veterans; Owner: New Care Health Corp; License: state

Golden Acres Living and Rehabilitation Center
2525 Centerville Rd., Dallas, TX 75228, (214) 327-4503; Facility type: Skilled care, Alzheimer's; Certified Beds: 264; Certified: Medicaid, Medicare, Veterans; Owner: Nonprofit; License: state

IHS at Doctor's Healthcare Center
9009 White Rock Tr., Dallas, TX 75238, (214) 348-8100; Facility type: Skilled care, Alzheimer's; Certified Beds: 280; Certified: Medicaid, Medicare; Owner: Proprietary/Public; License: state

ManorCare Health Services
3326 Burgoyne St., Dallas, TX 75233, (214) 330-9291; Facility type: Skilled care, Alzheimer's; Certified Beds: 204; Certified: Medicaid, Medicare, Veterans; Owner: HCR ManorCare; License: state

Presbyterian Village North Special Care Center
8600 Skyline Dr., Dallas, TX 75243, (214) 355-9600; Facility type: Skilled care, Alzheimer's; Certified Beds: 88; Owner: Nonprofit; License: state

Walnut Place
5515 Glen Lakes Dr., Dallas, TX 75231, (214) 361-8923; Facility type: Skilled care, Alzheimer's; Certified Beds: 177; Owner: Nonprofit; License: state

Denton

Cottonwood Nursing and Rehabilitation LP
2224 N Carroll Blvd., Denton, TX 76201, (940) 387-6656; Facility type: Skilled care, Alzheimer's; Certified Beds: 60; Certified: Medicaid, Medicare, Veterans; Owner: Proprietary/Public; License: state

El Paso

Good Samaritan Society–White Acres
7304 Good Samaritan Ct., El Paso, TX 79912, (915) 581-4683; Facility type: Skilled care, Alzheimer's; Certified Beds: 60; Certified: Medicaid, Medicare; Owner: Nonprofit; License: state

Health Center at the MonteVista at Coronado
1575 Belvidere St., El Paso, TX 79912, (915) 833-2229; Facility type: Skilled care, Alzheimer's; Certified Beds: 75; Certified: Medicaid, Medicare; Owner: Marriott Senior Living Services; License: state

Oasis Nursing & Rehabilitation Center
9001 N Loop Rd., El Paso, TX 79907, (915) 859-1650; Facility type: Skilled care, Alzheimer's; Certified Beds: 130; Certified: Medicaid, Medicare, Veterans; Owner: Healthco, Inc.; License: state

Ennis

Ennis Care Center
1200 S Hall St., Ennis, TX 75119, (972) 875-9051; Facility type: Skilled care, Alzheimer's; Certified Beds: 155; Certified: Medicaid, Medicare, Veterans; Owner: Integrated Health Services; License: state

Odd Fellow & Rebekah Nursing Home
2300 Oak Grove Rd., Ennis, TX 75119, (972) 875-8643; Facility type: Skilled care, Alzheimer's; Certified Beds: 136; Certified: Medicaid, Medicare; Owner: Nonprofit; License: state

Farwell

Farwell Convalescent Center
305 5th St., Farwell, TX 79325, (806) 481-9027; Facility type: Skilled care, Alzheimer's; Certified Beds:

75; Certified: Medicaid, Medicare; Owner: Evangelic Lutheran Good Samaritan Society; License: state

Fort Worth

The Courtyards at Fort Worth
8001 Western Hills Blvd., Fort Worth, TX 76108, (817) 246-4953; Facility type: Skilled care, Alzheimer's; Certified Beds: 255; Certified: Medicaid, Medicare, Veterans; Owner: Integrated Health Services; License: state

Haltom Convalescent Center
2936 Markum Dr., Fort Worth, TX 76117, (817) 831-0545; Facility type: Skilled care, Alzheimer's; Certified Beds: 127; Certified: Medicaid, Medicare; Owner: State & Local Gov.; License: state

Lake Lodge Nursing and Rehabilitation LP
3899 Marina Dr., Fort Worth, TX 76135, (817) 237-7231; Facility type: Skilled care, Alzheimer's; Certified Beds: 148; Certified: Medicaid, Medicare; Owner: Proprietary/Public; License: state

Renaissance Park Multi-Care Center
4252 Bryant Irvin Rd., Fort Worth, TX 76109, (817) 738-2975; Facility type: Skilled care, Alzheimer's; Certified Beds: 120; Certified: Medicare; Owner: Life Care Centers of America; License: state

Southwest Nursing and Rehabilitation Center
5300 Alta Mesa Blvd., Fort Worth, TX 76133, (817) 346-1800; Facility type: Skilled care, Alzheimer's; Certified Beds: 160; Certified: Medicaid; Owner: Proprietary/Public; License: state

Friona

Prairie Acres
201 E 15th St., Friona, TX 79035, (806) 250-3922; Facility type: Skilled care, Alzheimer's; Certified Beds: 83; Certified: Medicaid, Medicare, Veterans; Owner: State & Local Gov.; License: state

Garland

Castle Manor
1922 Castle Dr., Garland, TX 75040, (972) 494-1471; Facility type: Skilled care, Alzheimer's; Beds: 90; Certified: Medicaid, Medicare; Owner: Mariner Post Acute Network; License: state

Georgetown

The Wesleyan at Scenic
2001 Scenic Dr., Georgetown, TX 78626, (512) 863-9511; Facility type: Skilled care, Alzheimer's; Certified Beds: 222; Certified: Medicaid, Medicare; Owner: Nonprofit; License: state

Giddings

Country Care Plex
1181 N Williamson, Giddings, TX 78942, (409) 542-3611; Facility type: Skilled care, Alzheimer's; Certified Beds: 88; Certified: Medicaid; Owner: Nonprofit; License: state

Oakland Manor Nursing Center
1400 N Main St., Giddings, TX 78942, (409) 542-1755; Facility type: Skilled care, Alzheimer's; Certified Beds: 120; Certified: Medicaid, Medicare, Veterans; Owner: Fountain View, Inc.; License: state

Goldthwaite

Goldthwaite Health & Rehabilitation Center
1207 Reynolds St., Goldthwaite, TX 76844, (325) 648-2258; Facility type: Skilled care, Alzheimer's; Certified Beds: 94; Certified: Medicaid, Veterans; Owner: Proprietary/Public; License: state

Hillview Manor
1110 Rice St., Goldthwaite, TX 76844, (915) 648-2247; Facility type: Skilled care, Alzheimer's; Certified Beds: 52; Certified: Medicaid, Medicare, Veterans; Owner: Mariner Post Acute Network; License: state

Hamilton

Dove Hill Care Center & Villas
1315 E Hwy. 22 E, Hamilton, TX 76531, (254) 386-3171; Facility type: Skilled care, Alzheimer's; Certified Beds: 78; Certified: Medicaid, Medicare, Veterans; Owner: Nonprofit; License: state

Harlingen

Harlingen Nursing & Rehabilitation Center
3810 Hale St., Harlingen, TX 78550, (956) 412-8660; Facility type: Skilled care, Alzheimer's; Certified Beds: 115; Certified: Medicaid, Medicare; Owner: Regency Nursing Centers; License: state

Houston

Beechnut Manor
12777 Beechnut St., Houston, TX 77072, (281) 879-8040; Facility type: Skilled care, Alzheimer's; Certified Beds: 146; Certified: Medicaid, Medicare, Veterans; Owner: Living Centers of America; License: state

Clarewood House Extended Care Center
7400 Clarewood Dr., Houston, TX 77036, (713) 774-5821; Facility type: Skilled care, Alzheimer's; Beds: Certified 60; Payer mix: 99% Private pay; Owner: Nonprofit; License: state

Heart of Texas Health Care & Rehabilitation Center–All Seasons
6150 S Loop E, Houston, TX 77087, (713) 643-2628;

Facility type: Skilled care, Alzheimer's; Beds: Certified 120; Certified: Medicaid, Medicare; Owner: Heart of TX Healthcare; License: state

ManorCare Health Services
7505 Bellerive, Houston, TX 77036, (713) 774-9611; Facility type: Skilled care, Alzheimer's; Certified Beds: 134; Certified: Medicare; Owner: HCR ManorCare; License: state

Parkway Place
1321 Park Bayou Dr., Houston, TX 77077, (281) 556-9200; Facility type: Skilled care, Alzheimer's; Certified Beds: 60; Certified: Medicaid; Owner: Religious, Capital Senior Management; License: state

Saint Dominic Nursing Home
2409 E Holcombe Blvd., Houston, TX 77021, (713) 741-8701; Facility type: Skilled care, Alzheimer's; Certified Beds: 158; Certified: Medicaid; Owner: Nonprofit; License: state

Irving

Ashford Hall
2021 Shoaf Dr., Irving, TX 75061, (972) 579-1919; Facility type: Skilled care, Alzheimer's; Certified Beds: 330; Certified: Medicaid, Medicare, Veterans; Owner: Lion Health Centers; License: state

Kerrville

Edgewater Care Center
1213 Water St., Kerrville, TX 78028, (830) 896-2411; Facility type: Skilled care, Alzheimer's; Certified Beds: 179; Certified: Medicaid, Medicare, Veterans; Owner: Mariner Post Acute Network; License: state

Levelland

Levelland Nursing & Rehabilitation Center
210 W Ave., Levelland, TX 79336, (806) 894-7011; Facility type: Skilled care, Alzheimer's; Certified Beds: 87; Certified: Medicaid, Medicare, Veterans; Owner: Mariner Post Acute Network; License: state

Lynwood Nursing and Rehabilitation LP
803 S Alamo, Levelland, TX 79336, (806) 894-2806; Facility type: Skilled care, Alzheimer's; Certified Beds: 120; Certified: Medicaid, Medicare, Veterans; Owner: Nonprofit; License: state

Lockhart

Chisholm Trail Living & Rehabilitation Center
107 N Medina, Lockhart, TX 78644, (512) 398-5213; Facility type: Skilled care, Alzheimer's; Certified Beds: 100; Certified: Medicaid, Medicare; Owner: Diversicare Management Services; License: state

Longview

The Clairmont Longview
3201 N 4th St., Longview, TX 75605, (903) 263-4291; Facility type: Skilled care, Alzheimer's; Certified Beds: 198; Certified: Medicaid, Medicare; Owner: Nonprofit; License: state

Havencare Nursing and Rehabilitation Center
111 Ruthlynn Dr., Longview, TX 75601, (903) 757-2557; Facility type: Skilled care, Alzheimer's; Certified Beds: 108; Certified: Medicaid, Medicare; Owner: Mariner Post Acute Network; License: state

Lubbock

Bender Terrace
4510 27th St. Lubbock, TX 79410, (806) 795-4368; Facility type: Skilled care, Alzheimer's; Certified Beds: 120; Certified: Medicaid, Medicare; Owner: For profit; License: state

Heritage Oaks Nursing & Rehabilitation Center
5301 University Ave., Lubbock, TX 79413, (806) 795-8792; Facility type: Skilled care, Alzheimer's; Certified Beds: 159; Certified: Medicaid, Medicare; Owner: For profit; License: state

Lubbock Hospitality House Nursing and Rehabilitation
4710 Slide Rd., Lubbock, TX 79414, (806) 797-3481; Facility type: Skilled care, Alzheimer's; Certified Beds: 117; Certified: Medicaid, Medicare; Owner: Fountain View, Inc.; License: state

Whisperwood Nursing & Rehabilitation Center
5502 W 4th St., Lubbock, TX 79416, (806) 793-1111; Facility type: Skilled care, Alzheimer's; Certified Beds: 117; Certified: Medicaid, Medicare, Veterans; Owner: Nonprofit; License: state

Lufkin

Pine Haven Nursing Home
1712 N. Timberland, Lufkin, TX 75901, (936) 632-3346; Facility type: Skilled care, Alzheimer's; Certified Beds: 92; Certified: Medicaid, Medicare; Owner: Medcare Cantex Healthcare; License: state

Pinecrest Retirement Community
1302 Tom Temple Dr., Lufkin, TX 75904, (409) 634-1054; Facility type: Skilled care, Alzheimer's; Certified Beds: 57; Owner: Nonprofit; License: state

Luling

Oakcreek Nursing and Rehabilitation
105 N. Magnolia, Luling, TX 78648, (830) 875-5606; Facility type: Skilled care, Alzheimer's; Certified Beds: 96; Certified: Medicaid; Owner: Private; License: state

Midland

Mabee Health Care Center
2208 N Loop 250 W, Midland, TX 79707, (915) 699-3401; Facility type: Skilled care, Alzheimer's; Certified Beds: 162; Certified: Medicaid; Owner: Nonprofit; License: state

Rockwood Manor
2000 N Main, Midland, TX 79705, (915) 686-1898; Facility type: Skilled care, Alzheimer's; Certified Beds: 112; Certified: Medicaid, Medicare, Veterans; Owner: Nonprofit; License: state

Mount Pleasant

Mount Pleasant Healthcare Center
1606 Memorial St., Mount Pleasant, TX 75455, (903) 572-3618; Facility type: Skilled care, Alzheimer's; Certified Beds: 128; Certified: Medicaid, Medicare, Veterans; Owner: Sun Healthcare; License: state

New Braunfels

Colonial ManorCare Center
821 Business 81 W, New Braunfels, TX 78130, (830) 625-7526; Facility type: Skilled care, Alzheimer's; Certified Beds: 154; Certified: Medicaid, Medicare, Veterans; Owner: Fountain View, Inc.; License: state

Eden Home
631 Lakeview Blvd., New Braunfels, TX 78130, (830) 625-6291; Facility type: Skilled care, Alzheimer's, Assisted Living; Certified Beds: 197; Certified: Medicaid, Medicare; Owner: Nonprofit; License: state

Odessa

Buena Vida Nursing and Rehab Odessa
3800 Englewood Ln., Odessa, TX 79762, (915) 362-2583; Facility type: Skilled care, Alzheimer's; Certified Beds: 117; Certified: Medicaid, Medicare, Veterans; Owner: Nonprofit; License: state

New Horizon Nursing Center
2510 W 8th St., Odessa, TX 79763, (915) 333-4511; Facility type: Skilled care, Alzheimer's; Certified Beds: 80; Certified: Medicaid, Medicare; Owner: Nonprofit; License: state

Pecos

Pecos Nursing Home
1819 Memorial Dr., Pecos, TX 79772, (915) 447-2183; Facility type: Skilled care, Alzheimer's; Certified Beds: 89; Certified: Medicaid; Owner: Private; License: state

Plano

Heritage Manor Healthcare Center
1621 Coit Rd., Plano, TX 75075, (972) 596-7930;

Facility type: Skilled care, Alzheimer's; Certified Beds: 160; Certified: Medicaid, Medicare; Owner: Integrated Health Services; License: state

San Antonio

The Grand Court II
5100 Newcome Dr., San Antonio, TX 78229, (210) 680-2280; Facility type: Skilled care, Alzheimer's; Certified Beds: 50; Certified: Medicare; Owner: Nonprofit; License: state

Meridian Care Monte Vista
616 W Russell, San Antonio, TX 78212, (210) 735-9233; Facility type: Skilled care, Alzheimer's; Certified Beds: 108; Certified: Medicaid, Medicare, Veterans; Owner: Nonprofit; License: state

Mission Oaks Manor
3030 Roosevelt Ave., San Antonio 78214, (210) 924-8151; Facility type: Skilled care, Alzheimer's; Certified Beds: 150; Certified: Medicaid, Medicare, Veterans; Owner: Proprietary/Public; License: state

Morningside Manor
602 Babcock Rd., San Antonio, TX 78201, (210) 731-1000; Facility type: Skilled care, Alzheimer's; Certified Beds: 119; Certified: Medicaid, Medicare; Owner: Nonprofit/Religious; License: state

Normandy Terrace Nursing & Rehabilitation Center
841 Rice Rd., San Antonio, TX 78220, (210) 648-0101; Facility type: Skilled care, Alzheimer's; Certified Beds: 320; Certified: Medicaid, Medicare, Veterans; Owner: Vencor; License: state

Oak Park Nursing and Rehabilitation Center
7302 Oak Manor Dr., San Antonio, TX 78229, (210) 344-8537; Facility type: Skilled care, Alzheimer's; Certified Beds: 138; Certified: Medicaid, Medicare, Veterans; Owner: Integrated Health Services; License: state

Tobius Hills Assisted Living
225 W Laurel, San Antonio, TX 78212, (210) 227-0267; Facility type: Skilled care, Alzheimer's; Certified Beds: 50; Certified: Medicaid, Medicare; Owner: Private; License: state

Trisun Care Center
8300 Wurzbach Rd., San Antonio, TX 78229, (210) 617-2200; Facility type: Skilled care, Alzheimer's; Certified Beds: 140; Certified: Medicaid, Medicare, Veterans; Owner: HCR ManorCare; License: state

San Marcos

Texan Nursing & Rehab of San Marcos LLC
1600 N IH 35, San Marcos, TX 78666, (512) 353-5026; Facility type: Skilled care, Alzheimer's; Certified Beds: 129; Certified: Medicaid, Medicare, Veterans; Owner: Proprietary/Public; License: state

Stephenville

Mulberry Manor
1670 Lingleville Rd., Stephenville, TX 76401, (254) 968-2158; Facility type: Skilled care, Alzheimer's; Certified Beds: 104; Certified: Medicaid, Medicare, Veterans; Owner: Mariner Post Acute Network; License: state

Tahoka

Tahoka Care Center
1829 S 7th St., Tahoka, TX 79373, (806) 998-5018; Facility type: Skilled care, Alzheimer's; Beds: 50; Certified: Medicaid; Owner: MSC Assoc; License: state; Activities: Arts & Crafts; Dances; Pet therapy; Group exercise; Outings; Support Groups; Other: Alzheimer's secured unit

Temple

Regency Manor Healthcare Center
3011 W Adams Ave., Temple, TX 76504, (254) 773-1626; Facility type: Skilled care, Alzheimer's; Certified Beds: 140; Certified: Medicaid, Medicare, Veterans; Owner: Complete Care Services; License: state

Temple Living Center East
1511 Marland Wood Rd., Temple, TX 765502, (254) 899-6500; Facility type: Skilled care, Alzheimer's; Certified Beds: 148; Certified: Medicaid; Owner: HCR ManorCare; License: state

Texarkana

Pine Haven Care Center
4808 Elizabeth St., Texarkana, TX 75503, (903) 794-3826; Facility type: Skilled care, Alzheimer's; Certified Beds: 90; Certified: Medicaid, Medicare; Owner: Proprietary/Public; License: state

Tyler

Briarcliff Health Center
3403 S Vine St., Tyler, TX 75701, (903) 581-5714; Facility type: Skilled care, Alzheimer's; Certified Beds: 230; Certified: Medicaid, Medicare; Owner: Briarcliff Mgt; License: state

Park Place Nursing & Rehabilitation Center
2450 E 5th St., Tyler, TX 592-6745; Facility type: Skilled care, Alzheimer's; Certified Beds: 120; Certified: Medicare; Owner: Nonprofit/Religious; License: state

Waco

Crestview Healthcare Residence LTD
1400 Lakeshore Dr., Waco, TX 76708, (254) 753-0291; Facility type: Skilled care, Alzheimer's; Certified Beds: 192; Certified: Medicaid, Medicare; Owner: Private; License: state

Saint Catherine Center
300 West Hwy 6, Waco, TX 76712, (254) 736-3177; Facility type: Skilled care, Alzheimer's; Certified Beds: 240; Certified: Medicaid, Medicare, Veterans; Owner: Nonprofit/Religious; License: state

Saint Elizabeth Center
400 Austin, Waco, TX 76703, (254) 756-5441; Facility type: Skilled care, Alzheimer's; Beds: 120; Certified: Medicaid, Medicare, Veterans; Owner: Nonprofit/Religious; License: state

Weatherford

Peach Tree Place
315 Anderson St. W, Weatherford, TX 76086, (817) 599-4181; Facility type: Alzheimer's; Certified Beds: 59; Certified: Medicaid; Owner: Living Centers of Texas; License: state

Weatherford Healthcare Center
521 W 7th St., Weatherford, TX 76086, (817) 594-8713; Facility type: Skilled care, Alzheimer's; Certified Beds: 122; Certified: Medicaid, Medicare, Veterans; Owner: Mariner Post Acute Network; License: state

Webster

ManorCare Health Services
750 W Texas Ave., Webster, TX 77598, (281) 332-3496; Facility type: Skilled care, Alzheimer's; Certified Beds: 113; Certified: Medicaid, Medicare; Owner: HCR ManorCare; License: state

Weimar

Parkview Manor
206 N Smith St., Weimar, TX 78962, (409) 725-8564; Facility type: Skilled care, Alzheimer's; Certified Beds: 100; Certified: Medicaid; Owner: Nonprofit/Religious; License: state

Wichita Falls

Southwest Parkway Nursing Center
2400 Southwest Pkwy, Wichita Falls, TX 76308, (940) 691-5301; Facility type: Skilled care, Alzheimer's; Certified Beds: 90; Certified: Medicaid; Owner: Nonprofit/Religious; License: state

Texhoma Christian Care Center
300 Loop 11, Wichita Falls, TX 76305, (940) 723-8420, Facility type: Skilled care, Alzheimer's; Certified Beds: 367; Certified: Medicaid, Medicare; Owner: Nonprofit/Religious; License: state

Winnsboro

Winnsboro Nursing Home
402 S Chestnut St., Winnsboro, TX 75494, (903) 342-6156; Facility type: Skilled care, Alzheimer's;

Certified Beds: 60; Certified: Medicaid; Owner: Private, Charapata Development; License: state

Woodville

Holiday Pines Nursing and Rehabilitation LP
1201 Cardinal Dr., Woodville, TX 75979, (409) 283-3397; Facility type: Skilled care, Alzheimer's; Certified Beds: 112; Certified: Medicaid, Medicare; Owner: Nonprofit/Religious; License: state

Yoakum

Stevens Health Care and Rehab Center
204 Walter St., Yoakum, TX 77955, (361) 293-3544; Facility type: Skilled care, Alzheimer's; Certified Beds: 106; Certified: Medicaid, Medicare; Owner: New Covenant Care of TX; License: state

UTAH

American Fork

Heritage Care Center
350 E 300 N, American Fork, UT 84003, (801) 756-5293; Facility type: Skilled care, Alzheimer's; Certified Beds: 106; Certified: Medicaid, Medicare; Owner: Heritage Mgt Co; License: state

Bountiful

Avalon Care Center–Bountiful
523 N Main St., Bountiful, UT 84010, (801) 951-2273; Facility type: Skilled care, Alzheimer's; Certified Beds: 122; Certified: Medicaid, Medicare, Veterans; Owner: Private; License: state

North Canyon Care Center
350 S 400 E, Bountiful, UT 84010, (801) 397-4700; Facility type: Skilled care, Alzheimer's; Certified Beds: 102; Certified: Medicaid, Medicare, Veterans; Owner: Rocky Mt Healthcare Services; License: state

Brigham City

Willow Glen Health and Rehab, LLC
775 N 200 E, Brigham City, UT, 84302, (435) 723-7777; Facility type: Skilled care, Alzheimer's; Certified Beds: 84; Certified: Medicaid, Medicare; Owner: Peak Medical Corp; License: state

Ferron

Emery County Care & Rehabilitation Center
455 W Mill Rd., Ferron, UT 84523, (435) 384-2301; Facility type: Skilled care, Alzheimer's; Certified Beds: 55; Certified: Medicaid, Medicare; Owner: State & Local Gov.; License: state

Heber City

Rocky Mountain Care Center
160 W 500 N, Heber City, UT, 84032, (435) 654-5500; Facility type: Skilled care, Alzheimer's; Certified Beds: 46; Certified: Medicaid, Medicare; Owner: Rocky Mt Healthcare Services; License: state

Logan

Logan Nursing & Rehabilitation Center
1480 N 400 E, Logan, UT 84341, (435) 750-5501; Facility type: Skilled care, Alzheimer's; Certified Beds: 118; Certified: Medicaid, Medicare; Owner: Private; License: state

Sunshine Terrace Foundation
248 West 300 N, Logan, UT 84321, (435) 725-0411; Facility type: Skilled care, Alzheimer's; Certified Beds: 172; Certified: Medicaid, Medicare, Veterans; Owner: Nonprofit/Religious; License: state

Milford

Milford Valley Memorial Long Term Care Center
451 N Main St., Milford, UT 84751, (435) 387-2411; Facility type: Skilled care, Alzheimer's; Beds: 50; Certified: Medicaid, Medicare, Veterans; Owner: State & Local Gov.; License: state; Activities: Arts & Crafts; Dances; Pet therapy; Group exercise; Outings; Support Groups; Other: Adult day care, Home health care

Ogden

Aspen Care Center
2325 Madison Ave., Ogden, UT 84401, (801) 399-5846; Facility type: Skilled care, Alzheimer's; Certified Beds: 72; Certified: Medicaid, Medicare; Owner: Nonprofit/Religious; License: state

Lomond Peak Care and Rehab
524 E 800 N, Ogden UT 84404, (801) 782-3740; Facility type: Skilled care, Alzheimer's; Certified Beds: 85; Certified: Medicaid, Medicare; Owner: Private; License: state

Mountain View Health Services
5865 S Wasatch Dr., Ogden, UT 84403, (801) 479-

8480; Facility type: Skilled care, Alzheimer's; Certified Beds: 155; Certified: Medicaid, Medicare; Owner: Private; License: state

Orem

Orem Rehabilitation & Nursing Center
575 E 1400 St., Orem, UT 84058, (801) 225-4741; Facility type: Skilled care, Alzheimer's; Certified Beds: 120; Certified: Medicaid, Medicare, Veterans; Owner: Utah Senior Services; License: state

Price

Pinnacle Nursing and Rehabilitation Center
1340 E 300 N, Price, UT 84501, (435) 637-9213; Facility type: Skilled care, Alzheimer's; Certified Beds: 100; Certified: Medicaid, Medicare, Veterans; Owner: Quality Healthcare; License: state

Provo

Provo Rehabilitation & Nursing
1001 N 500 W, Provo, UT 84601, (801) 377-9661; Facility type: Skilled care, Alzheimer's; Certified Beds: 220; Certified: Medicaid, Medicare; Owner: Quality Healthcare; License: state

Richfield

Richfield Care Center
83 E 1100 N, Richfield, UT 84701, (435) 896-8211; Facility type: Skilled care, Alzheimer's; Certified Beds: 98; Certified: Medicaid, Medicare, Veterans; Owner: Nonprofit/Religious; License: state

Salt Lake City

Bennion Care Center
6246 South Redwood RD., Salt Lake City, UT 84123, (801) 969-1420; Facility type: Skilled care, Alzheimer's; Certified Beds: 104; Certified: Medicaid, Medicare, Veterans; Owner: Health Care Consulting; License: state

Christus St. Joseph Villa
451 Bishop Federal Ln., Salt Lake City, UT 84115, (801) 487-7557; Facility type: Skilled care, Alzheimer's; Certified Beds: 221; Certified: Medicaid, Medicare; Owner: Nonprofit/Religious; License: state

Fairview Care Center East
455 S 900 E, Salt Lake City, UT 84102, (801) 355-6891; Facility type: Skilled care, Alzheimer's; Certified

Beds: 36; Certified: Medicaid; Owner: Private; License: state

Highland Care Center
4285 South Highland Dr., Salt Lake City, UT 84124, (801) 278-2839; Facility type: Skilled care, Alzheimer's; Certified Beds: 95; Certified: Medicare; Owner: Nonprofit/Religious; License: state

Millcreek Health Center
3520 S Highland Dr., Salt Lake City, UT 84106, (801) 484-7638; Facility type: Skilled care, Alzheimer's; Certified Beds: 61; Certified: Medicaid, Medicare; Owner: Private; License: state

Sandy

Sandy Regional Health Center
50 E 9000 S, Sandy, UT 84070, (801) 561-9839; Facility type: Skilled care, Alzheimer's; Certified Beds: 154; Certified: Medicaid, Medicare; Owner: Horizon West, Inc.; License: state

Tooele

Rocky Mountain Care–Tooele
140 E 200 S, Tooele, UT 84074, (801)-397-4200; Facility type: Skilled care, Alzheimer's; Certified Beds: 84; Certified: Medicaid, Medicare; Owner: State & Local Gov.; License: state

Vernal

Uintah Care Center
510 S 500 W, Vernal, UT 84078, (435) 789-8851; Facility type: Skilled care, Alzheimer's; Certified Beds: 110; Certified: Medicaid, Medicare, Veterans; Owner: State & Local Gov.; License: state

West Jordan

Copper Ridge Health Care
3706 W 9000 S, West Jordan, UT 84088, (801) 280-2273; Facility type: Skilled care, Alzheimer's; Certified Beds: 120; Certified: Medicaid, Medicare, Veterans; Owner: Proprietary/Public; License: state

West Valley City

Hazen Nursing Home
2520 S Redwood Rd., West Valley City, UT 84119, (801) 972-1050; Facility type: Skilled care, Alzheimer's; Certified Beds: 2; Certified: Veterans; Owner: Proprietary/Public; License: state

VERMONT

Barre

Berlin Health & Rehabilitation Center
98 Hospitality Dr., Barre, VT 05641, (802) 229-0308; Facility type: Skilled care, Alzheimer's; Certified Beds: 141; Certified: Medicaid, Medicare, Veterans; Owner: Subacute Mgt Corp of America; License: state

Barton

Maple Lane Nursing Home
60 Maple Hill Rd., Barton, VT 05822, (802) 754-8575; Facility type: Skilled care, Alzheimer's; Certified Beds: 71; Certified: Medicaid, Medicare; Owner: Private; License: state

Bennington

Bennington Health & Rehabilitation
2 Blackberry Ln., Bennington, VT 05201, (802) 442-8525; Facility type: Skilled care, Alzheimer's; Certified Beds: 100; Certified: Medicaid, Medicare; Owner: Proprietary/Public; License: state

Crescent ManorCare Centers
312 Crescent Blvd., Bennington, VT 05201, (802) 447-1501; Facility type: Skilled care, Alzheimer's; Certified Beds: 90; Certified: Medicaid, Medicare; Owner: Private; License: state

Vermont Veterans' Home
325 North St., Bennington, VT 05201, (802) 442-6353; Facility type: Skilled care, Alzheimer's; Certified Beds: 177; Certified: Medicaid, Medicare, Veterans; Owner: State & Local Gov.; License: state

Burlington

Burlington Health & Rehabilitation
300 Pearl St., Burlington, VT 05401, (802) 658-4200; Facility type: Skilled care, Alzheimer's; Certified Beds: 126; Certified: Medicaid, Medicare, Veterans; Owner: Vermont Subacute Corp; License: state

Glover

Union House Nursing Home
3086 Glover St., Glover, VT 05839, (802) 525-6600; Facility type: Skilled care, Alzheimer's; Certified Beds: 44; Certified: Medicaid, Medicare; Owner: Private; License: state

Northfield

Mayo Healthcare Inc.
71 Richardson Ave., Northfield, VT 05663, (802) 485-3161; Facility type: Skilled care, Alzheimer's; Certified Beds: 50; Certified: Medicaid, Medicare, Veterans; Owner: Nonprofit/Religious; License: state

Rutland

Mountain View Center Genesis Healthcare
9 Haywood Ave., Rutland, VT 05701, (802) 775-0007; Facility type: Skilled care, Alzheimer's; Certified Beds: 158; Certified: Medicaid, Medicare, Veterans; Owner: Genesis ElderCare

Rutland Healthcare & Rehabilitation Center
46 Nichols St., Rutland, VT 05701, (802) 775-2941; Facility type: Skilled care, Alzheimer's; Certified Beds: 123; Certified: Medi-Cal, Medicare; Owner: Private; License: state

Saint Albans

Redstone Villa
7 Forest Hill Dr., Saint Albans, VT 05478, (802) 524-3498; Facility type: Skilled care, Alzheimer's; Certified Beds: 30; Certified: Medicaid, Medicare; Owner: Nonprofit/Religious; License: state

Shelburne

The Arbors & The Pillars
687 Harbor Rd., Shelburne, VT 05482, (802) 985-8600; Facility type: Skilled care, Alzheimer's; Beds: 6; Payer mix: 90% Private pay; Owner: Nonprofit/Religious; License: state; Activities: Arts & Crafts; Dances; Pet therapy; Group exercise; Outings; Support Groups; Other: Alzheimer's secured unit

Townshend

Stratton House Nursing Home
PO Box 216, Townshend, VT 05353, (802) 365-7344; Facility type: Skilled care, Alzheimer's; Beds: 40; Certified: Medicaid, Medicare; Owner: Nonprofit/Religious; License: state; Activities: Arts & Crafts; Dances; Pet therapy; Group exercise; Outings; Support Groups; Other: Adult day care

Vernon

Vernon Green Nursing Home
61 Greenway Dr., Vernon, VT 05354, (802) 254-6041; Facility type: Skilled care, Alzheimer's; Certified Beds: 60; Certified: Medicaid, Medicare; Owner: Nonprofit/Religious; License: state

Windsor

Cedar Hill Health Care Center
49 Cedar Hill Dr., Windsor, VT 05089, (802) 674-6609; Facility type: Skilled care, Alzheimer's; Certified Beds: 39; Certified: Medicaid, Medicare, Veterans; Owner: Proprietary/Public; License: state

VIRGINIA

Alexandria

Hermitage in Northern Virginia
500 Fairbanks Ave., Alexandria, VA 22311, (703) 820-2434; Facility type: Skilled care, Alzheimer's; Beds: 120; Payer mix: 100% Private pay; Owner: United Methodist Homes; License: state; Activities: Arts & Crafts; Dances; Pet therapy; Group exercise; Outings; Support Groups

Mount Vernon Nursing &Rehabilitation Center
8111 Tiswell Dr., Alexandria, VA 22306, (703) 360-4000; Facility type: Skilled care, Alzheimer's; Certified Beds: 98; Certified: Medicaid, Medicare; Owner: Nonprofit/Religious; License: state

Woodbine Rehabilitation & Healthcare Center
2729 King St., Alexandria, VA, 22302, (703) 836-8838; Facility type: Skilled care, Alzheimer's; Certified Beds: 307; Certified: Medicaid, Medicare, Veterans; Owner: Proprietary/Public; License: state

Annandale

Leewood Health Care Center
7120 Braddock Rd., Annandale, VA 22003, (703) 256-9770; Facility type: Skilled care, Alzheimer's; Certified Beds: 132; Certified: Medicaid; Owner: Private; License: state

Arlington

Cherrydale Health Care Center
3710 Lee Hwy., Arlington, VA 22207, (703) 243-7640; Facility type: Skilled care, Alzheimer's; Certified Beds: 240; Certified: Medicaid, Medicare, Veterans; Owner: Medical Facilities of America; License: state

ManorCare Health Services–Arlington
550 S Carlin Springs Rd., Arlington, VA 22204, (703) 379-7200; Facility type: Skilled care, Alzheimer's; Certified Beds: 171; Certified: Medicaid, Medicare, Veterans; Owner: HCR ManorCare; License: state

Potomac Center Genesis ElderCare Network
1785 S Hayes St., Arlington, VA 22202, (703) 920-5700; Facility type: Skilled care, Alzheimer's; Certified Beds: 240; Certified: Medicaid, Medicare, Veterans; Owner: Genesis Elder Care; License: state

Blacksburg

Heritage Hall Blacksburg
3610 S Main St., Blacksburg, VA 24060, (540) 951-7000; Facility type: Skilled care, Alzheimer's; Certified Beds: 194; Certified: Medicaid, Veterans; Owner: Nonprofit/Religious; License: state

Blackstone

Heritage Hall Blackstone
900 S Main St., Blackstone, VA 23824, (434) 292-5301; Facility type: Skilled care, Alzheimer's; Certified Beds: 180; Certified: Medicaid, Veterans; Owner: Nonprofit/Religious; License: state

Burkeville

Burkeville Piedmont Geriatric Hospital
Hwy. 360, Burkeville, VA 23922, (804) 767-4401; Facility type: Skilled care, Alzheimer's; Beds: 200; Certified: Medicaid, Medicare; Owner: State & Local Gov.; License: state; Activities: Arts & Crafts; Dances; Pet therapy; Group exercise; Outings; Support Groups; Other: Alzheimer's secured unit

Charlottesville

Charlottesville Health & Rehabilitation Center
505 W Rio Rd., Charlottesville, VA 22901, (434) 978-7015; Facility type: Skilled care, Alzheimer's; Certified Beds: 120; Certified: Medicaid, Medicare, Veterans; Owner: Nonprofit/Religious; License: state

Our Lady of Peace
751 Hillsdale Dr., Charlottesville, VA 22901, (434) 973-1155; Facility type: Skilled care, Alzheimer's; Certified Beds: 30; Certified: Medicaid; Owner: Nonprofit/Religious; License: state

Chesapeake

Sentara Village
778 Oak Grove Rd., Chesapeake, VA 23320, (757) 547-5666; Facility type: Skilled care, Alzheimer's, Assisted Living; Beds: 100; Certified: Medicaid, Medicare, Veterans; Owner: Sentara Life Care License: state; Activities: Arts & Crafts; Dances; Pet therapy; Group exercise; Outings; Support Groups

Chesterfield

Chesterfield County Health Center Commission
6800 Lucy Corr Blvd., Chesterfield, VA 23832, (804) 748-1511; Facility type: Skilled care, Alzheimer's; Certified Beds: 240; Certified: Medicaid, Medicare; Owner: Nonprofit; License: state

Culpeper

Culpeper Health & Rehabilitation Center
602 Madison Rd., Culpeper, VA 22701, (540) 825-2884; Facility type: Skilled care, Alzheimer's; Certified Beds: 180; Certified: Medicaid, Medicare, Veterans; Owner: Medical Facilities of America; License: state

Fairfax

Commonwealth Health & Rehab Center
4315 Chain Bridge Rd., Fairfax, VA 22030, (703)
934-5000; Facility type: Skilled care, Alzheimer's;
Certified Beds: 143; Certified: Medicaid, Medicare;
Owner: Nonprofit/Religious; License: state

Fairfax Nursing Center
10701 Main St., Fairfax, VA 22030, (703) 273-7705;
Facility type: Skilled care, Alzheimer's; Certified Beds:
198; Certified: Medicaid, Medicare, Veterans; Owner:
Genesis Elder Care; License: state

The Virginian Health
9229 Arlington Blvd., Fairfax, VA 22031, (703) 385-
0555; Facility type: Skilled care, Alzheimer's; Certified
Beds: 49; Certified: Medicare; Owner: Nonprofit/Re-
ligious; License: state

Falls Church

**Goodwin House West Nursing Bailey's
  Crossroads**
3440 S Jefferson St., Falls Church, VA 22041, (703)
578-7262; Facility type: Skilled care, Alzheimer's;
Certified Beds: 73; Certified: Medicaid, Medicare;
Owner: Nonprofit/Religious; License: state

Fredericksburg

Fredericksburg Nursing Home
3900 Plank Rd., Fredericksburg, VA 22407, (540)
786-8351; Facility type: Skilled care, Alzheimer's;
Certified Beds: 177; Certified: Medicaid, Medicare,
Veterans; Owner: Beverly Enterprises; License: state

Front Royal

Warren Memorial Hospital–Lynn Care Center
1000 Shenandoah Ave., Front Royal, VA 22630, (540)
636-0300; Facility type: Skilled care, Alzheimer's;
Certified Beds: 120; Certified: Medicaid, Medicare;
Owner: Nonprofit/Religious; License: state

Harrisonburg

Oak Lea Nursing Home
1475 Virginia Ave., Harrisonburg, VA 22802, (540)
564-3500; Facility type: Skilled care, Alzheimer's;
Certified Beds: 120; Certified: Medicaid; Owner: Virginia Mennonite Retirement Community; License:
state

Sunnyside Presbyterian Retirement Community
3935 Sunnyside Dr., Harrisonburg, VA 22801, (540)
568-8200; Facility type: Skilled care, Alzheimer's;
Certified Beds: 84; Certified: Medicaid; Owner: Non-
profit/Religious; License: state

Lawrenceville

Envoy of Lawrenceville, LLC
1722 Lawrenceville Plank Rd., Lawrenceville, VA
23868, (804) 848-4766; Facility type: Skilled care,
Alzheimer's; Certified Beds: 77; Certified: Medicaid,
Medicare; Owner: Mariner Post Acute Network; License: state

Leesburg

Heritage Hall Nursing & Rehabilitation Center
122 Morven Park Rd., NW, Leesburg, VA 20176,
(703) 777-8700; Facility type: Skilled care, Alzheimer's; Certified Beds: 164; Certified: Medicaid, Medicare, Veterans; Owner: HCMF Corp; License: state

Sunrise Assisted Living
246 W Market St., Leesburg, VA 20176, (703) 777-
1971; Facility type: Skilled care, Alzheimer's; Beds:
50; Owner: Sunrise Terrace; License: state; Activities:
Arts & Crafts; Dances; Pet therapy; Group exercise;
Outings; Support Groups; Other: Adult day care

Lynchburg

Medical Care Center
2200 Landover Pl., Lynchburg, VA 24501, (434) 846-
4626; Facility type: Skilled care, Alzheimer's; Certified
Beds: 118; Certified: Medicaid, Medicare; Owner:
HCR ManorCare; License: state

Saint John's Nursing Home
3500 Powhatan St., Lynchburg, VA 24501, (804)
845-6045; Facility type: Skilled care, Alzheimer's;
Beds: 50; Payer mix: 91% Private pay; Owner: Agape
Healthcare; License: state; Activities: Arts & Crafts;
Dances; Pet therapy; Group exercise; Outings; Support Groups; Other: Alzheimer's secured unit

Manassas

Birmingham Green
8605 Centreville Rd., Manassas, VA 20110, (703)
257-0935; Facility type: Skilled care, Alzheimer's;
Certified Beds: 180; Certified: Medicaid; Owner:
Nonprofit/Religious; License: state

Marion

**Southwestern Virginia Mental Health
  Institute–Geriatric Services**
340 Bagley Cir, Marion, VA 24354, (276) 783-1209;
Facility type: Skilled care, Alzheimer's; Certified Beds:
25; Certified: Medicaid; Owner: State & Local Gov.;
License: state

Martinsville

Beverly Healthcare
1607 Spruce St., Martinsville, VA 24112, (276) 632-

7146; Facility type: Skilled care, Alzheimer's; Certified Beds: 142; Certified: Medicaid, Medicare, Veterans; Owner: Beverly Enterprises; License: state

McLean

Arleigh Burke Pavilion
1739 Kirby Rd., McLean VA 22101, (703) 506-6900; Facility type: Skilled care, Alzheimer's; Beds: 50; Certified: Medicare; Owner: Nonprofit/Religious; License: state; Activities: Arts & Crafts; Dances; Pet therapy; Group exercise; Outings; Support Groups; Other: Alzheimer's secured unit

Mechanicsville

Meadowbridge Transitional Care Unit
826 Atlee, Mechanicsville, VA 23116, (757) 764-6421; Facility type: Skilled care, Alzheimer's; Beds: 40; Certified: Medicaid, Medicare; Owner: Health Corp of VA; License: state; Activities: Arts & Crafts; Dances; Pet therapy; Group exercise; Outings; Support Groups; Other: Alzheimer's secured unit, Home health care

Montvale

Woodhaven Nursing Home
13055 W Lynchburg-Salem Tpke., Montvale, VA 24122; (540) 947-2207; Facility type: Skilled care, Alzheimer's; Beds: 50; Payer mix: 100% Private pay; Owner: Proprietary/Public; License: state; Activities: Arts & Crafts; Dances; Pet therapy; Group exercise; Outings; Support Groups; Other: Alzheimer's secured unit

Nassawadox

Heritage Hall Nursing Home
9468 Hospital Rd., Nassawadox, VA 23413, (757) 442-5600; Facility type: Skilled care, Alzheimer's; Certified Beds: 145; Certified: Medicaid, Medicare, Veterans; Owner: HCMF Corp; License: state

Newport News

The Gardens at Warwick Forest
1000 Old Denbigh Blvd., Newport News, VA 23602, (757) 875-2000; Facility type: Skilled care, Alzheimer's; Certified Beds: 242; Certified: Medicaid, Medicare; Owner: Riverside Health System; License: state

James Pointe Care Center
5015 Huntington Ave., Newport News, VA 23607, (757) 244-1734; Facility type: Skilled care, Alzheimer's; Beds: 90; Certified: Medicaid, Medicare, Veterans; Owner: Private; License: state; Activities: Arts & Crafts; Dances; Pet therapy; Group exercise; Outings; Support Groups; Other: Alzheimer's secured unit

The Newport
11141 Warwick Blvd., Newport News, VA 23601, (757) 595-3733; Facility type: Skilled care, Alzheimer's; Certified Beds: 45; Owner: Proprietary/Public; License: state

Norfolk

Autumn Care of Norfolk
1401 Halstead Ave., Norfolk, VA 23502, (757) 857-0481; Facility type: Skilled care, Alzheimer's; Certified Beds: 120; Certified: Medicaid, Medicare, Veterans; Owner: Autumn Corp; License: state

Envoy of Thornton Hall
827 Norview Ave., Norfolk, VA 23509, (757) 853-6281; Facility type: Skilled care, Alzheimer's; Certified Beds: 60; Certified: Medicaid, Medicare; Owner: Genesis ElderCare; License: state

Harbor Point M & R Center
1005 Hampton Blvd., Norfolk, VA 23507, (757) 623-5602; Facility type: Skilled care, Alzheimer's; Certified Beds: 169; Certified: Medicaid, Medicare; Owner: Vencor, Inc.; License: state

Sentara Nursing Center
249 S Newton Rd., Norfolk, VA 23502, (757) 892-5500; Facility type: Skilled care, Alzheimer's; Certified Beds: 193; Certified: Medicaid, Medicare, Veterans; Owner: Sentara Life Care; License: state

Richmond

Beth Sholom Home of Virginia
1600 John Rolf Pkwy, Richmond, VA 23233, (804) 750-2183; Facility type: Skilled care, Alzheimer's; Certified Beds: 116; Certified: Medicaid, Medicare; Owner: Nonprofit/Religious; License: state

Envoy of Westover Hills
4403 Forest Hill Ave., Richmond, VA 23225, (804) 231-0231; Facility type: Skilled care, Alzheimer's; Certified Beds: 198; Certified: Medicaid, Medicare, Veterans; Owner: Convalescent Care Inc.; License: state

Glenburnie Rehab & Nursing Center
1901 Libbie Ave., Richmond, VA 23226, (804) 281-3500; Facility type: Skilled care, Alzheimer's; Certified Beds: 125; Certified: Medicaid, Medicare, Veterans; Owner: Capitol Care Mgt Co; License: state

ManorCare Health Services Stratford Hall
2125 Hilliard Rd., Richmond, VA 23228, (804) 266-9666; Facility type: Skilled care, Alzheimer's; Certified Beds: 194; Certified: Medicaid, Medicare; Owner: HCR ManorCare; License: state

Roanoke

Friendship Health and Rehab Center
327 Hershberger Rd., NW, Roanoke, VA 24012,

(540) 265-2123; Facility type: Skilled care, Alzheimer's; Certified Beds: 373; Certified: Medicaid, Medicare; Owner: Nonprofit/Religious; License: state

Staunton

Envoy of Staunton, LLC
512 Houston St., Staunton, VA 24402, (540) 886-2335; Facility type: Skilled care, Alzheimer's; Certified Beds: 170; Certified: Medicaid, Medicare, Veterans; Owner: Nonprofit/Religious; License: state

Suffolk

Bon Secours-Maryview Nursing Care Center
4775 Bridge Rd., Suffolk, VA 23435, (757) 686-0488; Facility type: Skilled care, Alzheimer's; Certified Beds: 120; Certified: Medicaid, Veterans; Owner: Nonprofit/Religious; License: state

Virginia Beach

Beacon Shores Nursing & Rehabilitation
340 Lynn Shores Dr., Virginia Beach, VA 23452, (757) 340-6611; Facility type: Skilled care, Alzheimer's; Certified Beds: 180; Certified: Medicaid, Medicare, Veterans; Owner: Nonprofit/Religious; License: state

Beth Sholom Home of Eastern Virginia
6401 Auburn Dr., Virginia Beach, VA 23464, (757) 420-2512; Facility type: Skilled care, Alzheimer's; Certified Beds: 120; Certified: Medicaid, Medicare; Owner: Nonprofit/Religious; License: state

Sentara NSG Center–Windermere
1604 Old Donation Pkwy, Virginia Beach, VA 23454,

(757) 496-3939; Facility type: Skilled care, Alzheimer's; Certified Beds: 90; Certified: Medicaid; Owner: Nonprofit/Religious; License: state

Warrenton

Oak Springs of Warrenton
614 Hastings Ln., Warrenton, VA 20186, (540) 347-4770; Facility type: Skilled care, Alzheimer's; Certified Beds: 130; Certified: Medicaid, Medicare; Owner: Private; License: state

Williamsburg

Woodhaven Hall at Williamsburg Landing
5700 Williamsburg Landing Dr., Williamsburg, VA 23185, (757) 258-2196; Facility type: Skilled care, Alzheimer's; Certified Beds: 15; Certified: Medicare; Owner: Williamsburg Landing Inc.; License: state

Yorktown

Regency Healthcare Center & Rehabilitation Center
112 N Constitution Dr., Grafton, VA 23692, (757) 890-0675; Facility type: Skilled care, Alzheimer's; Certified Beds: 60; Certified: Medicaid, Medicare, Veterans; Owner: Medical Facilities of America; License: state

York Convalescent Center
113 Battle Rd., Yorktown, VA 23692, (757) 898-1491; Facility type: Skilled care, Alzheimer's; Certified Beds: 60; Certified: Medicaid; Owner: Nonprofit/Religious; License: state

WASHINGTON

Anacortes

Fidalgo Care Center
1105 27th St., Anacortes, WA 98221, (360) 293-3174; Facility type: Skilled care, Alzheimer's; Certified Beds: 44; Certified: Medicaid, Medicare; Owner: HMH Management; License: state

Arlington

Regency Care Center & Arlington
620 S Hazel St., Arlington, WA 98223, (360) 403-8247; Facility type: Skilled care, Alzheimer's; Certified Beds: 96; Certified: Medicaid, Medicare; Owner: Regency Northwest; License: state

Bainbridge Island

Messenger House Care Center
10861 Manitou Park Blvd., NE, Bainbridge Island, WA 98110, (206) 842-2654; Facility type: Skilled care, Alzheimer's; Certified Beds: 96; Certified: Medicaid, Medicare; Owner: Proprietary/Public; License: state

Bellevue

Care Center at Kelsey Creek
2210 132nd Ave., Se, Bellevue, WA 98005, (425) 957-2400; Facility type: Skilled care, Alzheimer's; Beds: 100; Certified: Medicaid, Medicare; Owner: Nonprofit/Religious; License: state; Activities: Arts & Crafts; Dances; Pet therapy; Group exercise; Outings; Support Groups; Other: Alzheimer's secured unit

Bellingham

Sehome Park Care Center
700 32nd St., Bellingham, WA 98225, (360) 734-9330; Facility type: Skilled care, Alzheimer's; Beds: 110; Certified: Medicaid, Medicare; Owner: Sunrise Healthcare Corp; License: state; Activities: Arts & Crafts; Dances; Pet therapy; Group exercise; Outings; Support Groups; Other: Alzheimer's secured unit

Bothell

North Creek Health and Rehabilitation Center
10909 NE 185th St., Bothell, WA 98011, (425) 486-7174; Facility type: Skilled care, Alzheimer's; Certified Beds: 100; Certified: Medicaid, Medicare, Veterans; Owner: Nonprofit/Religious; License: state

Burlington

SunRise Care & Rehabilitation
1036 Victoria Ave., Burlington, WA 98233, (360) 755-0711; Facility type: Skilled care, Alzheimer's; Certified Beds: 49; Certified: Medicaid, Medicare; Owner: Proprietary/Public; License: state

Cathlamet

Columbia View Care Center
155 Adler, Cathlamet, WA 98612, (360) 795-3140; Facility type: Skilled care, Alzheimer's; Certified Beds: 36; Certified: Medicaid, Medicare, Veterans; Owner: Sun Healthcare Group; License: state

Centralia

Liberty Country Place
917 S Scheuber Rd., Centralia, WA 98531, (360) 736-9384; Facility type: Skilled care, Alzheimer's; Certified Beds: 128; Certified: Medicaid, Medicare; Owner: Nonprofit/Religious; License: state

Riverside Nursing & Rehabilitation Center
1305 Alexander Rd., Centralia, WA 98531, (360) 736-2823; Facility type: Skilled care, Alzheimer's; Certified Beds: 91; Certified: Medicaid, Medicare, Veterans; Owner: ExtendiCare Health Services; License: state

Sharon Care Center
1509 Harrison Ave., Centralia, WA 98531, (360) 736-0112; Facility type: Skilled care, Alzheimer's, Assisted Living; Certified Beds: 42; Certified: Medicaid, Medicare; Owner: Proprietary/Public; License: state

Chelan

Regency Manor
726 N Markeson, Chelan, WA 98816, (509) 682-2551; Facility type: Skilled care, Alzheimer's; Certified Beds: 55; Certified: Medicaid, Medicare, Veterans; Owner: Regency Pacific; License: state

Colville

Pinewood Terrace Nursing Center
1000 E Elep St., Colville WA 99114, (509) 684-2573; Facility type: Skilled care, Alzheimer's; Certified Beds: 92; Certified: Medicaid, Medicare, Veterans; Owner: Beverly Enterprises; License: state

Everett

Bethany at Silver Lake
2235 Lake Heights Dr., Everett, WA 98208, (425) 338-3000; Facility type: Skilled care, Alzheimer's; Certified Beds: 120; Certified: Medicaid, Medicare; Owner: Evangelical Lutheran Church; License: state

SunRise View Convalescent Center
2520 Madison St., Everett, WA 98203, (425) 353-4040; Facility type: Skilled care, Alzheimer's; Certified Beds: 59; Certified: Medicaid, Medicare; Owner: Private; License: state

Grand Coulee

Coulee Community Hospital
411 Fortuyn Rd., Grand Coulee, WA 99133, (509) 633-1753; Facility type: Skilled care, Alzheimer's; Beds: 30; Certified: Medicaid; Owner: Brim Healthcare; License: state; Activities: Arts & Crafts; Dances; Pet therapy; Group exercise; Outings; Support Groups; Other: Alzheimer's secured unit

Grandview

Grandview Healthcare Center
912 Hillcrest Ave., Grandview WA 98930, (509) 882-1200; Facility type: Skilled care, Alzheimer's; Certified Beds: 60; Certified: Medicaid, Medicare, Veterans; Owner: Nonprofit/Religious; License: state

Walnut Grove Boarding Home
5305 N Hicks Rd., Grandview, WA 98930, (509) 882-2400; Facility type: Skilled care, Alzheimer's; Beds: 70; Certified: Medicaid, Medicare, Veterans; Owner: Nonprofit/Religious; License: state; Activities: Arts & Crafts; Dances; Pet therapy; Group exercise; Outings; Support Groups; Other: Adult day care

Issaquah

Issaquah Nursing and Rehabilitation Center
805 Front St. S, Issaquah, WA 98027, (425) 392-1271; Facility type: Skilled care, Alzheimer's; Certified Beds: 140; Certified: Medicaid, Medicare, Veterans; Owner: Vencor; License: state

Providence Marianwood
3725 Providence Point Dr., SE, Issaquah, WA 98029, (425) 391-2800; Facility type: Skilled care, Alzheimer's; Certified Beds: 120; Certified: Medicaid, Medicare; Owner: Nonprofit/Religious; License: state

Kent

Benson Heights Rehabilitation Center
22410 Benson Rd., SE, Kent, WA 98031, (253) 852-7755; Facility type: Skilled care, Alzheimer's; Certified Beds: 91; Certified: Medicaid, Medicare, Veterans; Owner: Beverly Enterprises; License: state

Long Beach

Ocean View Convalescent Center
211 W Pioneer Rd., Long Beach, WA 98631, (360) 642-3123; Facility type: Skilled care, Alzheimer's; Beds: 60; Certified: Medicaid, Medicare, Veterans; Owner: Life Care Centers of America; License: state; Activities: Arts & Crafts; Dances; Pet therapy; Group exercise; Outings; Support Groups; Other: Alzheimer's secured unit, Adult day care

Lynden

Christian Health Care Center
855 Aaron Dr., Lynden, WA 98264, (360) 354-4434; Facility type: Skilled care, Alzheimer's; Certified Beds: 142; Certified: Medicaid, Medicare, Veterans; Owner: Christian Home for the Aged & Infirm, Inc.; License: state

Lynnwood

ManorCare Health Services
3701 188th St., SW, Lynnwood, WA 98037, (425) 775-9222; Facility type: Skilled care, Alzheimer's; Certified Beds: 113; Certified: Medicare; Owner: HCR ManorCare; License: state

Monroe

Regency Care Center at Monroe
1355 W Main St., Monroe, WA 98272, (360) 794-4011; Facility type: Skilled care, Alzheimer's; Certified Beds: 92; Certified: Medicaid, Medicare, Veterans; Owner: Regency Pacific; License: state

Moses Lake

Lake Ridge Solana Alzheimer's Care Center
817 E Plum St., Moses Lake, WA 98837, (509) 765-7835; Facility type: Skilled care, Alzheimer's; Certified Beds: 74; Certified: Medicaid, Medicare, Veterans; Owner: Sun Healthcare Group; License: state

Olympia

Providence Mother Joseph Care Center
3333 Ensign Rd., NE, Olympia, WA 98506, (360) 493-4900; Facility type: Skilled care, Alzheimer's; Certified Beds: 152; Certified: Medicaid, Medicare; Owner: Nonprofit/Religious; License: state

Port Orchard

Life Care Center of Port Orchard
2031 Pottery Ave., Port Orchard, WA 98366, (360) 876-8035; Facility type: Skilled care, Alzheimer's; Certified Beds: 125; Certified: Medicaid, Medicare, Veterans; Owner: Life Care Centers of America; License: state

Puyallup

Linden Grove Health Care Center
400 29th St. NE, Puyallup, WA 98372, (253) 841-4400; Facility type: Skilled care, Alzheimer's; Certified Beds: 130; Certified: Medicaid, Medicare; Owner: Genesis ElderCare; License: state

Rainier Vista Care Center
920 12th Ave. SE, Puyallup, WA 98372, (253) 841-3422; Facility type: Skilled care, Alzheimer's; Certified Beds: 117; Certified: Medicaid, Medicare, Veterans; Owner: Vencor, Inc.; License: state

Seattle

Bayview Manor
11 W Aloha St., Seattle, WA 98119, (206) 284-7330; Facility type: Skilled care, Alzheimer's; Certified Beds: 50; Certified: Medicaid, Medicare; Owner: Nonprofit/Religious; License: state

Bessie Burton Sullivan
1020 E Jefferson, Seattle, WA 98122, (206) 323-1028; Facility type: Skilled care, Alzheimer's; Beds: 140; Certified: Medicaid, Medicare; Owner: Nonprofit/Religious; License: state; Activities: Arts & Crafts; Dances; Pet therapy; Group exercise; Outings; Support Groups; Other: Alzheimer's secured unit, Adult day care; Affiliations: Catholic Church

Caroline Kline Galland Home
7500 Seward Park Ave. S, Seattle, WA 98118, (206) 725-8800; Facility type: Skilled care, Alzheimer's; Certified Beds: 206; Certified: Medicaid, Medicare; Owner: Nonprofit/Religious; License: state

Columbia Lutheran Home
4700 Phinney Ave. N, Seattle, WA 98103, (206) 632-7400; Facility type: Skilled care, Alzheimer's; Certified Beds: 116; Certified: Medicaid, Medicare, Veterans; Owner: Nonprofit/Religious; License: state

Crista Senior Community
19303 Fremont Ave. N, Seattle, WA 98133, (206) 546-7400; Facility type: Skilled care, Alzheimer's; Beds: 180; Certified: Medicaid, Medicare; Owner: Nonprofit/Religious; License: state; Activities: Arts & Crafts; Dances; Pet therapy; Group exercise; Outings; Support Groups; Other: Alzheimer's secured unit, Affiliations: Christian

Health and Rehabilitation of North Seattle
13333 Greenwood Ave. N, Seattle, WA 98133, (206)

362-0303; Facility type: Skilled care, Alzheimer's; Certified Beds: 151; Certified: Medicaid, Medicare, Veterans; Owner: Evergreen Healthcare Mgt; License: state

Horizon House
900 University St., Seattle, WA 98101, (206) 624-3700; Facility type: Skilled care, Alzheimer's; Beds: 60; Certified: Medicare; Payer mix: 86% Private pay; Owner: Nonprofit/Religious; License: state; Activities: Arts & Crafts; Dances; Pet therapy; Group exercise; Outings; Support Groups; Other: Alzheimer's secured unit

Jacobsen House
1810 11th Ave., Seattle, WA 98122, (206) 323-5321; Facility type: Skilled care, Alzheimer's; Beds: 40; Owner: Nonprofit/Religious; License: state; Activities: Arts & Crafts; Dances; Pet therapy; Group exercise; Outings; Support Groups; Other: Alzheimer's secured unit

Leon Sullivan Health Care Center
2611 S Dearborn, Seattle, WA 98144, (206) 325-6700; Facility type: Skilled care, Alzheimer's; Certified Beds: 165; Certified: Medicaid, Medicare, Veterans; Owner: Nonprofit/Religious; License: state

Magnolia Health Care Center
4646 36th Ave. W, Seattle. WA 98199, (206) 283-9322; Facility type: Skilled care, Alzheimer's; Beds: 70; Certified: Medicaid, Medicare, Veterans; Owner: Private; License: state; Activities: Arts & Crafts; Dances; Pet therapy; Group exercise; Outings; Support Groups; Other: Alzheimer's secured unit

Seattle Keiro
1601 E Yesler Way, Seattle, WA 98122, (206) 323-7100; Facility type: Skilled care, Alzheimer's; Certified Beds: 150; Certified: Medicaid, Medicare; Owner: Nonprofit/Religious; License: state

Washington Center for Comprehensive Rehabilitation
2821 S Walden St., Seattle, WA 98144, (206) 725-2800; Facility type: Skilled care, Alzheimer's; Certified Beds: 165; Certified: Medicaid, Medicare, Veterans; Owner: Nonprofit/Religious; License: state

Wedgewood Rehabilitation Center
9132 Ravenna Ave. NE, Seattle, WA 98115, (206) 524-6535; Facility type: Skilled care, Alzheimer's; Beds: 70; Certified: Medicaid, Medicare; Owner: Sunrise Healthcare; License: state; Activities: Arts & Crafts; Dances; Pet therapy; Group exercise; Outings; Support Groups; Other: Alzheimer's secured unit

Shoreline

Park Ridge Care Center
1250 NE 145th, Seattle, WA 98155, (206) 363-5856; Facility type: Skilled care, Alzheimer's; Certified Beds:

115; Certified: Medicaid, Medicare; Owner: All Season Living Centers; License: state

Richmond Beach Medical & Rehabilitation
19235 15th Ave. W, Seattle, WA 98177, (206) 546-2666; Facility type: Skilled care, Alzheimer's; Certified Beds: 140; Certified: Medicaid, Medicare, Veterans; Owner: Sun Healthcare; License: state

Snohomish

Mercy Haven Health Care Center LLC
800 10th St., Snohomish, WA 98291, (360) 568-3161; Facility type: Skilled care, Alzheimer's; Certified Beds: 91; Certified: Medicaid, Medicare; Owner: Nonprofit/Religious; License: state

Spokane

Garden Terrace Manor W
424 7th Ave., Spokane, WA 99204, (509) 838-8223; Facility type: Skilled care, Alzheimer's; Beds: 60; Certified: Medicaid, Medicare, Veterans; Owner: Nonprofit/Religious; License: state; Activities: Arts & Crafts; Dances; Pet therapy; Group exercise; Outings; Support Groups; Other: Alzheimer's secured unit

The Gardens on University
414 University Rd., Spokane, WA 99206, (509) 924-4650; Facility type: Skilled care, Alzheimer's; Certified Beds: 124; Certified: Medicaid, Medicare, Veterans; Owner: ExtendiCare; License: state

Loganhurst Health Care
1515 E Illinois Ave., Spokane, WA 99207, (509) 484-3132; Facility type: Skilled care, Alzheimer's; Beds: 50; Certified: Medicaid, Medicare; Owner: Proprietary/Public; License: state; Activities: Arts & Crafts; Dances; Pet therapy; Group exercise; Outings; Support Groups

Royal Park Care Center
7411 N Nevada, Spokane, WA 99208, (509) 489-2273; Facility type: Skilled care, Alzheimer's; Certified Beds: 164; Certified: Medicaid, Medicare; Owner: Private; License: state

Sunshine Gardens
10410 E 9th Ave., Spokane, WA 99206, (509) 926-3547; Facility type: Skilled care, Alzheimer's; Certified Beds: 84; Certified: Medicaid, Medicare, Veterans; Owner: Nonprofit/Religious; License: state

Tacoma

Franke Tobey Jones Retirement Estates
5340 N Bristol, Tacoma, WA 98407; Facility type: Skilled care, Alzheimer's; Beds: 50; Payer mix: 100% Private pay; Owner: Nonprofit/Religious; License: state; Activities: Arts & Crafts; Dances; Pet therapy; Group exercise; Outings; Support Groups; Other: Alzheimer's secured unit

Georgian House
8407 Steilacoom Blvd., SW, Tacoma, WA 98498, (253) 588-2146; Facility type: Skilled care, Alzheimer's; Certified Beds: 73; Certified: Medicaid, Medicare; Owner: Genesis ElderCare; License: state

The Highlands Healthcare Center
5954 N 26th St., Tacoma, WA 98407, (253) 752-7713; Facility type: Skilled care, Alzheimer's; Beds: 90; Certified: Medicaid, Medicare, Veterans; Owner: Genesis ElderCare; License: state; Activities: Arts & Crafts; Dances; Pet therapy; Group exercise; Outings; Support Groups; Other: Alzheimer's secured unit

Orchard Park
4755 S 48th St., Tacoma, WA 98409, (253) 475-4611; Facility type: Skilled care, Alzheimer's; Certified Beds: 147; Certified: Medicaid, Medicare, Veterans; Owner: Genesis ElderCare; License: state

Tukwila

Highline Community Hospital
12844 Military Rd., S, Tukwila, WA 98168, (206) 248-4520; Facility type: Skilled care, Alzheimer's; Certified: Certified Beds: 30; Medicaid, Medicare; Owner: Nonprofit/Religious; License: state

Vancouver

Fort Vancouver Convalescent Center
8507 NE 8th Way, Vancouver, WA 98664, (360) 254-5335; Facility type: Skilled care, Alzheimer's; Certified Beds: 92; Certified: Medicare; Owner: Nonprofit/Religious; License: state

Rose Vista Nursing Center
5001 Columbia View Dr., Vancouver, WA 98661, (360) 696-0161; Facility type: Skilled care, Alzheimer's; Beds: 60; Certified: Medicaid, Medicare, Veterans; Owner: Prestige Care Co; License: state; Activities: Arts & Crafts; Dances; Pet therapy; Outings; Support Groups; Other: Alzheimer's secured unit

Walla Walla

Park Manor Rehabilitation Center
1710 Plaza Way, Walla Walla, WA 99362, (509) 529-4218; Facility type: Skilled care, Alzheimer's; Beds: 99; Certified: Medicaid, Medicare, Veterans; Owner: Vencor, Inc.; License: state

Wapato

Emerald Circle
209 N Ahtanum Ave., Wapato, WA 98951, (509) 877-3175; Facility type: Skilled care, Alzheimer's; Certified Beds: 82; Certified: Medicaid, Medicare, Veterans; Owner: Nonprofit/Religious; License: state

Wenatchee

Parkside Rehabilitation & Care Center
1230 Monitor Ave., Wenatchee, WA 98801, (509) 663-1628; Facility type: Skilled care, Alzheimer's; Beds: 140; Certified: Medicaid, Medicare, Veterans; Owner: Triple C Convalescent Co; License: state; Activities: Arts & Crafts; Dances; Pet therapy; Group exercise; Outings; Support Groups; Other: Alzheimer's secured unit

Yakima

Heritage Garden Care Center
115 N 10th St., Yakima, WA 98901, (509) 248-4173; Facility type: Skilled care, Alzheimer's; Beds: 100; Certified: Medicaid; Owner: Proprietary/Public; License: state; Activities: Arts & Crafts; Dances; Pet therapy; Group exercise; Outings; Support Groups; Other: Alzheimer's secured unit

Landmark Care Center
710 N 39th Ave., Yakima, WA 98902, (509) 248-4102; Facility type: Skilled care, Alzheimer's; Certified Beds: 93; Certified: Medicaid, Medicare; Owner: Proprietary/Public; License: state

Summitview Healthcare Center
3801 Summitview Ave., Yakima, WA 98902, (509) 966-6240; Facility type: Skilled care, Alzheimer's; Certified Beds: 68; Certified: Medicaid, Medicare; Owner: Nonprofit/Religious; License: state

WEST VIRGINIA

Buckhannon

Holbrook Nursing Home
346 S Florida St., Buckhannon, WV 26201, (304) 472-3280; Facility type: Skilled care, Alzheimer's; Certified Beds: 120; Certified: Medicaid, Medicare; Owner: Proprietary/Public; License: state

Charleston

Arthur B Hodges Center
500 Morris St., Charleston, WV 25301, (304) 435-6560; Facility type: Skilled care, Alzheimer's; Beds: 120; Certified: Medicaid, Medicare; Owner: Private; License: state; Activities: Arts & Crafts; Dances; Pet therapy; Group exercise; Outings; Support Groups; Other: Alzheimer's secured unit

Cowen

Webster Nursing & Rehabilitation Center, LLC
Erbacon Road, PO Box 989, Cowen, WV 26206, (304) 226-5301; Facility type: Skilled care, Alzheimer's; Certified Beds: 60; Certified: Medicaid, Medicare, Veterans; Owner: American Medical Facility Mgt; License: state

Fairmont

Tygart Center at Fairmont Campus
1539 Country Club Rd., Fairmont, WV 26554, (304) 366-9100; Facility type: Skilled care, Alzheimer's; Certified Beds: 119; Certified: Medicaid, Medicare; Owner: Private; License: state

Harrisville

Pine View Nursing and Rehabilitation Center
400 McKinley St., Harrisville, WV 26362, (304) 643-2712; Facility type: Skilled care, Alzheimer's; Certified Beds: 56; Certified: Medicaid; Owner: Proprietary/Public; License: state

Morgantown

The Madison
161 Bakers Bridge Rd., Morgantown, WV 26505, (304) 285-0692; Facility type: Skilled care, Alzheimer's; Certified Beds: 62; Certified: Medicaid, Medicare; Owner: Proprietary/Public; License: state

Moundsville

Mound View Health Center
2200 Floral St., Moundsville, WV 26041, (304) 843-1035; Facility type: Skilled care, Alzheimer's; Certified Beds: 129; Certified: Medicaid, Medicare, Veterans; Owner: Private; License: state

Petersburg

Grant County Nursing Home
27 Early Ave., Petersburg, WV 26847, (304) 257-4233; Facility type: Skilled care, Alzheimer's; Certified Beds: 110; Certified: Medicaid, Medicare; Owner: Nonprofit; License: state

Princeton

Princeton Health Care Center
315 Court House Rd., Princeton, WV 24740, (304) 487-3458; Facility type: Skilled care, Alzheimer's; Certified Beds: 120; Certified: Medicaid, Medicare, Veterans; Owner: Private; License: state

Thomas

Courtland Acres Nursing Home
HC 60, Thomas, WV 26292, (304) 463-4181; Facility type: Skilled care, Alzheimer's; Certified Beds: 94; Certified: Medicaid, Medicare, Veterans; Owner: Nonprofit; License: state

---

WISCONSIN

Arpin

Bethel Center
8014 Bethel Rd., Arpin, WI 54410, (715) 652-2103; Facility type: Skilled care, Alzheimer's Certified Beds: 111; Certified: Medicaid; Owner: Genesis ElderCare; License: state

Beloit

Premier Care
2121 Pioneer Dr., Beloit, WI 53511, (608) 365-9526; Facility type: Skilled care, Alzheimer's; Certified Beds: 120; Certified: Medicaid, Medicare, Veterans; Owner: Proprietary/Public; License: state

Black River Falls

Pine View Care Center
400 County Rd., Black River Falls, WI 54615, (715) 284-5396; Facility type: Skilled care, Alzheimer's; Certified Beds: 95; Certified: Medicaid, Medicare, Veterans; Owner: State & Local Gov.; License: state

Bloomer

Hetzel Care Nursing & Rehabilitation Center LLC
1840 Priddy St., Boomer, WI 54724, (715) 568-2503; Facility type: Skilled care, Alzheimer's; Certified Beds: 31; Certified: Medicaid, Medicare, Veterans; Owner: Private; License: state

Boscobel

Boscobel Care and Rehab
207 Parker St., Boscobel, WI 53805, (608) 375-6342; Facility type: Skilled care, Alzheimer's; Certified Beds: 50; Certified: Medicaid, Medicare; Owner: Private; License: state

Burlington

Mount Carmel Medical & Rehabilitation Center
677 E State St., Burlington, WI 53105, (262) 763-

9531; Facility type: Skilled care, Alzheimer's; Certified Beds: 155; Certified: Medicaid, Medicare; Owner: Vencor, Inc.; License: state

Chetek

Knapp Haven Nursing Home
725 Knapp St., Chetek, WI 54728, (715) 924-4891; Facility type: Skilled care, Alzheimer's; Certified Beds: 97; Certified: Medicaid, Veterans; Owner: Private; State & Local Gov: state

Chippewa Falls

Wissota Health and Regional Vent Center
2815 County Highway I, Chippewa Falls, WI 54729, (715) 723-9341; Facility type: Skilled care, Alzheimer's; Certified Beds: 120; Certified: Medicaid, Medicare, Veterans; Owner: ExtendiCare Health Services; License: state

Crandon

The Crandon Nursing Home
105 W. Pioneer, Crandon, WI 54520, (715) 478-3324; Facility type: Skilled care, Alzheimer's; Certified Beds: 50; Certified: Medicaid, Medicare, Veterans; Owner: Arizconsin Group; License: state

Eau Claire

Clairemont Nursing and Rehab
2120 Heights Rd., Eau Claire, WI 54701, (715) 832-1681; Facility type: Skilled care, Alzheimer's; Certified Beds: 161; Certified: Medicaid, Medicare, Veterans; Owner: Real Property Health Facilities Corp; License: state

Dove Healthcare West
1405 Truax Blvd., Eau Claire, WI 54703, (715) 552-1030; Facility type: Skilled care, Alzheimer's; Beds: 190; Certified: Medicaid, Medicare, Veterans; Owner: Private; License: state; Activities: Arts & Crafts; Dances; Pet therapy; Group exercise; Outings; Support Groups

Elkhorn

Lakeland Nursing Home of Walworth County
W3930 County Rd. NN, Elkhorn, WI 53121, (262) 741-3600; Facility type: Skilled care, Alzheimer's; Certified Beds: 160; Certified: Medicaid; Owner: State & Local Gov.; License: state

Elmwood

Heritage of Elmwood Nursing Home
232 E Springer Ave., Elmwood, WI 54740, (715) 639-2911; Facility type: Skilled care, Alzheimer's; Certified Beds: 46; Certified: Medicare; Owner: State & Local Gov.; License: state

Fond Du Lac

Fond Du Lac Lutheran Home
244 N Macy St., Fond Du Lac, WI 54935, (920) 921-9520; Facility type: Skilled care, Alzheimer's; Certified Beds: 133; Certified: Medicaid; Owner: State & Local Gov.; License: state

ManorCare Health Services
265 S National Ave., Fond Du Lac, WI 54935, (920) 922-7342; Facility type: Skilled care, Alzheimer's; Certified Beds: 108; Certified: Medicaid, Medicare; Owner: HCR ManorCare; License: state

Saint Francis Home
33 Everett St., Fond Du Lac, WI 54935, (920) 923-7980; Facility type: Skilled care, Alzheimer's; Certified Beds: 107; Certified: Medicaid, Medicare, Veterans; Owner: Private; License: state

Glendale

Golden LivingCenter Colonial Manor
1616 W Bender Rd., Glendale, WI 53209, (414) 228-8700; Facility type: Skilled care, Alzheimer's; Certified Beds: 141; Certified: Medicaid, Medicare, Veterans; Owner: Senior Community Services; License: state

Seven Oaks
6263 N Green Bay Ave., Glendale, WI 53209, (414) 351-0543; Facility type: Skilled care, Alzheimer's; Certified Beds: 94; Certified: Medicaid, Medicare, Veterans; Owner: Private; License: state

Green Bay

Grancare Nursing Center
1155 Dousman St., Green Bay, WI 54303, (920) 494-4525; Facility type: Skilled care, Alzheimer's; Certified Beds: 75; Certified: Medicaid, Medicare; Owner: Proprietary/Public; License: state

Parkview Manor Health Rehabilitation Center
2961 St. Anthony Dr., Green Bay, WI 54311, (920) 468-0861; Facility type: Skilled care, Alzheimer's; Certified Beds: 136; Certified: Medicaid, Veterans; Owner: State & Local Gov.; License: state

Greenfield

Clement Manor Health Care
3939 S 92nd St., Greenfield, WI 53228; (414) 321-1800; Facility type: Skilled care, Alzheimer's; Certified Beds: 166; Certified: Medicaid, Medicare; Owner: Benedictine Health Systems; License: state

Southpointe Healthcare Center
4500 W Loomis Rd., Greenfield, WI 53220, (414) 325-5300; Facility type: Skilled care, Alzheimer's; Certified Beds: 174; Certified: Medicaid, Medicare, Veterans; Mariner Post Acute Network: Private; License: state

Janesville

Rocky County Health Care Center
N Parker Dr., Janesville, WI 53547, (608) 757-5000; Facility type: Skilled care, Alzheimer's; Beds: 300; Certified: Medicaid, Medicare; Owner: State & Local Gov.; License: state; Activities: Arts & Crafts; Dances; Pet therapy; Group exercise; Outings; Support Groups; Other: Alzheimer's secured unit, Adult day care; Affiliations: American Assn. of Homes & Services for the Aging

Saint Elizabeth's Nursing Home
109 S Atwood, Janesville, WI 53545, (608) 752-6709; Facility type: Skilled care, Alzheimer's; Certified Beds: 43; Certified: Medicaid, Medicare, Veterans; Owner: Private; License: state

Kenosha

Brookside Care Center
3506 Washington Rd., Kenosha, WI 53144, (262) 653-3800; Facility type: Skilled care, Alzheimer's; Certified Beds: 154; Certified: Medicaid, Medicare; Owner: State & Local Gov.; License: state

Woodstock Health & Rehabilitation Center
3415 N Sheridan Rd., Kenosha, WI 53140, (262) 657-6175; Facility type: Skilled care, Alzheimer's; Certified Beds: 159; Certified: Medicaid, Medicare, Veterans; Owner: Vencor, Inc.; License: state

Kewaunee

Kewaunee Health Care Center
1308 Lincoln St., Kewaunee, WI 54216, (920) 388-4111; Facility type: Skilled care, Alzheimer's; Certified Beds: 66; Certified: Medicaid, Medicare, Veterans; Owner: Private; License: state

King

Wisconsin Veterans Home
N2665 County Rd. QQ, King, WI 54946, (715) 258-5586; Facility type: Skilled care, Alzheimer's; Certified Beds: 205; Certified: Medicaid, Veterans; Owner: Private; License: state

La Crosse

Hillview Healthcare Center
3501 Park Lane Dr., La Crosse, WI 54601, (608) 789-4800; Facility type: Skilled care, Alzheimer's; Certified Beds: 199; Certified: Medicaid, Medicare, Veterans; Owner: State & Local Gov.; License: state

Lancaster

Lancaster Care Center
1350 S Madison St., Lancaster, WI 53813, (608) 723-4143; Facility type: Skilled care, Alzheimer's; Certified Beds: 70; Certified: Medicaid, Medicare, Veterans; Owner: Rice Health Care Facilities; License: state

Orchard Manor
8800 Hwy. 61 S, Lancaster, WI 53813, (608) 723-2113; Facility type: Skilled care, Alzheimer's; Certified Beds: 117; Certified: Medicaid, Medicare; Owner: State & Local Gov.; License: state

Laona

Nu-Roc Community Healthcare
3576A Nu Roc Ln, Laona, WI 54541, (715) 674-4477; Facility type: Skilled care, Alzheimer's; Certified Beds: 50; Certified: Medicaid, Veterans; Owner: Private; License: state

Lodi

Lodi Good Samaritan Center
700 Clark St., Lodi, WI 53555, (608) 592-3241; Facility type: Skilled care, Alzheimer's; Certified Beds: 72; Certified: Medicaid, Medicare; Owner: Evangelical Lutheran Good Samaritan Society; License: state

Madison

Belmont Nursing & Rehabilitation Center
110 Belmont Rd., Madison, WI 53714, (608) 249-7391; Facility type: Skilled care, Alzheimer's; Certified Beds: 90; Certified: Medicaid, Medicare, Veterans; Owner: Genesis ElderCare; License: state

ManorCare Health Services
801 Braxton Pl., Madison, WI 53715, (608) 251-1010; Facility type: Skilled care, Alzheimer's; Beds: 170; Certified: Medicaid, Medicare; Owner: HCR Manor-Care; License: state; Activities: Arts & Crafts; Dances; Pet therapy; Group exercise; Outings; Support Groups; Other: Alzheimer's secured unit

Oakwood Lutheran Homes Assoc.
6201 Mineral Point Rd., Madison, WI 53705, (608) 230-4325; Facility type: Skilled care, Alzheimer's; Certified Beds: 95; Certified: Medicaid, Medicare; Owner: Private; Nonprofit: state

Manitowoc

Manitowoc Health Care Center
2021 S. Alverno Rd., Manitowoc, WI 54220, (920) 683-4100; Facility type: Skilled care, Alzheimer's; Certified Beds: 150; Certified: Medicaid, Medicare, Veterans; Owner: State & Local Gov.; License: state

River's Bend Health & Rehabilitation Center
960 S Rapids Rd., Manitowoc, WI 54220, (920) 684-1144; Facility type: Skilled care, Alzheimer's; Certified

Beds: 124; Certified: Medicaid, Medicare; Owner: Wisconsin Health Services; License: state

Shady Lane Nursing Care Center
1235 S 24th St., Manitowoc, WI 54220, (920) 682-8254; Facility type: Skilled care, Alzheimer's; Certified Beds: 161; Certified: Medicaid, Medicare, Veterans; Owner: Nonprofit; License: state

Milwaukee

Alexian Village of Milwaukee
9255 N 76th St., Milwaukee, WI 53223, (414) 355-9300; Facility type: Skilled care, Alzheimer's; Certified Beds: 108; Certified: Medicaid, Medicare; Owner: Private; License: state

Jewish Home & Care Center
1414 N Prospect Ave., Milwaukee, WI 53202, (414) 276-2627; Facility type: Skilled care, Alzheimer's; Certified Beds: 160; Certified: Medicaid, Medicare; Owner: Nonprofit/Religious; License: state

Luther Manor
4545 N 92nd St., Milwaukee, WI 53225, (414) 464-3880; Facility type: Skilled care, Alzheimer's; Certified Beds: 223; Certified: Medicaid, Medicare; Owner: Private; License: state

Milwaukee Catholic Home
2330 N Prospect Ave., Milwaukee, WI 53211, (414) 220-4610; Facility type: Skilled care, Alzheimer's; Certified Beds: 122; Certified: Medicaid, Medicare; Owner: Private; License: state

Milwaukee Protestant Home for Aged Health Center
2449 N Downer Ave., Milwaukee, WI 53211, (414) 332-8610; Facility type: Skilled care, Alzheimer's; Beds: 50; Certified: Medicaid; Owner: Nonprofit Corp; License: state; Activities: Arts & Crafts; Dances; Pet therapy; Group exercise; Outings; Support Groups

Saint John's on the Lake
1840 N Prospect Ave., Milwaukee, WI 53202, (414) 272-2022; Facility type: Skilled care, Alzheimer's; Certified Beds: 56; Certified: Medicaid, Medicare; Owner: Private; License: state

Trinity Village
7500 W Dean Rd., Milwaukee, WI 53223, (414) 354-7300; Facility type: Skilled care, Alzheimer's; Certified Beds: 70; Certified: Medicaid, Medicare; Owner: Nonprofit; License: state

Wellspring of Milwaukee
9350 W Fond Du Lac Ave., Milwaukee, WI 53225, (414) 438-4360; Facility type: Skilled care, Alzheimer's; Certified Beds: 185; Certified: Medicaid, Medicare, Veterans; Owner: Beverly Enterprises; License: state

Wisconsin Lutheran Care Center
6800 N 76th St., Milwaukee, WI 53223, (414) 353-5000; Facility type: Skilled care, Alzheimer's; Certified Beds: 144; Certified: Medicaid, Medicare; Owner: Private; License: state

Monroe

Pleasant View Nursing Home N
3150 Hwy., 81, Monroe, WI 53566, (608) 325-2171; Facility type: Skilled care, Alzheimer's; Certified Beds: 130; Certified: Medicaid, Medicare; Owner: Private; License: state

New Richmond

Saint Croix Health Center
1445 N 4th St., New Richmond, WI 54017; (715) 246-6991; Facility type: Skilled care, Alzheimer's; Certified Beds: 72; Certified: Medicaid, Medicare; Owner: State & Local Gov.; License: state

Oconomowoc

Shorehaven Health & Rehab Center
1305 W. Wisconsin Ave, Oconomowoc, WI 53066, (262) 567-8341; Facility type: Skilled care, Alzheimer's; Certified Beds: 135; Certified: Medicaid, Medicare; Owner: Nonprofit; License: state

Oconto Falls

Sharpe Care Nursing & Rehabilitation Center, LLC
1000 E Highland Dr., Oconto Falls, WI 54154, (920) 848-3272; Facility type: Skilled care, Alzheimer's; Certified Beds: 99; Certified: Medicaid, Medicare, Veterans; Owner: Proprietary/Public; License: state

Oshkosh

Evergreen Health Center
1130 N Westfield St., Oshkosh, WI 54902, (920) 233-2340; Facility type: Skilled care, Alzheimer's; Certified Beds: 108; Certified: Medicaid; Owner: Private; License: state

Northpoint Med and Rehab Center
1850 Bowen St., Oshkosh, WI 54901, (920) 233-4011; Facility type: Skilled care, Alzheimer's; Certified Beds: 120; Certified: Medicaid, Medicare, Veterans; Owner: Private; License: state

Phelps

Lillian E Kerr Healthcare Center
2383 Hwy. 17, Phelps, WI 54554, (715) 545-2589; Facility type: Skilled care, Alzheimer's; Certified Beds: 64; Certified: Medicaid, Medicare, Veterans; Nonprofit; License: state

Racine

The Becker-Shoop Center
6101 16th St., Racine, WI 53406, (262) 637-7486;
Facility type: Skilled care, Alzheimer's; Certified Beds:
110; Certified: Medicaid; Owner: Private; License:
state

Lincoln Lutheran Care Center
1600 Ohio St., Racine, WI 53405, (262) 637-7491;
Facility type: Skilled care, Alzheimer's; Beds: 230;
Certified: Medicaid, Medicare; Owner: Private; License: state; Activities: Arts & Crafts; Dances; Pet
therapy; Group exercise; Outings; Support Groups;
Other: Alzheimer's secured unit; Affiliations: Lincoln
Lutheran of Racine Ecumenical

Reedsburg

Sauk County Health Care Center
1051 Clark St. Reedsburg, WI 53959, (608) 524-
7500; Facility type: Skilled care, Alzheimer's; Certified
Beds: 82; Certified: Medicaid, Medicare; Owner:
State & Local Gov.; License: state

Rhinelander

Taylor Park & Rehabilitation Center
903 Boyce Dr., Rhinelander, WI 54501, (715) 365-
6816; Facility type: Skilled care, Alzheimer's; Certified
Beds: 100; Certified: Medicaid, Medicare; Owner:
Private; License: state

Rice Lake

Heritage Manor
19 W Newton St., Rice Lake, WI 54868, (715) 234-
2161; Facility type: Skilled care, Alzheimer's; Certified
Beds: 92; Certified: Medicaid, Medicare, Veterans;
Owner: First American Care Facility; License: state

Richland Center

Pine Valley Health Care
25951 Circle View Dr., Richland Center, WI 53581,
(608) 647-2138; Facility type: Skilled care, Alzheimer's; Certified Beds: 104; Certified: Medicaid, Medicare, Veterans; Owner: State & Local Gov.; License:
state

Shawano

Maple Lane Health Care Facility
N4231 State Hwy 22, Shawano, WI 54166, (715) 526-
3158; Facility type: Skilled care, Alzheimer's; Certified
Beds: 74; Certified: Medicaid; Owner: State & Local
Gov.; License: state

Sheboygan

Sunny Ridge Health & Rehab Center
3014 E Erie Ave., Sheboygan, WI 53081, (920) 459-
3028; Facility type: Skilled care, Alzheimer's; Certified
Beds: 140; Certified: Medicaid, Medicare; Owner:
Private; License: state

Sheboygan Falls

**Sheboygan County Comprehensive Health
Center N**
3790 CTH VN, Sheboygan Falls, WI 53085, (920)
467-4648; Facility type: Skilled care, Alzheimer's;
Beds: 150; Certified: Medicaid, Medicare; Owner:
Nonprofit; License: state; Activities: Arts & Crafts;
Dances; Pet therapy; Group exercise; Outings; Support Groups; Other: Alzheimer's secured unit

Sister Bay

Good Samaritan Society Scandia Village
10560 Applewood Rd., Sister Bay, WI 54234, (920)
854-2317; Facility type: Skilled care, Alzheimer's;
Certified Beds: 60; Certified: Medicaid, Medicare;
Owner: Evangelical Lutheran Good Samaritan Society; License: state

Sparta

Rolling Hills Rehabilitation Center
14345 County Hwy. B, Sparta, WI 54656, (608) 269-
8800; Facility type: Skilled care, Alzheimer's; Certified
Beds: 90; Certified: Medicaid, Medicare, Veterans;
Owner: Private; License: state

Superior

Colonial Health Care Services
3120 N 21st St., Superior, WI 54880, (715) 393-2922;
Facility type: Skilled care, Alzheimer's; Beds: 40; Certified: Medicaid; Owner: Proprietary/Public; License:
state; Activities: Arts & Crafts; Dances; Pet therapy;
Group exercise; Outings; Support Groups; Other:
Alzheimer's secured unit

Waukesha

Lindengrove Waukesha
425 N University Dr., Waukesha, WI 52188, (262)
524-6400; Facility type: Skilled care, Alzheimer's;
Certified Beds: 135; Certified: Medicaid, Medicare;
Owner: Private; License: state

Waukesha Springs Health & Rehabilitation
1810 Kensington Dr., Waukesha, WI 53188, (262)
548-1400; Facility type: Skilled care, Alzheimer's;
Certified Beds: 177; Certified: Medicaid, Medicare;
Owner: Proprietary/Public; License: state

West Allis

Maplewood Center
8615 W Beloit Rd., West Allis, WI 53227, (414) 607-
4100; Facility type: Skilled care, Alzheimer's; Certified

Beds: 150; Certified: Medicaid, Medicare; Owner: Nonprofit; License: state

Mary Jude Nursing Home
9806 W Lincoln Ave., West Allis, WI 53227, (414) 543-5330; Facility type: Skilled care, Alzheimer's; Certified Beds: 50; Certified: Medicaid, Medicare; Owner: Private; License: state

West Bend

Cedar Lake Health & Rehab Center
5595 County Rd. Z, West Bend, WI 53095, (262) 306-2100; Facility type: Skilled care, Alzheimer's; Certified Beds: 229; Certified: Medicaid, Medicare; Owner: Nonprofit/Religious; License: state

West Salem

Lakeview Health Center
902 E Garland St., West Salem, WI 54669, (608) 786-1400; Facility type: Skilled care, Alzheimer's; Certified Beds: 142; Certified: Medicaid, Veterans; Owner: State & Local Gov.; License: state

Whitehall

Trempealeau County Health Care Center W
20298 State Rd. 121, Whitehall, WI 54773, (715) 538-4312; Facility type: Skilled care, Alzheimer's; Certified Beds: 34; Certified: Medicaid; Owner: State & Local Gov.; License: state

WYOMING

Basin

Wyoming Retirement Center
890 Hwy. 20 S, Basin, WY 82410, (307) 568-2431; Facility type: Skilled care, Alzheimer's; Certified Beds: 90; Certified: Medicaid, Medicare, Veterans; Owner: State & Local Gov.; License: state

Cheyenne

Mountain Towers Healthcare & Rehabilitation Center
3128 Boxelder Dr., Cheyenne, WY 82001, (307) 634-7901; Facility type: Skilled care, Alzheimer's; Certified Beds: 146; Certified: Medicaid, Medicare, Veterans; Owner: Vencor, Inc.; License: state

Greybull

Bonnie Bluejacket Memorial Nursing Home
388 S US Hwy. 20, Greybull, WY 82426, (307) 568-3311; Facility type: Skilled care, Alzheimer's; Certified Beds: 37; Certified: Medicaid, Medicare, Veterans; Owner: State & Local Gov.; License: state

Jackson

Saint John's Living Center
625 E Broadway, Jackson, WY 8300, (307) 739-7450; Facility type: Skilled care, Alzheimer's; Certified Beds: 60; Certified: Medicaid, Medicare; Owner: Private; License: state

Laramie

Ivinson Memorial Hospital–Extended Care Facility
255 N 30th, Laramie, WY 82072, (307) 742-2141; Facility type: Skilled care, Alzheimer's; Certified Beds: 9; Certified: Medicaid, Medicare; State & Local Gov: Private; License: state

Lovell

New Horizons Care Center
1111 Lane 12, Lovell, WY 82431, (307) 548-5200; Facility type: Skilled care, Alzheimer's; Certified Beds: 85; Certified: Medicaid, Medicare; Owner: Nonprofit/Religious; License: state

Newcastle

Weston County Manor
1124 Washington Blvd., Newcastle, WY, 82701, (307) 746-4491; Facility type: Skilled care, Alzheimer's; Certified Beds: 54; Certified: Medicaid, Medicare, Veterans; Owner: Private; License: state

Powell

Powell Nursing Home
777 Avenue H, Powell, WY 82435, (307) 754-2267; Facility type: Skilled care, Alzheimer's; Certified Beds: 100; Certified: Medicaid, Medicare; Owner: Private; License: state

Riverton

Wind River Healthcare & Rehabilitation Center
1002 Forest Dr., Riverton, WY 82501, (307) 856-9471; Facility type: Skilled care, Alzheimer's; Certified Beds: 81; Certified: Medicaid, Medicare, Veterans; Owner: Vencor, Inc.; License: state

Rock Springs

Sage View Care Center
1325 Sage St., Rock Springs, WY 82901, (307) 362-3780; Facility type: Skilled care, Alzheimer's; Certified

Beds: 101; Certified: Medicaid, Medicare, Veterans; Owner: Vencor, Inc.; License: state

Worland

Worland Healthcare and Rehabilitation Center
1901 Howell Ave., Worland, WY 82401, (307) 347-4285; Facility type: Skilled care, Alzheimer's; Certified Beds: 87; Certified: Medicaid, Medicare; Owner: Integrate Health Services, Inc.; License: state

Research Facilities

The following institutions are associated with government funded research efforts. Many of these institutions are involved in clinical trials. Information on clinical trials can be found in the Resources section following this section.

ADSC next to the institution name designates members of the Alzheimer's Disease Cooperative Study. ADC indicates institutions that are affiliated with and funded by the National Institute on Aging.

Alabama

Alzheimer's Disease Research Center
Daniel Marson, J.D., Ph.D., Director
University of Alabama at Birmingham
Sparks Research Center
1720 7th Avenue South, Ste. 650K
Birmingham, AL 35233-7340
Information Line: (205) 934-3847
Director's Tel: (205) 934-2334
Director's Fax: (205) 975-3094
Director's e-mail: dmarson@uab.edu
Website: www.uab.edu/adc

Arizona

Arizona Alzheimer's Disease Center/Sun Health Research Institute
Eric Reiman, M.D., Director
Arizona Alzheimer's Disease Center
Banner Alzheimer's Institute
901 E. Willeta Street
Phoenix, AZ 85006
Information Line: (602) 239-6500
Director's Tel: (602) 239-6999
Director's Fax: (602) 239-6253
Director's e-mail: eric.reiman@bannerhealth.com
Website: www.azalz.org/

California

Stanford University (ADCS, ADC)
Jerome, A. Yesavage, M.D., Director
Alzheimer's Disease Research Center
Department of Psychiatry and Behavioral Science
Stanford, CA 94305-5550
(650) 852-3827
Fax: (650) 852-3297

University of California, Davis (ADCS, ADC)
Charles S. DeCarli, M.D., Director
Alzheimer's Disease Center
University of California, Davis Medical Center
4860 Y Street, Suite 3700
Sacramento, CA 95817
ADCS Information: (925) 372-2485
ADC Information: (916) 734-5496
Director's e-mail: charles.decarli@ucdmc.ucdavis.edu

University of California, Irvine (ADCS, ADC)
Carl W. Cotman, Ph.D., director
Alzheimer's Disease Center
Institute for Brain Aging and Dementia
1113 Gillespie Neuroscience Research Facility
Irvine, CA 92697
(949) 824-5847
Director's e-mail: cwcotman@uci.edu
Website: www.alz.uci.edu

University of California, Los Angeles (ADC)
John Ringman, M.D., Interim Director
Alzheimer's Disease Center
Department of Neurology
University of California, Los Angeles
10911 Weyburn Avenue, Ste.200
Los Angeles, CA 90095-1769
(310) 794-3231
Director's e-mail: jringman@mednet.ucla.edu

University of California, San Diego (ADCS, ADC)
Douglas R. Galasko, M.D., Director
Alzheimer's Disease Center
Department of Neurosciences
UCSD School of Medicine
9500 Gilman Drive
La Jolla, CA 92093-0948
(858) 622-5820
ADC: (858) 622-5800
Director's e-mail: dgalasko@ucsd.edu
Website: http://adrc.ucsd.edu

University of California, San Francisco
Bruce Miller, M.D., Director
Alzheimer's Disease Research Center
University of California, San Francisco, Box 1207
350 Parnassus Avenue, Suite 905
San Francisco, CA 94143-1207
Information Line: (415) 476-6880
Director's Tel: (415) 476-5569
Director's Fax: (415) 476-4800
ADC e-mail: adrc@memory.ucsf.edu
Director's e-mail: bmiller@memory.ucsf.edu
Website: http://memory.ucsf.edu

University of Southern California
Helena Chui, M.D., Director
University of Southern California
Health Consultation Center
1510 San Pablo St, HCC643
Los Angeles, CA 90033
(323) 442-7686
Fax: (323) 442-7689
E-mail: chui@usc.edu
Website: http://www.usc.edu/dept/gero/ADRC

University of Southern California (ADCS, ADC)
Caleb E. Finch, Ph.D., Director
Andrus Gerontology Center
University Park, MC 0191
3715 McClintock Avenue
Los Angeles, CA 90089-0191
(323) 442-3715, (213) 740-7777
E-mail: cfinch@almaak.usc.edu

Connecticut

Yale University School of Medicine (ADCS)
New Haven, CT
(203) 764-8100

District of Columbia

Georgetown University Medical School (ADCS)
Georgetown University
Washington, DC
(202) 784-6671

Florida

Florida ADRC
Huntington Potter, Ph.D., Director
Byrd Alzheimer's Institute
4001 E Fletcher Avenue
Tampa, FL 33613
(813) 866-1600
Fax: (813) 866-1601
E-mail: hpotter@health.usf.edu
Website: http://www.floridaadrc.org

Mayo Clinic, Jacksonville (ADCS)
Jacksonville, FL
(904) 953-7103

University of South Florida, Tampa (ADCS)
Tampa, FL
(813) 974-4355

Georgia

Emory University (ADCS, ADC)
Allan I. Levey, M.D., Director
Neurology Department
101 Woodruff Circle #6000
Atlanta, GA 30322
(404) 727-7220
Fax: (404) 727-3999
E-mail: alevey@emory.edu
Website: http://www.med.Emory.edu/ADRC

Illinois

Northwestern University (ADCS, ADC)
Marsel Mesulam, M.D., Director and Principal Investigator ADC Program
Cognitive Neurology and Alzheimer Disease
675 N St Clair, Galter 20-100
Chicago, IL 60611
ADCS: (312) 695-2343
ADC: (312) 908-9339
E-mail: mmesulam@northwestern.edu
Website: http://www.brain.northwestern.edu

Rush University Medical Center
Rush Alzheimer's Disease Core Center
David A. Bennett, M.D., Director
Rush University Medical Center
Armour Academic Center
600 S Paulina St, Suite 1026
Chicago, IL 60612
(312) 942-4823
Fax: (312) 563-4605
E-mail: dbennett@rush.edu
Website: http://www.rush.edu/rumc/page-12909955
62913.html

Indiana

Indiana University (ADCS, ADC)
Bernardino Ghetti, M.D., Director
Indiana Alzheimer's Disease Center
Department of Pathology and Laboratory Medicine
635 Barnhill Drive, MS-A142
Indianapolis, IN 46202-5120
(317) 274-7818
Fax: (317) 274-4882
E-mail: bghetti@iupui.edu
Website: http://iadc.iupui.edu

Kansas

University of Kansas Medical Center (ADC)
Charles DeCarli, M.D., Director
Department of Neurology
3901 Rainbow Boulevard
Kansas City, KS 66160-7314
(913) 588-6979

Kentucky

University of Kentucky, Lexington (ADCS, ADC)
Richard Kryscio, Ph.D., Interim Director
Sanders-Brown Research Center on Aging
101 Sanders-Brown Building
Lexington, KY 40536-0230
ADCS: (859) 257-6508
ADC: (859) 257-4064
E-mail: kryscio@email.uky.edu
Website: http://www.mc.uky.edu/coa/clinicalcore/
alzheimercenter.html

Maryland

Johns Hopkins University School of Medicine
Marilyn Albert, Ph.D., Director
Johns Hopkins University School of Medicine
Reed Hall 2226
1620 McElderry St
Baltimore, MD 21205
(410) 614-3040
Fax: (410) 502-2189
Email: malbert9@jhmi.edu
Website: http://www.alzresearch.org

Massachusetts

Harvard Medical School/Massachusetts General Hospital (ADC)
John Growdon, M.D., Director
Alzheimer's Disease Center
Department of Neurology
Massachusetts General Hospital
15 Parkman Street

Boston, MA 02114
(617) 726-1728
E-mail: growdon@helix.mgh.harvard.edu

Massachusetts ADRC
Bradley T. Hyman, M.D., Ph.D., Director
Massachusetts General Hospital
Department of Neurology
CNY 114-2009, 16th Street
Charlestown, MA 02129
(617) 726-2299
Fax: (617) 724-1480
E-mail: b_hyman@helix.mgh.harvard.edu
Website: http://www.madrc.org

Memorial Veterans Hospital ADCS, ADC
Boston University
Neil W. Kowall, M.D., Director
150 S Huntington Avenue
Jamaica Plain, MA 02130
(857) 364-4831
Fax: (857) 364-4454
E-mail: nkowall@bu.edu
Website: http://www.bu.edu/alzresearch/

Michigan

University of Michigan (ADCS, ADC)
Sil Gilman, M.D., Director
300 N Ingalls 3D15
Ann Arbor, MI 48109-0489
ADCS: (734) 936-8764
ADC: (734) 764-2190, (734) 936-1808
E-mail: sgilman@umich.edu
Website: http://www.med.umich.edu/alzheimers/

Minnesota

Mayo Clinic, Rochester (ADCS, ADC)
Ronald Petersen, M.D., Director
Department of Neurology
200 First Street, SW
Rochester, MN 55905
(507) 538-0487
Fax: (507) 538-6012
E-mail: peter8@mayo.edu
Website: http://mayoresearch.mayo.edu/mayo/re
search/alzheimers_center

Missouri

Washington University (ADCS, ADC)
Eugene M. Johnson, Jr., Co-Director
John C. Morris, M.D., Co-Director
Alzheimer's Disease Research Center
4488 Forest Park Avenue
St. Louis, MO 63108-2293
ADCS: (314) 286-2364

ADC: (314) 286-2881
E-mail: morrisj@abraxas.wustl.edu
Website: http://alzheimer.wustl.edu/

New York

Columbia University (ADCS, ADC)
Michael L. Shelanski, M.D., Director
Alzheimer's Disease Research Center
Department of Pathology
630 West 168th Street
New York, NY 10032
ADCS: (212) 305-3300
ADC: (212) 305-6553
E-mail: mls7@columbia.edu
Website: http://www.alzheimercenter.org

Mt. Sinai School of Medicine (ADCS, ADC)
Mary Sano, Ph.D., Director
Department of Psychiatry, Box 1230
One Gustave L. Levy Place
New York, NY 10029-6574
(718) 741-4228
Fax: (718) 562-9120
E-mail: mary.sano@mssm.edu
Website: http://www.mssm.edu/psychiatry/adrc/

New York University, ADC
Steven H. Ferris, Ph.D., Director
Alzheimer's Disease Center
New York University School of Medicine
560 First Avenue, Room THN 312V
New York, NY 10016
(212) 241-8329
E-mail: steven.ferris@med.nyu.edu
Website: http://www.med.nyu.edu/adc/

Taub Institute on Alzheimer's Disease and the Aging Brain
Richard Mayeaux, M.D., Director
Columbia University Medical Center
630 West 168th Street
New York, NY 10032
(212) 305-1818
Website: http://www.cumc.columbia.edu/dept/taub/

University of Rochester Medical Center (ADCS, ADC)
Paul Coleman, Ph.D., Director
Alzheimer's Disease Center
Center for Aging and Developmental Biology
601 Elmwood Avenue, Box 645
Rochester, NY 14642
ADCS: (716) 760-6561
ADC: (716) 275-2581
E-mail: paulcoleman@urmc.rochester.edu

North Carolina

Duke University (ADC)
Kathleen A. Welsh-Bohmer, Ph.D., ABPP, Director

Joseph and Kathleen Bryan Alzheimer's Disease Research Center
2200 West Main Street, Suite A-200
Durham, NC 27705
(919) 668-0820
Fax: (919) 668-0828
E-mail: kathleen.welshbohmer@duke.edu
Website: http://adrc.mc.duke.edu

Ohio

University Hospitals of Cleveland (ADCS, ADC)
Case Western University
Karl Herrup, Ph.D., Director
12200 Fairhill Road
Cleveland, OH 44120-1013
ADCS: (216) 844-6419
ADC: (216) 844-6400

Oregon

Oregon Health Sciences University (ADCS, ADC)
Jeffrey Kaye, M.D., Director
Alzheimer's Disease Center
Department of Neurology, CR 131
3181 SW Sam Jackson Park Road
Portland, OR 97239-3098
ADCS: (503) 494-7615
ADC: (503) 494-6976
E-mail: kaye@ohsu.edu
Website: http://www.ohsu.edu/research/alzheimers/

Pennsylvania

University of Pennsylvania Medical School (ADCS, ADC)
John Q. Trojanowski, M.D., Director
Alzheimer's Disease Center
Center for Neurodegenerative Disease Research
3rd Floor Maloney Building
3600 Spruce Street
Philadelphia, PA 19104-4283
ADCS: (215) 349-5903
ADC: (215) 662-4708
E-mail: trojanow@mail.med.upenn.edu
Website: http://www.pennadc.org

University of Pittsburgh
Oscar Lopez, M.D., Director
University of Pittsburgh
Department of Neurology
3501 Forbes Avenue, Suite 830
Pittsburgh, PA 15213
shipping address: ADRC 4-West UPMC Montefiore
3459 Fifth Avenue
Pittsburgh, PA 15213
(412) 246-6869

Fax: (412) 246-6873
E-mail: lopezol@upmc.edu
Website: http://www.adrc.pitt.edu

University of Pittsburgh (ADCS, ADC)
Steven DeKosky, M.D., Director
Alzheimer's Disease Research Center
4-West Mentefiore University Hospital
200 Lothrop Street
Pittsburgh, PA 15213
ADCS: (412) 692-2705
ADC: (412) 692-2700
E-mail: dekosyky@vms.cls.pitt.edu

Rhode Island

Memorial Hospital of Rhode Island (ADCS)
Brown University
Pawtucket, RI
(401) 729-3752

South Carolina

Medical University of South Carolina (ADCS)
North Charleston, SC
(843) 740-1592, ext. 17

Texas

Baylor College of Medicine (ADCS, ADC)
Stanley Appel, M.D., Director
Alzheimer's Disease Research Center
6501 Fannin Street, NB 302
Houston, TX 77030-3498
ADCS: (713) 798-5325
ADC: (713) 798-6660
E-mail: lappel@bum.tmc.edu

Southwestern Medical Center (ADCS, ADC)
University of Texas
Roger Rosenberg, M.D., Director
Alzheimer's Disease Research Center
5323 Harry Hines Boulevard

Dallas, TX 75390-9036
(214) 648-3239
Fax: (214) 648-6824
E-mail: Roger.Rosenberg@UTSouthwestern.edu
Website: http://www.utsouthwestern.edu/alzheimers/
research

Washington

University of Washington (ADCS, ADC)
Murray Rasking, M.D., Director
Alzheimer's Disease Center
Department of Psychiatry, VA Medical Center
GRECC (116A)
1660 S. Columbian Way
Seattle, WA 98108
(206) 768-5375
Fax: (206) 764-2573
E-mail: murray.raskind@med.va.gov
Website: http://depts.washington.edu/adrcweb/

University of Washington, Department of Pathology (ADC)
George A. Martin, M.D., Director
Alzheimer's Disease Research Center
Box 357470, HSB K-543
1959 NE Pacific Avenue
Seattle, WA 98195-7470
(206) 543-6761
E-mail: gmmartin@U.washington.edu
Website: http://weber.u.washington.edu/~adrcweb/

Wisconsin

University of Wisconsin
Sanjay Asthana, M.D., Director
University of Wisconsin
2870 University Ave, Suite 106
Madison, WI 53705
(608) 263-9969
Fax: (608) 280-7165
E-mail: sa@medicine.wisc.edu
Website: http://www.wcmp.wisc.edu/

Resources

This section is divided into the following categories: Books. Booklets and Pamphlets. Subscription Newsletters. Internet Forums, Bulletin Boards and Blogs. Clinical Trials. Finding and Evaluating Nursing Homes. Minority Aging Organizations. Diet and Nutrition Resources. Caregiver Resources. National, Regional and Government Organizations. AoA Long-Term Care Resource Centers. AoA Legal Assistance and Service and Support Centers for the Elderly. Internet Educational Resources. Internet Caregiver Resources. Medicare and Other Health Insurance Resources. Assistance in Finding Nursing Home Ombudsman and Licensure Programs, by State. National Long Term Care Accreditation Agencies.

Books

American Psychiatric Association. *Diagnostic and Statistical Manual of Mental Disorders*, Fourth Edition, Text Revision. Washington, DC: American Psychiatric Association, 2000.

Becker, Robert, and Ezio Giacobini, eds. *Alzheimer Disease: From Molecular Biology to Therapy*. Boston: Birkhäuser, 1996.

Davidson, Ann. *Alzheimer's. A Love Story: One Year in My Husband's Journey*. Secaucus, NJ: Carol Publishing Group, 1997.

Davidson, Frena Gray. *The Alzheimer's Sourcebook for Caregivers: A Practical Guide for Getting Through the Day*. 3rd edition. New York: McGraw-Hill, 1999.

Davis, Helen D., and Michael P. Jensen. *Alzheimer's: The Answers You Need*. Forest Knolls, CA: Elder Books, 1997.

Davis, Robert. *My Journey into Alzheimer's Disease*. Wheaton, IL: Tyndale House Publishers, 1989.

Doraiswamy, P. Muraly, Lisa P. Gwyther, and Tina Adler. *The Alzheimer's Action Plan: What You Need to Know — and What You Can Do — About Memory Problems, from Prevention to Early Intervention and Care*. New York: St. Martin's Griffin Press, 2009.

Genova, Lisa. *Still Alice: A Novel*. New York: Simon & Schuster, 2007.

Granet, Roger, and Eileen Fallon. *Is It Alzheimer's? What to Do When Loved Ones Can't Remember What They Should*. New York: Avon Books, 1998.

Grubbs, William M. *In Sickness & In Health: Caring for a Loved One with Alzheimer's*. Forest Knolls, CA: Elder Books, 1996.

Haisman, Pam, R.N. *Alzheimer's Disease Caregivers Speak Out*. Fort Myers, FL: Chippendale House, 1998.

Hilden, Julie. *The Bad Daughter*. Chapel Hill, NC: Algonquin Books, 1998.

Kandel, Eric, James Schwartz, and Thomas Jessell. *Principles of Neural Science*. 4th Edition. New York: McGraw Hill, 2000.

Khachaturian, Zaven, and Teresa Radebaugh. *Alzheimer's Disease: Cause(s), Diagnosis, Treatment and Care*. Sanford, FL: InSync Communications, 1996.

Kuhn, Daniel, and David A. Bennett. *Alzheimer's Early Stages: First Steps in Caring and Treatment*. New York: Publishers Group West, 1999.

Mace, Nancy, and Peter V. Rabins. *The 36-Hour Day: A Family Guide to Caring for Persons with Alzheimer Disease, Other Dementias, and Memory Loss in Later Life*. 4th Edition. Baltimore, MD: Johns Hopkins University Press, 2006.

McDermott, Terry. *101 Theory Drive: A Neuroscientist's Quest for Memory*. New York: Pantheon Books, 2010.

Nolte, John. *The Human Brain: An Introduction to its Functional Anatomy*. 5th Edition. St. Louis: Mosby, 2002.

Perlmutter, David, and Albert Villold. *Power Up Your Brain: The Neuroscience of Enlightenment*. Carlsbad, CA: Hay House, 2011.

Perlmutter, David, and Carol Colman. *The Better Brain Book*. New York: Riverhead Books, 2005.

Pynoos, J. E., et al. *Strategies for Alzheimer's Caregivers.* Los Angeles: Program in Policy and Services Research, Andurs Gerontology Center, University of Southern California, 1988.

Seegmiller, Judy. *Life with Big Al (Early Alzheimer's): A Caregivers Diary.* El Dorado Hills, CA: Alexander's Publishing, 2000.

Shenk, David. *The Forgetting: Alzheimer's: Portrait of an Epidemic.* New York: Anchor, 2003.

Snowdon, David, Ph.D. *Aging with Grace: What the Nun Study Teaches Us About Leading Longer, Healthier and More Meaningful Lives.* New York: Bantam Books, 2002.

Tanzi, Rudolph, and Ann B. Parson. *Decoding Darkness: The Search for the Genetic Causes of Alzheimer's Disease.* Cambridge, MA: Perseus Book Group, 2000.

Taylor, Richard. *Alzheimer's from the Inside Out.* Baltimore, MD: Health Professions Press, 2006.

Terry, R.D., et al., eds. *Alzheimer's Disease.* Philadelphia: Lippincott/Williams and Wilkins, 1999.

Booklets and Pamphlets

Alzheimer's Association 24/7 Helpline: (800) 272-3900. http://www.alz.org/alzheimers_disease_publications.asp

Alzheimer's Disease: Availability of Specialized Nursing Home Programs, Intramural Research Highlights, NMES: National Medical Expenditure Survey, Number 1. AHCPR Publication Number 91-0100, Agency for Health Care Policy and Research, free of charge by calling (800) 358-9295, or ordering online at http://www.ahcpr.gov

"Alzheimer's Disease: Unraveling the Mystery." This well-illustrated online booklet published by the National Institutes of Health provides basic information about Alzheimer's disease and current research efforts. http://www.nia.nih.gov/Alzheimers/Publications/Unraveling/

Alzheimer's Library. The Alzheimer's library has many different downloadable pamphlets from various organizations on Alzheimer's disease and caregiving. http://alzheimers.boomja.com/Caregiving-Booklets-and-Pamphlets-26608.html

Care for Advanced Alzheimer's Disease. Publication of the Alzheimer's Association, 919 Michigan IL 60611.

Developmental Disabilities and Alzheimer's Disease ... What You Should Know. 1995. The Arc of the Unites States, National Headquarters, 500 TX 76010, (817) 261-6003.

Early Alzheimer's Disease: A Guide for Patients and Families. Agency for Health Care Policy and Research, U.S. Department of Health and Human Services, free of charge by calling (800) 358-9295.

Elder Locator Resources: "Adult Day Care"; "Home Health Care"; "Preventing Falls at Home"; "Caring for a Patient with Alzheimer's disease." These four pamphlets are available at Elder Locator service of the NIA. 24-hour hotline in English and Spanish (800) 677-1116. http://www.eldercare.gov/ELDERCARE.NET/Public/Resources/Topic/Alzheimer_Disease.aspx

Facts and Figures 2010 Alzheimer's Disease of the Alzheimer's Association. Information on statistics, causes, costs, prevalence, ethnicity, caregiver resources and more. The 74-page report can be downloaded at http://www.alz.org/documents_custom/report_alzfactsfigures2010.pdf

From Theory to Therapy: The Development of Drugs for Alzheimer's Disease (information kit on current drug therapies and therapies currently under testing). Publication of the Alzheimer's Association, 919 Michigan, Chicago, IL 60611. http://www.alz.org

Frontotemporal Lobe Dementia Information, Jan 2011/ Comprehensive information on Pick's disease and other types of frontotemporal lobe dementia. National Institute of Neurological Disorders and Stroke. http://www.ninds.nih.gov/disorders/picks/picks.htm

Guidelines for Dignity (guidelines for specialized Alzheimer's disease care in nursing homes and other residential settings). Publication of the Alzheimer's Association, 919 Michigan, Chicago, IL 60611. http://www.alz.org

Hospitalization Happens. Publication of the North Carolina Division of Aging; available free of charge through website, http://www.dhhs.state.nc.us/aging/ad.htm or by calling (800) 228-8738.

Janicki, M., Heller, T., et al. *Practice Guidelines for the Clinical Assessment and Care Management of Alzheimer and other Dementias among Adults with Mental Retardation.* 1995. American Association on Mental Retardation — Aging Special Interest Group, 444 Suite 846, Washington (800) 424-3668.

Living with Alzheimer's Disease. Publication of TriAD, 888-TriADHELP.

Living with Early-Onset Alzheimer's Disease. 1999. Brochure #ED206Z, The Alzheimer's Association, (800) 272-3900.

Lott, I. *Alzheimer's Disease and Down Syndrome.* 1995. National Down Syndrome Society, 666 Broadway, New York, NY 10012, (800) 221-4602 or (212) 460-9330.

Mental Health Information Network. Information on Alzheimer's disease and other forms of dementia provided by various organizations including the Alzheimer's Association of Canada. http://mhin.bu.edu/quick.cfm?title=brochure&div=body&font=2

Subscription Newsletters

Early Alzheimer's: A Forum for Early Stage Dementia Care. Santa Barbara, CA, Chapter of the Alzheimer's Association, Published quarterly, annual subscription $55.00, (805) 563-0020.

Perspectives: A newsletter for individuals diagnosed with

Alzheimer's disease. Alzheimer's Disease Research Center, La Jolla, CA, published quarterly, annual subscription $24.00, (858) 622-5800.

JOURNALS

Alzheimer's and Dementia. Journal of the American Medical Directors Association. www.alzheimer-sanddementia.org

Alzheimer's Care Today. This quarterly journal describes the latest treatment advances for Alzheimer's and it has articles dealing with Alzheimer's disease and its care; http://www.nursingcenter.com/library/journalissue.asp?Journal_ID=515681&Issue_ID=1103692

Alzheimer's Research & Therapy. The major forum for translational research into Alzheimer's disease. An international peer-reviewed journal, it publishes open access research articles of outstanding quality. Alzheimer's Research & Therapy publishes basic research with a translational focus, as well as clinical trials, research into drug discovery and development, and epidemiologic studies. Although the primary focus is Alzheimer's dementia, the scope will encompass translational research into other neurodegenerative diseases. http://www.alzres.com

American Journal of Alzheimer's Disease and Other Dementias. http://aja.sagepub.com/

International Journal of Alzheimer's Disease. Open access journal for research articles from around the world. http://www.sage-hindawi.com/journals/ijad/

Journal of Alzheimer's Disease. IOS Press (MetaPress). http://iospress.metapress.com/content/105656/

Journal of Alzheimer's Disease. This international multidisciplinary journal is designed to facilitate progress in understanding the etiology and pathogenesis of Alzheimer's. http://www.j-alz.com/

Medical Journal/Article Search Engines for Conventional and Alternative Medicine in Alzheimer's Disease

Article abstracts and articles from many medical journals can also be accessed often at no charge through the following websites:

Agency for Health Care Quality and Research: http://www.ahrq.gov

Alternative Medicine Digest: http://www.alternative-medicine-digest.com/

Alzheimer's Association Alternative Medicine. Information on Tramiprosate, Omega-3 Oils, Herbal Medicine and More: http://www.alz.org/alzheimers_disease_alternative_treatments.asp

Alzheimer's Disease Research: http://www.alternative-medicine-digest.com/alzheimers-treatment.html

Alzheimer's Disease Weekly. This organization has a large library of research articles on Alzheimer's disease, including information on alternative medical therapies, and an email list that sends out the latest reports to subscribers weekly. http://alzheimersweekly.com

Amedeo Free Medical Journals: http://www.freemedicaljournals.com

BioMed Central. Open access journal articles, abstracts and full text: http://www.biomedcentral.com

Biomed Central for Complementary and Alternative Medicine: www.biomedcentral.com/bmccomplementalternmed/

Complementary Medicine for Alzheimer's Disease. University of Maryland Medical Center. Information on Diet, Lifestyle Changes, Herbal Medicine, Energy Medicine and More: http://www.umm.edu/altmed/articles/alzheimers-disease-000005.htm

Life Extension Foundation: http://www.lef.org

National Center for Complementary and Alternative Medicine. Division of the National Library of Medicine, National Institutes of Health: http://nccam.nih.gov/

National Library of Medicine PubMed: http://www.ncbi.nlm.nih.gov/pubmed

Internet Forums, Bulletin Boards and Blogs

Alzheimer Research Forum. The Alzheimer Research Forum is an Internet organization devoted to advances, research publications and news about Alzheimer's disease. http://www.alzforum.org/

Alzheimer's Discussion Board at About.Com. An online discussion board where individuals can learn from other caregivers and those with Alzheimer's about how to cope more effectively with the disease. http://forums.about.com/n/pfx/forum.aspx?webtag=ab-alzheimers

Alzheimer's Society Message Forum. The society hosts a number of different bulletin boards according to topics such as caregiving. http://www.alzheimer.ca/english/forums/intro.htm

Dementia Advocacy and Support Network International (DASNI). DASN International is an internet-based support network established to: promote respect; provide a forum for exchanging news and information; encourage support mechanisms such as local groups, counseling groups, internet resources; advocate for services with individuals with dementia; assist people in connecting with their local Alzheimer's Association. DASNI activities currently include an Internet-based support group for people with various dementias and those concerned with patient well-being. Twice-daily Internet chats help ease the isolation of dementia and educate participants about living with their disease. http://www.dasninternational.org/

Elder Care's Alzheimer Caregivers Blog. A wealth of information on Alzheimer's disease research and disease management, includes a 24-hour crisis line at (800) 209-4342. http://alzheimerscareathome. com/

HBO Alzheimer's Project. This website and television series features a four-part documentary series, 15 short supplemental films, a robust website, and a nationwide community-based information and outreach campaign. A book published by Public Affairs Books was developed as a companion to the project. http://www.hbo.com/alzheimers/index.html

MD Junction Alzheimer's Q&A Boards. This board supports multiple forums with up to date information. http://www.mdjunction.com/forums/alzheim ers-disease-discussions

Clinical Trials

A number of organizations are involved in clinical trials for Alzheimer's disease. The purpose of clinical trials is to improve the understanding of certain conditions. Patients participating in clinical trial for neurological conditions will continue receiving medical care, routine laboratory tests and diagnostic tests from their primary physicians. Information on ongoing trials can be obtained from the following agencies:

The Alzheimer's Disease Clinical Trials Database. A joint project of the Food and Drug Administration and the National Institute on Aging, it provides clinical trial information by state along with contact information. Here you can search a database of clinical trials on Alzheimer's disease and dementia currently in progress at sites throughout the U.S. http://www.nia.nih.gov/Alzheimers/ResearchInfor mation/ClinicalTrials/

The Alzheimer's Disease Cooperative Study (ADCS). University of California, San Diego, La Jolla, CA, (323) 442-3715. The ADCS consortium is a network of 83 university affiliated research facilities coordinated by the University of California, San Diego. Individual facilities are listed as ADCS centers in the resource section describing *Research Facilities.* http://www.adcs.org/

Alzheimer's Disease Education and Referral (ADEAR) Center, (800) 438-4380. ADEAR provides information to the public about ongoing clinical trials and opportunities for participation. http://www. nia.nih.gov/alzheimers

CenterWatch Clinical Trials Listing Service. Lists clinical trials for Alzheimer's disease that aren't included in the Alzheimer's Disease Clinical Trials Database. http://www.centerwatch.com/studies/CAT11.htm.

Clinical Trials Service of the National Institutes of Health and the National Institute of Neurological Disorders and Stroke (NINDS). 9000 Rockville Pike, Bethesda, Maryland, 20892, (800) 411-1222. This web site, through its National Library of Med-

icine, shows all trials for Alzheimer's disease, including those that are no longer recruiting patients. http://www.clinicaltrials.gov

Cochrane Database, a Collaborative Review of Clinical Trials. http://www2.cochrane.org/. An internet search can be performed on any drug therapy under review attached to the words Cochrane database; for instance, "Cochrane review of cholinesterase inhibitors" = http://www2.cochrane.org/reviews/ en/ab005593.html.

Ethnic Elder Care's Drugs Undergoing Clinical Trials. Information on Clinical Trials for Alzheimer's Drugs: http://www.ethnicelderscare.net/clinical trials.htm

Fourth Annual Alzheimer's Disease Clinical Trial Conference to be held Nov 3–6, 2011, at the U.S. Grant Hotel in San Diego, CA. http://www.ctad. fr/

Info.com Alzheimer's Disease Clinical Trials. This website contains ten different search engines with comprehensive clinical trial information. http:// www.info.com/alzheimer's%20trials?cb=27&cmp= 3974

Life Extension Foundation Studies. The Life Extension Foundation is conducting a clinical trial (CL025) to measure the effects of weekly medication injections and nutritional supplements that may help suppress the inflammatory factor implicated in the neuronal degeneration of Alzheimer's disease. This study requires weekly visits and runs approximately 17 weeks. Subjects receive blood tests, evaluations, blood pressure checks and study medication at no cost. For more information call (866) 517-4536, http://www.lef.org

Oxon Publications of Clinical Trial Results. Information on completed phase IV clinical trials: http:// www.oxonepi.com/index.php?option=com_con tent&view=article&id=80&Itemid=95

San Francisco Alzheimer's and Dementia Clinic, (415) 673-4600, http://www.sfcrc.com

University of California, Davis, Alzheimer's Disease Centers. Martinez, CA, (925) 372-2485, contact: Joan Webb, RN. Sacramento, CA, (916) 734-5496, contact: Bobbi Henk, RN. http://alzheimer.uc davis.edu

Veritas Medicine. A company that helps to link patients with clinical trials, including Alzheimer's disease trials. Veritas helps patients, their family members and physicians find National Institutes of Health (NIH) sponsored trials based on their location and medical profile through partnerships with pharmaceutical companies and research organizations. http://www.veritasmedicine.com

Wikipedia Alzheimer's Disease Clinical Trial Information. Regularly updated, this website entry provides information on therapies that have been evaluated or are under current evaluation for Alzheimer's disease. http://en.wikipedia.org/wiki/Alz heimer's_disease_clinical_research

Finding and Evaluating Nursing Homes

Advancing Excellence in America's Nursing Homes is a national campaign to encourage, assist and empower nursing homes to improve the quality of care and life for residents. The mission of the campaign is to help nursing homes achieve excellence in the quality of care and quality of life for the more than 1.5 million residents of America's nursing homes. (800) 272-3900. http://www.nhqualitycampaign. org/

American Association for Homes and Services for the Aging (AAHSA) is a national nonprofit organization representing 5,000 not-for-profit nursing homes, retirement communities, assisted living residences and senior housing. http://www.aahsa. org/

Assisted Living Federation of America (ALFA) is the largest national association exclusively dedicated to professionally operated assisted living communities for seniors. ALFA's member-driven programs promote business and operational excellence through national conferences, research, publications, and executive networks. ALFA works to influence public policy by advocating for informed choice, quality care, and accessibility for all Americans. http://www.alfa.org

Brown University's Long Term Care Focus, Brown University Center for Gerontology and Healthcare Research. Supported by the National Institute on Aging, LTCFocUS.org provides data on nursing home care in the U.S. Their goal is to allow researchers to trace relationships between state policies, local market forces and the quality of long-term care and enable policymakers to craft state and local guidelines that promote high-quality, cost-effective, equitable care for older Americans. http://ltcfocus.org/default.aspx

Cite Health Nursing Homes' website allows individuals to search specific nursing homes by state; includes detailed report on a nursing home including information on quality, staffing, deficiencies, reviews, ratings and more. http://citehealth.com/ nursing-homes

Continuing Care Accreditation Commission, (202) 783-7286. http://www.aging.pitt.edu/seniors/re sources/long-term.asp

Eldercare Locator of the National Institute on Aging runs a 24-hour hotline for services in English and Spanish at (800) 677-1116. http://www.eldercare. gov/ELDERCARE.NET/Public/Resources/Topic/ Alzheimer_Disease.aspx

Medicare.Gov Nursing Home Comparisons. Maintained and regularly updated by Medicare, this website allows individuals to compare nursing home facilities in specific locations by rankings based on inspections and report reviews. Website also has information on finding and paying for nursing homes. http://www.medicare.gov/nhcom pare/

National Adult Day Services Association (NADSA) is the leading voice of the rapidly growing adult day services (ADS) industry and the national focal point for ADS providers. Members include adult day center providers, state associations of providers, corporations, educators, students, retired workers and others interested in working to build better lives for adults in adult day programs. http://www. nadsa.org

National Association for Homecare and Hospice (NAHC) is the nation's largest trade association representing the interests and concerns of home care agencies, hospices, home care aide organizations, and medical equipment suppliers. http://www. nahc.org

National Citizens' Coalition for Nursing Home Reform (NCCNHR) was formed because of public concern about substandard care in nursing homes. NCCNHR provides information and leadership on federal and state regulatory and legislative policy development and models and strategies to improve care and life for residents of nursing homes and other long term care facilities. http://www.nccnhr. org/

Nursing Home Abuse. This website, established in 2004 and maintained by a law firm, offers suggestions for evaluating nursing homes and preventing patient abuse; it includes articles on current legal challenges and information on nursing homes that have been cited. http://www.elderly-abuse.com

Nursing Home Ratings Abuse and Neglect Report. Through a partnership with ElderCare, this website provides a free referral service with information on finding home care and assisted living as well as financial planning and personal emergency responses. http://www.nursing-homes-ratings.com/

A Place for Mom. Assistance with finding resources in local areas. http://www.aplaceformom.com

Senior Living.com. This informational website is solely owned and operated by the activism company MGroup LLC, headquartered in Nashville, Tennessee. This resource aims to serve the needs of individuals living in or searching for nursing homes. Website is affiliated with member nursing homes. http://www.seniorliving.com/about

Minority Aging Organizations

Asociación Nacional Pro Personas Mayores [National Association for Hispanic Elderly] has been serving the needs of Hispanic elderly and other low income persons since 1975. Recognized as the pioneer and the leading organization in the field of Hispanic aging, today, it is one of the broadest based Hispanic organizations in the nation. As a private, nonprofit 501(c)(3) corporation with both public and private funding, it has earned a national reputation for its work with the elderly and for its increasingly significant role in the larger Hispanic community.

National Aging Pacific Center on Aging (NAPCA). The NAPCA's mission is to serve as the nation's leading advocacy organization committed to the dignity, well-being, and quality of life of Asian Pacific Americans (APA) in their senior years. http://www.napca.org

National Caucus and Center on Black Aging (NCBA) was established in 1972. The Caucus existed as an advocacy group until 1973 when it received a grant from the Administration on Aging (AoA) to conduct research, train personnel and serve as a technical resource. The NCBA was established to administer the AoA grant. http://www.ncba-aged.org

National Hispanic Council on Aging (NHCOA) is the nation's premier constituency-based organization dedicated to improving the quality of life for the Hispanic/Latino elderly, their families, and their communities. Now in its 28th year, NHCOA represents a network of 42 community-based organizations across the continental U.S., the District of Columbia, and Puerto Rico. http://www.nhcoa.org

National Indian Council on Aging, Inc. (NICOA), a non-profit organization, was founded in 1976 by members of the National Tribal Chairmen's Association that called for a national organization to advocate for improved, comprehensive health and social services to American Indian and Alaska Native Elders. For more than 30 years, the organization has provided service as the nation's foremost advocate for American Indians and Alaska Native elders. http://www.nicoa.org

Diet and Nutrition Resources

Meals on Wheels Association of America (MOWAA) the oldest and largest organization in the United States representing those who provide meal services to people in need. MOWAA works toward the social, physical, nutritional, and economic betterment of vulnerable Americans. As a national organization, MOWAA focuses on those issues that can best assist its member programs in achieving their individual missions of providing quality meals and nutrition services to as many vulnerable people as possible in the most efficient and effective manner, all "so no senior goes hungry." http://www.mowaa.org

National Association of Nutrition and Aging Services Programs (NANASP) is a national membership organization for persons across the country working to provide older adults healthful food and nutrition through community-based services. NANASP's mission is to strengthen through advocacy and education those who help older Americans. http://www.nanasp.org

Natural News Drug Watch Database. This division of Natural News lists nutrient deficiencies caused by specific over-the-counter and prescription drugs, and it provides information on nutrients that interfere with drug absorption. http://www.NaturalNews.com/DrugWatch_Home.html

Perlmutter, David, M.D., is an expert on nutrient deficiencies as well as other environmental factors that contribute to cognitive changes in Alzheimer's Disease. http://drperlmutter.com/

Caregiver Resources

Alzheimer's Disease.com for Caregivers. Caregiver tips and support. http://www.alzheimersdisease.com/index.jsp

Caregiver Information. http://www.caregiver-information.com/

Caregivers web-site, Alzheimer's Disease International. http://www.alz.co.uk/carers/

Elder Care Alzheimer's Caregivers Blog and Crisis Hotline, (800) 209-4342. http://alzheimerscareathome.com/

Family Caregiver Alliance (FCA), 180 Montgomery Street, Suite 900, San Francisco, CA 94104, (415) 434-3388, (800) 438-4380. http://www.caregiver.org

Family Caregiving 101. The National Family Caregivers Association (NFCA) and the National Alliance for Caregiving (NAC) run a site designed to provide caregivers with the basic tools, skills and information they need to protect their own physical and mental health while they provide high quality care for their loved one. http://www.familycaregiving101.org

Medline Plus Resources for Alzheimer's Disease Caregivers, provided by the National Library of Medicine. Numerous articles and tip sheets in both English and Spanish. http://www.nlm.nih.gov/medlineplus/alzheimerscaregivers.html

National Alliance for Caregiving. Established in 1996, The National Alliance for Caregiving is a non-profit coalition of national organizations focusing on issues of family caregiving. Alliance members include grassroots organizations, professional associations, service organizations, disease-specific organizations, a government agency, and corporations. http://www.caregiving.org/

National Family Caregivers Association, (800) 896-3650. http://www.nfcacares.org

Resources for Enhancing Alzheimer's Caregiver Health (REACH). Coordinating Center: University Center for Social and Urban Research, University of Pittsburgh, 121 University Place, Pittsburgh, PA 15260. http://www.edc.pitt.edu/reach/

Right at Home, assistance for caregivers and Alzheimer's disease resources. http://www.rightathome.net/winstonsalem/blog/great-resources-for-coping-with-emotions-of-alzheimers/

National, Regional and Government Organizations

The following organizations provide educational resources and support for patients with Alzheimer's disease and their families. Many of these organizations have local chapters, free newsletters, current research news, and affiliated support groups:

Administration on Aging, U.S. Department of Health and Human Services. http://www.aoa.gov

Ageless Design, Smarter Safer Living for Seniors, 126 159th Court North, Jupiter, FL 33478. (561) 745-0210. http://www.agelessdesign.com

Alzheimer's Association National Headquarters (member of Alzheimer's Disease International). 919 North Michigan Avenue, Suite 1000, Chicago, IL 60611-1676, (800) 272-3900. Email: info@alz.org. http://www.alz.org. The Alzheimer's Association has local chapters around the country.

Alzheimer's Disease Education and Referral (ADEAR) Center. P.O. Box 8250, Silver Spring, MD 20907-8250, (800) 438-4380. Email: adear@alzheimers.org. http://www.nia.nih.gov/alzheimers

Alzheimer's Disease International. 64 Great Suffolk Street, London, SE1 0BL, UK. Tel: +44 20 7981 0880, Fax: +44 20 79282357. Email: info@alz.co.uk. Alzheimer's Disease International is an umbrella organization of 57 national Alzheimer Associations located around the world whose main purpose is to improve the quality of life of people with dementia and their caregivers and to raise awareness of the disease.

American Association of Retired Persons (AARP). 601 E St., NW, Washington, DC 20049, (888) 687-2277. http:// www.aarp.org

American Geriatrics Society. 350 Fifth Avenue, Suite 801, New York, NY 10118, (212) 308-1414.

American Health Assistance Foundation. 22512 Gateway Center Drive, Clarksburg, Maryland 20871, (800) 437-2423. This organization provides funding for Alzheimer's disease research, educational resources to families and caregivers, and emergency financial support for Alzheimer's disease patients and caregivers. http://www.ahaf.org

American Health Care Association. This site has links to the organization's state associations. http://www.ahca.org

American Psychiatric Association Public Information on Alzheimer's Disease. 1400 K Street, NW, Washington, DC 20005. http://www.apa.org/topics/alzheimers/index.aspx

Clearinghouse on Aging and Developmental Disabilities, RRTC on Aging and Developmental Disabilities (M/C 626). The University of Illinois at Chicago, 7640 West Roosevelt Rd., Chicago, IL 60608-6904, (800) 996-8845. http://www.rrtcadd.org/

Duke University Family Support Program. (800) 672-4213

Disability, Aging and Long-Term Care Policy, Office of the Assistant Secretary for Planning and Evaluation, Department of Health and Human Services. http://aspe.hhs.gov

ElderCare Locator Service of the National Institute on Aging. Provides information on Alzheimer's disease and services in local communities. 24 hr. hotline in English and Spanish at (800) 677-1116. http://www.eldercare.gov/ELDERCARE.NET/Public/Resources/Topic/Alzheimer_Disease.aspx

Government Resources on Medicaid Long-Term Care Waivers. Department of Elder Affairs. Medicaid Long-Term Care Waivers; the purpose of Medicaid Long-Term Care Waiver programs is to avoid or delay unnecessary and costly nursing home placement and enhance quality of life by providing alternative, less restrictive long-term care options for seniors who qualify for Medicaid skilled nursing home care. These options include care in the home, or in a community setting such as an assisted living facility or adult day care center. http://www.oppaga.state.fl.us/profiles/5023/

Indiana National Cell Repository for Alzheimer's Disease (NCRAD). Headquartered at the University of Indiana and funded by the National Institutes of Health, the National Institute on Aging has in place a Genetics Initiative to assist in the identification of the risk factor genes for Alzheimer's disease. To this end, NIA supports the National Cell Repository for Alzheimer's Disease (NCRAD) at Indiana University as a national repository in order to facilitate access by qualified investigators to samples and Associated Phenotypic Data for the study of the genetics of late-onset Alzheimer's disease. Contact information at alzstudy@iupui.edu. http://ncrad.iu.edu/forResearchers/sampleTransfer.asp

National Alzheimer's Coordinating Center, University of Washington School for Public Health. 4225 Roosevelt Way NE, Suite 301, Seattle, WA 98105, (206) 543-8637. This center facilitates collaborative research among the 30 Alzheimer's Disease Centers funded by the National Institute on Aging. In its scope of activities, the center provides public access to clinical trial data, information about news and events and a variety of educational resources. http://ww.alz.washington.edu

National Council of Senior Citizens. 8403 Colesville Rd., Suite 1200, Silver Spring, Maryland 20910, (301) 578-8800. http://www.ncscinc.org

National Council on the Aging. 409 Third Street, SW, 2nd Floor, Washington, DC 20024, (202) 479-1200. http://www.ncoa.org

National Institute of Neurological Disorders and Stroke, National Institutes of Health. Bethesda, MD 20892. http://wwwninds.nih.gov

National Institute on Aging (NIA). 9000 Rockville

Pike, Building 31, Room 2C-02, Bethesda, MD 20205, (301) 469-1752. http://www.nia.nih.gov/

National Senior Citizens Law Center. 1101 14th Street, NW, Suite 400, Washington, DC 20005. http://www.nsclc.org

Neuroscience and Neuropsychology of Aging Program, National Institute on Aging. Gateway Building, Suite 3C307, 7201 Wisconsin Avenue MSC 9205, Bethesda, Maryland 20892-9205, (301) 496-9350. Director, Brad Wise, M.D., email: by86y@nih.gov.

NIHSeniorHealth. This website from the National Institutes of Health features basic health and wellness information for older adults. The site contains modules on Alzheimer's disease and caring for someone with the disease. http://nihseniorhealth.gov/index.html

North Carolina Division of Aging, Alzheimer's Association-Eastern NC Chapter. 4000 Oberlin Road, Suite 208, Raleigh, NC 27605, (800) 228-8738, (919) 832-3732. http://www.alznc.org/

Suncoast Gerontology Center at the University of South Florida. 12901 Bruce B. Down Boulevard, MDC 50, Tampa, FL 33612, (800) 633-4563 (813) 974-4355. http://health.usf.edu/medicine/suncoast alzheimers/index.htm

TriAD, National Association of Triads, Inc. (NATI). Triad is a partnership of law enforcement, senior citizens, and community groups. The sole purpose of Triad is to promote senior safety and to reduce the fear of crime that seniors often experience. Information can be found at the website on organizing a Triad program at the grass-roots level, and provides ideas and programs to implement in communities, as well as training materials for law enforcement, senior volunteers, and community groups. (888) TriADHELP. http://www.national triad.org/About_NATI.htm

U.S. Department of Health and Human Services, Centers for Disease Control and Prevention. Hyattsville, MD 20782, (301) 458-4636. http://www.hhs.gov/open/contacts/cdc.html

AoA Long-Term Care Resource Centers

National Rural Long Term Care Resource Center
University of Kansas Medical Center
University of Kansas Center on Aging
3901 Rainbow Boulevard
Kansas City, KS 66160
(913) 588-1201

This center focuses on rural long-term care issues. Its major goal is to improve the availability of and access to effective long-term care and community services for the rural elderly.

National Resource Center: Diversity and Long Term Care

Brandeis University
Waltham, MA 02254
(800) 456-9966

This center supports the development and operation of long-term care ombudsman programs within each state; provides Stat ombudsman programs with educational support and training.

National Center on Elder Abuse (NCEA)
c/o Center for Community Research and Services
University of Delaware
297 Graham Hall
Newark, DE 19716
http://www.ncea.aoa.gov/ncearoot/Main_Site/index.aspx

This center is a consortium of six partners headed by the National Association of State Units on Aging. The NDEA provides elder abuse information to professionals and the public and offers technical assistance and training to elder abuse agencies. The center also conducts short-term research and assists in policy development.

National Policy and Resource Center on Nutrition and Aging
Florida International University
Department of Dietetics and Nutrition, OE200
Florida International University
Miami, FL 33199
(305) 348-1517
http://nutritionandaging.fiu.edu/

This center serves as a national focal point for issues related to nutrition and aging, with emphasis on the prevention of malnutrition and food insecurity.

AoA Legal Assistance and Service and Support Centers for the Elderly

ABA Commission on Law and Aging. The mission of the ABA Commission on Law and Aging is to strengthen and secure the legal rights, dignity, autonomy, quality of life, and quality of care of elders. It carries out this mission through research, policy development, technical assistance, advocacy, education, and training. The Commission consists of a 15-member interdisciplinary body of experts in aging and law, including lawyers, judges, health and social services professionals, academics, and advocates. http://www.abanet.org/aging/

Black Elderly Legal Assistance Support Project. National Bar Association, 1225 11th Street, NW, Washington, DC 20001, (202) 842-3900. This project encourages the involvement of local chapters of the National Bar Association in establishing and expanding African American and other minority community care coalitions in four sites throughout the U.S. The group also works to meet the needs of low income, vulnerable African American and minority older persons. http://www.nationalbar.org/nba/history3.shtml

The Center for Social Gerontology (TCSG). 2307 Shelby Avenue, Ann Arbor, MI 48103-3895, (734) 665-1126. Since its inception in 1972, TCSG has been a non-profit research, training and social policy organization dedicated to promoting the individual autonomy of older persons and advancing their well-being in society. TCSG has pursued this goal through a wide variety of projects, including serving since 1985 as an Administration on Aging-funded National Support Center in Law & Aging. TCSG's mission is to help society adapt to the dramatic increase in the numbers of old and very old, and to insure that older persons at all socio-economic and health levels are able to meet their needs and use their talents and abilities in a changing society. http://www.tcsg.org/

International Network for the Prevention of Elder Abuse. Acknowledging the diversity of culture, background, and lifestyle of the world population, the International Network for the Prevention of Elder Abuse aims to increase society's ability, through international collaboration, to recognize and respond to the mistreatment of older people in whatever setting it occurs, so that the latter years of life will be free from abuse, neglect and exploitation. http://www.inpea.net/

Legal Counsel for the Elderly. American Association of Retired Persons (AARP). 601 E Street NW, Suite A1-200, Washington, DC 20049, (202) 434-7700. This group provides training and technical assistance to states on substantive law and advocacy skills, on protective services law and on the expansion of legal service programs for disability and Medicare benefits. The Legal Counsel also publishes a bi-monthly newsletter, the *Elder Law Forum*, which is distributed to 4,500 agencies and advocates. Member website for legal services: http://www.aarplsn.com/lsn/ui/jsp/benefits.jsp

The National Clearinghouse on Abuse in Later Life (NCALL) provides training and technical assistance on abuse in later life. Staff will respond to requests received via telephone, e-mail, regular mail and in person about specific cases or services. Staff members are also available to review materials and participate on state and national advisory committees. In addition, NCALL staff members are available to train audiences including professionals from domestic violence and sexual assault programs, the aging network, adult protective services, criminal justice, health care, faith based and other areas. http://www.ncall.us/

National Consumer Law Center (NCLC) is the nation's consumer law expert, helping consumers, their advocates, and public policy makers use powerful and complex consumer laws on behalf of low-income and vulnerable Americans seeking economic justice. http://www.consumerlaw.org/

National Eldercare Legal Assistance Project Members. National Senior Citizens Law Center (NSCLC), 1444 Eye St., NW, Suite 1100, Washington, DC 20005, (202) 289-6976, Email: nsclc@nsclc.org. The NSCLC provides case consultation, technical assistance, training and legal assistance support services to local and state aging legal service networks for the purpose of enhancing their capabilities. This group publishes newsletters with current changes in laws affecting the elderly and training materials. http://www.nsclc.org/

National Legal Assistance Support Agency. American Bar Association, Commission on Legal Problems of the Elderly. 1800 M Street, NW. Washington, DC 20036, (202) 331-2630. The National Legal Assistance Support Agency helps in developing accessible and responsible legal resources for the elderly.

National Legal Assistance Support and Information. National Clearinghouse for Legal Services, Inc., 205 W. Monroe St., 2nd Floor, Chicago, IL 60606-5013, (312) 263-3830. The National Clearinghouse provides legal information and research services to providers of legal assistance to older persons. http://pview.findlaw.com/view/1648095_1

National Legal Support for Elderly People with Mental Disabilities Project. Judge David L. Bazelon Center for Mental Health Law, 1101 15th Street, NW, Suite 1212, Washington, DC 20005-5730, (202) 467-5730. This project trains advocates to meet the needs of the elderly with mental disabilities, ensuring they can age at home with supports that strengthen individual capabilities. The project publishes reports dealing with legal issues facing this population and sponsors workshops on advocacy systems for the elderly with mental disabilities. http://www.bazelon.org/

National Senior Citizens Law Center (NSCLC). Since 1972, the NSCLS has worked to promote the independence and well-being of low-income elderly and disabled Americans, especially women, people of color, and other disadvantaged minorities. The NSCLC advocates nationwide to promote the independence and well-being of low-income elderly and disabled Americans. http://www.nsclc.org/

Strengthening Legal Assistance Project. The Center for Social Gerontology, Inc. expands and improves the delivery of legal assistance to vulnerable elderly by providing training, technical assistance and educational support in areas of law such as disabilities, self-determination and the right to refuse treatment, elder abuse, and guardianship and alternatives. http://www.tcsg.org/

Internet Educational Resources

The following websites have been developed to help those facing the challenge of managing Alzheimer's disease find more information and available resources.

Action for Healthy Aging & Elder Care. The Novartis Gerontology Foundation's educational support web site. http://www.healthandage.com

Administration on Aging. This site has links to state Area Agencies on Aging and federal agency consumer web sites. http://www.aoa.gov

Alternative Natural Medical Protocols. This site has numerous links to research articles discussing the role of aluminum, antioxidant therapy, estrogen therapy, melatonin therapy, amalgam fillings and many other topics. http://www.natmedpro.com/nmp/Refs-Alzheim.htm

Alzheimer Support.com, (800) 366-5924 This web site provides educational resources related to Alzheimer's disease. This organization focuses on three primary objectives: reporting the latest news in Alzheimer's disease treatment and research, making top quality nutritional supplements available at low prices, and donating profits from these supplements to Alzheimer's disease research. This site also has an affiliated chat board. http://www.prohealth.com/alzheimers/?b1=AZWEBO

Alzheimer's Disease Brain. This government sponsored web site includes illustrations of degenerative brain neurons, pinpointing disturbances in the areas responsible for motion, vision, sensory, speech and memory. http://search.usa.gov/search?affiliate=pueblo.gsa.gov&query=alzheimers&x=16&y=4

Alzheimer's disease website at the National Institute for Neurological Disorders and Stroke. http://www.ninds.nih.gov/

Alzheimer's Disease Society. www.alzheimers.org.uk/

Alzheimer's Disease Solution; Alzheimer's Disease Prevention and Education. http://www.thealzheimerssolution.com/

American Health Assistance Foundation. This nonprofit organization is dedicated to research, education and emergency financial assistance for Alzheimer's disease patients. http://www.ahaf.org

Centers for Disease Control, National Center for Health Statistics Alzheimer's Disease. http://www.cdc.gov/nchs/fastats/alzheimr.htm

ElderWeb. This site contains information about eldercare topics and state-specific Medicaid regulations. http://www.elderweb.com

Fisher Center for Alzheimer's Research Foundation. Provides comprehensive local information by zip code on available resources such as physical therapy, insurance appeals, Medicaid services, physicians and other services for Alzheimer's disease patients and caregivers. http://www.alzinfo.org/resource-locator

HealingWell.com Alzheimer's Disease Resource Center. This site provides information and articles as well as a directory listing organizations, support groups, chat rooms, and books on Alzheimer's disease; online support group and chat room. http://www.healingwell.com/alzheimers/

Health Care Financing Administration. This site offers information about federal regulations, quality care initiatives, Medicare and Medicaid. http://www.hcfa.gov

Lewy Body Dementia Association, Inc. http://www.lbda.org/

The Massachusetts General Hospital Memory Disorder Units. http://www.mgh.harvard.edu/neurology/services/treatmentprograms.aspx?id=1088

Mayo Clinic. http://www.mayoclinic.com/

Med Grasp. http://www.alzheimers-support.com

Medline Plus Health Information for Alzheimer's disease. This site has links to latest news and studies, clinical trials, alternative therapy, caregiver information and specific problems. This site provides information in both English and Spanish. http://www.nlm.nih.gov/medlineplus/alzheimersdisease.html

Murphy's Unofficial Medicaid Page. This site serves as a resource guide to Medicaid. It offers information about Medicaid-specific resources and links to state-specific Medicaid informational sites. http://.geocites.com/CapitolHill/5974

National Aging Information Center. Links to major web resources on topics related to aging and available services for seniors. http://www.aoa.gov/naic/Main_Site/Search.aspx

Normal and Alzheimer Brain Comparison. This web site includes lateral and overhead scans of a normal brain and an Alzheimer brain with the areas of memory, understanding, hearing, speech, temper, personality and brain atrophy clearly labeled. http://www.ALZBRAIN.org

Novartis Foundation for Gerontology. Dedicated to promoting healthy aging. The Alzheimer's disease center funded by this organization provides educational support related to Alzheimer's disease. http://www.halthandage.com

Partners Program of Excellence in Alzheimer's and Other Neurodegenerative Diseases. Array of resources in basic and clinic neurosciences with links to current research, patient and caregiver resources and scientific accomplishments. http://www.pslgroup.com/dg/d455e.htm

Physicians Committee for Responsible Medicine. This group is dedicated to the responsible reporting of both conventional and alternative therapies. Their web site includes news reports, clinical research, controversies and issues, links to their journal, a resource sections and a search engine. http://www.pcrm.org

Psychiatry Resources. Psychiatry24x7 offers extensive information on dementia and Alzheimer's disease. http://www.Psychiatry24x7.com/

WebMD Alzheimer's Disease Health Center. General information on Alzheimer's disease diagnosis, symptoms and treatment; current research news; videos; caregiver information. http://www.webmd.com/alzheimers/default.htm

Internet Caregiver Resources

About.com Alzheimer's Disease. This site includes educational resources, an online support group and a list of top nursing homes. http://www.alzheimers.about.com

Alzheimer's Caregivers Speak Out. This site provides resources to help answer questions about Alzheimer's disease and provides information about the book of this title, which is dedicated to the problems of caring for Alzheimer's disease patients. http://www.chpublishers.com

ALZwell Caregiver Support. http://alzwell.com

The American Geriatrics Society. http://www.americangeriatrics.org/

ElderCare Online. ElderCare is an online community for people caring for loved ones with Alzheimer's disease. This site offers a comprehensive library of practical articles, educational modules and supportive discussion groups. http://www.ec-online.net

The Family Caregiver's Alliance. (800) 445-8106. http://www.caregiver.org

The National Family Caregivers Association. (800) 896-3650. http://www.nfcacares.org

Nursing Home Medicine. This site has articles and news highlights relating to nursing home care. http://www.mmhc.com/nhm/

Massachusetts General Hospital Memory Disorders Unit. http://www.mgh.harvard.edu/neurology/services/treatmentprograms.aspx?id=1088

TriAD. (888) TriADHELP. This organization provides information, support and local services for patients with Alzheimer's disease and their caretakers. http://lifecenter.ric.org/index.php?tray=content&tid=top1&cid=2845

Medicare and Other Health Insurance Resources

Department of Regulatory Agencies, Division of Insurance. (800) 930-3745

Medicare Assistance. (800) 638-6833. http://www.medicare.gov

Social Security Administration. (800) 772-1213. http://www.ssa.gov

Veterans Benefits. (800) 733-8387

Assistance in Finding Nursing Home Ombudsman and Licensure Programs, by State

State Ombudsman Programs offer assistance in resolving problems with nursing homes and in helping find a suitable nursing home. Departments of Health and Human Services or Public Health provide information on certifying and licensing nursing homes by state. States who have received grants under the Alzheimer's Disease Demonstration Grants to States

(ADDGS) program are designated by the addition of ADDGS next to their name.

ALABAMA

State Long-Term Care Ombudsman
Alabama Department of Senior Services, ADDGS
770 Washington Avenue
RSA Plaza, Suite 470
Montgomery, Alabama 99503-5209
http://www.alabamaageline.gov/
(334) 242-5743

Executive Director, Certification Division of Provider Services
Department of Public Health
P.O. Box 303017
Montgomery, Alabama 36130-5175
(334) 206-5175

ALASKA

State Long-Term Care Ombudsman
http://www.akoltco.org/
Alaska Commission on Aging, ADDGS
http://www.hss.state.ak.us/acoa/
3601 C Street, Suite 260
Anchorage, Alaska 99503-5209
(907) 563-6393, (800) 478-9996

Director, Health Facilities Licensing and Certification
Department of Health and Social Services
4730 Business Park Boulevard, Suite 18
Building H
Anchorage, Alaska 50399
(907) 561-8081

ARIZONA

State Long-Term Care Ombudsman
https://www.azdes.gov/common.aspx?menu=36&menuc=28&id=2464
Aging and Adult Administration
Department of Economic Security
1789 W. Jefferson Street, 950 A
Phoenix, Arizona, 85007
(602) 542-4446

Program Director, Division of Assurance and Licensure Services
Arizona Department of Human Services
1647 E. Morten Avenue, Suite 130
Phoenix, Arizona 85020-4610
(602) 674-9705

ARKANSAS

State Long-Term Care Ombudsman
http://www.arombudsman.com/
Division of Aging and Adult Services

Arkansas Department of Human Services
P.O. Box 1437, Slot 1412
Little Rock, Arkansas 72203-1437
(501) 682-2441
http://www.arkansas.gov/dhs/homepage.html

Director, Division of Medical Services
Office of Long-Term Care
Arkansas Department of Human Services, ADDGS
Division of Aging and Adult Services
P. O. Box 8059, Mail Slot 400
Little Rock, Arkansas 72203-8059
(501) 682-8430
http://www.agingcare.com/Find-Senior-Care/Assisted-Living/Arkansas-AR/

CALIFORNIA

State Long-Term Care Ombudsman
Department of Aging, ADDGS
1600 K Street
Sacramento, California 95814
(916) 322-6681
http://www.aging.ca.gov/programs/ombudsman.asp

Deputy Director, Licensing and Certification Programs
Department of Health Services
P.O. Box 942732
1800 Third Street, Suite 210
Sacramento, California 94234-7320
(916) 445-3054

COLORADO

State Long-Term Care Ombudsman
The Legal Center
455 Sherman Street, Suite 130
Denver, Colorado 80203
(303) 722-0300
http://www.cdhs.state.co.us/aas/adultprotection_omb
program.htm

Director, Health Facilities Division
Colorado Department of Public Health and Environment
4300 Cherry Creek Drive S.
Denver, Colorado 80246
(303) 692-2835

CONNECTICUT

State Long-Term Care Ombudsman
Elderly Services Division
25 Sigourney Street, 10th Floor
Hartford, Connecticut 06106-5033
(806) 247-4080
http://www.ct.gov/LTCOP/site/default.asp

Director, State of Connecticut Department of Public
Health

410 Capitol Avenue, Mail Slot 12HSR
P.O. Box 340308
Hartford, Connecticut 06134
(860) 509-7406

DELAWARE

State Long-Term Care Ombudsman
Division of Services for the Aging and Adults with
Physical Disabilities
Division of Aging
18 North Walnut Street
Milford, DE 19963
(302) 422-1386, (800) 223-9074
http://dhss.delaware.gov/dhss/main/ltcop.html

Director, Division of Long-Term Care Residents Protection
Delaware Department of Health and Social Services
3 Mill Road, Suite 308
Wilmington, Delaware 19806
(302) 577-6661
http://dhss.delaware.gov/dhss/main/contacts.htm

DISTRICT OF COLUMBIA

State Long-Term Care Ombudsman
Legal Counsel for the Elderly, AARP Foundation
601 E. Street N.W.
Washington, DC 20049
(202) 662-4933
http://www.theconsumervoice.org/

Director, Health Regulation Administration
Department of Health
899 N. Capitol Street, N.E.
Washington, DC 20002
(202) 442-5955
http://dchealth.dc.gov/doh/site/default.asp

FLORIDA

State Long-Term Care Ombudsman
LTC Ombudsman Counsel
Department of Elder Affairs, ADDGS
4040 Esplanade Way
Tallahassee, Florida 32399-7000
(850) 414-2000
http://ombudsman.myflorida.com/

Secretary, Long-Term Care Unit
Florida Agency for Health Care
2727 Mahan Drive
Tallahassee, Florida 32308
(850) 448-5861
http://ahca.myflorida.com/

GEORGIA

State Long-Term Care Ombudsman
Division of Aging Services

132 Mitchell Street
Atlanta, Georgia 30303-3176
(404) 730-0184
(888) 454-5826
http://www.georgiaombudsman.org/

Director, Office of Regulatory Service of Long-Term
   Care
Department of Human Resources
Two Peachtree Street N.W., Suite 31-447
Atlanta, Georgia 30303
(404) 657-5850
http://dhs.georgia.gov/portal/site/DHS/

HAWAII

State Long-Term Care Ombudsman
Executive Office on Aging
250 S. Hotel Street, Suite 107
Honolulu, Hawaii 96813-2831
(808) 586-0100
http://hawaii.gov/health/eoa/LTCO.html

Director, Office of Health Care Assurance
Department of Health
1250 Punchbowl Street
Honolulu, Hawaii 96813
(808) 586-4080
http://hawaii.gov/health/

IDAHO

State Long-Term Care Ombudsman
Commission on Aging
P.O. Box 83720
Boise, Idaho 837 06
(208) 334-2220
http://www.idahoaging.com/IdahoCommissionon
   Aging/ICOAProgramsandServices/Ombudsmen/
   tabid/134/Default.aspx

Director, Bureau of Facility Standards
P.O. Box 83720
Boise, Idaho 83720-0036
(208) 334-6626
http://www.healthandwelfare.idaho.gov/Medical/
   LicensingCertification/FacilityStandards/tabid/223/
   Default.aspx

ILLINOIS

State Long-Term Care Ombudsman
Illinois Department on Aging
421 E. Capitol Avenue, Springfield, Illinois 62701-
   1789
(217) 785-3143; in-state (800) 252-8966
http://www.state.il.us/aging/1abuselegal/ombuds.htm

Director, Office of Quality Assurance
Illinois Department of Public Health, ADDGS
525–535 W. Jefferson Street

Springfield, Illinois 62761-0001
(217) 782-4977
http://www.idph.state.il.us/

INDIANA

State Long-Term Care Ombudsman
Aging and Rehabilitation Services, ADDGS
P.O. Box 7083-W454
402 W. Washington Street, Room W-454
Indianapolis, Indiana 46207
(317) 232-7134
http://www.in.gov/fssa/da/3474.htm

Director, Bureau of Aging and In-Home Services
Mail Stop 21-10
P.O. Box 7083
402 W. Washington Street, Room W-454
Indianapolis, Indiana 46204-7083
(317) 232-7020
http://www.in.gov/fssa/ddrs/2872.htm

IOWA

State Long-Term Care Ombudsman
Department of Elder Affairs, ADDGS
200 Tenth Street, 3rd Floor
Clemens Building
Des Moines, Iowa 50309-3609
(515) 242-3328
http://www.aging.iowa.gov/advocacy/ombudsman.
   html

Executive Director, Health Facilities Division
Department of Inspections and Appeals
Lucas State Office Building
Des Moines, Iowa 50319-0083
(515) 281-7102
http://dia.iowa.gov/

KANSAS

State Long-Term Care Ombudsman
900 S.W. Tenth Avenue, Suite 1041
Topeka, Kansas 66612-1616
(877) 662-8362
http://armada.websitewelcome.com/~kansasom/

Secretary, Health Facilities
Landon State Office Building
1000 S.W. Jackson,
Topeka, Kansas 66612
(785) 296-1500
http://www.kdheks.gov/

KENTUCKY

State Long-Term Care Ombudsman
Office of Aging Services
275 E. Main Street
Frankfort, Kentucky 40621

(502) 564-6930
http://chfs.ky.gov/dail/kltcop.htm

Director, Licensing and Regulation
Office of the Inspector General
609 Wilkinson Blvd.
Frankfort, Kentucky 40601
(502) 564-1985
http://eppcoig.ky.gov/Pages/default.aspx

LOUISIANA

State Long-Term Care Ombudsman
Governor's Office of Elderly Affairs
P.O. Box 61
Baton Rouge, Louisiana 70821
(225) 342-7100; in-state (866) 632-0922
http://goea.louisiana.gov/index.cfm?md=pagebuilder
&tmp=home&pid=4&pnid=2&nid=15

Director, State of Louisiana Health Standards
P.O. Box 3767
Baton Rouge, Louisiana 70821-3767
(225) 342-0138
http://www.dhh.louisiana.gov/offices/?id=112

MAINE

State Long-Term Care Ombudsman
P.O. Box 128
Augusta, Maine 04332
(207) 621-1079
http://www.maineombudsman.org/

Director, Bureau of Medical Services
Division of Licensing and Certification
Department of Human Services, ADDGS
Bureau of Elder and Adult Services
32 Blossom Lane
11 State House Station
Augusta, Maine 04333-0011
(207) 287-9200
http://www.maine.gov/dhhs/oes/contact.htm

MARYLAND

State Long-Term Care Ombudsman
Maryland Department of Aging, ADDGS
301 W. Preston Street, Room 1007
Baltimore, Maryland 21201
(410) 767-1100
http://www.mdoa.state.md.us/senior.html

Secretary, Office of Health Care Quality
Spring Grove Hospital Center
BB Building
55 Wade Avenue
Baltimore, Maryland 21228
(410) 402-6000
http://www.springgrove.com/

MASSACHUSETTS

State Long-Term Care Ombudsman
Commonwealth of Massachusetts
Executive Office of Elder Affairs, ADDGS
One Ashburton Place, 5th Floor
Boston, Massachusetts 02108-1518
(617) 727-7750
http://www.mass.gov/?pageID=elderssubtopic&L=3&
L0=Home&L1=Service+Organizations+and+Advo
cates&L2=Long+Term+Care+Ombudsman&sid=
Eelders

Secretary, Licensure and Certification
Division of Health Care Quality
99 Chauncy Street
Boston, Massachusetts 02111
(617) 753-8000
http://www.mass.gov/dph/dhcq

MICHIGAN

State Long-Term Care Ombudsman
Citizens for Better Care
Suite 211 6105 W. Street Joseph Highway
Lansing, MI 48917
(517) 886-6797, Toll Free (800) 292-7852
http://www.michigan.gov/mdch/

Director, MDCIS Bureau of Health Systems
Division of Nursing Home Monitoring
Capitol View Building
201 Townsend Street
Lansing, MI 48913
(517) 373-3740
http://www.michigan.gov/mdch/0,1607,7-132-27417_
27655_27662---,00.html

MINNESOTA

State Long-Term Care Ombudsman
Office of Ombudsman for Older Minnesotans
Board on Aging, ADDGS
444 Lafayette Road
St. Paul, MN 55155
(651) 296-0382
http://www.dhs.state.mn.us/main/idcplg?IdcService=
GET_DYNAMIC_CONVERSION&Revision
SelectionMethod=LatestReleased&dDocName=id_
000269

Executive Secretary, Long-Term Care and Certification
Division of Facility and Provider Compliance
85 E. Seventh Place, Suite 300
St. Paul, Minnesota 57101
(651) 215-8701
http://www.health.state.mn.us/

MISSISSIPPI

State Long-Term Care Ombudsman
Division of Aging and Adult Services
750 N. State Street
Jackson, Mississippi 39202
(601) 359-4927
http://www.nursinghomepatientrights.com/Missis
    sippi_Nursing_Home_Abuse_Assistance.htm

Director, Licensure and Certification
35 East Woodrow Wilson Avenue
Jackson, Mississippi 39216
(601) 359-2629
http://msdh.ms.gov/msdhsite/_static/30,0,83.html

MISSOURI

State Long-Term Care Ombudsman
Department of Social Services, Division of Aging,
    ADDGS
P.O. Box 1337
Jefferson City, Missouri 65102
(573) 751-3082; (800) 309-3282
http://www.cmaaa.net/ombud.htm

Director, Division of Aging
615 Howerton Court
P.O. Box 1337
Jefferson City, Missouri 65109
(573) 751-6400
http://health.mo.gov/seniors/aaa/

MONTANA

State Long-Term Care Ombudsman
Office on Aging, Senior and Long-Term Care Divi-
    sion
Department of Public Health and Human Services
P.O. Box 4210
Helena, Montana 59604-4210
(406) 444-4676
http://www.dphhs.mt.gov/sltc/index.shtml

State Aging Coordinator, Quality Assurance Division
Department of Public Health and Human Services
2401 Colonial Drive
Helena, Montana 59620
(406) 444-2037
http://www.dphhs.mt.gov/

NEBRASKA

State Long-Term Care Ombudsman
Department of Health and Human Services, ADDGS
Division of Aging and Disability Services
P.O. Box 95026
Lincoln, Nebraska 68509-5026
(402) 471-2307
http://www.hhs.state.ne.us/ags/ltcombud.htm

Administrator, Regulation and Licensure
Credentialing Division, Department of Health and
    Human Services
301 Centennial Mall S.
P.O. Box 94986
Lincoln, Nebraska 68509-4986
(402) 471-3651
http://www.hhs.state.ne.us/crl/crlindex.htm

NEVADA

State Long-Term Care Ombudsman
Department of Human Resources, Division for Aging
    Services, ADDGS
340 N. Eleventh Street, Suite 203
Las Vegas, Nevada 89101
(702) 486-3545
http://www.nvaging.net/ltc.htm

Administrator, Bureau of Licensure and Certification
727 Fairview Drive Suite E
Carson City, Nevada 89701
(775) 684-1030
http://health.nv.gov/HCQC.htm

NEW HAMPSHIRE

State Long-Term Care Ombudsman
Health and Human Services
129 Pleasant Street
Concord, New Hampshire 03301-6505
(603) 271-4375
http://www.dhhs.nh.gov/oltco/index.htm

Director, Office of Program Support
Health Facilities Administration
Department of Health and Human Services
Division of Elderly and Adult Services, ADDGS
129 Pleasant Street
Concord, New Hampshire 03301-3857
(603) 271-4968
http://www.dhhs.nh.gov/dcbcs/beas/

NEW JERSEY

State Long-Term Care Ombudsman
Office of the Ombudsman for the Institutionalized
    Elderly
101 S. Broad Street CN807
Trenton, New Jersey 08625-0807
(609) 292-8016
http://www.state.nj.us/publicadvocate/seniors/elder/

Assistant Commissioner
Division of Long-Term Care Systems
New Jersey Department of Health Services
P.O. Box 360
Trenton, New Jersey 08625
(609) 292-7837
http://www.state.nj.us/health/

New Mexico

State Long-Term Care Ombudsman
State Agency on Aging, ADDGS
228 E. Palace Avenue
Santa Fe, New Mexico 87501
(505) 827-7640
http://www.nmaging.state.nm.us/Ombudsman_bu
reau.html

Director, Health Facilities Licensing and Certification
Bureau
525 Camino de los Marquez, Suite 2
Santa Fe, New Mexico 78501
(505) 476-9028
http://dhi.health.state.nm.us/HFLC/index.php

New York

State Long-Term Care Ombudsman
New York State Office for the Aging
Two Empire State Plaza
Albany, New York 12223-0001
(518) 408-1469
http://www.aging.ny.gov/

Executive Director, Office of Continuing Care
New York State Department of Health
166 Delaware Avenue
Delmar, New York 12054
(518) 478-1020
http://www.health.state.ny.us/

North Carolina

State Long-Term Care Ombudsman
Division of Aging
2101 Mail Service Center
Raleigh, North Carolina 27699-2101
(919) 733-8395

Director, Division of Facilities Services
Licensure and Certification Section
Department of Health and Human Services, ADDGS
2711 Mail Service Center
Raleigh, North Carolina 27699-2711
(919) 733-3983
http://www.dhhs.state.nc.us/aging/ombud.htm

North Dakota

State Long-Term Care Ombudsman
Department of Health and Human Services
Aging Services Division
1237 W Divide Ave Suite 6
Bismarck, North Dakota 58501
(701) 328-4617
http://www.nd.gov/dhs/services/adultsaging/ombuds
man.html

Director, Division of Health Facilities
North Dakota Department of Health

600 E. Boulevard Avenue
Bismarck, North Dakota 58505-0200
(701) 328-2352
http://www.ndhealth.gov/

Ohio

State Long-Term Care Ombudsman
Ohio Department of Aging
50 W. Broad Street, 9th Floor
Columbus, Ohio 43215-3363
(614) 466-1221; (800) 282-1206
http://www.aging.ohio.gov

Director, Licensure Program
Ohio Department of Health
246 N. High Street
Columbus, Ohio 43215-2412
(614) 466-7857
http://www.odh.ohio.gov/

Oklahoma

State Long-Term Care Ombudsman
Aging Services Division
Department of Human Services
2401 NW 23rd Street Suite 40
Oklahoma City, Oklahoma 73107
(405) 521-2327
http://www.okdhs.org/divisionsoffices/visd/asd/ltc/

Division Administrator, Special Health Services
Oklahoma State Health Department
1000 N.E. Tenth Street
Oklahoma City, Oklahoma 73117
(405) 271-6868
http://www.ok.gov/health/

Oregon

State Long-Term Care Ombudsman
3855 Wolverine N.E., Suite 6
Salem, Oregon 97305-1251
(800) 522-2602
http://www.oregon.gov/LTCO/index.shtml

Administrator, Long-Term Care Quality Section
Senior and Disabled Services Division
500 Summer Street N.E.
Salem, Oregon 97301
(503) 945-5767
http://www.oregon.gov/DHS/

Pennsylvania

State Long-Term Care Ombudsman
Pennsylvania Department of Aging
555 Walnut Street, 5th Floor
Harrisburg, Pennsylvania 17101-1919
(717) 783-7247
http://www.aging.state.pa.us

Secretary, Bureau of Facility Licensure and Certification
Division of Nursing Care Facilities
Pennsylvania Department of Health
P.O. Box 90
Harrisburg, Pennsylvania 17108
(717) 787-1816
www.health.state.pa.us

RHODE ISLAND

State Long-Term Care Ombudsman
Alliance for Better Long-Term Care
422 Post Road, Suite 204
Warwick, Rhode Island 02888
(401) 785-3340

Director, Rhode Island Department of Health
Division of Facilities Regulation
Department of Elderly Affairs, ADDGS
3 Capitol Hill, Room 306
Providence, Rhode Island 09908
(401) 222-4537
http://www.health.state.ri.us/

SOUTH CAROLINA

State Long-Term Care Ombudsman
Division on Aging
1301 Gervais St. Suite 350
Columbia, South Carolina 29201
(803) 734-9900
http://www.state.sc.us/dmh/ombud_program.htm

Office of Senior and Long-Term Care Services
Division of Health Licensing
Department of Health and Environmental Control
2600 Bull Street
Columbia, South Carolina 29201-8206
(803) 545-4205
http://www.scdhec.gov/

SOUTH DAKOTA

State Long-Term Care Ombudsman
Department of Social Services
Office of Adult Services and Aging
700 Governors Drive
Pierre, South Dakota 57501-2291
(605) 773-3656
http://www.state.sd.us/social/ASA/services/ombuds
  man.htm

Administrator, Licensure and Certification
South Dakota Department of Health
615 E. Fourth Street
Pierre, South Dakota 57501-1700
(605) 773-5273
http://doh.sd.gov/

TENNESSEE

State Long-Term Care Ombudsman
Commission on Aging, ADDGS
500 Deaderic Street, STE. 825
Nashville, Tennessee 37243
(615) 741-2056
http://www.tn.gov/comaging/ombudsman.html

Executive Director, Office of Health Licensure and
  Regulation
Division of Health Care Facilities
Tennessee Department of Health
426 Fifth Avenue N.
Cordell Hull Building, 1st Floor
Nashville, Tennessee 37247
(615) 741-7532
http://health.state.tn.us/

TEXAS

State Long-Term Care Ombudsman
Texas Department on Aging
P.O. Box 149030
Mail Code W250
Austin, Texas 78714
(512) 438-4265
http://www.dads.state.tx.us/news_info/ombudsman/
  index.html

Executive Director, Long-Term Care Regulatory
Mail Code E-342, Texas Department of Human Serv-
  ices, ADDGS
P.O. Box 149030
Austin, Texas 78714-9030
(512) 438-2633; in-state (800) 458-9858

UTAH

State Long-Term Care Ombudsman
Aging and Adult Services
195 North 1950 West
Salt Lake City, Utah 84116
(801) 538-3924
http://www.hsdaas.utah.gov/ombudsman/index.html

Director, Bureau of Licensing
Department of Health
P.O. Box 143101
Salt Lake City, Utah 84114
(801) 538-6406
http://health.utah.gov/

VERMONT

State Long-Term Care Ombudsman
Vermont Legal Aid, Inc.
P.O. Box 1367

264 N. Winooski Avenue
Burlington, Vermont 05402
(802) 863-5620
http://www.dail.state.vt.us/ltcinfo/ombudsman.html

Commissioner, Division of Licensing and Protection
Department of Aging and Disabilities, ADDGS
103 S. Main Street, Ladd Hall
Waterbury, Vermont 05671-2301
(802) 241-2401
http://dail.vermont.gov/

VIRGINIA

State Long-Term Care Ombudsman
24 E Cary Street, Suite 100
Richmond, Virginia 23219
(804) 565-1600
http://www.vda.virginia.gov/ombudsman.asp

Commissioner, Division of Long-Term Care Services
Center for Quality Health Care Services and Consumer Protection
Department for the Aging, ADDGS
Virginia State Department of Health
1600 Forest Avenue Suite 102
Richmond, Virginia 23229-5007
(804) 662-9333
http://www.arlingtonva.us/Departments/humanser
    vices/services/aging/HumanServicesServicesAging
    AgingDisability.aspx

WASHINGTON

State Long-Term Care Ombudsman
South King County Multi-Services Center
P.O. Box 23699
1200 S. 336th Street
Federal Way, Washington 98003
(253) 838-6810; in state (800) 422-1384
http://www.ltcop.org

Assistant Secretary, Residential Care Services
Department of Social and Health Services
P.O. Box 45050
1111 Washington St. S.E.
Olympia, Washington 98504-5050
(360) 725-2260
http://www.aasa.dshs.wa.gov/

WEST VIRGINIA

State Long-Term Care Ombudsman
West Virginia Bureau of Senior Services
Commission on Aging
1900 Kanawha Boulevard E.
Holly Grove Building 10
Charleston, West Virginia 25305-0160

(304) 558-3317
http://www.wvseniorservices.gov

Commissioner, Licensure and Certification
Office of Health Facilities
350 Capitol Street
Charleston, West Virginia 25301
(304) 558-1700
http://www.wvdhhr.org/bms

WISCONSIN

State Long-Term Care Ombudsman
Board on Aging and Long-Term Care
1402 Pankratz Street, Suite 111
Madison, Wisconsin 53704-4001
(608) 246-7014
http://www.dhs.wisconsin.gov/aging/boaltc/ltcom
    bud.htm

Director, Bureau of Quality Assurance
Department of Health and Family Services
Bureau of Aging and Long Term Care Resources,
    ADDGS
One W. Wilson Street,
Madison, Wisconsin, 53707
(608) 266-3840
http://www.dhs.wisconsin.gov/aging/

WYOMING

State Long-Term Care Ombudsman
Wyoming Long-Term Care Ombudsman Program
865 Gilchrist
P.O. Box 94
Wheatland, Wyoming 82201
(307) 322-5553
http://www.wyomingseniors.com/services/long-term-
    care-ombudsman

Administrator, Office of Health Quality
Department of Health
6101 Yellowstone Road Suite 400
Cheyenne, Wyoming 82002
(307) 777-7123
http://wdh.state.wy.us/

National Long Term Care Accreditation Agencies

Continuing Care Accreditation Commission
2519 Connecticut Avenue, NW
Washington, DC 20008-1520
(202) 783-2242
http://www.aahsa.org/
    Founded in 1985 and sponsored by the American Association of Homes & Services for the Aging, this is the nation's only accrediting body for continuing care retirement communities.

Joint Commission's Home Care Accreditation Program
Joint Commission on Accreditation of Healthcare Organizations
   ganizations
(630) 792-5000
http://www.jointcommission.org/

Joint Commission accreditation is widely recognized as an important seal of approval in the healthcare marketplace. Surveys are conducted by professionals with administrative and clinical experience in home care organization.

Index

References in ***bold italics*** indicate illustrations.

A2M 7
Abbeville Nursing Home, Abbeville, SC 355
The Abbey Care Center, St. Louis, MO 313
Abbey Delray South, Delray Beach, FL 221
Abbey Delray, Delray Beach, FL 221
Abbey Rehabilitation & Nursing Center, St. Petersburg, FL 227
Abbott Terrace Health Center, Waterbury, CT 217
Aberdeen Health & Rehabilitation, Aberdeen, SD 357
Abeta (A) 7, 20, 50, 54, 61, 150
Abeta 42 7
Abilene Convalescent Center, Abilene, TX 362
Abington of Glenview, Glenview, IL 249
Abington Place Health and Rehab Center, Little Rock, AR 194
ABSMC Summit Campus, Oakland, CA 202
Abstract reasoning 7
Acacia Park Nursing and Rehabilitation Center, Modesto, CA 201
Academy Manor, Andover, MA 293
Acadia Nursing & Rehab, Baton Rouge, LA 282
Acetylcholine 8, 71, 90, 91, 97, 101, 133; deficiency 8
Acetylcholinesterase 8–9, *36*, 118, 133, 170
Acetylcholinesterase inhibitors 8, 9–10, 56, 145, 154
Acetyl-L-carnitine 7–8, 61
Acquired immune deficiency syndrome (AIDS) 10, 100
Activation imaging 10
Activities of daily living 10
Activity therapy 11
Acupuncture 11
AD7C 11, 34
Adams County Nursing Center, Natchez, MS 308–9
Adams Lane Care Center, Zanesville, OH 342
Addison's disease 65
Adenosine triphosphate 7
Administration on Aging 11, 75
Adult day care 11

Advance directives 12, 75
Advanced Rehabilitation & Healthcare Center, Clearwater, FL 220
Adventist Care Centers-Courtland, Inc., Orlando, FL 226
Advocacy 12
Affect 12
Affective disorders 12
Afferent nerve fibers 12, 45
A.G. Rhodes Home Inc., Atlanta, GA 231
A.G. Rhodes Home Inc.— Cobb, Marietta, GA 235
A.G. Rhodes Home, Wesley Woods, Atlanta, GA 231
Age-associated memory impairment 12–3
Agency for Health Care Policy and Research 7
Agency of Healthcare Research and Quality 7
Aggression 13, 83, 139, 158
Aging 13, 161, 167, 171
Agitation 13, 17, 32, 40, 41, 56, 66, 174, 176
Agnosia 13–4, 64, 147
Agraphia 14
AIDS dementia complex 10
Aisen, Paul 14
Akathisia 14
Alameda Care Center, Burbank, CA 197
Alameda County Medical Center, San Leandro, CA 205
Alameda Healthcare and Wellness Center, Alameda, CA 196
Alameda Oaks Nursing Center, Corpus Christi, TX 364
Alamitos Belmont Rehabilitation Hospital, Long Beach, CA 200
Alamo Nursing Home, Kalamazoo, MI 302
Albany Care, Evanston, IL 248
Albany Health Care Inc., Albany, GA 231
Albert, Marilyn 389
Alcott Rehabilitation Hospital, Los Angeles, CA 200
Alden Alma Nelson Manor, Rockford, IL 254
Alden Des Plaines Rehabilitation & Healthcare, Des Plaines, IL 246

Alden Estates of Evanston, Evanston, IL 248
Alden-Lincoln Rehabilitation & Health Care Center, Inc., Chicago, IL 243
Alden Northmoor Rehabilitation & Healthcare, Chicago, IL 243
Alden Nursing Center–Lakeland, Chicago, IL 243
Alden Princeton Rehabilitation & Healthcare, Chicago, IL 243
Alden Terrace Convalescent Hospital, Los Angeles, CA 200–201
Alden Valley Ridge, Bloomingdale, IL 242
Alden Wentworth Rehab & Healthcare Center, Chicago, IL 243
Aldersgate Village Health Unit, Topeka, KS 277
Aledo Rehab & Healthcare Center, Aledo, IL 242
Alexandria Care Center, Alexandria, IN 256
Alexandria Care Center, Los Angeles, CA 201
Alexandria Manor, Bloomfield, CT 214
Alexia 14, 24
Alexian Brothers Lansdowne Village, Saint Louis, MO 313
Alexian Village of Milwaukee, Milwaukee, WI 383
Algona Good Samaritan Center, Algona, IA 265–6
Algona ManorCare Center, Algona IA 265
Alice Manor, Baltimore, MD 290
All-American Care of Little Rock, Little Rock, AR 194
All American Nursing Home, Chicago, IL 243–4
All Faith Pavilion, Chicago, IL 244
All Saint Healthcare Subacute, North Hollywood, CA 202
All Saints Catholic Nursing & Rehabilitation Center, Jacksonville, FL 223
All Saints Subacute and Rehab Center, San Leandro, CA 205
Allegent Health Immanuel Fontenelle Home, Omaha, NE 317
Allele 14

Allenbrooke Nursing & Rehabilitation Center, Memphis, TN 361
Alliance Good Samaritan Village, Alliance, NE 316
Alliance Nursing and Rehabilitation Center, El Monte, CA 198
Allied Services Skilled Nursing Center, Scranton, PA 351
Aloha Nursing & Rehabilitation Center, Kaneohe, HI 238–9
Alpha lipoic acid 14
Alpha Manor Nursing Home, Detroit, MI 299–300
Alpha secretase enzyme 14, *22*
Alpha synuclein 14, 129, 144
Alpine Care Center, LLC, Ruston, LA 287
Alpine Living Center, Thornton, CO 213
Altamaha Healthcare Center, Jesup, GA 234
Altercare of Bucyrus, Bucyrus, OH 334
Altercare of Navarre, Navarre, OH 340
Altercare of Wadsworth, Wadsworth, OH 342
Alternative medicine 14–5, 90
Altoona ManorCare Center, Altoona, IA 266
Aluminum 15, 76, 82, 119
Alvarado LTC Partners, Inc., Alvarado, TX 362–3
Alz–50 15
Alzheimer, Alois 15–6, 135
Alzheimer Research Forum 16, 395
Alzheimer's Association 16, 25, 42
Alzheimer's Disease Anti-inflammatory Prevential Trial (ADAPT) 16, 61
Alzheimer's Disease Assessment Scale Cognition Component (ADAS–Cog) 16
Alzheimer's Disease Centers of the NIA 16–7
Alzheimer's Disease Clinical Trials Database 17
Alzheimer's Disease Cooperative Study (ADCS) 17–8, 53
Alzheimer's Disease Cooperative Study–Clinical Global Impression of Change (ADCS–CGIC) 18
Alzheimer's Disease Demonstration Grants to States (ADDGS) Program 18
Alzheimer's Disease Education and Referral (ADEAR) Center 18
Alzheimer's Disease International 18
Alzheimer's Disease Neuroimaging Initiative 18–9
Alzheimer's Disease Research Program 19
Alzheimer's Living Center at Elim, Fresno, CA 199
Amara Healthcare & Rehabilitation, Augusta, GA 231
Ambassador Manor Nursing Center LLC, Tulsa, OK 344
Ambassador Nursing & Rehab Center, Chicago, IL 244
Ambassador Nursing & Rehabilitation, Detroit, MI 300
Amberwood Convalescent Hospital, Los Angeles, CA 201

Ambulation 19
Amelia Manor Nursing Home Inc., Lafayette, LA 285
American Association of Homes and Services for the Aging 19, 58
American Convalescent Center of Detroit, Detroit, MI 300
American Finnish Nursing Home, Lake Worth, FL 224
American Health Assistance Foundation 19
American Journal of Alzheimer's Disease 19
American Psychiatric Association 12, 64, 65, 67, 72
American River Care Center, Carmichael, CA 197
American Village, Indianapolis, IN 261
Americare Convalescent Center of Detroit, Detroit, MI 300
Amino Acids 19
Amnesia 30, 72
Ampakines 20, 109, 119
Ampalex *see* CX516
Amsterdam Nursing Home Corp., New York, NY 326
Amvid 20
Amy 117 20
Amygdaloid nucleus (amygdala) 20, *55, 115*
Amyloid 20
Amyloid angiopathy 20
Amyloid beta peptide 20, 105
Amyloid beta peptide antibody 20
Amyloid beta protein 20–1
Amyloid hypothesis 21, 22
Amyloid plaque formation 13, *22*
Amyloid plaques 22, *39*
Amyloid precursor protein (APP) 21, 22, 105
Amyloidosis 22
AN–1792 Vaccine 22
Anaheim Crest Nursing Center, Anaheim, CA 196
Anaheim Healthcare Center, LLC, Anaheim, CA 196
Anaheim Terrace Care Center, Anaheim, CA 196
Anavex 22–3
Anchor Lodge Nursing Home, Lorain, OH 338
The Anderson, Cincinnati, OH 335
Andover Village Retirement Community, Andover, OH 332
Andrew Residence, Minneapolis, MN 306
Andrus Gerontology Center 350
Aneta Parkview Health Center, Aneta, ND 330
Angels Care Center, Cannon Falls, MN 305
Angiography 23, 57, 69
Animal models 23
Ann Maria of Aurora Inc., Aurora, OH 332
Ann Pearl Nursing Facility, Kaneohe, HI 239
Anomia 23, 75
Anorexia 12, 23, 71, 170
Anosmia 23
Anoxia 117

Anthocyanins 23–4, 34
Antibodies 24
Anti-inflammatory drugs 24, 31, 56, 61, 76
Antioxidant therapy 18, 24, 82
Antioxidants 18
Anti-psychotic medications 29–30
Apache Junction Health Center, Apache Junction, AZ 187
Apathy 10, 11, 24, 132, 134, 145, 152, 153, 168
Aphasia 14, 24
Apoaequorin 24–5
APOE2 allele 25–6
APOE3 allele 25–6
APOE4 allele 25–6, 85
Apolipoprotein A 25
Apolipoprotein E 14, 82, 106
Apolipoprotein E genotype 26, 94
Apolipoprotein J *see* Clusterin
Apolipoproteins 26–7
Apollo Health & Rehabilitation Center, St. Petersburg, FL 227
Apoptosis 27, 43
Apoptosis Related Gene 27
Apostolic Christian Home of Eureka, Eureka, IL 248
Apostolic Christian Resthaven, Elgin, IL 247
Apostolic Christian Skyline, Peoria, Peoria, IL 253
APP *see* Amyloid precursor protein
Appearance 27
Appel, Stanley 391
Appetite 7, 23, 66, 158, 168
Apple Rehab Avon, Avon, CT 214
Apple Rehab Colchester, Colchester, CT 214
Apple Rehab Middletown, Middletown, CT 215
Apple Rehab Rocky Hill, Rocky Hill, CT 216
Apple Rehab Saybrook, Old Saybrook, CT 216
Applewood Living Center, Longmont, CO 212
Applewood Nursing Center, Woodhaven, MI 304
Apraxia 27, 60
Arachidonic acid 70–1
Arachnoid mater 27, *116*
Aransas Pass Nursing & Convalescent Center, Aransas Pass, TX 363
Arbor Hills Nursing Center, La Mesa, CA 200
Arbor Oaks Healthcare and Rehabilitation Center, Malvern, AR 194
The Arbor of Itasca, Itasca, IL 249–50
Arbor Place, Festus, MO 310–1
Arbor Springs Health & Rehab Center, LTD, Opelika, AL 186
Arbor Trace Health and Living, Richmond, IN 263–4
Arbor Trail Rehab & Skilled Nursing, Inverness, FL 223
Arbor View Rehabilitation & Wellness Center, Santa Monica, CA 205
The Arbors & The Pillars, Shelburne, VT 371
Arbors at Fairlawn, Fairlawn, OH 336–7

Arbors at Michigan City, Michigan City, IN 262
Arbors Care Center. Toms River. NJ 322
Arbour Healthcare Center, Chicago, IL 244
Archicortex 27
Archie Hendricks Senior Skilled Nursing Facility, Sells, AZ 191
Archstone Care Center, Chandler, AZ 188
Arden House Rehabilitation & Nursing Center, Hamden, CT 215
Arden Rehab and Health Center, Sacramento, CA 203
Ardmore on Main Care & Rehabilitation, Ardmore, TN 359
Arginine 134, 135
Aricept see Donepezil hydrochloride
Aristocrat Berea, Berea, OH 333
Aristocrat West Nursing Home, Cleveland, OH 335
Arizona State Veterans' Home — Phoenix, Phoenix, AZ 189
Arkansas Convalescent Center, Pine Bluff, AR 195
Arleigh Burke Pavilion, McLean, VA 374
Armenian Nursing & Rehabilitation, Boston, MA 293
Armstrong County Health Center, Kittanning, PA 350
Arrowhead Healthcare, Jonesboro, GA 234
Arsenic 65, 94, 105
Art therapy 27
Arthur B Hodges Center, Charleston, WV 379
Artman Community, Ambler, PA 347–8
Arvada Care and Rehabilitation Center, Arvada, CO 206–7
Asbury Health Center, Pittsburgh, PA 351
Asbury Park Nursing and Rehabilitation Center, Sacramento, CA 203
Ash Flat Convalescent Center, Ash Flat, AR 192
Ash Grove Healthcare Facility, Ash Grove, MO 309
Ashbrook Nursing Home, Scotch Plains, NJ 322
Ashby Care, Berkeley, CA 197
Ashford Hall, Irving, TX 366
Ashland Care Center, Ashland, NE 316
Ashley Health and Rehabilitation, Rogers, AR 195
Ashtabula County Nursing Home, Kingsville, OH 338
Ashton Court Care/Rehabilitation Center, Liberty, MO 312
Ashton Hall Nursing & Rehabilitation Center, Philadelphia, PA 351
Ashwaganda 27–8, 31
Aspartame 61, 135
Aspen Care Center, Ogden, UT 369
Aspen Living Center, Colorado Springs, CO 208
Aspen Park Health Care, Moscow, ID 240
Aspirin 28
Assisted living 28

Assisted living costs 28
Assisted living facility 28
The Assumption Village, North Lima, OH 340
Asta Care Center of Elgin, Elgin, IL 247–8
Asthana, Sanjay 391
Aston Park Health Care Center Inc., Asheville, NC 328
Astoria Park, Bridgeport, CT 214
Astoria Place Living & Rehab, Chicago, IL 244
Astrocytes 28–9, 88
At Home Assisted Living 29
Atapryl see Selegiline hydrochloride
Ataxia 29, 35, 45
Atherosclerosis 26, 29
Atlantic Memorial Healthcare Center, Long Beach, CA 200
Atlantic Shores Nursing & Rehabilitation, Melbourne, FL 224
Atria Briarcliff Village Health Center, Tyler, TX 368
The Atrium at Wayne, Wayne, NJ 323
Atrium Healthcare Center, Chicago, IL 244
Atrophy 29, 36
Attleboro Nursing & Rehabilitation center, Langhorne, PA 350–1
Auburn Hills Nursing & Rehabilitation Center, Mountain Home, AR 194–5
Auburn Manor, Chaska, MN 305
Auditory area of the brain 82
Augsburg Lutheran Home, Baltimore, MD 290
Augustana Chapel View Care Center, Hopkins, MN 306
Augustana Healthcare of Minneapolis, Minneapolis, MN 306
Aurora Care Center, Aurora, CO 207
Aurora Manor Special Care Center, Aurora, OH 332
Autoantibodies 30, 88, 92, 103, 117, 123
Autoimmune disease 30, 45, 96
Autoimmune encephalopathy 30
Autonomic nervous system 30
Autopsy 16, 17, 30, 141, 149, 180
Autumn Care of Norfolk, Norfolk, VA 374
Autumn Heights Health Care Center, Denver CO 209
Autumn Hills Health & Rehab Center, Demotte, IN 258
Autumn Meadows Healthcare, Linn, MO 312
Autumn Oaks Caring Center, Mountain Grove, MO 313
Autumn Ridge, Wabash, IN 265
Autumn Village, LLC, Worcester, MA 297
Autumnwood of Livonia, Livonia, MI 302
Avalon Care Center — Bountiful, Bountiful, UT 369
Avalon Care Center — Honolulu, Honolulu, HI 238
Avalon Care Center — Shadow Mountain, Scottsdale, AZ 190
Avalon Health and Rehabilitation Center — Tucson, Tucson, AZ 191

Avalon Place, Monroe, LA 285
Avamere at Three Fountains, Medford, OR 346
Avamere Court at Keizer, Keizer, OR 345
Avante at Boca Raton Inc., Boca Raton, FL 219
Avante at Inverness Inc., Inverness, FL 223
Avante at Lake Worth, Lake Worth, Fl 224
Avante at Wilson, Wilson, NC 330
Aventura Nursing Center, North Miami Beach, FL 226
Avera Eureka Health Care Center, Eureka, SD 358
Avera Prince of Peace, Sioux Falls, SD 359
Avera Rosebud Country Care Center, Gregory, SD 358
Avery Nursing Home, Hartford, CT 215
Avlosulfon see Dapsone
Avon Health & Rehabilitation, Avon, IN 257
Avon Health Center, Avon, CT 214
Avon Oaks Nursing Facility, Avon, OH 332
Axon 31, 46, 51
Axona 31
Ayurveda 31
Azalea Trace Nursing Center, Columbus, GA 232
Azalea Woods Rehabilitation & Nursing Center, LLC, Aiken, SC 355
Azalealand Nursing Home Inc., Savannah, GA 236
Azalia Gardens Nursing Center, Wiggins, MS 309
Azura of Lakewood, Lakewood, CO 211

Babinski's sign 31
BACE1 enzyme 31
Bacterial meningitis 65
Baisch Nursing Center, De Soto, MO 310
Baker Katz Nursing Home, Haverhill, MA 295
Bakersfield Healthcare Center, Bakersfield, CA 196
Balanced Budget Refinement Act 31
Balanced Care, Springfield, MO 244
Balboa Nursing & Rehabilitation, San Diego, CA 204
Ball Pavilion, Erie, PA 349
Ballard Nursing Center, Des Plaines, IL 246
Balmoral Home, Chicago, IL 244
Baltic Country Manor, Baltic, OH 332–3
Baltimore Longitudinal Study of Aging 23
Banner Boswell Rehabilitation Center, Sun City, AZ 191
Bannister House, Providence, RI 354
Baptist 31–2
Baptist Home Inc., Bismarck, ND 330
Baptist Homes of Western PA, Pittsburgh, PA 351–2
Baptist Manor, Pensacola, FL 227

Baptist Village — Sun Ridge, Surprise, AZ 191

Barbourville Health and Rehab Center, Barbourville, KY 279

Barclay Friends, West Chester, PA 353

Barfield Health Care, Guntersville, AL 184

Barn Hill Care Center, Newton, NJ 321

Barrington Terrace of Boynton Beach, Boynton Beach, FL 220

Barron Center, Portland, ME 289

Basal forebrain 32, *55*, *115*

Basal ganglia 32

Basal nuclei 32

Bashford East Health Care, Louisville, KY 280

Batavia Nursing & Convalescent Inn, Batavia, OH 333

Bath Manor Special Care Center, Akron, OH 331

Baton Rouge Health Care Center, Baton Rouge, LA 282

Baton Rouge Heritage House II, Baton Rouge, LA 282

Bay Center, Panama City, FL 226

Bay Crest Care Center, Torrance, CA 206

Bay Point Healthcare Center, Hayward, CA 199

Bay View Nursing & Rehabilitation Center, Alameda, CA 196

Bay Village of Sarasota, Sarasota, FL 228

Baya Pointe Nursing & Rehabilitation Center, Lake City, FL 223

Bayley Place, Cincinnati, OH 335

Baylor University 352

Bayou Chateau Nursing Center, Simmesport, LA 288

Bayshore Health Center, Duluth, MN 305

Bayside Manor, Pensacola, FL 227

Bayside Rehabilitation & Health Center, St. Petersburg, FL 227

Bayview Manor, Seattle, WA 377

Baywood Nursing Center, St. Petersburg, FL 227

Bazelon Center and Fund 23

Beachwood Point, Beachwood, OH 333

Beacon Manor, Indiana, PA 350

Beacon Shores Nursing & Rehabilitation, Virginia Beach, VA 375

Beartooth Manor, Columbus, MT 315

Beatitudes Campus, Phoenix, AZ 189

Beatrice Good Samaritan Center, Beatrice, NE 316

Beaumont at Bryn Mawr, Bryn Mawr, PA 348

Beaumont at University Campus, Worcester, MA 297

Beaumont Rehabilitation & Skilled Nursing Center, Westborough, MA 297

Beauvais Manor Healthcare & Rehab Center, St. Louis, MO 313

Beck Anxiety Inventory 32

Beck Depression Index (BDI) 32

The Becker—Shoup Center, Racine, WI 384

Becket House at New Concord, New Concord, OH 340

Bedford Hills, Bedford, NH 319

Beech Tree Manor, Jellico, TN 360–1

Beechnut Manor, Houston, TX 365

Behavior 24, 53, 72, 74, 80, 113–114, 129, 135, 146

Behavioral and Social Research Program 32

Behavioral Pathology in Alzheimer's Disease 32

Behavioral Rating Scale for Dementia 32

Behcet's syndrome 65

Bel Air Health & Rehab, Bel Air, ME 291

Bel-Arbor Health Care, Macon, GA 234

Belcourt Terrace Nursing Home, Nashville, TN 361–2

Bell Minor Home, Gainesville, GA 233

Bell Nursing Home, Belmont, OH 267

Bell Trace Health and Living Center, Bloomington, IN 257

Belle Maison Nursing Home, Hammond, LA 284

Belle Manor Nursing Home, New Carlisle, OH 340

Belle Meade Home, Greenville, KY 280

Belle Teche, New Iberia, LA 286

Belleaire Healthcare Center, Clearwater, FL 220–221

Belleview Valley Nursing Home, Belleview, MO 309

Bellevue Care Center, Bellevue, OH 333

Belmont Lodge Health Care Center, Pueblo, CO 212

Belmont Nursing & Rehabilitation Center, Madison, WI 382

Bel-Wood Nursing Home, Peoria, IL 253

Bender Terrace, Lubbock, TX 366

Benedictine Health Center of Minneapolis, Minneapolis, MN 320

Benedictine Living Center of Garrison, Garrison, ND 331

Beneva Lakes Healthcare & Rehab, Sarasota, FL 228

Benjamin Health Care Center, Boston, MA 293

Bennett, David 388

Bennett Hills Care & Rehabilitation Center, Gooding, ID 240

Bennington Health & Rehabilitation Center, Bennington, VT 371

Bennion Care Center, Salt Lake City, UT 370

Benson Heights Rehabilitation Center, Kent, WA 377

Bent County Memorial Nursing Home, Las Animas, CO 211

Benton Visual Retention Test 32–3

Benzodiazepines 163, 174

Berg, Leonard 33

Berkley East Convalescent Hospital, Santa Monica, CA 205

Berkley ManorCare Center, Denver CO 209

Berkley Valley Convalescent Hospital, Van Nuys, CA 206

Berkshire Manor, North Miami, FL 225

Berlin Health & Rehabilitation Center, Barre, VT 371

Bernice Nursing & Rehabilitation Center, Bernice, LA 283

Berrien Nursing Center, Nashville, GA 235

Bessie Burton Sullivan, Seattle, WA 377

Beta amyloid protein (BAP) 7, 14, 20, 21, *22*, 31, 33, 43, 102

Beta secretase (BACE) *22*, 33, 92

Beta 2 microglobulin 33

Beth Abraham Health Services, Bronx, NY 324

Beth Haven Nursing Home, Hannibal, MO 311

Beth Israel at Shalom Park, Aurora, CO 207

Beth Sholom Home of Eastern Virginia, Virginia Beach, VA 375

Beth Sholom Home of Virginia, Richmond, VA 374

Bethany at Silver Lake, Everett, WA 376

Bethany Healthplex, Lakewood, CO 211

Bethany Home, Fargo, ND 331

Bethany Home, Inc., Alexandria, MN 305

Bethany Lutheran Home, Council Bluffs, IA 266

Bethany Lutheran Home, Sioux Falls, SD 359

Bethany Lutheran Village, Dayton, OH 336

Bethany Manor, Story City, IA 271

Bethany Nursing Home, Canton, OH 334

Bethany Terrace Nursing Care, Morton Grove, IL 250

Bethel Care Center, St. Paul, Minnesota 307

Bethel Center, Arpin, WI 380

Bethel Lutheran Home Inc., Williston, ND 331

Bethel Lutheran Home, Madison, SD 358

Bethel Manor, Evanston, IN 258–9

Bethesda Care Center, Fremont, OH 337

Bethesda Dilworth Memorial Home, Saint Louis, MO 313

Bethesda Health & Rehab Center, Bethesda, ME 291

Bethesda Home, Hayward, CA 199

Bethesda South Gate, St. Louis, MO 313–4

Bethlehem Woods, Fort Wayne, IN 259

Betsy Ross Health Related Facility, Rome, NY 327

Betty Ann Nursing Center, Grove, OK 343

Betty Dare Good Samaritan Center, Alamogordo, NM 255

Beverly Healthcare Center, Bessemer, AL 183

Beverly Healthcare, Fair Hope, AL 184

Beverly Healthcare, Martinsville, VA 373–4

Beverly Healthcare — Hillview, Altoona, PA 347

Bezalel Nursing Home, Far Rockway, NY 325

Big Sandy Medical Center, Big Sandy, MT 315

Big Sky Care Center, Helena, MT 315

Big Springs Specialty Care Center, Huntsville, AL 185

Bill Nichols State Veterans Home, Alexander City, AL 183

Binswanger's disease 33–4

Birch View Nursing Center, Birch Tree, MO 309

Birchwood Nursing Center, Traverse City, MI 304

Birchwood Plaza Nursing Home, Chicago, IL 244

Birmingham Green Nursing Facility, Manassas, VA 373

Bishop Drumm Care Center, Johnston, IA 269

Bishop's Corner Skilled Nursing & Rehabilitation, West Hartford, CT 217

Bixby Manor Nursing Home, Bixby, OK 342

Black Mountain Center–Alzheimer's Unit, Black Mountain, NC 328

Bladder function 4; see also Incontinence

Blaine Manor, Hailey, ID 240

Blaire House of Worcester, Worcester, MA 298

Blaire House of Milford, Milford, MA 296

Blakeley Care Center, North Baltimore, OH 340

Blaylock, Russell, M.D. 79

Bleomycin hydrolase 34

Blessed, G. 34

Blessed Dementia Rating Scale 34

Blessed Test 34

Blevins Retirement & Care Center, McAlester, OK 343

Blood brain barrier 34

Blood pressure see Hypertension

Blood tests 34

Bloomfield Care Center, Bloomfield, IA 205

Bloomfield Health Care Center, Bloomfield, CT 214

Blossom Health Care Center, Rochester, NY 326

Blough Health Care Center, Bethlehem, PA 348

Blue Ridge East, Harrisburg, PA 350

Blue Ridge Healthcare Center, Raleigh, NC 329

Blue River Health & Rehabilitation, Kansas City, MO 311

Blue Valley Nursing Home, Hebron, NE 317

Blueberries 34

Bluegrass Care & Rehabilitation Center, Lexington, KY 280

Board-and-care homes 34–5

Boca Raton Rehabilitation Center, Boca Raton, FL 219–20

Bolingreen Nursing Center, Macon, GA 234

Bon Harbor Nursing & Rehabilitation Center, Owensboro, KY 281

Bon Secours—Maria Manor Nursing & Rehabilitation Center, St. Petersburg, FL 228

Bon Secours—Maryview Nursing Care Center, Suffolk, VA 375

Bonnie Bluejacket Memorial Nursing Home, Greybull, WY 385

Bonterra Nursing Center, East Point, GA 233

Booker T. Washington Nursing Center, Shreveport, LA 287

Borderview Manor Inc., Van Buren, ME 290

Boscobel Care and Rehab, Boscobel, WI 380

Boston Naming Test (BNT) 35

Boston University 97, 389

Boswell–Parker Nursing Center, Greensboro, GA 234

Boulder Manor Progressive Care Center, Boulder, CO 207

Boulevard Rehabilitation Center, Boynton Beach, FL 220

Boulevard Temple Care Center, Detroit, MI 300

Bourgeois, Michelle 116

Bovine spongiform encephalopathy (BSE) 35

Bowling Green Manor, Bowling Green, OH 333

Boyd Nursing & Rehabilitation Center, Ashland, KY 279

Boynton Beach Rehabilitation Center, Boynton Beach, FL 220

Bozeman Health & Rehabilitation Center, Bozeman, MT 315

BR12 mutations 63

Braak and Braak Staging 35, 131

Brac View Manor Health Care Facility, Euclid, OH 336

Braden River Care Center, Bradenton, FL 220

Bradford Guest Care, LLC, Shreveport, LA 287–8

Bradford Nursing Pavilion, Bradford, PA 348

Bradley Bay Health Center, Bay Village, OH 333

The Bradley Gardens, San Jacinto, CA 205

Bradley Healthcare & Rehabilitation Center, Cleveland, TN 359–60

Brahmi 31

Brain abscess 65

Brain anatomy 35, *36, 37*

Brain derived neurotrophic factor (BDNF) 35, 84, 108

Brain exercise 35

Brain imaging studies 35, 56

Brain in Alzheimer's disease 17, 35–6

Brain injuries 37, 44, 65, 93

Brain plasticity 35, 37, 114

Brain tumors 37–8

Brainstem 38

Brainstem Auditory Evoked Responses (BAER) 38

Braintree Manor Nursing & Rehabilitation, Braintree, MA 294

Brakeley Park Center, Phillipsburg, NJ 322

Brandon Woods at Alvamar, Lawrence, KS 275

Brandon Woods of Dartmouth, South Dartmouth, MA 297

Brandon Woods of New Bedford, New Bedford, MA 296

Brandywine Nursing & Rehabilitation Center, Wilmington, DE 218

Brandywyne Health Care Center, Winter Haven, FL 230

Brentwood Extended Care & Rehabilitation, Muskogee, OK 343–4

Brentwood North Nursing Rehabilitation & Special Care, Riverwoods, IL 254

Brentwood Rehabilitation & Nursing Center, Yarmouth, ME 290

Brethren Care Inc., Ashland, OH 332

Brewer Rehabilitation & Living Center, Brewer, ME 289

Brewster Health Center, Topeka, KS 277

Brian Center Health & Rehabilitation, Hendersonville, Hendersonville, NC 329

Brian Center Health & Retirement, Charlotte, NC 328

Brian Center Nursing Care–Yanceyville, Yanceyville, NC 330

Briarcliff Health Center, Texarkana, TX 368

Briarcliffe Manor, Johnston, RI 354

Briarleaf Nursing & Convalescent Center, Doylestown, PA 349

The Briarwood, Stow, OH 341

Briarwood Health Care Center, Denver, CO 209

Briarwood Health Care, Sacramento, CA 203

Briarwood Nursing and Rehabilitation, Little Rock, AR 194

Bridge at Bay Saint Joe, Port St. Joe, FL 227

Bridge Point Care & Rehabilitation Center, Florence, KY 280

Bridgepark Center for Rehabilitation & Nursing Services, Akron, OH 331

Bridgeport Health Care Center Inc., Bridgeport, CT 214

Bridgeport Manor, Bridgeport, CT 214

Bridgeview Estates, Twin Falls, ID 241

Bridgewood Health Care Center, Kansas City, MO 311

Brief Cognitive Rating Scale 39, 90

Brier Oak on Sunset, Los Angeles, CA 201

Bright Glade Convalescent Center, Memphis, TN 361

Bright light therapy 39–40

Brighton at Ambler, Ambler, PA 348

Brighton Convalescent Center, Pasadena, CA 202

Brighton Gardens of Sun City, Sun City, AZ 191
Brighton Place—East, Spring Valley, CA 205
Brighton Place—San Diego, San Diego, CA 204
Brighton Ridge Nursing Center, Eureka Springs, AR 193
Brightview Care Center, Inc., Chicago, IL 244
Britany Manor, Midland, MI 302
Britthaven of Bowling Green, Bowling Green, KY 279
Britthaven of New Bern, New Bern, NC 329
Britthaven of Piedmont, Albemarle, NC 328
Broadlawn Manor Nursing & Rehabilitation center, Amityville, NY 324
Broadview Health Center, Columbus, OH 335
Broca's aphasia 24, 40
Broca's area 40
Brodmann's area 82
Bronzeville Park Nursing & Living Center, Chicago, IL 244
Brookhaven Medical Care Facility, Muskegon, MI 303
Brooking Park, Chesterfield, MO 310
Brooklyn Center for Rehabilitation & Residential Care, Brooklyn, NY 325
Brookshire House, Denver, CO 209
Brookside Care Center, Kenosha, WI 382
Brookside Health and Rehabilitation Center, Little Rock, AR 194
Brookside Inn, Castle Rock, CO 208
Brooksville Healthcare Center, Brooksville, FL 220
Broomall Presbyterian Village, Broomall, PA 348
Bruce McCandless Colorado State Veterans Nursing Center, Florence, CO 210
Bryan County Health & Rehabilitation Center, Richmond Hill, GA 235
Bryn Mawr Healthcare Center, Minneapolis, MN 306
Bryn Mawr Terrace Convalescent Center, Bryn Mawr, PA 348
Brynwood Center, Monticello, FL 225
Buck's Hill Nursing & Rehabilitation, Waterbury, CT 217
Buckingham Pavilion, Chicago, IL 244
Buckner Villa Siesta Home, Austin, TX 363
Budd Terrace Intermediate Care Home, Atlanta, GA 231
Buena Vida Nursing and Rehabilitation Odessa, Odessa, TX 367
Buena Vista Care Center, Anaheim, CA 196
Burbank Healthcare and Rehab, Burbank, CA 197
Burcham Hills Retirement Center II, East Lansing, MI 300
Burgin Nursing Manor, Olney, IL 252–3

Burkeville Piedmont Geriatric Hospital, Burkeville, VA 372
Burlington Health & Rehabilitation, Burlington, VT 371
Buschke-Fuhl selective Reminding Test 32
Bush, Ashley 50
Busipirone 40
Butterfield Trail Village, Fayetteville, AR 193
Byron Health Care Center, Fort Wayne, IN 259

Cabrini Center for Nursing and Rehab, New York, NY 325
CADASIL 40, 69
Caffeine 41
Calcium 41, 77, 90, 102, 120
Calcium channel blockers 41
Calhoun County Medical Care Facility, Battle Creek, MI 299
California Gardens Nursing & Rehab, Chicago, IL 244
California Healthcare and Rehabilitation, Van Nuys, CA 206
California Home for the Aged, Fresno, CA 199
California Pacific Medical Center—California East Campus, San Francisco, CA 204
California Special Care Center, La Mesa, CA 200
California Verbal Learning Tests 41
Callaway Nursing Home, Sulphur, OK 344
Calvary Fellowship Homes, Lancaster, PA 350
Cambridge Care Center Inc., Lakewood, CO 211
Cambridge Examination for Mental Disorders of the Elderly (CAMDEX) 41
Cambridge Health & Rehabilitation Center, Cambridge, OH 334
Cambridge Neuropsychological Test Automated Battery (CANTAB) 41
Cambridge North Health Care Center, Clawson, MI 299
Cambridge Place, Lexington, KY 280
Cambridge Rehabilitation & Nursing Home, Cambridge, MA 294
Camelia Gardens of Life Care, Thomasville, GA 237
Camelia Health Care Center, Aurora, CO 207
Camellia Gardens, Pasadena Gardens, CA 202
Camelot Hall Convalescent Center, Livonia, MI 302
Camelot Leisure Living, Ferriday, LA 283
Camelot Nursing and Rehabilitation Center, Farmington, MO 310
Canadian Study of Health and Aging (CSHA) 41
Canon Lodge Care Center, Canon City, CO 207
Canterbury Manor, Waterloo, IL 255
Canterbury Place, Pittsburgh, PA 352
Canterbury Towers, Tampa, FL 229

Canterbury Villa of Alliance, Alliance, OH 332
Canton Health Care Center, Canton, OH 334
Canyon Oaks Nursing and Rehabilitation Center, Canoga Park, CA 197
Capases 27
Capital Care Center, Springfield, IL 255
Capitol Care Center, Boise, ID 239
Capitol Healthcare Services, Dover, DE 218
Capitol Hill Healthcare Center, Montgomery, AL 185–6
Capitol Hill Nursing Center, Washington, DC 219
Capitol House Nursing & Rehab Center, Baton Rouge, LA 282
Capri at the Pointe Rehab, Phoenix, AZ 189
Carbamazepine 41
Carbon monoxide 64, 65
Cardiac failure 64
Cardinal Nursing & Rehabilitation Center, South Bend, IN 264
Cardiopulmonary resuscitation 12, 70, 107
Care and Rehabilitation at Glacier Hills, Ann Arbor, MI 298
Care Center at Jacksonville, Jacksonville, IL 250
Care Center at Kelsey Creek, Bellevue, WA 375
Care Manor, Mountain Home, AR 195
Care Pavilion of Walnut Park, Philadelphia, PA 351
Care with Dignity Convalescent Hospital, San Diego, CA 204
Careage of Clarion, Clarion, IA 266
Careage of Fort Dodge, Fort Dodge, IA 268
Careage of Newton, Newton, IA 270
Caregiver Bill of Rights 42
Caregiver resources 42
Caregiver training 42
Caregivers 18, 32, 42
Caribou Nursing Home, Caribou, ME 289
Caring House, Sacaton, AZ 190
Carleton-Willard Village Nursing Center, Bedford, MA 293
Carlinville Rehab & Healthcare, Carlinville, IL 243
Carlisle Manor Health Care, Carlisle, OH 334
Carlton at the Lake, Chicago, IL 244
Carlyle House Inc., Framingham, MA 295
Carmel Hills Care Center, Monterey, CA 202
Carmichael Care and Rehabilitation Center, Carmichael, CA 197
Carnegie Gardens Nursing Center, Melbourne, FL 224
Carnitine see Acetyl-L-carnitine
Caroline Kline Galland Home, Seattle, WA 377
Carolyn Boone Lewis Healthcare Center, Washington, DC 219
Carriage Hill Bethesda, Bethesda, ME 291

Carriage Inn of Dayton, Dayton, OH 336

Carriage Square Health Care Center Inc., Saint Joseph, MO 313

Carrington Park Nursing Home, Ashtabula, OH 332

Carrington Place Nursing & Rehabilitation Center, St. Petersburg, FL 228

Carroll Health Care Center, Carrollton, OH 334

Carroll Manor Nursing & Rehabilitation, Washington, DC 219

Carrollton Manor, Carrollton, GA 232

Carrollton Nursing & Rehabilitation Center, Carrollton, GA 232

Carrollwood Care Center, Tampa, FL 229

Casa De Oro Care Center, Las Cruces, NM 324

Casa Mora Rehabilitation & Extended Care, Bradenton, FL 220

Casa Real Health Care Center, Santa Fe, NM 324

Cascade View Nursing & Alzheimer's Care Center, Bend, OR 345

Case Western University 351

Casein kinase–1 (CK–1) 43

Caspase inhibitors 43

Caspases 43

Castle Manor, Garland, TX 365

Castle Rock Care Center, Castle Rock, CO 208

Catalina Health Care Center, Tucson, AZ 191

Catecholamines 43

Catered Manor Nursing Center, Long Beach, CA 200

Cathedral Gerontology Center, Jacksonville, FL 223

Cathepsin D inhibitors 43

Catholic Eldercare on Main, Minneapolis, MN 306

Catholic Memorial Home, Fall River, MA 294

Caton Manor, Baltimore, MD 290

Catonsville Commons, Catonsville, MD 291

Causes of Alzheimer's Disease 43

CC Young Memorial Home–Young Health Center, Dallas, TX 364

Cedar Crest Nursing & Rehabilitation Center, Sunnyvale, CA 206

Cedar Falls Health Care Center, Cedar Falls, IA 266

Cedar Falls Lutheran Home, Cedar Falls, IA 266

Cedar Hill Health Care Center, Windsor, VT 371

Cedar Hills Healthcare Center, Jacksonville, FL 223

Cedar Lake Healthcare, West Bend, WI 385

Cedar Ridge Center for Health Care & Rehabilitation, Skowhegan, ME 289

Cedar Wood Villa, Red Lodge, MT 316

Cedarbrook Nursing Home, Allentown, PA 347

Cedarcrest Manor, Washington, MO 315

Cedarglen Healthcare, Danvers, MA 294

The Cedars Inc., McPherson, KS 275

Cedars of Lebanon, Lebanon, OH 338

Cedarwood Health Care Center, Inc., Colorado Springs, CO 208

Celecoxib 16

Cells 43

Centella asiatica 43–4

Centennial Health Care Center, Greeley, CO 211

Center for Extended Care at Amherst, Amherst, MA 293

Center for Mental Health Services (CMHS) 44

Center for Nursing & Rehabilitation Inc., Brooklyn, NY 325

Center Home Hispanic Elderly, Chicago, IL 244

Centers for Medicare & Medicaid Services 44

Centracare Health System Melrose Health Villa, CC, Melrose, MN 306

Central Gardens, San Francisco, CA 204

Central nervous system (CNS) 8, 20, 23, 24, 28, 29, 37, 38

Central Oklahoma Christian Home, Oklahoma City, OK 344

Central sulcus 44

Centre Crest, Bellefonte, PA 348

Centrophenoxine 44–5

Centura Health Care Center at Centennial, Colorado Springs, CO 208

Centura Health Namaste Alzheimer Center, Colorado Springs, CO 208

Centura Health Pavilion at Villa Pueblo, Pueblo, CO 212

Centura Health Progressive Care Center, Canon City, CO 207

Century Oak Care Center, Middleburg Heights, OH 339

CERAD 108

CERE110 45

Cerebellar ataxia 45

Cerebellar disease 73, 139

Cerebellum 45, 49

Cerebral atrophy 45

Cerebral blood flow studies 10, 45, 162

Cerebral blood vessels 45, 46, 47

Cerebral circulation 45

Cerebral cortex 45–6, 49, 55

Cerebral hemispheres 36, 47, 48

Cerebral ischemia 48

Cerebral thrombosis 48

Cerebrolysin 48

Cerebrospinal fluid (CSF) 7, 48–9

Cerebrovascular disease 49

Cerebrovascular system 49

Cerebrum 49

Cerenity Care Center on Humboldt, St. Paul, Minnesota 307

Certificate in Dementia Care 49

Chalet Village Health & Rehab, Berne, IN 257

Champaign-Urbana Rehabilitation Center, Savoy, IL 255

Chandler Convalescent Hospital, North Hollywood, CA 202

Chandler Hall Health Services, Newton, PA 351

Chapel Hill Community, Canal Fulton, OH 334

Chapel Pointe at Carlisle, Carlisle, PA 348

Chapin Hill at Red Bank, Red Bank, NJ 322

Chariton Park Healthcare Center, Salisbury, MO 314

Charlene Manor Extended Care Facility, Greenfield, MA 295

Charlesgate Nursing Center, Providence, RI 354

Charleston Manor Skilled Nursing Facility by Americare, Charleston, MO 310

Charlottesville Health & Rehabilitation Center, Charlottesville, VA 372

Charlwell House Skilled Nursing Facility, Norwood, MA 296–7

Chase Care Center, El Cajon, CA 198

Chateau at Moorings Park, Naples, FL 225

Chateau Center, Willowsbrook, IL 256

Chateau De Notre Dame, New Orleans, LA 286

Chateau Terrebonne Healthcare, Houma, LA 284

Chatsworth Health Care Center, Chatsworth, GA 232

Cheboygan Memorial LTC, Cheboygan, MI 299

Chelation therapy 14, 50

Chelsea Jewish Nursing Home, Chelsea, MA 294

Chelsea Place Care Center, Hartford, CT 215

Chelsea Retirement Community, Chelsea, MI 299

Cheltenham Nursing & Rehabilitation Center, Philadelphia, PA 351

Chenal Heights Nursing and Rehabilitation, Little Rock, AR 194

Chenal Rehabilitation and Health Care Center, Little Rock, AR 194

Cherokee County Nursing Home, Centre, AL 184

Cherokee Village Assisted Living, Centre, AL 184

Cherreelynn Health Care Center, Littleton, CO 211

Cherry Creek Nursing Center, Aurora, CO 207

Cherry Hills Healthcare Center, Englewood, CO 210

Cherry Lane Nursing Center, Laurel, MD 292

Cherry Ridge at Emmett Care & Rehab, Emmett, ID 239–40

Cherry Village, Great Bend, KS 273

Cherry Wood Rehabilitation at Mount Tabor, Portland, OR 345

Cherrydale Health & Rehabilitation Center, Arlington, VA 372

Cherryvale Care Center, Cherryvale, KS 272

Chesapeake Woods Center, Cambridge, MD 291

Cheshire House Health Care Facility

& Rehabilitation Center, Waterbury, CT 217

Chester River Manor, Chestertown, MD 291

Chesterfield County Health Center Commission, Chesterfield, VA 372

Cheyenne Mountain Care & Rehabilitation Center, Colorado Springs, CO 208

Chicago Ridge Nursing Center, Chicago Ridge, IL 246

Chicagoland Christian Village, Crown Point, IN 258

Chino Valley Health Care Center, Pomona, CA 203

Chisolm Trail Living & Rehabilitation Center, Lockhart, TX 366

Chlamydia pneumoniae 50

Chlorpromazine 50

Cholesterol 50

Cholesterol lowering drugs 18, 54, 174

Choline 50

Choline acetyltransferase *9*, 51

Cholinergic basal forebrain 50

Cholinergic deficit 69, 163

Cholinergic hypothesis 50

Cholinergic neurons 50

Cholinergic synapses 50

Cholinergic system 51

Cholinesterase 9, 51

Cholinesterase inhibitors *see* Acetylcholinesterase inhibitors

Chorea 51

Choroid plexus 51

Christian City Convalescent Center, Union City, GA 237

Christian Health Care Center, Corbin, KY 279

Christian Health Care Center, Lynden, WA 377

Christian Health Care Center, Wyckoff, NJ 323

Christian Health Center, Louisville, KY 280

Christian Healthcare of Springfield West, Springfield, MO 314

Christian Nursing Home, Lincoln, IL 251

Christian Park Village, Escanaba, MI 300

Christian Rest Home Association, Grand Rapids, MI 301

Christopher East Health Care Center, Louisville, KY 280

Christopher House, Wheat Ridge, CO 213

Christopher House, Worcester, MA 298

Christus Saint Joseph, Monroe, LA 285

Christus St. Joseph Villa, Salt Lake City, UT 370

Chromosome 1 51, 74, 84

Chromosome 2 20

Chromosome 10 51

Chromosome 12 106

Chromosome 14 52, 74, 84

Chromosome 17 82

Chromosome 19 52, 106

Chromosome 21 33, 52, 72, 73, 84

Chromosomes 51, 84

Chui, Helena 388

Chula Vista Care Center, Mesa, AZ 188

Chulio Hills Health & Rehab, Rome, GA 236

Circadian rhythm 52

Citadel Care Center, Mesa, AZ 188

Citicoline 52

City of Oaks Health & Rehab, Raleigh, NC 329

Claiborne & Hughes Health Center, Franklin, TN 360

The Clairmont Longview, Longview, TX 366

Clairmont Nursing and Rehab, Eau Claire, WI 381

Clara Baldwin Stocker Home, West Covina, CA 206

Clara Maass Medical Center, Belleville, NJ 320

The Claremont, Eau Claire, WI 340

Claremont Beaumont LP, Beaumont, TX 363

Claremont ManorCare Center, Claremont, CA 197

Claremont Nursing & Rehabilitation Center, Carlisle, PA 348

Claremont Rehabilitation & Living Center, Buffalo Grove, IL 243

Clarewood House Extended Care Center, Houston, TX 365

Claridge Healthcare Center, Lake Bluff, IL 250

Claridge House Nursing Center, North Miami, FL 225

Clark-Lindsey Village, Urbana, IL 255

Clark Manor Convalescent Center, Chicago, IL 244

Clark Retirement Community, Grand Rapids, MI 301

Clement Manor Health Care, Greenfield, WI 381

Clermont Park Skilled Nursing, Denver, CO 209

Cleveland Care & Rehabilitation, Cleveland, TN 360

Cleveland Scale for Activities of Daily Living 52

Clifford Chester Sims State Veterans Home, Panama City, FL 226

Clinical Dementia Rating Scale (CDRS) 52

Clinical Global Impression (CGI) 53

Clinical Global Impression of Change Scale (CGIC) 53

Clinical trials 53, 74, 81

Clinician Interview Based Impression of Change (CIBI) 53

Clinician Interview Based Impression of Change with Caregiver Input (CIBIC +) 53–4

Clioquinol 54

Clock Draw Test 54

Clozapine 54

Clusterin 54

Coastal Health & Rehabilitation, Daytona Beach, FL 221

Coastal Manor, Yarmouth, ME 290

Cobblestone Crossings, Terre Haute, IN 264

Cochrane Dementia Group Registry of Clinical Trials 54

Coenzyme Q-10 54–5, 98

Coexisting illness 54

Cogburn Health & Rehabilitation, Inc., Mobile, AL 185

Cognex *see* Tacrine hydrochloride

Cognision System 55

Cognitive ability 55

Cognitive assessment 55–6

Cognitive defects 83, 121

Cognitive impairment 56; *see also* Mild cognitive impairment

Cognitive reserve 56

Cohen-Mansfield Agitation Inventory (CMAI) 56

Coleman, Paul 390

College Hill Nursing, Wichita, KS 278

Collingswood Nursing & Rehabilitation Center, Rockville, MD 292

Colonial Care Center, Long Beach, CA 160

Colonial Columns Health Care Center, Colorado Springs, CO 208

Colonial Health Care Services, Superior, WI 384

Colonial ManorCare, Bowling Green, KY 279

Colonial ManorCare Center, New Braunfels, TX 367

Colonial Manor Guest House, Rayville, LA 219

Colonial Manor Nursing & Rehabilitation Center, New Braunfels, TX 321

Colonial Manor Nursing & Rehabilitation Center, Rayville, LA 287

Colonial Manor II, Hollis, OK 343

Colonial Oaks Care Center, Bossier City, LA 283

Colonial Oaks Living Center, Metairie, LA 285

Colony House Nursing & Rehabilitation Center, Abingon, MA 293

Colorado State Veterans Home — Homelake, Monte Vista, CO 212

Colorado State Veterans Home — Walsenburg, Walsenburg, CO 213

Colorado State Veterans Home at Fitzsimmons, Aurora, CO 207

Colorado State Veterans Nursing Home Walsenburg, Walsenburg, CO 213

Columbia Care Center, Scappoose, OR 346

Columbia Lutheran Home, Seattle, WA 377

Columbia University 56, 171, 390

Columbia University Scale of Psychopathology in Alzheimer's disease (CUSPAD) 56

Columbia View Care Center, Cathlamet, WA 376

Columbine ManorCare Center, Salida, CO 213

Columbus Alzheimer Care Center, Columbus, OH 335

Columbus Health and Rehab Center, Columbus, IN 257

Combativeness 56

Combination therapy 56

Commissures 56

The Commons, Enid, OK 343

Commons at Orlando Lutheran Towers, Orlando, FL 226
Commonwealth Health & Rehab Center, Fairfax, VA 373
Communication 56-7
Community Care, Chicago, IL 244
Community Convalescent Hospital of La Mesa, La Mesa, CA 200
Community Healthcare Center, Marion, OH 339
Community Hospital of San Bernardino, San Bernardino, CA 204
Community Northview Care Center, Anderson, IN 256
Community Nursing & Rehabilitation, Indianapolis, IN 261
Community Parkview Care Center, Elwood, IN 258
Community Skilled Nursing Centre of Warren, Warren, OH 342
Community Springs Healthcare Facility, El Dorado Springs, MO 310
Compere's Nursing Home, Jackson, MS 308
Competence 56
Complement 56
Comprehensive Healthcare of Clearwater, Clearwater, FL 221
Computed axial tomography (CAT scan) 56
Computed tomography (CT scan) 56
Concord Care Center of Toledo, Toledo, OH 341
Concord Healthcare & Rehabilitation, Lakewood, NJ 321
Concord Nursing and Rehab, Oak Lawn, IL 252
Concordia at Rebecca Residence, Allison Park, PA 347
Conestoga View, Lancaster, PA 350
Confrontations 57-8
Confusion Assessment Method Diagnostic Algorithm (CAM) 45
Consciousness 58, 167
Consolata Home, New Iberia, LA 286
Consortium to Establish a Registry for Alzheimer's disease (CERAD) 45, 89
Constructional praxis 58
Consulate Healthcare of Kissimmee, Kissimmee, FL 223
Consulate Healthcare of Lakeland, Lakeland, FL 224
Consulate Healthcare of Melbourne, Melbourne, FL 225
Consulate Healthcare of North Fort Meyers, Fort Meyers, FL 222
Consulate Healthcare of Sarasota, Sarasota, FL 228
Consulate Healthcare at West Altamonte, Altamonte Springs, FL 219
Consulate Healthcare of West Palm Beach, West Palm Beach, FL 229
Continuing Care Accreditation Commission 58
Continuing Care Communities 58-9
Continuum of Care 59
Convalescent Center of Honolulu, Honolulu, HI 238

Cook Health Care, Youngstown, AZ 192
Coos County Nursing Hospital, West Stewartstown, NH 319
Copper 50, 59, 77, 82
Copper Mountain Inn, Globe, AZ 188
Copper Ridge Health Care, West Jordan, UT 370
Coral Reef Nursing & Rehabilitation Center, Miami, FL 225
Corbin Nursing Home, Corbin, KY 279
Cori Manor Skilled & Residential Center, Fenton, MO 310
Corinthian Gardens Health Care Center, Bakersfield, CA 196
Cornell Scale for Depression 47
Corner Brook Place, Kansas City, MO 311
Coronado Healthcare Center, Phoenix, AZ 189
Coronado Nursing Center, Abilene, TX 362
Corpus callosum *48*, *49*, 56, 59
Cortex 59
Cortex Pharmaceuticals 61
Cortical atrophy 35, 127, 147
Corticosteroids *see* Prednisone
Cortisol 63
Cortland Healthcare Center, Cortland, OH 336
Cortlandt Nursing Care Center Inc., Cortlandt Manor, NY 325
Corvallis Manor, Corvallis, OR 345
Cost of care 60
Cotman, Carl 387
Cottage of the Shoals Care & Rehabilitation Center, Tuscumbia, AL 186
Cottonwood Canyon Healthcare Center, El Cajon, CA 198
Cottonwood Nursing & Rehabilitation, LP, Denton, TX 364
Coulee Community Hospital, Grand Coulee, WA 376
Council Grove Healthcare, Council Grove, KS 272
Country Care Plex, Giddings, TX 365
Country Club Center II, Mount Vernon, OH 339
Country Club Retirement Center, Ashtabula, OH 332
Country Hills Health Center, El Cajon, CA 198
Country Lawn Nursing Home, Navarre, OH 340
Country View, Waterloo, IA 272
Country Villa Hacienda Healthcare, San Bernardino, CA 204
Country Villa La Mesa Healthcare Center, La Mesa, CA 200
Country Villa Mar Vista Nursing Center, Los Angeles, CA 201
Country Villa Merced Nursing & Rehabilitation Center, Merced, CA 201
Country Villa Modesto Nursing & Rehabilitation Center, Modesto, CA 201
Country Villa Park Avenue Nursing

and Health Center, Pomona, CA 203
Country Villa Plaza, Santa Ana, CA 205
County Villa West Covina Healthcare Center, West Covina, CA 206
Countryside Manor, Stokesdale, NC 329
Court House Manor, Washington Court House, OH 342
Courtland Acres Nursing Home, Thomas, WV 380
Courtland Gardens Health Center, Stamford, CT 216
Courtland Healthcare Center Fairfax Nursing Home, Berwyn, IL 242
Courtland Manor Nursing & Convalescent Home, Dover, DE 218
Courtland Manor Nursing & Rehabilitation Center, Baltimore, ND 290
Courtland Rehabilitation & Living Center, Ellsworth, ME 289
Courtlands of Orlando Rehabilitation & Healthcare Center, Orlando, FL 226
Courtyard Healthcare Center Fairfax Nursing Home, Inc., Berwyn, IL 242
Courtyard Healthcare Center, Goshen, IN 260
Courtyard Manor, Lafayette, LA 285
Courtyard of Natchitoches, Natchitoches, LA 286
Courtyards at Fort Worth, Fort Worth, TX 365
Covenant Nursing Home, New Orleans, LA 286
Covenant Village Care Center, Plantation, FL 227
Coventry Meadows, Fort Wayne, IN 260
Coventry Skilled Nursing & Rehabilitation, Coventry, RI 354
Coyne Healthcare Center, Rockland, MA 297
Craighead Nursing Center, Jonesboro, AR 193
Cranbury Center, Monroe Township, NJ 321
The Crandon Nursing Home, Crandon, WI 381
Cranial bones 48
Cranial nerves 60
Cranium 60
Creek Care Center, Westminster, CO 213
Crescent ManorCare Centers, Bennington, VT 371
Crestview Health & Rehab Center, Atlanta, GA 231
Crestview Home Inc., Bethany, MO 309
Crestview Manor Healthcare, LTD, Waco, TX 368
Crestwood Healthcare, LLC, Florissant, MO 311
Crestwood Manor 112, Modesto, CA 201
Crete Manor, Crete, NE 317
Creutzfeldt-Jakob disease 60, 68, 75, 100

Cripple Creek Rehabilitation & Wellness Center, Cripple Creek, CO 209

Crista Senior Community, Seattle, WA 377

Critically attained threshold of cerebral hypoperfusion (CATCH) 60

Cross Landings Health & Rehab Center, Monticello, FL 225

Crowley Ridge Care Center, Dexter, MO 310

Crown Bay Nursing and Rehabilitation, Alameda, CA 196

Crowne Health Care of Mobile, Mobile, AL 185

Crowne Health Care of Montgomery, Montgomery, AL 186

Crying 66, 71

Crystal Care Center, Crystal, MN 305

Crystal Care Center of Mansfield, Mansfield, OH 338

Crystal Creek Health & Rehabilitation Center, Florissant, MO 311

Crystallin, Alpha B 60–1

Cueing 61

Cullman Health Care Center, Cullman, AL 184

Culpeper Healthcare Center, Culpeper, VA 372

Cultural variables 68

Cumbernauld Village, Winfield, KS 278

Curcumin 61

Cushing syndrome 65

Cuyahoga Falls Country Place, Cuyahoga Falls, OH 336

CX516 (Ampalex) 61

CX1632 61–2

Cyclin-dependent kinase 5 (cdk5) 104

Cyclooxygenase enzymes 24, 62

Cyclooxygenase-2 62

Cyclooxygenase-2 inhibitor 62

Cypress Cove, Muscle Shoals, AL 186

Cypress Point Nursing & Rehabilitation Center, Bossier City, LA 283

Cytochrome-c oxidase 62

Cytokines 62, 101

Cytoskeletal abnormalities 62

D'Adamio, Luciano 62–3

Dallas Nursing & Rehabilitation Center, Dallas, TX 364

Danbury Health Care Center, Danbury, CT 214

Dandridge Burgundi Manor, Youngstown, OH 342

Daniel Health Care Complex, Fulton, MS 308

Dapsone 63

Darcy Hall of Life Care, West Palm Beach, FL 229

Daughters of Israel, West Orange, NJ 323

Daughters of Jacob Nursing Home Co Inc., Bronx, NY 324

Dauphin Manor, Harrisburg, PA 350

Davenport Good Samaritan Center, Davenport, IA 267

Davenport Lutheran Home, Davenport, IA 267

David Place, David City, NE 317

Davis County Hospital, Bloomfield, IA 266

Davis East, Pine Bluff, AR 195

Davis Life Care Center, Pine Bluff, AR 195

Dawson Pointe, LLC, Dawson Springs, KY 279–80

Daytona Beach Health & Rehabilitation Center, Daytona Beach, FL 221

Deanwood Healthcare & Rehabilitation Center, Washington, DC 219

DeCarli, Charles 387, 389

Deep brain stimulation 63

Deer Meadows Retirement Community, Philadelphia, PA 351

Deerbrook Care Centre, Joliet, IL 250

Deerfield Beach Health and Rehabilitation Center, Pompano Beach, FL 227

Dehydroepiandrosterone (DHEA) sulfate 63

DeKosky, Steven T. 63

Delaware Veterans Home, Milford, DE 218

Delhaven Manor, St. Louis, MO 314

Delirium 11, 63–4

Delmar Gardens, Overland Park, KS 276

Delmar Gardens of Green Valley, Henderson, NV 318

Delusions 64, 68, 69, 83, 114

Dementia 11, 64–5, 115, 116, 117, 119, 120, 121

Dementia of the Alzheimer's type 65

Dementia pugilistica 26, 65–6, 128

Dementia Trialists' Collaboration 66

Denali Center, Fairbanks, AK 187

Dendrite 22, 66

Dentate nucleus 66

Deoxyribonucleic acid (DNA) 66

Department of Social Security 81, 137, 141, 163

Depression 12, 66, 163, 165, 168, 174

DeRidder Rehabilitation & Retirement Center, DeRidder, LA 283

Deseret Nursing, Onaga, KS 276

Deseret Nursing & Healthcare, Oswego, KS 276

Deseret Nursing and Rehab at Smith Center, Smith Center, KS 278

Deseret Nursing Center, Wellington, KS 278

Desert Cove Nursing Center, Chandler, AZ 188

Desert Haven Care Center, Phoenix, AZ 189

Desert Highlands Care Center, Kingman, AZ 188

Desert Life Rehabilitation and Care Center, Tucson, AZ 192

Desferrioxamine 67, 103

Devereux House Nursing Home, Marblehead, MA 296

The DeVille House Nursing Home, Donaldsonville, LA 283

Devon Gables Health Care Center, Tucson, AZ 192

Dewitt Rehab and Healthcare Center, New York, NY 326

Diabetes 34, 55, 77, 78, 102

Diagnosis of Alzheimer's disease 17, 37

Diagnostic and Statistic Manual of Mental Disorders, 4th Edition revised (DSM IV-R) 67–8, 72–3

Diagnostic criteria for Alzheimer's disease 67–8

Dialysis 15

Dick, Malcolm Boyne 68

Diencephalon 49, 55, 68, 115

Diet and Nutrition 68, 76

Dietary restriction 68

Dietary supplements 68–9

Differential diagnosis 69

Diffuse Lewy body dementia (DLBD) 69

Digital subtraction angiography (DSA) 69

Dignity 69–70

Disability Assessment for Dementia (DAD) 70

Disease course 17

Disorientation 70

Distraction 70

Dixon Health Care Center, Dixon, IL 246–7

DNR see Do not resuscitate

Do not resuscitate 12, 70

Dobson Plaza, Evanston, IL 191

Dr. WF & Mada Dunaway Manor Nursing Home of Guymon, Guymon, OK 343

Dodge City Good Samaritan Center, Dodge City, KS 272

Don Orione Healthcare Center, Boston, MA 293

Donaldson Assisted Living, Fayetteville, TN 360

Donepezil 10, 50, 71, 118, 145

Dopamine 51, 71, 84

Doppler imaging 71–2

Douglas Rehabilitation, Mattoon, IL 252

Dove Healthcare at Lake Wales, Lake Wales, FL 223

Dove Healthcare West, Eau Claire, WI 381

Dove Hill Care Center & Villas, Hamilton, TX 365

Down Syndrome 72, 77, 86

Downey Care Center, Downey, CA 198

Downey Community Health Center, Downey, CA 198

Dress 101, 102, 156, 165

Driftwood Healthcare, Hayward, CA 199

Driftwood Healthcare Center, Torrance, CA 206

Driftwood Nursing Center, Gulfport, MS 308

Driving 72

Drug interactions 72

Drug intoxication 72

Drug therapy 72

Drugs contributing to dementia 72, 85, 113

Du Page Convalescent Center, Wheaton, IL 256

Dugan Memorial Home, West Point, MS 309

Duke University 49, 87, 135, 390, 399

Dunwoody Village, Newton Square, PA 351

Dura mater 73, *116*

Durable power of attorney 73

Durable power of attorney for health care 73

D'Youville Senior Care Center, Lowell, MA 296

Dysarthria 73

Dysdiadochokinesis 73

Dysphasia 73

Eagle Cliff Manor, Billings, MT 315

Eagle Health & Rehabilitation, Statesboro, GA 236

Eagle Pond Rehabilitation & Living Center, South Dennis, MA 297

Eagle Ridge at Grand Valley, Grand Junction, CO 210

Eagle Valley Meadows, Indianapolis, IN 261

Eaglecrest Nursing & Rehab Center, Ash Flat, AR 192

Early onset familial Alzheimer's disease (EOFAD) 73–4

East Jefferson, Metairie, LA 285

East Lake Nursing & Rehab, Elkhart, IN 258

East Lansing Healthcare Center, East Lansing, MI 300

East Liverpool Convalescent Center, East Liverpool, OH 336

East Longmeadow Skilled Nursing Center, East Longmeadow, MA 294

East Mesa Emeritus Healthcare Center, Mesa, AZ 189

East Moline Nursing & Rehab, East Moline, IL 247

Eastern Idaho Regional Medical Center, Idaho Falls, ID 240

Eastern Pines Convalescent Center, Atlantic City, NJ 319

Eastgate Village Retirement Center, Muskogee, OK 344

Easton Nursing Center, Easton, PA 349

Eastpointe Nursing Center, Chelsea, MA 294

Eastside Rehabilitation & Living Center, Bangor, ME 289

Eastview Nursing Center, Macon, GA 234

Eaton County Medical Care Facility, Charlotte, MI 299

Eben Ezer Lutheran Care Center, Brush, CO 207

Ebony Lake Healthcare Center, Brownsville, TX 363

Echoencephalography (ECHO) scan 74

Echolalia 74

Eden alternative 74

Eden Home, New Braunfels, TX 367

Eden Park Nursing Home, Utica, NY 327

Eden Village Care Center, Glen Carbon, IL 249

Edgehill Nursing & Rehabilitation Center, Glenside, PA 349

Edgewater Care Center, Kerrville, TX 366

Edgewater Convalescent Hospital, Long Beach, CA 200

Edgewood Manor Nursing Center, Port Clinton, OH 341

Edinborough Healthcare Center, Dunedin, FL 222

Edmond Healthcare Center, Edmond, OK 343

Education 155, 158, 159, 168, 180

Edward J. Healey Nursing & Rehabilitation, West Palm Beach, FL 229–30

Edwardsville Nursing & Rehab, Edwardsville, IL 247

Efferent nerve fibers 74

Efficacy of treatment 74

Effingham Rehabilitation & Healthcare Center, Effingham, IL 247

Egb 74

Egret Cove Center, St. Petersburg, FL 228

Eisenhower Nursing & Convalescent Hospital, Pasadena, CA 202–3

El Monte Convalescent Hospital, El Monte, CA 198

Elan Corporation 22

Eldepryl *see* Selegiline hydrochloride

Elder Books 74

Elder Law Attorneys 75

Eldercare Locator 75

Eldora Nursing & Rehabilitation Center, Eldora, IA 268

Eldorado Care Center, LLC, El Cajon, CA 198

Electroencephalogram (EEG) 75

Electromagnetic fields 77

Elk City Nursing Center, Elk City, OK 343

Ellis Manor, Hartford, CT 215

Elm Brook Health Care & Rehabilitation, Elmhurst, IL 248

Elmcrest Care Center, El Monte, CA 198

Elmhaven East, Parsons, KS 276

Elmhaven West, Parsons, KS 276

Elmhurst Extended Care Center Inc., Elmhurst, IL 248

Elmora Hills Health & Rehabilitation Center, Elizabeth, NJ 320

Elms Haven Care Center, Thornton, CO 213

Elmwood, Green Springs, OH 337

Elmwood Care Center, Berkeley, CA 197

Elmwood Geriatric Center, Detroit, MI 300

Elyria United Methodist Village, Elyria, OH 336

Emanuel Convalescent Hospital, San Jose, CA 205

Emanuel County Nursing Home, Swainsboro, GA 236

The Embassy Care Center, Wilmington, IL 256

Emerald Circle Convalescent Center, Wapato, WA 379

Emery County Care & Rehabilitation Center, Ferron, UT 369

Emmanuel Nursing Home, Detroit Lakes, MN 305

Emmetsburg Care Center, Emmetsburg, IA 268

Emmett Care & Rehabilitation, Emmett, ID 240

Emotional changes 24, 32, 45, 142

Emporia Presbyterian Manor, Emporia, KS 273

Encephalitis 30, 75

Encephalopathy 30, 75

End of life care *see* Advance directives

Endoplasmic reticulum associated binding protein (ERAB) 76

England Manor Nursing Home Inc., England, AR 193

English Oaks Convalescent and Rehabilitation Hospital, Modesto, CA 201

Ennis Care Center, Ennis, TX 364

Entorhinal cortex 76, 108

Environmental factors 76–7, 88

Envoy of Lawrenceville, Lawrenceville, VA 373

Envoy of Staunton, Staunton, VA 375

Envoy of Thornton Hall, Norfolk, VA 374

Envoy of Westover Hills, Richmond, VA 374

Enzymes 77

Ependyma 77

Epidemiology 77

Episcopal Church Home, Louisville, KY 280

Episcopal Church Home, Rochester, NY 326

Episcopal Church Home of Minnesota, St. Paul, Minnesota 307

Epoch Senior Healthcare of Harwich, Harwich, MA 295

Eptastigmine (MF0201) 77–8

Ergoloid mesylate (Hydergine) 78

Escondido Care Center, Escondido, CA 198

Eskaton Care Center — Greenhaven, Sacramento, CA 203

Eskaton Village Care Center, Carmichael, CA 197

Estes Nursing Home — Northway, Birmingham, AL 183

Esther Marie Nursing Center, Geneva, OH 337

Estherville Good Samaritan Center, Estherville, IA 268

Estrella Care and Rehabilitation Center, Avondale, AZ 187

Estrogen 78, 103, 172, 174, 177

Estrogen replacement therapy 78

Ethics committees 78

Ethnicity 78

Etiology of Alzheimer's Disease 78–9

Etowah Health Care Center, Etowah, TN 360

Etowah Landing Care & Rehab, Rome, GA 236

Eugene Rehabilitation & Specialty Care, Eugene, OR 345

Euphoria 12, 132

Evans, Denis 388

Evans Memorial Home, Cresco, IA 267

Evanston Nursing & Rehab, Evanston, IL 248

Event Related Potentials 55

Eventide Lutheran Home, Moorhead, MN 307

Everett Nursing & Rehab Center, Everett, MA 294

Evergreen Care Center, Owasso, OK 344

Evergreen Health and Living Center, Southfield, MI 303–4

Evergreen Health Care Center Inc., Bakersfield, CA 196

Evergreen Health Center, Oshkosh, WI 383

Evergreen Hillsboro Health & Rehabilitation center, Hillsboro, OR 345

Evergreen Milton Freewater Health & Rehabilitation Center, Milton Freewater, OR 345

Evergreen Nursing & Rehabilitation Center, Effingham, IL 247

Evergreen Nursing Home, Alamosa, CO 206

Evergreen Retirement Community, Oshkosh, WI 383

Evergreen Terrace Care Center, Lakewood, CO 211

Excel Rehabilitation & Healthcare, Tampa, FL 229

Excell Healthcare, Oakland, CA 202

Exceptional Living Care Center Holly Hill, Bloomington, IN 257

Excitation of nerve cells 79

Excitotoxicity 79–80

Excitotoxins 79–80, 135

Exelon see Rivastigmine

Exempla/Colorado Lutheran Care, Arvada, CO 207

Exercise 79

Exocytosis 80

Fahr's disease 80

Fairacres Manor Inc., Greeley, CO 211

Fairburn Health Care, Fairburn, GA 233

Fairfax Nursing Center, Fairfax, VA 373

Fairhaven Inc., Sykesville, MD 292

Fairhaven Nursing, Lowell, MA 296

Fairhaven Retirement & Health Care Community, Upper Sandusky, OH 341

Fairland Nursing & Rehabilitation Center, Silver Spring, MD 292

Fairlane Senior Care & Rehabilitation, Detroit, MI 300

Fairmont Care Center, Chicago, IL 244

Fairview Baptist Home, Downer's Grove, IL 247

Fairview Care Center, Joliet, IL 250

Fairview Care Center East, Salt Lake City, UT 370

Fairview Commons, Great Barrington, MA 295

Fairview Fellowship Home for Senior Citizens, Fairview, OK 343

Fairview Health & Rehabilitation Center, Birmingham, AL 183–4

Fairview Skilled Nursing & Rehabilitation, Toledo, OH 341

Faith Haven Senior Care Center, Jackson, MI 302

Falling Spring Nursing & Rehabilitation Center, Chambersburg, PA 348

Falmouth, Care & Rehabilitation Falmouth, MA 295

Falx cerebelli 80

Falx cerebri 80

Familial Alzheimer's disease (FAD) 80, 84

Familial fatal insomnia 80

Family Health West Nursing Home, Fruita, CO 210

Farwell Convalescent Center, Farwell, TX 364–5

Fayette Health & Rehabilitation Center, Baltimore, MD 290

Fayetteville City Hospital and Geriatric Center, Fayetteville, AR 193

Fayetteville Health and Rehabilitation, Fayetteville, AR 193

Fayetteville Veterans Home, Fayetteville, AR 193

Feeding problems 80

Fern Crest Manor Living Center, New Orleans, LA 286

Ferris, Steven 390

FHN Freeport Memorial Hospital, Freeport, IL 249

Fidalgo Care Center, Anacortes, WA 375

Fidelity Healthcare, El Monte, CA 198

Filosa Convalescent Home Inc., Danbury, CT 215

Financial burden 80–1

Financial Capacity 81

Financing long-term care 81

Finch, Caleb 388

First Community Village Healthcare Center, Columbus, OH 335

Five Oaks Manor, Concord, NC 328

Flannery Oaks Guest House, Baton Rouge, LA 282

Fleet Landing, Atlantic Beach, FL 219

Fletcher Health & Rehab Center, Tampa, FL 229

Flint Ridge Nursing & Rehabilitation Center, Newark, OH 340

Florence Comprehensive Care Center, Florence, AL 184

Florence Hand Home, LaGrange, GA 234

Florence Park Care Center, Florence, KY 280

Florida Club Care Center, Miami, FL 225

Flushing ManorCare, Flushing, NY 325

Folic acid 81, 177

Folic acid deficiency 81

Fond Du Lac Lutheran Home, Fond Du Lac, WI 381

Food and Drug Administration (FDA) 81

Forbes Nursing Center, Pittsburgh, PA 352

Forebrain 9, 31

Forest Creek Village, Indianapolis, IN 261

Forest Hill Health Rehabilitation, East Moline, IL 247

Forest Manor, Northport, AL 186

Forest Park Health Center, Carlisle, PA 348

Fort Dodge Villa Care Center, Fort Dodge, IA 268–9

Fort Lauderdale Health & Rehabilitation Center, Fort Lauderdale, FL 222

Fort Pierce Healthcare, Fort Pierce, FL 222

Fort Scott Manor, Fort Scott, KS 273

Fort Tyron Rehab & Healthcare Facility, New York, NY 326

Fort Valley Healthcare Center, Fort Valley, GA 233

Fort Vancouver Convalescent Center, Vancouver, WA 379

Forum at Desert Harbor, Peoria, AZ 189

Foundation Park Dementia Care Center, Toledo, OH 337

Fountain City Care & Rehabilitation, Columbus, GA 232

Fountain Inn Nursing Home, Fountain Inn, SC 356

Fountain Springs Healthcare, Rapid City, SD 358

Fountain View Subacute and Nursing Center, Los Angeles, CA 201

Fountain View Village, Fountain Hills, AZ 188

Fountainview, Eldorado, IL 247

Fountainview Center for Alzheimer's Disease, Atlanta, GA 231

Four Seasons Nursing & Rehab, Brooklyn, NY 325

Fourth ventricle 81

The Franciscan at Saint Leonard Center, Centerville, OH 335

Franciscan Convalescent Hospital, Merced, CA 201

Franciscan Health Care Center, Louisville, KY 281

Franciscan Village, Lemont, IL 250

Franke Tobey Jones Retirement Estates, Tacoma, WA 378

Frankford Nursing & Rehabilitation Center, Baltimore, MD 290

Franklin Plaza Extended Care, Cleveland, OH 335

Franklin Ridge, Franklin, OH 337

Fraser Health Center, Hilton Head Island, SC 356

Frasier Meadows Manor Health Care Center, Boulder, CO 207

Frazee Care Center, Frazee, MN 305

Fredericksburg Nursing Home, Fredericksburg, VA 373

Free radicals 62, 81, 90, 103

Freedom Plaza Care Center, Peoria, AZ 189

Freeport Rehabilitation, Freeport, IL 249

Fremont Center Genesis Eldercare, Fremont, OH 337

French Park Care Center, Santa Ana, CA 205

Frene Valley Health Center, Hermann, MO 311

Friends Life Care at Home 82

Friends Village at Woodstown, Woodstown, NJ 323

Friendship Haven, Fort Dodge, IA 269
Friendship Health & Rehabilitation, Cleveland, GA 232
Friendship Health and Rehabilitation, Roanoke, VA 374–5
Friendship Home, Audubon, IA 266
Friendship Home, Carlinville, IL 243
Friendship Manor Nashville, Nashville, IL 252
Friendship Manor of Saint Elmo, Saint Elmo, IL 254
Friendship Villa Care Center, Miles City, MT 316
Friendship Village of Schaumburg, Schaumburg, IL 255
Friendship Village of South Hills, Upper Saint Clair, PA 352
Friendship Village of Sunset Hills, Saint Louis, MO 314
Friendship Village Retirement, Waterloo, IA 272
Friendship Village Sunset Hills, St. Louis, MO 314
Fritz Reuter Altenheim, North Bergen, NJ 321
Frontal cortex 82
Frontal lobe *36*, 82
Frontotemporal dementia 52, 82–3, 128
Functional MRI 110–1
Fungal meningitis 65
Future Care & Charles Village, Baltimore, MD 290–1
Future Care Pineview Nursing, Clinton, MD 291

Gainesville Healthcare Center, Gainesville, FL 222
Gait 66, 83, 98, 135
Galantamine 10, 83
Galasko, Douglas 388
Galtier Health Center, St. Paul, Minnesota 307
Gamma-aminobutyric acid (GABA) 84, 133
Gamma secretase 84
Gamma secretase inhibitors 84
Gammagard 84, 103
Gammaglobulin Alzheimer's Partnership (GAP) Study 103
Ganglia 84
Garden Court Health & Rehabilitation Center, Bossier City, LA 283
Garden of the Gods Care Center, Colorado Springs, CO 208
Garden Park Nursing Home, Shreveport, LA 288
Garden Terrace Alzheimer's Center of Excellence, Aurora, CO 207
Garden Terrace at Overland Park, Overland Park, KS 276
Garden Terrace Manor W, Spokane, WA 378
Garden Valley Nursing & Rehabilitation, Kansas City, MO 311–2
Garden Valley Retirement Village, Garden City, KS 273
Garden Villa, Bloomington, IN 257
Gardena Convalescent Center, Gardena, CA 199

The Gardens at Warwick Forest, Newport News, VA 374
Gardens Care Center, Kingman, AZ 188
The Gardens on University, Spokane, WA 378
Garfield Neurobehavioral Center, Oakland, CA 202
Gateway Care Center, Eatontown, NJ 320
Gateway Community Living Center, Cleveland, GA 232
Gaymont Nursing Center, Norwalk, OH 340
Genes 84, 108, 122, 150, 153, 154
Genes in Alzheimer's disease 84–5, 86–7
Genese County Nursing Home, Batavia, NY 324
Genesis Health Care of New York, Watertown, NY 327
Genetic counseling 86
Genetic mapping 86
Genetic mutations 86, 122
Genetic testing 86
Georgetown University 14, 388
Georgia Regional Hospital, Decatur, GA 233
Georgian House, Tacoma, WA 379
Gerald Nursing & Rehabilitation, Gerald, MO 311
Geriatric Depression Scale 87
German Center for Extended Care, Boston, MA 293
Germantown Home, Philadelphia, PA 351
Gerontology 87
Gerstmann-Straussler-Scheinker Disease 87
Ghetti, Bernardino 389
Ghost cells 131
Gillette Nursing Home, Warren, OH 341
Gilman, Sil 389
Gingko biloba 87–8
Glacier Hills Nursing Center, Ann Arbor, MI 320
Gladeview Health Care Center, Old Saybrook, CT 216
Gladstone Institute 118, 143, 163, 173
Glen Ayr Health Center, Lakewood, CO 211
Glen Cove Nursing Pavilion, Panama City, FL 226–7
Glen Haven Health and Rehabilitation, LLC, Northport, AL 186
Glen Oaks Health Campus, New Castle, IN 263
Glenburnie Rehab & Nursing Center, Richmond, VA 374
Glencrest Nursing Rehabilitation Center Ltd., Chicago, IL 244
Glenn-Mor Nursing Home, Thomasville, GA 237
Glenshire Nursing & Rehabilitation Center, Richton Park, IL 254
Glenview Terrace Nursing Center, Glenview, IL 249
Glenwood Healthcare, Inc., Florence, AL 184
Glial cells 88

Glial fibrillary acid protein (GFAP) 88
Gliosis 88
Glisan Care Center, Portland, OR 346
Global assessments 88
Global Deterioration Scale (GDS) 88–9
Glorified Health & Rehabilitation of Greenville, Greenville, SC 356
Glucose 15, 29, 34, 43, 101, 123
Glutamate 61, 90
Glutathione 90, 123
Glyceryl-l-phosphorylcholine 90–1
Glyosaminoglycans 91
Goerlic Center, Sylvania, OH 341
Gold City Community Living Center, Dahlonega, GA 232
Golden Acres Living and Rehabilitation Center, Dallas, TX 364
Golden Acres Lorain County Nursing Home, Amherst, OH 332
Golden Age Nursing Home, Denham Springs, LA 283
Golden Crest Nursing Center, North Providence, RI 354
Golden Gate Care Center, San Francisco, CA 204
Golden Hills Subacute and Rehab Center, San Diego, CA 204
Golden LivingCenter – Bella Vista, Rapid City, SD 358
Golden LivingCenter – Brandywine, Greenfield, IN 260
Golden LivingCenter – Briarwood, Tucker, GA 237
Golden LivingCenter – Camelot, Louisville, KY 281
Golden LivingCenter – Chase County, Cottonwood Falls, KS 272
Golden LivingCenter – Colonial Manor, Glendale, WI 381
Golden LivingCenter – Dexter House, Malden, MA 296
Golden LivingCenter – Elkhart, Elkhart, IN 258
Golden LivingCenter – Frederick, Frederick, MD 291–2
Golden LivingCenter – Fresno, Fresno, CA 199
Golden LivingCenter – Glenwood, Decatur, GA 233
Golden LivingCenter – Golden Rule, Richmond IN 264
Golden LivingCenter – Hagerstown, Hagerstown, MD 292
Golden LivingCenter – Hillcreek, Louisville, KY 281
Golden LivingCenter – Hillcrest of Wayzata, Wayzata, MN 308
Golden LivingCenter – Hopkins, Hopkins, MN 306
Golden LivingCenter – Jesup, Jesup, GA 234
Golden LivingCenter – Kennestone, Marietta, GA 235
Golden LivingCenter – Lake Norden, SC 358
Golden LivingCenter – Lake Ridge, Roseville, MN 307
Golden LivingCenter – Maryville, Maryville, MO 312

Golden LivingCenter — Meadow-brook, Rapid City, SD 358

Golden LivingCenter — Montgomery, Montgomery, AL 186

Golden LivingCenter — Mount Lebanon, Pittsburgh, PA 352

Golden LivingCenter — Mountain View, Winchester, TN 362

Golden LivingCenter — Muncie, Muncie, IN 263

Golden LivingCenter — Northside, Atlanta, GA 231

Golden LivingCenter — Oil City, Oil City, PA 351

Golden LivingCenter — Petersburg, Petersburg, IN 263

Golden LivingCenter — Pierre, Pierre, SD 358

Golden LivingCenter — Plattsmouth, Plattsmouth, NE 318

Golden LivingCenter — Redfield, Redfield, SD 358

Golden LivingCenter — Richmond, Richmond, IN 264

Golden LivingCenter — Rome, Rome, GA 236

Golden LivingCenter — Saint James, Saint James, MO 313

Golden LivingCenter — Saint Louis Park Plaza, St. Louis Park, MN 307

Golden LivingCenter — Salem, Salem, SD 358

Golden LivingCenter — Slayton, Slayton, MN 308

Golden LivingCenter — Sorensen, Omaha, NE 317

Golden LivingCenter — Southaven, Southaven, MS 309

Golden LivingCenter — Spring Hill, Spring Hill, KS 277

Golden LivingCenter — Valparaiso, Valparaiso, IN 265

Golden LivingCenter — Waynesburg, Waynesburg, PA 353

Golden LivingCenter — Wellington, Wellington, KS 278

Golden LivingCenter — West Newton, West Newton, MA 297

Golden LivingCenter — Windermere, Augusta, GA 231

Golden Oaks Medical Care Facility, Pontiac, MI 303

Golden Peaks Care & Rehabilitation Center, Fort Collins, CO 210

Golden Plains Healthcare Center, Hutchinson, KS 274

Golden Rule Home, Shawnee, OK 344

Golden Years Homestead Inc., Fort Wayne, IN 259

Goldenrod ManorCare Center, Clarinda, IA 266

Goldsmith, Harry 91

Goldstar Rehabilitation & Nursing Center of San Monica, Santa Monica, CA 205

Goldthwaithe Senior Health Center, Goldthwaite, TX 365

Good Samaritan Center — Idaho Falls Village, Idaho Falls, ID 240

Good Samaritan Center — Silver Hills Village, Silverton, ID 241

Good Samaritan Center — Valentine, Valentine, NE 318

Good Samaritan Home Inc., Evansville, IN 258

Good Samaritan Home Inc., Oakland City, IN 263

Good Samaritan Home Inc., Quincy, IL 254

Good Samaritan Moscow Village, Moscow, ID 240

Good Samaritan Nursing Home, Avon, OH 332

Good Samaritan Society — Auburn, Auburn, NE 316

Good Samaritan Society — Beatrice, Beatrice, NE 316

Good Samaritan Society — Betty Dare, Alamogordo, NM 323

Good Samaritan Society — Boise Village, Boise, ID 239

Good Samaritan Society — Bonnell County, Greeley, CO 211

Good Samaritan Society — Callaway, Callaway, NE 316

Good Samaritan Society — Canton, SD 357–8

Good Samaritan Society — Daytona, Daytona Beach, FL 221

Good Samaritan Society — DeSmet, DeSmet, SC 358

Good Samaritan Society — Hays, Hays, KS 273

Good Samaritan Society — Holstein, Holstein, IA 269

Good Samaritan Society — Hutchinson Village, Hutchinson, KS 274

Good Samaritan Society — Indianola, IA 269

Good Samaritan Society — Live Oak, FL 224

Good Samaritan Society — Mesa Good Shepherd, Mesa, AZ 189

Good Samaritan Society — Moscow Village, Moscow, ID 240–1

Good Samaritan Society — Mountain Home, Mountain Home, AR 195

Good Samaritan Society — New Orleans, New Orleans, LA 286

Good Samaritan Society — Peoria Good Shepherd, Peoria, AZ 189

Good Samaritan Society — Prescott Village Good Shepherd, Prescott, AZ 190

Good Samaritan Society — Sioux Falls Village, Sioux Falls, SD 359

Good Samaritan Society — University Specialty Care, Minneapolis, MN 306

Good Samaritan Society — White Acres, El Paso, TX 364

Good Samaritan Village of Hastings, Hastings, NE 317

Good Shepherd Home, Fostoria, OH 337

Goodwill Nursing Home, Inc. Macon, GA 234

Goodwin House West Nursing Care Unit, Falls Church, VA 373

Gordon Health & Rehabilitation, Calhoun, GA 232

Gotu kola see Centella asiatica

Govalle Care Center, Austin, TX 363

Governor's House Rehabilitation & Nursing Center, Simsbury, CT 216

Grace Barker Nursing Center, Warren, RI 355

Grace Healthcare of Clarksville, Clarksville, TN 359

Grace Healthcare of Cordova, Cordova, TN 360

Grace Healthcare of Phoenix, Phoenix, AZ 190

Grace Healthcare of Tucker, Tucker, GA 237

Gracelen Terrace, Portland, OR 346

Gracy Woods Nursing Center, Austin, TX 363

Gracy Woods II Nursing Center, Austin, TX 363

Grafton County Home, North Haverhill, NH 319

Gramercy Court, Sacramento, CA 203

Grancare Nursing Center, Green Bay, WI 381

Grancell Village, Reseda, CA 203

The Grand Court II, San Antonio, TX 367

Grand Cove Nursing & Rehabilitation Center, Lake Charles, LA 285

Grand Junction Regional Care Center, Grand Junction, CO 210

Grand Park Convalescent Hospital, Los Angeles, CA 201

The Grand Traverse Pavilions, Traverse City, MI 304

Grand Village, Grand Rapids, MN 306

Grandview Convalescent Center, Martinsville, IN 262

Grandview Healthcare Center, Grandview, WA 376

Grandview Healthcare Center, Jasper, GA 234

Grandview Healthcare Center, Oelwein, IA 270

Grandview Heights, Inc., Marshalltown, IA 270

Grandview ManorCare Center, Grandview, MO 311

Grant County Nursing Home, Petersburg, WV 380

Grant Manor Inc., Williamstown, KY 282

Granulovacuolar degeneration 91

Grapeseed oil extract 24

Graves' disease 92, 172, 173

Gray and white matter of the brain 46–7, *116*

Gray matter of the brain 91, 95, 110, 125, 128, 136

Great Bend Health & Rehab Center, Great Bend, KS 273

Green Acres Manor, Toms River, NJ 322

Green Knoll Care & Rehabilitation, Bridgewater, NJ 319

Green Meadows Health & Wellness Center, Louisville, OH 338

Green tea 91–2

Greenbriar Health Care Center of Hammonton, Hammonton, NJ 320–1

Greenbriar Nursing Center, Eaton, OH 336

Greencroft Health Care, Goshen, IN 260

Greene Oaks Health Center, Xenia, OH 342

Greenfield Care Center of Gardena, Gardena, CA 199

Greenhills Health & Rehab Center, Nashville, TN 362

Greenwich Woods Health Care Center, Greenwich, CT 215

Greenwood Care, Evanston, IL 248

Greenwood Health and Living Community, Greenwood, IN 260

Greenwood Health Care Community, LLC, Greenwood, IN 260

Greenwood Manor, Iowa City, IA 269

Grooved Pegboard Test 74

The Grove, Columbia, MS 308

Grove Manor, Grove City, PA 349

Grove of Evanston, Evanston, IL 249

Grove Street Extended Care and Living Center, San Francisco, CA 204

The Groves Center, Lake Wales, FL 223–4

Growdon, John 389

Growth hormone 60

Guam amyotrophic lateral sclerosis-parkinsonism-dementia complex 64, 96, 128

Guarana 92

Guardian Care Convalescent Center, Orlando, FL 226

Guardian Center, Brockton, MA 294

Guest Care at Spring Lake, LLC, Shreveport, LA 288

The Guest Home, Shreveport, LA 288

Guest House of Baton Rouge, Baton Rouge, LA 282

Hacienda Rehabilitation and Care Center, Sierra Vista, AZ 191

Haldol see Haloperidol

Hale Anuenue Restorative Care, Hilo, HI 238

Hale Nani Rehabilitation & Nursing Center, Honolulu, HI 238

Hallervorden-Spatz disease 92

Hallmark Park Nursing Center, Denver, CO 209

Hallucinations 10, 11, 15, 92, 139, 143, 152, 160, 165, 168

Haloperidol 92

Haltom Convalescent Center, Fort Worth, TX 365

Hamden Health Care Center, Hamden CT 215

Hamilton Plaza Nursing & Rehabilitation Center, Passaic, NJ 322

Hammond Nursing Home, Hammond, LA 284

Hammonds Lane, Brooklyn Park, MD 291

Hampton Court Nursing & Rehabilitation, North Miami Beach, FL 226

Hanceville Nursing & Rehabilitation Center, Hanceville, AL 184

Hancock Manor Nursing Home, Sneedville, TN 362

Hanover Hall, Hanover, PA 350

Hanover Hill Health Care Center, Manchester, NH 319

Hanover Nursing Center, Hanover, IN 260

Hanover Terrace Healthcare, Hanover, NH 319

Happy Siesta Nursing Home, Remsen, IA 271

Harbor Beach Nursing & Rehabilitation Center, Fort Lauderdale, FL 222

Harbor Convalescent Hospital, Torrance, CA 206

Harbor Point M & R Center, Norfolk, VA 374

Harbor View Care Center, Corpus Christi, TX 364

Harbor View Nursing & Rehabilitation Center, Memphis, TN 361

Harbor Villa Care Center, Anaheim, CA 196

Harborside Healthcare — Beachwood, Beachwood, OH 333

Harborside Healthcare — Broadview Heights, Broadview Heights, OH 333

Harborside Healthcare — Pheasant Wood, Petersborough, NH 319

Harborside Nursing & Rehabilitation Center, Baltimore, MD 291

Harbour's Edge Health Center, Delray Beach, FL 221

Harlingen Nursing Center, Harlingen, TX 365

Harmony Health Care Center, Miami, FL 225

Harmony Manor Skilled Nursing, Winnemucca, NV 318

Harmony Nursing & Rehabilitation Center, Chicago, IL 244–5

Harmony Point Nursing Center, Lakewood, CO 211

Harold and Grace Upjohn Community, Kalamazoo, MI 233

Harper, David 52

Harrington Court, Colchester, CT 214

Harris Health Care Center North, Central Falls, RI 354

Harris Health Center, East Providence, RI 354

Harrison House of Georgetown, Georgetown, DE 218

Harry, Jean 92, 118

Harry and Jeannette Weinberg Care Center, Kaneohe, HI 239

Hartford Healthcare, Hartford, AL 185

Hartford Nursing & Rehabilitation, Detroit, MI 300

Harts Harbor Healthcare Center, Jacksonville, FL 223

Harvard University 14, 46, 52, 54, 95, 174, 181, 389, 402

Harvest Manor Nursing Home, Denham Springs, LA 283

Hashimoto's encephalitis/encephalopathy 30, 92–3, 105

Hathaway Manor Extended Care Facility, New Bedford, MA 296

Hattie Ide Chaffe Home, East Providence, RI 354

Hattiesburg Health & Rehabilitation Center, Hattiesburg, MS 308

Havasu Nursing Center, Lake Havasu, AZ 188

Haven Convalescent Home, New Castle, PA 351

Haven Nursing Center Inc., Columbia, LA 283

Havencare Nursing & Rehabilitation, Longview, TX 366

Havenwood, Concord, NH 319

Hawaii Medical Center East, Honolulu, HI 238

Hawthorne Convalescent Center, Hawthorne, CA 199

Hawthorne Health & Rehabilitation of Ocala, Ocala, FL 226

Hawthorne House, Freeport, ME 289

Haym Salomon Home for the Aged, Brooklyn, NY 325

Haysville Healthcare Center, Haysville, KS 274

Hayward Convalescent Hospital, Hayward, CA 199

Hayward Hills Healthcare Center, Hayward, CA 199–200

Hazel I. Findlay Country Manor, Saint Johns, MI 303

Hazen Nursing Home, West Valley City, UT 370

HBO Alzheimer's Project 93

HCFA see Health Care Financing Administration

Head injuries and trauma 51, 61, 63, 75, 130–131

Health and Rehabilitation of North Seattle, Seattle, WA 377–8

Health Care Center at Richland Place, Nashville, TN 362

Health Care Center of Tampa, Tampa, FL 229

Health Care Financing Administration 5, 34, 75

Health care proxy 93

Health Center at Standifer Place, Chattanooga, TN 359

Health Center at Wesley Glen, Columbus, OH 335

Health Center of Daytona Beach, Daytona Beach, FL 221

Health Center of Lake City, Lake City, FL 223

Health Center of Pensacola, Pensacola, FL 227

Health Center of Windermere, Orlando, FL 226

Health Center at the MonteVista at Coronado, El Paso, TX 364

Health Insurance Association of America 111

Health Insurance Portability and Accountability Act 93–4

Health maintenance organization (HMO) v94

Healthaven Nursing Home, Akron, OH 331

Healthcare and Rehabilitation of Sanford, Sanford, FL 228

Healthcare Community, Coventry, RI 354

Healthcare Inc, Ashville, AL 183
Healthpark Care Center, Fort Meyers, FL 222
Healthsource Saginaw, Inc., Saginaw, MI 303
Healthwin, South Bend, IN 264
Hearing 56, 177
Heart of Georgia Nursing Home, Eastman, GA 233
Heart of Texas Health Care & Rehabilitation Center–All Seasons, Houston, TX 365–6
Hearthside Care Center, Coos Bay, OR 345
The Hearthstone, York, NE 318
Hearthstone Manor, Medford, OR 346
Heartland Care & Rehabilitation Center, Cape Girardeau, MO 309–10
Heartland Care Center, McAlester, OK 343
Heartland Health Care & Rehabilitation Center, Sarasota, FL 228
Heartland Health Care Center — Adelphi, Adelphi, ND 290
Heartland Health Care Center — Ann Arbor, Ann Arbor, MI 298
Heartland Health Care Center — Georgian Bloomfield, Bloomfield Hills, MI 299
Heartland Health Care Center — Grand Rapids, Grand Rapids, MI 301
Heartland Health Care Center — Kalamazoo, MI 302
Heartland Health Care Center — Knollview, Muskegon, MI 303
Heartland Health Care Center, Moline, IL 252
Heartland Health Care Center, Pittsburgh, PA 352
Heartland Health Care Center — Saginaw, Saginaw, MI 303
Heartland Health Care Center — University, Livonia, MI 301
Heartland Health Care Center of Boca Raton, Boca Raton, FL 220
Heartland Health Care Center of Boynton, Boynton Beach, FL 220
Heartland Health Care Center of Hyattsville, Hyattsville, MD 283
Heartland Healthcare — Hyattsville, Hyattsville, MD 292
Heartland Healthcare at Briarwood, Flint, MI 300–301
Heartland Healthcare Center, Moline, IL 252
Heartland of Brooksville, Brooksville, FL 220
Heartland of Champaign, Champaign, IL 243
Heartland of Holland, Holland, MI 301
Heartland of South Jacksonville, S. Jacksonville, FL 223
Heartland of Urbana, Urbana, OH 341
Heartland of West Ashley, Charleston, SC 355
Heartland of Zephyrhills, Zephyrhills, FL 230
Heat shock proteins 61, 163
Heat stroke 65
Heather Hill Inc., Chardon, OH 335

Heavy metal toxicity 94
Hebrew Home & Hospital Inc., West Hartford, CT 217
Helia Healthcare of Champaign, Champaign, IL 243
Helping Our Mobile Elderly (HOME) 76, 86
Hennis Care Center, Dover, OH 336
Herbal therapy 15, 94
The Heritage, Corbin, KY 279
Heritage Care Center, American Fork, UT 369
Heritage Center, Evansville, IN 258
Heritage Convalescent Center, Amarillo, TX 363
Heritage Garden Care Center, Yakima, WA 379
Heritage Hall, Blacksburg, VA 372
Heritage Hall, Blackstone, VA 372
Heritage Hall, Nassawadox, VA 374
Heritage Hall Nursing & Rehabilitation Center, Leesburg, VA 373
Heritage Health, Jacksonville, IL 250
Heritage Health Care Center — Venice, Venice, FL 229
Heritage Healthcare, Hammond, LA 284
Heritage Healthcare at Crestwood, Valdosta, GA 237
Heritage Healthcare at Holly Hill, Valdosta, GA 237
Heritage Healthcare at Lakehaven, Valdosta, GA 237
Heritage Healthcare at Magnolia Manor, Moultrie, GA 235
Heritage Healthcare at Spring Valley, Elberton, GA 233
Heritage Healthcare at West Lafayette, West Lafayette, IN 265
Heritage Healthcare Center, Globe, AZ 188
Heritage Healthcare of Franklin, Franklin, GA 233
Heritage Healthcare of Jasper, Jasper, GA 234
Heritage Healthcare of Macon, Macon, GA 234
Heritage Healthcare of Savannah, Savannah, GA 236
Heritage Healthcare of Toomsboro, Toomsboro, GA 237
Heritage Healthcare of Valdosta, Valdosta, GA 237
Heritage Hills Nursing Center, McAlester, OK 343
Heritage House Convalescent Center, Shelbyville, IN 264
Heritage Inn Health & Rehab, Statesboro, GA 236
Heritage Manor, Plano, TX 367
Heritage Manor, Rice Lake, WI 384
Heritage ManorCare Center of Newton, Newton 270
Heritage Manor Carlinville, Carlinville, IL 243
Heritage Manor Elgin, Elgin, IL 248
Heritage Manor Health & Rehabilitation Center, Ferriday, LA 283–4
Heritage Manor Health Care Center, Flint, MI 301
Heritage Manor of Baton Rouge, Baton Rouge, LA 282

Heritage Manor of Houma, Houma, LA 284
Heritage Manor of Mandeville, Mandeville, LA 285
Heritage Manor of Napoleonville, Napoleonville, LA 286
Heritage Manor of Opelousas, Opelousas, LA 287
Heritage Manor South, Shreveport, LA 288
Heritage Nursing Home Inc., Chicago, IL 245
Heritage Oaks Nursing & Rehabilitation, Lubbock, TX 366
Heritage of Elmwood Nursing Home, Elmwood, WI 381
Heritage of Wauneta, Wauneta, NE 318
Heritage Park, Dade City, FL 221
Heritage Park, Fort Wayne, IN 259
Heritage Park Care & Rehabilitation Center, Bradenton, FL 220
Heritage Park Care Center, Carbondale, CO 208
Heritage Park Nursing Center, Rogers, AR 195
Heritage Park Rehabilitation & Healthcare Center, Fort Meyers, FL 222
Heritage Rehabilitation & Living Center, Winthrop, ME 290
Heritage Rehabilitation Center, Torrance, CA 206
Heritage Square, Dixon, IL 247
Heritage Square Nursing & Rehabilitation Center — Blytheville, Blytheville, AR 192
Hermitage Care & Rehabilitation Center, Owensboro, KY 281
Hermitage in Northern Virginia, Alexandria, VA 372
Herpes encephalitis 65
Herpes viruses 65, 93, 94, 95
Herrup, Karl 390
Hetzel Care Center, Bloomer, WI 380
Hialeah Shores, Miami, FL 225
Hickory Creek at Lebanon, Lebanon, IN 262
Hickory Pointe Care & Rehabilitation Center, Oskaloosa, KS 276
High density lipoprotein (HDL) 95
High Valley Lodge, Sunland, CA 205
Highland Care Center, Salt Lake City, UT 370
Highland Care Center, Inc., Jamaica, NY 325
Highland Community Hospital, Tukwila, WA 379
Highland House Nursing & Rehabilitation Center, Grants Pass, OR 345
Highland House of Fayetteville Inc., Fayetteville, NC 329
Highland Nursing & Rehabilitation Center, Kansas City, MO 312
Highland Pines Rehabilitation Center, Clearwater, FL 221
The Highlands, Fitchburg, MA 295
The Highlands Healthcare Center, Tacoma, WA 379
Highlands Lake Center, Lakeland, FL 224
Highlands Nursing & Rehab Center, Louisville, KY 281

Highline Community Hospital, Tukwila, WA 337–338
Highline Rehabilitation and Care Center, Denver, CO 209
Highmore Healthcare Center, Highmore, SD 358
Hilderbrand Care Center, Canon City, CO 207
Hill Haven Nursing Home, Commerce, GA 232
Hillcress Commons Nursing & Rehab, Pittsfield, MA 297
Hillcrest Care, San Bernardino, CA 204
Hillcrest Care and Rehab, Prescott, AR 195
Hillcrest Care Center, Long Beach, CA 200
Hillcrest Haven Convalescent Center, Pocatello, ID 241
Hillcrest Health Care Center, Owensboro, KY 281
Hillcrest Nursing & Rehab, Joliet, IL 250
Hillcrest Nursing Home, Corbin, KY 279
Hillsborough County Nursing Home, Goffstown, NH 319
Hillside Center, Wilmington, DE 218
Hillside Manor Healthcare & Rehab Center, St. Louis, MO 314
Hillside Nursing Center of Wake Forest, Wake Forest, NC 330
Hilltop Estates, Gothenburg, NE 317
Hilltop Rehabilitation & Nursing Center, Cincinnati, OH 335
Hillview Healthcare Center, La Crosse, WI 382
Hillview Manor, Goldthwaite, TX 365
Hillview Terrace, Montgomery, AL 186
Hilo Medical Center, Hilo, HI 238
Hindbrain see Rhombencephalon
Hippocampus 55, 82, 95, 115
Hiram Shaddox Geriatric Center, Mountain Home, AR 195
Hirano bodies 91, 96
Histology 95
HLA 2 allele 76, 96
Hoarding 96
Hobbs Health Care Center, Hobbs, NM 323
Holbrook Nursing Home, Buchanannon, WV 379
Holgate Quality Care Nursing & Rehabilitation Center, Holgate, OH 337
Holiday ManorCare Center, Canoga Park, CA 197
Holiday Pines Nursing & Rehabilitation LP, Woodville, TX 369
Holiday Resort, Emporia, KS 273
The Holiday Retirement Home, Manville, RI 354
Holladay Park Plaza, Portland, OR 346
Holland Home — Fulton Manor, Grand Rapids, MI 301
Hollidaysburg Veterans Home, Hollidaysburg, PA 350

Holly Heights Nursing Center, Denver, CO 209
Holly Manor Center, Mendham, NJ 321
Holly Nursing Care Center, Holly, CO 211
Holmes Lake Manor, Lincoln, NE 317
Holy Family Nursing and Rehab, Des Plaines, IL 246
Holy Rosary Extended Care Unit, Miles City, MT 316
Holyoke Geriatric & Convalescent Center, Holyoke, MA 295
Holyoke Rehabilitation Center, Holyoke, MA 295
Home and Community Based Programs 78
Home Association, Tampa, FL 229
Home Bridge Center, Belvidere, IL 242
Home care 96
Home care accreditation program 96
Home Health Care 96–7
Homeland Center, Harrisburg, PA 350
Homestead Care and Rehabilitation, Lancaster, OH 338
Homestead Health, Garden City, KS 273
Homestead Manor, Stamps, AR 195
Homestead Nursing Center, Lexington, KY 280
Homewood at Hanover, PA, Hanover, PA 350
Homewood at Williamsport Maryland Inc., Williamsport, MD 293
Homocysteine 77, 97
Hong, Jau-Shyong 118
Hooverwood Nursing Home, Indianapolis, IN 261
Hope Creek Care Center, East Moline, IL 247
Hope Health Care Center, Westland, MI 304
Hopewell Healthcare Center, Sumter, SC 357
Hopkins Manor, North Providence, RI 354
Horizon Care Center, Arverne, NY 324
Horizon Health & Rehabilitation Center, Fresno, CA 199
Horizon House, Seattle, WA 378
Horizons Health Care & Retirement Community, Eckert, CO 210
Howell Care Center at Howell, Howell, MI 301
Hoyt Nursing & Rehab Center, Saginaw, MI 303
Hubbard Care Center, Hubbard, IA 269
Hudson Point at Riverdale, Bronx, NY 324
Hudson View Care & Rehabilitation Center LLC, North Bergen, NJ 322
Human immunodeficiency virus (HIV) 10
Hunt Nursing & Retirement Center, Danvers, MA 294
Hunter Acres Care Center, Sikeston, MO 314

Hunter Creek Health & Rehabilitation, Northport, AL 186
Hunter Woods, Charlotte, NC 328
Huntington Park Care Center, Papillion, NE 318
Huntington's chorea disease 75, 97, 106, 108
Huperzine A 94, 97, 135
Huron County Medical Care Facility, Bad Axe, MI 298
Hurstbourne Care Center at Stony Brook, Louisville, KY 281
Hydergine see Ergoloid mesylate
Hydrocephalus 97–8
Hydrogen peroxide 50, 98
Hyman, Bradley 389
Hypercapnia 65
Hypernatremia 65
Hypertension 98, 136, 176
Hypoglycemia 65
Hypothalamus 32, 49, 68, 71, 98
Hypothyroidism 105, 117

Ibuprofen 24, 98
Idaho Falls Care & Rehab Center, Idaho Falls, ID 240
Idaho State Veterans Home — Boise, Boise, ID 239
Idaho State Veterans Home — Lewiston, Lewiston, ID 240
Idaho State Veterans Home — Pocatello, Pocatello, ID 241
Ideal Senior Living Center, Endicott, NY 325
Idebenone 98
Idylwood Care Center, Sunnyvale, CA 206
IHS at Doctor's Healthcare Center, Dallas, TX 364
IHS of Manchester, Manchester, NH 319
IHS of Williamston, Williamston, NC 330
Imaging studies 98–9, 107
Immanuel Campus of Care, Peoria, AZ 189
Immobility 90
Immune response 82
Immune system 82, 98
Imperial Grove Pavilion, Chicago, IL 245
Imperial Healthcare Center, Naples, FL 225
Inanition 99, 165
Incidence 90, 99
Incontinence 99
Independence 99
Indian Creek Healthcare Center & Rehabilitation Center, Overland Park, KS 276
Indian Hills Manor, Ogallala, NE 317
Indiana Alzheimer's Disease Center 389
Indiana Alzheimer's Disease National Cell Repository 99
Indiana University 389, 399
Indiana Veterans Home, West Lafayette, IN 265
Indigo Manor, Daytona Beach, FL 221
Indole-3-Proprionic Acid (IPA) 99–100

Infectious agents 75, 76, 100, 151
Infectious dementia 100
Inflammation 100–1
Informant Questionnaire on Cognitive Decline in the Elderly (IQCODE) 101
Ingraham Manor, Bristol, CT 214
Inheritance 101; see also Genes in Alzheimer's Disease
Inland Valley Care and Rehabilitation Center, Pomona, CA 203
The Inn at Freedom Village, Holland, MI 301
Innisfree Nursing and Rehabilitation, Rogers, AR 195
Inositol 50, 123
Insomnia 12, 66, 68, 71, 80
Instrumental Activities of Daily Living (IADL) 101
Insulin 101–2
Integrins 102
Intercommunity Care Center, Long Beach, CA 200
Interleukin 1 (IL–1) 102
Interlochen Health and Rehabilitation Center, Arlington, TX 363
Internal capsule 102
International Classification of Diseases, 10th revision (ICD-10) 102
International Genomics of Alzheimer's Project 102
Interview for Deterioration in Daily Living Activities in Dementia (IDDD) 102
Intracranial area of the brain 102
Intracranial pressure 38, 45
Intravenous immunoglobulin (IVIG) therapy 102–3
IOOF Home of Ohio, Springfield, OH 341
Iosco County Medical Care Facility, Tawas City, MI 304
Iowa City Rehabilitation & Health Care Center, Iowa City, IA 269
Iowa Veterans Home, Marshalltown, IA 270
The Iroquois Residents Home, Watseka, IL 256
Iron County Medical Care Facility, Crystal Falls, MI 299
Iron deposits 82, 103, 119
Ironwood Health & Rehabilitation Center, South Bend, IN 264
Isabella County Medical Care Facility, Mount Pleasant, MI 303
Isabella Geriatric Center, New York, NY 326
Isabelle Ridgeway Nursing Center, Columbus, OH 335
Ischemia 38, 103
Ischemia Scores 103
Island Nursing Home, Honolulu, HI 238
Island Nursing Home Inc., Deer Isle, ME 289
Issaquah Care Center, Issaquah, WA 376
Ivinson Memorial Hospital — Extended Care Facility, Laramie, WY 385
Ivy Court, Coeur D' Alene, ID 239
Ivy Woods Manor, North Lima, OH 340

Jacaranda Manor, St. Petersburg, FL 228
Jackson Memorial Longterm Care Center, Miami, FL 225
Jacksonville Convalescent Center, Jacksonville, IL 250
Jacobsen House, Seattle, WA 378
James Pointe Care Center, Newport News, VA 374
James S. Taylor Memorial Home, Louisville, KY 281
James Square Health & Rehabilitation Center, Syracuse, NY 327
Jamestown Health and Rehab, Rogers, AR 195
Janesville Nursing Home, Janesville, MN 306
JB Johnson Nursing Center, Washington, DC 219
Jefferson City Nursing & Rehabilitation, LLC, Jefferson City, MO 311
Jefferson Health Care Center, Jefferson, LA 284
Jefferson Manor Nursing & Rehab, Baton Rouge, LA 282
Jefferson Regional Medical Center, Pine Bluff, AR 195
Jennings Hall, Garfield Heights, OH 337
Jesup Healthcare, Jesup, GA 234
Jewell Care Center of Denver, Denver, CO 209
Jewish Healthcare Center, Worcester, MA 297
Jewish Home, San Francisco, CA 204
Jewish Home & Care Center, Milwaukee, WI 383
Jewish Home and Hospital for the Aged, New York, NY 326
Jewish Home of Greater Harrisburg, Harrisburg, PA 350
Jewish Home of Rochester Inc., Rochester, NY 327
JF Hawkins Nursing Home, Newberry, SC 356–7
JFK Hartwyck at Edison Estates, Edison, NJ 320
JML Care Center Inc., Falmouth, MA 295
Jo Ellen Smith Convalescent Center, New Orleans, LA 286
Job Haines Home for Aged People, Bloomfield, NJ 319
John J. Hainkel Jr. Home and Rehabilitation Center, New Orleans, LA 286
John Knox Village Health Center, Pompano Beach, FL 227
John Knox Village Medical Center, Tampa, FL 229
Johns Hopkins University 389, 398
Johnson, Eugene 389
Johnson County Care Center, Warrensburg, MO 314–5
Joint Commission on Accreditation of Healthcare Organizations (JCAHO) 103
Joliet Terrace, Joliet, IL 250
Jonesboro Healthcare Center, Jonesboro, AR 194
Jonesboro Nursing & Rehab Center, Jonesboro, GA 234

Joplin Health & Rehabilitation Center, Joplin, MO 311
Jordan Creek Nursing & Rehabilitation, Springfield, MO 314
The Joseph L. Morse Geriatric Center Inc., West Palm Beach, FL 230
Journal of Alzheimer's Disease 103
Joyce Eisenberg Keefer Medical Center, Reseda, CA 203
Judgment 11, 17, 55, 64, 72, 103, 132, 141
Julia Temple Center, Englewood, CO 210
Juniper Village — The Spearman Center, Denver, CO 209
Juniper Village at Monte Vista, Monte Vista, CO 212

Kade Nursing Home, Washington, PA 352–3
Kahl Home for the Aged & Infirm, Davenport, IA 268
Kaiser Permanente Post Acute, San Leandro, CA 205
Kansas Christian Home, Newton, KS 276
Kansas City Presbyterian Manor, Kansas City, KS 274
Kaplan Heathcare Center, Kaplan, LA 284
Karcher Estates, Nampa, ID 241
Karen Acres Care Center, Urbandale, IA 271
Kateri Residence, New York, NY 326
Katherine's Place at Weddington, Fayetteville, AR 193
Kathleen Daniel Rehabilitation Nursing Center, Framingham, MA 295
Kaye, Jeffrey 390
Keepsake Program 84–85
Keiro Nursing Home II, Los Angeles, CA 201
Keller Landing Care & Rehabilitation Center, Tuscumbia, AL 186
Kendal at Oberlin, Oberlin, OH 341
Kennebunk Nursing Home, Kennebunk, ME 289
Kennedy Care Center, Los Angeles, CA 201
Kennedy Health Care Center, Sewell, NJ 322
Kent Center, Kent, OH 338
Kent Regency Center, Warwick, RI 355
Kenwood Healthcare Center, Chicago, IL 245
Keswick Multicare Center, Baltimore, MD 291
Ketoglutarate dehydrogenase enzyme complex (KGDHC) 103–4
Kewaunee Health Care Center, Kewaunee, WI 382
Keysville Nursing & Rehabilitation Center, Keysville, GA 234
Khachaturian, Zaven 104, 151
Khalsa, Dharma Singh 114
Kidney disease 33, 65, 166
Kimberly Hall North, Windsor, CT 217
Kimberly Hall South Center, Windsor, CT 217

Kimwell Rehabilitation & Nursing, Fall River, MA 294–5

Kinases 104–5

Kindred Hospital Cleveland Subacute Unit, Cleveland, OH 335

King's Daughters Medical Center, Ashland, KY 279

Kings Harbor Multi-Care Center, Bronx, NY 324–5

King's ManorCare Center, Neptune, NJ 321

Kingsbrook Lifecare Center, Ashland, KS 279

Kingston of Ashland, Ashland, OH 332

Kirby Pines Manor, Memphis, TN 361

Kittanning Care Center, Kittanning, PA 350

Knapp Haven Nursing Home, Chetek, WI 381

Knox County Hospital, Barbourville, KY 279

Kohala Hospital, Kapaau, HI 239

Komanoff Center for Geriatric & Rehabilitative Medicine, Long Beach, NY 326

Korean ginseng 104

Korsakoff's syndrome 65, 104–5

Kowall, Neil 389

Kresson View Center, Voorhees, NJ 322

Kryscio, Richard 389

Kuakini Geriatric Care, Honolulu, HI 238

Kungholmen Project 65

Kunitz protease inhibitor (KPI) domain 105

La Belle ManorCare Center, La Belle, MO 312

La Colina Care Center, Tucson, AZ 191

La Crosse Health & Rehab, Coeur D' Alene, ID 239

La Estancia Nursing & Rehabilitation Center, Phoenix, AZ 189–90

La Grange Nursing & Rehab Center, La Grange, GA 234

La Hacienda at La Posada, Green Valley, AZ 188

La Mesa Healthcare Center, La Mesa, CA 200

La Mesa Healthcare Center, Yuma, AZ 192

La Paz at Paramount, Paramount, CA 202

La Villa Grande Care Center, Grand Junction, CO 211

Laboratory tests 11, 105

Lackawanna County Health Care Center, Olyphant, PA 351

Lacombe Nursing Centre, Lacombe, LA 284

Laconia Center Genesis ElderCare Network, Laconia, NH 319

LaCrosse Health & Rehabilitation Center, Coeur D'Alene, ID 239

Lafon Nursing Facility of the Holy Family, New Orleans, LA 286

Laguna Honda Hospital and Rehabilitation Center, San Francisco, CA 204

Lahser Hills Care Center, Southfield, MI 304

Laisure, Linda 105

Lake Balboa Care Center, Van Nuys, CA 206

Lake County Nursing 7 Rehab, East Chicago, IL 258

Lake Hills Inn, Lake Havasu, AZ 188

Lake Lodge Nursing & Rehabilitation LP, Fort Worth, TX 365

Lake Pointe Health Care, Lorain, OH 338

Lake Ridge Solana Alzheimer's Care Center, Moses Lake, WA 377

Lake Shore Healthcare and Rehab, Chicago, IL 245

Lake View Care Center at Delray, Delray Beach, FL 221–2

Lakeland Health Care Center, Effingham, IL 247

Lakeland Hills Center, Lakeland, FL 224

Lakeland Nursing & Rehabilitation Jackson, MS 308

Lakeland Nursing Home of Walworth County, Elkhorn, WI 381

Lakeland Skilled Nursing, Angola, IN 257

Lakepoint Nursing & Rehabilitation Center of El Dorado, El Dorado, KS 273

Lakeshore Skilled Nursing & Specialty Care, Detroit, MI 300

Lakeshore Villas Healthcare Center, Tampa, FL 229

Lakeshore Wedgewood, Nashville, TN 362

Lakeside Living Center, Quitman, MS 309

Lakeside Lutheran Home, Emmetsburg, IA 268

Lakeside Pavillion Healthcare, Naples, FL 225

Lakeview Center–Genesis Healthcare, Lakewood, NJ 314

Lakeview Health Center, West Salem, WI 385

Lakeview Healthcare & Rehabilitation, Lamar, MO 287

Lakeview Manor Inc., Indianapolis, IN 261

Lakeview Manor Nursing Home, New Road, LA 287

Lakeview Nursing Home, Inc., Birmingham, AL 184

Lakewood Care Center, Baudette, MN 305

Lakewood Park Health Center, Downey, CA 198

Lakewood Quarters Rehabilitation & Nursing Center, Baton Rouge, LA 282

Lancaster Care Center, Lancaster, WI 382

Lancaster Manor, Lincoln, NE 317

Landmark Care Center, Yakima, WA 379

Landmark Nursing Center — Hammond, Hammond, LA 284

Landmark of Lake Charles, Lake Charles, LA 285

Language/verbal skills 105–6, 147, 151, 159, 162, 165, 174, 179

Lanier Manor, Jacksonville, FL 223

Lanterman Developmental Center, Pomona, CA 203

Larchwood Inns, Grand Junction, CO 210

Largo Rehabilitation & Spa, Largo, FL 224

Larned Healthcare Living Center, Larned, KS 274–5

Las Flores Convalescent Hospital, Gardena, CA 199

Las Fuentes Care Center, Prescott, AZ 190

Las Villas Del Norte Health Care Center, Escondido, CA 199

LaSalle County Nursing Home, Ottawa, IL 253

Late-onset Alzheimer's Disease 106

Late-stage Alzheimer's Disease 106

Lateral sulcus 106

Lauderdale Christian Nursing Home, Killen, AL 185

Laurel ManorCare Center, Colorado Springs, CO 208

Laurel Wood Care Center, Johnstown, PA 350

Laurelhurst Village, Portk=land, OR 346

Laurell Point Healthcare & Rehabilitation, Fort Pierce, FL 222

The Laurels of Bedford, Battle Creek, MI 299

The Laurels of Mt. Pleasant, Mount Pleasant, MI 302

Laurelton Village, Brick, NJ 319

Lawrence Nursing Care Center, Arverne, NY 324

Lawrence Presbyterian Manor, Lawrence, KS 275

Lawton and Brody Scale for Instrumental Activities of Daily Living (IADL) 87

Lead 107

Leahi Hospital, Honolulu, HI 238

Learning/Thought Process 55, 64

Lecithin 50, 174

Lee County Constant Care Inc., Beatyville, KY 279

Lee Manor, Des Plaines, IL 246

Leewood Health Care Center, Annandale, VA 372

Legacy Park, Peabody, KS 277

Legacy Rehab and Care Center, Bullhead City, AZ 187

Leisure Court Nursing Center, Anaheim, CA 196

Leisure Oaks Convalescent Center, Defiance, OH 336

Leisure Park Health Center, Lakewood, NJ 321

Lemay Avenue Heath & Rehabilitation, Fort Collins, CO 210

Lemont Nursing & Rehab, Lemont, IL 250

Lenawee Medical Care Facility, Adrian, MI 298

Lenoir Health Care Center, Columbia, MO 310

Leon Sullivan Health Care Center, Seattle, WA 378

Leprosy 63, 157
Leroy Manor, Le Roy, IL 250
Levelland Nursing Home, Levelland, TX 366
Levey, Allan 388
Levindale Hebrew Geriatric Center & Hospital, Inc., Baltimore, MD 291
Lewis Memorial Christian Village, Springfield, IL 255
Lewy bodies 107
Lewy body dementia 14, 69, 107
Lewy body variant of Alzheimer's disease 107
Lexington Care Center, Lexington, MO 312
Lexington Health Care Center, Bloomington, IL 242
Lexington of Chicago Ridge, Chicago Ridge, IL 246
Lexington of Elmhurst, Elmhurst, IL 248
Lexington of LaGrange, LaGrange, IL 252
Lexington of Schaumburg, Schaumburg, IL 255
Lexington Park, Topeka, KS 277
Liberal Good Samaritan Center, Liberal, KS 275
Liberty Commons Nursing & Rehabilitation Center, Wilmington, NC 330
Liberty Country Place, Centralia, WA 376
Liberty Nursing & Rehabilitation of Mecklenburg City, Charlotte, NC 328
Liberty Retirement Community, Middleton, OH 339
Libertyville Manor Extended Care, Libertyville, IL 250
Life Care Center at Health Mountain, Phoenix, AZ 190
Life Care Center of Altamonte Springs, Altamonte Springs, FL 219
Life Care Center of Boise, Boise, ID 239
Life Care Center of Bruceton — Hollow Rock, Bruceton, TN 357
Life Care Center of Charleston, North Charleston, SC 357
Life Care Center of Colorado Springs, Colorado Springs, CO 208
Life Care Center of Columbia, Columbia, SC 355–6
Life Care Center of Columbia, Columbia, TN 360
Life Care Center of Crossville, Crossville, TN 360
Life Care Center of East Ridge, East Ridge, TN 359
Life Care Center of Escondido, Escondido, CA 198–9
Life Care Center of Grandview, Grandview, MO 311
Life Care Center of Greeley, Greeley, CO 211
Life Care Center of Hilo, Hilo, HI 238
Life Care Center of Hilton Head, Hilton Head Island, SC 356

Life Care Center of Idaho Falls, Idaho Falls, ID 240
Life Care Center of Kona, Kailua Kona, HI 238
Life Care Center of Lewiston, Lewiston, ID 240
Life Care Center of Littleton, Littleton, CO 211
Life Care Center of Longmont, Longmont, CO 212
Life Care Center of Medina, Medina, OH 339
Life Care Center of Michigan City, IN 262
Life Care Center of Osawatomie, Osawatomie, KS 276
Life Care Center of Paradise Valley, Phoenix, AZ 190
Life Care Center of Port Orchard, Port Orchard, WA 377
Life Care Center of Pueblo, Pueblo, CO 212
Life Care Center of Red Rock, Chattanooga, TN 359
Life Care Center of Sandpoint, Sandpoint, ID 241
Life Care Center of Scottsdale, Scottsdale, AZ 190
Life Care Center of Sierra Vista, Sierra Vista, AZ 191
Life Care Center of Treasure Valley, Boise, ID 239
Life Care Center of Tucson, Tucson, AZ 192
Life Care Center of Westminster, Westminster, CO 213
Life Care Center of Winter Haven, Winter Haven, FL 230
Life Care Center of Yuma, Yuma, AZ 192
Life Care Centers of Wichita, Wichita, KS 278
Life prolonging interventions 107
Life sustaining treatment 107
Lillian E. Kerr Healthcare Center, Phelps, WI 383
Lily Pond Nursing Home, Staten Island, NY 327
Lima Convalescent Home, Lima, OH 338
Limbic system 20, 30, 95, 107, 142
Lincoln Donaldson Care Center, Fayetteville, TN 360
Lincoln Lutheran Care Center, Racine, WI 384
Lincoln Park Manor, Kettering, OH 338
Lincoln Park Manor, Lincoln, KS 275
Linden Grove, Puyallup, WA 377
Lindengrove, Waukesha, WI 384
Lingenfelter Center, Kingman, AZ 188
Linwood Care Center, Linwood, NJ 321
Linwood Nursing & Rehabilitation Center, Scranton, PA 352
Linwood Village Nursing, Cushing, OK 343
Lipid disorders 26, 50, 52, 65
Lipid peroxidation 82, 107–8
Lipofuscin 45, 107

Litchfield Woods Health Care Center, Torrington, CT 216
Little Creek Sanitarium, Knoxville, TN 361
Little Flower Manor & St. Therese Residence, Scranton Diocese, Wilkes-Barre, PA 353
Little Sisters of the Poor, Louisville, KY 281
Live Oak Retirement Center, Shreveport, LA 288
Liver disease 107, 108
Living trust 107
Living will 12, 70, 75, 108
Lobar distribution 107
Lobes of the brain 47, *48*
Lodi Good Samaritan Center, Lodi, WI 382
Logan Manor Community Health Services, Logan, KS 275
Logan Nursing & Rehabilitation Center, Logan, UT 369
Loganhurst Health Care, Spokane, WA 378
Logical Memory Delayed Recall 107
Lomond Peak Care & Rehab, Ogden, UT 369
Long Beach Care Center, Inc., Long Beach, CA 200
Long Ridge of Stamford, Stamford, CT 216
Long-term care 107
Long-term care insurance 107–8
Long Term Care of Greenfield, Greenfield, OH 337
Longmeadow Nursing Center — Camden, Camden, AR 192–3
Longmeadow Nursing Center — Malvern, Malvern, AR 194
Longview Nursing Home, Manchester, MD 292
Longwood Manor Convalescent Hospital, Los Angeles, CA 201
Lopez, Oscar 390
Lorantffy Care Center Incorporated, Akron, OH 331
Louisiana War Veterans Home, Jackson, LA 285
Lourdes Health Care Center, Inc., Wilton, CT 217
Lourdes-Noreen McKeen Residence for Geriatric Care, West Palm Beach, FL 230
Loveland Health Care Center, Loveland, OH 338
Lovestone, Simon 54
Low dose naltrexone (LDN) 109
Lowell Healthcare Center, Lowell, MA 296
Lowman Home Nursing Home, White Rock, SC 357
Lubbock Hospitality House, Lubbock, TX 366
Lumbar puncture 109
Luther Crest Nursing Facility, Allentown, PA 347
Luther Manor, Dubuque, IA 268
Luther Manor, Milwaukee, WI 383
Luther Manor Nursing Home, Saginaw, MI 303
The Lutheran Home, Belle Plaine, MN 305

Lutheran Home — Monroe, Monroe, MI 302
Lutheran Home, Strawberry Point, IA 271
Lutheran Home for the Aged, Arlington Heights, IL 242
Lutheran Home Hickory, Hickory, NC 329
Lutheran Life Villages, Fort Wayne, IN 259
Lutheran Memorial Home, Sandusky, OH 341
Lutheran Village of Columbus Care Center, Columbus, OH 335
Luverne Nursing Facility, Luverne, AL 185
Lynch, Gary 109
Lyngblomstem Care Center, St. Paul, Minnesota 307–8
Lynwood Nursing Home, Mobile, AL 185
Lyons Good Samaritan Center, Lyons, KS 275

M266 109
Mabee Health Care Center, Midland, TX 367
Macneal Memorial Hospital, Berwyn, IL 242
Macroglia *29*
Mad cow disease *see* Bovine spongiform encephalopathy
The Madison, Morgantown, WV 380
Madison Health and Rehabilitation LLC, Little Rock, AR 194
Madison memory study 25
Madison Valley Manor, Ennis, MT 315
Madrid Home for the Aging, Madrid, IA 270
Magnesium 109
Magnetic resonance imaging (MRI) *49*, 109–11
Magnetic resonance spectroscopy (MRS) 111
Magnolia Estates, Lafayette, LA 285
Magnolia Haven Nursing Home, Tuskegee, AL 187
Magnolia Health Care Center, Seattle, WA 378
Magnolia Manor Nursing Home Inc., Shreveport, LA 288
Magnolia Manor of Columbus Nursing Center, Columbus, GA 232
Magnolia Special Care Center, El Cajon, CA 198
Magnolia Village Care & Rehabilitation Center, Bowling Green, KY 279
Magnum Care of Adrian, Adrian. MI 298
Magnum Care of Albion, Albion, MI 298
Maine General Rehab & Nursing at Glenridge, Augusta, ME 288
Maine General Rehab & Nursing at Graybirch, Augusta, ME 288
Maine Veteran's Home, Augusta, ME 289
Maine Veteran's Home — Bangor, Bangor, ME 289

Maison Aine, Stow, OH 341
Maison De Lafayette, Lafayette, LA 285
Maison De Ville Nursing Home of Harvey, Harvey, LA 284
Maison De Ville of Houma, Houma, LA 284
Majora Lane Care Center, Millersburg, OH 339
Malnutrition 111
Maluhia, Honolulu, HI 238
Malvern Nursing and Rehabilitation, Malvern, AR 194
Managed Care 111–2
Manchester and Oxford Universities Scale for the Psychopathological Assessment of Dementia (MOUSEPAD) 112
Manderley Health Care Center, Osgood, IN 263
Manitowoc Health Care Center, Manitowoc, WI 382
Manor Oaks Nursing & Rehabilitation National Healthcare, Fort Lauderdale, FL 222
Manor of Battle Creek, Battle Creek, MI 299
Manor of Farmington Hills, Farmington Hills, MI 300
Manor of Northwest Detroit Skilled Nursing & Rehab, Detroit, MI 300
Manor of the Plains, Dodge City, KS 272
Manor of Wayne Skilled Nursing & Rehab, Wayne, MI 304
Manor on the Green, Daytona Beach, FL 221
Manor Pines Convalescent Center, Fort Lauderdale, FL 222
ManorCare, Canton, OH 334
ManorCare at Elk Grove Village, Elk Grove Village, IL 248
ManorCare at Hinsdale, Hinsdale, IL 249
ManorCare at Kankakee, Kankakee, IL 250
ManorCare at Libertyville, Libertyville, IL 251
ManorCare at Oak Lawn — East, Oak Lawn, IL 252
ManorCare at Oak Lawn — West, Oak Lawn, IL 252
ManorCare at Palos Heights — East, Palos Heights, IL 253
ManorCare at Palos Heights — West, Palos Heights, IL 252
ManorCare at Rolling Meadows, Rolling Meadows, IL 254
ManorCare Health Services, Aberdeen, SD 357
ManorCare Health Services, Akron, OH 332
ManorCare Health Services, Anderson, IN 256–7
ManorCare Health Services, Arlington, VA 372
ManorCare Health Services, Barberton, OH 333
ManorCare Health Services — Bethel Park, Bethel Park, PA 348
ManorCare Health Services, Boca Raton, FL 220

ManorCare Health Services — Boulder, Boulder, CO 207
ManorCare Health Services, Chambersburg, PA 348
ManorCare Health Services, Dallas, TX 364
ManorCare Health Services, Davenport, IA 267
ManorCare Health Services, Delray Beach, FL 222
ManorCare Health Services, Dubuque, IA 268
ManorCare Health Services — Dunedin, Dunedin, FL 222
ManorCare Health Services, Elizabethtown, PA 349
ManorCare Health Services, Fond Du Lac, WI 381
ManorCare Health Services, Houston, TX 366
ManorCare Health Services — Kingston Court, York, PA 353
ManorCare Health Services, Lynnwood, WA 377
ManorCare Health Services, Madison, WI 382
ManorCare Health Services — New Providence, NJ 321
ManorCare Health Services — North, York, PA 353
ManorCare Health Services, North Olmsted, OH 340
ManorCare Health Services — Pike Creek, Wilmington, DE 218
ManorCare Health Services — Plantation, FL 227
ManorCare Health Services — Pottstown, Pottstown, PA 352
ManorCare Health Services — Prestwick, Avon, IN 257
ManorCare Health Services, Reno, NV 318
ManorCare Health Services — Ruxton, Towson, MD 292
ManorCare Health Services, Sarasota, FL 228
ManorCare Health Services, Silver Spring, MD 292
ManorCare Health Services — South Holland, South Holland, IL 255
ManorCare Health Services, Springfield, MO 314
ManorCare Health Services Stratford Hall, Richmond, VA 374
ManorCare Health Services — Summer Trace, Carmel, IN 257
ManorCare Health Services, Venice, FL 229
ManorCare Health Services, Webster, TX 368
ManorCare Health Services — West Reading North, West Reading, PA 353
ManorCare Health Services — Williamsport North, Williamsport, PA 353
ManorCare Health Services — Williamsport South, Williamsport, PA 353
ManorCare Health Services — Wilmington, Wilmington, DE 218
ManorCare Nursing & Rehab Center, Winter Park, FL 230

ManorCare Nursing Center, Denver CO 209

ManorCare of Elgin, Elgin, IL 248

ManorCare of Wilmette, Wilmette, IL 256

ManorCare Rehabilitation Center — Decatur, Decatur, GA 233

ManorCare Rehabilitation Center — Marietta, Marietta, GA 235

Mansfield Memorial Home, Mansfield, OH 338

Maple Crest Care Center, Belvidere, IL 242

Maple Lane Health Care Facility, Shawano, WI 384

Maple Lane Nursing Home, Barton, VT 371

Maple Lawn Health Center, Eureka, IL 248

Maple Park Village, Westfield IN 265

Maple Ridge Care Centre, Lincoln, IL 251

Maple View Manor, Rocky Hill, CT 216

Maples Benzie Co Medical Center, Frankfort, MI 301

Maplewood Center, West Allis, WI 384–5

Maravilla Care Center, Phoenix, AZ 190

Marchiafava-Bignami disease 51

Margaret Manor, Chicago, IL 245

Margaret McLaughlin McCarrick Care, Somerset, NJ 322

Margaret Tietz for Nursing Care Inc., Jamaica, NY 325

The Maria-Joseph Center, Dayton, OH 336

Marian Estates, Sublimity, OR 346

Marian Manor, Boston, MA 293

Marian Manor Corp, Pittsburgh, PA 352

Marietta Center for Health & Rehabilitation, Marietta, GA 235

Marietta Center for Health & Rehabilitation, Marietta, OH 338

Marion County Nursing Home, Yellville, AR 195

Marion House Health Care Center, Ocala, FL 226

Markle Health Care, Markle, IN 262

Marlinda Imperial Convalescent Hospital, Pasadena, CA 203

Marquette County Medical Care Facility, Ishpeming, MI 301–2

Marquette Manor, Indianapolis, IN 261

Marquis Care at Oregon City, Oregon City, OR 346

Marquis Care at Plum Ridge, Klamath Falls, OR 346

Marshall Manor Nursing Home, Guntersville, AL 184

Marson, Daniel 387

Martha Franks Baptist Retirement Center, Laurens, SC 356

Martin, George 391

Martin Luther Care Center, Bloomington, MN 305

Mary Ann Morse Nursing & Rehabilitation Center, Natick, MA 296

Mary Anna Nursing Home Inc., Wisner, LA 288

Mary Goss Nursing Home, Monroe, LA 285

Mary Jude Nursing Home, West Allis, WI 385

Mary Lee DePugh Nursing Home, Winter Park, FL 230

Mary Manning Walsh Nursing Home, New York, NY 326

Maryhaven Nursing & Rehab, Glenview, IL 249

Marymount Manor SNF, Eureka, MO 310

Maryville Healthcare & Rehabilitation, Maryville, TN 361

Maryville Nursing Home, Beaverton, OR 345

Masonic Care Health Center, Wallingford, CT 217

Masonic Village at Elizabethtown, Elizabethtown, PA 349

Massage therapy and physical therapy 112

Masters Healthcare Center, Algood, TN 359

Mather Pavilion, Evanston, IL 249

Mattoon Healthcare & Rehab, Mattoon, IL 252

Mayfair Manor, Lexington, KY 280

Mayflower Health Care Center, Grinnell, IA 269

Mayflower Health Care Center, Winter Park, FL 230

Mayo Clinic 63, 119, 388, 389, 402

Mayo Healthcare Inc., Northfield, VT 371

McAuley Center, Urbana, OH 341

McAuley Hall, Watchung, NJ 322

McCrea Manor Nursing & Rehabilitation Center, Alliance, OH 332

McCrite Plaza Health Center, Topeka, KS 277

McGivney Health Care Center, Carmel, IN 257

McIntosh Manor, McIntosh, MN 306

McKendree Village, Hermitage, TN 360

McKinley Health Care, Canton, OH 334

McLean Health Center, Simsbury, CT 216

McMahon-Tomlinson Nursing Center, Lawton, OK 343

McPherson Care Center, LLC, McPherson, KS 275

Meadow Green Nursing & Rehabilitation Center, Waltham, MA 297

Meadowbridge Transitional Care Unit, Mechanicsville, VA 374

Meadowbrook Golden LivingCenter, Rapid City, SD 358

Meadowbrook Manor — Bolingbrook, Bolingbrook, IL 242–3

Meadowbrook Manor — Hartford, Fowler, OH 337

Meadowbrook Nursing Home, Pulaski, TN 362

Meadowbrook Nursing Home, Tucker, GA 237

Meadowcrest Nursing Center, Bethel Park, PA 348

Meadowlark Hills, Manhattan, KS 275

The Meadows, Nashville, TN 362

Meadows Manor, Terre Haute, IN 264

Meadows Mennonite Home, Chenoa, IL 243

Meals on Wheels 167, 398

Medco Center of Bowling Green, Bowling Green, KY 279

Medial temporal lobe 10, 57, 95, 107, 110

Medicaid 44, 93, 112, 136, 137, 152, 161, 165

Medical Care Center, Lynchburg, VA 373

Medical ethics 112

Medical problems 112

Medicalodge of Eudora, Eudora, KS 273

Medicalodge of Fort Scott, Fort Scott, KS 273

Medicalodge Post Acute Center of Kansas City, Kansas City, KS 274

Medicalodges Butler, Butler, MO 309

Medicalodges of Arkansas City, Arkansas City, KS 272

Medicalodges of Douglass, Douglass, KS 273

Medicare 112–3

Medicare HMOs 113

Medicare Payment Advisory Commission (MedPAC) 113

Medications that may cause or worsen cognitive impairment 72, 85, 113

Medi-Home Inc. of Arkoma, Arkoma, OK 342

Medilodge of Southfield, Inc., Southfield, MI 304

Medilodge of Taylor, Inc., Taylor, MI 304

Medina Village Retirement Community, Medina, OH 339

Meditation 113–4

Medulla oblongata **49**, 114

Mega, Michael 114

Melancholia 12, 66, 114

Melanin 114

Melanotransferrin 103, 141

Melatonin 114

MEM1003 114

Memantine 90, 114–5

Memorial Delirium Assessment Scale (MDAS) 115

Memorial Hospital Transitional Care, Abilene, KS 272

Memorial Veterans Hospital, Boston University 389

Memory 108, 109, 110, **115**–116, 118, 119, 123, 125, 128, 132

Memory aids 116

Memory impairment 64, 87, 98, 115, 116

Memory storage 115

Memory tests 78, 153

Memphis Jewish Home, Cordova, TN 360

Meninges of the brain 116

Meningitis 65, 97, 98, 116

Menno Haven, Chambersbury, PA 348

Mennonite Memorial Home, Bluffton, OH 333

Menorah House, Boca Raton, FL 220

Menorah Park Center for Seniors, Beachwood, OH 333

Mercer County Nursing Home, Aledo, IL 242

Mercury 105, 107, 116

Mercy Haven Health Care Center, Snohomish, WA 378

Mercy Hospital of the Franciscan Sisters, Oelwein, IA 270

Mercy Medical, Daphne, AL 184

Mercy Retirement & Care Center, Oakland, CA 202

Mercy St. John's Center, Springfield, OH 341

Meridian Care Monte Vista, San Antonio, TX 367

Meridian Nursing, Ocean Grove, NJ 322

Meridian Village Care Center, Glen Carbon, IL 249

The Merriman of Akron, Akron, OH 332

Merry Manor, Marion, IN 262

Mesa Christian Health and Rehabilitation Center, Mesa, AZ 189

Mesa Vista of Boulder, Boulder, CO 207

Mesencephalon 117

Mesial temporal lobe 117

Messenger House Care Center, Bainbridge Island, WA 375

Messiah Village, Mechanicsburg, PA 351

Mesulam, Marsel 388

Metabolic causes of dementia 117

Metabolism 117, 120, 148, 149

Metacom Manor Health Center, Bristol, RI 354

Metairie Health Care Center, Metairie, LA 285

Metalloproteinases 117

Metals see Minerals and Heavy metal toxicity

Methodist Home, Chicago, IL 245

Metrifonate 10, 117–8

Metropolitan Jewish Geriatric Center, Brooklyn, NY 325

Mi Casa Nursing Center, Mesa, AZ 189

MI Nursing & Restorative Center, Lawrence, MA 295–6

Miami Jewish Home & Hospital for the Aged, Inc., Miami, FL 225

Michigan Christian Home, Grand Rapids, MI 301

Michigan Masonic Home, Alma, MI 298

Microglial cells 22, 28, 29, 118

Microtubule-associated protein tau (MAPT) 118

Microtubules 118, 127

Mid-America Convalescent Centers Inc., Chicago, IL 245

Mid-Atlantic of Cumberland, LLC, Cumberland, MD 291

Middle Georgia Nursing Home, Eastman, GA 233

Middlebelt Health Care Center, Livonia, MI 302

Middletown Nursing, Middletown, IN 262

Midlands Living Center, LLC, Council Bluffs, IA 267

Midmichigan Stratford Village, Midland, MI 302

Midsagittal section of the brain 49

Midsouth Health & Rehabilitation Center, Memphis, TN 361

Milan Health Care Center, Milan, IN 262

Milbank Memorial Fund 118

Mild cognitive impairment (MCI) 118–9

Milford Center Genesis ElderCare Network, Milford, DE 218

Milford Valley Memorial Long Term Care Center, Milford, UT 369

Millcreek Health Center, Salt Lake City, UT 370

Mille Lacs Health System, Onamia, MN 307

Miller Healthcare Center, Kankakee, IL 250

Miller's Merry Manor, Huntington, IN 260

Miller's Merry Manor, Middletown, IN 262

Miller's Merry Manor, Wabash, IN 265

The Millhouse, Trenton, NJ 322

Milton & Hattie Kutz Home, Wilmington, DE 218

Milwaukee Catholic Home, Milwaukee, WI 383

Milwaukee Protestant Home for Aged Health Center, Milwaukee, WI 383

Mineral Springs of North Conway, Healthcare & Rehabilitation, North Conway, NH 319

Minerals 24, 129, 181

Minerva Elder Care, Minerva, OH 339

Mini-Mental Status Examination (MMSE) 119

Minnequa Midcenter, Inc., Pueblo, CO 212

Minnesota Valley Health Center, Le Sueur, MN 306

Mission Arch Care, Roswell, NM 324

Mission Carmichael Healthcare Center, Carmichael, CA 197

Mission Nursing Home, Plymouth, MN 307

Mission Oaks Manor, San Antonio, TX 367

Mississippi Care Center of Dekalb, LLC, De Kalb, MS 308

Missoula Health & Rehabilitation Center, Missoula, MT 316

Mitchell Manor Convalescent Home, McAlester, OK 343

Mitchell's Nursing Home Inc., Danville, AR 193

Mitochondria 120

Mitochondrial DNA polymorphisms 120

Mixed forms of dementia 120

MM Ewing Continuing Care Care Center, Canandaigua, NY 325

Moberly Nursing & Rehabilitation, Moberly, MO 313

Mobile Nursing and Rehabilitation Center, Mobile, AL 185

Mobridge Care Center, Mobridge, SC 358

Modified Mini-Mental Status Examination 120

Modified Scales of Psychological Development (M–OSOD) 98

Molecular genetics 120

Molokai General Hospital, Kaunakakai, HI 239

Monarda 120

Monoamine oxidase 120

Monoamine oxidase inhibitors (MAO inhibitors) 120–1

Monoclonal antibody therapy 121

Monosodium glutamate 121, 135

Monroe Community Hospital, Rochester, NY 327

Monroe Manor, Jay, OK 343

Monte Vista Grove Homes, Pasadena, CA 203

Montebello on Academy Healthcare Center, Albuquerque, NM 323

Montello Manor, Lewiston, ME 289

Monterey Pines Skilled Nursing Facility, Monterey, CA 202

MonteVista at Coronado, El Paso, TX 364

Montgomery Care & Rehabilitation, Clarksville, TN 359

Montgomery Place, Chicago, IL 245

Monticello Nursing & Rehabilitation, Monticello, IA 270

Mood 12, 121

Moore-Few Care Center, Nevada, MO 313

Moravian Manor, Lititz, PA 351

Morning View Care Center of Centerburg, Carrollton, OH 335

Morningside Manor, Alcester, SD 357

Morningside Manor, San Antonio, TX 367

Morris, John 119

Morris Hills Center, Morristown, NJ 321

Morrison-Bogorad, Marcelle 121

Morrow Manor Nursing Center, Chesterville, OH 335

Mortality 17, 121

Morton Bakar Center, Hayward, CA 200

Motor fibers 121

Motor skills/Movement disorders 21, 37, 67, 160

Mound View Health Center, Moundsville, WV 380

Mount Carmel Home — Keens Memorial, Kearney, NE 317

Mount Carmel Medical & Rehabilitation Center, Burlington, WI 380

Mount Miguel Covenant Village Health Facility, Spring Valley, CA 205

Mount Olivet Careview Home, Minneapolis, MN 306

Mount Pleasant Healthcare Center, Mount Pleasant, TX 367

Mount Pleasant Manor, Mount Pleasant, SC 356

Mount Pleasant Retirement Village, Monroe, OH 339

Mount Saint Francis Health Center, Woonsocket, RI 355

Mount Saint Francis Nursing Center, Colorado Springs, CO 208

Mount Saint Joseph Nursing Home, Waterville, ME 290

Mount Saint Vincent Nursing Home, Holyoke, MA 295
Mount Vernon Nursing Center, Alexandria, VA 372
Mountain Ridge Wellness Center, Black Mountain, NC 328
Mountain Towers Healthcare & Rehabilitation Center, Cheyenne, WY 385
Mountain Valley Rehabilitation Center, Kellogg, ID 240
Mountain View Care Center, Colorado Springs, CO 208
Mountain View Care Center, Tucson, AZ 371
Mountain View Center Genesis Healthcare, Rutland, VT 371
Mountain View Health & Rehabilitation, Carson City, NV 318
Mountain View Health Services, Ogden, UT 369–70
Mountain View Manor, Prescott, AZ 190
Mountain View Nursing Home, Ossipee, NH 319
Mountain Vista Health Center, Wheat Ridge, CO 213
Mountainview Health Care Center, Birmingham, AL 184
Muhlenberg Community Hospital, Greenville, KY 280
Mulberry Manor, Stephenville, TX 368
Multi-infarct dementia (MID) 100
Multi-Medical Center, Towson, MD 293
Multiple sclerosis 65, 122, 123
Muscarinic acetylcholine receptor 122
Muscle weakness 71, 158
Muscogee Manor & Rehabilitation Center, Columbus, GA 232
Music therapy 122
Mutations see Gene mutations
Mycoplasma fermentens 122
Myelin basic protein (MBP) 122
Myelin basic protein (MBP) antibodies 123
Myelin 26, 38, 88
Myelin sheath 123
Myelinated nerve fibers 123
Myoclonus 123
Myrtle Beach Manor, Myrtle Beach, SC 356
Myxedema coma 65, 117

N-acetylcysteine (NAC) 123
Naming deficits 106
Nampa Care Center, Nampa, ID 241
Nancy Hart Nursing Center, Elberton, GA 233
Naproxen 16, 123
Natchitoches Community Health Center, Natchitoches, LA 286
Natchitoches Nursing & Rehabilitation, LLC, Natchitoches, LA 286
Nathaniel Witherell, Greenwich, CT 215
National Alzheimer's Coordinating Center 123
National Center for Complementary and Alternative Medicine (NCCAM) 14

National Center on Caregivers Division 123
National Citizens' Coalition for Nursing Home Reform (NCCNHR) 123–4
National Institute of Allergy & Infectious Disease (NIAD) 124
National Institute of Mental Health (NIMH) 124
National Institute of Neurogical Disorders and Stroke (NINDS) 124
National Institute on Aging (NIA) 123, 124, 132
National Institutes of Environmental Health Sciences 118, 141
National Institutes of Health (NIH) 124
National Library of Medicine (NLM) 124
National Senior Citizens Law Center (NSCLC) 124
Nazareth Home, Louisville, KY 281
Nebraska Skilled Nursing & Rehabilitation, Omaha, NE 317
Nefiracetam 124
The Neighbors, Byron, IL 243
Nentwic Convalescent Home Incorporated, East Liverpool, OH 336
Neocortex 37, 124
Neostigmine 125
NeoTrofin (AIT–082) 125
Nerve fibers 125
Nerve growth factor 125, 132, 133
Nerve impulse 125, *126*
Nervous system 8, 125
Neshaminy Manor Home, Warrington, PA 352
Neural thread protein (NTP) 125
Neurites 125
Neuritic plaques see Senile plaque
Neurodegenerative disease 125–7, 149, 152, 159, 166, 178
Neurofibrillary tangles (NFTs) 36–7, *38*, *39*, *127*, 128
Neurofilament inclusion body disease (NIBD) 128–9
Neurogenesis 129
Neuroglia 129
Neuroleptic medications 129
Neurological disorder 129
Neurology 129
Neuroma 129
Neuromodulator 129
Neuromuscular junction 129
Neuronal damage and destruction 14, 32, 40, 71, 73, 78, 96, 108
Neuronal growth 38, 64
Neurons 8, *39*, 89, 129–31
Neuropathological staging of Alzheimer's disease 131
Neuropathology 131
Neuropathy 131
Neuropeptides 131
Neuropil threads 36
Neuropraxia 131–2
Neuroprotective agents 132
Neuropsychiatric inventory (NPI) 132
Neuropsychiatric testing 69
Neuropsychologic symptoms in Alzheimer's disease 132
Neuropsychological tests 132

Neuro-Rehab Center of Worcester, Worcester, MA 297
Neuroscience and Neuropsychology of Aging (NNA) Program of the NIA 132
Neurosyphilis 65, 73
Neurotoxicity 21, 61
Neurotoxin 133
Neurotransmitters 78, 79, 80, 84, *126*, 133
Neurotrophic factors 48, 133
Neurotrophins 133
New Harmonie Healthcare Center, New Harmony, IN 263
New Hope Health and Rehabilitation, LLC, Rogers, AR 195
New Horizon Nursing Center, Odessa, TX 367
New Horizons Care Center, Lovell, WY 385
New Horizons North, Gainesville, GA 233
New Iberia Manor South, New Iberia, LA 286
New Light Nursing Home, Detroit, MI 300
New London Healthcare Center, Snellville, GA 236
New Mark Care Center, Kansas City, MO 312
New Vista Nursing & Rehabilitation Center, Sunland, CA 205–6
New York University 79, 88, 149, 390
Newark Healthcare Center, Newark, OH 340
Newkirk Nursing Center, Newkirk, OK 344
The Newport, Newport News, VA 374
Newport Nursing & Rehabilitation, Jersey City, NH 321
Newton Healthcare Center, Newton, IA 270
Newton Presbyterian Manor, Newton, KS 276
NHC Health Care, Chattanooga, Chattanooga, TN 359
NHC Health Care — Hillview Health Care Center, Columbia, TN 360
NHC Health Care, Laurens, SC 356
NHC Health Care — Maryland Heights, Maryland Heights, MO 312
NHC Health Care — McMinnville, McMinnville, TN 361
NHC Health Care, Pulaski, TN 362
NHC Healthcare — Sumter, Sumter, SC 357
NHC Healthcare — Town and Country, Town and Country, MO 314
NHC McMinville Health Care Center, McMinnville, TN 362
Niacinamide 133–4
Nicotinamide adenine dinucleotide (NADH) 112
Nicotine 134
Nicotinic acetylcholine receptor 134
Nightingale Health Care Center, Warren, MI 301
NINCDS/ADRA criteria for Alzheimer's disease 134
Nineteenth Avenue Healthcare Center, San Francisco, CA 204

Nitric oxide (NO) 134–5
Nitric oxide synthase 135
NMDA (N-methyl-d-aspartate) receptor 90, 115, 135
NMS Healthcare of Hagerstown, Hagerstown, MD 292
Noncognitive behavioral abnormalities 135
Non-steroidal anti-inflammatory drugs 61, 84, 135
Norepinephrine 133, 135–6
Normal pressure hydrocephalus 97–8, 136
Normandy Terrace Nursing & Rehabilitation Center, San Antonio, TX 367
North Canyon Care Center, Bountiful, UT 369
North Central Good Samaritan Center, Mohall, ND 331
North Church Nursing & Rehab, Jacksonville, IL 250
North Creek Health and Rehabilitation Center, Bothell, WA 376
North Florida Rehabilitation & Specialty Care, Gainesville, FL 222
North Gate Health Care Facility, North Tonawanda, NY 326
North Hills Life Care and Rehabilitation, Fayetteville, AR 193
North Las Vegas Care Center, North Las Vegas, NV 318
North Mountain Medical and Rehabilitation Center, Phoenix, AZ 190
North Ridge Care Center, New Hope, MN 307
Northampton Nursing Home Inc., Northampton, MA 296
Northeast Atlanta Health & Rehab Center, Atlanta, GA 231
Northeast LA War Veteran's Home, Monroe, LA 285–6
Northern Lakes Nursing & Rehab, Angola, IN 257
Northern Manhattan Rehab & Nursing Center, New York, NY 326
Northfield Center for Health & Rehabilitation, Louisville, KY 281
Northgate Unit of Lakeview Christian Home, Carlsbad, NM 323
Northpoint Lexington Healthcare Center, Lexington, KY 280
Northpoint Med and Rehab Center, Oshkosh, WI 383
Northridge Care Center, Baker, LA 282
Northview Village, St. Louis, MO 314
Northwest Louisiana War Veterans Home, Bossier City, LA 283
Northwestern University 388
Northwood Care Center, Belvidere, IL 242
Northwoods Health Care Center, Belvidere, IL 242
Norwell Knoll Nursing Home, Norwell, MA 296
Norwichtown and Care Center, Norwich, CT 215
Norwood Pines Alzheimers Center, Sacramento, CA 203
Novartis Foundation for Gerontology 136

Nucleus basalis of Meynert 136
Nun Study 136, 180
Nu-Roc Community Healthcare, Laona, WI 382
Nurse Care of Buckhead, Atlanta, GA 231
Nursecare Nursing & Rehabilitation Center,, Shreveport, LA 288
Nursing and Rehabilitation Center at Good Shepherd, Little Rock, AR 194
Nursing Center at Freedom Village, Bradenton, FL 220
Nursing Center at University Village, Tampa, FL 229
Nursing home accreditations 136–7
Nursing home costs 137
Nursing home facilities 137
Nursing home Medicaid alternatives to long term care 137
Nursing home options 137–8
Nursing home violations 138
Nutrient deficiencies 138–9
NYC Healthcare Joplin, Joplin, MO 311
Nymox Pharmaceutical Corporation 125
Nystagmus 139

Oahe Manor — Gettysburg Medical Center, Gettysburg, SD 358
Oak Grove Rehabilitation & Living Center, Waterville, ME 290
Oak Hill, Waterloo, IL 255–6
Oak Lea Nursing Home, Harrisonburg, VA 373
Oak Manor Healthcare & Rehabilitation Center, Largo, FL 224
Oak Park Nursing & Rehabilitation, San Antonio, TX 367
Oak Springs of Warrenton, Warrenton, VA 375
Oak Trace Care and Rehabilitation Center, Bessemer, AL 183
Oak View Home, Waverly Hall, GA 237
Oakbridge Healthcare Center, Lake Worth, FL 224
Oakcreek Nursing & Rehabilitation, Luling, TX 366
Oakdale Care Center, Poplar Bluff, MO 313
Oakland Manor Nursing Center, Giddings, TX 365
Oakland Nursing & Rehabilitation Center, Oakland, MD 292
Oaklawn Nursing & Rehabilitation Center, Louisville, KY 281
Oakmont West Nursing Center, Greenville, SC 356
Oaknoll Retirement Residence, Iowa City, IA 269
The Oaks, Monroe, LA 286
The Oaks at Avon, Avon Park, FL 219
The Oaks at Limestone, Gainesville, GA 233
The Oaks at Peake, Macon, GA 234
The Oaks of Carrollton, Carrollton, GA 232
The Oaks of Houma, Houma, LA 284
Oaks of Kissimmee, Kissimmee, FL 223

The Oaks of West Kettering, Kettering, OH 338
Oakton Pavillion, Des Plaines, IL 246
Oakview Heights, Mount Carmel, IL 252
Oakwood Lutheran Home, Madison, WI 382
Oasis Health & Rehabilitation Center, Lake Worth, FL 224
Oasis Nursing & Rehabilitation, El Paso, TX 364
Oberg, Gary 77
Occipital lobe 139
Ocean View Convalescent Center, Long Beach, WA 377
Oceana Rehabilitation Center, Cape May Court House, NJ 320
Oceanside Nursing Home, Tybee Island, GA 237
Ochoco Care Center, Prineville, OR 346
Odd Fellow & Rebekah Home, Mattoon, IL 252
Odd Fellow & Rebekah Nursing Home, Ennis, TX 364
Odor Identification Test 139
Ohio State University 43, 51, 116
Olanzapine 30, 139
Old Jefferson Community Care Center, Baton Rouge, LA 282
Older American Act 139–40
Oligodendrocytes 140
Olmsted Decision for Americans with Disabilities Act 140
Olmsted Manor Skilled Nursing Center, North Olmsted, OH 340
Ombudsman 140
Omega-3 fatty acids 140–1
Omentum 91, 141
Omnibus Reconciliation Act (OBRA) regulations 141
Opiod peptides 141
Opp Health & Rehabilitation, Opp, AL 186
Orchard Health & Rehabilitation, Pulaski, GA 235
Orchard Manor, Lancaster, WI 382
Orchard Park Health Care, Tacoma, WA 379
Orchard Park Health Care Center, Littleton, CO 211
Orchard View Manor, East Providence, RI 354
The Orchards Rehabilitation & Care Center, Lewiston, ID 240
Oregon Health Sciences University 390
Orem Nursing & Rehabilitation Center, Orem, UT 370
Organic brain syndrome 11, 37–8, 142
Organic solvents 142
Orientation 142
Orlando Health & Rehabilitation Center, Orlando, FL 226
Osborn Health and Rehabilitation, Scottsdale, AZ 190
Osceola Nursing Home, Ocilla, GA 235
Ottawa County Nursing, Minneapolis, KS 276
Ottawa County Riverview Nursing Home, Oak Harbor, OH 341

Otterbein–Lebanon Retirement Community, Lebanon, OH 338
Ottumwa Good Samaritan Health & Rehabilitation Center, Ottumwa, IA 270–1
Ouachita Nursing and Rehabilitation Center, Camden, AR 193
Our Lady of Angels Retirement Home, Joliet, IL 250
Our Lady of Consolation, West Islip, NY 327
Our Lady of Peace, Charlottesville, VA 372
Our Lady of Prompt Succor, Opelousas, LA 287
Our Lady of Wisdom Healthcare Center, New Orleans, LA 287
Our Lady's Residence Health Care Center, Pleasantville, NJ 322
Owensboro Place Care & Rehabilitation Center, Owensboro, KY 281
The Oxford, Haverhill, MA 295
Oxidation 81
Oxidative stress 81, 90
Ozark Mountain Regional Healthcare Center, Crane, MO 310
Ozark Nursing & Care Center, Ozark, MO 313

P.A. Peterson Center for Health, Rockford, IL 254
P substance 97, 167
P97 142
Pacific Care Center Inc., Pacific, MO 313
Pacific Gardens Nursing and Rehabilitation Center, Fresno, CA 199
Pacing 142
Paclitaxel 142
Page Rehabilitation & Healthcare Center, Fort Meyers, FL 222
Pain 142
Paired helical filaments 127, 128
Palace at Kendall Nursing & Rehabilitation Center, Miami, FL 225
Palemon Gaskin Memorial Nursing Home, Ocilla, GA 235
Paleocortex 142
Paleomammalian brain 142
Palisade Living center, Palisade, CO 212
Palliative care 143
Palm Garden of Aventura, North Miami Beach, FL 226
Palm Garden of Ocala, Ocala, FL 226
Palm Garden of Sun City, Sun City Center, FL 228
Palm Garden of Tampa, Tampa, FL 229
Palm Garden of West Palm Beach, West Palm Beach, FL 230
Palm View Rehabilitation and Care Center, Yuma, AZ 192
Palmer Pioneers' Home, Palmer, AK 187
Palms at Park Place, Kissimmee, FL 223
Palmyra Nursing Home, Albany, GA 231
Palo Duro Care Center, Amarillo, TX 363

Paloman Gaskin Memorial Nursing Home, Ocilla, GA 235
Palomar Continuing Care Center, Escondido, CA 199
Paradigm Health Care Center at Waterbury, Waterbury, CT 217
Paramount Convalescent Hospital, Paramount, CA 202
Paramount Meadows, Paramount, CA 202
Paraneoplastic disease 30
Paranoia 143
Parasympathetic nervous system 143
Parietal lobe 143
Park Anaheim Healthcare Center, Anaheim, CA 196
Park Avenue Health and Rehabilitation Center, Tucson, AZ 192
Park Forest Care Center Inc., Westminster, CO 213
Park Haven Home, Ashtabula, OH 332
Park Manor Health and Rehabilitation Center, LLC, Northport, AL 186
Park Manor Rehabilitation Center, Walla Walla, WA 379
Park Meadows Health & Rehabilitation, Gainesville, FL 222–3
Park Place Nursing & Rehabilitation, Tyler, TX 368
Park Place Nursing and Rehabilitation, LLC, Selma, AL 186
Park Place Nursing Facility, Monroe, GA 235
Park Ridge Care Center, Shoreline, WA 378
Park Springs Health Center, Stone Mountain, GA 236
Park View Rehabilitation & Heath Center, Springfield, MA 297
Parker Oaks Community, Winnebago, MN 308
Parkinsonian symptoms 143
Parkinson's disease 14, 90, 143–4
Parkside Rehabilitation & Care Center, Wenatchee, WA 379
Parkside Special Care Centre, El Cajon, CA 198
Parkside Towers, St. Louis, MO 314
Parkview Care & Rehabilitation Center, Inc., Massapequa, NY 326
Parkview Healthcare Center, Bakersfield, CA 196
Parkview Manor, Weimar, TX 368
Parkview Manor Health Rehabilitation Center, Green Bay, WI 381
Parkview Nursing & Rehab, Wilmington, DE 218
Parkview Nursing & Rehabilitation, Big Spring, TX 363
Parkway Medical Center, Louisville, KY 281
Parkway Place, Houston, TX 366
Parkwood Health Care Center, Lebanon, IN 262
Parkwood Nursing & Rehabilitation Center, Snellville, GA 236
Parsons Good Samaritan Center, Parsons, KS 276
Parsons Hill Nursing & Rehabilitation Center, Worcester, MA 297

Pathogenesis of Alzheimer's disease 8, 101, 103, 135
Pathology 144
Patty Elwood Center, Cresco, IA 267
Paul Oliver Memorial Hospital–Long Term Care Unit, Frankfort, MI 301
The Pavilion at Saint Luke, Hazleton, PA 350
Payson Care Center, Payson, AZ 189
Peabody Glen Nursing Center, Peabody, MA 297
Peach Tree Place, Weatherford, TX 368
The Peaks Care Center, Longmont, CO 212
Pearl Street Health & Rehabilitation Center, Englewood, CO 210
Pecos Nursing Home, Pecos, TX 367
Pekin Manor, Pekin, IL 253
Pembrooke Health & Rehabilitation Residence, West Chester, PA 353
Penick Village, Southern Pines, NC 329
Peninsula Center for Extended Care & Rehabilitation, Far Rockaway, NY 325
Pepper Hill Nursing & Rehabilitation Center, LLC, Aiken, SC 355
Peripheral nervous system 8
Perlmutter, David, M.D. 114, 144
Pernicious anemia 117
Perry County Nursing Home, Marion, AL 185
Perry Oaks Nursing & Rehab, Perryville, MO 313
Pershing Convalescent Home, Berwyn, IL 242
Personality changes 144
Petersburg Healthcare & Rehabilitation, Petersburg, IN 203
Petersburg Medical Center Long Term Care Petersburg, AK 187
Petersen, Ronald 389
Peterson Park Health Care Center, Chicago, IL 245
Phenserine 144–5
Phoebe Home, Allentown, PA 347
Phoenix Mountain Nursing Center, Phoenix, AZ 190
Phosphatidylserine 15, 145
Phosphorylation 25, 121, 138, 142, 14, 153
Physostigmine 144, 146
Phytochemicals 146–7
Pia mater 89, *116*
Pick's disease 147–8
Pickway ManorCare Center, Circleville, OH 335
Piedmont Crossing, Thomasville, NC 329–30
Piedmont Health Care Center Piedmont, AL 186
Piedmont Nursing & Rehabilitation Center, Greer, SC 356
Pierce Manor, Pierce, NE 318
Pierremont Healthcare Center, Shreveport, LA 288
Pikes Peak Care & Rehabilitation Center, Colorado Springs, CO 208
Pilgrim Manor, Grand Rapids, MI 301

Pilgrim Manor Guest Care Services, Bossier City, LA 283
Pilgrim Place Health Services Center, Claremont, CA 197
Pillaging 148
Pillars of North County Health & Rehab Center, Florissant, MO 311
Pine Haven Care Center, Texarkana, TX 368
Pine Haven Nursing Home, Lufkin, TX 366
Pine Hills Health and Rehabilitation LLC, Camden, AR 193
Pine Kirk Care Center, Kirkersville, OH 338
Pine Lane Therapy and Living Center, Inc, Mountain Home, AR 195
Pine Ridge Care Center, Elizabethton, TN 360
Pine Run Health Center, Doylestown, PA 349
Pine Valley Health Care, Richland Center, WI 384
Pine View Care Center, Black River Falls, WI 380
Pine View Nursing & Rehabilitation Center, Harrisville, WV 380
Pinecrest Medical Care Facility, Powers, MI 303
Pinecrest Nursing Home, Humboldt, KS 274
Pinecrest Retirement Community, Lufkin, TX 366
Pinehill Nursing Center, Byromville, GA 231
Pines at Bristol for Nursing & Rehabilitation, Bristol, CT 214
The Pines Nursing & Convalescent Home, Dillon, SC 356
Pines of Sarasota, Sarasota, FL 228
Pinewood Care Center, Coeur D'Alene, ID 239
Pinewood Terrace, Colville, WA 376
Pinnacle Nursing, Price, UT 370
Pioneer Care Center, Fergus Falls, MN 305
Pioneer Health Care Center, Rocky Ford, CO 213
Pioneer Memorial Nursing Home, Viborg, SD 359
Pisgah Manor Health Care Center, Candler, NC 328
Pituitary disease 49
Plantation Nursing & Rehabilitation Center, Plantation, FL 227
Plantation Oaks Nursing & Rehabilitation Center, Wisner, LA 288
Plaque see Neuritic plaque and Senile Plaque
Platelet activation studies 148
Plaza Del Rio Care Center, Peoria, AZ 189
Plaza Healthcare, Scottsdale, AZ 190–1
Plaza Manor, Kansas City, MO 312
Plaza Nursing Home Co. Inc., Syracuse, NY 327
Plaza West, Sun City Center, FL 228
Pleasant Care Living Center, Pleasantville, IA 271
Pleasant Valley Nursing and Rehabilitation, Little Rock, AR 194

Pleasant View Luther Home, Ottawa, IL 253
Pleasant View Nursing Home N, Monroe, WI 383
Pleasantview Home, Kalona, IA 269–70
Plum Creek Care Center, Lexington, NE 317
Plum Creek Healthcare Center, Amarillo, TX 363
Pneumonia 11, 153
Pocatello Care & Rehab Center, Pocatello, ID 241
Pocopson Home, West Chester, PA 353
Point Loma Convalescent Hospital, San Diego, CA 204
Pointe Coupee Parish Nursing Home, New Roads, LA 287
Pomona Vista Alzheimer's Center, Pomona, CA 203
Pompano Beach Health & Rehab Center, Pompano Beach, FL 227
Ponca City Nursing & Rehabilitation Center, Ponca City, OK 344
Ponderosa Pines Care and Rehab, Inc., Chandler, AZ 188
Pons 49
Pontchartrain Health Care Centre, Mandeville, LA 285
Pope John Paul II Center for Health, Danbury, CT 215
Poplar Heights Care & Rehabilitation, Elizabethtown, NC 328
Porter Hills Health Center, Grand Rapids, MI 301
Porteus Mazes 148
Posado Del Sol Health Care Center, Tucson, AZ 192
Positron emission tomography (PET) 10, 67, 98, 99, 141, 148–9
Postville Good Samaritan Center, Postville, IA 271
Potomac Center Genesis ElderCare Network, Arlington, VA 372
Potomac Valley Nursing & Wellness Center, Rockville, MD 292
Potter, Huntington 388
Powder Springs Nursing & Rehabilitation Center, Powder Springs, GA 235
Powell Nursing Home, Powell, WY 385
Poydras Manor Nursing Facility, Saint Bernard, LA 287
Prairie Acres, Friona, TX 365
Prairie Manor, Chicago Heights, IL 246
Prairieview Lutheran Home, Danforth, IL 246
Praxis Alzheimer's Facility, Easton, PA 349
Preclinical phase of Alzheimer's disease 56, 150
Prednisone 150
Premier Care, Beloit, WI 380
Premier Place at the Glenview, Naples, FL 225
Prenatal genetic testing 150
Presbyterian Community Care Center, Ontario, OR 345

Presbyterian Manor of Farmington, Farmington, MO 310
Presbyterian Village North Special Care Center, Dallas, TX 364
Prescott House Nursing Home, North Andover, MA 296
Prescott Manor Nursing Center, Prescott, AR 195
Presenile dementia 121, 147, 150
Presenilin-1 (PS-1) gene 52, 74, 84, 85, 86
Presenilin therapy 150
Presenilin-2 (PS-2) gene 51, 63, 84, 85, 86
Presidential Pavilion, Chicago, IL 245
Presidio Health Care Center, Spring Valley, CA 205
Prestige Care and Rehab Center of Anchorage, Anchorage, AK 187
Presynaptic vesicles 150–1
Prevalence of Alzheimer's Disease 77, 151
Primary progressive aphasia 151
Princeton Health Care Center, Princeton, WV 380
Princeton Place, Albuquerque, NM 323
Princeton Place, Ruston, LA 287
Prions 35, 60, 87
Program for All-Inclusive Care for the Elderly (PACE) 112, 113, 152
Progressive Deterioration Scale (PDS) 152
Progressive multifocal leukoencephalopathy 65
Progressive supranuclear palsy (PSP) 64, 107, 128, 152
Propentofylline 152
Prosencephalon 152
Prostate apoptosis response-4 (Par-4) protein 127
Proteolysis 91
Provena Geneva Care Center, Geneva, IL 249
Provena Heritage Village, Kankakee, IL 250
Provena St. Joseph Center, Freeport, IL 249
Provena Villa Franciscan, Joliet, IL 250
Providence Christian Healthcare & Rehab Center, Zeeland, MI 304
Providence Downer's Grove, Downer's Grove, IL 247
Providence Extended Care Center, Anchorage, AK 187
Providence Marianwood, Issaquah, WA 376
Providence Mother Joseph Care Center, Olympia, WA 377
Providence Place, Minneapolis, MN 306
Providence South Holland, South Holland, IL 255
Provincial House of Adrian, Adrian, MI 298
Provo Rehabilitation & Nursing, Provo, UT 370
Pseudodementia 152
Psychologist, clinical 152
Psychology 152
Psychometric testing 49
Psychomotor activity 63

Psychosis 13, 30, 65, 105, 107, 153, 158, 174, 176
Psychotropic agent 13, 72, 153–4
Pterostilbene 34
Pueblo Care & Rehabilitation Center, Pueblo, CO 212
Pulmonary edema 70
Pupil dilation test 153
Purkinje cells 45
Putnam Acres Care Center, Ottawa, OH 341
Puxico Nursing & Rehabilitation Center, Puxico, MO 313

Quabbin Valley Health Care, Athol, MA 293
Quail Run Health Center, Cameron, MO 309
Quality Care Health Center, Lebanon, TN 361
Quatrain 30
Quetiapine fumarate 153–4
Quinn Meadows Rehabilitation & Care Center, Pocatello, ID 241
Quinton Memorial Healthcare & Rehabilitation Dalton, GA 232–3

Radionuclide Brain Scan 154
Radius Healthcare, Danvers, MA 294
Rainbow Beach Care Center, Chicago, IL 245
Rainier Vista Care Center, Puyallup, WA 377
Raintree Manor, McMinnville, TN 361
Raleigh Rehab and Healthcare Center, Raleigh, NC 329
Ramona Care Center, El Monte, CA 198
Rancho Mesa Care Center, Alta Loma, CA 196
Randolph Hills Nursing Center, Wheaton, MD 293
Rapid eye movement (REM) 154
Rapidly progressive dementia 154
Rasking, Murray 391
Ray E. Dillon Living Center, Hutchinson, KS 274
Rayville Nursing & Rehabilitation Center, Rayville, LA 287
Receptor 154
Recombinant DNA technology 154
Red Oak Good Samaritan Center, Red Oak, IA 271
Red Rock Care and Rehab Center, Inc., Cottonwood, AZ 188
Red Rose Health & Rehab, Cassville, MO 310
Red Wing Health Center, Red Wing, MN 307
Redeemer Residence, Inc., Minneapolis, MN 307
Redford Geriatric Village, Detroit, MI 300
Redstone Villa, Saint Albans, VT 371
Redwood Extended Care Center, Portland, OR 346
Reelfoot Manor, Tiptonville, TN 362
Reflex disturbances 154–5
Regal Estate, Independence, KS 274
Regal Heights Healthcare & Rehab Center, Hockessin, DE 218

Regency Care Center, Arlington, WA 375
Regency Care Center, Monroe, WA 377
Regency Healthcare Center and Rehabilitation Center, Yorktown VA 375
Regency Heights of Norwich, LLC, Norwich, CT 215
Regency House of Wallingford, Wallingford, CT 217
Regency Manor, Chelan, WA 376
Regency Manor, Temple, TX 368
Regency Manor Healthcare & Rehabilitation Center, Temple, TX 368
Regency Manor Rehabilitation & Subacute Center, Columbus, OH 335
Regency Place Nursing & Rehab Center, Baton Rouge, LA 283
Regency Place of Fort Wayne, Fort Wayne, IN 259
Regency Place of Greenfield, Greenfield, IN 260
Regency Place of Lafayette, Lafayette, IN 261
Regency Place of South Bend, South Bend, IN 264
Regent Care Center, Hackensack, NJ 320
Regents Park Nursing & Rehabilitation Center, Boca Raton, FL 220
Regents Park of Winter Park, Winter Park, FL 230
Regis Woods Care & Rehabilitation Center, Louisville, KY 281
Rehabilitation & Care Center of Jackson County, Murphysboro, IL 252
Rehabilitation & Healthcare Center of Tampa, Tampa, FL 229
Rehabilitation & Nursing Center at Firelands, New London, OH 340
Rehabilitation & Nursing Center of Monroe, Monroe, NC 329
Rehabilitation & Nursing Center of the Rockies, Fort Collins, CO 210
Rehabilitation Center of Bakersfield, Bakersfield, CA 196
Rehabilitation Center of St. Petersburg, St. Petersburg, FL 228
Reiman, Eric 387
Reisberg's Seven Stages of Alzheimer's 55–6
Remacemide 156
Reminyl see Galantamine hydrobromide
Renaissance at 87th Street, Chicago, IL 245
Renaissance at Midway, Chicago, IL 245
Renaissance Health & Rehab, West Palm Beach, FL 230
Renaissance Park Multi-Care Center, Fort Worth, TX 365
Renaissance Park South, Chicago, IL 245
Renown Skilled Nursing, Sparks, NV 318
Rensselaer Care Center, Rensselaer, IN 263
Reo Vista Healthcare Center, San Diego, CA 204
Repetitive behavior 156
Reptilian brain 156

Research 156
Residence at Kensington, Middletown, OH 339
Residence at McCormick's Creek, Spencer, IN 264
Resident-Centered Care 156
Resources for Enhancing Alzheimer's Caregiver's Health (REACH) 156
Respite care 11, 42, 96, 112, 113, 156–7
Restoration Healthcare of Commerce, Commerce, GA 232
Resurrection Life Center, Chicago, IL 245
Resveratrol 157
Retention and Immediate Recall 157
Rex Rehab and Nursing Care Center, Raleigh, NC 329
Rey-Osterreith complex figure 157
Rhombencephalon 157
Richfield Health Center, Richfield, MN 307
Richfield Rehabilitation & Care Center, Richfield, UT 370
Richmond Healthcare and Rehab Center, Richmond, KS 277
Richmond Place, Lexington, KY 280
Rickman Nursing Care Center, Asheville, NC 328
Ridge Crest Care Center, Warren, OH 342
Ridge Crest Nursing Center, Warrensburg, MO 315
Ridge Pavilion, Cincinnati, OH 335
Ridge View Manor LLC, Buffalo, NY 325
Ridgecrest Health and Rehabilitation, Jonesboro, AR 194
Ridgecrest Healthcare, Phoenix, AZ 190
Ridgecrest Nursing & Rehabilitation Center, DeLand, FL 221
Ridgeview Health Care Center, Jasper, AL 185
Ridgewood Manor, Dalton, GA 233
Ridgewood Place, Akron, OH 332
Rifamycin 157
Rim County Health and Rehabilitation Center, Payson, AZ 189
Ringman, John 387
Rio Rancho Nursing & Rehabilitation Center, Rio Rancho, NM 324
Ripley Crossing, Milan, IN 263
Risen Son Christian Village, Council Bluffs, IA 267
Risk factors 157–8
Risperidone 158
Rivastigmine 10, 56, 69, 79, 146, 158, 176
River Front Nursing & Rehabilitation Center, Bradenton, FL 220
River Gardens Rehab and Care Center, Bullhead City, AZ 187
River Oaks and Rehabilitation Center, Columbus, TX 363
River Oaks Retirement Manor, Lafayette, LA 285
River Ridge Care & Rehabilitation Center, Twin Falls, ID 241–2
Riverbluff Nursing Home, Rockford, IL 254
Riverdell Health Care Center, Boonville, MO 309

Rivergate Terrace, Riverview, MI 303
River's Bend Health & Rehabilitation Center, Manitowoc, WI 382–3
Riverside Nursing & Rehabilitation Center, Centralia, WA 376
Riverside Nursing Home, Monroe, LA 286
Riverview Health & Rehab, Savannah, GA 236
Riverview Rehab & Health Center, Baltimore, MD 291
Riverwoods at Exeter, Exeter, NH 319
Riviera Manor Inc., Chicago Heights, IL 246
Robinson Home, Portland, OR 346
Rock Creek Manor Nursing Center, Washington, DC 219
Rock Island Nursing & Rehab, Rock Island, IL 254
Rock View Good Samaritan Center, Parshall, ND 331
Rockwood Manor, Midland, TX 367
Rocky Count Health Care Center, Janesville, WI 382
Rocky Hill Skilled Nursing & Rehabilitation, Rocky Hill, CT 216
Rocky Mountain Care Center, Heber City, UT 369
Rocky Mountain Care Center, Helena, MT 316
Rocky Mountain Care Center — Tooele, Tooele, UT 370
Rofecoxib 158
Rogue Valley Manor, Medford, OR 346
Rolling Green Village Mildred L. Smith Health Center, Greenville, SC 356
Rolling Hills Health Center, Topeka, KS 277
Rolling Hills Rehabilitation Center, Sparta, WI 384
Ronald and Nancy Reagan Research Institute 104
Rose Brook Care Center, Edgar, NE 317
Rose City Nursing Home, Portland, OR 346
Rose Haven Nursing Facility, Thomasville, GA 237
Rose Linn Care Center, West Linn, OR 347
Rose Manor Healthcare Center, Durham, NC 328
Rose Mountain Care Center, New Brunswick, NJ 321
Rose Vista Nursing Center, Vancouver, WA 379
Rosecrans Care Center, Gardena, CA 199
Rosegate Village, Richmond, IN 264
Rosemary 158
Rosemont at Stone Mountain, Stone Mountain, GA 236
Rosenberg, Roger 391
Rosewalk Village at Indianapolis, Indianapolis, IN 261
Rosewood Care Center Inc. — Peoria, Peoria, IL 253
Rosewood Care Center of Joliet, Joliet, IL 250

Rosewood Care Center of Moline, Moline, IL 252
Rosewood Care Center of Swansea, Swansea, IL 255
Rosewood Care of Edwardsville, Edwardsville, IL 247
Rosewood Health Care, Bowling Green, KY 279
Rosewood Manor, Pensacola, FL 227
Rosewood Nursing Center, Lake Charles, LA 285
Ross Manor, Bangor, ME 289
Rouse-Warren County Home, Youngsville, PA 353
Routines 158–9
Rowan Community, Denver CO 210
Royal Care of Avon Park, Avon Park, FL 219
Royal Care Skilled Nursing Center, Long Beach, CA 200
Royal Nursing Center, LLC, Falmouth, MA 295
Royal Oak Nursing & Rehabilitation, Middleburg Heights, OH 339
Royal Oak Nursing Center, Dade City, FL 221
Royal Oaks Health Care & Rehabilitation Center, Terre Haute, IN 264–5
Royal Park Care Center, Spokane, WA 378
Royal Plaza Retirement & Care Center, Lewiston, ID 240
Royal Rehabilitation and Nursing Center, Braintree, MA 294
Royale Gardens Health & Rehabilitation Center, Grants Pass, OR 345
Royale Health Care Center, Santa Ana, CA 205
Ruffin Care Center of Bloomville, Bloomville, OH 333
Ruleville Health Care Center, Ruleville, MS 309
Runnells County Nursing & Rehabilitation Center I, Ballinger, TX 363
Rush University Medical Center 388
Russell Regional Medical Center, Salina, KS 278
Ruston Nursing & Rehabilitation Center, LLC, Ruston, LA 287
Rutland Healthcare & Rehabilitation Center, Rutland, VT 327
The Riverwood Center, Jacksonville, FL 223

S 100 beta 102
Sabal Palms Health Care Center, Largo, FL 224
Sacks, Oliver, M.D. 122, 128
Sacred Heart Home, Chicago, IL 245
Sacred Heart Village, Louisville, KY 281
S-adenosylmethionine (SAMe) 159
Safe Haven Care Center of Pocatello, Pocatello, ID 241
Safe Return Program 159
Safety 159
Sage View Care Center, Rock Springs, WY 385–6
Saint Agnes Healthcare & Rehabilitation, Chicago, IL 245

Saint Andre Health Care Facility, Biddeford, ME 289
Saint Andrew's Bay Skilled Nursing & Rehab, Panama City, FL 227
Saint Andrew's Village, Indiana, PA 350
Saint Anne Home, Greensburg, PA 349
Saint Anne's Nursing Center Residence, Miami, FL 225
Saint Ann's Home for the Aged, Jersey City, NJ 321
Saint Ann's Nursing Home Co Inc., Rochester, NY 327
Saint Anthony Home Inc., Crown Point, IN 258
Saint Anthony Nursing Home, Inc., Metairie, LA 285
Saint Anthony Park Home, Saint Paul, MN 308
Saint Anthony's Continuing Care Center, Rock Island, IL 254
Saint Anthony's Memorial Hospital, Effingham, IL 247
Saint Benedict's Health Center, Dickinson, ND 330
Saint Bernard's Medical Center, Jonesboro, AR 194
Saint Camillus Rehabilitation and Nursing Center, Stamford, CT 216
Saint Catherine Center, Waco, TX 368
Saint Catherine Healthcare and Rehab, Albuquerque, NM 323
Saint Catherine's Care Center, Washington Court House, OH 342
Saint Catherine's Care Center of Findlay, Findlay, OH 337
Saint Catherine's Center of Fostoria, Fostoria, OH 337
Saint Catherine's Living Center, Wahlpeton, ND 331
Saint Catherine's Residence, North Bend, OR 345
Saint Charles Health Center, New Orleans, LA 287
Saint Clara's Manor, Lincoln, IL 251
Saint Clare Manor, Baton Rouge, LA 283
Saint Croix Health Center, New Richmond, WI 383
Saint Dominic Nursing Home, Houston, TX 366
Saint Edward Home, Fairlawn, OH 337
Saint Elizabeth Center, Waco, TX 368
Saint Elizabeth Rehab & Nursing CE, Baltimore, MD 291
Saint Elizabeth's Hospital, Wabasha, MN 308
Saint Elizabeth's Nursing Home, Janesville, WI 382
Saint Elizabeth's Place, Jonesboro, AZ 194
Saint Francis Care Center at Brackenville, Hockessin, DE 218
Saint Francis Country House, Darby, PA 349
Saint Francis Extended Care, Hayward, CA 200
Saint Francis Home, Fond Du Lac, WI 381
Saint Francis Home, Saginaw, MI 303

Saint Francis Manor, Farmington, MO 310

Saint Francis Manor, Grinnell, IA 269

Saint Francis Nursing & Rehabilitation Center, Oberlin, LA 287

Saint Francis Nursing Center, Detroit, MI 300

St. George-Hyslop, Peter, M.D. 159

Saint John of God Retirement & Care Center, Los Angeles, CA 201

Saint John Rest Home, Victoria, KS 278

Saint John Senior Community, Detroit, MI 300

Saint John's Home of Milwaukee, Milwaukee, WI 343

Saint John's Living Center, Jackson, WY 385

Saint John's Lutheran Home, Billings, MT 315

Saint John's Nursing Home, Lynchburg, VA 373

Saint John's of Hays, Hays, KS 273–4

Saint John's on the Lake Health Care Center, Milwaukee, WI 383

Saint John's Place of Arkansas, LLC, Fordyce, AR 193

Saint Joseph's Hospital, Yonkers, NY 327

Saint Jude Care Center, Portland, OR 346

Saint Lucas Care Center, Faribault, MN 305

Saint Luke Hospital West, Florence, KY 280

Saint Luke Lutheran Home for the Aging, North Canton, OH 340

St. Martin De Porres Multi-Care Center, Lake Charles, LA 285

St. Martins in the Pines, Birmingham, AL 184

Saint Mary Health Care, Lafayette, IN 261

Saint Mary Health Care, Worcester, MA 298

Saint Mary Home, West Hartford, CT 217

Saint Mary's Alzheimer's Center, Columbiana, OH 335

Saint Mary's D' Youville Pavilion, Lewiston, ME 289

Saint Mary's Health & Rehab Center of Campbell County, La Follette, TN 361

Saint Mary's Home of Erie, Erie, PA 349

Saint Mary's Home, St. Paul, Minnesota 308

Saint Mary's Nursing Home, Saint Clair Shores, MI 303

Saint Matthew Lutheran Home, Park Ridge, IL 253

Saint Patrick's Manor Inc., Framingham, MA 295

Saint Paul's Tower, Oakland, CA 202

Saint Peter Villa Rehabilitation & Nursing Center, Memphis, TN 361

Saint Sophia Healthcare, Florissant, MO 311

Saint Vincent's Care Center, Bismarck, ND 330

Salem Nursing & Rehabilitation Center of Tuskegee, Tuskegee, AL 187

Salem Village, Joliet, IL 250

Salemtowne Retirement Community, Winston-Salem, NC 330

Salina Presbyterian Manor, Salina, KS 277

Salisbury Center, Salisbury, MD 292

Saluda Nursing Center, Saluda, SC 357

San Diego Healthcare Center, San Diego, CA 204

San Juan Living Center, Montrose, CO 212

San Luis Care Center, Alamosa, CO 206

Sancta Maria Nursing Center, Cambridge, MA 294

Sanctuary at Holy Cross, South Bend, IN 264

Sanctuary at McCauley, Muskegon, MI 303

Sanctuary at St. Mary's, Grand Rapids, MI 301

Sanctuary at the Park, Muskegon, MI 303

Sanders-Brown Center on Aging 55, 136, 389

Sandoz Clinical Assessment — Geriatric (SCAG) 159

Sandpiper Convalescent Center, Mount Pleasant, SC 356

Sandrock Ridge Care & Rehabilitation, Craig, CO 209

Sandy Regional Health Center, Sandy, UT 370

Sano, Mary 390

Santa Fe Care Center, Santa Fe, NM 324

Santa Monica Convalescent Center II, Santa Monica, CA 205

Santa Rita Nursing & Rehabilitation Center, Green Valley, AZ 188

Santa Rosa Care Center, Tucson, AZ 192

Sarah A Reed Retirement Center, Erie, PA 349

Saugus Care & Rehabilitation Center, Saugus, MA 297

Sauk County Health Care Center, Reedsburg, WI 384

Savannah Beach Nursing & Rehab, Tybee Island, GA 237

Savannah Rehab & Nursing Center, Savannah, GA 236

Savannah Square Health Care, Savannah, GA 236

Saxony Health Center, Saxonburg, PA 352

Saylor Lane Health Care Center, Sacramento, CA 203

Scalabrini Villa, Newport, RI 354

SCAN Health Plan of Long Beach, California 159–60

Scandia Village Good Samaritan, Sister Bay, WI 384

Scenic Hills Nursing Center, Bidwell, OH 333

Schizophrenia 7, 19, 61, 72, 176

Schoellkopf Health Center, Niagra Falls, NY 326

Schome Park Care Center, Bellingham, WA 333

Schuylkill Center, Pottsville, PA 352

Schuylkill County Home — Rest Haven, Schuylkill Haven, PA 352

Scotland Count Care Center, Memphis, MO 312–3

Scottsdale Heritage Court, Scottsdale, AZ 191

Scottsdale Nursing and Rehab Center, Scottsdale, AZ 191

Scottsdale Village Square, Scottsdale, AZ 191

Seaside Rehabilitation & Healthcare Center, Portland, ME 289

Seattle Keiro, Seattle, WA 378

Seaview Nursing & Rehabilitation Center, Pompano Beach, FL 227

Secretase enzymes 160

Sedatives 65, 113, 160

Sedgewood Commons, Falmouth, ME 289

Sehome Park Care Center, Bellingham, WA 376

Selective Serotonin Reuptake Inhibitors (SSRIs) 160

Selegiline hydrochloride (Eldepryl, Atapryl) 160

Semagacestat 160

Seneca Health & Rehabilitation Center, Seneca, SC 357

Seneca Place, Verona, PA 352

Senile dementia/Alzheimer's type (SDAT) 160

Senile plaque 20, 26, 29, 30, 33, 36, 43, 59, 96, 103, 160–1, 167, 176

Senility 161

Senior Medicare Patrol Project 161

Sentara Nursing Center, Norfolk, VA 374

Sentara Nursing Center — Windermere, Virginia Beach, VA 375

Sentara Village, Chesapeake, VA 372

Sentinel Event Alert 161

Sequencing 161

Serotonin 19, 40, 66, 84, 133, 141, 159, 160, 161, 162

Seven-Minute Screen 162

Seven Oaks, Glendale, WI 381

Seven Springs Health and Rehabilitation, LLC, Heber Springs, AR 193

Severe Impairment Battery 162

Sexuality 162

Shadecrest Health Care Center, Jasper, AL 185

Shadowing 162

Shady Lane Nursing Care Center, Manitowoc, WI 383

Share Medical Center, Alva, OK 342

Sharon Care Center, Centralia, WA 376

Sharon Care Center, Los Angeles, CA 201

Sharon Health Care Pines Inc., Peoria, IL 253

Sharpe Care Nursing & Rehabilitation Center, LTD, Oconto Falls, WI 383

Shawnee Colonial Estates Nursing Home, Shawnee, OK 286

Sheboygan County Comprehensive Health Center N, Sheboygan Falls, WI 384

Shelanski, Michael 390

Shell Point Nursing Pavilion, Fort Meyers, FL 222

Shepherd's Choice, Gettysburg, PA 349

Sheridan Care Center, Sheridan, OR 346

Sheriden Woods Health Care Center, Bristol, CT 214

Sherman County Good Samaritan Center, Goodland, KS 273

Sherrill House, Inc., Boston, MA 293–4

Sherwin Manor Nursing Center, Chicago, IL 246

Sherwood Manor Nursing & Rehabilitation Center, Baton Rouge, LA 283

Sherwood Park Nursing & Rehabilitation Center, Keizer, OR 345

Shook Home, Chambersburg, PA 348–9

Shorehaven Health Center, Oconomowoc, WI 383

Short-term memory 82, 118, 119, 121, 122, 128, 165

Sierra Healthcare Community, Lakewood, CO 211

Signature Healthcare at Mallard Bay, Cambridge, ME 291

Signature Healthcare of Buckhead, Atlanta, GA 231

Signature Healthcare of Columbia, Columbia, TN 360

Silver Care Healthcare Center, Cherry Hill, NJ 320

Silver Creek Manor, Bristol, RI 354

Silver Lake Center, Dover, DE 218

Silver Lake Nursing & Rehabilitation Center, Bristol, PA 348

Silver Oaks Health and Rehabilitation Center, Camden, AR 193

Silver Oaks Health Campus, Columbus, IN 258

Silver Oaks Nursing Center, New Castle, PA 351

Silver Wood Good Samaritan Center, Silverton, ID 241

Single-nucleotide polymorphisms (SNPs) 162

Single photon emission tomography (SPECT) 162, 173, 179

Sioux Falls Good Samaritan Village, Sioux Falls, SD 310

Siuslaw Care Center, Florence, OR 345

Skilcare Nursing Center, Jonesboro, AR 194

Skilled nursing care 137, 163

Skyline Ridge Nursing & Rehabilitation Center, Canon City, CO 207

Skyview Nursing Center, Oklahoma City, OK 286

Sleep disturbances 114, 135, 154, 156, 158, 159, 162, 163

Smith House Health Care Center, Stamford, CT 216

Smoking 77, 163, 170

Snowdon, D.H. 136

Social HMOs see Medicare HMOs

Social Security benefits 81, 112, 137, 141, 163

Sodium 21, 65, 79, 121, 172

Soldiers' Home in Massachusetts, Chelsea, MA 294

South Heritage Health & Rehabilitation Center, St. Petersburg, FL 228

South Hills Health Car Center, Eugene, OR 345

South Jersey Health Care Center, Camden, NJ 319

South Park Rehabilitation & Nursing Center, Corpus Christi, TX 364

South Shore Nursing & Rehabilitation Center, Chicago, IL 246

South Shore Nursing & Rehabilitation Center, South Shore, KY 282

South Tampa Health & Rehabilitation Center, Tampa, FL 229

South Windsor Nursing & Rehabilitation, South Windsor, CT 216

Southeast Colorado Hospital & Long Term Care Center, Springfield, CO 213

Southern Acres Care Center, Monroe, LA 286

Southern Care LLC, Guin, AL 184

Southern Oaks Rehabilitation and Care Center, Pensacola, FL 227

Southern Ocean Center, Manahawkin, NJ 321

Southland Nursing Home, Marion, AL 185

Southland Nursing Home, Peachtree City, GA 235

Southpointe Healthcare Center, Greenfield, WI 381

Southridge Village Nursing and Rehabilitation Center, Heber Springs, AR 193

Southwest Medical Center, Liberal, KS 275

Southwest Nursing & Rehabilitation Center, Fort Worth, TX 365

Southwest Parkway Nursing Center, Wichita Falls, TX 368

Southwestern Virginia Mental Health Institute–Geriatric Services, Marion VA 373

Space occupying lesions 23, 64, 65, 69, 76, 154

Spaulding Nursing & Therapy Center — North End, Boston, MA 294

Spaulding Nursing & Therapy Center — West Roxbury, West Roxbury, MA 287

Spearman's rank order correlation coefficient 163

Special care units (SCUs) 163

Specialty Care of Pensacola, Pensacola, FL 227

SPECT see Single photon/positron emission computed tomography scan

Spectrum Health, Nursing & Rehab — Fuller Ave., Grand Rapids, MI 301

Speech problems 132, 141, 142, 151, 174

Spinal cord 163–4, 167

Spinal nerves *164*

Sporadic Alzheimer's disease 186, 149, 164

Sprain Brook Manor Nursing Home, Scarsdale, NY 327

Spring Creek Health Care Center, Fort Collins, CO 210

Spring Hill Health & Rehabilitation Center, Brooksville, FL 220

Spring Lake Rehabilitation Center, Winter Haven, FL 230

Springbrook Center, Westbrook, ME 290

Springdale West, Mesa, AZ 189

Springfield Care Center Springfield, IL 255

Springhurst Health & Rehabilitation Center, Louisville, KY 281

Springs at Watermark, Bridgeport, CT 214

Springs Meadow Health Care Center, Clarksville, TN 359

Springs Village Care Center, Colorado Springs, CO 208

Stages of Alzheimer's disease 128, 131, 139–40, 144, 155, 164–5, 168, 173, 176

Stanford University 78, 145, 175, 387

Stanley Manor, Albemarle, NC 328

Stanton Health Center, Stanton, NE 318

State policies on mental health care 165–6

Statins 166

Steere House Nursing & Rehabilitation Center, Providence, RI 355

Stem cell differentiation *166*

Stem cells 21, 43, 84, 166–7

Stephens County Hospital Transitional Care, Hugoton, KS 274

Stephenson Nursing Center, Freeport, IL 249

Sterling Place, Baton Rouge, LA 283

Stevens Health Care & Rehab, Yoakum, TX 369

Stoddard Baptist Nursing Home, Washington, DC 219

Stonebrook Nursing, New Castle, IN 263

Stonehill Care Center, Dubuque, IA 268

Stratford ManorCare & Rehab, West Orange, NJ 323

Stratford Nursing & Rehabilitation Center, Stratford, IA 271

Stratton House Nursing Home, Townshend, VT 371

Stress 13, 23, 31, 37, 42, 54, 167, 178

Stroke 62, 65, 67, 69, 72, 76, 83, 90, 91, 112, 117, 141, 148, 166, 167

Stroop Color Interference Test 167

Stroud Oakview Care Center South, Stroud, OK 286

Structural magnetic resonance imaging 110–1

Subarachnoid hemorrhage 98, 136

Subarachnoid space 167

Subdural hematoma/hemorrhage 58, 139–140, 167

Subsidized senior housing 167

Substance P 167

Substantia nigra 167

Sugar Creek Rest & Meadow Lake Manor, Worthington, PA 353

Summerfield Health & Rehabilitation Center, Louisville, KY 281

Summit Commons, skilled Nursing & Rehabilitation, Providence, RI 355

Summit Healthcare, Okeene, OK 344

Summit Manor, Columbia, KY 279–80

Summit Ridge Center, West Orange, NJ 323

Summit View of Farragut, Knoxville, TN 361

Summitview Healthcare Center, Yakima, WA 379

Sun City Health and Rehabilitation Center, Sun City, AZ 191

Sun Dial Manor, Bristol, SD 357

Sun Grove Village Care Center, Peoria, AZ 189

Sun Terrace Health Care Center, Sun City Center, FL 228–9

SunBridge Bear Creek Care & Rehabilitation, Morrison, CO 212

SunBridge Care & Community Center, Jackson, TN 360

SunBridge Care & Rehabilitation for Elmore, Elmore, AL 184

SunBridge Care & Rehabilitation for New Lexington, New Lexington, OH 340

Suncrest Healthcare Center, Phoenix, AZ 190

Sundowning 167

Sunny Ridge, Sheboygan, WI 384

Sunnybrook Alzheimer & Healthcare, Raleigh, NC 329

Sunnybrook Health Care Center, Corpus Christi, TX 364

Sunnyside Nursing Center, Torrance, CA 206

Sunnyside Presbyterian Retirement Community, Harrisonburg, VA 373

Sunrise Assisted Living 29, 167–8

Sunrise Assisted Living, Leesburg, VA 373

SunRise Care & Rehabilitation, Burlington, WA 376

SunRise View Convalescent Center, Everett, WA 376

Sunset Health Care Center, Union, MO 314

Sunset Hills Care & Rehab, Inc., Safford, AZ 190

Sunset Hills Health & Rehabilitation Center, St. Louis, MO 314

Sunset Manor, Brush, CO 207

Sunset Manor, Irene, SD 358

Sunset Nursing Home, Cleveland, OH 335

Sunset Point Care & Rehabilitation Center, Clearwater, FL 221

Sunshine Gardens, Spokane, WA 378

Sunshine Terrace Foundation, Logan, UT 369

Sunview Health and Rehabilitation Center, Youngstown, AZ 192

Superior saggital sinus 80

Support groups 168

Suspiciousness 168

Susquehanna Nursing Home & Health Related Facility, Johnson City, NY 325–6

Suwannee Health Care Center, Live Oak, FL 224

Swansea Rehabilitation & Healthcare, Swansea, IL 255

Sweden Valley Manor, Coudersport, PA 349

Sweet Brook Care Centers Inc., Williamstown, MA 297

Swiss Village Inc., Berne, IN 257

Swope Ridge Geriatric Center, Kansas City, MO 312

Sylvan Court, Canby, MN 305

Sylvester Health Care Inc., Sylvester, GA 237

Sympathetic nervous system 149, 168

Symptoms of Alzheimer's disease 150, 152, 155, 158, 159, 161, 165, 167, 168

Synapses 110, 131, 133, 168–9

Synaptic cleft 51, 80, 131, 133, 151, 169

Synaptic connections 169

Synaptic density 169

Synaptic spines 169

Synaptic strengths 169

Synaptic vesicle *126*, 169

Synapton *see* Physostigmine salicylate

Synaptophysin 169

Syphilis See Neurosyphilis

Systemic lupus erythematosus 30, 65

Tabitha Nursing Home, Lincoln, NE 317

Tablerock Healthcare, Kimberling City, MO 312

Tacrine hydrochloride (THA) 4, 79, 142–143

Tahoka Care Center, Tahoka, TX 368

Talahi Care Center, Saint Cloud, MN 307

Tall Pines Care and Rehab, Inc., Show Low, AZ 191

Tangles *see* Neurofibrillary tangles

Tanzi, Rudolph 7

Tarpon Point Nursing & Rehabilitation, Sarasota, FL 228

Taste 79, 82, 121

Tau gene 82

Tau protein 26, 36, 43, 82, 104, 118, 122, 171

Taub Institute on Alzheimer's and the Aging Brain 13, 171, 390

Tauists 31, 171

Taxol *see* Paclitaxel

Taylor Care Center, Jacksonville, FL 223

Taylor Park & Rehabilitation, Rhinelander, WI 384

Tel Hai Nursing Center, Honey Brook, PA 350

Tela choroidea 171

Telencephalon *see* Cerebrum

Telomerase 171

Temple Living Center East, Temple, TX 368

Temporal lobe 117, 132, 139, 147, 171

Tendercare Alpena, Alpena, MI 298

Tendercare Green View, Alpena, MI 298

Tendercare Health Care of Cheboygan, Cheboygan, MI 299

Tendercare Health Centers — Birchwood, Traverse City, MI 304

Tendercare Kalamazoo, Kalamazoo, MI 302

Tendercare Midland, Midland, MI 302

Tendercare West, Lansing, MI 302

Tendercare Westwood, Kalamazoo, MI 302

Tennessee State Veterans Home, Humboldt, TN 360

Teresian House Nursing Home Co Inc., Albany, NY 324

Terminal illness 172

Terrace Gardens Health Care Center, Colorado Springs, CO 208–9

Terraces of Lake Worth, Lake Worth, FL 224

Terrebonne General Medical Center, Houma, LA 284

Terrence Cardinal Cook Rehabilitation Center, New York, NY 326

Testosterone 172

Teton Nursing Home, Choteau, MT 315

Texan Nursing & Rehab of Amarillo, Amarillo, TX 363

Texan Nursing & Rehab of San Marcos, San Marcos, TX 367

Texas Functional Living Scale (TFLS) 172

Texhoma Christian Care Center, Wichita Falls, TX 368

Thal, Leon, M.D. 172

Thalamus 172

Thiamine 65, 66, 104, 177

Think Gum 172

Third ventricle 172

Thornton Terrace Health Center, Hanover, IN 260

Thought process 55, 173

Thyroid disease 30, 52, 65, 172–3

Tierra Pines Center, Largo, FL 224

Timberridge Nursing & Rehab Center, Ocala, FL 226

Tobacco Root Mountains Care Center, Sheridan, MT 316

Tobius Hills Assisted Living, San Antonio, TX 367

Topanga Terrace, Canoga Park, CA 197

Topeka Community Health Center, Topeka, KS 277

Topeka Presbyterian Manor, Topeka, KS 277–8

Torrington Health & Rehabilitation Center, Torrington, CT 216

Touch therapy 173

Toxin exposure 65, 173

Toxin 173

Tradewater Pointe, Dawson Springs, KY 280

Traditions Health and Rehabilitation, Lithonia, GA 234

Trailmaking B 173

Transcutaneous electrical nerve stimulation 173

Transforming growth factor beta-1 (TGF-β1) 62, 118, 173

Transitional Care Center of Owensboro, Owensboro, KY 282

Transitional Health Services of Fremont, Fremont, MI 301

Transitional Health Services of Wayne, Wayne, MI 304

Transitions Health Care at Sykesville, Sykesville, MD 292

Traumatic head injury 174; *see also* Brain injury
Treatment for Alzheimer's disease 148, 153, 158, 160, 163, 170, 172, 174
Tremont Health & Rehabilitation Center, Tremont, PA 352
Trempealeau County Health Care Center W, Whitehall, WI 385
Trevecca Health Care Center, Nashville, TN 362
Trevila of Golden Valley, Golden Valley, MN 305–6
Tri-County Care Center, Vandalia, MO 314
Tri-County Extended Care Center, Fairfield, OH 336
Tri-County Manor Living Center, Horton, KS 274
Tricyclic antidepressants 52, 70, 93, 135
Trillium Specialty Hospital — West Valley, Sun City, AZ 191
Trinidad State Nursing Home, Trinidad, CO 213
Trinity Center at Lutheran Park, Des Moines, IA 268
Trinity Living Center, Grove City, PA 349–50
Trinity Lutheran Manor, Merriam, KS 275
Trinity Manor, Dodge City, KS 273
Trinity Mission Nursing & Rehab of Holly, Moscow, ID 241
Trinity Mission Nursing & Rehab of Midland, Nampa, ID 241
Trinity Nursing Home, Minot, ND 331
Trinity Saint Elizabeth Care Services, Baker, OR 345
Trinity Village, Milwaukee, WI 383
Trinity Village Medical Center, Pine Bluff, AR 195
Trisun Care Center, San Antonio, TX 367
Trisun Care Center — Westwood, Corpus Christi, TX 364
Triune brain 174–5
Trojanowski, John 390
Trophic factors 175
Truman Healthcare & Rehabilitation, Lamar, MO 312
Truman Medical Center Lakewood, Kansas City, MO 312
Tumor necrosis factor (TNF) 175
Tumor necrosis factor inhibitors 175
Tunnel Center for Rehabilitation and Healthcare, San Francisco, CA 204
Twin Falls Care & Rehabilitation Center, Twin Falls, ID 242
Twin Maples Home, Durham, CT 215
Twin Oaks Convalescent Center Inc., Alma, GA 231
Twin Oaks Nursing Home, Mobile, AL 185
Tygart Center at Fairmont Campus, Fairmont, WV 380

Ubiquinone *see* Coenzyme Q-10
Uintah Care Center, Vernal, UT 370
Ultrasonography 175
Umpqua Valley Nursing & Rehabilitation, Roseburg, OR 346

Unihealth Magnolia Manor South, Moultrie, GA 235
Unihealth Post-Acute Care — Aiken, LLC, Aiken, SC 355
Unihealth Post-Acute Care — Augusta Hills, Augusta, GA 231
Unihealth Post-Acute Care — Bamberg, SC 355
Unihealth Post-Acute Care — Columbia, SC 356
Unihealth Post-Acute Care — Durham, Durham, NC 328
Unihealth Post-Acute Care — Fairburn, Fairburn, GA 233
Unihealth Post-Acute Care — Swainsboro, Swainsboro, GA 236
Union House Nursing Home, Glover, VT 371
Union Printers Home, LTC, Colorado Springs, CO 209
United Methodist Health Care Center, Clinton, OK 342–3
The United Methodist Village, Lawrenceville, IL 250
Unity Health & Rehabilitation Center, Miami, FL 225
University Center West, DeLand, FL 221
University Hospitals of Cleveland 390
University Manor Health & Rehabilitation Center, Cleveland, OH 335
University Nursing & Rehab, Des Moines, IA 268
University of Alabama at Birmingham 81, 387
University of California, Davis 153, 387, 396
University of California, Irvine 68, 109, 133, 175, 387
University of California, Los Angeles 114, 149, 387
University of California, San Diego 14, 18, 143, 173, 388, 396
University of California, San Francisco 118, 144, 154, 388
University of Kansas 389, 400
University of Kentucky at Lexington 55, 136, 389
University of Miami 400
University of Michigan 62, 389
University of Pennsylvania's Center for Neurodegenerative Diseases 65, 95, 390
University of Pittsburgh 38, 63, 77, 390, 391, 398
University of Rochester Medical Center 390
University of South Carolina 391
University of Texas Southwestern Medical Center 172, 391
University of Washington 37, 74, 79, 123, 391, 399
University of Wisconsin 391
University Park Care Center, Pueblo, CO 212
University Park Nursing Center, Fort Wayne, IN 260
Uptown Health Care Center Inc., Denver CO 210
Urbandale Healthcare — Urbandale, Urbandale, IA 271

Vaccines 20, 24, 33, 68, 124, 175–6
Valencia Hills Health & Rehab Center, Lake Worth, FL 224
Valerie Manor, Torrington, CT 216
Valle Vista Manor, Lewistown, MT 316
Valley Grande Manor, Brownsville, TX 363
Valley Healthcare Center, San Bernardino, CA 204
The Valley Inn, Mancos, CO 212
Valley ManorCare Center, Montrose, CO 212
Valley Manor Convalescent Hospital, N. Hollywood, CA 202
Valley View Alzheimer's Care Center, Frankfort, OH 337
Valley View Health Care Center, Canon City, CO 207–8
Valley View Health Care Center, Elkhart, IN 258
Valley View Senior Life, Junction City, KS 274
Valley View Villa, Fort Morgan, CO 210
Valley Vista Care Center, Saint Maries, ID 241
Valley Vista Care Center of Sandpoint, Sandpoint, ID 241
Valley West Health Care Center, Eugene, OR 345
Valparaiso Care & Rehabilitation Center, Valparaiso, IN 265
Valproate 18, 176
Val66Met polymorphism 176
Van Ayer Manor Nursing Center, Martin, TN 361
Van Buren Good Samaritan Center, Keosauqua, IA 270
Vascular dementia 176–7
Vascular disease 23, 32, 49, 69, 79, 83, 176
Vasculitis 30, 65, 92
Ventricles of the brain 36, 51, 57, 74, 95, 177
Verde Vista Care & Rehab, Inc., Camp Verde, AZ 187–8
Vermilion Health Care Center, Kaplan, LA 284
Vermis 45
Vermont Veterans Home, Bennington, VT 371
Vernon Green Nursing Home, Vernon, VT 371
Vernon Manor Health Care Center, Vernon CT 216
Verrazano Nursing Home, Staten Island, NY 327
Veterans Administration 79, 172, 177
Via Christi Village, Manhattan, KS 212
Victory Lakes Continuing Care Center, Lindenhurst, IL 193
Villa Cascade Care Center, Lebanon, OR 346
Villa Crest Nursing & Retirement Community, Manchester, NH 319
Villa Feliciano Chronic Disease, Jackson, LA 284
Villa Las Palmas Healthcare Center, El Cajon, CA 198
Villa ManorCare Center, Lakewood, CO 211

Villa Maria, Fargo, ND 331
Villa Marie Elena Healthcare, Compton, CA 197
Villa Marie Nursing Center, North Miami, FL 226
Villa Saint Joseph, Overland Park, KS 276
Village at Victory Lakes, Lindenhurst, IL 251–2
Village Care & Rehabilitation Center, Westminster, CO 213
Village Green of Wallingford, Wallingford, CT 217
Village Health Care, Gresham, OR 345
The Village Health Care Center, Missoula, MT 316
Village House Nursing & Rehabilitation Center, Newport, RI 354
Village Manor, Wood Village, OR 291
Village on the Isle, Venice, FL 229
Villas at Sunny Acres, Thornton, CO 213
Villisca Good Samaritan Center, Villisca, IA 272
Vincentian Home, Pittsburgh, PA 352
Vinpocetine 177
The Virginian Health, Fairfax, VA 373
Viruses 76, 85, 94, 102, 122, 151
Vista Grande Rehabilitation & Care Center, Cortez, CO 209
Vista Specialty Care, LaGrande, OR 345
Visuo-spatial skills 130, 134–135
Vitamin B 134, 172, 178, 179
Vitamin B12 deficiency 65, 66, 73, 87, 97, 105, 144, 145, 177–8, 179
Vitamin D 178
Vitamin E 18, 24, 69, 82, 132, 160, 178, 179
Vitamins 69, 174, 178–9

Wabash Skilled Care Center, Wabash, IN 265
Wadsworth Glen Health Care & Rehabilitation Center, Middletown, CT 215
Wagoner Care Center, Wagoner, OK 344
Wakefield Care & Rehabilitation Center, Wakefield, MA 297
Walker Methodist Health Center, Minneapolis, MN 307
Walnut Creek Nursing Center, Kettering, OH 338
Walnut Grove Boarding Home, Grandview, WA 376
Walnut ManorCare Center, Anaheim, CA 196
Walnut Place, Dallas, TX 364
Walsenburg Care Center, Walsenburg, CO 213
Walton Regional Nursing Home, Monroe, GA 235
Wandering 179
Warning signs 179
Warr Acres Nursing Center, Oklahoma City, OK 344
Warren Barr Pavilion, Chicago, IL 246
Warren Manor Health & Rehabilitation Center, Selma, AL 186

Warren Memorial Hospital — Lynn Care Center, Front Royal, VA 373
Warren Woods Health & Rehab Center, Warren, MI 304
Washington Center for Aging Services, Washington, DC 219
Washington Center for Comprehensive Rehabilitation, Seattle, WA 378
Washington County Health Center, Washington, PA 353
The Washington Home, Washington, D.C. 219
Washington University 13, 33, 84, 119, 121, 389, 391
Waterfront Terrace, Chicago, IL 246
Water's Edge Center for Health & Rehab, Middletown, CT 215
Water's Edge Healthcare Center, Trenton NJ 322
Waters of Summit County, Fort Wayne, IN 260
Waterview Center, Cedar Grove, NJ 320
Waterview Villa, East Providence, RI 354
Watseka Rehabilitation & Health Care Center, Watseka, IL 256
Waukesha Springs Health & Rehabilitation, Waukesha, WI 384
Waveny Care Center, New Canaan, CT 215
Wayne Healthcare, Newark, NY 326
Weatherford Healthcare Center, Weatherford, TX 368
Webb City Health & Rehabilitation Center, Webb City, MO 315
Webster Nursing & Rehabilitation Center LLC, Cowen, WV 380
Wechsler Adult Intelligence Scale (WAIS) 179
Wechsler Memory Scale 179
Wedgewood Rehabilitation Center, Seattle, WA 378
Wellington Manor HealthCare Center, Indianapolis, IN 261
Wellington Parc of Owensboro, Owensboro, KY 282
Wellness recommendations 179–80
Wellspring of Milwaukee, Milwaukee, WI 383
Welsh-Bohmer, Kathleen 390
Wernicke area 180
Wernicke's aphasia 180
Wernicke's encephalopathy 180
Wesley Manor Nursing Center & Retirement Community, Louisville, KY 281
Wesley Pines — Methodist Retirement Community, Lumberton, NC 329
Wesley Towers, Hutchinson, KS 274
Wesleyan at Scenic Nursing Home, Georgetown, TX 365
Wesleyan Health Care Center, Marion, IN 262
West Anaheim Extended Care, Anaheim, CA 196
West Hartford Health & Rehabilitation Center, West Hartford, CT 217
West Hills Health and Rehab Center, Canoga Park, CA 197

West Jefferson Healthcare Center, Harvey, LA 284
Westchester Care Center, Tempe, AZ 191
Westchester Gardens Rehabilitation & Care Center, Clearwater, FL 221
Westerly Nursing Home, Westerly, RI 355
Western MD Healthcare Center, Hagerstown, MD 292
Westford House, Westford, MA 297
Westgate Manor, Bangor, ME 289
Westminster Place, Evanston, IL 249
Westminster Towers, Orlando, FL 226
Westminster Village Health Care, Dover, DE 218
Westmoreland Care & Rehab Center Westmoreland, TN 362
Westmoreland Manor, Greensburg, PA 349
Westmoreland Place, Chillicothe, OH 335
Weston County Manor, Newcastle, WI 385
Westpark Health Care Center, Cleveland, OH 335
Westridge Health Care, Terre Haute, IN 265
Westridge Nursing Center, Clarinda, IA 266
Westview Care Center, Britt, IA 266
Westwind Special Care Center, Pueblo, CO 212
Westwood Manor Nursing Home, Inc., DeRidder, LA 283
Westwood Nursing Center, Detroit, MI 300
Wheat Ridge Manor, Wheat Ridge, CO 213
Wheatcrest Hills, Britton, SD 357
Wheatland Nursing & Rehabilitation Center, Russell, KS 277
The Wheatlands Health Care Center, Kingman, KS 274
Whipple disease 65
Whispering Oaks, Ardmore, OK 342
Whispering Oaks, Tampa, FL 229
Whispering Pines Nursing Home, Fayetteville, NC 329
Whisperwood Nursing & Rehabilitation, Lubbock, TX 366
White Acres Good Samaritan Retirement Village & Nursing Center, El Paso, TX 364
White Hall Nursing & Rehab Center, White Hall, IL 256
White matter of the brain 28, 33, 40, 44, *47*, 49, 56, 60, 63, 66, 101, 180
White Oak Manor, Burlington, NC 328
White Oak Manor, Lancaster, SC 356
White Oak Manor — Rock Hill, Rock Hill, SC 357
Whitehall Boca Raton, Boca Raton, FL 220
Whitehall Healthcare Center of Ann Arbor, Ann Arbor, MI 298
The Whitehall North, Deerfield, IL 246

Whitehills Health Care Center, East Lansing, MI 300

Whitesburg Gardens Healthcare, Huntsville, AL 185

Whitey Manor Convalescent Center, Hamden, CT 215

Whiting Health Care Center, Whiting, NJ 323

Whitney Oaks Care Center, Carmichael, CA 197

Wichita Nursing Center, Wichita, KS 278

Wilkins Nursing Center, Duncan, OK 343

William Bremen Jewish Home, Atlanta, GA 231

Williams County Hillside Country Living, Bryan, OH 333

Williamson Appalachian Regional–Skilled Nursing, South Williamson, KY 282

Willow Care Nursing Inc., Willow Springs, MO 315

Willow Glen Health & Rehab, Brigham City, UT 369

Willow Wood at Woldenberg Center, New Orleans, LA 287

Willowbrook Court at Brittany, Lansdale, PA 351

Willowbrook Health Care Center, Yadkinville, NC 330

Willowbrook Nursing & Rehab Center, St. Louis, MO 314

Willows at Winchester Care & Rehabilitation Center, Winchester, TN 362

Willows Health Center, Rockford, IL 254

Wilmed Nursing Care Center, Wilson, NC 330

Wilson's disease 105

Wilton Meadows Health Care Center, Wilton, CT 217

Winchester House, Libertyville, IL 251

Wind Crest Alzheimer's Care Center, Abilene, TX 362

Wind River Healthcare & Rehabilitation Center, Riverton, WY 385

Windsor Convalescent Center of North Long Beach, Long Beach, CA 200

Windsor El Camino Care Center, Carmichael, CA 197

Windsor Elk Grove Care & Rehabilitation Center, Elk Grove, CA 198

Windsor Gardens Convalescent Center of Anaheim, Anaheim, CA 196

Windsor Gardens Convalescent Hospital, Los Angeles, CA 201

Windsor Gardens of Hawthorne, Hawthorne, CA 199

Windsor Health Care Center, Windsor, CO 213–4

Windsor House, Huntsville, AL 185

Windsor Monterey Care Center, Monterey, CA 202

Windsor Place of Independence, LLC, Independence, KS 274

Windsor Terrace Health Care, Van Nuys, CA 206

Winfield Good Samaritan Village, Winfield, KS 278

Winfield Rest Haven, Winfield, KS 278

Wingate at Andover Skilled Nursing, Andover, MA 293

Wingate at Belvidere Rehab & Nursing Center, Lowell, MA 296

Winner Regional Healthcare Center, Winner, SD 359

Winnsboro Nursing Home, Winnsboro, TX 368–9

Winter Haven Health, Winter Haven, FL 230

Winter Park Towers, Winter Park, FL 230

Winthrop Health & Rehab, Rome, GA 236

Wintobury Care Center, Bloomfield, CT 214

Wisconsin Card Sort Test 180

Wisconsin Lutheran Care Center, Milwaukee, WI 383

Wisconsin Veterans Home, King, WI 382

Wise, Brad, M.D. 400

Wishek Home for the Aged, Wishek, ND 331

Wissota Health & Regional Vent Center, Chippewa Falls, WI 381

Wittenberg Lutheran Village, Crown Point, IN 258

Wolcott Hall for Special Care, Torrington, CT 216

Wood Glen Alzheimer's Community, Dayton, OH 336

Wood Mill Care & Rehabilitation Center, Lawrence, MA 296

Woodbine Rehabilitation & Healthcare Center, Alexandria, VA 372

Woodbridge Park Nursing & Rehabilitation, Commerce City, CO 209

Woodbridge Terrace Nursing & Rehabilitation, Commerce City, CO 209

Woodcrest Nursing Center, Decatur, IN 258

Woodhaven Hall at Williamsburg Landing, Williamsburg, VA 375

Woodhaven Nursing & Alzheimer Care Center, Lumberton, NC 329

Woodhaven Nursing Home, Montvale, VA 374

Woodland Care Center, Reseda, CA 203

Woodland Hills — A Stonebridge Community, Marble Hill, MO 312

Woodland Hills Healthcare and Rehabilitation, Little Rock, AR 194

Woodland Manor, Springfield, MO 314

Woodland Oaks Health Care Facility, Ashland, KY 279

Woodland Village Nursing & Rehabilitation Center, New Orleans, LA 287

Woodruff Manor, Woodruff, SC 357

Woodstock Health & Rehabilitation Center, Kenosha, WI 382

Woodview Home, Ardmore, OK 342

Woodward Hills Nursing Center, Bloomfield Hills, MI 299

Woonsocket Health Center, Woonsocket, RI 355

Word pairing 136

Worland Healthcare and Rehabilitation Center, Worland, WY 386

World Alzheimer's day 180

Wrightsville Manor, Inc., Wrightsville, GA 237

Writing 14, 24, 29, 116, 147, 151, 165, 168, 180

Writing studies 180–1

Wyeth Ayerst Laboratories 15

Wyoming County Nursing Home, Warsaw, NY 327

Wyoming Retirement Center, Basin, WY 385

Wyss-Coray, Tony, Ph.D. 118, 175

Xanomeline 181

Xenobiotics 181

Yale University 388

York Convalescent Center, Yorktown, VA 375

York County Nursing Home, York, PA 353

Yorkland Park Care Center, Columbus, OH 335–6

Yukio Okutso State Veterans Home, Hilo, HI 238

Yuma Nursing Center, Yuma, AZ 192

Zephyr Haven Nursing Home, Zephyrhills, FL 230

Zinc 50, 54, 59, 77, 82, 116, 119, 174, 181

Zyprexa see Olanzapine